Revelations
of the
Restoration

Revelations of the Restoration

A COMMENTARY ON THE DOCTRINE AND COVENANTS
AND OTHER MODERN REVELATIONS

JOSEPH FIELDING MCCONKIE

CRAIG J. OSTLER

DESERET
BOOK

Visit us at www.deseretbook.com

Library of Congress Cataloging-in-Publication Data

McConkie, Joseph F.
  Revelations of the Restoration / Joseph Fielding McConkie and Craig J. Ostler.
    p. cm.
  Includes bibliographical references and index.
  ISBN 1-57345-785-X
    1. Doctrine and Covenants—Commentaries. I. Ostler, Craig J. 1954– II. Title.

BX8628.M39 2000
289.3'2—dc21   00-058922

Printed in the United States of America   18961-6676

10 9   8   7   6   5   4   3   2   1

CONTENTS

PREFACE

Each revelation or document considered in this work is given a doctrinal and historical introduction to help in understanding the particular circumstances that called it forth. General commentary follows with a detailed consideration of words or phrases that are important to a meaningful understanding of the text under consideration. It is intended that this volume be used as a study aid in conjunction with the scriptures.

In both historical and doctrinal issues we have drawn liberally on the best thinking and insights of latter-day prophets and apostles and Latter-day Saint scholars. In some instances our understanding has been extended by secular sources. We acknowledge indebtedness to the hundreds of sources we have cited. We have attempted to properly credit them in a manner that is easy for the reader to follow in seeking either the source or additional information. Whether the thought was borrowed or originated with us, we assume responsibility for it. Shortcomings that may be found in this work are our own.

We are not vain enough to suppose that we have given the best possible explanation of everything covered in the length and breadth of these revelations. We hope, however, that our efforts enlighten and are thus in harmony with the Spirit of him of whom the revelations testify.

We extend special appreciation to our friend and colleague Robert L. Millet for his helpful counsel in the preparation of this manuscript and to Suzanne Brady of Deseret Book for her valuable contribution in its preparation for publication. We also extend thanks to Robert J. Matthews for his Church sense and understanding, particularly of the revelations on the priesthood; and to Lee Ann Lavender and Rebecca Sybrowsky, who spent countless hours laboring on and improving the tedious and thankless parts of this manuscript. Rachel Strain contributed significantly in historical research and content review. Greg Giauque also aided in researching and reviewing the manuscript.

As always, we are particularly indebted to our wives, Brenda and Sandra, who picked up the slack while we were lost in the labor.

INTRODUCTION

Were our modern day to produce a Moses, who among the world's throngs would accept him? Who today would believe a man claiming to have stood face to face with the God of Abraham, Isaac, and Jacob, to have received commandments by which the people were to be governed, and to have been charged with the responsibility to gather Israel from the ends of the earth and establish God's covenant people once again in their lands of promise? Among the Catholics, Protestants, Jews, and Muslims, all of whom profess an acceptance of the ancient Moses as a prophet, who would accept a modern successor? Surely the announcement that such a prophet again walked the earth could only be received with rejoicing among people of faith and goodness.

What if we were to learn that this very prophet had been foreseen and described by Moses, that Israel's ancient lawgiver had come to him and instructed him, and that Moses himself had laid his hands upon the head of his modern successor and given him the very keys and authority he had received from the great Jehovah on the heights of Sinai? Surely we would then know with perfect assurance that the God of heaven, that same God who gathered the Israelites anciently and led them out of their Egyptian bondage, had not forgotten his people nor the promises made to them by so many of the ancient prophets.

If the ancient revelations are true, modern revelations and heavenly visitations must follow. If we are to believe that God was a God of miracles in ancient times, are we not justified in believing that he is a God of miracles in our day? If he could speak in that ancient day with both the voice of thunder and the voice of perfect stillness, if he could stand face to face with his chosen prophet, if he could reveal to him his mind and will, if he could commission him to stand in his stead and labor in his behalf, if he could gather his people and put his name and blessing upon them, could he not do so today? If such a course represented a God of wisdom and love in that day long ago, would it not represent the same

1

in our day? Or are we to suppose that God has come to realize the futility and folly of such a course?

Latter-day Saints worship a God who speaks to his children, who of his own accord chooses men to mark the path he would have us follow. In our day God has chosen Joseph Smith as a modern-day Moses. Like his ancient counterpart, this latter-day prophet is a great revelator of Christ for his dispensation. If Moses stands approved by us for his word and works, certainly one whose fruits are the same should merit the same approbation. The testimony of this book is that the God who called and spoke to the prophets of the Old and New Testaments is the same God who called and spoke to Joseph Smith. Their doctrines, priesthood, works, and opposition are the same, as are the rewards for faithful discipleship to them.

The revelations of the Restoration stand as the perfect evidence that God is the same yesterday, today, and forever. All who believe that he spoke anciently are bound to believe that he speaks in our day, for such was the promise of his ancient prophets. And all who have come to know that he speaks with authority today know in turn that he spoke to his chosen people anciently. Thus Moses revealed the role to be played by Joseph Smith in the latter-day gathering of Israel, and Joseph Smith in turn revealed much about his ancient counterpart (Moses 1).

This volume places the revelations of the Restoration in their historical and doctrinal context in order that we might see more clearly their purpose and meaning. In it we see how one revelation builds upon another, and we are invited to advance from grace to grace, following the path of our Lord and Master.

Joseph Smith–History 1:1–26, The First Vision

Date: 23 December 1805–Spring 1820
Place: Sharon, Vermont; Palmyra and Manchester, New York

"The greatest event that has ever occurred in the world," declared President Joseph F. Smith, "since the resurrection of the Son of God from the tomb and his ascension on high, was the coming of the Father and of the Son to that boy Joseph Smith, to prepare the way for the laying of the foundation of his kingdom—not the kingdom of man—never more to cease nor to be overturned. Having accepted this truth, I find it easy to accept of every other truth that he enunciated and declared during his mission of fourteen years in the world. He never taught a doctrine that was not true. He never practiced a doctrine that he was not commanded to practice. He never advocated error. He was not deceived. He saw; he heard; he did as he was commanded to do; and, therefore, God is responsible for the work accomplished by Joseph Smith—not Joseph Smith. The Lord is responsible for it, and not man" (*Gospel Doctrine*, 495–96).

For those who live in the latter days, all other events pale in significance to the bright splendor of the Father and the Son appearing to the young boy, Joseph Smith Jr. Centuries after the testimony of ancient prophets and apostles had been recorded in the Holy Bible, another could testify that he had seen God with his own eyes.

Joseph Smith–History 1:1–2

JS–H 1:1 *Many reports . . . in circulation by evil-disposed and designing persons.* Truth and virtue are never without their opposites. Were this not the case ours would not be a fallen world, and were it not a fallen world there would be no need for a Sacred Grove that represents the search for light and truth in a mist of darkness. It is the destiny of the Church, as it was of the Prophet Joseph Smith, to "be both good and evil spoken of among all people" (Joseph Smith–History 1:33). History attests that the path of the true saint is marked by rejection, opposition, and persecution. As smoke betrays the fire, so the rancorous hollering of the adversary betrays the truths of heaven.

In the hope of dousing the flames of misrepresentation and falsehood, Joseph Smith tells his own story. All who have listened to one tale or another and all who seek after truth are obligated to give him a fair hearing. The traditional Christian world ought be reminded that faith rests upon a willingness to accept the testimony of Matthew, Mark, Luke, and John, each a devout disciple of Christ. Had the ancients chosen instead to hear only the testimonies of Judas, Caiaphas, Pilate, and Herod, there would be no professing Christians today. Thus Christians could not in the name of loyalty to Christian principles do other than give the testimony of Joseph Smith an honest and prayerful hearing.

I have been induced to write this history. In December 1841 the Prophet Joseph Smith lamented: "Since I have been engaged in laying the foundation of the Church of Jesus Christ of Latter-day Saints, I have been prevented in various ways from continuing my journal and history in a manner satisfactory to myself or in justice to the cause. Long imprisonments, vexatious and long-continued law-suits, the treachery of some of my clerks, the death of others, and the poverty of myself and brethren from continued plunder and driving, have prevented my handing down to posterity a connected memorandum of events desirable to all lovers of truth; yet I have continued to keep up a journal in the best manner my circumstances would allow, and dictate for my history from time to time, as I have had opportunity so that the labors and suffering of the first Elders and Saints of this last kingdom might not wholly be lost to the world" (*History of the Church*, 4:470). The history of the Church begun in 1838 was the first fully organized attempt to place the events that had transpired in relation to the restoration of the gospel into a comprehensive and chronologically arranged record.

The Smith Family
JOSEPH SMITH–HISTORY 1:3–4

JS–H 1:3 It is evident that God directed the movements of Joseph Smith Sr.'s family, eventually guiding them to the area of Palmyra and Manchester, New York, so that they would be near the Hill Cumorah. During the first twenty years of his and Lucy's marriage, they relocated nine times. Throughout this period Joseph Sr. farmed, operated a mercantile business, crystallized ginseng root to be exported to China, and taught school.

While the family was living in Lebanon, New Hampshire, typhus fever spread throughout New England. Young Joseph Jr. contracted this disease, and an abscess spread into the tibia of his left leg. The common medical practice of the day prescribed amputation of the afflicted limb; however, a short distance from the Smith home at Dartmouth Medical College, Dr. Nathan Smith taught another method for treating the abscess that saved the leg of afflicted individuals. The providence of the Lord placed the Smith family in the only known location in the world where such a procedure was practiced. The result was that young Joseph's leg was not amputated.

Three years of crop failure in Norwich, Vermont, precipitated the family's eventual move to Palmyra, New York. The year 1816 is known as "the year without summer." The eruption of the volcanic Mount Tambora on the island of Sumbawa, east of Java, in 1815 caused changes in the atmosphere. The volcanic ash and debris shaded the sun's rays, and many believed that this caused snow to fall in June and July in the New England states. "Coming after several years of hardships, the crop failure was more than the Smith family could handle. This, with other factors, caused them to leave Vermont. Packing their belongings, they moved to Palmyra, New York, where young Joseph was to receive a series of remarkable visions and the Book of Mormon" (Bellville, "Year without a Summer," 65).

JS–H 1:4 *His family consisting of eleven souls.* At the time of the First Vision, the Joseph Smith Sr. family consisted of Joseph Sr., forty-eight; Lucy, forty-three; Alvin, twenty-two; Hyrum, twenty; Sophronia, sixteen; Joseph Jr., fourteen; Samuel, twelve; William, nine; Catherine, seven; and Don Carlos, four.

In an earlier account of his formative years, the Prophet wrote that he was born "of goodly Parents who spared no pains to instructing me in the christian religion" (Backman, *First Vision*, 155). Thus, although they generally were not associated with any particular denomination, the Smith family studied the Bible and lived by Christian principles.

An Unusual Excitement about Religion
JOSEPH SMITH–HISTORY 1:5–10

JS–H 1:5 *Unusual excitement on the subject of religion.* It is likely that the young Joseph attended camp meetings promoted by Methodists to spread their faith. These meetings "were usually held on the edge of a grove of trees or in a small clearing in the midst of a forest. After traveling many miles along dusty or water-logged roads, the settlers would locate their wagons and pitch their tents on the outskirts of the encampment. Farmers' markets and grog or liquor shops often sprang up near the camp grounds, thereby providing some farmers with unusual economic opportunities. The meetings frequently continued for several days, and sometimes one session would last nearly all day and into the night. Ministers would rotate preaching assignments so that one minister would immediately be followed by another, and at times two or three ministers would preach simultaneously in different parts of the camp ground. Itinerants not only preached lengthy sermons but devoted much of their time to counseling and to directing prayer circles and group singing" (Backman, *First Vision*, 71–72).

Joseph's account seems to describe a similar series of meetings in which the clergy promoted "this extraordinary scene of religious feeling, in order to have everybody converted" (Joseph Smith–History 1:6). Enthusiastic and emotional demonstrations, including falling to the ground and crying out for mercy, were not uncommon. Years later Joseph told a group in Nauvoo that at one of the revival meetings his mother, brother, and sisters got religion. "He wanted to get Religion too, wanted to feel and shout like the rest but could feel nothing" (*Alexander Neibaur's Recording of Joseph Smith's Testimony*, cited in Backman, *First Vision*, 177).

The whole district of country. At this time there was an awakening of religious fervor among the population of western New York (Backman, *First Vision*, 53–89). The early settlers that came into the area were largely "unchurched." However, many of them were religious people who desired to join God's church.

JS–H 1:6 *A scene of great confusion.* "Where there is no vision, the people perish" (Proverbs 29:18). Because plain and precious things were "taken away out of the gospel of the Lamb," an angel explained to Nephi, "an exceedingly great many do stumble" (1 Nephi 13:29). Further, Nephi taught, "Because of the greatness of their stumbling block . . . they have built up many churches" (2 Nephi 26:20). The Apostasy and the Reformation left Christianity squabbling over the proper path to salvation.

The Prophet Joseph Smith wrote to Mr. John Wentworth, editor and proprietor of the *Chicago Democrat* newspaper, that disagreements between the various religious sects led him to examine their claims in greater earnest. "Considering that all could not be right," wrote the

Prophet, "and that God could not be the author of so much confusion, I determined to investigate the subject more fully, believing that if God had a Church it would not be split up into factions, and that if He taught one society to worship one way, and administer in one set of ordinances, He would not teach another, principles which were diametrically opposed" (*History of the Church*, 4:536). See Wentworth Letter, page 1003.

Good feelings . . . were entirely lost in a strife of words and a contest about opinions. The Savior taught this principle to the Nephites: "He that hath the spirit of contention is not of me, but is of the devil, who is the father of contention" (3 Nephi 11:29). See commentary on Doctrine and Covenants 71:7.

JS–H 1:7 *My father's family was proselyted to the Presbyterian faith.* Joseph experienced the results of the Apostasy and the attendant Reformation in his own family. His parents, brothers, and sisters were divided in their beliefs concerning which church to join. While his mother, Hyrum, Samuel, and Sophronia joined the Presbyterian faith, he, his father, and Alvin remained unchurched.

JS–H 1:8 *Called up to serious reflection and great uneasiness.* "From the age of twelve years to fifteen," Joseph Smith said, "I pondered many things in my heart concerning the situation of the world of mankind, the contentions and divisions, the wickedness and abominations, and the darkness which pervaded the minds of mankind. My mind became exceedingly distressed, for I became convicted of my sins, . . . for I looked upon the sun, the glorious luminary of the earth, and also the moon rolling in their majesty through the heavens, and also the stars shining in their courses, and the earth also upon which I stood, and the beast of the field, and the fowls of heaven, and the fish of the waters, and also man walking forth upon the face of the earth in majesty and in the strength of beauty, whose power and intelligence in governing the things which are so exceeding great and marvelous, even in the likeness of him who created them. And when I considered upon these things, my heart exclaimed, 'Well hath the wise man said it is a fool that saith in his heart there is no God.' My heart exclaimed, 'All these bear testimony and bespeak an omnipotent and omnipresent power, a being who maketh laws and decreeeth and bindeth all things in their bounds, who filleth eternity, who was and is and will be from all eternity to eternity'" (Backman, *First Vision*, 156–57; spelling and punctuation standardized).

I attended their several meetings. Joseph most likely would have attended meetings of the Presbyterian Church, the only religious

denomination with a building in Palmyra village before 1823. Yet, he
indicated that he "became somewhat partial to the Methodist sect, and
(he) felt some desire to be united with them" (Joseph Smith–History 1:8).

JS–H 1:10 *Are they all wrong together?* "By searching the Scriptures,"
Joseph explained, "I found that mankind did not come unto the Lord but
that they had apostatized from the true and living faith and there was no
society or denomination that built upon the Gospel of Jesus Christ as
recorded in the New Testament. And I felt to mourn for my own sins and
for the sins of the world. For I learned in the scriptures that God was the
same yesterday, today, and forever" (Backman, *First Vision*, 156; spelling
and punctuation standardized).

Joseph Sought Wisdom
JOSEPH SMITH–HISTORY 1:11–14

JS–H 1:11 *I was one day reading the Epistle of James.* This was not
Joseph's first appeal to the Bible for answers to his questions. He wrote:
"At about the age of twelve years my mind became seriously impressed
with regard to the all-important concerns for the welfare of my immortal
soul, which led me to searching the scriptures, believing as I was taught,
that they contained the word of God, thus applying myself to them"
(Backman, *First Vision*, 156; spelling and punctuation standardized).

In an interview in 1893, the year before his death, William Smith,
younger brother of the Prophet, recalled the background to Joseph's reading this passage of scripture. "There was a joint revival in the neighborhood between the Baptists, Methodists and Presbyterians and they had
succeeded in stirring up quite a feeling, and after the meeting the question arose which church should have the converts. Rev. Stockton was
the president of the meeting and suggested it was their meeting and
under their care and they had a church there and they ought to join the
Presbyterians, but as father did not like Rev. Stockton very well, our folks
hesitated and the next evening a Rev. Mr. Lane of the Methodists
preached a sermon on 'what church shall I join?' And the burden of
the discourse was to ask God, using as a text, 'If any man lack wisdom
let him ask of God who giveth to all men liberally.'" And of course
when Joseph went home and was looking over the text he was impressed
to do just what the preacher had said, and going out in the woods with
child-like, simple, trusting faith, believing that God meant just what He

said, he kneeled down and prayed" (*Deseret Semi-Weekly News*, 23 January 1894, 6).

JS–H 1:12 In the description of his feelings as he read James 1:5, Joseph Smith gives us a perfect description of the Spirit of revelation. The key elements in that description include the force with which the message of the text entered his heart, the attendant feelings, and the manner in which he reflected upon it again and again. It is an everlasting pattern that revelation begets revelation. Here Joseph Smith receives a revelation directing him to what we now know as the Sacred Grove.

This may well be the most instructive passage in holy writ on how truth is found and how we as a people should present our message to those not of our faith. There is no end to the argument over the meaning of Bible texts. Those who most vehemently oppose the idea of continuous revelation while declaring that all answers are to be found in the Bible are the least able to agree with each other on its meaning.

Satan Attempts to Prevent Joseph from Praying
Joseph Smith–History 1:15–16A

JS–H 1:15 *Retired to the place where I had previously designed to go.* The First Vision, as it is now known, took place in a grove of trees that the Smiths were clearing near their log home in Palmyra, New York. Recounting the experience, Joseph Smith said that he went to "a clearing, and went to the stump where I had struck my axe when I had quit work, and I kneeled down, and prayed" (Backman, *First Vision*, 176).

JS–H 1:16 *The power of some actual being.* Joseph was not wrestling with a formless power void of body but with a spirit being whose body is in the form and likeness of man. Devils are spirit beings that followed Satan in his rebellion against God in pre-mortality. In one account of this experience, Joseph said, "I heard a noise behind me like some one walking towards me. I strove again to pray, but could not; the noise of walking seemed to draw nearer, I sprang upon my feet and looked around, but saw no person or thing that was calculated to produce the noise of walking" (Backman, *First Vision*, 159).

Telling the story of the First Vision, Orson Hyde said, "The adversary benighted his [Joseph's] mind with doubts, and brought to his soul all kinds of improper pictures and tried to hinder him in his efforts and the accomplishment of his goal" (Backman, *First Vision*, 174).

The Father and the Son Appear
JOSEPH SMITH–HISTORY 1:16B–17

JS–H 1:16 *I saw a pillar of light.* We have no language that can adequately describe the glories of heaven. Joseph also used the phrases "pillar of fire" and "pillar of flame" to describe the light which appeared as part of his vision. Orson Pratt wrote the earliest published account of the First Vision in 1840. Assuming that he has accurately reflected the way Joseph Smith told the story, his account is very instructive. "While thus pouring out his soul," he wrote, "anxiously desiring an answer from God, he at length saw a very bright and glorious light in the heavens above; which, at first, seemed to be a considerable distance. He continued praying, while the light appeared to be gradually descending towards him; and as it drew nearer, it increased in brightness and magnitude, so that, by the time that it reached the tops of the trees, the whole wilderness, for some distance around was illuminated in a most glorious and brilliant manner. He expected to have seen the leaves and boughs of the trees consumed, as soon as the light came in contact with them; but perceiving that it did not produce that effect, he was encouraged with the hope of being able to endure its presence. It continued descending slowly, until it rested upon the earth, and he was enveloped in the midst of it. When it first came upon him, it produced a peculiar sensation throughout his whole system; and immediately his mind was caught away, from the natural objects with which he was surrounded; and he was enwrapped in a heavenly vision" (Backman, *First Vision*, 172).

JS–H 1:17 *I saw two Personages.* On another occasion Joseph Smith said, "A personage appeared in the midst of this pillar of flame, which was spread all around and yet nothing consumed. Another personage soon appeared like unto the first" (Backman, *First Vision*, 159). Alexander Neibaur heard Joseph Smith tell about the First Vision in Nauvoo just two months before the Prophet's martyrdom. According to his account, Joseph "saw a personage in the fire, [of] light complexion, blue eyes, a piece of white cloth drawn over his shoulders, his right arm bare. After a while another person came to the side of the first" (Backman, *First Vision*, 177; spelling and punctuation standardized). In the Wentworth Letter, Joseph wrote that he "saw two glorious personages, who exactly resembled each other in features, and likeness" (Smith, *History of the Church*, 4:536). See Wentworth Letter, page 1003.

When Joseph walked away from the grove of trees near his home, he

knew more about the Father and his Son, Jesus Christ, than any other living soul. The heresy of the great apostasy concerning the trinity was dispelled in a moment of vision. No amount of philosophical debate can
hold a flicker of light to the revelatory flame, brighter than noonday sun,
that Joseph witnessed.

One of them spake unto me. The Father is identified as the first to
address Joseph. This rare occurrence of the Father appearing to man on
earth is consistent with the doctrine revealed by John that "no man hath
seen God [the Father] at any time, except he hath borne record of the
Son" (JST John 1:19). In addition to the words of the Father, Joseph
revealed that the Savior also addressed him, "saying Joseph, my son, thy
sins are forgiven thee. Go thy way, walk in my statutes and keep my commandments. Behold, I am the Lord of glory. I was crucified for the world
that all those who believe on my name may have eternal life" (Backman,
First Vision, 157; spelling and punctuation standardized). See commentary on Doctrine and Covenants 20:5.

This is My Beloved Son. Hear Him! With the fall of Adam came the
need for a Redeemer or Savior. He is the Only Begotten of the Father and
the only source of salvation for all of Adam's posterity. Thus, all revelations for the salvation of Adam's children must come through him. By
having the Son answer Joseph Smith's question, the Father pointed our
attention to Christ as the source of all saving doctrine. He it is that we
must hear!

Scripture records three other occasions upon which the Father has
spoken from the heavens. These are the Savior's baptism and on the
Mount of Transfiguration in the Old World as well as the introduction of
Christ to the Nephites in the New World.

Joseph's Prayer Is Answered
JOSEPH SMITH–HISTORY 1:18–20

JS–H 1:19 *Their creeds.* See commentary on Doctrine and Covenants
123:7–8.

They were all wrong. The vineyard of the Lord had "become corrupted
every whit" (D&C 33:4). Thus, the need for the Restoration rests upon
the doctrine of the universal apostasy of the meridian-day church, for if
the true church were found on the earth, there would be no need for the
Restoration. During the centuries that preceded the First Vision, the
world was enveloped in spiritual darkness. The authority that Jesus

bestowed during his mortal ministry to act in his name was lost, and saving truths were perverted. All of this had been foretold in prophecy. The
apostle Paul warned the early members of the Church saying, "Take heed
therefore unto yourselves, and to all the flock, over the which the Holy
Ghost hath made you overseers, to feed the church of God, which he
hath purchased with his own blood. For I know this, that after my departing shall grievous wolves enter in among you, not sparing the flock. Also
of your own selves shall men arise, speaking perverse things, to draw away
disciples after them. Therefore watch, and remember, that by the space of
three years I ceased not to warn every one night and day with tears" (Acts
20:28–31).

Paul was not alone in addressing the problems that crept into the
Church. Peter also mentioned the false teachers who were among the
meridian-day saints. "But there were false prophets also among the people,
even as there shall be false teachers among you, who privily shall bring in
damnable heresies, even denying the Lord that bought them, and bring
upon themselves swift destruction. And many shall follow their pernicious
ways; by reason of whom the way of truth shall be evil spoken of. And
through covetousness shall they with feigned words make merchandise of
you: whose judgment now of a long time lingereth not, and their damnation slumbereth not" (2 Peter 2:1–3).

Jude wrote an exhortation to the meridian-day members of the
Church of Jesus Christ that they "should earnestly contend for the faith
which was once delivered unto the saints. For there are certain men crept
in unawares, . . . denying the only Lord God, and our Lord Jesus Christ"
(Jude 1:3–4).

After the death of Peter, John was the presiding apostle or president
of the Church. Yet, there were those in his day who rejected him and
taught their own doctrines and commandments. One such was
Diotrephes. He rebelled against John and other properly appointed
church leaders. Further, he mutinied in usurping authority over an area
of the Church, taking the members under his own control. John addressed
this rebellion in an epistle to the saints. "I wrote unto the church: but
Diotrephes, who loveth to have the preeminence among them, receiveth
us not. Wherefore, if I come, I will remember his deeds which he doeth,
prating against us with malicious words: and not content therewith, neither doth he himself receive the brethren, and forbiddeth them that
would, and casteth them out of the church" (3 John 1:9–10).

In addition, John fought against some of the learned men of the

Church in his day. These false brethren desired to replace the doctrine of the bodily resurrection with Greek philosophies concerning God. The Greeks argued in their speculative philosophy that all matter is essentially evil. As the mutinous leaders taught this concept, the bodily resurrection of Jesus Christ was discarded. Some, known as docetists, even taught that Jesus did not really have a body of flesh and bone as a mortal, but only seemed, or appeared, to have come in the flesh. John confronted such heresies: "Brethren, this is the testimony which we give of that which was from the beginning, which we have heard, which we have seen with our eyes, which we have looked upon, and our hands have handled, of the Word of life" (JST 1 John 1:1). "For many deceivers are entered into the world, who confess not that Jesus Christ is come in the flesh" (2 John 1:7).

Though the gospel spread quickly throughout the Roman Empire after the resurrection of Christ, an insidious mutiny was fomenting among some. Embarrassed by the simple doctrine taught by the Apostles, they sought for something more acceptable in a sophisticated Greek world. This transformation of the faith was obviously complete by the writing of the Nicene Creed in A.D. 325. "It is impossible for any one, whether he be a student of history or no, to fail to notice a difference of both form and content between the Sermon on the Mount and the Nicene Creed. The Sermon on the Mount is the promulgation of a new law of conduct; it assumes beliefs rather than formulates them; the theological conceptions which underlie it belong to the ethical rather than the speculative side of theology; metaphysics are wholly absent. The Nicene Creed is a statement partly of historical facts and partly of dogmatic inferences; the metaphysical terms which it contains would probably have been unintelligible to the first disciples; ethics have no place in it. The one belongs to a world of Syrian peasants, the other to a world of Greek philosophers" (Hatch, *Influence of Greek Ideas,* 1).

Long after they had declared the heavens sealed and prophets and apostles to be a thing of the past, the leaders of what called itself the Christian faith met in Nicaea to determine the nature of the God they worshipped. The event is known as the church's first ecumenical council, and out of it came the first formal Christian creed. Everything associated with this council is strangely at odds with the pattern of faith preserved in holy writ. Here prophets were formally replaced by scholars and the revelations of heaven by philosophical speculations. The council was called not by religious leaders but by the Roman emperor Constantine, himself a sun worshipper, who presided over it in regal splendor. His motive lay in the power that he saw within the church to unite his fractured kingdom. The council represented the beginning of an alliance between church and state and the end of religious freedom that would reap untold misery in years to come. Those not acquiescing to the religious decisions of the council were to be banished from their homes by the authority of the state. Indeed, there was nothing in the nature of this council to suggest a purity of purpose.

The council of Nicaea determined that God was incomprehensible and that Jesus of Nazareth, who claimed to be the Son of God, was Logos, meaning that he was the manifestation of the mind of the Father and as such was neither older nor younger than his Father. The new God of Christianity was then denominated as a majestic mystery, both unknown and unknowable. The creed announcing these determinations became the standard by which all doctrine was to be measured. Failure to accept it became a greater bar to acceptance in the traditional Christian world than rejection of the New Testament.

Thus a mist of darkness filled the earth in what we have come to call a universal apostasy. It engulfed the priesthood, its keys, all the ordinances of salvation and the ordinances of blessing, and the offices of the priesthood and its officers. Plain and precious things were taken from holy writ, and other things were added in their place. The purity of every doctrine and principle of salvation was lost. In their stead came an oppressive tyranny over the hearts and minds of men. Where once there had been love unfeigned, now there was a blood-stained sword. Where there had been robes of righteousness, now there were silks, and scarlets, and fine-twined linen, and precious clothing. Worship was replaced by ritual; the prayer of faith, by gold and silver. So darkness covered the earth and gross darkness the minds of the people (Isaiah 60:2).

In the darkness of the night, the stars of heaven shine forth with greater brilliance. So it was that an unnumbered host of wise and good people reflected such light as they had among those who would look heavenward. In a distant day, brighter lights were to be seen that would chase away the powers of fear, ignorance, and superstition that had ruled for so long. Elder Bruce R. McConkie stated: "There was a Calvin, a Zwingli, a Luther, a Wesley; there were wise and good men—morning stars who shone more brightly than their fellows—who arose in every nation. There were men of insight and courage who were sickened by the sins and evils of the night. These great souls hacked and sawed at the chains with which the masses were bound. They sought to do good and to help their fellowmen—all according to the best light and knowledge they had.

"In Germany and France and England and Switzerland and elsewhere groups began to break away from the religion of centuries past. A few rays of light were parting the darkness of the eastern sky.

"Many who sought freedom to worship God according to the dictates of their conscience migrated to America. And in due course, by the power of the Father, a new nation was created, a nation 'conceived in liberty, and dedicated to the proposition that all men were created equal' (Abraham Lincoln, Gettysburg Address.) The United States of America came into being. Beyond the mountains, now not many leagues away, a new day was gestating in the womb of nature.

"As the earth continued to turn slowly and steadily on its decreed course, as the dawn brightened and the morning light increased, as the Constitution of the United States guaranteed religious freedom, as men were tempered in their feelings and began to view each other with more equity and fairness, as the Bible was published and read by more people, as darkness fled and light increased, the time for the rising of the gospel sun was at hand" (Conference Report, April 1978, 17).

Such was the setting in which the youthful Joseph Smith went into a quiet grove not far from his parents' log home in the spring of 1820 to inquire of the Lord which of all the churches he should join. In response to his humble prayer, both the Father and the Son appeared to him. Calling him by name, the Father said, "This is My Beloved Son. Hear Him!" (Joseph Smith–History 1:17). Everything that Joseph Smith was told and witnessed in the grove that day stood as a rejection of Christian tradition and placed him at odds with it. He learned that the heavens were not sealed and that God could and did speak directly to mankind as he had done in ages past. He learned that both the Father and the Son were personal beings and that they had, contrary to the creeds of Christendom, body, parts, and passions. He learned that they were separate and distinct and that they were offended by both the creeds and the churches of men.

JS–H 1:20 *When the light had departed, I had no strength.* The Prophet Joseph Smith had been transfigured that he might endure the presence of God. The Spirit of God had overshadowed him, causing a divine transformation in his body. Physical exhaustion is a natural attendant to such an experience. "I was left alone, and saw this great vision, and there remained no strength in me," Daniel recounted, "for my comeliness was turned in me into corruption, and I retained no strength. Yet heard I the voice of his words: and when I heard the voice of his words, then was I in a deep sleep on my face, and my face toward the ground" (Daniel 10:8–9).

Similarly, Nephi wrote concerning his father's experience, when "as he prayed unto the Lord, there came a pillar of fire and dwelt upon a rock before him; and he saw and heard much; and because of the things which he saw and heard he did quake and tremble exceedingly. And it came to pass that he returned to his own house at Jerusalem; and he cast himself upon his bed, being overcome with the Spirit and the things which he had seen" (1 Nephi 1:6–7).

Likewise, Moses also experienced similar weakness. Following his experiences when he was caught up to a high mountain where he saw God face to face and talked with him, "the presence of God withdrew from Moses, that his glory was not upon Moses; and Moses was left unto himself. And as he was left unto himself, he fell unto the earth. And it came to pass that it was for the space of many hours before Moses did again receive his natural strength like unto man" (Moses 1:9–10). Concerning this experience Moses explained, "But now my own eyes have beheld God; but not my natural, but my spiritual eyes, for my natural eyes could not have beheld; for I should have withered and died in his presence; but his glory was upon me; and I beheld his face, for I was transfigured before him" (Moses 1:11). See commentary on Doctrine and Covenants 76.

Joseph Smith Is Persecuted
JOSEPH SMITH–HISTORY 1:21–26

JS–H 1:21–26 Persecution is the heritage of the Lord's servants. "Blessed are ye, when men shall revile you, and persecute you, and shall say all manner of evil against you falsely, for my sake," declared the Savior. "Rejoice, and be exceeding glad: for great is your reward in heaven: for so persecuted they the prophets which were before you" (Matthew 5:11–12).

"Persecution has not stopped the progress of truth," the Prophet Joseph Smith avowed, "but has only added fuel to the flame, it has spread with increasing rapidity. Proud of the cause which they have espoused, and conscious of our innocence, and of the truth of their system, amidst calumny and reproach, have the Elders of this Church gone forth, and planted the Gospel in almost every state in the Union; it has penetrated our cities, it has spread over our villages, and has caused thousands of our intelligent, noble, and patriotic citizens to obey its divine mandates, and be governed by its sacred truths. It has also spread into England, Ireland, Scotland, and Wales, where, in the year 1840, a few of our missionaries were sent, and over five thousand joined the Standard of Truth; there are numbers now joining in every land" (*History of the Church*, 4:540).

JS–H 1:21 *No such things as visions or revelations in these days.* As light is the great enemy of darkness, so revelation is the arch enemy of false religion. Nothing so threatens the prince of darkness as the light of heaven. Continuous revelation is as important to true religion as breath is to life or constant nourishment is to the body.

"The message left with the youthful seer by the God of heaven was most drastic," explained Joseph Fielding Smith. "It had been declared in language that could be clearly understood, that the creeds of men were not in accord with his Gospel. This was not a message to please the religious teachers of the day. Moreover, the vision had shattered the traditions of the times. The doctrines taught in the churches were emphatically contradicted and disproved. The world was teaching and believing that the canon of scripture was full; that there was not to be and could not be, more revelation; that the visitation of angels had ceased with the early Christian fathers, and such things as these had passed away forever. Again, the doctrine was taught that the Father, Son and Holy Ghost were incomprehensible, without body, parts and passions. A revelation of the Father and the Son as separate persons, each with a body tangible and in the form of the body of man, was destructive of this doctrine, as revelation was of the doctrine of the closed heavens. The world had held that perfection in religion and the organization of the Church of Christ was not to be expected, but that men were led by their own human reason to interpret the word of the Lord as set forth in the scriptures" (*Essentials in Church History*, 42).

JOSEPH SMITH–HISTORY 1:27–54; DOCTRINE AND COVENANTS 2

DATE: 21 SEPTEMBER 1823
PLACE: MANCHESTER, NEW YORK

To believe in the Bible is to believe in the ministry of angels. From Genesis to Revelation, angels declared the saving principles of the gospel of Jesus Christ to men chosen of God. These men in turn were to declare the message given them by the angels of the Lord to those of their generation. "I, the Lord God, gave unto Adam and unto his seed, that they should not die as to the temporal death, until I, the Lord God, should send forth angels to declare unto them repentance and redemption, through faith on the name of mine Only Begotten Son" (D&C 29:42). "Thus," we are told, "the Gospel began to be preached, from the beginning, being declared by holy angels sent forth from the presence of God, and by his own voice, and by the gift of the Holy Ghost" (Moses 5:58). And four thousand years later when the angel appeared to John on the Isle of Patmos, he introduced himself, saying, "I am thy fellowservant, and of thy brethren the prophets" (Revelation 22:9). We do not know which of the ancient prophets it was who came to instruct John. We do know that he came from a great quorum of prophets all of whom he said had "the testimony of Jesus" which he identified as the "spirit of prophecy" (Revelation 19:10).

To believe in the life and ministry of Christ is to believe in angels. It was an angel who announced to Mary that she had been chosen to be the mother of the Son of God (Luke 1:26–33); it was an angel who told Joseph to take Mary as his wife for her child had been conceived by divine power (Matthew 1:20); it was an angel who told the shepherds of the birth of the Christ, and a heavenly host who rejoiced in song on the night of his birth (Luke 2:10–14). The promise was given to Christ long before his birth that the angels of heaven would be charged to protect him against the designs of evil spirits (Psalm 91:11–12). So it was that an angel strengthened Christ when he sweat drops of blood in Gethsemane

(Luke 22:43–44), and angels announced his resurrection (Luke 24:4–6) and his ascension into heaven (Acts 1:10–11).

The testimony of Christ affirmed the prominent role of angels in the plan of salvation. "Whosoever shall confess me before men, him shall the Son of man also confess before the angels of God: but he that denieth me before men shall be denied before the angels of God," he said (Luke 12:8–9). Of those young in the faith he said, "Take heed that ye despise not one of these little ones; for I say unto you, That in heaven their angels do always behold the face of my Father which is in heaven" (Matthew 18:10). The reapers in the great day of harvest, Christ said, will be angels to whom will be given the charge to separate the tares from the wheat. "The Son of man shall send forth his angels, and they shall gather out of his kingdom all things that offend, and them which do iniquity" (Matthew 13:41). When Christ comes in his glory he has promised to bring all his holy angels with him (Matthew 25:31). Prior to that great day he has promised to "send his angels with a great sound of a trumpet," who shall then "gather together his elect from the four winds, from one end of heaven to the other" (Matthew 24:31). Such is the story that now unfolds before us.

The Angel Moroni Brings Joseph a Message from God
JOSEPH SMITH–HISTORY 1:27–33

JS–H 1:30 *A personage appeared.* Reference is to the angel Moroni, a resurrected being. That is an exalted man, having a body of flesh and bones. His power over the elements and the laws of this earth was the same as that of the resurrected Christ.

The only angels who administer to this earth either did or will live upon it (D&C 130:5). Their appearance is essentially the same as that by which they will be known here (D&C 77:2). The Bible speaks of Abraham, Manoah's wife, and Joshua as mistaking an angel for a man (Genesis 18:1–16; Joshua 5:13–15; Judges 13:6). Describing the angels that guarded the tomb of Christ, Mark says that the women "saw a young man" (16:5), and Luke that "two men stood by them" (24:4).

JS–H 1:33 *My name should be had for good and evil among all nations.* This may well be the most remarkable prophecy of our dispensation. Well might it be asked, "What is the probability that this unknown and uneducated farm boy, destined to eke out a living on the very edge of civilization will be known to both great and small throughout the length and breadth of the earth?" Further, the prophecy states his name will be known for both good and evil; that is, at its very mention there will be those who step forward to testify that he is the great prophet of the Restoration, while others will claim him to be an impostor and a worker of iniquity. It is an eternal verity that the greater the truth the greater the heresy that will stand opposite it. So it is with those called of God to hold the torch of light and truth. The greater the light they hold the louder the prince of darkness and his legions will howl.

When Joseph went the first time to Cumorah to see in person that which he had seen in vision, Moroni again appeared to continue his instruction. Oliver Cowdery, who recorded a detailed account of what transpired, tells us that Moroni promised Joseph a sign by which he could know that the things of which he spoke would come to pass. "This is the sign: When these things begin to be known, that is, when it is known that the Lord has shown you these things, the workers of iniquity will seek your overthrow: they will circulate falsehoods to destroy your reputation, and also will seek to take your life; but remember this, if you are faithful, and shall hereafter continue to keep the commandments of the Lord, you shall be preserved to bring these things forth; for in due time he will again give you a commandment to come and take them. When they are interpreted the Lord will give the holy priesthood to some, and they shall begin to proclaim this gospel and baptize by water, and after that they shall have power to give the Holy Ghost by the laying on of their hands. Then will persecution rage more and more; for the iniquities of men shall be revealed, and those who are not built upon the Rock will seek to overthrow this church; but it will increase the more opposed, and spread farther and farther" (*Messenger and Advocate*, 2:199).

Moroni Informs Joseph of the Gold Plates and the Urim and Thummin
JOSEPH SMITH–HISTORY 1:34-35

JS–H 1:34 *The fulness of the everlasting Gospel was contained in it.* The Book of Mormon contains the fulness of the everlasting gospel (D&C 20:9; 42:12). This is not to say that it contains all gospel truths. The idea that all that we can learn from God can be contained within the covers of a book demeans both God and man. "That which is of God is light; and he that receiveth light, and continueth in God, receiveth more light; and that light groweth brighter and brighter until the perfect day" (D&C

50:24). The Book of Mormon itself vigorously opposes the notion that a book of scripture, or even a collection of scriptural works would be sufficient for salvation. "Wo be unto him that saith: We have received, and we need no more!" wrote Nephi. "Wo be unto him that shall say: We have received the word of God, and we need no more of the word of God, for we have enough! For behold, thus saith the Lord God: I will give unto the children of men line upon line, precept upon precept, here a little and there a little; and blessed are those who hearken unto my precepts, and lend an ear unto my counsel, for they shall learn wisdom; for unto him that receiveth I will give more; and from them that shall say, We have enough, from them shall be taken away even that which they have" (2 Nephi 28:27, 29–30).

In saying that the Book of Mormon contains "the fulness of the gospel," what is meant is that it contains those fundamental truths upon which all saving principles must build. These are the principles one should understand before baptism. To be baptized we need not understand all there is to know about the gospel. We simply need to have laid a foundation of faith and understanding upon which we can continue to build until we have received a fulness of all that the Father has (D&C 93:19–20).

JS–H 1:35 *The Urim and Thummim.* From the Old Testament we learn that the Urim and Thummim was used by priests to receive revelation. Though no clear explanation has been preserved for us we can deduce that this device consisted of ocular objects belonging to the ephod or vestment of the high priest. The Urim and Thummim was carried in the breastplate of judgment, which bore the names of the twelve tribes of Israel on twelve precious stones so as to be on the high priest's heart when he went before the Lord (Exodus 28:15–30; Leviticus 8:8; cf. Ecclesiasticus 45:10; Bible Dictionary, 610). Possession of the Urim and Thummim "was one of the greatest distinctions conferred upon the priestly family" and was connected with the priest's right to stand in the presence of God and to speak in his behalf (*International Standard Bible Encyclopedia*, 4:3040; Exodus 28:30). Through apostasy, the use of the Urim and Thummim was lost to Israel. Thus, as the Jews returned from their Babylonian captivity, when they were faced with a question they could not answer, it was agreed to postpone their decision until there should rise up "a priest with Urim and with Thummim" (Ezra 2:63; Nehemiah 7:65). Hosea described their plight, saying, "For the children of Israel shall abide many days without a king, and without a prince, and without a sacrifice, and without an image, and without an ephod, and without teraphim." Commenting on this verse, one Bible dictionary observed that "it seems natural to infer that the teraphim were, in these instances, the unauthorized substitutes for the Urim" (Smith, *Dictionary of the Bible*, 4:3358).

Given that the Book of Mormon was ordained in the councils of heaven to be the scriptural record to gather Israel to the true Messiah, it seems most appropriate that its translator would do so with the aid of the same type of seeric device by which revelation was given to the twelve tribes anciently. As the spokesman of the Lord was identified by the possession of the Urim and Thummim before the day of Israel's dispersion so he is identified by the possession of the Urim and Thummim in the great day of gathering.

In the Wentworth Letter Joseph Smith said, "With the records was found a curious instrument, which the ancients called 'Urim and Thummim,' which consisted of two transparent stones set in the rim of a bow fastened to a breast plate. Through the medium of the Urim and Thummim I translated the record by the gift and power of God" (*History of the Church*, 4:537). For further information on the breastplate, see commentary on Doctrine and Covenants 17:1, "The breastplate"; on the Urim and Thummim, see commentary on Doctrine and Covenants 9:7–10; 10:1.

Moroni's Discourse on Bible Prophecy
JOSEPH SMITH–HISTORY 1:36–41

JS–H 1:37–41 In this brief account of the appearance of Moroni, Joseph Smith recounts five of the scriptural texts quoted to him by the angel, all of which come from the Bible, four from the Old Testament and one from the New. Thus the Book of Mormon is introduced to Joseph Smith as fulfilling Bible prophecy. The two great doctrinal threads that bind the Book of Mormon together—the promises made to the fathers and the divine sonship of Christ—perfectly reflect the prophecy and teachings of the prophets of the Old World. As one cannot truly understand the message of the Old Testament and reject the New Testament, neither can one truly understand the message of the Bible and reject the message of the Book of Mormon. They are companion volumes and were introduced as such to Joseph Smith by Moroni.

Though Moroni quoted liberally from the Bible in his instruction to

Joseph Smith, it is interesting to note that he did not quote the litany of Bible texts used so often by Latter-day Saint missionaries to prove the Book of Mormon to be true (Ezekiel 37; John 10:16; Revelation 14:6–7). The idea that the Book of Mormon is to be given credence or defended with the use of Bible texts simply did not occur to him. Rather, Moroni centered the youthful prophet's attention on the Lord's promise to gather Israel and restore his Church and kingdom in the last days. "This messenger," Joseph observed, "proclaimed himself to be an angel of God, sent to bring the joyful tidings that the covenant which God made with ancient Israel was at hand to be fulfilled" (Smith, *History of the Church,* 4:536–37). "He then proceeded and gave a general account of the promises made to the fathers, and also gave a history of the aborigines of this country, and said they were literal descendants of Abraham" (*Messenger and Advocate,* 1:80).

JS–H 1:37 *The day cometh that shall burn as an oven.* Sectarian commentaries consistently argue that Malachi's prophecy relative to the return of Elijah found fulfillment in his appearance on the Mount of Transfiguration (Matthew 17:1–3). This, however, was not the day in which the earth burned as an oven and the wicked were left as stubble. That appearance of Elijah was but a precursor of yet another which would take place in our own dispensation. See commentary on Doctrine and Covenants 110:13–14.

For they that come shall burn them. Reference here is to the angels of heaven who will come in the authority of the Lord to separate the wheat from the tares and to burn the latter (Matthew 13:39–41). In a revelation given to Joseph Smith in December 1832, the Lord said: "The angels are crying unto the Lord day and night, who are ready and waiting to be sent forth to reap down the fields; but the Lord saith unto them, pluck not up the tares while the blade is yet tender (for verily your faith is weak), lest you destroy the wheat also. Therefore, let the wheat and the tares grow together until the harvest is fully ripe; then ye shall first gather out the wheat from among the tares, and after the gathering of the wheat, behold and lo, the tares are bound in bundles, and the field remaineth to be burned" (D&C 86:5–7). See commentary on Doctrine and Covenants 86:5.

It shall leave them neither root nor branch. Those who are cut off will be left without family connections. Having rejected that authority restored by Elijah—the sealing power by which families are bound eternally—they

will be left without root (progenitors) or branch (posterity) in the worlds
to come.

JS–H 1:38 *I will reveal unto you the Priesthood.* Moroni is saying not
that the priesthood will be restored by Elijah but rather that its great function and purpose, which centers in the perpetuation of the family unit, will
be revealed through the authority restored by Elijah (D&C 110:13–16).

Before the coming of the great and dreadful day of the Lord. This reference is to the Second Coming, which will be a great day for the righteous
and a dreadful day for the wicked.

JS–H 1:39 *He shall plant in the hearts of the children the promises made
to the fathers.* The fathers spoken of in this text are Abraham, Isaac, and
Jacob. The promise given them was that of the continuation of seed or the
continuation of the family unit (Genesis 12:1–3; 13:16; 15:2–6; 16:2–4;
17:2–7; 21:12–13; 22:18; 24:60; 25:23; 28:1–4). The emphasis of Malachi
centered in the power that rested with those who had received the fulness
of the blessings of the priesthood to labor for and bless their posterity even
after they had departed this life. Moroni, on the other hand, emphasized
the spirit, known to us as the spirit of Elijah, which he prophesied would be
known to the descendants of Abraham as they are gathered in the last
days. It is this spirit that creates within the gathering remnant of Israel the
desire to extend the blessings of the gospel to their progenitors who died
without them. Thus Moroni in his paraphrase of Malachi ties the return
of Elijah to the covenant God made with Abraham.

If it were not so, the whole earth would be utterly wasted at his coming.
Moroni uses the phrase "utterly wasted" relative to the purpose of earth
life rather than "a curse" as used by Malachi. If we do not accomplish the
primary purpose for which we came to mortality, namely the forming of
an eternal family unit, we have wasted our lives on matters that are not
of eternal importance.

JS–H 1:40 *He quoted the eleventh chapter of Isaiah, saying that it was
about to be fulfilled.* This chapter prophetically describes the gathering of
Israel in the last days. It speaks of an ensign or great prophet of the
Restoration who will by birth have right to preside over gathering Israel
and to be both priest and king. This prophet, Isaiah tells us, is to be a
descendant of both Jesse and Ephraim. In quoting this text to Joseph
Smith, Moroni links the youthful prophet with his destiny. See commentary on Doctrine and Covenants 113:1–6.

*He quoted also the third chapter of Acts, twenty-second and twenty-third
verses.* Here Moroni is quoting Peter, who in turn is quoting Moses

(Deuteronomy 18:18–19). In this prophecy of the coming of Christ, Israel was told that the messenger would be a prophet like Moses and that all who failed to accept him would "be destroyed from among the people" (Acts 3:23). Speaking to the Nephites, the resurrected Christ said "that whosoever will not believe in my words, who am Jesus Christ, which the Father shall cause him [Joseph Smith] to bring forth unto the Gentiles, and shall give unto him power that he shall bring them forth unto the Gentiles, (it shall be done even as Moses said) they shall be cut off from among my people who are of the covenant" (3 Nephi 21:11).

The principle involved is that all people must accept Christ as he is revealed to them through the prophet chosen to stand at the head of the dispensation of which they are a part. Moses was the great revelator of Christ for his dispensation. To accept Christ in that day the people had to accept the testimony of Moses. In like manner, God's children could not accept Christ in the meridian dispensation without accepting the testimony of Peter, to whom Christ had given the keys of the kingdom. Thus Christ told the Nephites that in the last days those who would not accept his words as they come through the Book of Mormon (which Joseph Smith would translate) would be cut off from among the people of the covenant. By rejecting Joseph Smith and the authority restored to him, they would not receive the blessings of the temple as promised to the seed of Abraham, Isaac, and Jacob, and would thus be left without root or branch in the worlds to come.

JS–H 1:41 He also quoted the second chapter of Joel, from the twenty-eighth verse to the last. Again the theme is the restoration of the gospel and the gathering of Israel. Joel told us that in the last days those who call on the name of the Lord will find refuge either in Mount Zion, meaning the New Jerusalem (D&C 84:2), or in the Jerusalem of old. Joel spoke also of signs in the heavens and of the Spirit of the Lord being poured out upon all flesh. He said, "Your sons and your daughters shall prophesy, your old men shall dream dreams, your young men shall see visions: and also upon the servants and upon the handmaids in those days will I pour out my spirit" (Joel 2:28–29).

Moroni told Joseph that this text had not yet been fulfilled but that it soon would be. In historical Christianity, Joel's prophecy is almost universally thought to have been fulfilled because Peter quoted it on the day of Pentecost, saying, "This is that which was spoken by the prophet Joel" (Acts 2:16). Though the events of the day of Pentecost constituted an appropriate application of the text, they did not constitute its fulfillment.

Joel spoke of wonders in the heaven, including "blood, and fire, and pillars of smoke" (Joel 2:30). These signs will attend the great and dreadful day of Christ's return. Nor could it be argued that the Saints of Peter's day were able to find deliverance in either Jerusalem or on Mount Zion. Theirs was a day of persecution, not a day of deliverance.

The fulness of the Gentiles was soon to come in. "After the house of Israel should be scattered they should be gathered together again," Lehi explained, "or, in fine, after the Gentiles [scattered Israel in the Gentile nations] had received the fulness of the Gospel, the natural branches of the olive-tree [the Jews], or the remnants of the house of Israel, should be grafted in, or come to the knowledge of the true Messiah, their Lord and their Redeemer" (1 Nephi 10:14).

Explaining this principle to his wayward brothers, Nephi said, "The thing which our father meaneth concerning the grafting in of the natural branches through the fulness of the Gentiles, is, that in the latter days, when our seed shall have dwindled in unbelief, yea, for the space of many years, and many generations after the Messiah shall be manifested in body unto the children of men, then shall the fulness of the gospel of the Messiah come unto the Gentiles, and from the Gentiles unto the remnant of our seed—

"And at that day shall the remnant of our seed know that they are of the house of Israel, and that they are the covenant people of the Lord; and then shall they know and come to the knowledge of their forefathers, and also to the knowledge of the gospel of their Redeemer, which was ministered unto their fathers by him; wherefore, they shall come to the knowledge of their Redeemer and the very points of his doctrine, that they may know how to come unto him and be saved" (1 Nephi 15:13–14). See commentary on Doctrine and Covenants 45:28.

He quoted many other passages of scripture. In letters published in the *Messenger and Advocate* (the Church newspaper published in Kirtland, Ohio, between 1834 and 1837), Oliver Cowdery gave a much more detailed account of the things Moroni taught Joseph Smith. He cited thirty texts from the Old and New Testaments that were a part of Moroni's instructions to the Prophet. Moroni quoted the following texts from the Bible to Joseph Smith during his visits during the night of 21 September 1823 and the next morning: Deuteronomy 32:23–24, 43; Psalms 91:6; 100; 107; 144; 146:10; Isaiah 1:7, 23–24, 25–26; 2:1–4; 4:5–6; 11; 13:10; 24:20; 28:21; 29:11, 13–14; 43:6; 59:20; Jeremiah 16:16, 19; 19:3; 30:18–21; 31:1, 6, 8–9, 27–28, 31–33; 50:5; Joel 2:28–32;

Malachi 3 (part); Malachi 4 (with variation); Matthew 19:30; John 10:27; Acts 3:22–23; Romans 11:25; 1 Corinthians 1:27–29; 1 Thessalonians 4:7 (*Messenger and Advocate*, 1:79–80).

The Second and Third Visits of Moroni
JOSEPH SMITH–HISTORY 1:42–47

JS–H 1:42 No principle is more fundamental to true religion than faith. Salvation simply cannot be found in scholarly debate. For this reason the Lord never intended that the plates from which the Book of Mormon was translated be put on display for the world to argue over their authenticity. The plates are not the issue. At issue—and it is one of eternal import—is the doctrine they teach, the testimony they bear, the prophecy they contain, and the inspiration and direction we receive from them.

If the book in its origin traces to God, the system by which we obtain it must also trace to God. It too must evidence the truth of the book and its message. And so it does. The divinely ordained system to establish the verity of spiritual truth centers in the law of witnesses. Paul stated that principle thus: "In the mouth of two or three witnesses shall every word be established" (2 Corinthians 13:1). Joseph, whose understanding came line upon line as it does to all men, learned of this principle from the plates themselves. From Nephi's rendering of Isaiah 29 the Prophet learned the following:

"Wherefore, at that day when the book shall be delivered unto the man of whom I have spoken, the book shall be hid from the eyes of the world, that the eyes of none shall behold it save it be that three witnesses shall behold it, by the power of God, besides him to whom the book shall be delivered; and they shall testify to the truth of the book and the things therein. And there is none other which shall view it, save it be a few according to the will of God, to bear testimony of his word unto the children of men; for the Lord God hath said that the words of the faithful should speak as if it were from the dead. Wherefore, the Lord God will proceed to bring forth the words of the book; and in the mouth of as many witnesses as seemeth him good will he establish his word; and wo be unto him that rejecteth the word of God!" (2 Nephi 27:12–14).

Restating this same principle, Moroni directed himself to the translator of the plates, saying: "Ye may be privileged that ye may show the plates unto those who shall assist to bring forth this work; and unto three shall they be shown by the power of God; wherefore they shall know of a surety that these things are true. And in the mouth of three witnesses shall these things be established; and the testimony of three, and this work, in the which shall be shown forth the power of God and also his word, of which the Father, and the Son, and the Holy Ghost bear record—and all this shall stand as a testimony against the world at the last day" (Ether 5:2–4).

JS–H 1:42–47 It is significant that Moroni came three times on the night of 21 September 1823 to deliver the same message. Peter's dream of the clean and unclean animals, which preceded the extending of the blessings of the gospel to the Gentiles, was also repeated three times (Acts 10:16). In the Old Testament we read that the youthful Samuel did not understand the voice of the Lord until he heard it the third time (1 Samuel 3:8). This was also the case with the Nephites when the voice of the Father spoke from the heavens to introduce his Son (3 Nephi 11:5). Similarly, during the imprisonment of Helaman's sons, Nephi and Lehi, a heavenly voice was heard three times commanding men to repent (Helaman 5:30–33).

The Fourth Visit of Moroni
JOSEPH SMITH–HISTORY 1:48–50

JS–H 1:48 *I found my strength so exhausted.* This was not simply the result of lack of sleep. It is a physically exhausting experience for those of a temporal nature to be brought into the presence of God or angels. See commentary on Joseph Smith–History 1:20, page 15; Doctrine and Covenants 76.

JS–H 1:50 *He replied to me that it was of God.* Joseph Smith Sr. was the first in this dispensation to hear and believe the testimony of his son. Being a visionary man himself, he had no difficulty believing that visions could be shared by those enjoying the purity of youth. His wife, Lucy Mack Smith, recorded seven dreams or visions her husband received prior to the restoration of the gospel (Smith, *History of Joseph Smith*, 1996, 62–67).

Joseph Visits the Hill Cumorah
JOSEPH SMITH–HISTORY 1:51–54

JS–H 1:53 Oliver Cowdery gave us a description of a very important lesson taught to the youthful prophet. When Joseph first attempted to take possession of the record, "a shock was produced upon his system, by an invisible power which deprived him, in a measure, of his natural strength. He desisted for an instant, and then made another attempt, but was more sensibly shocked than before. What was the occasion of this he knew not—there was the pure unsullied record, as had been described—he had heard of the power of enchantment, and a thousand like stories, which held the hidden treasures of the earth, and supposed that physical exertion and personal strength was only necessary to enable him to yet obtain the object of his wish. He therefore made the third attempt with an increased exertion, when his strength failed him more than at either of the former times, and without premeditating he exclaimed, 'Why can I not obtain this book?' 'Because you have not kept the commandments of the Lord,' answered a voice, within a seeming short distance. He looked, and to his astonishment, there stood the angel who had previously given him the directions concerning this matter. In an instant, all the former instructions, the great intelligence concerning Israel and the last days, were brought to his mind: he thought of the time when his heart was fervently engaged in prayer to the Lord, when his spirit was contrite, and when his holy messenger from the skies unfolded the wonderful things connected with this record. He had come, to be sure, and found the word of the angel fulfilled concerning the reality of the record, but he had failed to remember the great end for which they had been kept, and in consequence could not have power to take them into his possession and bear them away.

"At that instant he looked to the Lord in prayer, and as he prayed darkness began to disperse from his mind and his soul was lit up as it was the evening before, and he was filled with the Holy Spirit; and again did the Lord manifest his condescension and mercy: the heavens were opened and the glory of the Lord shone round about and rested upon him. While he thus stood gazing and admiring, the angel said, 'Look!' and as he thus spake he beheld the prince of darkness, surrounded by his innumerable train of associates. All this passed before him, and the heavenly messenger said, 'All this is shown, the good and the evil, the holy and impure, the glory of God and the power of darkness, that you may know hereafter the two powers and never be influenced or overcome by that wicked one. Behold, whatever entices and leads to good and to do good, is of God, and whatever does not is of that wicked one: It is he that fills the hearts of men with evil, to walk in darkness and blaspheme God; and you may learn from henceforth, that his ways are to destruction, but the way of holiness is peace and rest. You now see why you could not obtain this record; that the commandment was strict, and that if ever these sacred things are obtained they must be by prayer and faithfulness in obeying the Lord. They are not deposited here for the sake of accumulating gain and wealth for the glory of this world: they were sealed by the prayer of faith, and because of the knowledge which they contain they are of no worth among the children of men, only for their knowledge. On them is contained the fulness of the gospel of Jesus Christ, as it was given to his people on this land, and when it shall be brought forth by the power of God it shall be carried to the Gentiles, of whom many will receive it, and after will the seed of Israel be brought into the fold of their Redeemer by obeying it also. Those who kept the commandments of the Lord on this land, desired this at his hand, and through the prayer of faith obtained the promise, that if their descendants should transgress and fall away, that a record might be kept and in the last days come to their children. These things are sacred, and must be kept so, for the promise of the Lord concerning them, must be fulfilled. No man can obtain them if his heart is impure, because they contain that which is sacred; and besides, should they be entrusted in unholy hands the knowledge could not come to the world, because they cannot be interpreted by the learning of this generation; consequently, they would be considered of no worth, only as precious metal. Therefore, remember, that they are to be translated by the gift and power of God'" (*Messenger and Advocate*, 2:197–98; *Times and Seasons*, 2:393).

General Commentary

We cannot share the faith of those about whom we read in holy writ without a belief in the ministry of angels. Nor can we profess to be the possessors of a restored gospel without also professing the same faith shown by Saints of former days. As they professed the ministry of angels in a world that was often incredulous, so must we. Indeed, the apostle Paul taught that all who are heirs of salvation must have angels minister unto them (Hebrews 1:14). In our day belief in angels who appear in bodily form and who teach and testify of Christ and the saving principles of his gospel, including the bestowal of authority, is virtually unheard of. Yet even in those instances in which others profess to have shared the companionship of angels, none introduced their angels to others as did Joseph Smith. It is profoundly significant that Joseph's testimony relative to the appearance of Moroni is collaborated by three witnesses: Oliver Cowdery, Martin

Harris, and David Whitmer, each of whom testified to having stood in the presence of Moroni, seen the plates, and heard the voice of God testify to the truthfulness of the book. Such a testimony cannot be discarded lightly. Indeed, we set it aside only at the peril of our eternal life.

JOSEPH SMITH–HISTORY 1:55–65

DATE: 19 NOVEMBER 1823–FEBRUARY 1829
PLACE: MANCHESTER, NEW YORK; HARMONY, PENNSYLVANIA;
SOUTH BAINBRIDGE, NEW YORK; NEW YORK CITY, NEW YORK

The Death of Alvin; Joseph's Marriage to Emma Hale
JOSEPH SMITH–HISTORY 1:55–58

JS–H 1:56 *My father's family met with a great affliction by the death of my eldest brother, Alvin.* "He was a very handsome man," wrote the Prophet, "surpassed by none but Adam and Seth, and of great strength" (Smith, *History of the Church,* 5:246). While in Nauvoo, Joseph reflected on Alvin's death: "I remember well the pangs of sorrow that swelled my youthful bosom and almost burst my tender heart when he died. He was the oldest and the noblest of my father's family. He was one of the noblest of the sons of men. Shall his name not be recorded in this book? Yes, Alvin, let it be had here and be handed down upon these sacred pages for ever and ever. In him there was no guile. He lived without spot from the time he was a child. From the time of his birth he never knew mirth. He was candid and sober and never would play; and minded his father and mother in toiling all day. He was one of the soberest of men, and when he died the angel of the Lord visited him in his last moments" (Smith, *History of the Church,* 5:126–27).

Lucy Mack Smith recorded the particulars concerning the death of her eldest son: "On the fifteenth of November, 1823, about ten o'clock in the morning, Alvin was taken very sick with the bilious colic. He came to the house in great distress and requested his father to go immediately for a physician, which he accordingly did. But the doctor who generally attended upon our family being absent, Mr. Smith was compelled to go further than he expected. However, he found in the next village one Dr. Greenwood, who, when he came, immediately administered a heavy dose of calomel to the patient, although he objected much against it. [Calomel was a mixture of mercury-oxide and arsenic. It was administered in a clay-like substance formed into bars. Pieces were broken from these bars to be ingested by the afflicted individual.]

"This calomel lodged in his stomach, and all the powerful medicine which was afterwards prescribed by skillful physicians could not remove it.

"On the third day of his sickness, Dr. McIntyre, the favorite of the family and a man of great skill and experience, was brought and with him four other professors of medicine. But all their exertions were of no avail, just as Alvin had declared would be the case. He said, 'The calomel is still lodged in the same place and you cannot move it. Consequently, it must take my life'" (*History of Joseph Smith*, 1996, 115).

Before his death, Alvin spoke to each of his brothers and sisters separately. Lucy Mack Smith recorded that he admonished his brother Joseph: "'I am going to die now. The distress which I suffer and the sensations that I have tell me my time is very short. I want you to be a good boy and do everything that lies in your power to obtain the record. Be faithful in receiving instruction and in keeping every commandment that is given you. Your brother Alvin must now leave you, but remember the example which he has set for you, and set a good example for the children that are younger than you. Always be kind to Father and Mother.'

"He then asked me to take his little sister Lucy up and bring her to him, for he wished to see her. This child was the youngest of the family, and he was extremely fond of her and was in the habit of taking her up and caressing her, which naturally attached her to him. She could not then talk plainly, and always called her brother 'Amby.' I went to her and said, 'Lucy, Amby wants to see you.' At this she started out of her sleep and screamed out, 'Oh, Amby, Amby.' We took her to him, and she sprang from my arms and caught him round the neck and cried out, 'Oh, my Amby,' and kissed him again and again.

"To Lucy he said, 'You must be the best girl in the world and take care of Mother. You can't have your Amby anymore. Amby is going away; he must leave little Lucy.' He then kissed her and said, 'Take her away. I think my breath offends her.' We took hold of the child, but she clenched hold of him with such a desperate grasp that it was very difficult to disengage her hands.

"As I turned with the child, Alvin said, 'Father, Mother, brothers, sisters, farewell! I can now breathe out my life as calmly as a clock,' and immediately closed his eyes in death.

"The child still cried to go back to Alvin. One present said to her,

'Alvin is gone. An angel has taken his spirit to heaven.' When the babe heard this, she renewed her cries, and as I bent over his corpse with her in my arms, she again threw her arms around him and kissed him repeatedly, screaming as before. And until the body was taken from the house, she continued constantly crying and showing such manifestation of affection mingled with terror at the scene before her as is seldom witnessed in a child.

"This harrowed up our feelings almost to distraction, for Alvin was a youth of singular goodness of disposition—kind and amiable manners, so much so that lamentation and mourning filled the whole neighborhood where we lived, and, of course, more than usual grief filled the hearts of those from whose immediate circle he was taken, those who felt and saw the effects of his nobleness and generosity every hour of his existence.

"It was the wish of the principal physician that Alvin's body should be cut open to ascertain, if possible, the cause of his disease and death. When this was done, they found the calomel still lodged in the upper bowels, untouched by anything which he had taken to carry it off. It was as near in its natural state as it could be, surrounded as it was with gangrene.

"Dr. McIntyre and Dr. Robinson performed the operation. The last named doctor was seventy years of age. He spoke long and earnestly to the younger physicians upon the danger of administering powerful medicine without the thorough knowledge of the practice of physic. 'Here,' he said 'is one of the loveliest youth that ever trod the streets of Palmyra destroyed, murdered as it were, by him at whose hand relief was expected, cast off from the face of the earth by a careless quack who even dared to trifle with the life of a fellow mortal.'

"When the time for interment arrived, the inhabitants of the surrounding country gathered together, and during the funeral obsequies they gave the most affectionate manifestations of their sympathy; but there was one that felt our grief more deeply than the rest—a lovely young woman who was engaged to be married to my son. The disconsolate girl was rendered most desolate by his unexpected death, and as long as we knew her, she never recovered her wonted animation and good spirits.

"Thus was our happiness blasted in a moment. When we least expected the blow, it came upon us. The poisoned shaft entered our very hearts' core and diffused to deadly effect throughout our veins. We were for a time almost swallowed up in grief, so much so that it seemed impossible for us to interest ourselves at all about the concerns of life. The feeling of every heart was to make speedy preparation to follow him who had been too much the idol of our hearts. And then if it pleased God to take us also, we would receive the call as a favor at his hands from whom it came.

"Alvin had ever manifested a greater zeal and anxiety, if it were possible, than any of the rest with regard to the record which had been shown to Joseph, and he always showed the most intense interest concerning the matter. With this before our minds, we could not endure to hear or say one word upon that subject, for the moment that Joseph spoke of the record it would immediately bring Alvin to our minds with all his kindness, his affection, his zeal, and piety. And when we looked to his place and realized that he was gone from it, to return no more in this life, we all wept with one accord over our irretrievable loss, and we could 'not be comforted, because he was not'" (Smith, *History of Joseph Smith*, 1996, 116–19). See commentary on Doctrine and Covenants 137:6, "And marveled how it was that he had obtained an inheritance in that kingdom."

JS–H 1:57–58 Lucy Mack Smith recorded that before he left for Pennsylvania, "Joseph called my husband and myself aside and said, 'I have been very lonely ever since Alvin died and I have concluded to get married, and if you have no objections to my uniting myself in marriage with Miss Emma Hale, she would be my choice in preference to any other woman I have ever seen.' We were pleased with his choice and not only consented to his marrying her, but requested him to bring her home with him and live with us" (*History of Joseph Smith*, 1996, 126).

Regarding the circumstances surrounding her marriage, Emma later related her perspective to her eldest son: "I had no intention of marrying when I left home; but during my visit at Mr. Stowell's, your father visited me there. My folks were bitterly opposed to him; and being importuned by your father, aided by Mr. Stowell, who urged me to marry him, and preferring to marry him to any other man I knew, I consented" (quoted in Bushman, *Joseph Smith*, 77).

Joseph Smith Receives the Gold Plates
JOSEPH SMITH–HISTORY 1:59–62

JS–H 1:59 *I should be responsible for them.* "When Joseph first took the plates into his hands, the angel of the Lord stood by and said:

"'Now you have got the record into your own hands, and you are but a man, therefore you will have to be watchful and faithful to your trust,

or you will be overpowered by wicked men, for they will lay every plan
and scheme that is possible to get them away from you. And if you do not
take heed continually, they will succeed. While they were in my hands I
could keep them, and no man had power to take them away, but now I
give them up to you. Beware, and look well to your ways, and you shall
have power to retain them until the time for them to be translated'"
(Smith, *History of Joseph Smith*, 1996, 145). See commentary on Doctrine
and Covenants 3:5.

JS–H 1:59 *If I would use all my endeavors to preserve them.* The
Prophet Joseph Smith had to actively protect the plates from the moment
he received them. He was creative in his choice of hiding places, and in
many instances he depended on inspiration from God to fulfill his responsibility. Lucy Mack Smith recorded that Joseph first hid the plates in a
hollow birch log. When he later returned to retrieve them, "Joseph took
the plates from their place and, wrapping them in his linen frock, put
them under his arm and started for the house. After walking a short distance in the road, he thought it would be safer to go across through the
woods. Traveling some distance after he left the road, he came to a large
windfall, and as he was jumping over a log, a man sprang up from behind
and gave him a heavy blow with a gun. Joseph turned around and
knocked him to the ground, and then ran at the top of his speed. About
half a mile further, he was attacked again in precisely the same way. He
soon brought this one down also and ran on again, but before he got
home, he was accosted the third time with a severe stroke with a gun.
When he struck the last one, he dislocated his thumb, which, however,
he did not notice till he came in sight of the house. He threw himself
down in the corner of the fence to recover his breath. As soon as he was
able, he rose and finished his race for the house, where he arrived altogether speechless from fright and exhaustion" (Smith, *History of Joseph
Smith*, 1996, 144).

After Joseph arrived home, the plates were placed in a chest and
secreted under a hearthstone in the Smith home. Later, Joseph hid the
plates in the Smiths' cooper shop across the street from the house. During
his and Emma's removal to Harmony, Pennsylvania, he hid them in barrel
of beans. One may wonder what those who sought the plates would have
done had they ever obtained them and whether their only purpose was to
obtain them for the gold of which they were made. Regardless, these
people were determined to destroy the work of God. Mormon wrote:
"Having been commanded of the Lord that I should not suffer the records

which had been handed down by our fathers, which were sacred, to fall into the hands of the Lamanites, (for the Lamanites would destroy them) therefore I . . . hid up in the hill Cumorah all the records which had been entrusted to me by the hand of the Lord" (Mormon 6:6).

JS–H 1:60 *By the wisdom of God, they remained safe in my hands.* "Joseph kept the Urim and Thummim constantly about his person, by the use of which he could in a moment tell whether the plates were in any danger" (Smith, *History of Joseph Smith*, 1996, 142).

Fulfillment of Isaiah's Prophecy
JOSEPH SMITH–HISTORY 1:63–65

JS–H 1:65 *Part of the plates were sealed.* Although various individuals have made estimates, it is not known exactly what portion of the plates was sealed. The sealed portion of the Book of Mormon contains a revelation given to the brother of Jared at the time the premortal Savior appeared to him on top of the mount Shelem. Moroni explained that "the Lord . . . showed unto the brother of Jared all of the inhabitants of the earth which had been, and also all that would be; and he withheld them not from his sight, even unto the ends of the earth" (Ether 3:25). The sealed part of the record is "a revelation from God, from the beginning of the world to the ending thereof" (2 Nephi 27:7).

Although it is true that "there never were greater things made manifest than those which were made manifest unto the brother of Jared" (Ether 4:4), it is also true that others were shown things equally great. Such noble souls as Adam, Enoch, Abraham, Moses, Nephi, John the Revelator, the Prophet Joseph Smith, and others were given views of things from the foundation of the world to the eternities. Elder Bruce R. McConkie expounded on the scriptural description of those things contained in the sealed part of the plates, indicating that "an account of life in preexistence; of the creation of all things; of the Fall and the Atonement and the Second Coming; of temple ordinances in their fulness; of the ministry and mission of translated beings; of life in the spirit world, in both paradise and hell; of the kingdoms of glory to be inhabited by resurrected beings, and many such things" must surely be recorded thereon (*Sermons and Writings*, 277).

Moroni wrote "the very things which the brother of Jared saw" (Ether 4:4), after which he sealed up his writings, along with the interpreters, according to the command of the Lord. This part of the record will come forth during the Millennium, for "the things which are sealed shall not be delivered in the day of the wickedness and abominations of the people" (2 Nephi 27:8).

I cannot read a sealed book. The words of Dr. Charles Anthon fulfill the prophecy as recorded in Isaiah 29:11 that "the vision of all is become unto you as the words of a book that is sealed, which men deliver to one that is learned, saying, Read this, I pray thee: and he saith, I cannot; for it is sealed."

Oliver Cowdery related that during Moroni's visits to Joseph on the night of 21 September 1823, the heavenly messenger referred to Isaiah's words and explained the importance of their fulfillment in the work of the Restoration. "'Yet,' said he [Moroni], 'the scripture must be fulfilled before it is translated, which says that the words of a book, which were sealed, were presented to the learned; for thus has God determined to leave men without excuse, and show to the meek that his arm is not shortened that it cannot save'" (*Messenger and Advocate*, 1:80).

DOCTRINE AND COVENANTS 1

DATE: 1 NOVEMBER 1831
PLACE: HIRAM, OHIO

Our dispensation began in the spring of 1820 with the First Vision. In this marvelous theophany, the Father, of whom Jesus of Nazareth testified and whom he worshipped, appeared to the youthful Joseph Smith. He did so to assert anew that this same Jesus, who also appeared in this vision, was both his Son and the source of our salvation. In response to Joseph's question about which church he should join, he was told, "None of them, for they are all wrong." Thereafter, Joseph Smith learned of an apostasy both in doctrine and authority that followed the death of Christ and his apostles. He also learned that he had been chosen to act as the agent of the Lord in the restoration of gospel truth and of priesthood authority by which the ordinances of salvation were to be preformed. As stones are quarried and set side by side in the building of a great temple, so revelations were granted to Joseph Smith one upon another as the great labor began to establish the mountain of the Lord's house upon the earth. By the time the Prophet received Doctrine and Covenants 1, he had recorded more than sixty revelations. The time had now come to bind them in a single volume so that their testimony might go forth to every nation, kindred, tongue, and people, declaring the beginning of the great and final dispensation of the gospel.

The matter of selecting revelations for publication was considered at a special council of high priests held in Hiram, Ohio, beginning 1 November 1831. This revelation, which affirmed the Lord's interest in the matter, was received between the sessions held that day. William Kelley, who was present, records the circumstances in which the revelation was received: "A committee had been appointed to draft a preface, consisting of O. Cowdery and, I think Sidney Rigdon, but when they made their report . . . the conference then requested Joseph to enquire of the Lord about it, and he said that he would if the people would bow in prayer with him. This they did and Joseph prayed.

"When they arose, Joseph dictated by the Spirit the preface found in the Book of Doctrine and Covenants while sitting by a window of the room in which the conference was sitting; and Sidney Rigdon wrote it down. Joseph would deliver a few sentences and Sidney would write them down, then read them aloud, and if correct, then Joseph would proceed and deliver more, and by this process the preface was given" (William Kelley, quoted in Backman, *Joseph Smith and the Doctrine and Covenants*, 2).

After Joseph received this revelation, a number of the brethren present at the conference arose and testified to the truthfulness of the Book of Commandments. Notwithstanding this, some of the brethren criticized the language in which the revelations were recorded. The Prophet did not take any notice of these critics; if the Lord should select some other instrument through whom to speak to the Church, it would be agreeable to him. But the Lord had no such intentions. A test was then given by way of revelation by which the Prophet's critics could test the legitimacy of his revelations (D&C 67).

It should be noted that the language of Doctrine and Covenants 1 and the previous revelations received by Joseph Smith (including the Book of Mormon) established the pattern for the revelations of this dispensation. Since the events they announce had long been prophesied in the Bible, and since the King James Bible was the Bible of the American frontier, where the Restoration took place, it was natural that the revelations be recorded in that language or style. In contrast to the colloquial or informal language of some modern translations, the King James Bible preserves a sense of reverence and dignity for the sacred with a choice of words that carry the feeling of Sunday go-to-meeting best dress.

The revelations in the Doctrine and Covenants repeatedly pick up phrases in the language of the King James translators in such a manner as to announce their fulfillment or to provide a significant commentary on them. Reading these phrases affirms our faith in the Bible, the Lord's approval of the labor of the King James translators, our unity with prophets of old, and the restoration of the faith of the ancients.

A host of Bible translations following the King James Version have announced themselves to be superior to it. After all, the modern translator has a thousandfold more ancient manuscripts to work with than the translators did in the days of King James, and many of these manuscripts are older and thus more reliable. It is also held that today's translator has a greater command of the ancient languages than those at the time of King James. Further, it is argued that in the interim period the language of the King James translators has in many instances become archaic. Despite such arguments, the Church retains loyalty to the Bible of Joseph Smith's day. In so doing we are not attempting to be another quaint sect that refuses to move forward with the times. We freely acknowledge the difficulties that exist in the Bible and are used to being criticized for having made that admission. However, what we retain from our loyalty to the King James Bible far outweighs what we might gain from more modern translations. We continue to use this "archaic" version for two primary reasons: first, because of the near countless instances in which the revelations of the Restoration pick up the language of the Bible of Joseph Smith's day, announcing its fulfillment or amplifying it by the Spirit of revelation; and second, because it was the King James Version of the Bible that Joseph Smith used to give us what is known as the "Inspired Version," or "The Joseph Smith Translation." This text adds immeasurably to our understanding of the gospel as it was known to those of both Old and New Testament times. At the same time, we have no hesitation in using any Bible translation that adds to our understanding.

Of particular importance is the understanding that ours is a restored Church and as such binds us in faith and practice to the peoples of the Bible. Indeed, we are the true old-time religion; we have no principles save they are eternal. We seek with great interest a knowledge and understanding of the ancient Saints and their faith and practices. Just as they called forth the revelations of heaven, worked miracles, entertained angels, and stood in the divine presence, we seek to do the same, standing where they stood and believing what they believed. It is through our faith that we will find salvation even as they found it. It follows that we cannot truly be students of the Doctrine and Covenants without also being students of the Old and New Testaments. In the Doctrine and Covenants many of the words of the prophets find fulfillment. As the New Testament is replete with prophecy from the Old Testament, is rendered in the language of the Old Testament, and stands in fulfillment of the Old Testament, so the revelations of the Doctrine and Covenants stand in relationship to the Bible. These revelations witness that the Bible is true and that all that has been spoken by God's prophets will find fulfillment.

The Voice of Warning to All People
DOCTRINE AND COVENANTS 1:1–7

1:1 *Hearken ye people from afar; and ye that are upon the islands of the sea, listen together.* The announcement that all are to listen to the voice of the servant of the Lord comes from the words of Isaiah as he propheti-cally described the latter-day gathering of Israel (Isaiah 49:1). Implicit in the text is the promise that the Lord will speak to the scattered remnants of Israel through a prophet just as he spoke to their fathers anciently through prophets. It is a perfect text to introduce the revelations of the Restoration and to show that they come in fulfillment of the words of the ancient prophets.

The text has a rich heritage. It can be and properly has been applied to the ministry of Christ. The early American colonials thought it a prophecy of their destiny. In their Bible it read, "Listen unto me ye Isles [or coastlands]." They applied this to their coming to this land and thought of themselves as those the Lord had gathered to build a New Jerusalem. As Nephi rendered it to his people: "Hearken, O ye house of Israel, all ye that are broken off and are driven out because of the wicked-ness of the pastors of my people; yea, all ye that are broken off, that are scattered abroad, who are of my people, O house of Israel. Listen, O isles, unto me, and hearken ye people from far" (1 Nephi 21:1). His language fits perfectly these refugees from the religious wars of Europe.

In the present text the Lord applies the words of Isaiah first to those of his church and then to the ends of the earth that will listen. In its first line this revelation links the announcement of the Restoration with Isaiah's prophecy of this event. The Isaiah text then goes on to describe a prophet known by name and ordained before he was in his mother's womb. This, of course, fits the Prophet Joseph Smith perfectly (2 Nephi 3:15; Smith, *Teachings of the Prophet Joseph Smith*, 365). Jesus of Nazareth and the nation of Israel also fulfill this prophecy.

1:2 *The voice of the Lord is unto all men.* "The voice of warning shall be unto all people" (v. 4). That is to say, this revelation and the entire compilation of revelations in the Doctrine and Covenants were intended to go to the world. The Doctrine and Covenants is to be used in mission-ary work! While it is true that the Book of Mormon is the book ordained in the councils of heaven to gather Israel, it is equally true that it was not intended that the Book of Mormon stand alone. The Book of Mormon would be of no benefit to the nations of the earth unless someone were ordained and given authority to preach the gospel and administer its ordi-nances. Thus the compilation of revelations in the Doctrine and Covenants assume a place of eminence among the revelations of the Restoration. The Doctrine and Covenants provides the framework for the Restoration. This compilation of revelations announces that the heavens have been opened and that God speaks to prophets today as he did anciently. It is here that we learn that the priesthood or authority to act in the name of God has been restored. In these revelations we learn of "the only true and living church upon the face of the whole earth" (D&C 1:30) being reestablished. We learn that the authority to baptize has been given again to the children of men as have all other ordinances necessary for their salvation.

1:3 *The rebellious.* No neutrality exists where the gospel of Jesus Christ is concerned. We sustain it, embrace it, and live it, or we stand in opposition to it. There is no middle ground. We number ourselves among the citizens of the kingdom of God, or we must march with those who are in rebellion against that kingdom.

1:4 *The voice of warning.* The voice of warning that is to go forth to all people cannot in the justice of God be confined to the writings of prophets who lived thousands of years ago. The promise of this text is that it will go forth by the mouth of those whom the Lord has chosen in our day. "It is only just," wrote Joseph Fielding Smith, "that the Lord would speak again from the heavens, before that great day shall come, and commission his servants and send them forth to proclaim repentance and once again say to the people, 'The kingdom of heaven is at hand.' Surely, the Lord would not depend entirely upon the predictions of his ancient prophets for this warning of his second coming. True it is, that the warnings given of old are to be heeded, but near the approach of these great events, it is right, and reason compels us to believe, that the Lord would again raise his voice through his appointed servants in a warning that the people might know that this great and dreadful day is even now at our doors" (*Restoration of All Things,* 302–3).

1:4 *By the mouths of my disciples.* It is commonly thought that the prophecies announcing that the gospel will be taught to those of every nation, kindred, tongue, and people can somehow be filled through radio, television, computers, or other forms of mass communication. This, however, cannot be the case. Only an ordained servant of the Lord can receive a confession of sins, baptize, and confer the gift of the Holy Ghost. Though the mass media can greatly help in the teaching of the gospel, it will never replace the need for missionaries to find, love, teach, and nurture those who are seeking the blessings of the gospel.

1:5 *None shall stay them.* No power can prevent the gospel from going forth. It is destined to be taught to those of every nation, kindred, and tongue. "The Standard of Truth," Joseph Smith said, "has been erected;

no unhallowed hand can stop the work from progressing; persecutions may rage, mobs may combine, armies may assemble, calumny may defame, but the truth of God will go forth boldly, nobly, and independent, till it has penetrated every continent, visited every clime, swept every country, and sounded in every ear, till the purposes of God shall be accomplished, and the Great Jehovah shall say the work is done" (*History of the Church*, 4:540).

1:6 *My preface unto the book of my commandments.* The revelations received by the Prophet Joseph Smith were first gathered and prepared for publication under the title the Book of Commandments. This revelation, recorded in section 1, was given as the preface to that compilation. Apparently, a committee had been appointed to write a preface but was unable to do so to the satisfaction of the conference. As noted in the introduction to this section, the Prophet was then requested to inquire of the Lord. He did so, and this revelation was the result. Hence we find the Lord saying this is "my preface" to the Book of Commandments.

"The publication was commenced by William W. Phelps and Co. in Jackson County, Missouri, but before the work was completed the press and type were destroyed by a mob, July 20, 1833, and only a few of the printed forms were preserved; these were bound and used by those fortunate enough to secure them in the uncompleted condition as the *Book of Commandments*. Later, in the year 1835, the revelations, now greatly increased in number, were again compiled and ordered printed as *The Doctrine and Covenants*" (*Teachings of the Prophet Joseph Smith*, 7n).

Wickedness Precedes the Second Coming
DOCTRINE AND COVENANTS 1:8–16

1:8 *Power given to seal.* Anciently, a seal was a hard substance formed into a particular emblem used to make an impression on wax or clay. Often a seal would be set in a signet ring and used like a signature to convey authority or to assure authenticity of a document. Figuratively, as used in a text such as this, it signifies the right of possession. Thus Alma speaking of the unrepentant says the devil "doth seal you his" (Alma 34:35), whereas the Lord told Joseph Smith that the faithful "are sealed by the Holy Spirit of promise, which the Father sheds forth upon all those who are just and true" (D&C 76:53). See commentary on Doctrine and Covenants 76:53, "Sealed by the Holy Spirit of promise."

It is not uncommon for Latter-day Saints to be asked by Protestants,

"Have you been saved?" A more proper expression on their part would be, "Have you been sealed?" That is, has the Holy Ghost placed the seal of his approval on your life and works? In the complete and proper sense, no one is saved in mortality. We seek to be saved from the effects of Adam's fall, which has estranged us from God. Only when we—through the atonement of Christ—have overcome death and sin are we saved, or fully reconciled to him. Thus to be saved is to obtain eternal life and live in the presence of God. We can, however, enjoy the assurance of heaven that the Lord approves of the course we are following as we work out our salvation in this mortal estate.

The unbelieving and rebellious. The priesthood has power over both the righteous and the wicked. By its authority the righteous are blessed and the wicked cursed. Blessings are the God-given reward for obedience; cursings are the God-given penalty for disobedience. To accept the gospel is to be blessed; to reject it is to be cursed. To receive the servants of the Lord is to receive their reward (Matthew 10:40–41). Those who reject the servants of the Lord have the promise that they will be "sealed up" according to the law and the testimony and be "delivered over unto darkness" (D&C 133:71–72). From him who does not repent, the Lord said, "shall be taken even the light which he has received" (D&C 1:33), and he shall be left to suffer the effects of darkness until the day of his redemption. "These are they who shall not be redeemed from the devil until the last resurrection" (D&C 76:85).

As the sealing of someone to eternal life requires both priesthood and keys, so does the sealing of one to the wrath of God. Today such authority is held only by the First Presidency and the Quorum of the Twelve and any to whom they specifically give it. It is not held by missionaries generally.

1:10 The Lord shall come to recompense unto every man according to his work. The scriptures repeatedly attest that judgment will be by works not by the profession of faith (Matthew 5:16; John 3:21; 8:39; Acts 10:35; Revelation 3:15–16; 20:12–13). "By their fruits ye shall know them," the Savior said. "Not every one that saith unto me, Lord, Lord, shall enter into the kingdom of heaven; but he that doeth the will of my Father which is in heaven." Then, of those who do not endure in faith to the end, he said, "Many will say to me in that day, Lord, Lord, have we not prophesied in thy name? and in thy name have cast out devils? and in thy name done many wonderful works? And then will I profess unto them, I never knew you: depart from me, ye that work iniquity" (Matthew 7:20–23).

Our devotion to the gospel cause is found in the way we choose to live. To believe a principle is to live the principle. James taught the doctrine well when he said, "For as the body without the spirit is dead, so faith without works is dead also" (James 2:26). We do not expect rewards for faith we have not exercised, answers to prayers we have not offered, strength in muscles we have not used, or talents we have not cultivated. We do not expect to harvest where we have not planted, understand books we have not read, hear that to which we will not listen, or see that to which we will not open our eyes. Indeed we believe that "there is a law, irrevocably decreed in heaven before the foundations of this world, upon which all blessings are predicated—and when we obtain any blessing from God, it is by obedience to that law upon which it is predicated" (D&C 130:20–21).

1:11 *That all that will hear may hear.* Contrary to the idea that some are born to heaven and others to hell, the announcement of heaven is that the gospel of Christ is "unto all men" (Joseph Smith–Matthew 1:46). No soul will be brought to judgment without having had the full chance to accept the saving truths of the gospel of Jesus Christ. All are entitled to hear the gospel declared, for all are capable of embracing it and receiving the fulness of its blessings. Were this not so we could not argue in behalf of the justice of heaven or the infinite nature of Christ's atonement.

1:12 *Prepare ye for that which is to come.* See commentary on Doctrine and Covenants 34:5–9; 65:1, 3.

1:13 *His sword is bathed in heaven.* This phrase comes from Isaiah. The full text reads: "For my sword shall be bathed in heaven: behold, it shall come down upon Idumea, and upon the people of my curse, to judgment" (Isaiah 34:5). Idumea is the symbol of the world, meaning the people of the world (D&C 36), all of whom have been cursed by their rejection of the gospel. Raising the warning voice, Isaiah announced that the Second Coming will be a day of vengeance and judgment, a day in which the indignation of the Lord shall come upon all nations and his fury upon their armies. In that day all that is worldly is destined to be destroyed (Isaiah 34:1–10).

1:14 Salvation can only be found by following a living voice and the direction of scripture as given to those of each dispensation. Those of our day cannot find salvation in the Bible while rejecting the revelations of the Restoration any more than those of Christ's day could find it in rejecting him and following the law of Moses. The true gospel always requires living ministers to perform its ordinances and living prophets to teach its truths. See commentary on verse 30.

The arm of the Lord shall be revealed. Again, the imagery is that of Isaiah. The ancient prophet promised that the Lord would make "bare his holy arm in the eyes of all the nations" (Isaiah 52:10). Commenting on this passage, Nephi said, "The Lord God will proceed to make bare his arm in the eyes of all the nations, in bringing about his covenants and his gospel unto those who are of the house of Israel. Wherefore, he will bring them again out of captivity, and they shall be gathered together to the lands of their inheritance; and they shall be brought out of obscurity and out of darkness; and they shall know that the Lord is their Savior and their Redeemer, the Mighty One of Israel" (1 Nephi 22:11–12). Missionaries, those commissioned of the Lord to gather scattered Israel to the covenants of salvation, are the arm of the Lord. See commentary on Doctrine and Covenants 35:13–14.

Shall be cut off from among the people. This language comes from Moses' prophecy to the children of Israel describing what would become of those who failed to accept Christ (Deuteronomy 18:18–19). "The people" to whom reference is made are the rightful heirs of Abraham, Isaac, and Jacob. To be cut off is to be left without family ties in the worlds to come. Peter quoted this same text on the day of Pentecost (Acts 3:22–23), as did Christ to the nation of the Nephites (3 Nephi 21:11). Moroni also quoted it to Joseph Smith, announcing that it was about to be fulfilled. See commentary on Joseph Smith–History 1:40, "He quoted also the third chapter of Acts, twenty-second and twenty-third verses," page???.

1:15–16 The language of verse 15 relates to another prophetic description of the last days given by Isaiah. "The earth also is defiled under the inhabitants thereof; because they have transgressed the laws, changed the ordinance, broken the everlasting covenant. Therefore hath the curse devoured the earth, and they that dwell therein are desolate: therefore the inhabitants of the earth are burned, and few men left" (Isaiah 24:5–6).

The earth was created for righteous purposes and is defiled by wickedness and rebellion against the truth. The word *ordinance* as used by Isaiah refers to laws or statutes, particularly those fixed in writing. To say that people have broken covenants and changed ordinances could well be intended to convey the idea that they have tampered with holy writ in order that others might stumble or stray from the laws of God, as the present revelation states (*Interpreter's Dictionary of the Bible*, 3:607). This is precisely what Nephi prophesied would happen (1 Nephi 13:29). To break the "everlasting covenant" suggests that there would be those who would seek salvation in supposed covenants of their own making or on their own terms without the necessity of priesthood covenants. The Lord said that such do not seek righteousness but seek to walk in their own way, after the image of their own god, who is in the image and likeness of the world.

1:16 *After the image of his own God.* All gospel principles are simply appendages to our understanding of the nature of God. No salvation is found in the worship of a false god. The crowning revelation of the New Testament is the fatherhood of God. Christ virtually never referred to Deity by any title other than Father, and the Father never refers to Christ by any title or name other than Son. While 240 references sustain this doctrine, the traditional Christian world declares it to be a metaphor. Thus the Christian world's great claim to truth is that it has a better metaphor for God than rival systems of salvation. Indeed, we are told that "all affirmations of Scripture and the Fathers [those who wrote after the death of the Apostles] are but metaphors devised for the ignorant" (Cross, *Oxford Dictionary*, 576). Further, we are told that "Eusebius is a faithful enough disciple of Origen to agree with Plato that it is sometimes necessary for the lawgiver to lie in order to persuade people rather than coerce them, and to suggest that this is an explanation of the anthropomorphism of the Old Testament" (ibid., 1:452). Or as the great Catholic scholar Erigena explained: "We know only *that* he is, we do not know *what* he is. Whatever we affirm in regard to him is true of him in a figurative sense only; hence, in reality he is not what we declare him to be" (Bavinck, *Doctrine of God*, 23). According to such scholars, the real reason God consistently appears to Old Testament prophets in the form of a man is that the people are better off believing a lie than being confronted with the truth. As to the truth, traditional Christianity tells us that God is underivable, unnameable, and incomprehensible. He is thus known best by those who know him not at all.

Fundamental to the Catholic and Protestant faiths is acceptance of the God of their creeds. Known to us today as the doctrine of the Holy Trinity, this teaching first found formal expression in the Nicene Creed and then in its successor, the Athanasian Creed. It reads as follows: "We worship one God in trinity and trinity in unity; neither confounding the persons; nor dividing the substance. For there is one person of the Father:

another of the Son; and another of the Holy Ghost. But the Godhead of the Father, of the Son, and of the Holy Ghost, is all one: the glory equal, the majesty coeternal.

"Such as the Father is: such is the Son: and such is the Holy Ghost. The Father uncreate: the Son uncreate: and the Holy Ghost uncreate. The Father incomprehensible: the Son incomprehensible: and the Holy Ghost incomprehensible.

"The Father eternal: The Son eternal: and the Holy Ghost eternal. And yet there are not three eternals: but one eternal. And also there are not three uncreated: nor three incomprehensibles, but one uncreated: and one incomprehensible. So likewise the Father is Almighty: the Son Almighty and the Holy Ghost Almighty. And yet they are not three Almighties: but one Almighty:

"So the Father is God: the Son is God: and the Holy Ghost is God; And yet they are not three Gods: but one God. So likewise the Father is Lord: the Son is Lord: and the Holy Ghost is Lord. And yet not three Lords: but one Lord. For like as we are compelled by the Christian verity: to acknowledge every person by himself to be God and Lord: so are we forbidden by the Catholic religion: to say, there be three Gods, or three Lords" (Smith, *Restoration of All Things*, 49).

The Nicene Creed is not found in any Gospel. It derives from no utterance of Christ nor from the words of any of his apostles. It directly contradicts the plain language of the New Testament. Its ideas cannot even be expressed in scriptural language; they are cloaked in that of the Greek philosophy from whence they came. Its best defense is the admission that it is a mystery and as such is indefensible. Edward Gibbon tells us: "The great Athanasius himself, has candidly confessed that whenever he forced his understanding to mediate on the divinity of the *Logos*, his toilsome and unavailing efforts recoiled on themselves; that the more he thought, the less he comprehended; and the more he wrote, the less capable was he of expressing his thoughts" (Gibbon, *Decline and Fall*, 392). Of the Athanasian Creed, which was formulated about a century after the Nicene Creed, James E. Talmage said, "It would be difficult to conceive of a greater number of inconsistencies and contradictions expressed in words as few" (*Articles of Faith*, 44).

In the midst of this great dispensation of darkness, a time would come according to Jeremiah in which people would awake, saying: "O Lord, my strength, and my fortress, and my refuge in the day of affliction, the Gentiles shall come unto thee from the ends of the earth, and shall say,

Surely our fathers have inherited lies, vanity, and things wherein there is no profit. Shall a man make gods unto himself, and they are no gods? Therefore, behold, I will this once cause them to know, I will cause them to know mine hand and my might; and they shall know that my name is The Lord" (Jeremiah 16:19–21).

As that day begins to dawn, we see on the horizon such noble spirits as Thomas Jefferson, who observed, "When we shall have done away with the incomprehensible jargon of the Trinitarian arithmetic, that three are one, and one is three; when we shall have knocked down the artificial scaffolding, reared to mask from view the very simple structure of Jesus; when, in short, we shall have unlearned everything which has been taught since his day, and got back to the pure and simple doctrines he inculcated, we shall then be truly and worthily his disciples" (quoted in McGrath, *Understanding the Trinity*, 110). Or as Parley P. Pratt would observe when once the light of the restored gospel had risen: "It is painful to the human mind to be compelled to admit that such wonderful inconsistencies of language or ideas have ever found place in any human creed. Yet, so it is. It is but another way of saying that there is a God who does not exist, a God who is composed of nonentity, who is the negative of all existence, who occupies no space, who exists in no time, who is composed of no substance, known or unknown, and who has no powers or properties in common with any thing or being known to exist or which can possibly be conceived of as existing either in the heavens or on the earth" (*Key*, 18).

The pantheon of false gods is a great and spacious building that provides room for all manner of social and political philosophies. It invites men to worship at the shrine of their own intellect and to worship science and the laws of nature. It honors false Christs and false prophets who teach their disciples to walk after their own devices and after the imagination of their own evil hearts (Jeremiah 18:12). The promise of our present text is that all such, like Babylon of old, will perish. See commentary on Doctrine and Covenants 20:28.

Joseph Smith to Restore Truths and Powers
DOCTRINE AND COVENANTS 1:17–23

1:17 Commencing in the spring of 1820 the Lord spoke to Joseph Smith and gave him commandments. By obedience to these commandments, recorded in the Doctrine and Covenants, we can prepare ourselves for the Second Coming and be spared the calamities that will precede it. See commentary on Doctrine and Covenants 5:19.

1:18 *Proclaim these things unto the world.* In an earlier revelation the Lord had said, "You shall declare the things which have been revealed to my servant, Joseph Smith, Jun. You shall begin to preach from this time forth, yea, to reap in the field which is white already to be burned" (D&C 31:4). It is the message of the Restoration that must go to those of every nation, kindred, tongue, and people. The heavens have been opened. God speaks! Angels have come to restore all the power and authority known to the faithful of the ancient world. The dispensation of the fulness of times has commenced.

1:19 In establishing his Church and kingdom during the meridian of time, Christ did not choose to convey the keys of that kingdom upon the twelve most learned scribes or rabbis of that generation; rather, he chose, with one exception, unlettered men from Galilee. Of his understanding of the gospel, Paul wrote, "I neither received it of man, neither was I taught it, but by the revelation of Jesus Christ" (Galatians 1:12). In his epistle to the Corinthians he explained: "Because the foolishness of God is wiser than men; and the weakness of God is stronger than men. For ye see your calling, brethren, how that not many wise men after the flesh, not many mighty, not many noble, are called: but God hath chosen the foolish things of the world to confound the wise; and God hath chosen the weak things of the world to confound the things which are mighty; and base things of the world, and things which are despised, hath God chosen, yea, and things which are not, to bring to nought things that are: that no flesh should glory in his presence" (1 Corinthians 1:25–29).

It is that same gospel known to the meridian Saints that the Lord restored through the Prophet Joseph Smith. Of necessity this means that the Church must be governed by the spirit of revelation as that spirit manifests itself through those whose knowledge and testimony stand independent of the wisdom and learning of the world.

1:20 *That every man might speak in the name of God.* Along with the restoration of the gospel comes the restoration of the priesthood, which is the power and authority to speak in the name of God. In the providence of God all men are entitled to hold the priesthood and preside over their family in righteousness.

1:22 *That mine everlasting covenant might be established.* The restoration of the gospel centers on the restoration of the "everlasting covenant," not in the restoration of the organization of the New Testament church.

Salvation is found in making and keeping covenants, not in the organizational structure of the Church.

1:23 *That the fulness of my gospel might be proclaimed by the weak and the simple.* See commentary on Doctrine and Covenants 35:13.

Book of Mormon Brought Forth and the Church Established
DOCTRINE AND COVENANTS 1:24–33

1:24 *After the manner of their language.* Revelations come in the language of those to whom they are given and according to their understanding. If an angel of the Lord speaks to a child he will speak according to the understanding of the child. Similarly, if our spiritual preparation is puny, the revelations we receive will in like manner be puny (2 Nephi 31:3).

1:25–27 We do not believe in the infallibility of prophets or any other set of men. All men err, sin, and are invited to repent (Romans 3:23). Lorenzo Snow observed: "I can fellowship the President of the Church if he does not know everything I know. . . . I saw the . . . imperfections in [Joseph Smith]. . . . I thanked God that He would put upon a man who had those imperfections the power and authority He placed upon him . . . for I knew that I myself had weakness, and I thought there was a chance for me. . . . I thanked God that I saw these imperfections" (quoted by Maxwell, in Conference Report, October 1984, 10). In so saying, Elder Snow reflected both the spirit and counsel of Moroni, who wrote: "Condemn me not because of mine imperfection, neither my father, because of his imperfection, neither them who have written before him; but rather give thanks unto God that he hath made manifest unto you our imperfections, that ye may learn to be more wise than we have been" (Mormon 9:31).

1:28 *Receive knowledge from time to time.* No one lives in a constant deluge of revelation. The treasures of heaven are not dispensed cheaply.

1:29 Joseph Smith did not translate according to the learning of men. He translated "by the gift and power of God" (D&C 135:3). At a Church conference in 1831, Hyrum Smith invited the Prophet to explain more fully how the Book of Mormon came forth. Joseph Smith responded that "it was not intended to tell the world all the particulars of the coming forth of the Book of Mormon; and it was not expedient for him to relate these things" (*History of the Church,* 1:220). See commentary on Doctrine and Covenants 6–9.

1:30 *Bring it forth out of obscurity and out of darkness.* The phrase comes from Isaiah wherein he described the coming forth of the Book of Mormon. "And in that day shall the deaf hear the words of the book, and the eyes of the blind shall see out of obscurity, and out of darkness" (Isaiah 29:18; 2 Nephi 27:29). Nephi used this language to describe the latter day gathering of Israel. "Wherefore, he [God] will bring them again out of captivity, and they shall be gathered together to the lands of their inheritance; and they shall be brought out of obscurity and out of darkness; and they shall know that the Lord is their Savior and their Redeemer, the Mighty One of Israel" (1 Nephi 22:12).

This text tells us that those who receive the Book of Mormon (referred to in this verse as "these commandments") will have power "to lay the foundation of this church" and "to bring it forth out of obscurity and out of darkness" (see commentary on D&C 18:4). The primary meaning of the word *obscure* is not that which is "little known" but rather that which is "devoid of light." It is the darkness of ignorance and unbelief to which this phrase makes reference (D&C 84:54). Nephi properly placed the phrase in the context of latter-day Israel being gathered to the light of the gospel, or more specifically to the knowledge and testimony of Christ, who is the Mighty One of Israel (1 Nephi 15:13–14; 2 Nephi 6:11; 10:7; 25:16–17). Thus the foundation of the Church becomes the truth and testimony of Christ as restored in the Book of Mormon.

Only true . . . church. Catholicism is founded on the idea that authority is necessary to represent God and that certain ordinances are essential to salvation. Those principles in turn dictate that there can be but one true church, meaning one church that has the right to speak for God and perform the ordinances of salvation. Protestantism, on the other hand, in breaking with the mother church, takes the only remaining position—rejecting the need for authority and ordinances. Having done so, Protestantism must of necessity argue that neither ordinances nor church membership is a tenet of salvation and that "the one true church doctrine" is narrow minded, bigoted, and even unchristian. This, of course, is what Protestantism does. Out of this chain of thought grows the popularized notion that it is not what you believe but how you believe that counts and the attendant idea that somehow all churches, even though they teach contradictory doctrines, are true—assuming, of course, that they are Protestant churches.

The idea that all churches are true, though satisfying to those who seek salvation on their own terms, defies every principle of truth and logic known to humankind. Let us briefly consider some of the ways it does so.

First, the essence of Christianity centers on the idea that salvation is in Christ. That being the case, everyone who truly embraces the Christian faith must at the same time embrace the idea that it is only in and through Christ that salvation comes. Christ himself said, "I am the way, the truth, and the life: no man cometh unto the Father, but by me" (John 14:6). The doctrine of all the holy prophets has been that there is "none other name under heaven given among men, whereby we must be saved" (Acts 4:12; see also D&C 18:23; 2 Nephi 25:20; 31:21). Within the ranks of those professing to be Christians may be differences on the require-ments of salvation, but all must agree on the acceptance of Christ as the source of salvation. At issue here is not whether a line must be drawn between the believer and the nonbeliever but simply where that line should be drawn. Historically Protestants do not hesitate to draw that line in such a manner as to exclude Catholics, Latter-day Saints, Seventh-day Adventists, and Jehovah Witnesses. In practice, then, it becomes a Christian duty for Protestants to draw that line, doing so in such a manner as to exclude all who dare disagree with them. It only becomes an unchristian practice when someone suggests that they are on the wrong side of the line.

Second, to argue that the power of salvation rests in the Protestant world is to argue that a live branch can be cut from a dead tree. Or, as James described it, it is to argue that a fountain can simultaneously bring forth sweet and bitter water or that a fig tree can bear olive berries (James 3:11–12). Protestants claim to have rejected corrupt Catholic traditions in a return to Bible religion. This argument raises two great difficulties. The first is that they simply do not do it. They have retained as founda-tional to their faith the most corrupting traditions of the old mother church, namely her creeds. The second great difficulty is that Bible reli-gion is itself unbiblical because no one within the covers of the Bible ever had a Bible. Their religion was one of prophets, apostles, and continuous revelation. Never in Bible times was the Church and kingdom of God governed by a book. Now it is important to get our history straight. Christian existence predates the Bible by more than three centuries. The great Christian creeds, the very foundation upon which Protestantism's whole concept of Deity rests, are Bible free. Their creation predates that of the Bible. Protestantism holds fast to these creeds, refusing to acknowl-edge that they are part of the Catholic tradition that they claim to have rejected. It is allegiance to these creeds that predetermines the manner in which they interpret the Bible. At the same time they claim the Bible to be the last word on all things. Thus traditions rooted in historical creeds rather than the Bible have been retained as the guiding revelations of the Protestant faith.

Third, the notion that salvation can be found in any of a host of contradictory doctrines defies reason and argues that God's kingdom is one of chaos and disorder. We are being asked to believe that if a dozen people add a column of figures and each arrives at a different sum, we must accept each of them as right. After all, it is not the sum that you come to that matters but the zeal with which you add the figures that counts. Similarly, this notion argues that all men, women, and children who receive a prescription from a doctor are entitled to go to the pharmacists and concoct their own mixture of drugs. Not even a fool could swallow such a thing. Yet this is exactly what we are asked to believe in the realm of spiritual things. We are told that laws govern everything in the universe except in the realm of the spirit. As to spiritual things, the argument must become that God leaves it to each man, woman, and child to determine for themselves which gospel principles apply to them and which do not. Salvation becomes a divine smorgasbord at which we all satisfy our own appetites.

To maintain that all churches are true—meaning that they possess the power of salvation and the authority to act as the agent of God—may have some resemblance to Christian tolerance. But upon examination such a notion reveals itself to be a deceptive ploy lulling people into the belief that it is for them to dictate the terms of salvation and to determine the nature and character of God. In such a god we have no interest.

True and living church. To be in possession of the doctrines of Christ is not of itself sufficient for salvation. Without living prophets there is no gospel and never has been. The gospel is not a book. "There is no salvation between the two lids of the Bible," Joseph Smith said, "without a legal administrator" (*Teachings of the Prophet Joseph Smith*, 319). Though the truths of salvation may be found in the Bible, the mere possession of the Bible brings neither the necessary authority to perform the ordinances of salvation nor the spirit of revelation necessary to appropriately apply those truths. One may possess the truth and yet be without the power to breathe life into it.

Some outside The Church of Jesus Christ of Latter-day Saints profess a belief in the revelations found in the Doctrine and Covenants, but they refuse to sustain those men whom Joseph Smith ordained to be his successors. Yet it is that priesthood held by his successors, according to the revelations Joseph Smith received, that "administereth the gospel" (D&C 84:19). The "only true and living church upon the face of the whole earth" must, by definition, possess not only the truths of salvation but also the necessary authority to perform the ordinances of salvation and the spirit of revelation by which those truths are properly applied.

1:33 *For my Spirit shall not always strive with man.* "The Holy Ghost will not dwell in unclean tabernacles nor strive with people unless they keep their minds as well as their bodies clean, and they are diligent before the Lord" (Smith, *Answers*, 4:88). The Holy Ghost does not strive with God's children but rather comes to teach, comfort, and edify only as they prepare themselves to receive his companionship. The light of Christ, on the other hand, will labor and strive with people to bring them to the additional light that comes from this member of the Godhead. People and individuals can, however, reach a state in which the light of Christ will cease striving with them. It was such a state that led to the destruction of the Nephite nation at the end of the Book of Mormon. In that context we find Mormon writing his son Moroni, saying, "My son, I fear lest the Lamanites shall destroy this people; for they do not repent, and Satan stirreth them up continually to anger one with another. Behold, I am laboring with them continually; and when I speak the word of God with sharpness they tremble and anger against me; and when I use no sharpness they harden their hearts against it; wherefore, I fear lest the Spirit of the Lord hath ceased striving with them" (Moroni 9:3–4). This proved to be the case as a nation of people turned against the light they had received and were destroyed.

Peace Shall Be Taken from the Earth
DOCTRINE AND COVENANTS 1:34–36

1:34 *Make these things known unto all flesh.* See commentary on verse 18.

1:35 *Peace shall be taken from the earth.* Doctrine and Covenants 87, a revelation on "war," states that peace would be taken from the earth with the beginning of the Civil War (vv. 1–2). See commentary on Doctrine and Covenants 63:32–35.

The devil shall have power over his own dominion. On all matters of light, virtue, and truth we make the choice to fight Satan or concede power to him. Joseph Smith said that "the devil has no power over us only as we permit him. The moment we revolt at anything which comes from God, the devil takes power" (*Teachings of the Prophet Joseph Smith*, 181).

1:36 *Judgment upon Idumea, or the world.* Idumea was the name given to the land of Edom by the Greeks and Romans. Since Israel had to pass through Idumea to obtain the promised land, it became a symbol of the world, or the worldly, through which we must pass to obtain our divine inheritance.

Search These Commandments
DOCTRINE AND COVENANTS 1:37–39

1:37 *Search these commandments.* The command is to search those things recorded in the Book of Commandments, or what we now have as the Doctrine and Covenants. It is the obligation of every faithful Saint.

They are true and faithful. The word "true" is derived from the Old English "treowe," which means faithful, trustworthy, or covenant. To be true is to be constant, steadfast, and faithful. The thrust of the meaning here is that the words of the Lord are completely reliable or trustworthy and that obedient acceptance of them constitutes a covenant with God that he cannot break (D&C 82:10). Teaching this principle, Nephi said, "I heard a voice from the Father, saying: Yea, the words of my Beloved are true and faithful. He that endureth to the end, the same shall be saved" (2 Nephi 31:15).

1:38 *Whether by mine own voice or by the voice of my servants, it is the same.* The Lord's agents, those holding his priesthood, have both the right and responsibility to speak in the first person for him. For instance, speaking to Moses, the Lord said, "Thou shalt be made stronger than many waters; for they shall obey thy command as if thou wert God" (Moses 1:25).

DOCTRINE AND COVENANTS 2

DATE: 21 SEPTEMBER 1823
PLACE: MANCHESTER, NEW YORK

Doctrine and Covenants 2 is one of two revelations in the Doctrine and Covenants that come entirely from the words of an angel; Doctrine and Covenants 13 is the other one. Chronologically, it is the first section in the Doctrine and Covenants. It contains a brief extract from the words of the angel Moroni to Joseph Smith on the night of 21 September 1823. In this revelation, Moroni, an angel, promises the return of Elijah, also an angel. For an account of the fulfillment of this prophecy, see commentary on Doctrine and Covenants 110:13–14, 16.

In his instruction to Joseph Smith, Moroni acquainted him with the covenant God made with Abraham concerning his seed and with the many prophecies about the latter-day gathering of Israel. All that Joseph Smith would restore in the coming years would build upon the foundation of this understanding. See commentary on Joseph Smith–History 1:38–39, page 22.

DOCTRINE AND COVENANTS 3

DATE: JULY 1828

PLACE: HARMONY, PENNSYLVANIA

After Martin Harris's return from New York, where he showed the transcribed characters of the Book of Mormon to Charles Anthon, he commenced again his labor as scribe for the prophet about 12 April 1828. The two men worked together until 14 June, by which time they had completed 116 pages of manuscript on foolscap paper.

Joseph Smith recalled, "Some time after Mr. Harris had begun to write for me, he began to importune me to give him liberty to carry the writings home and show them; and desired of me that I would inquire of the Lord, through the Urim and Thummim, if he might not do so. I did inquire, and the answer was that he must not. However, he was not satisfied with this answer, and desired that I should inquire again. I did so, and the answer was as before. Still he could not be contented, but insisted that I should inquire once more. After much solicitation I again inquired of the Lord, and permission was granted him to have the writings on certain conditions; which were, that he show them only to his brother, Preserved Harris, his own wife, his father and his mother, and a Mrs. Cobb, a sister to his wife. In accordance with this last answer, I required of him that he should bind himself in a covenant to me in a most solemn manner that he would not do otherwise than had been directed. He did so. He bound himself as I required of him, took the writings, and went his way. Notwithstanding, however, the great restrictions which he had been laid under, and the solemnity of the covenant which he had made with me, he did show them to others, and by stratagem they got them away from him, and they never have been recovered unto this day.

"In the meantime, while Martin Harris was gone with the writings, I went to visit my father's family at Manchester. I continued there for a short season, and then returned to my place in Pennsylvania. Immediately after my return home, I was walking out a little distance, when, behold, the former heavenly messenger appeared and handed to me the Urim and

Thummim again—for it had been taken from me in consequence of my
having wearied the Lord in asking for the privilege of letting Martin
Harris take the writings, which he lost by transgression—and I inquired
of the Lord through it, and obtained the following . . ." (*History of the
Church*, 1:21–22).

The Lord's Course
DOCTRINE AND COVENANTS 3:1–4

3:1 *The purposes of God cannot be frustrated.* As God cannot be
deceived, neither can he be surprised, caught unaware, or unprepared.
Provisions were made for the loss of the 116 pages even while the Book
of Mormon was being engraved on the gold plates. Thirty years after arriving in the promised land, Nephi was commanded by the Lord to make
another record in addition to the general record he had been keeping.
Nephi said, "I have received a commandment of the Lord that I should
make these [the small] plates, for the special purpose that there should be
an account engraven of the ministry of my people" (1 Nephi 9:3). Nephi
did not know why, but he was obedient because he trusted that "the Lord
hath commanded me to make these plates for a wise purpose in him,
which purpose I know not" (1 Nephi 9:5). These small plates were passed
to Jacob, his sons, and eventually King Benjamin and the judges until
they came into Mormon's hands. Mormon was inspired to insert these
small plates after having abridged the large plates. He admitted that he
did not know why but said he knew they would be "choice unto my
brethren. And I do this for a wise purpose; for thus it whispereth me,
according to the workings of the Spirit of the Lord which is in me . . . but
the Lord knoweth all things which are to come" (Words of Mormon
1:6–7). See commentary on Doctrine and Covenants 10.

3:4 *Sets at naught the counsels of God.* More anxious to be heard than
to hear, Joseph disregarded the Lord's counsel that he not entrust the 116
pages to Martin Harris. Having been twice refused by the Lord, he asked
yet a third time and received the answer he sought. The stage was set for
him to learn a lesson as important as it was painful.

No office or calling can excuse either man or woman from the responsibility of following the Lord's counsel and direction. For this reason, the
life of Christ becomes such a perfect example for us. In all things he
sought only to do the will of his Father (Mosiah 15:7). See commentary
on Doctrine and Covenants 24:2.

Fear God More Than Man
DOCTRINE AND COVENANTS 3:5–8

3:5 *You have been entrusted with these things.* Properly the responsibility for the loss of the 116 pages rested with Joseph Smith even though Martin Harris failed to keep his covenant with the Prophet. Concerning the plates, Moroni told Joseph Smith that he "should be responsible for them; that if [he] should let them go carelessly, or through any neglect of [his], [he] should be cut off" (Joseph Smith–History 1:59). In principle these same instructions applied to the translation text. Lucy Mack Smith explained that "the Lord permitted Martin Harris to take the manuscript home with him, on the condition that my son was responsible for its safety. This my son was willing to do, as he could not conceive it possible for so kind a friend to betray the trust reposed in him" (*History of Joseph Smith*, 1996, 160–61).

3:5 *Remember also the promises which were made to you.* Moroni told the Prophet that if he would make every effort to preserve the plates, he would be able to keep them safe (Joseph Smith–History 1:59). Oliver Cowdery said Moroni instructed Joseph after his first unsuccessful attempt to obtain the plates, saying, "You now see why you could not obtain this record; that the commandment was strict, and that if ever these sacred things are obtained they must be by prayer and faithfulness in obeying the Lord. . . . No man can obtain them if his heart is impure, because they contain that which is sacred. . . . Now, go thy way, remembering what the Lord has done for thee, and be diligent in keeping his commandments, and he will deliver thee from temptations and all the arts and devices of the wicked one.—Forget not to pray, that thy mind may become strong, that when he shall manifest unto thee, thou mayest have power to escape the evil, and obtain those precious things" (*Messenger and Advocate*, 2:198–99).

3:7 *You should not have feared man more than God.* It is not difficult to see why Joseph Smith was eager to grant the request of Martin Harris to show the translation to his wife and family. Martin was Joseph's senior by more than twenty years. He was a wealthy land owner while Joseph was but a day laborer. In giving much by way of time and support to Joseph, Martin had become estranged from his wife and had become the laughing stock of Palmyra.

Martin's wife, Lucy Harris, had given her husband an ultimatum that he either bring the manuscript home for her to see or she would leave

him, taking the children with her. After her husband's first visit to
Harmony to serve as Joseph's scribe, Martin's wife "prepared a bed and
room for him alone, which she refused to enter" (Smith, *History of Joseph
Smith*, 1996, 155).

The Prophet's mother gave the following account of events in the
Harris home after Mrs. Harris returned from visiting the Prophet in
Harmony: "When she returned home, which was about two weeks from
the time she arrived in Harmony, she endeavored to dissuade Mr. Harris
from having anything further to do with the writing or translating of the
record. But Mr. Harris paid but little attention to her, and as he had
agreed to go back and write for a season at least, he did so.

"After Mr. Harris left again for Pennsylvania, his wife went from place
to place, and from house to house, telling her grievances to everyone she
met, but particularly bewailing that the deception which Joe Smith was
practicing upon the people was about to strip her of all that she possessed.
'But,' said the woman, 'I know how to take care of my property, and I'll
let them see that pretty shortly.' So she carried away her furniture, linen
and bedding, and other movable articles, till she well-nigh divested the
premises of everything which could conduce to comfort or convenience.
These things she deposited with her friends in whom she reposed sufficient confidence to assure her of the safety of her property" (Smith,
History of Joseph Smith, 1996, 157–58). See commentary on Doctrine and
Covenants 19:25.

Notwithstanding these things, Joseph was to learn to fear God more
than man. He was to trust the Lord to reward his servants and to make
right all that in his wisdom should be corrected. See commentary on
Doctrine and Covenants 5:21.

Joseph Is Warned to Repent
DOCTRINE AND COVENANTS 3:9–15

3:9 *Thou wast chosen to do the work of the Lord.* "The Prophet Joseph
Smith . . . [was] reserved to come forth in the fulness of times to take part
in laying the foundations of the great latter-day work" (D&C 138:53).
Regardless of this foreordination, the Church is the Lord's and it is for him
to run it. Neither Joseph Smith nor any other man in this church is
greater than the calling to which they have been ordained.

Because of transgression, if thou art not aware thou wilt fall. When
Martin informed Joseph that he had lost the manuscript, Lucy Mack

Smith said that Joseph clinched his hands together and exclaimed, "'All is lost, is lost! What shall I do? I have sinned. It is I who tempted the wrath of God by asking him for that which I had no right to ask, as I was differently instructed by the angel.' And he wept and groaned, walking the floor continually.

"At last he told Martin to go back to his house and search again. 'No,' said Mr. Harris, 'it is all in vain, for I have looked in every place in the house. I have even ripped open beds and pillows, and I know it is not there.'

"'Then must I,' said Joseph, 'return to my wife with such a tale as this? I dare not do it lest I should kill her at once. And how shall I appear before the Lord? Of what rebuke am I not worthy from the angel of the Most High?'

"I besought him not to mourn so, for it might be that the Lord would forgive him, after a short season of humiliation and repentance on his part. But what could I say to comfort him, when he saw all the family in the same situation of mind that he was? Our sobs and groans, and the most bitter lamentations filled the house. Joseph, in particular, was more distressed than the rest, for he knew definitely and by sorrowful experience the consequence of what would seem to others to be a very trifling neglect of duty. He continued walking backwards and forwards, weeping and grieving like a tender infant until about sunset, when we persuaded him to take a little nourishment" (*History of Joseph Smith*, 1996, 165–66).

3:10 *But remember, God is merciful; therefore, repent.* God is not a vengeful master bent on the punishment of his servants. He is firm but also merciful. Because he desires to bless his children, he will prepare a way to deliver them, if they will repent and obey.

As published in the *Book of Commandments*, this verse included an additional phrase. "Therefore, repent of that which thou hast done, *and he will only cause thee to be afflicted for a season.*" By turning his heart to the Lord, Joseph lost the gift of translation and the peace of the Spirit for only a short time (v. 14).

3:12–13 *A wicked man . . . has broken the most sacred promises.* The Lord had placed "certain conditions" on the permission that was granted to Martin Harris when he took the manuscript to Palmyra. The conditions were "that he show them only to his brother, Preserved Harris, his own wife, his father and his mother, and a Mrs. Cobb, a sister to his wife. In accordance with this last answer, I required of him that he should bind himself in a covenant to me in a most solemn manner that he would not do otherwise than had been directed. He did so. He bound himself as I required of him, took the writings, and went his way. Notwithstanding, however, the great restrictions which he had been laid under, and the solemnity of the covenant which he had made with me, he did show them to others, and by stratagem they got them away from him, and they never have been recovered unto this day" (Smith, *History of the Church*, 1:21). Lucy Mack Smith indicated that Martin "bound himself in *a written covenant* of the most solemn nature" (Smith, *History of Joseph Smith*, 1979, 124).

3:14 *Thou hast lost thy privileges for a season.* Moroni took both the plates and the Urim and Thummim from the Prophet before Joseph received this revelation. Speaking of the events following his return to Harmony, Joseph said: "After I arrived here, I commenced humbling myself in mighty prayer before the Lord, and as I poured out my soul in supplication to him, that if possible I might obtain mercy at his hands and be forgiven of all that I had done which was contrary to his will, an angel stood before me, and answered me, saying, that I had sinned in delivering the manuscript into the hands of a wicked man, and as I had ventured to become responsible for this man's faithfulness, I would of necessity suffer the consequences of his indiscretion, and I must now give back the Urim and Thummim into his (the angel's) hands.

"This I did as I was directed, and as I handed them to him he remarked, 'If you are very humble and penitent, it may be you will receive them again; if so, it will be on the twenty-second of next September'" (Smith, *History of Joseph Smith*, 1996, 173–74).

The Book of Mormon to Save the Seed of Lehi
DOCTRINE AND COVENANTS 3:16–20

3:19 *For this very purpose are these plates preserved.* On the title page of the Book of Mormon, Moroni indicates that the book was written "to show unto the remnant of the House of Israel what great things the Lord hath done for their fathers; and that they may know the covenants of the Lord, that they are not cast off forever—And also to the convincing of the Jew and Gentile that JESUS is the Christ, the ETERNAL God." From beginning to end, the book is true to its announced purpose. In one of many examples that could be cited, Nephi spoke prophetically of a day in which the gospel would be taken to Lehi's seed, saying, "At that day shall the remnant of our seed know that they are of the house of Israel, and that they are the covenant people of the Lord; and then shall they know and come to the knowledge of their forefathers, and also to the knowledge of the gospel of their Redeemer, which was ministered unto their fathers by him; wherefore, they shall come to the knowledge of their Redeemer and the very points of his doctrine, that they may know how to come unto him and be saved" (1 Nephi 15:14).

The story unfolding here is that Moroni, the son of Mormon, who identified himself as "a pure descendant of Lehi" (3 Nephi 5:20), is bringing a sacred history to Joseph Smith in order that the Prophet might translate it and see that it is taken to the posterity of those who wrote it. For some reason it is of great importance to the writers of the book that their descendants, though many generations removed, receive it. It witnesses that the hearts of the fathers are turned to their children—that death and the distance of time have not lessened their love and concern for them. It is a bold declaration that the enforced separation brought by death was not intended to bring an end to the family unit. It testifies that righteous parents watch over their children and their children's children through the generations, praying and laboring in their behalf.

DOCTRINE AND COVENANTS 4

DATE: FEBRUARY 1829
PLACE: HARMONY, PENNSYLVANIA

During the month of February 1829, Joseph Smith Sr. and his wife, Lucy, traveled to Harmony, Pennsylvania, to visit with their son Joseph and his wife, Emma. They had not seen Joseph since he left in the sorrowful circumstances following the loss of the 116 pages of the Book of Mormon manuscript. After receiving the news that the Lord had restored the ancient record and the gift of translation to his son, Joseph Smith Sr. asked his son to inquire in his behalf relative to his duty. This revelation is the result of that inquiry.

Valiant Service Saves the Lord's Ministers
DOCTRINE AND COVENANTS 4:1–4

4:1 A marvelous work is about to come forth. The marvelous work to which reference is made is the Book of Mormon and the restored Church. The language is that of Isaiah, the great prophet of the Restoration. Speaking for the Lord, he wrote, "Therefore, behold, I will proceed to do a marvellous work among this people, even a marvellous work and a wonder: for the wisdom of their wise men shall perish, and the understanding of their prudent men shall be hid" (Isaiah 29:14).

4:2 The measure of our love for God is found in the way we live his gospel and labor in his cause. Our service to him ought to always represent the "first fruits" or the best we have to offer. Surely, we would not give Christ the scraps from our table but rather the seat of honor. Anciently, the law of sacrifice required the best of one's flocks—the breeding stock—and the best of their fruits, the prized seed. Such an offering attested that God and the things of his kingdom came first, that our first love was not for the earth and its goodness but rather for the goodness of heaven. So it must ever be among his people.

4:3 This text is not intended to suggest that we can assume the right to act in the name of the Lord without having been called by prophecy and the laying on of hands. Rather, it explains that the desire to serve—the willingness to serve as needed—will give birth to the opportunity to serve.

4:4 *Field is white already to harvest.* The hearts of many are ready to accept the gospel and unite themselves with the house of faith.

He that thrusteth in his sickle. After returning home to the Palmyra-Manchester, New York, area, Father Smith had opportunity to thrust his sickle into fields that were ripe for the gospel harvest. It was around this time that Oliver Cowdery came to stay in the Smith home and, from there, went to Harmony, Pennsylvania, to offer his help to the Prophet as a scribe. Joseph Smith Sr. also helped to strengthen the testimonies of Thomas B. Marsh, Solomon Chamberlain, and Parley P. Pratt in the days that immediately followed (McConkie, *Father of the Prophet,* 113–16).

In October and November 1830 Father Smith was unable to pay a fourteen-dollar debt. The holder of the note was a Quaker who hoped that he could persuade Joseph Sr. to renounce his testimony of the Book of Mormon at the promise of being set free. In addition to laboring in the jail's cooper shop to earn money to pay off the debt, Father Smith preached every Sunday that he was in jail. After his release, he baptized two individuals who were incarcerated with him and whose hearts had been pricked by the message of the marvelous work that had come forth in the latter-days as expounded by Father Smith (Smith, *History of Joseph Smith,* 1996, 238–43).

He perisheth not, but bringeth salvation to his soul. Those who dedicate their efforts to bringing others to salvation save their own souls in the process. The Savior provided the perfect example of this process in his mortal ministry and invited all to follow him. Those who take upon them the name of Jesus Christ and covenant to enter into a partnership of caring about others and serving God with all of their souls receive grace for grace. The Lord strengthens them and enlarges their capacity to bless the lives of those they serve. The spiritual growth and testimony that comes through experiences gained in the service of God can be stored up, like summer wheat for the winter season. When winter storms blow in the paths of people who have faithfully served and developed this spiritual strength, they are able to endure in faith to the end.

Revelation identifies that faithful service and obedience have a direct relationship with the remission of sins: "Blessed are you who are now hearing these words of mine from the mouth of my servant, for your sins are forgiven you" (D&C 50:36). "Ye are blessed, for the testimony which ye have borne is recorded in heaven for the angels to look upon; and they rejoice over you, and your sins are forgiven you" (D&C 62:3). "I will forgive you of your sins with this commandment—that you remain steadfast in your minds in solemnity and the spirit of prayer" (D&C 84:61). "Verily thus saith the Lord unto you, my servant Lyman: Your sins are forgiven you, because you have obeyed my voice in coming up hither this morning to receive counsel of him whom I have appointed" (D&C 108:1).

Qualifying to Serve God
DOCTRINE AND COVENANTS 4:5-7

4:6 *Remember faith . . . charity.* These same qualities are mentioned by the apostle Peter in 2 Peter 1:5–10. He indicates that there is an additive order to the attaining of these attributes. Virtue is added to faith, knowledge is added to virtue, and so on. These characteristics are also mentioned in the instructions on priesthood in Doctrine and Covenants 107:30. In both instances, readers are promised that "if these things abound in them they shall not be unfruitful in the knowledge of the Lord" (D&C 107:31). Of these qualities Peter says, "If ye do these things, ye shall never fall" (2 Peter 1:10).

DOCTRINE AND COVENANTS 5

DATE: MARCH 1829

PLACE: HARMONY, PENNSYLVANIA

After repenting of the vanity and foolishness that resulted in the loss of the 116 pages, Martin Harris requested the Prophet to inquire of the Lord in his behalf. The content of this revelation suggests that he still desired to see the plates.

Martin Harris Desires to See the Plates

DOCTRINE AND COVENANTS 5:1–4

5:1 *Martin Harris has desired a witness.* More than seven months had passed since the Lord sorely chastened the Prophet Joseph Smith for the lost manuscript episode. It appears that Martin Harris, identified in an earlier revelation as a wicked man who broke sacred promises (D&C 3:12–13), requested this witness because he had not seen the plates and was troubled about whether Joseph actually had them.

5:4 *You have a gift to translate the plates.* Joseph's ability to translate the plates, while requiring great faith and mental discipline, was a gift of God. The gift had been given for the Lord's purpose and was to be used only for that purpose. All references to the translation of the Book of Mormon in holy writ affirm that it was translated by "the gift and power of God" (Preface to the Book of Mormon; Testimony of the Three Witnesses; D&C 135:3).

The Lord's Word to This Generation

DOCTRINE AND COVENANTS 5:5–10

5:6 *Hereafter you shall be ordained.* Common thought in the Protestant world is that spiritual experiences constitute the authority to declare the word of God. This is not the case. As the Prophet would yet write, "We believe that a man must be called of God, by prophecy, and by the laying on of hands by those who are in authority, to preach the

Gospel and administer in the ordinances thereof" (Article of Faith 5). At this point in time, the authority to act in the name of God had not been restored. It was while the Prophet was laboring on the translation of the Book of Mormon that the Aaronic and Melchizedek Priesthoods were restored.

5:7 Modern history knows no book more criticized or vehemently damned by priests and clergy than the Book of Mormon. What is of interest is that there has never been a single instance in which these critics of the book have attempted to use the standard given by the Savior to discern whether it is true. Never has one of these spiritual leaders stood before their congregations or suggested to those to whom they write that they apply the simple test suggested by the book itself—read it and pray about it. On the contrary, countless efforts have been made to discredit the book through the use of bad history or poor reasoning.

The idea of discerning something by its fruits (content or message) comes from Christ. But from whence comes the idea of discerning by roots (authorship, antiquity, etc.)? Is it not significant that those choosing to judge the Bible by its roots have never come to faithful conclusions about its origins? Do we really want to reject the Book of Mormon with a standard that is equally, if not more, damaging to the credibility of the Bible? For example, try to find a higher critic who believes that Moses wrote the books of Moses, that Isaiah actually wrote the sixty-six chapters attributed to him, that David wrote the psalms ascribed to him, that Solomon is the author of Proverbs, or that Matthew and John wrote the books bearing their names. If you want to quibble with scholars over this matter according to their rules of scholarship, you will lose—the Bible is not what it professes to be. But if you want to apply the test of the Savior and taste the fruits of the Bible, you will win—it is all that it professes to be and more.

We cannot all be scholars and know all that our schools have to teach, but we can all be spiritual and learn those things that the Spirit has to teach. Again we turn to Christ for a standard by which all men might know truth. His words were as follows: "My doctrine is not mine, but his that sent me. If any man will do his will, he shall know of the doctrine, whether it be of God, or whether I speak of myself" (John 7:16–17).

5:10 *This generation shall have my word through you.* As used in the text, the word *generation* can properly be understood to mean "dispensation." Just as there is no valid priesthood authority on the earth today that does not trace to the Lord through the Prophet Joseph Smith—to whom that priesthood was restored—so is there no valid testimony or knowledge of the truths of salvation that does not in like manner trace to him. As one cannot legitimately accept the Father while rejecting the testimony of his divine Son, so one cannot in truth profess to accept the Son while rejecting those upon whom he has placed his name. In the meridian day one could not profess to accept Christ while rejecting Peter or the other apostles; so it is in our day. One cannot profess to accept Christ while rejecting Joseph Smith, for he is the great revelator of Christ for this dispensation.

Each dispensation has followed this divinely appointed pattern. Those of all past dispensations were required to accept the testimony of the prophet called of God to lead them. Thus their faith was to be centered in the words of a living prophet rather than those of a dead one. In the days of Adam, then, to reject Adam as the Lord's spokesman was to close the door of salvation in one's own face. Yet if, in the name of loyalty to Adam or another of the dead prophets, individuals living in the days of Moses had rejected him and the gospel he received on Sinai, they too would have closed the door of salvation. In all generations, the faith of the true Saints has been a living one which manifests itself in the Saints' acceptance of the revelations of heaven as they are given for their own time and circumstances.

The Testimony of Three Witnesses
DOCTRINE AND COVENANTS 5:11–20

5:11 *The testimony of three.* More than twenty-three hundred years before the plates came forth in 1827, the Lord revealed to the prophet Nephi, "The book shall be hid from the eyes of the world, that the eyes of none shall behold it save it be that three witnesses shall behold it, by the power of God, besides him to whom the book shall be delivered; and they shall testify to the truth of the book and the things therein" (2 Nephi 27:12). Oliver Cowdery, David Whitmer, and Martin Harris were chosen by the Lord to be witnesses of the gold plates (D&C 17). This was consistent with the law to determine truth as declared to ancient Israel: "at the mouth of two witnesses, or at the mouth of three witnesses, shall the matter be established" (Deuteronomy 19:15).

Each of the Three Witnesses remained true throughout their lives to their testimony of the Book of Mormon. "When he reiterated his testimony [of the Book of Mormon] in the closing days of his life, David

Whitmer said: 'I tell you of these things that you may tell others that what I have said is true, and I dare not deny it; I heard the voice of God commanding me to testify to the same'" (Anderson, *Investigating*, 118).

5:11 *I will show these things.* The Three Witnesses saw the plates and other sacred objects by the power of God. Joseph Smith did not show the plates to the Three Witnesses, the angel of God did. These men were not Joseph's witnesses, but they were witnesses commissioned by God to bear testimony to the world that they had seen the plates and the other sacred objects.

Shall go forth with my words. Beginning with the first edition of the Book of Mormon, each copy of the book has contained the testimony of the Three Witnesses (The Testimony of Three Witnesses, introductory pages of the Book of Mormon). The first edition of the book concluded with their testimony. Subsequent editions placed their testimony in the front of the book as a preface or introduction to it.

5:12 *They shall know of a surety that these things are true.* In addition to testifying that they had seen the plates, the Three Witnesses also included the following as their testimony to the world: "And we also know that they have been translated by the gift and power of God, for his voice hath declared it unto us; wherefore we know of a surety that the work is true" (The Testimony of Three Witnesses, introductory pages of the Book of Mormon).

5:14 *To none else will I grant this power, to receive this same testimony.* The experience of the Three Witnesses is distinct from both the experience of the Eight Witnesses and the reported experience of Mary Whitmer in seeing the plates. While the Prophet Joseph Smith showed the eight men the plates and a messenger outside the Whitmer barn showed Mary Whitmer the plates, the Three Witnesses were shown the plates in vision by the power of God. In addition, they saw other sacred objects (D&C 17:1), beheld an angel, and heard the voice of God from heaven. No other witnesses have been granted such a powerful confirmation of the verity of the book.

The coming forth of my church out of the wilderness. This phrase comes from the revelation that John the Revelator received while on the Isle of Patmos (Revelation 12:1–6). He saw a woman who had given birth to a child and was afterward driven into the wilderness. Later, in the Joseph Smith Translation, the interpretation of the woman as representing "the church of God" driven into the wilderness was confirmed (JST Revelation 12:7).

The Church being driven into the wilderness represents the great apostasy that occurred in the meridian day, when the Church was both literally and figuratively driven into the wilderness. In this revelation the Lord announced that the time had come for his Church to come out of the wilderness. The First Vision and the translation of the Book of Mormon constitute the beginning of the restoration of the kingdom of God on the earth.

Clear as the moon, and fair as the sun, and terrible as an army with banners. The Church is to come out of the "wilderness of darkness, and shine forth" (D&C 109:73). It will rise up as the sun that dissipates the darkness of the long night of apostasy with its light. It will shine as the clear whiteness of the moon in contrast to the darkness of the night. It will announce its arrival openly, with banners unfurled, and cause emotions of terror in the breasts of the armies of Lucifer. The rising light of the Restoration, symbolically embodied in the sun and moon, causes the hounds of hell to howl. The restoration of the kingdom of God in the dispensation of the fulness of times indicates that the dawning of the Millennium is near. Therefore, Satan "knoweth that he hath but a short time" (Revelation 12:12) before he will be bound and unable to tempt the children of men. Thus the Church is likened to a mighty army that has come to reclaim the earth for its rightful king.

In 1834 the Lord indicated that before Zion or Jackson County could be redeemed, the Saints must fulfill this description by becoming sanctified through receiving their endowment in the Lord's house at Kirtland, Ohio (D&C 105:31–33).

5:16 The promise here is that those who believe in the Book of Mormon will also experience other manifestations of the Spirit of the Lord. The knowledge obtained from the Book of Mormon brings with it greater faith in the God of heaven, which faith in turn brings a greater yield in the blessings of the Spirit.

5:19 *A desolating scourge shall go forth.* Since the time of this revelation, the world has suffered from the chastisement of cholera, small pox, and, more recently, AIDS. The continuation and extent of the sicknesses that shall yet plague the world are dependent upon mankind's response to the Lord's command to repent of their sins. Isaiah prophesied: "The earth also is defiled under the inhabitants thereof; because they have transgressed the laws, changed the ordinance, broken the everlasting covenant. Therefore hath the curse devoured the earth, and they that dwell therein are desolate: therefore the inhabitants of the earth are burned, and few men left" (Isaiah 24:5–6). In this revelation the Lord specifically states that the scourge awaiting the world is a result of people hardening their hearts against the testimony of the Book of Mormon and of the restoration of the Church of Jesus Christ. See commentary on Doctrine and Covenants 1:17.

5:20 *As I also told the people of the destruction of Jerusalem.* On the last day of his mortal ministry as the Savior taught on the temple mount, he prophesied its destruction, saying that not so much as one stone would be left standing upon another. That evening, surrounded by his disciples in a private garden on the Mount of Olives, he responded to their questions about his prophecy and told them that the nation of the Jews would be destroyed and that its survivors would be scattered among those of every nation, kindred, tongue, and people. See commentary on Doctrine and Covenants 45:16; Joseph Smith–Matthew 1:1–4, page 340.

It is now a matter of history that the Roman armies destroyed Jerusalem in A.D. 70. As impossible as the Master's prophecy must have appeared in the day in which it was uttered, every jot and tittle has been fulfilled.

Here we are told that if the inhabitants of the earth do not repent, the destruction of the wicked inhabitants of the earth by a desolating scourge in the latter-days is equally as sure as the destruction that came upon Jerusalem.

Martin Harris as One of the Witnesses
DOCTRINE AND COVENANTS 5:21-29

5:21 *Yield to the persuasions of men no more.* The Prophet is reminded of the difficult lesson learned when he yielded to Martin Harris's requests regarding the 116-page manuscript. See commentary on Doctrine and Covenants 3:7.

5:22 *Even if you should be slain.* This is the first hint in the revelations given to Joseph Smith that a martyr's death awaited him. While incarcerated in Liberty Jail, he was told that "there is a time appointed for every man, according as his works shall be" (D&C 121:25), and that "bounds" had been set beyond which his enemies could not go. "Thy days are known, and thy years shall not be numbered less; therefore, fear not what man can do, for God shall be with you forever and ever" (D&C 122:9).

5:24 *If he will bow down before me.* Martin's wickedness in breaking his covenant regarding the 116-page manuscript was known to all those who were involved. Martin acknowledged to the Prophet Joseph Smith that he had sinned. Indeed, his first words to Joseph after losing the manuscript were, "Oh! I have lost my soul. I have lost my soul" (Smith, *History of Joseph Smith*, 1996, 165). Martin had not approached God concerning his sins, however. Like Martin Harris, all who transgress the commandments of God must bow themselves before the God of heaven to seek his forgiveness. The truly repentant must humble themselves before God in acknowledging their sins and covenant with him to keep his commandments (v. 28).

Then will I grant unto him a view of the things which he desires to see. Martin was given a conditional promise that he would be one of the three special witnesses to be shown the plates by the power of God. To be granted this privilege Martin must humble himself before the Lord. See commentary on Doctrine and Covenants 17:2.

5:29 *Nor trouble me any more concerning this matter.* Earlier, when the Lord revealed that Martin Harris could not take the 116-page manuscript to show to his wife and others, he persisted in the request like a young child pestering a parent until Joseph wearied and gave in to his request. Here the Lord announced that he would give his answer but once. Having so done it was then up to Martin Harris to repent and qualify himself to be one of the special witnesses of the Book of Mormon.

The Lord Directs Joseph Concerning the Translation
DOCTRINE AND COVENANTS 5:30–35

5:30–34 *I will provide means whereby thou mayest accomplish the thing which I have commanded thee.* The Lord is directing the work of the translation of the Book of Mormon. When Martin Harris broke his covenant and subsequently lost the 116-page manuscript, he no longer served as a scribe. Emma, Joseph's wife, stated that she and her brother, Reuben Hale, both aided as scribes for part of the translation (*Saints Herald*, 26:289). The Lord did not intend for either Emma or Reuben to be the primary scribe for the Book of Mormon translation. Within a few weeks Oliver Cowdery would be led by the hand of the Lord to Harmony, where he would offer his help to the Prophet. See introduction to commentary on Doctrine and Covenants 6.

DOCTRINE AND COVENANTS 6–9
TRANSLATING THE BOOK OF MORMON

In April 1829 the Prophet recorded four revelations. Each is a part of the same story—the translation of the Book of Mormon—and each involves the same two men, Joseph Smith and Oliver Cowdery. These sections are the four most important documents extant today from which we can learn how the Book of Mormon was translated.

In Doctrine and Covenants 6 Oliver Cowdery is told that he has been given a special gift—even the gift of revelation—by which he may know mysteries and by which he might bring many to a knowledge of the truth (D&C 6:10–12). Oliver is also told that he will be given another gift, the gift of translation, that he might translate even as Joseph (D&C 6:25). He is further told that this is necessary for the process of translation to comply with the divine law of witnesses. Testimony that the Book of Mormon was translated by the gift and power of God would not rest on the word of Joseph Smith alone. Oliver was to be the second witness to the process by which it was translated (D&C 6:28).

Section 7 centers on a difference of opinion between Joseph and Oliver over the meaning of a text in the Gospel of John. They agreed to settle the matter by inquiring of God through the use of the Urim and Thummim. The revelation is a translated version of a parchment written and hidden up by John. The Prophet describes the experience in such a manner as to suggest that the revelation was jointly received. It is surely more than coincidence that in the previous revelation Oliver had been told he would receive the gift of translation and assist in bringing forth ancient scriptural records. This experience, as well as his participation in the translation of the parchment written by John, appears to be orchestrated by the Lord to prepare Oliver for his role in translating the Book of Mormon.

Section 8 affirms that Oliver Cowdery will be granted the opportunity to translate. It instructs him in the manner of receiving revelation, this being fundamental to the process of translation. It will be given you "in your mind and in your heart" (v. 2), he is told. Then the promise is also renewed relative to his second gift, the ability to use the Urim and Thummim. Again he is reminded that he must—even with the use of these divine instruments—ask in faith.

Section 9 affirms that Oliver did in fact translate but that he lost confidence and, like Peter as he walked on water, lost the power to continue translating (Matthew 14:31). Two reasons for his failure are given in this revelation: first, he had not studied or prepared himself properly; second, his fear had caused the moment to be lost to him (vv. 8, 11).

Often in the telling of this story it is general practice to emphasize Oliver's failure to translate rather than point out that for a few glorious moments he did so. Perhaps our purposes would be better served by emphasizing his success rather than his failure. With Peter as a point of reference, we ask, Is not the fact that he actually walked on water of greater significance than the fact that he feared for a moment and lost the capacity to do so? That Oliver translated—even briefly—is of great importance, for it made him a participant in the process of translation. He could now stand at Joseph's side and testify that the Book of Mormon was indeed translated by the gift and power of God and in no other way.

DOCTRINE AND COVENANTS 6

DATE: APRIL 1829 (ON OR AFTER 7 APRIL)
PLACE: HARMONY, PENNSYLVANIA

While teaching school in the community of Palmyra, New York, in the year 1829, Oliver Cowdery heard reports about Joseph Smith and his gold plates. Because the families that sent children to the school were expected to provide lodgings for the teacher, Oliver looked forward to staying with the Smiths, where he hoped to gain the truth of the story. Upon coming to live with the Smith family, Oliver gained the confidence of the Prophet's father and learned about the labor in which Joseph was involved. With that knowledge came an impression that he must go and write for Joseph. As soon as he could be excused from his obligations as a teacher, Oliver traveled to Harmony with the Prophet's younger brother Samuel. They arrived Sunday evening, 5 April 1829. Oliver was then able to receive a firsthand account of the events of the Restoration. He began his labors as the Prophet's scribe on Tuesday, 7 April.

Mother Smith recorded that after Oliver's conversation with Joseph Smith Sr., Oliver indicated that the matter had worked upon his bones, and he couldn't get it out of his mind. Finally, he resolved to accompany Samuel, who was apparently going to Harmony to help Joseph with his spring planting. "I have made it a subject of prayer, and I firmly believe that if it is the will of the Lord that I should go, and that there is a work for me to do in this thing, I am determined to attend to it" (as cited in Smith, *History of Joseph Smith*, 1996, 182). Oliver and Samuel covered the 140 miles on foot together.

Further, Mother Smith notes that "[Joseph] had been so hurried with business and writing, etc., that he could not proceed with the work as fast as it was necessary for him to do. There was also another disadvantage under which he had to labor. Emma had so much of her time taken up with the care of her house that she could write but little for him. Accordingly, two or three days before the arrival of Oliver and Samuel, Joseph called upon his Heavenly Father to send him a scribe as the angel had promised, and he was informed that the same should be forthcoming in a few days.

"When Oliver was introduced to Joseph, he said, 'Mr. Smith, I have come for the purpose of writing for you.' This was not at all unexpected to Joseph, for although he had never seen Mr. Cowdery before, he knew that the Lord was able to perform, and that he had been faithful to fulfill, all his promises" (*History of Joseph Smith*, 1996, 184).

Of these events, the Prophet recorded: "The Lord appeared unto a young man by the name Oliver Cowdery and shewed unto him the plates in a vision and also the truth of the work and what the Lord was about to do through me, his unworthy servant. Therefore he was desirous to come and write for me to translate" (Jessee, *Papers of Joseph Smith*, 1:10; spelling standardized).

Laborers in the Lord's Field Gain Salvation
DOCTRINE AND COVENANTS 6:1–5

6:1 *A great and marvelous work is about to come forth.* See commentary on Doctrine and Covenants 4:1.

6:2 It is not the voice of God of which we speak here but the word of God. There is power in the word—the truth, which is light. It can cut through the darkness of ignorance and unbelief; it can pierce the soul, cut to the core, bring the mighty to their knees, and humble the proud.

Describing the Spirit that attends the word of God, Joseph Smith said it "pierceth all things, and often times it maketh my bones to quake" (D&C 85:6). It lifts, edifies, inspires, enlightens, ennobles, and empowers. "For the word of the Lord is truth, and whatsoever is truth is light, and whatsoever is light is Spirit, even the Spirit of Jesus Christ" (D&C 84:45; see Hebrews 4:12; D&C 11:2; 12:2; 14:2; 33:1).

6:3 *The field is white.* See commentary on Doctrine and Covenants 4:4.

6:5 The promise that those who ask will receive is given to those who have taken up the sickle to harvest for the Lord. Those who are in the Lord's service have special claim on his attention.

Salvation Is the Greatest of God's Gifts
DOCTRINE AND COVENANTS 6:6–13

6:9 *Say nothing but repentance unto this generation.* Repentance is the doctrine that marks the true messenger of the Lord. Jeremiah identified the distinguishing doctrine of false prophets when he said, "They say unto every one that walketh after the imagination of his own heart, No evil shall come upon you" (Jeremiah 23:17). Thus the Lord typified apostate religion, saying, "For they have strayed from mine ordinances, and have broken mine everlasting covenant; they seek not the Lord to establish his righteousness, but every man walketh in his own way, and after the image of his own god, whose image is in the likeness of the world, and whose substance is that of an idol, which waxeth old and shall perish in Babylon, even Babylon the great, which shall fall" (D&C 1:15–16).

This expression does not indicate that the gospel consists of the doctrine of repentance alone; rather, the implication is that without the doctrine of repentance one cannot have the true gospel. No gospel principle can be properly understood without the purity of heart and soul that must first come from repentance (D&C 11:9; 19:21).

6:10–12 Oliver Cowdery had been given two gifts. The first was the gift of revelation by which he could obtain a knowledge of the mysteries of the kingdom, and the second was the gift to translate (D&C 6:25–28). In the realm of spiritual things, few men have been so richly favored.

6:13 *The gift of salvation.* Salvation in its fullest meaning is synonymous with exaltation, or eternal life. To be saved is to obtain a place in the celestial kingdom. In most instances, this is the way the word is

used in scripture. This is the salvation the Saints seek, and it is of this
which the Lord says, "There is no gift greater than the gift of salvation"
(D&C 6:13).

The Witness of Truth Comes by the Spirit
DOCTRINE AND COVENANTS 6:14–24

6:14–15 These verses, which describe the experience of Oliver
Cowdery as he was led by the Spirit to assume the important role that
would be his in the translation of the Book of Mormon, also typify the
experience of countless truth seekers. The Spirit leads seekers of truth to
the places where they will hear the truths of salvation preached. But even
as their prayers are answered, they often do not know it. It is only as they
grow in the things of the Spirit that they are able to look back on a
sequence of events and begin to realize how completely their course was
directed by the powers of heaven.

Here the Lord affirms for Oliver Cowdery that his prayers have been
answered. It is in effect a revelation, telling him that he has been receiving revelations. Similar experiences are common among those who are
growing up spiritually. We are told that the Lamanites, after their conversion, "were baptized with fire and with the Holy Ghost, and they knew
it not" (3 Nephi 9:20). Christ's companions on the road to Emmaus did
not realize who it was who taught them until the day's end and his departure from them. Only then did one of them say to the other, "Did not our
heart burn within us, while he talked with us by the way, and while he
opened to us the scriptures" (Luke 24:32).

6:14 Though he did not realize it, Oliver had been led by the hand of
providence to Palmyra, where he was teaching school. From there he was
led to take lodgings with the Smith family. Responding to this Spirit that
guided his destiny—as sure as the star of heaven guided the wise men of
old to the child Jesus—Oliver was led to Harmony, Pennsylvania, where
he offered his services to Joseph as a scribe.

6:16 God alone, in the full sense of the word, knows the hearts of
men. This, however, does not suggest that the prince of darkness cannot
discern friend from foe or that he cannot sense men's susceptibility to
yield to temptations.

6:17 The effect of this revelation was to affirm for Oliver that Joseph
Smith was a prophet. That in turn would add to his confidence relative

to the Book of Mormon. See commentary on Doctrine and Covenants 17:6; 18:2.

6:19 *Admonish him in his faults.* Nothing in any of the revelations of the Restoration suggest that Joseph Smith was either above the law, infallible, or not subject to any of the foibles common to men in this fallen world (D&C 3:4).

6:23 *Did I not speak peace to your mind?* Those seeking to become conversant in the language of the Spirit, who wish to know when their prayers are being answered and when the Spirit is directing them, must learn to identify the feelings of peace, comfort, and assurance that are characteristic of the spirit of revelation. Each time Oliver had prayed, he had experienced a quiet assurance. Unfamiliar with the nature of such prompting, he had not recognized that those feelings came in response to his prayers. His experience is instructive to all who are in the process of growing up in the things of the Spirit.

Oliver Is Granted the Key of Translation
DOCTRINE AND COVENANTS 6:25–28

6:25 *A gift . . . to translate, even as . . . Joseph.* Here Oliver is promised that he will have the gift of translation in the same portion and manner as enjoyed by the Prophet Joseph Smith.

6:27 This promise found a partial fulfillment in the revelation recorded in Doctrine and Covenants 7.

6:28 *Keys of this gift.* Both Joseph and Oliver had been given the gift to translate. The imagery of keys suggests the ability to unlock that which would otherwise remain hidden.

The mouth of two or three witnesses. According to divine plan, both Joseph and Oliver were to be involved in the process of translating the Book of Mormon. Thus, both men would be able to testify that the book had been translated by the gift and power of God. Oliver did, in fact, translate a small portion of the book. See commentary on Doctrine and Covenants 9:5.

Look to Christ and Do Good Continually
DOCTRINE AND COVENANTS 6:29–37

6:29–37 In these verses both Joseph and Oliver are admonished to be faithful in the labors to which they have been called. The Lord, who knows the unspoken thoughts of our hearts, understood Joseph and Oliver's anxiety about the translation and its acceptance in an unbelieving world. The Lord assures them that if men reject his message, Joseph and Oliver will still be blessed. He also reminds them of his own rejection and suffering at the hands of men. They are told that should men accept the Book of Mormon there will be great cause to rejoice and though they are only two in number, he will be with them. Joseph and Oliver need but do that which is good, and in so doing they will reap that which is good.

DOCTRINE AND COVENANTS 7

DATE: APRIL 1829 (ON OR AFTER 7 APRIL)
PLACE: HARMONY, PENNSYLVANIA

This revelation was received in April 1829. Of it, Joseph Smith said: "I continued to translate and he [Oliver] to write, with little cessation, during which time we received several revelations. A difference of opinion arising between us about the account of John the Apostle, mentioned in the New Testament, as to whether he died or continued to live, we mutually agreed to settle it by the Urim and Thummim and the following is the word which we received . . ." (*History of the Church*, 1:35–36).

The preface to this revelation, in both the Book of Commandments and the 1835 edition of the Doctrine and Covenants, reads as follows: "A Revelation given to Joseph Smith, Jun., and Oliver Cowdery, in Harmony, Pennsylvania, April 1829, when they desired to know whether John, the beloved disciple, tarried on earth or died. Translated from parchment, written and hid up by himself."

In the previous revelation Oliver was promised the gift of translation (D&C 6:25). He was also promised that he would be involved as a translator in bringing forth revelations that had been hidden up because of the wickedness of men (D&C 6:27). This revelation appears to be at least a partial fulfillment of those promises. It would also appear that this experience was preparatory to fulfillment of the promise that had been made to Oliver that he would aid in the translation of the Book of Mormon.

John the Beloved and the Gathering of Israel
DOCTRINE AND COVENANTS 7:1–3

7:1 *You shall ask what you will.* We read accounts of spiritually noble men who have received the Lord's promise that they may ask whatever they will of him and it will be given them. Nephi, son of Helaman, was such a man. Because of his tireless service in the cause of truth, the Lord said to him, "I will bless thee forever; and I will make thee mighty in word and in deed, in faith and in works; yea, even that all things shall be done unto thee according to thy word, for thou shalt not ask that which is contrary to my will" (Helaman 10:5). In like manner the Lord told Enoch, "My Spirit is upon you, wherefore all thy words will I justify; and the mountains shall flee before you, and the rivers shall turn from their course; and thou shalt abide in me, and I in you; therefore walk with me" (Moses 6:34). Such was the promise here accorded by Christ to his beloved cousin John the Revelator.

7:2 *Lord, give unto me power over death.* See commentary on Doctrine and Covenants 49:8, "Holy men that ye know not of."

7:3 *Shall prophesy before nations.* See commentary on Doctrine and Covenants 77:9, "This is Elias"; 77:14, "It was a mission, and an ordinance, for him to gather the tribes."

Peter, James, and John Hold Gospel Keys
DOCTRINE AND COVENANTS 7:4–8

7:6 John was promised that he would not taste of death until the time of Christ's return. During the interim period he would be a translated being like unto Enoch and those of his city. "Many have supposed," Joseph Smith explained, "that the doctrine of translation was a doctrine whereby men were taken immediately into the presence of God, and into an eternal fullness, but this is a mistaken idea. Their place of habitation is that of the terrestrial order, and a place prepared for such characters He held in reserve to be ministering angels unto many planets, and who as yet have not entered into so great a fullness as those who are resurrected from the dead" (*Teachings of the Prophet Joseph Smith,* 170).

I will make him as flaming fire. This language, though used by Paul (Hebrews 1:7), traces to Psalm 104:4. It is part of the imagery used to describe the splendor and glory in which God clothes himself and his servants. Though John as a translated being could appear in glory, "as flaming fire," much of his labor could be accomplished while his glory was withheld.

A ministering angel. Paul taught that "angels are ministering spirits" (JST Hebrews 1:7). Speaking of angels, Mormon explained that "the office of their ministry is to call men unto repentance, and to fulfil and to do the work of the covenants of the Father, which he hath made unto the children of men, to prepare the way among the children of men, by declaring the word of Christ unto the chosen vessels of the Lord, that they may bear testimony of him" (Moroni 7:31).

He shall minister for those who shall be heirs of salvation who dwell on the earth. Again, the language is that of the apostle Paul, who said that angels are "sent forth to minister for them who shall be heirs of salvation" (Hebrews 1:14). A modern rendering of this text reads, "The angels are only spirit-messengers sent out to help and care for those who are to receive his salvation" *(Living New Testament).* The ministering of angels has been common to those of the household of faith in all ages. "Thus the Gospel began to be preached, from the beginning, being declared by holy angels sent forth from the presence of God, and by his own voice, and by the gift of the Holy Ghost" (Moses 5:58). So it would be that John, who was himself ministered to by angels (Revelation 22:9), would now be called upon to administer in like fashion to others. At a conference of the Church, held June 1831, Joseph Smith said "John the Revelator was then among the Ten Tribes of Israel who had been led away by Shalmaneser, king of Assyria, to prepare them for their return from their long dispersion" *(History of the Church,* 1:176).

7:7 The text affirms that Peter, James, and John constituted "a quorum of three presidents" according to the ancient order (D&C 107:29), and as such they presided over the meridian-day Church. A little more than a month after this revelation was received, John the Baptist would explain to Joseph and Oliver that in restoring the Aaronic Priesthood he had acted under the direction of these three men who "held the keys of the Priesthood of Melchizedek" (Joseph Smith–History 1:72), also known as "the Presidency of the High Priesthood" (D&C 81:2). We know their office today as that of the First Presidency (D&C 107:22).

DOCTRINE AND COVENANTS 8

DATE: APRIL 1829 (ON OR AFTER 7 APRIL)
PLACE: HARMONY, PENNSYLVANIA

Oliver Cowdery is here given permission to use the gift of translation that he had been promised and told that he may aid in the labor of translating the Book of Mormon. Preparatory to that, the Lord teaches Oliver two principles: the spirit of revelation is essential to the translation process, and faith is also a part of that process, for should he give way to doubt, he will lose the power of God and be unable to proceed.

Revelation Comes by the Holy Ghost
DOCTRINE AND COVENANTS 8:1–5

8:1–5 In these verses Oliver Cowdery is told that he has been given the gift of revelation. If he asks in faith, doing so with an honest heart, he is promised that he will be able to translate ancient records. From the Book of Mormon we learn that there are many records which are yet to come forth. These records will also contain a witness of Christ and the assurance of the promises made to the posterity of Abraham. And like the Book of Mormon, these sacred records can be translated only by the gift and power of God (2 Nephi 29:10–14; 3 Nephi 26:6–11; Ether 3:22–28; 4:5–7).

8:2 Though we would not seek to limit the ways in which the Lord can communicate his mind and will to his children, we would be well within the mark to say that most revelation comes in the form of thoughts and feelings that the Lord places in the hearts and minds of those he chooses to instruct. They in turn are left to clothe those thoughts with words that might be shared with others. This stands in sharp contrast with the sectarian world, where the prevailing doctrine—known as divine dictation—maintains that when the Lord chooses to speak through someone, all his or her bodily functions are suspended. The recipient of the revelation becomes as a dummy in the lap of the divine ventriloquist, voicing only those words that are given it. This, it is reasoned, must be the case so that the culture, understanding, and temperament of the revelation's recipient do not influence its expression. Thus, it is argued that revelation is both inerrant and infallible. Here we learn that the Lord gave us as his children both minds and hearts, with the intent that they be used to converse with him. As we grow in spiritual understanding, our capacity to receive and understand revelation increases accordingly, just as a child's ability to converse with others increases as that child grows in understanding.

There are no mindless revelations, nor are there any heartless ones. Indeed, we would say that the more disciplined and informed the mind and the more refined and purified the heart, the greater the portion of heavenly light forthcoming. As parents speak to their children according to the level of their understanding, so does our Heavenly Father speak to his children. For this reason, the Lord reminds Oliver (v. 5) to keep his commandments. One cannot do those things that alienate the Spirit of the Lord and at the same time draw upon the light and strength that it brings.

Mysteries of God and the Power to Translate
DOCTRINE AND COVENANTS 8:6–11

8:6 *The gift of Aaron.* In the Book of Commandments this was called the "rod of nature," which has caused considerable speculation that Oliver Cowdery had some kind of a divining rod by which he could receive revelation. Then comes the supposition that in changing this text to read "the gift of Aaron," Joseph Smith decided he was telling more than he intended. Such conclusions do not seem to represent good doctrine, good history, or a correct appraisal of the Prophet's purpose in making this change. Consider the following:

First, there is no record or statement tracing to either Joseph Smith or Oliver Cowdery that so much as hints that Oliver had or used any sort of a rod to receive revelation.

Second, the divinely ordained system by which the Book of Mormon was to be translated was the Urim and Thummim. There is no justification for the supposition that Oliver, when granted the privilege of translating, would do so by some other means. Here the Lord said he had been given the "gift of Aaron." True it is that Aaron had a rod which became a serpent when he cast it down before Pharaoh (Exodus 7:10), but he did not use it to receive revelation. Aaron had another gift, the Urim and Thummim, for that purpose (Exodus 28:30; Leviticus 8:6–9).

Third, in Doctrine and Covenants 6, Oliver was told that he had a gift by which he could ask and receive and even obtain a knowledge of the mysteries of heaven (D&C 6:3–12). He was also told that he would be given the gift by which he could translate "even as my servant Joseph" (D&C 6:25). If he was to translate even as Joseph, he would have to translate by the same means used by the Prophet, the Urim and Thummim.

Fourth, in this section, Oliver is again told that he would be granted the spirit of revelation, and in addition to that he would be given another gift, the "gift of Aaron," by which he had already learned many things. Certainly the things he had learned included that which is contained in Doctrine and Covenants 6 and 7, both of which were received by the use of the Urim and Thummim.

Fifth, it would be difficult to suppose that Joseph was attempting to obscure anything in making the change from "rod of nature" (Book of Commandments) to "gift of Aaron" (1835 Doctrine and Covenants), given that he left intact the promise that Oliver would hold this gift in his hands. We know of no seeric device that Oliver could have held in his hands except the Urim and Thummim.

Finally, both Joseph and Oliver had been promised the "keys of this gift" (D&C 6:28). Joseph never used a rod in translation. The gift he used, in common with Oliver, was the Urim and Thummim. Lucy Mack Smith said that Joseph referred to the Urim and Thummim as "a key." It was by this key that "the angel manifested those things to him that were shown him in vision; by which also he could at any time ascertain the approach of danger, either to himself or the record, and for this cause he kept these things constantly about his person" (Smith, *History of Joseph Smith*, 1996, 145). In yet another instance, Lucy Mack Smith recorded that Joseph told her he had "a key" by which he translated. She said she did not know what he meant, but he placed the "article in [her] hands and, examining it with no covering but a silk handkerchief, found that it consisted of two smooth three-cornered diamonds set in glass, and the glasses were set in silver bows connected with each other in much the same way that old-fashioned spectacles are made" (Smith, *History of Joseph Smith*, 1996, 139).

We conclude, therefore, that the gift promised to Oliver Cowdery could be nothing other than the Urim and Thummim and that Joseph's purpose in making this change was to clarify rather than conceal its meaning. This change assumes that the reader will know that the gift given the high priest in ancient times was the Urim and Thummim, but then the whole story of the Restoration assumes knowledge of the ancient order of things.

It may be that the Urim and Thummim were referred to as a rod because they were connected by a rod to the breastplate Joseph received with the plates. The Prophet's brother William described the means by which the Urim and Thummim were attached to the breastplate, saying "A pocket was prepared in the breastplate on the left side, immediately over the heart. When not in use the Urim and Thummim was placed in the pocket, the rod being of just the right length to allow it to be deposited. This instrument could, however, be detached from the breast-plate when away from home, but Joseph always used it in connection with the breastplate when translating, as it permitted him to have both hands free to touch the plates" (Smith, *Rod of Iron* 1, 3 [February 1924]: 7). See commentary on Doctrine and Covenants 10:1. As to "nature" in the phrase "rod of nature," the dictionary of Joseph Smith's day defined *nature* as comprehending "the works of God" (Webster, *Dictionary*, 1828).

8:9 *By means of the Urim and Thummin.* Oliver receives the promise that he too will be able to translate as did Joseph.

8:10 It appears that the Urim and Thummim functioned according to the same principles as did the Liahona—according to the "faith and diligence" of those using it (Alma 37:41).

DOCTRINE AND COVENANTS 9

DATE: APRIL 1829 (ON OR AFTER 7 APRIL)
PLACE: HARMONY, PENNSYLVANIA

This revelation, which confirms that Oliver Cowdery had for a moment been able to translate, explains why he was unable to continue doing so. The two key words denoting his inability to do so are "study" and "fear." Oliver is told that he was to have studied the matter out in his mind, come to a conclusion, and then sought the confirmation of the Lord. He is also told that because he feared, the moment was lost to him, and it was no longer expedient for him to translate.

The lessons growing out of Oliver Cowdery's experience are of immense value to all who seek answer to prayers. For that purpose, sec-tion 9 should be thoughtfully studied. It is the most authoritative and instructive source we have—particularly when studied in concert with the previous three revelations—in helping us to understand how the Book of Mormon was translated.

Oliver Loses Confidence to Translate
DOCTRINE AND COVENANTS 9:1–6

9:2 Further scriptural records will be given to the Latter-day Saints when their faith becomes such as Oliver's was supposed to have been.

9:5 *You began to translate.* Peter walked on water for a short period before his faith failed him. Oliver Cowdery translated for a like period of time before he lost the confidence to continue.

9:6 *It is wisdom in me.* Countless souls seeking to understand the principles upon which the truths of heaven are dispensed will find helpful instruction in Oliver Cowdery's efforts to translate. Here we learn that answers come to those who have prepared themselves to receive them. It is not enough for us to simply ask. Study, thought, pondering, and prayerful searching are very much a part of the revelatory process. In the earlier revelation (D&C 8:2), Oliver was told that the process of revelation would include the use of both his mind and his heart. Surely, what we can do we must do. We do not ask for our daily bread with the idea in mind that angels will be sent to prepare our soil, plant the seeds, nurture the plants, and then do the work of the harvest. Faith is not a substitute for indolence. So it is that in seeking an answer we study the matter, make the best possible conclusion, and then take it to the Lord for confirmation or for redirection. In like manner, when we are called to serve in the Church, we do not shift the responsibility of receiving necessary revelation for our callings to those who preside over us. Spiritually, we are to stand on our own feet. As appropriate, we may seek counsel from others and their confirmation of the course we feel impressed to follow, but we do not properly shift the burden of our office back to them.

The Process by Which the Book of Mormon Was Translated
DOCTRINE AND COVENANTS 9:7–14

9:7–10 Explanations as to how the Book of Mormon was translated have become the source of considerable speculation and misinformation. There appears to be little interest on the part of some writers to distinguish between what might be called historical prattle and competent testimony. For instance, scripture, statements by the Prophet himself, and the collaborative testimony of Oliver Cowdery—the only firsthand sources we have on the matter—are not, among some, accorded the same attention or credence as things said by secondhand witnesses who in thought and spirit were clearly out of harmony with the Prophet and the Church.

The matter of how the Book of Mormon was translated has been of considerable interest and discussion virtually from the time the book became public. This is illustrated in an exchange that took place between the Prophet and his brother Hyrum in a conference of the Church held 25 October 1831. On that occasion Hyrum said "that he thought best that the information of the coming forth of the book of Mormon be related by Joseph himself to the Elders present that all might know for themselves." In response, Joseph Smith said that "it was not intended to tell the world all the particulars of the coming forth of the book of Mormon, & also said that it was not expedient for him to relate these things &c" (Cannon and Cook, *Far West Record*, 23).

Yet, it was not intended that we be entirely ignorant of the process of translation; otherwise, the revelation recorded in Doctrine and Covenants 9 would not have been included in a compilation of revelations intended for the eyes of the entire world. There are principles involved here of which every faithful Latter-day Saint ought to be a competent witness. There are also counterfeit notions about how the Book of Mormon was translated that enhance neither our understanding of how revelation is received nor our appreciation for the labor and faith involved so that we might have the Book of Mormon. Perhaps the matter can be treated most directly in a question and answer format. We will proceed in that manner.

Question: Why was Joseph Smith so reluctant to disclose details relative to the process of translation?

Answer: Because of its sacred nature. It is an "awful responsibility," Joseph Smith said, "to write in the name of the Lord" (*History of the Church*, 1:226). Nor would we suppose it a small thing to be entrusted with a seeric device such as the Urim and Thummim. Just as the instrument itself was not to be held up to the gaze of the world, neither was the process by which it functioned. It seems more than coincidence that one of the first things translated by Joseph Smith after Oliver Cowdery became his scribe was the story of King Limhi asking Ammon if he could translate the records in his possession. Ammon responded that he could not, but he knew one who could. Ammon then explained, "For he has wherewith that he can look, and translate all records that are of ancient date; and it is a gift from God. And the things are called interpreters, and no man can look in them except he be commanded, lest he should look for that he ought not and he should perish. And whosoever is commanded to look in them, the same is called seer" (Mosiah 8:13).

The earliest known description of the process of translating the Book of Mormon is found in an article titled "History of the Mormonites," published 9 June 1831, in Kirtland, Ohio. The writer, Josiah Jones, claims as his source the first Latter-day Saint missionaries to that territory—Elders Cowdery, Pratt, Whitmer, and Peterson, from whom he learned that the book was translated by "looking into a stone or two stones, when put into a dark place, which stones he said were found in the box with the plates. They affirmed while [Joseph] looked through the stone spectacles another sat by and wrote what he told them, and thus the book was written. . . .

"A few days after these men appeared again, a few of us went to see them and Cowdery was requested to state how the plates were found, which he did. He stated that Smith looked onto or through the transparent stones to translate what was on the plates. I then asked him if he had ever looked through the stones to see what he could see in them; his reply was that he was not permitted to look into them. I asked him who debarred him from looking into them; he remained sometime in silence, then said that he had so much confidence in his friend Smith, who told him that he must not look into them, that he did not presume to do so lest he should tempt God and be struck dead" (Allen, "Historian's Corner," 308).

Though the article fails to acknowledge Oliver's frustrating experience in attempting to translate, it does emphasize the feeling of sacredness that was associated with the use of the Urim and Thummim. Similarly, in another early article, Martin Harris was recorded as having said that Joseph had been directed "not to let any mortal being examine them [the interpreters], under no less penalty than instant death" ("Golden Bible," 3).

Oliver was twice cautioned not to trifle with sacred things, having reference to the seeric aids that would be used in translation. "Do not ask," he was warned, "for that which you ought not" (D&C 8:10; see 6:12). And again, Joseph Smith was told that "if they [meaning the world] will not believe my words, they would not believe you, my servant Joseph, if it were possible that you should show them all these things which I have committed unto you" (D&C 5:7).

A testimony of the Book of Mormon must of necessity embrace the understanding that it came as a "gift" of God, by the "power of God." It is both the foundation upon which the modern Church is to rest and a miracle. To suppose that in its origin the Book of Mormon is less than a miracle is to attempt to build the house of one's understanding upon something other than the foundation upon which the Lord placed it. It is not expected that miracles be explained.

Question: Did Joseph Smith say anything about the process of translation?

Answer: Yes. Joseph affirmed that he "translated from the plates," and that he used the Urim and Thummim to do so. After the loss of the 116 pages by Martin Harris, both the plates and the Urim and Thummim were taken from him. Without the Urim and Thummim he could not translate. During this period Joseph made a short visit to his parents in Manchester, New York, and then returned again to Pennsylvania. "Immediately after my return home," he recounted, "I was walking out a little distance, when, behold, the former heavenly messenger appeared and handed to me the Urim and Thummim again—for it had been taken from me in consequence of my having wearied the Lord in asking for the privilege of letting Martin Harris take the writings, which he lost by transgression—and I inquired of the Lord through it, and obtained the following [section 3]" (Smith, *History of the Church*, 1:21–22).

"After I had obtained the above revelation," the Prophet continued, "both the plates and the Urim and Thummim were taken from me again; but in a few days they were returned to me, when I inquired of the Lord, and the Lord said thus unto me:

"Now, behold, I say unto you, that because you delivered up those writings which you had power given unto you to translate by the means of the Urim and Thummim, into the hands of a wicked man, you have lost them. And you also lost your gift at the same time, and your mind became darkened" (Smith, *History of the Church*, 1:23–24).

In the Wentworth Letter, the Prophet wrote: "With the records was found a curious instrument, which the ancients called "Urim and Thummim," which consisted of two transparent stones set in the rim of a bow fastened to a breast plate. Through the medium of the Urim and Thummim I translated the record by the gift and power of God" (*History of the Church*, 4:537).

Question: What was the testimony of Oliver Cowdery on the matter?

Answer: In the October 1834 *Messenger and Advocate*, Oliver Cowdery wrote: "These were days never to be forgotten—to sit under the sound of a voice dictated by the inspiration of heaven, awakened the utmost gratitude of this bosom! Day after day I continued, uninterrupted, to write from his mouth, as he translated, with the Urim and Thummim, or, as the Nephites would have said, 'Interpreters,' the history or record called 'The book of Mormon'" (*Messenger and Advocate*, 1:14).

The testimony borne by Oliver Cowdery upon his return to the Church was as follows: "Friends and Brethren: My name is Cowdery, Oliver Cowdery. In the early history of this Church, I stood identified with her, and one in her councils. True it is that the gifts and callings of God are without repentance; not because I was better than the rest of mankind was I called, to fulfill the purposes of God. He called me to a high and holy calling. I wrote with my own pen, the entire Book of Mormon (save a few pages) as it fell from the lips of the Prophet Joseph Smith, as he translated it by the gift and power of God, by means of the Urim and Thummim, or, as it is called by the book, 'holy interpreters.' I beheld with my eyes, and handled with my hands, the gold plates from which it was translated. I also saw with my eyes and handled with my hands the 'holy interpreters'" (as cited in Smith, *Restoration of All Things*, 113).

Question: What should we know about the process of translation?

Answer: Certainly each member of the Church should have a meaningful understanding of that which the Lord has revealed to us on the matter. Our query then becomes, to what revelation do we turn? The answer is Doctrine and Covenants 9, in which we learn that Oliver Cowdery commenced to translate and then lost his courage and could not continue (vv. 5, 11).

"You must study it out in your mind," the Lord told him, "then [that is after having arrived at your own best determination as to what the proper meaning is] you must ask me if it be right, and if it is right I will cause that your bosom shall burn within you; therefore, you shall feel that it is right. But if it be not right you shall have no such feelings, but you shall have a stupor of thought that shall cause you to forget the thing which is wrong; therefore, you cannot write that which is sacred save it be given you from me" (D&C 9:8–9).

In this context let us give at least brief consideration to the preparation that Joseph Smith made in order to have the sense and feel of this ancient record he was translating. First, it would be well to observe that he had received considerable tutoring from Moroni and other prophets from the Book of Mormon. In the Wentworth Letter Joseph Smith tells us that Moroni told him about the original inhabitants of this country and gave him "a sketch of their origin, progress, civilization, laws, governments, of their righteousness and iniquity, and the blessings of God being finally withdrawn from them as a people" (*History of the Church*, 4:537). Illustrating the understanding that Joseph obtained of these things long before he began the labor of translation, his mother tells us how "every evening we gathered our children together and gave our time up to the discussion of those things which he instructed to us. I think that we presented the most peculiar aspect of any family that ever lived upon the earth, all seated in a circle, father, mother, sons, and daughters, listening in breathless anxiety to the religious teachings of a boy eighteen years of age who had never read the Bible through by course in his life. For Joseph was less inclined to the study of books than any child we had, but much more given to reflection and deep study.

"We were convinced that God was about to bring to light something that we might stay our minds upon, something that would give us a more perfect knowledge of the plan of salvation and the redemption of the human family than anything which had been taught us heretofore, and we rejoiced in it with exceeding great joy. The sweetest union and happiness pervaded our house. No jar nor discord disturbed our peace, and tranquility reigned in our midst.

"In the course of our evening conversations, Joseph gave us some of the most amusing recitals which could be imagined. He would describe the ancient inhabitants of this continent, their dress, their manner of traveling, the animals which they rode, the cities that they built, and the structure of their buildings with every particular, their mode of warfare, and their religious worship as specifically as though he had spent his life with them. It will be recollected by the reader that all that I mentioned and much more took place within the compass of one short year" (Smith, *History of Joseph Smith*, 1996, 111–12).

In this respect the testimony of Lorenzo Brown about the preparation the Prophet made for his translation of the Bible may be instructive. He records the Prophet as saying: "After I got through translating the Book of Mormon, I took up the Bible to read with the Urim and Thummim. I read the first chapter of Genesis and I saw the things as they were done. I turned over the next and the next, and the whole passed before me like a grand panorama; and so on chapter after chapter until I read the whole of it. I saw it all!" (as cited in Matthews, *Plainer Translation*, 25).

The kind of knowledge thus suggested seems to have been requisite to the labor of translation. For Joseph to properly render the sense of the characters recorded on the plates entrusted to him, he had to both know and feel what stood behind them. Perhaps the point is best illustrated with the Bible, for there seems to be no end of Bible translations. Why, we would ask, is the labor of Bible translation never done? Because, we are told, that as our knowledge of ancient civilizations—their laws, governments, cultures, and languages—increases so does our ability to give meaningful and accurate translations to that which they wrote. As it is with the manuscripts from which the Bible comes, so it is with the characters recorded on the plates of gold from which Joseph Smith translated.

Question: In addition to statements of the Prophet, the text of Doctrine and Covenants 9, and the testimony of Oliver Cowdery, who else has described the process by which the Book of Mormon was translated?

Answer: Perhaps prime among their number would be David Whitmer.

Question: What light does he shed on the matter?

Answer: Precious little. The testimony of David Whitmer, which is laid forth below, clearly contradicts the principles established by the Lord in this revelation. It is also at odds with the testimonies of both Joseph Smith and Oliver Cowdery. In our judgment, Mr. Whitmer is not a reliable source on this matter. We are entirely respectful of and grateful for the testimony to which he appended his name as one of the three witnesses of the truthfulness of the Book of Mormon and its divine origin. That, however, does not make him a competent witness to the process of translation. We too, like countless others, are competent witnesses of the truthfulness of the Book of Mormon. Our knowledge of how it was translated, however, is limited to that which has come through the channels ordained by the Lord for that purpose. As to David Whitmer's explanation, it should be remembered that he never looked into the Urim and Thummim nor translated anything. His testimony of how the Book of Mormon was transltated is hearsay.

Spanning a period of twenty years (1869–1888), some seventy recorded testimonies about the coming forth of the Book of Mormon claim David Whitmer as their source. Though there are a number of inconsistencies in these accounts, David Whitmer was repeatedly reported to have said that after the loss of the 116 pages, the Lord took both the plates and the Urim and Thummim from the Prophet, never to be returned. In their stead, David Whitmer maintained, the Prophet used an oval-shaped, chocolate-colored seer stone slightly larger than an egg. Thus, everything we have in the Book of Mormon, according to Mr. Whitmer, was translated by placing the chocolate-colored stone in a hat into which Joseph would bury his head so as to close out the light. While doing so he could see "an oblong piece of parchment, on which the hieroglyphics would appear," and below the ancient writing, the translation would be given in English. Joseph would then read this to Oliver Cowdery, who in turn would write it. If he did so correctly, the characters and the interpretation would disappear and be replaced by other characters with their interpretation (Cook, *David Whitmer Interviews*, 115, 157–58).

Such an explanation is, in our judgment, simply fiction created for the purpose of demeaning Joseph Smith and to undermine the validity of the revelations he received after translating the Book of Mormon. We invite the reader to consider the following:

First, for more than fifty years David Whitmer forthrightly rejected Joseph Smith, declaring him to be a fallen prophet. Though he never denied his testimony of the Book of Mormon, he rejected virtually everything else associated with the ministry of Joseph Smith and the restoration of the gospel. His rejection included both the Aaronic and Melchizedek Priesthoods, which were restored during the time the Book of Mormon was being translated and, of course, the revelations which would eventually constitute the Doctrine and Covenants.

Second, according to David Whitmer's account of how the Book of Mormon was translated, Joseph Smith was the instrument of transmission, while translation rested solely with the Lord. This is simply a reflection of the notion of divine dictation, which holds that every word of scripture comes from God himself. If David Whitmer's account is to be accepted, revelation also includes spelling and punctuation. This notion is at odds with the explanation found in Doctrine and Covenants 8 and 9, which details how revelation comes. In this respect, Richard Anderson observed that Whitmer "after decades of reflection outside of the Church, concluded that no modification could possibly be made in any revelation. This highly rigid view of these revelations matched his highly rigid view of the origin of the Book of Mormon" ("By the Gift and Power of God," 84). By contrast Brigham Young observed, "Should the Lord Almighty send an angel to re-write the Bible, it would in many places be very different from what it now is. And I will even venture to say that if the Book of Mormon were now to be re-written, in many instances it would materially differ from the present translation" (*Journal of Discourses*, 9:311).

David Whitmer repeatedly said that if a word was misspelled, the translator would not be able to go on until it had been corrected. This hardly allows for the 3,913 changes that have been made between the first edition of the Book of Mormon and the edition presently in use.

Third, if the process of translation was simply a matter of reading from a seer stone in a hat, surely Oliver Cowdery could do that as well, if not better, than Joseph Smith. After all, Oliver was a schoolteacher. How then do we account for Oliver's inability to translate? Further, regarding the use of a hat in translation, Joseph's brother William Smith explained that the Prophet used the Urim and Thummim attached to the breastplate by a rod that held the seer stones set in the rims of a bow before his eyes. "The instrument caused a strain on Joseph's eyes, and he sometimes resorted to covering his eyes with a hat to exclude the light in part" (Smith, *Rod of Iron* 1, 3 [February 1924]: 7).

Fourth, Joseph Smith repeatedly testified to having both the plates and the Urim and Thummim returned to him. He further testified that he translated from the plates by the use of the Urim and Thummim.

Fifth, David Whitmer gave inconsistent accounts of the instrument used to translate. Thomas Wood Smith, in a published response about an interview he had with David Whitmer, who told him that Joseph Smith used the Urim and Thummim in translating the Book of Mormon, wrote, "When I first read Mr. Traughber's paper in the *Herald* of November 15th, I thought that I would not notice his attack at all, as I supposed that I was believed by the Church to be fair and truthful in my statements of other men's views, when I have occasion to use them, and I shall make this reply only: That unless my interview with David Whitmer in January, 1876, was only a dream, or that I failed to understand plain English, I believed then, and since, and now, that he said that Joseph possessed, and used the Urim and Thummim in the translation of the inscriptions referred to, and I remember of being much pleased with that statement, as I had heard of the 'Seer stone' being used. And unless I dreamed the interview, or very soon after failed to recollect the occasion, he described the form and size of the said Urim and Thummim. The nearest approach to a retraction of my testimony as given . . . publicly in many places from the stand from January, 1876, till now, is, that unless I altogether misunderstood 'Father Whitmer' on this point, he said the translation was done by the aid of the Urim and Thummim. If he says he did not intend to convey such an impression to my mind, then I say I regret that I misunderstood him, and unintentionally have misrepresented him. But that I understood him as represented by me frequently I still affirm" (as cited in Cook, *David Whitmer Interviews*, 56).

Finally, the testimony of David Whitmer simply does not accord with the divine pattern. If Joseph Smith translated everything that is now in the Book of Mormon without using the gold plates, we are left to wonder why the plates were necessary in the first place. It will be remembered that possession of the plates placed the Smith family in considerable danger, causing them a host of difficulties. If the plates were not part of the translation process, this would not have been the case. It also leaves us wondering why the Lord directed the writers of the Book of Mormon to make a duplicate record of the plates of Lehi. This provision—which compensated for the loss of the 116 pages—would have served no purpose either. Further, we would be left to wonder why it was necessary for Moroni to instruct Joseph each year for four years before he was entrusted with the plates. We would also wonder why it was so important for Moroni to show the plates to the three witnesses, including David Whitmer. And why did the Lord have the Prophet show the plates to the eight witnesses? Why all this flap and fuss if the Prophet didn't really have the plates and if they were not used in the process of translation? What David Whitmer is asking us to believe is that the Lord had Moroni seal up the plates and the means by which they were to be translated hundreds of years before they would come into Joseph Smith's possession and then decided to have the Prophet use a seer stone found while digging a well so that none of these things would be necessary after all. Is this, we would ask, really a credible explanation of the way the heavens operate?

When asked how the labor of translation was accomplished, the Prophet declined to answer, saying, "It was not intended to tell the world all the particulars of the coming forth of the book of Mormon" (Cannon and Cook, *Far West Record*, 23). Surely we do not look to the world or the understanding of the world for an answer. We would expect to find that understanding only as we come to understand in greater measure the operations of the Spirit of revelation. See commentary on Joseph Smith–History 1:35, page 21; Doctrine and Covenants 10:1.

9:7 You took no thought. Without works there can be no faith. We pray for our daily bread knowing that our prayers must be sustained by the sweat of our brow. So it is in the realm of spiritual things. We pray for knowledge, knowing that our prayers must be sustained by the labors of both our hearts and our minds.

9:8 *You must study.* Every revelation requires a labor of its own. For example, a young man seeking an eternal companion must court young women with whom he is most likely to find the kind of companionship he seeks. It is for him, not the angels of heaven, to choose his wife. Having made his choice, he can then seek and obtain the confirmation of heaven that he has chosen wisely; but it is not for the heavens to make that choice for him.

The inspiration sought by those who would write good books or compose good music requires much by way of preparation. So it is with art or artistry of all kinds; the heavens reward those who school and prepare themselves well.

You shall feel that it is right. Feelings are the language of the Spirit. All true religion is a feeling. "Ye were past feeling, that ye could not feel his [the Lord's] words," Nephi said to his brothers Laman and Lemuel, who were given up to wickedness (1 Nephi 17:45). Having taught truth, Joseph Smith said: "This is good doctrine. It tastes good. I can taste the principles of eternal life, and so can you. They are given to me by the revelations of Jesus Christ; and I know that when I tell you these words of eternal life as they are given to me, you taste them. . . . I can also taste the spirit of eternal life. I know it is good; and when I tell you to these things which were given me by inspiration of the Holy Spirit, you are bound to receive them as sweet, and rejoice more and more" (*Teachings of the Prophet Joseph Smith*, 355).

9:9 *Stupor of thought.* Lack of confidence, a sense of uncertainty, mental sluggishness—such phrases describe our feelings when we have as yet to obtain the mind and will of heaven. By contrast, Joseph Smith said, "A person may profit by noticing the first intimation of the spirit of revelation; for instance, when you feel pure intelligence flowing into you, it may give you sudden strokes of ideas, so that by noticing it, you may find it fulfilled the same day or soon; (i.e.). those things that were presented unto your minds by the Spirit of God, will come to pass; and thus by learning the Spirit of God and understanding it, you may grow into the principle of relation, until you become perfect in Christ Jesus" (*Teachings of the Prophet Joseph Smith*, 151).

9:10 If Oliver Cowdery had understood his responsibility in the process of receiving revelation—that is, had he understood the principles just enumerated by the Lord in this revelation—he would have been able to translate.

It is not expedient that you should translate now. Though Oliver had lost the privilege to translate for a time and season, this statement implies that it will be accorded to him again. However, we are not aware of any evidence that Oliver, after this occasion, did in fact act as a translator.

9:11 *You feared, and the time is past.* Fear has been the culprit of many a lost opportunity. The experience is common to us all. Those who have learned to trust that the Lord will give them that which they should say or do in such situations have been and will continue to be the instruments through which great good is accomplished.

9:14 Having called us to the labor, it is for the Lord to sustain us in it. As it is his inspiration and direction that we seek, so it is his hand that protects us.

DOCTRINE AND COVENANTS 10

DATE: SUMMER 1828
PLACE: HARMONY, PENNSYLVANIA

Doctrine and Covenants 3 and 10 are companion revelations. In Doctrine and Covenants 3, the Prophet learned of the provisions the Lord had made many generations earlier, even while the Book of Mormon was being written, to provide for the loss of the 116 pages which he had translated from the book of Lehi. Perhaps more is involved in this story than a dramatic lesson on obedience by the youthful prophet. It could well be that the experience obtained while translating this portion of the ancient record was also foreseen as a necessary part of his schooling as he prepared himself for the sacred task of translating.

Doctrine and Covenants 3 was obtained by the use of the Urim and Thummim, after which it and the plates were again taken from the Prophet. In a few days they were returned. Again, through the Urim and Thummim, the Prophet inquired of the Lord and received the revelation recorded in section 10.

There has been considerable discussion concerning the date this revelation was given. Current editions of the Doctrine and Covenants place the date as the summer of 1828; editions prior to 1921 give the date as 1829. It appears that the revelation was given in 1828 and that some additions were made in 1829. For instance, early in the revelation, the Lord stated that the power to translate "is now restored" to the Prophet Joseph Smith. Later, the Lord referred to the translation of the books of Mosiah through Moroni in the past tense (D&C 10:3, 41).

The Gift of Translation Is Restored to the Prophet
DOCTRINE AND COVENANTS 10:1–4

10:1 *By the means of the Urim and Thummim.* The reference to the "Urim and Thummim" in this text was added in the 1835 edition of the Doctrine and Covenants. Prior to that, the word *interpreters* was used (see commentary on D&C 8:6). It appears that while Joseph Smith was laboring on the translation of the Old Testament, he became acquainted with the revelatory device known to the ancients as the Urim and Thummim. Recognizing this term to be the same as the instrument that he had been given to translate the Book of Mormon and use in the receipt of revelation, he adopted the Bible term and added clarification by inserting "Urim and Thummim" in the approprate texts.

The Book of Mormon spoke of "two stones" fastened into the "two rims of a bow" as the "interpreters" (Mosiah 28:13, 20; Ether 3:23). Thus it was natural for the earliest members of the Church to speak of the "interpreters" (later to be called Urim and Thummim) as seer stones.

The description of the Urim and Thummim being fastened to the breastplate of the high priest of Israel, as recorded in Exodus 28, most likely opened the Prophet's mind to association between the two. The translation of the material in this chapter of Exodus was recorded sometime between 2 February and 2 July 1833 (Matthews, *Plainer Translation*, 79). Earlier references to the interpreters as the Urim and Thummim are tentative. For example, in January 1833 William W. Phelps, editor of the Church newspaper, *The Evening and the Morning Star*, wrote regarding the Book of Mormon: "It was translated by the gift and power of God, by an unlearned man, through the aid of a pair of interpreters, or spectacles– (known perhaps, in ancient days as Teraphim, or Urim and Thummim)" (1:58).

After the Prophet's experience with translating the Old Testament, references to the Nephite interpreters as the Urim and Thummim were more definite. For instance, in October 1834, Oliver Cowdery testified: "Day after day I continued, uninterrupted, to write from his [Joseph's] mouth, as he translated, with the Urim and Thummim, or, as the Nephites would have said, 'Interpreters,' the history, or record, called 'The book of Mormon'" (*Messenger and Advocate*, 1:14). See also the note following the end of Joseph Smith–History, 58.

At the time of the publication of the Doctrine and Covenants in 1835, wording of the revelations was reviewed by the publication committee, which included the Prophet Joseph Smith. Three years later, when the Prophet dictated his history, he made clear the association between the interpreters, or seer stones, and the Urim and Thummim. He explained that "these stones, fastened to a breastplate, constituted what is called the Urim and Thummim" (Joseph Smith–History 1:35).

The night that Moroni first appeared to Joseph, he explained to him "that there were two stones in silver bows . . . deposited with the plates;

and the possession and use of these stones were what constituted 'seers' in ancient or former times; and that God had prepared them for the purpose of translating the book" (Joseph Smith–History 1:35). Previously, these stones were given to the brother of Jared to be included with his writings. At that time, the Lord told the brother of Jared, "The language which ye shall write I have confounded; wherefore I will cause in my own due time that these stones shall magnify to the eyes of men these things which ye shall write" (Ether 3:24). In Doctrine and Covenants 17 the connection between the stones given to the brother of Jared and the Urim and Thummim is confirmed. That revelation stated that the Three Witnesses would view "the Urim and Thummim, which were given to the brother of Jared upon the mount, when he talked with the Lord face to face" (D&C 17:1).

The Book of Mormon tells us that Limhi's people discovered the plates of Ether, which contained the brother of Jared's writings. Subsequently, the plates were given to King Mosiah who "translated them by the means of those two stones which were fastened into the two rims of a bow" (Mosiah 28:13). How Mosiah received the stones is not known. Neither is it evident who placed them in the rims of a bow. Mormon wrote that over the centuries the stones had "been kept and preserved by the hand of the Lord" (Mosiah 28:15). The interpreters were passed from one record keeper to the next until Mormon gave them to Moroni. Moroni then placed them in the Hill Cumorah with the plates and the breastplate in the stone box specially prepared to contain these items.

The Prophet Joseph Smith described the Urim and Thummim as "two transparent stones set in the rim of a bow fastened to a breastplate" (*History of the Church*, 4:537). Lucy Mack Smith was able to inspect the Urim and Thummim the morning after Joseph had obtained them from the Hill Cumorah. She stated that she "took the article in [her] hands and, examining it with no covering but a silk handkerchief, found that it consisted of two smooth three-cornered diamonds set in glass, and the glasses were set in silver bows connected with each other in much the same way that old-fashioned spectacles are made" (Smith, *History of Joseph Smith*, 1996, 139). See commentary on Joseph Smith–History 1:35, page 21; Doctrine and Covenants 9:7–10.

10:2 *Your mind became darkened.* The mental faculties of the Prophet Joseph Smith were affected by his disobedience in allowing the 116-page manuscript to leave his possession. "That wicked one cometh and taketh away light and truth, through disobedience, from the children of men"

(D&C 93:39). Once the Spirit, or light, had been taken away, Joseph could no longer translate.

10:3 *It is now restored unto you again.* Both the Urim and Thummim and the plates were taken from Joseph as a consequence of losing the 116-page manuscript. Later, both were returned to him, and the Lord granted the gift of translation once again. "I continued my supplications to God, without cessation," Joseph explained, "and on the twenty-second of September [1828], I had the joy and satisfaction of again receiving the Urim and Thummim, with which I have again commenced translating, and Emma writes for me, but the angel said that the Lord would send me a scribe, and I trust that it will be so. The angel was rejoiced when he gave me back the Urim and Thummim, and he told me that the Lord was pleased with my faithfulness and humility, and loved me for my penitence and diligence in prayer, in the which I had performed my duty so well as to receive the Urim and Thummim and was able to enter upon the work of translation again" (Smith, *History of Joseph Smith*, 1996, 176).

Continue on unto the finishing of the remainder of the work of translation. Joseph Smith was not to retranslate the engravings from the plates of Lehi. He commenced translating where he left off. He had already translated the abridgment made by Mormon up to the book of Mosiah. This means that he had translated the accounts from the time of Lehi leaving Jerusalem through the time of King Benjamin. The renewed efforts of translation began with Mosiah chapter one. After finishing the translation of the plates through the book of Moroni, Joseph then continued as instructed in this revelation to translate the small plates of Nephi, or what we know as First and Second Nephi, Jacob, Enos, Jarom, Omni, and the Words of Mormon. See commentary on Doctrine and Covenants 10:35–43.

10:4 *Means provided to enable you to translate.* See commentary on Doctrine and Covenants 5:30–34; introduction to commentary on Doctrine and Covenants 6–9.

Satan Seeks Joseph's Destruction
DOCTRINE AND COVENANTS 10:5–9

10:5 *The hands of the servants of Satan that do uphold his work.* All who work evil are servants of the adversary. "That which is evil cometh of the devil," taught Mormon, "for the devil is an enemy unto God, and fighteth against him continually, and inviteth and enticeth to sin, and to do that which is evil continually" (Moroni 7:12).

10:6 *They have sought to destroy you.* When Martin Harris violated the covenant he made with the Prophet, his actions became those of a servant of the devil. "The moment we revolt at anything which comes from God, the devil takes power," the Prophet said (*Teachings of the Prophet Joseph Smith*, 181).

10:8–9 *You have delivered them up.* See commentary on Doctrine and Covenants 3:5, "You have been entrusted with these things."

Satan's Plan to Destroy the Work of God
DOCTRINE AND COVENANTS 10:10–34

10:10–13 *Satan hath put it into their hearts to alter the words.* The practice of distorting the words of God and tampering with scripture is as old as the written word. Those who will deceive with the spoken word will also deceive with the written word. Such has ever been the case. In the 1980s, Mark Hoffman, through the use of forged documents, convinced some people not to believe the account of the Prophet Joseph Smith concerning the coming forth of the Book of Mormon. He cunningly insinuated that Joseph Smith had altered his story concerning the details of the manner in which he received the plates from which the Book of Mormon was translated. He forged documents that had superstitious references to the occult and claimed them to be written by those close to the Prophet. His ploy centered in the infamous "salamander letter," in which Martin Harris was purported to have written that a white salamander appeared to Joseph to inform him about the plates in the Hill Cumorah. Moreover, Hoffman planned to produce a forgery of the lost 116 pages with "references to money-digging and folk magic that were consistent with the letters" (Lindsey, *Gathering of Saints*, 381). In like manner, historical Christianity has been deluged with pseudepigraphic (writings falsely attributed to biblical characters, and alleged to have been written in biblical times) and apocryphal works that, during periods of debate, sustain their writers' views. Thus it is as the Prophet told us: things would be both taken from and added to the holy book (1 Nephi 13:23–30; D&C 91).

10:14 *I will not suffer that Satan shall accomplish his evil design.* By revealing Satan's designs, the Lord thwarted those designs. The following was published in the first edition of the Book of Mormon: "To the reader—As many false reports have been circulated respecting the following work, and also many unlawful measures taken by evil designing persons to destroy me, and also the work, I would inform you that I translated, by the gift and power of God, and caused to be written, one hundred and sixteen pages, the which I took from the book of Lehi, which was an account abridged from the plates of Lehi, by the hand of Mormon; which said account, some person or persons have stolen and kept from me, notwithstanding my utmost exertions to recover it again—and being commanded of the Lord that I should not translate the same over again, for Satan had put it into their hearts to tempt the Lord their God, by altering the words, that they did read contrary from that which I translated and caused to be written; and if I should bring forth the same words again, or, in other words, if I should translate the same over again, they would publish that which they had stolen, and Satan would stir up the hearts of this generation, that they might not receive this work; but behold, the Lord said unto me, I will not suffer that Satan shall accomplish his evil design in this thing; therefore thou shalt translate from the plates of Nephi, until ye come to that which ye have translated, which ye have retained; and behold ye shall publish it as the record of Nephi; and thus I will confound those who have altered my words. I will not suffer that they shall destroy my work; yea, I will show unto them that my wisdom is greater than the cunning of the devil" (Smith, *History of the Church*, 1:56–57).

By publishing this information, it became futile for the men who had the pages of translation and had altered them to carry out their plans. Indeed, if the men revealed that they had the pages, they would also reveal that not only were they thieves but also that they were the designing men identified in the preface of the Book of Mormon.

10:20–26 *He draggeth their souls down to hell.* In Satan's attempt to destroy Joseph and the work of the Restoration, he was able to take a few souls captive. Through his "great hold upon their hearts" (D&C 10:20) he was able to make them like unto himself, liars that oppose the work of God. This was possible because these individuals "love[d] darkness rather than light" (D&C 10:21). These hapless souls were caught in the traps they had dug for another (1 Nephi 22:14).

10:28 *Wo be unto him that lieth to deceive because he supposeth that another lieth to deceive.* The idea that lying is justified if its purpose is to catch someone in a lie is a revelation as dark as the kingdom from which it came. It is a common experience for missionaries to be confronted by efforts born of such darkness on the part of priests and ministers whose purpose is to keep their parishioners from reading the Book or Mormon, listening to the message of the Restoration, or from being baptized. The servant of light cannot advance his cause with darkness. We cannot fight the adversary with his own spirit or his methods; to do so is to give him the victory.

10:32 *Satan will harden the hearts of the people to stir them up to anger against you.* "The devil has great power to deceive," taught the Prophet Joseph Smith; "he will so transform things as to make one gape at those who are doing the will of God" (*Teachings of the Prophet Joseph Smith,* 227). "Woe unto them," wrote Isaiah, "that call evil good, and good evil; that put darkness for light, and light for darkness; that put bitter for sweet, and sweet for bitter!" (Isaiah 5:20; 2 Nephi 16–20).

The Lord's Plan Regarding the 116-Page Manuscript
DOCTRINE AND COVENANTS 10:35–45

10:35–43 More than two thousand three hundred years before the loss of that which Joseph Smith had translated from the plates of Lehi, the Lord inspired his prophet to make a provision for that event. Nephi was commanded to make two sets of records concerning the Lord's dealings with his family. The first set of records was "an account of the reign of the kings, and the wars and contentions of [the] people" (1 Nephi 9:4). Nephi wrote that the second set was made "for [a] special purpose" not understood by him (1 Nephi 9:3). "But the Lord knoweth all things from the beginning; wherefore, he prepareth a way to accomplish all his works among the children of men" (1 Nephi 9:6).

Both sets of plates, known as the large and the small plates of Nephi, were handed down from generation to generation for nearly one thousand years until they were committed into the hands of the prophet Mormon. While Mormon labored on his abridgment of the ancient records, he felt impressed to include Nephi's second set of plates, the small plates of Nephi, in their entirety. This is all the more remarkable because Mormon had already finished an abridgment of the same time period covered on this second set of plates as it was contained on the large plates of Nephi and had indicated that he could not include nearly as much as he would have liked to.

"After I had made an abridgment from the plates of Nephi," Moroni said, "down to the reign of this king Benjamin, of whom Amaleki spake, I searched among the records which had been delivered into my hands, and I found these plates, which contained this small account of the prophets, from Jacob down to the reign of this king Benjamin, and also many of the words of Nephi. And the things which are upon these plates pleasing me, because of the prophecies of the coming of Christ; . . . wherefore, I chose these things, to finish my record upon them. . . . And I do this for a wise purpose; for thus it whispereth me, according to the workings of the Spirit of the Lord which is in me. And now, I do not know all things; but the Lord knoweth all things which are to come; wherefore, he worketh in me to do according to his will" (Words of Mormon 1:3–5, 7).

Thus, the Lord instructed his servants, Nephi and Mormon, to prepare a similar account of the same time period covered in the 116-page manuscript that was lost. These preparations allowed the Prophet Joseph Smith to translate from a separate record than the one whose translation had been altered by the wicked men who had the manuscript. It appears that the Savior was referring to these events in his instructions to the Nephites during his visit to the Americas following his resurrection. "But behold, the life of my servant shall be in my hand; therefore they shall not hurt him, although he shall be marred because of them. Yet I will heal him, for I will show unto them that my wisdom is greater than the cunning of the devil" (3 Nephi 21:10).

Significantly, the entire plan of salvation, as announced in the councils of heaven, rests on similar foreknowledge. The atoning sacrifice of Jesus Christ was foreordained to come in answer to the fall of Adam. Knowing that Adam would fall and that all would sin, the Lord made provisions for us to be redeemed through the atonement of Christ.

10:37 *You cannot always tell the wicked from the righteous.* The wisdom of God far surpasses that of mortal man. Even prophets and apostles do not always discern the intents of those who would betray them. The Lord warned the early Saints, "Behold, verily I say unto you, there are hypocrites among you, who have deceived some, which has given the adversary power; but behold such shall be reclaimed; But the hypocrites shall be detected and shall be cut off, either in life or in death, even as I will; and wo unto them who are cut off from my church, for the same are overcome of the world. Wherefore, let every man beware lest he do that which is not in truth and righteousness before me" (D&C 50:7–9).

10:41 See commentary on verse 3, "Continue on unto the finishing of the remainder of the work of translation."

10:44 *An abridgment of the account of Nephi.* In the introductory material published with the first edition of the Book of Mormon, the

Prophet Joseph Smith indicated that the account lost in the 116-page manuscript was taken "from the book of Lehi, which was an account abridged from the plates of Lehi, by the hand of Mormon." Nephi made an abridgment of his father Lehi's record before he wrote an account of his own life on the small plates of Nephi. Today, the Book of Mormon contains a translation of Nephi's abridgment (1 Nephi 1:16–17).

10:45 *The plates of Nephi which do throw greater views upon my gospel.* The books of First and Second Nephi along with the writings of Jacob are in doctrinal content virtually without peer in scripture.

Book of Mormon Prophets Wrote to Their Descendants
DOCTRINE AND COVENANTS 10:46–55

10:46 *All the remainder of this work.* This phrase refers to Mormon's abridgment of the large plates of Nephi, Moroni's abridgment of the plates of Ether, and Moroni's writings. These include the books of Mosiah through Moroni in the Book of Mormon.

My disciples, desired in their prayers should come forth unto this people. See commentary on Doctrine and Covenants 3:19.

10:48 *All that had become Lamanites because of their dissensions.* During the time of the Zion society that followed the visit of the Savior to the Americas, there were no divisions among the people, "neither were there Lamanites, nor any manner of -ites; but they were in one, the children of Christ" (4 Nephi 1:17). The previous designations of Nephites and Lamanites lost their meaning and importance. Sometime before one hundred and ninety-four years had passed since the signs were given in the Americas of the Savior's birth, "a small part of the people who had revolted from the church and taken upon them the name of Lamanites; therefore there began to be Lamanites again in the land" (4 Nephi 1:20). It was not until two hundred and thirty-one years after Christ's birth that "there was a great division among the people. Therefore the true believers in Christ, and the true worshipers of Christ, . . . were called Nephites, and Jacobites, and Josephites, and Zoramites. And it came to pass that they who rejected the gospel were called Lamanites, and Lemuelites, and Ishmaelites" (4 Nephi 1:35, 37–38). During the great last battles of his people, Mormon indicated that among the Nephites there were "a few who had deserted over unto the Lamanites" (Mormon 6:15).

Because of dissensions, some of those who were descendants of Nephi had become Lamanites. The Book of Mormon prophets prayed that their words might come to their descendants in the latter days. Those who are known today as Lamanites may very well have the blood of Nephi in their veins but are considered Lamanites because of the dissension practiced by their forefathers.

The Lord Establishes His Gospel
DOCTRINE AND COVENANTS 10:53–63

10:54–62 In response to his critics, who were threatened by the presence of a living prophet and new revelation, the Lord declared, "Think not that I am come to destroy the law, or the prophets: I am not come to destroy, but to fulfil" (Matthew 5:17). Similarly, those threatened for the same reasons in our day have attacked the Book of Mormon as their ancient counterparts did the Christ, saying it destroys the Bible. When indeed, one of its chief purposes is to fulfill Bible prophecy. In addition, it stands as an independent witness of Bible truths. In similar fashion, the Restoration did not destroy the community of believers in Christ but built up the true and living church to which the honest in heart gather.

Those who harden their hearts against the Lord and his work declare, "A Bible! A Bible! We have got a Bible, and there cannot be any more Bible" (2 Nephi 29:3). On the other hand, those who truly receive Christ's words will receive the Book of Mormon with thankful hearts and willing minds. Writing of the Book of Mormon, Nephi taught, "And if ye shall believe in Christ ye will believe in these words, for they are the words of Christ, and he hath given them unto me" (2 Nephi 33:10).

10:63 *They do wrest the scriptures and do not understand them.* It is the ploy of devils to use the scriptures to stir up the hearts of people to contend against the Restoration. As the religious leaders in the days of Christ used scripture to reject him, so the words of Christ and his ancient apostles are used to reject their modern counterparts. The true intent of the words of the Lord and his servants is twisted and misconstrued to create a counterfeit gospel. Like Paul, before his conversion, these cynics "kick against the pricks," meaning that they find in their religious traditions justification to reject and persecute the Saints, while their hearts are pricked with the knowledge that that which they war against is the truth.

Those Whose Hearts Are Right

DOCTRINE AND COVENANTS 10:64–70

10:67 *The same is my church.* This phrase refers to those whose hearts are right and ready to receive the fulness of the gospel. Though the Church had not yet been organized, there were those whose love of truth was such that they are spoken of as if they were members of that church, for indeed they yet will be. See commentary on Doctrine and Covenants 18:4, "Concerning the foundation of my church;" 137:7–9.

10:69 *My rock.* See commentary on Doctrine and Covenants 18:4, "My gospel, and my rock;" 128:10, "Upon this rock."

The gates of hell shall not prevail against them. See commentary on Doctrine and Covenants 21:6, "The gates of hell shall not prevail against you;" 128:10, "The gates of hell shall not prevail."

DOCTRINE AND COVENANTS 11

DATE: MAY 1829 (AFTER 25 MAY)
PLACE: HARMONY, PENNSYLVANIA

This revelation appears to have been given after the restoration of the Aaronic Priesthood, which took place 15 May 1829. Joseph Smith recounted, "We were forced to keep secret the circumstances of having received the Priesthood and our having been baptized, owing to a spirit of persecution which had already manifested itself in the neighborhood. We had been threatened with being mobbed from time to time, and this, too, by professors of religion. And their intentions of mobbing us were only counteracted by the influence of my wife's father's family (under Divine providence), who had become very friendly to me, and who were opposed to mobs, and were willing that I should be allowed to continue the work of translation without interruption; and therefore offered and promised us protection from all unlawful proceedings as far as in them lay.

"After a few days, however, feeling it to be our duty, we commenced to reason out of the Scriptures with our acquaintances and friends, as we happened to meet with them. About this time my brother Samuel H. Smith came to visit us. We informed him of what the Lord was about to do for the children of men, and began to reason with him out of the Bible. We also showed him that part of the work which we had translated, and labored to persuade him concerning the Gospel of Jesus Christ, which was now about to be revealed in its fulness. He was not, however, very easily persuaded of these things, but after much inquiry and explanation he retired to the woods, in order that by secret and fervent prayer he might obtain of a merciful God, wisdom to enable him to judge for himself. The result was that he obtained revelation for himself sufficient to convince him of the truth of our assertions to him; and on the twenty-fifth day of that same month in which we had been baptized and ordained, Oliver Cowdery baptized him; and he returned to his father's house, greatly glorifying and praising God, being filled with the Holy Spirit.

"Not many days afterwards, my brother Hyrum Smith came to us to inquire concerning these things, when at his earnest request, I inquired of the Lord through the Urim and Thummim, and received for him the following . . ." (*History of the Church*, 1:43–45).

The Lord Extends Similar Callings to His Servants
DOCTRINE AND COVENANTS 11:1–9

11:1–9 Verses 1 through 9 in Doctrine and Covenants 11 are identical to verses 1 through 9 in section 6. Verses 1 through 5 are also repeated in sections 12 and 14. Such repetition is no more unusual than a teacher saying the same thing to different classes or a missionary responding to different people in the same way when they have asked the same question. See commentary on Doctrine and Covenants 4:1–4; 6:1–9.

The Pattern by Which All Spiritual Truths Are Discerned
DOCTRINE AND COVENANTS 11:10–14

11:10 *Thou shalt have a gift.* The gift referred to here is the gift of the Holy Ghost. This, surely one of the greatest of all the gifts of God, comes by the laying on of hands after the ordinance of baptism. Hyrum was baptized 29 June 1829 in Seneca Lake by Joseph Smith. He received the gift of the Holy Ghost at the meeting at which the Church was organized on 6 April 1830. Thereafter, other gifts followed, including the gifts of prophecy and revelation, which would attend his ministry (vv. 21–22).

11:12–14 These verses give us the standard by which we discern spirits. That which comes from God will always lead us to do good, to do justly, to walk humbly, and to judge with a righteous judgment. Any spirit or influence that fails to do this does not come from the God of heaven. A minister of another faith caught doing something very dishonest to dissuade a member of his congregation from joining with the Latter-day Saints defiantly responded, "God approves of any tactics we use to fight Mormonism." One is left to wonder just what kind of god it is who uses lies and deception to accomplish his work.

The Spirit of the Lord will always bring light, not darkness; understanding, not confusion; joy, not sorrow; peace and assurance, not uncertainty. It is by this Spirit, Hyrum is told, that he can know all things pertaining to righteousness.

Keep the Commandments and Study the Gospel
DOCTRINE AND COVENANTS 11:15–22

11:15 *You need not suppose that you are called to preach until you are called.* See commentary on Doctrine and Covenants 42:11.

11:16 This verse was written in May 1829 before the publication of the Book of Mormon, the organization of the Church, or before Hyrum had been baptized or had the gift of the Holy Ghost confirmed upon him.

11:19 We do not understand the text to be saying that Hyrum would play a role in translating the Book of Mormon but rather that he would assume a prominent role in proclaiming the book and its truths. It appears to be this assistance in bringing forth the Book of Mormon that qualified Hyrum Smith to become one of the Eight Witnesses (Ether 5:2; Testimony of the Eight Witnesses).

11:21–22 The special gift given Hyrum would center in his ability to declare with great power the message of the Restoration. Given that we cannot teach that which we do not know, it was required that he prepare himself that he might be a suitable companion of the Holy Spirit. The scriptures were to constitute the foundation of his understanding. Hyrum was to become a student of the Bible ("my word which hath gone forth among the children of men") and the Book of Mormon ("my word which shall come forth among the children of men"). Building upon the foundation of these books, he would enjoy the Spirit of revelation and much would be added to his understanding that reached beyond the written word.

Explaining the principle here involved, Elder Bruce R. McConkie has said, "Those who preach by the power of the Holy Ghost use the scriptures as their basic source of knowledge and doctrine. They begin with what the Lord has before revealed to other inspired men. But it is the practice of the Lord to give added knowledge to those upon whose hearts the true meanings and intents of the scriptures have been impressed. Many great doctrinal revelations come to those who preach from the scriptures. When they are in tune with the Infinite, the Lord lets them know, first, the full and complete meaning of the scriptures they are expounding, and then he ofttimes expands their views so that new truths flood in upon them, and they learn added things that those who do not follow such a course can never know. Hence, as to 'preaching the word,' the Lord commands his servants to go forth 'saying none other things than that which the prophets and apostles have written, and that which is taught them by the Comforter through the prayer of faith' (D&C 52:9). In a living, growing, divine church, new truths will come from time to time and old truths will be applied with new vigor to new situations, all under the guidance of the Holy Spirit of God" (*Promised Messiah*, 515–16).

Do not Deny the Spirit of Revelation
DOCTRINE AND COVENANTS 11:23–30

11:25 *Deny not the spirit of revelation.* To deny the Spirit of revelation is not only to close the windows of heaven to further light and knowledge but also to lose the understanding of the divine word already given. "I will give unto the children of men line upon line, precept upon precept, here a little and there a little; and blessed are those who hearken unto my precepts, and lend an ear unto my counsel, for they shall learn wisdom; for unto him that receiveth I will give more; and from them that shall say, We have enough, from them shall be taken away even that which they have" (2 Nephi 28:30).

11:30 Hyrum's position was much like that of the meridian twelve of whom the Savior said that they would "receive power" after that the Holy Ghost had come upon them (Acts 1:8). He is promised that he will be given power to become a son of God. That is, he will be spiritually adopted by covenant into the family of God, thus he becomes an heir of God and joint-heir with Christ (Romans 8:17), having rightful claim upon all that the Father has (D&C 76:95; 84:38; 93:19).

Believe on my name. To believe on the name of Christ is to accept those who come in his name, those who hold his priesthood and have been authorized to act in his name. See commentary on Doctrine and Covenants 18:29.

DOCTRINE AND COVENANTS 12

DATE: MAY 1829
PLACE: HARMONY, PENNSYLVANIA

The following revelation was received by the Prophet for Joseph Knight at Harmony, Susquehanna County, Pennsylvania, in May 1829. "An old gentleman came to visit us," the Prophet noted, "of whose name I wish to make honorable mention—Mr. Joseph Knight, Sen., of Colesville, Broome county, New York, who, having heard of the manner in which we were occupying our time, very kindly and considerately brought us a quantity of provisions, in order that we might not be interrupted in the work of translation by the want of such necessaries of life; and I would just mention here, as in duty bound, that he several times brought us supplies, a distance of at least thirty miles, which enabled us to continue the work when otherwise we must have relinquished it for a season.

"Being very anxious to know his duty as to this work, I inquired of the Lord for him, and obtained the following . . ." (Smith, *History of the Church*, 1:47–48).

Qualified to Assist in the Lord's Work
DOCTRINE AND COVENANTS 12:1–9

12:1–6 See commentary on Doctrine and Covenants 4:1–4; 6:1–5; 11:1–9.

12:8 Wealth, intelligence, or other qualities held in high honor by the world do not qualify one to be of service in the kingdom of God. Rather, such simple virtues as humility, love, faith, hope, charity, and temperance prove attractive to the light of heaven and the companionship of the Holy Ghost.

DOCTRINE AND COVENANTS 13;
JOSEPH SMITH–HISTORY 1:66–75

DATE: 15 MAY 1829
PLACE: HARMONY, PENNSYLVANIA

Doctrine and Covenants 13, which announces the restoration of the Aaronic Priesthood, is an extract from the Prophet's history as recorded in Joseph Smith–History 1:66–75.

Asking God about Baptism
JOSEPH SMITH–HISTORY 1:66–68

JS–H 1:68 *Baptism for the remission of sins, that we found mentioned in the translation of the plates.* From this statement and from Oliver Cowdery's account of the restoration of the Aaronic Priesthood, it can be reasonably deduced where Joseph and Oliver were in the process of translation when they went into the woods to inquire of the Lord relative to the necessity of baptism. Oliver said that it took place "after writing the account given of the Savior's ministry to the remnant of the seed of Jacob, upon this continent" (note following the end of Joseph Smith–History, 59). This would place the work of translation in 3 Nephi 11. It will be remembered that Nephi's discourse on baptism (2 Nephi 31) was recorded on the small plates of Nephi, which were not translated until after the account of the ministry of the Savior and the books that followed it had been translated.

It was consistently argued by David Whitmer and others that Joseph Smith did not use the plates in the translation process. Joseph Smith, however, consistently maintained that the translation process involved the use of the plates. For further information on the translation process, see commentary on Doctrine and Covenants 6–9.

Laid his hands upon us. There could be little surprise that when the priesthood was lost the knowledge of how it was properly obtained was lost also. Here we learn that the way the priesthood is conferred is by the laying on of hands. This symbolizes the placing of God's hands upon those who are being commissioned to act in his stead (D&C 36:1–2). The same Hebrew word for *hand* means "power." Thus, symbolically, the laying on of hands represents the conferring of power.

Aaronic Priesthood Restored
JOSEPH SMITH–HISTORY 1:69–72

JS–H 1:69 My *fellow servants*. The angel who ministered to John the Revelator said of himself, "I am thy fellowservant, and of thy brethren the prophets" (Revelation 22:9). Such salutations illustrate the sense of oneness that exists between the servants of the Lord in all gospel dispensations.

The keys of the ministering of angels. As the Melchizedek Priesthood holds the keys or authority to perform the ordinances by which men come into the presence of God, so the Aaronic Priesthood holds the authority to perform the ordinances by which we are prepared to receive the ministration of angels. For instance, Joseph Smith said, "All Priesthood is Melchizedek, but there are different portions or degrees of it. That portion which brought Moses to speak with God face to face was taken away; but that which brought the ministry of angels remained" (*Teachings of the Prophet Joseph Smith*, 180–81).

Elder Dallin H. Oaks explained: "In general, the blessings of spiritual companionship and communication are only available to those who are clean. . . . Through the Aaronic Priesthood ordinances of baptism and the sacrament, we are cleansed of our sins and promised that if we keep our covenants we will always have His Spirit to be with us. I believe that promise not only refers to the Holy Ghost but also to the ministering of angels, for 'angels speak by the power of the Holy Ghost; wherefore, they speak the words of Christ' (2 Nephi 32:3). So it is that those who hold the Aaronic Priesthood open the door for all Church members who worthily partake of the sacrament to enjoy the companionship of the Spirit of the Lord and the ministering of angels" (Conference Report, October 1998, 51).

It becomes the right of all who are of the household of faith to enjoy this blessing. We need not suppose that the ministering of angels is always known or seen by those to whom they have ministered. It was the apostle Paul who said that "some have entertained angels unawares" (Hebrews 13:2). "Angelic messages can be delivered by a voice or merely by thoughts or feelings communicated to the mind. President John Taylor described 'the action of the angels or messengers of God, upon our minds, so that the heart can conceive . . . revelations from the eternal world'" (Oaks, Conference Report, October 1998, 51).

This shall never be taken again from the earth. According to Oliver Cowdery's recollection, the words of the Baptist were, "Upon you my fellow-servants, in the name of Messiah, I confer this Priesthood and this authority, which shall remain upon the earth, that the Sons of Levi may yet offer an offering unto the Lord in righteousness!" (note following the end of Joseph Smith–History, 59). The law of sacrifice, as known from the days of Adam, will as a part of the restoration of all things be brought back at least for a time and season, the length of which we do not know.

Until the sons of Levi do offer again an offering unto the Lord in righteousness. This language ties the restoration of the Aaronic Priesthood to the prophecy in Malachi 3:1–4. The prophecy begins with the promise that the Lord will send his messenger to prepare the way before him and announces that he will come "suddenly" to his temple. Sectarian commentaries are in universal agreement that the messenger was John the Baptist and that this prophecy was filled in the manner in which he prepared the nation of Israel to accept Christ and his ministry. Indeed, Christ himself affirms that Malachi had reference to the Baptist (Mark 1:2). We part company with such commentary, however, in their assumption that Malachi's prophecy found fulfillment in the mortal ministry of John. Christ is to come again, and it will be in his second coming that he will "suddenly come to his temple" when the rest of Malachi's prophecy will find fulfillment. Of that day Malachi asked, "Who may abide the day of his coming? and who shall stand when he appeareth? for he is like a refiner's fire, and like fuller's soap: and he shall sit as a refiner and purifier of silver: and he shall purify the sons of Levi, and purge them as gold and silver, that they may offer unto the Lord an offering in righteousness" (Malachi 3:2–3). No one had any difficulty abiding the presence of the mortal Christ, though the unclean certainly will in the day of his return. In his mortal ministry he was not like a refiner's fire nor was he like fuller's soap. He certainly did not purify the sons of Levi at that time nor was their offering (the sacrifices of the temple) acceptable to him. These are millennial events of which Malachi spoke, and as Christ is to return, so must the Baptist return, again to prepare the way for Him.

The Aaronic Priesthood is a preparatory priesthood. As it was intended to prepare the nation of Israel for the coming of Christ in the meridian of time, so it is to prepare the covenant people of the Lord for the return of their King and the establishment of the millennial kingdom. What Malachi is telling us is that as the sons of Levi were to do a labor to prepare their people for the coming of Christ, in like manner they are to do a special labor in the last days to prepare those of the house of faith to receive that same Christ. Thus, John restores to Joseph and Oliver the very authority by which the sons of Levi will be purified and by which they will perform the same ordinances performed by their ancient counterparts.

Amplifying what is involved here, Joseph Smith explained: "It is generally supposed that sacrifice was entirely done away when the Great Sacrifice [i.e.,] the sacrifice of the Lord Jesus was offered up, and that there will be no necessity for the ordinance of sacrifice in future; but those who assert this are certainly not acquainted with the duties, privileges and authority of the Priesthood, or with the Prophets.

"The offering of sacrifice has ever been connected and forms a part of the duties of the Priesthood. It began with the Priesthood, and will be continued until after the coming of Christ, from generation to generation. We frequently have mention made of the offering of sacrifice by the servants of the Most High in ancient days, prior to the law of Moses; which ordinances will be continued when the Priesthood is restored with all its authority, power and blessings. . . .

"These sacrifices, as well as every ordinance belonging to the Priesthood, will, when the Temple of the Lord shall be built, and the sons of Levi be purified, be fully restored and attended to in all their powers, ramifications, and blessings. This ever did and ever will exist when the powers of the Melchizedek Priesthood are sufficiently manifest; else how can the restitution of all things spoken of by the Holy Prophets be brought to pass. It is not to be understood that the law of Moses will be established again with all its rites and variety of ceremonies; this has never been spoken of by the prophets; but those things which existed prior to Moses' day, namely, sacrifice, will be continued.

"It may be asked by some, what necessity for sacrifice, since the Great Sacrifice was offered? In answer to which, if repentance, baptism, and faith existed prior to the days of Christ, what necessity for them since that time? The Priesthood has descended in a regular line from father to son through their succeeding generations" (*Teachings of the Prophet Joseph Smith*, 172–73; see also Smith, *History of the Church*, 4:207–12).

JS–H 1:70 *Holy Ghost . . . conferred on us hereafter.* The Holy Ghost was first conferred upon men in this dispensation in the meeting at which the Church was organized which took place 6 April 1830. See commentary on Doctrine and Covenants 20:41, "Laying on of hands."

I should baptize Oliver, . . . he should baptize me. Neither the God of heaven nor those angels who act under his direction do for men that which they can do for themselves. Joseph and Oliver had just had the priesthood of Aaron conferred upon them. They now held the authority to baptize by water and were directed to do so by the Baptist.

JS–H 1:71 Immediately after they had baptized each other Joseph and Oliver were directed by John to reordain each other. Though no explanation is given it would appear that the Baptist was establishing the order of the kingdom—that is, that baptism must precede receipt of the priesthood. Their so doing also reaffirms the principle that angels do not do for us what we can do for ourselves.

JS–H 1:72 *The same that is called John the Baptist in the New Testament.* It was not uncommon in the meridian day for people to be named or renamed according to significant things they did or for a prominent event of which they were apart. Thus, John the son of Zacharias became known among the children of Israel as John the Baptist though this obviously was not the name given him by his father in his infancy (Luke 1:63).

The keys of the Priesthood of Melchizedek. See commentary on Doctrine and Covenants 7:7.

Priesthood of Melchizedek . . . conferred on us. See commentary on Doctrine and Covenants 20:2.

I should be called the first Elder of the Church, and he (Oliver Cowdery) the second. See commentary on Doctrine and Covenants 20:2, "The first elder."

The Holy Ghost Reveals the Meaning of the Scriptures
JOSEPH SMITH–HISTORY 1:73–75

JS–H 1:73–75 Immediately after their baptism, Joseph Smith and Oliver Cowdery were immersed in the spirit of prophecy and revelation. They did not receive the gift of the Holy Ghost at this time, for that would come, as noted, after the Melchizedek Priesthood was conferred upon them. They did, however, enjoy a rich outpouring of that Spirit whereby they discovered meanings otherwise hidden to them in their scripture study and their labor with the scriptures.

DOCTRINE AND COVENANTS 14–16

DATE: JUNE 1829
PLACE: FAYETTE, NEW YORK

These revelations were given through Joseph Smith to David, John, and Peter Whitmer Jr., in June 1829. Joseph and his scribe Oliver had recently relocated from Harmony, Pennsylvania, to reside with the Whitmer family in Fayette, New York, where the revelations were received.

During the translation of the Book of Mormon, Oliver Cowdery corresponded with the Peter Whitmer Sr. family about the work in which he was engaged. In her history, Joseph's mother wrote that the Lord instructed Joseph and Oliver by means of the Urim and Thummim to request to live with the Whitmers. "One morning as he applied it to his eyes to look upon the record, instead of the words of the book being given to him, he was commanded to write a letter to one David Whitmer, who lived in Waterloo. This man Joseph had never seen, but he was instructed to say to him that he must come with his team immediately, in order to convey Joseph and Oliver back to his house, that they might remain with him there until the translation should be completed, as an evil-designing people were seeking to take away Joseph's life in order to prevent the work of God from going forth among the world" (Smith, *History of Joseph Smith*, 1996, 192).

David arrived with a wagon in early June to transport Joseph and Oliver to his family's home in Fayette. During this move, Joseph entrusted the plates to Moroni for safekeeping. David Whitmer recorded an interesting event that occurred en route. "When I was returning to Fayette, with Joseph and Oliver, all of us riding in the wagon, Oliver and I on an old fashioned wooden spring seat and Joseph behind us; while traveling along in a clear open place, a very pleasant, nice-looking old man suddenly appeared by the side of our wagon and saluted us with, 'good morning, it is very warm,' at the same time wiping his face or forehead with his hand. We returned the salutation, and by a sign from Joseph, I invited him to ride if he was going our way. But he said very pleasantly, 'No, I am going to Cumorah.' This name was something new to me, I did not know what Cumorah meant. We all gazed at him and at each other, and as I looked enquiringly of Joseph, the old man instantly disappeared, so that I did not see him again" (*Millennial Star*, 49:772).

Shortly after the three men arrived in Fayette, Moroni delivered the plates to Joseph in the Whitmer garden. Describing the circumstances at the Whitmer farm, Joseph said, "It was arranged that we should have our board free of charge, and the assistance of one of his brothers to write for me, and also his own assistance when convenient. Having much need of such timely aid in an undertaking so arduous, and being informed that the people in the neighborhood of the Whitmers were anxiously awaiting the opportunity to inquire into these things, we accepted the invitation, and accompanied Mr. Whitmer to his father's house, and there resided until the translation was finished and the copyright secured. Upon our arrival, we found Mr. Whitmer's family very anxious concerning the work, and very friendly toward ourselves. They continued so, boarded and lodged us according to arrangements; and John Whitmer, in particular, assisted us very much in writing during the remainder of the work.

"In the meantime, David, John and Peter Whitmer, Jun., became our zealous friends and assistants in the work; and being anxious to know their respective duties, and having desired with much earnestness that I should inquire of the Lord concerning them, I did so, through the means of the Urim and Thummim, and obtained for them in succession the following revelations . . ." (Smith, *History of the Church*, 1:49).

DOCTRINE AND COVENANTS 14

Spiritual and Temporal Blessings Promised
DOCTRINE AND COVENANTS 14:1–11

14:1–6 See commentary on Doctrine and Covenants 6:1–5; 11:1–9.

14:7 *If you keep my commandments and endure to the end.* Many of the revelations in the Doctrine and Covenants, such as this one, were first given as personal instructions, warnings, and encouragement to early investigators and members of the Church. They can be likened to patriarchal blessings, which often give similar counsel and warning. This admonition was of special importance to David Whitmer. Even though he was one of the three witnesses to the Book of Mormon, he lost the Spirit and was excommunicated from the Church in 1838. Although he never denied his testimony of the Book of Mormon, he was a constant critic of Joseph Smith and died outside the Church. We note with particular interest that when Moroni showed the Three Witnesses the plates, he turned directly to David Whitmer and said, "David, blessed is he that endureth to the end" (Roberts, Conference Report, October 1926, 126).

14:8 *That you may stand as a witness of the things of which you shall both hear and see.* See commentary on Doctrine and Covenants 6:28; 17; 135:1–3.

14:11 *Ye shall be blessed both spiritually and temporally.* David Whitmer had already received a witness to the Lord's promise. In the preparation to move the Prophet Joseph Smith and Oliver Cowdery to his father's farm, there were several manifestations of divine intervention, which brought both spiritual and temporal blessings. When Oliver Cowdery's letter arrived at the Whitmer home requesting that David travel to Harmony, Pennsylvania, to transport him and Joseph to Fayette, the family was not certain how to respond. David Whitmer explained, "I did not know what to do, I was pressed with my work. I had some 20 acres to plow, so I concluded I would finish plowing and then go. I got up one morning to go to work as usual, and on going to the field, found between five and seven acres of my ground had been plowed during the night.

"I don't know who did it; but it was done just as I would have done it myself, and the plow was left standing in the furrow" (*Millennial Star*, 49:772).

Describing this event, Lucy Mack Smith recalled: "When he [David] informed his father of the fact, his father could not believe it till he examined for himself and ascertained that it was actually true. 'Well,' said his father, 'there must be some overruling power in this thing, and I think you had better go as soon as you get your plaster of paris sown [a common fertilizer of the day] and bring up the man with his scribe.'

"To this also David agreed. The next morning, as soon as breakfast was over, he took the half-bushel measure under his arm and went out to the place where he supposed the plaster to be, as he knew exactly where he had left it twenty-four hours earlier. But when he came to look for it, behold, it had entirely disappeared! Every vestige of it was gone from the spot where he left it. He ran to his sister's house a few yards distant and inquired if she knew what had become of it.

"'Why?' she said, in surprise. 'Was it not all spread yesterday?'

"'Not to my knowledge,' answered David.

"'I am astonished at that,' replied his sister, 'for the children came to me in the forenoon and begged of me to go out and see the men sow plaster in the field, saying that they never saw anybody sow plaster so fast in their lives. I accordingly went and saw three men at work in the field, as the children said, but, supposing that you had hired some help on account of your hurry, I went immediately into the house and gave the subject no further attention.'

"David made considerable inquiry in regard to the matter, both among his relatives and neighbors, but was not able to learn who had done it. However, the family were convinced that there was an exertion of supernatural power connected with this strange occurrence" (Smith, *History of Joseph Smith*, 1996, 193–94).

As if this was not enough to convince the Whitmers that the Lord had chosen Joseph Smith to be his servant, David related: "When I arrived at Harmony, Joseph and Oliver were coming toward me, and met me some distance from the house. Oliver told me that Joseph had told him when I started from home, where I had stopped the first night, how I read the sign at the tavern, where I stopped the next night, etc., and that I would be there that day before dinner, and this was why they had come out to meet me; all of which was exactly as Joseph had told Oliver, at which I was greatly astonished" (*Millennial Star*, 49:772).

DOCTRINE AND COVENANTS 15

The Thing of Most Worth
DOCTRINE AND COVENANTS 15:1–6

15:6 *The thing which will be of the most worth . . . declare repentance.* As a woman grows in grace and goodness by giving birth to a child and then raising it to maturity, so the elders of Israel grow in like manner by teaching the gospel of repentance and nurturing those newly born into the faith. Such a course brings with it its own reward—not just in the worlds to come but in the present estate—for as they aid in the spiritual development of others so they sustain their own growth. Such a course is the most perfect illustration of the principle that one reaps as he has sown (D&C 6:3).

DOCTRINE AND COVENANTS 16

Revelations Held in High Esteem
DOCTRINE AND COVENANTS 16:1–6

16:1–6 Doctrine and Covenants 15 and 16 are identical save the names John and Peter in verse one and the word "unto" in verse 5 of section 16, which was inserted after 1843. They are the only known revelations to have been given in exactly the same wording. Similar to the first six verses of sections 6, 11, 12, and 14, the parallel wording indicates that the messages were directed intimately to the recipients but also to "all those who have desires to bring forth and establish this work" (D&C 12:7). Like mission calls that are extended today, the wording of each call is identical. Nonetheless, the recipients esteemed the call as an intimate revelation giving direction to their service in the kingdom of God.

The publication of these three sections (D&C 14–16) illustrates the importance that Joseph Smith and those who assisted in the Restoration attached to the Lord's words. Elder John A. Widtsoe explained: "The Doctrine and Covenants is a compilation of the revelations received by Joseph Smith to individuals and for the guidance of the Church. From the first years of the work the Prophet kept every scrap of paper pertaining to the progress of the work. In fact this care of things that must have seemed trivial is one of the evidences of the sincerity of the man. For example, when John and Peter Whitmer asked for help, he received for each of them a revelation, substantially the same. . . .

"This simple revelation is directed to the individual and at first sight has no permanent value for the Church. Yet as a revelation from God it was preserved and published. An insincere man could have eliminated this and other similar revelations as of little consequence. Not so with Joseph. The Lord had spoken. The words were part of the building of the kingdom of God, and the same advice would be useful to many men then and now" (*Joseph Smith*, 251–52).

DOCTRINE AND COVENANTS 17

DATE: JUNE 1829
PLACE: FAYETTE, NEW YORK

"In the course of the work of translation," wrote the Prophet Joseph Smith, "we ascertained that three special witnesses were to be provided by the Lord, to whom He would grant that they should see the plates from which this work (the Book of Mormon) should be translated; and that these witnesses should bear record of the same, as will be found recorded [Ether 5:2–4; 2 Nephi 11:3]. Almost immediately after we had made this discovery, it occurred to Oliver Cowdery, David Whitmer, and the afore-mentioned Martin Harris (who had come to inquire after our progress in the work) that they would have me inquire of the Lord to know if they might not obtain of him the privilege to be these three special witnesses; and finally they became so very solicitous, and urged me so much to inquire at length I complied; and through the Urim and Thummim, I obtained of the Lord for them the following . . ." (*History of the Church*, 1:52–53).

Three Witnesses to See Sacred Relics
DOCTRINE AND COVENANTS 17:1

17:1 Why did the Lord insure that the plates and the other sacred objects were passed down from generation to generation? Further, why were they preserved to be seen by the Three Witnesses? One reason is that they serve as evidence that the events of the Book of Mormon are true. Each of the sacred objects that were seen by the Three Witnesses stands as proof to the world that the Book of Mormon people and events are real. There are those who have argued that the events recounted in the Book of Mormon are simply a story told to illustrate various points or doctrines. Such a view would discount the reality of the appearance of Moroni to the youthful Joseph Smith. Similarly, the brass plates and the sword of Laban as seen by the witnesses evidenced the existence of Nephi and the account he wrote concerning his obtaining the brass plates by beheading Laban with Laban's own sword. Lehi's journey through the wilderness and his travels to the Americas are evidenced by the witnesses viewing the Liahona. The many records, along with the Urim and Thummim and the breastplate witnessed that the translation of the Book of Mormon occurred just as the Prophet Joseph Smith declared.

These physical objects and the presence of Moroni also indicate the importance of records and angels in the perpetuation of spiritual knowledge and the development of faith on the earth. Throughout the Book of Mormon, emphasis is given to the importance of keeping records and bestowing sacred objects from one generation to the next. While entrusting his son Helaman with the plates, the interpreters, and the Liahona, Alma taught, "By small and simple things are great things brought to pass; and small means in many instances doth confound the wise . . . and bringeth about the salvation of many souls" (Alma 37:6–7). The testimonies of Joseph Smith and the Three Witnesses that they saw an angel and these sacred objects "prepareth the way that the residue of men may have faith in Christ, that the Holy Ghost may have place in their hearts" (Moroni 7:32).

You shall have a view of the plates. David Whitmer described, "We not only saw the plates of the Book of Mormon, but also the brass plates, the plates of the Book of Ether, the plates containing the record of the wickedness and secret combinations of the people of the world down to the time of their being engraved, and many other plates. The fact is, it was just as though Joseph, Oliver and I were sitting just here on a log, when we were overshadowed by a light. It was not like the light of the sun nor like that of a fire, but more glorious and beautiful. It extended away round us, I cannot tell how far, but in the midst of this light about as far off as he sits (pointing to John C. Whitmer, sitting a few feet from him), there appeared, as it were, a table with many records or plates upon it, besides the plates of the Book of Mormon" (*Millennial Star*, 49:772).

The plates of Mormon, which were delivered by Moroni to the Prophet Joseph Smith, received particular attention. Joseph wrote, "we beheld a light above us in the air, of exceeding brightness; and behold, an angel stood before us. In his hands he held the plates which we had been praying for these to have a view of. He turned over the leaves one by one, so that we could see them, and discern the engravings thereon distinctly" (Smith, *History of the Church*, 1:54). David Whitmer indicated that the angel did not turn over all of the leaves because part of the plates were sealed. He described the plates as being "about eight inches wide and six or seven inches long, as they appeared a little wider than long, and three rings kept the plates together; one above, one in the middle and one below, so that the angel could turn every leaf entirely over. The thickness was about of a common sheet of tin used by tinsmiths" (Cook, *David Whitmer Interviews*, 21).

Relative to the things that the Lord promised the Three Witnesses that they were entitled to see, we have this interesting account preserved for us by Brigham Young: "When Joseph got the plates, the angel instructed him to carry them back to the hill Cumorah, which he did. Oliver says that when Joseph and Oliver went there, the hill opened, and they walked into a cave, in which there was a large and spacious room. He says he did not think, at the time, whether they had the light of the sun or artificial light; but that it was just as light as day. They laid the plates on a table; it was a large table that stood in the room. Under this table there was a pile of plates as much as two feet high, and there were altogether in this room more plates than probably many wagon loads; they were piled up in the corners and along the walls. The first time they went there the sword of Laban hung upon the wall; but when they went again it had been taken down and laid upon the table across the gold plates; it was unsheathed, and on it was written these words: 'This sword will never be sheathed again until the kingdoms of this world become the kingdom of our God and his Christ'" (*Journal of Discourses*, 19:38).

The breastplate. The breastplate was contained in the stone box that held the plates. Lucy Mack Smith had the privilege of handling the breastplate soon after Joseph received it from the Hill Cumorah. She said that Joseph "handed me the breastplate spoken of in his history.

"It was wrapped in a thin muslin handkerchief, so thin that I could see the glistening metal and ascertain its proportions without any difficulty.

"It was concave on one side, and convex on the other, and extended from the neck downwards, as far as the center of the stomach of a man of extraordinary size. It had four straps of the same material for the purpose of fastening it to the breast, two of which ran back to go over the shoulders, and the other two were designed to fasten to the hips. They were just the width of two of my fingers (for I measured them), and they had holes in the end of them to be convenient in fastening" (Smith, *History of Joseph Smith*, 1996, 148–49).

The Urim and Thummim were attached to the breastplate by means of a rod. William Smith, the Prophet's brother, explained that "a pocket was prepared in the breastplate on the left side, immediately over the heart. When not in use the Urim and Thummim was placed in this pocket, the rod being of just the right length to allow it to be so deposited. This instrument could, however, be detached from the breastplate . . . when away from home, but [Joseph] always used it in connection with the breastplate when receiving official communications, and usually so when translating, as it permitted him to have both hands free to hold the plates" (Smith, in *Rod of Iron* 1, 3 [February 1924]: 7).

Anciently, Aaron, the brother of Moses, was given a breastplate. Considering William's description of the breastplate, it is instructive to note the similarity, both in appearance as well as purpose regarding the Urim and Thummim, with the ancient breastplate. "And thou shalt make the breastplate of judgment with cunning work. . . . And thou shalt make upon the breastplate chains at the ends . . . and . . . two rings on the two ends" (Exodus 28:15, 22–23) to fasten the breastplate to the shoulder pieces of the priestly ephod. Further, Moses was instructed, "And thou shalt put in the breastplate of judgment the Urim and Thummim; and they shall be upon Aaron's heart" (Exodus 28:30).

The sword of Laban. Nephi described the sword thus: "The hilt thereof was of pure gold, and the workmanship thereof was exceedingly fine, and I saw that the blade thereof was of the most precious steel" (1 Nephi 4:9). As this was the sword that Nephi used to slay Laban in order to obtain the brass plates, it is a symbol that "the Lord slayeth the wicked to bring forth his righteous purposes" (1 Nephi 4:13). It served as evidence to the Three Witnesses of the truthfulness of the account concerning Laban and the obtaining of the brass plates as recorded in the Book of Mormon.

The Urim and Thummim. See commentary on Joseph Smith–History 1:35, page 21; Doctrine and Covenants 9:7–10; 10:1.

Miraculous directors. Alma stated that these directors were identified by his fathers as the "Liahona, which is, being interpreted, a compass" (Alma 37:38). As the description suggests, this sacred object gave instructions to the family of Lehi as to the direction they were to travel in the wilderness and across the waters. Nephi recorded that "as my father arose in the morning, and went forth to the tent door, to his great astonishment he beheld upon the ground a round ball of curious workmanship; and it was of fine brass. And within the ball were two spindles; and the one pointed the way whither we should go into the wilderness" (1 Nephi 16:10). Further, the Lord chose to reveal his will to Lehi and his family by means of writings that appeared upon the ball. The pointers and the writings "did work according to the faith and diligence and heed" (1 Nephi 16:28) which were given to the commandments of the Lord. This sacred relic was handed down with the plates kept by the prophetic writers of the Nephite records. There is no other account of anyone else seeing the Liahona in the latter days except for the vision given to the Prophet Joseph Smith and the Three Witnesses on this occasion.

Three Witnesses to Testify by the Power of God
DOCTRINE AND COVENANTS 17:2–9

17:2 *It is by your faith that you shall obtain a view of them.* Sacred experiences do not come but by faith. The election to be one of the three special witness was simply a calling until it was made sure by the individual and collective faith of those who sought the witness. Joseph Smith explained that "not many days after the above commandment was given, we four, viz., Martin Harris, David Whitmer, Oliver Cowdery and myself, agreed to retire into the woods, and try to obtain, by fervent and humble prayer, the fulfilment of the promises given in the above revelation—that they should have a view of the plates. We accordingly made choice of a piece of woods convenient to Mr. Whitmer's house, to which we retired, and having knelt down, we began to pray in much faith to Almighty God to bestow upon us a realization of these promises.

"According to previous arrangement, I commenced vocal prayer to our Heavenly Father, and was followed by each of the others in succession. We did not at the first trial, however, obtain any answer or manifestation of divine favor in our behalf. We again observed the same order of prayer, each calling on and praying fervently to God in rotation, but with the same result as before.

"Upon this, our second failure, Martin Harris proposed that he should withdraw himself from us, believing, as he expressed himself, that his presence was the cause of our not obtaining what we wished for. He accordingly withdrew from us" (*History of the Church*, 1:54).

Earlier that morning Joseph exhorted Martin, "*You* have got to humble yourself before your God this day and obtain, if possible, a forgiveness of your sins. If you will do this, it is God's will that you and Oliver Cowdery and David Whitmer should look upon the plates" (Smith, *History of Joseph Smith*, 1996, 199; emphasis in original).

It was after Martin Harris had separated himself from the others that Moroni appeared and showed to them the things mentioned in this revelation. Thereafter, Joseph went in search of Martin. He found him some distance away engaged in prayer. "I found [Martin] at a considerable distance, fervently engaged in prayer. He soon told me, however, that he had not yet prevailed with the Lord, and earnestly requested me to join him in prayer, that he also might realize the same blessings which we had just received. We accordingly joined in prayer, and ultimately obtained our desires, for before we had yet finished, the same vision was opened to our view, at least it was again opened to me, and I once more beheld and heard the same things; whilst at the same moment, Martin Harris cried out, apparently in an ecstasy of joy, "'Tis enough; 'tis enough; mine eyes have beheld; mine eyes have beheld;' and jumping up, he shouted, 'Hosanna,' blessing God, and otherwise rejoiced exceedingly" (Smith, *History of the Church*, 1:55). See commentary on Doctrine and Covenants 5:24.

17:3 *You shall testify of them, by the power of God.* Nephi wrote that "when a man speaketh by the power of the Holy Ghost the power of the Holy Ghost carrieth it unto the hearts of the children of men" (2 Nephi 33:1). As these men lived worthy of that companionship, there was a great power that attended their testimony. Those who were privileged to hear one or more of the Three Witnesses bear testimony also had opportunity to have that testimony confirmed by the power of the Holy Ghost. William H. Homer visited with Martin Harris in the Kirtland Temple about the last of December 1869. He asked Martin, "'What about your testimony to the Book of Mormon? Do you still believe that the Book of Mormon is true and that Joseph Smith was a Prophet?' Again, the effect was electric. A changed old man stood before me. It was no longer a man with an imagined grievance. It was a man with a message, a man with a noble conviction in his heart, a man inspired of God and endowed with divine knowledge. Through the broken window of the Temple shone the winter sun, clear and radiant.

"'Young man,' answered Martin Harris with impressiveness, 'Do I believe it! Do I see the sun shining! Just as surely as the sun is shining on us and gives us light, and the . . . [moon] and stars give us light by night, just as surely as the breath of life sustains us, so surely do I know that Joseph Smith was a true prophet of God, chosen of God to open the last dispensation of the fulness of times; so surely do I know that the Book of Mormon was divinely translated. I saw the plates; I saw the Angel; I heard the voice of God. I know that the Book of Mormon is true and that Joseph Smith was a true Prophet of God. I might as well doubt my own existence as to doubt the divine authenticity of the Book of Mormon or the divine calling of Joseph Smith.' *It was a sublime moment. It was a wonderful testimony. We were thrilled to the very roots of our hair.* The shabby, emaciated little man before us was transformed as he stood with hand outstretched toward the sun of heaven. A halo seemed to encircle him. A divine fire glowed in his eyes. His voice throbbed with the sincerity and the conviction of his message. It was the real Martin Harris whose burning testimony no power on earth could quench. *It was the most thrilling moment of my life*" (Homer, "Passing of Martin Harris," 469–70; emphasis added).

Following this experience, William Homer said that James A. Crockett, his nonmember cousin, placed his hands on William's shoulders and said, "'Wait a minute.' Looking me squarely in the eyes he said, 'I can testify that the Book of Mormon is true. There is something within me that tells me that the old man told the truth. I know the Book of Mormon is true'" (Homer, "Passing of Martin Harris," 471).

David Henry Cannon met with both Martin Harris and David Whitmer in 1861. Concerning the testimony he heard Martin Harris bear, he stated, "There was a feeling accompanied his testimony, when he bore it, that I have never experienced either before or since in any man that I ever heard bear testimony" (Evans, *Cannon Family Historical Treasury*, 250). Regarding the experience with David Whitmer, he explained, "There was a feeling accompanied this testimony which was similar to the one I experienced with Martin Harris" (Evans, *Cannon Family Historical Treasury*, 251).

Similarly, George A. Smith expressed, "We loved to hear brother Oliver testify, we were blessed with his witness" (*Journal of Discourses*, 17:200). Wilford Woodruff concurred, "I have seen Oliver Cowdery when it seemed as though the earth trembled under his feet. I never heard a man bear a stronger testimony than he did when under the influence of the Spirit" (*Collected Discourses*, 1:220).

17:4 *That my servant Joseph Smith, Jun., may not be destroyed.* Joseph was overwhelmed with joy that others now had the responsibility to bear witness that he had told the truth concerning the angel and the plates. His mother explained, "When they returned to the house, it was between three and four o'clock. Mrs. Whitmer, Mr. Smith, and myself were sitting in a bedroom, myself on a bedside. When Joseph came in, he threw himself down beside me and exclaimed, 'Father! Mother! You do not know how happy I am. The Lord has caused the plates to be shown to three

more besides me. They have also seen an angel and will have to testify to
the truth of what I have said, for they know for themselves that I do not
go about to deceive the people. I do feel as though I was relieved of a
dreadful burden which was almost too much for me to endure. But they
will now have to bear a part, and it does rejoice my soul that I am not any
longer to be entirely alone in the world.'

"Martin Harris then came in. He seemed almost overcome with an
excess of joy. He then testified to what he had seen and heard, as did also
the others, Oliver and David, who added that no tongue could express the
joy of their hearts and the greatness of the things which they had both
seen and heard" (Smith, History of Joseph Smith,1996, 199).

The strength and importance of the testimony of the Three Witnesses
of the Restoration is immeasurable. It is significant that not only did the
Prophet Joseph Smith testify truthfully of his sacred revelatory experiences but others shared these experiences with him. Many articles and
books have been written to explain away or refute the testimony of Joseph
Smith. Indeed, the authors of these articles have sought to destroy the
Prophet by destroying the credibility of his testimony. However, these
critics curiously leave the testimony of the Three Witnesses alone. It has
been the common practice for detractors of the Restoration to stick their
heads in the sand and ignore the special witness of these three men. One
cannot get around their testimony nor undermine it. Notwithstanding
their struggles and trials, each of these men remained true to their testimony of these events to their deaths. Their testimony gives great credibility to the testimony of Joseph Smith.

17:5 *Ye shall testify that you have seen them.* See The Testimony of
Three Witnesses, introductory pages to the Book of Mormon.

17:6 *As your Lord and your God liveth it is true.* Bruce R. McConkie
said, "This is God's testimony of the Book of Mormon. In it Deity himself has laid his godhood on the line. Either the book is true or God ceases
to be God" (Conference Report, April 1982, 50). See commentary on
Doctrine and Covenants 6:17; 18:2.

17:8 "And we know," testified the Three Witnesses, "that if we are
faithful in Christ, we shall rid our garments of the blood of all men, and
be found spotless before the judgment-seat of Christ, and shall dwell with
him eternally in the heavens" (Testimony of Three Witnesses).

DOCTRINE AND COVENANTS 18

DATE: JUNE 1829
PLACE: FAYETTE, NEW YORK

As promised by John the Baptist, the Melchizedek Priesthood was restored to the earth by the ancient apostles Peter, James, and John. This occurred sometime after the restoration of the Aaronic Priesthood on 15 May 1829, and the first part of June 1829, when this revelation was given. Oliver Cowdery and David Whitmer were with the Prophet when the revelation was received. When the higher priesthood was restored, Joseph and Oliver were given "the keys of the kingdom," meaning the authority to preside over the Church, and the keys of "the dispensation of the fulness of times" (D&C 27:13; 128:20). In preparation for the organization of the Church, the Prophet had directed Oliver Cowdery to prepare a foundational document for that purpose. Frustrated in his efforts to do so, Oliver asked the Prophet to inquire of the Lord for direction on that matter. This section came in response to that request.

Describing these events, Joseph Smith said, "We had for some time made this matter a subject of humble prayer, and at length we got together in the chamber of Mr. Whitmer's house, in order more particularly to seek of the Lord what we now so earnestly desired; and here, to our unspeakable satisfaction, did we realize the truth of the Savior's promise— 'Ask, and it shall be given you; seek, and ye shall find; knock, and it shall be opened unto you'—for we had not long been engaged in solemn and fervent prayer, when the word of the Lord came unto us in the chamber, commanding us that I should ordain Oliver Cowdery to be an Elder in the Church of Jesus Christ; and that he also should ordain me to the same office; and then to ordain others, as it should be made known unto us from time to time. We were, however, commanded to defer this our ordination until such times as it should be practicable to have our brethren, who had been and who should be baptized, assembled together, when we must have their sanction to our thus proceeding to ordain each other, and have them decide by vote whether they were willing to accept us as spiritual teachers or not; when also we were commanded to bless bread and break it with them, and to take wine, bless it, and drink it with them; afterward proceed to ordain each other according to commandment; then call out such men as the Spirit should dictate, and ordain them; and then attend to the laying on of hands for the gift of the Holy Ghost, upon all those whom we had previously baptized, doing all things in the name of the Lord" (*History of the Church*, 1:60–61). As a consequence of the instructions given in this revelation, the document known as the "Articles and Covenants of the Church" (D&C 20), which led to the organization of The Church of Jesus Christ of Latter-day Saints, was written.

Instructions on Building Up the Church of Christ
DOCTRINE AND COVENANTS 18:1–9

18:2 *The things which you have written are true.* These words constitute a testimony by the God of heaven that the Book of Mormon is true. To say that the book is true means that it is a reliable representation of the truths of salvation. No equivalent statement from the God of heaven exists relative to either the Old or New Testaments or any of the books within them. See commentary on Doctrine and Covenants 6:17; 17:6.

18:3 *Rely upon the things which are written.* Oliver is instructed to rely upon the truths concerning the building up of the Church of Christ as they are written in the Book of Mormon. The inspired document that resulted is now recorded in Doctrine and Covenants 20. It is apparent that the Lord inspired Oliver's mind as he searched the Book of Mormon manuscript for information regarding the foundational document of the Church and that the Prophet Joseph Smith received revelation in refining that document. See commentary on Doctrine and Covenants 20.

18:4 *Concerning the foundation of my church.* Of necessity the Church was to be founded on correct principles, principles distinctive to the restoration, not principles borrowed from some other source. That source is here identified as the Book of Mormon. It is of particular importance to note that the Book of Mormon had to come forth before the organization of the Church, for it was to constitute the foundation of the same. So it was that the first copies of the Book of Mormon—five thousand in number, a rather remarkable expression of confidence—were completed in March 1830, and the Church was organized the next month on 6 April.

My *gospel, and my rock.* Reference is to the first principles and ordinances of the gospel of Jesus Christ, which are faith, repentance, baptism, and the gift of the Holy Ghost (3 Nephi 11:31–39). The rock upon which the Church is to be built is the revealed testimony that Jesus is the Christ, the Son of the living God (Helaman 5:12; D&C 33:12–13). See commentary on Doctrine and Covenants 128:10, "Upon this rock."

18:8 *And his name is Joseph.* Thousands of years ago, Joseph of Egypt had prophesied that the choice seer of the last days destined to restore the gospel and gather Israel would bear his name (JST Genesis 50:33; 2 Nephi 3:15). The etymology of the name *Joseph* is usually given as "the Lord addeth," "may [God] add," or "increaser." Though appropriate, such renderings have veiled a richer meaning associated with the name. In Genesis 30:23 at the birth of her son Joseph, Rachel proclaims, "God hath taken away my reproach." It has been suggested that *Joseph* is derived from the Hebrew word for reproach, *Asaph,* which carries the meaning of "he who gathers," or "he who causes to return." Thus the great prophet of the Restoration was given the name that most appropriately describes his divine calling.

18:9 *As unto Paul mine apostle, for you are called even with that same calling.* An apostle, as understood today, is an office of the priesthood within the Church of Jesus Christ. There was no Quorum of the Twelve at the time of this revelation. Indeed, there was not even an elder since none had been or would be ordained to offices in the priesthood until the members of the soon-to-be-organized Church could vote on or sustain such action. This reference to Oliver and David as apostles could only mean that they were special witnesses of events associated with the Restoration but not to an office in the priesthood. Emphasizing this distinction, the Lord referred to Joseph, as well as Oliver, as "an apostle of Jesus Christ" and as "an elder of the church" (D&C 20:2, 3; 21:1). Both Oliver Cowdery and David Whitmer were called as special witnesses. This witness was given them when the voice of God declared to them that the Book of Mormon was translated by his power as they gazed upon the plates and the Lord's messenger (D&C 17). However, neither of these men ever served as members of the Quorum of the Twelve Apostles. In like manner, to a group of faithful high priests, the Lord said, "And as I said unto mine apostles, even so I say unto you, for you are mine apostles, even God's high priests; ye are they whom my Father hath given me; ye are my friends" (D&C 84:63).

The Worth of Souls Is Great
DOCTRINE AND COVENANTS 18:10–16

18:10 *The worth of souls is great.* There is no means of measurement that can adequately place a value on a human soul. As created by God they are immortal; as redeemed by the blood of Christ they can become as God is. That which is eternal denies measurement.

Save life itself, nothing in all eternity is of greater worth than the atonement of Christ. Thus it follows that the greatest work in which anyone could be involved is that labor that brings souls to Christ, that they might receive in full measure the blessings that come only because of his sacrifice and only to those who are obedient to the laws and ordinances of his gospel. The Lord had already emphasized this principle to John and Peter Whitmer Jr. by way of revelation (D&C 15, 16). Joseph Smith explained that this revelation illustrated the nature of their calling to the priesthood (*History of the Church*, 1:62). In the same spirit, Alma taught that it was the responsibility of those who are "ordained unto the high priesthood of the holy order of God, to teach his commandments unto the children of men, that they also might enter into his rest" (Alma 13:6).

18:12 *On conditions of repentance.* There is nothing in all the eternities—both the love and grace of Christ included—to which conditions are not attached. That which is without conditions is without existence. So it is that we understand that Christ came to save us from our sins not in them (Helaman 5:11). Through his atonement, Christ brings "salvation to all those who shall believe on his name; this being the intent of this last sacrifice, to bring about the bowels of mercy, which overpowereth justice, and bringeth about means unto men that they may have faith unto repentance. And thus mercy can satisfy the demands of justice, and encircles them in the arms of safety, while he that exercises no faith unto repentance is exposed to the whole law of the demands of justice; therefore only unto him that has faith unto repentance is brought about the great and eternal plan of redemption" (Alma 34:15–16). Repentance is the condition on which the receipt of all blessings is predicated (D&C 138:19).

18:15 *How great shall be your joy.* The Book of Mormon recounts the experiences of the sons of Mosiah and their companions who taught the Lamanites the gospel. After toiling for fourteen years (Alma 17:4), they rejoiced in the success which they had in teaching repentance among them (Alma 26). Ammon said, "Yea, I know that I am nothing; as to my strength I am weak; therefore I will not boast of myself, but I will boast of my God, for in his strength I can do all things; yea, behold, many mighty miracles we have wrought in this land, for which we will praise his name forever" (Alma 26:12). Such is the joy known to those who labor to bring souls into the kingdom of God.

The Church and the Saints Bear the Name of Christ
DOCTRINE AND COVENANTS 18:17–25

18:18 *Holy Ghost, which manifesteth all things which are expedient.* Christ promised the Nephites that they would receive whatever they asked of the Father "which is right" (3 Nephi 18:20). In like manner, we have the promise that the Comforter will teach us "all things that are expedient" (D&C 75:10), and we have been cautioned that if we ask for that which "is not expedient" that it will turn unto our "condemnation" (D&C 88:65).

18:20 *Contend against no church, save it be the church of the devil.* Elder Joseph Fielding Smith explained, "When we are commanded to 'contend against no church save it be the church of the devil,' we must understand that this is instruction to us to contend against all evil, that which is opposed to righteousness and truth. James declares, that 'every good gift and every perfect gift is from above, and cometh down from the Father of lights, with whom is no variableness, neither shadow of turning,' and the scriptures also teach, 'for there is nothing which is good save it comes from the Lord; and that which is evil cometh from the devil.' (Omni 25.) All who go forth to teach should do so in wisdom and not contend with the churches or engage in profitless debates, but teach in the spirit of kindness and try to persuade people to receive the truth" (*Church History and Modern Revelation,* 1:83).

The word *contend* as used here has reference to our making earnest efforts to teaching and persuading as opposed to quarrelling.

18:21 *Take upon you the name of Christ.* See commentary on Doctrine and Covenants 20:77.

18:24 *For in that name shall they be called at the last day.* If it is Christ's church, it must of necessity bear his name. Teaching this principle to the Nephites, Christ said, "And whoso taketh upon him my name, and endureth to the end, the same shall be saved at the last day. Therefore, whatsoever ye shall do, ye shall do it in my name; therefore ye shall call the church in my name; and ye shall call upon the Father in my name that he will bless the church for my sake. And how be it my church save it be called in my name? For if a church be called in Moses' name then it be Moses' church; or if it be called in the name of a man then it be the church of a man; but if it be called in my name then it is my church, if it so be that they are built upon my gospel. Verily I say unto you, that ye are built upon my gospel; therefore ye shall call whatsoever things ye do call, in my name; therefore if ye call upon the Father, for the church, if it be in my name the Father will hear you; And if it so be that the church is built upon my gospel then will the Father show forth his own works in it" (3 Nephi 27:6–10).

The Mission of the Twelve
DOCTRINE AND COVENANTS 18:26–33

18:26 *Called to declare my gospel, both unto Gentile and unto Jew.* Later the Quorum of the Twelve would be given "the keys, to open the door by the proclamation of the gospel of Jesus Christ, and first unto the Gentiles and then unto the Jews" (D&C 107:35).

18:27 *Take upon them my name with full purpose of heart.* All who enter the waters of baptism take upon themselves the name of Christ and thus the obligation to live worthy of that name.

18:29 *They are they who are ordained of me to baptize in my name.* In all dispensations the Lord has commanded his disciples to baptize in his name. Beginning with Adam, the Lord said, "If thou wilt turn unto me, and hearken unto my voice, and believe, and repent of all thy transgressions, and be baptized, even in water, in the name of mine Only Begotten Son, who is full of grace and truth, which is Jesus Christ, the only name which shall be given under heaven, whereby salvation shall come unto the children of men, ye shall receive the gift of the Holy Ghost, asking all things in his name, and whatsoever ye shall ask, it shall be given you" (Moses 6:52). This instruction takes on added meaning when it is remembered that it was quoted by Enoch to his people, that it was preserved by Moses, and given anew to us through the Prophet Joseph Smith. From Adam to Enoch and from Enoch to Moses and from Moses to Joseph Smith, who restored the text to us, the principle has been the same.

To baptize in the Lord's name, or to perform any ordinance in his name, is to do that work by his authority or priesthood. After Peter and John healed a lame man, the Pharisees, in an attempt to ascertain the source of the miracle, questioned Peter, "By what power, or by what name, have ye done this?" (Acts 4:7). Peter declared, "By the name of Jesus Christ of Nazareth . . . doth this man stand here before you whole. . . . Neither is there salvation in any other: for there is none other name under heaven given among men, whereby we must be saved" (Acts 4:10, 12). Thus, the name of Jesus Christ is equated with the priesthood authority to perform ordinances for the salvation of men (Abraham 1:18). See commentary on Doctrine and Covenants 11:30.

18:30 *According to the words which are written.* See commentary on verse 3.

18:31 *My grace is sufficient for you.* The Twelve are able to fulfill their calling as they rely on the Savior. Under the direction of the Twelve, the gospel has gone forth and the Church of Christ has been built up, attended by the divine help of the Lord Jesus Christ among "every nation, kindred, tongue, and people, working mighty miracles, signs, and wonders, among the children of men according to their faith" (2 Nephi 26:13). Iron curtains have crumbled, despots and tyrants have fled their seats of government, and in it all the hand of the Lord has not been shortened. As Nephi testified, the Lord will "prepare a way for them that they [the Twelve] may accomplish the thing which he commandeth them" (1 Nephi 3:7).

Reading the Scriptures by the Spirit
DOCTRINE AND COVENANTS 18:34–36

18:35 *It is my voice . . . for they are given by my Spirit.* See commentary on Doctrine and Covenants 88:66.

18:36 *You can testify that you have heard my voice, and know my words.* This revelation was given in June 1829; the Twelve were not called until February 1835. Nevertheless, the Twelve are told that if they will read this revelation (and for that matter any revelation) under the direction or influence of the Holy Ghost, they will be able to testify that they have heard the voice of the Lord. The principle applies to all who read the word of the Lord under the direction of the Spirit. To read under the direction of the Spirit is to hear that voice. This principle is repeated in Doctrine and Covenants 84, in which the Lord says, "Verily, verily, I say unto you who now hear my words, *which are my voice*, blessed are ye inasmuch as you receive these things" (v. 60; emphasis added).

Searching Out the Twelve

DOCTRINE AND COVENANTS 18:37-47

18:37 *You shall search out the Twelve.* Oliver Cowdery and David Whitmer were given the charge to "search out" or find those worthy and capable of holding the office of an apostle. As one of the Three Witnesses, Martin Harris would share in this responsibility. Following the experiences of Zion's Camp, the time for choosing arrived. In Kirtland on 14 February 1835, Joseph paid tribute to those who had marched with Zion's Camp and then proposed that the time had come to ordain twelve men to the office of an apostle. "President Joseph Smith, Jun., said that the first business of the meeting was, for the Three Witnesses of the Book of Mormon, to pray, each one, and then proceed to choose twelve men from the Church, as Apostles, to go to all nations, kindreds, tongues, and people.

"The Three Witnesses, viz., Oliver Cowdery, David Whitmer, and Martin Harris, united in prayer.

"These three witnesses were then blessed by the laying on of the hands of the [First] Presidency.

"The Witnesses then, according to a former commandment [the present revelation], proceeded to make choice of the Twelve. Their names are as follows:

"1. Lyman E. Johnson

"2. Brigham Young

"3. Heber C. Kimball

"4. Orson Hyde

"5. David W. Patten

"6. Luke S. Johnson

"7. William E. M'Lellin

"8. John F. Boynton

"9. Orson Pratt

"10. William Smith

"11. Thomas B. Marsh

"12. Parley P. Pratt" (Smith, *History of the Church*, 2:186–87).

These men were ordained in the quorum according to age, from oldest to youngest.

18:42 *Who have arrived at the years of accountability.* See Doctrine and Covenants 68:27.

DOCTRINE AND COVENANTS 19

DATE: MARCH 1830
PLACE: MANCHESTER, NEW YORK

This revelation came in response to Martin Harris's inquiry to the Prophet regarding his standing before the Lord. Troubled in spirit by his transgression, concerned about his farm, which he had mortgaged to finance the printing of the Book of Mormon, and perhaps sobered by the responsibility attendant to the remarkable vision shown to him and the other special witnesses of the Book of Mormon, Martin was desirous to receive both confirmation and direction from the Lord.

From the personal recollections of Joseph Knight, a participant in these events, we have the following story: "In the Spring of 1830 I went with my Team and took Joseph out to Manchester to his Father. When we was on our way he told me that there must be a Church formed But did not tell when. Now when we got near to his fathers we saw a man some Eighty Rods Before us run acros the street with a Bundle in his hand. 'There,' says Joseph, 'there is Martin going a Cros the road with some thing in his hand.' Says I, 'how Could you know him so far? Says he, 'I Believe it is him,' and when we Came up it was Martin with a Bunch of morman Books. He Came to us and after Compliments he says, 'The Books will not sell for no Body wants them.' Joseph says, 'I think they will sell well.' Says he, 'I want a Commandment.' 'Why,' says Joseph, 'fullfill what you have got.' 'But,' says he, 'I must have a Commandment.' Joseph put him off. But he insisted three or four times he must have a Commandment.

"We went home to his fathers and Martin with us. Martin stayed at his Fathers and slept in a Bed on the flor with me. Martin awoke me in the nite and asked me if I felt any thing on the Bed. I told him no. Says I, 'Did you?' 'Yes, I felt some thing as Big as a grat Dog Sprang upon my Brest.' Says I, 'Was you not mistekened.' 'No,' says he. 'It was so.' I Sprang up and felt, But I Could see nor feal nothing. In the morning he got up and said he must have a Commandment to Joseph and went home. And

143

along in the after part of the Day Joseph and Oliver Received a Commandmant which is in Book of Covenants Page 174 [D&C 19]" (Jessee, "Joseph Knight," 36–37; spelling and punctuation as in original).

In this revelation we obtain insights relative to the suffering of Christ not given in other scriptural texts. We are also granted an expanded understanding relative to the nature of divine punishment and the suffering awaiting the unrepentant. This section ranks among the most instructive of our doctrinal revelations.

God's Judgments and Punishments
DOCTRINE AND COVENANTS 19:1–12

19:1 "The death on Calvary," said Elder Orson F. Whitney, "was no more the ending of that divine career, than the birth at Bethlehem was its beginning" (Conference Report, April 1927, 101). Christ is an eternal being. He has existed from the beginning and will continue to live in glory throughout all eternity. See commentary on Doctrine and Covenants 76:4.

Alpha and Omega. The first and last letters of the Greek alphabet are used as name-titles for Christ. Figuratively, they represent the timeless and eternal nature of the attributes of Deity.

19:2 *Having accomplished and finished the will of him whose I am.* Having explained the plan of salvation to all his children and the central place of the One who would make of himself an offering for their sins, the Father in the Grand Council of Heaven asked, "Whom shall I send?" (Abraham 3:27). He whom we know as Jesus of Nazareth responded, saying, "Father, thy will be done, and the glory be thine forever" (Moses 4:2). As he hung upon the cross, the suffering of Gethsemane and Calvary now behind him, the Savior declared, "Father, it is finished, thy will is done" (JST Matthew 27:54).

19:3 *The destroying of Satan and his works at the end of the world.* See commentary on Doctrine and Covenants 88:114.

The last great day of judgment. Reference is to the time that follows the Millennium—a period of one thousand years of righteousness. It is instructive in the context of this revelation to note that the scriptures do not speak of a *final judgment* in which all people of the earth are brought before God at one time to receive rewards and punishments. Rather, the Lord speaks of judgment that has a great last day in which he will banish Satan and his hosts into their own place. At that time all of God's children who belong to this earth will have had judgment passed upon them. Statements, such as those found in the Book of Mormon, that "the day cometh that all shall rise from the dead and stand before God, and be judged according to their works" (Alma 11:41) do not intend to convey the idea that all will be judged on one final day of judgment any more than all will be resurrected the same day. The principle being taught is that there will be judgment for each individual's works and that there is a time at the end of the Millennium when all will have received that judgment.

19:5 *Weeping, wailing and gnashing of teeth.* This phrase is a proverbial way of dramatizing the intensity of the sorrow, anguish, and bitterness that are the fruits of sin.

19:6 *It is not written that there shall be no end to this torment, but it is written* endless torment. The phrase "endless torment" is not found in the Bible, though it appears seven times in the Book of Mormon (2 Nephi 9:19, 26; 28:23; Jacob 6:10; Mosiah 3:25; 28:3; Moroni 8:21). Martin Harris must have read of *endless torment* in a Book of Mormon manuscript. He apparently understood the phrase to mean that his suffering was of necessity to be endless in duration. Had the opportunity been his to study the text of the book more carefully, he would have discovered that this was not the case. The Book of Mormon clearly states that people may be delivered from hell, or endless torment. "O the greatness of the mercy of our God, the Holy One of Israel! For he delivereth his saints from that awful monster the devil, and death, and hell, and that lake of fire and brimstone, which is endless torment" (2 Nephi 9:19; see also v. 26). Jacob's message in referring to endless torment is that such would be the state of all mankind, if there had been no atonement made.

Similarly, Alma declared, "I was racked with eternal torment, for my soul was harrowed up to the greatest degree and racked with all my sins" (Alma 36:12). Yet, this torment, which he described as "inexpressible horror," "exquisite" in its bitterness, lasted only three days, or until the time that Alma called upon the mercy of Christ to deliver him from his awful state (Alma 36:14, 21). See commentary on Doctrine and Covenants 19:17.

19:7 *It is written* eternal damnation . . . *that it might work upon the hearts of the children of men.* Just as the righteous will be raised up in the resurrection unto eternal life, so the wicked will be cast into outer darkness in the great and last day of judgment. "And thus did I, the Lord God, appoint unto man the days of his probation—that by his natural death he might be raised in immortality unto eternal life, even as many as would believe; And they that believe not unto eternal damnation; for they cannot be redeemed from their spiritual fall, because they repent not; for they love darkness rather than light, and their deeds are evil" (D&C 29:43–45).

During his mortal ministry the Savior declared, "But he that shall blaspheme against the Holy Ghost hath never forgiveness, but is in danger of eternal damnation" (Mark 3:29). Eternal damnation is the punishment of those who remain unrepentant and, consequently, are eternally cast out of God's presence. The contrast between rewards and punishments makes plain the greatness of God's blessings as well as the severity of his punishments. This clear distinction works on their hearts "to choose liberty and eternal life, through the great Mediator of all men" rather than "to choose captivity and death, according to the captivity and power of the devil" (2 Nephi 2:27).

19:10–13 Here we are told that both *eternal* and *endless* are nouns rather than adjectives used in many texts to describe the punishment that comes from God. By way of illustration, in the Salt Lake Valley near what is known as the Point of the Mountain is a large institution designed to confine law breakers. It bears the name Utah State Penitentiary because it belongs to the State of Utah and is used to punish those who have broken the laws of the state. In like manner, the Lord has a place to confine those who have broken his laws. It bears the name "eternal punishment" or "endless punishment," which denote ownership, not the duration of the punishment involved.

Elder James E. Talmage explained: "To hell there is an exit as well as an entrance. Hell is no place to which a vindictive judge sends prisoners to suffer and to be punished principally for his glory; but it is a place prepared for the teaching, the disciplining of those who failed to learn here upon the earth what they should have learned. True, we read of everlasting punishment, unending suffering, eternal damnation. That is a direful expression; but in his mercy the Lord has made plain what those words mean. 'Eternal punishment,' he says, is God's punishment, for he is eternal; and that condition or state or possibility will ever exist for the sinner who deserves and really needs such condemnation; but this does not mean that the individual sufferer or sinner is to be eternally and everlastingly made to endure and suffer. No man will be kept in hell longer than is necessary to bring him to a fitness for something better. When he reaches that stage the prison doors will open and there will be rejoicing among the hosts who welcome him into a better state. The Lord has not abated in the least what he has said in earlier dispensations concerning the operation of his law and his gospel, but he has made clear unto us his goodness and mercy through it all, for it is his glory and his work to bring about the immortality and eternal life of man" (Conference Report, April 1930, 97).

Christ Suffered for the Sins of All Who Will Repent
DOCTRINE AND COVENANTS 19:13–24

19:16 *I, God, have suffered these things.* Only a God can atone for the sins of another. Referring to the atoning sacrifice of the Savior, Amulek explained that "it must be an infinite and eternal sacrifice" (Alma 34:10). Further, Christ was able to offer himself a sacrifice for sin, explained Lehi, because of his "merits, and mercy, and grace" (2 Nephi 2:8). The Savior uniquely merited the ability to suffer for the sins of others because he was sinless, and justice, therefore, could not demand that he suffer punishment for sin. When he suffered for sin, it was not for his own sins; rather, his suffering met the demands of justice for the sins of others. He was not constrained by law to suffer for the sins of others but did so out of his mercy and loving kindness to them. The concept of grace indicates aid that comes from a divine source. Therefore, Christ was uniquely qualified to offer grace through the atoning sacrifice because as a member of the Godhead he condescended to become the Only Begotten Son of God in the flesh. His divine sonship as the Only Begotten Son of God enabled him to suffer "more than man can suffer, except it be unto death" (Mosiah 3:7).

19:17 *If they would not repent they must suffer even as I.* If they do not repent, "the wicked remain as though there had been no redemption made, except it be the loosing of the bands of death" (Alma 11:41). Thus, the unrepentant suffer a spiritual death in which they are cut off from the presence of God, and the Spirit of the Lord is withdrawn from them. Those who inherit the telestial kingdom are numbered among those who must suffer the demands of justice for sin in the spirit world. "These are they who are cast down to hell and suffer the wrath of Almighty God" (D&C 76:106).

The suffering referred to by the Savior is not a quantity of punishment meted out and experienced for a predetermined length of time. Individuals suffer as long as they remain in sin. When they repent, the atonement of Christ has claim upon them. "Hence the salvation of Jesus Christ was wrought out for all men," taught the Prophet Joseph Smith, "in order to triumph over the devil; for if it did not catch him in one place, it would in another; for he stood up as a Savior. All will suffer until they obey Christ himself" (*Teachings of the Prophet Joseph Smith,* 357). Therefore, the suffering continues until individuals repent and forsake their sins. See commentary on Doctrine and Covenants 19:6.

There are those who have falsely supposed that Christ's suffering supplants suffering on the part of those who repent. This simply is not the case. There is no repentance without suffering. Teaching this principle to his son Corianton, Alma said, "Now, repentance could not come unto men except there were a punishment, which also was eternal as the life of the soul should be, affixed opposite to the plan of happiness, which was as eternal also as the life of the soul. Now, how could a man repent except he should sin? How could he sin if there was no law? How could there be a law save there was a punishment? Now, there was a punishment affixed, and a just law given, which brought remorse of conscience unto man" (Alma 42:16–18). What the present text means is that the repentant soul will not have to suffer "even as" the Savior suffered. But it does not mean that they will not have to suffer. Nor should it be supposed that their suffering is confined to the natural consequences of their actions. In addition to those consequences, he or she must experience the anguish associated with true repentance.

President Spencer W. Kimball said of personal suffering that it "is a very important part of repentance. One has not begun to repent until he has suffered intensely for his sins. . . . If a person hasn't suffered, he hasn't repented. . . . He has got to go through a change in his system whereby he suffers and then forgiveness is a possibility" (*Teachings of Spencer W. Kimball,* 88, 99).

Elder Dallin H. Oaks explained that "some Latter-day Saints who wrongly think repentance is easy maintain that a little sinning will not hurt. Young people of this persuasion may say, 'It is okay to have a few free ones, because it is easy to repent before your mission or marriage.' The adult versions are more sophisticated and more pernicious. Perhaps some would even assert that a person is better off after he has sinned and repented. 'Get a little experience with sin,' one argument goes, 'and then you will be better able to counsel and sympathize with sinners. You can always repent.'

"I plead with my brothers and sisters, my young friends and my older friends, avoid transgression! The idea that one can deliberately sin and easily repent or that one is better off after sinning and repenting are devilish lies of the adversary. Would anyone seriously contend that it is better to learn firsthand that a certain blow will break a bone or that a certain mixture of chemicals will explode and burn off our skin? Are we better off after we have sustained and then scarred over from such injuries? It is obviously better to heed the warnings of wise persons who know the effects of certain traumas on our bodies" ("Sins, Crimes, and Atonement," 7).

Responding to the issue as to why it is necessary for one to suffer when serious transgression is involved, Elder Oaks said, "We often think of the results of repentance as simply cleansing us from sin. But that is an incomplete view of the matter. A person who sins is like a tree that bends easily in the wind. On a windy and rainy day the tree bends so deeply against the ground that the leaves become soiled with mud, like sin. If we only focus on cleaning the leaves, the weakness in the tree that allowed it to bend and soil its leaves may remain. Merely cleaning the leaves does not strengthen the tree. Similarly, a person who is merely sorry to be soiled by sin will sin again in the next high wind. The susceptibility to repetition continues until the tree has been strengthened" ("Sin and Suffering," 150).

19:18 *Which suffering caused myself . . . to tremble because of pain.* This revelation is unique among all scripture in its intimacy. Jesus Christ speaks of his suffering and of the feelings attending it. No one else shared this experience with him. Elder Bruce R. McConkie explained: "We do not know, we cannot tell, no mortal mind can conceive the full import of what Christ did in Gethsemane. We know he sweat great gouts of blood from every pore as he drained the dregs of that bitter cup his Father had given him.

"We know he suffered, both body and spirit, more than it is possible for man to suffer, except it be unto death.

"We know that in some way, incomprehensible to us, his suffering satisfied the demands of justice, ransomed penitent souls from the pains and penalties of sin, and made mercy available to those who believe in his holy name.

"We know that he lay prostrate upon the ground as the pains and agonies of an infinite burden caused him to tremble and would that he might not drink the bitter cup.

"We know that an angel came from the courts of glory to strengthen him in his ordeal, and we suppose it was mighty Michael, who foremost fell that mortal man might be.

"As near as we can judge, these infinite agonies—this suffering beyond compare—continued for some three or four hours" (Conference Report, April 1985, 9–10).

Bleed at every pore. "Blood cometh from every pore," prophesied King Benjamin, "so great shall be his anguish for the wickedness and the abominations of his people" (Mosiah 3:7; see also Luke 22:44). The Savior confirmed the declarations of Luke and King Benjamin concerning the extent of his suffering. Elder Neal A. Maxwell offered insight into the symbolic significance of the Savior's anguish: "His infinite atonement affected every age, every dispensation, and every person (see 2 Nephi 9:7; 25:16). Hence the appropriate symbolism of His bleeding at each and every pore—not just some" (Conference Report, October 1988, 41).

Would that I might not drink the bitter cup. "Later, in Gethsemane," observed Elder Neal A. Maxwell, "the suffering Jesus began to be 'sore amazed' (Mark 14:33), or, in the Greek, 'awestruck' and 'astonished.'

"Imagine, Jehovah, the Creator of this and other worlds, 'astonished'! Jesus knew cognitively what He must do, but not experientially. He had never personally known the exquisite and exacting process of an atonement before. Thus, when the agony came in its fulness, it was so much, much worse than even He with his unique intellect had ever imagined! No wonder an angel appeared to strengthen him! (See Luke 22:43.)

"The cumulative weight of all mortal sins—past, present, and future—pressed upon that perfect, sinless, and sensitive Soul! All our infirmities and sicknesses were somehow, too, a part of the awful arithmetic of the Atonement. (See Alma 7:11–12, Isaiah 53:3–5, Matthew 8:17.) The anguished Jesus not only pled with the Father that the hour and cup might pass from Him, but with this relevant citation. 'And he said, Abba, Father, all things are possible unto thee; take away this cup from me' (Mark 14:35–36)" (Conference Report, April 1985, 92).

19:19 *Finished my preparations unto the children of men.* The way is prepared for all to come back into the presence of God through Christ's atoning for the transgression of Adam and Eve in the Garden of Eden and through his resurrection from the dead. Further, the Atonement and the Resurrection completed the Savior's preparation of the way in which we can be redeemed from spiritual death caused by our own sins and return to our Father again to dwell with him throughout eternity.

19:20 *In the smallest, yea, even in the least degree you have tasted at the time I withdrew my Spirit.* This is the only revelation in which the Savior has unveiled that his suffering for sin included the withdrawal of the Spirit. This fact is intimated in the Savior's soul-wrenching cry from

Golgotha, "My God, my God, why hast thou forsaken me?" (Matthew 27:46). With reference to that moment on the cross, Elder James E. Talmage wrote: "What mind of man can fathom the significance of that awful cry? It seems, that in addition to the fearful suffering incident to crucifixion, the agony of Gethsemane had recurred, intensified beyond human power to endure. In that bitterest hour the dying Christ was alone, alone in most terrible reality. That the supreme sacrifice of the Son might be consummated in all its fulness, the Father seems to have withdrawn the support of His immediate Presence, leaving to the Savior of men the glory of complete victory over the forces of sin and death" (*Jesus the Christ*, 661).

President Brigham Young provided increased understanding regarding the withdrawal of the Spirit from the Savior as part of the atoning sacrifice: "The Father withdrew His spirit from His son, at the time he was to be crucified. . . . At the very moment, at the hour when the crisis came for him to offer up his life, the Father withdrew Himself, withdrew His Spirit, and cast a vail over him. That is what made him sweat blood. If he had had the power of God upon him, he would not have sweat blood; but all was withdrawn from him, and a veil was cast over him, and he then plead with the Father not to forsake him" (*Journal of Discourses*, 3:206).

The immediate context of the Savior's reference to Joseph Smith and Martin Harris was the loss of the 116-page manuscript (D&C 3). At that time Joseph and Martin suffered excruciating spiritual pain. The Lord indicated in this revelation that this suffering resulted from the withdrawal of his Spirit. These men in some measure had experienced that. Yet, even that anguish was but a sliver of pain in comparison to the suffering for sin that Jesus Christ experienced.

Lucy Mack Smith gave insight to the punishment that Joseph and Martin tasted on the occasion. She wrote that on hearing that the manuscript was lost, her son Joseph clenched his hands together, crying that all was lost. "He wept and groaned, walking the floor continually. . . .

"I besought him not to mourn so, for it might be that the Lord would forgive him, after a short season of humiliation and repentance on his part. But what could I say to comfort him when he saw all the family in the same state of mind that he was? Our sobs and groans and the most bitter lamentations filled the house. Joseph, in particular, was more distressed than the rest. . . . He continued walking backwards and forwards, weeping and grieving like a tender infant until about sunset, when we persuaded him to take a little nourishment. . . .

"I well remember that day of darkness, both within and without. To us, at least, the heavens seemed clothed with blackness, and the earth shrouded with gloom. I have often said within myself that if a continual punishment, as severe as that which we experienced on that occasion, were to be inflicted upon the most wicked characters who ever stood upon the footstool of the Almighty—if even their punishment were no greater than that, I should feel to pity their condition" (Smith, *History of Joseph Smith*, 1996, 165–66, 171).

19:21 *Show not these things unto the world.* A loving Father does not reveal truths to his children that they are not prepared to receive but, rather, gives them milk until they can bear meat. The Prophet Joseph Smith taught that "the Lord deals with his people as a tender parent with a child, communicating light and intelligence and the knowledge of his ways as they can bear it" (*History of the Church*, 5:402). Alma explained that "it is given unto many to know the mysteries of God; nevertheless they are laid under a strict command that they shall not impart only according to the portion of his word which he doth grant unto the children of men, according to the heed and diligence which they give unto him" (Alma 12:9).

Instructions Concerning the Printing of the Book of Mormon
DOCTRINE AND COVENANTS 19:25–41

19:25 *Thou shalt not covet thy neighbor's wife.* It is not known why Martin Harris would receive this particular warning. Martin's marriage was unhappy, due in part to his wife's decided opposition to his involvement in the translation and publication of the Book of Mormon. It may be that problems in his marriage were opening the door to temptation. See commentary on Doctrine and Covenants 3:7.

19:26–35 On 25 August 1829, more than six months previous to this revelation, Martin Harris mortgaged 240 acres of his farm to pay for the printing of five thousand copies of the Book of Mormon. E. B. Grandin, who was also the publisher of the book, held the contract for three thousand dollars. Martin agreed to deed a sufficient amount of his farm to pay the debt if the money could not be raised within eighteen months by the sale of the Book of Mormon to interested parties. As we have noted, Martin was concerned about losing his farm. His concern proved to be well-founded because the citizens near Palmyra voted to boycott purchasing the Book of Mormon. To pay the debt, Martin sold 151 acres of the family farm, which included the frame home he had built earlier in his married life. His wife, Lucy, had made preparations to provide for herself and the children, if she ever deemed it necessary to end the marriage. "When the property was about to be sold, [she] left him, taking their children, and never again returned to live with Martin Harris" (Tuckett and Wilson, *Martin Harris Story*, 51).

19:27 *The Jew, of whom the Lamanites are a remnant.* The Lamanites can be considered Jews in the sense that the families of Lehi and Ishmael were citizens of the southern kingdom and thus were Jewish naturals. As to blood lineage, Lehi was a descendant of Manasseh; Ishmael was a descendant of Ephraim (Erastus Snow, *Journal of Discourses*, 23:184).

19:30 *Reviling not against revilers.* This admonition became very practical advice for Martin a short time after the Book of Mormon came off the press. The *Palmyra Courier* reported: "Shortly after the completion of the printing of the Book of Mormon, Martin Harris began (his effort) to sell the work, and was daily seen on the street, inviting his friends and neighbors to buy. His form was conspicuous, with a grey suit of homespun, his head surmounted by a large stiff hat, while under his arm he carried several copies of the book" (31 May 1872, 2). During one of these occasions Martin had opportunity to practice this counsel. "Harris was proverbially a peaceful as well as an honest man. He was slow to retaliate an offence. . . . Urging the sale of the book . . . he fell into debate about its character with a neighbor of an irascible temperament. His opponent became angry, and struck him a severe blow upon the right side of his face. Instantly turning toward the assailant the other cheek, he [Harris] quoted the Christian maxim, reading it from the book in his hand [Book of Mormon] page 481 [as it also appears in Matthew 5:39], 'Whosoever shall smite thee on the right cheek, turn to him the other also'" (Tucker, *Progress of Mormonism*, 61).

19:31 *Of tenets thou shalt not talk.* Tenets are doctrinal beliefs that distinguish those of various denominations from one another. This verse instructs us that in presenting our message we are to avoid peripheral discussions—be they to establish common ground or to find fault—and instead center on the message of the Restoration.

DOCTRINE AND COVENANTS 20 AND 22

The Articles and Covenants of the Church

DATE: APRIL 1830

PLACE: FAYETTE AND MANCHESTER, NEW YORK

On Tuesday, 6 April 1830, in upstate New York, a small group of people gathered in the log home of Peter Whitmer Sr. They did so according to divine command, for the time had come to establish the Church of Jesus Christ once again upon the earth. The meeting began with solemn prayer. Those present were then invited to sustain Joseph Smith Jr. and Oliver Cowdery as "their teachers in the things of the kingdom of God" and to organize the Church. This was done unanimously. Joseph Smith then ordained Oliver Cowdery an elder in the Church, and Oliver ordained Joseph to the same office. The sacrament of bread and wine was then administered to those constituting the formal organization of the Church. By name they were Joseph Smith Jr., Oliver Cowdery, Hyrum Smith, Peter Whitmer Jr., Samuel H. Smith, and David Whitmer. Though Joseph, Oliver, Samuel, and Hyrum had previously been baptized, they were baptized again, most likely before the meeting here described. They were then confirmed members of the Church and given the gift of the Holy Ghost by the laying on of hands. Joseph Smith noted, "The Holy Ghost was poured out upon us to a very great degree—some prophesied, whilst we all praised the Lord, and rejoiced exceedingly" (*History of the Church*, 1:78). The revelation recorded in section 21 of the Doctrine and Covenants was then received. Following this, others were ordained to various offices in the priesthood and made expressions of faith. The meeting was then concluded with prayer. At that point several of those present desired to be united with the Church and were baptized. Among them were the Prophet's parents, Joseph Sr. and Lucy Mack Smith, as well as Martin Harris and Orrin Porter Rockwell.

As early as June 1829 Joseph Smith asked Oliver Cowdery to

formulate an expression of basic principles and practices of the soon-to-be-organized Church. Oliver in turn asked the Prophet to inquire of the Lord about what he should do. Doctrine and Covenants 18 was given in response to that request. In the revelation Oliver was directed to rely upon the teachings "concerning the foundation of my church, my gospel, and my rock" (D&C 18:4) as contained in the Book of Mormon. Drawing upon the principles in the Book of Mormon, Oliver submitted a manuscript to the Prophet. "Then Joseph Smith, or both he and Oliver Cowdery, revised that document. They put it in the format now found in section 20" (Woodford, "Articles and Covenants," 264–65).

Section 20 binds together a number of separate revelations. It appears that verses 1 through 4, which designate the day upon which the Church was to be organized, were given early in April 1830. Other sections of the revelation were at least influenced by Oliver's draft and may have existed before that date. Section 20 is divided into distinct discussions concerning the brief history that preceded the Church organization, a declaration of beliefs, requirements for baptism, duties of priesthood offices and members, ordinances of the Church, and record keeping. This revelation and section 22 became known among the early members as the Articles and Covenants of the Church.

Organization of the Church Directed
DOCTRINE AND COVENANTS 20:1–4

20:1 The day upon which Joseph Smith was to organize the Church is here identified as 6 April 1830. This identification of the date, expressed in the manner customary at the time, should probably not be understood as a confirmation that the organization of the Church took place 1,830 years after the birth of Christ. If, as we learn in the Gospel of Matthew, the wise men visited Herod before finding the Christ child, we can with some certainty identify the year of his birth. History shows that Herod died before the Passover of 750 A.U.C. (750 years after the founding of Rome), which corresponds to the year 4 B.C. in our reckoning of time. Herod's order to slay the children in and around Bethlehem "from two years old and under" (Matthew 2:16) suggests that Christ was born in 5 or 6 B.C. (McConkie, *Mortal Messiah*, 1:349–50). Both history and the testimony of our modern prophets indicate that Christ was born on April 6 (see Lee, Conference Report, April 1973, 4; Kimball, Conference Report, April 1974, 4).

The Church of Christ. The name "The Church of Jesus Christ of Latter-day Saints" was given in a revelation on 26 April 1838. See commentary on Doctrine and Covenants 115:4.

20:2 Joseph Smith and Oliver Cowdery received the Melchizedek Priesthood at the hands of Peter, James, and John almost a year before the organization of the Church. They had not, however, been ordained to an office within the priesthood; one cannot hold an office in a non-existent organization. They were apostles in the sense that they were special witnesses of Christ, having translated the Book of Mormon, been instructed by Moroni, and received both the Aaronic and Melchizedek Priesthoods at the hands of divine messengers. In the meeting in which the Church was organized, Joseph and Oliver were ordained elders. If they had already held the office of apostle, this ordination would have been unnecessary.

Ordained an apostle. The word *ordained* is frequently used in the Doctrine and Covenants to mean "designated" or "appointed." For instance, revelations speak of "the beasts of the field and the fowls of the air, and that which cometh of the earth" as being ordained (D&C 49:19). In section 89 we are told that "wholesome herbs God hath ordained" for the use of man, as were fruits in their season and all grains (D&C 89:10). Emma Smith is spoken of as having been ordained (D&C 25:7). Those who become sons of perdition are spoken of as having been "ordained unto this condemnation" (D&C 76:48).

The first elder. The designation of Joseph and Oliver as "first" and "second" elders of the Church was added to the original document which simply read "elders." This denomination helps dramatize their role as the presiding officers in the Church during its early years when its size did not justify the organizational structure known to us today. See commentary on Doctrine and Covenants 21:10, 12.

The Book of Mormon Proves the Divinity of the Restoration
DOCTRINE AND COVENANTS 20:5–12

20:5 *He had received a remission of his sins.* This alludes to the First Vision in which Joseph was told that his sins were forgiven him (McConkie and Millet, *Joseph Smith,* 371). See commentary on Joseph Smith–History 1:17, page 10.

He was entangled again in the vanities of the world. Joseph Smith explained: "During the space of time which intervened between the time I had the vision and the year eighteen hundred and twenty-three—having been forbidden to join any of the religious sects of the day, and being of very tender years, and persecuted by those who ought to have been my friends and to have treated me kindly, and if they supposed me to be deluded to have endeavored in a proper and affectionate manner to have reclaimed me—I was left to all kinds of temptations; and, mingling with all kinds of society, I frequently fell into many foolish errors, and displayed the weakness of youth, and the foibles of human nature; which, I am sorry to say, led me into divers temptations, offensive in the sight of God. In making this confession, no one need suppose me guilty of any great or malignant sins. A disposition to commit such was never in my nature. But I was guilty of levity, and sometimes associated with jovial company, etc., not consistent with that character which ought to be maintained by one who was called of God as I had been. But this will not seem very strange to any one who recollects my youth, and is acquainted with my native cheery temperament" (Joseph Smith–History 1:28).

20:6 *An holy angel.* The angel referred to here is Moroni.

20:8 The "means" prepared by which the Book of Mormon was translated were the Urim and Thummim. See commentary on Joseph Smith–History 1:35, page 21; Doctrine and Covenants 9:7–10; 10:1.

20:9 *The fulness of the gospel of Jesus Christ.* See commentary on Joseph Smith–History 1:34, page 20.

20:10 The writers of the Book of Mormon wrote by the spirit of inspiration; their words are scripture. Moroni, and others of their number, have testified of the truthfulness of the Book of Mormon to many. The best known illustration of this is found in the testimony of the three witnesses (introductory pages to the Book of Mormon).

20:11–12 Three reasons for which the Lord gave us the Book of Mormon are stated in these verses. First, in an age when the reliability of the Bible is constantly questioned, the Book of Mormon comes forth as proof of the Bible's credibility. It is an independent witness of the principle of revelation, of the prophetic office as known to the ancients, of the ministry of angels, and of the saving principles of the gospel. The Book of Mormon reaffirms the promises made to the fathers relative to the redemption of Israel. It fulfills biblical prophecy concerning the visit of Christ to these "other" sheep (John 10:16). It also fulfills prophecy about a book that would come forth to aid in the gathering of Israel (Isaiah 29:11–12, 14, 18; Ezekiel 37:15–28). Second, the Book of Mormon constitutes a sure proof that Joseph Smith is a prophet. A host of internal evidences verify that the book is not the work of men, not the least of which is the invitation given to all honest seekers of truth to inquire of God relative to the book's truthfulness (Moroni 10:3–5). Third, the Book of Mormon evidences that God is the same yesterday, today, and forever. Thus Nephi described the Holy Ghost as "the gift of God unto all those who diligently seek him, as well in times of old as in the time that he should manifest himself unto the children of men. . . . For he that diligently seeketh shall find; and the mysteries of God shall be unfolded unto them, by the power of the Holy Ghost, as well in these times as in times of old, and as well in times of old as in times to come; wherefore, the course of the Lord is one eternal round" (1 Nephi 10:17, 19).

20:11 *Proving to the world that the holy scriptures are true.* Here we are told that one of the primary purposes of the Book of Mormon is to prove that the Bible is true. This same message was given to Joseph of Egypt when the Lord told him of the mission and ministry of the Prophet Joseph Smith. "Unto him will I give power to bring forth my word unto the seed of thy loins," the ancient Joseph was told, "and not to the bringing forth of my word only, saith the Lord, but to the convincing them of my word, which shall have already gone forth among them in the last days" (JST Genesis 50:30; 2 Nephi 3:11). Curiously, it is a common practice among Latter-day Saint missionaries to attempt to prove the Book of Mormon is true using Bible texts. In contrast, the Lord directs that we do the reverse, showing to those not of our faith how the Book of Mormon proves the Bible true. It is the knowledge and testimony restored to us through the Book of Mormon that unlock the greatness of the Bible.

All to Be Judged by Their Acceptance or Rejection of the Book of Mormon
DOCTRINE AND COVENANTS 20:13–16

20:13–16 Speaking to the Nephites, the resurrected Christ said that those of the last days who would not accept his words as they came to them through the Book of Mormon would be "cut off from among my people who are of the covenant" (3 Nephi 21:11). That is to say they will not receive the blessings of salvation found in the house of the Lord because they rejected the gospel as it came to them through the Book of Mormon and the Prophet Joseph Smith.

Many profess to accept Christ and his gospel as found in the Bible while rejecting that gospel as it comes to them through those the Lord has chosen to be his agents in this dispensation. There is not and never can be salvation in such a course. The food eaten by the ancients will not strengthen our bodies, nor will their baptisms cleanse our spirits. Those of whom we read in the Bible found salvation through their allegiance to gospel principles taught by the living oracles of their own day, not through the faith of a people who lived long before them, and so must we. For our day, those accepting the testimony of Christ as found in the Book of Mormon and complying with the laws and ordinances of the gospel as directed by living prophets are promised crowns of glory. Those rejecting the Book of Mormon and the direction of those the Lord has appointed as his messengers in this day have no such promise.

Creation, Fall, Atonement, Baptism
DOCTRINE AND COVENANTS 20:17–28

20:17 *By these things we know that there is a God in heaven.* The antecedents to "by these things" as found in the previous verses are the First Vision (v. 5) and the Book of Mormon (vv. 6–16). In effect, this verse announces a new gospel dispensation. "Gospel dispensations are those periods of time during which the Lord reveals or dispenses the doctrines of the gospel to men so that reliance need not be placed on past ages for this saving knowledge" (McConkie, *Mormon Doctrine*, 200–201). Our testimony is to stand on revelation that is immediate and personal to us and to our day. Thus we profess to know that there is a God in heaven because he revealed himself in our day. We believe that he speaks because he has spoken to us, and we trace all ordinances of salvation through that authority revealed to the Prophet Joseph Smith.

From everlasting to everlasting. See commentary on Doctrine and Covenants 132:20.

20:18 The biblical declaration that man is created in the image and likeness of God has been robbed of its purpose and meaning by historical Christianity (Genesis 1:27). Having determined that God has no corporeal image, apostate Christianity can only conclude that this biblical passage cannot possibly mean what it says. This text is argued to have reference to some part of the mind or spirit of man rather than the body as the context clearly suggests. The revelations of the Restoration leave no question on the matter. In Moses 6:9 we read: "In the image of his own body, male and female, created he them, and blessed them, and called their name Adam." In the Book of Mormon, Abinadi taught that Christ would "take upon him the image of man, and it should be the image after

which man was created in the beginning; or in other words, he said that
man was created after the image of God, and that God should come down
among the children of men, and take upon him flesh and blood, and go
forth upon the face of the earth" (Mosiah 7:27).

20:19 *That he should be the only being whom they should worship.* In the
most proper sense the true Saint, in all gospel dispensations, has worshiped but one God. He is the Father of our spirits. Christ, through his
atonement, reconciles us to the Father. Because we are "saved" (meaning
reconciled to the Father) only through the merits and mercy of Christ,
we pray to the Father in his name. All that Christ does is done "according
to the will of the Father" (v. 24). Thus when the plan of salvation was
presented in the Grand Council of Heaven and the need for a redeemer
explained, the Father asked, "Whom shall I send?" (Abraham 3:27), and
it was Christ who responded, saying: "Father, thy will be done, and the
glory be thine forever" (Moses 4:2).

20:21 *The Almighty God gave his Only Begotten Son.* Though the
Almighty God is the Father of the spirits of all humankind, Christ alone
was begotten of him in the flesh and is known as the Only Begotten Son.

As it is written in those scriptures which have been given of him. The King
James Version of the Bible attests that Christ was the Only Begotten of
the Father. Most modern translations reject this doctrine. Where we are
accustomed to reading that "God so loved the world, that he gave his only
begotten Son, that whosoever believeth in him should not perish, but
have everlasting life" (John 3:16), we now read that "God so loved the
world, that he gave his only Son," or that "God so loved the world that
he gave his one and only Son." These translations deny us our divine
inheritance and are supported by a theology that holds Christ as the Son
of God only in a metaphorical sense.

20:25–27 Peter testified that there was but one name under heaven
whereby men could be saved (Acts 4:12). In his instruction to the
Ephesians, Paul reminded them that there was but "one Lord, one faith,
one baptism, one God and Father of all" (Ephesians 4:5–6). This text
announces another singular truth, one long lost to traditional
Christianity: there is but one plan of salvation. Further, this plan was first
known to Adam and has been known to the faithful Saints of all dispensations. This plan requires faith in Christ as the Only Begotten of the
Father, repentance from sin, baptism by those in authority, receipt of the
Holy Ghost, and endurance in faith to the end. God spoke to Adam, saying: "If thou wilt turn unto me, and hearken unto my voice, and believe,

and repent of all thy transgressions, and be baptized, even in water, in the name of mine Only Begotten Son, who is full of grace and truth, which is Jesus Christ, the only name which shall be given under heaven, whereby salvation shall come unto the children of men, ye shall receive the gift of the Holy Ghost, asking all things in his name, and whatsoever ye shall ask, it shall be given you" (Moses 6:52).

Teaching this principle, Joseph Smith said: "For our own part we cannot believe that the ancients in all ages were so ignorant of the system of heaven as many suppose, since all that were ever saved, were saved through the power of this great plan of redemption, as much before the coming of Christ as since; if not, God has had different plans in operation (if we may so express it), to bring men back to dwell with Himself; and this we cannot believe, since there has been no change in the constitution of man since he fell; and the ordinance or institution of offering blood in sacrifice was only designed to be performed till Christ was offered up and shed His blood—as said before—that man might look forward in faith to that time. It will be noticed that, according to Paul, (Galatians 3:8) the Gospel was preached to Abraham. We would like to be informed in what name the Gospel was then preached, whether it was in the name of Christ or some other name. If in any other name, was it the Gospel? And if it was the Gospel, and that preached in the name of Christ, had it any ordinances? If not, was it the Gospel? And if it has ordinances what were they? Our friends may say, perhaps, that there were never any ordinances except those of offering sacrifices before the coming of Christ, and that it could not be possible before the Gospel to have been administered while the law of sacrifices of blood was in force. But we will recollect that Abraham offered sacrifice, and notwithstanding this, had the Gospel preached to him. That the offering of sacrifice was only to point the mind forward to Christ, we infer from these remarkable words of Jesus to the Jews: 'Your Father Abraham rejoiced to see my day: and he saw it, and was glad' (John 8:56). So, then, because the ancients offered sacrifice it did not hinder their hearing the Gospel; but served, as we said before, to open their eyes, and enable them to look forward to the time of the coming of the Savior, and rejoice in His redemption. We find also, that when the Israelites came out of Egypt they had the Gospel preached to them, according to Paul in his letter to the Hebrews, which says: 'For unto us was the Gospel preached, as well as unto them: but the word preached did not profit them, not being mixed with faith in them that heard it' (Hebrews 4:2). It is said again, in Galatians 3:19, that the law (of Moses, or the Levitical law) was 'added' because of transgression. What, we ask, was this law added to, if it was not added to the Gospel? It must be plain that it was added to the Gospel, since we learn that they had the Gospel preached to them. From these few facts, we conclude that whenever the Lord revealed Himself to men in ancient days, and commanded them to offer sacrifice to Him, that it was done that they might look forward in faith to the time of His coming, and rely upon the power of that atonement for a remission of their sins. And this they have done, thousands who have gone before us, whose garments are spotless, and who are, like Job, waiting with an assurance like his, that they will see Him in the latter day upon the earth, even in their flesh" (*Teachings of the Prophet Joseph Smith*, 59–61).

20:28 There is no thought in such passages to suggest that the Father, Son, and Holy Ghost are of the same essence as is declared in the creeds of apostate Christianity. It is the perfect unity of the Godhead that is stressed here. The whole system of salvation consists of our becoming one with the Father, Son, and Holy Ghost. We are saved to the extent that we have learned to believe as they believe, think as they think, and act as they would act. Thus in his great intercessory prayer, Christ said: "Neither pray I for these alone [referring to the Twelve], but for them also which shall believe on me through their word; that they all may be one; as thou, Father, art in me, and I in thee, that they also may be one in us: that the world may believe that thou hast sent me. And the glory which thou gavest me I have given them; that they may be one, even as we are one: I in them, and thou in me, that they may be made perfect in one; and that the world may know that thou hast sent me, and hast loved them, as thou hast loved me" (John 17:20–23). See commentary on Doctrine and Covenants 1:16.

Laws Governing Repentance, Justification, Sanctification, and Baptism
DOCTRINE AND COVENANTS 20:29–37

20:29 *All men must repent and believe.* The expression of belief can never replace the need to repent. Both devils and scoundrels believe in Christ, but neither will have place in the kingdom of heaven (James 2:19).

Believe on the name of Jesus Christ. The charge here is to believe in Christ and, moreover, to believe on the "name" of Christ, which is placed on those he has chosen to act in his stead (Abraham 1:18). It is one thing to say one has faith in Christ and quite another to demonstrate it by sustaining those he has appointed to lead his Church.

Worship the Father in his name. See commentary on Doctrine and Covenants 20:19.

20:30 *Justification.* There cannot be a kingdom of God without a system of government and laws. To hold citizenship in that kingdom we must abide by the laws of that kingdom. We are justified when we have complied with the requirements of the law. If our actions are in question, we are justified if those actions, as judged by God, are ratified or approved. Thus we stand innocent or vindicated by the law. The purpose of this verse is to sustain the necessity of the laws and ordinances of the gospel. It is to affirm that the grace of Christ does not dispense with the necessity of obedience to the laws of God. Rather, it states that in and through the atonement of Christ all may be saved by obedience to the laws and ordinances of the gospel (Article of Faith 3).

The principle of justification is illustrated in the baptism of Christ. It will be remembered that when Christ sought baptism at the hands of the Baptist, John "forbad him, saying, I have need to be baptized of thee, and comest thou to me?" Taking advantage of the teaching moment, Christ responded, "Suffer it to be so now: for thus it becometh us to fulfil all righteousness" (Matthew 3:14–15). That is to say, though I do not need baptism for a remission of sins, I must still comply with the law in order to be justified. This is precisely what Nephi is teaching us when he said: "Now, if the Lamb of God, he being holy, should have need to be baptized by water, to fulfil all righteousness, O then, how much more need have we, being unholy, to be baptized, yea, even by water!" Then in response to the question of how Christ fulfilled all righteousness in his baptism, he said that he humbled himself before the Father and witnessed to him that he would be obedient in keeping his commandments. By his willing obedience to the law he is vindicated by the law and becomes an example to all men showing them "the straitness of the path, and the narrowness of the gate," by which they too must obtain citizenship in his Father's kingdom (2 Nephi 31:5, 9).

The great revelation on the law of justification for our dispensation is found in Doctrine and Covenants 132:5–20.

20:31 *Sanctification.* Through the grace of Christ those who have been justified can be cleansed from sin and be made holy. The text extends this promise to those who serve God with all their might, mind, and strength. Sanctification comes through the Holy Ghost, who purges from the souls of men both the desire for sin and its dreadful effects (Alma 13:12). Teaching this principle, the scriptures repeatedly speak of the necessity of our being baptized not only by water but by "fire and by the Holy Ghost" (2 Nephi 31:17; see also 31:13; Luke 3:16; 3 Nephi 9:20; D&C 19:31; 33:11; 39:6). See commentary on Doctrine and Covenants 84:33.

20:32–34 All who are subject to death, all who have blood coursing through their veins, are heirs to the effects of the fall of Adam. All such must labor and pray continually that they do not fall. None are excused from the charge to endure in faith to the end. Nephi stated it thus: "Wherefore, ye must press forward with a steadfastness in Christ, having a perfect brightness of hope, and a love of God and of all men. Wherefore, if ye shall press forward, feasting upon the word of Christ, and endure to the end, behold, thus saith the Father: Ye shall have eternal life" (2 Nephi 31:20).

Brigham Young said: "Do not suppose that we shall ever in the flesh be free from temptations to sin. Some suppose that they can in the flesh be sanctified body and spirit and become so pure that they will never again feel the effects of the power of the adversary of truth. Were it possible for a person to attain to this degree of perfection in the flesh, he could not die neither remain in a world where sin predominates. Sin has entered into the world, and death by sin. I think we shall more or less feel the effects of sin so long as we live, and finally have to pass the ordeals of death. Do not understand that in the flesh we shall ever overcome the power of sin to such a degree that we shall never taste death" (*Journal of Discourses*, 10:173).

20:35 The Articles and Covenants of the Church, which we now know as sections 20 and 22, were read by the Prophet to those assembled at the first conference of the Church held 9 June 1830 at Fayette, New York. They became the first revelations received by Joseph Smith to be formally sustained by the body of the Church. The reading of these revelations became the practice at early Church conferences (Cannon and Cook, *Far West Record*, 2n). Zebedee Coltrin, Orson Hyde, A. Sidney Gilbert, Orson Pratt, and others had copies of the revelations that they used for this purpose (Woodford, "Historical Developments," 265). In order to do so these men had to make their own longhand copy of the revelations. As those copies are compared we find the same problem that existed in the meridian Church: no two were exactly the same. The possibility existed for those making their own copy of the revelation to add to or take from it. This verse comes as a warning, like that given to those of old (Revelation 22:18–19), that they were neither to take from or add to the revelations. This does not suggest that the Prophet himself could not edit his own revelations.

With the formal publication of the revelations in our day we are not in a position to add to or take from holy writ as was done anciently (1 Nephi 13:23–29). We can, however, add to or take from their intended meaning in the interpretation we place on them. All scriptural commentary is a measure of the spiritual maturity and integrity of those making it. The same, of course, is true of the manner in which we choose to apply the teachings of holy writ in our lives.

20:37 This verse restates the prerequisites for baptism as given in Moroni 6:1–3.

"And truly manifest by their works that they have received of the Spirit of Christ unto the remission of their sins." Our faith in Christ is measured by the extent to which we pattern our lives after him. The things we choose to do evidence for whom we have chosen to labor. The truly repentant will bring forth, as Luke stated it, "fruits worthy of repentance" (Luke 3:8), or as Alma said it, bring forth "works which are meet for repentance" (Alma 5:54).

Having listed many of the attributes of godliness, Peter said, "If these things be in you, and abound, they make you that ye shall neither be barren nor unfruitful in the knowledge of our Lord Jesus Christ. But he that lacketh these things is blind, and cannot see afar off, and hath forgotten that he was purged from his old sins" (2 Peter 1:8–9).

One of the dramatic experiences of the young church centered on this phrase. Telling the story, Joseph Smith said: "Shortly after we had received the above revelations, Oliver Cowdery returned to Mr. Peter Whitmer's, Sen., and I began to arrange and copy the revelations, which we had received from time to time; in which I was assisted by John Whitmer, who now resided with me.

"Whilst thus employed in the work appointed me by my Heavenly Father, I received a letter from Oliver Cowdery, the contents of which gave me both sorrow and uneasiness. Not having that letter now in my possession, I cannot of course give it here in full, but merely an extract of the most prominent parts, which I can yet, and expect long to, remember.

"He wrote to inform me that he had discovered an error in one of the commandments—Book of Doctrine and Covenants: 'And truly manifest

by their works that they have received of the Spirit of Christ unto a remission of their sins.'

"The above quotation, he said, was erroneous, and added: 'I command
you in the name of God to erase those words, that no priestcraft be
amongst us!'

"I immediately wrote to him in reply, in which I asked him by what
authority he took upon him to command me to alter or erase, to add to
or diminish from, a revelation or commandment from Almighty God.

"A few days afterwards I visited him and Mr. Whitmer's family, when
I found the family in general of his opinion concerning the words above
quoted, and it was not without both labor and perseverance that I could
prevail with any of them to reason calmly on the subject. However,
Christian Whitmer at length became convinced that the sentence was
reasonable, and according to Scripture; and finally, with his assistance, I
succeeded in bringing, not only the Whitmer family, but also Oliver
Cowdery to acknowledge that they had been in error, and that the sentence in dispute was in accordance with the rest of the commandment.
And thus was this error rooted out, which having its rise in presumption
and rash judgment, was the more particularly calculated (when once fairly
understood) to teach each and all of us the necessity of humility and
meekness before the Lord, that He might teach us of His ways, that we
might walk in His paths, and live by every word that proceedeth forth
from His mouth" (Smith, *History of the Church*, 1:104–5).

Duties of Elders, Priests, Teachers, and Deacons
DOCTRINE AND COVENANTS 20:38–67

20:38 An apostle is an elder. All holders of the Melchizedek
Priesthood are properly referred to as "elder." Such usage helps preserve
the sacred nature of such offices as high priest, patriarch, or apostle.

20:41 *Laying on of hands*. Rich symbolism is associated with all gospel
ordinances. The hand is a symbol of power or authority, the extended
hand a symbol of friendship, confidence, and trust. The laying on of hands
represents the placing of God's hand or power upon the head of the one
being blessed (D&C 36:1–2).

In restoring the Aaronic Priesthood to Joseph Smith and Oliver
Cowdery, John the Baptist told them that the Aaronic Priesthood was
without "the power of laying on hands for the gift of the Holy Ghost."
This authority, he explained, would be given to them by Peter, James, and

John who would restore the "Priesthood of Melchizedek" (Joseph Smith–History 1:70, 72). This evidences that the laying on of hands to confer blessings or authority reaches back to ancient times. Indeed, whenever the higher priesthood has been on the earth the authority to bestow the gift of the Holy Ghost has existed also. See commentary on Joseph Smith–History 1:70, page 120; Doctrine and Covenants 20:41, "Laying on of hands."

Baptism of fire and the Holy Ghost. To obtain salvation all accountable persons must receive two baptisms. They must be baptized of water and of the Spirit (D&C 76:51–52). The baptism of the Spirit is called the baptism of fire and of the Holy Ghost (Matthew 3:11; Luke 3:16; 2 Nephi 31:13–14; 3 Nephi 11:35; 12:1–2; Mormon 7:10; D&C 33:11; 39:6). Fire is an agent of purification and symbolizes the cleansing of the soul (Alma 13:12). Thus sanctification comes by the reception of the Holy Ghost (3 Nephi 27:19–21).

"The baptism of fire is not something in addition to the receipt of the Holy Ghost; rather, it is the actual enjoyment of the gift which is offered by the laying on of hands at the time of baptism. 'Remission of sins,' the Lord says, comes 'by baptism and by fire, yea, even the Holy Ghost.' (D. & C. 19:31; 2 Ne. 31:17.) Those who receive the baptism of fire are 'filled as if with fire.' (Hela. 5:45)" (McConkie, *Mormon Doctrine*, 73).

20:43 *To confirm the church.* In the same ordinance in which someone is given the gift of the Holy Ghost they are also confirmed a member of The Church of Jesus Christ of Latter-day Saints. Membership in the Church can be obtained in no other way.

20:45 The Holy Ghost should direct what we say and do in all meetings in which the gospel is taught or in which the affairs of the Church are administered. Such meetings should always accord themselves with the "commandments and revelations" already given. See commentary on Doctrine and Covenants 46.

20:46 In the early history of the Church, those holding the office of a priest were, on occasion, called to serve as missionaries. This was the case with Wilford Woodruff, who observed, "I went out as a priest, and my companion as an elder, and we traveled thousands of miles, and had many things manifested to us. I desire to impress upon you the fact that it does not make any difference whether a man is a priest or an apostle, if he magnifies his calling. A priest holds the key of the ministering of angels. Never in my life, as an apostle, as a seventy, or as an elder, have I ever had more of the protection of the Lord than while holding the office as a priest"

(*Discourses*, 300). Again Woodruff testifed, "I had the administration of angels while holding the office of a priest" (*Discourses*, 298).

20:47 *To pray vocally.* Occasionally we hear it said that we should not pray vocally because Satan can hear our prayers. Satan has no power to interfere with a heartfelt prayer be it vocal or silent. Vocal and public prayers are very much a part of our faith. For such occasions as a temple dedication a written prayer is also appropriate (D&C 109).

20:60 *Ordained by the power of the Holy Ghost.* As all meetings are to be conducted under the direction of the Holy Ghost (v. 45) so are all gospel ordinances. This text repeats the instruction of Moroni on how men are to be ordained to the priesthood (Moroni 3:1–4).

20:61 *This church of Christ.* This reference is to the branch in Fayette, New York, where the Church was organized.

20:65 Verses 65 through 67, which reflect a church organization that exceeds what was necessary in April of 1830, were added by the Prophet some time after the rest of the revelation was given (Smith, *History of the Church*, 1:68n).

20:65 *Without the vote of that church.* See commentary on Doctrine and Covenants 26:2.

20:66 *Traveling bishops.* In February 1831 Edward Partridge became the first man called to serve as a bishop in this dispensation (D&C 41:9). In December of that same year Newel K. Whitney was also called to serve in that capacity (D&C 72). These men served as regional or traveling bishops: Whitney for Ohio and the eastern states, Partridge for Missouri. Congregations of the Saints were not divided into what are now called wards, presided over by a standing bishop, until the early 1840s in Nauvoo.

20:67 *President of the high priesthood.* This phrase lends itself to two distinctive usages. Anyone holding a position of presidency in the Melchizedek Priesthood, that is if they are the presiding officer, could properly be addressed as the "president of the high priesthood" in the context of their calling or office. In its fullest and most proper sense the title applies alone to the president of the Church. Only he presides over all other priesthood officers. Of his office revelation states: "The duty of the President of the office of the High Priesthood is to preside over the whole church, and to be like unto Moses—Behold, here is wisdom; yea, to be a seer, a revelator, a translator, and a prophet, having all the gifts of God which he bestows upon the head of the church" (D&C 107:91–92). See commentary on Doctrine and Covenants 84:29.

To be ordained by. As used here the phrase "ordained by" means approved by and should not be confused with ordination to a priesthood office.

Duties of Members
DOCTRINE AND COVENANTS 20:68–69

20:68 Between baptism and the conferral of the Holy Ghost and the partaking of the sacrament appropriate instruction should be given the new member. We cannot live a covenant if we do not understand that covenant.

20:69 *A godly walk and conversation.* In Webster's 1828 Dictionary, *conversation* is defined as, the "general course of manners; behavior; deportment; especially as it respects morals."

Blessing of Children
DOCTRINE AND COVENANTS 20:70–71

20:70 *Bring them unto the elders before the church.* As there are to be no private interpretations of scripture (2 Peter 1:20) so there are no private ordinances of the gospel. All gospel ordinances belong to the Church and are to be performed at the invitation and under the direction of those who preside. For instance, even though a man holds the office of an elder he has no right to baptize his own children and give them the gift of the Holy Ghost save he receives that direction from his own bishop. This text applies this principle to the blessing of little children.

20:71 To father Abraham the Lord said, "I will establish a covenant of circumcision with thee, and it shall be my covenant between me and thee, and thy seed after thee, in their generations; that thou mayest know for ever that children are not accountable before me until they are eight years old" (JST Genesis 17:11). To those of our dispensation the Lord said, "Inasmuch as parents have children in Zion, or in any of her stakes which are organized, that teach them not to understand the doctrine of repentance, faith in Christ the Son of the living God, and of baptism and the gift of the Holy Ghost by the laying on of the hands, when eight years old, the sin be upon the heads of the parents" (D&C 68:25).

None are to be baptized save they are "accountable and capable of committing sin." The baptism of little children, or anyone else who is not accountable for their acts, in the words of Mormon "setteth at naught the atonement" of Christ "and the power of his redemption" (Moroni 8:10, 20).

Mode of Baptism
DOCTRINE AND COVENANTS 20:72–74

20:72–74 For nearly two thousand years the historical Christian world has debated the necessity, mode, and purpose of baptism. Among their number the matter remains hopelessly unresolved. Indeed, the only possible resolution of this and a host of other issues can be found in a new dispensation of the gospel. That is, the simple truths of salvation must be dispensed anew from the heavens. This, of course, is precisely what happened with this revelation and the organization of the Church under the direction of Joseph Smith. Given that the God of the historical Christian world has surrendered both speech and the attendant right to give revelation, such a solution is rejected by them. Yet, despite all of their objections, John the Baptist has indeed returned to earth and restored the authority by which he baptized the Son of God and a host of other faithful souls. He conferred that authority upon the heads of Joseph Smith and Oliver Cowdery and had them baptize each other. Now in this revelation, in concert with the revelation on baptism given to the Nephites (3 Nephi 11:23–27), the mode of baptism is restored. This instruction, of necessity, preceded the organization of the Church.

The Sacrament
DOCTRINE AND COVENANTS 20:75–79

20:77 *Willing to take upon them the name of thy Son.* Commenting on this text, Elder Dallin H. Oaks observed, "It is significant that when we partake of the sacrament we do not witness that we *take upon us* the name of Jesus Christ. We witness that we are *willing* to do so. . . . The fact that we only witness to our willingness suggests that something else must happen before we actually take that sacred name upon us in the most important sense.

"What future event or events could this covenant contemplate? The scriptures suggest two sacred possibilities, one concerning the authority of God, especially as exercised in the temples, and the other—closely related—concerning exaltation in the celestial kingdom. . . .

"Willingness to take upon us the name of Jesus Christ can therefore be understood as willingness to take upon us the authority of Jesus Christ. According to this meaning, by partaking of the sacrament we witness our willingness to participate in the sacred ordinances of the temple and to receive the highest blessings available through the name and by the authority of the Savior when he chooses to confer them upon us" (Conference Report, April 1985, 102–3).

20:78 *The wine.* See Doctrine and Covenants 27:2–3.

Regulations for Governing Church Membership
DOCTRINE AND COVENANTS 20:80–84

20:81 *The several churches, composing the church of Christ.* The terms *ward* and *stake* as units of Church organization had not yet come into use. The first stake was organized in 1834. The term *ward* as a unit of Church organization came in the Nauvoo era.

20:84 *Take a letter certifying that they are regular members in good standing.* In our worldwide Church, membership records are kept on a computer network administered from the headquarters of the Church in Salt Lake City.

DOCTRINE AND COVENANTS 22

In the Book of Commandments this section appeared immediately before section 20, suggesting the possibility that it had been received prior to the organization of the Church. This seems a reasonable assumption given that it requires those who had been baptized by either Joseph Smith or Oliver Cowdery to be baptized again as members of the Church. It was first published in the *The Evening and the Morning Star* as the concluding part of what we know as section 20 (June 1832, 1). Together these revelations now recorded in sections 20 and 22 were known as the Articles and Covenants of the Church.

Baptism Is a New and Everlasting Covenant
DOCTRINE AND COVENANTS 22:1

22:1 *All old covenants have I caused to be done away in this thing.* With the restoration of the priesthood and the organization of the Church and kingdom of God once again upon the earth, the Church alone possesses the authority to speak for God and to perform the ordinances of salvation. Similarly, before the coming of Christ in the flesh, faithful Israelites were duty bound to honor the proscriptions of the law of Moses. After Christ's coming they were to let go of the law of Moses and embrace the order instituted by the Savior.

A *new and an everlasting covenant*. The covenants of salvation are new in that they have been restored anew in this dispensation. They are everlasting in that they remain the same in all gospel dispensations and their effects are everlasting.

Baptism is *a* new and *an* everlasting covenant. The composite of all gospel covenants constitutes *the* new and everlasting covenant. See commentary on Doctrine and Covenants 132:4–6.

That which was from the beginning. The ordinance of baptism for the remission of sins has existed from the days of Adam (D&C 20:25–26; Moses 6:52–53), as have all gospel ordinances. Teaching this principle, Joseph Smith said: "Now taking it for granted that the scriptures say what they mean, and mean what they say, we have sufficient grounds to go on and prove from the Bible that the gospel has always been the same; the ordinances to fulfill its requirements, the same; and the officers to officiate, the same; and the signs and fruits resulting from the promises, the same" (*Teachings of the Prophet Joseph Smith*, 264).

Baptism by Authority Necessary
DOCTRINE AND COVENANTS 22:2–4

22:2 *The law of Moses*. Joseph Smith, Oliver Cowdery, and a number of others were baptized by the authority restored by John the Baptist prior to the organization of the Church. With the organization of the Church the question arises, Did they need rebaptism? In response the Lord said, "You cannot enter in at the strait gate by the law of Moses." That is to say, as the law of Moses was legal and binding until the time of fulness came with Christ, so the baptisms performed by the authority restored by John the Baptist were legal and binding until the organization of the Church on 6 April 1830. Those baptized prior to this time were baptized for the remission of sins but not for admission into a then nonexistent church.

By your dead works. This refers to those baptisms that were performed by those not having priesthood authority. Such baptisms, even if performed "a hundred times" are dead. That is, they have no life in them because they were performed without authority.

22:3 Because there were no legal administrators upon the earth, the Lord restored both the priesthood and the Church through which the ordinances of salvation could again be administered.

22:4 Those who were arguing against the need of their rebaptism are invited to conform to the order instituted by the God of heaven.

DOCTRINE AND COVENANTS 21

DATE: 6 APRIL 1830
PLACE: FAYETTE, NEW YORK

In all gospel dispensations the true Saint has followed living prophets. By contrast it is characteristic of false religion to pay homage to the prophets of ages past while distorting and twisting their words to justify rejecting the living oracles. For instance, in our day it is common to hear people say, "My religion is Bible religion," not realizing that the statement itself is unbiblical. No one living during Bible times ever had a Bible, because it was compiled at a later date. The faithful of whom we read in the Bible are identified by their willingness to following the particular prophet sent to them. Nothing could illustrate more perfectly the principles involved than to have Joseph Smith receive a revelation in the very meeting at which the Church was organized, which defined his role as a prophet and seer and the role of those who would place themselves under covenant to sustain him. This is the revelation the Prophet received.

The Role of the Prophet
DOCTRINE AND COVENANTS 21:1–3

21:1 A *record kept among you.* Both as a Church and as families we are a record-keeping people. The Church of Jesus Christ of Latter-day Saints has a more complete and perfect history than any other organization of comparable size upon the face of the earth. Virtually without exception those events for which adequate records do not exist are the result of the persecution of the Saints, not their lack of discipline or obedience in keeping this commandment.

Seer. In Old Testament times a prophet was called a seer, from the Hebrew *re'eh*, meaning "one who sees" (1 Samuel 9:9). Contextually this definition carried the idea of seeing that which was hidden to others. The Hebrew *hozen*, meaning "one who sees a vision," was also translated "seer." Among Book of Mormon peoples a prophet was understood to be a man "chosen of God" to speak his words (Helaman 9:16; Alma 5:11). He was one to whom God had given great power and authority (Helaman 11:18) to act in his name (Alma 19:4). The Book of Mormon makes a clear distinction between a seer and a prophet. Ammon declares a seer to be greater than a prophet. By way of explanation he states: "A seer is a revelator and a prophet also; and a gift which is greater can no man have, except he should possess the power of God, which no man can; yet a man may have great power given him from God. But a seer can know of things which are past, and also of things which are to come, and by them shall all things be revealed, or, rather, shall secret things be made manifest, and hidden things shall come to light, and things which are not known shall be made known by them, and also things shall be made known by them which otherwise could not be known" (Mosiah 8:16–17).

A prophet. Defining the office and call of a prophet, Anthony W. Ivins explained, "A careful study of the etymology of the word and of the lives, works and character of the prophets of old makes clear the fact that a prophet was, and is, one called to act as God's messenger. He is to teach men the character of God, and define and make known to the people, his will. He is to denounce sin, and declare the punishment of transgression. He is to be above all else a preacher of righteousness, and when the people depart from the path which he has marked out for them to follow, is to call them back to the true faith. He is an interpreter of the scripture, and declares its meaning and application. When future events are to be declared he predicts them, but his direct, and most important calling is to be a forth-teller, or director of present policy, rather than a foreteller of that which is to come" (Conference Report, October 1925, 20).

An apostle of Jesus Christ. See commentary on Doctrine and Covenants 20:2.

Through the will of God the Father. God chooses his prophets. Our Father in Heaven foreordained that Joseph Smith should be the prophet to open the dispensation of the fulness of times.

Through . . . the grace of your Lord Jesus Christ. The call of every prophet is dependent upon divine help. Only through the direction and power of the Savior was the Prophet Joseph Smith able to be a seer, translator, and revelator.

21:2–3 This revelation, which was given during the meeting at which the Church was organized, identifies the importance of the principle of revelation—upon which principle the Lord's Church has been built in all gospel dispensations (Matthew 16:18). "What constitutes the kingdom of God?" Joseph Smith asked. In response the Lord said, "Where there is a prophet, a priest, or a righteous man unto whom God gives His oracles, there is the kingdom of God; and where the oracles of God are not, there the kingdom of God is not" (*Teachings of the Prophet Joseph Smith*, 272).

The Role of the Member
DOCTRINE AND COVENANTS 21:4–8

21:4–5 *Walking in all holiness before me*. With the restoration of the gospel comes the restoration of the charge to be a holy people. To the children of Israel at the time of Moses the Lord said, "Sanctify yourselves, and ye shall be holy; for I am holy" (Leviticus 11:44), and again, "Ye shall be unto me a kingdom of priests, and an holy nation" (Exodus 19:6). Peter repeated this charge to the meridian Saints, saying, "As he which hath called you is holy, so be ye holy in all manner of conversation [meaning conduct]" (1 Peter 1:15), and, "Ye are a chosen generation, a royal priesthood, an holy nation, a peculiar people; that ye should shew forth the praises of him who hath called you out of darkness into his marvellous light" (1 Peter 2:9).

21:4 *Meaning the church*. This phrase links or ties that which follows to all who are members of the Church. It is directed to those who are members of the Church today as much as it was to those to whom it was given in April of 1830.

21:5 *His word ye shall receive as if from mine own mouth*. See commentary on Doctrine and Covenants 1:38.

In all patience and faith. It is not to be expected that the wisdom in the direction given by our prophets will always be immediately apparent. Faith must always be a part of the life of the Latter-day Saint. President Harold B. Lee explained this principle: "There will be some things that take patience and faith. You may not like what comes from the authority of the Church. . . . It may contradict your social views. It may interfere with some of your social life. But if you listen to these things, as if from the mouth of the Lord himself, with patience and faith, the promise is that 'the gates of hell shall not prevail against you; yea, and the Lord God will disperse the powers of darkness from before you, and cause the heavens to shake for your good, and his name's glory' (D&C 21:6)" (Conference Report, October 1970, 152).

21:6 *By doing these things.* The promises given in this verse are given to those who follow the living prophet and walk in holiness.

The gates of hell shall not prevail against you. A gate prevails when it keeps us in from or out of the place we desire to go. Because of the atonement of Christ the gates of hell—that is the place of departed spirits—will not prevail. Ultimately all spirits will be reunited with their bodies in a union that is inseparable.

The promise given in this verse is that the prince of darkness and all the legions of hell cannot prevail over the Saints of God. As the Lord would yet tell Joseph Smith of his enemies, "Their bounds are set, they cannot pass. Thy days are known, and thy years shall not be numbered less; therefore, fear not what man can do, for God shall be with you forever and ever" (D&C 122:9). Such is the promise here granted to all the household of faith. See commentary on Doctrine and Covenants 128:10 "The gates of hell shall not prevail."

Disperse the powers of darkness from before you. The battle for the souls of men is between light and darkness, truth and error, righteousness and wickedness. The promise given here is that darkness will be dispelled by light, falsehood by truth, and wickedness by righteousness for those who trod the path of holiness. To the extent that they heed the voice of the living prophet they too will become prophets, and light and truth will be their companions.

Cause the heavens to shake for your good. As we choose to march with the armies of heaven, they choose to march with us. "The rights of the priesthood," Joseph Smith taught, "are inseparably connected with the powers of heaven." These powers, he said, "cannot be controlled nor handled only upon the principles of righteousness" (D&C 121:36).

21:7 *The cause of Zion.* "Zion is the name given by the Lord to his Saints; it is the name by which the Lord's people are always identified. Of the Saints in Enoch's day the record says: 'And the Lord called his people ZION, because they were of one heart and one mind, and dwelt in righteousness; and there was no poor among them' (Moses 7:18). 'This is Zion—The pure in heart—,' he said in this day (D&C 97:21). Thus The Church of Jesus Christ of Latter-day Saints is Zion. Joining the Church is becoming a citizen of Zion" (McConkie, *Mormon Doctrine*, 854).

21:8 *Unto the remission of his sins.* Through his faith and works Joseph Smith stood clean before the Lord.

The Saints Will Be Loyal to the Prophet
DOCTRINE AND COVENANTS 21:9–12

21:9 *They shall believe on his words.* This phrase constitutes the test of discipleship for a Latter-day Saint. Elder Bruce R. McConkie stated it thus, "The test of discipleship is how totally and completely and fully we believe the word that was revealed through Joseph Smith, and how effectively we echo or proclaim that word to the world" ("This Generation," 7).

21:10–12 During the meeting at which this revelation was given Joseph Smith ordained Oliver Cowdery an elder; Oliver Cowdery then ordained Joseph Smith to the same office. See commentary on Doctrine and Covenants 20:2.

21:12 *The first preacher.* In Nauvoo Joseph Smith was a confident and powerful speaker; in Fayette he was not. As with all men he had to grow up into the office that was his. Oliver Cowdery was called on to deliver the first public discourse in this dispensation. That took place five days later, on Sunday, at the home of Peter Whitmer Sr., where this revelation was received on the day the Church was organized.

DOCTRINE AND COVENANTS 23

DATE: APRIL 1830
PLACE: MANCHESTER, NEW YORK

Doctrine and Covenants 23 brings together five separate revelations as published in the Book of Commandments. The date given in that publication is 6 April 1830. All but Joseph Knight were told that they were "under no condemnation," meaning that the course they were pursuing was pleasing to the Lord. Oliver Cowdery, with Hyrum and Samuel Smith, was numbered among the six original members of the Church and as such would have been baptized that morning. Joseph Smith Sr. and his wife, Lucy, were baptized after the meeting. As indicated in the revelation given to him, Joseph Knight was resisting the responsibility to pray—both publicly and in private—and had not been baptized. Thus he does not receive the assurance given the others.

Revelation to Oliver Cowdery
DOCTRINE AND COVENANTS 23:1–2

23:1 *Beware of pride.* This warning proved to be most telling; pride was, in the words of Joseph Fielding Smith, "one of Oliver Cowdery's besetting sins" (*Church History and Modern Revelation*, 1:120–21). Oliver Cowdery stood at the side of Joseph Smith during some of the most important events of this dispensation. He was the Prophet's primary scribe in the translation of the Book of Mormon. He was shown by Moroni the plates from which it was translated and heard the God of heaven testify that it was true. He was with the Prophet when both the Aaronic and Melchizedek Priesthoods were restored. At the organization of the Church he was sustained as its second elder and later was sustained as an assistant or associate president of the Church. He was with the Prophet in the Kirtland Temple when Christ appeared to acknowledge his acceptance of that edifice as his house. Oliver there received with the Prophet power and authority at the hands of Moses, Elias, and Elijah. In the earth's

180 REVELATIONS OF THE RESTORATION

history few men have been so honored, and yet, he lost the spirit of his calling and left the Church for a time.

"If he could have humbled himself in the troubled days of Kirtland he would not have lost his place and membership in the Church," Joseph Fielding Smith explained. "That which had been bestowed upon him was exceedingly great and had he been willing to humble himself, it was his privilege to stand with the Prophet Joseph Smith through all time and eternity, holding the keys of the Dispensation of the Fulness of Times. However, at this particular time when this word was sought [D&C 23], he was free from condemnation. He was commanded to make known his calling to both the Church and also to the world, and while doing this his heart would be opened to teach them the truth from henceforth and forever. His great mission was to stand shoulder to shoulder with the Prophet Joseph Smith holding the keys of salvation for this dispensation. It was also his duty to bear witness to all mankind of the restoration of the Gospel" (Smith, *Church History and Modern Revelation*, 1:121).

Wilford Woodruff said he heard Joseph Smith say that Oliver Cowdery . . . said to him, "'If I leave this Church it will fall.'

"Said Joseph, 'Oliver, you try it.' Oliver tried it. He fell, but the kingdom of God did not" (*Discourses*, 123).

Revelation to Hyrum Smith
DOCTRINE AND COVENANTS 23:3

23:3 *Thy tongue loosed.* Nearly a year prior to this revelation, Hyrum had sought the privilege of declaring the gospel. In response to that desire the Lord told him that there was much that he needed to do to receive such a calling. The simple reality is that we cannot teach what we do not know, and the Holy Ghost cannot call to our remembrance that which we have not learned. "Seek not to declare my word," Hyrum was told, "but first seek to obtain my word, and then shall your tongue be loosed; then, if you desire, you shall have my Spirit and my word, yea, the power of God unto the convincing of men. But now hold your peace; study my word which hath gone forth among the children of men, and also study my word which shall come forth among the children of men, or that which is now translating, yea, until you have obtained all which I shall grant unto the children of men in this generation, and then shall all things be added thereto" (D&C 11:21–22). Having more fully prepared himself, Hyrum is now entitled to the companionship of the Spirit and the direction that comes from it.

Thy duty is unto the church forever, and this because of thy family. Like many things in patriarchal blessings this promise could not have been fully understood at the time it was given. It would be three years before the office of church patriarch would be restored and Joseph Smith Sr. identified as the man through whom this lineal office would descend. At his death in September of 1840, that office fell to Hyrum, his oldest living son. Thus Hyrum was destined because of his family to serve in the Church. At the time of his death he was serving both as church patriarch and as an associate president of the Church with his brother the Prophet (D&C 124:94–96).

Revelation to Samuel Smith
DOCTRINE AND COVENANTS 23:4

23:4 *Samuel.* "The last of the Eight Witnesses was a younger brother of the Prophet's. He was born in the year 1808, hence was twenty-two years of age when he beheld and handled the Nephite plates. He was of a serious, religious nature, even in his youth; and with three others of his father's family joined the Presbyterian church. While Joseph the Prophet was engaged with Oliver Cowdery in translating the Nephite record, in Harmony, Pennsylvania, Samuel paid him a visit in the month of May 1829, about the time that the Aaronic Priesthood was conferred upon the Prophet and Oliver by the ministration of John the Baptist. Samuel had come to inquire about the work and Joseph bore testimony of its truth and showed him some of the translation of the Book of Mormon. Samuel seems not to have been easily converted, but after much inquiry he retired to the woods and sought, by secret and fervent prayer, for wisdom to enable him to judge for himself concerning the things of which his brother had testified. The result was that he obtained a revelation for himself sufficient to convince him of the truth, and on the 25th day of May, 1829, he was baptized by Oliver Cowdery and returned to his father's house, in Manchester, New York, greatly glorifying and praising God. He was the third person baptized by divine authority in the new dispensation, Joseph Smith and Oliver Cowdery being the first two. He was also one of the six members by whom the organization of the Church was effected on the 6th day of April, 1830" (Roberts, *New Witnesses for God,* 2:293–94).

Not as yet called to preach. In time, Samuel was called as the first missionary of the Restoration. He traveled to the areas of Victor-Mendon, New York. The copies of the Book of Mormon that he left in that area were instrumental in the conversion of Brigham Young and Heber C. Kimball, as well as their extended families.

Revelation to Joseph Smith Sr.
DOCTRINE AND COVENANTS 23:5

23:5 Joseph Smith Sr. was the father of the Prophet Joseph Smith and the first patriarch in this dispensation. In the language of the Prophet he was "the oldest man of the blood of Joseph or of the seed of Abraham" (Smith, *History of the Church*, 3:381), meaning he was the oldest living firstborn son of Joseph of Egypt and thus the rightful heir to the office of church patriarch (*Teachings of the Prophet Joseph Smith*, 38–39, 151).

Revelation to Joseph Knight
DOCTRINE AND COVENANTS 23:6–7

23:6 *You must take up your cross.* The Savior himself explained this phrase saying, "For a man to take up his cross, is to deny himself all ungodliness, and every worldly lust, and keep my commandments" (JST Matthew 16:26; D&C 56:2; 112:14).

23:7 *It is your duty to unite with the true church.* Because he was reluctant to pray, Joseph Knight had not obtained the witness of the Spirit to which he was entitled and thus was not baptized on the day the Church was organized. On the 9th of June of the same year he and his wife were baptized by Oliver Cowdery. In the last years of his life the Prophet spoke affectionately of Joseph Knight: "While I contemplate the virtues and the good qualities and characteristics of the faithful few, which I am now recording in the Book of the Law of the Lord, 'of such as have stood by me in every hour of peril, for these fifteen long years past,' say, for instance, my aged and beloved brother, Joseph Knight, Sen., who was among the number of the first to administer to my necessities, while I was laboring in the commencement of the bringing forth of the work of the Lord, and of laying the foundation of the Church of Jesus Christ of Latter-day Saints. For fifteen years he has been faithful and true, and even-handed and exemplary, and virtuous and kind, never deviating to the right hand or to the left. Behold he is a righteous man, may God

Almighty lengthen out the old man's days; and may his trembling, tortured, and broken body be renewed, and in the vigor of health turn upon
him, if it be Thy will, consistently, O God; and it shall be said of him, by
the sons of Zion, while there is one of them remaining, that this man was
a faithful man in Israel; therefore his name shall never be forgotten"
(Smith, *History of the Church*, 5:124–25).

MOSES 1; DOCTRINE AND COVENANTS 24

DATE: JUNE AND JULY 1830

PLACE: HARMONY, PENNSYLVANIA

As the seed of the gospel began to take root and the tender plant broke ground, the enemy of all righteousness made every imaginable effort to destroy it. In June 1830 a conference was held in Fayette where several of the brethren were ordained to the priesthood. After this meeting Joseph Smith returned with his family to Harmony, Pennsylvania. Shortly thereafter he and his wife, in company with Oliver Cowdery, John Whitmer, and David Whitmer, visited the branch of the Church at Colesville, New York. There on a Saturday afternoon a stream was dammed to create a place for baptisms the next day. Learning of this, a mob, incited by local clergy, tore the dam down during the night. The Saints responded by rebuilding the dam early Monday morning and baptizing thirteen people before the mob could reassemble. Upon their return the mob surrounded the home of Joseph Knight where Joseph Smith confronted them. Later that evening the Prophet was arrested on the charge of setting the country in an uproar by his preaching and teaching the Book of Mormon.

Joseph was tried and acquitted in South Bainbridge and immediately arrested again and taken to Colesville for trial. Again he was acquitted. A few days later he and Oliver returned to the home of the Knights to confirm those who had been baptized; however, they found it necessary to flee to avoid conflict with the mob which was again assembling.

It was in the midst of all this harassment that the Prophet recorded Moses 1. Of these events he said, "Amid all the trials and tribulations we had to wade through, the Lord, who well knew our infantile and delicate situation, vouchsafed for us a supply of strength, and granted us 'line upon line of knowledge—here a little and there a little,' of which the following was a precious morsel . . ." (Smith, *History of the Church*, 1:98).

MOSES 1

Moses 1 constitutes the beginning of the Prophet's labor known to us as the Joseph Smith Translation of the Bible. It is a revelation given to Moses sometime after his experience at the burning bush yet before he led the children of Israel out of Egypt (Moses 1:17, 26). Coming in the midst of so many difficulties, this revelation was received by the members of the Church as an expression of God's love for them.

The Revelation of God and His Glory to Moses
MOSES 1:1–11

Moses 1:1–11 From these verses, which recount Moses' experience when he was caught up into the presence of God, we learn a very singular truth about the nature of man. To endure the presence of God, it was necessary for Moses to be transfigured—that is transformed from his natural state to a higher state of glory. In this glorified state he was able to witness the visions of eternity. This privilege was accorded him because he was a son of God in the similitude of his Only Begotten and because it was preparatory to the work to which he had been called. After Moses returned to his natural state, with a great sense of amazement he said, "Now, for this cause I know that man is nothing, which thing I never had supposed" (v. 10). Thus we learn that natural or fallen man is "nothing," while that same man, clothed in the glory which comes only from God, becomes a being of infinite worth.

Moses' Confrontation with Satan
MOSES 1:12–24

Moses 1:12–24 Having been clothed in the glory of God and having learned that he himself was indeed a son of God, Moses then learned to judge between the God of light and glory and the prince of darkness. Satan came before him and demanded to be worshiped as the Only Begotten of the Father. Moses detected the great counterfeiter of all saving truths for Satan is devoid of glory. "Where is thy glory, that I should worship thee?" (v. 13) Moses asked. Here we have the second great lesson to be found in this revelation—the truths of salvation require both teacher and student to be clothed in the robes of righteousness. That which can be taught or learned without the aid of the Spirit is not of God.

It may hold sway in earthly kingdoms—bring power and influence among men—but it has no place in the gospel of Christ nor in the kingdom of his Father.

Moses Again Receives the Glory of God
MOSES 1:25–42

Moses 1:25–42 Moses is now told that he will enjoy the power of God, even that he will "be made stronger than many waters" (v. 25) that he might deliver the Lord's people from bondage. With the glory of God upon him, he was then shown a series of visions. First came the creation of the earth—even every particle of it. This was preparatory to his writing the account of the creation. Then came the history that would follow: Moses was shown every soul destined to come to this earth. The vision of countless worlds followed—each created by Christ under the direction of the Father. Nevertheless, Moses was told "only an account of this earth, and the inhabitants thereof" (v. 35). In this setting the Lord explained to Moses, and to everyone with the faith to accept his words, "This is my work and my glory—to bring to pass the immortality and eternal life of man" (v. 39).

DOCTRINE AND COVENANTS 24

"After our departure from Colesville, after the trial, the Church there were very anxious, as might be expected, concerning our again visiting them, during which time Sister Knight, wife of Newel Knight, had a dream, which enabled her to say that we would visit them that day, which really came to pass, for a few hours afterwards we arrived; and thus was our faith much strengthened concerning dreams and visions in the last days, foretold by the ancient Prophet Joel; and although we this time were forced to seek safety from our enemies by flight, yet did we feel confident that eventually we should come off victorious, if we only continued faithful to Him who had called us forth from darkness into the marvelous light of the everlasting Gospel of our Lord Jesus Christ.

"Shortly after our return home, we received the following commandments . . ." (Smith, *History of the Church*, 1:101).

Joseph Smith's Calling

DOCTRINE AND COVENANTS 24:1–9

24:1 As the night follows the day, so opposition follows truth. The promised "restoration of all things" has witnessed the revival of all past arguments against God's earthly kingdom along with the spirit of antagonism known to the Saints of all dispensations past. "It seems," said Joseph Smith, "as though the adversary was aware, at a very early period of my life, that I was destined to prove a disturber and an annoyer of his kingdom; else why should the powers of darkness combine against me?" (Joseph Smith–History 1:20).

The Church was but weeks old when Joseph Smith was arrested on charges of being a disorderly person and setting the country in an uproar by preaching the Book of Mormon. The arresting constable was to have delivered him into a mob ambush, but, impressed with his character, instead aided his escape. "James Davidson and John Reid, Esqrs., respectable farmers, men renowned for their integrity, and well versed in the laws of their country," were retained to defend the Prophet, which they did successfully (Smith, *History of the Church*, 1:89). "But alas!" as Reid told the story, "the devil, not satisfied with his defeat, stirred up a man not unlike himself" (Smith, *History of the Church*, 6:394) to go to the adjoining county and obtain a writ against Joseph there. Allowed neither food nor rest, Joseph was immediately taken captive by the arresting officer. "He took me to a tavern," Joseph recounted, "and gathered in a number of men, who used every means to abuse, ridicule and insult me. They spit upon me, pointed their fingers at me, saying, 'Prophesy, prophesy!' and thus did they imitate those who crucified the Savior of mankind, not knowing what they did" (Smith, *History of the Church*, 1:91).

Friends of the Prophet again sought Davidson and Reid to defend him. "I made every reasonable excuse I could," John Reid said, "as I was nearly worn down through fatigue and want of sleep, as I had been engaged in law suits for two days, and nearly the whole of two nights. . . . While Mr. Knight was pleading with me to go, a peculiar impression or thought struck my mind, that I must go and defend him, for he was the Lord's *anointed*. I did not know what it meant, but thought I must go and clear the Lord's *anointed*. I said I would go, and started with as much faith as the Apostles had when they could remove mountains, accompanied by Father Knight, who was like the old patriarchs that followed the ark of

188 REVELATIONS OF THE RESTORATION

God to the city of David" (Smith, *History of the Church*, 1:95; emphasis added).

Of the second trial Joseph Smith said: "Many witnesses were again called forward and examined, some of whom swore to the most palpable falsehoods, and like the false witnesses which had appeared against me the day previous, they contradicted themselves so plainly that the court would not admit their testimony. Others were called, who showed by their zeal that they were willing enough to prove something against me, but all they could do was to tell something which somebody else had told them" (*History of the Church*, 1:92). These trials were but the pattern, the prototype, of that which the future would witness a thousand times over, though the enemies of the Church would quickly learn that printer's ink was safer than public cross-examination.

Of his attorneys the Prophet said: "They spoke like men inspired of God, whilst those who were arrayed against me trembled under the sound of their voices, and quailed before them like criminals before a bar of justice" (Smith, *History of the Church*, 1:94). This too prefigured many a future scene.

"Whilst I was engaged in the case, . . . and when I came to speak upon it," said John Reid, "I was inspired with an eloquence which was altogether new to me, and which was overpowering and irresistible. I succeeded, as I expected, in obtaining the prisoner's discharge" (Smith, *History of Joseph Smith*, 1996, 234).

Called and chosen. One does not choose to be the Lord's servant. The choice of who will serve him and what and where that service will be rests with God alone. It was not the church of Joseph Smith that was being restored but the Church of Jesus Christ. Joseph Smith was his servant, first called and ordained in the councils of heaven to the ministry that was his.

24:2 *Thou art not excusable in thy transgressions*. No one is above the law. Joseph Smith was as accountable for misdeeds as anyone else, perhaps more so because of his office and calling. We are reminded of the charge given by the Savior to the Nephite Twelve. "Ye must watch and pray always," he said, "lest ye be tempted by the devil, and ye be led away captive by him" (3 Nephi 18:15). See commentary on Doctrine and Covenants 3:4.

24:3 *Magnify thine office*. See commentary on Doctrine and Covenants 84:33.

The church which is in Colesville, Fayette, and Manchester. During this period there were three main branches of the Church: Manchester, consisting primarily of the Smith family; Fayette, consisting primarily of the Whitmer family; and Colesville, consisting primarily of the Knight family.

They shall support thee. Reference is to the branches of the Church previously mentioned. There is no thought of a paid ministry here. The Prophet was not being allocated a salary, yet he would require food and lodging while he labored in behalf of the Lord. See commentary on Doctrine and Covenants 43:13.

24:4 To sustain those whom the Lord has called and chosen is to be blessed; to oppose them is to be cursed (D&C 121:16–23).

24:5 The Prophet began at this time to arrange and copy the revelations he had received for publication (Smith, *History of the Church,* 1:104). It was also at this time that he received the revelation known to us as Moses 1, which was the beginning of his work on the Inspired Version of the Bible.

24:6 By the power of the Holy Ghost one can speak or write spontaneously. Joseph Smith did both. He commonly received revelations in meetings with others present. Indeed, we would be within the mark to say that most of his revelations were received in this manner. Initially, he did not record revelations as he received them; he had, however, the ability to recall them at will (Smith, *History of the Church,* 5:xxxii). This revelation directed him to prepare the revelations he had received so that copies could be made of them.

Parley P. Pratt, who was present when several revelations were received, described the process thus: "Each sentence was uttered slowly and very distinctly, and with a pause between each, sufficiently long for it to be recorded, by an ordinary writer, in long hand.

"This was the manner in which all his written revelations were dictated and written. There was never any hesitation, reviewing or reading back, in order to keep the run of the subject" (Pratt, *Autobiography,* 48). William E. McLellin, in like manner, said: "I, as scribe, have written revelations from the mouth of [the Prophet]. And I have been present many times when others wrote for Joseph; therefore I speak as one having experience. The scribe seats himself at a desk or table, with pen, ink, and paper. The subject of enquiry being understood, the Prophet and Revelator enquires of God. He spiritually sees, hears, and feels, and then speaks as he is moved upon by the holy Ghost, the 'thus saith the Lord,' sentence after sentence, and waits for his amanuenses to write and then read aloud each sentence. Thus they proceed until the revelator says

Amen, at the close of what is then communicated. I have known [Joseph], without premeditation, to thus deliver off in broken sentences, some of the most sublime pieces of composition which I ever perused in any book" (in Backman, *Joseph Smith and the Doctrine and Covenants*, 1–2).

I will send unto them a cursing instead of a blessing. One cannot accept the servants of God without at the same time accepting the message they have been commissioned to bear. One could not, for instance, profess to accept Joseph Smith as a prophet and at the same time reject the Book of Mormon. As with the servants of God so with the revelations of God: we are blessed by accepting them and cursed by rejecting them.

24:7–9 Joseph's call was to labor in the things of the Spirit. In this he was to be blessed. Others would be granted the ability to accumulate the wealth of the world. He would not. Those so blessed are expected to contribute liberally of their means to the building of the kingdom of God. Critics of the Prophet have accused him of attempting to obtain power and wealth. Such charges expose only their own desires and ignorance. Every key, power, and authority that Joseph ever received he gave to others. The same was true of temporal things—all that he had he freely gave to those in need.

Brigham Young described Joseph's nature: "You that have lived in Nauvoo, in Missouri, in Kirtland, Ohio, can you assign a reason why Joseph could not keep a store, and be a merchant? Let me just give you a few reasons, and there are men here who know how matters went in those days. Joseph goes to New York and buys 20,000 dollars' worth of goods, comes into Kirtland and commences to trade. In comes one of the brethren, 'Brother Joseph, let me have a frock pattern for my wife.' What if Joseph says, 'No, I cannot without the money.' The consequence would be, 'He is no Prophet,' says James. Pretty soon Thomas walks in. 'Brother Joseph, will you trust me for a pair of boots?' 'No, I cannot let them go without the money.' 'Well,' says Thomas, 'Brother Joseph is no Prophet; I have found that out, and I am glad of it.' After a while, in comes Bill and sister Susan. Says Bill, 'Brother Joseph, I want a shawl, I have not got the money, but I wish you to trust me a week or a fortnight.' Well, brother Joseph thinks the others have gone and apostatized, and he don't know but these goods will make the whole Church do the same, so he lets Bill have a shawl. Bill walks off with it and meets a brother. 'Well,' says he, 'what do you think of brother Joseph?' 'O he is a first-rate man, and I fully believe he is a Prophet. See here, he has trusted me this shawl.' Richard says, 'I think I will go down and see if he won't trust me some.' In walks

Richard. 'Brother Joseph, I want to trade about 20 dollars.' 'Well,' says Joseph, 'these goods will make the people apostatize; so over they go, they are of less value than the people.' Richard gets his goods. Another comes in the same way to make a trade of 25 dollars, and so it goes. Joseph was a first-rate fellow with them all the time, provided he never would ask them to pay him. In this way it is easy for us to trade away a first-rate store of goods, and be in debt for them" (*Journal of Discourses*, 1:215).

Oliver Called to Preach
DOCTRINE AND COVENANTS 24:10–12

24:10–12 Oliver is charged to be tireless in defense of the faith. In so doing he is promised great strength and the power of God unto the convincing of men. He is also reminded that his strength is in the Lord not himself. Future events would prove that to be the case.

Miracles
DOCTRINE AND COVENANTS 24:13–14

24:13–14 We do not trifle with that which is sacred. Miracles are not to be called for save the Spirit of the Lord directs. No revealed direction is necessary, however, to rebuke the devil or to administer to the sick or those bitten by poisonous serpents. See commentary on Doctrine and Covenants 63:8–9.

Dusting of the Feet
DOCTRINE AND COVENANTS 24:15–17

24:15–17 Those who go forth in the service of the Lord also go forth with the promise of his protection. "Their arm shall be my arm, and I will be their shield and their buckler; and I will gird up their loins, and they shall fight manfully for me; and their enemies shall be under their feet; and I will let fall the sword in their behalf, and by the fire of mine indignation will I preserve them" (D&C 35:14).

24:15 *Casting off the dust of your feet.* The same injunctions given in this revelation were given by the Savior to the Twelve in the meridian day. Luke records it thus: "Then he called his twelve disciples together, and gave them power and authority over all devils, and to cure diseases. And he sent them to preach the kingdom of God, and to heal the sick. And he said unto them, Take nothing for your journey, neither staves, nor scrip, neither bread, neither money; neither have two coats apiece. And whatsoever house ye enter into, there abide, and thence depart. And whosoever will not receive you, when ye go out of that city, shake off the very dust from your feet for a testimony against them" (Luke 9:1–5). Commenting on this verse, Elder James E. Talmage observed: "To ceremonially shake the dust from one's feet as a testimony against another was understood by the Jews to symbolize a cessation of fellowship and a renunciation of all responsibility for consequences that might follow. It became an ordinance of accusation and testimony by the Lord's instructions to His apostles as cited in the text. In the current dispensation, the Lord has similarly directed His authorized servants to so testify against those who wilfully and maliciously oppose the truth when authoritatively presented (D&C 24:15; 60:15; 75:20; 84:92; 99:4). The responsibility of testifying before the Lord by this accusing symbol is so great that the means may be employed only under unusual and extreme conditions, as the Spirit of the Lord may direct" (*Jesus the Christ*, 345).

After the call of the Twelve in our day, we would understand this authority to rest with them, as it did anciently, or to those to whom they directly give it. The authority to perform the same has not been given to missionaries generally. Those performing this ordinance are further directed that it not be done in the presence of those they are testifying against "lest thou provoke them, but in secret; and wash thy feet, as a testimony against them in the day of judgment" (D&C 60:15). See commentary on Doctrine and Covenants 75:20–21.

Take Neither Purse nor Scrip
DOCTRINE AND COVENANTS 24:18–19

24:18 *Purse nor scrip.* To travel without purse or scrip is to travel without money or food. A "scrip" was a bag made from skins that was often used to carry scraps of food.

DOCTRINE AND COVENANTS 25

DATE: JULY 1830
PLACE: HARMONY, PENNSYLVANIA

Numbered among the revelations contained in the Doctrine and Covenants are those given to people collectively and individually. This, however, is the only revelation given specifically to a woman. What is of greatest significance here is that this revelation given to the Prophet's wife, Emma Smith, is intended in principle and purpose for the instruction and blessing of faithful women everywhere. It is a revelation on the role of women.

Emma an Elect Lady
DOCTRINE AND COVENANTS 25:1–6

25:1 *Emma Smith, my daughter.* Emma had recently been baptized. In this revelation Christ acknowledges her as his daughter. All who have taken upon themselves the name of Christ in the waters of baptism and covenanted to live worthy of that name may be adopted into the family of Christ and are in a figurative sense his sons and daughters (Mosiah 5:7; D&C 39:4).

As recorded in the Book of Commandments, this revelation simply read, "Emma, my daughter." "Smith" was added in the 1835 edition of the Doctrine and Covenants, apparently to aid the reader.

25:2 Here Emma receives the promise that if she continues in the path of faith and virtue her life will be preserved to accomplish all that she was ordained to do in the councils of heaven. The Lord has said, "What I say unto one I say unto all" (D&C 93:49), from which we can conclude that this same promise is shared by every virtuous and faithful woman who has taken upon herself the name of Christ and lived according to that covenant. They have the promise that they will receive an everlasting inheritance in Zion (D&C 59:2–3).

25:3 *Thou art an elect lady.* This designation, which is used in only one other instance in scripture (2 John 1:1), identifies a woman who is called and chosen as a servant of the Lord even before her birth. Emma would yet become the first woman in this dispensation to receive the fulness of temple blessings and to preside over the Relief Society. On the day of the organization of the Relief Society, the Prophet recorded that "elect" meant to be "elected to a certain work, &c., and that the revelation was then fulfilled by Sister Emma's election to the Presidency of the Society, she having previously been ordained to expound the scriptures" (Smith, *History of the Church*, 4:552–53).

25:4 Apparently Emma had been disgruntled because she had not been permitted to see the plates and other things shown to the special witnesses of the Book of Mormon (D&C 17).

25:5 Many would look to Emma for an example. She would have the opportunity to do much good. It was her destiny to be a leader among the daughters of Zion, yet her greatest call and office was to be that of wife and companion to her husband.

25:6 *Go with him.* Emma is directed not to remain behind in Harmony, Pennsylvania. Emma's parents had been turned against the Prophet by Nathaniel Lewis, a local minister and brother to her mother. Once Emma left Harmony with Joseph, she never saw her parents again.

Be unto him for a scribe. Emma had served for a short period as Joseph's scribe in the translation of the Book of Mormon. She would yet act in a similar capacity as the Prophet labored on the Inspired Version of the Bible.

Emma to Write, Expound Scripture, and Select Hymns
DOCTRINE AND COVENANTS 25:7–11

25:7 *Thou shalt be ordained.* To avoid confusing this action with a priesthood ordination, today we would say "set apart." See commentary on Doctrine and Covenants 20:2.

Expound scripture. To "expound" is to interpret. Emma was to have a special gift in making plain that which the prophets and apostles had written.

25:8 Emma was baptized on 28 June 1830 at Colesville, New York. Before she could be confirmed and given the gift of the Holy Ghost, Joseph was arrested "for setting the country in an uproar by preaching the Book of Mormon." Vilified by his captors, he was subjected to two spurious trials before being released. It was not until August that Emma was able to be confirmed.

25:9 *Thy husband shall support thee in the church.* In the Book of Commandments this read, "Thy husband shall support thee from the church," conveying the idea that she need not worry about Joseph's expending all his time and energy in the service of the Lord because the Church would provide for them.

25:11 *Make a selection of sacred hymns.* The singing of hymns has been an important part of worship among the Lord's people in all dispensations. Of the peoples of the Book of Mormon we are told that "their meetings were conducted by the church after the manner of the workings of the Spirit, and by the power of the Holy Ghost; for as the power of the Holy Ghost led them whether to preach, or to exhort, or to pray, or to supplicate, or to sing, even so it was done" (Moroni 6:9). Emma was directed to compile the first collection of hymns in this dispensation. This selection of sacred hymns was published in Kirtland, Ohio, in 1835. It consisted of ninety hymns printed without music, only a few of which were written by Latter-day Saint authors.

Principles Applicable to All
DOCTRINE AND COVENANTS 25:8–16

25:12 By tradition our worship services begin with a hymn. We do so because of the great power in music to attract the Spirit of the Lord. Generally, all are invited to participate in the singing. "The song of the righteous," the Lord said, "is a prayer unto me." Significantly, it is the heart to which the Lord listens, not the beauty of the voice.

25:13 *Cleave unto the covenants which thou hast made.* Marriage vows superseded Emma's allegiance to her parents. As the Lord told Adam, "Therefore shall a man leave his father and his mother, and shall cleave unto his wife; and they shall be one flesh" (Moses 3:24).

25:14 *Beware of pride.* As the wife of Joseph Smith and as a woman of great ability, Emma is especially warned against pride. Perhaps the murmuring for which she was admonished (v. 4) included envy of the circle of faithful brethren that had with Joseph entertained angels, received revelations, and performed miracles. Of necessity they had shared confidences and counsel to which she could not be privy.

25:16 *This is my voice unto all.* Although this revelation was given to Emma Smith, it is true that all faithful women will be well served by its admonitions and blessed in like manner by its promises. Through Emma the Lord is saying to all women of faith that if they will walk in paths of

virtue they will be preserved to accomplish their life's mission and they
will be assured an inheritance in Zion (v. 2). They too have the promise
that their sins have been forgiven (v. 3). Those who have husbands are
charged to be a comfort to them (v. 5); indeed, the greatest labor they will
perform will be that which they find at their husbands' side. Their husbands will find strength in their strength, courage in their courage, and
faith in their faith (v. 5). It is also their right to expound scripture and,
for that matter, to interpret and apply the various manifestations of the
Spirit to their families and in their various assignments in the Church
(v. 7). Following the instruction to give time to writing and learning
(v. 8), would enhance the ability of every woman to bless others.
President Spencer W. Kimball observed that "children may not recover
from the ignorance of their mothers" (*Teachings of Spencer W. Kimball*,
320). Few blessings are of greater worth to a child than a well-read
mother. The admonition of the Lord also includes the direction that a
faithful woman lay aside the things of this world in preference to those
things of a better world (v. 10). Also included in the instruction from the
Lord is the direction for Emma—and all women—to lift up her heart and
rejoice, cleave to her covenants, beware of pride, and continue in the
spirit of meekness (vv. 13–14), and finally to "keep [the] commandments
continually" (v. 15).

DOCTRINE AND COVENANTS 26

DATE: JULY 1830
PLACE: HARMONY, PENNSYLVANIA

This revelation was given at Harmony, Pennsylvania, in July of 1830 to Joseph Smith, Oliver Cowdery, and John Whitmer. Though but two verses in length, this revelation is of particular importance in establishing the law of common consent. The manner in which it is referred to in the revelation assumes that those receiving it are already familiar with the principle. The principle, which is associated with the restoration of the Melchizedek Priesthood, finds expression as early as May of 1829. Joseph Smith recorded: "The word of the Lord came unto us in the chamber [the upper floor of Peter Whitmer's log home], commanding us that I should ordain Oliver Cowdery to be an Elder in the Church of Jesus Christ; and that he also should ordain me to the same office; and then to ordain others, as it should be made known unto us from time to time. We were, however, commanded to defer this our ordination until such times as it should be practicable to have our brethren, who had been and who should be baptized, assembled together, when we must have their sanction to our thus proceeding to ordain each other, and have them decide by vote whether they were willing to accept us as spiritual teachers or not" (*History of the Church*, 1:60–61).

Instruction to Study and Preach
DOCTRINE AND COVENANTS 26:1

26:1 *Studying of the scriptures.* The direction to Joseph Smith, Oliver Cowdery, and John Whitmer to "study of the scriptures" apparently referred to the work they had commenced on the translation of the Bible (Matthews, *Plainer Translation*, 27).

Confirming the church at Colesville. There was both great interest in the Church and great opposition to it at Colesville. The intervention of mobs had prevented the confirmation of those who had been baptized there.

197

Go to the west to hold the next conference. The second conference of the Church was held at Fayette, New York, about one hundred miles north-west of Harmony, Pennsylvania. It commenced 26 September 1830 and continued for three days.

The Law of Common Consent

DOCTRINE AND COVENANTS 26:2

26:2 Agency is one of the fundamental laws of heaven. There can be no forced righteousness, nor can laws and leaders be imposed upon us. As Latter-day Saints we maintain that it is the right of every man or woman to "worship how, where, or what they may" (Article of Faith 11). In the churches of men it is the right of those who formed them to determine their doctrines and choose their leaders. By contrast, the Lord restored the Church of Jesus Christ, and because the Church belongs to Christ it is his right to run it. It is for him to decree its laws and choose its officers; nevertheless, true religion always preserves to its adherents the right of conscience and freedom of choice. Thus the Lord has instituted in his Church a principle known as the law of common consent. According to this law those who lead can do so only with the consent of those who are expected to follow. In like manner, it is the right of those who are to be bound by that scripture and law to consent to do so. Every offering within the Church and kingdom of God must be a free will offering.

The consent of those so governed is obtained by the simple act of rais-ing one's hand in an affirmative or negative vote when the proposition is put forward in the appropriate meeting. A negative vote is appropriate if the one making it is aware that something in the life of the individual being sustained is out of harmony with the standards of the Church. Negative votes are not given simply because the one called is not the pref-erence of those voting or does not appear to be the most qualified. It has been said that in some instances pigeons are called to preside over eagles. In such cases the eagle must learn to fly in formation under the direction of the pigeon or wander off and be lost.

In the meeting at which the Church was organized, Joseph Smith and Oliver Cowdery were sustained by those who constituted its membership to preside as the first and second elders of the Church. The question is asked, What would have happened had they not received that sustaining vote? In answer we would respond that the refusal of those present to sus-tain them would not take from them either the Aaronic or Melchizedek

Priesthood or the keys which had been conferred upon them. This authority would still have rested with them and thus the Lord would have led them to another people willing to sustain them. Those having rejected them would have closed the door of salvation to themselves. In like manner, the question is asked, What would happen if we as a people chose not to have a particular principle binding upon us? The answer, of course, is that it would not be binding and thus we would have closed the door in our own faces to the blessings that were associated with it. We could choose, for instance, not to be bound by the prohibitions of the Word of Wisdom, but in so choosing we would forfeit all blessings associated with that law (D&C 89:18–21; 28:10). See commentary on Doctrine and Covenants 72:7; 73:2.

DOCTRINE AND COVENANTS 27

DATE: AUGUST 1830

PLACE: HARMONY, PENNSYLVANIA

"Early in the month of August [1830]," Joseph Smith stated, "Newel Knight and his wife paid us a visit at my place in Harmony, Pennsylvania; and as neither his wife nor mine had been as yet confirmed, it was proposed that we should confirm them, and partake together of the Sacrament, before he and his wife should leave us. In order to prepare for this I set out to procure some wine for the occasion, but had gone only a short distance when I was met by a heavenly messenger, and received the following revelation, the first four paragraphs [D&C 27:1–5a, 14, 15a, 18b] of which were written at this time, and the remainder in the September following" (*History of the Church*, 1:106).

Emblems to Be Used in Partaking of the Sacrament

DOCTRINE AND COVENANTS 27:1–4

27:2–3 Because of this revelation we as a Church use water in place of wine in the sacrament. Two and a half years after this revelation was given Joseph Smith received a health law known as the Word of Wisdom. Relative to the use of wine or strong drink it states: "That inasmuch as any man drinketh wine or strong drink among you, behold it is not good, neither meet in the sight of your Father, only in assembling yourselves together to offer up your sacraments before him. And, behold, this should be wine, yea, pure wine of the grape of the vine, of your own make. And, again, strong drinks are not for the belly, but for the washing of your bodies" (D&C 89:5–7). "Strong drinks" is a biblical phrase which has reference to any drink with intoxicating qualities. When Christ returns, we are told that he will again partake of the "fruit of the vine" (Matthew 26:29) with us in a great sacrament meeting.

Recounting the events that followed this experience, Joseph recorded the following: "In obedience to the above commandment, we prepared some wine of our own making, and held our meeting, consisting only of five, viz., Newel Knight and his wife, myself and my wife, and John Whitmer. We partook together of the Sacrament, after which we confirmed these two sisters into the Church, and spent the evening in a glorious manner. The Spirit of the Lord was poured out upon us, we praised the Lord God, and rejoiced exceedingly" (Smith, *History of the Church,* 1:108).

Christ and His Servants from All Dispensations to Partake of the Sacrament Together
DOCTRINE AND COVENANTS 27:5–14

27:5–14 In the judgment of many students of the Doctrine and Covenants, these verses are descriptive of the great meeting yet to be held at Adam-ondi-Ahman. Expressing this view, Elder Bruce R. McConkie wrote as follows: "Before the Lord Jesus descends openly and publicly in the clouds of glory, attended by all the hosts of heaven; before the great and dreadful day of the Lord sends terror and destruction from one end of the earth to the other; before he stands on Mount Zion, or sets his feet on Olivet, or utters his voice from an American Zion or a Jewish Jerusalem; before all flesh shall see him together; before any of his appearances, which taken together comprise the second coming of the Son of God— before all these, there is to be a secret appearance to selected members of his Church. He will come in private to his prophet and to the apostles then living. Those who have held keys and powers and authorities in all ages from Adam to the present will also be present. And further, all the faithful members of the Church then living and all the faithful saints of all the ages past will be present. It will be the greatest congregation of faithful saints ever assembled on planet earth. It will be a sacrament meeting. It will be a day of judgment for the faithful of all the ages. And it will take place in Daviess County, Missouri, at a place called Adam-ondi-Ahman" (*Millennial Messiah,* 578–79).

"With reference to the use of sacramental wine in our day, the Lord said to Joseph Smith: 'You shall partake of none except it is made new among you; yea, in this my Father's kingdom which shall be built up on the earth.' In so stating, he is picking up the language he used in the upper room. Then he says: 'The hour cometh that I will drink of the fruit of the vine with you on the earth.' Jesus is going to partake of the sacrament again with his mortal disciples on earth. But it will not be with mortals only. He names others who will be present and who will participate in the sacred ordinance. These include Moroni, Elias, John the Baptist, Elijah, Abraham, Isaac, Jacob, Joseph (who was sold into Egypt), Peter, James, and John, 'and also with Michael, or Adam, the father of all, the prince of all, the ancient of days.' Each of these is named simply by way of illustration. The grand summation of the whole matter comes in these words: 'And also with all those whom my Father hath given me out of the world' (D&C 27:4–14). The sacrament is to be administered in a future day, on this earth, when the Lord Jesus is present, and when all the righteous of all ages are present. This, of course, will be a part of the grand council at Adam-ondi-Ahman" (McConkie, *Millennial Messiah*, 587).

27:5 At the Last Supper, when Jesus instituted the sacrament, he explained the symbolism of the wine that the apostles drank, saying, "This is my blood of the new testament, which is shed for many for the remission of sins. But I say unto you, I will not drink henceforth of this fruit of the vine, until that day when I drink it new with you in my Father's kingdom" (Matthew 26:28–29). Doctrine and Covenants 27:5 states that Moroni will be in attendance at that meeting. The verses that follow expand the list of those who are invited to partake of the sacrament with the Savior to include all who have been faithful to their testimony of him.

Fulness of my everlasting gospel. See commentary on Joseph Smith–History 1:34, page 20.

The stick of Ephraim. The stick of Ephraim is the Book of Mormon—the testimony of Christ written by the descendants of Joseph who was sold into Egypt as prophesied by Ezekiel (Ezekiel 37:15–28).

27:6 *Elias, to whom I have committed the keys of bringing to pass the restoration of all things.* The 1835 edition of the Doctrine and Covenants includes the phrase "or restorer of all things." In this sense the name *Elias* is a title, which properly belongs to all the ancient prophets who came to aid in the restoration of all things. No single messenger from the presence of God restored all things; rather the composite of all messengers is properly referred to as Elias. Each of the individual messengers is also referred to as such. "Who is Elias?" the Savior asked. He then responded to his own question, saying, "Behold, this is Elias, whom I send to prepare the way before me" (JST Matthew 17:13).

The specific messenger mentioned in this verse is identified in the verse that follows. The Elias who appeared to Zacharias was Gabriel, who in turn was identified by the Prophet Joseph Smith as Noah (*Teachings of the Prophet Joseph Smith,* 157).

27:10 *By whom the promises remain.* Reference is to the promises made to Abraham, Isaac, and Jacob (Abraham 2:9–11). See commentary on Doctrine and Covenants 110:12.

27:11 *Michael, or Adam.* The name *Michael,* which means "who is like God," is the name by which Adam was known in the councils of heaven (D&C 128:21).

27:12 This text confirms the restoration of the Melchizedek Priesthood, for which we have no date or official account. Erastus Snow, who served as an apostle for nearly forty years, gives the following account of the restoration of the higher priesthood: "In due course of time, as we read in the history which he [Joseph Smith] has left, Peter, James and John appeared to him—it was at a period when they were being pursued by their enemies and they had to travel all night, and in the dawn of the coming day when they were weary and worn who should appear to them but Peter, James and John, for the purpose of conferring upon them the Apostleship, the keys of which they themselves had held while upon the earth, which had been bestowed upon them by the Savior. This Priesthood conferred upon them by those three messengers embraces within it all offices of the Priesthood from the highest to the lowest. As has been often taught us that the keys of the presidency of this Apostleship represent the highest authority conferred upon man in the flesh. And by virtue of these keys of Priesthood the Prophet Joseph from time to time proceeded to ordain and set in order the Priesthood in its various quorums as we see it today in the Church" (*Journal of Discourses,* 23:183).

27:13 *The keys of my kingdom.* Peter, James, and John committed three things to Joseph Smith and Oliver Cowdery: the Melchizedek Priesthood; the keys of that priesthood, meaning the right to preside over all of its functions and offices; and the keys of the dispensation of the fulness of times. The holding of such keys is properly referred to as the apostleship, for keys are the distinctive characteristic of that office.

A dispensation of the gospel for the last times. A gospel dispensation is a period of time in which the truths of salvation are dispensed anew from the heavens so that there is no dependency on the revelations given to those of an earlier age. If priesthood has not come down by descent, it too must be restored. Ours is the final dispensation of the gospel. In it all priesthood, keys, powers, authorities, and doctrines known to any of the Lord's people in a previous day must be restored. Thus the Church stands completely independent of the doctrine and practices of historical

Christianity. We do not borrow from their doctrine nor their practices. Neither do we seek their approval of our doctrine or practices.

I will gather together in one all things. This language traces to the apostle Paul, who prophesied that in the dispensation of the fulness of times the Father would "gather together in one all things in Christ, both which are in heaven, and which are on earth; even in him" (Ephesians 1:10). The first among those things restored from the heavens came through the First Vision. It was the knowledge of God and his willingness to reveal his mind and will to men. Then came the priesthood, both Aaronic and Melchizedek. After that, "divers angels, from Michael or Adam down to the present time, all declaring their dispensation, their rights, their keys, their honors, their majesty and glory, and the power of their priesthood; giving line upon line, precept upon precept; here a little, and there a little; giving us consolation by holding forth that which is to come, confirming our hope!" (D&C 128:21).

Thereafter the tribes of Israel are to be gathered from among every nation, kindred, tongue, and people, as are the scriptural records kept by their fathers (2 Nephi 29:14), and "the islands shall become one land; and the land of Jerusalem and land of Zion shall be turned back into their own place, and the earth shall be like as it was in the days before it was divided" (D&C 133:23–24). This, the dispensation of the fulness of all past dispensations, will enjoy the restoration of all the glory, power, and knowledge known to any dispensation in the past. In addition to which the Lord said, "I deign to reveal unto my church things which have been kept hid from before the foundation of the world, things that pertain to the dispensation of the fulness of times" (D&C 124:41).

27:14 This verse constitutes the invitation to all faithful Latter-day Saints to attend the great sacrament meeting over which the Savior will preside in Adam-ondi-Ahman.

Gird Up Your Loins
DOCTRINE AND COVENANTS 27:15–18

27:15 *Gird up your loins.* The long loose dress of the ancient world made it necessary for men who were going to run or make a journey to put a belt or band around their waist. This was also thought to give the body strength, and it provided an ideal place for carrying weapons.

27:18 *Be agreed as touching all things whatsoever ye ask of me.* There is a strength in unified prayer that is not found otherwise. For instance, we read that the Nephite Twelve were "united in mighty prayer and fasting" when Jesus appeared to them (3 Nephi 27:1). Similarly, Joseph Smith and six elders united in prayer and were rewarded with one of the greatest revelations on priesthood given in this dispensation (D&C 84:1). "Whatsoever ye shall ask in faith," the Lord said, "being united in prayer according to my command, ye shall receive" (D&C 29:6).

DOCTRINE AND COVENANTS 28

DATE: SEPTEMBER 1830
PLACE: FAYETTE, NEW YORK

During the summer of 1830 Joseph Smith recorded that "a spirit of persecution began again to manifest itself against us in the neighborhood where I now resided [Harmony, Pennsylvania]," which he said began with "a man of the Methodist persuasion, who professed to be a minister of God. This man had learned that my father-in-law and his family had promised us protection, and were friendly, and inquiring into the work; and knowing that if he could get him turned against me, my friends in that place would be but few, he visited my father-in-law, and told him falsehoods concerning me of the most shameful nature, which turned the old gentleman and his family so much against us, that they would no longer promise us protection nor believe our doctrines" (*History of the Church*, 1:108).

It appears that the Methodist minister mentioned by Joseph Smith was Nathaniel C. Lewis, brother to Emma Smith's mother (Porter, "Study of the Origins," 169). Joseph and Oliver had been threatened by mobs from time to time, but the influence of Isaac Hale, Emma's father, had served as a protection to them. Now that he and Emma's mother had been soured against the Prophet, it became necessary for Joseph and Oliver to seek protection elsewhere.

"Towards the latter end of August," Joseph wrote, "in company with John and David Whitmer, and my brother Hyrum Smith, I visited the Church at Colesville, New York. Well knowing the determined hostility of our enemies in that quarter, and also knowing that it was our duty to visit the Church, we had called upon our Heavenly Father, in mighty prayer, that He would grant us an opportunity of meeting with them, that he would blind the eyes of our enemies, so that they would not know us, and that we might on this occasion return unmolested. Our prayers were not in vain, for when within a little distance of Mr. Knight's place, we encountered a large company at work upon the public road, amongst whom were several of our most bitter enemies. They looked earnest at us, but not knowing us, we passed on without interruption. That evening we assembled the Church, and confirmed them, partook of the Sacrament, and held a happy meeting, having much reason to rejoice in the God of our salvation, and sing hosannas to His holy name. Next morning we set out on our return home, and although our enemies had offered a reward of five dollars to any one who would give them information of our arrival, yet did we get out of the neighborhood, without the least annoyance, and arrived home in safety. Some few days afterwards, however, Newel Knight came to my place, and from him we learned that, very shortly after our departure, the mob came to know of our having been there, when they immediately collected together, and threatened the brethren, and very much annoyed them during all that day.

"Meantime, Brother Knight had come with his wagon, prepared to move my family to Fayette, New York. Mr. Whitmer, having heard of the persecutions against us at Harmony, Pennsylvania, had invited us to go and live with him; and during the last week in August we arrived at Fayette, amidst the congratulations of our brethren and friends.

"To our great grief, however, we soon found that Satan had been lying in wait to deceive, and seeking whom he might devour. Brother Hiram Page had in his possession a certain stone, by which he had obtained certain 'revelations' concerning the upbuilding of Zion, the order of the Church, etc., all of which were entirely at variance with the order of God's house, as laid down in the New Testament, as well as in our late revelations. As a conference meeting had been appointed for the 26th day of September, I thought it wisdom not to do much more than to converse with the brethren on the subject, until the conference should meet. Finding, however, that many, especially the Whitmer family and Oliver Cowdery, were believing much in the things set forth by this stone, we thought best to inquire of the Lord concerning so important a matter; and before conference convened, we received the following . . ." (Smith, *History of the Church*, 1:108–10).

Joseph Smith Holds the Keys of the Mysteries
DOCTRINE AND COVENANTS 28:1–7

28:1–7 It was Oliver Cowdery's right and responsibility as the second elder of the Church to teach, as directed by the Spirit. He was to teach those things revealed through Joseph Smith the Prophet. It was not his right, however, to receive revelation for the Church. The Lord's house is a house of order, and there can never be more than one man on earth at a time who can speak by way of revelation to the whole Church. Teaching this principle, Joseph Smith said: "I will inform you that it is contrary to the economy of God for any member of the Church, or any one, to receive instruction for those in authority, higher than themselves; therefore you will see the impropriety of giving heed to them; but if any person have a vision or a visitation from a heavenly messenger, it must be for his own benefit and instruction; for the fundamental principles, government, and doctrine of the Church are vested in the keys of the kingdom" (*History of the Church*, 1:338; *Teachings of the Prophet Joseph Smith*, 21). This principle was an important clarification for many early members of the Church who had come from a congregational background in which any member of the congregation could proclaim doctrine. Such misunderstanding led to an earlier error on the part of Oliver Cowdery. See commentary on Doctrine and Covenants 20:37.

28:2 *For he receiveth them even as Moses.* Miriam and Aaron, the sister and brother of Moses and themselves great leaders in Israel, were critical of Moses' marriage to an Ethiopian woman. "Hath the Lord indeed spoken only by Moses? hath he not spoken also by us?" they asked. Then we read: "And the Lord came down in the pillar of the cloud, and stood in the door of the tabernacle, and called Aaron and Miriam: and they both came forth. And he said, Hear now my words: If there be a prophet among you, I the Lord will make myself known unto him in a vision, and will speak unto him in a dream. My servant Moses is not so, who is faithful in all mine house. With him will I speak mouth to mouth [face to face as one man speaketh with another], even apparently, and not in dark speeches; and the similitude of the Lord shall he behold: wherefore then were ye not afraid to speak against my servant Moses? And the anger of the Lord was kindled against them; and he departed. And the cloud departed from off the tabernacle; and, behold, Miriam became leprous, white as snow: and Aaron looked upon Miriam, and, behold, she was leprous." Aaron, in a repentant spirit, plead with Moses to seek a healing blessing for their sister. Thus Aaron and Miriam were required to seek the blessing of heaven through the very mediator whom they had murmured against. The healing blessing was granted, nevertheless it was required that Miriam remain seven days outside the camp of Israel before they could again resume their march (Numbers 12:2, 5–10).

Both Moses and Joseph Smith were dispensation heads and as such enjoyed an intimacy with God not known to many other prophets.

28:7 *Keys of the mysteries, and the revelations.* To hold the keys of the mysteries and revelations is to possess the right to turn the key that opens the heavens to us. In the theological sense, a mystery is something that can only be known by revelation. Sacred rituals are referred to as mysteries because participation in them also has the effect of unlocking the heavens to us, bringing an understanding that could not otherwise be had.

Until I shall appoint unto them another in his stead. As long as Joseph Smith was the presiding officer in the Church he alone could receive revelation for the Church. If the Prophet proved unworthy, the Saints had the assurance that the Lord would call another in his stead. In accordance with the law the Lord had established that only the presiding officer of the Church can receive revelation for the Church, the revelation announcing that at some time someone else would replace Joseph Smith, of necessity, could come only through him (D&C 35:18; 43:3–4; 90:2–4).

Oliver Cowdery to Preach to the Lamanites
DOCTRINE AND COVENANTS 28:8–10

28:8 Shortly after Oliver's call to preach to the Lamanites, Peter Whitmer Jr., Parley P. Pratt, and Ziba Peterson were also called to accompany him (D&C 30:5; 32:1–3). Despite their lack of success among the Lamanites, the mission itself proved to be of great importance to the young Church. The missionaries set out on their 1,500 mile journey on foot. Near Buffalo, New York, they visited the Catteraugus Indians and left the Book of Mormon with them. From there they proceeded to Kirtland, Ohio. There they met Sidney Rigdon, a popular Campbellite minister and former friend and instructor of Elder Pratt's. After learning of the Book of Mormon and being convinced that he had no authority to minister the ordinances of the gospel, Sidney Rigdon and many of his congregation were baptized. Thereafter the missionaries found themselves teaching day and night. "In two or three weeks from our arrival in the neighborhood with the news, we had baptized one hundred and twenty-seven souls," noted Elder Pratt, "and this number soon increased to one thousand. The disciples were filled with joy and gladness; while rage and lying was abundantly manifested by gainsayers; faith was strong, joy was great, and persecution heavy" (Pratt, *Autobiography*, 36). Among the converts who quickly established themselves as men of unusual capacity were Isaac Morley, John Murdock, and Lyman Wight.

Near Sandusky, Ohio, the missionaries visited the Wyanddot tribe and preached the gospel to them. In January of 1831 the missionaries passed through St. Louis and St. Charles where little interest was taken in their message. "We travelled," Elder Pratt recounted, "on foot for three hundred miles through vast prairies and through trackless wilds of snow—no beaten road; houses few and far between; and the bleak northwest wind always blowing in our faces with a keenness which would almost take the skin off the face. We traveled for whole days, from morning till night, without a house or fire, wading in snow to the knees at every step, and the cold so intense that the snow did not melt on the south side of the houses, even in the mid-day sun, for nearly six weeks. We carried on our backs our changes of clothing, several books, and corn bread and raw pork. We often ate our frozen bread and pork by the way, when the bread would be so frozen that we could not bite or penetrate any part of it but the outside crust" (Pratt, *Autobiography*, 40).

After traveling four months and suffering untold hardships the missionaries arrived in Jackson County, Missouri, which was then the western frontier. They rested at Independence, then crossed the frontier and visited the Shawnee and the Delaware Indians. These tribes exhibited great interest in the Book of Mormon, which aroused the ire of ministers of other faiths who prevailed upon the Indian agents to expel the missionaries from that part of the country. They returned to Jackson County, where they labored with measurable success.

28:9 From the Book of Mormon (Ether 13) the Saints learned that a New Jerusalem was to be established upon this the American continent. This prophecy caused some speculation among them as to where the City of Zion would be established. The revelation answering that question would come in July of 1831. See commentary on Doctrine and Covenants 57:2.

Satan Deceived Hiram Page
DOCTRINE AND COVENANTS 28:11–16

28:11–16 The Lord directed that Oliver Cowdery, rather than the Prophet, labor to correct Hiram Page. This was to be done privately.

28:11 *That stone.* A "peepstone" appearing to be the one used by Hiram Page to receive his revelations is now in the possession of the

RLDS Church. It is a flat stone about seven inches long and four inches wide and one-quarter inch thick. It is dark gray in color with waves of brown and purple. It also has a small hole drilled through one end so that it could be worn on a chain around Hiram's neck (Wright, "Hiram Page Stone," 85).

28:12 *Contrary to the church covenants.* The Articles and Covenants of the Church (D&C 20 and 22) placed Joseph Smith as the first, or presiding, elder of the Church. As this revelation affirms, it would be for him and him alone to receive revelations for the Church. Thus the revelation concerning the location of the New Jerusalem, of necessity, had to come through Joseph.

28:13 *By common consent.* See commentary on Doctrine and Covenants 26:2; 72:7; 73:2.

MOSES 3–5

DATE: JUNE–OCTOBER 1830
PLACE: HARMONY, PENNSYLVANIA, AND FAYETTE, NEW YORK

"The subjects of these chapters of Genesis translated by the Prophet have to do with the spiritual and temporal creations, agency, the rebellion of Lucifer, the fall of Adam, and the introduction of the gospel to Adam and his posterity," explained Robert J. Matthews. "The doctrinal emphasis is clear and prominent in the Joseph Smith Translation but is almost totally lacking in any other Bible.

"In the Prophet's translation of Genesis 1–5, principles are woven into a story line relating the events of the Garden of Eden, Satan's rebellion, his temptation of Adam and Eve, their eating the forbidden fruit, and their being ushered out of the garden. In contrast, the material in Doctrine and Covenants 29:30–45 is a brief statement of doctrinal principles—without the story—actually a summary of the doctrine found in the longer narrative of Joseph Smith's translation of Genesis 1–5. Thus, for maximum comprehension, the Prophet's translation of Genesis 1–5 (Moses 2–5) should be read just prior to a study of Doctrine and Covenants 29, since that appears to be the order in which they were received.

"The historical relationship between these two revelations begins a pattern repeated in later revelations, a pattern which shows that many of the concepts contained in the Doctrine and Covenants were first presented to the mind of the Prophet during his translation of the Bible and actually were recorded first in that translation. Later many of these subjects were enlarged upon and appeared as parts of various sections of the Doctrine and Covenants" (*Bible! A Bible!* 151).

Prior to and following the reception of Doctrine and Covenants 29, the Prophet Joseph Smith worked on the inspired translation of the Bible. He began with Genesis, from which we received the selections published in the Pearl of Great Price as Moses 1 through 8. Moses 3 and 4 appear to have been received while the Prophet Joseph Smith resided in Harmony,

Pennsylvania, between June and August 1830. Moses 5 was received after Joseph and Emma moved to Fayette, New York, during the last week of August. Doctrinal connections between Moses 5 and Doctrine and Covenants 29 suggest that the translation of Moses 5 most likely preceded the reception of section 29.

Moses 3

Nephi wrote that "my father, Lehi, took the records which were engraven upon the plates of brass, and he did search them from the beginning. And he beheld that they did contain the five books of Moses, which gave an account of the creation of the world, and also of Adam and Eve, who were our first parents" (1 Nephi 5:10–11). It is evident from Lehi's teachings that he had a more complete record than is found in our modern Bible. This would accord with Nephi's statement that many plain and precious things, including covenants of the Lord, were taken from the Bible before it went forth to the nations of the earth (1 Nephi 13:20–29). It is also significant that many of the items of doctrine and prophecy to which Lehi refers and upon which he gives commentary are found in the Joseph Smith Translation of Genesis (2 Nephi 2; Moses 3–4).

God Created All Things Spiritually before They Were Naturally upon the Earth
Moses 3:1–9

Moses 3:5 *I . . . created all things . . . spiritually, before they were naturally upon the face of the earth.* The state of creation before the fall of Adam is herein revealed. The events described in the Creation account in Genesis are of a spiritual-physical nature. Adam and Eve were created in a physical state from the dust of the earth, but they could not die. Death did not enter the world until after the Fall. "Now what is a spiritual body?" asked President Joseph Fielding Smith. "It is one that is quickened by spirit and not by blood" (*Doctrines of Salvation*, 1:76). Thus, the spirit that flows through the body gives it the description of being "spiritual." All creations were sustained by spirit element before the fall of Adam. Hence, the spiritual creation and organization of element in a paradisiacal state required the fall to mortality to bring to pass God's purposes. After Adam and Eve partook of the forbidden fruit, blood formed in their bodies, and other changes were introduced into the world, by which all of creation became natural (McConkie, *Mormon Doctrine*, 268–69). The means by which plants and animals were changed to a natural state has not yet been revealed; however, "in that day when the Lord shall come, he shall reveal all things—*Things which have passed, and hidden things which no man knew, things of the earth, by which it was made, and the purpose and the end thereof*— Things most precious, things that are above, and things that are beneath, things that are in the earth, and upon the earth, and in heaven" (D&C 101:32–34; emphasis added). Meanwhile, it seems to have been necessary for Christ to work out a blood atonement because Adam made a blood fall.

I . . . had created all the children of men; . . . for in heaven created I them. The earth is not the first home of any of God's creations. All living things were created spiritually before being placed on earth. They were composed of spirit matter or more refined element (D&C 131:7), waiting for the time when they might come to earth and take upon them a physical body—one which would be permanently theirs in the Resurrection. The reference in this verse to the spirit creation concerns an event that had already taken place before the spiritual-physical creation that was revealed to Moses. "There is no account of the creation of man," explained Joseph Fielding Smith, "or other forms of life when they were created as spirits. There is just the simple statement that they were so created before the physical creation. The statements in Moses 3:5 and Genesis 2:5 are interpolations into the account of the physical creation, explaining that all things were first created in the spirit existence in heaven before they were placed upon this earth.

"We were all created untold ages before we were placed on this earth. We discover from Abraham 3:22–28, that it was before the earth was formed that the plan of salvation was presented to the spirits, or 'intelligences.' This being true, then man, animals and plants were not created in the spirit at the time of the creation of the earth, but long before" (*Doctrines of Salvation*, 1:75–76).

Although this revelation refers specifically to plants and the children of men as having been created in a spirit state before coming to earth, animals were also created in this manner. The spirits of all creations are in the likeness of their earthly bodies. See commentary on Doctrine and Covenants 77:2.

There was not yet flesh upon the earth. Reference is to mortal flesh in which "the life of the flesh is in the blood" (Leviticus 17:11). In the sense that blood had not yet been introduced into the spiritual-physical creation "there was not yet flesh on the earth."

Moses 3:7 *The first flesh upon the earth.* This is not to say that Adam was the first of all God's creations. Indeed, all of the creative accounts (Genesis, Moses, Abraham, and the temple) make a point of the fact that the earth was created for Adam and that he was the last of God's creations placed here. The phrase "first flesh" means that he was the first living thing to be subject to death. "Since flesh often means mortality Adam is spoken of as the 'first flesh' upon the earth, meaning he was the first mortal on the earth, all things being created in a non-mortal condition, and becoming mortal through the fall of Adam. Jesus is the 'Only Begotten of the Father' in the flesh, meaning he is the only one begotten of the Father into mortality" (Bible Dictionary, 675–76).

The first man also. There were no pre-Adamites. Adam was the "first man" created by the Father (Moses 1:34) and declared by him to be his son (Moses 6:22).

Moses 3:9 *It became also a living soul.* As "the spirit and the body are the soul of man" (D&C 88:15), so plants became living souls as spirit matter and the dust of the earth combined in their creation.

It remaineth in the sphere in which I, God, created it. Lehi, commenting on this principle as recorded on the plates of brass, stated: "All things which were created must have remained in the same state in which they were after they were created; and they must have remained forever, and had no end" (2 Nephi 2:22). Thus, there was no death among all of the life on earth before the fall of Adam.

I, the Lord God, planted the tree of life . . . and also the tree of knowledge. The tree of life and tree of knowledge were of supreme importance to the plan of God in furthering the progression of his children. "To bring about his eternal purposes in the end of man" explained Lehi, "after he had created our first parents, and the beasts of the field and the fowls of the air, and in fine, all things which are created, it must needs be that there was an opposition; even the forbidden fruit in opposition to the tree of life; the one being sweet and the other bitter" (2 Nephi 2:15). As recounted in the passages that follow, the choices offered by these two trees help to bring to pass the immortality and eternal life of man. The fruit of the tree of life represents eternal life, and the fruit of the tree of knowledge offers the changes by which Adam and Eve became mortal and provided physical bodies to God's spirit children. See Doctrine and Covenants 29:39.

Woman a Helpmeet for Man
MOSES 3:10–25

Moses 3:17 *Thou mayest choose for thyself.* Conflicting commandments were given to Adam and Eve. They were told to multiply and replenish the earth (Moses 2:28). They were also told not to partake of the tree of the knowledge of good and evil (Moses 3:17). They could not keep the first commandment without breaking the second (2 Nephi 2:25; Moses 5:11). "Just why the Lord would say to Adam that he forbade him to partake of the fruit of that tree is not made clear in the Bible account, but in the original as it comes to us in the Book of Moses it is made definitely clear. [The Lord told] Adam that if he wished to remain as he was in the garden, then he was not to eat the fruit, but if he desired to eat it and partake of death he was at liberty to do so" (Smith, *Answers*, 4:81). As the Fall came by free choices of man, so salvation through the Atonement must come in the same manner. See commentary on Doctrine and Covenants 29:39, "Agents unto themselves."

In the Garden of Eden there was no sin, pain, disease, decay, aging, corruption, or evil of any sort. For these to exist it would be necessary for Adam to do something to change the nature of the world over which God had given him dominion. Adam chose to do so, that is "Adam fell that men might be" (2 Nephi 2:25). Corruption in all its forms and evil in all its variety entered the world. In effecting the fall Adam created the need for a redeemer and thus placed the plan of salvation in motion (Moses 5:11).

Thou shalt surely die. By partaking of the forbidden fruit Adam and Eve became subject to both a physical death (separation of body and spirit) and a spiritual death (estrangement from the presence of God). See Doctrine and Covenants 29:39.

Moses 3:19 *They were also living souls.* As "the spirit and the body are the soul of man" (D&C 88:15), so animals have a dual nature of spirit and body. The spirits of all animals are in the likeness of their earthly bodies (D&C 77:2).

Moses 3:21–23 The imagery used to veil the account of Eve's birth is most beautiful, particularly so in a day when there is so much confusion about the role of women. Symbolically, Eve is created from Adam. She was not taken from the bones of Adam's head nor from the bones of his heel, for it is not the place of woman to be either above man or beneath him. Her place is at his side, and so she is taken, in the figurative sense, from his rib—the bone that girds the side and rests closest to the heart. Thus we find Adam declaring: "This I know now is bone of my bones, and flesh of my flesh; she shall be called Woman, because she was taken out of man" (v. 23). Eve, unlike the rest of God's creations, was of Adam's bone and of his flesh, meaning that she was equal to him in powers, faculties, and rights. See commentary on Moses 5:1–2, page 224.

Moses 3:25 *The man and his wife.* Adam and Eve were married before the Fall brought death into the world. The marriage covenant is not restricted to the bounds of mortality but was designed to be eternal from the beginning. The Savior revealed to the Prophet Joseph Smith that marriage is part of "the law of my Holy Priesthood, as was ordained by me and my Father before the world was" (D&C 132:28).

MOSES 4

How Satan Became the Devil
MOSES 4:1–4

Moses 4:1 *I will redeem all mankind, that one soul shall not be lost.* The Prophet Joseph Smith explained: "The contention in heaven was—Jesus said there would be certain souls that would not be saved; and the devil said he could save them all, and laid his plans before the grand council, who gave their vote in favor of Jesus Christ. So the devil rose up in rebellion against God, and was cast down, with all who put up their heads for him" (*Teachings of the Prophet Joseph Smith*, 357).

Perhaps some irony is to be found in the fact that those who embraced the cause wherein none were to be lost became the only ones who are everlastingly lost. They alone become "perdition," or hopelessly lost. They are "the only ones on whom the second death shall have any power; yea, verily, the only ones who shall not be redeemed in the due time of the Lord, after the sufferings of his wrath. For all the rest shall be brought forth by the resurrection of the dead, through the triumph and the glory of the Lamb, who was slain, who was in the bosom of the Father before the worlds were made" (D&C 76:37–39).

Give me thine honor. The Father's honor is his "everlasting dominion," which flows unto him "without compulsory means" (D&C 121:46). His children freely honor him, as he ordains only that which will bring to pass immortality and eternal lives. He is the author of the plan of salvation. He reigns in heaven with the scepter of righteousness and truth (D&C 121:46).

Pride, arrogance, haughtiness, lust for power, and lack of faith in God are manifested in the presumptuous offer of Lucifer. He desired to set up his own priesthood order. The order was designed to set himself up at its head and none would preside over him, not even God. Isaiah expressed Lucifer's desire in poetic verse: "For thou hast said in thine heart, I will ascend into heaven, I will exalt my throne above the stars of God: I will sit also upon the mount of the congregation, in the sides of the north: I will ascend above the heights of the clouds; I will be like the most High" (Isaiah 14:13–14). Those who are willing to give Lucifer honor as their father form his priesthood order and are known as sons of perdition.

Moses 4:2 *Father, thy will be done.* The Son had no plan of his own. The Father is the author of the plan of salvation. The Prophet Joseph Smith taught, "God himself, finding he was in the midst of spirits and glory, because he was more intelligent, saw proper to institute laws whereby the rest could have a privilege to advance like himself. The relationship we have with God places us in a situation to advance in knowledge. He has power to institute laws to instruct the weaker intelligences, that they may be exalted with himself" (*Teachings of the Prophet Joseph Smith*, 354).

The will of the Only Begotten Son has always been the will of the Father in all things. We learn of the Father's plan from the teachings of the Savior. "Behold I have given unto you my gospel, and this is the gospel which I have given unto you—that I came into the world to do the will of my Father, because my Father sent me. And my Father sent me that I might be lifted up upon the cross; and after that I had been lifted up upon the cross, that I might draw all men unto me, that as I have been lifted up by men even so should men be lifted up by the Father, to stand before me, to be judged of their works, whether they be good or whether they be evil" (3 Nephi 27:13–14).

Moses 4:3 *Satan . . . sought to destroy the agency of man.* The salvation guaranteed by Satan to all of the children of God would have come at the cost of their agency. The right of choice would have been lost to them. Without the right of choice there can be neither righteousness nor wickedness and therefore no purpose in our mortal probation. For God to have accepted such a proposal would in itself have destroyed the purpose of our creation.

Satan rebelled against me. When he was not chosen as the promised Messiah, Lucifer "was angry, and kept not his first estate" (Abraham 3:28). He sought to openly rebel against the authority of the Father. "A third part of the hosts of heaven turned he away from [God] because of their agency" (D&C 29:36). "And there was war in heaven" (Revelation 12:7).

Moses 4:4 *He became Satan, yea, even the devil.* Lucifer had been a bearer of light, as his name, son of the morning, implies. He was "an angel of God who was in authority in the presence of God . . . a son of the morning" (D&C 76:25–26). However, his rebellion led him to become Satan, meaning the slanderer and "the accuser of our brethren" (Revelation 12:10). He became a liar and "sought that which was evil before God. And because he had fallen from heaven, and had become miserable forever, he sought also the misery of all mankind" (2 Nephi 2:17–18).

Satan Tempts Eve
MOSES 4:5–11

Moses 4:5 *The serpent was more subtle than any beast of the field.* In this verse the serpent symbolizes Lucifer. Similar symbolism was used in the revelation given to John the apostle. He beheld "a great red dragon, having seven heads and ten horns, and seven crowns upon his heads. And his tail drew the third part of the stars of heaven, and did cast them to the earth: . . . And the great dragon was cast out, that old serpent, called the Devil, and Satan, which deceiveth the whole world: . . . and his angels were cast out with him" (Revelation 12:3–4, 9). Commenting on the account of the fall of Adam as recorded on the brass plates, Lehi explained, "According to the things which I have read, [I] must needs suppose that an angel of God, according to that which is written, had fallen from heaven; wherefore, he became a devil, having sought that which was evil before God. And because he had fallen from heaven, and had become miserable forever, he sought also the misery of all mankind. Wherefore, *he said unto Eve, yea, even that old serpent, who is the devil,* who is the father of all lies, wherefore he said: Partake of the forbidden fruit, and ye shall not die, but ye shall be as God, knowing good and evil" (2 Nephi 2:17–18; emphasis added).

Moses 4:6 *The serpent, (for he had drawn away many after him).* Again, reference to the serpent is symbolic of Lucifer and those spirits that followed him in rebellion against God. However, the possibility that there was also an actual serpent or snake in the garden, through which the devil spoke, remains. Such is hinted at in verse 7: "he spake by the mouth of the serpent." An example of devils entering into the bodies of animals is recorded in the New Testament wherein evil spirits were permitted to enter into the bodies of swine (Luke 8:32–33). It may be that as "angels speak by the power of the Holy Ghost" (2 Nephi 32:3), so devils speak by the power of Satan. That is, the serpent may signify that Satan spoke by the mouth of his angels.

He sought also to beguile Eve. Eve did not rebel against God in partaking of the forbidden fruit. She was innocent, like a little child, not knowing good from evil. Satan deceived her by lying to her, telling her that she would not surely die if she partook of the fruit of the tree of knowledge of good and evil. Thus, a law was transgressed, but a sin was not committed.

He knew not the mind of God. As is true of those whom the devil takes captive, so it is true of Lucifer and his fall to perdition: "They that will harden their hearts, to them is given the lesser portion of the word until they know nothing concerning his mysteries" (Alma 12:11). All apostates are in a similar situation of having lost light and truth. "Strange as it may appear at first thought," expressed the Prophet Joseph Smith, "yet it is no less strange than true, that notwithstanding all the professed determination to live godly, apostates after turning from the faith of Christ, unless they have speedily repented, have sooner or later fallen into the snares of the wicked one, and have been left destitute of the Spirit of God, to manifest their wickedness in the eyes of multitudes. . . . There is a superior intelligence bestowed upon such as obey the Gospel with full purpose of heart, which, if sinned against, the apostate is left naked and destitute of the Spirit of God. . . . When once that light which was in them is taken from them, they become as much darkened as they were previously enlightened" (*Teachings of the Prophet Joseph Smith,* 67).

He sought to destroy the world. Referring to Lucifer, Lehi explained: "Because he had fallen from heaven, and he had become miserable forever, he sought also the misery of all mankind" (2 Nephi 2:18). Lucifer believed that the fall of Adam would lead to the eventual captivity of all God's children. Lucifer was cut off from the presence of God, becoming spiritually dead. He believed that by tempting Eve to partake of the forbidden fruit that she too would be cut off from the presence of God. In this plan Lucifer was correct. Lehi further explained that God "gave commandment that all men must repent; for he showed unto all men that they were lost, because of the transgression of their parents" (2 Nephi 2:21). In addition, the consequence of temporal death, as pronounced by God upon Adam and Eve if they partook of the forbidden fruit, was the separation of the body and spirit. In such a situation Adam and Eve, and their posterity, would become disembodied spirits after death, thus becoming like Lucifer. Because Lucifer has no faith and no light to comprehend Christ's atoning sacrifice, he believed, as Jacob described in the Book of Mormon, that "our spirits must have become like unto him, and we become devils, angels to a devil, to be shut out from the presence of our God, and to remain with the father of lies, in misery, like into himself" (2 Nephi 9:9).

Adam and Eve's Fall; Death Enters the World
MOSES 4:12–25

Moses 4:12–25 The apostle Paul explained that "Adam was not deceived, but the woman being deceived was in the transgression" (1 Timothy 2:14). In other words, Eve partook of the fruit due to her innocent and trusting nature, not knowing good and evil. On the other hand, there was no deception involved when Adam partook of the forbidden fruit. It appears that Adam purposely fell that he might remain with Eve, according to the commandment of the Lord (v. 18). Further, they were commanded to multiply and replenish the earth, which they could not do in their immortal or paradisiacal state.

"What is meant by partaking of the fruit of the tree of knowledge of good and evil," explained Elder Bruce R. McConkie, "is that our first parents complied with whatever laws were involved so that their bodies would change from their state of paradisiacal immortality to a state of natural mortality" (*Sermons and Writings*, 189).

Moses 4:13 *They sewed fig-leaves together and made themselves aprons.* The fig is a symbol of fertility. In clothing the sexual parts of their bodies—which represent the power of creation—with fig leaves, Adam and Eve announced that they now had the power to procreate.

Moses 4:20 *Because thou hast done this thou shalt be cursed.* This curse, placed upon the serpent, symbolizes the curse placed upon those that followed Lucifer in the premortal life. Throughout eternity they will remain lower than the cattle or the beasts of the field, for even the beasts have bodies of flesh and bone and enjoy the privilege of resurrection, whereas the devil and his angels remain unembodied spirits forever.

Moses 4:21 *He shall bruise thy head, and thou shalt bruise his heel.* "He" to whom reference is made is Christ. The biblical text, rather sadly, reads "it" (Genesis 3:15). It is Christ who will "bruise" (in Hebrew, "crush") Satan's head. Satan will have his moment of victory in the crucifixion of Christ (spoken of as bruising Christ's heel), but the ultimate victory over death and sin will rest with Christ (described here as bruising Satan's head).

Moses 4:22 *I will greatly multiply thy sorrow and thy conception.* This could have been translated "your pain in childbearing," or "your labor and groaning." The pain of childbearing rests with the woman. It seems also a part of the nature of women to feel a greater sorrow or pain in the improper actions of wayward children.

He shall rule over thee. "I have a question about the word *rule*," stated President Spencer W. Kimball. "It gives the wrong impression. I would prefer to use the word *preside* because that's what he does. A righteous husband presides over his wife and family" ("Blessings and Responsibilities," 72). President Howard W. Hunter taught, "A man who holds the priesthood accepts his wife as a partner in the leadership of the home and family with full knowledge of and full participation in all decisions relating thereto. Of necessity there must be in the Church and in the home a presiding officer (D&C 107:21). By divine appointment, the responsibility to preside in the home rests upon the priesthood holder (Moses 4:22). The Lord intended that the wife be a helpmeet for man . . . that is, a companion equal and necessary in full partnership. Presiding in righteousness necessitates a shared responsibility between husband and wife; together you act with knowledge and participation in all family matters. For a man to operate independently of or without regard to the feelings and counsel of his wife in governing the family is to exercise unrighteous dominion" (Conference Report, October 1994, 68).

Adam and Eve Are Sent Forth from the Garden of Eden
MOSES 4:26–32

Moses 4:26 *Mother of all living; . . . the first of all women, which are many.* "Adam and Eve, who were our first parents" (1 Nephi 5:11) are the mortal progenitors of all men and women. It would appear that the first parents on each earth would properly bear the names Adam and Eve (Abraham 3:3).

Moses 4:27 *Make coats of skins, and clothed them.* After Adam and

Eve had partaken of the fruit of the tree of knowledge of good and evil, after they had blood flowing in their veins, after all things in the world of which they were a part had become subject to death, the God of Heaven taught them the law of sacrifice. This law required the death—by the shedding of blood—of two lambs whose skins were then placed on Adam and Eve. These special garments were worn by them when they went out into the lone and dreary world. The garments constituted a constant reminder of the protection they would enjoy (through the blood of the Lamb, even the Son of God) from all the effects of the Fall.

Moses 4:31 *Cherubim and a flaming sword.* Cherubim are usually depicted as winged animals, such as bulls and lions. Sometimes they are composite creatures of several animals and have the face of a man. They are utilized in many cultures to represent the guardians of sacred buildings, treasures, trees, etc. All who return to the presence of God must be able to "pass by the angels, and the gods, which are set there" to guard the way so that those who have not been properly prepared may not enter (D&C 132:19).

When asked, "What does the scripture mean, which saith that God placed cherubim and a flaming sword on the east of the garden of Eden, lest our first parents should enter and partake of the fruit of the tree of life, and live forever?" (Alma 12:21), the prophet Alma explained, "Now we see that Adam did fall by the partaking of the forbidden fruit, according to the word of God; and thus we see, that by his fall, all mankind became a lost and fallen people. And now behold, I say unto you that if it had been possible for Adam to have partaken of the fruit of the tree of life at that time, there would have been no death, and the word would have been void, making God a liar, for he said: If thou eat thou shalt surely die. And we see that death comes upon mankind, yea, the death which has been spoken of by Amulek, which is the temporal death; nevertheless there was a space granted unto man in which he might repent; therefore this life became a probationary state; a time to prepare to meet God; a time to prepare for that endless state which has been spoken of by us, which is after the resurrection of the dead. . . . And now behold, if it were possible that our first parents could have gone forth and partaken of the tree of life they would have been forever miserable, having no preparatory state; and thus the plan of redemption would have been frustrated, and the word of God would have been void, taking none effect. But behold, it was not so; but it was appointed unto men that they must die; and after death, they must come to judgment, even that same judgment of which we have spoken, which is the end" (Alma 12:22–24, 26–27).

MOSES 5

Adam and Eve Bring Forth Children
MOSES 5:1–3

Moses 5:1–3 Adam and Eve were the parents of many children and may have been grandparents before Cain and Abel were born.

Moses 5:1 *Adam began to till the earth.* Adam and Eve were neither ignorant nor helpless when they left Eden to begin life in this fallen world. While in Eden they had learned to dress and keep a garden (Moses 3:15) and undoubtedly learned much about animals and their various uses (Moses 2:26).

Moses 5:1–2 *Eve, also, his wife, did labor with him . . . and she bare unto him sons and daughters.* Created in the image and likeness of God, Adam and Eve became in their marriage the prototype of manhood and womanhood. They labored together, taught their children together, prayed together, and heard the voice of the Lord together. Indeed, according to the divine command, they became one flesh (Moses 3:24).

Adam Offers Sacrifice and Serves God
MOSES 5:4–15

Moses 5:4 *For they were shut out from his presence.* See commentary on Doctrine and Covenants 29:41, "The first death, even that same death which is the last death."

Moses 5:6 *I know not.* Obedience often precedes understanding. This, however, is not blind faith, for faith can only be exercised in principles that are true (Alma 32:21) and requires a knowledge of God, his commandments, and his power.

Moses 5:7 *Is a similitude of the sacrifice of the Only Begotten of the Father.* Elder Bruce R. McConkie observed, "A long, wearisome road runs from Eden to Gethsemane, from the garden in which the promise of a Redeemer was first given to the garden in which the promised redemption was wrought. Long, wearisome centuries—forty periods of one hundred years each—separated the promise of a Redeemer from his destined crucifixion. During all these slow-passing years millions upon millions of faithful souls looked forward, with an eye of faith, to that day when Messiah's infinite and eternal atoning sacrifice would free them from their sins. Lest they forget, the Lord gave them the ordinance of sacrifice, an ordinance perfectly designed to keep them in remembrance of that which was to be" (*Promised Messiah*, 383).

Moses 5:8 *Do all that thou doest in the name of the Son.* No more perfect evidence of apostasy could be cited than the notion in the historical Christian world that Christianity—that is the belief that salvation is in Christ—began in the meridian of time, thus leaving those who lived in the first half of earth's history without claim upon the redeeming blood of Christ. That this simply was not the case is amply attested to in the Book of Mormon. The robbing of the Old Testament of this understanding is the classical illustration of plain and precious things having been taken from that record. Conversely, no more perfect evidence could be cited that Joseph Smith was a prophet than the restoration of the knowledge that from the days of Adam the knowledge of Christ and his gospel were known to the children of men.

From the first man to the last, salvation comes only in the name of Christ. The Prophet Joseph Smith observed that "we cannot believe that the ancients in all ages were so ignorant of the system of heaven as many suppose, since all that were ever saved, were saved through the power of this great plan of redemption, as much before the coming of Christ as since; if not, God has had different plans in operation (if we may so express it), to bring men back to dwell with Himself; and this we cannot believe, since there has been no change in the constitution of man since he fell" (*Teachings of the Prophet Joseph Smith*, 59–60).

Call upon God in the name of the Son forevermore. Each prayer offered in the name of Christ strengthens faith in the Only Begotten. By command we have been directed to pray only to the Father, doing so in the name of his Beloved Son.

The practice of the Saints and prophets of all ages was first given to Adam by the angel. They prayed to the Father in the name of his Only Begotten. Enoch prayed, "I ask thee, O Lord, in the name of thine Only Begotten, even Jesus Christ, that thou wilt have mercy upon Noah and his seed, that the earth might never more be covered by the floods" (Moses 7:50). The Lord said to Moses, "Call upon God in the name of mine Only Begotten" (Moses 1:17). The Nephite prophet Jacob declared, "We knew of Christ, and we had a hope of his glory many hundred years before his coming; and not only we ourselves had a hope of his glory, but also all the holy prophets which were before us. Behold, they believed in Christ and worshiped the Father in his name, and also we worship the Father in his name" (Jacob 4:4–5). All of the prophets worshiped the Father in the name of the Son.

Moses 5:9 *The Holy Ghost.* See commentary on Doctrine and Covenants 130:22–23.

Saying: I am the Only Begotten. This is a classic example of the principle of divine investiture of authority. Here, the Holy Ghost speaks in the first person for Christ. Similarly, in many instances Christ speaks in the first person for the Father (Moses 1:6).

Moses 5:10 *Adam blessed God.* For Adam to bless God means that he praised God and that he rejoiced in his goodness and mercy. "And in nothing doth man offend God, or against none is his wrath kindled, save those who confess not his hand in all things, and obey not his commandments" (D&C 59:21).

Because of my transgression. We do not properly speak of Adam's sin but of his transgression. The distinction being made is that sin represents willful disobedience. Adam broke a law and thus transgressed, but he did so to comply with a greater command of God. Adam is heir to the consequence of the broken law, but he is not guilty of sinful rebellion (Moses 6:53; Article of Faith 2).

In this life I shall have joy. Without a knowledge of good and evil there could be no happiness. If Adam and Eve had not fallen, explained Lehi, "they would have remained in a state of innocence, having no joy, for they knew no misery; doing no good, for they knew no sin" (2 Nephi 2:23).

Moses 5:11 Here Eve, a prophetess in her own right, utters one of the most perfect expressions of the plan of salvation ever uttered. Their transgression was necessary in order that they might have seed, know good from evil, be redeemed by Christ from their fallen state, and obtain eternal life, which is the privilege of all who are obedient to the laws and ordinances of the gospel.

We never should have had seed. If Adam and Eve had not partaken of the forbidden fruit they "would have had no children" (2 Nephi 2:23; Moses 6:48). Among the changes that the bodies of Adam and Eve experienced because of the Fall was the power to have children. Perhaps, as well as the blood of mortality forming in their bodies, something similar to hormonal changes enabled the bodies of Adam and Eve to produce seed. Immature children have blood, but they do not have the power to beget children.

Moses 5:13 *I am also a son of God.* Satan was born a spirit son of

God, yet through his rebellion he was cast out of heaven and lost all claim to a divine inheritance. He received the name *Perdition* and is no longer numbered among those who may bear the name of God, nor be known as one of his sons.

Believe it not. From the time that Adam was the first prophet and preacher of righteousness, Satan has sent false prophets and preachers to oppose the truth. The Prophet Joseph Smith said: "In relation to the kingdom of God, the devil always sets up his kingdom at the very same time in opposition to God" (*Teachings of the Prophet Joseph Smith,* 365). Here Satan told those of the children of Adam who would listen to him to not believe the things that their parents were teaching them. That same practice is as common in our day as it was at the time of our first parents.

They loved Satan more than God. They loved the things of the world more than the things of God.

Carnal, sensual, and devilish. Fleshly pursuits can never bring lasting happiness but rather lead to captivity according to "the captivity and power of the devil; for he seeketh that all men might be miserable like unto himself" (2 Nephi 2:27).

Cain and Abel Offer Sacrifice—Cain Rebels, Loves Satan More Than God, and Becomes Perdition
MOSES 5:16–41

Moses 5:16–21 The Prophet Joseph Smith gave inspired commentary on these verses: "By faith in this atonement or plan of redemption, Abel offered to God a sacrifice that was accepted, which was the firstlings of the flock. Cain offered of the fruit of the ground, and was not accepted, because he could not do it in faith, he could have no faith, or could not exercise faith contrary to the plan of heaven. It must be shedding the blood of the Only Begotten to atone for man; for this was the plan of redemption; and without the shedding of blood was no remission; and as the sacrifice was instituted for a type, by which man was to discern the great Sacrifice which God had prepared; to offer a sacrifice contrary to that, no faith could be exercised, because redemption was not purchased in that way, nor the power of atonement instituted after that order; consequently Cain could have no faith; and whatsoever is not of faith, is sin. But Abel offered an acceptable sacrifice, by which he obtained witness that he was righteous, God himself testifying of his gifts. Certainly, the shedding of the blood of a beast could be beneficial to no man, except it

228 REVELATIONS OF THE RESTORATION

was done in imitation, or as a type, or explanation of what was to be offered through the gift of God Himself; and this performance done with an eye looking forward in faith on the power of that great Sacrifice for a remission of sins.

"But however various may have been, and may be at the present time, the opinions of men respecting the conduct of Abel, and the knowledge which he had on the subject of atonement, it is evident in our minds, that he was instructed more fully in the plan than what the Bible speaks of, for how could he offer a sacrifice in faith, looking to God for a remission of his sins in the power of the great atonement, without having been previously instructed in that plan? And further, if he was accepted of God, what were the ordinances performed further than the offering of the firstlings of the flock?

"It is said by Paul in his letter to the Hebrew brethren, that Abel obtained witness that he was righteous, God testifying of his gifts. To whom did God testify of the gifts of Abel, was it to Paul? We have very little on this important subject in the forepart of the Bible. But it is said that Abel himself obtained witness that he was righteous. Then certainly God spoke to him: indeed, it is said that God talked with him; and if He did, would He not, seeing that Abel was righteous deliver to him the whole plan of the Gospel? And is not the Gospel the news of the redemption? How could Abel offer a sacrifice and look forward with faith on the Son of God for a remission of his sins, and not understand the Gospel? The mere shedding of the blood of beasts or offering anything else in sacrifice, could not procure a remission of sins, except it were performed in faith of something to come; if it could, Cain's offering must have been as good as Abel's. And if Abel was taught of the coming of the Son of God, was he not taught also of His ordinances? We all admit that the Gospel has ordinances, and if so, had it not always ordinances, and were not its ordinances always the same?" (*Teachings of the Prophet Joseph Smith*, 58–59).

Moses 5:21 *But unto Cain, and to his offering, he had not respect.* God does not accept offerings made in unrighteousness. "The power, glory and blessings of the Priesthood could not continue with those who received ordination only as their righteousness continued," explained the Prophet Joseph Smith; "for Cain also being authorized to offer sacrifice, but not offering it in righteousness, was cursed. It signifies, then, that the ordinances must be kept in the very way God has appointed; otherwise their

Priesthood will prove a cursing instead of a blessing" (*Teachings of the Prophet Joseph Smith*, 169).

Moses 5:23 *Thou shalt rule over him.* "All beings who have bodies," taught the Prophet Joseph Smith, "have power over those who have not" (*Teachings of the Prophet Joseph Smith*, 81). The Prophet further taught that "When those (spirits in the eternal world) have come into this world and received tabernacles, then died and again have risen and received glorified bodies, they will have an ascendancy over the spirits who have received no bodies, or kept not their first estate, like the devil" (*Teachings of the Prophet Joseph Smith*, 305–6). Therefore, following the last resurrection of those "who shall remain filthy still" (D&C 88:102), Cain, as well as others that become perdition, will have power over Lucifer, a personage of spirit only.

Moses 5:24 *Thou shalt be called Perdition; for thou wast also before the world.* Referring to Cain's choice to keep his first estate, Elder Bruce R. McConkie explained: "That son of Adam, though a friend of Lucifer in pre-existence, did manage to gain mortal birth. He could have hearkened to his Father Adam and walked in the strait and narrow path. But instead he chose to follow a course which he had already charted, in a very real sense, in his first estate, an estate where he had been known as perdition. Coming from this background, Cain elected to use his agency to fight the truth in this life, and in his case he became a son of perdition" (*Doctrinal New Testament Commentary*, 1:715). See commentary on Doctrine and Covenants 76:26, 35.

Moses 5:25 *He rejected the greater counsel which was had from God.* Cain's status was such that he enjoyed personal conversation with the Lord. No one in earth's history has received a more direct call to repentance than that which was given to Cain, for it had been his privilege to walk and talk with God. The Lord revealed that "he who sins against the greater light shall receive the greater condemnation" (D&C 82:3). Thus, in consequence of Cain's love for Satan and rejection of the counsel given him by God, his punishment was meted out of equal nature. See commentary on Moses 5:38.

A cursing which I will put upon thee, except thou repent. In the improper offering he made, Cain had abused both the priesthood and the knowledge that was his. Of necessity he must repent or be cursed—which cursing would result in the loss of both the knowledge of God that was his and the right to approach him in sacrifice or to perform any priesthood function.

230 REVELATIONS OF THE RESTORATION

Moses 5:26 *Abel, . . . who walked in holiness before the Lord.* "If, then Abel was a righteous man he had to become so by keeping the commandments," wrote the Prophet Joseph Smith (*Times and Seasons,* 3:905). Abel "received the priesthood by the commandments of God, by the hand of his father Adam" (D&C 84:16). The Prophet taught that Abel "magnified the Priesthood which was conferred upon him, and died a righteous man, and therefore has become an angel of God by receiving his body from the dead, holding still the keys of his dispensation; and was sent down from heaven unto Paul to minister consoling words, and to commit unto him a knowledge of the mysteries of godliness" (*Teachings of the Prophet Joseph Smith,* 169). In killing Abel, Cain was killing the Lord's anointed.

Moses 5:31 *Cain was called Master Mahan.* The name *Mahan* means master of a great secret. Lucifer had been the "Mahan" or master of the secret that one might murder for gain in mortality. He taught this secret to Cain as part of the oath that he made with him (v. 30). In gaining power over Satan (v. 23) by killing his brother, Cain became the master of him who had mastery over all evil.

Moses 5:32 *Cain rose up against Abel, his brother, and slew him.* President George Q. Cannon explained: "The power of Satan from the beginning of time until the present has been directed against the Priesthood of the Son of God. Every effort of his has been for the destruction of that Priesthood or the weakening of its influence. He has not only sought to weaken the influence of the servants of God, but he has sought to take their lives. Hence the Savior said concerning him, that he was a murderer and a liar from the beginning. That has been his spirit" (*Collected Discourses,* 4:398).

Moses 5:33 *I am free.* In so saying, Cain illustrates the kind of dark distortion that is always associated with evil. Cain, who had known no bondage, will now never be without it. His sentence will be that of a fugitive and a vagabond, one who will never again know peace and happiness (v. 37). Repentance is beyond his reach, and he has forfeited all gospel blessings.

Moses 5:38 *My punishment is greater than I can bear.* Rather than being a recipient of Satan's promised freedom, Cain found himself in eternal bondage. See commentary on Moses 5:24.

Moses 5:39 *From thy face shall I be hid.* Cain chose a course that turned the blessings he had received into a cursing. He would now lose the authority or priesthood that had been his. No longer would Cain be able to stand in the presence of God as he had previously done (vv. 22–24). Those blessings promised him and his posterity through him were now lost. Of those who pursue such a course in our dispensation the Lord said, "They shall not have right to the priesthood, nor their posterity after them from generation to generation" (D&C 121:21).

Moses 5:40 *I the Lord set a mark upon Cain.* The mark, which we understand to be a black skin, was not a curse but was placed on Cain at his request for his own protection.

Murder and Wickedness Spread
MOSES 5:42–55

Moses 5:42–55 The descendants and followers of Cain continued the wickedness associated with secret conspiracies, murdering for gain.

Moses 5:50 *He slew him for the oath's sake.* In order to keep their wicked works of darkness hidden, those belonging to the secret combination swore oaths of secrecy. When Irad, the grandson of Cain, revealed the secrets to the sons of Adam, he broke his oath. The oath was originally revealed to Cain by Satan: "Swear unto me by thy throat, and if thou tell it thou shalt die; and swear thy brethren by their heads, and by the living God, that they tell it not; for if they tell it, they shall surely die" (Moses 5:29). Therefore, Irad was killed for the "oath's sake."

The Gospel Preached from the Beginning
MOSES 5:56–59

Moses 5:58 *The Gospel . . . preached, from the beginning.* All true religion is revealed religion. In all ages and in all dispensations in which the gospel has been taught, it has been taught by angels, by the voice of God—meaning revelation that is immediate and personal to those of that day—and by the Holy Ghost.

Moses 5:59 *An holy ordinance.* The holy ordinance to which reference is made was animal sacrifice. As the previous chapter ended, we were told that God taught that law to Adam and Eve while they were yet in Eden. We also learned that he clothed them in "coats of skins" (D&C 4:27), which were to act as a garment of protection, protecting them from all of the effects of the Fall—that is, through the blood of the Lamb, meaning the Atonement of Christ, all the effects of the Fall would be rectified.

This is followed by the story of Abel offering an acceptable sacrifice and thus gaining the approval of God, while his brother, Cain, refused to conform to the order of God and deliberately offered an unacceptable sacrifice. Angered at the Lord's rejection of his sacrifice and now having entered into league with Satan, he killed his brother, Abel. As a consequence he lost the spiritual privileges that were his, chief among which was the right to come unto the presence of the Lord. As the story continues into the next chapter, we read that God gave another son to Adam and Eve—Seth, to whom he revealed himself because Seth offered an acceptable sacrifice. From all of this we can but conclude that the holy ordinance, through which all the promises made by the Lord to those of that ancient day were confirmed, was that law that promised them redemption in and through the blood of the Lamb.

DOCTRINE AND COVENANTS 29

DATE: SEPTEMBER 1830
PLACE: FAYETTE, NEW YORK

"In these early days of the Church the Lord revealed to the Prophet for the benefit of the members, line upon line and precept upon precept, thus unfolding to them the great truths of the Gospel. This revelation was given a few days before the conference of September 26, 1830, and in anticipation of that gathering. The Lord had commanded Oliver Cowdery to tarry (Sec. 28:10) until after this conference should be held, before departing on his mission to the Lamanites. The wonderful doctrines explained in this revelation were of such importance that it was well for Oliver and his companions to know them, that they might teach the people on their way, and to the Lamanites when they arrived at their destination, with a more complete comprehension of the plan of Salvation than they otherwise would have had" (Smith, *Church History and Modern Revelation*, 1:139–40).

The Gathering of the Elect

29:1 *Jesus Christ, your Redeemer, the Great I AM.* Here Jesus Christ declares himself to be both our Redeemer and the same God who appeared to Moses on Sinai. The title "I AM" is derived from the third person singular form of the Hebrew verb "to be" and is transliterated by four letters YHWH. When directly translated, YHWH means "he is" or "he exists." Therefore, the very use of the title "I AM" affirms faith in the existence of God. The tetragrammaton YHWH was probably pronounced Yahweh. Later renditions of the name of God included attempts to pronounce the name of God from these letters. King James translators used the anglicized name Jehovah, but most often preferred to use the title LORD (with capital letters) to indicate where the biblical text contained YHWH, the name of Deity.

When Christ appeared to Moses on Mt. Sinai, he used the title

"I AM" to identify himself as the God of the ancient patriarchs. "And Moses said unto God, Behold, *when* I come unto the children of Israel, and shall say unto them, The God of your fathers hath sent me unto you; and they shall say to me, What *is* his name? what shall I say unto them? And God said unto Moses, I AM THAT I AM: and he said, Thus shalt thou say unto the children of Israel, I AM hath sent me unto you. And God said moreover unto Moses, Thus shalt thou say unto the children of Israel, The LORD [YWHW] God of your fathers, the God of Abraham, the God of Isaac, and the God of Jacob, hath sent me unto you: this is my name for ever, and this is my memorial unto all generations" (Exodus 3:13–15).

29:5 *Your advocate with the Father.* See commentary on Doctrine and Covenants 45:3.

29:7 *Mine elect.* Many noble and great spirits were in mortality as the Restoration unfolded (Abraham 3:22–23; D&C 138:53–55). They were elected, or, in other words, foreordained by God, to be born in the lineage of Abraham. Bible and Book of Mormon prophets both spoke of the great and marvelous work that would take place in the last days that would result in the gathering of the elect in fulfillment of the covenants that God had made with their ancient fathers. Having proven themselves valiant in the cause of the Lord in premortality, they brought to earth the characteristics that distinguished them as faithful in that sphere. They are among those whom the Savior identified as his sheep who, he said, would know his voice (John 10:27).

29:8 *Gathered in unto one place.* See commentary on Doctrine and Covenants 57:1–3; 101:21–22; 115:5–6.

Destruction of the Wicked Will Precede the Millennium
DOCTRINE AND COVENANTS 29:9–21

29:9 The destruction of the wicked at the end of the world is a theme that prevailed in the Restoration beginning with the instructions of Moroni to the youthful Joseph Smith. See commentary on Joseph Smith–History 1:37, page 23.

29:12 Isaiah prophesied of the time when Christ the "king shall reign in righteousness, and princes shall rule in judgment" (Isaiah 32:1). Likewise, Daniel saw the day in which all other "thrones were cast down, and the Ancient of days did sit, . . . the judgment was set, and the books were opened" (Daniel 7:9–10; Revelation 20:4). Commenting on these verses, Elder Bruce R. McConkie wrote: "Thrones are cast down: the kingdoms of this world cease; it is the day when the Lord makes a full end of all nations. He alone shall be exalted in that day. The Ancient of Days, the oldest and most ancient of men, Adam our father, sits in judgment over the righteous of his race. Be it remembered that the Twelve Apostles of the Lamb, who were with the Lord in his ministry in Jerusalem, shall judge the whole house of Israel, meaning that portion of Israel who have kept the commandments, 'and none else' (D&C 29:12). There will be a great hierarchy of judges in that great day, of whom Adam, under Christ, will be the chief of all. Those judges will judge the righteous ones under their jurisdiction, but Christ himself, he alone, will judge the wicked" (*Millennial Messiah*, 584).

The second coming of the Savior also inaugurates the time of judgment for the righteous. It will be presided over by Adam, the Ancient of days. The meridian Twelve will judge the house of Israel under his direction. During his mortal ministry, the Savior told the Twelve in Jerusalem that when he came again, he would "sit in the throne of his glory," and he identified them as the princes mentioned by Isaiah who would "sit upon twelve thrones, judging the twelve tribes of Israel" (Matthew 19:28). While in the Americas, the resurrected Lord instructed the Nephite Twelve that they would judge their people. Further, he explained that the Nephite Twelve, as a remnant of the House of Israel, would be judged of the Twelve Apostles at Jerusalem and that they in turn would judge their people (1 Nephi 12:9; Mormon 3:17–19).

During the millennial day the kingdom of heaven will become one with the kingdom of God on earth (D&C 65:5–6), and the Saints will reign with the Savior. The governing princes and judges of the kingdom will be under the direction of the holy priesthood. Many will preside in righteousness during that time. The original Twelve will preside over the whole house of Israel under the direction of Adam, who will act under the direction of Christ (D&C 78:16).

Clothed with robes of righteousness, with crowns upon their heads. Those who are exalted in celestial glory receive robes and crowns, even as the Savior Jesus Christ, to rule and reign with him in eternity as a royal priesthood.

29:14 These signs that the Second Coming is near are to take place immediately after the destruction of the wicked and the desolation of abomination in Jerusalem. See Joseph Smith–Matthew 1:31–32, 33, page 349.

29:16 *A great hailstorm.* Apparently, this will be one of several hailstorms sent by the Lord to call his children to repentance (D&C 43:25).

Isaiah prophesied of hail that would bring the proud and wicked low prior to the time of peace and righteousness (Isaiah 32:15–19). In addition, Ezekiel spoke of the destruction of the armies of Gog by "overflowing rain, and great hailstones, fire, and brimstone" (Ezekiel 38:22) in the latter-day war against the people of Israel. The apostle John saw in vision that at the opening of the seventh seal and after the testimony of thunderings, lightnings, and earthquakes, "there followed hail and fire mingled with blood" (Revelation 8:7), which destroyed a third part of both trees and grass. Further, John saw a time when "there fell upon men a great hail out of heaven, *every stone* about the weight of a talent: and men blasphemed God because of the plague of the hail; for the plague thereof was exceeding great" (Revelation 16:21). This hailstorm, which will destroy the crops of the earth, as with all of the predicted natural disasters, will come as vengeance upon the wicked.

29:17 *The cup of mine indignation is full.* The symbolism is a graphic means of portraying the destruction of the wicked. It is the same as shown in the apocalyptic vision given to the apostle John recorded in the book of Revelation in which plagues filled cups to the brim and were poured out upon the inhabitants of the earth.

29:19 *Their flesh shall fall from off their bones, and their eyes from their sockets.* The prophet Zechariah placed the fulfillment of this plague at a time when all nations will have gathered to battle against Jerusalem. "Then shall the Lord go forth, and fight against those nations. . . . And this shall be the plague wherewith the Lord will smite all the people that have fought against Jerusalem; Their flesh shall consume away while they stand upon their feet, and their eyes shall consume away in their holes, and their tongue shall consume away in their mouth" (Zechariah 14:3, 12).

29:21 *Abominations shall not reign.* Regarding the scene portrayed in these verses, Wilford Woodruff declared, "No man can contemplate the truth concerning the nations of the earth without sorrow, when he sees the wailing, the mourning, and death, that will come in consequence of judgments, plagues, and war. It has already begun, and it will continue to multiply and increase until the scene is ended, and wound up.

"Do I delight in the destruction of the children of men? No. Does the Lord? No. He gives them timely warning, and if they do not listen to His counsel, they must suffer the consequences" (*Journal of Discourses*, 2:201).

The Last Resurrection and Final Judgment Follow the Millennium

DOCTRINE AND COVENANTS 29:22–29

29:22 *Men again begin to deny their God.* At the end of the Millennium those who are sons of perdition will again defy the power of God. That is, those individuals who were overcome by Lucifer while in mortality will stand upon the earth in the flesh as resurrected beings for a short season (D&C 88:32). They will oppose Christ's right to rule and reign. They will seek to place Lucifer in his stead. "The devil and his armies shall be cast away into their own place, that they shall not have power over the saints any more at all. For Michael shall fight their battles, and shall overcome him who seeketh the throne of him who sitteth upon the throne, even the Lamb" (D&C 88:114–15).

29:23 *A new heaven.* "This earth will be rolled back into the presence of God," declared the Prophet Joseph Smith, "and crowned with celestial glory" (*Teachings of the Prophet Joseph Smith*, 181). Brigham Young taught that the earth will move through space to "return again unto the presence of the Father" (*Journal of Discourses*, 17:143). Thus, the heavens will literally become new for those who inhabit the earth as celestial beings.

A new earth. Following the Millennium the earth will "be prepared for the celestial glory; For after it hath filled the measure of its creation, it shall be crowned with glory, even with the presence of God the Father; that bodies who are of the celestial kingdom may possess it forever and ever" (D&C 88:18–20). Further, the Prophet Joseph Smith taught that "this earth, in its sanctified and immortal state, will be made like unto crystal and will be a Urim and Thummim to the inhabitants who dwell thereon" (D&C 130:9).

29:24 *Beasts, the fowls of the air, and the fishes of the sea.* Regarding the salvation of beasts, fowls, and fishes, the Prophet Joseph Smith taught that those that fill the measure of their creation are resurrected and dwell in the celestial kingdom. See commentary on Doctrine and Covenants 77:2.

29:26 *Michael, mine archangel, shall sound his trump.* Michael is Adam, the first man (D&C 27:11). He is chief among God's sons and has been given "the keys of salvation under the counsel and direction of the Holy One" (D&C 78:16), who is Jesus Christ. The sounding of Michael's trump is to announce the resurrection of the dead. The Son of God loosed the bands of death for all through his atoning sacrifice and resurrection.

The prophet Daniel associated Adam with the time of the resurrection of his people (Daniel 12:1–2). Thus, it appears that the trump with which Adam announces the resurrection from the dead also signifies keys that Adam possesses in directing the resurrection. It is altogether appropriate that Adam, who imposed death upon all of his posterity, be the one to call them forth from their graves.

Concepts from the Translation of the Bible Explained: All Things Are Spiritual unto the Lord
DOCTRINE AND COVENANTS 29:30–35

29:30–35 This revelation was given to clarify concepts revealed to the Prophet in his labor in translating the Bible. These verses and those that follow speak of the premortal existence, the creation of the earth, the fall of Adam, and the preaching of the plan of redemption during the first dispensation of the gospel.

29:30 *The first shall be last.* The state of the body in the first creation of man upon the earth will also be the state of the body in the last creation. That is, both will be immortal. True mortality will reign for a season and temporal death shall make its demands on all of God's creations upon this earth. Yet because Adam was created in a spiritual state (meaning one in which there was no death), so shall the resurrection bring to pass a similar state. Thus, the first state of man will also be the last. See commentary on Doctrine and Covenants 29:32.

I have created by the word of my power. The word of the Father's power is his Son, Jesus Christ. The word of the Son's power is his Spirit, the light of Christ. The words and power of Christ are those of the Father. The Father and the Son are one in their creative endeavors. Concerning his creations, the Lord explained, "And by the word of my power, have I created them, which is mine Only begotten Son, who is full of grace and truth. And worlds without number have I created; and I also created them for mine own purpose; and by the Son I created them, which is mine Only Begotten" (Moses 1:32–33). Excepting the birth of spirits, all the labor of creation is done by Christ under the direction of the Father.

Which is the power of my Spirit. The power by which the worlds were and are made is the light of Christ. Likewise, it is by that same power that the moon and stars have their existence. As our revelations read, "This is the light of Christ. As also he is in the sun, and the light of the sun, and the power thereof by which it was made" (D&C 88:7).

29:31 *Both spiritual and temporal.* Spiritual creation refers to the physical creation of Adam and Eve in an immortal state. That is, they could not die until after they partook of the fruit of the tree of knowledge of good and evil, which caused the Fall and introduced corruption into their bodies. After the Fall their bodies were temporal, or in other words they were in a temporary state. The Lord declared, "I . . . created all things . . . spiritually before they were naturally upon the face of the earth" (Moses 3:5).

29:32 *First temporal, and secondly spiritual.* The temporal, or mortal life upon the earth that will end in death, precedes life that is spiritual, or the resurrected state. In both instances, before the Fall and after the Resurrection, "spiritual bodies" are bodies that are not subject to death or corruption. Speaking of the body placed in a grave and its subsequent resurrection, the apostle Paul explained, "It is sown a natural body; it is raised a spiritual body" (1 Corinthians 15:44).

Which is the last of my work. The phrase "last of my work" has reference to the Resurrection, which is the completion of the Lord's work, his crowning achievement.

29:33 *My works have no end, neither beginning.* All of God's creations are eternal. The Lord revealed to Moses, "for my works are without end, and also my words, for they never cease" (Moses 1:4). Similarly, they did not begin with their mortal creation, but existed before this earth was created. The Prophet Joseph Smith further explained: "Element had an existence from the time [God] had. The pure principles of element are principles which can never be destroyed; they may be organized and reorganized, but not destroyed. They had no beginning, and can have no end" (*Teachings of the Prophet Joseph Smith*, 351–52). God's eternal work is to create and "to bring to pass the immortality and eternal life" (Moses 1:39) of his creations.

29:34 *Not at any time have I given unto you a law which was temporal.* That which is "temporal" is limited by time; it is temporary. The laws of God are eternal. They are everlastingly the same. It could also be observed that because every action has its consequence, there is nothing we do that does not affect who and what we are, which in turn determines who and what we will be in the worlds to come. See commentary on Doctrine and Covenants 29:41.

Jedediah M. Grant explained the eternal nature of laws and the power which governs those laws: "If Joseph had a right to dictate me in relation to salvation, in relation to a hereafter, he had a right to dictate me in relation to all my earthly affairs, in relation to the treasures of the earth, and in relation to the earth itself. He had a right to dictate in relation to the cities of the earth, to the natives of the earth, and in relation to everything on land and on sea. That is what he had a right to do, if he had any right at all. If he did not have that right, he did not have the Priesthood of God, he did not have the endless Priesthood that emanates from an eternal being. A priesthood that is clipped, and lacks length, is not the Priesthood of God; if it lacks depth, it is not the Priesthood of God; for the Priesthood in ancient times extended over the wide world, and coped with the universe, and had a right to govern and control the inhabitants thereof, to regulate them, give them laws, and execute those laws. That power looked like the Priesthood of God. This same Priesthood has been given to Joseph Smith, and has been handed down to his successors" (*Journal of Discourses*, 2:13–14).

29:35 *An agent unto himself.* See commentary on verse 39.

The Devil and His Hosts Were Cast Out of Heaven to Tempt Man
DOCTRINE AND COVENANTS 29:36–39

29:36 *He rebelled against me, saying, Give me thine honor, which is my power.* It is in the Joseph Smith translation that we find the earliest references to the rebellion of Lucifer in the councils of heaven. From it we learn that in the premortal life Satan came before the Father, "saying— Behold, here am I, send me, I will be thy son, and I will redeem all mankind, that one soul shall not be lost, and surely I will do it; wherefore give me thine honor" (Moses 4:1).

Thus, Lucifer "sought to destroy the agency of man" and "became Satan, yea, even the devil, the father of all lies, to deceive and to blind men, and to lead them captive at his will" (Moses 4:3–4). The Lord reiterated in this revelation to Joseph Smith that he gave unto man "that he should be an agent unto himself" (D&C 29:35). By deception Lucifer used that very agency to induce others to follow him until they lost their right of choice and the light that could enable them to seek repentance and forgiveness. Those who followed Lucifer made him their father in place of the true Father of their spirits and gave honor to the usurper of the true God. See commentary on Moses 4:1, page 217; Doctrine and Covenants 76:25.

Also a third part of the hosts of heaven. These are the spirits who followed Lucifer in the premortal sphere. They came out in open rebellion against God and his Only Begotten Son. As Lucifer is called perdition, they are the sons of perdition. They receive the same punishment as did the devil himself. That is, they will never obtain a physical body and thus will not be resurrected. They are referred to as "devils, angels to a devil, to be shut out from the presence of our God, and to remain with the father of lies, in misery, like unto himself" (2 Nephi 9:9).

Because of their agency. See commentary on Doctrine and Covenants 58:28.

29:39 *It must needs be that the devil should tempt the children of men.* Like Adam and Eve before the Fall, all humanity are "in their infant state, innocent before God" (D&C 93:38). They know neither good nor evil. In a world in which both good and evil exist, God commands that we be righteous. By persuading men to do evil Satan presents opposition to the plan of God. Thus, the children of men become agents to choose of their own free will who they will follow, God or the devil.

Agents unto themselves. Agency is the gift of God. For agency to exist there must be laws, knowledge of the laws, freedom of choice in living the laws, and consequences appended to our actions.

We are given the responsibility to determine for whom and for what we will be agents. "For behold, ye are free; ye are permitted to act for yourselves; for behold, God hath given unto you a knowledge and he hath made you free. He hath given unto you that ye might know good from evil, and he hath given unto you that ye might choose life or death; and ye can do good and be restored unto that which is good, or have that which is good restored unto you; or ye can do evil, and have that which is evil restored unto you" (Helaman 14:30–31). The devil, through his tempting, heightens our awareness of the decision that must be made; will we "do all things whatsoever the Lord [our] God shall command" us? (Abraham 3:25; 2 Nephi 2:11–16). See commentary on Doctrine and Covenants 58:28.

Concepts from the Translation of the Bible Explained: Spiritual Death
DOCTRINE AND COVENANTS 29:40–45

29:40 *The devil tempted Adam, and he partook of the forbidden fruit.* See commentary on Moses 4:5–25, page 219.

29:41 *Because of his transgression.* See commentary on Moses 5:10, page 226.

The first death, even that same death which is the last death. God warned

Adam and Eve that if they partook of the forbidden fruit they would die. However, the death of the body was not the first death. The first death to come upon them was a "spiritual death" in which they were cast out of the presence of God. Later they also suffered a temporal or physical death in which their temporal bodies returned to the dust of the earth. Through the resurrection of Jesus Christ all mankind will be redeemed and brought back into the presence of God to be judged (Alma 42:23; Helaman 14:17). For the wicked "there cometh upon them again a spiritual death, yea, a second death, for they are cut off again as to things pertaining to righteousness" (Helaman 14:18) and are cast out of God's presence. Thus, the first death that came upon mankind will also be the last death to come upon the wicked.

29:42 *Send forth angels to declare unto them repentance and redemption.* See Moses 6:58.

29:43 *Appoint unto man the days of his probation.* Alma explained that "there was a space granted unto man in which he might repent; therefore this life became a probationary state; a time to prepare to meet God; a time to prepare for that endless state . . . which is after the resurrection of the dead" (Alma 12:24).

29:45 *They receive their wages of whom they list to obey.* See commentary on Moses 5:23, page 229.

Little Children Are Redeemed through the Atonement
DOCTRINE AND COVENANTS 29:46–50

29:47 *They cannot sin.* Little children are innocent because they do not comprehend the difference between good and evil. Lucifer cannot entice any soul to sin who does not comprehend good and evil. Thus, they are not accountable to God for their actions. Laws that might be transgressed or broken by little children are atoned for by Jesus Christ. If little children die "before they arrive at the years of accountability, [they] are saved in the celestial kingdom of heaven" (D&C 137:10).

Begin to become accountable before me. Becoming accountable is a process. Considerable accountability must be obtained a measurable time before baptism at eight years of age. The process then continues as the child grows to adulthood.

29:48 *That great things may be required at the hand of their fathers.* See Doctrine and Covenants 68:25–29.

29:50 *He that hath no understanding.* Speaking of those who are mentally disabled, President Joseph Fielding Smith explained: "[They] shall receive blessings just like little children who die in infancy. They are free from sin, because their minds are not capable of a correct understanding of right and wrong. Mormon, when writing to his son Moroni on the subject of baptism places deficient children in the same category with little children who are under the age of accountability, they do not require baptism, for the atonement of Jesus Christ takes care of them equally with little children who die before the age of accountability" (*Answers*, 3:20).

DOCTRINE AND COVENANTS 30

DATE: SEPTEMBER 1830
PLACE: FAYETTE, NEW YORK

Section 30 is a combination of three revelations received following a three-day conference of the Church. Among other things, the concern over false revelations received by Hiram Page through his "peep-stone" was resolved during the conference (D&C 28:11–13). The Prophet Joseph Smith wrote: "At length our conference assembled. The subject of the stone previously mentioned was discussed, and after considerable investigation, Brother Page, as well as the whole Church who were present, renounced the said stone, and all things connected therewith, much to our mutual satisfaction and happiness. We now partook of the Sacrament, confirmed and ordained many, and attended to a great variety of Church business on the first and the two following days of the conference, during which time we had much of the power of God manifested amongst us; the Holy Ghost came upon us, and filled us with joy unspeakable; and peace, and faith, and hope, and charity abounded in our midst. Before we separated we received the following . . ." (*History of the Church*, 1:115). See introduction to Doctrine and Covenants 28.

David Whitmer Is Chastened

DOCTRINE AND COVENANTS 30:1–4

30:1 *Feared man and have not relied on me.* The Prophet and his wife, Emma, were dependent on David and Julia Whitmer for lodgings when this revelation was received. For him to give the revelation to the Whitmers, which he did without hesitation, evidences that his trust was in God, not man. David Whitmer, on the other hand, had chosen to support his brother-in-law, Hiram Page, in the use of his peepstone in order to maintain peace in the family.

30:2 *You have not given heed unto my Spirit, and to those who were set over you.* The seeds of David Whitmer's disaffection with the Prophet and the Church were sown very early. It appears that, with the exception of the Book of Mormon, he struggled with everything that came by revelation through Joseph Smith. His loyalty to the revelations received by his brother-in-law through his peepstone, in this instance, over that which had been revealed to the Prophet was but the foreshadowing of future difficulties he would have with revelations received by the Prophet. In future years we find him arguing that Joseph Smith originally taught that the Bible and the Book of Mormon contained "God's law in its completeness." He considered the Doctrine and Covenants unnecessary as its revelations were "purely personal." He categorically denied the coming of John the Baptist to restore the Aaronic Priesthood and the coming of Peter, James, and John to restore the higher priesthood. Similarly, he denied the coming of Moses, Elias, and Elijah in the Kirtland Temple (Cook, *David Whitmer Interviews*, xviii-xx).

30:3 *You are left to inquire for yourself at my hand.* The meaning here is that since you will not accept that which I have given through the Prophet, you will be left to that which you yourself can obtain from me.

Peter Whitmer Is Called As Oliver Cowdery's Companion on a Mission to the Lamanites
DOCTRINE AND COVENANTS 30:5–8

30:5 *Take your journey with your brother Oliver.* See commentary on Doctrine and Covenants 28:8.

30:7 *None have I appointed to be his counselor over him in the church.* Oliver Cowdery jointly held all the keys of the kingdom with Joseph Smith. When the Church was organized, he was sustained as the second elder or the second leading officer in the Church. See commentary on Doctrine and Covenants 20:2.

Concerning church matters. This clarification of the extent of Joseph Smith's and Oliver Cowdery's authority to give direction to the Saints was not included in the 1833 Book of Commandments but was added in the 1835 edition of the Doctrine and Covenants. It was not intended that officers in the priesthood or in the Church be responsible to give direction outside their sphere of authority. See commentary on Doctrine and Covenants 29:34.

John Whitmer Called to Preach the Gospel
DOCTRINE AND COVENANTS 30:9–11

30:10 *At your brother Philip Burroughs'*. Philip Burroughs was a farmer who lived in Fayette, New York. Thus, John Whitmer was called to serve at the house of a neighbor utilizing the Burroughs's home as the place where meetings were held. Earlier in the month, on 5 September 1830, Parley P. Pratt preached to a large audience at the Burroughs's home. He wrote, "On the next Sabbath I preached to a large concourse of people, assembled at the house of a Mr. Burroughs. The Holy Ghost came upon me mightily. I spoke the word of God with power, reasoning out of the Scriptures and the Book of Mormon. The people were convinced, overwhelmed in tears, and four heads of families came forward expressing their faith, and were baptized" (Pratt, *Autobiography*, 27).

DOCTRINE AND COVENANTS 31

DATE: SEPTEMBER 1830
PLACE: FAYETTE, NEW YORK

This is the last of the four revelations given by the Prophet in September of 1830 while in Fayette, New York, where the first conference of the Church had been held. The revelation was given to Thomas B. Marsh, who with his wife was converted to the Church by the Book of Mormon. This revelation announces how we as a people are to present our message to the world. Though it is a common practice among members of the Church to seek common ground with those who profess faith in Christ by an appeal to the Bible, the direction given in this revelation is that we declare the things that have been revealed through the Prophet Joseph Smith. The message of the Restoration centers on the idea that it is not common ground we seek in sharing the gospel. There is nothing common about our message. The way we answer questions about our faith ought to be by finding the quickest and most direct route to the Sacred Grove. That is our ground. It is sacred ground. It is where testimonies are born and the greatest truths of heaven are unveiled.

We claim no priesthood, keys, power, authority, or doctrines that do not trace themselves directly to heaven. We have not built upon the theological rubble of the past. All that we have, and this includes our faith in the Bible and our understanding of it, has come to us by direct revelation in this dispensation. Doctrines from any other source are without authority among the Latter-day Saints. All doctrine and authority must come through the channels the Lord has ordained for our dispensation, and that channel is the priesthood and keys restored to the Prophet Joseph Smith.

Blessing and Assurances Given to Thomas B. Marsh
DOCTRINE AND COVENANTS 31:1–8

31:1 *Because of your faith in my work.* Thomas Marsh was a man of spiritual sensitivity. He followed the promptings of the Spirit as he traveled from Boston, Massachusetts, where he worked in a type foundry, to northwestern New York. He later wrote, "I believed the Spirit of God dictated me to make a journey west. I started in company with one Benjamin Hall, who was also led by the Spirit. I went to Lima, Livingston county, New York, where I staid [stayed] some three months, and then left for home. I called on my return at Lyonstown, on a family, whose names I do not recollect. On leaving there next morning the lady enquired if I had heard of the Golden Book found by a youth named Joseph Smith. I informed her I never heard anything about it, and became very anxious to know concerning the matter. On enquiring, she told me I could learn more about it from Martin Harris, in Palmyra.

"I returned back westward and found Martin Harris at the printing office, in Palmyra, where the first sixteen pages of the Book of Mormon had just been struck off, the proof sheet of which I obtained from the printer and took with me. As soon as Martin Harris found out my intentions he took me to the house of Joseph Smith, sen., where Joseph Smith, jun. resided, who could give me any information I might wish. Here I found Oliver Cowdery, who gave me all the information concerning the book I desired. After staying there two days I started for Charleston, Mass., highly pleased with the information I had obtained concerning the new found book.

"After arriving home and finding my family all well, I showed my wife the sixteen pages of the Book of Mormon which I had obtained, with which she was well pleased, believing it to be the work of God. From this time for about one year I corresponded with Oliver Cowdery and Joseph Smith, jun., and prepared myself to move west.

"Learning by letter that the Church of Jesus Christ had been organized on the 6th day of April, 1830, I moved to Palmyra, Ontario co., in September following, and landed at the house of Joseph Smith, sen., with my whole family. During the month [on 3 September 1830] I was baptized by David Whitmer, in Cayuga lake, and in a few days I was ordained an Elder by Oliver Cowdery with six Elders, at Father Whitmer's house" (*Millennial Star*, 26:375; spelling as in original).

31:2 *The day cometh that they will believe and know the truth.* Sister Marsh believed in the work of the Restoration when her husband first brought home the printer's proof sheet of the Book of Mormon. Their children were young at this time, being nine, seven, and three years of age. The particular challenge they had faced is unknown.

31:3 *Your tongue shall be loosed.* Hyrum M. Smith and Janne M.

Sjodahl noted: "As long as Thomas B. Marsh was faithful he was an elo-
quent speaker. At the time of the troubles in Clay County, Mo., he was
elected a member of a committee to lay the grievances of the Saints
before the authorities of the State. On that occasion he spoke so impres-
sively that General Atchison, who was present, shed tears, and the meeting passed resolutions to assist the Saints in finding a new location"
(*Doctrine and Covenants Commentary*, 165).

You shall declare glad tidings of great joy unto this generation. Just as the
angelic announcement to the shepherds of the Savior's birth was a declaration of "good tidings of great joy" (Luke 2:10), so the proclamation that
the Lord has restored the fulness of the gospel in these latter days is a declaration of "glad tidings." Significantly, the restoration of the gospel in
this dispensation heralds the second coming of Christ and his millennial
reign. Those called to go forth and declare the gospel go forth to declare
"good tidings of great joy" as did their ancient counterparts. "Now, what
do we hear in the gospel which we have received? A voice of gladness! A
voice of mercy from heaven; and a voice of truth out of the earth; glad
tidings for the dead; a voice of gladness for the living and the dead; glad
tidings of great joy. How beautiful upon the mountains are the feet of
those that bring glad tidings of good things, and that say unto Zion:
Behold, thy God reigneth!" (D&C 128:19).

31:4 *Declare the things which have been revealed to my servant, Joseph
Smith, Jun.* Our charge, as given here to Thomas B. Marsh, is to declare
the truths revealed in our day, not just the truths revealed in ages past. As
we go forth as missionaries, we have been commanded to teach from the
Book of Mormon and the Doctrine and Covenants rather than from that
which was revealed to Isaiah, Jeremiah, Peter, or Paul.

The field which is white already to be burned. In previous revelations the
field has also been referred to as being white, but in those revelations it
was an indication that it was ready for harvest not destruction (D&C 4:4;
6:3; 11:3; 12:3, 14:3). The Lord explained that the kingdom of God is
going forth upon the face of the earth to harvest the honest in heart and
those "who are ready to receive the fulness of my gospel" (D&C 35:12).
The Lord also announced that the world is ripening in iniquity and is
ready for the destruction of the wicked. Before the field is burned, the
wheat, or the righteous, must be harvested. The Lord revealed that "this
Gospel of the Kingdom shall be preached in all the world, for a witness
unto all nations, and then shall the end come, or the destruction of the
wicked" (Joseph Smith–Matthew 1:31).

Counsel and Warnings Given to Thomas B. Marsh
DOCTRINE AND COVENANTS 31:9–13

31:9 *Revile not against those that revile.* To revile is to do that which is vile; that is, it is to speak to or about someone with abusive language. Obviously, such behavior is offensive to the Spirit of the Lord. We can never fight the adversary with the spirit of the adversary, for to do so is to give him the victory (Jude 1:9).

Govern your house in meekness, and be steadfast. Because he failed to heed this warning, Thomas B. Marsh lost his faith and experienced great difficulties in his family. See commentary on Doctrine and Covenants 112:10, 15.

DOCTRINE AND COVENANTS 32

DATE: OCTOBER 1830
PLACE: PROBABLY MANCHESTER, NEW YORK

This revelation given to Parley P. Pratt and Ziba Peterson addressed their desires to preach the gospel to the Lamanites. On 26 September 1830 Oliver Cowdery was called to declare the gospel to the Native Americans, who had been identified as descendants of Book of Mormon peoples. A few days later Peter Whitmer Jr. was called to accompany Oliver as his companion on that mission (D&C 30:5–6). In this revelation, Parley P. Pratt and Ziba Peterson are called to preach the gospel to the Lamanites and to accompany Oliver Cowdery and Peter Whitmer Jr. See commentary on Doctrine and Covenants 28:8.

Parley P. Pratt and Ziba Peterson Are Called As Missionaries to the Lamanites
DOCTRINE AND COVENANTS 32:1–5

32:1 *My servant Parley P. Pratt.* The calling of Parley P. Pratt to accompany Oliver Cowdery and Peter Whitmer on their mission to the Lamanites proved to have a great influence on the Restoration and the gathering of Israel. Parley's earlier association with a group of Reformed Baptists in the Kirtland, Ohio, area influenced him to stop in that vicinity, where Sidney Rigdon, along with two other important preachers in the Reformed Baptist movement—Alexander Campbell and Walter Scott—had begun a religious group known as Disciples of Christ, or Campbellites. They had established several congregations near Kirtland that sought to live as the early Christians of the New Testament had. The four missionaries to the Lamanites requested to teach at one of the churches where Sidney preached. The missionaries soon found that their knapsacks would not carry enough copies of the Book of Mormon to satisfy the desires of the many who wanted to read it. Sidney Rigdon was given a copy, which he intently studied. He received a witness of its truthfulness. His conversion to the Restoration caused quite a stir in northern Ohio and throughout Pennsylvania and New York, where the Campbellites also had a strong influence.

In less than one month, 127 individuals were convinced of the truthfulness of the Restoration and were baptized. Not only did this double the total membership of the Church at that time but it also provided a number of the future leaders for the Church. Among those early members of the Church were Sidney Rigdon and Frederick G. Williams, future members of the First Presidency (D&C 35, 81, 90:6), and Edward Partridge, future presiding bishop (D&C 41:9). In addition, Kirtland, near the area where these conversions took place, became a gathering place for the Saints and the location of the first temple dedicated in this dispensation.

The Lord surely knew at the time that Elder Pratt was called to this missionary journey that he would influence his companions to stop in the Kirtland area. The hand of the Lord is easily discerned in the unusual collection of truth seekers gathered in that area. "The same God that placed that star in a precise orbit millennia before it appeared over Bethlehem in celebration of the birth of the Babe," observed Elder Neal A. Maxwell, "has given at least equal attention to placement of each of us in precise human orbits so that we may, if we will, illuminate the landscape of our individual lives, so that our light may not only lead others but warm them as well" (*That My Family Should Partake*, 86). The remarkable collection of men and women in and around Kirtland, like those in upstate New York, defies any thought of chance. The situation parallels that of the group of men assembled by the hand of the Lord to give birth to this nation.

32:2 *Go with my servants, Oliver Cowdery and Peter Whitmer, Jun.* At this time, Oliver Cowdery stood second only to Joseph Smith as a witness of the great events associated with the Restoration. While preaching in Mayfield, Ohio, on the way to Kirtland, he had the opportunity to bear his testimony of the coming forth of the Book of Mormon. So powerful was the testimony that he bore in Mayfield, Ohio, that a young lawyer, Varnum Card, turned to his friend begging him to lead him away. "Card's face was 'pale,' and 'his frame trembled as we walked away and mounted our horses.' Regaining his composure, Varnum Card evaluated his experience: ' "Mr. Barr, if you had not been there, I certainly should have gone into the water." He said the impulse was irresistible'" (Anderson, "Impact of the First Preaching," 491–92).

In like manner, the second witness, borne by Peter Whitmer Jr. as one of the eight witnesses of the gold plates, must have been cause for serious reflection on the part of their listeners.

32:3 *Ziba Peterson also shall go with them.* This missionary journey served to be of special importance for Ziba Peterson, who met and converted Rebecca Hooper who became his wife on 11 August 1831.

And I myself will go with them and be in their midst. See commentary on Doctrine and Covenants 50:43.

DOCTRINE AND COVENANTS 33

DATE: OCTOBER 1830
PLACE: FAYETTE, NEW YORK

The instruction to raise a warning voice, given here to newly ordained elders Ezra Thayre and Northrop Sweet, constitutes the pattern to be followed by all missionaries. Their boldness is to match that of their message. The two missionaries are directed three times to open their mouths, with the promise that they will be filled and "laden with sheaves" upon their backs. Their message is to be one of faith, repentance, and baptism. Such is the gospel they have been commissioned to bear. They are also to remember the Articles and Covenants (D&C 20 and 22) and bestow the gift of the Holy Ghost upon those they baptize. They are also instructed to teach from the Book of Mormon and to be prepared in all that they do for the return of Christ.

Laborers Called for the Eleventh Hour

DOCTRINE AND COVENANTS 33:1–4

33:1 Ezra Thayre and Northrop Sweet were both citizens of the Palmyra, New York, area. They were baptized in October 1830 by Parley P. Pratt. Brother Thayre, a builder of bridges, dams, and mills, had employed members of the Smith family (Cook, *Revelations*, 47). Ezra Thayre is mentioned later in the Doctrine and Covenants among those brethren who were called to travel to Missouri, where the Lord would designate the spot for the latter-day temple in Zion (D&C 52:22). Due to difficulties with covetousness, the Lord later revoked the command that he travel to Zion (D&C 56:5, 8). He marched with Zion's Camp and in 1835 was chosen as one of the Seventy. Following the martyrdom of the Prophet Joseph Smith, Thayre chose not to support the Quorum of the Twelve. Remaining in the Midwest, he eventually joined the Reorganized Church of Jesus Christ of Latter-Day Saints.

Northrop Sweet faltered from the faith a few months after his conversion. After moving to Kirtland, Ohio, he became involved with manifestations of strange spirits. Elder George A. Smith recalled: "Joseph Smith came to Kirtland, and taught that people in relation to their error. He showed them that the Spirit of God did not bind men nor make them insane, and that the power of the adversary which had been manifested in many instances was visible even from that cause, for persons under its influence became helpless, and were bound hand and foot as in chains, being as immovable as a stick of timber. When Joseph came to instruct these Saints in relation to the true Spirit, and the manner of determining the one from the other, in a short time a number of those who had been influenced by those foul manifestations, apostatized. Among the number was Wycom Clark; he got a revelation that he was to be the prophet— that he was the true revelator; and himself, Northrop Sweet and four other individuals retired from the Church, and organized the 'Pure Church of Christ,' as they called it, composed of six members, and commenced having meetings, and preaching, but that was the extent of the growth of his early schism" (*Journal of Discourses*, 11:4).

Whose word is quick and powerful. The Lord likens the power of the Spirit, which carries his words to the hearts of his children, to a force "quick and powerful, sharper than a two-edged sword." Nephi explained to his brothers that "the guilty taketh the truth to be hard, for it cutteth them to the very center" (1 Nephi 16:2). Ezra Thayre wrote concerning his personal experience, which illustrates these phrases: "When Hyrum [Smith] began to speak, every word touched me to the inmost soul. I thought every word was pointed to me. God punished me and riveted me to the spot. I could not help myself. The tears rolled down my cheeks, I was very proud and stubborn. There were many there who knew me, I dare not look up. I sat until I recovered myself before I dare look up. They sung some hymns and that filled me with the Spirit. When Hyrum got through, he picked up a book and said, 'here is the Book of Mormon.' I said, let me see it. I then opened the book, and I received a shock with such exquisite joy that no pen can write and no tongue can express. I shut the book and said, what is the price of it? 'Fourteen shillings' was the reply. I said, I'll take the book. I opened it again, and I felt a double portion of the Spirit, that I did not know whether I was in the world or not. I felt as though I was truly in heaven. Martin Harris rushed to me to tell me that the book was true. I told him that he need not tell me that, for I knew that it is true as well as he" (Cook, *Revelations*, 47–48).

Discerner of the thoughts and intents of the heart. God cannot be deceived. He alone can discern all the thoughts of men (D&C 6:16;

1 Kings 8:39). This knowledge causes the wicked to tremble when their evil intentions are made known. Such was the case of Zeezrom when he attempted to deceive Alma and Amulek. Alma declared to him that God "knows all thy thoughts, and thou seest that thy thoughts are made known unto us by his Spirit" (Alma 12:3).

33:3–4 The Lord expounds "all the scriptures in one" (3 Nephi 23:14). In this instance he illustrated the relationship between the parable of the laborers in the vineyard (Matthew 20:1–16); the allegory of Zenos (Jacob 5); and the vision of John the Beloved concerning the Apostasy and the restoration of the Church of Christ in the latter days (Revelation 12:1–6).

33:3 *It is the eleventh hour.* In the era of the Bible, division of time designated that the first hour of a day began at sunrise, or approximately 6:00 A.M. The eleventh hour came at about 5:00 P.M., or towards the end of the workday. "The kingdom of heaven is like unto a man that is an householder," the Savior taught, "which went out early in the morning to hire labourers into his vineyard" (Matthew 20:1). In the parable of the laborers we learn that at "about the eleventh hour he went out, and found others standing idle, and saith unto them, Why stand ye here all the day idle? They say unto him, Because no man hath hired us. He saith unto them, Go ye also into the vineyard" (Matthew 20:6–7). In symbolic fashion, the restoration of the gospel came in the eleventh hour. The laborers of all dispensations have served as coworkers in the vineyard of the Lord, some receiving their commission to work in the early hours that followed the Creation and others to work in these the last days.

33:4 *My vineyard has become corrupted every whit.* This image is drawn from the allegory of the olive trees as found in Jacob 5. "And it came to pass that they went down into the nethermost parts of the vineyard. And it came to pass that they beheld that the fruit of the natural branches had become corrupt also; yea, the first and the second and also the last; and they had all become corrupt" (Jacob 5:39). The vineyard is representative of the workplace of the Lord's servants. The complete corruption of the vineyard represents the apostate conditions of the world. As revealed through the prophet Zenos, the Lord's solution to the decay in his vineyard is to prune it one last time and to graft in the lost branches of the house of Israel. He will send forth his servants to gather his people before he burns the world.

Repent, for the Kingdom of Heaven Is at Hand, and the Bridegroom Comes
DOCTRINE AND COVENANTS 33:5–18

33:5 *Called forth out of the wilderness.* See commentary on Doctrine and Covenants 5:14.

33:6 *Will I gather mine elect.* See commentary on Doctrine and Covenants 29:7.

33:7 *Reap with all your might.* See commentary on Doctrine and Covenants 4:4.

33:10 *Prepare ye the way of the Lord, and make his paths straight.* Similar to John the Baptist's mission to prepare the way for the mortal ministry of the Savior, the Saints of the latter-days are to prepare the way for the millennial ministry of Jesus Christ. Authors Hyrum M. Smith and Janne M. Sjodahl observed: "Eastern potentates, when traveling from one part of the kingdom to another, would proclaim their coming and order their subjects to prepare the way for them, by building roads where there were none, if necessary; by leveling hills and filling up depressions, and straightening out the winding paths. . . . To prepare the way of the Lord and make His paths straight is to acknowledge His sovereignty and to make all necessary preparations for His reception. He will not come to reign until all necessary preparations for his coming have been made" (*Doctrine and Covenants Commentary,* 174). "Hear this, O Earth!" declared the Prophet Joseph Smith. "The Lord will not come to reign over the righteous, in this world, in 1843, nor until everything for the Bridegroom is ready" (*Teachings of the Prophet Joseph Smith,* 280).

33:13 *Upon this rock I will build my church.* See commentary on Doctrine and Covenants 128:10, "Upon this rock."

The gates of hell. See commentary on Doctrine and Covenants 128:10, "The gates of hell shall not prevail."

33:14 *Church articles and covenants.* Reference is to Doctrine and Covenants sections 20 and 22.

33:17 *Having your lamps trimmed and burning, and oil with you.* This reference is to the parable of the ten virgins (Matthew 25:1–13). In this case the Bridegroom was to arrive at midnight. A lamp would do no good if it were not providing light to the individual who awaited his coming. The symbolism of the parable is simple: one must remain prepared for the coming of the Savior through righteous living. Just as the light shines outwardly, so the energy for the light comes from the olive oil, which is within the lamp. It is the same with our individual preparation for the coming of the Lord: the strength to endure is an inner strength that comes from the Spirit of God.

Anciently, lamps were small clay containers filled with oil and provided with cotton wicks that needed trimming after each use so that they would not smoke when lit again. It was best to keep the lamp continuously burning day and night, for it was a difficult labor to rekindle the flame, and the burning lamp could provide fire for whatever purpose was necessary, thus symbolizing our constant companion in the gift of the Holy Ghost.

33:18 *I come quickly.* The reference to the Savior coming quickly does not indicate the nearness of his second coming. Rather, as illustrated in the context of the parable of the ten virgins, it indicates that there will not be time to prepare for the separation of the righteous and the wicked after the Savior comes. Such preparation must have been made previous to his appearances.

DOCTRINE AND COVENANTS 34

DATE: 4 NOVEMBER 1830

PLACE: FAYETTE, NEW YORK

The Prophet recorded in his journal that "in the forepart of November, Orson Pratt, a young man nineteen years of age, who had been baptized at the first preaching of his brother, Parley P. Pratt, September 19th (his birthday), about six weeks previous, in Canaan, New York, came to inquire of the Lord what his duty was, and received the following answer" (Smith, *History of the Church*, 1:127–28).

Orson Pratt, along with his elder brother, Parley, was one of the original members called to the Quorum of the Twelve Apostles in this dispensation. Concerning his early life and the events that led to his request that the Prophet Joseph Smith inquire of the Lord in his behalf, Orson wrote: "From the age of ten to nineteen I saw much of the world, and was tossed about without any permanent abiding place; but through the grace of God, I was kept from many of the evils to which young people are exposed; the early impressions of morality and religion, instilled into my mind by my parents, always remained with me; and I often felt a great anxiety to be prepared for a future state; but never commenced, in real earnest, to seek after the Lord, until the autumn of 1829. I then began to pray very fervently, repenting of every sin. In the silent shades of night, while others were slumbering upon their pillows, I often retired to some secret place in the lonely fields or solitary wilderness, and bowed before the Lord, and prayed for hours with a broken heart and contrite spirit; this was my comfort and delight. The greatest desire of my heart was for the Lord to manifest his will concerning me. I continued to pray in this fervent manner until September, 1830, at which time two elders of the Church of Jesus Christ of Latter-day Saints, came into the neighborhood, one of which was my brother Parley. They held several meetings which I attended.

"Being convinced of the divine authenticity of the doctrine they taught, I was baptized September 19, 1830. This was my birthday, being nineteen-years old. I was the only person in the country [region] who received and obeyed the message. Shortly after my baptism the Elders left.

"In October, 1830, I traveled westward over two hundred miles to see Joseph Smith, the Prophet. I found him in Fayette, Seneca County, N.Y., residing at the house of Mr. Whitmer. I soon became intimately acquainted with this good man, and also with the witnesses of the Book of Mormon. By my request, on the 4th of November, the Prophet Joseph inquired of the Lord for me, and received the revelation published in the Doctrine and Covenants" (as cited in Watson, *Orson Pratt Journals*, 8–9).

The Faithful Become the Sons of God
DOCTRINE AND COVENANTS 34:1–4

34:1–4 Through his faith in Christ, repentance, and obedience to the ordinances of baptism by water and fire, Orson Pratt was born of the Spirit. In order to enter into the kingdom of God all people "must be born again; yea, born of God," testified Alma, "changed from their carnal and fallen state, to a state of righteousness, being redeemed of God, becoming his sons and daughters" (Mosiah 27:25). King Benjamin explained that those who make the covenants associated with baptism "shall be called the children of Christ, his sons, and his daughters" for their "hearts are changed" through faith on the name of Christ and thus they "become his sons and his daughters" (Mosiah 5:7). To be born again is to be adopted as a son or daughter of Christ.

"Temporally speaking, only members of the family abide permanently in the house; servants come and go in their menial ministrations; they cannot abide forever in the house unless freed from their station as bondsmen; they remain outside the inner circle unless adopted as members of the family, thus being made legal heirs of all its privileges" (McConkie, *Mortal Messiah*, 3:159).

Preaching the Gospel Prepares the Way for the Second Coming
DOCTRINE AND COVENANTS 34:5–9

34:6 *Lift up your voice as with the sound of a trump, both long and loud.* At the time of his death on 3 October 1881, Orson Pratt had served as an apostle for more than forty-five years. He filled at least eleven missions to the Eastern States and crossed the Atlantic Ocean to Great Britain and the European continent another sixteen times to preach the gospel. In addition to his missionary labors, Orson Pratt was a tireless writer and defender of the faith. He authored several books and fifteen missionary tracts and served as editor of the *Millennial Star*, the Church's newspaper in England. He arranged the Book of Mormon and the Doctrine and Covenants in chapters and verses with footnotes and references, and prepared the first American edition of the Pearl of Great Price for publication.

34:7 *I shall come in a cloud.* When the Lord returns it will be in light and glory, here described as a cloud. His coming is also described as "a pillar of fire" (D&C 29:12). Of his appearances anciently, we read that he "came down in a cloud" (Numbers 11:25) or "in the pillar of the cloud" (Numbers 12:5). Likewise, when he spoke with the brother of Jared, he "stood in a cloud" (Ether 2:14). The experiences of Peter, James, and John on the Mount of Transfiguration were described by Matthew as a "bright cloud" (Matthew 17:5). Hebrew sources refer to the glory that attends the Lord as "The Presence" or the *Shechinah*.

34:9 *The sun shall be darkened.* See commentary on Doctrine and Covenants 45:42.

Prophecy Comes by the Power of the Holy Ghost
DOCTRINE AND COVENANTS 34:10–12

34:10 *Prophesy, and it shall be given by the power of the Holy Ghost.* Of this prophecy, Elder Orson Pratt modestly observed: "This was a particular point in the revelation that seemed to me too great for me ever to attain to, and yet there was a positive command that I should do it. I have often reflected upon this revelation, and have oftentimes inquired in my heart—'Have I fulfilled that commandment as I ought to have done? Have I sought as earnestly as I ought to obtain the gift of prophecy, so as to fulfill the requirement of Heaven?' And I have felt sometimes to condemn myself because of my slothfulness and because of the little progress that I have made in relation to this great, heavenly, and divine gift" (*Journal of Discourses*, 17:290–91). See commentary on Doctrine and Covenants 68:4.

DOCTRINE AND COVENANTS 35

DATE: DECEMBER 1830
PLACE: NEAR FAYETTE, NEW YORK

Doctrine and Covenants 35 addresses the preparation of Sidney Rigdon to be a servant of the Lord. Sidney served as the Prophet's scribe in the translation of the Bible and as the first counselor in the First Presidency of the Church. Of this revelation Joseph Smith recorded: "In December Sidney Rigdon came to inquire of the Lord, and with him came Edward Partridge; the latter was a pattern of piety, and one of the Lord's great men. Shortly after the arrival of these two brethren, thus spake the Lord" (*History of the Church*, 1:128).

Through the Atonement of Jesus Christ
Men May Become One with God
DOCTRINE AND COVENANTS 35:1–2

35:1 *Alpha and Omega.* See commentary on Doctrine and Covenants 19:1.

Whose course is one eternal round. "As one earth shall pass away," the Lord revealed to Moses, "and the heavens thereof even so shall another come; and there is no end to my works, neither to my words. For behold, this is my work and my glory—to bring to pass the immortality and eternal life of man" (Moses 1:38–39).

35:2 A volume could be written about the truths announced in this verse, though it consists of but a single sentence. First, it introduces Jesus Christ as the source of the revelation. Indeed, every revelation for the salvation of men must come through Jesus Christ, his being the only name under heaven whereby salvation can come. Second, it affirms that he is the Son of God. It is the divine inheritance obtained thereby that enabled him to lay down his life in our behalf and to take it up again. Third, it reminds us that he died for our sins, not for sins he committed. Indeed, he is our Savior and we are saved by his goodness and grace. Fourth, it declares that the promise of salvation is only to those who choose to believe not simply in him but also "in his name," meaning they will reverence and accept those that have been commissioned to act in his behalf. For Sidney Rigdon that meant Joseph Smith. For us it means his legal and lawful successors. Fifth, it further confines the blessings of salvation to those who become sons of God, meaning those who are born again and live according to the things of the Spirit. Sixth, it reminds us, as John taught, that Christ, in order to obtain his own salvation, had to become one with God. That is he had to learn to think as God thinks, feel as God feels, and act as God acts. To do so is the system and process of salvation. No one who is unlike God can be saved (D&C 93:6–20). Thus, the obvious conclusion is then drawn that we must become one with Christ and thus one with the Father. This process of surrendering our will to that of our Father—as did Christ—constitutes the system and plan of salvation.

We note with interest that the same principles given here, in essentially the same order, are developed in the Lectures on Faith. Some have credited Sidney Rigdon with the writing of these lectures. Such a conclusion overstates the role played by Elder Rigdon, though he did work closely with the Prophet on them. The instruction in this verse may well have constituted a source of direction to them in that labor.

Sidney Rigdon Was Prepared for His Greater Work in the Restoration
DOCTRINE AND COVENANTS 35:3–7

35:4–6 Joseph Fielding Smith wrote: "A great number of forceful, intelligent men who became leaders in the Church had been gathered by Sidney Rigdon, with the help of the Lord, in this part of the land. Without any question, the Spirit of the Lord had rested upon these men, as it did on Sidney Rigdon and Parley P. Pratt, to direct them to gather in Kirtland at that early day. When, therefore, Parley P. Pratt, Ziba Peterson and their companions came to Kirtland they found the way prepared for them through the preaching, very largely, of Sidney Rigdon, so that it was not a difficult matter for these missionaries to convince this group of the truth. While Sidney was preaching and baptizing by immersion without authority, which the Lord informed him in this revelation, yet it all resulted in good when the Gospel message reached them. These men were not only convinced and ready for baptism, but were in a condition by which the Priesthood could be given them, and this was done" (*Church History and Modern Revelation*, 1:160).

Miracles, Signs, and Wonders Come by Faith
DOCTRINE AND COVENANTS 35:8–12

35:8 *Mine arm is not shortened.* Reference to the arm of the Lord symbolizes his power in working with the children of men. A shortened arm would suggest that his power had in some way been diminished. The Lord walked among mortal men, healing the sick, giving sight to the blind, unstopping deaf ears and dumb lips. At his word the lame took up their beds and walked. He promised his disciples, "He that believeth on me, the works that I do shall he do also; and greater works than these shall he do; because I go unto my Father" (John 14:12). The restoration of the fulness of the gospel included the power and authority of God to work great miracles. Ministers of that day and our own commonly teach that the power of God manifest in the miracles of the New Testament were a blessing bestowed on the Saints of an earlier day, but were not intended for our day. Here the Lord declares that his power is available to men on earth today and it is their faith that determines the miracles, signs, and wonders that will be manifest. See commentary on Doctrine and Covenants 84:64–72.

35:12 *None that doeth good.* Missionaries who go out to share the gospel meet many people who profess spiritual experiences. Such experiences are easily discerned by ascertaining their purpose. If the experience opens their hearts and minds to accept the fulness of the gospel when it comes to them, it is obviously of God. If, on the other hand, their purpose is to excuse themselves from any responsibility to accept additional light and truth and the blessings that come from it, their experiences obviously come from some other source. See commentary on D&C 84:45–46.

The message taken by these early missionaries to the Ohio Valley had just that effect. Many who were involved in back-to-the-Bible movements were more prepared to accept the message of the Restoration. On the other hand, this same message provided others with an excuse for refusing to listen to their message. The difference here was not the Bible but rather the ears of men.

Ready to receive the fulness of my gospel. In a later revelation, the Lord explains that the Spirit gives light to every individual that is born into the world. Those that will hearken to the voice of the Spirit will come into the kingdom and covenant with God to serve him. Those who do not hearken to the Spirit and instead reject the fulness of the gospel do so because they are "under the bondage of sin" (D&C 84:50).

The Lord Chooses the Weak of the World to Be His Servants

DOCTRINE AND COVENANTS 35:13–19

35:13 *I call upon the weak things of the world.* It is the degree of understanding one has received from the Spirit, not the degrees awarded by the understanding of men, that prepares an individual to teach or receive the gospel. We live in a world of information and knowledge, much of which has no power to save mankind, inspire faith, or encourage repentance. Only that which comes from God will bring men to God.

The perfect expression of this principle is found in the lives of those God calls to serve as missionaries. The latter-day missionary force is largely comprised of young men and women who are unacquainted with the ways of the world but who quickly learn to depend on the direction of the Spirit. The apostle Paul explained, "For ye see your calling, brethren, how that not many wise men after the flesh, not many mighty, not many noble, are called: but God hath chosen the foolish things of the world to confound the wise; and God hath chosen the weak things of the world to confound the things which are mighty; and base things of the world, and things which are despised, hath God chosen" (1 Corinthians 1:26–28).

This principle was manifest in the calling of the unlearned boy, Joseph Smith, to be the servant of the Lord in restoring the fulness of the gospel in the latter days. When Sidney Rigdon first received the Book of Mormon and studied its contents, he was impressed by the fact that this powerful testament of Christ came through an unlearned man. Illustrating this point, A. W. Cowles records the following: "After a few days Cowdery returned and held a long interview with Rigdon. Rigdon had read a considerable portion of the book. He questioned Cowdery about Smith and found that he was entirely illiterate. Rigdon expressed the utmost amazement that such a man should write a book which seemed to shed a flood of light on all the old scriptures, open all their profoundest mysteries, and give them perfect consistency and complete system. In his fresh enthusiasm he exclaimed that if God ever gave a revelation, surely this must be divine" (as cited in Anderson, "Impact of the First Preaching," 479).

35:14 *They shall fight manfully for me.* Courage and faith will be the companions of every successful missionary. In June 1835 Elders David W. Patten, Wilford Woodruff, and Warren Parrish were together preaching the gospel in Tennessee. A local sheriff arrested them on false pretenses at the urging of a Methodist priest. A mock trial was held in which the defendants were not allowed to say a word in their own behalf. They were pronounced guilty. "Brother Patten, being filled with the Holy Ghost, arose to his feet, and by the power of God bound them fast to their seats while he addressed them. He rebuked them sharply for their wicked and unjust proceedings. Bro. Parrish afterwards said, 'My hair stood up straight on my head, for I expected to be killed.' When Patten closed, the Judge addressed him, saying, 'You must be armed with concealed weapons, or you would not treat an armed court as you have this.' Patten replied, 'I am armed with weapons you know not of, and my weapons are the Holy Priesthood and the power of God. God is my friend, and he permits you to exercise all the power you have, and he bestows on me all the power I have'" (in Jenson, *LDS Biographical Encyclopedia*, 1:78). Saints in the area paid the court costs, and the missionaries were set free. That evening a heavenly messenger appeared to Elder Patten and warned him that the mob at the courthouse was in a rage because their prisoners had been freed. These brethren escaped unharmed by heeding this angelic warning.

35:15 *The poor and the meek shall have the gospel preached unto them.* The experiences of virtually all missionaries show them that wealth brings with it a sense of self-sufficiency. It seems that the more individuals have accumulated of the things of this world, the less likely they will have an interest in the things of another world. Among those who have little of this world's goods, there exists a greater chance for missionaries to find individuals with an interest in the things of an eternal world. During his mission to England in 1840, Brigham Young wrote, "Almost without exception it is the poor that receive the Gospel" (as cited in Smith, *History of the Church*, 4:126).

35:18 *I have given unto him the keys of the mystery of those things which have been sealed.* See commentary on Doctrine and Covenants 28:7.

The Bible Will Be Restored and Israel Will Be Saved

DOCTRINE AND COVENANTS 35:20–27

35:20 *Thou shalt write for him; and the scriptures shall be given.* Sidney Rigdon was called of the Lord to be Joseph Smith's scribe for the translation of the Bible. Oliver Cowdery, who had previously served in this capacity, was in Missouri among the Lamanites. Elder Rigdon was the Prophet's scribe when the heavens were opened to them and they saw what we now know as the revelation on the degrees of glory (D&C 76).

Even as they are in mine own bosom. Much in the Old and New Testaments has not come to us as it was originally penned. The promise here is that the spirit of revelation will rest upon the Prophet with sufficient sureness to enable these ancient records to reflect those things that constitute the mind and will of the Lord.

To the salvation of mine own elect. Scripture is of little interest and thus of little worth to those of little faith. The greater our faith in God, the greater attention we give to his word.

35:23 *It shall be given unto him to prophesy.* The Prophet Joseph Smith taught the truths of the restored gospel by the spirit of prophecy. He had the same Spirit as those prophets who came before him. He was not dependent on the knowledge of past dispensations but received the truths from the author of our salvation.

Prove his words. Sidney Rigdon was to "prove" that the revelations given to Joseph Smith were in harmony and, indeed, came in fulfillment of that which is found in the Bible.

35:24 *I will cause the heavens to shake for your good.* See commentary on Doctrine and Covenants 21:6.

Zion shall rejoice upon the hills and flourish. See commentary on Doctrine and Covenants 49:24.

35:25 *By the keys which I have given shall they be led.* The house of Israel, including the lost ten tribes, is under the direction of those who hold the keys of the kingdom. "The keys of the kingdom, which belong always unto the Presidency of the High Priesthood" (D&C 81:2), were bestowed on the Prophet Joseph Smith and Oliver Cowdery by Peter, James, and John. See commentary on Doctrine and Covenants 27:13.

DOCTRINE AND COVENANTS 36

DATE: DECEMBER 1830
PLACE: NEAR FAYETTE, NEW YORK

Sidney Rigdon and Edward Partridge traveled to New York to meet the Prophet Joseph Smith following Sidney's conversion and baptism in Ohio. After his baptism in November 1830, Sidney Rigdon left almost immediately from Kirtland, Ohio, to go to Fayette, New York, to meet Joseph Smith. His traveling companion was a young hat-maker by the name of Edward Partridge, who shared his interest in meeting the Prophet but had not yet been baptized. While the previous revelation (section 35) was given to Sidney Rigdon, this one was given to Edward Partridge.

Regarding the arrival of Edward and Sidney at the Smith home, Lucy Mack Smith wrote: "In December of the same year, Joseph appointed a meeting at our house. While he was preaching, Sidney Rigdon and Edward Partridge came in and seated themselves in the congregation. When Joseph had finished his discourse, he gave all who had any remarks to make the privilege of speaking. Upon this, Mr. Partridge arose, and stated that he had been to Manchester with the view of obtaining further information respecting the doctrine which we preached; but, not finding us, he had made some inquiry of our neighbors concerning our characters, which they stated had been unimpeachable, until Joseph deceived them relative to the Book of Mormon. He also said that he had walked over our farm, and observed the good order and industry which it exhibited; and, having seen what we had sacrificed for the sake of our faith, and having heard that our veracity was not questioned upon any other point than that of our religion, he believed our testimony and was ready to be baptized, 'if,' said he, 'Brother Joseph will baptize me.'

"'You are now,' replied Joseph, 'much fatigued, Brother Partridge, and you had better rest today and be baptized tomorrow.'

"'Just as Brother Joseph thinks best,' replied Mr. Partridge, 'I am ready at any time.'

"He was accordingly baptized the next day" (*History of Joseph Smith,* 1996, 249–50). Apparently it was soon after his baptism that he asked the Prophet to inquire of the Lord in his behalf, and the revelation recorded in Doctrine and Covenants 36 was received.

Whether by the Hand of the Lord or of His Servants It Is the Same
DOCTRINE AND COVENANTS 36:1–3

36:2 *I will lay my hand upon you by the hand of my servant Sidney Rigdon.* Edward Partridge was baptized by the Prophet 11 December 1830 in the Seneca River. He was ordained an elder by Sidney Rigdon.

When the Lord's servants act in his behalf, it is as if the Lord himself has personally acted. Great symbolism is associated with the laying on of hands. The hand is a symbol of power and is associated with the idea of strength, providence, or blessings. Priesthood, keys, ordinations, offices, blessings, and so on are granted by the laying on of hands. This symbolizes the placing of God's hand or power upon the one so blessed. It also provides an orderly, observable, and documented way to convey offices or authority. See commentary on Doctrine and Covenants 42:11, "Known to the Church . . . regularly ordained."

The Duty of Every Priesthood Bearer Is to Preach the Gospel
DOCTRINE AND COVENANTS 36:4–8

36:5–7 The clear thrust of these verses is that every man who has the Melchizedek Priesthood conferred upon him is obligated to serve as a missionary. President Kimball illustrated this principle when he said, "The question has been often asked, 'Is the mission program one of compulsion?' And the answer, of course, is no. Everyone is given his free agency. The question is asked: Should every young man fill a mission? And the answer of the Church is yes, and the answer of the Lord is yes. Enlarging this answer we say: Certainly every male member of the Church *should* fill a mission, like he *should* pay his tithing, like he *should* attend his meetings, like he *should* keep his life clean and free from the ugliness of the world and plan a celestial marriage in the temple of the Lord" ("Planning for a Full and Abundant Life," 87). In like manner, Elder A. Theodore Tuttle commented: "I talked with a young man about a mission. He said,

'I don't want to go.' I asked, 'What has that got to do with it? We need you'" (Conference Report, October 1974, 100).

36:6 *Come forth out of the fire.* This phrase comes from Jude 1:23. The thought it conveys is that in the Day of Judgment every corruptible thing will be consumed (D&C 101:24), and the wicked shall be burned with unquenchable fire (Malachi 4:1). If the erring Saints are to be saved they must be pulled, as it were, from the coming fire, even as God said of Israel: "Ye were as a firebrand plucked out of the burning" (Amos 4:11).

Hating even the garments spotted with the flesh. Again, the phrase comes from Jude 1:23. To put an end to disease in ancient Israel, clothing spotted by contagious diseases was destroyed by burning (Leviticus 13:47–59; 15:4–17). Here the thought is to liken the dreaded disease to sin. The Saints are to avoid the remotest contact with it; the very garments, as it were, of the sinners are to be burned with fire, meaning that anything which has had contact with the pollutions of the wicked must be shunned, and so also with those yet in the world who are invited to join the kingdom.

36:8 *I will suddenly come to my temple.* Among the passages of scripture that the angel Moroni quoted in tutoring the Prophet Joseph Smith was Malachi's prophecy that "the Lord, whom ye seek, shall suddenly come to his temple" (Malachi 3:1). The Lord will make numerous appearances at his temples. The first of these occurred when the Lord appeared to his servants in the Kirtland Temple on 3 April 1836 (see commentary on D&C 110:1–3). There are many temples, and it is, of course, the right of the Savior to appear in any or all of them as often as suits his purposes. Reference is made to his future appearance in the temple yet to be built in the New Jerusalem (D&C 42:35–36). We would understand this to be but the pattern of a host of other such appearances in his temples.

DOCTRINE AND COVENANTS 37

DATE: DECEMBER 1830
PLACE: CANANDAIGUA, NEW YORK

Though this revelation was given to Joseph Smith and Sidney Rigdon, it was directed to the Church, which consisted of small congregations in Fayette, Manchester, and Colesville. Given in December 1830, it was the last of nineteen revelations received by Joseph Smith that year. It was also the first revelation in this dispensation to direct a gathering of the Saints. Constant harassment in upstate New York, contrasted with the warm reception the missionaries to the Lamanites had received in the Ohio Valley, precipitated the revelation.

The Saints Are Called to Gather at the Ohio
DOCTRINE AND COVENANTS 37:1–4

37:1 *Translate.* Joseph Smith was laboring on his translation of the Bible, known to us today as the Joseph Smith Translation.

The Ohio. Reference is to the Ohio Valley and more particularly to the city of Kirtland, where the first missionaries, Oliver Cowdery, Peter Whitmer, Parley P. Pratt, and Ziba Peterson, had enjoyed so much success.

37:3 *They should assemble together at the Ohio.* Though unknown to the Saints at this time, it would be in Kirtland, Ohio, that some of the most important events of this dispensation would take place. Their gathering there was necessary for the construction of a temple and the subsequent appearance of Christ—to accept that edifice as his house—and then the appearance of Moses, Elias, and Elijah to restore the keys, powers, and majesties they held when on earth. It would be here that the Saints would be "endowed with power from on high" (D&C 38:32). Almost half of the revelations in the Doctrine and Covenants were given in Ohio. It was here that the school of the prophets was formed, the Lectures on Faith given, most of the work on the Joseph Smith Translation completed, and the Abraham papyrus purchased. It was also here that the law of consecration was revealed and revelations relative the establishment of Zion received. No period in the history of the Church equals the Ohio era for the outpouring of divine knowledge. See commentary on Doctrine and Covenants 110.

Oliver Cowdery shall return. The reference is to Oliver's return from his mission to the Lamanites (D&C 28:8).

37:4 *Let every man choose for himself.* There is no compulsion in the Lord's Church. To sell all that they owned and move from upstate New York to Kirtland, Ohio, a distance of some three hundred miles in the midst of a bitter winter, would be very difficult and required considerable faith. It was necessary that it be their own choice to go, if for no other reason than that the kingdom of God rests upon the foundation of faith. It is the prince of darkness who builds upon the principle of compulsion.

MOSES 6–7

DATE: DECEMBER 1830

PLACE: FAYETTE, NEW YORK

Truths restored through Joseph Smith about Enoch and his city of Zion, which was taken up into heaven, greatly interested the early Saints of this dispensation. The Prophet's faithful followers could not help but see in him something of an Enoch figure and likened their situation to that of their ancient counterparts. Moses 6 records the lineage of Enoch, who was the seventh in a chain of patriarchs extending back to Adam (vv. 10–22). Joseph Smith stood at the head of the seventh and final great gospel dispensation. Both men taught the same doctrines and held the same priesthood; both were seers, having had a magnificent vision of future events; both were opposed by great wickedness; both had performed miracles; and both had stood in the presence of God. Each prophet had gathered the faithful for the purpose of building a great temple city, and each of them taught a doctrine that would prepare the faithful to enter into God's presence while yet in the flesh.

Against fierce opposition Enoch converted many to the gospel of Jesus Christ (Moses 7:12–13). In so doing he was granted great power to protect the Lord's people. By his words "the earth trembled, and the mountains fled, . . . and the rivers of water were turned out of their course" (Moses 7:13). Stricken by fear, Enoch's enemies and the giants of the land stood far off, and "the Lord came and dwelt with his people, and they dwelt in righteousness" (Moses 7:16).

With Enoch at their head, the faithful became of one heart and one mind with no poor among them (Moses 7:18). Their lives were based on "the order of him who was without beginning of days or end of years," even Jesus Christ (Moses 6:67), and "after the order of the covenant which God made with Enoch" (JST Genesis 14:27). He and his people built a great city known to us as the "City of Holiness, even Zion" (Moses 7:19). After 365 years of preparation, this city was caught up into heaven (Moses 7:69).

273

Enoch left a prophetic description of our dispensation, as recorded in Moses 7.

The Restoration in the Latter Days
MOSES 7:62–65

Moses 7:62 Four key events are cited by Enoch in his prophetic description of this the final gospel dispensation. First, righteousness, he said, would come down out of heaven. Previous to this he had spoken of Christ as "the Righteous" (Moses 7:47), which suggests that this text could be an allusion to the First Vision. Certainly Enoch's prophecy embraced that singular event along with the appearance of a host of angels, each to restore their "rights, their keys, their honors, their majesty and glory, and the power of their priesthood; giving line upon line, precept upon precept; here a little, and there a little; giving us consolation by holding forth that which is to come, confirming our hope!" (D&C 128:21). Along with the heavenly messengers spoken of by Enoch came a great outpouring of revelation through the Prophet Joseph Smith, much of which finds expression in the volume known to us as the Doctrine and Covenants.

Second, Enoch spoke of truth coming forth from the earth to testify of God's Only Begotten Son, his resurrection from the dead, and the resurrection of all the inhabitants of the earth. The Book of Mormon fits this description perfectly. Thus the testimony of heaven and earth combines in the third event, which is the gathering of the elect from the four quarters of the earth. The message that we are to proclaim, the message that will gather the honest of heart from every nation is to center in Christ as he was known to those of dispensations past. The testimony we are to bear and the truths we are to teach as we go forth to gather Israel are found in the Book of Mormon and the Doctrine and Covenants. The fourth prophecy centered in the place to which Israel is to be gathered, a holy city, patterned after that of Enoch's city, a city destined to become a New Jerusalem with a great temple of the Lord standing in its center.

My tabernacle. Reference is to the house of the Lord (Ezekiel 37:27).

Moses 7:63–64 Further revelation is granted on this matter in the Joseph Smith Translation of Genesis 9:21–24. It reads as follows: "And the bow shall be in the cloud; and I will look upon it, that I may remember the everlasting covenant, which I made unto thy father Enoch; that, when men should keep all my commandments, Zion should again come on the earth, the city of Enoch which I have caught up unto myself. And this is mine everlasting covenant, that when thy posterity shall embrace the truth, and look upward, then shall Zion look downward, and all the heavens shall shake with gladness, and the earth shall tremble with joy. And the general assembly of the church of the first-born shall come down out of heaven, and possess the earth, and shall have place until the end come. And this is mine everlasting covenant, which I made with thy father Enoch. And the bow shall be in the cloud, and I will establish my covenant unto thee, which I have made between me and thee, for every living creature of all flesh that shall be upon the earth."

DOCTRINE AND COVENANTS 38

DATE: 2 JANUARY 1831
PLACE: FAYETTE, NEW YORK

This revelation, given at Fayette, New York, 2 January 1831, is an extension of the revelation given to Joseph Smith about Enoch and the establishment of his city of Zion. It built on the knowledge there and worked to increase the desire of the Saints to establish the New Jerusalem spoken of in the book of Ether. See commentary on Moses 7:62–65, page 273.

The Omniscience of God
DOCTRINE AND COVENANTS 38:1–3

38:1 *Great I Am.* See commentary on Doctrine and Covenants 29:1. *Alpha and Omega.* See commentary on Doctrine and Covenants 19:1. *Seraphic hosts of heaven, before the world was made.* The hosts of heaven referred to here are unembodied spirits yet to be born into mortality (D&C 45:1; Genesis 2:1; Moses 3:1; Abraham 5:1). *Seraphim* is the plural form of the Hebrew word *seraph*, which means "burning."

38:2 *Knoweth all things.* Scripture testifies that all three members of the Godhead have all knowledge—past, present, and future. This stands in sharp contrast with the idea held by some that God is forever learning. To suppose this is also to admit that God is forever ignorant. It is the testimony of all the standard works that God—meaning the Father, the Son, and the Holy Ghost—knows all things both in heaven and on earth (Mosiah 4:9). Joseph Smith explained that unless God had all the attributes of godliness in perfection, including knowledge, we could not be expected to exercise faith in him. "Without the idea of the existence of these attributes in the Deity men could not exercise faith in him for life and salvation; seeing that without the knowledge of all things, God would not be able to save any portion of his creatures; for it is by reason of the knowledge which he has of all things, from the beginning to the end, that enables him to give that understanding to his creatures by which they are made partakers of eternal life; and if it were not for the idea existing in

276

the minds of men that God had all knowledge it would be impossible for them to exercise faith in him" (Smith, *Lectures on Faith*, 4:11). See commentary on *Lectures on Faith*, 4:11, page 840.

The following are representative of the declaration of scripture:

"Great is our Lord, and of great power: his understanding is infinite" (Psalm 147:5).

"But the Lord knoweth all things from the beginning; wherefore, he prepareth a way to accomplish all his works among the children of men; for behold, he hath all power unto the fulfilling of all his words. Thus it is. Amen" (1 Nephi 9:6).

"O how great the holiness of our God! For he knoweth all things, and there is not anything save he knows it" (2 Nephi 9:20).

"Believe in God; believe that he is, and that he created all things, both in heaven and in earth; believe that he has all wisdom, and all power, both in heaven and in earth; believe that man doth not comprehend all the things which the Lord can comprehend" (Mosiah 4:9).

"Therefore, I would that ye should be steadfast and immovable, always abounding in good works, that Christ, the Lord God Omnipotent, may seal you his, that you may be brought to heaven, that ye may have everlasting salvation and eternal life, through the wisdom, and power, and justice, and mercy of him who created all things, in heaven and in earth, who is God above all. Amen" (Mosiah 5:15).

"He comprehendeth all things, and all things are before him, and all things are round about him; and he is above all things, and in all things, and is through all things, and is round about all things; and all things are by him, and of him, even God, forever and ever" (D&C 88:41).

The omniscience of God troubles some because they suppose it to be in conflict with agency. If God knows that something is going to happen, they argue, we have no power of choice to prevent it. They assume that foreknowledge has a causal effect, reasoning that if God knows we are going to do something wrong, we are predetermined to do it. Were that the case, it would also follow that God's ignorance of future events would have a preventive effect. That is, if God did not know something was going to happen, then it wouldn't happen. If that were true, it would follow that we have agency or freedom of choice in direct proportion to God's ignorance. Thus, rather than rejoice in the knowledge of God, scripture should exult in his ignorance. The whole chain of thought is threadbare. Ignorance about the cause of cancer never prevented it, and knowledge of it never caused it. Our knowledge that one season follows

another, that the tides come and go, that the sun rises and sets, has nothing to do with their happening; nor will our ignorance of these events
deter them in any way. Our ignorance or knowledge of either the laws of
nature or the laws of the gospel is without causal effect. True it is that God
has the power to intervene and prevent certain things from happening,
but he will not do so to contravene the agency that he himself gave us.

For all things are present before mine eyes. To Moses the Lord said, "All
things are present with me, for I know them all" (Moses 1:6). For God
past, present, and future are always before him as one. Exalted beings
"reside in the presence of God, on a globe like a sea of glass and fire,
where all things for their glory are manifest, past, present, and future, and
are continually before the Lord. The place where God resides is a great
Urim and Thummim. This earth, in its sanctified and immortal state, will
be made like unto crystal and will be a Urim and Thummim to the
inhabitants who dwell thereon, whereby all things pertaining to an inferior kingdom, or all kingdoms of a lower order, will be manifest to those
who dwell on it; and this earth will be Christ's" (D&C 130:7–9).

38:3 *All things came by me.* Under the direction of the Father, Christ
has created worlds without number. "By the word of my power, have I created them, which is mine Only Begotten Son, who is full of grace and
truth. And worlds without number have I created; and I also created them
for mine own purpose; and by the Son I created them, which is mine Only
Begotten" (Moses 1:32–33). When Christ says, "all things came by me,"
as he does in this text, he is speaking by divine investiture of authority.
That is, he is speaking in the first person for his Father. Although the
great labor of creation rested with Christ, he is not the father of the spirits of men, nor did he create himself. In the premortal realm Christ was
the firstborn of all the spirit children of our eternal Father. In mortality
he is the Only Begotten of the Father, meaning the only Son begotten of
God in the flesh, or with blood.

Enoch's City of Zion
DOCTRINE AND COVENANTS 38:4–6

38:4 The promise in Ether 13 of a New Jerusalem piqued the early
Saints' interest in the establishment of that city and of a Zion society.
They had undoubtedly inherited a keen interest in establishing such a
society from their forebears, who had fled Europe and come to America
for the very purpose of establishing a covenant society and reinstating the

ancient order of things. It is significant that in this revelation, given just after the announcement that the Lord's people were to gather, reference is made to Enoch's Zion.

I am the same which have taken the Zion of Enoch into mine own bosom. While laboring on the Joseph Smith Translation a few weeks previous to this revelation, the Prophet learned that Enoch, one of the greatest of the Old Testament prophets and yet one for whom the Bible preserves the barest of references (Genesis 5:21–24), established a city of holiness, or Zion. In that revelation we learn that the Lord called his people Zion "because they were of one heart and one mind, and dwelt in righteousness; and there was no poor among them" (Moses 7:18). Joseph further learned that "all the days of Zion, in the days of Enoch, were three hundred and sixty-five years. And Enoch and all his people walked with God, and he dwelt in the midst of Zion; and it came to pass that Zion was not, for God received it up into his own bosom; and from thence went forth the saying, Zion Is Fled" (Moses 7:68–69). Our immediate text tells us that those of Enoch's city were taken into heaven because they believed in the name of Christ and because he became their advocate with the Father. These revelations were obviously announcing the principles upon which the Zion of the last days is to be built and to which the city of Enoch will, in a millennial day, yet return.

Bosom. The bosom is naturally associated with the idea of embracing in love and fellowship. In the East it had an extended meaning associated with the manner of dress. Long, flowing garments bound at the waist by a girdle provided a convenient carrying place, like a bag, in the fold of material over the breast. Thus the bosom became a carrying place used by shepherds to carry helpless lambs (Isaiah 40:11).

38:5–6 Those who rejected the testimony of Christ as it was declared to them by Enoch and others of the prophets of that day gave themselves up to such wickedness that the Lord said: "Wherefore, I can stretch forth mine hands and hold all the creations which I have made; and mine eye can pierce them also, and among all the workmanship of mine hands there has not been so great wickedness as among thy brethren. . . . But behold, these which thine eyes are upon shall perish in the floods; and behold, I will shut them up; a prison have I prepared for them. And That which I have chosen hath pled before my face. Wherefore, he suffereth for their sins; inasmuch as they will repent in the day that my Chosen shall return unto me, and until that day they shall be in torment;

Wherefore, for this shall the heavens weep, yea, and all the workmanship of mine hands" (Moses 7:36–40).

38:5 *The wicked have I kept in chains of darkness until the judgment of the great day.* Among the things in Enoch's panoramic vision of future dispensations are the events that surrounded the resurrection of Christ. "As many of the spirits as were in prison came forth," he said, "and stood on the right hand of God; and the remainder where reserved in chains of darkness until the judgment of the great day" (Moses 7:57). All are to be resurrected, each in his or her order. That order will be determined by the law by which they lived. The first to come forth from the grave will be those who are to be celestial, only then will those who are to be terrestrial be resurrected, and then those who are telestial, and last of all those who are filthy still, meaning those who are perdition (D&C 88:16–32, 99–104).

The Wicked Will Not Abide the Coming of Christ
DOCTRINE AND COVENANTS 38:7–12

38:8 *The veil of darkness shall soon be rent.* See commentary on Moses 7:62–65, page 274.

He that is not purified shall not abide the day. Reference is to the millennial day in which the earth "will be renewed and receive its paradisiacal glory" (Article of Faith 10). Prior to that day, the earth will be cleansed of all that is telestial. See commentary on Doctrine and Covenants 101:22–41.

38:9 *The enemy shall not overcome.* Joseph Fielding Smith wrote: "He has given to us the kingdom. He has made us the promise that the enemy of the kingdom shall not overcome. We may have trouble. We have had trouble. We may meet with opposition, but that opposition shall fail in its endeavor to destroy the work of God . . .

"The gospel has been restored, and the kingdom given to his saints according to the prophecy of Daniel. It is not again to be removed, destroyed, or given to other people, and in his own way and time he is going to break down all other systems, that his kingdom may prevail and that he may come and reign as Lord of lords and King of kings upon the face of the whole earth . . .

"The Lord has called attention to the fact that he is going to destroy systems and organizations and combinations that are false. And how is he going to do it? By giving their members the truth, if they will receive it; by giving them the privilege of coming out of those organizations to receive the truth and have every opportunity to come into his kingdom, for his hand is outstretched ready to greet them. If they will not come; if they will not receive his message; then, of course, they must fall with their systems. Truth will prevail; truth will stand when all else is removed, and it is destined to cover the face of the earth" (*Doctrines of Salvation*, 1:241).

Gird up your loins. See commentary on Doctrine and Covenants 27:15.

38:10 *But not all.* Some members of the Church were in need of repentance (D&C 1:30).

38:11 *All flesh is corrupted.* By its very definition, a universal apostasy, like the darkness of night, leaves nothing unaffected. This is not to say, for instance, that there was no truth or goodness to be found in the Dark Ages or in the churches of the world. It is, however, to say that there was no truth or goodness that was not affected by that darkness. To flourish, the flowering plant requires the light of the sun, without which it will wilt away. Likewise, every good thing needs heaven's light to grow and is hindered by the lack of that light.

The powers of darkness prevail. Describing the establishment of Zion and the latter-day New Jerusalem, Isaiah wrote: "Arise, shine; for thy light is come, and the glory of the Lord is risen upon thee. For, behold, the darkness shall cover the earth, and gross darkness the people: but the Lord shall arise upon thee, and his glory shall be seen upon thee" (Isaiah 60:1–2). In this text Isaiah contrasts the light of Zion with the darkness of the world. An epistle written by the elders in Kirtland amplifies the language of Isaiah: "Consider for a moment, brethren, the fulfillment of the words of the prophet; for we behold that darkness covers the earth, and gross darkness the minds of the inhabitants thereof—that crimes of every description are increasing among men—vices of great enormity are practiced—the rising generation growing up in the fullness of pride and arrogance—the aged losing every sense of conviction, and seemingly banishing every thought of a day of retribution—intemperance, immorality, extravagance, pride, blindness of heart, idolatry, the loss of natural affection; the love of this world, and indifference toward the things of eternity increasing among those who profess a belief in the religion of heaven, and infidelity spreading itself in consequence of the same—men giving themselves up to commit acts of the foulest kind, and deeds of the blackest dye, blaspheming, defrauding, blasting the reputation of neighbors, stealing, robbing, murdering; advocating error and opposing the truth, forsaking the covenant of heaven, and denying the faith of Jesus—and in the midst of all this, the day of the Lord fast approaching when none except those who have won the wedding garment will be permitted to eat and drink in the presence of the Bridegroom, the Prince of Peace!" (*Teachings of the Prophet Joseph Smith*, 47).

In the presence of all the hosts of heaven. We have no secrets from the hosts of heaven. They are quite mindful of our doings. "The spirits of the just . . . ," said Joseph Smith, "are not far from us, and know and understand our thoughts, feelings, and motions and are often pained therewith" (*Teachings of the Prophet Joseph Smith*, 326). Those who are on the Lord's errand do not walk alone. To such he said, "I have given the heavenly hosts and mine angels charge concerning you" (D&C 84:42). "And whoso receiveth you, there I will be also, for I will go before your face. I will be on your right hand and on your left, and my Spirit shall be in your hearts, and mine angels round about you, to bear you up" (D&C 84:88).

38:12 *Which causeth silence to reign.* See commentary on Doctrine and Covenants 88:95.

Angels are waiting . . . to gather the tares that they may be burned. See commentary on Doctrine and Covenants 88:1–13.

The Covenant of Gathering

DOCTRINE AND COVENANTS 38:13–22

38:13 Repeated attempts had been and yet would be made to destroy Joseph Smith. Of his enemies the Lord said, "Their bounds are set, they cannot pass." To the Prophet he said, "Thy days are known, and thy years shall not be numbered less; therefore, fear not what man can do, for God shall be with you forever and ever" (D&C 122:9).

38:17 *I have made the earth rich.* "The earth is full," the Lord said, "and there is enough and to spare" (D&C 104:17).

Again I will stand upon it. Reference is to the Millennium, when the Lord will again abide upon the earth.

38:18–20 Promised lands are given with a covenant that is everlasting. Those to whom the lands are given will be blessed to enjoy them through time and eternity. The psalmist tells us that the "meek shall inherit the earth" and "dwell therein for ever" (Psalm 37:11, 29, 34). Christ reaffirmed this promise in what is known as the Sermon on the

Mount (Matthew 5:5). By revelation Joseph Smith has assured us that the promise was literal not figurative (D&C 88:17–18). Ancient Israel was commanded to honor its fathers and mothers that their days would be long upon the land which the Lord had given them (Exodus 20:12). This does not suggest that Israel would live longer than other people, but rather that throughout the generations she and her posterity would live in peace and prosperity upon the land the Lord had given her and that she would lay claim to that same land in an eternal world. Consider the language of the covenant: "Therefore shall ye keep all the commandments which I command you this day, that ye may be strong, and go in and possess the land, whither ye go to posses it; and that ye may prolong your days in the land, which the Lord sware unto your fathers to give unto them and to their seed, a land that floweth with milk and honey" (Deuteronomy 11:8–9). This land, first promised to Abraham, was given as an "everlasting possession" (Genesis 17:8; 48:4; Abraham 2:6). John Taylor explains: "Men have conquered, and taken, bought and sold, the earth without God. But their possessions will perish with them; they may perpetuate them by law for a season to their descendants, but the Saints of God will finally inherit the earth for ever, in time, and in eternity, Abraham held his possessions on a very different footing from the above. The Lord appeared unto him, and made a covenant with him, and said, 'And I will give unto thee, and to thy seed after thee, the land wherein thou art a stranger, all the land of Canaan, for an *everlasting possession.*' [Genesis 17:8.] This covenant was an eternal one; yet Abraham did not possess the land, for Stephen says, 'he gave him none inheritance in it, no, not so much as to set his foot on.' [Acts 7:5.] And Paul says, 'By faith Abraham, when he was called to go out into a place which he should after receive for an inheritance, obeyed; and he went out, not knowing whither he went. By faith he sojourned in the land of promise, as in a strange country, dwelling in tabernacles with Isaac and Jacob, the heirs with him of the same promise; for he looked for a city which hath foundations, whose builder and maker is God.' [Hebrews 11:8–10.] Here, then, we find land given to Abraham by promise, a land that he did not possess; but he will do so, 'for he looked for a city which hath foundations, whose builder and maker is God.' He looked forward to the redemption of his seed, the establishment of the kingdom of God, and the inheritance of those blessings eternally. If any one doubts this, let them read the [31st] chapter of Jeremiah, and the [36th] to [39th] chapters of Ezekiel; wherein it is stated that Israel is to be gathered to their own land, that it is to become as the

Garden of Eden, and to be no more desolate. Ezekiel speaks of the resurrection of the dead, and the coming together of the bones, flesh, sinews, and skin, of a living army; of the uniting of the nations of Judah, and Israel, in one; and in consequence of the great development of the powers of God, the heathen would be filled with astonishment; and finally, that God's tabernacle should be planted in their midst for evermore. Then let them read from the [47th] to the last chapter of Ezekiel; and they will find an account, not only of the restoration of the Jews, and ten tribes, but that the land is actually divided to them by inheritance, in their different tribes, according to the promise made thousands of years before to Abraham. In the 13th and 14th verses of the [47th] chapter, he refers to this, and says, 'Thus saith the Lord God, This shall be the border whereby ye shall inherit the land according to the twelve tribes of Israel: Joseph shall have two portions. And ye shall inherit it, one as well as another; concerning the which I *lifted up mine hand to give it unto your fathers*; and this land shall fall unto you for an inheritance.' Thus we find that the promise unto Abraham concerning territory will be literally fulfilled" (Taylor, *Government of God*, 43, 45; emphasis in original).

38:18 *No curse when the Lord cometh.* The curse placed upon the earth at the time of Adam's fall will be lifted during the millennial day. Of that day, Elder Bruce R. McConkie wrote: "Adam in his ancient Eden was denied the privilege of partaking of the fruit of the tree of life, lest doing so he should live forever in his sins. But now, all who are freed from sin through the blood of the Lamb shall partake forever of that fruit of which men eat and never hunger more. 'And there shall be no more curse: but the throne of God and of the Lamb shall be in it; and his servants shall serve him.' Whereas the earth was cursed so that it brought forth thorns, thistles, briers, and noxious weeds, whereas man was required to eat his bread in the sweat of his face; whereas sorrow and death passed upon all men—all this in the beginning—now the ransom has been paid and all things have become new" (*Millennial Messiah*, 704–5).

38:21–22 The prophetic word declares that with the return of Christ there will be "a full end of all nations" (D&C 87:6), meaning all man-made governments will surrender their authority to the Lord of lords and King of kings, who "will reign personally upon the earth" (Article of Faith 10). Joseph Smith explained that "Christ and the resurrected Saints will reign over the earth during the thousand years. They will not probably dwell upon the earth, but will visit it when they please, or when it is necessary to govern it" (*Teachings of the Prophet Joseph Smith*, 268). Having lost the glory of David's day, Israel took great solace in the prophecies that such glory would be restored to her. For instance, Zechariah testified, "And the Lord shall be king over all the earth: in that [millennial] day shall there be one Lord, and his name one" (Zechariah 14:9). Describing that day, Zephaniah wrote: "The Lord hath taken away thy judgments, he hath cast out thine enemy: the king of Israel, even the Lord, is in the midst of thee: thou shalt not see evil any more. In that day it shall be said to Jerusalem, Fear thou not: and to Zion, Let not thine hands be slack. The Lord thy God in the midst of thee is mighty; he will save, he will rejoice over thee with joy; he will rest in his love, he will joy over thee with singing. . . . I will undo all that afflict thee: and I will save her that halteth, and gather her that was driven out; and I will get them praise and fame in every land where they have been put to shame. At that time will I bring you again, even in the time that I gather you: for I will make you a name and a praise among all people of the earth, when I turn back your captivity before your eyes, saith the Lord" (Zephaniah 3:15–17, 19–20). And again Hosea wrote, "I am the Lord thy God . . . for there is no saviour beside me. . . . I will be thy king: where is any other that may save thee in all thy cities?" (Hosea 13:4, 10).

"When the Lord reigns, how will he do it? John says: 'He shall rule them with a rod of iron.' (Rev. 19:15). What is the rod of iron? Nephi says: 'I beheld that the rod of iron . . . was the word of God, which led to the fountain of living waters, or to the tree of life.' (1 Ne. 11:25). Thus, Christ reigneth in and through and by means of the gospel. There is no other way. Men will be subject to him because they believe the gospel. The gospel is his law. He has no other. And so we read relative to his coming: 'And another trump shall sound, which is the fifth trump, which is the fifth angel who committeth the everlasting gospel—flying through the midst of heaven, unto all nations, kindreds, tongues, and people; and this shall be the sound of his trump, saying to all people, both in heaven and in earth, and that are under the earth—for every ear shall hear it, and every knee shall bow, and every tongue shall confess, while they hear the sound of the trump, saying: Fear God, and give glory to him who sitteth upon the throne, forever and ever; for the hour of his judgment is come.' (D&C 88:103–4). Every knee shall bow! The Lord reigneth! He is King over all the earth!" (McConkie, *Millennial Messiah*, 590–91).

Saints Commanded to Be One and Esteem Each Other
DOCTRINE AND COVENANTS 38:23–27

38:23 *Teach one another.* It has ever been the system in the Lord's kingdom that we "teach one another." In a revelation given a month later the Lord said: "And now, behold, I give unto you a commandment, that when ye are assembled together ye shall instruct and edify each other, that ye may know how to act and direct my church, how to act upon the points of my law and commandments, which I have given" (D&C 43:8).

38:24 *Let every man esteem his brother as himself.* Teaching this same principle, the apostle James wrote: "For if there come unto your assembly a man with a gold ring, in goodly apparel, and there come in also a poor man in vile raiment; and ye have respect to him that weareth the gay clothing, and say unto him, Sit thou here in a good place; and say to the poor, Stand thou there, or sit here under my footstool: are ye not then partial in yourselves, and are become judges of evil thoughts? Hearken, my beloved brethren, Hath not God chosen the poor of this world rich in faith, and heirs of the kingdom which he hath promised to them that love him? But ye have despised the poor. Do not rich men oppress you, and draw you before the judgment seats? Do not they blaspheme that worthy name by the which ye are called? If ye fulfil the royal law according to the scripture, Thou shalt love thy neighbour as thyself, ye do well: But if ye have respect to persons, ye commit sin, and are convinced of the law as transgressors" (James 2:2–9).

38:27 *Be one; and if ye are not one ye are not mine.* Salvation comes in our obtaining the mind of Christ and thus being one with him (1 Corinthians 2:16). We are saved to the extent that we have learned to believe as he believes, feel as he feels, and act as he acts. This is the sense in which the Father, Son, and Holy Ghost are spoken of as being one God. The intent of scripture is not to suggest three manifestations of the same God, but rather three persons who are one in thought and deed. To the extent that we do not believe, feel, or act as Christ would, we are not one with him, and thus the Lord would say of us, "Ye are not mine."

The Wicked Seek the Saints' Lives
DOCTRINE AND COVENANTS 38:28–29

38:28 The adversary and his legions have always sought the lives of the Lord's anointed. Elder Joseph F. Smith explained: "It has ever been the desire of the wicked to destroy the people of God. They have never slackened their efforts, nor failed to use all the means in their power, nor hesitated to resort to the most cruel, foul and fiendish acts to accomplish their nefarious purpose. This same cruel enmity, although for the time being, to some extent subdued or held in check by the Almighty, still smoulders and rankles in their hearts, awaiting a favorable opportunity to burst forth as fiercely as at any time during the life of the Prophet Joseph. This is one of the strongest evidences we can have of the divine mission of President Brigham Young. Because of the inspiration of the Almighty and power of God which has rested upon him and accompanied his administrations, he has been the very centre of the target at which all the deadly weapons of the enemy has been aimed ever since the death of the Prophet Joseph. I say this is one of the strongest evidences we can have of this fact, aside from the testimony of the Holy Spirit, which bringeth knowledge. It is unmistakable. The hatred of the wicked always has and always will follow the Priesthood and the Saints. The devil will not lose sight of the power of God vested in man—the Holy Priesthood. He fears it, he hates it, and will never cease to stir up the hearts of the debased and corrupt in anger and malice towards those who hold this power, and to persecute the Saints, until he is bound. He delights in apostacy and in apostates, and uses them for his purpose, but what does he or his emissaries care for their organizations? Do they hate them? Is the world moved with anger or malice against them? No. They become a part of the world, fraternize with the people of the world and lose their distinction or identity, as the people of God notwithstanding their claims and pretentions to being believers in the Prophet Joseph Smith, and the Gospel which he was instrumental in restoring to the earth" (*Journal of Discourses,* 19:24–25).

38:29 Prophetically, this is the earliest allusion to the Civil War. See Doctrine and Covenants 87.

The Saints Are to Be Endowed with Power and Go Forth to All Nations
DOCTRINE AND COVENANTS 38:30–33

38:32 *There I will give unto you my law.* See commentary on Doctrine and Covenants 42.

You shall be endowed with power from on high. The endowment is an ordinance of protection and blessing normally given in a temple. A partial endowment was given in the Kirtland Temple, but the full endowment was not revealed until the Saints were in Nauvoo.

The elders of Israel—like their ancient counterparts—were not to go to the nations of the earth until they had received this heavenly endowment (Luke 24:49; Acts 1:4, 8; D&C 95:8–9). See commentary on Doctrine and Covenants 39:15, "And from thence men shall go forth into all nations."

38:33 *Israel shall be saved.* The Lord made the covenant of salvation with Abraham and his seed, meaning the literal seed of his body. All who receive it must do so at the hands of those who are rightful heirs of that covenant (Abraham 2:9, 11). Those not of the house of Israel who embrace the gospel are adopted into his lineage. The Holy Ghost must "purge out the old blood" from these, Joseph Smith explained, "and make [them] actually of the seed of Abraham" (*Teachings of the Prophet Joseph Smith*, 150).

No power shall stay my hand. See commentary on Doctrine and Covenants 1:5.

Care for the Poor and Seek Riches of Eternity
DOCTRINE AND COVENANTS 38:34–42

38:34 *Appointed by the voice of the church.* Those who serve in positions of authority over others in the Church do so only with the consent of those over whom they preside (D&C 26:2; 28:12).

38:38 *Endowed with power from on high.* See commentary on verse 32.

38:39 *Lest ye become as the Nephites of old.* After the ministry of Christ among the Nephites, they lived for two hundred years in perfect peace and harmony. "And now, in this two hundred and first year there began to be among them those who were lifted up in pride, such as the wearing of costly apparel, and all manner of fine pearls, and of the fine things of the world. And from that time forth they did have their goods and their substance no more common among them. And they began to be divided into classes; and they began to build up churches unto themselves to get gain, and began to deny the true church of Christ. And it came to pass that when two hundred and ten years had passed away there were many churches in the land; yea, there were many churches which professed to know the Christ, and yet they did deny the more parts of his gospel, insomuch that they did receive all manner of wickedness, and did administer that which was sacred unto him to whom it had been forbidden because of unworthiness. And this church did multiply exceedingly because of iniquity, and because of the power of Satan who did get hold upon their hearts" (4 Nephi 1:24–28).

38:41 *Let your preaching be the warning voice.* The voice of warning will always be the voice of the true messenger of the Lord. The Lord does not send out his servants to assure the world that the course they are following is acceptable to him. Their purpose is to declare repentance, the need for baptism both for the remission of sins and for entrance into the Church and kingdom of God. Those who reject this message forfeit all the knowledge and blessings that would come to those who have received an inheritance in Zion.

38:42 *And go ye out from among the wicked.* The Saints are to leave upstate New York and go to Ohio.

Be ye clean that bear the vessels of the Lord. The phrase comes from Isaiah (Isaiah 52:11) and was directed to those who held the priesthood and thus had the responsibility to tend the sacred vessels of the temple. In order to perform their temple duties, the priests cleansed themselves in a three-part ritual. They were washed, anointed, and then clothed in the garment of the priesthood (Leviticus 8). The symbolism of this ritual is instructive. Priesthood holders must first be clean to act in the name of the Lord. Those who are clean can be anointed with oil, which symbolizes the outpouring of the Spirit. When they possess the Spirit, they can then be clothed in the garment of the priesthood, which represents the power and authority of God. This text seems particularly appropriate in the context of the endowment that had been promised the Saints (D&C 38:8).

DOCTRINE AND COVENANTS 39

DATE: 5 JANUARY 1831
PLACE: FAYETTE, NEW YORK

Religious traditions can be a major stumbling block to receiving Jesus Christ and the restoration of his gospel in the latter days. Many doors are closed to missionaries throughout the world in the name of loyalty to another faith or church. What should be our approach in proclaiming the Restoration to members of other Christian churches? In this revelation the Lord addressed a Baptist preacher about entrance into the kingdom of God. The Lord's words and message to this man are an example of how the Lord would have us address sincere members of other Christian faiths. Prefacing this revelation, the Prophet Joseph Smith recorded, "Not long after this conference of the 2nd of January closed, there was a man came to me by the name of James Covill, who had been a Baptist minister for about forty years, and covenanted with the Lord that he would obey any command that the Lord would give to him through me, as His servant, and I received the following" (*History of the Church*, 1:143).

The Saints Have Power to Become the Sons of God
DOCTRINE AND COVENANTS 39:1–4

39:1–4 Jesus Christ established his gospel during his mortal ministry, and he has come in these latter days to offer salvation to all who will come unto him (John 1:12). By echoing John's testimony, the Lord intimates that those who profess to receive the Lord Jesus Christ as their Savior are in a similar situation to that of the Jews of Jesus' day. Like their Jewish counterparts of the meridian day, they are put to the test of discipleship. In the early Church, those who left the apostate conditions of Judaism and received Jesus Christ were given the power of spiritual rebirth. Those who stubbornly held to false traditions that had developed among the once-vibrant faith of the covenant people remained in darkness.

39:4 *Power to become my sons.* The sonship here spoken of does not have reference to man's existence as a spirit offspring of the Eternal Father. Rather, through faith and righteousness, men have the power to become (1) the sons of Christ (D&C 39:1–6), and (2) sons of God, meaning the Father, by adoption into the family of Christ.

"Through 'the covenant' of baptism, those who are actually born again become 'the children of Christ, his sons, and his daughters'; they are 'spiritually begotten' by him; their 'hearts are changed through faith on his name'; thus they 'are born of him and have become his sons and his daughters.' (Mosiah 5:7.) Baptism and church membership standing alone do not make men sons of Christ, but through them, as he said, men have 'power to become my sons.' (D&C 39:4; Rev. 21:7.)

"Those who are sons of God (meaning the Father) are persons who, first, receive the gospel, join the true Church, obtain the priesthood, marry for eternity, and walk in obedience to the whole gospel law. They are then adopted into the family of Jesus Christ, become joint-heirs with him, and consequently receive, inherit, and possess equally with him in glorious exaltation in the kingdom of his Father (D&C 76:54–60; 84:33–41; 88:107; 132:15–25; Rom. 8:14–18; Gal. 3:26–29; 4:1–7)" (McConkie, *Doctrinal New Testament Commentary,* 1:73–74).

To Receive the Gospel Is to Receive Christ
DOCTRINE AND COVENANTS 39:5–6

39:5 *He that receiveth my gospel receiveth me.* As "the messenger of salvation" (D&C 93:8), Jesus Christ taught the gospel which he received from the Father. The true test of discipleship lies in receiving his message, especially when it entails forsaking former false religious principles. It is self-deception for individuals to say that they have received Jesus into their life if they then reject his gospel. Many ask themselves the question, "If I had lived on the earth at the time of Jesus, would I have been one of his disciples?" The correct and indisputable response is simple. What is our response to the restoration of his gospel in the latter days? How we answer that question is a sure indication of what our response would have been had we dwelt in Judea or Galilee during the lifetime of the Savior.

39:6 *This is my gospel—repentance and baptism by water.* All who receive the Savior must have "faith unto repentance" (Alma 34:16). They must be willing to be baptized "as a witness before him that ye have entered into a covenant with him, that ye will serve him and keep his commandments" (Mosiah 18:10). Those who confess that the Restoration is the work of God but are unwilling to covenant in the waters of baptism will not receive the blessings of the gift of the Holy Ghost or enter the gate to eternal life.

James Covill Is Commanded to Be Baptized
DOCTRINE AND COVENANTS 39:7–14

39:10 *The days of thy deliverance are come, if thou wilt hearken to my voice.* All blessings of the gospel are predicated upon obedience, and deliverance from the captivity of sin and error is dependent upon obedience. Elder Harold B. Lee referred to the Lord's promises to his servants, if they would hearken to his voice: "I sat in a class in Sunday School in my own ward one day, and the teacher was the son of a patriarch. He said he used to take down the blessings of his father, and he noticed that his father gave what he called 'iffy' blessings. He would give a blessing, but it was predicated on 'if you will not do this' or 'if you will cease doing that.' And he said, 'I watched these men to whom my father gave the 'iffy' blessings, and I saw that many of them did not heed the warning that my father as a patriarch had given, and the blessings were never received because they did not comply.

"You know, this started me thinking. I went back into the Doctrine and Covenants and began to read the 'iffy' revelations that have been given to the various brethren in the Church. If you want to have an exercise in something that will startle you, read some of the warnings that were given through the Prophet Joseph Smith to Thomas B. Marsh, Martin Harris, some of the Whitmer brothers, William E. McLellin—warnings which, had they heeded, some would not have fallen by the wayside. But because they did not heed, and they didn't clear up their lives, they fell by the wayside, and some had to be dropped from membership in the Church" (Conference Report, October 1972, 130).

The blessings offered to James Covill were of great import. Because he returned to his life as a Baptist minister, none of these blessings were secured. Although these blessings were personally directed to James Covill, they are available to all who will receive the fulness of the restored gospel of Jesus Christ.

You shall receive my Spirit. Individuals may enjoy the guidance of the Spirit in their lives and may receive a witness of the Holy Ghost, but the gift of the Holy Ghost is a greater blessing. Alma explained that the blessing given to those who are baptized is that the Lord "may pour out his Spirit more abundantly upon" them (Mosiah 18:10). The Spirit of Christ, which "is given to every man, that he may know good from evil" (Moroni 7:16), was previously available to James Covill. The power of the Holy Ghost surely came upon him as he heard the message of the restored gospel. However, the gift of the Holy Ghost, received by the laying on of hands by one in authority, could not be his unless he acted upon the witness that he received. It is one thing to have the Holy Ghost visit an individual. It is another for an individual to receive the right to have the Holy Ghost as a constant companion. "There is a difference between the Holy Ghost and the gift of the Holy Ghost," taught Joseph Smith. "Cornelius received the Holy Ghost before he was baptized, which was the convincing power of God unto him of the truth of the Gospel, but he could not receive the gift of the Holy Ghost until after he was baptized. Had he not taken this sign or ordinance upon him, the Holy Ghost which convinced him of the truth of God, would have left him" (*Teachings of the Prophet Joseph Smith*, 199).

A *blessing so great as you never have known.* See commentary on verse 15, "I have kept in store a blessing."

A Special Blessing Is to Be Given Those Who Go Forth to Preach
DOCTRINE AND COVENANTS 39:15–21

39:15 *Inasmuch as my people shall assemble themselves at the Ohio.* "It was the design of the councils of heaven before the world was," said Joseph Smith, "that the principles and laws of the priesthood should be predicated upon the gathering of the people in every age of the world. . . . Ordinances instituted in the heavens before the foundation of the world, in the priesthood, for the salvation of men, are not to be altered or changed. All must be saved on the same principles" (*Teachings of the Prophet Joseph Smith*, 308). It was in Ohio that the first temple of this last dispensation would be built.

I have kept in store a blessing. Three days before this revelation was given, the Lord revealed to the Church that in Ohio they would "be endowed with power from on high" (D&C 38:32). Should James Covill choose to assemble with the Saints in Ohio, this endowment, a blessing that had been lost to the world for nearly two millennia, would likewise be available to him. See commentary on Doctrine and Covenants 38:32; 105:11.

And from thence men shall go forth into all nations. The resurrected Christ instructed the meridian-day apostles to "tarry ye in the city of Jerusalem, until ye be endued with power from on high" and then preach "in his name among all nations" (Luke 24:47, 49). In like manner, modern-day missionaries are not sent to all the world until they have received this same endowment in the house of the Lord.

After the elders received the gift of the Holy Ghost, the Lord began to reveal that he had an endowment in store for the faithful (D&C 38:22; 43:16), "a blessing such as is not known among the children of men" (D&C 39:15.) He said in June 1830, "I gave unto you a commandment that you should build a house, in the which house I design to endow those whom I have chosen with power from on high; for this is the promise of the Father unto you; therefore I command you to tarry, even as mine apostles at Jerusalem" (D&C 95:8–9; 105:11–12, 18, 33).

Servants of the Lord are not fully qualified to go forth to preach the gospel and build up the kingdom unless they have the gift of the Holy Ghost and have been endowed with power from on high, meaning that they have received the knowledge, powers, and blessings normally given only in the temple, the house of the Lord.

39:17–18 See commentary on Doctrine and Covenants 43:17–28.

Those Who Receive the Gospel Shall Be Gathered in Time and in Eternity
DOCTRINE AND COVENANTS 39:22–24

39:22 *They shall be gathered unto me in time and in eternity.* Joseph Smith wrote: "The main object [of gathering] was to build unto the Lord a house whereby He could reveal unto His people the ordinances of His house and the glories of His kingdom, and teach the people the way of salvation; for there are certain ordinances and principles that, when they are taught and practiced, must be done in a place or house built for that purpose. . . . It is for the same purpose that God gathers together His people in the last days, to build unto the Lord a house to prepare them for the ordinances" (*Teachings of the Prophet Joseph Smith*, 308).

DOCTRINE AND COVENANTS 40

DATE: JANUARY 1831
PLACE: FAYETTE, NEW YORK

This is the first revelation to be given jointly to the Prophet Joseph Smith and Sidney Rigdon. Of this revelation Joseph Smith recorded, "As James Covill rejected the word of the Lord, and returned to his former principles and people, the Lord gave unto me and Sidney Rigdon the following revelation explaining why he obeyed not the word . . ." (*History of the Church*, 1:145).

40:2 *He received the word with gladness.* The words of explanation concerning James Covill's rejection of the restored gospel are rooted in the Savior's parable of the sower, or better entitled, the parable of the soil, as recorded in Matthew 13. In the meridian day the Lord explained to his disciples that "he that received the seed into stony places, the same is he that heareth the word, and anon with joy receiveth it; Yet hath he not root in himself, but dureth for a while: for when tribulation or persecution ariseth because of the word, by and by he is offended. He also that received seed among the thorns is he that heareth the word; and the care of this world, and the deceitfulness of riches, choke the word, and he becometh unfruitful" (Matthew 13:20–22).

DOCTRINE AND COVENANTS 41

DATE: 4 FEBRUARY 1831
PLACE: KIRTLAND, OHIO

Doctrine and Covenants 41 is of special importance because it restored the office of bishop in the Church of Christ. Though it would not be until the Church had established itself in the Salt Lake Valley that bishops would function in wards as they do in our day, those holding the office of bishop played an important role in directing temporal affairs in this early period.

This is the first of many revelations that were received in Ohio, where more sections of the Doctrine and Covenants were given than in any other location. Kirtland was designated by the Lord as the first place of gathering for the Saints in this dispensation.

The Prophet Joseph Smith wrote: "The latter part of January, in company with Brothers Sidney Rigdon and Edward Partridge, I started with my wife for Kirtland, Ohio, where we arrived about the first of February, and were kindly received and welcomed into the house of Brother Newel K. Whitney. My wife and I lived in the family of Brother Whitney several weeks, and received every kindness and attention which could be expected, and especially from Sister Whitney" (*History of the Church*, 1:145–46).

The Lord Will Bless His Church with His Law
DOCTRINE AND COVENANTS 41:1–6

41:1 *I delight to bless with the greatest of all blessings.* It was here in Kirtland that the first temple would be built in this dispensation; the beginning of the endowment would be restored; the keys for gathering Israel would be restored; the keys necessary for eternal marriage would be brought back; and the keys of the sealing power would be committed again to men on the earth. It is out of these events that the promises made to the fathers will find fulfillment and that the fulness of all gospel blessings will be extended to all willing to receive them.

296

Ye that hear me not will I curse, that have professed my name, with the heaviest of all cursings. The greatest of heaven's blessings are reserved for those who accept Christ and his gospel, and those who choose to walk in other paths can expect only to receive wages of him whom they have chosen to serve. Of note here is Christ's displeasure with those who reject the restored gospel while feigning loyalty to him and his word. Just as those who put Christ to death in the name of loyalty to the law of Moses were condemned by that law, so too will those who reject the message of the Restoration be condemned by that law they profess to represent.

41:2 *Assemble yourselves together to agree upon my word.* There is no suggestion here that it is the prerogative of the elders of the Church to get together and determine among themselves what is and what is not the gospel. It is the Lord's Church, to which they are members only. He runs it. All gospel principles come from him. In this particular instance, five days after this revelation had been given, Joseph Smith, in company with twelve elders, received a revelation on Church government which included instruction about dealing with transgressions (D&C 42).

41:3 *Ye shall receive my law.* Reference is to Doctrine and Covenants 42, which is known as "the Law" or "the law of the Church."

41:5 *He that receiveth my law and doeth it, the same is my disciple.* In historical Christianity, there exists the notion that one can receive Jesus Christ as Savior without receiving him as Lord and Master. These are they who are willing to accept the saving grace of the Son of God but who see no need to conform to any particular discipline or standard of behavior. Within the Protestant world, these individuals refer to themselves as "carnal Christians." No such notion can exist among the true Saints.

This concept is essentially the same as expressed by the Master in the Sermon on the Mount when he said: "Not every one that saith unto me, Lord, Lord, shall enter into the kingdom of heaven; but he that doeth the will of my Father which is in heaven. Many will say to me in that day, Lord, Lord, have we not prophesied in thy name? and in thy name have cast out devils? and in thy name done many wonderful works? And then will I profess unto them, I never knew you: depart from me, ye that work iniquity" (Matthew 7:21–23).

Shall be cast out from among you. This is the first revelation of the Restoration to teach the Saints that those who will not keep the law of the Lord are to be severed from membership in his Church. Further instructions concerning those who are to be cut off were revealed as part

of the law that the Lord promised to give to his Church. See commentary
on Doctrine and Covenants 42:20–26.

The First Bishop of the Restoration Is Called
DOCTRINE AND COVENANTS 41:7–12

41:7 *My servant Joseph Smith, Jun., should have a house built.* Lucy
Diantha Morley Allen indicated that "the first time the Prophet and his
family came to Kirtland they lived with Isaac Morley, Lucy's father. Later
'Father Morley' built a small house for them on his farm." It was at this
home that Emma gave birth to twins, both of whom died soon after birth.
"Lucy and her elder sister kept house for Emma Smith while she was ill,"
recovering from the physical and emotional drain of losing the twins
("Joseph Smith, the Prophet," 537).

41:8 *Sidney Rigdon should live as seemeth him good.* In all but the most
unusual instances, the choice of vocation and place of residence is left to
the individual. It is not a matter of Church assignment or of revelation.
This principle was revealed when Sidney Rigdon lost his employ as a minister because he accepted the restored gospel and was baptized at the
hands of Oliver Cowdery.

41:9 The pattern of callings in the Church was reiterated in the
restoration of the office of bishop: (1) The Lord extends the call through
the presiding authority, one known to the Church, as recognized in the
person of the Prophet Joseph Smith. (2) The members of the Church sustain the appointment by their voice. (3) The individual, so called and
sustained, is ordained to the office by those in authority. These principles
were given to the Church as the Lord's law (D&C 42:11).

Ordained a bishop. The duties of a bishop were not revealed at this
time. As the restoration of priesthood offices unfolded, responsibilities and
instructions concerning bishops were received. The office to which
Edward Partridge was called would be somewhat equivalent to that of presiding bishop of the Church today. The presiding bishop was responsible
for overseeing the Lord's storehouses for the poor, a function considered to
be full-time employment. In addition he was "appointed to be a judge in
Israel, like as it was in ancient days, to divide the lands of the heritage of
God unto his children" (D&C 58:17) within the law of consecration.
Further, he was to judge members of the Church with the assistance of
two counselors. The Lord instructed that Edward Partridge, as the presiding bishop, was to live in Zion, which was later identified as Jackson

County, Missouri. He was responsible for the purchase of lands that were given as inheritances to the Saints and for church buildings, specifically the temple. See commentary on Doctrine and Covenants 68:15–18; 72:9–11; 107:15.

Spend all his time in the labors of the church. Edward Partridge was the second person called to full-time service in the kingdom. Earlier, the Prophet Joseph Smith was called to devote all of his labors in Zion and told that he should receive his support from the Church (D&C 24:3, 7). By appointment Bishop Partridge was to oversee the Lord's storehouse for the poor and "be employed in doing this business" (D&C 51:14). It was by this means that he was to provide for the needs of his own family.

41:11 *Like unto Nathanael of old, in whom there is no guile.* See John 1:45–47.

DOCTRINE AND COVENANTS 42

DATE: 9 FEBRUARY 1831
PLACE: KIRTLAND, OHIO

At a conference of the Church held in Fayette, New York, in January 1831, the Lord commanded the Saints to go to "the Ohio," where he would give them his law and where they would be endowed with power from on high (D&C 38:32). In February of the following year, after their arrival in Ohio, this revelation, known as the law or "the law of the Church," was received.

Doctrine and Covenants 42 illustrates the importance of revelation immediate to our day. For example, particular attention is given to correcting misconceptions growing out of the New Testament practice of having "all things common" (Acts 4:32). Some of those baptized in Kirtland, Ohio, had belonged to a system called "common stock," in which all property was held jointly as a community. The experience had not always been a good one. John Whitmer explained: "The disciples had all things common, and were going to destruction very fast as to temporal things; for they considered from reading the scripture that what belonged to a brother, belonged to any of the brethren. Therefore they would take each others clothes and other property and use it without leave which brought on confusion and disappointment, for they did not understand the scripture" ("Book of John Whitmer," 37).

The primary purpose of this revelation was to bring order to the Church. It begins with direction about how the missionaries were to go forth and what they were to teach. It announces the manner in which the missionaries, and all Church officers, were to be called and set apart. It also restores those parts of the gospel that were incorporated in the law of Moses as the Ten Commandments and the principles that determine whether a particular transgression is to be disciplined by the Church or addressed by the civil courts.

300

Elders Are Authorized to Build Up the Church Abroad
DOCTRINE AND COVENANTS 42:1–10

42:1 *Assembled yourselves together.* In response to the Lord's direction (D&C 41:2), twelve elders met together.

42:2 *Obey the law which I shall give unto you.* "The law of heaven is presented to man," observed the Prophet Joseph Smith, "and as such guarantees to all who obey it a reward far beyond any earthly consideration; though it does not promise that the believer in every age should be exempt from the afflictions and troubles arising from different sources in consequence of the acts of wicked men on earth. Still in the midst of all this there is a promise predicated upon the fact that it is the law of heaven, which transcends the law of man, as far as eternal life the temporal; and as the blessings which God is able to give, are greater than those which can be given by man. Then, certainly, if the law of man is binding upon man when acknowledged, how much more must the law of heaven be! And as much as the law of heaven is more perfect than the law of man, so much greater must be the reward if obeyed. The law of man promises safety in temporal life; but the law of God promises that life which is eternal, even an inheritance at God's own right hand, secure from all the powers of the wicked one" (*Teachings of the Prophet Joseph Smith*, 50).

42:4 *Go forth in my name, every one of you, excepting my servants Joseph Smith, Jun., and Sidney Rigdon.* Just as missionaries are necessary to spread the faith, so is leadership necessary among those who have found it. Joseph Smith and Sidney Rigdon's primary responsibilities were to those who had joined the Church and to the continuation of their work on the translation of the Bible. They were to go forth to declare the word for a short season as directed by the Spirit (v. 5), but returned to give leadership to the body of the Church.

42:6 *Two by two.* During his mortal ministry, the Savior organized the Twelve and the Seventy to go forth two by two (Mark 6:7 and Luke 10:1). The Lord's wisdom is evident in sending forth missionaries in companionships. Such a system allows that two witnesses bear testimony of the truthfulness of the restored gospel and encourage and protect each other.

Declaring my word like unto angels of God. The commission of missionaries and of angels is one and the same. Both have been called by God to teach the same gospel. Referring to angels and, by implication, to missionaries, Mormon taught: "The office of their ministry is to call men unto repentance, and to fulfil and to do the work of the covenants of the Father, which he hath made unto the children of men, to prepare the way among the children of men, by declaring the word of Christ unto the chosen vessels of the Lord, that they may bear testimony of him. And by so doing, the Lord God prepareth the way that the residue of men may have faith in Christ, that the Holy Ghost may have place in their hearts, according to the power thereof; and after this manner bringeth to pass the Father, the covenants which he hath made unto the children of men" (Moroni 7:31–32).

42:9 *The city of the New Jerusalem.* This is the first reference in the Doctrine and Covenants to the city of the New Jerusalem. Book of Mormon and biblical references teach that Saints in the latter days will gather to build a city to which the Lord will come. Further, Ether indicated that "a New Jerusalem should be built up upon this land, unto the remnant of the seed of Joseph" (Ether 13:6). Two months previous to receiving the law of the Church, while the Prophet Joseph Smith was engaged in the translation of the Bible, the Lord revealed, "Righteousness and truth will I cause to sweep the earth as with a flood, to gather out mine elect from the four quarters of the earth, unto a place which I shall prepare, an Holy City, that my people may gird up their loins, and be looking forth for the time of my coming; for there shall be my tabernacle, and it shall be called Zion, a New Jerusalem" (Moses 7:62).

In addition the Lord revealed in the Bible translation that Enoch and his people established a city called Zion, based on the principles of righteousness. This work laid the foundation for the laws of consecration revealed in this section which, in connection with the other laws revealed herein, are the foundation for the city of New Jerusalem. Not long after this revelation had been received, the site of the city of New Jerusalem was designated as Independence, Missouri. See commentary on Doctrine and Covenants 57:3, "Independence is the center place."

The Law of Authority and Teaching
DOCTRINE AND COVENANTS 42:11–17

42:11 *Known to the church . . . regularly ordained.* Previous revelation indicated that "no person is to be ordained to any office in this church, where there is a regularly organized branch of the same, without the vote of that church" (D&C 20:65). It is equally important that the person performing the ordinance be known to the Church to have authority. There are no secret ordinations to offices within the Church, nor are there any secrets as to who has been sent to preach the gospel to the world. Such a system is divine and protects the Saints and investigators of the gospel from deception by self-appointed teachers and leaders. This principle protects the Church against the activities of apostate groups who obviously are without the authority to teach the gospel or administer its ordinances, as are the priests and ministers of other faiths.

42:12 *Teach the principles of my gospel, which are in the Bible and the Book of Mormon.* Our charge is to teach the principles of the gospel using the scriptures as our primary text. At the time this revelation was given, the Doctrine and Covenants and the Pearl of Great Price had not yet been compiled or they would have been included with the Bible and the Book of Mormon. There is a spirit and power in teaching from the scriptures that cannot be found in other sources. In the Church today we have a great dependency on dramatic stories to illustrate principles we design to teach. As popular and helpful as such teaching devices are, they do not have the power to expand the mind and bring additional revelation that is found in the scriptures.

In the which is the fulness of the gospel. See commentary on Joseph Smith–History 1:34, page 20.

42:13 *The covenants and church articles.* Refers to Doctrine and Covenants 20 and 22, which were known by the title "Articles and Covenants of the Church." See commentary on Doctrine and Covenants 20 and 22.

42:14 *If ye receive not the Spirit ye shall not teach.* It is the Spirit that carries the message of the gospel teacher to the hearts of the listener. "For when a man speaketh by the power of the Holy Ghost," Nephi taught, "the power of the Holy Ghost carrieth it unto the hearts of the children of men" (2 Nephi 33:1). It naturally follows that teachers must live the gospel, or they cannot enjoy the companionship of the Spirit. The Lord indicated that those who obtain both his word and his Spirit have "the power of God unto the convincing of men" (D&C 11:21). Illustrating this principle, President Brigham Young said: "You have frequently heard me say that I would rather hear an Elder, either here or in the world, speak only five words accompanied by the power of God, and they would do more good than to hear long sermons without the Spirit. That is true, and we know it" (*Journal of Discourses*, 5:327). Further, he explained, "When a man rises up to speak in the name of the Lord, and is filled with the

light, and the intelligence and power which cometh from God, his countenance alone will convey more, to those who are inspired by the same
spirit, than can possibly be conveyed, by the words of any language now
used by mankind" (Young, *Journal of Discourses*, 10:353).

42:15 *Until the fulness of my scriptures is given.* Refers to the translation of the Bible. See commentary on Doctrine and Covenants 42:56–57.

42:17 *The Comforter . . . beareth record of the Father and of the Son.*
See 3 Nephi 11:32–36.

Moral Laws Renewed
DOCTRINE AND COVENANTS 42:18–29

42:18 *I speak unto the church.* "Unto whom much is given much is
required," the Lord declared; "and he who sins against the greater light
shall receive the greater condemnation" (D&C 82:3). Thus, the principles and laws revealed in this revelation have particular application to
members of the Church, and not necessarily to those who have not
covenanted with God in the waters of baptism to keep his commandments. Regarding those who do not have the law given to them, the
Prophet Joseph Smith taught, "The Great Parent of the universe looks
upon the whole human family with a fatherly care and paternal regard;
He views them as His offspring. . . . He will judge them, 'not according to
what they have not, but according to what they have,' those who have
lived without law, will be judged without law, and those who have a law,
will be judged by that law" (*Teachings of the Prophet Joseph Smith*, 218).

Thou shalt not kill. The Lord interpreted this commandment as, "Thou
shalt do no murder" (Matthew 19:18).

Shall not have forgiveness in this world, nor in the world to come. Cold-
blooded murder is sin unto death, meaning that the murderer cannot
obtain the glory of the celestial world. Such murderers, after properly suffering for their sins, will eventually find place in the telestial kingdom.
They will come forth from the grave in the last resurrection following the
Millennium. Although they can never be granted entrance into celestial
glory, their sins *can* be blotted out. They can be pardoned and removed
from spirit prison as long as they have not committed the unpardonable
sin of blasphemy against the Holy Ghost.

42:19 *He that killeth shall die.* Sinning against the Holy Ghost, which
would make one a son of perdition, is the only sin more grievous than murder (Alma 39:5–6). Murder, according to the law of God, is punishable by

death. As noted in verse 79, any who have taken life in such a manner are to be delivered up to and dealt with by the laws of the land. No Church court or disciplinary council would adjudicate such a matter.

It has been a common practice in anti-Mormon literature to accuse the Church of "blood atonement," meaning taking the life of apostates and transgressors. Addressing this accusation, Elder Bruce R. McConkie wrote: "There simply is no such thing among us as a doctrine of blood atonement that grants a remission of sins or confers any other benefit upon a person because his own blood is shed for sins. Let me say categorically and unequivocally that this doctrine can only operate in a day when there is no separation of Church and State and when the power to take life is vested in the ruling theocracy as was the case in the day of Moses. From the day of Joseph Smith to the present there has been no single instance of so-called blood atonement under any pretext" (letter to Mr. Thomas B. McAffee, 18 October 1978). See commentary on Doctrine and Covenants 42:79.

42:20 *Shall be cast out.* To be cast out is to be excommunicated. See commentary on verses 23, 24, and 26.

42:22 *And none else.* President Spencer W. Kimball explained: "The words *none else* eliminate everyone and everything. The spouse then becomes pre-eminent in the life of the husband or wife and neither social life nor occupational life nor political life nor any other interest nor person nor thing shall ever take precedence over the companion spouse" (*Miracle of Forgiveness*, 250).

Likewise, Paul wrote that men should "love their wives as their own bodies" (Ephesians 5:28).

42:23 *Shall deny the faith, and shall not have the Spirit.* The Spirit cannot dwell with adulterers. Without exception, those who commit adultery will lose the Spirit and the witness and testimony which it brings. George A. Smith stated: "I believe, if you will take the whole circle of the history of apostates from this Church, that in ninety-nine cases out of every hundred you will find that the spirit of adultery or covetousness was the original cause.

"There was a man named John Smith came into the Church, and was somewhat prominent in the State of Indiana. He preached some little, and was considered quite zealous; but he said he had proved that the Book of Doctrine and Covenants was not true; 'For it says,' said he, 'that if a man shall commit adultery, and not repent of it, he shall lose the Spirit of God, and shall deny the faith. Now, I have done it, and have not denied the faith; and so I have proved that the revelation in the Book of Doctrine and Covenants is not from God.' The spirit of blindness had so taken possession of him that he could not see that when he was proclaiming that the revelations were not true, he was denying the faith. That spirit has such an effect over the human mind as totally to blind them in relation to their own acts and the spirit that governs them" (*Journal of Discourses*, 7:114).

42:26 *If he doeth it again, he shall not be forgiven, but shall be cast out.* As stated in the previous verses of this revelation, unrepentant adulterers are to be excommunicated from the Church (vv. 22–24). There is the possibility that a member of the Church may be repentant and forsake adultery for a time and then commit the sin again. Such a person is likely to be cast out, which may be done by either excommunication or disfellowshipment from the Church.

This verse has caused some concern in connection with Joseph Smith's instructions, given 25 November 1843, on the occasion of a Brother Harrison Sagers's disciplinary court before the high council of Nauvoo. Charged with seduction, he said Joseph Smith had approved his course. The Prophet said: "I was present with several of the Twelve, and gave an address tending to do away with every evil, and exhorting them to practice virtue and holiness before the Lord; told them that the Church had not received any permission from me to commit fornication, adultery, or any corrupt action; but my every word and action has been to the contrary. If a man commit adultery, he cannot receive the celestial kingdom of God. Even if he is saved in any kingdom, it cannot be the celestial kingdom. I did think that the many examples that have been made manifest, such as John C. Bennett's and others, were sufficient to show the fallacy of such a course of conduct" (Smith, *History of the Church*, 6:81).

Elder Bruce R. McConkie explained: "The Prophet Joseph Smith in these words is addressing himself to those, and those only, whose calling and election has been made sure. The words do not refer to any others, either in or out of the Church. Having received the added light and knowledge that come in being sealed up unto eternal life, those whose calling and election has been made sure are subject to greater penalties if they transgress. Adulterers, as many scriptures attest and as the practice of the Church confirms, can repent and gain full salvation" (*New Witness*, 231).

Laws Governing Consecration

DOCTRINE AND COVENANTS 42:30–39

42:30–39 The Savior commanded the Saints to become one and to be "united according to the union required by the law of the celestial kingdom" (D&C 105:4). "For if ye are not equal in earthly things," the Lord declared, "ye cannot be equal in obtaining heavenly things" (D&C 78:6). Such equality and unity lead to becoming one with God and Christ. Those who live the law of consecration learn to esteem others as themselves. Consecrating temporal property is an outward manifestation of the innermost feelings of one's heart toward others. It tutors the soul in consecrating stores of spiritual knowledge to the building up of Zion and bringing "to pass the immortality and eternal life of man" (Moses 1:39). Similarly, the Saints of Alma's day "did walk uprightly before God, imparting to one another both temporally and spiritually according to their needs and their wants" (Mosiah 18:29).

The portion of the law of consecration revealed and restored at this time was limited to consecrating personal property. Like the Saints in the days of Enoch, Melchizedek, Peter, and Nephi after the visit of the risen Lord to the Americas, the Saints of the latter days were commanded to have all things in common and to see that there were no poor among them (Moses 7:18; JST Genesis 14:33–40; Acts 2:44–45; 4:34–5:11; 4 Nephi 1:3; D&C 38:24–27). The laws regarding consecration and stewardship of property were revealed through the Prophet Joseph Smith, line upon line.

The Saints of God in all ages consecrate their time, talents, strength, properties, and monies to establish the Lord's work and kingdom in their days. As circumstances require, these Saints are called to serve missions, colonize, build temples, and magnify their callings in a host of different ways.

42:30 *Consecrate of thy properties.* To consecrate property is to set it aside or devote it for sacred purposes. In this case the sacred work is to provide for the poor. Consecration of property teaches the Saints that they are stewards over the earth for the Lord. The foundational principle upon which this law rests is recognition that the Lord is the creator of the earth and, therefore, all property is his. "Behold, the Lord hath created the earth that it should be inhabited," Nephi explained; "and he hath created his children that they should possess it" (1 Nephi 17:36). All worldly wealth, whether it be lands or gold, is provided for the benefit of God's

children during their mortal sojourn. In commanding his Saints to consecrate their temporal earthly goods to the building up of his kingdom,
the Lord is not interested in real estate, precious ores, jewels, or houses.
Rather, consecration is a godly activity, and those who devote their
property, time, and talents to blessing others become more godlike.

With a covenant and a deed which cannot be broken. To dramatize the
seriousness of breaking this covenant the Lord said, "It had been better
for him that he had been drowned in the depth of the sea" (D&C 54:5).
The deed was a legally binding document, written and signed by both the
member consecrating his property and by the bishop who received the
property as the Lord's authorized agent. Thus, the covenant was binding
according to both the laws of God and the laws of the land.

42:32 *A steward over his own property.* After consecrating his properties the member received another legal, signed document from the bishop
listing the lands, furniture, tools, and so on that were being deeded to him
as his personal property. This property was held as a stewardship for the
Master, Jesus Christ, Lord of the earth. This arrangement recognized that
we are but stewards for the Lord and are accountable to him for the use
of our talents to bless the lives of others.

Sufficient for himself and family. The personal property deeded to the
member was to be adequate to enable him to provide for his family
according to the number of children and other dependents in the household. See commentary on Doctrine and Covenants 51:3.

42:34 *The residue shall be kept in my storehouse.* Anciently, the Lord
declared, "Bring ye all the tithes into the storehouse, that there may be
meat in mine house" (Malachi 3:10). The keeping of the Lord's storehouse to provide for the poor was restored with this revelation. One of
the most sacred trusts that is placed in the bishop's hands is that of providing for the poor and needy. In this law the bishop uses the property or
goods that are surplus to provide for the needs of the members. Although
sometimes referred to as a "bishop's storehouse," the bishop is but a servant of the Lord in distributing goods from the Lord's storehouse. These
storehouses containing food and wares are part of the Church welfare program. In addition, much of the burden of providing for the poor rests with
the fast offering monies collected as a free-will offering from the Saints
each fast day. See commentary on Doctrine and Covenants 78:3–4.

42:35 *Building up of the New Jerusalem.* In time the land will be purchased and the city of the New Jerusalem will be built, from which the
Lord will reign on earth.

42:36 *My covenant people.* The Lord's people have always been a covenant people. Their covenants are both individual and communal. There is no implication in the plan of salvation that we are saved separately and singly. We are not saved alone. Salvation is a community affair, as is the redemption of Zion or the building of a temple. The covenants we make with God on an individual basis require that we also be a part of a covenant community.

Anciently, Israel was chosen to be a covenant people, a holy nation, and a royal priesthood (Exodus 19:5–6). Likewise, the law of consecration is not simply a covenant made by an individual with God. Rather, it includes a covenant people or, in this case, a church whose members have covenanted to bring to pass the care of the poor and the establishment of Zion. Zion can be built up only by a community of Saints who are "of one heart and one mind, and [dwell] in righteousness; and there [is] no poor among them" (Moses 7:18).

42:39 One fulfillment of this verse is manifest in the work of building chapels and temples throughout Latin America. The Lord has proceeded to take the riches of the Gentiles (as defined by Book of Mormon writers) in the United States and Canada and consecrated them for the blessing of those whose circumstances are more humble.

Laws Governing Clothing and Work
DOCTRINE AND COVENANTS 42:40–42

42:40 *Let all thy garments be plain.* The true saint does not chase after the fashions of the world. The statement that their "garments be plain" does not preclude their wearing things that are richly colored but rather suggests an appropriate standard of modesty. The Nephite prophets repeatedly identified the wearing of costly clothing with apostasy and failure to live gospel standards (Jacob 2:13; Alma 1:6, 32; 4:6; 5:53; 31:27–28; 4 Nephi 24; Mormon 8:36–37). Jacob warned, "Because some of you have obtained [riches] more abundantly than that of your brethren ye are lifted up in the pride of your hearts, and wear stiff necks and high heads because of the costliness of your apparel, and persecute your brethren because ye suppose that ye are better than they" (Jacob 2:13).

42:42 *He that is idle shall not eat the bread nor wear the garments of the laborer.* This principle has been a guiding light in the restored gospel. The welfare program, for which the Church is renowned, is based on the dignity of working for what is received. Heber J. Grant read a message from the First Presidency that stated: "Our primary purpose was to set up in so far as it might be possible, a system under which the curse of idleness would be done away with, the evils of a dole abolished, and independence, industry, thrift and self respect be once more established amongst our people. The aim of the Church is to help the people to help themselves. Work is to be re-enthroned as the ruling principle of the lives of our Church membership" (Conference Report, October 1936, 3). J. Reuben Clark testified, "From the foundation of the Church until now, idleness has been condemned as unworthy of Church members, as destructive of character, as violative of the true Christian life, as contrary to the command given to Adam as the law of this world 'In the sweat of thy brow, thou shalt eat bread'" (Conference Report, October 1936, 2–3).

The Sick and Those That Die
DOCTRINE AND COVENANTS 42:43–52

42:43 In the early 1800s herbs were the common means by which physicians ministered to the sick. Rather than being an admonition against the medicines found in nature, this revelation finds a place for both the skillful administration of herbs and the healing blessing at the hands of the priesthood. Being ill and unable to raise his head from his pillow, the Prophet Joseph Smith, on 14 June 1837, recorded: "I continued to grow worse and worse until my sufferings were excruciating, and although in the midst of it all I felt to rejoice in the salvation of Israel's God, yet I found it expedient to call to my assistance those means which a kind Providence had provided for the restoration of the sick, in connection with the ordinances; and Dr. Levi Richards, at my request, administered to me herbs and mild food, and nursed me with all tenderness and attention; and my heavenly Father blessed his administrations to the easing and comforting of my system, for I began to amend in a short time, and in a few days I was able to resume my usual labors.

"This is one of the many instances in which I have suddenly been brought from a state of health, to the borders of the grave, and as suddenly restored, for which my heart swells with gratitude to my heavenly Father, and I feel renewedly to dedicate myself and all my powers to His service.

"While I was thus afflicted, the enemy of all righteousness was suggesting, apostates reporting, and the doubtful believing that my afflictions were sent upon me, because I was in transgression, and had taught the Church things contrary to godliness; but of this the Lord judge between me and them, while I pray my Father to forgive them the wrong they do" (*History of the Church*, 2:493).

The Book of Mormon speaks "of the excellent qualities of the many plants and roots which God had prepared to remove the cause of diseases" (Alma 46:40). In the *Times and Seasons* the question was asked, "Who is to administer those herbs?" The answer: "We presume that nine tenths of the human family, neither understand the physiology of the human system, the nature and effects of disease, nor the medicinal properties of herbs; and under such circumstances would not be competent to administer at all. Herbs are to be used, and mild food; but those herbs are to be used by skillful hands. . . . We should judge, then, from the above, that a person who is acquainted with the physiology of the human system, and the nature and medicinal properties of herbs, is more competent to judge of those things, and to administer with judgment and skill, than the one who is ignorant, both of the organization of the human system, of the medicinal properties of herbs, and of the nature and effects of disease.

"It is also evident that, if there is any danger, or wrong, in the administration of herbs, it is from their being in the hands of unskillful men, and particularly in the hands of an enemy.

"On reviewing the whole subject, we cannot but regret that, as saints, we have not all faith, either to be healed, or to cast ourselves into the hands of God, and 'whether we live, live unto God, or whether we die, die unto the Lord.' But—inasmuch as all have not faith, those that are strong ought not to condemn the weak, inasmuch as they make a judicious means of those things which the Lord, in his mercy, has been pleased to provide, and appoint for the infirmities and diseases of human nature.

"We are aware that this community have been a good deal imposed upon by quacks; that nostrums of all kinds have been administered by injudicious hands, producing the most deleterious effects; and that many have slept in the dust, who, if they had been let alone, would still have been in the land of the living" (*Times and Seasons*, 4:325–26).

42:44 *Elders of the church . . . shall pray for and lay their hands upon them in my name.* The practice of healing by the laying on of hands has been given by the Lord as one of the signs that would follow them that believe. During the Savior's mortal ministry "all they that had any sick with divers diseases brought them unto him; and he laid his hands on every one of them, and healed them" (Luke 4:40). The apostle James instructed the meridian-day Saints, asking, "Is any sick among you? let him call for the elders of the church; and let them pray over him, anointing him with oil in the name of the Lord" (James 5:14).

Administrations have two parts: anointings and sealings; both are accompanied by the laying on of hands.

It is the practice of the Church that administering to the sick be done at the request of the sick or someone closely involved with the sick person, so that it will be done in answer to faith. Those called on to perform the ordinance should encourage the sick person to rely on the Lord's promise, "Whatsoever thing ye shall ask the Father in my name, which is good, in faith believing that ye shall receive, behold, it shall be done unto you" (Moroni 7:26). The sick person may be encouraged to keep the commandments so that he or she can have faith and be entitled to the blessings of the Lord.

In performing the administration, one elder anoints the sick person with oil on or near the crown of the head for the restoration of health. Pure olive oil which has been consecrated for that purpose should be used. Taking consecrated oil internally, or using it for anointing or rubbing afflicted parts of the body, is not part of the ordinance of administering to the sick.

After the anointing two or more elders lay their hands on the head of the sick person. One of them acts as voice to seal the anointing. The one speaking offers prayers, pronounces blessings, or gives promises as the Spirit directs.

42:46 *Shall not taste of death, for it shall be sweet unto them.* Joseph Fielding Smith explained: "To some members of the Church the saying that those who die in the Lord shall not taste of death has been a hard saying. They have seen good faithful men and women suffer days and at times for months before they were taken. But here the Lord does not say they shall not suffer pain of body, but that they shall be free from the anguish and torment of soul which will be partaken of by the wicked, and although they may suffer in body, yet death to them will be sweet in that they will realize that they are worthy before the Lord. The Savior said to Martha: 'And whosoever liveth and believe in me shall never die.' That is to say, they shall never die the second death and feel the torment of the wicked when they come face to face with eternity" (*Church History and Modern Revelation*, 1:186).

With reference to this phrase, Spencer W. Kimball added: "I think that means they are not going into the other world feeling resentment and reticence. After they get past a certain point they go with happiness, peace and contentment" (*Teachings of Spencer W. Kimball*, 38). The Prophet Joseph Smith demonstrated such a view of imminent death. Apostle John Taylor recorded, "When Joseph went to Carthage to deliver himself up to the pretended requirements of the law, two or three days previous to his assassination, he said: 'I am going like a lamb to the slaughter; but I am calm as a summer's morning; I have a conscience void of offense towards God, and towards all men'" (D&C 135:4).

The greatest example of meeting death with sweetness amidst excruciating pain and agony is the Savior Jesus Christ. We sense in him, as he approached the hour of greatest suffering attendant to his crucifixion, a peace and calmness. He did not fear death for he knew it to be a prelude to triumph over the grave. Those who have received a testimony of the truthfulness of the restored gospel know death to be part of the plan of an all-knowing, wise, and loving God. They look forward to reunion with loved ones in the spirit world and to embrace family and friends in the flesh following the resurrection. Moreover, at the moment of death the anticipated reunion may begin as evidenced in the accounts of those who have been greeted by angels. For example, referring to his brother Alvin, the Prophet Joseph Smith wrote, "He was one of the soberest of men, and when he died the angel of the Lord visited him in his last moments" (*History of the Church*, 5:127).

With reference to the death of Heber C. Kimball, George Q. Cannon described how death is pleasant: "It was sweet with him. There was nothing repulsive, nothing dreadful or terrible in it, but on the contrary it was calm, peaceful and sweet. There were heavenly influences there, as though angels were there, and no doubt they were, prepared to escort him hence to the society of those whom he loved and who loved him dearly. I thought of the joy there would be in the spirit land, when Joseph, and Hyrum, and David, and Willard, and Jededia, and Parley would welcome him to their midst, and the thousands of others who have gone before, and like them have been faithful. What a welcome to their midst will brother Heber receive! to labor and toil with them in the spirit world in the great work in which we are engaged" (*Journal of Discourses*, 12:184).

Alma the younger testified, "Behold, it has been made known unto me by an angel, that the spirits of all men, as soon as they are departed from this mortal body, yea, the spirits of all men, whether they be good or evil, are taken home to that God who gave them life. And then shall it come to pass, that the spirits of those who are righteous are received into a state of happiness, which is called paradise, a state of rest, a state of peace, where they shall rest from all their troubles and from all care, and sorrow" (Alma 40:11–12).

42:48 *Faith in me to be healed.* See commentary on Doctrine and Covenants 46:19–20.

Not appointed unto death. We labor in this life according to divine appointment, some for great lengths of time and others for shorter periods. While in jail at Liberty after repeated attempts had been made to take his life, the Prophet Joseph Smith was told by the Lord, "Thy days are known, and thy years shall not be numbered less; therefore, fear not what man can do, for God shall be with you forever and ever" (D&C 122:9).

Our faith exercised to extend the lives of loved ones is always subject to the overriding will of the Lord. If he wills to take one of his children from this life to the next, then his will prevails.

The principle that men are appointed to die does not necessarily mean that each individual has a predestined moment in mortality when death is to occur. Neither does it mean that God will intervene to prevent all accidents, carelessness, or wicked choices that bring sorrow and death. The Lord indicated that death for many of his children is on a flexible time schedule. "There is a time appointed for every man, according as his works shall be" (D&C 121:25). President Wilford Woodruff elaborated on the means by which the righteous might be appointed unto death: "The Prophet Joseph Smith held the keys of this dispensation on this side of the vail, and he will hold them throughout the countless ages of eternity. He went into the spirit world to unlock the prison doors and to preach the Gospel to the millions of spirits who are in darkness, and every Apostle, every Seventy, every Elder, etc., who has died in the faith as soon as he passes to the other side of the vail, enters into the work of the ministry, and there is a thousand times more to preach there than there is here. I have felt of late as if our brethren on the other side of the vail had held a council, and that they had said to this one, and that one, 'Cease thy work on earth, come hence, we need help,' and they have called this man and that man. It has appeared so to me in seeing the many men who have been called from our midst lately. Perhaps I may be permitted to relate a circumstance with which I am acquainted in relation to Bishop Roskelley, of Smithfield, Cache Valley. On one occasion he was suddenly taken very sick—near to death's door. While he lay in this condition, President Peter Maughan, who was dead, came to him and said: 'Brother Roskelley, we held a council on the other side of the vail. I have had a great deal to do, and I have the privilege of coming here to appoint one man to come and help. I have had three names given to me in council, and you are one of them. I want to inquire into your circumstances.' The Bishop told him what he had to do, and they conversed together as one man would converse with another. President Maughan then said to him: 'I think I will not call you. I think you are wanted here more than perhaps one of the others.' Bishop Roskelley got well from that hour. Very soon after, the second man was taken sick, but not being able to exercise sufficient faith, Brother Roskelley did not go to him. By and by this man recovered, and on meeting Brother Roskelley he said: 'Brother Maughan came to me the other night and told me he was sent to call one man from the ward,' and he named two men as had been done to Brother Roskelley. A few days afterwards the third man was taken sick and died. Now, I name this to show a principle. They have work on the other side of the vail; and they want men, and they call them. And that was my view in regard to Brother George A. Smith. When he was almost at death's door, Brother Cannon administered to him, and in thirty minutes he was up and ate breakfast with his family. We labored with him in this way, but ultimately, as you know, he died. But it taught me a lesson. I felt that man was wanted behind the vail. We labored also with Brother Pratt; he, too, was wanted behind the vail" (*Journal of Discourses*, 22:333–34).

42:52 *They who have not faith to do these things, but believe in me, have power to become my sons.* To be blind, deaf, or lame is not evidence that an individual does not have faith unto salvation. See commentary on Doctrine and Covenants 34:1–4.

Clarifications Regarding the Law of Consecration
DOCTRINE AND COVENANTS 42:53–55

42:53 *Stand in the place of thy stewardship.* See commentary on Doctrine and Covenants 42:32.

42:54 Fellowship with the Saints does not give leave to take advantage of another's goodness. "There were some of the disciples," wrote John Whitmer, "who were flattered into the Church because they thought that all things were to be common, therefore they thought to glut themselves upon the labors of others" ("Book of John Whitmer," 42). Within the covenant community of the law of consecration material goods were not communal property. Each individual received a deed to his own personal property and did not have claim on another's property for his personal use.

This aberration of the true law of God was practiced by a group of Sidney Rigdon's followers who were living on the property of Isaac Morley. Soon after joining the Church in the winter of 1831, Levi Hancock traveled to Kirtland to gather with the Saints. He wrote: "The next morning brother Harvey Redfield took us to Brother Isaac Morleys who was a cooper by trade and one of the most honest patient men I ever saw. The company he maintained looked large enough to bring on a famine. I do not know if they lived on him all the time or not.

"While I was in the room at 'Father Morleys' as we all called him, this same Hermon Bassett came to me and took my watch out of my pocket and walked off as though it was his. I thought he would bring it back soon but was disappointed as he sold it. I asked him what he meant by selling my watch.

"'Oh, said he, I thought it was all in the family.' I told him I did not like such family doings and I would not bear it" (*Autobiography of Levi Ward Hancock*, 42).

Scriptures of the Restoration to Govern the Church
DOCTRINE AND COVENANTS 42:56-61

42:56 *Thou shalt ask.* Many revelations of the Restoration came in answer to questions by members of the infant Church. Real life situations were the seedbed of revelation. Thus, the restored gospel as revealed in the latter days is a practicable application of the principles of salvation and the building up of the kingdom of God on earth as needed during mortality. Mankind seeks for instruction to guide them through this world and for enlightenment to understand the purposes of mortality in relation to that which came before and that which will follow in the eternities. In addition to the real-life situations from which the revelations came forth, the Lord appointed the Prophet Joseph Smith to translate the Bible, which work restored the truths and wisdom of all past dispensations. As Joseph sought to understand the biblical record, the Lord "[poured] down knowledge from heaven upon the heads of the Latter-day Saints" (D&C 121:33) in accordance with the promises found in these verses.

42:56 *My scriptures shall be given as I have appointed.* The Lord determined that the Restoration would include the dispensing of new scripture and of perfecting scripture already available to mankind.

"*Question: How and in what way is the new knowledge being restored?*

"Answer: By revelation. Our doctrine is not handed down, in the sectarian sense; it is revealed. It is revealed directly as in the case of the Doctrine and Covenants; or by the process of translation, as in the case of the Book of Mormon; or by the process of perfecting ancient scriptures, as in the case of the Joseph Smith Translation. . . .

"*Question: What are the vehicles of the restoration?*

"Answer: First, the Book of Mormon, which was translated by the gift and power of God; second, the Doctrine and Covenants, whose contents are revealed, coupled with such inspired utterances as the King Follett Sermon; and, third, the so-called Translations, which include the book of Abraham, the book of Moses (itself part of the Inspired Version), and the whole Joseph Smith Translation of the Bible.

"None of these vehicles have given us their full load. We have only about a third of the Book of Mormon; the field of revelation is without bounds or limits; and the Bible restoration has scarcely been commenced.

"*Question: When will we receive more of the mind and will of the Lord, and when will the great doctrinal restoration be completed?*

"We have a revealed answer as to when we shall receive the sealed portion of the Book of Mormon. What we have so far received is to test our faith. When we repent of all our iniquity and become clean before the Lord, and when we exercise faith in him like unto the brother of Jared, then the sealed portion of the ancient word will be translated and read from the housetops.

"The same is certainly true of the brass plates and the lost portions of the Bible. What we have received so far is to test our faith. Why should the Lord give us more of the biblical word if we are indifferent to what he has already revealed? Does anyone think the Lord should give us the words of Zenos when we are ignoring the words of Isaiah?

"There are revelations without end that are available to the faithful at any time they are prepared to receive them.

"As a matter of practical reality, however, the great doctrinal restoration is to be Millennial. Of that day Nephi said: Then 'the earth shall be full of the knowledge of the Lord as the waters cover the sea. Wherefore, the things of all nations shall be made known; yea, all things shall be made known unto the children of men. There is nothing which is secret save it shall be revealed; there is no work of darkness save it shall be made manifest in the light; and there is nothing which is sealed upon the earth save it shall be loosed. Wherefore, all things which have been revealed unto the children of men shall at that day be revealed; and Satan shall have

REVELATIONS OF THE RESTORATION

power over the hearts of the children of men no more, for a long time.'
(2 Nephi 30:15–18)" (McConkie, "Doctrinal Restoration," 20–21).

They shall be preserved in safety. During the six-month period that the
Prophet was held at Liberty Jail, his papers (among which was the New
Translation of the Bible, which we call the Joseph Smith Translation)
were left in the hands of his secretary, James Mulholland. Mulholland and
his family discussed in private what might happen if the mob were to
obtain the manuscript. They feared that Mulholland might be attacked
by a mob, and that the mob would destroy the papers he possessed just for
the sake of ruining them. The family also felt the manuscript would not
be safe in Far West.

Knowing that the life of Mulholland was in constant danger and out
of concern for the safety of the papers that were left in his care, it was
decided that Mulholland's sister-in-law, Ann Scott, should take care of
the materials. She has written of this event in Far West as follows:

"[The mob] frequently searched my father's house, and were very
insulting in their deportment. They also searched other houses of the
saints, including that of President Joseph Smith, who at the time was confined in Liberty Jail. Joseph's confinement in jail, coupled with the ruthless invasions of the mob, caused his scribe, Elder James Mulholland, to
seek a place of safety for important church papers in his possession.
Among the papers in Mulholland's keeping was the manuscript of the
Inspired Translation of the Bible, the revelation on the rebellion [D&C
87], etc., etc. Brother Mulholland requested me to take charge of the
papers, as he thought they would be more secure with me, because I was a
woman, and the mob would not be likely to search my person.
Immediately on taking possession of the papers, I made two cotton bags
of sufficient size to contain them, sewing a band around the top ends of
sufficient length to button around my waist; and I carried those papers on
my person in the day-time, when the mob was around, and slept with
them under my pillow at night. I cannot remember the exact length of
time I had those papers in my possession; but I gave them to sister Emma
Smith, the prophet's wife, on the evening of her departure for Commerce"
(as cited in Matthews, *Plainer Translation*, 99).

"Emma Smith left Far West, en route to Commerce, Illinois, on
February 15, 1839, and according to the report, she 'wore the bags just as
Ann Scott had done'" (Matthews, *Plainer Translation*, 100).

42:57 *Not teach them until ye have received them in full.* This commandment refers to the translation of the Bible. Similar counsel was given to the

Prophet Joseph Smith at other times during the translation process. Some confusion concerning the appropriate use of the Joseph Smith Translation of the Bible has arisen due to this passage. The question is, "Did the Prophet Joseph Smith ever finish the revelatory translation of the Bible?" The difficulty in answering this question is that none of the standard works are completed in their fulness. For example, there is much more to come forth from the Nephite records from which we received the abridged edition of Mormon's writings. A large portion of the plates upon which the Book of Mormon was written is sealed, and there are books of the Bible that were lost. Not all revelations received by the Prophet Joseph Smith have been placed in the Doctrine and Covenants. The Pearl of Great Price has undergone additions and deletions since it compilation and publication in the nineteenth century. Yet we consider these scriptural texts to be complete enough for publication. The translation of the Bible may be considered as complete as the other books of scripture within the Restoration.

In addition we have the Lord's word that the inspired translation of the Bible was deemed completed to the degree that he commanded that it be published. William Law, as a member of the First Presidency of the Church, was commanded to "publish the new translation of my holy word unto the inhabitants of the earth" (D&C 124:89). The opportunity to publish the translation was lost with the failure of William Law to abide in the covenant. After the martyrdom of the Prophet Joseph Smith, his wife, Emma, retained the manuscripts of the translation, which went to the Reorganized Church of Jesus Christ of Latter Day Saints through the Smith family.

The Location of the New Jerusalem and Mysteries of the Kingdom to Be Revealed
DOCTRINE AND COVENANTS 42:62–69

42:62 *Where the New Jerusalem shall be built.* See commentary on Doctrine and Covenants 57:2–3.

42:64 *Teach them that shall be converted to flee to the west.* The point of reference to this command is that the Saints should gather to Ohio, which at this time was considered the west to the many who were in the eastern regions of the United States. The movement of the Saints, as a gathered body of people, was in a general western direction throughout the early history of the Church. Each such removal to another place of gathering was "for a defense, and for a refuge from the storm" (D&C 115:6) of persecution and evil designs of the Saint's enemies.

42:69 *The kingdom, or in other words, the keys of the church.* Where the keys are, there the kingdom is. The doctrine of priesthood keys separates the true Church of God from all other claimants to that title. The Prophet Joseph Smith received keys of the Church, the power delegated from God to direct the work of the kingdom, from heavenly messengers. John the Baptist restored the keys of the Aaronic Priesthood, and Peter, James, and John restored the keys of the Melchizedek Priesthood, consisting of the keys of the kingdom. See commentary on Doctrine and Covenants 27:12–13.

Church Officers Are to Be Supported from Consecrated Properties
DOCTRINE AND COVENANTS 42:70–73

42:70–73 Reference to the bishop and his counselors in this passage refers to the presiding bishopric. This is the first mention of counselors to assist the bishop and surely restores that which existed anciently. On 4 February 1831 Edward Partridge was called to the office of bishop, being the first so called in this dispensation. On 6 June 1831 Isaac Morley and John Corrill were set apart as counselors to Bishop Partridge.

Justification for full-time employees of the Church being remunerated for their labor is found in this verse. Earlier, the Lord revealed that the Prophet Joseph Smith should be supported in his temporal needs by the Church. See commentary on Doctrine and Covenants 24:3; 43:13, "Provide for him food and raiment."

Laws for Dealing with Adulterers
DOCTRINE AND COVENANTS 42:74–93

42:74–93 The fundamental laws of the Church, as recorded in the first 73 verses of Doctrine and Covenants 42, were revealed on 9 February 1831. Undoubtedly, concerns arose as to what steps should be taken if members transgressed the revealed laws. As a result, two weeks later the Lord revealed the remainder of this section on 23 February, as recorded in verses 74 through 93. The latter portion of the law makes known the proper way to deal with transgressors.

42:74 *Put away their companions.* Reference is to obtaining a divorce. In the case referred to the innocent spouse should not bear any shame or discipline on the part of the Church.

42:75 *Left their companions for the sake of adultery.* Reference is to individuals who leave their husbands or wives because they themselves are committing adultery and wish to live with the adulterous companion. *And their companions are living.* Adulterers who abandon their wives for an adulterous alliance are not dealt with in the same manner as those who remain with their wives and family, repenting and seeking forgiveness as previously explained in this revelation. "He that has committed adultery and repents with all his heart, and forsaketh it, and doeth it no more, thou shalt forgive" (D&C 42:25). In contrast, the man or woman who leaves a spouse to live with the companion in sin has placed himself or herself in a more serious situation—complicating the ability to repent "with all his heart" and to forsake adultery. In such cases the Lord indicates that such individuals are to be excommunicated, losing their membership in the Church of Jesus Christ.

42:76 *Be watchful and careful, with all inquiry, that ye receive none such among you if they are married.* The Church must be clean, like a virtuous bride, to be acceptable to the bridegroom, Jesus Christ. The general law of the Church is that any couple, whose union was initiated by an adulterous relationship, is not to be sealed in the house of the Lord for time and eternity. The proper beginning to marriage is not abandonment of a previous marriage because of adultery. Any exceptions to this law need to be addressed directly by the First Presidency of the Church. Because adulterers are also liars and, thus, will cover their iniquity with all manner of deception, the Church is commanded to carefully examine the reasons for forsaking marriage. Time and careful inquiry will reveal the true offenders within the marriage covenant.

Nearly ten years after this law was revealed, the importance of these instructions evidenced itself in the case of John C. Bennett. Mr. Bennett came to Nauvoo, Illinois, and was extended a cordial welcome by the Prophet Joseph Smith. In the course of time it was learned that he had left a wife and three children in the East and was a man of gross sexual immorality. Following the revelation of his true character, John C. Bennett was excommunicated from the Church.

Laws for Dealing with Murderers and Adulterers Contrasted
DOCTRINE AND COVENANTS 42:78–83

42:79 *If any persons among you shall kill they shall be delivered up and dealt with according to the laws of the land.* The Lord commanded that his

Saints maintain the separation of church and state according to the laws of the land. Already set forth in the law is that murderers shall be cast out of the Church. However, that does not end the responsibility of the Church. Neither known nor accused murderers should be harbored in their crimes by claiming religious privileges of providing sanctuary for criminals. Indeed, just the opposite is the case. The Church should deliver murderers up to be dealt with by civil authorities according to the law of the land in which the Church members reside.

42:80 *Tried before two elders of the church, or more.* The priesthood presides at disciplinary councils for Saints whose membership in the Church is in jeopardy. In these early days of the Restoration the organization of wards and stakes was not yet revealed. In time the Lord revealed the disciplinary council system in which bishops and stake presidents preside in administering the laws revealed herein. See Doctrine and Covenants 102.

By two witnesses. This command restored and clarified appropriate application of the law given to Israel anciently that the Saints were to be condemned "at the mouth of two witnesses, or three witnesses [to] . . . put the evil away from among you" (Deuteronomy 17:6–7).

42:82 *It is necessary that the bishop be present.* See commentary on Doctrine and Covenants 107:77–84.

Laws for Dealing with Thieves and Liars
DOCTRINE AND COVENANTS 42:84–87

42:84–87 The robber, the thief, and the liar are to be delivered up to the law of the land, whereas those who commit iniquity are to be tried by a Church disciplinary council. In this way the Church sustains the government and its laws designed to protect itself and its citizens. As to matters of improper behavior, immorality, and apostasy, these constitute an offence against the Church and its members and are thus the prerogative of a Church council to decide. In doing so the Church does not, and has not, inflicted corporeal punishment or confiscated property. The only penalties the Church can impose are loss of fellowship or loss of the privileges that accompany members in good standing.

42:87 *He or she shall be delivered up unto the law, even that of God.* President James E. Faust instructed priesthood leaders concerning the seriousness of carrying out the Lord's law to discipline those Saints who commit serious transgressions: "Those who have keys, which include the judicial or disciplinary authority, have the responsibility for keeping the Church cleansed from all iniquity (D&C 20:54; 43:11). Bishops, stake presidents, mission presidents, and others who have the responsibility of keeping the Church pure must perform this labor in a spirit of love and kindness. It should not be done in a spirit of punishment, but rather of helping. However, it is of no kindness to a brother or sister in transgression for their presiding officers to look the other way. Some words on this subject come from President John Taylor:

"'Furthermore, I have heard of some Bishops who have been seeking to cover up the iniquities of men; I tell them, in the name of God, they will have to bear . . . that iniquity, and if any of you want to partake of the sins of men, or uphold them, you will have to bear them. Do you hear it, you Bishops and you Presidents? God will require it at your hands. You are not placed in a position to tamper with the principles of righteousness, nor to cover up the infamies and corruptions of men' (Conference Report, April 1880, 78).

"On this matter, we urge you presiding brethren to seek the Spirit of God, to study and be guided by the scriptures and the *General Handbook of Instructions.* Church discipline is not limited to sexual sins but includes other acts such as murder, abortions, burglary, theft, fraud, and other dishonesty, deliberate disobedience to the rules and regulations of the Church, advocating or practicing polygamy, apostasy, or any other unchristianlike conduct, including defiance or ridicule of the Lord's anointed, contrary to the law of the Lord and the order of the Church" ("Keeping Covenants," 37).

Laws for Dealing with Private and Public Offenses
DOCTRINE AND COVENANTS 42:88–93

42:89 *Not before the world.* Church disciplinary councils are conducted in private chambers. Everything that takes place in these councils is regarded with the strictest confidence. The sanctity of these councils is recognized by civil authority, and those involved are granted priest-penitent privilege, meaning that they cannot be required to divulge what took place even in a court of law. See commentary on Doctrine and Covenants 102.

DOCTRINE AND COVENANTS 43

DATE: FEBRUARY 1831
PLACE: KIRTLAND, OHIO

No truth of salvation stands unopposed. When the Lord calls a prophet, false prophets arise. In New York, Satan deceived Hiram Page and the Whitmer family with a counterfeit seer stone. Similarly, in Ohio, Lucifer temporarily misled new converts into accepting his imitation of a prophet. Therefore, the lessons previously learned in New York regarding false spirits needed to be taught again. See introduction to Doctrine and Covenants 28.

The Prophet Joseph Smith recorded that soon after the law of the Church (D&C 42) was received, "a woman came making pretensions of revealing commandments, laws and other curious matters" (*History of the Church*, 1:154). John Whitmer identified the intruder as "a woman by the name of Hubble who professed to be a prophetess of the Lord and professed to have many revelations, and knew the Book of Mormon was true, and that she should become a teacher in the Church of Christ. She appeared to be very sanctimonious and deceived some who were not able to detect her in her hypocracy: others however had the spirit of discernment, and her follies and abominations were made manifest" ("Book of John Whitmer," 42). Mrs. Hubble's sanctimonious conduct added to the difficulty of dealing with the errors introduced at this time. Ezra Booth, an early member and eventual apostate, stated as part of his attack on the Church that Mrs. Hubble, "professing to be a prophetess, made her appearance in Kirtland, and so ingratiated herself into the esteem and favor of some of the Elders that they received her as a person commissioned to act a conspicuous part in Mormonizing the world. [Sidney] Rigdon, and some others, gave her the right hand of fellowship, and literally saluted her with what they called the 'kiss' of charity. But [Joseph] Smith . . . declared her an imposter, and she returned to the place from whence she came. Her visit, however, made a deep impression on the minds of many, and the barbed arrow which she left in the hearts of some, is not as yet eradicated" (in Cook, *Revelations*, 61–62).

We face similar ploys today, and it is essential that every member of the Church has the power of discernment and knows the spiritual laws by which spiritual counterfeiters are detected. Unlike true messengers—who always focus on the need for repentance—these self-ordained prophets and prophetesses come to tell us that all that really matters is that we love one another, thus subverting the discipline of true discipleship. These deceivers disguise false doctrine by dipping it in honey. The errors they introduce are difficult to confront because these counterfeiters promote themselves as being more accepting and loving than those who defend the kingdom against such false intruders.

The masks and costumes of false prophets may change, but the doctrine of the kingdom as reiterated in this revelation remains enduring and true. If followed, the simple guidelines revealed herein protect the Saints from deceivers, false revelators, and false spirits.

Revelations and Commandments Come Only through the One Appointed
DOCTRINE AND COVENANTS 43:1–7

43:2 *Ye have received a commandment for a law unto my church.* See commentary on Doctrine and Covenants 42:11.

43:3 *None other appointed unto you to receive commandments and revelations.* The words "none other" exclude any pretenders or deceivers that might seek to lead the Saints astray. The Lord avoids confusion in his kingdom by appointing one individual, the president of The Church of Jesus Christ of Latter-day Saints, to receive revelations and commandments for the Church. Even though other members of the First Presidency and the Quorum of Twelve Apostles are sustained as prophets, seers, and revelators, they are under the direction of the president of the Church. In his instructions on the priesthood, Joseph Smith explained, "And again, the duty of the President of the office of the High Priesthood is to preside over the whole church, and to be like unto Moses" (D&C 107:91), who was the spokesman for God to ancient Israel. See commentary on Doctrine and Covenants 28:2.

43:4 *He shall not have power except to appoint another.* At this early date in the Restoration, the Lord made provision to protect his little flock from the deception of false prophets in the event that even Joseph Smith fell into transgression. The law remains that there is but one on the earth who receives commandments and revelations for the Church. Had the responsibility of being the Lord's mouthpiece been taken from the Prophet Joseph Smith, the last authorized act he would be called on to perform would have been to confer the keys of the kingdom on another. See commentary on Doctrine and Covenants 90:3.

43:6 *That you may not be deceived.* During his mortal ministry the Savior warned his disciples: "Beware of false prophets, which come to you in sheep's clothing, but inwardly they are ravening wolves" (Matthew 7:15). The sanctimonious cloak of "the kiss of charity" hid the true intentions of Mrs. Hubble. Likewise, over the many years since this revelation was given, others have clothed themselves in apparel of various deceptive colors and styles. Some wear the claim of special manifestations or commissions that authorize them to perpetuate plural marriage. Others attire themselves in beguiling raiment of a commission from Enoch to set up the united order; power to translate the sealed portion of the Book of Mormon; scholarly insight to tell the "true Mormon history;" visions that reveal the feminine identity of the Holy Ghost; keys to gather the Saints to Zion; near-death experiences that make known the previously unrevealed mysteries of the post-mortal spirit world; and a host of other distractions to the true issue at hand. The Lord warned of their deception. Let this simple truth ring in the ears of all Saints: They are deceivers and are not authorized to give commandments or revelations to the Church nor to any individual member who seeks to follow the truth of the restored gospel!

This warning is of special importance to those that live in the latter days. "For in those days there shall also arise false Christs, and false prophets, and shall show great signs and wonders, insomuch, that, if possible, they shall deceive the very elect, who are the elect according to the covenant" (Joseph Smith–Matthew 1:22). Deception can be avoided by following this law as revealed by the Lord to the Church, for "whoso treasureth up my word, shall not be deceived" (Joseph Smith–Matthew 1:37).

43:7 *He that is ordained of me shall come in at the gate.* "He that entereth not by the door into the sheepfold," the Savior taught, "but climbeth up some other way, the same is a thief and a robber. But he that entereth in by the door is the shepherd of the sheep" (John 10:1–2). True servants of the Lord will always be known to the Church, having been called, sustained by the voice of the Church, and properly ordained. See commentary on Doctrine and Covenants 42:11.

Saints Assemble to Instruct and Edify Each Other
DOCTRINE AND COVENANTS 43:8–10

43:8 *Edify each other.* See commentary on Doctrine and Covenants 50:23.

That ye may know how to act and direct my church. The Church of Jesus Christ of Latter-day Saints is the Lord's Church, and he leads it. We seek our instruction from him. Tremendous energy is expended in the kingdom of God to instruct the Saints in the discharge of their duties. Regular councils and training meetings are held to aid each of us in keeping our covenants and magnifying the offices and callings that are ours.

43:10 *Inasmuch as ye do it not, it shall be taken, even that which ye have received.* Saints who stop attending or who are lax in attending Church meetings lose the Spirit. Attaining and retaining spiritual knowledge is governed by eternal law. We must continue to receive line upon line in the manner that the Lord directs, or we will fall prey to that spirit which robs us of testimony and faith. "He that will harden his heart," Alma explained, "the same receiveth the lesser portion of the word; and he that will not harden his heart, to him is given the greater portion of the word, until it is given unto him to know the mysteries of God until he know them in full. And they that will harden their hearts, to them is given the lesser portion of the word until they know nothing concerning his mysteries; and then they are taken captive by the devil, and led by his will down to destruction. Now this is what is meant by the chains of hell" (Alma 12:10–11).

Saints Are to Provide Financial Assistance for the Work of the Kingdom
DOCTRINE AND COVENANTS 43:11–14

43:13 *The mysteries of the kingdom.* Mysteries are those principles and doctrines that can be understood only by revelation.

Provide for him food and raiment. The Master could have chosen another way to provide for his servant. He might have rained manna from heaven, sent quail to his doorstep, or commanded Joseph to let his nets down to capture a school of fish, as occurred on other occasions. In this instance he chose to do as had been done before with the prophet Elijah. During a famine the Lord sent Elijah to a widow woman in Zarephath. She and her son prepared for Elijah their last handful of meal and a little cruse of oil with which to make a cake. Elijah stayed with these two

faithful souls for the duration of the famine, in which the Lord provided
that neither the meal nor the oil ran out (1 Kings 17:8–23). Similarly, the
Saints were to provide Joseph with life's temporal necessities so that he
might continue to do the work of the kingdom. The work of the
Restoration required all of the Prophet's attention at this time. Without
the assistance of the Saints, he would have been unable to do the work of
restoring the gospel of Jesus Christ to the earth. That work will bless the
lives of all who embrace the gospel in this dispensation and will, in turn,
aid them in blessing the lives of their progenitors who lived before the
gospel was restored. See commentary on Doctrine and Covenants 24:3,
"They shall support thee," and commentary on Doctrine and Covenants
41:7.

Missionaries Are to Teach, Not Be Taught
DOCTRINE AND COVENANTS 43:15–16

43:15 *Ye are not sent forth to be taught.* In teaching the gospel we are
to follow the example of Christ. Of him we read, "He served under his
father, and he spake not as other men, neither could he be taught; for he
needed not that any man should teach him" (JST Matthew 3:25). The
text is not suggesting that Joseph, Jesus' earthly father, could not teach
him, but rather that his understanding must be rooted in the revelation
of heaven, not the wisdom of men. The same principle was to be true of
all who went forth in Jesus' name. Teaching this principle to those of the
meridian church, John the Revelator said, "The anointing which ye have
received of him abideth in you, and ye need not that any man teach you:
but as the same anointing teacheth you of all things, and is truth, and is
no lie, and even as it hath taught you, ye shall abide in him" (1 John
2:27).

43:16 *Ye are to be taught from on high.* Distinct from academic knowledge imparted in earthly schools, the Lord imparts knowledge of eternal
verities by his Spirit and confirms the truthfulness of the Restoration. Paul
illustrated this principle perfectly when he said: "And I, brethren, when I
came to you, came not with excellency of speech or of wisdom, declaring
unto you the testimony of God. For I determined not to know any thing
among you, save Jesus Christ, and him crucified. And I was with you in
weakness, and in fear, and in much trembling. And my speech and my
preaching was not with enticing words of man's wisdom, but in demonstration of the Spirit and of power: that your faith should not stand in the

wisdom of men, but in the power of God" (1 Corinthians 2:1–5). See commentary on Doctrine and Covenants 50:10–20.

43:16 *Endowed with power.* See commentary on Doctrine and Covenants 88:74–75.

Elders Are to Warn and Prepare Men for the Great Day of the Lord
DOCTRINE AND COVENANTS 43:17–28

43:17–28 The message of this dispensation is that the Savior will return to the earth and that all must repent in preparation for that event. The Lord has commissioned his servants to call upon the people. These servants have been accepted by some and rejected and hated by others. After the testimony of the Lord's servants "cometh wrath and indignation upon the people" (D&C 88:88). The voices of men may be ignored and the Lord's servants cast aside by many of the earth's inhabitants without temporal consequence. Doors can be closed in the faces of missionaries and their message left unheard. No door, however, can be closed to the voice of thunders, the flashes of lightning, tempests, earthquakes, hailstorms, famines, and pestilence. Such messages cannot go unheard. Men are powerless to hide from the wrath of God, and the time will come when the elements shall testify against them.

43:17 *The great day of the Lord.* The day of Satan's power is limited and will soon end, for the "the great day of the Lord" will come, Satan will be bound, and righteousness will rule and reign.

Millennial Conditions Revealed
DOCTRINE AND COVENANTS 43:29–35

43:29 "It has been the design of Jehovah," taught the Prophet Joseph Smith, "from the commencement of the world, and is His purpose now, to regulate the affairs of the world in His own time, to stand as head of the universe, and take the reins of government in His own hand. When that is done, judgment will be administered in righteousness; anarchy and confusion will be destroyed, and 'nations will learn war no more'" (*Teachings of the Prophet Joseph Smith*, 250).

My people shall be redeemed and shall reign with me on earth. "Christ and the resurrected Saints will reign over the earth during the thousand years," the Prophet Joseph Smith explained. "They will not probably

dwell upon the earth, but will visit it when they please, or when it is necessary to govern it" (*Teachings of the Prophet Joseph Smith*, 268). It will be a
glorious time to be instructed more perfectly in the government of God
by Adam, Enoch, Moses, King Benjamin, Captain Moroni, Brigham
Young, the Prophet Joseph Smith, and others.

43:31 *For Satan shall be bound.* Nephi taught that Satan will be
bound because the wicked will be destroyed and Christ will come to rule
and reign. "For behold, saith the prophet, the time cometh speedily that
Satan shall have no more power over the hearts of the children of men;
for the day soon cometh that all the proud and they who do wickedly
shall be as stubble; and the day cometh that they must be burned. . . . And
because of the righteousness of his people, Satan has no power; wherefore,
he cannot be loosed for the space of many years; for he hath no power
over the hearts of the people, for they dwell in righteousness, and the
Holy One of Israel reigneth" (1 Nephi 22:15, 26). Thus we see that in the
Savior's millennial kingdom Satan will be bound by the power of God and
thereafter kept in check by the righteousness of the Lord's people.

When he is loosed again he shall only reign for a little season. See commentary on Doctrine and Covenants 29:22.

Then cometh the end of the earth. It is at this time that "the heaven and
the earth shall be consumed and pass away, and there shall be a new
heaven and a new earth" (D&C 29:23). See commentary on Doctrine
and Covenants 88:26.

43:32 *Changed in the twinkling of an eye.* See commentary on Doctrine
and Covenants 101:31.

43:33 *Unquenchable fire.* This is a metaphor for the anguish of soul
to be suffered by the wicked. King Benjamin tells us that their torment
"is as a lake of fire and brimstone" (Mosiah 3:27).

43:35 *Be sober.* Similarly, Alma instructed his son Corianton, a missionary, to "declare the word with truth and soberness," that souls might
be brought to repentance and the plan of mercy have claim upon them"
(Alma 42:31). Again the missionaries of our day have been charged to
"remain steadfast in your minds in solemnity and the spirit of prayer, in
bearing testimony to all the world of those things which are communicated unto you" (D&C 84:61).

JOSEPH SMITH TRANSLATION GENESIS 14:26–40

DATE: BETWEEN DECEMBER 1830 AND MARCH 1831

In this priceless restoration of an ancient text, which is in itself worth all the effort associated with the Joseph Smith Translation, we learn of the man Melchizedek and of the nature of the higher or holy priesthood as it functioned from the days of Adam to Abraham.

Few events in earth's history match in importance the restoration of the Aaronic and Melchizedek Priesthoods to the Prophet Joseph Smith and his companion, Oliver Cowdery. Simply stated, without priesthood there is no salvation. All the faith and goodness in the world cannot substitute for the necessary power and authority to perform the ordinances necessary to return to the presence of God. Without it sins cannot be remitted, the gospel taught, or the kingdom of the adversary held in check. "The Melchizedek Priesthood," Joseph Smith said, "is the channel through which all knowledge, doctrine, the plan of salvation and every important matter is revealed from heaven" (*Teachings of the Prophet Joseph Smith*, 166–67). Given the importance of this priesthood that bears the name Melchizedek, there has to be some surprise on the part of the student of the Bible to discover that all that the Bible has to say about this man whose name is synonymous with the powers of heaven can be read orally in two minutes (Genesis 14:18; Psalm 110:4; Hebrews 5:6–10; 7:1–4, 10, 15–21).

Melchizedek, Man of Faith
JOSEPH SMITH TRANSLATION GENESIS 14:26–29

JST Genesis 14:26–29 Melchizedek is an enigma to both the Jewish and the Christian worlds. Without introduction or explanation he appears on the scene in the Valley of Shaveh (Kidron) when Abram is returning from rescuing his nephew, Lot, from the four kings who had carried him off. He brings with him bread and wine, blesses Abram, and receives tithes from him. The text refers to him as the king of Salem (Jerusalem) and as the priest of the most high God (Genesis 14:18–20).

Yet for a thousand years no mention of his name is found on the pages of holy writ. Then he appears as suddenly as he disappeared, and we find mention of him in a single psalm of David's. "The Lord hath sworn, and will not repent, Thou art a priest for ever after the order of Melchizedek" (Psalm 110:4). It appears that both David and Melchizedek as priest-kings are figures of the promised Messiah possessing the same order or priesthood that would belong to him. Again the scriptures fall silent for a period of a thousand years in which no reference is found to the name Melchizedek. Then Paul in his epistle to Hebrews tells us that Christ received the Melchizedek Priesthood and was ordained to the office of high priest. His purpose being to sustain the fact that Christ held a priesthood that was superior to that of Aaron and the Levites (Hebrews 5–7).

Scriptural silence provides a fertile field for legends. From books with discolored pages and covers that flake like piecrust we learn that ancient writers thought Melchizedek to be the patriarch Shem, his brother Ham, or Enoch, whose city was taken into heaven. Others have held that he was an angel, the Holy Ghost, the Messiah, or the Son of God (*Smith's Bible Dictionary*, 3:1876). The matter becomes more confused, for the book of Hebrews declares him to be "without father, without mother, without descent, having neither beginning of days, nor end of life; but made like unto the Son of God; abideth a priest continually" (Hebrews 7:3).

If, as prophecy assures us, the apostasy was to be universal, we could not expect other than that the knowledge and understanding of the priesthood would be lost along with all other saving truths. And so it was. The restoration of the priesthood requires the enigma of Melchizedek to be erased and a knowledge of this great preacher of righteousness to be restored. Such also has been the case. From the Book of Mormon we learn that "Melchizedek was a king over the land of Salem; and his people had waxed strong in iniquity and abomination; yea, they had all gone astray; they were full of all manner of wickedness; But Melchizedek having exercised mighty faith, and received the office of the high priesthood according to the holy order of God, did preach repentance unto his people. And behold, they did repent; and Melchizedek did establish peace in the land in his days; therefore he was called the prince of peace, for he was the king of Salem; and he did reign under his father. Now, there were many before him, and also there were many afterwards, but none were greater; therefore, of him they have more particularly made mention" (Alma 13:17–19).

In the current text we learn that, from his childhood, Melchizedek had been faithful and righteous and that he had been blessed and preserved by the power of the priesthood. By that power he had defended himself from both lions and fire. We also learn that it is the priesthood that is without father, mother, or end of days, not Melchizedek, as suggested in Hebrews 7:3.

The Power of the Priesthood
JOSEPH SMITH TRANSLATION GENESIS 14:30–32

JST Genesis 14:30–32 Nowhere in holy writ do we find a more graphic description of the power of God as possessed by those who have been called and chosen to stand in his stead than in these verses. Mighty men of God in ancient days have caused mountains to flee and rivers of water to turn out of their course; they have called a land to come up out of the sea and caused armies to flee (Moses 7:13–14); they have divided the earth into various continents (Genesis 10:25) and parted the waters (Moses 1:25); they have sealed the heavens that there would be no rain and opened them again (James 5:17–18). Such was the faith and power known to them. As Nephi said, "If God had commanded me to do all things I could do them. If he should command me that I should say unto this water, be thou earth, it should be earth; and if I should say it, it would be done" (1 Nephi 17:50). Further, we have been promised that "this same Priesthood, which was in the beginning, shall be in the end of the world also" (Moses 6:7).

Melchizedek and His City Were Taken into Heaven
JOSEPH SMITH TRANSLATION GENESIS 14:33–34

JST Genesis 14:33 Melchizedek is a classic type for Christ, that is, his life was a prophetic foreshadowing of that of the Savior's. He was both priest and king. He taught repentance and ruled in righteousness. He brought peace to a once wicked people who were then caught up into heaven, and as Alma tells us he served under his father (Alma 13:18).

JST Genesis 14:34 Here we are told that Melchizedek's people sought for the city of Enoch and were taken into heaven. The inhabitants of Enoch's city were translated beings. It would be hard to understand this text as saying anything other than that Melchizedek translated the inhabitants of his city as Enoch had translated those of his city. The one went up from the place of the New Jerusalem; the other, from the place of the Jerusalem of old. Knowing that Enoch's city will return during the millennial day to join the New Jerusalem, we are left to wonder if Melchizedek and his people might in like manner return to join the inhabitants of the Jerusalem of old.

Abraham Was Blessed by Melchizedek
JOSEPH SMITH TRANSLATION GENESIS 14:35-40

JST Genesis 14:37 Abraham received great blessings at the hands of Melchizedek.

JST Genesis 14:40 *According to the covenant which he had made.* For the covenant God made with Abraham, see Abraham 2:9–11.

DOCTRINE AND COVENANTS 44

DATE: LATTER PART OF FEBRUARY 1831
PLACE: KIRTLAND, OHIO

This revelation, calling for a conference of the elders of the Church, led to the expansion of missionary work. It was also at this conference that the office of high priest was restored. It would be the fourth conference of the Church since its organization a little more than one year earlier in upstate New York and the first conference in Ohio.

In obedience to the Lord's command, the elders met in Kirtland on 3 through 6 June 1831. At the end of the conference, Doctrine and Covenants 52 was received, directing the elders to travel to Missouri, where they were to gather for yet another conference. The effort and sacrifice in making such a journey emphasizes the importance of the spirit and power that come when the Saints gather together.

After the missionaries' arrival in Missouri, sections 57 through 59 were received, which give instructions concerning the site of the temple in the New Jerusalem and the building up of Zion.

The Lord Pours Out His Spirit on Assemblies of the Saints
DOCTRINE AND COVENANTS 44:1-3

44:1–3 Since the time of this command to gather in Kirtland, Ohio, for a Church conference, thousands of conferences have been held in the Church. Whether they are conferences of the general membership or are held on regional, mission, stake, or ward levels, the promise of receiving an outpouring of the Spirit remains the same.

More Converts Are Needed to Organize According to God's Law
DOCTRINE AND COVENANTS 44:4-6

44:4–6 Until there was a sufficient number of Saints it would not be possible to implement the laws of consecration and stewardship that the

Lord revealed. Funds were needed for legal deeds that would give the Saints lawful claim to the lands that were settled. These laws were not to be carried individually but rather as communities of covenant people.

44:6 *Ye must visit the poor and the needy.* Less fortunate members were not to be neglected until such time as living the laws of consecration could provide surplus from the bishop's storehouse to provide for them. See commentary on Doctrine and Covenants 42:30.

DOCTRINE AND COVENANTS 45;
JOSEPH SMITH–MATTHEW

DATE: 7 MARCH 1831 AND BETWEEN 7 APRIL AND 19 JUNE 1831
PLACE: KIRTLAND, OHIO

The arrival of the Prophet in Kirtland, Ohio, marked the beginning of a period of rapid growth in the young Church. By June of 1831 its membership numbered more than two thousand. As was to be expected, this growth excited a great deal of opposition. Civic leaders, ministers, newspaper editors, and others labored to put a stop to the progress of the Church. Joseph Smith recorded that "many false reports, lies, and foolish stories, were published in the newspapers, and circulated in every direction, to prevent people from investigating the work, or embracing the faith" (*History of the Church,* 1:158).

During these times of slander and abuse the Lord rewarded the Saints with light and knowledge far beyond the understanding of the historical Christian world. Doctrine and Covenants 45 and Joseph Smith–Matthew are prime examples of this. These two revelations dealing with the s igns of the times reach back to the instruction given by the Savior to his disciples on the Mount of Olives during the last week of his public ministry.

Christl Is Our Advocate with the Father
DOCTRINE AND COVENANTS 45:1–9

45:1 *All the hosts thereof.* Scripture speaks of Christ as the creator of all things (Moses 1:32–33; D&C 93:10). Such statements emphasize his role in the Creation and his unity and oneness with the Father. In the literal sense he is not the creator of humankind. Like us, he too is the Father's offspring. Yet in and through his atoning sacrifice, Christ becomes savior to us all and thus the father of our hope for eternal life.

45:2 *Lest death shall overtake you; in an hour when ye think not.* "Take heed, and beware of covetousness:" warned the Savior, "for a man's life consisteth not in the abundance of the things which he possesseth. And he spake a parable unto them, saying, The ground of a certain rich man brought forth plentifully: And he thought within himself, saying, What shall I do, because I have no room where to bestow my fruits? And he said, This will I do: I will pull down my barns, and build greater; and there will I bestow all my fruits and my goods. And I will say to my soul, Soul, thou hast much goods laid up for many years; take thine ease, eat, drink, and be merry. But God said unto him, Thou fool, this night thy soul shall be required of thee: then whose shall those things be, which thou hast provided? So is he that layeth up treasure for himself, and is not rich toward God" (Luke 12:15–21).

This revelation was addressed to members of the Church to whom has been given sufficient truth to obtain eternal life, which pursuit must not be allowed to suffer at the expense of temporal concerns.

45:3 *Advocate with the Father.* Christ is the advocate with the Father, meaning that he pleads the cause of the righteous in the courts of heaven.

45:6 *While it is called today.* "Behold, now it is called today until the coming of the Son of Man" (D&C 64:23).

45:9 *Mine everlasting covenant . . . to be a standard for my people.* The restoration of the fulness of the gospel constitutes the everlasting covenant (D&C 133:57). When the standard, or in Isaiah's words, the "ensign," is lifted, the house of Israel—meaning those of believing blood—gathers to it. An ensign is a banner or flag that serves to rally armies in battle. It identifies the place of gathering. "The Lord shall set his hand again the second time to recover the remnant of his people," prophesied Isaiah, "And he shall set up an ensign for the nations, and shall assemble the outcasts of Israel, and gather together the dispersed of Judah from the four corners of the earth" (Isaiah 11:11–12). The Lord speaks from the heavens anew in the dispensation of the fulness of times, and his voice and words are as a standard to which his people gather.

Enoch's City Will Return in the Millennium
DOCTRINE AND COVENANTS 45:10–14

45:10–14 All the holy prophets since the world began have prophesied of the second coming of Christ when he will establish the "times of refreshing" (Acts 3:19), or millennial rule. First among their number was father Adam, who "predicted whatsoever should befall his posterity unto the latest generation" (D&C 107:56). Enoch also "saw the day of the coming of the Son of Man, in the last days, to dwell on the earth in righteousness for the space of a thousand years; but before that day he saw great tribulations among the wicked; and he also saw the sea, that it was troubled, and men's hearts failing them, looking forth with fear for the judgments of the Almighty God, which should come upon the wicked. And the Lord showed Enoch all things, even unto the end of the world; and he saw the day of the righteous, the hour of their redemption, and received a fulness of joy" (Moses 7:65–67).

45:12 *Reserved until a day of righteousness.* The Lord promised Enoch that as part of the Restoration in the last days a holy city would be built upon the earth. "It shall be called Zion, a New Jerusalem. And the Lord said unto Enoch: Then shalt thou and all thy city meet them there, and we will receive them into our bosom, and they shall see us; and we will fall upon their necks, and they shall fall upon our necks, and we will kiss each other; And there shall be mine abode, and it shall be Zion, which shall come forth out of all the creations which I have made; and for the space of a thousand years the earth shall rest" (Moses 7:62–64). See commentary on Joseph Smith Translation Genesis 14:34, page 333.

45:13 *Strangers and pilgrims on the earth.* Among the faithful in Old Testament times were those who were translated and separated from the earth. Chief among these were those of the city of Enoch (Moses 7:21). After that city had been translated, others who sought to emulate their faith and righteousness were also caught up into heaven (Moses 7:27). Still others confessing themselves to be "strangers and pilgrims" on the earth—meaning that their hearts and minds were set upon the things of a better world—sought like privilege but did not obtain that blessing while in mortality.

The Lord Reveals Anew the Olivet Discourse

DOCTRINE AND COVENANTS 45:15–17; JOSEPH SMITH–MATTHEW 1:1–4

45:15 *As unto men in days of old.* The scope of prophecies concerning tribulations to precede Christ's second coming were not first revealed in this dispensation or during the generation of the meridian-day apostles. Indeed, prophets such as Enoch were shown in vision that following great tribulation the Lord would return upon the earth to reign in righteousness. It appears that the prelude to this revelation concerning the tribulations to precede the Savior's return and the establishment of the city of Zion, or the New Jerusalem, was the inspired translation of the record of Enoch as recorded in Moses 7:60–67: "And the Lord said unto Enoch: As I live, even so will I come in the last days, in the days of wickedness and vengeance, to fulfil the oath which I have made unto you concerning the children of Noah; And the day shall come that the earth shall rest, but before that day the heavens shall be darkened, and a veil of darkness shall cover the earth; and the heavens shall shake, and also the earth; and great tribulations shall be among the children of men, but my people will I preserve; And righteousness will I send down out of heaven; and truth will I send forth out of the earth, to bear testimony of mine Only Begotten; his resurrection from the dead; yea, and also the resurrection of all men; and righteousness and truth will I cause to sweep the earth as with a flood, to gather out mine elect from the four quarters of the earth, unto a place which I shall prepare, an Holy City, that my people may gird up their loins, and be looking forth for the time of my coming; for there shall be my tabernacle, and it shall be called Zion, a New Jerusalem. . . . And it came to pass that Enoch saw the day of the coming of the Son of Man, in the last days, to dwell on the earth in righteousness for the space of a thousand years; But before that day he saw great tribulations among the wicked; and he also saw the sea, that it was troubled, and men's hearts failing them, looking forth with fear for the judgments of the Almighty God, which should come upon the wicked. And the Lord showed Enoch all things, even unto the end of the world; and he saw the day of the righteous, the hour of their redemption, and received a fulness of joy."

45:16 *As I showed it unto my disciples.* On Tuesday of the Passion Week, Jesus took his disciples apart to teach them privately. He chose as his setting the hillside east of Jerusalem known as the Mount of Olives. This location gave the title "Olivet Discourse" to the Savior's teachings on the destruction of Jerusalem and the signs of his second coming. There are several accounts of this discussion in the scriptures. Matthew, Mark, and Luke each included portions of the Olivet Discourse in their testimonies, or Gospels, of the Lord. Today, in addition to the accounts recorded in the Gospels, we are privileged to have this discourse included in section 45 and in the inspired translations of Matthew, Mark, and Luke.

The revelation recorded in Doctrine and Covenants 45 led the Prophet Joseph Smith to set aside the translation of the Old Testament, in which he was engaged at the time, and begin the translation of the New Testament. See commentary on Doctrine and Covenants 45:60–61.

45:17 *Ye have looked upon the long absence of your spirits from your bodies to be a bondage.* See Doctrine and Covenants 93:33–34.

The day of redemption. To be redeemed is to be freed from the dominion and power of the adversary. Such will be the case for those who live during that period in which Satan is bound, the period known to us as the Millennium.

The restoration of the scattered Israel. The ancient kingdom of Israel will be reestablished again. Both the Northern Kingdom and the kingdom of Judah were destroyed and their citizens scattered among all of the nations of the earth. The Lord promised the house of Israel that he would not forsake them but would gather and restore them as a nation in the last days. The priesthood is to preside over this gathering, which will first bring hearts and souls to Christ and then lead the house of Israel to promised lands of inheritance. See commentary on Doctrine and Covenants 110:11.

JST–M 1:1–4 Joseph Smith's translation of Matthew 24 is our most helpful commentary on the Savior's discourse on the signs of the times. It was the receipt of this revelation (D&C 45) that stimulated the Prophet to leave his translation of the Old Testament and move to a consideration of Matthew 24. Because these two revelations are so closely related in time and content we will consider them together in this work. While Matthew's account intertwines and combines events surrounding the destruction of Jerusalem with the signs of the last days, the Joseph Smith Translation separates the two. As clarified in the Joseph Smith Translation, the Savior first addressed the destruction of Jerusalem and the Jewish nation. He then answered his disciples' questions regarding the signs of his coming, which will usher in the Millennium and the restoration of the house of Israel. Thus we see how the events of the one are a prophetic prefigure of the other. The disciples apparently understood that the restoration of the Jewish nation, along with the house of Israel, was associated with the end of the world, or the destruction of the wicked at the second coming of Jesus Christ. Therefore, it was natural that they would unite these two events in the questions that they posed to the Lord.

The Destruction of Jerusalem Foretold
DOCTRINE AND COVENANTS 45:18–23;
JOSEPH SMITH–MATTHEW 1:5–20

45:18 *This temple which is in Jerusalem, which ye call the house of God.* The temple in Jerusalem had become "a den of thieves." On two occasions Christ had cleansed its sacred precincts of money-changers and those who would make it a house of merchandise (John 2:13–17; Matthew 21:12–13). He said, "Ye call [it] the house of God," but God would hardly regard it as such.

45:19 *Desolation shall come upon this generation.* The Savior referred to this as "the abomination of desolation, spoken of by Daniel the prophet, concerning the destruction of Jerusalem" (Joseph Smith–Matthew 1:12). The destruction of Jerusalem and the Jewish nation came, as had their earlier destruction by the Babylonians, because of wickedness that reigned among the people. Less than forty years from the time that the Savior foretold the destruction of that generation, a Roman army led by Titus laid siege to the walled city of Jerusalem. Hunger within the city exceeded human endurance and, as Moses had prophesied, in the severity of the siege mothers ate their own children (Deuteronomy 28:57). Within the city itself, warring factions of thieves and murderers sought to rule the citizenry and rob them of food and anything they thought of value. The temple and city caught fire in the fight over the desecrated mount upon which Herod had built a house of the Lord to win favor with the Jews. During the ensuing slaughter—numbered in the hundreds of thousands—blood literally flowed in the streets in adequate measure to dowse the flames. The remnant of the Jews not destroyed in this desolation were scattered to all nations. Jerusalem was ploughed under and rebuilt as a Roman city devoid of true worship.

45:20 *Not be left one stone upon another.* The desecrated house of God, Jesus declared, would not be allowed to stand in mocking hypocrisy. In literal fulfillment of the Lord's prophecy, Roman soldiers under the command of Titus dismantled the buildings associated with the temple, stone by stone, following the siege of Jerusalem in A.D. 70. The temple was left a heap of rubble. During the late twentieth century archaeologists uncovered the ancient road that ran at the base of the retaining wall built by Herod when he extended the original platform of the temples built under the direction of Solomon and Zerubbabel. They discovered that the massive stones of the temple had been pushed over the precipice of the temple mount down onto the road below. Huge ashlars, or hand-dressed stones, were broken on the road and revealed in the excavations. Today an archaeological garden stands as a witness to the Savior's words.

Symbolically, the announcement that not one stone would be left standing on another meant that the house of Israel would be scattered among those of every nation, kindred, and tongue, that no two families would be left side by side when the end of their nation came. Conversely, in the last days, the gathering of Israel—family by family—will token God's favor resting upon them once again, the crowning event of that latter-day gathering being the restoration of their temple and their nation.

45:21 *Every desolation which I have told you concerning them shall come to pass.* Joseph Smith–Matthew delineates this desolation in verses 5 through 20.

JS–M 1:5–20 "I saw under the altar the souls of them that were slain for the word of God, and for the testimony which they held: And they cried with a loud voice, saying, How long, O Lord, holy and true, dost thou not judge and avenge our blood on them that dwell on the earth? And white robes were given unto every one of them; and it was said unto them, that they should rest yet for a little season, until their fellowservants also and their brethren, that should be killed as they were, should be fulfilled" (Revelation 6:9–11).

Not only did the wicked slay the apostles and righteous Saints but they also fought against the doctrine of Christ as taught by the apostles. "And the multitude of the earth was gathered together," wrote Nephi of his vision concerning this time period. "And I beheld that they were in a large and spacious building, like unto the building which my father saw. And the angel of the Lord spake unto me again, saying: Behold the world and the wisdom thereof; yea, behold the house of Israel hath gathered together to fight against the twelve apostles of the Lamb. And it came to pass that I saw and bear record, that the great and spacious building was the pride of the world" (1 Nephi 11:35–36). See commentary on Joseph Smith–History 1:19, page 11.

JS–M 1:12 *Stand in the holy place.* Elder Bruce R. McConkie explained: "The counsel that the saints should then 'stand in the holy place' means that they should assemble together where they could receive prophetic guidance that would preserve them from the desolations of the day. The place of their assembly became holy because of the righteousness of the holy ones who comprised the Lord's congregation. . . . And when that day came, the true saints, guided as true saints always are by the spirit of revelation, fled to Pella in Perea and were spared" (*Mortal Messiah*, 3:430).

45:22 *The heavens and the earth shall pass away.* See commentary on Doctrine and Covenants 29:23.

Apostasy to Intervene between the Destruction of Jerusalem and the Second Coming

JOSEPH SMITH–MATTHEW 1:21–26

JS–M 1:21–22 *After the tribulation of those days . . . there shall also arise false Christs, and false prophets.* The era that followed the destruction of Jerusalem was rife with false Christs and false prophets that sought to lead the meridian-day Saints. Apostasy enveloped the church. In verse 5 Christ warned his apostles not to be deceived by false Christs. It is hard to suppose that these men who knew Christ, traveled with him, and in some cases, were related to him, would be deceived by impersonators. The thrust of this warning centers in false representations of what Christ, and those who come in his name, teach. Isaiah said of the Savior that "his visage was so marred more than any man" (Isaiah 52:14). We can suppose that Isaiah was telling us that his image, person, and purpose would be distorted or misused more than any other man in earth's history. See commentary on Joseph Smith–History 1:19, page 11.

JS–M 1:22 *The very elect, who are the elect according to the covenant.* Those who enter into the covenants of salvation become the Lord's elect, or chosen. It will be to them that he turns to act as his agents, bear his priesthood, and lead his people. Even before they were born, these people developed spiritual sensitivities to discern between truth and error. These elect will have the ability to discern the false doctrines attributed to Christ from those that are true. However, the signs and wonders that are brought forth by Lucifer and those he has overcome are of such a nature that even the elect must take care or they will be deceived. Many of those through whom coursed the blood of Israel, the covenant people of the Lord, were deceived. Christianity was engulfed in a flood of apostasy that spread across the earth and drowned the truths taught by Christ and his apostles.

JS–M 1:23 *You also shall hear of wars, and rumors of wars.* The followers of Christ found it necessary to flee the sword. Apostate Christianity took up the sword as the persecuted became the persecutors. It was Constantine who forged the union of the Bible and the sword when he adopted apostate Christianity as the official religion of the realm. The wrestle between Rome and Constantinople over which was to be the chief city brought with it the threat of war between these two cities, both of which aptly fit the Revelator's description of the woman (city) built upon seven mountains (Revelation 17:9). The followers of Mohammed spread the Islamic faith by the sword, which in time was met by equally ferocious means of conversion by Christians. Banners emblazoned with the cross led armies into battle. Europe was set aflame with religious fervor to defend Jerusalem from the infidel as rumor and false prophets led ill-prepared Christians to war against the Muslim world. Europe divided into nations, and each warred against the other through the succeeding centuries.

But the end is not yet. The events of the era of apostasy are not the signs concerning which the disciples inquired of the Lord regarding his return and the end of the world. Those signs will yet follow in the Savior's discourse.

JS–M 1:25 The path of seclusion does not bring souls to Christ. Qualities of love, patience, temperance, virtue and godliness are attained by serving others. Reading this inspired verse, one cannot help but sorrow over the many devout Christians who through the ages mistakenly sought the Lord in secluded chambers or desert monasteries.

JS–M 1:26 *So shall also the coming of the Son of Man be.* Jesus Christ will return in as glorious a manner as the rising sun. When the Savior makes his public appearance to the world, it will be universally known. In addition, as the light of the morning sun shines from the east to the west across the expanse of the earth, there will be many hours of visitation to the world until all nations have received their rightful king. Indicative of this metaphor describing his second coming, Christ identified that he would come to various locations: Mount Zion, or the city of the New Jerusalem, the Mount of Olives, the islands of the sea, and upon the land of Zion (D&C 133:18–20).

Signs That the Times of the Gentiles Are Fulfilled

DOCTRINE AND COVENANTS 45:24–33; JOSEPH SMITH–MATTHEW 1:27–32

45:25 *They [the Jews] shall remain until the times of the Gentiles be fulfilled.* The gathering of the Jews to Jerusalem is one of the most easily identifiable signs of the times. It signals the fulfillment of the "times of the

Gentiles," the present era in which we live. The gathering to Jerusalem foreshadows the period in which the times of the Jews will begin. In that era the Jews will begin to accept the gospel and enjoy the blessings that flow therefrom.

The gospel has been given at various times to different peoples on a priority basis. The Savior's mortal mission was not to the Gentiles "but unto the lost sheep of the house of Israel" (Matthew 15:24). He foretold that the time would come when the gospel covenant and knowledge of the true Messiah would be taken from the Jews and given to another people (Matthew 21:33–22:14). In fulfillment of the Lord's words, Peter received a vision indicating that the times of the Gentiles had commenced (Acts 10:9–11:18).

As the Jews who were dispersed throughout the Roman Empire increasingly rejected the gospel of Jesus Christ, greater emphasis was placed on taking the gospel to the Gentiles. The apostle Paul was in the forefront of this marvelous work. He and Barnabas explained to a congregation of Jews gathered to hear them in a synagogue at Antioch of Pisidia, "It was necessary that the word of God should first have been spoken to you: but seeing ye put it from you, and judge yourselves unworthy of everlasting life, lo, we turn to the Gentiles" (Acts 13:46).

The Lord indicated that in the latter days the restored gospel would "go forth unto the ends of the earth, unto the Gentiles first, and then, behold, and lo, they shall turn unto the Jews" (D&C 90:9). The Second Coming ushers in the time when the Jewish nation will once again receive opportunity to hear the gospel and enter into the covenant of God on a priority basis. When the emphasis changes, and the fulness of the gospel is brought to the Jews instead of to the Gentile nations, it may be said that the times of the Gentiles is fulfilled. Before that change in emphasis occurs, the Savior prophesied, the Jews will again gather in preparation to receive their King. "Judah must return," explained the Prophet Joseph Smith, "Jerusalem must be rebuilt, and the temple, and water come out from under the temple, and the waters of the Dead Sea be healed. It will take some time to rebuild the walls of the city and the temple, &c.; and all this must be done before the Son of Man will make His appearance" (*Teachings of the Prophet Joseph Smith*, 286).

Luke's account of the Olivet Discourse indicates that "Jerusalem shall be trodden down of the Gentiles, until the times of the Gentiles be fulfilled" (Luke 21:24). After centuries of non-Jewish domination of the holy city, war brought Jerusalem under Jewish control in 1967. The Six-day

War, which began 5 June 1967, was a turning point in history. The holy city was annexed, and shortly thereafter the state of Israel declared Jerusalem to be its capital.

The miracle of the rebuilding of Jerusalem by the Jews has been under the direction of the Almighty. The Prophet Joseph Smith directed Orson Hyde to travel to Jerusalem to dedicate the land for the return of the Jews. Elder Hyde knelt on the Mount of Olives and fulfilled this assignment 24 October 1841. Since that time Jews have been stirred in spirit to return to the land of their forefathers. This is not to say that the Lord condones the bloodshed that has occurred in the Jewish redemption of the land of Palestine. Applicable to the Jewish nation are the words of the Lord to the Saints concerning the establishment of Zion in Jackson County, Missouri: "Wherefore, the land of Zion shall not be obtained but by purchase or by blood, otherwise there is none inheritance for you. And if by purchase, behold you are blessed; and if by blood, as you are forbidden to shed blood, lo, your enemies are upon you, and ye shall be scourged from city to city, and from synagogue to synagogue, and but few shall stand to receive an inheritance" (D&C 63:29–31).

The events cited have transpired over a number of years. There is yet more to take place. The fulfilling of the times of the Gentiles is not to be measured in a particular moment; rather it will take place naturally and gradually over an extended period of time, the dawn of which is not far from us.

JS–M 1:30; D&C 45:27 *Because iniquity shall abound, the love of men shall wax cold.* The deluge of divorce, abuse, and abandoned wives and children is the result of wickedness engulfing the world. Today, sins of immorality have led to legalization and increase in abortions. Pornography, sexual perversions, and abundant adulteries have paved the way to broken hearts and homes. And often, through it all, the wicked parties are past feeling. Their hearts are cold in solid indifference to the sorrow they cause and the judgments of God they bring upon themselves. Iniquity and coldness form a vicious circle in which one feeds off the other until the wicked of the earth are ripened in their corruption. As a result, the Lord will come out in his wrath to destroy the hardened wicked from off the face of the earth at his coming.

45:28 Moroni referred to the times of the Gentiles coming in as "the fulness of the Gentiles" (Joseph Smith–History 1:41). The restoration of the fulness of the gospel was foreordained to occur during the era of the times of the Gentiles. The condemnation of the Gentile nations occurs "because that which was from the beginning is plainly manifest unto them, and they receive not the light" (D&C 93:31). The times of the Gentiles will be fulfilled, or come to an end, in the generation in which they reject the restoration of the gospel. See commentary on Joseph Smith–History 1:41, page 25.

45:31 *For a desolating sickness shall cover the land.* See commentary on Doctrine and Covenants 1:17; 5:19.

45:32 *My disciples shall stand in holy places.* Where are the holy places in which Christ intended his disciples to stand? In this dispensation the Lord has directed the Saints to gather to Zion. He indicates in Doctrine and Covenants 57 that the site of the city of the New Jerusalem is in the area of Independence, Missouri.

Will all of the Saints gather to Missouri? "Behold, there is none other place appointed," explained the Lord, "than that which I have appointed; neither shall there be any other place appointed than that which I have appointed, for the work of the gathering of my saints—Until the day cometh when there is found no more room for them; and then I have other places which I will appoint unto them, and they shall be called stakes, for the curtains or the strength of Zion. Behold, it is my will, that all they who call on my name, and worship me according to mine everlasting gospel, should gather together, and stand in holy places; And prepare for the revelation which is to come, when the veil of the covering of my temple, in my tabernacle, which hideth the earth, shall be taken off, and all flesh shall see me together" (D&C 101:20–23).

Clearly, the Lord ordained the stakes of Zion to be the holy places in which the Saints will stand in preparation for the Second Coming. The Lord gave further direction "that the gathering together upon the land of Zion, and upon her stakes, may be for a defense, and for a refuge from the storm, and from wrath when it shall be poured out without mixture upon the whole earth" (D&C 115:6).

There is strength in the organization of a stake. Stake presidents and bishops are ordained and set apart with keys to guide the Saints in righteousness. Further, members of the Church are organized into quorums and Relief Societies, in which they better learn the doctrines of the kingdom and their individual duties. Zion is built up one stake at a time. As members are sanctified and receive the blessings of the temple, Zion puts on her beautiful garments. Thus, each stake in Zion may become a holy place for a defense against wickedness and tribulations of the latter days. See commentary on Doctrine and Covenants 45:67.

JS–M 1:27 The gathering of Israel commences before the Second Coming. The carcass to which Israel gathers symbolizes the restored Church of Christ. Israel is attracted to the truths of the Restoration as eagles are drawn to a carcass.

JS–M 1:28–29 "The coming of the Son of Man never will be— never can be till the judgments spoken of for this hour are poured out: which judgments are commenced" (*Teachings of the Prophet Joseph Smith,* 286).

JS–M 1:31 *This Gospel of the Kingdom shall be preached in all the world.* "The time was at hand that the Gospel in all its fullness must be preached in power, unto all nations," explained the Prophet Joseph Smith, "that a people might be prepared for the Millennial reign" (*History of the Church,* 4:537).

JS–M 1:32 That which took place in the destruction of Jerusalem anciently will occur again in the latter days. Zechariah revealed in further detail that "the city shall be taken, and the houses rifled, and the women ravished; and half of the city shall go forth into captivity" (Zechariah 14:2). See commentary on Doctrine and Covenants 45:19, 47.

Be Not Troubled, but Look Forth for the Great Day of the Lord
DOCTRINE AND COVENANTS 45:34–42; JOSEPH SMITH–MATTHEW 1:33–40

45:35 *Be not troubled.* The signs of the times herald glorious days to come. The second coming of the Lord will usher in the Millennium of one thousand years of peace and righteousness. Appropriate are the words of the Savior, "Ye are little children, and ye have not as yet understood how great blessings the Father hath in his own hands and prepared for you; and ye cannot bear all things now; nevertheless, be of good cheer, for I will lead you along" (D&C 78:17–18).

45:36 *The light shall begin to break forth.* The reference is to the restoration of the fulness of the gospel.

45:39 *Shall be looking forth for the great day.* "I will prophesy," stated the Prophet Joseph Smith on 2 July 1839, "that the signs of the coming of the Son of Man are already commenced. One pestilence will desolate after another. We shall soon have war and bloodshed. The moon will be turned into blood. I testify of these things, and that the coming of the Son of Man is nigh, even at your doors. If our souls and our bodies are not looking forth for the coming of the Son of Man; and after we are dead, if we are not looking forth, we shall be among those who are calling for the rocks to fall upon them" (*Teachings of the Prophet Joseph Smith*, 160).

45:42; JS–M 1:33 Elder Bruce R. McConkie observed: "We learn that the signs promised . . . are to occur after the abomination of desolation sweeps Jerusalem for the second time. They will thus come almost at the very hour of the Second Coming. From other scriptural accounts of these same signs we learn that 'the earth shall tremble and reel to and fro as a drunken man' (D. & C. 88:87), and 'shall remove out of her place' (Isa. 13:10–13); that 'the islands shall become one land' (D. & C. 133:23); and that 'the stars shall be hurled from their places.' (D. & C. 133:49). Thus it would seem, when the Lord makes his appearance and the earth is restored to its paradisiacal state, that there will be great physical changes. When the continents become one land and the earth reels to and fro, with all that then occurs, it will surely appear unto men as though the very stars of heaven were being hurled from their places, and so they will be as far as their relationship to the earth is concerned. That there may be other heavenly bodies, having the appearance of stars, that shall fall on the earth may also well be. Truly the scriptures testify of many signs and wonders in the heavens above (D. & C. 29:14; Joel 2:31; Rev. 6:12–17)" (*Doctrinal New Testament Commentary*, 1:678).

JS–M 1:36 *The sign of the Son of Man.* At the April 1843 conference of the Church the Prophet Joseph Smith testified: "There will be wars and rumors of wars, signs in the heavens above and on the earth beneath, the sun turned into darkness and the moon to blood, earthquakes in divers places, the seas heaving beyond their bounds; then will appear one grand sign of the Son of Man in heaven. But what will the world do? They will say it is a planet, a comet, etc. But the Son of Man will come as the sign of the coming of the Son of Man, which will be as the light of the morning cometh out of the east" (*Teachings of the Prophet Joseph Smith*, 286–87).

JS–M 1:37 *Whoso treasureth up my word, shall not be deceived.* The prophetic word is for our salvation. It is not enough to simply read the scriptures. An occasional listening ear in meetings of the Church will not provide the necessary weapons against the adversary in the last days. The words of the scriptures must be esteemed in the vaults of the heart like priceless jewels. The Spirit must impress upon the soul the meaning and import of the words written.

It is the rod of iron, or the word of God, that leads to the tree of life. Nephi observed that "whoso would hearken unto the word of God, and would hold fast unto it, they would never perish; neither could the temptations and the fiery darts of the adversary overpower them unto blindness, to lead them away to destruction" (1 Nephi 15:24).

The scriptures are our best source for avoiding deception. This is especially true of nonscriptural expositions that fill the soul with opinions and wild assertions. "There are among us many loose writings predicting the calamities which are about to overtake us," counseled President Harold B. Lee. "Some of these have been publicized as though they were necessary to wake up the world to the horrors about to overtake us. Many of these are from sources upon which there cannot be unquestioned reliance.

"Are you priesthood bearers aware of the fact that we need no such publications to be forewarned, if we were only conversant with what the scriptures have already spoken to us in plainness?

"Let me give you the sure word of prophecy on which you should rely for your guide instead of these strange sources which may have great political implications.

"Read the twenty-fourth chapter of Matthew—particularly that inspired version as contained in the Pearl of Great Price (Joseph Smith–Matthew).

"Then read the forty-fifth section of the Doctrine and Covenants where the Lord, not man, has documented the signs of the times.

"Now turn to section 101 and section 133 of the Doctrine and Covenants and hear the step-by-step recounting of events leading up to the coming of the Savior.

"Finally, turn to the promises the Lord makes to those who keep the commandments when these judgments descend upon the wicked, as set forth in the Doctrine and Covenants, section 38.

"Brethren, these are some of the writings with which you should concern yourselves, rather than commentaries that may come from those whose information may not be the most reliable and whose motives may be subject to question. And may I say, parenthetically, most of such writers are not handicapped by having any authentic information on their writings" (*Teachings of Harold B. Lee*, 399). See commentary on Doctrine and Covenants 43:3, 6.

JS–M 1:37 *He shall send his angels before him . . . and they shall gather together the remainder of his elect.* In the last days missionaries will comb the earth to fulfill their commission to gather Israel. They will not be alone in this great labor. Those on the other side of the veil will aid them in finding their scattered kin and in preparing their hearts and minds to receive the fulness of the gospel.

JS–M 1:39 *Mine elect, when they shall see all these things, they shall know.* Faithful Saints, the children of light, will not be taken by surprise at the Second Coming. It is abundantly evident to those with eyes to see and ears to hear that the signs are appearing. "The coming of the Lord draweth nigh, and it overtaketh the world as a thief in the night" (D&C 106:4). The world will focus on the temporal concerns of the day: "For it shall be with them, as it was in the days which were before the flood; for until the day that Noah entered into the ark they were eating and drinking, marrying and giving in marriage; And knew not until the flood came, and took them all away; so shall also the coming of the Son of Man be. Then shall be fulfilled that which is written, that in the last days, two shall be in the field, the one shall be taken, and the other left; Two shall be grinding at the mill, the one shall be taken, and the other left" (Joseph Smith–Matthew 1:42–45).

JS–M 1:40 *That day, and hour, no one knoweth.* See Doctrine and Covenants 130:14–17.

The Resurrection Attends the Second Coming
DOCTRINE AND COVENANTS 45:43–46

45:43 The Jewish nation shall gather to Jerusalem. See commentary on verse 25.

45:45 The resurrection of the just will begin before the destruction of the wicked takes place. "For the Lord himself shall descend from heaven with a shout, with the voice of the archangel, and with the trump of God: and the dead in Christ shall rise first: Then they who are alive, shall be caught up together into the clouds with them who remain [the dead], to meet the Lord in the air" (JST 1 Thessalonians 4:16). See commentary on Doctrine and Covenants 88:96–98.

An angel shall sound his trump. See commentary on Doctrine and Covenants 29:26.

Christ Shall Stand on the Mount of Olives; Jews Shall See the Wounds in His Hands and Feet

DOCTRINE AND COVENANTS 45:47–53

45:47–53 Among the more mysterious passages of the Old Testament are the writings of the prophet Zechariah. For reasons unknown, the Savior's illumination of Zechariah's prophecies is not found in the New Testament accounts of the Olivet Discourse. The clarity of Doctrine and Covenants 45, then, is of immense value to understanding the conversion of the Jewish remnant spoken of in Zechariah. Indeed, once individuals study this revelation they might bear testimony, "Our minds being now enlightened, we began to have the scriptures laid open to our understandings, and the true meaning and intention of their more mysterious passages revealed unto us in a manner which we never could attain to previously, nor ever before had thought of" (Joseph Smith–History 1:74).

45:47 Those who fight against the gathered Jewish remnant in Jerusalem will be destroyed at the Lord's coming. "Behold, I will make Jerusalem a cup of trembling unto all the people round about," revealed the Lord, "when they shall be in the siege both against Judah and against Jerusalem. And in that day will I make Jerusalem a burdensome stone for all people: all that burden themselves with it shall be cut in pieces, though all the people of the earth be gathered together against it. . . . And it shall come to pass in that day, that I will seek to destroy all the nations that come against Jerusalem. . . . And this shall be the plague wherewith the Lord will smite all the people that have fought against Jerusalem; Their flesh shall consume away while they stand upon their feet, and their eyes shall consume away in their holes, and their tongue shall consume away in their mouth" (Zechariah 12:2–3, 9; 14:12).

45:48 *Then shall the Lord set his foot upon this mount.* The Savior shall descend "upon the mount of Olives, which is before Jerusalem on the east, and the mount of Olives shall cleave in the midst thereof toward the east and toward the west, and there shall be a very great valley; and half of the mountain shall remove toward the north, and half of it toward the south" (Zechariah 14:4).

45:51–53 This is the great day when the Savior will reclaim the outcasts of Judah and accomplish his glorious plan for their redemption. It is his Spirit that now prompts many to gather to their ancient homeland. And it is the spirit of the devil that inspires the wicked to assemble against Jerusalem to destroy the gathered Jewish remnant. The spirit of messianic anticipation will once again fill the hearts of the persecuted and hopeful nation. In glory and great power the Lord will descend to save them from destruction at the hands of their enemies. And, undoubtedly, they will see the unexpected wounds in the Messiah's hands, feet, and side, and ask, in fulfillment of Zechariah's words, "What are these wounds in thy hands? Then he shall answer, Those with which I was wounded in the house of my friends" (Zechariah 13:6). "Then the Jews who have only partly believed in Christ and who have not been willing to accept him as their Redeemer, will be converted and forgiven on their repentance and a nation will be born in a day" (Smith, *Church History and Modern Revelation*, 1:197).

Isaiah gloried in the day of Jewish redemption, when finally the scales of tradition will fall from their eyes allowing them to be enlightened. "Hear the word of the Lord, ye that tremble at his word; Your brethren that hated you, that cast you out for my name's sake, said, Let the Lord be glorified: but he shall appear to your joy, and they shall be ashamed. A voice of noise from the city, a voice from the temple, a voice of the Lord that rendereth recompence to his enemies. Before she travailed, she brought forth; before her pain came, she was delivered of a man child. Who hath heard such a thing? who hath seen such things? Shall the earth be made to bring forth in one day? or shall a nation be born at once? for as soon as Zion travailed, she brought forth her children" (Isaiah 66:5–8).

In that day the righteous Jews will be as their ancient counterpart, Saul of Tarsus, when the Lord appeared to him on the road to Damascus. They too will turn from the traditions of their fathers by which means "that wicked one cometh and taketh away light and truth" (D&C 93:39). The Lord promised: "And I will pour upon the house of David, and upon the inhabitants of Jerusalem, the spirit of grace and of supplications: and they shall look upon me whom they have pierced, and they shall mourn for him, as one mourneth for his only son, and shall be in bitterness for him, as one that is in bitterness for his firstborn. . . . In that day there shall be a fountain opened to the house of David and to the inhabitants of Jerusalem for sin and for uncleanness" (Zechariah 12:10; 13:1).

The Lord Shall Reign during the Millennium
DOCTRINE AND COVENANTS 45:54–59

45:54 *The heathen nations be redeemed.* The heathen nations are those which, in general, are neither Jewish nor Christian. The righteous

Muslim, Hindu, Buddhist, agnostic, and those righteous of any other class or persuasion will be spared in the destruction of the wicked and dwell upon the earth in its paradisiacal state. "To say that the heathens would be damned because they did not believe the Gospel would be preposterous," explained the Prophet Joseph Smith, "and to say that the Jews would all be damned that do not believe in Jesus would be equally absurd; for 'how can they believe on him of whom they have not heard, and how can they hear without a preacher, and how can he preach except he be sent;' consequently neither Jew nor heathen can be culpable for rejecting the conflicting opinions of sectarianism, nor for rejecting any testimony but that which is sent of God, for as the preacher cannot preach except he be sent, so the hearer cannot believe without he hear a 'sent' preacher, and cannot be condemned for what he has not heard, and being without law, will have to be judged without law" (*Teachings of the Prophet Joseph Smith*, 221).

Freedom of worship will be enjoyed by all in that great millennial day. Agency will be prized by all who love and seek the truth. There will be those who cling to false notions and retain their loyalty to false churches. Missionary work and the teaching of the gospel will of necessity continue until all shall know the Lord (Jeremiah 31:34).

Not all wickedness will cease at the beginning of the Millennium. Some will reject the testimony of Jesus Christ and his divine mission. The Prophet Joseph Smith taught that "there will be wicked men on the earth during the thousand years. The heathen nations who will not come up to worship will be visited with the judgments of God, and must eventually be destroyed from the earth" (*Teachings of the Prophet Joseph Smith*, 268–69). Those who knew no law or sinned in ignorance because of the traditions of their fathers will be given opportunity to receive the testimony of Jesus and be numbered among the Saints.

45:55 *Satan shall be bound.* See commentary on Doctrine and Covenants 43:31.

45:59 *He will be their king and their lawgiver.* "The Lord has at various times commenced this kind of government," the Prophet Joseph Smith explained, "and tendered His services to the human family. . . . When the children of Israel were chosen with Moses at their head, they were to be a peculiar people, among whom God should place His name; their motto was: 'the Lord is our lawgiver; the Lord is our Judge; the Lord is our King; and He shall reign over us.' While in this state they might truly say, 'Happy is that people, whose God is the Lord.' Their government was a theocracy; they had God to make their laws, and men chosen by Him to administer them; He was their God, and they were His people. Moses received the word of the Lord from God Himself; he was the mouth of God to Aaron, and Aaron taught the people, in both civil and ecclesiastical affairs; they were both one, there was no distinction; so will it be when the purposes of God shall be accomplished: when 'the Lord shall be King over the whole earth' and 'Jerusalem His throne.' 'The law shall go forth from Zion, and the word of the Lord from Jerusalem.'

"This is the only thing that can bring about the 'restitution of all things spoken of by all the holy Prophets since the world was'—'the dispensation of the fullness of times, when God shall gather together all things in one.' Other attempts to promote universal peace and happiness in the human family have proved abortive; every effort has failed; every plan and design has fallen to the ground; it needs the wisdom of God, the intelligence of God, and the power of God to accomplish this. The world has had a fair trial for six thousand years; the Lord will try the seventh thousand Himself; 'He whose right it is, will possess the kingdom, and reign until He has put all things under His feet;' iniquity will hide its hoary head, Satan will be bound, and the works of darkness destroyed; righteousness will be put to the line, and judgment to the plummet, and 'he that fears the Lord will alone be exalted in that day'" (*Teachings of the Prophet Joseph Smith*, 251–52).

The Prophet to Begin the Translation of the New Testament
DOCTRINE AND COVENANTS 45:60–62

45:60–62 The translation of the book of Matthew in the New Testament commenced while Genesis was still being translated. The day following the reception of these instructions, 8 March 1831, the Prophet Joseph Smith began the translation of Matthew. In time the work of translation arrived at Matthew 24, in which the restored truths examined in this section of commentary were revealed. Thus, the Lord's promise to the Saints was fulfilled. In addition, other truths of the Restoration were revealed during the work of the translation of the New Testament and had profound influence on the revelations received and compiled in the Doctrine and Covenants. Of particular influence and interest are sections 74, 76, 77, 86, 88, and 93.

The Saints Are to Gather and Build the New Jerusalem, to Which People from All Nations Will Come

DOCTRINE AND COVENANTS 45:63–75

45:63 *Wars in your own lands.* The Lord knows the hearts of men and knew beforehand the eventual carnage that would result due to the Civil War. Two years following this revelation, the Prophet Joseph Smith stated, "I am prepared to say by the authority of Jesus Christ, that not many years shall pass away before the United States shall present such a scene of bloodshed as has not a parallel in the history of our nation" (*Teachings of the Prophet Joseph Smith*, 17). See commentary on Doctrine and Covenants 38:29; 87:1.

45:65–75 The early Saints were unable to live according to the laws and principles upon which Zion must be built. The promises and blessings offered by the Lord were not bestowed in that day due to wickedness. The timetable of the Lord in fulfillment of the promises given is somewhat dependent on us. This principle was reflected in a discourse that the Prophet Joseph Smith gave to the Relief Society sisters assembled in Nauvoo, Illinois: "I now deliver it as a prophecy, if the inhabitants of this state, with the people of the surrounding country, will turn unto the Lord with all their hearts, ten years will not roll around before the kings and queens of the earth will come unto Zion, and pay their respects to the leaders of this people; they shall come with their millions, and shall contribute of their abundance for the relief of the poor, and the building up and beautifying of Zion" (*Teachings of the Prophet Joseph Smith*, 227).

Until the time arrives that we, the covenant people of the Lord, increase in numbers and are able to abide the laws of the celestial kingdom as a community, we will not see the fulfillment of these verses. See commentary on Doctrine and Covenants 105:3–5.

45:65 *With one heart and with one mind.* The Saints are given the opportunity to establish Zion on the earth, even as the righteous people of Enoch's day were: "And the Lord called his people Zion, because they were of one heart and one mind, and dwelt in righteousness; and there was no poor among them. And Enoch continued his preaching in righteousness unto the people of God. And it came to pass in his days, that he built a city that was called the City of Holiness, even Zion" (Moses 7:18–19).

45:66 *The New Jerusalem.* See commentary on Doctrine and Covenants 42:9; 57:2.

45:67 *It shall be called Zion.* Zion is not limited to one city or land. Although the concept of Zion may be understood in its infant state as a city, Isaiah prophesied that Zion "shalt break forth on the right hand and on the left" (Isaiah 54:3). "You know there has been great discussion in relation to Zion," taught the Prophet Joseph Smith, "where it is, and where the gathering of the dispensation is, and which I am now going to tell you. The prophets have spoken and written upon it; but I will make a proclamation that will cover a broader ground. The whole of America is Zion itself from north to south, and is described by the Prophets, who declare that it is the Zion where the mountain of the Lord should be, and that it should be in the center of the land" (*Teachings of the Prophet Joseph Smith*, 362).

When the early Saints "first heard the fullness of the Gospel preached by the first Elders," explained Elder Erastus Snow, "and read the revelations given through the Prophet Joseph Smith, our ideas of Zion were very limited. But as our minds began to grow and expand, why we began to look upon Zion as a great people, and the Stakes of Zion as numerous. . . . We ceased to set bounds to Zion and her Stakes" (*Journal of Discourses*, 25:30–31).

45:68 *Take his sword against his neighbor.* The wicked have no respect for life. Those who thirst for the shedding of blood create scenes incomprehensible to the minds of most Saints. Mormon lamented the fallen conditions and depravity of his people in the last battles between the Nephites and the Lamanites. The wicked of the last days will surpass the iniquity of the Book of Mormon peoples who fought in large national armies. The prophet Ezekiel wrote that among the armies of the wicked in the wars of the last days, even the battle of Gog and Magog, "every man's sword shall be against his brother" (Ezekiel 38:21).

In the revelation under consideration, the Savior continued to expound upon the words of Zechariah. During the siege of Jerusalem that precedes the Lord's appearance to the Jews on the Mount of Olives the wicked will turn upon one another. "And it shall come to pass in that day, that a great tumult from the Lord shall be among them; and they shall lay hold every one on the hand of his neighbour, and his hand shall rise up against the hand of his neighbour" (Zechariah 14:13).

Flee unto Zion for safety. See commentary on Doctrine and Covenants 45:32.

45:71 *The righteous shall be gathered out from among all nations.* There are good people among all nations. In time the Lord will seek out each of his children, and they will be given the blessings of knowing the fulness of the gospel. In the dedicatory prayer of the Kirtland Temple, the Prophet Joseph Smith plead with God: "And whatsoever city thy servants shall enter, and the people of that city receive their testimony, let thy peace and thy salvation be upon that city; that they may gather out of that city the righteous, that they may come forth to Zion, or to her stakes, the places of thine appointment, with songs of everlasting joy; and until this be accomplished, let not thy judgments fall upon that city" (D&C 109:39–40).

In particular, the gathering of the righteous seeks to find and save the house of Israel scattered among all nations. The Savior also referred to this work as gathering the wheat from among the tares before the field is burned. Thus, before the destruction of the wicked, the gospel "[must] be preached in all the world" (Joseph Smith–Matthew 1:31).

DOCTRINE AND COVENANTS 46

DATE: 8 MARCH 1831
PLACE: KIRTLAND, OHIO

This revelation was given through the Prophet Joseph at Kirtland, Ohio, 8 March 1831. It addresses two matters of considerable importance to the infant Church. First, the matter of who, if any, should be excluded from meetings. Second, the discerning of spirits so that the Saints might avoid the host of spiritual counterfeits common in the world. Its doctrinal significance, however, reaches far beyond these two issues in that it restores to the earth the doctrine of spiritual gifts.

By the second half of the second century a noticeable change had taken place in the Church organized by Christ and his apostles. Spiritual gifts were no longer to be found. As one sympathetic church historian observed, "The church was no longer a place where the Spirit of prophecy could be heard. More and more people were joining the churches, but the distinction between church and world was fading. The church was becoming secularized; it was coming to terms with heathen thought and culture and philosophy" (Shelley, *Church History in Plain Language*, 64–65). Thus as the Holy Ghost quietly withdrew from the ancient church the voice of the philosopher boisterously took its place. Nephi aptly described what would follow. Priests, he said, teaching with their own learning, will contend one with another while denying the power of God, the spirit of revelation, and the working of miracles. Such things, they will say, have been done away with (2 Nephi 28:4–6). It follows as a great evidence of the Restoration that these gifts—which were so much a part of the faith of the Saints in dispensations past—would once again find their rightful place in the Church of Christ.

Truth Seekers Not to Be Excluded from Public Meetings
DOCTRINE AND COVENANTS 46:1–6

46:1–6 In these early days, when the order of the Church was new to everyone, the practice of excluding nonbelievers from sacrament and confirmation meetings developed. This caused some discussion because the Book of Mormon directed the Nephite Twelve not to exclude those unworthy to partake of the sacrament from sacrament meetings (3 Nephi 18:28–32). The correctness of that principle is confirmed in this revelation in its announcement that truth seekers are welcome in all public meetings held by the Church.

Moroni informs us that, among his people, meetings were conducted "after the manner of the workings of the Spirit, and by the power of the Holy Ghost; for as the power of the Holy Ghost led them whether to preach, or to exhort, or to pray, or to supplicate, or to sing, even so it was done" (Moroni 6:9). This same instruction found expression in the direction given to the restored Church (D&C 20:45) and is repeated again in the present text.

46:2 *Notwithstanding those things which are written.* In the context of this revelation, this phrase means "in accordance with that which has been written." The text is occasionally used to sustain the idea that immediate revelation supersedes written policy. Though this does not reflect the original purpose or meaning of this text, it is a correct principle (D&C 52:9; 68:4; 121:33).

Ask of God and Seek the Gifts of the Spirit
DOCTRINE AND COVENANTS 46:7–12

46:7 *Ye are commanded in all things to ask of God.* There is nothing optional here. It is a command that we "ask of God," and that we do so "in all things." When blessings are needed, we are to "ask of God." Where understanding is required, we are to "ask of God." When testimony or confirmation is needed, we are to "ask of God." If false spirits need detecting, we are to "ask of God." In matters both temporal and spiritual we are to importune the heavens and align ourselves with their direction. This is not to suggest that we can move neither to the right nor to the left without divine command. It is, however, to say that the spirit of "prayer and thanksgiving" be a part of all that we do. "Whatsoever thing ye shall ask the Father in my name, which is good, in faith believing that ye shall receive, behold, it shall be done unto you" (Moroni 7:26). "Counsel with the Lord in all thy doings," Alma directed his son Helaman, with the appended promise that "he will direct thee for good; yea, when thou liest down at night lie down unto the Lord, that he may watch over you in your sleep; and when thou risest in the morning let thy heart be full of thanks unto God; and if ye do these things, ye shall be lifted up at the last day" (Alma 37:37).

That which the Spirit testifies unto you even so I would that ye should do. The specific context of this direction pertains to the manner in which meetings are conducted in the name of the Lord (v. 2). In principle it applies to all that is done in his name. As the Spirit directs, so we should respond. For instance, the Lord said, "Speak the thoughts that I shall put into your hearts, and you shall not be confounded before men; for it shall be given you in the very hour, yea, in the very moment, what ye shall say" (D&C 100:5–6). If we choose to ignore such prompting, we will quickly find that the Spirit will in like manner choose to ignore us.

Considering the end of your salvation. In all of our choices and decisions we might well ask, Is this in harmony with the covenants I have made, does this lead me closer to God? If our answer is in the affirmative, we have, in the language of this revelation, considered the end of our salvation.

Doing all things with prayer and thanksgiving. As we have been directed to counsel with the Lord in all things, so we have been directed to render thanks for all that we have been given. In a subsequent revelation the Prophet was told, "In nothing doth man offend God, or against none is his wrath kindled, save those who confess not his hand in all things, and obey not his commandments" (D&C 59:21).

Doctrines of devils, or the commandments of men. It is a sad commentary that the "doctrines of devils" and the "commandments of men" have so often paraded as the principles of salvation taking refuge in the churches of the world. Such doctrines have been used to support murder, tyranny, and oppression. In his vision of the Middle Ages, Nephi saw and described the formation of a church which he said would slay the Saints of God, torture them, and bind them down with a yoke of iron. "I beheld," he said, "this great and abominable church; and I saw the devil that he was the founder of it. And I also saw gold, and silver, and silks, and scarlets, and fine-twined linen, and all manner of precious clothing; and I saw many harlots. And the angel [Nephi's guide and mentor during the vision] spake unto me, saying: Behold the gold, and the silver, and silks, and the scarlets, and the fine-twined linen, and the precious clothing, and the harlots, are the desires of this great and abominable church. And also for the praise of the world do they destroy the saints of God, and bring them down into captivity" (1 Nephi 13:6–9). It was to escape that captivity that many of our forefathers left Europe and came to the New World. We cannot in wisdom suppose that the prince of darkness was the father of but one such church. Describing the churches that would oppose the restored gospel in the last days, Nephi said: "Yea, and there shall be many which shall say: Eat, drink, and be merry, for tomorrow we die; and it shall be well with us. And there shall also be many which shall say: Eat, drink, and be merry; nevertheless, fear God—he will justify in committing a little sin; yea, lie a little, take advantage of one because of his words, dig a pit for thy neighbor; there is no harm in this; and do all these things, for tomorrow we die; and if it so be that we are guilty, God will beat us with a few stripes, and at last we shall be saved in the kingdom of God. Yea, and there shall be many which shall teach after this manner, false and vain and foolish doctrines, . . . their churches have become corrupted, and their churches are lifted up; because of pride they are puffed up. They rob the poor because of their fine sanctuaries; they rob the poor because of their fine clothing; and they persecute the meek and the poor in heart, because in their pride they are puffed up" (2 Nephi 28:7–9, 12–13). Joseph Smith described the creeds of these churches as "the very mainspring of all corruption," and as the "handcuffs, and chains, and shackles, and fetters of hell" (D&C 123:7–8).

Though the doctrines of devils will always be found parading as the truths of salvation, we would be both foolish and naïve to suppose that the adversary limits his proselytizing to the sphere of religion. As the darkness of night knows no bounds, so the influence of the adversary reigns wherever the light of the gospel has been forced to flee. Politics, academics, and entertainment are among the fields that have reaped a rich harvest for the father of all lies. While one man may lose his soul in the quest for power, another will choose to worship at the shrine of his own intellect, and still another will surrender all that is decent in the quest for pleasure. Each will have devils at his side parroting the litanies of hell, their chief doctrines centering in the right of individuals to do as they please—either because they are above the law or because there is no law—and the promise of an all-loving and nonjudgmental god whose unconditional love assures salvation to all.

As to the commandments of men, it need only be observed that if one's faith is perfectly in line with the wisdom of the day it will be out of line with the wisdom of tomorrow. Surely a faith that does not reach beyond the wisdom of this world will be of little benefit in the worlds to come.

46:8 *Seek ye earnestly the best gifts.* Well might it be asked, Of all the gifts of the Spirit which are the "best" or the ones most to be desired? To which we readily answer, The gift or gifts most needed in your circumstances and situation. The best gift is the gift best suited to enable you to bless those with whom you have been called to labor. To the young mother, it may be patience, love, and understanding; to the aged woman, the ability to endure; to the newly called missionary, the gift of tongues; to the bishop, the gift of discernment; to the teacher, knowledge; to the priesthood leader, the gift of administration, and so forth.

46:9 *And him that seeketh so to do.* Who has rightful claim to the gifts of the Spirit? The Lord teaches us that it is those who love him and keep all of his commandments. The difficulty here is that none of us keep all of the commandments; at least we do not keep them perfectly. Attesting to the mercy and grace of heaven comes this phrase, which extends hope to all: "And him [or her] that seeketh so to do." Each of heaven's gifts is within our grasp, if we will but reach.

Not for a sign that they may consume it upon their lusts. There are no private gifts, each is given that we might aid and serve others. To seek gifts for self-gratification is contrary to the Spirit from which they come and the purpose for which they have been ordained. Similarly, Joseph F. Smith said: "Show me Latter-day Saints who have to feed upon miracles, signs and visions in order to keep them steadfast in the Church, and I will show you members of the Church who are not in good standing before God, and who are walking in slippery paths. It is not by marvelous manifestations unto us that we shall be established in the truth, but it is by humility and faithful obedience to the commandments and laws of God" (Conference Report, April 1900, 40).

46:10–12 Spiritual gifts are given by the Holy Ghost to those who have rightful claim upon his companionship through the waters of baptism and by the laying on of hands. Thus they are the exclusive providence of members of the Church (v. 10). These are spiritual talents given to bless those of the household of faith and to aid in the declaration of the gospel. They find their manifestation in service to others. By contrast, the myriad of talents with which the generality of humankind have been blessed can be used in a host of ways and for a great variety of purposes. Talents can be used in any cause, be it good or evil.

Spiritual gifts are talents given and consecrated for the Lord's purpose. All spiritual gifts edify the soul and testify of Christ. The talents of men may or may not be used for such purposes. In the world, artists, musicians, and writers labor for different masters and for different rewards. Whereas righteousness and obedience are requisites for the use of spiritual gifts, this is not always the case with other talents. Talents may find expression without the attendant aid of the Spirit, and even in opposition to it. Certainly, there are gifted artists in many fields outside of the Church who have responded to the light of Christ and to revelation from the Holy Ghost. We would liken the expression of such gifts to the labors of the great reformers who paved the way for the Restoration. We can only suppose that their offering will find acceptance by the God of heaven. We would further suppose that such gifts, as marvelous as they may be, will in a future day be enhanced by the greater light and power that the fulness of the gospel brings with it.

Gifts of the Spirit Enumerated
DOCTRINE AND COVENANTS 46:13–26

46:13–14 Every member of the Church is expected to have a personal assurance or testimony that Jesus is the Christ, the Son of the living God. Such a testimony comes only by the spirit of revelation; and thus when shared with others in company with the Spirit by which it came it may have a very electrifying effect. Nevertheless, there are those who are specially gifted in the bearing of testimony, who, like the soloists in a great choir, thrill our souls and raise the level of our faith beyond that which others can do.

In like manner, to some it has been given to testify with special power of the mission and ministry of the Prophet Joseph Smith, of the truthfulness of the Book of Mormon, or of some particular gospel principle in such a manner that it has a more powerful effect upon our souls than that which we normally experience when others bear like testimony.

46:14 *To others it is given to believe on their words.* Some are granted the privilege of penning scripture, while the generality of humankind are given the gift to "believe on their words." Virtually everyone has been edified by the words of others and has edified others with their own expressions. To some has been granted the gift of expression and to others has been given the ability to believe on their words.

46:15 *The differences of administration.* There is much to administer and govern in a great kingdom. So it is that if the house of the Lord is to be a house of order the labor of many officers and servants is required. In the kingdom of God there are of necessity "differences of administration," meaning a great variety of services that must be rendered.

46:16 *The diversities of operations.* The diversity of gifts found in the community of Saints suggests that there are a host of tasks that need doing and a variety of ways in which they can be done. It is expected that all faithful Saints will labor in their callings, using the gifts that God has given them. For this reason people are called to serve in various capacities for a time when their gift or gifts are particularly needed. We find the apostle Paul saying, "I have planted, Apollos watered" (1 Corinthians 3:6), to which it might be added, another pruned, and still another harvested, each doing that for which he was best suited. Surely, this has been true with those men called to stand at the head of the Church. Each has been endowed with the particular gifts needed during the time of his administration. The Prophet Joseph laid the foundation of this dispensation as no other man could. Yet, perhaps he would not have been Brigham's match in leading the Saints across the plains and colonizing the Great Basin. And so it has been with one prophet after another, each specially prepared to meet the challenges of that time for which he was called.

The "diversity of operations" could also be understood to embrace different ways particular gifts are manifest. The gift of healing, for instance, finds expression in one person's ability to administer healing herbs, the ability of another to heal through a priesthood blessing, and in still another the power to say, "Rise up and walk" (Acts 3:6). Indeed, we read of one who was healed by simply touching the hem of the Master's garment (Matthew 9:20–23).

46:17 *The word of wisdom.* Some have been blessed not just with wisdom but also with the ability to articulate the same in such a manner that it impresses itself upon those in need of it.

46:18 The question has often been asked, Are teachers born, or are they made? Some are born to teach just as others are born to a thousand other things: some to sing, others to write, still others to lead, to heal, to build, to nurture, and so on, each with talents enhanced by good training but not originating in that training. Gifts do not originate in books or in classes. True it is that such efforts may well improve a particular person's ability to do one thing or another, but they cannot grant them that ability in the first place. So it is in the realm of spiritual things. Teaching is a spiritual gift and, as this revelation suggests, some have received it and others have not. Teaching this principle, Moroni said, "For behold, to one is given by the Spirit of God, that he may teach the word of wisdom; and to another, that he may teach the word of knowledge by the same Spirit"

(Moroni 10:9–10). Similarly, we might say to one it is given to teach children of Primary age, to another to teach teenagers, and to yet another to teach adults. What then happens when we are called to labor in an assignment in which we have no gift? We can but respond that if the call came from the Lord—and such calls do—and if we thrust in our sickle with all our might, he will sustain us and bless our efforts so that his purposes will be accomplished.

46:19–20 It is expected that every member of the Church have sufficient faith to be healed and that every holder of the Melchizedek Priesthood have sufficient faith to utilize the power of that priesthood to heal those who are sick. To say that some have the gift to be healed and others the gift to heal is to say that they have power beyond that known to the generality of faithful Saints. It is supposed among some that the higher the office one holds in the priesthood the greater the blessing they can give. This is simply not the case. To illustrate this principle Brigham Young said that he was hounded constantly by people asking if he would come and give a blessing; "I only go occasionally, because it is the privilege of every father, who is an Elder in Israel, to have faith to heal his family, . . . and if he does not do it he is not living up to his privilege. It is just as reasonable for him to ask me to cut his wood and maintain his family, for if he had faith himself he would save me the trouble of leaving other duties to attend to his request" (*Journal of Discourses*, 3:46).

It is not expected that the faithful Saint will be relieved from every illness or the effects of every injury. Christ did not heal every sick or infirm soul in Israel, even within the household of faith. The elders of Israel do not wander through hospitals seeking the opportunity to give blessings. The faithful are always entitled to a blessing though that blessing may not always be the restoration of health and strength. As it takes faith to be healed, it also takes faith to accept the fact that it is not the intent or design of heaven that every sick soul be raised from its bed of affliction. Sooner or later all must die and, as the Prophet Joseph Smith said, "The only difference between the old and young dying is, one lives longer in heaven and eternal light and glory than the other, and is freed a little sooner from this miserable wicked world" (*Teachings of the Prophet Joseph Smith*, 197). See commentary on Doctrine and Covenants 42:43–48.

46:23 *The discerning of spirits.* "Nothing is a greater injury to the children of men," said Joseph Smith, "than to be under the influence of a false spirit when they think they have the Spirit of God" (*Teachings of the*

Prophet Joseph Smith, 205). A bishop is called to be "a judge" in Israel (D&C 64:40) and thus by virtue of his office has a special right to importune the heavens for this gift in order that he judge wisely and not be deceived by counterfeit gifts.

46:24–25 The gift of tongues is given for the purpose of testifying of Christ and teaching the gospel. The interpretation of tongues is given in order that language will not be a barrier to hearing and understanding the heaven-sent message. Joseph F. Smith said: "There is perhaps no gift of the spirit of God more easily imitated by the devil than the gift of tongues. Where two men or women exercise the gift of tongues by the inspiration of the spirit of God, there are a dozen perhaps who do it by the inspiration of the devil. . . .

"I believe in the gifts of the Holy Spirit unto men, but I do not want the gift of tongues, except when I need it. . . .

"So far as I am concerned, if the Lord will give me ability to teach the people in my native tongue, or in their own language to the understanding of those who hear me, that will be sufficient gift of tongues to me. Yet if the Lord gives you the gift of tongues, do not despise it, do not reject it. For if it comes from the Spirit of God, it will come to those who are worthy to receive it, and it is all right" (Conference Report, April 1900, 41).

46:24 *To speak with tongues.* "Be not so curious about tongues," the Prophet Joseph Smith counseled, "do not speak in tongues except there be an interpreter present; the ultimate design of tongues is to speak to foreigners, and if persons are very anxious to display their intelligence, let them speak to such in their own tongues. The gifts of God are all useful in their place, but when they are applied to that which God does not intend, they prove an injury, a snare and a curse instead of a blessing" (*History of the Church*, 5:31–32).

46:20–26 The working of miracles, prophecy, the discernment of spirits, and speaking in tongues are here listed as illustrations of spiritual gifts. It is not to be supposed that these, with the other gifts mentioned in this revelation, constitute an exhaustive list of the gifts that God has chosen to give his children. That is not the design or purpose of the revelation. The gifts of God are as diverse as are those to whom they have been given. Like fingerprints, they are individual and distinctive. The genius of this is that it binds us together as a community of Saints, everyone having something to contribute that no one else can do as well. Each of us is in a position to bless and to be blessed. For this reason we have been commanded to "meet together often" that we might succor and strengthen each other. It is not intended in the gospel plan that we be saved separate and singly. Salvation is in many respects a community affair.

Directing the Use of Spiritual Gifts
DOCTRINE AND COVENANTS 46:27–33

46:27 *Unto the bishop of the church.* This revelation was given some years before the development of wards and stakes. The bishop referred to would be the equivalent of the presiding bishop today. In like manner, the reference to elders would be to those holding positions of presidency. The idea is that those in positions of presidency must be able to discern the legitimate gifts of God from counterfeit gifts common to false religion and to discipline and direct the proper use of the gifts given of God to the Saints.

46:29 The president of the Church not only presides over all of its members but also over all of the gifts given them of God to aid in the building of his earthly kingdom. Under the direction of the prophet countless calls are made to utilize those gifts in sharing the gospel with all the nations and peoples of the earth and in teaching and strengthening those already in the Church.

46:30–32 When we are in tune with the Spirit so that it gives direction to our heavenly petitions, we may also have the perfect assurance that our prayers will be answered. By contrast the Lord has said, "If ye ask anything that is not expedient for you, it shall turn unto your condemnation" (D&C 88:65).

46:33 *Practice virtue and holiness.* See commentary on Doctrine and Covenants 121:45–46.

DOCTRINE AND COVENANTS 47

DATE: 8 MARCH 1831
PLACE: KIRTLAND, OHIO

The Lord had charged Joseph Smith to keep an accurate history of the Church. Accordingly, Oliver Cowdery acted as Church historian and recorder. When Oliver was called to serve as a missionary among the Lamanites (D&C 28:8; 30:5; 32:2), John Whitmer was called to replace him in these assignments. John was reluctant to accept this assignment but agreed to do as the Lord directed. This revelation, given 8 March 1831, came in response to his request that the call be manifest through the Prophet.

John Whitmer Called to Serve as Historian and Scribe
DOCTRINE AND COVENANTS 47:1–4

47:1–4 John Whitmer was Church historian for about seven years. Then on 10 March 1838, he lost his membership in the Church. At that time he was serving as a counselor to his brother David in the Missouri presidency. "Because he and W. W. Phelps, the other counselor, had taken personal title to the gathering site of Far West, the resentment of the Missouri members resulted in criticism and then formal suspension of that presidency from office. Declining to be called to account economically or to personally appear at high council trials," they were excommunicated (Anderson, *Investigating*, 127). When he left the Church, John Whitmer refused to surrender the history he had written. Later, when the brethren were compiling the history of the Church in Nauvoo he advised them that his history could be acquired "at a fair price." He was advised that they could get along quite well without it. In 1893, some years after his death, the Church obtained a copy of his history. His writings, which included revelations given by Joseph Smith during that seven-year period, were only eighty-five pages in length.

47:1 *Keep a regular history.* Joseph Smith in a meeting with the

Twelve some years after this revelation spoke as follows about the importance of accurate records and the writing of the history of the Church:

"If I now had in my possession, every decision which had been had
upon important items of doctrine and duties since the commencement of
this work, I would not part with them for any sum of money; but we have
neglected to take minutes of such things, thinking, perhaps, that they
would never benefit us afterwards; which, if we had them now, would
decide almost every point of doctrine which might be agitated. But this
has been neglected, and now we cannot bear record to the Church and
to the world, of the great and glorious manifestations which have been
made to us with that degree of power and authority we otherwise could, if
we now had these things to publish abroad.

"Since the Twelve are now chosen, I wish to tell them a course which
they may pursue, and be benefited thereafter, in a point of light of
which they are not now aware. If they will, every time they assemble,
appoint a person to preside over them during the meeting, and one or
more to keep a record of their proceedings, and on the decision of every
question or item, be it what it may, let such decision be written, and such
decision will forever remain upon record, and appear an item of covenant
or doctrine. An item thus decided may appear, at the time, of little or no
worth, but should it be published, and one of you lay hands on it after,
you will find it of infinite worth, not only to your brethren, but it will be
a feast to your own souls.

"Here is another important item. If you assemble from time to time,
and proceed to discuss important questions, and pass decisions upon the
same, and fail to note them down, by and by you will be driven to straits
from which you will not be able to extricate yourselves, because you may
be in a situation not to bring your faith to bear with sufficient perfection
or power to obtain the desired information; or, perhaps, for neglecting to
write these things when God had revealed them, not esteeming them of
sufficient worth, the Spirit may withdraw and God may be angry; and
there is, or was, a vast knowledge, of infinite importance, which is now
lost. What was the cause of this? It came in consequence of slothfulness,
or a neglect to appoint a man to occupy a few moments in writing all
these decisions.

"Here let me prophesy. The time will come, when, if you neglect to
do this thing, you will fall by the hands of unrighteous men. Were you
to be brought before the authorities, and be accused of any crime or mis-
demeanor, and be as innocent as the angels of God, unless you can prove

yourselves to have been somewhere else, your enemies will prevail against you; but if you can bring twelve men to testify that you were in a certain place, at that time, you will escape their hand. Now, if you will be careful to keep minutes of these things, as I have said, it will be one of the most important records ever seen; for all such decisions will ever after remain as items of doctrine and covenants" (*History of the Church*, 2:198–99).

DOCTRINE AND COVENANTS 48

DATE: MARCH 1831
PLACE: KIRTLAND, OHIO

This revelation is introduced in the Book of Commandments as "A Revelation to the bishop, and the church in Kirtland, Ohio, March, 1831." It came in response to the Prophet's inquiry as to where those coming from the east should settle and how they should obtain the necessary lands (see Smith, *History of the Church*, 1:166). The revelation is interesting for both what it does and does not reveal. All are anxious to know where the city of Zion will be built. The Lord will not be rushed in answering. His response is confined to the immediate moment. Those arriving from upstate New York are instructed to purchase lands in eastern Ohio "as seemeth them good."

Gathering Saints Are to Purchase Lands and Follow the Counsel of Their Presiding Officers
DOCTRINE AND COVENANTS 48:1-6

48:2 When the Colesville Saints arrived in Ohio, they settled in the township of Thompson, as Leman Copley had offered to let the Saints occupy his land there; at Thompson they were to be organized under the law of consecration and stewardship (D&C 54).

48:5 *The place is not yet to be revealed.* The place of gathering referred to in this revelation was subsequently revealed to be the land of Missouri (D&C 57:1–4).

48:6 *Presidency and the bishop of the church.* As published in the Book of Commandments, this phrase read, "Bishop and elders of the church." It would be another year before the first presidency was formed (D&C 81; 90). Thus in the Doctrine and Covenants, which was published in August 1835, the Prophet changed this section to reflect that development in the organization of the Church.

DOCTRINE AND COVENANTS 49

DATE: MARCH 1831
PLACE: KIRTLAND, OHIO

About fifteen miles from Kirtland, Ohio, where the body of the Church resided, was a community of Shaking Quakers, or Shakers. They were called Shaking Quakers because their dress resembled that of the Society of Friends, or Quakers, and because their system of worship included shaking and physical contortions. One of their number, Leman Copley, joined the Church though he still held to some of his former beliefs which he persisted in teaching. In this revelation, given 7 March 1831, he along with Sidney Rigdon and Parley P. Pratt were directed to take the message of the Restoration to the Shakers. Some months previously, Elder Pratt had spent two days with them and left them seven copies of the Book of Mormon. This revelation, which Sidney Rigdon read in its entirety to the Shakers, was given so that the missionaries might respond by the spirit of revelation to the matters of particular interest to the Shakers. Those beliefs included the idea that Christ had already returned, doing so in the form of a woman, Ann Lee, who had died in 1784. They held that baptism and the Lord's Supper ceased with the apostolic age, that there was no vicarious atonement, nor was there to be a bodily resurrection. The eating of pork was rejected, and some of their number rejected the eating of any meat at all. They also felt that a celibate life was superior to marriage and that having children reduced their standing with God.

Although this revelation (D&C 49) was rejected by the Shakers, its doctrinal announcements remain important. Also of importance is the pattern it established for missionary work. The elders did not engage the Shakers in a doctrinal debate over the peculiar tenets of their faith but invited them to hear the word of the Lord as it was given to them. It was then for them to choose whether they would accept that word as it came to them through a living prophet or reject it. Sadly, they rejected it.

How the Gospel Is to Be Declared
DOCTRINE AND COVENANTS 49:1–4

49:1 The missionaries sent to the Shakers are directed to declare the message of the Restoration even as they received it. That is, they are to testify that Joseph Smith is a prophet and that the gospel in its pristine purity has been restored again to the earth through him. As evidence of his prophetic call, they are to read this revelation in which the Lord responds to their key doctrinal concerns.

49:2 Like many with whom our missionaries share the message of the gospel, the Shakers reveled in certain truths while rejecting those requiring change and repentance on their part.

49:3 Leman Copley, a recent convert from the Shakers, is cautioned not to reason with his former colleagues on their ground. His commission now is to declare the message of the Restoration. If he is true to the message he has been given he is assured success; if he fails to follow this counsel he is told that he will not prosper. The principle is applicable to all missionary work. Our commission is to declare the message of the Restoration from the revelations of the Restoration. Such a course is consistently rewarded with a marvelous outpouring of the Spirit and a rich harvest of souls. Those insisting on giving credence to the restored gospel by "proving" it, as it were, from Old and New Testament texts or arguing for its credibility in some other way do not enjoy the same outpouring of the Spirit or the same power of conversion.

The Day and Hour of Christ's Return Is Unknown
DOCTRINE AND COVENANTS 49:5–7

49:5–6 There is some measurable power associated with these verses. In them we have the testimony of the Father that Christ is, indeed, his Only Begotten Son and that he is the Redeemer of mankind. Relative to this testimony, there is no middle ground; in the great day of judgment all will be called upon to either accept or reject it, which they do at the peril of their eternal lives. To the Shakers, this revelation affirms that Christ reigns in the heavens and has done so since his resurrection. Thus, it refutes the false doctrine that he dwelt upon the earth as a woman, Ann Lee, founder of the Shaker faith. See commentary on Doctrine and Covenants 49:22.

49:7 Though it is the duty of the Saints to be prepared for and to know the approximate time of Christ's return, none, not even the angels of heaven, will be trusted with the knowledge of the day and hour in which he will come. See commentary on Doctrine and Covenants 130:14–17.

Salvation Comes Only through Obedience
DOCTRINE AND COVENANTS 49:8-14

49:8 *All men shall repent.* Just as all men must exercise faith, so they must repent. "For all have sinned," said the apostle Paul, "and come short of the glory of God" (Romans 3:23).

Holy men that ye know not of. During his mortal ministry Christ said, "Verily I say unto you, There be some standing here, which shall not taste of death, till they see the Son of man coming in his kingdom" (Matthew 16:28; Mark 9:1; Luke 9:27). Commenting on this verse, Bruce R. McConkie said: "It is apparent that on a previous occasion, of which we have no present scriptural record, Jesus taught his disciples the truths about the doctrine of translation and promised that some of them would continue to live on earth until his Second Coming. John the Beloved is the only known one of these disciples who has continued to live without tasting death (John 21:20–24). Until the identity of any others is revealed, we have no way of knowing who they are or what mission they have been able to perform because of their translation" (*Doctrinal New Testament Commentary*, 1:396–97).

Similarly, we read that in the New World Christ empowered three of the Nephites so they might continue their earthly ministries until the time of his second coming (3 Nephi 28:4–12). See commentary on Doctrine and Covenants 7.

49:9 Joseph Smith restored the "new and everlasting covenant" (D&C 132:6). That is to say, the covenant he restored was new to those of his day, yet it had been everlastingly the same.

49:10 *The nations of the earth shall bow to it.* See commentary on Doctrine and Covenants 87:6.

49:12 *Believe on the name of the Lord.* See commentary on Doctrine and Covenants 112.

Marriage and Posterity Are Ordained of God

DOCTRINE AND COVENANTS 49:15-17

49:15 *Whoso forbiddeth to marry is not ordained of God.* Paul in his epistle to Timothy identified "forbidding to marry" as a sign of apostasy and a doctrine of the devil (1 Timothy 4:3). Marriage, we are assured in this text, is ordained of God. In a proclamation to the world, issued in 1995, the First Presidency and the Quorum of the Twelve asserted that "marriage between a man and a woman is ordained of God and that the family is central to the Creator's plan for the eternal destiny of His children" ("Family: A Proclamation to the World").

49:16–17 Here we are told that the very reason that God created the earth was so that we, his children, might come to it and marry and then as couples become "one flesh." Subsequent revelation would bring an understanding of the eternal nature of the marriage covenant and of the family unit.

God Sanctions Eating Meat

DOCTRINE AND COVENANTS 49:18-21

49:18–19 Another of the distinctive characteristics of the Shakers was that they were vegetarians. Here the Lord asserts that no authorized servant of his has ever been directed to command that we abstain from the use of meat. See commentary on Doctrine and Covenants 59:15–21.

49:20 Of the Zion society established by Enoch we read, "And the Lord called his people Zion, because they were of one heart and one mind, and dwelt in righteousness; and there was no poor among them" (Moses 7:18).

49:21 The killing of animals for sport finds no justification in scripture. "Surely, blood shall not be shed," the Lord told those in ancient days, "only for meat, to save your lives; and the blood of every beast will I require at your hands" (JST Genesis 9:11).

Zion to Flourish and the Lamanites to Blossom as a Rose

DOCTRINE AND COVENANTS 49:22-28

49:22 *Not in the form of a woman.* Shakers believed that Ann Lee, the founder of their faith, was the second embodiment of Christ's spirit. In "Mother Ann," as they called her, God's spirit had been incarnated in female form as they believed Jesus was God's spirit incarnated in male form (Foster, "Lee, Ann," *Encyclopedia of Religion*, 8:491).

49:23 The Shakers' notion that the Second Coming had taken place overlooked the prophetic promise that his coming was to be preceded by all manner of signs in the heavens (Joel 2:28–32; Matthew 24:29–30). The prophetic word also promises great physical changes on the earth. For example, the mountains are to be made low and the rough places are to be made smooth (Isaiah 40:4; JST Luke 3:10).

49:24 *Jacob shall flourish in the wilderness, and the Lamanites shall blossom as the rose.* The physical gathering alluded to is the assembling of the Latter-day Saints in the tops of the mountains in western America. There Zion shall flourish upon the hills and rejoice upon the mountains. The "wilderness" included areas that were colonized under the direction of Brigham Young. The day when the Lamanites shall blossom as the rose has scarcely commenced. They are only beginning to be the pure and delightsome people they will yet become.

49:25 *The place which I have appointed.* See commentary on Doctrine and Covenants 57:1–3; 101:21.

49:28 *I come quickly.* The reference is to the manner of his coming, not the time of his coming.

DOCTRINE AND COVENANTS 50

DATE: 9 MAY 1831
PLACE: KIRTLAND, OHIO

In the spring of 1831 several individuals in and around Kirtland, Ohio, claimed revelations for the guidance of the infant Church. Confusion was the result. Parley P. Pratt and other elders called on Joseph Smith to find out how members of the Church were to discern such spirits. This revelation came in response to that request.

Describing these events, Parley P. Pratt said: "As I went forth among the different branches, some very strange spiritual operations were manifested, which were disgusting, rather than edifying. Some persons would seem to swoon away, and make unseemly gestures, and be drawn or disfigured in their countenances. Others would fall into ecstacies, and be drawn into contortions, cramp, fits, etc. Others would seem to have visions and revelations, which were not edifying, and which were not congenial to the doctrine and spirit of the Gospel. In short, a false and lying spirit seemed to be creeping into the Church.

"All these things were new and strange to me, and had originated in the Church during our absence, and previous to the arrival of President Joseph Smith from New York.

"Feeling our weakness and inexperience, and lest we should err in judgment concerning these spiritual phenomena, myself, John Murdock, and several other Elders, went to Joseph Smith, and asked him to inquire of the Lord concerning these spirits or manifestations.

"After we had joined in prayer in his translating room, he dictated in our presence the following revelation" (*Autobiography*, 48).

Many False Spirits Are Abroad in the Earth
DOCTRINE AND COVENANTS 50:1–5

50:2 The April 1842 edition of the *Times and Seasons* contained an article written by the Prophet titled "Try the Spirits." Among other things, the Prophet said: "It is evident from the Apostles' writings, that many false spirits existed in their day, and had 'gone forth into the world,' and that it needed intelligence which God alone could impart to detect false spirits, and to prove what spirits were of God" (*Teachings of the Prophet Joseph Smith*, 202). The world is ignorant of such things, he said, because they are known only by the Spirit.

"The Egyptians were not able to discover the difference between the miracles of Moses and those of the magicians until they came to be tested together; and if Moses had not appeared in their midst, they would unquestionably have thought that the miracles of the magicians were performed through the mighty power of God, for they were great miracles that were performed by them—a supernatural agency was developed, and great power manifested. . . .

"There always did, in every age, seem to be a lack of intelligence pertaining to this subject. Spirits of all kinds have been manifested, in every age, and almost among all people. If we go among the pagans, they have their spirits; the Mohammedans, the Jews, the Christians, the Indians—all have their spirits, all have a supernatural agency, and all contend that their spirits are of God. Who shall solve the mystery? 'Try the spirits,' says John. . . .

" . . . But no one can try his own, and what is the reason? Because they have not a key to unlock, no rule wherewith to measure, and no criterion whereby they can test it. Could any one tell the length, breadth or height of a building without a rule? Test the quality of metals without a criterion, or point out the movements of the planetary systems, without a knowledge of astronomy? Certainly not; and if such ignorance as this is manifested about a spirit of this kind, who can describe an angel of light? If Satan should appear as one in glory, who can tell his color, his signs, his appearance, his glory, or what is the manner of his manifestation?" (*Teachings of the Prophet Joseph Smith*, 202–4). In answer to this question, the Prophet said it could not be done without the priesthood and a knowledge of the laws by which spirits are governed.

50:4 *Abominations in the church.* In addition to Parley P. Pratt's description of the false spirits that had deceived some few of the Saints, as given in the introduction to this section, John Whitmer recorded as follows: "Some had visions and could not tell what they saw. Some would fancy to themselves that they had the sword of Laban, and would wield it as expert as a light dragoon, some would act like an Indian in the act of scalping, some would slide or scoot on the floor, with the rapidity of a serpent, which [they] termed sailing in the boat to the Lamanites, preaching the gospel. And many other vain and foolish manoevers that are unmeaning and unprofitable to mention" ("Book of John Whitmer," 62).

Hypocrites Warned
DOCTRINE AND COVENANTS 50:6–9

50:6–9 As Latter-day Saints we make no pretense of being a perfect people. There are those among our number who know nothing of the things of the Spirit; there are others in whose lives the gospel once burned as fire and now is but an ember; there are others who are embarrassed by one gospel principle or another and who sneer and speak evil of the Lord's anointed; there are still others hiding behind the cloak of piety who privately violate virtually every commandment the Lord has given. Of a certainty there are hypocrites among us! To all these we say: Come share our fellowship, know of our love, and worship with us. In that process it is hoped that the desire will be found to improve, to repent, and to live like a Latter-day Saint ought to. Hypocrisy, whatever its form, always blocks the light of heaven and gives the spirit of the evil one a place to fester and grow. In some cases the innocent or unaware will be deceived by the hypocrite. The Lord freely forgives such of their innocent or foolish errors. This, however, will not be the case with hypocrites, whom the Lord will hold fully accountable for their deliberate and practiced deception.

The Gospel Must Be Taught by the Spirit
DOCTRINE AND COVENANTS 50:10–20

50:10–20 It is the Spirit that gives life and meaning to all gospel principles. Thus the gospel must be both taught and learned by the Spirit. Anything less than this, however well intended it may be, is not of God. Scripture, in order to be scripture, must be read and interpreted by the Spirit. Of the revelations of the Restoration the Lord said, "It is my voice which speaketh them unto you; for they are given by my Spirit unto you, and by my power you can read them one to another; and save it were by my power you could not have them; wherefore, you can testify that you have heard my voice, and know my words" (D&C 18:35–36). The same words when read by of those devoid of the Spirit may well be received as nothing but the voice of delusion or a pious fraud. Even the well intended may misuse the revelations of heaven when they fail to read and understand them by the light of heaven. Again, scripture is scripture only when

it is attended by the Spirit through which it came. Many an evil design
has been cloaked in scripture. Devils and false prophets draw freely upon
the words of holy writ to sustain and justify their purposes. The words of
the Savior in the parable of the great supper, "Compel them to come in"
(Luke 14:23), were used to justify the ruthless acts of the Inquisition
against those accused of heresy, as the expulsion of Adam and Eve from
the Garden of Eden was used to justify the confiscation of property and
wealth.

If scripture cannot be read and understood without the light of
heaven, then certainly the principles that grow out of its fertile soil must
be equally dependent on that light to produce good fruits. Does it not,
therefore, seem strange that we seek to give credibility to the word of God
by quoting those who have not embraced it? That some expend more
time and energy seeking external evidences to support the revelations of
heaven than they do to gain an understanding of them? That we seek to
sustain eternal principles with logic that reaches no higher than the tower
of Babel? If we are to lay a foundation upon which we can build the
temple of our understanding so that it does indeed reach to heaven, it
cannot be done upon any other principle than the principle of revelation.
Of any substitutes for that principle the word of the Lord states, "It is not
of God."

50:13 *Unto what were ye ordained?* The mistakes of youth were not
uncommon to the infant Church. Much instruction was necessary to protect the purity of the restored gospel from spiritual counterfeits common
to the unsophisticated Christianity of the American frontier. Levi
Hancock reported that while engaged in preaching the gospel three young
missionaries, Heman Basset, age sixteen (D&C 52:37); Edson Fuller, age
twenty-one (D&C 52:28); and Burr Riggs, age twenty (D&C 75:17), purported to receive revelations and see angels and would fall down frothing
at the mouth. "One of them who acted the worst was Burr Riggs, I have
seen him jump up from the floor, strike his head against the joist in the
Baldwins new house and swing some minutes, then fall like he was dead.
After an hour or two he would come to, he would prophesy and tell what
he had seen. At other times he appeared to be so honest and sincere I was
led to believe all he said, but concluded that all could not be blessed and
perhaps I was not as pure as those young men . . .

"Edson Fuller would fall and turn black in the face. Heman Bassett
would behave like a baboon. He said he had a revelation he had received
in Kirtland from the hand of an angel, he would read it and show pictures

of a course of angels declared to be Gods, then would testify of the truth of the work and I believed it all, like a fool.

"I dare not come out against any thing that an Elder should say for fear I should speak against the Holy Ghost" (*Autobiography of Levi Ward Hancock*, 41).

The gospel must be taught with a dignity and decorum appropriate to the kingdom of heaven. To teach it in any other way, as this revelation states, is "not of God." In like manner, an understanding of the gospel must be obtained according to that same Spirit. The testimony of the truths of heaven cannot be obtained nor nourished by any means other than the spirit of truth.

That Which Does Not Edify Is Not of God
DOCTRINE AND COVENANTS 50:21-25

50:21–22 The truths of heaven cannot be taught by a teacher who does not stand in the light of heaven, nor can they be learned by a student who does not bask in that same light. Standing together in that light, both are edified and rejoice together.

50:23 Anciently, the verb "to edify" meant to build sacred edifices such as temples. Through the years the word *edify* has come to describe the process of improving character or building spirituality. All that is of God edifies—that is, it lifts, builds, and improves; conversely, to edify is to eschew that which demeans, belittles, or excuses. To edify is to make the body and soul of man a holy tabernacle, a temple to God. If a doctrine does not offer the opportunity to reach, to build, or to improve, it is not of God.

50:24 Many in the religious world of our day profess to having been saved as a result of a particular religious experience. Their assumption is that because someone once stood in the light they will always stand in the light. This does not always prove to be the case. The greater flaw in such reasoning, however, is found in the assumption that whatever light they stood in constitutes the fulness of the light of heaven. Such an assumption would at best be foolish. Even then, to bask in gospel light is one thing; to follow the light of the gospel quite another. For those choosing to follow the light it becomes "brighter and brighter until the perfect day." Thus salvation becomes a journey rather than an event. The journey requires us to advance from grace to grace and refuses us the right to say that any religious experience is of itself sufficient. It was Nephi who wisely warned that from them that say, "We have enough . . . shall be taken away even that which they have" (2 Nephi 28:30).

The Faithful Will Possess All Things
DOCTRINE AND COVENANTS 50:26–27

50:26 *The servant of all.* In every gospel dispensation there have been those who have falsely claimed to be called of God. Often they betray themselves in their desire to be served rather than to serve. Responding to this problem in the early days of Christianity, the following direction is given in a work known as *The Didache*. "Welcome every apostle on arriving, as if he were the Lord. But he must not stay beyond one day. In case of necessity, however, the next day too. If he stays three days, he is a false prophet. On departing, an apostle must not accept anything save sufficient food to carry him till his next lodging. If he asks for money, he is a false prophet" (Ehrman, *New Testament*, 316).

50:27 *Possessor of all things.* When a man is properly sent forth in the name of the Lord it is to be expected that the fulness of God's power stands in readiness to sustain and aid him in accomplishing the task to which he has been called (JST Genesis 14). Those who obtain the glory of the celestial world are "they into whose hands the Father has given all things—they are they who are priests and kings, who have received of his fulness, and of his glory; . . . all things are theirs, whether life or death, or things present, or things to come, all are theirs and they are Christ's, and Christ is God's" (D&C 76:55–59).

The Pure to Obtain Divine Answers
DOCTRINE AND COVENANTS 50:28–36

50:28–29 No unclean thing can enter the presence of God, nor can any unclean thing receive the fulness of the Father. To possess all things, one must "be purified and cleansed from all sin." Hence the command to all who would be servants of God: "Prepare yourselves, and sanctify yourselves; yea, purify your hearts, and cleanse your hands and your feet before me, that I may make you clean; that I may testify unto your Father, and your God, and my God, that you are clean from the blood of this wicked generation" (D&C 88:74–75). Christ alone can make us clean. In the full and proper sense, according to the order he has established, those of our day are invited to go to the temple where the ritual here described is performed. Those professing to possess all things by virtue of their accept-ance of Christ but who refuse to honor the priesthood he has restored cannot be sanctified and thus are not endowed with power from on high (D&C 43:16). It is in the house of the Lord that those so endowed learn the order whereby answers are obtained.

50:29 *Ye shall ask whatsoever you will in the name of Jesus and it shall be done.* See commentary on Doctrine and Covenants 46:30–32.

50:30 When the Lord places individuals in a position of presidency, he also endows them with the capacity to discern spirits so that they do not lead astray those who sustain them in faith.

50:31 Any spirit emanating from the God of heaven is subject to confirmation by both those in a position of leadership and those who have placed themselves under covenant to follow that leader. If no confirma-tion is obtained the spirit does not come from God.

50:32–33 We cannot fight darkness with darkness, evil with evil, or that which is petty with pettiness, for by so doing we concede the victory to the very influence that we oppose. Teaching this principle, Jude tells that "Michael the archangel, when contending with the devil he disputed about the body of Moses, durst not bring against him a railing accusation, but said, The Lord rebuke thee" (Jude 1:9). In this story we find Michael, the commanding general in the army of the Lord, standing face to face with the prince of darkness to contend over the soul of Moses. Apparently, Satan claimed Moses to be under his dominion because he had killed an Egyptian taskmaster, while Michael claimed him a citizen of the kingdom of God as a great prophet and prototype of Christ. In this confrontation, Michael sets the example for all who fight in the army of the Lord by refusing to respond to the adversary in his own spirit.

50:33 *Boasting nor rejoicing.* Luke records that the Seventy returned from their missionary labors rejoicing, having discovered that they had power over serpents, scorpions, and evil spirits. To their surprise Christ directed that rather than glory in such things they should rejoice that their names were written in heaven (Luke 10:17–20). Similarly, in our dispensation, having described the power that would be given "them that believe," the Lord said, "A commandment I give unto them, that they shall not boast themselves of these things, neither speak them before the world; for these things are given unto you for your profit and for salvation" (D&C 84:73). As the Spirit is offended when we bring a "railing accusa-tion" against the adversary, so it is offended when we boast in what we have accomplished in the name of the Lord or when we glory in the power that is ours over the kingdom of darkness. We cannot "rail" and retain the Spirit, nor can we boast or rejoice exceedingly over that which we have been able to accomplish in the name of the Lord. Such labors are not done to be seen of men.

50:35 The servants of the Lord have been given power over all that stands in opposition to the kingdom of the Father. "They shall go forth and none shall stay them, for I the Lord have commanded them" (D&C 1:5). Thus by the power of his Spirit they can discern those spirits that are for them and those that are against them.

50:36 To receive the voice of the Lord always brings its attendant blessings, which include the remission of sins (D&C 62:3; 84:61; 108:1; 132:50, 56).

Strength Is Found in the Word
DOCTRINE AND COVENANTS 50:37–42

50:37 *Joseph Wakefield, in whom I am well pleased.* Shortly after this statement was made, Joseph Wakefield was called on a mission with Solomon Humphrey. On this mission they baptized George A. Smith, who would become the youngest apostle to be called in this dispensation. Thereafter, Wakefield became critical of the Prophet, having seen him leave his sacred studies and play with some children. Feeling that this was incompatible with the prophetic office, Wakefield left the Church.

Among the churches. Reference is to the various branches of the Church. This was before the creation of wards and stakes.

Strengthen them by the word of exhortation. The vitality of the gospel is in its doctrines. "Faith comes," Joseph Smith said, "by hearing the word of God," (*Teachings of the Prophet Joseph Smith,* 148). Faith cannot be exercised in a God of whom we have not heard or in doctrines that we have not been taught anymore than strength can be found in food we have not eaten or in renewal from rest we did not receive. Spiritual strength comes through learning and teaching of the saving principles of the gospel. There is no acceptable substitute for such exhortation.

50:38 *John Corrill.* Here John Corrill is called to labor in the Lord's vineyard. A month after this he was called to travel to Missouri with Lyman Wight (D&C 52:7). Prominent in the affairs of the Church, Corrill faltered during the Missouri persecutions and was excommunicated in 1839.

50:39 *Edward Partridge is not justified; . . . let him repent.* Apparently

Edward Partridge was doing or had done something to interfere with the elders filling the missions to which they had been called.

50:40 When the Church was first organized and its doctrines and practices were new to everyone, it was necessary for the Lord to use men who, like unseasoned timber, had not obtained the kind of spiritual maturity common to those offices where it has now existed for generations. Like seeds cast on rich but shallow soil, the Joseph Wakefields and John Corrills sprouted up with a burst of energy only to wither in the first storm or on the first scorching day. Time and experience are as necessary to spiritual growth as they are to the growth of the mind or the body. Thus the Lord speaks of the newly baptized as little children whom he will nurture and protect if they will stay close to him.

50:41–42 "My sheep hear my voice," Christ said in the meridian day, "and I know them, and they follow me: and I give unto them eternal life; and they shall never perish, neither shall any man pluck them out of my hand" (John 10:27–28). How is it then that some who were faithful cease to be so? It is true that no power can "pluck them out" of the hand of the Savior, but it is equally true that he will not prevent them from leaving should they choose to do so. While the commitment of the Father never wavers in the blessing and sustaining of his children, the commitment of his children often falters in their loyalty to him.

Those Who Have Built upon the Rock Are Promised That They Will See the Savior
DOCTRINE AND COVENANTS 50:43–46

50:43 The unity between the Father and the Son is perfect. Our salvation consists in becoming one with them. Here we are told that to the extent that our hearts and minds have become one with them they are in our midst.

50:45 *You shall hear my voice and see me.* As subsequent revelation will affirm, the promise to hear the voice of the Lord and to see him is literal not figurative (D&C 67:13; 76:117–18; 84:20–22; 88:68; 93:1; 107:19).

DOCTRINE AND COVENANTS 51

DATE: MAY 1831
PLACE: THOMPSON, OHIO

In response to the Lord's earlier command for the Church to move to Ohio, approximately two hundred Saints living in New York sold their properties and made the move west (D&C 37). Their arrival called attention to the need for further instructions to implement the law of consecration and stewardship as previously revealed (D&C 42:30–37). In preparation, an earlier revelation had directed the Saints to purchase lands in the region near Kirtland (D&C 48:3). In Thompson, Ohio, a new convert, Leman Copley, owned a large tract of land, some 759 acres, which he consecrated for the settlement of the newly arrived Saints. Bishop Edward Partridge was responsible for dividing this property among the Saints. Consequently, he requested the Prophet Joseph Smith to inquire of the Lord for direction on the matter.

This section was not included in the Book of Commandments. However, it is recorded in a manuscript containing forty-one revelations entitled "Kirtland Revelation Book." Verse five appears to be an inspired addition, which clarified the earlier written revelation. This revelation was first published in the 1835 edition of the Doctrine and Covenants.

Edward Partridge Is Appointed to Regulate Stewardships and Properties
DOCTRINE AND COVENANTS 51:1–8

51:2 *They will be cut off.* That is, they will be excommunicated, or lose their membership in the Church.

51:3 *Let my servant Edward Partridge . . . appoint unto this people their portions.* It was the responsibility of the bishop to give each family its stewardship. Instructing the bishop in the principles that would direct his decision, the Prophet explained in a letter to Bishop Partridge: "To condescend to particulars, I will tell you that every man must be his own judge how much he should receive and how much he should suffer to remain in the hands of the Bishop. I speak of those who consecrate more than they need for the support of themselves and their families.

"The matter of consecration must be done by the mutual consent of both parties; for to give the Bishop power to say how much every man shall have, and he be obliged to comply with the Bishop's judgment, is giving to the Bishop more power than a king has; and upon the other hand, to let every man say how much he needs, and the Bishop be obliged to comply with his judgment, is to throw Zion into confusion, and make a slave of the Bishop. The fact is, there must be a balance or equilibrium of power, between the Bishop and the people, and thus harmony and good will may be preserved among you.

"Therefore, those persons consecrating property to the Bishop in Zion, and then receiving an inheritance back, must reasonably show to the Bishop that they need as much as they claim. But in case the two parties cannot come to a mutual agreement, the Bishop is to have nothing to do about receiving such consecrations; and the case must be laid before a council of twelve High Priests, the Bishop not being one of the council, but he is to lay the case before them" (Smith, *History of the Church*, 1:364–65).

Those whom he has chosen. Bishop Partridge had chosen Isaac Morley and John Corrill to serve as his counselors. They were set apart on 6 June 1831.

Every man equal according to his family. No two families have exactly the same needs. In the division of properties, the number of children in a family, as well as the ages and abilities of the children, are taken into consideration. A farmer would receive farm land as his stewardship; a printer, a printing office; a tanner, a tannery; and a businessman, a mercantile establishment (D&C 57:8, 11; 104:19–42). "And all this," reads a later revelation, "for the benefit of the church of the living God, that every man may improve upon his talent, that every man may gain other talents" (D&C 82:18). In this manner the needs of the poor were provided for and individuals were placed in a position in which they could supply their own wants and aid others in doing the same thing.

51:4 *Give unto him a writing.* A few of these writings have survived to our day. Most deeds—which consisted of both printed and hand-written text—granted property, on the left-hand side, to "Edward Partridge, bishop of the Church." A description of the consecrated property followed in hand-written form. The deed stipulated that this transaction was "for the purpose of purchasing lands, and building up the New Jerusalem, even Zion, and for relieving the wants of the poor and needy." Where the name of the individual was written, it stated that they covenanted and bound themselves and their heirs forever, "to release all" their "right and interest in the above described property" (photocopy in Arrington, *Building the City of God*, 28).

The right-hand side of the document read, "Be it known that I, (Edward Partridge [name written by hand]) Of Jackson county, and state of Missouri, bishop of the church of Christ, organized according to law, and established by revelations of the Lord, on the 6th day of April, 1830, have leased, and by these present do lease unto [individual's name written by hand] of Jackson county, and state of Missouri, a member of said church, the following described piece or parcel of land . . . [description of property written by hand] to have and to hold the above property . . . And it is agreed by the parties that this lease and loan shall be binding during the life of the said [individual's name written by hand] unless he transgresses, and is not deemed worthy by the authority of the church, according to its laws, to belong to the church. And in that case I the said [individual's name written by hand] do acknowledge that I forfeit all claim to the above described leased and loaned property, and hereby bind myself to give back the leased, and also pay an equivalent for the loaned, for the benefit of said church" (photocopy in Arrington, *Building the City of God*, 29). Thus, the member leased the land and material goods as an individual stewardship, recognizing that the Church retained ownership of the property. Therefore, should an individual leave the Church, the Church held right to the leased land and loaned property.

51:5 Revelation is subject to clarification and adaptation to meet the needs of the Saints. For example, this verse reads differently in the Doctrine and Covenants than it does in the "Kirtland Revelation Book." Joseph Smith revised the original revelation in order to clarify the principles of the law of consecration. In the original text, Bishop Partridge was instructed to retain deeds for the Church to property consecrated by its members. It read thus:

"Wherefore let my servant Edward receive the properties of this people which have covenanted with me to obey the laws which I have given and let my servant Edward receive the money as it shall be laid before him according to the covenant and go and obtain a deed or article of this land unto himself of him who holdeth it 'if he harden not his heart for I have appointed him' to receive these things and thus through him the properties of the church shall be consecrated unto me" ("Kirtland Revelation Book", 87–88).

Accordingly, Edward Partridge, as bishop of the Church, was appointed the Lord's representative to receive property and money from the Saints that was to be used in purchasing land. Further, he divided inheritances among the Saints in Missouri by lending and leasing property to them. That is, Bishop Partridge held title to the land for the Church, but members received the leased land as a stewardship. If an individual left the Church after receiving property as a stewardship, the inheritance reverted back to the hands of the Church (v. 4). It was determined, however, that this practice did not accord with the law because individuals could not be deprived of property by a religious organization. Hence, the Prophet changed the instructions concerning the implementing of the deeded land.

"This is the principle on which the government of heaven is conducted," explained the Prophet, "by revelation adapted to the circumstances in which the children of the kingdom are placed" (*Teachings of the Prophet Joseph Smith*, 256). Consequently, principles of consecration were adapted to meet the circumstances of the Saints. In a letter to the Saints in Zion the Prophet Joseph Smith wrote, "On the subject of giving deeds, and receiving contributions from the brethren, I have nothing further to say on the subject than to recommend that you make yourselves acquainted with the commandments of the Lord, and the laws of the state, and govern yourselves accordingly" (*History of the Church*, 1:341).

The Saints Are to Deal Honestly and Establish a Storehouse
DOCTRINE AND COVENANTS 51:9–15

51:9 *Let every man deal honestly.* The seriousness of this command is illustrated in the account of the deceitful Ananias and his wife, Sapphira. As a member of the meridian-day Church, Ananias "sold a possession, and kept back part of the price, his wife also being privy to it, and brought a certain part, and laid it at the apostles' feet. But Peter said, Ananias, why hath Satan filled thine heart to lie to the Holy Ghost, and to keep back part of the price of the land? Whiles it remained, was it not thine own? and after it was sold, was it not in thine own power? why hast thou conceived this thing in thine heart? thou hast not lied unto men, but unto God. And Ananias hearing these words fell down, and gave up the ghost: . . . And the young men arose, wound him up, and carried him out, and buried him. And it was about the space of three hours after, when his wife, not knowing what was done, came in. And Peter answered unto her, Tell me whether ye sold the land for so much? And she said, Yea, for so much. Then Peter said unto her, How is it that ye have agreed together to tempt the Spirit of the Lord? behold, the feet of them which have buried thy husband are at the door, and shall carry thee out. Then fell she down straightway at his feet, and yielded up the ghost: and the young men came in, and found her dead, and, carrying her forth, buried her by her husband. And great fear came upon all the church, and upon as many as heard these things" (Acts 5:1–11).

51:11 *If another church.* Reference is to another branch of The Church of Jesus Christ of Latter-day Saints.

51:13 *Let the bishop appoint a storehouse unto this church.* See commentary on Doctrine and Covenants 42:34; 78:3.

51:15 *A privilege of organizing themselves according to my laws.* Man-made experiments and government programs forever fall short in their attempt to solve the problems associated with poverty and the economic inequality common to humanity. The Saints were given an opportunity to live in a society like that enjoyed by Enoch and his people. The Lord properly places his instructions regarding the law of consecration in the context of a blessing and a privilege.

Ohio Is to Be a Temporary Gathering Place
DOCTRINE AND COVENANTS 51:16–20

51:16 *For a little season.* Those who thought that Kirtland was the site of the city of the New Jerusalem learn here that this was not the case. Later, the Lord revealed that the Saints were to "retain a strong hold in the land of Kirtland, for the space of five years." See commentary on Doctrine and Covenants 64:20–21.

51:17 *Act upon this land as for years.* The work of the Lord should not be approached with tentativeness. Such an attitude inhibits both our faith and our actions. The Lord commanded the Saints to work with all their might, as if they were remaining in Ohio for years and not "a little season." The Saints from Colesville, New York, who settled the land in Thompson, followed the Lord's command. They cleared the land for farms and built homes, which were left behind when they traveled to Missouri. See commentary on Doctrine and Covenants 54.

51:18 *This shall be an example.* The instructions regarding the law of consecration were to serve as an example that would be implemented in other branches of the Church. "So it was not confined to any particular locality," explained Elder Lorenzo Snow, "but in that revelation [D&C 51] it was told the Bishop that this should be an example unto him in organizing in all Churches. So that wherever Edward Partridge should find a Church, he would have the privilege of organizing them according to the United Order, the Celestial Law, or the Order of Enoch" (*Journal of Discourses*, 19:344).

DOCTRINE AND COVENANTS 52

DATE: 7 JUNE 1831 (6 JUNE)
PLACE: KIRTLAND, OHIO

On 3 June 1831 the elders of Israel, then scattered throughout the country to declare the gospel, assembled in Kirtland for a priesthood conference. They came with the promise that the Lord would pour out his Spirit upon them (D&C 44:2). The minutes of the first day of the conference list sixty-two present and tell us that their time was spent in ordaining and giving exhortation. It was at this conference that men were ordained to the office of high priest for the first time in this dispensation. The conference lasted for three days. This revelation was given after the conference had concluded (whether that was June 6 or 7 is not entirely clear).

According to John Whitmer, who had been charged to keep the history of the Church, "The Spirit of the Lord fell upon Joseph in an unusual manner," and he prophesied many things. Having done so he "laid his hands upon Lyman Wight and ordained him to the High Priesthood, . . . after the holy order of God. And the Spirit fell upon Lyman and he prophesied concerning the coming of Christ (in Smith, *History of the Church,* 1:176 fn). For a consideration of the nature of the office of high priest see commentary on Doctrine and Covenants 84:29.

At this conference Brothers Lyman Wight, John Murdock, Reynolds Cahoon, Harvey Whitlock, and Hyrum Smith were ordained high priests by the Prophet. Lyman Wight in turn ordained Parley P. Pratt, Thomas B. Marsh, Isaac Morley, Edward Partridge, Joseph Wakefield, Martin Harris, Ezra Thayer, Ezra Booth, John Corrill, Samuel H. Smith, Solomon Hancock, Simeon Carter, Wheeler Baldwin, Jacob Scott, Joseph Smith Sr., John Whitmer, Joseph Smith Jr., and Sidney Rigdon, to the same office (Cannon and Cook, *Far West Record,* 7).

John Whitmer also notes that Joseph Smith said "that the man of sin would be revealed" at this conference. "While the Lord poured out His Spirit upon His servants," he noted, "the devil took a notion to make known his power. He bound Harvey Whitlock and John Murdock so that they could not speak, and others were affected but the Lord showed to Joseph, the seer the design of the thing; he commanded the devil in the name of Christ, and he departed, to our joy and comfort" (in Smith, *History of the Church*, 1:175, fn).

"In this conference much instruction was given by President Smith, who spake in great power, as he was moved upon by the Holy Ghost," recalled Parley P. Pratt, "and the spirit of power and of testimony rested down upon the Elders in a marvelous manner. Here also were some strange manifestations of false spirits which were immediately rebuked" (*Autobiography*, 68).

The Next Conference of the Church to Be in Missouri
DOCTRINE AND COVENANTS 52:1–2

52:2 *Missouri*. This is the first reference to the state of Missouri in the revelations of the Restoration. In September 1830 the Lord had stated that no man knew the place where the city of Zion would be built but that it would be located on the "borders by the Lamanites" (D&C 28:9). This revelation tells us it would be in Missouri. Independence, Missouri, was identified as the center place of the city of Zion in a revelation received six weeks later on 20 July 1831 (D&C 57:1–3).

A remnant of Jacob. As used in scripture, the remnant of Jacob generally refers to the twelve tribes collectively. A remnant of Jacob could be any of the various scattered parts of Jacob's family. In this instance the reference is to the descendants of Lehi, who was a rightful heir of all the promises made by God to Abraham, Isaac, and Jacob (D&C 19:27).

Heirs according to the covenant. All of Abraham's seed are heirs according to the covenant. They have a right to all the promises made to their ancient father on condition of righteousness. "I give unto thee a promise," the Lord told Abraham, "that this right shall continue in thee, and in thy seed after thee (that is to say, the literal seed, or the seed of the body) shall all the families of the earth be blessed, even with the blessings of the Gospel, which are the blessings of salvation, even of life eternal" (Abraham 2:11). See commentary on Doctrine and Covenants 86:8–11.

Elders Assigned to Travel Together
DOCTRINE AND COVENANTS 52:3-8

52:3-4 The revelation necessary for us to accomplish what we have been commanded to do will in most instances come as we proceed, not before. Echoing the same principle, Nephi said, "I was led by the Spirit, not knowing beforehand the things which I should do" (1 Nephi 4:6).

52:7 *Lyman Wight.* See commentary on Doctrine and Covenants 103:29–40; 124:18, 62–83.

John Corrill. See commentary on Doctrine and Covenants 50:38.

52:8 *John Murdock.* See commentary on Doctrine and Covenants 99.

The Elders to Declare What the Apostles
and Prophets Have Written
DOCTRINE AND COVENANTS 52:9-13

52:9 Some have suggested that those commissioned to teach the gospel should confine their teaching to holy writ. The present text does not sustain such an idea. Here, those going forth in the name of the Lord are directed to teach from the words of the prophets and apostles and "that which is taught them by the Comforter through the prayer of faith." True gospel teachers begin with the declaration of scripture, which they then teach under the direction of the Spirit. With the aid of that same Spirit they apply their message to those they are teaching. In many instances the Spirit will then unfold additional light and understanding to them (Alma 5:43–49). The supposition that the Spirit cannot reach beyond what has already been revealed denies the prophetic spirit of their message and suggests that they do not enjoy its companionship.

The Pattern by Which Spirits Are Discerned
DOCTRINE AND COVENANTS 52:14-21

52:14 *A pattern in all things.* The principles given here constitute a pattern or standard by which all who come professing to represent the Lord can be discerned.

52:15–21 Indecorous behavior is never attractive to the Spirit of the Lord, be it in prayer, preaching, music, or any other form. It is evident from the instructions given here that the irreverent spirit does not like to conform to the ordinances of the Lord. *Ordinances* here means all divine standards, not simply such rituals as baptism and receipt of the priesthood. If the spirit is good, the fruits will be good; they will always edify and be associated with dignity, purity, and modesty. Those spirits will always maintain the discipline associated with a house of order and can be trusted to conform to the pattern and standard of scripture.

Saints Are Expected to Provide for Their Own Needs
DOCTRINE AND COVENANTS 52:22–44

52:39 *Let them labor with their own hands that there be no idolatry nor wickedness practised.* It has ever been the practice among the true servants of the Lord to provide for themselves. In the Lord's Church there is no paid ministry, no professional clergy, as commonly found in other churches. More significantly there is no laity, for all are expected to serve. Under normal circumstances, all active members of the Church expect to serve in whatever capacity or position to which they are called by those whom they have sustained as their leaders.

DOCTRINE AND COVENANTS 53

DATE: JUNE 1831
PLACE: KIRTLAND, OHIO

This revelation illustrates the propriety of our inquiring of the Lord as to where he would have us serve. Though we do not seek particular callings or positions in the Church, we should seek to serve. Often the kind of direction sought by Sidney Gilbert in this revelation is given to us in patriarchal blessings—a privilege not then available to him.

Sidney Gilbert Is Called to Be Ordained an Elder and as the Bishop's Agent

DOCTRINE AND COVENANTS 53:1–7

53:1 *Concerning your calling and election in the church.* Brother Gilbert was not among the many called at the Kirtland conference to serve as a missionary traveling to Zion (D&C 52). Naturally, when he learned that others received instructions regarding their service, he wondered where he was to serve. Hence, the Prophet recorded that "at the request of Algernon Sidney Gilbert I inquired, and obtained the following" (Smith, *History of the Church*, 1:179). By revelation Elder Gilbert was directed to accompany the Prophet as he journeyed to Zion (D&C 53:5).

53:2 *Crucified for the sins of the world.* See commentary on Doctrine and Covenants 19:16–17.

Forsake the world. To "forsake the world" is to forsake that which is worldly, not to shun relationships with those of the world as the Jews did anciently. We have been called to be a light and an example to all who have not yet embraced the gospel. We can do this only as we interrelate with such individuals.

53:5 Edward Partridge and Martin Harris had been commanded to go to Missouri with Joseph Smith and Sidney Rigdon (D&C 52:24). Soon after this revelation was received, W. W. Phelps was also called to travel in company with this group (D&C 55:5).

53:6 *The first ordinances.* Instructions of the Lord are command-ments—as in city ordinances or laws. In this instance the Lord com-manded that Sidney Gilbert be ordained an elder and travel with the Prophet to Zion, where he would be given an appointment by Bishop Partridge.

DOCTRINE AND COVENANTS 54

DATE: JUNE 1831
PLACE: KIRTLAND, OHIO

Though this revelation was given to Newel Knight, it was intended for all those who were a part of the branch of the Church in Thompson, Ohio. This same group of people had joined the Church together in Colesville, New York, and had responded to the commandment to go to Ohio. Having settled in Thompson, they were directed by revelation to embrace the law of consecration and receive their stewardships as noted in section 51. Problems grew out of their effort to do so. It appears that pettiness and selfishness hindered their efforts. Although the full story has not been preserved, it appears that a recent convert from the Shakers by the name of Leman Copley, who owned a large tract of land in Thompson, became disaffected with the Church and returned to the Shakers. When he did so he demanded the return of his property and expelled the Saints who were living on it. Joseph Knight Jr. recalled, "The man was turned out of the church for bad conduct; . . . he then began to persecute us and we had to leave his farm and pay sixty dollars damage for putting up his houses and planting his ground" (as quoted in Porter, "Colesville Branch," 383).

The Saints Must Keep the Gospel
Covenant to Obtain Mercy
DOCTRINE AND COVENANTS 54:1–6

54:2 Newel Knight had been called to preside over the Saints at Thompson. Difficulties in the branch caused him to wonder if he ought to be released. Here the Lord tells him to stand in the office to which he was appointed.

54:4–5 Salvation is found in keeping the covenants we make with the Lord and is lost in breaking them. Here Leman Copley broke his covenants with the Church, returned to the Shakers, and expelled from their homes the Saints who had been given inheritances on his land. Of such a course, the Lord said, "It had been better for him that he had been drowned in the depth of the sea."

The Saints Must Be Patient in Tribulation
DOCTRINE AND COVENANTS 54:7–10

54:7–8 At least twelve families, composed of twenty-three adults and thirty-nine children, took their journey from Thompson to Missouri (Porter, "Study of the Origins," 299–303). In so doing they became the first community of Saints to travel to the land of Zion.

54:9 *Seek ye a living like unto men.* The Thompson Saints were to stop living the law of consecration. They were to provide for themselves until directed otherwise.

DOCTRINE AND COVENANTS 55

DATE: JUNE 1831
PLACE: KIRTLAND, OHIO

"About the middle of June, while we were preparing for our journey to Missouri," wrote Joseph Smith, "William W. Phelps and his family arrived among us—'to do the will of the Lord,' he said: so I inquired of the Lord concerning him and received the following" (*History of the Church*, 1:184–85).

William Wines Phelps, born 17 February 1792, at Hanover, New Jersey, became interested in the message of the Restoration while residing in Canandaigua, New York, about twelve miles south of Palmyra. His interest in the Book of Mormon led him to purchase a copy in April of 1830. He read the book and was convinced of its truthfulness. His further investigation of the Restoration took him to Ohio with the intent of becoming a member of the Church.

Previous to this time he was very involved in politics as editor of a partisan newspaper. He had sought nomination of the Anti-Mason Party for the office of lieutenant governor of the state of New York. Concerning the influence that he had in the Church, historian Bruce Van Orden observed: "Excluding Sidney Rigdon, W. W. Phelps was the most publicly well-known convert to the early Church. However, unlike Elder Rigdon, his contributions to the Kingdom of God were not for just a few years, but lasted throughout his life. As editor of *The Evening and the Morning Star* and as a frequent contributor to other Church publications (*Latter Day Saints' Messenger and Advocate*, the *Times and Seasons*, and the *Deseret News*) and also as a powerful orator, Brother Phelps was one of the most influential early exponents of LDS doctrines and practices. No one was better educated and more articulate than he in the early days of the Church" ("By That Book," 204).

W. W. Phelps Is Called and Chosen to Be Baptized, Ordained an Elder, and Preach the Gospel

DOCTRINE AND COVENANTS 55:1–3

55:1–3 The singular privilege is here accorded to W. W. Phelps, a nonmember of the Church, of having the Prophet inquire of the Lord in his behalf. This revelation comes in response to that request. W. W. Phelps is told to be baptized and receive the gift of the Holy Ghost by the laying on of hands. Thus the revelation, like many given under the hands of priesthood leaders, personalizes principles that apply to all accountable persons. The same message would be given to any honest truth seeker who in like manner sought a revelation from the Lord through the living oracle of his or her day.

W. W. Phelps is then told that he will be ordained an elder and called to preach the principles he has complied with, namely faith, repentance, baptism, and the receipt of the Holy Ghost by the laying on of hands.

55:1 *Thou art called and chosen.* In modern revelation the Lord confirms the doctrine of his ancient apostles, speaks of our "calling and election in the church" (D&C 53:1; 55:1), and declares that we "are called" to his "everlasting gospel" (D&C 101:39). He names the elders of his Church as among those "whom he hath called and chosen in these last days" (D&C 52:1; 41:2).

Because all are foreordained to gain exaltation and because no man can be exalted without the priesthood, it is self-evident that worthy brethren were foreordained to receive the priesthood. Alma taught that those who were ordained high priests in this life were "called and prepared from the foundation of the world according to the foreknowledge of God" (Alma 13:3). Joseph Smith declared, "Every man who has a calling to minister to the inhabitants of the world," which could include all who hold the Melchizedek Priesthood, "was ordained to that very purpose in the Grand Council of heaven before this world was. I suppose that I was ordained to this very office in that Grand Council" (*Teachings of the Prophet Joseph Smith*, 365).

He Is Also to Write Books for Children in Church Schools

DOCTRINE AND COVENANTS 55:4

55:4 *The work of printing.* Previous to joining the Church, Brother Phelps worked as editor of three newspapers and was familiar with printing.

Schools in this church, that little children also may receive instruction. This is the first reference in the revelations of the Restoration to Church schools. Ignorance and the gospel of Jesus Christ are incompatible, and the necessity of the Church to teach its members—particularly the children—will ever be with it. Many revelations would follow that dealt with this subject (D&C 88:77–80, 118, 127; 90:7, 13–15; 93:53; 95:17; 97:3–5; 109:7–8; 130:18–19).

The importance of teaching children to read and write was revealed during the translation of the Bible. "A book of remembrance was kept, in the which was recorded, in the language of Adam, for it was given unto as many as called upon God to write by the spirit of inspiration; and by them their children were taught to read and write, having a language which was pure and undefiled" (Moses 6:5–6).

President Joseph F. Smith taught, "The object, I may say almost the only purpose, for the maintenance of Church schools is that true religion and undefiled before God the Father, may be inculcated in the minds and hearts of our children while they are getting an education, to enable the heart, the soul and the spirit of our children to develop with proper teaching, in connection with the secular training that they receive in schools" (*Gospel Doctrine*, 353).

In the first edition of *The Evening and Morning Star*, the Church-owned newspaper in Independence, Missouri, William W. Phelps, as editor of the paper, wrote: "The disciples should lose no time in preparing schools for their children, that they may be taught as is pleasing unto the Lord, and brought up in the way of holiness. Those appointed to select and prepare books for the use of schools, will attend to that subject as soon as more weighty matters are finished. But the parents and guardians in the Church of Christ need not wait—it is all-important that children to become good should be taught [good]. Moses, while delivering the words of the Lord to the congregation of Israel, that is, to the parents, says, 'And these words which I command thee this day, shall be in thy heart: and thou shalt teach them diligently unto thy children, and shalt talk of them when thou sittest in thy house, and when thou walkest by the way, and when thou liest down, and when thou risest up. And thou shalt bind them for a sign upon thy hand, and they shall be as frontlets between thine eyes.' If it were necessary then to teach their children diligently, how much more necessary is it now, when the Church of Christ is to be an ensign, yea, even an ensample to the world, for good? A word to the wise ought to be sufficient, for children soon become men and women. Yes, they are they that must follow us, and perform the duties which not only appertain to this world, but to the second coming of the Savior, even preparing for the Sabbath of creation, and for eternity" (as quoted in Smith, *History of the Church*, 1:276–77).

He Is to Travel to Missouri, Which Will Be the Area of His Labors

DOCTRINE AND COVENANTS 55:5–6

55:5 W. W. Phelps was informed that his work would be in the soon-to-be designated site of latter-day Zion. His journey to Kirtland, Ohio, to be baptized was only the beginning of his travels. Once he put his hand to the plow there was to be no turning back. His talents were needed in Independence, Missouri, where he would become editor for the Church newspaper, *The Evening and the Morning Star,* and where he would be called to supervise the printing of the revelations to be published as the Book of Commandments (D&C 57:11).

DOCTRINE AND COVENANTS 56

DATE: JUNE 1831

PLACE: KIRTLAND, OHIO

Ezra Thayre (see commentary on D&C 33:1) was commanded to consecrate his property and travel to the western borders of Missouri with Thomas B. Marsh (D&C 52:22). He refused to leave until he had received compensation for his property, thus leaving Thomas B. Marsh without a companion. Elder Marsh inquired of the Prophet about what he should do. The Prophet said, "I inquired of the Lord, and received the following . . . " (Smith, *History of the Church*, 1:186).

The Lord Commands and Revokes, and the Disobedient Are Cast Off

DOCTRINE AND COVENANTS 56:1–13

56:1–2 Salvation comes to those who obey the word of the Lord. Mere confession of the Lord's name has never led to the faith unto repentance required for a forgiveness of sins. True faith in Christ leads to obedience and willingness to sacrifice for the kingdom of God. In this manner true Saints follow the Savior in taking up their cross, looking to his example.

56:4 *I, the Lord, command and revoke, as it seemeth me good.* The Lord explained, "I command and men obey not; I revoke and they receive not the blessing" (D&C 58:32). To illustrate, the children of Israel were commanded to posses the land of Canaan. They feared the people of the land and their mighty walled cities as reported by the spies sent to scout Canaan. In their rebellion "all the children of Israel murmured against Moses and against Aaron: . . . and they said one to another, Let us make a captain, and let us return into Egypt" (Numbers 14:2, 4). Because of the Israelites' rebellion, the Lord revoked his command that they enter the Promised Land. Instead the Lord commanded that they wander in the wilderness for forty years until the rebellious generation had all died. See commentary on Doctrine and Covenants 124:49–55.

56:5–10 New commands are given to compensate for and adjust to the consequences of the choices made by the rebellious who have failed to fulfill their responsibilities. Accordingly, the innocent and repentant are given new assignments within the Lord's vineyard. In this instance, the mission assignments of four individuals—Thomas B. Marsh, Ezra Thayre, Newel Knight, and Selah J. Griffin—are revised. In an earlier revelation, Thomas B. Marsh had been called to journey to Missouri with Ezra Thayre (D&C 52:22). Similarly, Newel Knight and Selah J. Griffin had been called to take their journey together as missionary companions (D&C 52:32). After Ezra Thayre's failure to prepare to leave in a timely manner and following the problems in the branch in Thompson, Ohio, over which Newel Knight presided, the Lord assigned Thomas B. Marsh to travel with Selah J. Griffin. Newell Knight was called to lead the Thompson Saints in their journey to Missouri. Ezra Thayre was left to determine whether he would join the Saints in Missouri or separate himself from the Church.

56:8 *The former commandment which I have given him.* The "former commandment" concerning farms in the Kirtland, Ohio, area was recorded in the "Kirtland Revelation Book." This revelation was not chosen for publication in the Book of Commandments or in the Doctrine and Covenants. It reads as follows:

"Hearken unto my words and behold I will make known unto you what ye shall do as it shall be pleasing unto me for verily I say unto you it must needs be that ye let the bargain stand that ye have made concerning those farms until it be so fulfilled behold ye are holden for the one even so likewise thine advisary is holden for the other. Wherefore it must needs be that ye pay no more money for the present time until the contract be fulfilled and let mine aged servant Joseph and his family go into the house after thine advisary is gone and let my servant Ezra board with him and let all the brethren immediately assemble together to put up an house for my servant Ezra and let my servant Fredericks family remain and let the house be prepared and their wants be supplied and when my servant Frederick returns from the west behold and lo he desireth to take his family in mine own due time unto the west let that which belongeth unto my servant Frederick be secured unto him by deed or bond and thus he willeth that the brethren reap the good thereof let mine aged servant Joseph govern the things of the farm and provide for the families and let him have help in as much as he standeth in need. Let my servant Ezra humble himself and at the conference meeting he shall be ordained unto power from on high and he shall go from thence (if he be obedient unto my commandments) and proclaim my gospel unto the western regions with my servants that must go forth even unto the borders by the Lamanites for behold I have a great work for them to do and it shall be given unto you to know what ye shall do at the conference meeting even so amen.

"What shall the brethren do with the monies. Ye shall go forth and seek diligently among the brethren and obtain lands and save the money that it may be consecrated to purchase lands in the west for an everlasting inheritance even so Amen" ("Kirtland Revelation Book", 91–92).

It is clear from this unpublished revelation that Ezra Thayre's concern did not regard the land in Thompson, Ohio, as has been commonly thought (see heading to this section in the current edition of the Doctrine and Covenants). Rather, it involved property in Kirtland, Ohio, upon which homes were located and in which the families of Joseph Smith Sr. and Frederick G. Williams resided.

Wo unto the Rich Who Will Not Help the Poor, and Wo unto the Poor Whose Hearts Are Not Broken

DOCTRINE AND COVENANTS 56:14–20

56:14 *You seek to counsel in your own ways.* The Nephite prophet Jacob declared: "O the vainness, and the frailties, and the foolishness of men! When they are learned they think they are wise, and they hearken not unto the counsel of God, for they set it aside, supposing they know of themselves, wherefore, their wisdom is foolishness and it profiteth them not. And they shall perish" (2 Nephi 9:28).

56:15 *Pleasure in unrighteousness.* This phrase comes from Paul's epistle to the Thessalonians. Speaking to those who "received not the love of the truth," Paul said that "God shall send them strong delusion, that they should believe a lie: That they all might be damned who believed not the truth, but had pleasure in unrighteousness" (2 Thessalonians 2:10–12).

56:16 Many are blinded by the deceitfulness of riches. Speaking to Joseph Smith, the Lord said: "There are many called, but few are chosen. And why are they not chosen? Because their hearts are set so much upon the things of this world" (D&C 121:34–35). To a wealthy young ruler who kept the laws of God, Christ said: "Yet lackest thou one thing: sell all that thou hast, and distribute unto the poor, and thou shalt have treasure in heaven: and come, follow me. And when he heard this, he was very sorrowful: for he was very rich. And when Jesus saw that he was very sorrowful, he said, How hardly shall they that have riches enter into the kingdom of God! For it is easier for a camel to go through a needle's eye, than for a rich man to enter into the kingdom of God" (Luke 18:22–25). In the Joseph Smith Translation the text reads, "It is impossible for them who trust in riches, to enter into the kingdom of God; but he who forsaketh the things which are of this world, it is possible with God, that he should enter in" (JST Luke 18:27). Riches, like talents, are given to us to share with others. The law of consecration revealed in the restoration of the gospel helps protect the Saints from the love of riches and teaches that this world's goods are to be used "to do good—to clothe the naked, and to feed the hungry, and to liberate the captive, and administer relief to the sick and the afflicted" (Jacob 2:19).

Your riches will canker your souls. Like slow-working poison, riches may rob individuals of eternal life. Jacob warned: "Wo unto the rich, who are rich as to the things of the world. For because they are rich they despise the poor, and they persecute the meek, and their hearts are upon their treasures; wherefore, their treasure is their god. And behold, their treasure shall perish with them also" (2 Nephi 9:30).

The harvest is past. See commentary on Doctrine and Covenants 45:2.

56:17 The poor who have their hearts set upon the riches that they wish they possessed are also in danger of losing their souls. King Benjamin taught, "I say unto the poor, ye who have not and yet have sufficient, that ye remain from day to day; I mean all you who deny the beggar, because ye have not; I would that ye say in your hearts that: I give not because I have not, but if I had I would give. And now, if ye say this in your hearts ye remain guiltless, otherwise ye are condemned; and your condemnation is just for ye covet that which ye have not received" (Mosiah 4:24–25).

56:20 *Their generations shall inherit the earth.* See commentary on Doctrine and Covenants 88:17.

DOCTRINE AND COVENANTS 57

DATE: 20 JULY 1831
PLACE: ZION, JACKSON COUNTY, MISSOURI

"On the 19th of June," wrote the Prophet Joseph Smith, "in company
with Sidney Rigdon, Martin Harris, Edward Partridge, William W. Phelps,
Joseph Coe, Algernon S. Gilbert and his wife, I started from Kirtland,
Ohio, for the land of Missouri, agreeable to the commandment before
received, wherein it was promised that if we were faithful, the land of our
inheritance, even the place for the city of the New Jerusalem, should be
revealed. We went by wagon, canal boats, and stages to Cincinnati. . . .
We left Cincinnati in a steamer, and landed at Louisville, Kentucky,
where we were detained three days in waiting for a steamer to convey us
to St. Louis. At St. Louis, myself, Brothers Harris, Phelps, Partridge and
Coe, went by land on foot to Independence, Jackson county, Missouri,
where we arrived about the middle of July, and the rest of the company
came by water a few days later. . . .

"The meeting of our brethren, who had long awaited our arrival, was
a glorious one, and moistened with many tears. It seemed good and pleasant for brethren to meet together in unity. But our reflections were many,
coming as we had from a highly cultivated state of society in the east, and
standing now upon the confines or western limits of the United States,
and looking into the vast wilderness of those that sat in darkness; how
natural it was to observe the degradation, leanness of intellect, ferocity,
and jealousy of a people that were nearly a century behind the times, and
to feel for those who roamed about without the benefit of civilization,
refinement, or religion; yea, and exclaim in the language of the Prophets:
'When will the wilderness blossom as the rose? When will Zion be built
up in her glory, and where will Thy temple stand, unto which all nations
shall come in the last days?'" (*History of the Church*, 1:188–89).

These questions couched in the imagery of the prophets bring to
mind the words of Isaiah wherein he said, "The wilderness and the solitary place shall be glad for them; and the desert shall rejoice, and blossom

as the rose" (Isaiah 35:1); "Arise, shine; for thy light is come, and the glory of the Lord is risen upon thee" (Isaiah 60:1); "And it shall come to pass in the last days, that the mountain of the Lord's house shall be established in the top of the mountains, and shall be exalted above the hills; and all nations shall flow unto it" (Isaiah 2:2).

Joseph Smith's question concerning the location of the latter-day temple is addressed in this section. The other two questions are answered in Doctrine and Covenants 58.

Independence, Missouri, Is the Place for the City of Zion and the Temple
DOCTRINE AND COVENANTS 57:1–3

57:1–2 The land for the city of Zion, or the New Jerusalem, was set apart from the time of the creation of the earth. The land near Independence, Missouri, encompasses the area of the garden planted eastward in Eden, in which Adam and Eve were placed. We learn from Brigham Young that "our God will finish his work where he commenced it, where the centre [place] of Zion is, and where the garden of Eden was" (*Journal of Discourses*, 8:72).

57:2 *The city of Zion.* The city of Zion—the New Jerusalem to be built in Independence, Missouri—and the Jerusalem of old will be the capitals of the millennial kingdom of Christ. The latter-day city of Zion shall be blessed with the presence of Enoch and his people, who were taken to heaven without tasting death (Moses 7:62–64). It shall expand its borders to include all of North and South America, until eventually the entire globe shall be called Zion. The Prophet Joseph Smith stated: "You know there has been great discussion in relation to Zion—where it is, and where the gathering of the dispensation is, and which I am now going to tell you. The prophets have spoken and written upon it; but I will make a proclamation that will cover a broader ground. The whole of America is Zion itself from north to south, and is described by the Prophets, who declare that it is the Zion where the mountain of the Lord should be, and that it should be in the center of the land. When Elders shall take up and examine the old prophecies in the Bible, they will see it" (*Teachings of the Prophet Joseph Smith*, 362). Further, "when Joseph first revealed the land where the Saints should gather," Brigham Young explained, "a woman in Canada asked if we thought that Jackson County would be large enough to gather all the people that would want to go to

Zion. I will answer the question really as it is. Zion will extend, eventually, all over this earth. There will be no nook or corner upon the earth but what will be in Zion. It will all be Zion" (*Journal of Discourses*, 9:138). See commentary on Doctrine and Covenants 133:21.

The building up of Zion began like a seed planted in parched soil. The Prophet expressed dismay at the lack of civilization and "leanness of intellect" of the inhabitants of the surrounding regions. As the kingdom of God on earth is like the stone cut out of the mountain without hands (Daniel 2:44–45), which rolled forth until it filled the earth, so is the beginning of the establishment of Zion the commencement of a new covenant community that will likewise fill the earth, in which the citizens are the pure in heart. A great change was and is required for the environs of Independence, Missouri, to become worthy of the divinely appointed appellation—Zion. In time, under the direction of his prophets, the city of Zion will be built upon the foundations laid at the dawn of this dispensation. It will be "Zion, because it is a place of righteousness," declared the Prophet Joseph Smith, "and all who build thereon, are to worship the true and living God—and all believe in one doctrine, even the doctrine of our Lord and Savior Jesus Christ" (*Teachings of the Prophet Joseph Smith*, 80).

57:3 *Independence is the center place.* There are many stakes in Zion in which the Saints will gather. However, the Lord singled out Independence, Missouri, as the center place of the millennial kingdom. Bruce R. McConkie taught: "Let Israel gather to the stakes of Zion in all nations. Let every land be a Zion to those appointed to dwell there. Let the fulness of the gospel be for all the saints in all nations. Let no blessing be denied them. Let temples arise wherein the fulness of the ordinances of the Lord's house may be administered. But still there is a center place, a place where the chief temple shall stand, a place to which the Lord shall come, a place whence the law shall go forth to govern all the earth in that day when the Second David reigns personally upon the earth. And that center place is what men now call Independence in Jackson County, Missouri, but which in a day to come will be the Zion of our God and the City of Holiness of his people. The site is selected; the place is known; the decree has gone forth; and the promised destiny is assured" (*New Witness*, 595). See commentary on Doctrine and Covenants 42:9.

The temple. Among all houses of the Lord, the temple to be built at the center place of Zion will stand supreme. It is destined to consist of a complex of twenty-four buildings, all dedicated as houses of the Lord.

The Lord revealed that the gathering to and building of the city of the New Jerusalem will have its beginning at the place of the temple (D&C 84:4). Along with the companion temple to be built in the Jerusalem of old, this is the temple in which Isaiah's words will find fulfillment: "And it shall come to pass in the last days, that the mountain of the Lord's house shall be established in the top of the mountains, and shall be exalted above the hills; and all nations shall flow unto it. And many people shall go and say, Come ye, and let us go up to the mountain of the Lord, to the house of the God of Jacob; and he will teach us of his ways, and we will walk in his paths: for out of Zion shall go forth the law, and the word of the Lord from Jerusalem" (Isaiah 2:2–3). Further, it is at the temple in the New Jerusalem that "the Lamb shall stand upon Mount Zion, and with him a hundred and forty-four thousand, having his Father's name written on their foreheads" (D&C 133:18). See commentary on Doctrine and Covenants 133:7–16, 18.

The twenty-four buildings aforementioned were located on a plot map of the future city of Zion. Joseph Smith wrote: "The names of the temples to be built on the painted squares as represented on the plot of the city of Zion, which is now about to be forwarded thither:—numbers 10, 11, and 12, are to be called, House of the Lord, for the Presidency of the High and most Holy Priesthood, after the order of Melchizedek, which was after the order of the Son of God, upon Mount Zion, City of the New Jerusalem. Numbers 7, 8, and 9, the Sacred Apostolic Repository, for the use of the Bishop. Numbers 4, 5, and 6, the Holy Evangelical House, for the High Priesthood of the Holy Order of God. Numbers 1, 2, and 3, the House of the Lord, for the Elders of Zion, an Ensign to the Nations. Numbers 22, 23, and 24, House of the Lord for the Presidency of the High Priesthood, after the Order of Aaron, a Standard for the People. Numbers 19, 20, and 21, House of the Lord, the Law of the Kingdom of Heaven, and Messenger to the People; for the Highest Priesthood after the Order of Aaron. Numbers 16, 17, and 18, House of the Lord for the Teachers in Zion, Messenger to the Church. Numbers 13, 14, and 15, House of the Lord for the Deacons in Zion, Helps in Government. Underneath must be written on each house—Holiness To The Lord" (*History of the Church*, 1:359). The Prophet Joseph Smith further instructed the Saints to commence by building temple number five as the beginning of the city of Zion, which temple was very similar to that built in Kirtland, Ohio (*History of the Church*, 1:359–62). Whether the

other buildings will be built before or after the Savior returns remains to
be revealed.

The Saints Are to Purchase Lands and
Receive Inheritances in That Area
DOCTRINE AND COVENANTS 57:4–7

57:4 *The land should be purchased by the saints.* The earth "and all
things therein are mine," declared the Lord (D&C 104:14). He has rightful title to the land of Zion. However, the Saints are peacemakers, who
obey the laws of the land. They are to obtain legal deed to the lands,
which will enable them to build up the city of Zion as they "carefully
gather together, as much in one region as can be, consistently with the
feelings of the people" (D&C 105:24).

"Here we pause for a moment," wrote the Prophet Joseph Smith at a
later time, "to make a few remarks upon the idea of gathering to this
place. It is well known that there were lands belonging to the government, to be sold to individuals; and it was understood by all, at least we
believed so, that we lived in a free country, a land of liberty and of laws,
guaranteeing to every man, or any company of men, the right of purchasing lands, and settling, and living upon them: therefore we thought no
harm in advising the Latter-day Saints, or 'Mormons,' as they are
reproachfully called, to gather to this place, inasmuch as it was their duty,
(and it was well understood so to be,) to purchase, with money, lands, and
live upon them, not infringing upon the rights of any individual, or community of people; always keeping in view the saying, 'Do unto others as
you would wish others to do unto you;' following also the good injunction: 'Deal justly, love mercy, and walk humbly with thy God.'

"These were our motives in teaching the people, or Latter-day Saints,
to gather together, beginning at this place; and inasmuch as there are
those who have had different views from this, we feel that it is a cause of
deep regret. Be it known unto all men, that our principles concerning this
thing, have not been such as have been represented by those who, we
have every reason to believe, are designing and wicked men, that have
said that this was our doctrine: 'To infringe upon the rights of a people
who inhabit our civil and free country: such as to drive the inhabitants of
Jackson County from their lands, and take possession thereof unlawfully.'
Far, yea, far be such a principle from our hearts. It never entered into our

minds; and we only say, that God shall reward such in that day when He shall come to make up His jewels" (*History of the Church*, 2:254–55).

The line running directly between Jew and Gentile. "This expression," wrote Joseph Fielding Smith, " . . . has reference to the line separating the Lamanites from the settlers in Jackson County. At this time the United States Government had given to the Indians the lands west of the Missouri, only later to take them away again. The Lamanites, who are Israelites, were referred to as Jews, and the Gentiles were the people, many of whom were of the lawless element, living east of the river" (*Church History and Modern Revelation*, 1:206).

57:5 *Every tract bordering by the prairies.* This phrase refers to the general area around Independence, Missouri, that was within the borders of the United States at that time. The land of western, central, and northern Missouri was covered with prairies.

57:7 *Divide unto the saints their inheritance.* See commentary on Doctrine and Covenants 58:17.

Sidney Gilbert, W.W. Phelps, and Oliver Cowdery Are Given Specific Callings
DOCTRINE AND COVENANTS 57:8–16

57:8–16 Authors Hyrum M. Smith and Janne M. Sjodahl record that "as soon as this Revelation had been received, Edward Partridge and the other brethren, appointed to 'plant' themselves in Zion, began the work of building. During the first winter the settlers put up with many inconveniences. In some log cabins, without windows and with the frozen ground for floor, several families were living together. They had very little to eat, but they were united, and their hearts were filled with brotherly love and a fervent desire to build up Zion. As a consequence, their meetings were times of refreshing, and in their family devotions they were blessed with the presence of the Holy Spirit. And as soon as the Saints in Ohio and elsewhere learned that the site of the City of Zion had been made known, the spirit of gathering was poured out upon them, and many sent money to Sidney Gilbert, the agent, and instructed him to secure land for them. So rapidly did they gather, that in 1832 there were 830 souls in the new settlements, and a certain degree of prosperity had begun to attend their efforts" (*Doctrine and Covenants Commentary*, 331).

57:10 *Those who sit in darkness and in the region and shadow of death.* The reference is to spiritual darkness. The wording is similar to that employed by Isaiah in prophesying of the Messiah: "The people that walked in darkness have seen a great light: they that dwell in the land of the shadow of death, upon them hath the light shined" (Isaiah 9:2). Various applications have been made of this text. Matthew saw the ministry of the Savior in Galilee as fulfilling Isaiah's words (Matthew 4:16). The Prophet Joseph Smith used this same phrase to refer to those who had died without receiving the fulness of the gospel. In *A Vision*, a poetical version of the visions revealing the qualifications and characteristics of those who will inherit the three kingdoms of glory, he wrote:

> Behold, these are they that have died without law;
> The heathen of ages that never had hope,
> And those of the region and shadow of death,
> The spirits in prison, that light has brought up.
> (*Times and Seasons*, 4:84; see commentary on D&C 76)

57:13 *Let my servant Oliver Cowdery assist him . . . to correct, and select, that all things may be right before me.* Apostle George A. Smith, cousin to the Prophet, capsulated the importance of the Lord's admonition that Oliver Cowdery preside over Brother Phelps's writing and editorializing: "Joseph asked my opinion of W. W. Phelps as an editor. I told him that I considered Phelps the sixth part of an editor, and that was the satirist. When it came to the cool direction necessarily intrusted to an editor in the control of public opinion—the soothing of enmity, he was deficient, and would always make more enemies than friends; but for my part, if I were able, I would be willing to pay Phelps for editing a paper, providing no body else should have the privilege of reading it but myself. Joseph laughed heartily—said I had the thing just right. Said he, 'Brother Phelps makes such a severe use of language as to make enemies all the time'" (in Smith, *History of the Church*, 5:390–91).

57:15 Reference here is particularly to members of the Colesville Branch, who traveled under the direction of Newel Knight. Obedient to the Lord's command that they relocate in Missouri (D&C 54:8), this group of Saints arrived in Independence 25 July 1831. Arrangements were made for them to settle near the Big Blue River in Jackson County, approximately twelve miles west of Independence.

DOCTRINE AND COVENANTS 58

DATE: 1 AUGUST 1831
PLACE: ZION, JACKSON COUNTY, MISSOURI

Twelve days prior to this revelation, Joseph Smith identified the place of the New Jerusalem and the building of the great temple of the latter days—that place being Independence, Missouri. Two days after this revelation was received, the Prophet dedicated the land for this purpose.

Introducing this revelation, he noted that "the first Sabbath after our arrival in Jackson county, Brother W. W. Phelps preached to a western audience over the boundary of the United States, wherein were present specimens of all the families of the earth; Shem, Ham and Japheth; several of the Lamanites or Indians—representative of Shem; quite a respectable number of negroes—descendants of Ham; and the balance was made up of citizens of the surrounding country, and fully represented themselves as pioneers of the West. At this meeting two were baptized, who had previously believed in the fulness of the Gospel.

"During this week the Colesville branch, referred to in the latter part of the last revelation, and Sidney Rigdon, Sidney Gilbert and wife and Elders Morley and Booth, arrived. I received the following" (Smith, *History of the Church*, 1:190–91).

Those Who Endure Tribulation Shall Be Crowned with Glory
DOCTRINE AND COVENANTS 58:1–5

58:2 *Blessed is he that keepeth my commandments, whether in life or in death.* Death is the temporary separation of the body and the spirit. The spirit goes to a world of spirits to await the day of resurrection, the inseparable union of body and spirit. These simple truths, lost to the Bible-believing world and restored to us in the Book of Mormon (Alma 40), bring with them the understanding that those who were prevented from complying with the full law of the gospel in this life will have that opportunity to do so in the worlds to come. Thus that world is an extension of the present world, to which the desires of our hearts follow us. Someone who kept the commandments here will keep them there. Those who loved light and truth here will love it there. Those who would have embraced the gospel here and valiantly defended the truth but died without the opportunity will have it there. Thus death enhances the righteous in the pursuit of godliness and grants light to all who desire to see the light.

58:3–5 These verses contain the Lord's answer to the Prophet's question as to when the wilderness would blossom as a rose and Zion be built up in her glory. The Lord knew that it would be "many years" before the Saints received inheritances in the land of Zion (D&C 58:44) and that only the path of tribulation would lead to the glory they sought. The Saints of the early 1830s could scarcely have conceived the ugly scenes that awaited them. Where the glory of heaven is destined to rest we can but expect the legions of the adversary to wage their best fight. See commentary on introduction to Doctrine and Covenants 57.

"In the true sense, the wilderness shall blossom as the rose when the earth is renewed and receives its paradisiacal glory. In the full sense, Zion shall regain her ancient glory, and attain that grandeur and might promised in the prophetic word, only during the Millennium, though the work of establishing Zion and building the New Jerusalem must precede our Lord's return. And as to the temple unto which all nations shall come in the last days, it shall be built in the New Jerusalem before the Second Coming, all as a part of the preparatory processes that will make ready a people for their Lord's return" (McConkie, *New Witness*, 595).

The Saints Are to Prepare for the Marriage of the Lamb and the Supper of the Lord
DOCTRINE AND COVENANTS 58:6–12

58:7 *That you might be honored in laying the foundation.* "The building up of Zion is a cause that has interested the people of God in every age," explained the Prophet Joseph Smith; "it is a theme upon which prophets, priests and kings have dwelt with peculiar delight; they have looked forward with joyful anticipation to the day in which we live; and fired with heavenly and joyful anticipations they have sung and written and prophesied of this our day; but they died without the sight; we are the favored people that God has made choice of to bring about the Latter-day glory; it is left for us to see, participate in and help to roll forward the Latter-day glory, 'the dispensation of the fulness of times, when God will gather together all things that are in heaven, and all things that are upon the earth,' 'even in one,' when the Saints of God will be gathered in one from every nation, and kindred, and people, and tongue, when the Jews will be gathered together into one, the wicked will also be gathered together to be destroyed, as spoken of by the prophets; the Spirit of God will also dwell with His people, and be withdrawn from the rest of the nations, and all things whether in heaven or on earth will be in one, even in Christ. The heavenly Priesthood will unite with the earthly, to bring about those great purposes; and whilst we are thus united in one common cause, to roll forth the kingdom of God, the heavenly Priesthood are not idle spectators, the Spirit of God will be showered down from above, and it will dwell in our midst. The blessings of the Most High will rest upon our tabernacles, and our name will be handed down to future ages; our children will rise up and call us blessed; and generations yet unborn will dwell with peculiar delight upon the scenes that we have passed through, the privations that we have endured; the untiring zeal that we have manifested; the all but insurmountable difficulties that we have overcome in laying the foundation of a work that brought about the glory and blessing which they will realize; a work that God and angels have contemplated with delight for generations past; that fired the souls of the ancient patriarchs and prophets; a work that is destined to bring about the destruction of the powers of darkness, the renovation of the earth, the glory of God, and the salvation of the human family" (*Teachings of the Prophet Joseph Smith,* 231–32).

    58:8 *A feast of fat things, of wine on the lees well refined.* "And in this mountain [Zion] shall the Lord of hosts make unto all people a feast of fat things," wrote Isaiah, "a feast of wines on the lees, of fat things full of marrow, of wines on the lees well refined" (Isaiah 25:6). It is a gospel feast of which the ancient prophet wrote, a meal worthy to be placed before the children of a King, even the Eternal Father. Anciently, meats with abundant fats were the privilege of the rich who could graze their animals to be served at banquets. The use of jellies and preserves from wines were also the diet of the rich. Thus these images are used to represent the goodness or richness of the gospel message that is to be taken to the poor.

That the earth may know that the mouths of the prophets shall not fail.
There is a unity of faith among the prophets. All have sworn allegiance
to the same principles and the same standards. The gospel known to
them is one and the same as the gospel revealed anew to us in this the
dispensation of the fulness of all past dispensations. So it is that their
faith is our faith, their doctrines our doctrines, their prophecies our
prophecies. We look to see the words of all the prophets find fulfillment
in the events of this the greatest of all gospel dispensations. We look to
the Book of Mormon to prove that the Bible is true (D&C 20:11;
1 Nephi 13:39; 2 Nephi 3:11; JST Genesis 50:30–31). Further, we find
the revelations of the Restoration to be the perfect evidence that the
God of heaven is the same yesterday, today, and forever.

58:9–11 The gospel has always been taught on a priority basis. Here
we are told that it is to go first to "the rich and the learned, the wise and
the noble." That is, the gospel was destined to come forth in a nation that
had sufficient natural resources and land to which the scattered remnants
of Israel could gather and find means to provide for themselves, a place
rich in the opportunity to learn and obtain wisdom, this so that it could in
turn send forth missionaries by the tens and hundreds of thousands to others. In so doing, this great army of missionaries went first to the literate
and comparatively rich nations of Europe, for here would be found a
people capable of providing the stability and learning necessary to lay the
foundations of the Church so that their sons and daughters could in turn
go to other nations here described as the "poor, the lame, the blind, and
the deaf." These, we are promised, will be lifted up, taught, and refined
that they might then take their rightful place in the quorums of the priesthood and the leadership of the Church.

"For it shall come to pass," declared the Lord, "that which I spake
by the mouths of my prophets shall be fulfilled; for I will consecrate of
the riches of those who embrace my gospel among the Gentiles unto
the poor of my people who are of the house of Israel" (D&C 42:39).
Those that accept the gospel among the rich in all nations of the world
are responsible to prepare the way for chapels and temples to be built
in the lands of the poor; for the Book of Mormon to be translated and
published in all languages; for missionaries to travel to the far reaches of
the world empowered with the authority of the priesthood to baptize
and administer the ordinances of the restored gospel. They are to see
that the supper of the Lord is well prepared for the lame, the blind, and
the deaf. Then the day will come when the Lord himself, who

ministered to the poor and afflicted, will return to reign as King in equity and righteousness. In that millennial day, all will be one, partakers of his goodness.

58:11 *Come in unto the marriage of the Lamb.* This New Testament imagery has reference to the ushering in of the Messiah's millennial kingdom. The invitation extended by missionaries to enter into the covenant of baptism is in effect the invitation to attend the marriage feast of the Lamb.

Bishops Are Judges in Israel
DOCTRINE AND COVENANTS 58:13–18

58:15 *Blindness of heart.* All true religion is a feeling. Describing the spirit of revelation, the Lord said, "I will tell you in your mind and in your heart, by the Holy Ghost, which shall come upon you and which shall dwell in your heart" (D&C 8:2). Again, the Lord has directed that his servants "speak the thoughts that I shall put into your hearts," with the attendant promise: "and you shall not be confounded before men" (D&C 100:5). To be insensitive to our feelings is to block the light and thus to reject the spirit of revelation.

58:17 *A judge in Israel.* Reference is to judges and officers that sat in the gates of the cities of ancient Israel. To them were brought the disputes and legal matters of the community, which they were to settle. Judges also taught the law of God to the Lord's people and instructed them in the ways of righteousness. Moses, the great judge among the Old Testament prophets, and his successor, Joshua, had the additional responsibility of dividing the land of Canaan among the various tribes of the house of Israel. The reception of the land of Canaan was in fulfillment of Abraham's covenant with God, wherein the Lord promised Abraham: "I will give unto thee, and to thy seed after thee, the land wherein thou art a stranger, all the land of Canaan, for an everlasting possession" (Genesis 17:8). In this revelation the Lord restored the principle of receiving a land inheritance that was integral to the Abrahamic covenant. Bishop Edward Partridge filled a similar role to the ancient judges when Saints received inheritances at his hand. This land assignment also prefigured the day when the Saints will literally inherit the earth. See commentary on Doctrine and Covenants 88:17.

The Saints Are to Obey the Laws of the Land
DOCTRINE AND COVENANTS 58:19–23

58:21–23 It is expected that Latter-day Saints will be obedient to the laws of the land. However, they are to hold forth the law received from Christ as an example to the governments of men. Hopefully, in this manner, they may influence the laws of respective nations to align more closely with the laws of God. Members of the Church are also encouraged to be actively involved in political processes, especially in areas where moral issues are concerned. "If this people live to the principles they have embraced," declared Brigham Young, "they will be capable of counseling the nations; for we build upon a just foundation, and our principles are truth, righteousness, and holiness. Let us stand by those principles until they crush out folly, . . . and we become teachers of wisdom to the nations" (*Journal of Discourses*, 7:66). See commentary on the Articles of Faith, page 1017.

Men Should Use Their Agency to Do Good
DOCTRINE AND COVENANTS 58:24–29

58:25 *Let them bring their families to this land.* Faith and sacrifice were required of all who came to the land of Zion. For example, members of Edward Partridge's family traveled from Ohio without the help of their father because of his duties in Missouri. Concerning their move to Zion, Emily Partridge, Bishop Partridge's daughter, wrote: "It seemed to him a very great undertaking for mother to break up her home and prepare for such a journey with a family of little children, without her husband to advise and make arrangements for her. For she was then young and inexperienced in such things. . . .

"The next season mother with her family started for Missouri, in a company of saints under the direction of W. W. Phelps and A. S. Gilbert. Mother must have had a great deal to try her on that journey that we as children knew nothing about. What little money she had with her to defray her expense, she was advised to put into the hands of W. W. Phelps and he cheated her out of it. We went down the Ohio River to Cincinnati in a keel boat. Then we took a steamboat and went up the Missouri River. It was on this boat that our provision chest was rifled and thrown over board. We saw it floating down stream and knew it at once. The lid was open and we could see that everything had been taken out but the papers that things were packed in. . . . When we were within about one hundred miles of our destination we met the ice coming down the river so thick that the boat could not proceed and we were forced to land at a place called 'Arrow Rock.' On the banks of the river there was a log cabin occupied by Negroes. There was two rooms, with no windows. The light was admitted through the open door, a common thing then in the negro cabins, and white folks too sometimes. These negroes let mother and Sister Morley have one room. There was about fifteen in number in both families. But there was a fire place in the room. We could have a good fire, and so keep from freezing. We remained here about two or three weeks, it being very cold weather. At the end of that time a large Kentucky wagon was procured and the two families and their effects were stowed into it and we started again for Independence. The weather was still very cold, so cold that we had to lay by again one day. That day my father and Brother Morley met us, and anybody that has been in like circumstances can understand how happy we were. . . . Whatever suffering and privation my mother had to endure she never murmured or complained, but rejoiced that she was counted worthy to endure tribulation for the Gospel's sake. She felt that she had enlisted in a good cause and she looked forward to the happy time that had been promised to the saints. Her religion compensated her for all the hardships she had to endure" ("Reminiscences," 8–9).

58:26 The desire to do that which is right and proper ought to be innate to the soul. "Virtue loveth virtue; light cleaveth unto light; mercy hath compassion on mercy" (D&C 88:40). To be devoid of such virtues is to be devoid of the Spirit. When we have been compelled to do a particular work, we typically do it according to the letter of the law, which "letter killeth"; but if our offering is freely given, that spirit will give it life (2 Corinthians 3:6). The virtue of all actions is in the motive behind them.

58:28 *For the power is in them, wherein they are agents unto themselves.* The doctrine of agency finds place among the plain and precious things lost from the text of the Bible. In his inspired translation of the book of Genesis, Joseph Smith first learned about our premortal estate, the Grand Council in heaven, Lucifer's rebellion and his desire to destroy the gift of agency that God had given to all of his spirit children (Moses 4:1–4).

In a revelation received in September 1830, the Prophet learned that the Lord charged Adam to be an agent unto himself while in Eden (D&C 29:35). After the Fall, when Adam and Eve became parents, the Lord said, "It is given unto them to know good from evil; wherefore they are agents unto themselves" (Moses 6:56).

As an agent unto yourself, you have the power of self-action. That is, you determine how you are going to act or what you are going to do. In the dictionary of Joseph Smith's day, agency was defined as "exerting power" or the "state of being in action." An "agent" was defined as one "entrusted with the concerns of another." The dictionary cited as examples an attorney or a minister (Webster, *Dictionary*, 1828, s.v. "agent"). There is no hint or intimation that the word has anything to do with choosing or the freedom of choice.

Teaching this principle, Joseph Fielding Smith said: "I have heard people say, and members of the Church too, 'I have a right to do as I please.' My answer is: No, you do not. You haven't any right at all to do just as you please. There is only one right that you have, and that is to do just what I read to you: keep the commandments of Jesus Christ. He has a perfect right to tell us so. We have no right to refuse. I do not care who the man is; I do not care where he lives, or what he is—when the gospel of Jesus Christ is presented to him, he has no right to refuse to receive it. He has the privilege. He is not compelled to receive it, because our Father in heaven has given to everyone of us, in the Church and out, the gift of free agency. That free agency gives us the privilege to accept and be loyal to our Lord's commandments, but it has never given us the right to reject them. Every man who rejects the commandments of our Father in heaven is rebellious" (Conference Report, April 1967, 120–21).

Scripture speaks of our being moral agents (D&C 101:78). A moral agent is someone who is obligated to act morally. To act morally is more than being moral. All infants are moral beings; they simply cannot do things that are wrong. They are not, however, moral agents because they do not have the power to act, the power to bring about change. The more mature the child, the greater his or her agency and ability to grow up into the power to act for himself, to make his own choices.

Similarly, as we grow in intelligence—meaning light and knowledge—in obedience, and faith, our agency grows proportionately. To increase in faith and knowledge of spiritual things is at the same time to increase in agency. Thus, God becomes the perfect example of a moral agent. No one has a greater power to act in a responsible and moral manner than he does.

Salvation can be granted only to moral agents, for only moral agents have the ability to distinguish between right and wrong and they alone have the capacity to be righteous.

The Lord Commands and Revokes
DOCTRINE AND COVENANTS 58:30–33

58:33 *I revoke and they receive not the blessing.* See commentary on Doctrine and Covenants 56:4.

To Repent, Men Must Confess and Forsake Their Sins
DOCTRINE AND COVENANTS 58:34–43

58:35–36 The gathering to the New Jerusalem was under the direction of the bishop of Zion and reserved for those that consecrated their property and goods to the Lord. It was the Saints' inability to live this very law that prevented them from redeeming Zion in the 1830s. See commentary on Doctrine and Covenants 105:1–10.

58:41 *He seeketh to excel.* In this context, the wickedness of excelling is that one seeks to be better than another for praise. The principle of unity upon which Zion must be built is sacrificed for the aggrandizement of the individual.

58:42 *I, the Lord, remember them no more.* The power of the Atonement is infinite and eternal. Those that are cleansed in the blood of the Lamb have every vestige of sin removed from their souls. The Lord promised: "Though your sins be as scarlet, they shall be as white as snow; though they be red like crimson, they shall be as wool" (Isaiah 1:18). In essence, they are perfected in Christ, and it is as though they had never sinned. The repentant sinner may receive every blessing that the Father has prepared for his children.

58:43 *He will confess them and forsake them.* "No one can ever be forgiven of any transgression until there is repentance," taught Spencer W. Kimball, "and one has not repented until he has bared his soul and admitted his intentions and weaknesses without excuses or rationalizations. He must admit to himself that he has grievously sinned. When he has confessed to himself without the slightest minimizing of the offense, or rationalizing its seriousness, or soft-pedaling its gravity, and admits it is as big as it really is, then he is ready to begin his repentance; and any other elements of repentance are of reduced value, until the conviction is established totally, and then repentance may mature and forgiveness may eventually come" (*Love Versus Lust*, 10).

To forsake is more than to refrain from sinning. It includes a mighty change that leads the individual to forsake the sins in his heart as well as to change his behavior. Those who are unable to root the desire to sin out of their hearts are like Lot's wife, who was unable to forsake Sodom and continued to look back upon her previous life until she returned to meet her own destruction. Thus, those who speak of their former sins with any degree of longing or attitude of boasting are in bondage to their sins. They have not yet fully repented.

The Saints Are to Purchase Their Inheritance and Gather in Missouri
DOCTRINE AND COVENANTS 58:44–58

58:50 Sidney Rigdon wrote a description of the land, which was not acceptable to the Lord. Concerning Rigdon's efforts, the Lord revealed: "I, the Lord, am not pleased with my servant Sidney Rigdon; he exalted himself in his heart, and received not counsel, but grieved the Spirit; Wherefore his writing is not acceptable unto the Lord, and he shall make another; and if the Lord receive it not, behold he standeth no longer in the office to which I have appointed him" (D&C 63:55–56). Our present records do not contain any further description of the land written by him.

58:56 *Let the work of the gathering be not in haste, nor by flight.* These words were first given by the Lord to the prophet Isaiah (Isaiah 52:12) and later taught to the Nephites by the Savior (3 Nephi 21:29). Sad experience taught the Saints the wisdom of the Lord's counsel. Those members that gathered to Zion before they had consecrated their property and, in turn, received an inheritance from the bishop, created confusion and lacked the Spirit of the Lord necessary to build up Zion. Today, unwise zeal should not influence Saints to gather to Jackson County, Missouri. The proper course is to follow counsel from the president of the Church in gathering. See commentary on Doctrine and Covenants 57:4; 63:24.

58:57 "On the second day of August," wrote the Prophet Joseph Smith, "I assisted the Colesville branch of the Church to lay the first log, for a house, as a foundation of Zion in Kaw township, twelve miles west of Independence. The log was carried and placed by twelve men, in honor of the twelve tribes of Israel. At the same time, through prayer, the land of Zion was consecrated and dedicated by Elder Sidney Rigdon for the gathering of the Saints. It was a season of joy to those present, and afforded a glimpse of the future, which time will yet unfold to the satisfaction of the faithful" (*History of the Church*, 1:196).

John Whitmer, in his *History of the Church*, gave further details about that date from a statement of Oliver Cowdery's: "'On the second day of August, 1831, Rigdon stood up and asked, saying,

"'Do you receive this land for the land of your inheritance with thankful hearts from the Lord?'

"Answer from all: 'We do.'

"'Do you pledge yourselves to keep the law of God in this land which you never have kept in your own lands?'

"'We do.'

"'Do you pledge yourselves to see that others of your brethren who shall come hither do keep the laws of God?'

"'We do.'

"After prayer, he arose and said: 'I now pronounce this land conse-crated and dedicated unto the Lord for a possession and inheritance for the Saints, and for all the faithful servants of the Lord to the remotest ages of time. In the name of Jesus Christ, having authority from Him. Amen'" (in Smith, *History of the Church*, 1:196, note).

Whitmer also recorded that on 3 August 1831, in obedience to these instructions, "eight elders, viz., Joseph Smith Jr., Oliver Cowdery, Sidney Rigdon, Peter Whitmer Jr., Frederick G. Williams, Wm. W. Phelps, Martin Harris, and Joseph Coe, assembled together where the Temple is to be erected. Sidney Rigdon dedicated the ground where the city is to stand: and Joseph Smith Jr. laid a stone at the northeast corner of the con-templated temple in the name of the Lord Jesus of Nazareth. After all present had rendered thanks to the great ruler of the universe, Sidney Rigdon pronounced this spot of ground wholly dedicated unto the Lord forever: Amen" ("Book of John Whitmer," 11).

Ziba Peterson Is Reprimanded
DOCTRINE AND COVENANTS 58:59–65

58:60 Four days after the receipt of this revelation, which includes a reprimand to Ziba Peterson, he again "was reprimanded publicly at a con-ference of the Church, and he subsequently confessed in a satisfactory manner. . . . On 11 August 1831, Ziba married Rebecca Hopper. . . . Because the marriage came so soon after the reprimand, some wondered if the two events were related; however, there is no historical evidence to support the relationship" (Garrett, "Ziba Peterson," 30).

DOCTRINE AND COVENANTS 59

DATE: 7 AUGUST 1831
PLACE: ZION, JACKSON COUNTY, MISSOURI

The weeks preceding this revelation had been very eventful. The Prophet and his party had arrived in Jackson County, Missouri; by the spirit of revelation he had designated the site for the temple, held conferences with the Saints in the area of Independence, directed the dedication of the land of Zion for the gathering of the Saints, and the day that this revelation was received he spoke at the funeral of a dear Saint and personal friend, Polly Knight, the aged wife of Joseph Knight Sr., who had died the day before. This revelation was received on Sunday, which it identifies as the day of worship for the Saints. It restored the law of the Sabbath as it had been given to ancient Israel. It was by this ancient covenant that the Lord's people were always to be known.

The Faithful Saints in Zion Shall Be Blessed
DOCTRINE AND COVENANTS 59:1–4

59:1–2 These verses have reference to Sister Polly Knight, wife of Joseph Knight Sr. She had traveled to Missouri with the Saints of the Colesville Branch from Ohio. Elder B. H. Roberts explained: "Polly Knight's health had been failing for some time, according to a statement made by her son, Newel. She was very ill during her journey from Kirtland to Missouri. 'Yet,' says her son, 'she would not consent to stop traveling; her only, or her greatest desire was to set her feet upon the land of Zion, and to have her body interred in that land. I went on shore and bought lumber to make a coffin in case she should die before we arrived at our place of destination—so fast did she fail. But the Lord gave her the desire of her heart, and she lived to stand upon that land'" (in Smith, *History of the Church*, 1:199 n). Concerning the day this revelation was received, the Prophet Joseph Smith wrote: "I attended the funeral of Sister Polly Knight, the wife of Joseph Knight, Sen. This was the first death in the

Church in this land, and I can say, a worthy member sleeps in Jesus till the resurrection" (*History of the Church*, 1:199).

59:4 *With commandments not a few.* This verse could have read, "with revelations not a few," because the words *commandment* and *revelation* were often used interchangeably. Thus the compilation of the Prophet's revelations was to be called the Book of Commandments (D&C 1:6), meaning the book of revelations. See commentary on Doctrine and Covenants 19.

Faithful Saints Are to Love and Serve the Lord and Keep His Commandments
DOCTRINE AND COVENANTS 59:5–8

59:5–9 This revelation not only reestablishes the law of the Sabbath for this dispensation but also reinstitutes the Decalogue, affirming that the Ten Commandments as given to Moses on Sinai were part of the higher law rather than the law of carnal commandments. As given in this dispensation, these commandments are as follows:

1. Thou shalt love the Lord thy God with all thy heart, with all thy might, mind, and strength.

2. In the name of Jesus Christ thou shalt serve him.

3. Thou shalt love thy neighbor as thyself.

4. Thou shalt not steal.

5. Neither commit adultery.

6. Nor kill.

7. Nor do anything like unto it.

8. Thou shalt thank the Lord thy God in all things.

9. Thou shalt offer a sacrifice unto the Lord thy God in righteousness, even that of a broken heart and a contrite spirit.

10. And that thou mayest more fully keep thy self unspotted from the world, thou shalt go to the house of prayer and offer up thy sacraments upon my holy day.

59:5 The true doctrine of worship is herein reiterated. We worship the Father in the name of his Son, Jesus Christ. The Savior taught the Samaritan woman, "True worshippers shall worship the Father in spirit and in truth" (John 4:23). All of God's children, the Son of Man included, are commanded to worship the Father. True worship is to emulate the life of the one worshipped. In this regard the plan of salvation is founded on the principle of worship, in which we do as our Heavenly

Father did before us that we might become like him. "Our relationship with the Father is supreme, paramount, and preeminent over all others," explained Elder Bruce R. McConkie. "He is the God we worship. It is his gospel that saves and exalts. He ordained and established the plan of salvation. He is the one who was once as we are now. The life he lives is eternal life, and if we are to gain this greatest of all the gifts of God, it will be because we become like him.

"Our relationship with the Father is one of parent and child. He is the one who gave us our agency. It was his plan that provided for a fall and an atonement. And it is to him that we must be reconciled if we are to gain salvation. He is the one to whom we have direct access by prayer, and if there were some need—which there is not—to single out one member of the Godhead for a special relationship, the Father, not the Son, would be the one to choose.

"Our relationship with the Son is one of brother or sister in the premortal life and one of being led to the Father by him while in this mortal sphere. He is the Lord Jehovah who championed our cause before the foundations of the earth were laid. He is the God of Israel, the promised Messiah, and the Redeemer of the world.

"By faith we are adopted into his family and become his children. We take upon ourselves his name, keep his commandments, and rejoice in the cleansing power of his blood. Salvation comes by him. From creation's dawn, as long as eternity endures, there neither has been nor will be any act of such transcendent power and import as his atoning sacrifice.

"We do not have a fraction of the power we need to properly praise his holy name and ascribe unto him the honor and power and might and glory and dominion that are his. He is our Lord, our God, and our King" (*Sermons and Writings*, 65). See commentary on Doctrine and Covenants 20:19.

Thou shalt love the Lord thy God with all thy heart. The love of God is the foundation for the purest form of worship. No one can have love for God fill his heart without also loving his fellowmen. The quality of our efforts to serve God and our treatment of others are a reflection of our feelings toward them. Anything less than a pure love of God, that empowers the soul to keep all of the commandments and to endure faithfully in tribulation, will not sustain an individual in the test of mortality to attain eternal life. Likewise, a love for our neighbors that falls short of esteeming them as ourselves will not kindle our kindest efforts in their behalf. Love for others must fill our hearts or, in the room that is left, the adversary will plant seeds of envy and selfishness. Further, and most important, our treatment of others is a measure of our love for God and his Son. The Savior declared, "Inasmuch as ye have done it unto one of the least of these my brethren, ye have done it unto me" (Matthew 25:40).

In the name of Jesus Christ thou shalt serve him. Our commandment is to worship the Father in the name of his Son.

59:6 *Anything like unto it.* When God placed Adam and Eve in the Garden of Eden, he told them that they could eat of the fruit of all the trees except the tree of the knowledge of good and evil. Of that tree he said, "Ye shall not eat of it, neither shall ye touch it, lest ye die" (Genesis 3:3). Sin is born in the touching stage. We court or flirt with sin before we commit ourselves to it. For instance, we may seek the exact demarcation or definition of a sin so that we can push up as close to it as possible, thinking that we can touch without tasting. This becomes particularly dangerous in sexual transgression, where sins are often simulated with the idea that no offense has been given to the Spirit. This simply is not the case. Toying with sin, simulating sin, and defining sin in such a manner that one can effectually touch it while still feigning innocence are each sins which can be as harmful, or in some instances even more harmful, than the sin itself.

59:7 All true worship of God includes gratitude to him for the blessings he bestows upon us. "O how you ought to thank your heavenly King!" exclaimed King Benjamin. "I say unto you, my brethren, that if you should render all the thanks and praise which your whole soul has power to possess, to that God who has created you, and has kept and preserved you, and has caused that ye should rejoice, and has granted that ye should live in peace one with another—I say unto you that if ye should serve him who has created you from the beginning, and is preserving you from day to day, by lending you breath, that ye may live and move and do according to your own will, and even supporting you from one moment to another—I say, if ye should serve him with all your whole souls yet ye would be unprofitable servants. . . . In the first place, he hath created you, and granted unto you your lives, for which ye are indebted unto him. And secondly, he doth require that ye should do as he hath commanded you; for which if ye do, he doth immediately bless you; and therefore he hath paid you. And ye are still indebted unto him, and are, and will be, forever and ever" (Mosiah 2:19–21, 23–24).

By Keeping the Lord's Day Holy, the Saints Are Blessed Temporally and Spiritually

DOCTRINE AND COVENANTS 59:9–19

59:9 *That thou mayest more fully keep thyself unspotted from the world.* James identified keeping oneself unspotted from the world as part of pure and undefiled religion (James 1:27). The Lord herein reveals that true religion includes observance of the Sabbath day—a holy day not a holiday—a day set apart upon which we rest from the cares of the other six days to offer up our "oblations and sacraments" and renew our souls. Countless discussions have centered on what constitutes proper observance of the Sabbath. The true test is here given. That which keeps us "unspotted from the world" is in harmony with the law of the Sabbath; that which does not so distinguish us is not in harmony with the spirit of the day. Our dress, our speech, and our behavior on this day should be such that it attests that we are a covenant people who love and honor the Lord. Anything less than this is less than the standard which ought to be ours.

Go to the house of prayer. Saints are to assemble together on the Sabbath day in buildings set apart for worship of the Lord. To seek solace in nature or at home does not fulfill the command. The Saints are to gather together to partake of the sacrament and to instruct one another.

Offer up thy sacraments. Sacraments are sacred oaths or covenants. Anciently, a sacrament was a ceremony in which a soldier swore an oath of allegiance to his king. So it is in the realm of spiritual things; a sacrament is a ceremony associated with a covenant in which we pledge loyalty to Christ and the standards of his gospel. Thus a sacrament is a formal expression of commitment and loyalty to our divinely sent King.

In the sacrament prayers, we remember the atonement of Christ, that we were bought with a price, and that we have covenanted to take his name upon us, thus doing and saying those things which he would do or say (D&C 20:77, 79). By doing so we obtain the promise that we might always have his Spirit to be with us.

My holy day. This revelation was received on a Sunday, the first day of the week, thus settling the issue for Latter-day Saints as to what day should be for the day of worship. In the first dispensations of the gospel, the seventh day was set apart to recall that the Lord rested on that day from his labors of creation (Genesis 2:1–3). During the Mosaic dispensation, the Lord affirmed that his people were to worship on the seventh day as a remembrance of his goodness in delivering them from their Egyptian bondage (Deuteronomy 5:12–15). Following the resurrection of Christ, the Saints were directed by revelation to observe the Sabbath on the first day of the week in remembrance of the day upon which the Lord rose from the tomb. This revelation affirms that this practice is to continue among his people.

59:10 *Pay thy devotions unto the Most High.* True religion centers in a reverence of respect shown to God. Out of this comes an understanding of his nature and purpose. As he chooses to rest and renew himself on the seventh day, we too, being in his image and likeness, are commanded to do likewise.

59:11 It is not enough to set the Sabbath apart as a day to do good or live properly. Such works do not distinguish the Sabbath from any other day. Proper works and devotions should be the labor of the Saints at all times. There are no gospel principles that apply alone to the Sabbath day, yet this day should be devoted alone to this purpose.

59:12 *Thou shalt offer thine oblations.* An oblation is an offering given in service to God. It may be our time, talents, or other means. "Offer your whole souls as an offering unto [God]," admonished Amaleki (Omni 1:26). The Lord's day is a day to "turn away thy foot . . . from doing thy pleasure on my holy day; and call the sabbath a delight, the holy of the Lord, honourable; and [thou] shalt honour him, not doing thine own ways, nor finding thine own pleasure, nor speaking thine own words: then shalt thou delight thyself in the Lord" (Isaiah 58:13–14).

Confessing thy sins. The Sabbath is a day of reconciliation with the Lord and with any against whom we may have sinned. The Lord exhorts his Saints that not one Sabbath day should pass without making the wrongs of the week right. Most sins would not be grievous, if attended to immediately. See commentary on Doctrine and Covenants 58:43.

Public confession is appropriate when the transgression is public. If our transgression involved but one or a few people, then it would be to them that the confession would be made and to none others. If our action is an offense to the ward, our confession should in like manner be made to the ward. Transgressions that are sufficiently serious that they call in question our standing in the Church should be made to the appropriate ecclesiastical officer, normally the bishop. All sins should be confessed to our Father in Heaven. Sins not involving Church standing or other people need be confessed only to God.

59:13 *Let thy food be prepared with singleness of heart.* The heart is to

be turned wholly to the Lord on his day. This is not a commandment pre-
cluding nice meals on the Lord's day, but rather that those that prepare
meals and those that receive of the bounty of the Lord recognize the hand
from whom all blessings flow. This was the practice of the meridian-day
Church of whom we read, "And they, continuing daily with one accord
in the temple, and breaking bread from house to house, did eat their meat
with gladness and singleness of heart" (Acts 2:46).

That thy fasting may be perfect. Each Sabbath day is a day of fasting.
This has no reference to abstaining from food. Rather, it refers to
abstaining from the things of the world, including the good things of
the world. Similar to the fact that we must eat good food to maintain
the strength of the body, yet on occasions we fast from that nourishment; likewise, the Sabbath is a day to refrain from worldly activities
regardless of how wholesome they may be. To justify participating in
worldly activities on the Sabbath because they are good activities is to
have an imperfect fast. The Savior's reference to doing well on the
Sabbath day dealt with loosing spiritual burdens, healings by the power
of God (Matthew 12:10–12; John 5:16–17, 21), and ultimately the resurrection during the great Sabbath of the earth—the Millennium.

59:15 *Do these things with thanksgiving.* Observance of the Lord's day is
a means by which we show our gratitude to the Lord. Children must be
taught gratitude for all that is given them. Likewise, we as the children of
God must render thanks to God for the many blessings received at his
hand. See commentary on verse 21.

With cheerful hearts and countenances. The Lord's day should be the
most joyful day of the week. The Saints are to gather together in joy and
gladness, rejoicing in that which they have received at the hand of the
Lord. The Sabbath should be a day of rest from worldly cares. Anciently,
the Lord admonished his people to "call the sabbath a delight," a day to
"delight thyself in the Lord" (Isaiah 58:13–14). True delight and joy
comes from the peace of the Spirit, which is to be sought with particular
attention on the Lord's day.

Not with much laughter, for this is sin. Activities that lead to excessive
laughter are not appropriate on the Sabbath. The Spirit of God is available to those who are cheerful, yet thoughtful and reflective. Fits of laughter were part of the false influences thought to be bestowed by the Spirit
of God in camp revivals during frontier days. Clearly, the Spirit of God
does not inspire Saints to break into uncontrollable laughter. "But the
fruit of the Spirit is love, joy, peace, longsuffering, gentleness, goodness,

faith, meekness, temperance" (Galatians 5:22–23). Similarly, the brethren who attended the School of the Prophets were admonished to "cast away your . . . excess of laughter far from you" (D&C 88:69) and to "cease from all your light speeches, from all laughter" (D&C 88:121).

59:16–19 Sabbath observance is a principle with a promise. Those living this principle are promised a richness and prosperity that will not be known to others. Similarly, the Lord blessed ancient Israel, saying, "Ye shall keep my sabbaths, and reverence my sanctuary: I am the Lord. If ye walk in my statutes, and keep my commandments, and do them; then I will give you rain in due season, and the land shall yield her increase, and the trees of the field shall yield their fruit. And your threshing shall reach unto the vintage, and the vintage shall reach unto the sowing time: and ye shall eat your bread to the full, and dwell in your land safely. And I will give peace in the land, and ye shall lie down, and none shall make you afraid: and I will rid evil beasts out of the land, neither shall the sword go through your land" (Leviticus 26:2–6).

The Saints Are to Acknowledge Their Blessings
DOCTRINE AND COVENANTS 59:20–24

59:20 *Unto this end were they made to be used.* See commentary on Doctrine and Covenants 104:17–18.

59:21 *Confess not his hand in all things.* "Beware that thou forget not the Lord thy God," Moses warned the children of Israel, "in not keeping his commandments, and his judgments, and his statutes, which I command thee this day: lest when thou hast eaten and art full, and hast built goodly houses, and dwelt therein; and when thy herds and thy flocks multiply, and thy silver and thy gold is multiplied, and all that thou hast is multiplied; then thine heart be lifted up, and thou forget the Lord thy God" (Deuteronomy 8:11–14). See commentary on Doctrine and Covenants 59:7).

DOCTRINE AND COVENANTS 60

DATE: 8 AUGUST 1831
PLACE: ZION, JACKSON COUNTY, MISSOURI

The time arrived for the elders gathered in Missouri to return to
Ohio. The Lord did not desire that they return with the same haste that
they traveled to Missouri (D&C 58:63). The Prophet Joseph Smith
recorded: "On the 8th, as there had been some inquiry among the Elders
what they were to do, I received the following . . ." (*History of the Church,*
1:201).

The Elders Are to Preach the Gospel
DOCTRINE AND COVENANTS 60:1–9

60:2 *They hide the talent which I have given unto them.* The truths of
the Restoration are not to be hoarded or hidden from others but shared
freely. In this passage, reference is to the Savior's parable of the talents
recorded in the New Testament. Three servants were given talents (pieces
of money) to improve upon. Two were faithful in doubling the amount
they received from their master. The third "went and digged in the earth,
and hid his lord's money" (Matthew 25:18). The first two were blessed for
their wisdom while the third was cursed for being a "wicked and slothful
servant" (Matthew 25:26). The message to the elders in Missouri was that
they must share the gospel and its saving ordinances with others or they
would lose the blessings the gospel offers.

60:5 *It mattereth not unto me.* Apparently, the elders petitioned the
Lord to know whether he desired that they construct canoes or purchase
them for their return to Ohio. Our decisions in such situations do not
matter to the Lord. "No answer is likely to come to a person who seeks
guidance in choosing between two alternatives that are equally acceptable to the Lord," explained Elder Dallin H. Oaks. "Thus, there are times
when we can serve productively in two different fields of labor. Either
answer is right. Similarly, the Spirit of the Lord is not likely to give us
revelations on matters that are trivial. I once heard a young woman in a

testimony meeting praise the spirituality of her husband, indicating that he submitted every question to the Lord. She told how he accompanied her shopping and would not even choose between different brands of canned vegetables without making his selection a matter of prayer. That strikes me as improper. I believe the Lord expects us to use the intelligence and experience He has given us to make these kind of choices. When a member asked the Prophet Joseph Smith for advice on a particular matter, the Prophet stated: 'It is a great thing to inquire at the hands of God, or to come into His presence: and we feel fearful to approach Him on subjects that are of little or no consequence' (*History of the Church*, 1:339)" ("Revelation," 46). In a revelation given a few days later, the Lord emphasized that he expects the Saints to make some decisions "according to their judgments" (D&C 61:22).

60:7 *Declare my word with loud voices, without wrath or doubting.* The tone and approach taken in teaching the word of God is as important as the words uttered. The sacred responsibility of priesthood bearers is to teach the gospel as the Lord Jesus Christ taught it. The gospel is to be taught not in anger but rather with the voice of hope in the salvation made available through the atoning blood of Christ. Further, the voice of God is one of assurance, not uncertainty.

They Should Not Idle Away Their Time, nor Bury Their Talents
DOCTRINE AND COVENANTS 60:10–17

60:12–14 These verses concern the companionships of elders that were commanded to teach the people on their routes to Missouri from Ohio, who had not yet arrived in Jackson County.

60:13 *Thou shalt not idle away thy time.* Revelation and inspiration from the Lord often comes as we are in the midst of doing. A common cliché states: "The Lord cannot steer a parked car!" The meaning is that we are guided as we are going about the Lord's business. It is better to get off one's knees after pleading for divine direction and to go forward full of faith that revelation will come in our moment of need than to wait on our knees unwilling to budge until the heavens resound with answers. Nephi understood this principle of revelation. Regarding his attempt to obtain the brass plates, he declared, "I was led by the Spirit, not knowing beforehand the things which I should do. Nevertheless I went forth" (1 Nephi 4:6–7). Likewise, the Lord instructed the brother of Jared that he was to propose means to light the barges of the Jaredites rather than expect God to solve the problem of crossing the ocean in darkness (Ether 2:25).

60:14 *Thou shalt speedily return, . . . not in haste.* How can these elders return speedily but not in haste? Simply, get up and move, but do not move so quickly that you are too busy to teach people the gospel.

60:15 *Shake off the dust of thy feet.* See commentary on Doctrine and Covenants 24:15.

DOCTRINE AND COVENANTS 61

DATE: 12 AUGUST 1831
PLACE: MCILWAINE'S BEND, ON THE MISSOURI RIVER

John the Revelator saw in vision that in the last days destruction would be upon the waters (Revelation 8:8–11; 16:3–4). This same principle was revealed to the Prophet Joseph Smith and his companions as they journeyed from Independence, Missouri, to Ohio in August 1831. They traveled in canoes on the Missouri River for two days, arriving near McIlwaine's Bend. "The canoe in which the Prophet and Sidney Rigdon were riding ran into a tree lodged and bobbing in the river. The canoe was upset, and the occupants almost drowned. With this near tragedy, the party of eleven decided to . . . encamp" (Cook, *Revelations*, 96).

Regarding this experience, the Prophet Joseph Smith recorded, "On the 9th, in company with ten Elders, I left Independence landing for Kirtland. We started down the river in canoes, and went the first day as far as Fort Osage, where we had an excellent wild turkey for supper. Nothing very important occurred till the third day, when many of the dangers so common upon the western waters, manifested themselves; and after we had encamped upon the bank of the river, at McIlwaine's Bend, Brother Phelps, in open vision by daylight, saw the destroyer in his most horrible power, ride upon the face of the waters; others heard the noise, but saw not the vision.

"The next morning after prayer, I received the following" (*History of the Church*, 1:203–4). The Prophet then recorded the revelation that we now have as Doctrine and Covenants 61.

The Elders Returning to Ohio Were to Preach Along the Way
DOCTRINE AND COVENANTS 61:1–12

61:2 *I . . . am merciful unto those who confess their sins.* B. H. Roberts explained that "during the three days upon the river some disagreements and ill feeling had developed among the brethren and explanations and reconciliations had become necessary" (*Comprehensive History of the*

Church, 1:262–63). See commentary on Doctrine and Covenants 58:42–43.

61:3 *The inhabitants on either side are perishing in unbelief.* This message reemphasizes the chastening the Lord gave these same elders before they departed from Independence, Missouri (D&C 60:1–9). They were in such a hurry that they neglected to raise the voice of warning to those people along their return route. Those who have received the fulness of the gospel have obligation to share the good news with others. The difficulties of mortality can be overwhelming, and "where there is no vision, the people perish" (Proverbs 29:18). The restored gospel provides the answers that give strength and purpose to life, but the work of the Restoration is vain if the people never hear the needed message because the Lord's servants are in a hurry to get home.

61:4 Good came of the elders' swift movement down the river because they were able to witness the power of the destroyer. Had that not been the case, the Lord might have intervened sooner to chastise them for their failure to teach the gospel along the way.

61:5 *I, the Lord, have decreed in mine anger many destructions upon the waters.* See commentary on Doctrine and Covenants 61:14–16.

61:7 The errand referred to was to obtain a printing press, since W. W. Phelps had been appointed to serve as "a printer unto the church" (D&C 57:11).

The Waters Were Cursed by John, and the Destroyer Rideth upon Their Face
DOCTRINE AND COVENANTS 61:13–22

61:14–16 In the Creation God blessed the waters to bring life forth abundantly (Genesis 1:20). Such conditions will not continue as we draw nearer to the days alluded to in these verses. Apparently, John the Beloved has been involved in bringing to pass the vision he was shown concerning destruction of life in the waters. He wrote that he saw in vision "as it were a great mountain burning with fire was cast into the sea: and the third part of the sea became blood; and the third part of the creatures which were in the sea, and had life, died; and the third part of the ships were destroyed. And the third angel sounded, and there fell a great star from heaven, burning as it were a lamp, and it fell upon the third part of the rivers, and upon the fountains of waters; and the name of the star is called Wormwood: and the third part of the waters became wormwood;

and many men died of the waters, because they were made bitter" (Revelation 8:8–11). There is no key given in scripture as to the details concerning the fulfillment of this destruction. Clearly, the devastating events are in the future.

61:17 *I, the Lord, in the beginning cursed the land.* This refers to the Lord's words to Adam after he partook of the forbidden fruit: "And unto Adam he said, Because thou hast hearkened unto the voice of thy wife, and hast eaten of the tree, of which I commanded thee, saying, Thou shalt not eat of it: cursed is the ground for thy sake; in sorrow shalt thou eat of it all the days of thy life; thorns also and thistles shall it bring forth to thee; and thou shalt eat the herb of the field; in the sweat of thy face shalt thou eat bread, till thou return unto the ground" (Genesis 3:17–19).

I blessed it, in its time, for the use of my saints. The fulfillment of this promise has come a little at a time. The Prophet Joseph Smith and the Saints turned a virtual, mosquito-infested swamp along the Mississippi River into Nauvoo, the City Beautiful. Later, those pioneers who settled the barren regions of the western United States saw the desert "rejoice, and blossom as the rose" (Isaiah 35:1). In both instances the faith and determination of the Saints was blessed from on high. A future millennial day will see greater changes, "for in the wilderness shall waters break out, and streams in the desert. And the parched ground shall become a pool, and the thirsty land springs of water" (Isaiah 35:6–7).

61:19 *The destroyer rideth upon the face thereof.* It is not clear if this destroyer is an angel of God or a devil. On other occasions when the destroyer is mentioned in scripture, he is a servant of God. For example, at the time of the first Passover in ancient Egypt, death was sent to all households that did not have the blood of a lamb upon their doorposts. But faithful Israelites were protected; the Lord promised them that he would "not suffer the destroyer to come in unto your houses to smite you" (Exodus 12:23). In our dispensation, when the Saints were being driven from Zion, the Lord declared, "Behold, the destroyer I have sent forth to destroy and lay waste mine enemies; and not many years hence they shall not be left to pollute mine heritage, and to blaspheme my name upon the lands which I have consecrated for the gathering together of my saints" (D&C 105:15). In a similar vein, "angels are crying unto the Lord day and night, who are ready and waiting to be sent forth to" destroy the wicked (D&C 86:5). Likewise, the revelation given to John the Beloved, referred to in this section, mentions several angels who send plagues and calamities upon the earth (Revelation 8–10, 15–18). Given that the destroyer rides upon the waters by the Lord's decree, it seems likely that the being seen in vision by William W. Phelps was a servant of God.

On the other hand, Joseph Fielding Smith wrote concerning this decree, "These brethren, while encamped at McIlwaine's Bend on the Missouri, beheld the power of the destroyer as he rode upon the storm. One of that number saw him in all his fearful majesty, and the Lord revealed to the entire group something of the power of this evil personage. It may seem strange to us, but it is the fact that Satan exercises dominion and has some control over the elements. . . . Paul speaks of Satan as the 'prince of the power of the air.' (Eph. 2:2.) The Lord revealed to these brethren some of the power of the adversary of mankind and how he rides upon the storm, as a means of affording them protection. They were commanded to use judgment as they traveled upon these waters, and the saints coming to Zion were instructed to travel by land on their way up to Zion. Moreover, notwithstanding the great power of Satan upon the waters, the Lord still held command and he could protect his people whether on land or by water as they journeyed" (*Church History and Modern Revelation*, 1:224–25).

61:22 *It mattereth not unto me.* See commentary on Doctrine and Covenants 60:5.

Some Have Power to Command the Waters

DOCTRINE AND COVENANTS 61:23–29

61:23 *The canal.* Travel on the waterways was a common mode of transportation in the 1830s. "The canal" refers to man-made waterways in the state of Ohio. Canal barges were towed by teams of mules or horses moving at fewer than five miles an hour. The Prophet Joseph Smith and other Saints used the canal system to travel to Missouri.

61:27 *Power to command the waters.* The priesthood is God's power on earth. God may instruct his servants to command the elements in his name. Such power comes only to those with faith. For example, Jacob informs us that those in his day received this power. "We search the prophets," he declared, "and we have many revelations and the spirit of prophecy; and having all these witnesses we obtain a hope, and our faith becometh unshaken, insomuch that we truly can command in the name of Jesus and the very trees obey us, or the mountains, or the waves of the sea" (Jacob 4:6). Other examples are Enoch, at whose command "rivers of water were turned out of their course" (Moses 7:13), and Moses, who commanded the parting of the Red Sea. LeGrand Richards shared an example of one in the latter days who had power given to him over the waters: "You will recall that in the early days of the gathering of the Saints it was considered as good as an insurance policy when a company of Latter-day Saints embarked on a vessel crossing the Atlantic. I recall reading in my grandfather's diary of a time when the boat upon which he was sailing was in great jeopardy, so much so that the captain of the boat came to him and pleaded with him to intercede with the Lord in behalf of the boat and her passengers; and Grandfather, remembering that he had been promised that he should have power over the elements, walked out on the deck of the boat and raised his hands to high heaven and rebuked the sea and the waves, and they were immediately calmed, and the appreciation of the captain of the boat was so great that he offered him the use of his private quarters during the balance of the journey" (Conference Report, April 1941, 84). In all of these instances the priesthood bearer followed the Master, who "rebuked the winds and the sea" (Matthew 8:26).

Elders Are Held Responsible to Preach the Gospel to the Wicked
DOCTRINE AND COVENANTS 61:30–35

61:30–31 "At the time of this revelation, Cincinnati was only a village, yet it was like other western towns such as Independence, the gathering place of many who had been forced to flee from the larger cities because of the violation of the law. In all the border towns in that day wickedness to a very great extent prevailed" (Smith, *Church History and Modern Revelation*, 1:225).

61:34 *They shall rid their garments.* The sins of the wicked symbolically stain the garment of the priesthood bearer who does not warn the wicked to repent (Ezekiel 3:16–21). This principle is illustrated in the explanation of Jacob, son of Lehi. He indicated that he and his brother Joseph "did magnify our office unto the Lord, taking upon us the responsibility, answering the sins of the people upon our own heads if we did not teach them the word of God with all diligence; wherefore, by laboring with our might their blood might not come upon our garments; otherwise their blood would come upon our garments, and we would not be found spotless at the last day" (Jacob 1:19). President John Taylor emphasized to the elders that they must serve with all their heart, might, mind, and strength or "God will hold you responsible for those whom you might have saved had you done your duty. How many of you can say, My garments are clean from the blood of this generation? I speak in behalf of the nations and the people thereof, and the honest in heart who are ignorant of God and his laws. He has called upon us to enlighten them, and to spread forth the truth, and send forth the principles of the Gospel, and point out the way of life. And it is for us to attend to these things, that we may secure the smiles and approbation of God" (*Journal of Discourses*, 20:23).

Prepare for the Coming of the Son of Man
DOCTRINE AND COVENANTS 61:36–39

61:36 *I have not forsaken you.* Tribulation is not evidence that the Lord has abandoned his people. This reassurance was especially comforting to the little band of elders following their harrowing experience on the Missouri River. See commentary on Doctrine and Covenants 122:9.

61:38 *Gird up your loins and be watchful and be sober.* The Prophet Joseph Smith stated, "When I contemplate the rapidity with which the great and glorious day of the coming of the Son of Man advances, when He shall come to receive His Saints unto Himself, where they shall dwell in His presence, and be crowned with glory and immortality: when I consider that soon the heavens are to be shaken, and the earth tremble and reel to and fro; and that the heavens are to be unfolded as a scroll when it is rolled up; and that every mountain and island are to flee away, I cry out in my heart, What manner of persons ought we to be in all holy conversation and godliness!" (*Teachings of the Prophet Jospeh Smith*, 29).

For he cometh in an hour you think not. The scriptures do not reveal the precise time of the Savior's return in glory. Those who are slothful will say in their heart that he "delayeth his coming" (D&C 45:26) and will indulge in sin, thinking that they will yet have a season to repent. The faithful servant will watch and be ready for the Master's return, regardless of when it is.

61:39 *Abide the day of his coming, whether in life or in death.* Preparation for the Lord's return is not exclusively reserved for those in mortality. The Second Coming will also be a reality and day of judgment for those in the spirit world. Those who have died will come forth from the grave in proper order, according to the law they abide. The righteous Saints, whether alive on the earth or in the grave, will "be caught up to meet him" (D&C 88:96). Those who are found under condemnation will be judged unworthy to be resurrected and to live upon the earth during the Millennium.

DOCTRINE AND COVENANTS 62

DATE: 13 AUGUST 1831

PLACE: CHARITON, MISSOURI, ON THE BANK OF THE MISSOURI RIVER

As the Prophet Joseph Smith and his company continued their return journey from Zion to Ohio, they met with another group of elders who were still on their way to Independence, Missouri. These two missionary companionships—Hyrum Smith and John Murdock, and David Whitmer and Harvey Whitlock (D&C 52:8, 25)—were about three weeks behind the elders that arrived with Joseph and dedicated the land for the building up of Zion. These latter four elders had invested their efforts in testifying to the people of the restoration of the gospel rather than traveling speedily to Zion. The Prophet Joseph Smith wrote, "On the 13th [August] I met several of the Elders on their way to the land of Zion, and after the joyful salutations with which brethren meet each other, who are actually 'contending for the faith once delivered to the Saints,' I received the following . . ." (*History of the Church*, 1:205).

Testimonies Are Recorded in Heaven

DOCTRINE AND COVENANTS 62:1–9

62:1 *Who knoweth the weakness of man and how to succor them who are tempted.* Temptations common to mortality were part of the Savior's mortal experience. The apostle Paul assured us that "we have not an high priest which cannot be touched with the feeling of our infirmities; but was in all points tempted like as we are, yet without sin. Let us therefore come boldly unto the throne of grace, that we may obtain mercy, and find grace to help in time of need" (Hebrews 4:15–16). "For in that he himself hath suffered being tempted," Paul further wrote, "he is able to succour them that are tempted" (Hebrews 2:18). This revelation reassures the Saints that Jesus Christ, by experience, is familiar with our mortal trials and temptations. Moreover, he knows how to help us to overcome our weaknesses and has made ample provision and preparation to cleanse us of our sins.

62:2 The elders that met with the Prophet's party, who had not had the privilege of going to Zion, were to complete their journey.

62:3 *The testimony which ye have borne is recorded in heaven for the angels to look upon.* The angels of heaven rejoice when we are filled with the Spirit and bear faithful testimony. Bearing Spirit-inspired testimony is an indication that we have received the power of the Holy Ghost into our lives. "A testimony of the truth is more than a mere assent of the mind," taught President Joseph F. Smith; "it is a conviction of the heart, a knowledge that fills the whole soul of its recipient" (*Gospel Doctrine*, 364). The Spirit bears witness to those who hear or read the words of truth in the message of the testimony. These powerful declarations of truth influence individuals on both sides of the veil. Further, they are recorded that they might strengthen the convictions of those who read them. Thus, "all who bear testimony by the power of the Holy Ghost are blessed," explained Elder Bruce R. McConkie; "their inspired utterances are recorded in heaven for the angels—their fellowservants—to look upon" (*Mortal Messiah*, 3:38).

Your sins are forgiven you. James taught: "Brethren, if any of you do err from the truth, and one convert him; let him know, that he which converteth the sinner from the error of his way shall save a soul from death, and shall hide a multitude of sins" (James 5:19–20). See commentary on Doctrine and Covenants 4:4; 61:33–34.

62:4 *Offer a sacrament unto the Most High.* The elders were instructed to stand upon the ground consecrated to be the center place of Zion and to make covenants with the Lord on that sacred site. See commentary on Doctrine and Covenants 59:9.

62:5 *It mattereth not unto me; only be faithful.* There are a multitude of decisions that pale in significance to keeping the commandments. Blessings of the greatest import are predicated upon obedience to God. See commentary on Doctrine and Covenants 60:5.

DOCTRINE AND COVENANTS 63

DATE: LATE AUGUST 1831
PLACE: KIRTLAND, OHIO

Revelations designating the location of Zion and the site for the temple brought a renewed excitement among the Saints in Ohio (D&C 57–58). The Prophet Joseph Smith wrote: "In these infant days of the Church, there was a great anxiety to obtain the word of the Lord upon every subject that in any way concerned our salvation; and as the land of Zion was now the most important temporal object in view, I enquired of the Lord for further information upon the gathering of the Saints, and the purchase of the land, and other matters, and received the following . . ." (*History of the Church*, 1:207).

A Day of Wrath Shall Come upon the Wicked
DOCTRINE AND COVENANTS 63:1–6

63:2 *Whose anger is kindled against the wicked and rebellious.* "Righteous anger is an attribute of Deity" (McConkie, *Mormon Doctrine*, 37). Unlike the anger of sinful men and women, the wrath of God does not consume his passions nor dominate his thoughts and actions. Often the Lord's anger is referred to as his wrath. Bruce R. McConkie explained: "Inherent in it is the purpose and intent of meting out a just punishment upon those whose acts have caused it to be aroused. The wrath of God does not fall upon the righteous, but upon the wicked (D&C 1:9; 59:21). 'Instead of blessings, ye, by your own works, bring cursings, wrath, indignation, and judgments upon your own heads, by your follies, and by all your abominations, which you practise before me, saith the Lord' (D&C 124:48)" (*Mormon Doctrine*, 851).

Those wicked and rebellious individuals upon whom the Lord was about to pour out his wrath called themselves "the people of the Lord" (D&C 63:1). They added to their sins that of hypocrisy and were like tares among the wheat, or a wolf among the flock. The Lord sought to bless the pure in heart by identifying the deceptions of predators and poisonous serpents that were posing as Saints in the Church.

63:3–4 The Lord knows that which is necessary for the salvation of each of his children. Some will die and work out their salvation in the world of spirits. Others will remain in mortality seeking to overcome the natural man while still in the flesh.

Signs Come by Faith
DOCTRINE AND COVENANTS 63:7–12

63:8 *There are those among you who seek signs.* These Saints sought signs because faith had been rooted out of their heart by the spirit of adultery. "He who seeketh a sign is an adulterous person," declared the Prophet Joseph Smith; "and that principle is eternal, undeviating, and firm as the pillars of heaven; for whenever you see a man seeking after a sign, you may set it down that he is an adulterous man" (*Teachings of the Prophet Joseph Smith*, 157).

63:9 *Faith cometh not by signs.* The idea that faith could come by seeing a sign is both a delusion and a contradiction. Such a notion supposed that a sign will substitute for faith. In effect that attitude says, Remove the need for faith and I will have faith. By contrast it is understood among those having the Spirit that faith precedes the miracle—that the miracle is the reward of faith, not the author of it.

Exercising faith brings spiritual strength, but sign seeking does not. Ezra Booth was present when Joseph Smith healed the arthritic arm of Alice (or Elsa) Johnson. As a result of this experience, he joined the Church. Soon after his baptism, however, he began to find fault with the Prophet, apostatized, and eventually published newspaper articles against the Church (D&C 71).

President Joseph F. Smith declared, "Show me Latter-day Saints who have to feed upon miracles, signs and visions in order to keep them steadfast in the Church, and I will show you members of the Church who are not in good standing before God, and who are walking in slippery paths. It is not by marvelous manifestations unto us that we shall be established in the truth, but it is by humility and faithful obedience to the commandments and laws of God. When I as a boy first started out in the ministry, I would frequently go out and ask the Lord to show me some marvelous thing, in order that I might receive a testimony. But the Lord withheld marvels from me, and showed me the truth, line upon line, precept upon precept, here a little and there a little, until he made me to know the truth from the crown of my head to the soles of my feet, and until doubt and fear had been absolutely purged from me. He did not have to send an angel from the heavens to do this, nor did he have to speak with the trump of an archangel. By the whisperings of the still small voice of the Spirit of the living God, he gave to me the testimony I possess" (*Gospel Doctrine*, 7).

63:11 *Unto such he showeth no signs, only in wrath unto their condemnation.* Sherem and Korihor are examples of those who demanded signs to their own detriment. Both were struck down by the power of God; Sherem fell to the earth and died a few days later, while Korihor was struck dumb (Jacob 7:13–20; Alma 30:48–50). "When the Church of Jesus Christ of Latter-day Saints was first founded," explained George A. Smith, "you could see persons rise up and ask, 'What sign will you show us that we may be made to believe?' I recollect a Campbellite preacher who came to Joseph Smith, I think his name was Hayden. He came in and made himself known to Joseph, and said that he had come a considerable distance to be convinced of the truth. 'Why,' said he, 'Mr. Smith, I want to know the truth, and when I am convinced, I will spend all my talents and time in defending and spreading the doctrines of your religion, and I will give you to understand that to convince me is equivalent to convincing all my society, amounting to several hundreds.' Well, Joseph commenced laying before him the coming forth of the work, and the first principles of the Gospel, when Mr. Hayden exclaimed, 'O this is not the evidence I want, the evidence that I wish to have is a notable miracle; I want to see some powerful manifestation of the power of God, I want to see a notable miracle performed; and if you perform such a one, then I will believe with all my heart and soul, and will exert all my power and all my extensive influence to convince others; and if you will not perform a miracle of this kind, then I am your worst and bitterest enemy.' 'Well,' said Joseph, 'what will you have done? Will you be struck blind, or dumb? Will you be paralyzed, or will you have one hand withered? Take your choice, choose which you please, and in the name of the Lord Jesus Christ it shall be done.' 'That is not the kind of miracle I want,' said the preacher. 'Then, sir,' replied Joseph, 'I can perform none, I am not going to bring any trouble upon any body else, sir, to convince you. I will tell you what you make me think of—the very first person who asked a sign of the Savior, for it is written, in the New Testament, that Satan came to the Savior in the desert, when he was hungry with forty days' fasting, and said, 'If you be the Son of God, command these stones to be made bread.' And now,' said Joseph, 'the children of the devil and his servants have been asking for signs ever since; and when the people in that day continued asking him for signs to prove the truth of the Gospel which he preached, the Savior replied, 'It is a wicked and an adulterous generation that seeketh a sign,' &c.

"But the poor preacher had so much faith in the power of the Prophet that he daren't risk being struck blind, lame, dumb, or having one hand withered, or any thing of the kind. We have frequently heard men calling for signs without knowing actually what they did want. Could he not have tested the principles, and thus have ascertained the truth? But this is not the disposition of men of the religious world" (*Journal of Discourses*, 2:326–27).

The Adulterous in Heart Shall Deny the Faith and Be Cast into the Lake of Fire
DOCTRINE AND COVENANTS 63:13–19

63:15 *Their folly shall be made manifest.* Often at the most inopportune time unrepented immorality is made known. Adultery may be hidden for a season, but all wicked acts kept in darkness are eventually drawn out into the light of day. Even if our unrepented sins are not revealed in this life, certainly at the judgment all will be made manifest.

63:16 *They . . . shall deny the faith.* "Those who are guilty and do not repent in a short time become fault-finders, criticizing their brethren, then the principles of the Gospel, and finally become bitter in their souls against the work and those who are engaged in it. The most bitter opponents of the Church and the Gospel many times have been proved to be immoral and leading unclean lives" (Smith, *Church History and Modern Revelation*, 1:230).

63:17–18 Adultery and its companion, lust, are among the most dangerous of soul-destroying sins. Those who are unable to overcome the temptations of immorality "suffer the wrath of God on earth. These are they who suffer the vengeance of eternal fire. These are they who are cast down to hell and suffer the wrath of Almighty God" (D&C 76:104–6). Thus, the excruciating agony of seared flesh, of burning pain without reprieve, typifies their suffering. At the coming of Christ such sinners will be judged and "found under condemnation . . . and they live not again until the thousand years [of the Millennium] are ended, neither again, until the end of the earth" (D&C 88:100–101).

63:17 *Whosoever loveth and maketh a lie.* "Some sins cannot be separated," declared Elder Bruce R. McConkie; "they are inseparably welded together. There never was a sign seeker who was not an adulterer, just as there never was an adulterer who was not also a liar. Once Lucifer gets a firm hold over one human weakness, he also applies his power to kindred weaknesses" (*Doctrinal New Testament Commentary*, 1:277).

The Faithful Shall Receive an Inheritance upon the Transfigured Earth
DOCTRINE AND COVENANTS 63:20–21

63:20 *The day of transfiguration.* This phrase refers to the change that will come upon those who live on earth during the Millennium, the seventh day of the earth's temporal existence (D&C 77:6–7). This change will be like that experienced by the Three Nephites. Mormon explained that transfiguration is not the same as resurrection but came upon the three disciples "that they might not taste of death . . . that they might not suffer pain nor sorrow" (3 Nephi 28:38).

63:21 *The earth shall be transfigured.* When the Lord comes again, "the earth will be renewed and receive its paradisiacal glory" (Article of Faith 10). Isaiah prophesied that there will be "a new earth" during the Millennium (Isaiah 65:17). All forms of life—be it plant or animal—that exist on the earth during the Millennium must abide that glory.

Shown unto mine apostles upon the mount. This refers to the events on "an high mountain apart" (Matthew 17:1) to which Jesus took Peter, James, and John. In this revelation we learn that both the Savior his three most trusted apostles were transfigured at that time.

Which account the fulness ye have not yet received. We look to a future day when we as a Church have reached sufficient spiritual maturity to be entrusted with the full account of what took place on the Mount of Transfiguration. "It appears that Peter, James, and John received their own endowments while on the mountain (Smith, *Doctrines of Salvation*, 2:165). Peter says that while there, they 'received from God the Father honour and glory,' seemingly bearing out this conclusion. It also appears that it was while on the mount that they received the more sure word of prophecy, it then being revealed to them that they were sealed up unto eternal life (2 Pet. 1:16–19; D&C 131:5)" (McConkie, *Doctrinal New Testament Commentary*, 1:400).

Subsequent to the revelation of Doctrine and Covenants 63, Joseph Smith learned further details regarding the events at the Mount of Transfiguration as he worked on his inspired translation of the Bible. From this work we learn that John the Baptist was present on the mount as a spirit being (JST Mark 9:3), and that Moses and Elijah spoke to the Savior "of his death, and also his resurrection, which he should accomplish at Jerusalem" (JST Luke 9:31).

The Obedient Receive the Mysteries of the Kingdom
DOCTRINE AND COVENANTS 63:22–23

63:22–23 In the context of the gospel, mysteries are truths that can be known only by revelation. "The key of the mysteries of the kingdom, even the key of the knowledge of God" is reserved for those Saints who enter the house of the Lord and are there endowed (D&C 84:19).

"It is given unto many to know the mysteries of God," taught Alma; "nevertheless they are laid under a strict command that they shall not impart only according to the portion of his word which he doth grant unto the children of men, according to the heed and diligence which they give unto him. And therefore, he that will harden his heart, the same receiveth the lesser portion of the word; and he that will not harden his heart, to him is given the greater portion of the word, until it is given unto him to know the mysteries of God until he know them in full" (Alma 12:9–10).

Inheritances in Zion Are to Be Purchased
DOCTRINE AND COVENANTS 63:24–31

63:24 *Not in haste, lest there should be confusion, which bringeth pestilence.* "Behold, mine house is a house of order, saith the Lord God, and not a house of confusion" (D&C 132:8). In their zeal some Saints were ready to gather to Zion with no thought of providing the necessities of life once they arrived. This problem was addressed in an epistle that was published in *The Evening and the Morning Star*, the official Church newspaper, and sent to the Church from the elders in Zion in July 1833. "To see numbers of disciples come to this land, destitute of means to procure an inheritance, and much less the necessaries of life, awakens a sympathy in our bosoms of no ordinary feeling; and we should do injustice to the Saints were we to remain silent, when, perhaps, a few words, by way of advice, may be the means of instructing them, that hereafter great difficulties may be avoided. For the disciples to suppose that they can come to this land without ought to eat, or to drink, or to wear, or anything to purchase these necessaries with, is a vain thought. For them to suppose that the Lord will open the windows of heaven, and rain down angel's food for them by the way, when their whole journey lies through a fertile country, stored with the blessings of life from His own hand for them to subsist upon, is also vain. For them to suppose that their clothes and shoes will not wear out upon the journey, when the whole of it lies through a country where there are thousands of sheep from which wool in abundance can be procured to make them garments, and cattle upon a thousand hills, to afford leather for shoes, is just as vain" (in Smith, *History of the Church*, 1:382).

63:27 *I the Lord will that you should purchase the lands.* See commentary on Doctrine and Covenants 57:4.

63:28–29 Satan desires to shed the blood of the Saints. He plotted with Cain to take the life of the righteous Abel. He entered the hearts of Judas and the Jewish leaders to crucify the Christ. In our day he seeks opportunity to turn the hearts of the people against the kingdom of God. Nephi prophesied of our day, saying, "At that day shall he rage in the hearts of the children of men, and stir them up to anger against that which is good" (2 Nephi 28:20). Nephi also said that "the blood of the saints" would "cry from the ground against" those who warred against them (2 Nephi 28:10).

In his wisdom the Lord warned the Saints that they should not give the wicked occasion against them because of the means by which they obtained the land of their inheritance in Zion.

The Lord Decrees Wars, and the Wicked Slay the Wicked
DOCTRINE AND COVENANTS 63:32–35

63:32 *I am holding my Spirit from the inhabitants of the earth.* See commentary on Doctrine and Covenants 1:33.

63:32–35 "God is not pleased either with war," declared President Heber J. Grant and his counselors in the First Presidency, "or with the wickedness which always heralds it. When He uses war, it is to wipe out sin and unrighteousness" (Conference Report, October 1940, 6).

Wickedness is the cause of all war. When men harden their hearts against the light of Christ, it will cease to strive with them. They then are left to themselves, and Satan has power and dominion over them. They rise up against one another in senseless wars and bloodshed. When the Lord says that he has "decreed wars on the face of the earth," we must not suppose that he condones war. Rather, the decree is that as men wax cold in iniquity, war will be the result, war in which the wicked will slay one another. Brigham Young explained, "God has decreed and foreordained many things that have come to pass, and he will continue to do so; but when he decrees great blessings upon a nation or upon an individual they are decreed upon certain conditions. When he decrees great plagues and overwhelming destructions upon nations or people, those decrees come to pass because those nations and people will not forsake their wickedness and turn unto the Lord" (*Journal of Discourses*, 10:324).

63:34 *The saints also shall hardly escape.* The Lord warned the Saints that they too would be affected by the ravages of inhumanity and destruction. Regarding the great wars of devastation that are prophesied, Nephi promised the Saints of the latter days: "For the time soon cometh that the fulness of the wrath of God shall be poured out upon all the children of men; for he will not suffer that the wicked shall destroy the righteous. Wherefore, he will preserve the righteous by his power, even if it so be that the fulness of his wrath must come, and the righteous be preserved, even unto the destruction of their enemies by fire. Wherefore, the righteous need not fear; for thus saith the prophet, they shall be saved, even if it so be as by fire" (1 Nephi 22:16–17).

The Saints Are to Gather to Zion and Provide Moneys to Build It Up
DOCTRINE AND COVENANTS 63:36–48

63:36–48 These verses refer to the Isaac Morley farm and the Whitney store. Before the missionaries arrived in Kirtland, Isaac Morley and Titus Billings had joined with others of like mind in a communal order. They lived together on the Morley farm in a group known as "the family." When the Prophet Joseph Smith relocated from New York to Ohio, he stayed the first few months on the Morley farm and had a small log house built for him and his wife (D&C 41:7). Apparently, while Brother Morley traveled to Missouri, Titus Billings was left in charge of the farm.

The second property of importance was the store owned by Newel K.

Whitney. This store became the headquarters for the Church after the Prophet's second journey to Missouri to set up a branch of the United Firm in Zion (D&C 82–83; for more on the United Firm, see commentary on D&C 78:3–4). The store was on the main floor; the Prophet and his family occupied the second level as their home. Many revelations of the Doctrine and Covenants were received in the store, and the School of the Prophets was first held there (D&C 84–98, 101).

We Live in the Latter Days and the Millennium Is Nigh
DOCTRINE AND COVENANTS 63:49–54

63:50 *The age of man.* Isaiah identifies this period of time as one hundred years (Isaiah 65:20).

63:51 *Changed in the twinkling of an eye.* See commentary on Doctrine and Covenants 101:31.

63:53 *Speaking after the manner of the Lord, they are now nigh at hand.* The Lord alludes to the fact that the time of the Second Coming and resurrection from the dead was not near as man measures time. In the grand scheme of things, however, the Saints are living in the latter days, during the last dispensation of the gospel before the ushering in of the Millennium.

63:54 *Until that hour there will be foolish virgins among the wise.* The Church will have members numbered among both the righteous and the wicked until the Lord returns in glory. The day of separation is a work directed by the Master and his angels and not left to mortal man. Thus, there is no guarantee of salvation for those who claim membership in the Lord's church. The foolish members of the kingdom who fail to live the laws revealed by God will be cut off with the rest of the wicked. This revelation, directed to the members of the Church, identifies two sins that the Saints are commanded to repent of or be cast down to hell—adultery and lying (vv. 14–19).

This Is a Day of Warning
DOCTRINE AND COVENANTS 63:55–58

63:56 *His writing is not acceptable.* See commentary on Doctrine and Covenants 58:50.

63:57 *In meekness, to warn sinners to repentance.* "Let the elders be exceedingly careful about unnecessarily disturbing and harrowing up the feelings of the people," the Prophet Joseph Smith wrote to the Saints. "Remember that your business is to preach the gospel in all humility and meekness, and warn sinners to repent and come to Christ.

"Avoid contentions and vain disputes with men of corrupt minds, who do not desire to know the truth. Remember that 'it is a day of warning, and not a day of many words.' If they receive not your testimony in one place, flee to another, remembering to cast no reflections, nor throw out any bitter sayings. If you do your duty, it will be just as well with you, as though all men embraced the gospel" (*Teachings of the Prophet Joseph Smith*, 43).

63:58 *This is a day of warning.* Elder Ezra Taft Benson explained, "The voice of warning is unto all people by the mouths of His servants [D&C 1:4]. If this voice is not heeded, the angels of destruction will increasingly go forth, and the chastening hand of Almighty God will be felt upon the nations, as decreed, until a full end thereof will be the result. Wars, devastation, and untold suffering will be your lot except you turn unto the Lord in humble repentance. Destruction, even more terrible and far-reaching than attended the last great war, will come with certainty unless rulers and people alike repent and cease their evil and godless ways. God will not be mocked [D&C 63:58]. He will not permit the sins of sexual immorality, secret murderous combinations, the killing of the unborn, and disregard for all His holy commandments and the messages of His servants to go unheeded without grievous punishment for such wickedness. The nations of the world cannot endure in sin. The way of escape is clear. The immutable laws of God remain steadfastly in the heavens above. When men and nations refuse to abide by them, the penalty must follow. They will be wasted away. Sin demands punishment" (*This Nation Shall Endure*, 11).

The Lord's Name Is Taken in Vain by Those Who Use It without Authority
DOCTRINE AND COVENANTS 63:59–66

63:62 *Use the name of the Lord, and use it in vain, having not authority.* Elder Spencer W. Kimball wrote: "Presumptuous and blasphemous are they who purport to baptize, bless, marry, or perform other sacraments in the name of the Lord while in fact lacking his specific authorization. And no one can obtain God's authority from reading the Bible or from just a desire to serve the Lord, no matter how pure his motives" (*Miracle of Forgiveness*, 55). "Although a man should be baptized an hundred times it availeth him nothing" (D&C 22:2), unless it is done by one having authority. "Will I accept of an offering, saith the Lord, that is not made in my name? Or will I receive at your hands that which I have not appointed?" (D&C 132:9–10).

In all societies and among all peoples, to act falsely in someone else's name is a serious wrongdoing. Be it in the form of plagiarism, counterfeiting, forgery, or even blasphemy, such acts are offensive to the spirit of truth. Many have mistakenly professed the authority to teach the gospel of Christ and administer the ordinances of salvation, but despite their sincerity, this is a grievous offense against the kingdom of God. Those who would usurp the sacred right to teach the gospel or administer its ordinances, professing the power to act in the name of Christ, do so without authority if they have not been properly called, ordained, and sent forth by him whose gospel it is—and their works are vain. They are administering adulterated truths, doctrinal forgeries, and counterfeited ordinances. However well intended, their works are profane, lacking validity in this life and, as the Lord himself declared, are without "efficacy, virtue, or force in and after the resurrection from the dead" (D&C 132:7).

63:64 In like manner the Savior counseled his disciples: "The mysteries of the kingdom ye shall keep within yourselves; for it is not meet to give that which is holy unto the dogs; neither cast ye your pearls unto swine, lest they trample them under their feet. For the world cannot receive that which ye, yourselves, are not able to bear; wherefore ye shall not give your pearls unto them, lest they turn again and rend you. Say unto them, Ask of God; ask, and it shall be given you; seek, and ye shall find; knock, and it shall be opened unto you. For every one that asketh, receiveth; and he that seeketh, findeth; and unto him that knocketh, it shall be opened" (JST Matthew 7:10–13). The truths of the restored gospel are like pearls that are treasured by the pure in heart. We should teach no more to our listeners than they are prepared to receive.

By constraint of the Spirit. By definition, in the dictionary of Joseph Smith's day, *constraint* describes that which "compels" one to act or "to forebear action." Thus the "constraint of the Spirit" could involve either boldness of speech or restrained silence (Webster, *Dictionary*, 1828). It means to trust in the promptings of the Spirit.

63:65 *Seek them a home.* The Prophet and Sidney Rigdon prepared to move to Hiram, Ohio, soon after receiving this revelation. Joseph and his family were welcomed into the home of John and Alice (or Elsa) Johnson. Sidney's family lived in a log home located across the street from the Johnsons.

DOCTRINE AND COVENANTS 64

DATE: 11 SEPTEMBER 1831
PLACE: KIRTLAND, OHIO

During this time the Church at Kirtland, Ohio, experienced a limited apostasy. In addition to the problems of the Saints in Ohio who were seeking after signs and suffering the spiritual weaknesses caused by immorality (see D&C 63), Ezra Booth returned from his mission to Missouri, discontented with imperfections he had observed in the conduct of the Prophet Joseph Smith during their sojourn together in the land of Zion. Booth accused the Prophet of "lightness and levity," a "proneness to jesting and joking," and a "temper easily irritated" (Roberts, *Comprehensive History of the Church*, 1:266). In a bitter spirit of opposition to the Prophet Joseph Smith, Booth convinced some members to join him in withdrawing from the Church and later wrote letters to local newspapers attacking the Prophet (see D&C 71). By revelation, the Lord acknowledged that Joseph had weaknesses and warned the Saints of the debilitating spirit of faultfinding that existed among them.

The day after this revelation was received, 12 September 1831, Joseph Smith, who had just returned from Missouri, moved with his family from Kirtland to Hiram, Ohio, which was approximately thirty-five miles south. There he and his family took residence with John Johnson, a prosperous farmer, with the hope that sufficient peace would be afforded him to continue his labor on the inspired translation of the Bible.

For the next six and one-half months the Johnson home would serve as the headquarters of the Church. Some of the greatest visions and revelations vouchsafed to this dispensation were received at this home, including "the vision" or revelation on the degrees of glory. Much work on the translation of the Bible was accomplished, and fifteen of the revelations in the Doctrine and Covenants were received here. Such a marvelous outpouring of divine truth did not go unnoticed by the prince of darkness. Opposition came swiftly, with apostates joining forces with other settlers in an attempt to interrupt the growth of the Church in the area. This organized resistance led to the mobbing of Joseph Smith and Sidney Rigdon and forced their departure.

In July 1833, when a mob destroyed the printing press in Missouri to prevent the publication of the Book of Commandments, a few copies of what had been printed were salvaged. They included this section down to the verse that reads, "For, verily I say that the rebellious are not of the blood of Ephraim" (D&C 64:36).

The Saints Must Forgive One Another
DOCTRINE AND COVENANTS 64:1–11

64:2 *That ye should overcome the world.* The vision of the degrees of glory identifies those who inherit the celestial kingdom as those "who overcome by faith" (D&C 76:53), that is, those whose first loyalty is to God and the principles of his gospel. Many are called, the Prophet taught, but few are chosen. That is because their hearts are set too much upon the things of the world (D&C 121:34–36). The world loves, honors, and rewards its own. We recall these classic lines from Shakespeare, in which Thomas Wolsey, chancellor to three kings, lamented when in his old age he found himself shorn of his office:

> Had I but served my God with half the zeal
> I served my king, he would not in mine age
> Have left me naked to mine enemies.
> *(Henry VIII, III:ii)*

"Ye are of God," John reminded the meridian Saints, "because greater is he that is in you, than he that is in the world." Of those not of the covenant he said, "They are of the world: therefore speak they of the world, and the world heareth them. We are of God: he that knoweth God heareth us; he that is not of God heareth not us. Hereby know we the spirit of truth, and the spirit of error" (1 John 4:4–6).

64:4 *I have given unto you the kingdom.* This refers to the Church and kingdom of God as it had been established once again upon the earth. See commentary on Doctrine and Covenants 65.

64:5 *The keys . . . of the kingdom shall not be taken from . . . Joseph Smith.* See commentary on Doctrine and Covenants 28:7; 43:3; 90:2–3.

Inasmuch as he obeyeth mine ordinances. To obey the ordinances is to keep the commandments. See commentary on Doctrine and Covenants 52:14–21.

64:6 "I will give you one of the Keys of the mysteries of the Kingdom," said the Prophet Joseph Smith. "It is an eternal principle, that has existed with God from all eternity: That man who rises up to condemn others, finding fault with the Church, saying that they are out of the way, while he himself is righteous, then know assuredly, that that man is in the high road to apostasy; and if he does not repent, will apostatize, as God lives" (*Teachings of the Prophet Joseph Smith*, 156–57). One of the first examples of this principle in this dispensation is Ezra Booth. Soon after finding fault in the Prophet Joseph Smith he left the Church, became the first to publish anti-Mormon material, and was part of the mob that tarred and feathered the Prophet. See commentary on Doctrine and Covenants 64:15–16; the introduction to Doctrine and Covenants 71; and the commentary on Doctrine and Covenants 78:9; 121:16–46; 122.

64:7 *Sinned unto death.* "Whosoever bringeth forth evil works, the same becometh a child of the devil, for he hearkeneth unto his voice, and doth follow him. And whosoever doeth this must receive his wages of him; therefore, for his wages he receiveth death, as to things pertaining unto righteousness, being dead unto all good works" (Alma 5:41–42).

We read the following in 1 John 5:16–17: "If any man see his brother sin a sin which is not unto death, he shall ask, and he shall give him life for them that sin not unto death. There is a sin unto death: I do not say that he shall pray for it. All unrighteousness is sin: and there is a sin not unto death." Modern revelation declares: "I, the Lord, forgive sins unto those who confess their sins before me and ask forgiveness, who have not sinned unto death" (D&C 64:7). "For if we sin wilfully after that we have received the knowledge of the truth, there remaineth no more sacrifice for sins, but a certain fearful looking for of judgment and fiery indignation, which shall devour the adversaries" (Hebrews 10:26–27). "All manner of sin and blasphemy shall be forgiven unto men: but the blasphemy against the Holy Ghost shall not be forgiven unto men, . . . neither in this world, neither in the world to come" (Matthew 12:31–32).

"In the sense that 'no murderer hath eternal life abiding in him' (1 John 3:15), that is, that none guilty of premeditated murder can ever gain the celestial kingdom, murder also is a sin unto death. Such persons can never again enjoy spiritual life. It appears that there are some special circumstances under which adultery, in this sense, is also a sin unto death, as witness the Prophet's declaration: "If a man commit adultery, he cannot receive the celestial kingdom of God. Even if he is saved in any kingdom, it cannot be the celestial kingdom" (Smith, *History of the Church*, 6:81).

64:8 With the exception of Judas, who was from Judah, the twelve apostles chosen by the Savior were from Galilee; a number of them were relatives, and all were neighbors. They would have been well acquainted with each other at the time of their call to the apostleship, and with that association would have come ample opportunity—for life always seems to afford such—to give and take offense. Some of these matters remained unresolved "in their hearts," which would both restrain the Spirit and canker the soul. For this, the Savior said, they were sorely chastened.

The same circumstances existed among these early brethren of the latter-day Church; such circumstances are common in small branches of the Church, as they are in small communities. Some of the early brethren had been living together in a communal organization in which they had attempted to own all things in common. The situation was rife with opportunity to either take or give offense. Thus the lesson learned by their counterparts in earlier generations seems most applicable.

In what we have come to know as the Sermon on the Mount, which was the ordination sermon for the newly called apostles in the meridian dispensation, Christ said, "If thou bring thy gift to the altar, and there rememberest that thy brother hath ought against thee; leave there thy gift before the altar, and go thy way; first be reconciled to thy brother, and then come and offer thy gift" (Matthew 5:23–24). The remembrance Christ speaks of is not that you have something against your brother, for the assumption is that you already would have corrected such feelings; instead, one coming to the altar may remember that his brother harbors bad feelings toward him. Such feelings may be unjustified; nevertheless, the responsibility rests with the true Saint to go to his brother and see that the matter is corrected.

64:8–9 Teaching the principles presented here, President Boyd K. Packer used the following illustration:

"There are spiritual disorders and spiritual diseases that can cause intense suffering.

"If you suffer from worry, from grief or shame or jealousy or disappointment or envy, from self-recrimination or self-justification, consider this lesson taught to me many years ago by a patriarch. He was as saintly a man as I have ever known. He was steady and serene, with a deep spiritual strength that many drew upon.

"He knew just how to minister to others who were suffering. On a number of occasions I was present when he gave blessings to those who were sick or who were otherwise afflicted. His was a life of service, both to the Church and to his community. . . .

"He grew up in a little community with a desire to make something of himself. He struggled to get an education.

"He married his sweetheart, and presently everything was just right. He was well employed, with a bright future. They were deeply in love, and she was expecting their first child.

"The night the baby was to be born, there were complications. The only doctor was somewhere in the countryside tending to the sick.

"After many hours of labor, the condition of the mother-to-be became desperate.

"Finally the doctor was located. In the emergency, he acted quickly and soon had things in order. The baby was born and the crisis, it appeared, was over.

"Some days later, the young mother died from the very infection that the doctor had been treating at another home that night. . . . Everything was not right now; everything was all wrong. He had lost his wife. He had no way to tend both the baby and his work.

"As the weeks wore on, his grief festered. 'That doctor should not be allowed to practice,' he would say. 'He brought that infection to my wife. If he had been careful, she would be alive today.'

"He thought of little else, and in his bitterness, he became threatening. Today, no doubt, he would have been pressed by many others to file a malpractice suit. And there are lawyers who would see in his pitiable condition only one ingredient—money!

"But that was another day, and one night a knock came at his door. A little girl said simply, 'Daddy wants you to come over. He wants to talk to you.'

"'Daddy' was the stake president. A grieving heartbroken young man went to see his spiritual leader.

"This spiritual shepherd had been watching his flock and had something to say to him.

"The counsel from that wise servant was simply, 'John, leave it alone. Nothing you do about it will bring her back. Anything you do will make it worse. John, leave it alone.'

"My friend told me then that this had been his trial—his Gethsemane. How could he leave it alone? Right was right! A terrible wrong had been committed and somebody must pay for it. It was a clear case.

"But he struggled in agony to get hold of himself. And finally, he determined that whatever else the issues were, he should be obedient.

"Obedience is powerful spiritual medicine. It comes close to being a cure-all.

"He determined to follow the counsel of that wise spiritual leader. He would leave it alone.

"Then he told me, 'I was an old man before I understood! It was not until I was an old man that I could finally see a poor country doctor— overworked, underpaid, run ragged from patient to patient, with little medicine, no hospital, few instruments, struggling to save lives, and suc-ceeding for the most part.

" 'He had come in a moment of crisis, when two lives hung in the bal-ance, and had acted without delay.

" 'I was an old man,' he repeated, 'before I finally understood! I would have ruined my life,' he said, 'and the lives of others.'

"Many times he had thanked the Lord on his knees for a wise spiri-tual leader who counseled simply, 'John, leave it alone'" ("Balm of Gilead," 17–18).

The Unrepentant Are to Be Tried in Church Disciplinary Councils
DOCTRINE AND COVENANTS 64:12–22

64:12 *Him that repenteth not of his sins, and confesseth them not.* See commentary on Doctrine and Covenants 58:42–43.

64:13 *That ye may be justified in the eyes of the law.* Compassion is not a godly virtue when used to excuse a transgressor's accountability before the law. Not only does it deny the sinner the opportunity to properly repent, but it also turns the supposedly compassionate person into a transgressor, because in such a course they too have disregarded God's law. On the other hand, to administer God's law without love and com-passion would be to misuse and misapply his law. Ours is a God both of law (3 Nephi 15:9) and of love (1 John 4:8) and neither attribute can be at odds with the other in the divine nature. To be justified in the eyes of the law is to have honored the law and by so doing to have honored the Lawgiver. To wink at the law is to have dismissed both the law and its Author as unwise and unjust.

64:15–16 Ezra Booth and Isaac Morley were called to serve as missionary companions in traveling to Independence, Missouri (D&C 52:23). They had angered the Lord in that they had "kept not the law, neither the commandment." A specific knowledge of what they did or did not do has not been preserved for us. It appears that they imbibed a selfish and critical spirit relative to what they had been asked to do. Isaac Morley repented of that spirit and became a valiant servant of the Lord. Ezra Booth, on the other hand, nurtured his association with the spirit of darkness until he became its servant. Six months later he joined the mob that tarred and feathered Joseph Smith (George A. Smith, *Journal of Discourses*, 11:6–7).

64:17 *Edward Partridge.* See commentary on Doctrine and Covenants 41:9, "Ordained a bishop."

64:20–21 When the revelation was given identifying Independence, Missouri, as the "center place" or "seat" of Zion (D&C 57:3), the place to which the Saints were to gather and build a temple to their God, the eyes and hearts of the Latter-day Saints turned to that place and they felt a natural anxiousness to unite with other Saints there. The time to leave Kirtland had not yet come, however, for it had not yet filled its destiny. Thus some were called to sell their land and leave while others were directed to stay.

Kirtland was, according to the language of this revelation, to remain a "strong hold" for the work of the Lord for another five years. Explaining why this was necessary, President Joseph Fielding Smith said: "It was in that land where the first temple in this dispensation was to be built. In that Temple the essential keys of restoration were to be revealed. It seems apparent that had all the people moved to Zion in Missouri at that time, the building of a temple would have been frustrated by the enemies of the people. . . . The restoration of the keys of the Priesthood held by the ancient prophets was essential to the progress of the Church. The Lord decreed that a house to his name should be reared in Kirtland where he could come and where he could send his messengers with these keys of power. The building of such a temple required time, and while the elders went to work with their might this house was not ready for dedication until March 27, 1836. It was on the third day of April 1836, that the Lord appeared in that house and where Elias, Moses and Elijah appeared and conferred the keys of their dispensations and authorities. How many other messengers came at that time we do not know. We know, however, that it was necessary that every key and authority should be revealed. Some were revealed, of necessity, before there was temple to which these messengers could come, but it was according to the divine plan that keys of this nature should be revealed in a house built to the name of the Lord. The revelation in which the Lord called upon the Saints to keep a strong hold in Kirtland, was given Sept. 11, 1831. It was in March 1836 that the house of the Lord was dedicated and the following April when the holy keys were bestowed. After this glorious event, the members of the Church were at liberty to remove to Zion. In fact there followed a few months later an apostasy, and many turned away from the Church, but some were saved, and they were under the necessity of fleeing from the place. However, the Spirit of the Lord prevailed until his work in that place was accomplished and the appointed time had passed" (*Church History and Modern Revelation*, 1:237).

It may well be that these verses have an important application in our day. Knowing that in time certain of the Saints will be called to return to Missouri, that the temple will be built there, and that Independence will become the "center place" of Zion, some acting independent of priesthood direction have chosen to return to that area in the attempt to assure themselves of some role in the events prophesied to take place there. We note with special interest that those who were to migrate to Zion in that early day were specifically named and called to do so by revelation given through the Prophet. Such was the order of things until Kirtland had fulfilled its purpose. Then the general invitation was given for all desiring to unite with the Saints in Missouri to do so. We would expect the same pattern to be followed in that future day of return and suggest that those who have acted on their own, going before they have been called, will find themselves more of a hindrance to the Lord's purpose than a help.

He That Is Tithed Shall Not Be Burned
DOCTRINE AND COVENANTS 64:23–25

64:23 *Now it is called today until the coming of the Son of Man.* We leave the past behind us; the future is in the hands of God; only the present, or "today," is given to us to act upon. The present is our stewardship, and we must prove ourselves wise stewards. With this thought in mind, Alma said, "The day of this life is the day for men to perform their labors." And thus he said, "I beseech of you that ye do not procrastinate the day of your repentance until the end; for after this day of life, which is given us to prepare for eternity, behold, if we do not improve our time while in this life, then cometh the night of darkness wherein there can be no labor performed" (Alma 34:32–33).

A *day for the tithing of my people.* This first reference to tithing in the revelations of the Restoration does not carry the same meaning we have given that principle in our day. This revelation was given while the Church was living the law of consecration and thus is being used in the broad and general sense of giving liberally, of sacrificing without counting the cost. The law of tithing as it is presently practiced among the Saints was revealed in 1838 after the Saints had been driven out of Zion and were no longer practicing the law of consecration as it applied to the stewardship of lands. See commentary on Doctrine and Covenants 119.

He that is tithed shall not be burned at his coming. That is to say, he that serves the Lord with all his heart, might, mind, and strength will find safety in that great and dreadful day. This text is not suggesting that all but faithful Latter-day Saints will be burned as stubble when Christ returns. The earth is at present subject to a telestial law. When Christ returns to usher in the millennial era, the earth will abide by a terrestrial and paradisiacal law. At that time all that is of a telestial order will be destroyed, while that which is terrestrial or celestial will be preserved.

64:24 *They that do wickedly shall be as stubble.* "The scriptures abound in declarations and reiterations, in repeated and solemn affirmations of the great fact that the day of the Lord's coming will be a day of glory and a day of terror—of glory and recompense unto those who are living righteously, and a day of terror unto the proud and unto all who do wickedly. Now, many have asked, do we interpret that scripture as meaning that in the day of the Lord's coming, all who are not members of the Church shall be burned, or otherwise destroyed, and only this little body of men and women, very small compared with the uncounted hosts of men now living, shall be spared the burning and shall escape destruction? I think not so. I do not think we are justified in putting that interpretation upon the Lord's word, for He recognizes every man according to the integrity of his heart, and men who have not been able to understand the Gospel or who have not had opportunity of learning it and knowing of it will not be counted as the willfully sinful who are fit only to be burned as stubble; but the proud, who lift themselves in the pride of their hearts and rise above the word of God and become a law unto themselves and who willfully and with knowledge deny the saving virtues of the atonement of Christ, and who are seeking to lead others away from the truth will be dealt with by

Him according to both justice and mercy" (Talmage, Conference Report, April 1916, 128).

The Saints Are Warned against Debt to Their Enemies
DOCTRINE AND COVENANTS 64:26–33

64:26–33 In these verses Newel K. Whitney and Sidney Gilbert are warned not to get into debt to their enemies. They are reminded that the Lord has power to provide for his own. Elders Whitney and Gilbert are acknowledged as his agents and can conduct business on his behalf, though they are to do so according to his will. They are to avoid discouragement as they lay the foundations of Zion, remembering that "out of small things proceedeth that which is great" (33).

64:31–32 Some members of the Church were losing faith because the redemption of Zion had not come according to their expectations. Here the Lord reminds us that his words are sure, and that he does not fail. Nevertheless, such things happen according to his timetable, not our own.

The Rebellious Shall Be Cut Off
DOCTRINE AND COVENANTS 64:34–36

64:34 *The Lord requireth the heart and a willing mind.* It was the desire of the Lord that his people establish Zion; to do so required a people of "one heart and one mind," a people who could dwell together "in righteousness," among whom there would be neither poverty nor idleness (Moses 7:18; D&C 68:30).

The measure of the worth of a man or woman, that is, their worth in the sight of God, is found in their hearts (1 Samuel 16:7). The true state of their hearts is expressed in their love of truth, their love of righteousness, and a desire to do those things that would please their Eternal Father. Christ, the "Beloved Son" of the Father, or as Mormon stated it the "most Beloved" of the Father, was beloved because of his willingness to do the will of the Father (3 Nephi 11:7; Mormon 5:14; Mosiah 15:7). Many profess a love for Christ, but as he said, "They draw near to me with their lips, but their hearts are far from me, they teach for doctrines the commandments of men, having a form of godliness, but they deny the power thereof" (Joseph Smith–History 1:19). To those of his own day he said, "If ye love me, keep my commandments" (John 14:15). He then added, "He that hath my commandments, and keepeth them, he it is that loveth me: and he that loveth me shall be loved of my Father, and I will love him, and will manifest myself to him" (John 14:21).

Only when we have given our hearts to God is anything else that we give acceptable to him. We must have the attitude encouraged by so many of our leaders: It is the kingdom of God or nothing. "Zion, first and foremost," said President Joseph F. Smith. "Seek first the kingdom of God and His righteousness, that all other things may be added in the due time of the Lord, and in accordance with His pleasure. These are principles that should pervade the minds and hearts of all the Latter-day Saints. . . .

"For my own part I would like to so live that with open heart and mind, before God and all men, if I were required to go to the ends of the earth and remain there proclaiming the Gospel of Christ, that I would be willing to do it; or if I were asked to give up what I possess in the world, for the building up of Zion, for some special necessary purpose, for advancing the cause of Zion in the world, that I would be prepared and ready to say, Father, here is all that I have; I place it upon the altar freely and give it for the benefit of Thy kingdom upon the earth and for the advancement of Thy cause. I would like to live so that this would indeed be my determination and that I would be able, if the requirement were made, to carry it out not only without regret but with pleasure. . . .

"I want to live so that, no matter what any other man in the world may do or say, so far as I am concerned there is but this one thing for me to do, and that is to be true to the covenants I have made with God and my brethren, to stand firm and steadfast for the advancement of Zion and for the building up of the kingdom of God in the earth" (Conference Report, April 1909, 3–5).

64:35 Zion was to be a holy and consecrated land. The Lord had expressly said, "My law shall be kept on this land" (D&C 58:19). Those who would not keep the law must of necessity be "cut off out of the land of Zion" (D&C 64:35), that is, they would have no right to an inheritance there, for the few can bring "the whole church under condemnation. . . . For shall the children of the kingdom pollute my holy land?" the Lord asked. "Verily, I say unto you, Nay" (D&C 84:55, 59).

All who will be a part of a covenant community must keep their covenants, for their failure is hurtful not just to themselves but to the whole of the community. These verses remind us that our covenants are not simply between ourselves and God, but they also involve promises to the community of Saints. Indeed, the Saints would yet learn that they had covenant obligations to the Saints of dispensations past and to those of their kindred who had lived when the gospel was not on the earth (D&C 128:15, 18).

The breaking of covenants not only hurts the transgressor but diminishes the community of believers of which they are a part. The oft-quoted text from Malachi is seen more clearly when we recognize that the Lord is addressing himself to the nation of Israel rather than particular individuals within that nation. "Even from the days of your fathers ye are gone away from mine ordinances, and have not kept them. Return unto me, and I will return unto you, saith the Lord of hosts. But ye said, Wherein shall we return? Will a man rob God? Yet ye have robbed me. But ye say, Wherein have we robbed thee? In tithes and offerings. *Ye are cursed with a curse: for ye have robbed me, even this whole nation.* Bring ye all the tithes into the storehouse, that there may be meat in mine house, and prove me now herewith, saith the Lord of hosts, if I will not open you the windows of heaven, and pour you out a blessing, that there shall not be room enough to receive it. And I will rebuke the devourer for your sakes, and he shall not destroy the fruits of your ground; neither shall your vine cast her fruit before the time in the field, saith the Lord of hosts. And all nations shall call you [the covenant people or nation of Israel] blessed: for ye shall be a delightsome land, saith the Lord of hosts" (Malachi 3:7–12; emphasis added).

64:36 *The rebellious are not of the blood of Ephraim.* As a host of scriptures attests, the great promise of the last days is both the gathering and redemption of Israel. Israel is gathered by embracing the covenant of salvation restored through the Prophet Joseph Smith. She will be redeemed when each of her tribes returns to its land of promise and temples are built in both the Jerusalem of old and in the New Jerusalem. The promise of an inheritance in the New World rests with the descendants of Joseph or his sons, Ephraim and Manasseh. This promise is real and rests with his literal seed. In them is to be found believing blood and a propensity to observe the statutes of the Lord. Thus those who rebel against the laws of the Lord as revealed to the inhabitants of Zion identify themselves as not being children of the covenant or "of the blood of Ephraim."

This was the last verse printed for the Book of Commandments before mobbers destroyed the press. The irony is poignant. Those seeking to destroy the Saints are here being told that in the due course of the Lord, they themselves will be driven from the land of Missouri and will have no claim upon it.

The Church Shall Judge the Nations
DOCTRINE AND COVENANTS 64:37–40

64:37–40 In an attempt to encourage the members of the Church at Corinth to solve their own difficulties rather than appeal to the secular courts, the apostle Paul asked, "Do ye not know that the saints shall judge the world?" And again he asked, "Know ye not that we shall judge angels?" (1 Corinthians 6:2–3). John the Revelator referred to this principle when he said, "And I saw thrones," referring to those who have been exalted, "and they sat upon them, and judgment was given unto them" (Revelation 20:4). Thus it appears that all who are to obtain a crown of glory will be placed in a position of judgment over those who fail to obtain such a crown.

However, before Zion will be placed in a position to judge the world she must first set her own house in order. If there are any not worthy of the offices to which they have been called, be they apostles, prophets, or those serving at any level in the Church, they must be replaced by those who will honor the call given to them. It will be remembered that Paul, writing to the Saints in Corinth, warned that there were "false apostles, deceitful workers, transforming themselves into the apostles of Christ" (2 Corinthians 11:13). The Church must cleanse itself before it can rightfully sit in judgment on the world.

Joseph Smith said, "It has been the design of Jehovah, from the commencement of the world, and is His purpose now, to regulate the affairs of the world in His own time, to stand as a head of the universe, and take the reins of government in His own hand. When that is done, judgment will be administered in righteousness; anarchy and confusion will be destroyed, and 'nations will learn war no more'" (*Teachings of the Prophet Joseph Smith*, 250–51).

Zion Shall Flourish
DOCTRINE AND COVENANTS 64:41–43

64:41 *Zion shall flourish.* "Who, let me ask, unless he was inspired of the Lord, speaking by the gift and power of God, at that remote period of the Church's history, when our numbers were few, when we had no influence, name or standing in the world—who, I would ask, under the circumstances in which we were placed when this prediction was made, could have uttered such words unless God inspired him?" So queried

Joseph F. Smith. To his own question he responded, "Zion is, indeed, flourishing on the hills, and it is rejoicing on the mountains, and we who compose it are gathering and assembling together unto the place appointed. I now ask this congregation if they cannot see that this pre-diction (which was made many years before the idea prevailed at all among this people that we should ever migrate and gather out to these mountain valleys) has been and is being literally fulfilled? If there were no other prophecy uttered by Joseph Smith, fulfilment of which could be pointed to, this alone would be sufficient to entitle him to the claim of being a true prophet" (*Gospel Doctrine*, 486–87).

On another occasion President Smith added to that prophecy of Joseph Smith his own prophetic words: "May Israel flourish upon the hills and rejoice upon the mountains, and assemble together unto the place which God has appointed, and there prosper, multiply and replenish the earth, and thence spread abroad throughout the land; for the time will come when we will find it necessary to fulfil the purposes of the Almighty by occupying the land of Zion in all parts of it. We are not destined to be confined to the valleys of the mountains. Zion is destined to grow, and the time will come when we will cry aloud, more than we do today, 'Give us room that we may dwell!'" (*Gospel Doctrine*, 75).

64:43 *Fear because of her terrible ones.* This prophecy is most remark-able, since it came in a day when the enemies of the Church inflicted pain and suffering upon the Saints with impunity. Yet, the promise was that sometime in the future all the nations of the earth would find reason to fear the power held by the elders of Israel. "Their arm shall be my arm," the Lord promised, "and I will be their shield and their buckler; and I will gird up their loins, and they shall fight manfully for me; and their enemies shall be under their feet; and I will let fall the sword in their behalf, and by the fire of mine indignation will I preserve them" (D&C 35:14).

DOCTRINE AND COVENANTS 65

DATE: 30 OCTOBER 1831
PLACE: HIRAM, OHIO

This revelation was designated by the Prophet as a "prayer" (Smith, *History of the Church*, 1:218). When we have so accorded our thoughts with those of heaven that our prayers are dictated by the Holy Ghost, we have the perfect assurance that our petitions will be honored. Such, for instance was the promise given to Nephi, son of Helaman, to whom the Lord said, "All things shall be done unto thee according to thy word, for thou shalt not ask that which is contrary to my will" (Helaman 10:5). A perfect illustration of this principle in our day is the prayer offered by President Spencer W. Kimball when he, the First Presidency, and the Quorum of the Twelve united in prayer in the house of the Lord to seek the privilege of granting the priesthood to all worthy male members of the Church. See commentary on Official Declaration 2, page 1154.

This revelation refers to the prophecy of Daniel that the God of heaven will set up his kingdom again upon the earth in the last days and announces that the fulfillment of that prophecy has commenced in the restoration of the gospel. Speaking of himself, the Prophet Joseph Smith said, "I calculate to be one of the instruments of setting up the kingdom of Daniel by the word of the Lord, and I intend to lay a foundation that will revolutionize the whole world" (*Teachings of the Prophet Joseph Smith*, 366). This section is also an important commentary on Matthew 6:10, wherein the Savior prayed, as part of the Lord's Prayer, that the kingdom of his Father, or "the kingdom of heaven," as it is here described, might be established on the earth. Thus the Prophet's prayer and the Lord's Prayer become one.

Keys of the Kingdom Are Committed to Man

DOCTRINE AND COVENANTS 65:1–2

65:1 *A voice as of one sent down from on high.* The "one" spoken of here is the Prophet Joseph Smith, whose testimony of the Father and the

472

Son and of the restoration of the gospel will yet go to those of every nation, kindred, tongue, and people. Every faithful missionary is to declare these truths and echo the testimony of the Prophet called to stand at the head of this, the greatest of all gospel dispensations.

Prepare ye the way of the Lord, make his paths straight. This language, which is Isaiah's, is descriptive of the ministry of John the Baptist and of Joseph Smith (Isaiah 40:3; Matthew 3:3; John 1:23; 1 Nephi 10:8). The path of the Lord is made "straight" by the declaration of "the gospel of repentance, and of baptism . . . for the remission of sins" (D&C 13:1; see also 133:17. As only a straight course will take us to the Lord, so only a straight course will bring the Lord to us. In all things pertaining to the Church and kingdom of God there must be discipline and order.

No message—save it be the gospel of Christ—can prepare the children of men to receive Christ. No messenger can declare that gospel unless the God of heaven has commissioned him. "I have sent mine everlasting covenant into the world," the Savior said, "to be a light to the world, and to be a standard for my people, and for the Gentiles to seek to it, and to be a messenger before my face to prepare the way before me" (D&C 45:9). And to Joseph Smith he said, "This generation [meaning dispensation] shall have my word through you" (D&C 5:10). See commentary on Doctrine and Covenants 33:10.

65:2 This verse announces that Daniel's prophecy of the establishment of God's kingdom in the last days is about to be fulfilled in the restoration of the gospel through Joseph Smith. This kingdom, the prophecy holds, is destined to "break in pieces and consume all" earthly kingdoms and "stand forever." Surely this would have seemed an awesome thing to the then-infant Church struggling for survival in Kirtland, Ohio, and Jackson County, Missouri.

It will be recalled that Nebuchadnezzar, the king of Babylon, in the second year of his reign "dreamed dreams" that greatly troubled him. His diviners could not tell him the dreams or interpret them for him (Daniel 2:5a). Angry, Nebuchadnezzar ordered that they be cut into pieces and their houses made into dunghills. Upon learning this, Daniel asked the king to give him time before he sought to give the interpretation. He then united in importuning the heavens with his companions (Shadrach, Meshach, and Abed-nego) and had the secret revealed to him in a night vision. Daniel then sought audience with the king, where he first rehearsed the particulars of Nebuchadnezzar's dream and then gave its interpretation.

That which the king had seen was "a great image" with a head of fine gold, breast and arms of silver, belly and thighs of brass, legs of iron, and feet of iron and clay. Then he saw a stone "cut out without hands" "which smote the image upon his feet," breaking them into pieces. "Then was the iron, the clay, the brass, the silver, and the gold, broken to pieces together, and became like the chaff of the summer threshing floors; and the wind carried them away, that no place was found for them: and the stone that smote the image became a great mountain, and filled the whole earth."

"Thou art this head of gold," Daniel explained to Nebuchadnezzar, "and after thee shall arise another kingdom inferior to thee, and another third kingdom of brass, which shall bear rule over all the earth." Then was to come a fourth kingdom with the strength of iron; that kingdom would be divided and the iron would be mixed with clay. "And in the days of these kings," Daniel explained, "shall the God of heaven set up a kingdom, which shall never be destroyed: and the kingdom shall not be left to other people, but it shall break in pieces and consume all these kingdoms, and it shall stand for ever. Forasmuch as thou sawest that the stone was cut out of the mountain without hands, and that it brake in pieces the iron, the brass, the clay, the silver, and the gold; the great God hath made known to the king what shall come to pass hereafter: and the dream is certain, and the interpretation thereof sure" (Daniel 2:1, 44–45).

By interpretation, we would understand that the kingdom of Nebuchadnezzar, which bore rule over all the earth, was the head of gold. Orson Pratt said, "'After thee shall come another kingdom represented by the breast and the arms of silver.' That is the Medo-Persian kingdom. After that another kingdom still inferior, called the kingdom of brass, forasmuch as gold is better than silver, silver more precious than brass, so these kingdoms that were to arise, to succeed each other, were to be inferior as time should pass along. The third kingdom, of brass, represented the Macedonian empire; then after that another kingdom, great and terrible, whose legs were of iron, strong and powerful. The fourth kingdom bore rule over the earth; that is admitted, by all commentators, to be the great Roman Empire, and by the division of the Roman empire into two divisions, representing the legs, and afterwards into the feet and toes. . . . The present modern kingdoms of Europe that have grown out from the Roman empire represent the last vestiges of that great and powerful empire of Rome; that is, it fills up and makes the image complete" (*Journal of Discourses*, 15:71).

The keys of the kingdom of God are committed unto man on the earth. The keys of the kingdom were committed to Joseph Smith and Oliver Cowdery in the spring of 1829 by Peter, James, and John, who received them at the hands of the Lord himself (D&C 27:12–13; 128:20–21).

The stone . . . cut out of the mountain. The stone cut out of the mountain is the latter-day kingdom of God as it was restored by the Prophet Joseph Smith.

As to how the stone is to fill the whole earth, Orson Pratt observed that the fulfillment of the prophecy would not come through the use of weapons of warfare, for the "kingdom or stone cut out of the mountain without hands is a power superior to that of carnal weapons—the power of truth, for the kingdom of God cannot be organized on the earth without truth being sent down from heaven, without authority being given from the Most High; without men again being called to the holy Priesthood and Apostleship, and sent forth to publish the truth in its naked simplicity and plainness to the inhabitants of the earth. This truth will be the weapon of warfare, this authority and power sent down from heaven will go forth and will proclaim the message of the everlasting Gospel, the Gospel of the latter-day kingdom, publishing it first among the nations that compose the feet and toes of the great image. Will they be broken to pieces? Yes, when this message is published to them. When they are sufficiently warned, when the servants of God have gone forth in obedience to his commandments, and published in their towns, villages, cities, States and governments these sacred and holy principles that God Almighty has sent down from heaven in the latter times, it will leave all people, nations and tongues that hear the Gospel, and the principles and message pertaining to that kingdom, without any excuse. It will be a warning that will be everlasting on the one hand, or on the other, either to the bringing of the people to repentance, reformation and obedience to the Gospel of the kingdom, or the judgments which are predicted in this prophecy of Daniel will be poured out upon the heads of those nations and kingdoms, and they will become like the chaff of the summer threshing floor, even all those kingdoms that compose the great image; for be it known that the remnants of the Babylonish kingdom, represented by the head of gold, still exist in Asia; the remnants of the silver kingdom, of the brass kingdom, and the kingdom of iron still have their existence; but when the Lord Almighty shall fulfil this prophecy, the toes and feet and legs of iron of that great image, or all these kingdoms, will be broken in pieces, and they will become like the chaff of the summer threshing floor; the wind will carry them away and no place will be found for them" (Journal of Discourses, 15:72).

Without hands. The expression "without hands," as found in the prophecy of Daniel, is intended to emphasize that the kingdom to be established in the last days will come by divine agency, not by the councils of men. It is to rest upon a new revelation, not upon the wisdom of ecumenical councils.

The Millennial Kingdom Shall Join the Kingdom of God on Earth

DOCTRINE AND COVENANTS 65:3–6

65:3 *Prepare ye the supper of the Lamb, make ready for the Bridegroom.* This imagery is that of the New Testament (Matthew 22:2; Revelation 19:9). Christ is both Lamb and Bridegroom; the bride is his Church, for whom the time of his coming will be a time of celebration. Missionaries now encompass the earth issuing the invitation to attend the marriage feast and rejoice with the King's Son. Those who clothe themselves in the robes of righteousness, or the wedding garment, will be accorded that privilege (Matthew 22:11–14).

65:4 *Make known his wonderful works among the people.* Isaiah described the restoration as a "marvellous work and a wonder" (Isaiah 29:14). Habakkuk described it by saying we would be called upon to "wonder marvelously" (Habakkuk 1:5; 3 Nephi 21:9).

65:6 It would be from this verse that the section obtains its name "the prayer." Here, the Prophet addresses the heavens with the plea that the stone seen by Daniel (meaning the kingdom of God) will go forth and fill the whole earth, that the day of the millennial kingdom (spoken of here as the kingdom of heaven) might come.

The kingdom of heaven. This refers to the political kingdom that will be established during the millennial era when the Lord has made a full end of all nations (Daniel 2:35, 44; D&C 87:6).

DOCTRINE AND COVENANTS 66

DATE: 29 OCTOBER 1831
PLACE: HIRAM, OHIO

In August 1831 William E. McLellin, then twenty-five years of age and recently widowed, was teaching school in Paris, Illinois. It was near this small town that he heard Harvey Whitlock and David Whitmer bear testimony of the Book of Mormon and the restored gospel in an outdoor meeting. Fascinated with their message, he closed his school with the idea of going to Missouri to meet the Prophet Joseph Smith. In Independence, Missouri, he met the Prophet's brother Hyrum, with whom he went into the woods and had a four-hour discussion about the events surrounding the Restoration. The following day he asked Hyrum to baptize him. Four days later he was ordained an elder. It was not, however, until he had traveled back to Kirtland, Ohio, to attend a conference that he first saw Joseph Smith. At this conference, held on 25 October 1831, McLellin was ordained a high priest. On Saturday, 29 October, he obtained the blessing from the Prophet here recorded. Of that occasion he said, "This day the Lord condescended to hear my prayer and give me a revelation of his will, through his prophet or seer (Joseph)—And these are the words which I wrote from his mouth." It is of particular interest that he recorded his own blessing (*Journals of William E. McLellin*, 45; spelling and syntax standardized).

In 1848 after McLellin's disaffection from the Church and after Brigham Young had led the Saints west, McLellin wrote of this occasion that "I had expected and believed that when I saw Bro. Joseph, I should receive [a revelation] and I went before the Lord in secret, and on my knees asked him to reveal the answer to five questions through his Prophet, and that too without his having any knowledge of my having made such request. I now testify in the fear of God, that every question which I had thus lodged in the ears of the Lord of Sabbaoth, were answered to my full and entire satisfaction. I desired it for a testimony of Joseph's inspiration. And I to this day consider it to me an evidence which I cannot refute" (*Journals of William E. McLellin*, 57; spelling and syntax standardized).

Although we have no record of the questions of which William E. McLellin speaks, they evidence themselves, at least in part, by a thoughtful reading of the revelation.

The Everlasting Covenant Is the Fulness of the Gospel
DOCTRINE AND COVENANTS 66:1–4

66:1 *Received my truths.* William E. McLellin had prayerfully sought the truth. "I rose early," he records in his journal on 20 August 1831, "and betook myself to earnest prayer to God to direct me into truth; and from all the light that I could gain by examinations, searches and researches I was bound as an honest man to acknowledge the truth and validity of the book of Mormon and also that I had found the people of the Lord—the living Church of Christ. Consequently as soon as we took breakfast I told Elder H. Smith that I wanted him to baptize me because I wanted to live among a people who were based upon pure principles and actuated by the Spirit of the Living God. I went with the Elders present to the water and was immersed according to the commandments of Jesus Christ by H[yrum] S[mith] and was confirmed by the water's edge by the laying on of the hands" (*Journals of William E. McLellin*, 33–34; spelling and syntax standardized).

The Savior . . . of as many as believe on my name. Though Christ saves all from death—making the separation of body and spirit but a temporary state—only those who believe on his name, that is, those who accept his gospel and honor those servants he has sent in his stead, are saved in the full and proper sense. They alone have claim upon the crown of eternal life here promised to William E. McLellin (D&C 66:12). See commentary on Doctrine and Covenants 138:19.

66:2 *Mine everlasting covenant, even the fulness of my gospel.* We err in supposing that the fulness of the gospel embraces all truth. Here we are told that William E. McLellin had embraced "the fulness" by being baptized. Yet such things as the Word of Wisdom, law of tithing, temple ordinances, and the organization of the Quorum of the Twelve were yet to be revealed.

As it was written by the prophets and apostles in days of old. Here William E. McLellin is assured that the restoration of the gospel comes in fulfillment of the promises made by the prophets and apostles of old and that the restored gospel is not simply in harmony with the Bible but in fulfillment of it.

66:3 *Repent . . . of those things which are not pleasing . . . for the Lord will show them unto you.* See commentary on verse 10.

Preach the Gospel, Heal the Sick, and Resist Temptation
DOCTRINE AND COVENANTS 66:5–13

66:5–8 Elder McLellin had obviously wanted to know the Lord's will concerning him. Should he go forth as a missionary? Should he go to Zion to seek an inheritance there? Or should he remain in Kirtland? The Lord responds, calling him to go back east, declaring the gospel from city to city, particularly in those places where it had not as yet been declared. He is to take Samuel Smith as his companion and be a mentor to him.

66:6 *But inasmuch as you can send, send.* Elder McLellin was to send whatever money he could spare to Zion, though he was not to go there as yet.

66:9 *Lay your hands upon the sick, and they shall recover.* In the short time he had been a member of the Church, Elder McLellin had been raised from affliction in a healing blessing administered to him by Hyrum Smith, he had assisted Hyrum in giving a blessing in which a sick child was instantly healed, and he had been healed of a severely sprained ankle by the Prophet. It would appear that among the blessings he had prayerfully sought from the Lord was that of the gift of healing, which is here promised him (*Journals of William E. McLellin,* 40, 43, 45; spelling and syntax standardized).

66:10 *Seek not to be cumbered.* Elder McLellin was not to concern himself with obtaining property, wealth, or earthly possessions.

Commit not adultery—a temptation with which thou hast been troubled. William E. McLellin's wife, Cinthia, and an infant child had died before the summer of 1831. Extant information suggests that he had a warm and tender relationship with her and that the temptation here mentioned came only after her death and before he married again (*Journals of William E. McLellin,* 251; spelling and syntax standardized).

66:11 *Push many people to Zion.* It will be recalled that Moses, in blessing the tribes of Joseph, promised that the thousands of Manasseh and the ten thousands of Ephraim would "push" scattered Israel "together to the ends of the earth" (Deuteronomy 33:17). Significantly, at the conclusion of McLellin's record of this revelation, he added, "A revelation given to William E. McLellin a true descendant from Joseph who was sold into Egypt down through the loins of Ephraim his Son—Given in Hiram, Portage Co. Ohio, 29th Oct 1831" (*Journals of William E. McLellin*, 46; spelling and syntax standardized).

With songs of everlasting joy upon their heads. See Doctrine and Covenants 45:71.

DOCTRINE AND COVENANTS 67

DATE: NOVEMBER 1831
PLACE: HIRAM, OHIO

This revelation was received at the same conference at which the
Church determined to publish the revelations received by the Prophet
Joseph Smith in the form of the Book of Commandments. What is known
to us today as section 1, or the Lord's preface, and section 133, the appendix, were also received at this conference. Of these events the *Far West
Record* records, "Br. Joseph Smith jr. said that inasmuch as the Lord has
bestowed a great blessing upon us in giving commandments and revelations, asked the Conference what testimony they were willing to attach
to these commandments which should shortly be sent to the world. A
number of the brethren arose and said that they were willing to testify to
the world that they knew that they were of the Lord" (Cannon and Cook,
Far West Record, 27). After the receipt of section 1 a discussion arose relative to the language of some of the revelations, and concern was expressed
as to whether those revelations suitably represented the mind of the Lord.
It was in response to this discussion that the following revelation was
given.

Fears and Doubt Cause Blessings to be Lost
DOCTRINE AND COVENANTS 67:1–3

67:1 *O ye elders of my church, who have assembled yourselves together.*
Those present numbered only ten: Joseph Smith Jr., Oliver Cowdery,
Sidney Rigdon, William E. McLellin, David Whitmer, John Whitmer,
Peter Whitmer Jr., Orson Hyde, Luke Johnson, and Lyman Johnson.

67:3 Apparently at least some of those present had come to the conference expecting spiritual manifestations that they did not receive. Two
of the three witnesses to the Book of Mormon, Oliver Cowdery and David
Whitmer, were present. They had been privileged to witness the appearance of Moroni, who personally showed them the plates from which the
Book of Mormon was translated and many other things prior to writing

their testimony which is published with the book. The anticipation that
such a written testimony would also be appended to the Book of
Commandments would have been most natural, as would the thought
that it might be preceded by some marvelous manifestation. The promise
that the time would come when such manifestations would be given
them, as given in verses 10–13 of this revelation, seems to affirm that this
was their expectation. See commentary on Doctrine and Covenants 17.

This verse affirms that the Spirit was restrained by their fears and
doubts. It would be necessary for them to strip themselves of "jealousies
and fears" and become more humble before they could enjoy such manifestations. Indeed, we are told that they were not "sufficiently humble" at
that time to be "quickened by the Spirit of God" that they might rend the
veil. See Doctrine and Covenants 67:10–11.

The Wisest among Them Challenged to
Duplicate the Least of the Revelations
DOCTRINE AND COVENANTS 67:4–9

67:4–9 Of these verses the Prophet said, "After the foregoing was
received, William E. M'Lellin, as the wisest man, in his own estimation,
having more learning than sense, endeavored to write a commandment
like unto one of the least of the Lord's, but failed; it was an awful responsibility to write in the name of the Lord. The Elders and all present that
witnessed this vain attempt of a man to imitate the language of Jesus
Christ, renewed their faith in the fulness of the Gospel, and in the truth
of the commandments and revelations which the Lord had given to the
Church through my instrumentality; and the Elders signified a willingness
to bear testimony of their truth to all the world. Accordingly I received
the following:

"The testimony of the witnesses to the book of the Lord's commandments, which He gave to His Church through Joseph Smith, Jun., who
was appointed by the voice of the Church for this purpose; we therefore
feel willing to bear testimony to all the world of mankind, to every creature upon the face of all the earth and upon the islands of the sea that the
Lord has borne record to our souls, through the Holy Ghost, shed forth
upon us, that these commandments were given by inspiration of God, and
are profitable for all men, and are verily true. We give this testimony unto
the world, the Lord being our helper; and it is through the grace of God,
the Father, and His Son, Jesus Christ, that we are permitted to have this

privilege of bearing this testimony unto the world, that the children of men may be profited thereby" (Smith, *History of the Church*, 1:226).

67:5 *His language you have known, and his imperfections you have known.* The revelations of scripture are not to be considered absolutely perfect, nor, with the single exception of Jesus, do we have infallible prophets. Of the revelations of the Restoration the Lord said, "These commandments are of me, and were given unto my servants in their weakness, after the manner of their language, that they might come to understanding" (D&C 1:24). In like manner Moroni said, "Condemn me not because of mine imperfection, neither my father, because of his imperfection, neither them who have written before him; but rather give thanks unto God that he hath made manifest unto you our imperfections, that ye may learn to be more wise than we have been" (Mormon 9:31).

Teaching this principle, Brigham Young said, "I am so far from believing that any government upon this earth has constitutions and laws that are perfect, that I do not even believe that there is a single revelation, among the many God has given to the Church, that is perfect in its fulness. The revelations of God contain correct doctrine and principle, so far as they go; but it is impossible for the poor, weak, low, grovelling, sinful inhabitants of the earth to receive a revelation from the Almighty in all its perfections. He has to speak to us in a manner to meet the extent of our capacities. . . .

"If an angel should come into this congregation, or visit any individual of it, and use the language he uses in heaven, what would we be benefitted? Not any, because we could not understand a word he said. When angels come to visit mortals, they have to condescend to and assume, more or less, the condition of mortals, they have to descend to our capacities in order to communicate with us" (*Journal of Discourses*, 2:314).

67:7 No one would ever be justified in saying that God did not live, that Jesus of Nazareth was not the Christ, or that Joseph Smith was not the great prophet of the Restoration. This text simply says that if someone could write something the equal of the puniest of the revelations to be found in the Book of Commandments (or today, the Doctrine and Covenants) they would be justified, for the moment, in saying that they did not yet know with perfect assurance that he was a Prophet. They would still be without excuse at the day of judgment if they did not proceed under the direction of the Spirit to obtain that witness of which the revelations of the Restoration contain more than ample evidence.

Make one like unto it. Illustrating the futility of man attempting to

imitate the revelations of heaven, Orson F. Whitney observed, "It is not
so easy to put the spirit of life into things. Man can make the body, but
God alone can create the spirit. You have heard, have you not, of the scientist who took a grain of wheat and endeavored to make one just like it?
First he separated the grain of wheat into its component parts, and found
that it contained so much lime, so much silica, so much of this element
and that; and then he took other parts corresponding thereto, brought
them together by means of his chemical skill, and produced a grain of
wheat so exactly similar to the other that the natural eye could not detect
any difference between them. But there was a difference, a vast difference,
and it was demonstrated when he planted the two grains. The one that
God made sprang up, and the one that man made stayed down. Why?
Because the man-made grain of wheat had no spirit—only a body, and the
body without the spirit is dead. Man cannot breathe into the body of
things the breath of life; that is a function and prerogative of Deity. It is
not so easy to frame revelations from God. A vain boaster making ridicule
of the proverbs of Solomon, said: 'Anybody can make proverbs.' His friend
answered, 'Try a few,' and the conversation ended" (Conference Report,
April 1917, 42). See commentary on Doctrine and Covenants 18:35–36.

67:9 *There is no unrighteousness in them.* Here we have one of the laws
by which that which is of God is discerned from that which is of men or
of devils. James stated it thus, "But the wisdom that is from above is first
pure, then peaceable, gentle, and easy to be intreated, full of mercy and
good fruits, without partiality, and without hypocrisy" (James 3:17).

Faithful Elders Shall Be Quickened by the Spirit and See the Face of God
DOCTRINE AND COVENANTS 67:10–14

67:10–14 It was not intended that the opening of the heavens be
only upon the head of Joseph Smith. As the glory of the sunrise is for all
who will get up to see it, so the glories of God's kingdom are there to bless
all who will receive them. "What power shall stay the heavens?" the
Prophet would yet ask. "As well might man stretch forth his puny arm to
stop the Missouri river in its decreed course, or to turn it up stream, as to
hinder the Almighty from pouring down knowledge from heaven upon
the heads of the Latter-day Saints" (D&C 121:33).

All who ask with an honest heart will receive. All who serve in faith
will be rewarded with greater faith. In the revelation that follows these

same elders are promised that their words will be scripture (D&C 68:1–5). The promise of the ministering of angels had already been given them (D&C 13). Indeed, the higher priesthood which they held was given to administer the gospel and held within it the "key of the mysteries of the kingdom, even the key of the knowledge of God" (D&C 84:19). It would be their right, as it is the right of every faithful Saint, "while in the flesh," to "bear his presence in the world of glory" (D&C 76:118).

67:11 The oft-quoted text in the Gospel of John stating that "no man hath seen God at any time" (John 1:18) was corrected by the Prophet in the Joseph Smith Translation to read, "And no man hath seen God at any time, except he hath borne record of the Son; for except it is through him no man can be saved" (JST John 1:19). Similarly, a statement in Timothy about the resurrected Lord says, "[He] only hath immortality, dwelling in the light which no man can approach unto; whom no man hath seen, nor can see: to whom be honour and power everlasting" (1 Timothy 6:16); this was changed to read, "Whom no man hath seen, nor can see, unto whom no man can approach, only he who hath the light and the hope of immortality dwelling in him" (JST 1 Timothy 6:16). And the text in 1 John 4:12 declaring that "no man hath seen God at any time" was corrected to read, "No man hath seen God at any time, except them who believe" (JST 1 John 4:12).

In each of these texts, the correction indicates that a person seeing the resurrected Christ must first demonstrate faith and devotion. We are reminded that Christ, who made many appearances after his resurrection, did so only to the faithful and devoted disciple. To those who had warred against him, such as the Sanhedrin, Caiaphas, Pilot, or Herod, the resurrected Lord did not appear. Nor did he appear to those who had been indifferent to him. Again, his only appearances were to his faithful disciples.

We find this same pattern in his brief but significant visit to those in the spirit world, of which our account says, "Unto the wicked he did not go, and among the ungodly and the unrepentant who had defiled themselves while in the flesh, his voice was not raised; neither did the rebellious who rejected the testimonies and the warnings of the ancient prophets behold his presence, nor look upon his face" (D&C 138:20–21). The same was of course true of his appearances in the New World. The wicked and unworthy were all destroyed before he made his appearance there.

DOCTRINE AND COVENANTS 68

DATE: NOVEMBER 1831
PLACE: HIRAM, OHIO

Doctrine and Covenants 68 has the appearance of combining three revelations, the first being the direction of the Lord to Orson Hyde, Luke S. Johnson, Lyman E. Johnson, and William E. McLellin, all of whom had been called to serve as missionaries (vv. 1–12). The revelation then turns our attention to the right of a direct lineal descendant of Aaron to hold the same keys of presidency that were held by John the Baptist and Aaron (vv. 13–24). The final section of the revelation deals with the responsibility of parents to teach the gospel to their children and warns against the evil of idleness among the Saints in Zion (vv. 25–35). Why these three concepts were placed together in the same revelation is not apparent.

Words of Elders When Moved upon by the Holy Ghost Are Scripture
DOCTRINE AND COVENANTS 68:1–7

68:1–7 In an earlier revelation the elders of Israel had been commanded to go forth "preaching the word by the way, saying none other things than that which the prophets and apostles have written, and that which is taught them by the Comforter through the prayer of faith" (D&C 52:9). That is, they were to preach from the scriptures, no other source for such writings being available to them, and then add to that as directed by the Comforter or the Holy Ghost.

Explaining these principles, Alma said, "For I am called to speak after this manner, according to the holy order of God, which is in Christ Jesus; yea, I am commanded to stand and testify unto this people the things which have been spoken by our fathers concerning the things which are to come" (Alma 5:44). The reference to the things spoken by their fathers would be the scriptural records available to them. "And this is not all,"

Alma continued. "Do ye not suppose that I know of these things myself? Behold, I testify unto you that I do know that these things whereof I have spoken are true. And how do ye suppose that I know of their surety? Behold, I say unto you they are made known unto me by the Holy Spirit of God. Behold, I have fasted and prayed many days that I might know these things of myself. And now I do know of myself that they are true; for the Lord God hath made them manifest unto me by his Holy Spirit; and this is the spirit of revelation which is in me" (Alma 5:45–56). Given that the things of the Spirit can be known only by the Spirit, it is the obligation of those who teach from the scriptures to know by revelation the verity of that which they teach (D&C 50:13–22). Then Alma added, "And moreover, I say unto you that it has thus been revealed unto me, that the words which have been spoken by our fathers are true, even so according to the spirit of prophecy which is in me, which is also by the manifestation of the Spirit of God" (Alma 5:47). To all of this Alma then says, "I say unto you, that I know of myself that whatsoever I shall say [future tense] unto you, concerning that which is to come, is true; and I say unto you, that I know that Jesus Christ shall come, yea, the Son, the Only Begotten of the Father, full of grace, and mercy, and truth. And behold, it is he that cometh to take away the sins of the world, yea, the sins of every man who steadfastly believeth on his name. And now I say unto you that this is the order after which I am called, yea, to preach unto my beloved brethren, yea, and every one that dwelleth in the land; yea, to preach unto all, both old and young, both bond and free; yea, I say unto you the aged, and also the middle aged, and the rising generation; yea, to cry unto them that they must repent and be born again" (Alma 5:48–49).

Thus the pattern established by Alma and called by him "the holy order of God," a Book of Mormon phrase for priesthood, which is interchangeable with the phrase "the order of his Son" (D&C 107:3), was to teach from the scriptures, testify of a personal knowledge born of the Spirit that the scriptures are true, and then add to that as the Spirit directs. This, he said, was the pattern to be followed in teaching the old, the young, the middle-aged, and the rising generation.

Teaching this same principle, Elder Bruce R. McConkie explained that "those who preach by the power of the Holy Ghost use the scriptures as their basic source of knowledge and doctrine. They begin with what the Lord has before revealed to other inspired men. But it is the practice of the Lord to give added knowledge to those upon whose hearts the true meanings and intents of the scriptures have been impressed. Many great doctrinal revelations come to those who preach from the scriptures. When they are in tune with the Infinite, the Lord lets them know, first, the full and complete meaning of the scriptures they are expounding, and then he ofttimes expands their views so that new truths flood in upon them, and they learn added things that those who do not follow such a course can never know. . . . In a living, growing, divine church, new truths will come from time to time and old truths will be applied with new vigor to new situations, all under the guidance of the Holy Spirit of God" (*Promised Messiah*, 515–16).

68:2–3 The four elders to whom this revelation was given are simply the example of the principle that applies to "all the faithful elders of my church" (v. 7). All are to teach by the power of the Holy Ghost, all are to know by the spirit of revelation that what they are teaching is true, and all are to be enlightened by the Spirit as they teach. Joseph Smith taught that "no man can receive the Holy Ghost without receiving revelations. The Holy Ghost is a revelator" (*Teachings of the Prophet Joseph Smith*, 328).

68:4 *Whatsoever they shall speak when moved upon by the Holy Ghost shall be scripture.* It must be remembered that this revelation was given to four elders sent forth to teach the message of the Restoration. They did not hold the office of apostle or seventy, for these offices had not yet been restored. By the world's standard they were too young to be learned in theology, but their God loved young men who had faith. The oldest of their number was twenty-six. None of them had been a member of the Church for more than a few months. The formal instruction they had received in its doctrines and practices could be counted in hours or days at the most. Their success depended on their companionship with the Holy Spirit. The path they marked would yet be followed by countless others.

Nowhere in the Bible is the spirit of revelation defined. Nowhere in that marvelous book do we find a definition of scripture. Here, with a single sentence, the Prophet sweeps away cobwebs woven of darkness and confusion that for centuries have blocked the light of heaven. Scripture is the mind of the Lord, the will of the Lord, the word of the Lord, the voice of the Lord, and the power of God unto salvation. Its source is the Holy Ghost, and all who by the laying on of hands have received the promise of the companionship of that member of the Godhead at the same time assume the obligation to witness of him and of his gospel—they are to speak scripture.

"Anything spoken by the Father, Son, or Holy Ghost, by the angels of heaven, or by mortal man when moved upon by the Holy Ghost, is scripture. Such spoken words are the will, mind, word, and voice of the Lord. (D. & C. 68:1–5.)

"Since it is a comparatively rare thing for mortal man to hear the personal voice of Deity, or to converse with angels, it follows that most scriptural utterances are given to man by revelation from the Holy Ghost. These statements, made by the power of the Holy Spirit, consist of the identical words which the Lord himself would speak under the same circumstances. They are indeed the Lord's words because he authorizes and directs the Holy Ghost to influence and guide men in giving utterance to them.

"It is by the power and guidance of the Holy Ghost—that Spirit Personage who, as a member of the Godhead, has power to speak with unerring certainty to the spirit within man—that the saints 'have the mind of Christ.' (1 Cor. 2:16.) That is, when moved upon by the Holy Ghost, the saints are enabled to think what our Lord thinks, to give voice to the very words he does or would speak, and to act as he would act in the same situation. What is true of the mortal saints is also true of the heavenly saints, for 'Angels speak by the power of the Holy Ghost; wherefore, they speak the words of Christ.' (2 Ne. 32:3.)

"All scripture is true. It is composed wholly and solely of pure, unvarnished, irrefutable, and eternal truth. 'Thy word,' O God, 'is truth.' (John 17:17.) 'By the power of the Holy Ghost ye may know the truth of all things.' (Moro. 10:5.)

"All scripture comes by revelation. Whenever any revealed truth is expressed in words, those words are scripture. 'The Holy Ghost is a revelator,' Joseph Smith said. 'No man can receive the Holy Ghost without receiving revelations.' (*Teachings of the Prophet Joseph Smith*, p. 328.) And when those revelations are either spoken or written, they are scripture.

"Most scripture has been, is now, and will continue to be oral and unrecorded. Throughout the length and breadth of his earthly kingdom, the Lord's agents are frequently moved upon to speak, testify, prophesy, exhort, expound, preach, and teach by the power of the Holy Ghost. Such inspired utterances benefit and bless those who speak them and the spiritually endowed among the hearers" (McConkie, *Doctrinal New Testament Commentary*, 1:55–56).

68:7 *All the faithful elders of my church.* "What I say unto one I say unto all" (D&C 93:49).

Elders Are to Preach and Baptize in All the World
DOCTRINE AND COVENANTS 68:8–12

68:8 *Go ye into all the world.* It was with this same language that Christ commissioned the meridian Twelve to go into "all the world" to declare his gospel (Mark 16:15). This is the first time that this express language appears in the revelations of the Restoration; in that sense, then, these words could be regarded as our commission to declare the gospel among all the nations of the earth. The phrase also finds expression in Doctrine and Covenants 84:62 and 112:28.

68:10 *He that believeth shall be blest with signs.* See commentary on Doctrine and Covenants 64:7–12; 88:64–70.

68:11 Though no man will know the day or the hour of Christ's return, his coming will not surprise the faithful Saints who, knowing the signs of the times, will have all things in readiness.

Firstborn among the Sons of Aaron May Serve as the Presiding Bishop
DOCTRINE AND COVENANTS 68:13–24

68:15–18 Explaining these verses, Elder Joseph Fielding Smith taught: "There are some men in the Church who have been blessed by patriarchs and pronounced descendants of Levi, but they have not made any claim to the office of bishop, for the revelation governing this situation says literal descendant of Aaron, not of Levi. There is evidently a great host of men who are descendants of Levi but not of Aaron.

"The person spoken of in the revelations as having the right by lineage to the bishopric is the one who is the firstborn. By virtue of his birth he is entitled to hold 'the keys or authority of the same.' This has reference only to the one who presides over the Aaronic Priesthood. It has no reference whatever to bishops of wards. Further, such a one must be designated by the First Presidency of the Church and receive his anointing and ordination under their hands. The revelation comes from the Presidency, not from the patriarch, to establish a claim to the right to preside in this office. In the absence of knowledge concerning such a descendant, any high priest, chosen by the Presidency, may hold the office of Presiding Bishop and serve with counselors" (*Doctrines of Salvation,* 3:92–93).

As the restoration of the Aaronic Priesthood is an absolutely essential part of the restoration of all things—particularly since that priesthood prepared the way for the first coming of Christ and must prepare the way for his return—so the office that presides over that priesthood is also an essential part of that restoration. Robert J. Matthews, in his work on the life of John the Baptist, observes that "the things of the law of Moses, especially with regard to the qualifications of the priests and their functions in the offering of various animal sacrifices, were designed by revelation to prefigure and typify the Messiah and to bear witness of him. Heavy penalties were affixed to the performance of sacred rites and duties without the proper authority. It was, therefore, essential that when the Messiah came in person as the Lamb of God, John, the forerunner and witness of the Lamb, should be of the proper lineage to qualify him for the mission. If it was necessary for a priest to be of the lineage of Aaron in order to labor with the sacrificial symbols, which were only prefigures of the Messiah, how much greater the necessity that John, the forerunner of the Messiah in person, be of the proper priestly lineage and authority" (*Burning Light*, 18).

So we ask, If it was absolutely essential that the one holding the keys of the Aaronic Priesthood in the meridian day be of the proper lineage, would not the same principle hold true in the dispensation of the fulness of all things? And would it not stand as a significant evidence of the divine calling of the Prophet Joseph Smith to discover that he had received a revelation foreshadowing that very thing? Certainly that is the case in the present revelation and in Doctrine and Covenants 107, another great revelation on priesthood (D&C 107:69–70, 76).

68:16 *A legal right to the bishopric.* As the descendants of Abraham have right by birth to the priesthood, assuming worthiness, so the firstborn son of Aaron and his posterity down through the generations have a right by birth to the office Aaron held. The word *bishopric*, as used in scripture, simply means "office," and in this case the office of bishop does not have reference to the presidency of three that presides over either the Aaronic Priesthood or wards (Acts 1:20; D&C 114:2).

Parents Are Commanded to Teach the Gospel to Their Children
DOCTRINE AND COVENANTS 68:25–28

68:25–28 We know of no society in which parents are not held responsible for the well-being of their children. To give life is to assume responsibility for that life. That responsibility reaches well beyond food, shelter, and clothing to embrace acceptable behavior and eventually the ability to provide for themselves. Here the Lord makes it a matter of divine responsibility for parents to teach their children the truths of salvation and to raise them in faith. There can be little surprise in this; they are his children too.

We are a covenant people, and when a man and a woman go to the house of the Lord to receive the promise that their love can be eternal— that they can continue as husband and wife in the worlds to come—and that their posterity can surround them, we can only expect that the Author of the covenant will require something of us in return. Certainly that which is required includes the responsibility to plant in the hearts of our children the desire to marry in the temple and the responsibility to raise our sons with a desire to serve as missionaries.

We occasionally hear parents say that it is for their children to decide whether they will attend church, be baptized, abide by the standards of the Church, serve missions, and so forth. We are left to wonder if these same parents give their children the same freedom of choice where their education is concerned, or in the choice of foods they eat, or the medicine they take when ill. That their right of agency must be protected is beyond question. What is not beyond question is the degree of agency or the extent of the choices that are granted to them as children. Is it for the junior high school student to choose not to go to school? Should elementary school children have complete freedom of choice as to the foods they eat or when they go to bed or what is acceptable behavior and what is not? The degree of responsibility to control such decisions in the temporal realm differs little from the responsibility parents have in the realm of spiritual things. Surely we would not want to argue that parents have responsibility for the physical well-being of their children but not their spiritual well-being.

68:27 *When eight years old.* The first scriptural reference to age eight as the age of accountability is found in the Joseph Smith Translation, Genesis 17:11. It reads, "And I will establish a covenant of circumcision with thee." God is speaking to Father Abraham: "*And it shall be* my covenant between me and thee, and thy seed after thee, in their generations; *that thou mayest know for ever that children are not accountable before me until they are eight years old.*" These truths must be understood in light of another revelation on the matter. In September 1830 a revelation was given in which we were told that "little children are redeemed from the foundation of the world" through Christ and that "they cannot sin, for power is not given unto Satan to tempt little children, *until they begin to become accountable before me*" (D&C 29:46–47; emphasis added). These revelations do not say that children cannot sin before they are eight years of age. Rather, they tell us that "little children" cannot sin "until they begin to become accountable." Accountability, which comes gradually, begins long before a child is eight. To suppose that a child can do nothing deliberately wrong before the age of eight is simply foolish. It is by becoming increasingly accountable that they prepare themselves for baptism. The unaccountable cannot be baptized.

The Saints Are to Observe the Sabbath, Labor Diligently, and Pray
DOCTRINE AND COVENANTS 68:29–35

68:29 *The inhabitants of Zion shall also observe the Sabbath.* See commentary on Doctrine and Covenants 59.

68:31–32 The principles involved in living the law of consecration, as it was being practiced in Zion (or Missouri) when this revelation was given, are one and the same with the principles upon which our present welfare system functions. In 1936 President Heber J. Grant read a message from the First Presidency that explained, "Our primary purpose was to set up, in so far as it might be possible, a system under which the curse of idleness would be done away with, the evils of a dole abolished, and independence, industry, thrift and self-respect be once more established amongst our people. The aim of the Church is to help the people to help themselves. Work is to be re-enthroned as the ruling principle of the lives of our Church membership" (Conference Report, October 1936, 3).

68:33 *He that observeth not his prayers before the Lord in the season thereof.* After having read this text, Joseph Fielding Smith observed that "we ought to be a praying people, and if there are in Zion those who do not observe their prayers in the season thereof, they are amenable to the law of the Church and may be brought before the judge, or in other words, the bishop, and he can try them for their fellowship, because the Lord himself has declared it in these words which I have read unto you" (Conference Report, October 1918, 57).

DOCTRINE AND COVENANTS 69

DATE: ON OR BEFORE 12 NOVEMBER 1831
PLACE: HIRAM, OHIO

By this time all necessary decisions for the publication of the Book of Commandments had been made, and this revelation directed Oliver Cowdery to carry the manuscript to Independence, Missouri, for printing. He was also to deliver funds that had been contributed to aid in the building of Zion. As the course of travel would take Oliver through a sparsely settled region to the frontier, John Whitmer was called to be his traveling companion.

The two men left Ohio on 20 November 1831, stopped in Winchester, Indiana, for about a week to regulate Church affairs in the branch, and arrived in Independence on 5 January 1832.

John Whitmer Called to Accompany Oliver Cowdery to Missouri

DOCTRINE AND COVENANTS 69:1–8

69:1 *The commandments.* This refers to the compilation of revelations received by the Prophet Joseph Smith that were to be published as the Book of Commandments.

The land of Zion. Jackson County, Missouri, had been identified by revelation as Zion (D&C 57:2–3).

69:2 *John Whitmer.* One of the eight witnesses to the Book of Mormon, John Whitmer is mentioned in four earlier revelations (D&C 15, 26, 30, and 47). He had previously been called to be the Church historian (D&C 47:2).

69:6 *The land of Zion shall be a seat.* Independence, Missouri, was to be "the center place" of Zion, the "seat" or headquarters of the Church. The day will yet come when this will be the case (Smith, *Doctrines of Salvation,* 3:66–79).

69:7 *From church to church.* To compile the history of the Church, John Whitmer was directed to travel from one congregation of the Saints to another to obtain information from them.

DOCTRINE AND COVENANTS 70

DATE: 12 NOVEMBER 1831
PLACE: KIRTLAND, OHIO

This revelation is directed to members of the Literary Firm. This firm concerned itself with the printing of official Church literature. "On 12 November, 1831, the last day of the Hiram, Ohio conferences, it was decided that inasmuch as Joseph Smith, Oliver Cowdery, Sidney Rigdon, John Whitmer, and Martin Harris had played such a conspicuous role in recording, preserving, and preparing the revelations for publication, they should 'have claim on the Church for recompense.' It was therefore voted by those present that the above-named brethren 'be appointed to manage [the sacred writings] according to the Laws of the Church and the Commandments of the Lord.' These men who were to 'manage' the revelations constituted the membership of the Literary Firm. Members of the partnership were consecrated in their respective responsibilities, and the profits from the sale of the Church publications were to benefit both the individual members as well as the Church at large." Publications were to include the Joseph Smith Translation, a Church hymnal, and a Church newspaper (Cook, *Revelations*, 112–13).

Stewards Appointed to Publish the Revelations
DOCTRINE AND COVENANTS 70:1–13

70:3 *Stewards over the revelations.* The brethren named in the first verse of this revelation were responsible before the Lord for the publication of the Book of Mormon and the Book of Commandments (now the Doctrine and Covenants).

70:6 *They shall not give these things unto the church, neither unto the world.* Neither the Book of Mormon nor the Book of Commandments were to be given away. They were to be sold at a fair price, with any profit from their sale going to compensate the members of the Literary Firm for their efforts and to the bishop's storehouse, where the money would be consecrated to the inhabitants of Zion.

70:10 *None are exempt from this law.* All who went to Zion were to be bound by the law of consecration.

70:12 Of the labor here involved Joseph Smith observed: "Brother Oliver has labored with me from the beginning in writing, etc. Brother Martin has labored with me from the beginning and Brother John Whitmer and Sidney Rigdon also for a considerable time, and as these sacred writings are now going to the Church for its benefit, that we may have claim on the Church for recompense—if this conference think these things worth prizing to be had on record to show hereafter—I feel that it will be according to the mind of the Spirit, for by it these things were put into my heart which I know to be the Spirit of truth" (*History of the Church*, 1:236).

This revelation recognizes that those who devoted themselves to bringing forth God's revelations for both the edification and salvation of the Saints had claim upon the Church for their temporal sustenance. Of necessity, establishing the kingdom of God required the establishment of a host of different kinds of stewardships. The Prophet and those mentioned in this revelation had a stewardship to publish the revelations and commandments (vv. 1–4), others had been given a stewardship involving the printing house (D&C 104:29–30), some were to work in a mercantile establishment (D&C 104:39–42), and so forth.

The Saints Should Be Equal in Temporal Things
DOCTRINE AND COVENANTS 70:14–18

70:14 *In your temporal things you shall be equal.* Again, the revelation is directed to those living the law of consecration as practiced in Zion. Both the laborer and the skilled craftsman would be rewarded according to their needs. The labors of one man were not to be valued above those of another. Each would receive "according to his family, according to his circumstances and his wants and needs" (D&C 51:3).

DOCTRINE AND COVENANTS 71

DATE: 1 DECEMBER 1831
PLACE: HIRAM, OHIO

This revelation directs Joseph Smith and Sidney Rigdon to set aside the labor of translation on the Bible for a time while they went forth in defense of the restored gospel. This was required by the deluge of falsehoods that had been spread by Ezra Booth, who has the dubious distinction of being the first apostate from the youthful Church to take up the pen against it (Smith, *History of the Church*, 1:175–221).

Joseph Smith and Sidney Rigdon Are to Go Forth and Proclaim the Gospel
DOCTRINE AND COVENANTS 71:1–4

71:1–4 The most effective way to defend the gospel is to declare it. Truth stands on its own and carries within itself the evidence of its own authenticity. As Christ will have the victory over Satan, so every truth will ultimately triumph over its counterpart, whatever its source may be. Knowing that falsehood cannot hold its own against the truth in open display, the ministers of darkness of necessity must first shade or distort the light of heaven. Only then do they dare attack it. It is for this reason that ministers of other faiths will never be found telling their congregations to read the Book of Mormon and then prayerfully ask God if it is true. Nor would they allow the other revelations of the Restoration to be tested by such a standard. For that matter, neither are their own doctrines to be subject to such an examination. Yet did not the apostle Paul counsel us to "prove all things" and hold fast to "that which is good"? (1 Thessalonians 5:21). And again we would ask, should we not hold in suspicion the merchant who will not allow his weights to be inspected?

71:1 *Expounding the mysteries thereof out of the scriptures.* The meaning of much that is in the scriptures remains a mystery to readers of holy writ. These "hidden treasures" are discovered only with the aid of that same

Spirit by which they were originally written. Those things that can properly be understood only by the spirit of revelation are thus spoken of as mysteries.

That portion of Spirit and power which shall be given unto you. The light of heaven descends upon us gradually as we grow in faith and understanding. In sharing the gospel we must learn to let the Spirit direct "that portion [which] shall be meted unto every man" (D&C 84:85), for the truths of heaven are dispensed only according to the preparation that has been made to receive them.

71:2–3 The Prophet recorded that "from this time [4 December 1831] until the 8th or 10th of January, 1832, myself and Elder Rigdon continued to preach in Shalersville, Ravenna, and other places, setting forth the truth, vindicating the cause of our Redeemer; showing that the day of vengeance was coming upon this generation like a thief in the night; that prejudice, blindness and darkness filled the minds of many, and caused them to persecute the true Church, and reject the true light; by which means we did much towards allaying the excited feelings which were growing out of the scandalous letters then being published in the *Ohio Star*, at Ravenna, by the before-mentioned apostate, Ezra Booth" (*History of the Church*, 1:241).

On 10 January 1832 a revelation was received directing Joseph Smith and Sidney Rigdon to return to the labor of translating the Bible (D&C 73:3).

71:4 *Prepare the way for the commandments and revelations which are to come.* Preparations were being made at this time for the publication of the Book of Commandments, the first compilation of revelations received in this dispensation (D&C 67). Virtually from the time of the death of the meridian Twelve Apostles, the historical Christian world began to teach that God no longer speaks, that revelation has ceased, and that no one can add to the canon of scripture. The announcement of a new canon of scripture, one that not only stands as an equal with the revelations of the Old and New Testament but that supercedes them as the voice of God to those of our day, is a spiritual earthquake the likes of which the world has rarely seen. If such a thing be admitted, then every doctrine given birth by either men or devils must "tumble to the dust" (1 Nephi 22:14), as indeed they will. No single doctrine poses a greater threat to priestcraft or false religion in any of its forms than the announcement that God has chosen a new Sinai on the American frontier and a modern Moses by the name of Joseph Smith.

The Enemies of the Saints Shall Be Confounded
DOCTRINE AND COVENANTS 71:5–11

71:6 "I will give unto the children of men," the Lord said through the prophet Nephi, "line upon line, precept upon precept, here a little and there a little; and blessed are those who hearken unto my precepts, and lend an ear unto my counsel, for they shall learn wisdom; for unto him that receiveth I will give more; and from them that shall say, We have enough, from them shall be taken away even that which they have" (2 Nephi 28:30). To the principle taught here by Nephi the Lord now adds the promise of "power," which is to be granted to those willing to hear his voice and continually add to their understanding. It naturally follows that as we grow in the knowledge of the things of the Spirit we will also grow in faith and in spiritual power. Thus our ability to discern and teach the truth will increase, as will the power with which we teach it. And again, by way of contrast, for those who say they have enough, from them shall be taken away even that which they have.

71:7 *Confound your enemies; call upon them to meet you both in public and in private.* As the experience of tens of thousands of missionaries attests, little, if any, gospel teaching is accomplished when we engage in debate or in "scripture bashing." Nevertheless, in some situations a confrontation may be unavoidable. The circumstances which called forth this revelation are one such instance. The directions given in this verse are understood to be confined to such instances and are not the standard way of presenting the gospel. In his instruction to the Nephites, Christ said: "There shall be no disputations among you, as there have hitherto been; neither shall there be disputations among you concerning the points of my doctrine, as there have hitherto been. . . . For verily, verily I say unto you, he that hath the spirit of contention is not of me, but is of the devil, who is the father of contention, and he stirreth up the hearts of men to contend with anger, one with another. Behold, this is not my doctrine, to stir up the hearts of men with anger, one against another; but this is my doctrine, that such things should be done away" (3 Nephi 11:28–30).

When we forthrightly declare the truths of salvation as restored through the Prophet Joseph Smith, it will generally have a much greater effect on the hearts of men than if we place our focus on refuting the many falsehoods that have been perpetuated against the Latter-day Saints or against our doctrines.

71:9 *No weapon that is formed against you shall prosper.* What success can one enjoy when fighting against the kingdom of God or the truths of salvation? Such victories will be but temporary, their glory but for a moment. Satan was granted power to bruise Christ's heel, but the sure promise is that God's Son will crush his head (Genesis 3:15, see fn). None who properly bear the name of Christ go forth with a promise that is less than that. The victory will always rest with truth over falsehood, light over darkness, good over evil, and love over hatred.

Subsequent to this revelation, the Prophet would yet pen these words: "The Standard of Truth has been erected; no unhallowed hand can stop the work from progressing; persecutions may rage, mobs may combine, armies may assemble, calumny may defame, but the truth of God will go forth boldly, nobly, and independent, till it has penetrated every continent, visited every clime, swept every country, and sounded in every ear, till the purposes of God shall be accomplished, and the Great Jehovah shall say the work is done" (Smith, *History of the Church*, 4:540).

71:11 *Keep my commandments; they are true and faithful.* See Doctrine and Covenants 1:38.

DOCTRINE AND COVENANTS 72

DATE: 4 DECEMBER 1831
PLACE: KIRTLAND, OHIO

Doctrine and Covenants 72 was the last revelation received in 1831, the year in which more of the revelations in the Doctrine and Covenants were received than any other. On 1 December Joseph Smith and Sidney Rigdon received a revelation (D&C 71) directing them to cease their labors on the translation of the Bible for a season. They were instructed to go throughout the "regions round about" to teach the gospel and confute the evil influence of the articles written against the Church by Ezra Booth in the *Ohio Star.* To that end they went to Kirtland, where on Sunday, 4 December, a number of the Saints assembled to learn their duty and to be instructed. It was in this setting that this revelation was received.

Doctrine and Covenants 72 combines two separate revelations from the "Kirtland Revelation Book"—verses 1–8, which deal with the call of Newel K. Whitney to serve as a bishop, and verses 9–26, which deal with the duties associated with that office.

Newel K. Whitney Called As a Bishop
DOCTRINE AND COVENANTS 72:1–8

72:2 *This part of the Lord's vineyard.* In February 1831 Edward Partridge was called to serve as a bishop in Kirtland (D&C 41:9) and given responsibility to operate a storehouse to help the poor (D&C 42:30–39) and to administer property transactions connected with the law of consecration (D&C 51). When Missouri was identified as the place for the gathering of the Saints, Bishop Partridge was appointed to labor there (D&C 58:14). This created the need for someone to fill the responsibilities that had been his in the Kirtland area. In August 1831 Newel K. Whitney was called to serve as an agent for the Church (D&C 63:42–45). Now, in this revelation, he is called to the office of bishop. Thus, these two men served as regional or traveling bishops (D&C 20:66), Bishop Whitney in Ohio and the eastern states, and Bishop Partridge in Missouri.

72:3 *Steward.* A steward is a guardian or keeper of that which belongs to another. In ancient times a steward's tasks could range from tending pigs to supervising the king's stores or leading his armies to battle. In all his actions, a steward was accountable to his master. In the gospel context, we are all stewards of our divine Master and will in a future day be called upon to give an accounting for what we did with the opportunities that were ours. See Doctrine and Covenants 42:32.

72:6 *The bishop in Zion.* This refers to Edward Partridge, the bishop in Zion, to whom those coming from Ohio were to bring a record certifying that they had faithfully embraced the law of consecration and thus were rightful heirs to an inheritance in Zion.

72:7 *The voice of the conference.* This refers to the consent of those present, indicated by a sustaining vote. The vote itself—which is given by raising the right hand—is a form of covenant with two parts: first, the sustaining assures acceptance of those whose names are being presented for approval, and second, it includes the promise of help and support as necessary for them to magnify the office to which they are being called.

Illustrating these principles, John Taylor observed, "We hold up our right hand when voting in token before God that we will sustain those for whom we vote. And if we cannot feel to sustain them, we ought not to hold up our hands, because to do this would be to act the part of hypocrites, And the question naturally arises, how far shall we sustain them? Or in other words, how far are we at liberty to depart from this covenant which we make before each other and before our God? For when we lift up our hands in this way, it is in token to God that we are sincere in what we do, and that we will sustain the parties we vote for. This is the way I look at these things. How far then should we sustain them, and how far should we not? This is a matter of serious importance to us. If we agree to do a thing and do not do it, we become covenant-breakers and violators of our obligations, which are, perhaps, as solemn and binding as anything we can enter into" (*Gospel Kingdom*, 174–75; Doctrine and Covenants 28:10). See commentary on Doctrine and Covenants 26:2.

72:8 Through this revelation Newel K. Whitney was identified as one whom the Lord had chosen to serve in the office of bishop. The instructions concerning this office were then given by way of revelation. On 10 February 1832 Hyrum Smith and Reynolds Cahoon were called and ordained as his counselors.

The Duties of the Bishop in Kirtland
DOCTRINE AND COVENANTS 72:9–26

72:9–23 The duties of the bishop in Kirtland are enumerated in these verses. The bishops involved here were not the bishops of wards. The Saints were not divided into the geographic divisions we know as wards until the Nauvoo period. These men, as noted earlier, were traveling or area bishops. As given here, the duties of Bishop Whitney included keeping the Lord's storehouse and receiving the contributions of the Saints in his jurisdiction. He was to look after the needy and be responsible for the Church's temporal affairs. He was further obligated to see that those who gathered with the Church in Missouri took with them a certificate or recommend (as we would call it today) certifying their faithfulness and right to lay claim upon an inheritance there.

72:9 *The law which has been given.* This refers to Doctrine and Covenants 42, known as the "law of the Church."

72:10 The first storehouse of the Church was Newel K. Whitney's store, in Kirtland, Ohio: "N. K. Whitney & Co."

72:11 *As before has been commanded.* See Doctrine and Covenants 42:31–36.

72:14 *Shall answer the debt unto the bishop in Zion.* See Doctrine and Covenants 42:71–73.

72:17 *A certificate.* See Doctrine and Covenants 20:64, 84; 72:19, 24–25.

Judge or bishop. A bishop is a "judge in Israel" (D&C 58:17; 64:40).

72:19–21 At a conference held the previous month (see head note to D&C 1) the Lord revealed his will that the Church publish the revelations that Joseph Smith had received in the form of the Book of Commandments. It was also determined that the Literary Firm (D&C 70) would be responsible for publishing Joseph Smith's New Translation of the Bible, when it was finished, along with a Church hymnal, children's literature, a Church almanac, and a newspaper (Garrett, "Coming Forth," 91).

72:24–25 See Doctrine and Covenants 72:17.

DOCTRINE AND COVENANTS 73

DATE: 10 JANUARY 1832
PLACE: HIRAM, OHIO

This revelation was given to Joseph Smith and Sidney Rigdon at Hiram, Ohio, 10 January 1832. It directed them to resume the labor of translating the Bible. That work had been interrupted for more than a month by the necessity of responding to the letters written by the apostate Ezra Booth. These letters, which were published in the *Ohio Star*, had caused considerable ill feeling against the Church. Joseph's and Sidney's labors had done much to ameliorate those feelings (Smith, *History of the Church*, 1:241–42).

Work Is to Begin Again on the Translation of the Bible
DOCTRINE AND COVENANTS 73:1–6

73:1 *Until conference.* This refers to the conference appointed to be held 25 January 1832 at Amherst, Ohio.

73:2 *By the voice of the conference.* This refers to the consent of those in attendance at the conference. See commentary on Doctrine and Covenants 26:2.

73:3–6 When Ezra Booth fled from Sidney Rigdon's challenge to meet him in public debate, the *Ohio Star* ceased publication of his scurrilous letters. At the same time the Prophet and Sidney befriended many through their public preaching. The best way to defend the gospel is simply to teach it, as Joseph and Sidney demonstrated in this instance. Such a course is here referred to as a "pattern unto the elders." See commentary on Doctrine and Covenants 71.

73:4 *Continue the work of translation until it be finished.* By divine commission Joseph Smith made the revision or translation of the King James Bible known to us today as the Joseph Smith Translation. He commenced that work in June 1830 and completed the major portion of it by July 1833. The work was constantly interrupted, and the Prophet was still making modifications in the text, while preparing it for publication, at

504

the time of his death in 1844. Changes had been made from Genesis through Revelation. Although this seems to highlight the flaws in the Bible as it has come to us, in a higher sense it should be understood that because revelation is a continuous process among the Lord's people, there is no revelation that could not be amplified by additional light from heaven.

73:6 *Gird up your loins.* See commentary on Doctrine and Covenants 27:5.

Be sober. While it is both appropriate and necessary for servants of the Lord to take time to relax and refresh themselves, it is not appropriate for them to be silly or light-minded. Such behavior becomes offensive to the Spirit, causing it to withdraw.

DOCTRINE AND COVENANTS 74

DATE: JANUARY 1832 (AFTER 10 JANUARY AND BEFORE 25 JANUARY)
PLACE: HIRAM, OHIO

Doctrine and Covenants 73, received 10 January 1832, directed Joseph Smith and Sidney Rigdon to resume the translation of the Bible. The Prophet noted: "Upon the reception of the foregoing word of the Lord, I recommenced the translation of the Scriptures, and labored diligently until just before the conference, which was to convene on the 25th of January. During this period, I also received the following [revelation], as an explanation of [1 Corinthians 7:14]" (Smith, *History of the Church*, 1:242).

Paul Counsels the Meridian Church Not to Keep the Law of Moses
DOCTRINE AND COVENANTS 74:1–5

74:1–5 Here Joseph Smith seeks and receives understanding relative to an expression of the apostle Paul that is, at best, difficult for the modern reader to understand. The greater issue Paul was addressing is whether a man or woman who is married to a non-Christian should remain in that marriage. Paul taught that the Christian partner should not in such a case take the initiative in seeking a divorce. If, on the other hand, the unbelieving partner desired to separate, the Christian, Paul felt, was not bound to remain in that union. At this point another question was raised relative to the status of children born of these mixed marriages. On this matter Paul made a statement that suggests that children born outside the faith are both unclean and unholy. His doing so may reflect his own Jewish background. "The Jews considered a child as born out of holiness whose parents were not proselytes at the time of the birth, though afterwards they became proselytes. On the other hand, they considered the children of heathens born in holiness provided the parents became proselytes before the birth. All the children of the heathens were reputed unclean by the Jews; and all their own children holy" (Clarke, *Clarke's Commentary*, 3:223). Paul's statement would naturally perplex the Prophet because he had already been taught that all little children are whole in Christ, they being incapable of committing sin (Moroni 8:8; D&C 29:46–47).

74:1 *Unbelieving husband . . . unbelieving wife.* This refers to a non-Christian or nonmember spouse.

The unbelieving husband is sanctified by the wife. As a man and a woman become one in the marriage union, all the virtues and blessings of the individual become the virtues and blessings of the union.

Else were your children unclean, but now are they holy. This notion (1 Corinthians 7:14), which represents a false tradition among the Jews, is currently used by many Christian commentators as a justification for infant baptism. If Paul, who made it plain that he was speaking by way of personal opinion and not by way of revelation (1 Corinthians 7:6; D&C 74:5), was intimating that a child would be unclean and thus unholy if not born to at least one Christian parent, he was clearly in error (D&C 74:6–7).

Little Children Are Holy and Are Sanctified through the Atonement
DOCTRINE AND COVENANTS 74:6–7

74:6–7 Among all the children on the face of the earth, not a single one is an enemy of Christ. It is true that countless numbers of their parents have yielded to the enticements of the flesh—and some even seek to crucify Christ afresh and put him to an open shame—yet even of their little children it can be said that they are holy. "The natural man is an enemy to God, and has been from the fall of Adam, and will be, forever and ever, unless he yields to the enticings of the Holy Spirit, and putteth off the natural man and becometh a saint through the atonement of Christ the Lord, and becometh as a child, submissive, meek, humble, patient, full of love, willing to submit to all things which the Lord seeth fit to inflict upon him, even as a child doth submit to his father" (Mosiah 3:19).

Because all little children are clean, pure, and holy, because they have been sanctified by the blood of Christ, if they were to die as children, that is, in this state of holiness, they have the sure promise of the Lord that they are rightful heirs of every blessing that heaven has to bestow (D&C 137:10; Moroni 8).

DOCTRINE AND COVENANTS 75

DATE: 25 JANUARY 1832
PLACE: AMHERST, OHIO

This revelation was given at a conference held in Amherst, Lorain County, Ohio. "At this conference," the Prophet observed, "much harmony prevailed, and considerable business was done to advance the kingdom, and promulgate the Gospel to the inhabitants of the surrounding country." It was at this conference that Joseph Smith was sustained and ordained President of the High Priesthood.

Joseph Smith also observed that "the Elders seemed anxious for me to inquire of the Lord that they might know His will, or learn what would be most pleasing to Him for them to do, in order to bring men to a sense of their condition; for as it was written, all men have gone out of the way, so that none doeth good, no, not one [Romans 3:12]. I inquired and received the following . . ." (*History of the Church*, 1:242–43).

A Command to Declare the Revelations of the Restoration
DOCTRINE AND COVENANTS 75:1–5

75:4 *Proclaiming the truth according to the revelations and commandments which I have given you.* The Church is charged with the responsibility to declare the message of the Restoration among those of every nation, kindred, tongue, and people. Here, the missionaries are reminded that they are to declare that message from the revelations given through the Prophet Joseph Smith. It is offensive to the Spirit when missionaries seek refuge and respectability in the Bible rather than declaring the message the Lord gave for our day. The Book of Mormon is the perfect evidence that Joseph Smith is a prophet, not the book of Isaiah, Jeremiah, or Daniel. The testimony of Christ as found in Matthew, Mark, Luke, and John is nothing short of marvelous, yet even their testimonies take on greater meaning when read by the light of modern revelation. While we value that which God spoke to the ancients, we treasure even more the knowledge that he has spoken again in our day, restored his priesthood, and given anew all the ordinances of salvation.

Ours is a testimony of a God who speaks, of prophets who live, of scripture penned in our day, of angels ministering in our midst. Indeed, "we believe in the gift of tongues, prophecy, revelation, visions, healing, interpretation of tongues, and so forth" (Article of Faith 7). Ours is a living Bible; it cannot be sealed; there can be no end to the revelations it contains. We profess ourselves to be Bible Christians in the true sense of the term. "Bible Christians were those who believed in having apostles and inspired prophets among them," Brigham Young explained. "Bible Christians could receive more revelation and add more books to the Bible; Bible Christians could converse with the Lord, and oftentimes beheld the face of Jesus; they could commune with holy angels; they had authority from God to lay hands upon those whom they baptized, for the reception or baptism of the Holy Ghost" (*Journal of Discourses*, 14:347). There is a spiritual power known to missionaries who teach and testify of the Restoration, doing so from its revelations, that is not experienced by those who seek to justify our doctrines or give credence to our message by the use of Bible texts (D&C 31:1–5; 49:1–4; 84:54–61).

Missionaries Directed to Pray for the Comforter
DOCTRINE AND COVENANTS 75:6–12

75:6–8 Earlier, William E. McLellin had been commanded in a revelation to go to the eastern states as companion of Samuel Smith (D&C 66:7–8). They served together for about one month. McLellin records that he then became ill and was confined to bed; however, Samuel Smith commented: "'We went a short distance, but because of disobedience, our way was hedged up before us'" (cited in *Journals of William E. McLellin*, 300; spelling and syntax standardized). Although Samuel does not indicate the nature of the disobedience, in this revelation the Lord chastised William McLellin for the murmurings of his heart. McLellin was reassigned to a new area of labor with Luke Johnson, but during that missionary sojourn, McLellin faltered in the faith. After he preached on the night of 25 February 1831, "McLellin's mind was filled with doubts and he debated whether his call to preach was by man or by 'the fountain of all wisdom.' Unable to resolve his dilemma, the missionary determined that he would 'cease proclaiming until I was satisfied in my own mind.' . . .

"Commenting on this sudden termination of their labors by his companion, Johnson stated, 'Brother McLellin got a situation behind a counter to sell tapes, &c., and I, preferring not to proceed alone, returned to the town of Hiram, and the Prophet appointed Seymour Brunson in his stead, with whom I travelled through Ohio, Virginia and Kentucky'" (*Journals of William E. McLellin*, 302; spelling and syntax standardized; see D&C 90:35).

75:10 In 3 Nephi we read that the newly called Nephite Twelve "did pray for that which they most desired; and they desired that the Holy Ghost should be given unto them." Further, we find Christ praying that the Holy Ghost would be given to all those who would believe on the words of the Twelve (3 Nephi 19:9, 21). Similarly, in this text those who go forth in the name of the Lord are enjoined to pray for the companionship of the Comforter, who will "teach [them] all things," as Christ promised he would teach the Twelve in the Old World (John 14:26).

That are expedient. See Doctrine and Covenants 18:18; 88:64–65.

Elders to Sit in Judgment on Those Who Reject Their Message

DOCTRINE AND COVENANTS 75:13–22

75:16 *He who is faithful shall overcome all things.* Faith in Christ as the Son of God will bring victory over all things. Only through such faith can we obtain victory over all that stands between us and a fulness in the Father. Thus we are told that those who obtain the crown of eternal life are those who "overcome by faith, and are sealed by the Holy Spirit of promise" (D&C 76:53). So it is that the promise of victory is not to those of strength or to those of great intellect but to those of faith.

75:19 *Leave your blessing upon that house.* This direction is as appropriate for the missionary of the present day as it was for missionaries in 1832. Indeed, the principle is timeless. To Abraham the Lord said, "I will bless them that bless thee, and curse them that curse thee" (Abraham 2:11). Wherever the servants of the Lord go they should leave their blessing.

75:20–21 The principles here announced find dramatic application in the experience of Samuel Smith, who went forth as the first missionary in this dispensation. Mother Smith records his experience as follows: "On the thirtieth of June, Samuel started on the mission to which he had been set apart by Joseph, and in traveling twenty-five miles, which was his first day's journey, he stopped at a number of places in order to sell his books, but was turned out of doors as soon as he declared his principles. When evening came on, he was faint and almost discouraged, but coming to an inn, which was surrounded with every appearance of plenty, he called to see if the landlord would buy one of his books. On going in, Samuel inquired of him, if he did not wish to purchase a history of the origin of the Indians.

"'I do not know,' replied the host; 'how did you get hold of it?'

"'It was translated,' rejoined Samuel, 'by my brother, from some gold plates that he found buried in the earth.'

"'You liar!' cried the landlord. 'Get out of my house—you shan't stay one minute with your books.'

"Samuel was sick at heart, for this was the fifth time he had been turned out of doors that day. He left the house and traveled a short distance and washed his feet in a small brook, as a testimony against the man. He then proceeded five miles further on his journey, and seeing an apple tree a short distance from the road, he concluded to pass the night under it; and here he lay all night upon the cold, damp ground. In the morning, he arose from his comfortless bed, and observing a small cottage at no great distance, he drew near, hoping to get a little refreshment. The only inmate was a widow, who seemed very poor. He asked her for food, relating the story of his former treatment. She prepared him victuals, and, after eating, he explained to her the history of the Book of Mormon. She listened attentively and believed all that he told her, but, in consequence of her poverty, she was unable to purchase one of the books. He presented her with one and proceeded to Bloomington, which was eight miles further.

"Here he stopped at the house of John P. Greene, who was a Methodist preacher and was at that time about starting on a preaching mission. He, like the others, did not wish to make a purchase of what he considered at that time to be a nonsensical fable; however, he said that he would take a subscription paper, and if he found anyone on his route who was disposed to purchase, he would take his name, and in two weeks Samuel might call again and he would let him know what the prospect was of selling. After making this arrangement, Samuel left one of his books with him, and returned home. At the time appointed, Samuel started again for the Reverend John P. Greene's, in order to learn the success which this gentleman had met with in finding sale for the Book of Mormon. This time, Mr. Smith and myself accompanied him, and it was our intention to have passed near the tavern where Samuel was so abusively treated a fortnight previous, but just before we came to the house, a sign of smallpox intercepted us. We turned aside, and meeting a citizen of the place, we inquired of him, to what extent this disease prevailed. He answered that the tavern keeper and two of his family had died with it not long since, but he did not know that anyone else had caught the disease, and that it was brought into the neighborhood by a traveler who stopped at the tavern overnight" (Smith, *History of Joseph Smith*, 1996, 225–26).

75:20 *Shake off the dust of your feet.* See commentary on Doctrine and Covenants 1:8; 24:15.

Families of Missionaries to Receive Help from the Church
DOCTRINE AND COVENANTS 75:23-36

75:29 In his instruction to Timothy, Paul wrote, "But if any provide not for his own, and specially for those of his own house, he hath denied the faith, and is worse than an infidel" (1 Timothy 5:8).

DOCTRINE AND COVENANTS 76

DATE: 16 FEBRUARY 1832
PLACE: HIRAM, OHIO

After returning to Hiram from the Amherst conference, Joseph Smith and Sidney Rigdon resumed their labors on the translation of the New Testament. The vision recorded in Doctrine and Covenants 76 was received while they were translating John 5:29.

Philo Dibble, one of a dozen men present when this vision was received, said that he saw the glory and felt the power but did not see the vision. He described the event by saying:

"Joseph would, at intervals, say: 'what do I see?' . . . Then he would relate what he had seen or what he was looking at. Then Sidney replied, 'I see the same.' Presently Sidney would say, 'what do I see?' and would repeat what he had seen or was seeing, and Joseph would reply, 'I see the same.'

"This manner of conversation was repeated at short intervals to the end of the vision, and during the whole time not a word was spoken by any other person. Not a sound nor motion made by anyone but Joseph and Sidney, and it seemed to me that they never moved a joint or limb during the time I was there, which I think was over an hour, and to the end of the vision.

"Joseph sat firmly and calmly all the time in the midst of a magnificent glory, but Sidney sat limp and pale, apparently as limber as a rag, observing which, Joseph remarked, smilingly, 'Sidney is not used to it as I am'" ("Recollections," 27:303–4).

Adding to that recollection on another occasion, Philo Dibble observed that "Joseph wore black clothes, but at this time seemed to be dressed in an element of glorious white, and his face shone as if it were transparent, but I did not see the same glory attending Sidney. Joseph appeared as strong as a lion, but Sidney seemed as weak as water, and Joseph, noticing his condition smiled and said, 'Brother Sidney is not as used to it as I am'" ("Philo Dibble's Narrative," 81).

"Nothing could be more pleasing to the Saints upon the order of the kingdom of the Lord, than the light which burst upon the world through the foregoing vision. Every law, every commandment, every promise, every truth, and every point touching the destiny of man, from Genesis to Revelation, where the purity of the scriptures remain unsullied by the folly of men, go to show the perfection of the theory [of different degrees of glory in the future life] and witnesses the fact that that document is a transcript from the records of the eternal world. The sublimity of the ideas; the purity of the language; the scope for action; the continued duration for completion, in order that the heirs of salvation may confess the Lord and bow the knee; the rewards for faithfulness, and the punishments for sins, are so much beyond the narrow-mindedness of men, that every honest man is constrained to exclaim: 'It came from God.'" (Smith, *History of the Church*, 1:252–53).

Initially, the revelation was not as well received by the Saints as would be supposed. Brigham Young explained, "When God revealed to Joseph Smith and Sidney Rigdon that there was a place prepared for all, according to the light they had received and their rejection of evil and practice of good, it was a great trial to many, and some apostatized because God was not going to send to everlasting punishment heathens and infants, but had a place of salvation, in due time, for all and would bless the honest and virtuous and truthful, whether they ever belonged to any church or not" (*Journal of Discourses*, 16:42).

On 1 February 1843 there appeared in the *Times and Seasons* (4:81–85) a short poem by W. W. Phelps addressed to Joseph Smith, entitled *Vade Mecum* ("go with me"), which was an appeal that in death he and the Prophet might go together to the paradise of God to find refuge there. Accompanying *Vade Mecum* was a much longer poetic response by the Prophet, *A Vision*, which consisted of a poetic rephrasing of Doctrine and Covenants 76 with some interpretive commentary. The Prophet's poetic response is perhaps the most authoritative and helpful commentary we have on this revelation (see page 540).

The Greatness of God
DOCTRINE AND COVENANTS 76:1–4

76:1 *Hear, O ye heavens, and give ear, O earth.* This revelation is for the inhabitants of both heaven and earth. The gospel is the same among the living and the dead. God is the same, the principles of salvation are the same, the necessity of faith, repentance, and baptism are the same, and the system by which those principles are taught is the same. Thus the revelation of those principles must also be the same. As the fulness of the gospel goes forth to those of every nation, kindred, tongue, and people by the Book of Mormon, so it must go forth in the same manner among their kindred dead. Indeed, its testimony is announced to be "a voice of gladness for the living and the dead" (D&C 128:19). The dead cannot be blessed by the authority restored to the living unless they are also blessed by the doctrines restored to them. So it is that "the dead speak forth anthems of eternal praise to the King Immanuel, who hath ordained, before the world was, that which would enable us to redeem them out of their prison; for the prisoners shall go free" (D&C 128:22; Isaiah 1:2; Deuteronomy 32:1).

The Lord is God. Jesus Christ is God. The God of the prophets of the Old Testament, the Lord Jehovah, was the promised Savior, Redeemer, Deliverer, and Messiah of the New Testament. He was and is the Lord Jesus Christ. This same truth is sustained by the prophets of the Book of Mormon. For instance, Nephi prophesied that when "the very God of Israel" dwelt among men, they would "set him at naught, and hearken not to the voice of his counsels" and would themselves "be scourged by all people, because they crucify the God of Israel" (1 Nephi 19:7, 13). A perfect witness that Israel's God and Mary's Son were one and the same was borne by the resurrected Jesus to the Nephites in these words: "I am Jesus Christ. . . . Come forth unto me, that ye may thrust your hands into my side, and also that ye may feel the prints of the nails in my hands and in my feet, that ye may know that I am the God of Israel, and the God of the whole earth, and have been slain for the sins of the world" (3 Nephi 11:10–14).

Beside him there is no Savior. See commentary on Doctrine and Covenants 76:14, 22, 23–24.

76:4 *From eternity to eternity he is the same.* "From eternity to eternity means from the spirit existence through the probation which we are in, and then back again to the eternal existence which will follow. Surely this is everlasting, for when we receive the resurrection, we will never die. We all existed in the first eternity. I think I can say of myself and others, we are from eternity; and we will be to eternity everlasting, if we receive the exaltation. The intelligent part of man was never created but always existed. That is true of each of us as well as it is of God, yet we are born sons and daughters of God in the spirit and are destined to exist forever. Those who become like God will also be from eternity to eternity" (Smith, *Doctrines of Salvation*, 1:12).

"In other words Christ, as an eternal, exalted Being, never varies; from one eternity to the next he is the same. From pre-existence to pre-existence his course goes on in one eternal round, and so will it be with all exalted beings. Those who become gods will then be from eternity to eternity, everlastingly the same, always possessing the fullness of all things and multiplying their race without end" (McConkie, *Mormon Doctrine*, 240).

All Things to Be Revealed to the Faithful
DOCTRINE AND COVENANTS 76:5–10

76:5–10 Those who serve God in righteousness and truth become heirs to the riches of his kingdom. The rewards he promises include an understanding of those things held to be of greatest worth in the heavenly realm. No mention is made here of the kind of things so often envied by those whose hearts are set upon the honors and riches of this world. Rather, the promise of heaven centers in a knowledge of things past and future as they pertain to the kingdom of God. Such knowledge embraces the wonders of eternity and the glory of things to come. It centers in wisdom beyond that known to the wisest and most prudent of men. The treasure least known to the world, and yet that which is of greatest worth, is that knowledge that comes only by way of revelation. It is God's alone to give, and he has promised the wisdom of heaven in full measure to his faithful servants. Truly, the "glory of God is intelligence" (D&C 93:36).

This promise extends to all faithful Saints. It stands independent of office or position, of gender or of age. Whether our position be high or low, whether we stand in the public view or are entirely shielded from it, it is the purity of our soul and of our service, not the position we hold, that opens the windows of heaven to us. To be righteous is to be justified; it is to follow a course that is approved by the Lord. It will be recalled, for instance, that Christ was baptized "to fulfil all righteousness" (Matthew 3:15). Those who are righteous comply with all the laws and ordinances of the gospel. They do the right thing for the right reason. They act out of a proper understanding of gospel principles. One cannot serve the Lord in ignorance or error. We must serve in "truth," that is, according to the light of heaven and in a course that is constant or steadfast. Those serving after this pattern will enjoy the companionship of the Holy Ghost, the spirit of revelation, and will have the heavens opened to them.

Elder Bruce R. McConkie illustrated the principles involved by sharing this experience: "When I was a mission president in Australia, I once said to those of my missionaries in Tasmania: 'Tomorrow we shall climb Mt. Wellington and hold our missionary meeting on the top. We shall there seek to commune with the Lord and partake of his Spirit.'

"We made the climb, and while on top of the peak we visited a television broadcasting station. A bright young man explained to us in words I had never heard, and using principles I could not and do not understand, how the sounds and scenes of television were broadcast into the valley below.

"That night, back in the city of Hobart, my two young sons and I sat before a television set that was tuned to the proper wave band, and we saw and heard and experienced what had been described to us in words.

"Now I think this illustrates perfectly what is involved in the receipt of revelation and the seeing of visions. We can read about visions and revelations in the records of the past, we can study the inspired writings of people who had the fullness of the gospel in their day, but we cannot comprehend what is involved until we see and hear and experience for ourselves.

"This Tabernacle is now full of words and music. Handel's *Messiah* is being sung, and the world's statesmen are propagandizing their people. But we do not hear any of it.

"This Tabernacle is full of scenes from Vietnam and Washington. There is even a picture of men walking on the surface of the moon. But we are not seeing these things. The minute, however, in which we tune a radio to the proper wave band and tune a television receiving set on the proper channel, we begin to hear and see and experience what otherwise remains completely unknown to us.

"And so it is with the revelations and visions of eternity. They are around us all the time. This Tabernacle is full of the same things which are recorded in the scriptures and much more. The vision of the degrees of glory is being broadcast before us, but we do not hear or see or experience because we have not tuned our souls to the wave band on which the Holy Ghost is broadcasting. . . .

"How this is done we do not know. We cannot comprehend God or the laws by which he governs the universe. But that it does happen we know because here in the valley below, when we attune our souls to the Infinite, we hear and see and experience the things of God.

"The laws governing radio and television have existed from the time of Adam to the present moment, but only in modern times have men heard and seen and experienced these miraculous things. And the laws have always existed whereby men can see visions, hear the voice of God, and partake of the things of the Spirit. But millions of people everywhere live and die without tasting the good word of God, because they do not obey the laws which implant the revelations of the Lord in their souls" (Conference Report, April 1971, 98–99).

76:5 *Fear me.* The fear of God has nothing to do with fright. It is rather a reverential awe that elicits the highest behavior from humankind.

Here the Lord tells us that he is "merciful and gracious" to those who fear him and serve him in "righteousness and in truth" to the end of their lives. The text attests that neither God's mercy nor his grace is unconditional. As to God's mercy, Alma testified that "whosoever repenteth shall find mercy," and again that "God is merciful unto all who believe on his name" (Alma 32:13, 22). From ancient times the Lord has promised his mercy to those who love him and keep his commandments (Exodus 20:6; Deuteronomy 5:10). We are told that the Lord showed mercy to David "according as he walked before [him] in truth, and in righteousness, and in uprightness of heart" (1 Kings 3:6). Standing before the altar of the Lord, Solomon declared, "Lord God of Israel, there is no God like thee, in heaven above, or on earth beneath, who keepest covenant and mercy with thy servants that walk before thee with all their heart" (1 Kings 8:23). As the Psalmist noted, "All the paths of the Lord are mercy and truth unto such as keep his covenant and his testimonies" (Psalm 25:10). Christ himself, speaking to his newly called apostles, said, "Blessed are the merciful: for they shall obtain mercy" (Matthew 5:7). Thus to enjoy the graciousness of God is to be blessed and favored by him.

76:7 *Will I reveal all mysteries.* In the theological sense, a mystery is something known by revelation. In some instances rituals are also referred to as mysteries because participation in them has the effect of unlocking the heavens. Without revelation, everything that pertains to God, to his kingdom, or to the life beyond this mortal sphere remains a mystery.

In the Prophet Joseph Smith's inspired poem *A Vision*, the stanza standing opposite this verse reads:

> From the council in Kolob, to time on the earth.
> And for ages to come unto them I will show
> My pleasure & will, what my kingdom will do:
> Eternity's wonders they truly shall know.
> (*Times and Seasons*, 4:82)

From this it would appear that the Grand Council in Heaven took place on Kolob, which we learn from the book of Abraham is the planet nearest to the throne of God (Abraham 3:3; Facsimile 2, Explanation, Figure 1). This stanza may suggest that Kolob was our place of residence during our premortal estate.

The Resurrections of the Just and the Unjust
DOCTRINE AND COVENANTS 76:11–18

76:13 *Who was in the bosom of the Father.* Christ was "Beloved and Chosen from the beginning" (Moses 4:2) because he "was in the bosom of the Father"; that is, he was perfectly at one with the Father.

76:14 *The record which we bear is the fulness of the gospel of Jesus Christ.* All that Joseph Smith taught in his role as a prophet, seer, and revelator about Christ becomes part of his testimony of Christ. Testimony is knowledge. One's competence as a witness is predicated on his or her knowledge. The fulness of Joseph Smith's testimony of Christ embraces all that the Prophet revealed, all that he taught, and all that he understood about the Only Begotten of the Father. Thus Joseph Smith becomes the great revelator, testator, and teacher of Christ for this dispensation. No man of whom we have record has revealed and taught more truth about Christ than Joseph Smith. The composite of all that he taught constitutes his testimony of Christ. This revelation (D&C 76) adds substantially to that testimony, particularly by the manner in which it extends his saving role to the inhabitants of worlds without number (v. 24).

With whom we conversed. To *converse* may also mean to dwell with or to associate with, as well as to have dialogue with.

76:15 *The work of translation.* This refers to the Joseph Smith Translation of the Bible.

76:16 *Son of Man.* Jesus Christ is the Son of Man, meaning the Son of "Man of Holiness," or God the Father (Moses 6:57; 7:35).

76:18 *This caused us to marvel.* As Joseph Smith worked on his inspired translation of the Bible, he read that those who had done "good" would come forth in the resurrection "of life," while those who had done "evil" were to come forth in the resurrection "of damnation" (John 5:29). At the bidding of the Spirit, the word *life* was changed to read *just* and the word *damnation* was changed to read *unjust.* Apparently it was this change that caused Joseph Smith and Sidney Rigdon to marvel. The context of the next verse suggests that they made the change at the direction of the Spirit without knowing why. Desirous to understand the reason for this change, they "meditated upon these things" (v. 19) and were granted this revelation. This in turn indicates that the Prophet's explanation in the introduction to this revelation that it was self-evident that much had been lost or taken from the writings of the ancient prophets before the Bible was compiled and that "Heaven" must include more kingdoms than one was the result of later reflection and not necessarily clear to him when this revelation was received.

The Atonement of Christ Applies to Other Worlds
DOCTRINE AND COVENANTS 76:19–24

76:21 *Holy angels, and them who are sanctified.* In his poetic rendering of this verse the Prophet wrote:

> I beheld round the throne, holy angels and hosts,
> And sanctified beings from worlds that have been,
> In holiness worshipping God and the Lamb,
> Forever and ever, amen and amen!
> (*Times and Seasons,* 4:82)

The reference to sanctified beings in this text thus seems to refer to the faithful of other worlds who, in their resurrected state, continue to worship both the Father and the Son.

76:22 *Last of all.* This phrase means "most recently." There is no suggestion here that this would be the last time that the Father and the Son would manifest themselves to men in the flesh. The whole purpose of the vision is to testify otherwise. It both begins and ends with the promise that the glories of eternity, including the vision of God, will continue to be manifest to those who serve him in truth and righteousness (vv. 5–10, 116–18).

76:23–24 That Christ, under the direction of the Father, created worlds without number, which were inhabited by the sons and daughters of God, was first revealed to Joseph Smith in June 1830 when he labored on the book of Moses (Moses 1:29–35). It could be reasoned that if Christ was their Creator he of necessity must be their Redeemer also. We need not rely only on reason, however. This revelation plainly states that through Christ the inhabitants of those worlds "are begotten [born again] sons and daughters unto God" (v. 24). In his poem *A Vision*, the Prophet stated the matter thus:

> By him, of him, and through him, the worlds were all made,
> Even all that career in the heavens so broad,
> Whose inhabitants, too, from the first to the last,
> Are sav'd by the very same Saviour of ours;
> And, of course, are begotten God's daughters and sons,
> By the very same truths, and the very same pow'rs.
> (*Times and Seasons*, 4:83)

In harmony with this doctrine, this revelation also emphatically teaches that "the Lord is God, and beside him there is no Savior" (v. 1). The poetic counterpart (stanza 2) reads, "And besides him there ne'er was a Saviour of men." Verse 13, which refers to Christ as the "Only Begotten Son," is changed in the poem to read, "Jesus the Maker and Saviour of all" (stanza 12).

Lucifer Fell and Became Perdition
DOCTRINE AND COVENANTS 76:25–27

76:25 With this verse the scene changes from the throne of the Father and Son, where they were worshiped by holy angels and sanctified beings, to that of our premortal estate.

In this setting in the Grand Council in Heaven, we find Lucifer, a son of the morning, rebelling against the Father and his Firstborn Son, who had been chosen to redeem men from their fallen state. Our understanding of these events has been restored to us line upon line. While translating the book of Genesis, the Prophet learned that Satan (here referred to as Lucifer) sought to be born into mortality as the Son of God and thus become the Redeemer of all humankind. His plan was to do so by contravening the principle of agency, promising that not one soul would be lost; then, having saved all, he would claim for himself the honor of God. In contrast, he who is referred to as the Beloved and Chosen of the Father stood forth and said, "Father thy will be done, and the glory be thine forever." Thus the Father explained, "Wherefore, because that Satan rebelled against me, and sought to destroy the agency of man, which I, the Lord God, had given him; and also, that I should give unto him mine own power; by the power of mine Only Begotten I caused that he should be cast down; and he became Satan. Yea, even the devil, the father of all lies, to deceive, and to blind men, and to lead them captive at his will, even as many as would not hearken unto my voice" (JST Genesis 3:4–5; Moses 4:1–4). In a revelation given shortly after the Prophet received this inspired translation of Genesis, attention was returned to these events when the Lord said, "He [Satan] rebelled against me, saying, Give me thine honor, which is my power; and also a third part of the hosts of heaven turned he away from me because of their agency; and they were thrust down, and thus came the devil and his angels; and, behold, there is a place prepared for them from the beginning, which place is hell" (D&C 29:36–38).

To that which had been revealed, this text adds the knowledge that Satan had been "in authority" in our premortal estate, meaning that an organization of some kind existed in which he held a position of considerable importance. Of this the inspired poetic version states:

> And I saw and bear record of warfare in heav'n;
> For an angel of light, in authority great,
> Rebell'd against Jesus and sought for his pow'r,
> But was thrust down to woe from his Godified state.

Of Christ the revelation simply says that he was "in the bosom of the Father," meaning that there was a closeness or oneness of purpose that existed between them.

Three years later, more of the story would be revealed in the book of Abraham. Here we learn that in the heavenly council our Father, having explained the necessity of a Redeemer, asked, "Whom shall I send? And one answered like unto the Son of Man: Here am I, send me. And another answered and said: Here am I, send me. And the Lord said: I will send the first. And the second was angry, and kept not his first estate; and, at that day, many followed after him" (Abraham 3:27–28).

76:26 Perdition. To be called *perdition* means one is hopelessly and irredeemably lost. It is to be so given up to wickedness and so filled with hatred of the gospel cause and of the Father and the Son that even the Atonement cannot extend the hope of salvation. Of those who come to the point of perdition, the Prophet said, "You cannot save such persons;

you cannot bring them to repentance; they make open war, like the devil, and awful is the consequence" (*Teachings of the Prophet Joseph Smith*, 358; D&C 132:27–28). See commentary on Doctrine and Covenants 76:35.

Lucifer. The name means "the Shining One" (Bible Dictionary, 726). Before his fall the devil was one of the great luminaries of heaven.

Sons of Perdition Suffer Eternal Damnation
DOCTRINE AND COVENANTS 76:28–49

76:29 *He maketh war with the saints of God.* The war that commenced in heaven now finds its battlefield on earth. Satan's animosity is toward the Saints of God, those who, like Christ, seek to do the will of the Father. One result of this ongoing war is that the truth of all things is established in the mouth of two witnesses: the quiet and peaceful whisperings of the Spirit, and, in opposition, the loud, ugly ranting of the adversary. He leaves unopposed no principle that leads to heaven.

76:30 *Sufferings.* Earlier renderings of this verse read "eternal suffering." This was also the case in verse 49 (Woodford, "Historical Development," 949, 950).

76:31 *Only those who have known the power of God and once were partakers thereof* can be numbered among the children of perdition. They must deny the truth, having a sure knowledge of it, and then defy or war against it. These are they who seek the blood of the Lord's anointed. They are partakers of that spirit that filled those who crucified Christ (v. 35).

76:35 *Having denied the Holy Spirit after having received it.* The issue here is denying the Holy Ghost. Christ said: "All manner of sin and blasphemy shall be forgiven unto men: but the blasphemy against the Holy Ghost shall not be forgiven unto men. And whosoever speaketh a word against the Son of man, it shall be forgiven him: but whosoever speaketh against the Holy Ghost, it shall not be forgiven him, neither in this world, neither in the world to come" (Matthew 12:31–32; Mark 3:29).

A perfect knowledge of the gospel comes only by the spirit of revelation, meaning the Holy Ghost. Those who are entrusted with such knowledge and then choose to deny it, coming out in open rebellion against God and his servants, will suffer perdition. These unite themselves with the legions of the devil who warred against God and Christ in the councils of heaven. For such a sin there is no forgiveness in this world or the world to come (*Teachings of the Prophet Joseph Smith*, 358). So it is that the Lord told the Jews that eventually—either in this world or in the world to come—all sins would be forgiven except blasphemy against the Holy Ghost. Blasphemy against the Holy Ghost is the unpardonable sin.

Forgiveness of sin, as this revelation teaches, does not in and of itself open the gate to the celestial kingdom. In the world to come the wicked will suffer until they choose to obey Christ, repent of their sins, and obtain forgiveness. Only then will they be resurrected, after which they will inherit the telestial kingdom (vv. 81–107). Those who have committed the unpardonable sin will not be redeemed from the devil, and after their resurrection, they will be cast out with the devil and his angels into everlasting darkness.

To commit the unpardonable sin, a person must receive the gospel, gain from the Holy Ghost by revelation the absolute knowledge of the divinity of Christ, and then deny "the new and everlasting covenant by which he was sanctified, calling it an unholy thing, and doing despite to the Spirit of grace" (*Teachings of the Prophet Joseph Smith,* 128). He thereby commits murder by assenting unto the Lord's death, that is, having a perfect knowledge of the truth, he comes out in open rebellion and places himself in a position wherein he would have crucified Christ, knowing perfectly that he was the Son of God. Christ is thus crucified afresh and put to open shame. See commentary on Doctrine and Covenants 132:27.

The Prophet further explained: "What must a man do to commit the unpardonable sin? He must receive the Holy Ghost, have the heavens opened unto him, and know God, and then sin against him. After a man has sinned against the Holy Ghost, there is no repentance for him. He has got to say that the sun does not shine while he sees it; he has got to deny Jesus Christ when the heavens have been opened unto him, and to deny the plan of salvation with his eyes open to the truth of it; and from that time he begins be an enemy. This is the case with many apostates of The Church of Jesus Christ of Latter-day Saints.

"When a man begins to be an enemy to this work, he hunts me, he seeks to kill me, and never ceases to thirst for my blood. He gets the spirit of the devil—the same spirit that they had who crucified the Lord of Life—the same spirit that sins against the Holy Ghost" (*Teachings of the Prophet Joseph Smith,* 358).

76:36 Fire and brimstone is a figure of speech representing the anguish associated with sin.

76:37 *The second death.* The second death is separation from the presence of God. The only souls throughout all eternity who will know no glory, no light, nor the presence of God in any form suffer perdition; they are hopelessly lost.

76:38 *Shall not be redeemed.* To be redeemed is to be freed from the dominion and power of Satan. Only those who become children of perdition are left without redemption.

After the sufferings of his wrath. Those who inherit the telestial kingdom will do so only after suffering the wrath of God and making full payment for their sins. All who inherit a degree of glory must eventually be free from sin. The children of perdition remain everlastingly without glory.

76:39 *For all the rest shall be brought forth by the resurrection of the dead.* This passage appears to say that sons of perdition will not be resurrected, yet that is not the case. Paul stated the matter succinctly: "For as in Adam all die, even so in Christ shall all be made alive" (1 Corinthians 15:22). The Book of Mormon repeatedly affirms that the resurrection is universal (2 Nephi 9:15, 22; Alma 11:42; 33:22; 40:4–5). Early manuscripts resolve this difficulty. For instance, *The Evening and The Morning Star*, the "Kirtland Revelation Book," and the "Book of Commandments, Laws, and Covenants," Book B, all read: "Who [or They] shall be brought forth by the resurrection of the dead," thus affirming that those who are destined to suffer perdition will be resurrected (Woodford, "Historical Development," 949–50). The poetic version of this verse reads:

> While all the rest are, through the triumph of Christ,
> Made partakers of grace, by the power of his word.
> (*Times and Seasons*, 4:83)

Thus, "all of the rest"—those inheriting celestial, terrestrial, or telestial glory—are redeemed from the second death, even spiritual death, through the resurrection. Samuel the Lamanite explained: "For behold, he surely must die that salvation may come; yea, it behooveth him and becometh expedient that he dieth, to bring to pass the resurrection of the dead, that thereby men may be brought into the presence of the Lord.

"Yea, behold, this death bringeth to pass the resurrection, and redeemeth all mankind from the first death—that spiritual death; for all mankind, by the fall of Adam being cut off from the presence of the Lord, are considered as dead, both as to things temporal and to things spiritual.

"But behold, the resurrection of Christ redeemeth mankind, yea, even all mankind, and bringeth them back into the presence of the Lord.

"Yea, and it bringeth to pass the condition of repentance, that whosoever repenteth the same is not hewn down and cast into the fire; but whosoever repenteth not is hewn down and cast into the fire; and there cometh upon them again a spiritual death, yea, a second death, for they are cut off again as to things pertaining to righteousness" (Helaman 14:15–18).

76:43 *Who deny the Son after the Father has revealed him.* Before a person can become one of the children of perdition, the Father and the Son must manifest themselves to them. They must have a perfect knowledge of the truthfulness of the gospel which they knowingly deny. See commentary on Doctrine and Covenants 76:35.

76:44 *Their worm dieth not, and the fire is not quenched.* This imagery is chosen to dramatize the endless or eternal nature of the punishment that will be known only to those who will join the devil and his angels in their never-ending punishment. This expression was used both by Isaiah (Isaiah 66:24) and by Christ (Mark 9:44–49). In this mortal world, the worms that prey upon the carcass of the dead must also die, as do fires when there is nothing left to fuel them. Conversely, in the place of eternal torment neither worm nor fire will ever die; that is, the torment will never end.

76:48 *Ordained.* The meaning of the word *ordained* as used in this instance is "appointed" (Webster, *Dictionary*, 1828). See commentary on Doctrine and Covenants 20:2.

Exaltation
DOCTRINE AND COVENANTS 76:50–70

76:50–70 These verses are descriptive of the rewards known to exalted beings. In a subsequent revelation it would be made known to Joseph Smith that within the celestial kingdom are three degrees of glory (D&C 131). These verses are descriptive of the highest of those three degrees (see commentary on D&C 76:71). Of the other two degrees within the celestial kingdom, we know only that their inhabitants will be ministering servants to those who have obtained the fulness of the Father, which can be done only through the ordinance of eternal marriage (D&C 132:15–19).

76:50–53 "We are not preaching a salvation for the inhabitants of the terrestrial or the telestial kingdoms. All of the ordinances of the gospel pertain to the celestial kingdom, and what the Lord will require by way of ordinances, if any, in the other kingdoms he has not revealed" (Smith, *Doctrines of Salvation*, 2:329).

76:50 *We saw and heard.* Not only were Joseph Smith and Sidney Rigdon permitted to see this marvelous vision, but they were also privileged to hear the voice of the Father testify that he who sat on his right hand was his Only Begotten Son.

The resurrection of the just. Two great resurrections await the inhabitants of the earth: the resurrection of the just and the resurrection of the unjust. These could also correctly be called the resurrection of the justified and the resurrection of the unjustified. The justified are those who stand approved of God and are thus heirs of his kingdom and his glory. See commentary on Doctrine and Covenants 88:97–104.

> These are they that arise in their bodies of flesh,
> When the trump of the first resurrection shall sound;
> These are they that come up to Mount Zion, in life,
> Where the blessings and gifts of the spirit abound.
> (*Times and Seasons*, 4:84)

76:51 *Received the testimony of Jesus, and believed on his name.* Two separate concepts are mentioned here. First, those who obtain a place in the celestial world will do so on the strength of their testimony of Christ. In addition to that testimony, they must also believe on the name of Christ. That is, they must also accept and reverence those who come in the authority, or the name, of Christ. They must respect the authority of the priesthood and all of its offices. Not only must they have accepted Christ, but they must also have complied with all the laws and ordinances of his gospel. They must accept and sustain the president of the Church, the Twelve Apostles, and all those who have been called to preside over them in the government of the kingdom of God. In the true and proper sense of things, one cannot accept Christ and at the same time reject those he has sent to act in his name. In the meridian day one could not truly profess to accept Christ while rejecting Peter, James, and John. Similarly, in our day people cannot genuinely profess to accept Christ but reject the testimony of Joseph Smith or his lawful successors in the presidency of the Church, nor can they reject the ordinances of salvation as they are found in that Church. Only by accepting these things can one take upon themselves the name of Christ or truly believe in his name.

Baptized after the manner of his burial. There is no true baptism except by immersion. Paul explained the symbolism of this sacred ordinance by saying, "Know ye not, that so many of us as were baptized into Jesus Christ were baptized into his death? Therefore we are buried with him by baptism into death: that like as Christ was raised up from the dead by the glory of the Father, even so we also should walk in newness of life. For if we have been planted together in the likeness of his death, we shall be also in the likeness of his resurrection: knowing this, that our old man is crucified with him, that the body of sin might be destroyed, that henceforth we should not serve sin" (Romans 6:3–6).

76:52 *By keeping the commandments they might be washed and cleansed from all their sins.* It is supposed by many that the remission of sins comes in the waters of baptism. Independent of keeping the commandments, this is not and cannot be the case. Moroni said in teaching this principle, "Baptism cometh by faith unto the fulfilling the commandments; and the fulfilling the commandments bringeth remission of sins" (Moroni 8:25). Baptism of water precedes the baptism of the Spirit, in which we are sanctified or cleansed. "Be baptized in my name," the Savior said, "that ye may be sanctified by the reception of the Holy Ghost, that ye may stand spotless before me at the last day" (3 Nephi 27:20).

76:53 *Who overcome by faith.* In an earlier revelation the Lord had said, "He that endureth in faith and doeth my will, the same shall overcome" (D&C 63:20). Only those of proven faith will inhabit the celestial kingdom. They will have met and conquered the great challenges of this mortal probation through faith in Christ (JST Genesis 14:30–32).

Sealed by the Holy Spirit of promise. It is not enough to receive an ordinance. For any ordinance to be valid, it must be ratified by the Holy Ghost, making it of efficacy, virtue, or force in and after the resurrection. For an ordinance and its promised blessings to stand approved in the eternal world it must pass a threefold test. First, it must have a divine origin—it must be of God's making, not of man's; second, it must be performed by one in authority, under the direction of the keys or presidency of the appropriate priesthood; third, it must receive the seal of the Holy Spirit of promise. That is, the Holy Ghost—who cannot be deceived—must attest that the one seeking the promised blessing lived in compliance with the terms of the covenant he or she made. "All covenants, contracts, bonds, obligations, oaths, vows, performances, connections, associations, or expectations" that we desire to have in a future world must be approved by the Holy Ghost (D&C 132:7).

This principle assures that there will be no unearned blessings in the heavenly realms. One might deceive a bishop or other ecclesiastical leader and thereby obtain the promise to a blessing in mortality for which he or she is not worthy (for instance, baptism, priesthood, the endowment, temple marriage), but no one will deceive the Holy Ghost. The promises given to those unworthy to receive them will have no effect on the other side of the veil, for the performance involved will not bear the approving seal of the Holy Ghost.

On the other hand, those who have received all the ordinances of salvation—each of them bearing the seal of the Holy Spirit of promise— have the sure promise of salvation. The Holy Ghost may place his approving seal on the various ordinances of salvation as we enter into them; then when we have received all the ordinances of salvation and have received the seal on all those ordinances, we have essentially received the sure promise of exaltation.

The poetic rendering of this verse reads:

> For these overcome, by their faith and their works,
> Being tried in their life-time, as purified gold,
> And seal'd by the spirit of promise, to life,
> By men called of God, as was Aaron of old.
> (*Times and Seasons*, 4:84)

Of this phrase, as it was used by Paul, *Clarke's Commentary* observes with surprising insight: "The Holy Spirit, which is promised to them who believe on Christ Jesus, was given to you, and thus you were *ascertained* to be the children of God, for God has no child who is not a partaker of the Holy Ghost, and he who has this Spirit has God's *seal* that he belongs to the heavenly family. It was customary among all nations, when a person purchased goods of any kind, to mark with his *seal* that which he had bought, in order that he might know it, and be able to claim it if mixed with the goods of others; to this custom the apostle may here allude but it was also customary to set a *seal* upon what was *dedicated to God*, or what was to be *offered to him in sacrifice*" (Clarke, *Clarke's Commentary*, 3:434; emphasis in original).

76:54 *Church of the Firstborn.* As baptism is the gate to the Church, celestial marriage is the gate to the Church of the Firstborn. Its membership is spoken of as "the inner circle of faithful saints who are heirs of exaltation and the fulness of the Father's kingdom" (McConkie, *Mormon*

Doctrine, 139). Members of the Church of the Firstborn are those who have been sealed by the Holy Spirit as described in the previous verse and in Doctrine and Covenants 88:3–5 (see also D&C 78:21). Those members of the Church of the Firstborn who dwell in heaven abide in the presence of God and are heirs of the fulness of the Father (D&C 107:19). They will be numbered with the church of Enoch and will "come down out of heaven" with them to possess the earth (JST Genesis 9:23).

> They are they, of the church of the firstborn of God,—
> And unto whose hands he committeth all things;
> For they hold the keys of the kingdom of heav'n
> And reign with the Saviour, as priests, and as kings.
> (*Times and Seasons*, 4:84)

76:55 *Given all things.* See commentary on Doctrine and Covenants 76:59, 94–95; see also Doctrine and Covenants 93:19, 20, 28.

76:56 *Who are priests and kings.* "Holders of the Melchizedek Priesthood have power to press forward in righteousness, living by every word that proceedeth forth from the mouth of God, magnifying their callings, going from grace to grace, until through the fulness of the ordinances of the temple they receive the fulness of the priesthood and are ordained kings and priests. Those so attaining shall have exaltation and be kings, priests, rulers, and lords in their respective spheres in the eternal kingdoms of the great King who is God our Father (Rev. 1:6; 5:10)" (McConkie, *Mormon Doctrine*, 425).

It naturally follows that if such privileges are accorded to men, women of similar faith will be endowed with similar blessings. Indeed, no man can become a king and priest without an eternal companion at his side, a wife who is a queen and priestess. President Joseph Fielding Smith observed that "women do not hold the priesthood, but if they are faithful and true, they will become priestesses and queens in the kingdom of God, and that implies that they will be given authority" (*Doctrines of Salvation*, 3:178). See commentary on Doctrine and Covenants 132:20.

It is in the house of the Lord that a husband and wife are prepared for such offices and callings, though the realization of the blessings will not come until after the resurrection.

76:57 *After the order of Melchizedek.* See Doctrine and Covenants

107:1–4; see also commentary on Joseph Smith Translation Genesis 14:26–40, page 331.

76:58 *They are gods.* This verse stands at the heart of Mormonism. It sets us apart from the world. It ennobles and exalts beyond the imagination of man. At the commencement of this revelation the Lord promised to reveal "the wonders of eternity," even wisdom and understanding that would "reach to heaven" and that would cause the wisdom of the worldly wise and prudent to "come to naught" (vv. 8–9). It is in such verses as this that the heavens are opened and we are invited to see as prophets saw. What soul can remain unstirred by such a vision! "God himself was once as we are now," declared the Prophet Joseph Smith, "and is an exalted man, and sits enthroned in yonder heavens! That is the great secret. If the veil were rent today, and the great God who holds this world in its orbit, and who upholds all worlds and all things by his power, was to make himself visible—I say, if you were to see him today, you would see him like a man in form—like yourselves in all the person, image, and very form as a man; for Adam was created in the very fashion, image and likeness of God, and received instruction from, and walked, talked and conversed with him, as one man talks and communes with another" (*Teachings of the Prophet Joseph Smith,* 345).

This verse immediately brings to mind the declaration of the Psalmist, who declared, "Ye are gods; and all of you are children of the most High" (Psalm 82:6). And again, the Psalmist asks, "What is man, that thou art mindful of him? and the son of man, that thou visitest him? For thou hast made him a little lower than the angels [gods], and hast crowned him with glory and honour. Thou madest him to have dominion over the works of thy hands; thou hast put all things under his feet" (Psalm 8:4–6).

So it is that we are the children of God, who is himself an exalted, glorified man. And thus it is our divine destiny as his heirs to stand at his side and become as he is. Such is the purpose of the plan of salvation, and for that purpose the faith of the ancients has been restored again in our time, in the dispensation of the fulness of all dispensations.

76:59 *All things are theirs.* "All those who keep his commandments shall grow up from grace to grace, and become heirs of the heavenly kingdom, and joint heirs with Jesus Christ; possessing the same mind, being transformed into the same image or likeness, even the express image of him who fills all in all; being filled with the fullness of this glory, and become one in him, even as the Father, Son and Holy Spirit are one" (Smith, *Lectures on Faith,* 5:2; see also D&C 84:38).

76:60 *They shall overcome all things.* In and through the atonement of Christ, the faithful and obedient will overcome all that is not rightfully a part of the celestial kingdom. Christ reconciles us not only to God but also to the fulness of his glory. Thus it is said of the man and woman who obtain that glory, "Then shall they be gods, because they have no end; therefore shall they be from everlasting to everlasting, because they con- tinue; then shall they be above all, because all things are subject unto them. Then shall they be gods, because they have all power, and the angels are subject unto them" (D&C 132:20).

76:63 When Christ returns to rule and reign upon the earth, he will bring with him all who have lived upon the earth who are worthy of a celestial glory (Joseph Smith–Matthew 1:1). Those living upon the earth who are worthy of that same glory will be caught up to meet them, as will their righteous counterparts in the world of spirits (D&C 88:96–98; 1 Thessalonians 4:13–17). Speaking of this same event, Jude quoted Enoch as promising that the "Lord cometh with ten thousands of his saints" (Jude 1:14).

76:64–65 The first resurrection is synonymous with the resurrection of the just. Patriarchal blessings commonly use the expression "morning of the first resurrection" to identify those who will be exalted. Doctrine and Covenants 45:54 indicates that heathens who knew no law shall come forth in the first resurrection. This resurrection, which is spoken of as being "tolerable," could properly be thought of as the afternoon of the first resurrection.

Abinadi said the first resurrection consisted of "all the prophets, and all those that have believed in their words, or all those that have kept the commandments of God." These, he said, would come forth with Christ in his resurrection (Mosiah 15:22). In like manner, Alma defined the first resurrection as the "resurrection of all those who have been, or who are, or who shall be, down to the resurrection of Christ from the dead" (Alma 40:16). Another resurrection, also termed a first resurrection, will include the righteous down to the time of Christ's return. Those righteous souls who are living when Christ returns, as well as the righteous who are born thereafter, will also come forth in what can properly be called a first res- urrection (D&C 132:19). The idea conveyed in the use of the expression "first resurrection" is that the righteous are resurrected first. The resurrection represents the order of heaven, which demands that the just be resurrected first and only thereafter will they who have been unjust be brought forth.

76:66 *Mount Zion.* In ancient days, Jerusalem, or the holy city, was sometimes referred to as Mount Zion, the place where God dwelled (Psalm 48:1–2). Thus the heavenly abode of God was also referred to as Mount Zion, or "the heavenly Jerusalem" (Hebrews 12:22). In the latter days the Lord revealed that he and his saints would "stand upon Mount Zion, which shall be the city of New Jerusalem. Which city shall be built, beginning at the temple lot, which is appointed by the finger of the Lord, in the western boundaries of the State of Missouri" (D&C 84:2–3; see also 133:18).

76:67 *An innumerable company of angels.* It is a false notion, one not worthy of the gospel of Jesus Christ, that only a few of God's children will be saved in the kingdom of God. In his vision of the redemption of the dead, President Joseph F. Smith saw an "innumerable company of the spirits of the just, who had been faithful in the testimony of Jesus while they lived in mortality" (D&C 138:12). All these awaited a glorious resurrection—and their number was limited to those who had lived from the days of Adam to the time of the crucifixion of Christ. Similarly, Alma spoke of "many, exceedingly great many, who were made pure and entered into the rest of the Lord their God" (Alma 13:12). Paul told the faithful of his day that they would join "an innumerable company of angels" in the heavenly place (Hebrews 12:22), while Daniel numbered the righteous who would stand before God as a "thousand thousands" who ministered to him, "and ten thousand times ten thousand" who stood before him (Daniel 7:10).

When Christ said, "In my Father's house [kingdom] are many mansions: if it were not so, I would have told you. I go to prepare a place for you" (John 14:2; see also Smith, *History of the Church*, 4:184), he was not suggesting that there were various degrees of glory. At that moment he was speaking to the Twelve, and though one of them would betray him, he was giving them the assurance that there was room for them and as many as would believe on their word in his Father's kingdom. There is no boundary to the heavenly city, no limit that needs to be put on its population. There is room in his Father's kingdom for every one of his children, if they will but choose to abide there. Were this not the case, were it true that God did not desire to save all of his children, Christ said, "I would have told you" (John 14:2).

The general assembly and church of Enoch. All those caught up into heaven with Enoch and his city will be numbered among those who eventually inhabit the celestial world. At the same time, all those who inherit the celestial kingdom will also come to a union with the people, or church, of Enoch.

Church . . . of the Firstborn. See commentary on verse 54.

76:69 *Just men made perfect through Jesus.* A just man is one whose course is justified or approved by the Holy Ghost; in the resurrection he will be made perfect because of the atonement of Christ. Thus the inhabitants of paradise are referred to as "just men made perfect" (D&C 129:3).

76:70 *Whose glory is that of the sun.* Speaking of those who will come forth in the morning of the first resurrection to inherit the celestial kingdom, Joseph Smith said, "They shall rise again to dwell in everlasting burnings in immortal glory, not to sorrow, suffer, or die any more; but they shall be heirs of God and joint heirs with Jesus Christ. What is it? To inherit the same power, the same glory and the same exaltation, until you arrive at the station of a God, and ascend the throne of eternal power, the same as those who have gone before" (*Teachings of the Prophet Joseph Smith*, 347).

Those Who Shall Inherit the Terrestrial Kingdom
DOCTRINE AND COVENANTS 76:71–80

76:71 *Fulness of the Father.* This verse affirms that the description in the previous verses (50–70) applies exclusively to the highest of the three degrees in the celestial kingdom (D&C 131). Only there do we find members of the Church of the Firstborn and those who have received the fulness of the Father.

76:72 *Died without law.* The law referred to here is the law of the gospel. Another four years would pass before Joseph Smith learned that the gospel will be taught to those who die without the opportunity to hear it in mortality. Among their number will be many who accept and live it. They, of course, will inherit the celestial kingdom. This phrase describes those who died without hearing the gospel and who did not accept it when it was taught to them in the spirit world, yet who lived worthy of a terrestrial glory. Every person will be rewarded according to the law he or she chooses to live. See commentary on Doctrine and Covenants 88:21–24; 137:7–9.

76:73–74 Those who rejected the gospel in mortality will have the opportunity to hear it again in the spirit world. Thus they receive a second chance to accept it. By so doing they are, of course, blessed—but not with the fulness of the Father. Rather, they receive the glory of the terrestrial order.

They receiv'd not the truth of the Savior at first;
But did, when they heard it in prison, again.
(*Times and Seasons*, 4:84)

76:73 *Spirits of men kept in prison, whom the Son visited, and preached the gospel unto them.* Peter told us that Christ preached the gospel to the "spirits in prison" who had been disobedient in an earlier age (1 Peter 3:19). He also said that the gospel was preached to them that are dead, that they might be judged by the same law or the same standard as those who heard the gospel while in the flesh (1 Peter 4:6). Notwithstanding the plainness of these expressions, most within the historical Christian world reject the idea that the gospel is taught in the spirit world. These verses, however, confirm the plain meaning of Peter's language—though they are greatly amplified in Joseph F. Smith's vision of the redemption of the dead. That vision affirms that all the dead, whether good or evil, are in spirit prison, for all are subject to the effects of Adam's fall, chief among them being death itself. Thus, though we learn in that vision that Christ did not go in person to the wicked, sending others in his name, he nonetheless preached to the spirits in prison, for the righteous too are prisoners who look upon the long absence of their spirits from their bodies as a bondage. See Doctrine and Covenants 138:50.

76:75 Only honorable men and women will inherit the terrestrial kingdom. Among their number will be those who were blinded to the message of the Restoration, either by their allegiance to the theories of men or because both the example and doctrines of apostate Christianity closed their minds to the possibility that such a thing as true religion could exist.

76:77 Those of the terrestrial order will be permitted to enjoy the glory of Christ's presence, but they will not have the privilege of becoming as he is.

76:78 The nature of our glory in the eternal worlds is determined by the nature of our bodies. As a celestial body is necessary to inherit the glories of a celestial world, so a terrestrial body is necessary to enjoy the glories of a terrestrial world and a telestial body those of a telestial world. All three degrees of glory are beyond the capacity of a mortal or fallen body to experience unaided by the power of God. See commentary on Doctrine and Covenants 88:21–32.

76:79 It is one thing to know the truth and quite another to accord one's life with it. In like manner, it is one thing to have a testimony of

Christ and quite another to live true and faithful to that knowledge. There will be those with testimonies who fail to live up to them and who find place in the terrestrial kingdom.

To be valiant is to be courageous, brave, and bold in the testimony of Jesus. It is to be valorous, gallant, and intrepid in that testimony. It is to be fully committed to the doctrines of the kingdom and the cause of Zion. Those who are not willing to give all their heart, might, mind, and strength in the service of their God will not be numbered in the worlds to come with those who do.

Those Who Shall Inherit the Telestial Kingdom
DOCTRINE AND COVENANTS 76:81–91

76:84–85 The citizenry of the telestial kingdom will at death be consigned to hell, where they must pay in full measure for their sins. Thereafter, they will come forth in the resurrection of the unjust to take their place in the telestial or lowest of the degrees of glory. "You cannot take a murderer, a suicide, an adulterer, a liar, or one who was or is thoroughly abominable in his life here, and simply by the performance of an ordinance of the gospel, cleanse him from sin and usher him into the presence of God," explained President Joseph F. Smith. "God has not instituted a plan of that kind, and it cannot be done. He has said you shall repent of your sins. The wicked will have to repent of their wickedness. Those who die without the knowledge of the gospel will have to come to the knowledge of it, and those who sin against light will have to pay the uttermost farthing for their transgression and their departure from the gospel, before they can ever get back to it. Do not forget that. Do not forget it, you elders in Israel, nor you, mothers in Israel, either; and, when you seek to save either the living or the dead, bear it in mind that you can only do it on the principle of their repentance and acceptation of the plan of life. That is the only way in which you can succeed" (*Gospel Doctrine*, 95).

76:86–87 Those in this kingdom will be ministered to by those in the terrestrial kingdom, who will be enlightened by the Holy Ghost. Those in the terrestrial kingdom, in turn, are ministered to by celestial beings.

76:89 *The glory of the telestial, which surpasses all understanding.* Here we are told that the glory of the telestial world will exceed anything known to this earth. In so saying, it is not the purpose of this revelation to encourage satisfaction in obtaining this rather than a greater glory. Instead, this promise evidences the love of God even for his errant children and his willingness to bless them with all that they are willing to receive. What are the blessings of this kingdom? Satan and his legions will have no power here. Death and suffering will be unknown. Hunger and pain will no longer exist. Oppression and injustices will have no place. Through Christ, all the effects of Adam's fall will have been rectified. This alone will create a world the glory and goodness of which will surpass all understanding. The nature of this world will be much like the one known to Adam and Eve prior to the fall.

The Glories of the Telestial, Terrestrial, and Celestial Kingdoms Contrasted
DOCTRINE AND COVENANTS 76:94–98

76:94–95 These verses speak of the glories to be enjoyed by all who inherit the celestial kingdom. They are heirs of God and joint-heirs with Christ. Explaining this phrase, Joseph Smith taught that they would "inherit the same power, the same glory and the same exaltation" as that enjoyed by Christ "until [they] arrive at the station of a God, and ascend the throne of eternal power, the same as those who have gone before. What did Jesus do? Why; I do the things I saw my Father do when worlds came rolling into existence. My Father worked out his kingdom with fear and trembling, and I must do the same; and when I get my kingdom, I shall present it to my Father, so that he may obtain kingdom upon kingdom, and it will exalt him in glory. He will then take a higher exaltation, and I will take his place, and thereby become exalted myself. So that Jesus treads in the tracks of his Father, and inherits what God did before; and God is thus glorified and exalted in the salvation and exaltation of all his children" (*Teachings of the Prophet Joseph Smith*, 347–48).

76:94 *Church of the Firstborn.* Faithful Saints who have received the fulness of temple blessings are members of the Church of the Firstborn. They are heirs of exaltation and of the fulness of the Father's kingdom. With the faithful of ages past, they become joint-heirs with Christ in receiving all that the Father has. See Doctrine and Covenants 93:20–22; see also commentary on Doctrine and Covenants 76:54.

They see as they are seen, and know as they are known. Those who obtain a celestial glory will no longer see and know in part. All things will be opened to their understanding. Developing this same thought, Paul said, "For now we see through a glass, darkly; but then face to face: now I know in part; but then shall I know even as also I am known"

(1 Corinthians 13:12). The word *glass* in this text refers to a mirror, which in that ancient day was made of polished metal that often gave an imperfect or distorted image. By analogy Paul is saying that in this life we often have an imperfect or distorted view of eternal things, but in a future day we will see things as they really are. *The Living New Testament* renders Paul's words thus, "We can understand only a little about God now, as if we were peering at his reflection in a poor mirror; but someday we are going to see him in his completeness, face to face" (1 Corinthians 13:12). In that day we will come to understand the majesty and glory with which God has endowed all his creations.

The Telestial Kingdom
DOCTRINE AND COVENANTS 76:99–113

76:99–101 The telestial kingdom is full of religions and priests and ministers of every kind. It is a battleground of ideas and ideologies. Professing Christians there will include self-claimed disciples of Paul declaring the gospel of salvation by grace alone; those loyal to Apollos, or the learning of men, as articulated by the suave and sophisticated; and those claiming to follow Peter (Cephas) and the church of Rome in thoughtless submission. "These are they who say they are some of one and some of another" (v. 100), some of Christ—or so they profess—some of John and the mystery of apocalypse, others of Moses and the law that he brought, some of Elias, and of Esaias, and of Isaiah, of Enoch and still more—

> These are they that came out for Apollos and Paul;
> For Cephas and Jesus, in all kinds of hope;
> For Enoch and Moses, and Peter, and John;
> For Luther and Calvin, and even the Pope.
>
> For they never received the gospel of Christ,
> Nor the prophetic spirit that came from the Lord;
> Nor the covenant neither, which Jacob once had;
> They went their own way, and they have their reward.
> (*Times and Seasons*, 4:85)

Mischief and the profession of piety have always gone hand in hand, as has the practice of picking and choosing among heaven's truths to find those that fit the professing believer's appetites and fancies. At the same time, such people turn a blind eye to the principles of sacrifice and obedience. So it is that living prophets are ignored in preference to dead ones and the spirit of revelation denied while the Bible is enshrined.

76:112 The question is often asked, Throughout the endless expanses of eternity will there eventually be advancement from degree to degree? That is, can those whose glory is telestial progress to a terrestrial order, while those of a terrestrial order become celestial? Though conflicting opinions have been given by men in positions of authority, the question is answered, in the judgment of the writers, by the very nature of the resurrection itself. If the resurrection is the inseparable union of body and spirit (Alma 11:45; D&C 138:17), then that which is telestial cannot be changed so that it could endure or abide a terrestrial law, "worlds without end," and that which is terrestrial for the same reason could not become celestial. See commentary on Doctrine and Covenants 88:17–32.

All the Faithful May See the Vision of the Degrees of Glory
DOCTRINE AND COVENANTS 76:114–19

76:114–19 Doctrine and Covenants 76 stands unrivaled as the greatest revelation of our dispensation. No other revelation reveals more of eternity past and eternity future than this revelation does. From it we learn of the role of Christ as creator and Savior of countless worlds, of the premortal life and the war in heaven, of the destiny of those who become children of perdition, and of the glories of the celestial, terrestrial, and telestial kingdoms. This combination of visions given to the Prophet and Sidney Rigdon stands unsurpassed in teaching the doctrine of heirship, with its testimony that mortal man in the course of the eternities can become equal in power, might, and dominion with God himself! The boldness of such a doctrine assures that we as a people will forever stand alone among those professing a faith in Christ. None want fellowship with us on doctrinal grounds, nor would we have reason to seek it with them. Plainly we stand alone. Yet in it all, no doctrine in this revelation matches in greatness the promise that every faithful soul is a rightful heir to all the mysteries of the kingdom, to every revelation and vision given or shown to the prophets, even to the manifestation of Christ himself.

There is but one gospel, and by that gospel all humankind will be saved or condemned. If that gospel allows one man to repent, it must in like manner allow all men the same privilege; and if it grants the visions of eternity to one man, it must, by the same principle, grant that same vision to all worthy Saints who seek it. Thus it is for each of us to choose that portion of heaven's light in which we will stand.

76:115 *He commanded that we should not write.* Joseph Smith later explained, "I could explain a hundred fold more than I ever have of the glories of the kingdoms manifested to me in vision, were I permitted, and were the people prepared to receive them" (*Teachings of the Prophet Joseph Smith*, 305).

76:118 *Bear his presence in the world of glory.* This revelation, which began with the promise that the faithful Saints may have the "wonders of eternity" (v. 8) revealed to them now, concludes with the promise that they might stand in the presence of God "while in the flesh." It is fundamental to our faith that if the God of heaven extends the promise of salvation to so much as a single soul he must in justice extend it to every soul on the same terms and conditions. If one can receive a remission of sins through faith, repentance, and baptism, so can all; if one can receive an answer to his prayers, so can all; if one can entertain angels, so can all; if one can stand in his presence while in the flesh, so can all. Such is the promise of the restored gospel; such is the declaration of this text. We do not have one gospel for prophets and another for their followers. There is but one gospel, and its covenants and promised blessings are alike for all.

A Vision
The Prophet's Response to a Poem by W. W. Phelps
February 1843

1 I will go, I will go, to the home of the Saints,
Where the virtue's the value, and life the reward;
But before I return to my former estate
I must fulfil the mission I had from the Lord.

2 Wherefore, hear, O ye heavens, and give ear O ye earth;
And rejoice ye inhabitants truly again;
For the Lord he is God, and his life never ends,
And besides him there ne'er was a Saviour of men.

3 His ways are a wonder; his wisdom is great;
The extent of his doings, there's none can unveil;
His purposes fail not; from age unto age
He still is the same, and his years never fail.

4 His throne is the heavens, his life time is all
  Of eternity *now*, and eternity *then;*
  His union is power, and none stays his hand,—
  The Alpha, Omega, for ever: Amen.

5 For thus saith the Lord, in the spirit of truth,
  I am merciful, gracious, and good unto those
  That fear me, and live for the life that's to come;
  My delight is to honor the saints with repose;

6 That serve me in righteousness true to the end;
  Eternal's their glory, and great their reward;
  I'll surely reveal all my myst'ries to them,—
  The great hidden myst'ries in my kingdom stor'd—

7 From the council in Kolob, to time on the earth.
  And for ages to come unto them I will show
  My pleasure & will, what my kingdom will do:
  Eternity's wonders they truly shall know.

8 Great things of the future I'll show unto them,
  Yea, things of the vast generations to rise;
  For their wisdom and glory shall be very great,
  And their pure understanding extend to the skies:

9 And before them the wisdom of wise men shall cease,
  And the nice understanding of prudent ones fail!
  For the light of my spirit shall light mine elect,
  And the truth is so mighty 't will ever prevail.

10 And the secrets and plans of my will I'll reveal;
  The sanctified pleasures when earth is renew'd,
  What the eye hath not seen, nor the ear hath yet heard;
  Nor the heart of the natural man ever hath view'd.

11 I, Joseph, the prophet, in spirit beheld,
  And the eyes of the inner man truly did see
  Eternity sketch'd in a vision from God,
  Of what was, and now is, and yet is to be.

12 Those things which the Father ordained of old,
Before the world was, or a system had run,—
Through Jesus the Maker and Saviour of all;
The only begotten, (Messiah) his son.

13 Of whom I bear record, as all prophets have,
And the record I bear is the fulness,—yea even
The truth of the gospel of Jesus—*the Christ*,
With whom I convers'd, in the vision of heav'n.

14 For while in the act of translating his word,
Which the Lord in his grace had appointed to me,
I came to the gospel recorded by John,
Chapter fifth and the twenty ninth verse, which you'll see.

Which was given as follows:
"Speaking of the resurrection of the dead,—
"Concerning those who shall hear the voice of
"the son of man—
"And shall come forth:—
"They who have done good in the resurrection
"of the just.
"And they who have done evil in the resurrection of the unjust."

15 I marvel'd at these resurrections, indeed!
For it came unto me by the spirit direct:—
And while I did meditate what it all meant,
The Lord touch'd the eyes of my own intellect:—

16 Hosanna forever! they open'd anon,
And the glory of God shone around where I was;
And there was the Son, at the Father's right hand,
In a fulness of glory, and holy applause.

17 I beheld round the throne, holy angels and hosts,
And sanctified beings from worlds that have been,
In holiness worshipping God and the Lamb,
Forever and ever, amen and amen!

18 And now after all of the proofs made of him,
By witnesses truly, by whom he was known,
This is mine, last of all, that he lives; yea he lives!
And sits at the right hand of God, on his throne.

19 And I heard a great voice, bearing record from heav'n,
He's the Saviour, and only begotten of God—
By him, of him, and through him, the worlds were all made,
Even all that career in the heavens so broad.

20 Whose inhabitants, too, from the first to the last,
Are sav'd by the very same Saviour of ours;
And, of course, are begotten God's daughters and sons,
By the very same truths, and the very same pow'rs.

21 And I saw and bear record of warfare in heav'n;
For an angel of light, in authority great,
Rebell'd against Jesus, and sought for his pow'r,
But was thrust down to woe from his Godified state.

22 And the heavens all wept, and the tears drop'd like dew,
That Lucifer, son of the morning had fell!
Yea, is fallen! is fall'n, and become, Oh, alas!
The son of Perdition; the devil of hell!

23 And while I was yet in the spirit of truth,
The commandment was: write ye the vision all out;
For Satan, old serpent, the devil's for war,—
And yet will encompass the saints round about.

24 And I saw, too, the suff'ring and mis'ry of those,
(Overcome by the devil, in warfare and fight,)
In hell-fire, and vengeance, the doom of the damn'd;
For the Lord said, the vision is further: so write.

25 For thus saith the Lord, now concerning all those
Who know of my power and partake of the same;
And suffer themselves, that they be overcome
By the power of Satan; despising my name:—

26 Defying my power, and denying the truth;—
They are they—of the world, or of men, most forlorn,
The Sons of Perdition, of whom, ah! I say,
'Twere better for them had they never been born!

27 They're vessels of wrath, and dishonor to God,
Doom'd to suffer his wrath, in the regions of woe,
Through the terrific night of eternity's round,
With the devil and all of his angels below:

28 Of whom it is said, no forgiveness is giv'n,
In this world, alas! nor the world that's to come;
For they have denied the spirit of God,
After having receiv'd it: and mis'ry's their doom.

29 And denying the only begotten of God,—
And crucify him to themselves, as they do,
And openly put him to shame in their flesh,
By gospel they cannot repentance renew.

30 They are they, who must go to the great lake of fire,
Which burneth with brimstone, yet never consumes,
And dwell with the devil, and angels of his,
While eternity goes and eternity comes.

31 They are they, who must groan through the great second death,
And are not redeemed in the time of the Lord;
While all the rest are, through the triumph of Christ,
Made partakers of grace, by the power of his word.

32 The myst'ry of Godliness truly is great;—
The past, and the present, and what is to be;
And this is the gospel—glad tidings to all,
Which the voice from the heavens bore record to me:

33 That he came to the world in the middle of time,
To lay down his life for his friends and his foes,
And bear away sin as a mission of love;
And sanctify earth for a blessed repose.

34 'Tis decreed, that he'll save all the work of his hands,
And sanctify them by his own precious blood;
And purify earth for the Sabbath of rest,
By the agent of fire, as it was by the flood.

35 The Savior will save all his Father did give,
Even all that he gave in the regions abroad,
Save the Sons of Perdition: They're lost; ever lost,
And can never return to the presence of God.

36 They are they, who must reign with the devil in hell,
In eternity now, and eternity then,
Where the worm dieth not, and the fire is not quench'd;—
And the punishment still, is eternal. Amen.

37 And which is the torment apostates receive,
But the end, or the place where the torment began,
Save to them who are made to partake of the same,
Was never, nor will be, revealed unto man.

38 Yet God shows by vision a glimpse of their fate,
And straightway he closes the scene that was shown:
So the width, or the depth, or the misery thereof,
Save to those that partake, is forever unknown.

39 And while I was pondering, the vision was closed;
And the voice said to me, write the vision: for lo!
'Tis the end of the scene of the sufferings of those,
Who remain filthy still in their anguish and woe.

40 And again I bear record of heavenly things,
Where virtue's the value, above all that's pric'd—
Of the truth of the gospel concerning the just,
That rise in the first resurrection of Christ.

41 Who receiv'd and believ'd, and repented likewise,
And then were baptis'd, as a man always was,
Who ask'd and receiv'd a remission of sin,
And honored the kingdom by keeping its laws.

42 Being buried in water, as Jesus had been,
And keeping the whole of his holy commands,
They received the gift of the spirit of truth,
By the ordinance truly of laying on hands.

43 For these overcome, by their faith and their works,
Being tried in their life-time, as purified gold,
And seal'd by the spirit of promise, to life,
By men called of God, as was Aaron of old.

44 They are they, of the church of the first born of God,—
And unto whose hands he committeth all things;
For they hold the keys of the kingdom of heav'n,
And reign with the Savior, as priests, and as kings.

45 They're priests of the order of Melchisedek,
Like Jesus, (from whom is this highest reward,)
Receiving a fulness of glory and light;
As written: They're Gods; even sons of the Lord.

46 So all things are theirs; yea, of life, or of death;
Yea, whether things now, or to come, all are theirs,
And they are the Savior's, and he is the Lord's,
Having overcome all, as eternity's heirs.

47 'Tis wisdom that man never glory in man,
But give God the glory for all that he hath;
For the righteous will walk in the presence of God,
While the wicked are trod under foot in his wrath.

48 Yea, the righteous shall dwell in the presence of God,
And of Jesus, forever, from earth's second birth—
For when he comes down in the splendor of heav'n,
All these he'll bring with him, to reign on the earth.

49 These are they that arise in their bodies of flesh,
When the trump of the first resurrection shall sound;
These are they that come up to Mount Zion, in life,
Where the blessings and gifts of the spirit abound.

50 These are they that have come to the heavenly place;
  To the numberless courses of angels above:
  To the city of God; e'en the holiest of all,
And the home of the blessed, the fountain of love:

51 To the church of old Enoch, and of the first born:
  And gen'ral assembly of ancient renown'd,
Whose names are all kept in the archives of heav'n,
  As chosen and faithful, and fit to be crown'd.

52 These are they that are perfect through Jesus' own blood,
  Whose bodies celestial are mention'd by Paul,
  Where the sun is the typical glory thereof,
And God, and his Christ, are the true judge of all.

53 Again I beheld the terrestrial world,
  In the order and glory of Jesus, go on;
'Twas not as the church of the first born of God
But shone in its place, as the moon to the sun.

54 Behold, these are they that have died without law;
  The heathen of ages that never had hope,
And those of the region and shadow of death,
  The spirits in prison, that light has brought up.

55 To spirits in prison the Savior once preach'd,
  And taught them the gospel, with powers afresh;
And then were the living baptiz'd for their dead,
  That they might be judg'd as if men in the flesh.

56 These are they that are hon'rable men of the earth;
  Who were blinded and dup'd by the cunning of men:
  They receiv'd not the truth of the Savior at first;
But did, when they heard it in prison, again.

57 Not valiant for truth, they obtain'd not the crown,
  But are of that glory that's typ'd by the moon:
They are they, that come into the presence of Christ,
  But not to the fulness of God, on his throne.

58 Again I beheld the telestial, as third,
The lesser, or starry world, next in its place,
For the leaven must leaven three measures of meal,
And every knee bow that is subject to grace.

59 These are they that receiv'd not the gospel of Christ,
Or evidence, either, that he ever was;
As the stars are all diff'rent in glory and light,
So differs the glory of these by the laws.

60 These are they that deny not the spirit of God,
But are thrust down to hell, with the devil, for sins,
As hypocrites, liars, whoremongers, and thieves,
And stay 'till the last resurrection begins.

61 'Till the Lamb shall have finish'd the work he begun;
Shall have trodden the wine press, in fury alone,
And overcome all by the pow'r of his might:
He conquers to conquer, and save all his own.

62 These are they that receive not a fulness of light,
From Christ, in eternity's world, where they are,
The terrestrial sends them the Comforter, though;
And minist'ring angels, to happify there.

63 And so the telestial is minister'd to,
By ministers from the terrestrial one,
As terrestrial is, from the celestial throne;
And the great, greater, greatest, seem's stars, moon, and sun.

64 And thus I beheld, in the vision of heav'n,
The telestial glory, dominion and bliss,
Surpassing the great understanding of men,—
Unknown, save reveal'd, in a world vain as this.

65 And lo, I beheld the terrestrial, too,
Which excels the telestial in glory and light,
In splendor, and knowledge, and wisdom, and joy,
In blessings, and graces, dominion and might.

66 I beheld the celestial, in glory sublime;
Which is the most excellent kingdom that is,—
Where God, e'en the Father, in harmony reigns;
Almighty, supreme, and eternal, in bliss.

67 Where the church of the first born in union reside,
And they see as they're seen, and they know as they're known;
Being equal in power, dominion and might,
With a fulness of glory and grace, round his throne.

68 The glory celestial is one like the sun;
The glory terrestr'al is one like the moon;
The glory telestial is one like the stars,
And all harmonize like the parts of a tune.

69 As the stars are all different in lustre and size,
So the telestial region, is mingled in bliss;
From least unto greatest, and greatest to least,
The reward is exactly as promis'd in this.

70 These are they that came out for Apollos and Paul;
For Cephas and Jesus, in all kinds of hope;
For Enoch and Moses, and Peter, and John;
For Luther and Calvin, and even the Pope.

71 For they never received the gospel of Christ,
Nor the prophetic spirit that came from the Lord;
Nor the covenant neither, which Jacob once had;
They went their own way, and they have their reward.

72 By the order of God, last of all, these are they,
That will not be gather'd with saints here below,
To be caught up to Jesus, and meet in the cloud:—
In darkness they worshipp'd; to darkness they go.

73 These are they that are sinful, the wicked at large,
That glutted their passion by meanness or worth;
All liars, adulterers, sorc'rers, and proud;
And suffer, as promis'd, God's wrath on the earth.

74 These are they that must suffer the vengeance of hell,
  'Till Christ shall have trodden all enemies down,
  And perfected his work, in the fulness of times:
  And is crown'd on his throne with his glorious crown.

75 The vast multitude of the telestial world—
  As the stars of the skies, or the sands of the sea;—
  The voice of Jehovah echo'd far and wide,
  Ev'ry tongue shall confess, and they all bow the knee.

76 Ev'ry man shall be judg'd by the works of his life,
  And receive a reward in the mansions prepar'd;
  For his judgments are just, and his works never end,
  As his prophets and servants have always declar'd.

77 But the great things of God, which he show'd unto me,
  Unlawful to utter, I dare not declare;
  They surpass all the wisdom and greatness of men,
  And only are seen, as has Paul, where they are.

78 I will go, I will go, while the secret of life,
  Is blooming in heaven, and blasting in hell;
  Is leaving on earth, and a budding in space:—
  I will go, I will go, with you, brother, farewell.

JOSEPH SMITH.
Nauvoo, February 1843.
(*Times and Seasons*, 4:81–85)

DOCTRINE AND COVENANTS 77

DATE: MARCH 1832
PLACE: HIRAM, OHIO

In the form of questions and answers, the Prophet unlocked the book of Revelation by the spirit of revelation. He recorded that "in connection with the translation of the Scriptures, I received the following explanation of the Revelation of St. John" (Smith, *History of the Church*, 1:253).

Beasts Have Spirits and Shall Dwell in Eternal Felicity on an Immortal Earth

DOCTRINE AND COVENANTS 77:1–4

77:1 The sea of glass was shown to John in vision when "a door was opened in heaven" (Revelation 4:1), revealing God sitting upon a throne. "And before the throne there was a sea of glass like unto crystal" (Revelation 4:6). John described heaven using earthly elements as likenesses. The Prophet Joseph Smith later explained that "angels do not reside on a planet like this earth; but they reside in the presence of God, on a globe like a sea of glass and fire, where all things for their glory are manifest, past, present, and future, and are continually before the Lord. The place where God resides is a great Urim and Thummim. This earth, in its sanctified and immortal state, will be made like unto crystal and will be a Urim and Thummim to the inhabitants who dwell thereon, whereby all things pertaining to an inferior kingdom, or all kingdoms of a lower order, will be manifest to those who dwell on it; and this earth will be Christ's" (D&C 130:6–9). The Lord revealed that the earth "must needs be sanctified from all unrighteousness, that it may be prepared for the celestial glory; for after it hath filled the measure of its creation, it shall be crowned with glory, even with the presence of God the Father" (D&C 88:18–19). John was privileged to see in vision that future day when the Father and the Son will crown the earth with the glory of their presence. This will take place after the Millennium, when the earth becomes the celestial kingdom for those who are worthy of that glory (D&C 88:17–20).

77:2 *The four beasts.* John's revelation reads: "Round about the throne, were four beasts full of eyes before and behind. And the first beast was like a lion, and the second beast like a calf, and the third beast had a face as a man, and the fourth beast was like a flying eagle. And the four beasts had each of them six wings about him; and they were full of eyes within: and they rest not day and night, saying, Holy, holy, holy, Lord God Almighty, which was, and is, and is to come" (Revelation 4:6–8). Animals not only find place in the celestial kingdom but also demonstrate an attitude of worship. Such worship is meaningful only to the extent that it represents an intelligent expression of faith on the part of the creatures involved. Animals, therefore, may have a natural intelligence beyond what has generally been supposed and may have the capacity to consciously choose to conform to the law by which their respective kingdoms are governed. They are very much a part of the gospel plan. They were created by God and occupied an important place in the earth's Edenic state. When Adam fell, animals fell too and thus stood as much in need of salvation through Christ as did our first parents. The restored gospel extends our understanding of the length and breadth of the Atonement to include all living things, not just the offspring of Adam and Eve.

John uses figurative expressions in describing heaven. The beasts shown to him represent different classes of beings. "John saw the actual beast in heaven," declared the Prophet Joseph Smith, "showing to John that beasts did actually exist there. . . . John saw curious looking beasts in heaven; he saw every creature that was in heaven,—all the beasts, fowls and fish in heaven,—actually there, giving glory to God. How do you prove it? (See Rev. 5:13.) 'And every creature which is in heaven, and on the earth, and under the earth, and such as are in the sea, and all that are in them, heard I saying, Blessing, and honor, and glory, and power, be unto Him that sitteth upon the throne, and unto the Lamb for ever and ever.'

"I suppose John saw beings there of a thousand forms, that had been saved from ten thousand times ten thousand earths like this,—strange beasts of which we have no conception: all might be seen in heaven. The grand secret was to show John what there was in heaven. John learned that God glorified Himself by saving all that His hands had made, whether beasts, fowls, fishes or men; and He will glorify Himself with them.

"Says one, 'I cannot believe in the salvation of beasts.' Any man who would tell you that this could not be, would tell you that the revelations are not true. John heard the words of the beasts giving glory to God, and understood them. God who made the beasts could understand every language spoken by them. The four beasts were four of the most noble animals that had filled the measure of their creation, and had been saved from other worlds, because they were perfect: they were like angels in their sphere. We are not told where they came from, and I do not know; but they were seen and heard by John praising and glorifying God" (*Teachings of the Prophet Joseph Smith,* 291–92).

It should be noted that not all beasts seen by John in vision were actual beasts dwelling in heaven. The Revelator, like Daniel and other prophets, was shown earthly events that were to come. The Prophet Joseph Smith taught that the fierce-looking beasts of the book of Revelation represented corrupt kingdoms on the earth: "When God made use of the figure of a beast in visions to the prophets He did it to represent those kingdoms which had degenerated and become corrupt, savage and beast-like in their dispositions, even the degenerate kingdoms of the wicked world; but He never made use of the figure of a beast nor any of the brute kind to represent His kingdom.

"Daniel says (chap. 7, v. 16) when he saw the vision of the four beasts, 'I came near unto one of them that stood by, and asked him the truth of all this,' the angel interpreted the vision to Daniel. . . . You there see that the beasts are spoken of to represent the kingdoms of the world, the inhabitants whereof were beastly and abominable characters; they were murderers, corrupt, carnivorous, and brutal in their dispositions. The lion, the bear, the leopard, and the ten-horned beast represented the kingdoms of the world, says Daniel; for I refer to the prophets to qualify my observations which I make" (*Teachings of the Prophet Joseph Smith,* 289).

The spirit of man in the likeness of his person. The mortal body was created in the image of the spirit body, or as this verse states, "that which is temporal in the likeness of that which is spiritual." The premortal Christ explained to the brother of Jared: "Seest thou that ye are created after mine own image? Yea, even all men were created in the beginning after mine own image. Behold, this body, which ye now behold, is the body of my spirit; and man have I created after the body of my spirit; and even as I appear unto thee to be in the spirit will I appear unto my people in the flesh" (Ether 3:15–16). Further, the spirit of each individual is in the likeness of God because "man, as a spirit, was begotten and born of heavenly parents, and reared to maturity in the eternal mansions of the Father" (Clark, *Messages*, 4:205). All things produce after their own kind whether in obtaining a body of spirit or a body of flesh.

The spirit of the beast, and every other creature. Each form of animal life is created after the image of a spirit body that, like humankind, existed before the temporal existence in mortality. In 1909 the First Presidency declared regarding God's creations: "By His almighty power He organized the earth, and all that it contains, from spirit and element, which exist co-eternally with Himself. He formed every plant that grows, and every animal that breathes, each after its own kind, spiritually and temporally—'that which is spiritual being in the likeness of that which is temporal, and that which is temporal in the likeness of that which is spiritual.' He made the tadpole and the ape, the lion and the elephant but He did not make them in His own image, nor endow them with Godlike reason and intelligence. Nevertheless, the whole animal creation will be perfected and perpetuated in the Hereafter, each class in its 'distinct order or sphere,' and will enjoy 'eternal felicity.' That fact has been made plain in this dispensation (Doctrine and Covenants 77:3)" (Clark, *Messages*, 4:206). Because creatures that fulfill the measure of their creation are resurrected in glory, it seems to follow that they will have power to beget spirits of their kind. The Prophet Joseph Smith reasoned, "Where was there ever a son without a father? And where was there ever a father without first being a son? Whenever did a tree or anything spring into existence without a progenitor? And everything comes in this way" (*Teachings of the Prophet Joseph Smith*, 373).

77:5 *Four and twenty elders.* We are told in verse five that these elders, who "had on their heads crowns of gold" (Revelation 4:4), were still in the paradise of God, waiting the day of their resurrection to crowns of glory. It would appear that John saw things in this instance not as they are but as they will be. Doctrine and Covenants 137 follows this same pattern. In this revelation, Joseph Smith saw a vision of his father and mother in the celestial kingdom, even though they were still living (v. 5).

This Earth Has a Temporal Existence of Seven Thousand Years
DOCTRINE AND COVENANTS 77:5-7

77:5 *The seven churches.* John addressed his account of the revelation received on the isle of Patmos to "the seven churches which are in Asia" (Revelation 1:11).

77:6–7 These verses help us understand when the events in the book of Revelation will be fulfilled. The book held "in the right hand of him that sat on the throne" (Revelation 5:1) contained the works of God from the time of Adam through the end of the Millennium. Each thousand-year period is represented by its respective seal. "John had the curtains of heaven withdrawn," explained the Prophet Joseph Smith, "and by vision looked through the dark vista of future ages, and contemplated events that should transpire throughout every subsequent period of time, until the final winding up scene" (*Teachings of the Prophet Joseph Smith*, 247). Further, the Lord's revealed timetable of John's vision indicates that most of the tribulations described by John will take place after the opening of the seventh seal, or during the seventh thousand years.

Various Angels Restore the Gospel and Minister on Earth

DOCTRINE AND COVENANTS 77:8–10

77:8 *The four angels.* John recorded, "I saw four angels standing on the four corners of the earth, holding the four winds of the earth, that the wind should not blow on the earth, nor on the sea, nor on any tree" (Revelation 7:1).

They who have the everlasting gospel to commit to every nation, kindred, tongue, and people. The restoration of the fulness of the gospel came to pass during the sixth thousand years through the instrumentality of the Prophet Joseph Smith. Various angels appeared to him, restoring keys and knowledge in opening the dispensation of the fulness of times.

77:9 *Till we have sealed the servants of our God in their foreheads.* Concerning this sealing, the Prophet Joseph Smith said: "Four destroying angels holding power over the four quarters of the earth until the servants of God are sealed in their foreheads, which signifies sealing the blessing upon their heads, meaning the everlasting covenant, thereby making their calling and election sure. When a seal is put upon the father and mother, it secures their posterity, so that they cannot be lost, but will be saved by virtue of the covenant of their father and mother" (*Teachings of the Prophet Joseph Smith*, 321).

This is Elias. "According to the plan and program of the Lord," Elder McConkie explained, "the dispensation of the fulness of times is 'the times of restitution of all things, which God hath spoken by the mouth of all his holy prophets since the world began.' (Acts 3:21.) This restoration is to be effected by Elias. Before the winding up of the Lord's work, the promise is: 'Elias truly shall first come, and restore all things.' (Matt. 17:11.) With these ancient scriptures before us, these questions arise: Who is the promised Elias who was to come and restore all things? Has this work of restoration taken place? Or is it something that is yet future?

"Correcting the Bible by the spirit of revelation, the Prophet restored a statement of John the Baptist which says that Christ is the Elias who was to restore all things. ([JST] John 1:21–28.) By revelation we are also informed that the Elias who was to restore all things is the angel Gabriel who was known in mortality as Noah. (D&C 27:6–7; Luke 1:5–25; *Teachings of the Prophet Joseph Smith*, 157.) From the same authentic source we also learn that the promised Elias is John the Revelator. (D&C 77:9, 14.) Thus there are three different revelations which name Elias as being three different persons. What are we to conclude?

"By finding answer to the question, by whom has the restoration been effected, we shall find who Elias is and find there is no problem in harmonizing these apparently contradictory revelations. Who has restored all things? Was it one man? Certainly not. Many angelic ministrants have been sent from the courts of glory to confer keys and powers, to commit their dispensations and glories again to men on earth. At least the following have come: Moroni, John the Baptist, Peter, James, and John, Moses, Elijah, Elias, Gabriel, Raphael, and Michael. (D&C 13; 110; 128:19–21.) Since it is apparent that no one messenger has carried the whole burden of the restoration, but rather that each has come with a specific endowment from on high, it becomes clear that Elias is a composite personage. The expression must be understood to be a name and a title for those whose mission it was to commit keys and powers to men in this final dispensation. (*Doctrines of Salvation*, vol. 1, pp. 170–174.)" (*Mormon Doctrine*, 221).

The Sealing of the 144,000

DOCTRINE AND COVENANTS 77:11

77:11 *High priests, ordained unto the holy order of God.* Those inheriting celestial glory are high priests or "priests of the Most High, after the order of Melchizedek" (D&C 76:57).

Ordained out of every nation. The twelve tribes of Israel have been "scattered upon all the face of the earth, and also among all nations" (1 Nephi 22:3). The gathering of Israel through the Restoration includes Saints of every nation who receive the highest ordinances of the priesthood. Temple blessings will be administered to these Saints by those of their own nation and in their own tongue (Revelation 5:9–10; D&C 90:11).

To bring as many as will come to the church of the Firstborn. Confirmed members of The Church of Jesus Christ of Latter-day Saints have been baptized and have received the gift of the Holy Ghost. Members of the Church of the Firstborn have received, in addition to these ordinances, all of the ordinances of the house of the Lord. They have entered into the new and everlasting covenant of marriage, which has been "sealed unto them by the Holy Spirit of promise" (D&C 132:19). They are therefore "sealed up unto eternal life . . . through the power of the Holy Priesthood" (D&C 131:5). The 144,000 high priests mentioned in this verse are set apart to minister the highest ordinances of the house of the Lord, bringing "as many as will come to the church of the Firstborn." The Prophet Joseph Smith taught: "It is not only necessary that you should be baptized for your dead, but you will have to go through all the ordinances for them, the same as you have gone through to save yourselves. There will be 144,000 saviors on Mount Zion, and with them an innumerable host that no man can number. Oh! I beseech you to go forward, go forward and make your calling and your election sure" (*Teachings of the Prophet Joseph Smith*, 366). "They who are the church of the Firstborn . . . are priests and kings . . . who overcome by faith and are sealed by the Holy Spirit of promise" (D&C 76:53–54, 56).

Christ Will Come in the Beginning of the Seventh Thousand Years

DOCTRINE AND COVENANTS 77:12–14

77:12 John recorded that "when he [Christ] had opened the seventh seal, there was silence in heaven about the space of half an hour. And I saw the seven angels which stood before God; and to them were given seven trumpets" (Revelation 8:1–2).

Judge all things, and shall redeem all things. Final judgment occurs for each person in the resurrection. All that are resurrected during the beginning of the seventh thousand years will be judged and receive either celestial or terrestrial glory.

Except that which he hath not put into his power. The atoning blood of the Lamb does not cleanse the wicked, who will not be redeemed from the dead until after the Millennium. Those who come forth from their graves after the Millennium will inherit a telestial glory or will be sons of perdition. The only people to enjoy the millennial peace will be the righteous.

The sounding of the trumpets of the seven angels are the preparing and finishing of his work. The seven angels announce desolation and wars at the sounding of their trumps. The destruction attendant to the return of the Lord both finishes his work in mortality among the wicked and prepares the world for the Millennium.

77:13 The ninth chapter of Revelation contains John's vision of wars and plagues. The Revelator saw that by this destruction "was the third part of men killed" (Revelation 9:18).

77:14 *The little book which was eaten by John.* The apostle John recorded, "And the voice which I heard from heaven spake unto me again, and said, Go and take the little book which is open in the hand of the angel which standeth upon the sea and upon the earth. And I went unto the angel, and said unto him, Give me the little book. And he said unto me, Take it, and eat it up; and it shall make thy belly bitter, but it shall be in thy mouth sweet as honey. And I took the little book out of the angel's hand, and ate it up; and it was in my mouth sweet as honey: and as soon as I had eaten it, my belly was bitter. And he said unto me, Thou must prophesy again before many peoples, and nations, and tongues, and kings" (Revelation 10:8–11).

By eating the book containing the word of God, John, in a symbolic sense, was eating the bread of life; he was feasting upon the word, which was in his "mouth sweet as honey." Yet it made his "belly bitter"; in other words, the judgments and plagues promised those who failed to eat that same word caused him great sorrow. "How sweet are thy words unto my taste! yea, sweeter than honey to my mouth!" (Psalm 119:103.) Such is the exulting cry of the psalmist. Conversely, how bitter is the penalty for rebellion and disobedience. Ezekiel in like circumstance had been commanded to eat a book, which was in his mouth "as honey for sweetness," but in the writing there was found "lamentations, and mourning, and woe" (Ezekiel 3:1–3; 2:6–10).

It was a mission, and an ordinance, for him to gather the tribes of Israel.

John requested of the risen Lord that he might have "power over death, that I may live and bring souls unto thee" (D&C 7:2). The Savior granted John his desire and promised him that he would "prophesy before nations, kindreds, tongues and people" (D&C 7:3). John's mission is to work with the scattered house of Israel in whatever capacity is necessary to prepare them to receive the restoration of the gospel. In that manner he will gather the family of Jacob. Remarks by the Prophet Joseph Smith indicate that John has been actively engaged in this commission. In June 1831 he declared "that John the Revelator was then among the Ten Tribes of Israel who had been led away by Shalmaneser, king of Assyria, to prepare them for their return from their long dispersion" (Smith, *History of the Church*, 1:176n).

The three Nephite disciples were given a similar mission. "And behold they will be among the Gentiles, and the Gentiles shall know them not. They will also be among the Jews, and the Jews shall know them not. And it shall come to pass, when the Lord seeth fit in his wisdom that they shall minister unto all the scattered tribes of Israel, and unto all nations, kindreds, tongues and people, and shall bring out of them unto Jesus many souls, that their desire may be fulfilled, and also because of the convincing power of God which is in them" (3 Nephi 28:27–29). Neither an account of John's work nor of the Nephite disciples' labor among the dispersed of Israel has yet been made known.

This is Elias. See commentary on verse 9, "This is Elias."

The Two Prophets Who Are to Be Slain in Jerusalem
DOCTRINE AND COVENANTS 77:15

77:15 The Lord revealed to John that "I will give power unto my two witnesses, and they shall prophesy a thousand two hundred and threescore days, clothed in sackcloth. . . . And if any man will hurt them, fire proceedeth out of their mouth, and devoureth their enemies: and if any man will hurt them, he must in this manner be killed. These have power to shut heaven, that it rain not in the days of their prophecy: and have power over waters to turn them to blood, and to smite the earth with all plagues, as often as they will. And when they shall have finished their testimony, the beast that ascendeth out of the bottomless pit shall make war against them, and shall overcome them, and kill them. And their dead bodies shall lie in the street of the great city, which spiritually is called Sodom and Egypt, where also our Lord was crucified. And they of the people and kindreds and tongues and nations shall see their dead bodies three days and an half, and shall not suffer their dead bodies to be put in graves. . . . And after three days and an half the Spirit of life from God entered into them, and they stood upon their feet; and great fear fell upon them which saw them. And they heard a great voice from heaven saying unto them, Come up hither. And they ascended up to heaven in a cloud; and their enemies beheld them" (Revelation 11:3, 5–9, 11–12).

Two prophets. The necessity of two prophets is to comply with the law of witnesses, which requires that the truth of all things be established by the testimony of two or more competent witnesses. These prophets will also of necessity have been called and commissioned by him who stands at the head of the earthly church and kingdom of God. Having established his Church once again upon the earth, the Lord has promised us that no true prophet will be called to function independent of that order he has established (D&C 42:11; Article of Faith 5).

Raised up to the Jewish nation. The two prophets do not come from the Jewish nation but are to prophesy to the Jewish nation. Similar to the biblical account of Jewish prophets such as Isaiah and Amos warning the other tribes of Israel, in the last days prophets will be sent to the Jews. The two witnesses will be like John the Baptist, preparing the Jewish people for the coming of the Messiah. Following their ministry the Lord will set his foot upon the Mount of Olives to personally minister to his people.

The mention of a Jewish nation in itself is prophetic. At the time of this revelation no Jewish nation existed in Palestine. See commentary on Doctrine and Covenants 45:48.

Built the city of Jerusalem in the land of their fathers. As the seed of Joseph is destined to build the city of New Jerusalem with its temple in the New World, so the seed of Judah is destined to build the city of Jerusalem with its temple in the Old World. This is to be done under the direction of the prophet who holds the keys of the gathering of Israel and the leading of the ten tribes from the lands of the North. Both cities with their temples must be built before Christ returns; nevertheless, the building of both cities will also continue after his coming.

DOCTRINE AND COVENANTS 78

DATE: BETWEEN 29 FEBRUARY AND 4 MARCH 1832
PLACE: HIRAM, OHIO

During the early part of 1832, the Prophet and Sidney Rigdon continued the work of revising the scriptures. At the time this revelation was given Joseph Smith was still residing at the home of John Johnson at Hiram, Ohio. This revelation was given to members of the "high priesthood" of the Church. They were assembled to impart instructions relative to the "united order," or "order of Enoch," the basis on which the promised Zion was to be built. The Lord had revealed that it was only through obedience to his heavenly order that Zion could be established.

The Saints Should Organize and Establish a Storehouse
DOCTRINE AND COVENANTS 78:1–4

78:1 *Ordained unto the high priesthood of my church.* See commentary on Doctrine and Covenants 84:29.

78:3–4 These verses are best understood in their immediate historical context. In earlier manuscript copies of this revelation, the phrase "in regulating and establishing the affairs of the storehouse for the poor of my people" (v. 3) was absent. The original words called for the organization of "the Literary and Mercantile establishments of my church." The Literary Firm referred to the group of elders that consecrated their property and talents for printing the scriptures and other Church publications (D&C 70:1–5). Further, the Lord called for the establishment of what is officially referred to in Church records as the United Firm, and later, the united order. Legal title to Church property and buildings was held in the name of the United Firm. It eventually included about a dozen Church leaders, specified by the Lord in revelation to receive responsibility as his stewards. Members of the order were governed by principles of the law of consecration. Surplus profits were used to operate the Church and to purchase lands for the inheritance of the Saints in Zion and Kirtland.

The decision was made to include several revelations received during councils of the Literary and United Firms in the first edition of the Doctrine and Covenants, published in 1835. By that time the United Firm, or United Order, had been reorganized with individual members receiving specific properties as stewardships (D&C 104). This reorganization took place after a mob in Jackson County, Missouri, destroyed much of the property owned by the firm and after an apostate named Doctor Philastus Hurlburt drained profits in Kirtland, Ohio, with a lawsuit to obtain firm-owned property. Additional financial burden stemmed from debt the Saints accrued on property purchased for the building of the houses of the Lord in Kirtland (D&C 94; 96). To protect firm members from claims against them, it was decided that references to the United Firm in the revelations be changed to refer to an order and that names of firm members and locations be replaced with unidentifiable designations, such as Enoch, Pelagoram, Mahemson, Shinehah, etc. Reflecting the changes made for the 1835 edition of the Doctrine and Covenants, the revelations continue to refer to the literary and mercantile establishments as "mine order" (D&C 96:4), "my order" (D&C 104:40), "the order" (D&C 104:1, 10, 21, 71) "this order" (D&C 78:8; 82:20; 92:2), and "united order" (D&C 92:1 104:1, 47, 53). The principles of stewardship emphasized in the revelation continue to guide the Church today in supplying funds for its operation and in providing for those in need.

78:3 *Both in this place and in the land of Zion.* This place refers to Ohio specifically Kirtland, and Zion refers to Independence, Missouri.

78:4 *The salvation of man.* God instituted the principles of the law of consecration for the blessing and welfare of the poor. These principle deal with temporal salvation. The attitude and spirit in which these principles are applied, however, is inseparably connected with the spiritual welfare of the Lord's people. Only when the Saints are of one heart and one mind can they dwell in righteousness having no poor among them (Moses 7:18).

Wise Use of Their Properties Will Lead to Salvation
DOCTRINE AND COVENANTS 78:5–12

78:5 *Equal in the bonds of heavenly things.* Elder Marion G. Romney explained the spiritual and temporal significance of the principles of the law of consecration as implemented in the welfare programs of the Church in bringing equality and unity among the Saints: "Church welfare is more than just a plan to provide for the physical needs of the

Saints. I am convinced that in addition to being a way of economic salvation in the days of necessity, it has deep spiritual significance; and that should other means always be available with which to supply the physical needs of the people, still the welfare plan, or some similar plan sponsored by the Church under the inspiration of the Lord, requiring us to serve and minister to one another in temporal affairs, would be necessary in order to bring us to that oneness, equality, and 'union required by the law of the celestial kingdom.' (D&C 105:4.)

"Unity, above all else, is the one thing characteristic of the Church of Christ. The burden of the Master's great prayer 'in the hour of his approaching death was, that the oneness subsisting between himself and the Father should also subsist between himself and his apostles, and . . . between them and all those who should receive the gospel through their teachings.' (B. H. Roberts, *The Falling Away*, 1–2.)

"The way to this oneness and unity has always been mutual consideration and helpfulness to one another. This the Lord declared to ancient Israel when he said, 'thou shalt love thy neighbor as thyself' (Leviticus 19:18), and during his earthly ministry he reaffirmed this command as one of the two great requirements upon which hang all the law and the prophets. (Matthew 22:37–39; Mark 12:29–31; Luke 10:27.)

"In this dispensation, the Lord has made it clear that loving one's neighbor as oneself includes administering to his temporal needs. He said to the members of the Church before it was a year old: 'be one; and if ye are not one ye are not mine.' (D&C 38:27.) . . .

"Keep in mind that this organization was to be built around a storehouse from which the needs of the poor among the Lord's people were to be supplied. Some folk regard this as a menial temporal activity; but the Lord said its purpose was to advance the cause which the saints had espoused for the salvation of men and to the glory of their Father in heaven. (D&C 78:4.) He thus associated it with his loftiest endeavor, that of bringing to pass the immortality and the eternal life of man, which he has declared to be his work and his glory. (Moses 1:39.)

"Who but the Lord himself could devise a way by which the members of his Church, rich and poor alike, can be so motivated that by the exercise of their own free agency they will administer to each other's needs in such a spirit of love as to move toward these great objectives? . . .

"To us and for our day, the Lord has given the welfare plan whereby we may demonstrate to him through mutual consideration and helpfulness to one another in temporal things, that we do love our neighbors as ourselves, rich and poor alike, and thereby move toward the equality, oneness, and unity which the Lord requires of us. This plan is not meant for any one class alone. We all need the training it affords. The day for the ushering in of the great millennium approaches, and for that day we must be prepared to live as one in perfect unity. We cannot come suddenly to that happy state. It will take training" (Conference Report, October 1945, 157–59).

78:9 The three brethren mentioned in verse 9 were the original members of the United Firm. They left to organize the firm in Missouri on 1 April 1832 accompanied by Peter Whitmer Jr. and Jesse Gause. The Prophet Joseph Smith suffered great persecution in the Hiram, Ohio, area previous to leaving in accordance with the Lord's counsel. A week earlier, on the evening of 24 March 1832, a mob came to the John Johnson home and dragged the Prophet from his bedroom. The mob had previously taken Sidney Rigdon from his home. After tarring and feathering the two men, the mob left them for dead. That evening Emma and Joseph had been taking turns caring for twin babies who were seriously ill with measles. Emma had nursed the children, and Joseph slept in the trundle bed with a baby boy lying on his chest. The mob took the Prophet, but left little Joseph behind to the ravages of the cold that swept into the room. On 29 March, due to the effects of the cold and the measles, the baby boy died. At the time the men departed for Missouri, others in Joseph's and Sidney's families were ill with the measles. The Prophet Joseph Smith wrote concerning the labor undertaken when "leaving our families in affliction amidst of death upon the mercy of mobs and of brethren who you know sometimes are found to be unstable, unbelieving, unmerciful and unkind and in this trying situation to keep the commandment of God we took our lives in our hands and traveled through every combination of wickedness to your country for your salvation" (Jessee, *Personal Writings of Joseph Smith*, 245; spelling standardized). The efforts of these men to fulfill the Lord's command to travel to Zion demonstrated their faith and diligence.

78:12 *Lose his office and standing in the church.* These brethren were given the responsibility to manage the finances of the Church. Any dishonesty in the use of the Lord's funds would bring a release from their calling and excommunication from the Church. Few matters in the Church today bring a more swift punishment than misuse of Church funds.

Delivered over to the buffetings of Satan. Elder Bruce R. McConkie explained: "To be turned over to the buffetings of Satan is to be given into his hands; it is to be turned over to him with all the protective power of the priesthood, of righteousness and of godliness removed, so that Lucifer is free to torment, persecute, and afflict such a person without let or hindrance. When the bars are down, the cuffs and curses of Satan, both in this world and in the world to come, bring indescribable anguish typified by burning fire and brimstone. The damned in hell so suffer" (*Mormon Doctrine*, 108).

"Apostates exhibit varying degrees of indifference and of rebellion," Elder McConkie further expounded, "and their punishment, in time and in eternity, is based on the type and degree of apostasy which is involved. Those who become indifferent to the Church, who simply drift from the course of righteousness to the way of the world, are not in the same category with traitors who fight the truth, and with those whose open rebellion destines them to eternal damnation as sons of perdition. All apostates are turned over to the buffetings of Satan in one degree or another, with the full wrath of Satan reserved for those who are cast into outer darkness with him in that kingdom devoid of glory.

"In this dispensation, those saints who broke the covenant of consecration by which they were bound in the united order were turned over to the buffetings of Satan. (D&C 78:3–12; 82:15–24; 104:1–10)" (*Doctrinal New Testament Commentary*, 3:75).

The day of redemption. Refers to the resurrection (D&C 88:16). This does not mean that those who are delivered to the buffetings of Satan will inherit celestial glory. Rather, they will be redeemed from hell to inherit a glory of which they are worthy. Those who become sons of perdition in mortality will be redeemed from Satan only in the sense that they will have power over him because they have resurrected bodies, for Satan is a personage of spirit.

The Church Should Be Independent of Earthly Powers
DOCTRINE AND COVENANTS 78:13–15

78:14–15 Joseph Fielding Smith wrote: "By the keeping of the covenant of consecration the Lord promised that the Church would stand independent above all other creatures beneath the celestial world. It is the will of the Lord, that eventually, the Church may take its rightful place above all other creatures upon the earth, or other spheres that are not celestial. This is the destiny of the Church, but the destiny of each of us individually depends on whether or not we will accept in faithfulness the covenants and obligations which are given us. The promise is that if we will be obedient we shall come up and be made rulers over many kingdoms. Those who receive the celestial exaltation will, without doubt, be made rulers over many kingdoms, and they will have power and authority to direct and to counsel those of lesser glories. Moreover, they will have the privilege of exaltation and of becoming creators in their own right as the sons of God" (*Church History and Modern Revelation*, 1:308).

78:14 *That the church may stand independent.* The temporal survival of the kingdom of God is not to be dependent on the success of worldly markets and merchandising. Neither is the ability of the Church to provide for the poor contingent on the ability of worldly governments to rebound from natural or manmade disasters. In recent years the strength of the kingdom has been evident in its independent capacity to reach areas of turmoil and catastrophe quickly and in an organized manner. Part of the latter-day mission of the Church is to demonstrate to the world that the Church has the ability to provide help to those in need.

As the Church is to stand independent in a temporal sense, so it must stand independent spiritually. The Church will not become part of the various ecumenical movements that unite the churches of men. It will join with other churches in helping the needy but will not seek agreement on the terms and conditions of salvation. We have no borrowed doctrines or authority. We are not beholden to other churches for our faith, nor do we seek favor or approval for any of our practices. In all things we stand independent.

78:15 *Be made rulers over many kingdoms.* The Lord declared, "To him who overcometh, and keepeth my commandments unto the end, will I give power over many kingdoms; and he shall rule them with the word of God" (JST Revelation 2:26–27). The faithful will be made rulers, not over earthly empires but in the household of God. They will inherit celestial glory and be made kings and queens, presiding over their posterity in eternity.

Adam-ondi-Ahman. See commentary on Doctrine and Covenants 116.

Michael (Adam) Serves under the Direction of the Holy One (Christ)

DOCTRINE AND COVENANTS 78:16

78:16 *Michael.* Adam, the first man, is the archangel Michael (D&C 107:54).

Given unto him the keys of salvation under the counsel and direction of the Holy One. Adam has the responsibility to supervise and direct the work of God on earth through all generations. "The Priesthood was first given to Adam," explained the Prophet Joseph Smith; "he obtained the First Presidency, and held the keys of it from generation to generation. He obtained it in the Creation, before the world was formed, as in Genesis 1:26, 27, 28. He had dominion given him over every living creature. He is Michael the Archangel, spoken of in the Scriptures. Then to Noah, who is Gabriel; he stands next in authority to Adam in the Priesthood; he was called of God to this office, and was the father of all living in his day, and to him was given the dominion. These men held keys first on earth, and then in heaven.

"The Priesthood is an everlasting principle, and existed with God from eternity, and will to eternity, without beginning of days or end of years. The keys have to be brought from heaven whenever the Gospel is sent. When they are revealed from heaven, it is by Adam's authority" (*Teachings of the Prophet Joseph Smith*, 157).

Adam presides over the entire human family on this earth under the direction of the Savior. Jesus Christ presides over all the Father's children on many earths. The Lord revealed to Moses: "Worlds without number have I created; and I also created them for mine own purpose; and by the Son I created them, which is mine Only Begotten. And the first man of all men have I called Adam, which is many. But only an account of this earth, and the inhabitants thereof, give I unto you" (Moses 1:33–35). The Lord has not revealed the order of the priesthood on any but this earth, but this text suggests that each world is presided over by the first man placed thereon. Further, Jesus Christ presides over each of these creations, giving his servants keys to preside under his direction.

Regarding Adam's position in the priesthood and his relationship to the priesthood order in the various dispensations of the gospel on earth, the Prophet Joseph Smith stated: "Commencing with Adam, who was the first man, who is spoken of in Daniel as being the 'Ancient of Days,' or in other words, the first and oldest of all, the great, grand progenitor of whom it is said in another place he is Michael, because he was the first and father of all, not only by progeny, but the first to hold the spiritual blessings, to whom was made known the plan of ordinances for the salvation of his posterity unto the end, and to whom Christ was first revealed, and through whom Christ has been revealed from heaven, and will continue to be revealed from henceforth. Adam holds the keys of the dispensation of the fullness of times; i.e., the dispensation of all the times have been and will be revealed through him from the beginning to Christ, and from Christ to the end of the dispensations that are to be revealed. . . .

"Therefore He set the ordinances to be the same forever and ever, and set Adam to watch over them, to reveal them from heaven to man, or to send angels to reveal them. . . . These angels are under the direction of Michael or Adam, who acts under the direction of the Lord. . . .

"This, then, is the nature of the Priesthood; every man holding the Presidency of his dispensation, and one man holding the Presidency of them all, even Adam; and Adam receiving his Presidency and authority from the Lord, but cannot receive a fullness until Christ shall present the Kingdom to the Father, which shall be at the end of the last dispensation" (*Teachings of the Prophet Joseph Smith*, 167–69).

The Prophet Joseph Smith and others who hold the keys of the kingdom in the last days are presided over by Adam. In a future day Adam will return to the earth and hold a council of those who have held keys. This meeting will be held at Adam-ondi-Ahman in northwest Missouri in preparation for the millennial reign of Jesus Christ. See commentary on Doctrine and Covenants 116.

Blessed Are the Faithful, for They Shall Inherit All Things
DOCTRINE AND COVENANTS 78:17–22

78:17–22 Saints who endure faithfully will return to the earth with the Savior "to reign on the earth over his people" during the Millennium (D&C 76:63). In eternity they will inherit all that the Father has and become "joint-heirs with Christ" (Romans 8:17). The Lord revealed further, "Wherefore, as it is written, they are gods, even the sons of God" (D&C 76:58). Such promises seem far from our immediate reach. "When you climb up a ladder," explained the Prophet Joseph Smith, "you must begin at the bottom, and ascend step by step, until you arrive at the top; and so it is with the principles of the Gospel—you must begin with the first, and go on until you learn all the principles of exaltation. But it will be a great while after you have passed through the veil before you will have learned them. It is not all to be comprehended in this world; it will be a great work to learn our salvation and exaltation even beyond the grave" (*Teachings of the Prophet Joseph Smith*, 348).

78:20 *Son Ahman.* This is the name of Jesus Christ in the pure language given to Adam. Orson Pratt stated: "There is one revelation that this people are not generally acquainted with. I think it has never been published, but probably it will be in the Church History. It is given in questions and answers. The first question is, 'What is the name of God in the pure language?' The answer says, 'Ahman.' 'What is the name of the Son of God?' Answer, 'Son Ahman'" (*Journal of Discourses*, 2:342). Elder McConkie explained, "In the pure language spoken by Adam—and which will be spoken again during the millennial era (Zephaniah 3:9)—the name of God the Father is Ahman, or possibly Ah Man, a name-title having a meaning identical with or at least very closely akin to Man of Holiness (Moses 6:57). God revealed himself to Adam by this name to signify that he is a Holy Man, a truth which man must know and comprehend if he is to become like God and inherit exaltation (1 John 3:1–3; D&C 132:19–24)" (*Mormon Doctrine*, 29). "Since Ahman is the name of God the Father in the pure language spoken by Adam, Son Ahman is the name of his Only Begotten Son" (McConkie, *Mormon Doctrine*, 740).

78:21 *Church of the Firstborn.* See commentary on Doctrine and Covenants 76:54–60, 94.

He will take you up in a cloud. The Lord revealed that at his coming "the saints that are upon the earth, who are alive, shall be quickened and be caught up to meet him. And they who have slept in their graves shall come forth, for their graves shall be opened; and they also shall be caught up to meet him in the midst of the pillar of heaven" (D&C 88:96–97).

DOCTRINE AND COVENANTS 79 AND 80

DATE: MARCH 1832
PLACE: HIRAM, OHIO

The Prophet Joseph Smith gave no background information concerning these two revelations. Apparently he received them near the same time. They teach and illustrate the distinct inspiration involved in calling the Saints to service in the kingdom. At times the Spirit directs that a particular person be called to a particular labor. At other times the Spirit indicates that many faithful souls could effectively serve. In both instances the callings are issued under the spirit of revelation.

Contrasting the mission call of Jared Carter with that of Stephen Burnett and Eden Smith illustrates the differences in inspired callings. Brother Carter was called to a specific area, whereas Brothers Burnett and Smith were told that their going in any direction would be approved of the Lord.

DOCTRINE AND COVENANTS 79

Jared Carter Is Called to Preach the Gospel by the Comforter
DOCTRINE AND COVENANTS 79:1–4

79:1 *Jared Carter should go again into the eastern countries.* Brother Carter had returned from serving a six-month mission (September 1831 through 29 February 1832) in this very area just a few weeks before this revelation was received. His new mission, which began 25 April 1832, took him to eastern New York and Vermont. He taught many relatives and friends on these missions.

The power of the ordination wherewith he has been ordained. Earlier, according to revelation, Jared Carter was ordained to the office of a priest in the Aaronic Priesthood (D&C 52:38). He received the Melchizedek

Priesthood and was ordained an elder prior to leaving on his first mission. After having received this revelation, he recorded: "The word of the Lord came forth that showed that it was his will that I should go forth to the Eastern country as in the power of ordinance where with I had been ordained, which was to the high privilege of administering in the name of Jesus Christ even to seal on earth, to build up the Church of Christ and to work miracles in the name of Christ" (*Journal of Jared Carter*; spelling standardized). It appears from Jared Carter's entry that he was ordained a high priest at this time (*Teachings of the Prophet Joseph Smith*, 20–21).

79:2 The Spirit of God may direct missionaries to the doors of those who are honest in heart and ready to hear the message of the Restoration.

79:3 *I will crown him again with sheaves.* Sheaves represent the fruits of missionary labor. The Lord emphasized the blessings that awaited Jared Carter if he would return to teach in the East. His experience in responding to this call illustrates the blessings that may come to those who are called to repeat assignments in the Church. After his service in this call ended, he recorded in his journal: "Now while I make this record, I remember the goodness of the Lord to me in the mission that I have lately been to in the East. I have enjoyed my health continually and the Lord, not withstanding the great opposition to the glorious work, has blessed me . . . in this mission in which I have been gone six months and two days. The Lord has permitted me to administer the gospel to 79 souls and many others by my instrumentality have been convinced of this most glorious work, where I have been in this mission" (*Journal of Jared Carter*; spelling standardized).

DOCTRINE AND COVENANTS 80

Stephen Burnett and Eden Smith Are Called to Preach in Whatever Place They Choose

DOCTRINE AND COVENANTS 80:1–5

80:3 *It mattereth not, for ye cannot go amiss.* Not every assignment is made because the Spirit dictates that specific people are to serve in specific areas. Many can serve effectively in various callings as needs dictate. Those called to serve may find that the spirit in which they fill the assignment is of greater importance than either the place they serve or the nature of the calling in which they serve. The Lord molds the lives of his servants like the master potter. If his servants follow the Spirit and do his will, he can make them the right persons in the right place at the right time.

DOCTRINE AND COVENANTS 81

DATE: 15 MARCH 1832
PLACE: HIRAM, OHIO

As this revelation currently reads, Doctrine and Covenants 81 calls Frederick G. Williams to serve as a counselor in the presidency of the Church. It was originally given, however, to Jesse Gause, who failed to live worthy of the appointment. Because the First Presidency had not yet been organized, this revelation became an important precursor to that event. Brother Williams was ordained to this office 18 March 1833.

The Keys of the Kingdom Are Always Held by the First Presidency
DOCTRINE AND COVENANTS 81:1–2

81:1 *To be a high priest in my church, and a counselor unto my servant Joseph Smith, Jun.* At a conference of the Church held at Amherst, Ohio, 25 January 1832, the Prophet Joseph Smith was sustained and then ordained president of the high priesthood, which ordination recognized his right to preside over the priesthood and serve as president of the Church. Jesse Gause and Sidney Rigdon were chosen as his counselors in the First Presidency and were ordained high priests on 8 March 1832.

Frederick G. Williams was subsequently called in the stead of Jesse Gause, at which time this revelation was addressed to Frederick G. Williams.

81:2 *Keys of the kingdom.* Keys, which are "the right of presidency," belong to those called to preside over the quorums of the priesthood (D&C 107:8). The kingdom is the church of God as established on the earth. Thus the "keys of the kingdom" constitute the authority to preside over the Church. The "right of presidency," or the keys of the Aaronic Priesthood, were restored to Joseph Smith and Oliver Cowdery by John the Baptist 15 May 1829 (Joseph Smith—History 1:69). John the Baptist told Joseph and Oliver that he acted under the direction of Peter, James, and John, who held the "keys" of the Melchizedek Priesthood (Joseph Smith—History 1:72).

"Unto you three," the Savior had promised Peter, James, and John, "I will give this power and the keys of this ministry until I come" (D&C 7:7). Peter, James, and John constituted the First Presidency in the meridian dispensation and they alone could restore that authority to those of our day. So it was that the meridian presidency appeared to Joseph Smith and Oliver Cowdery, "declaring themselves as possessing the keys of the kingdom, and of the dispensation of the fulness of times" (D&C 128:20), which keys they committed to these two men (D&C 27:12–13; 132:45). See commentary on Doctrine and Covenants 128:10, "The Keys of the Kingdom of Heaven."

Presidency of the High Priesthood. To hold the "Presidency of the High Priesthood" is to preside over the high priests or to preside over all who hold the priesthood, be it Aaronic or Melchizedek. "The Presidency of the High Priesthood, after the order of Melchizedek, have a right to officiate in all the offices of the church" (D&C 107:9). They "form a quorum of the Presidency of the Church" (D&C 107:22). Groups that have broken from the Church, claiming keys of a greater nature than those conferred on the Prophet or keys conferred to them through secret ordinations, are at odds with these revelations.

Joseph Fielding Smith explained the relationship between the "Presidency of the High Priesthood" and the presidency of the Church: "There is a difference between the office of President of the Church and President of the High Priesthood; however, these two offices cannot be separated and must be held by the same person duly appointed and sustained by proper vote. As President of the Church the presiding officer presides over all the membership of the Church. As President of the High Priesthood he presides over all the Priesthood of the Church and has authority to regulate it, for he holds the keys of that Priesthood. . . .

". . . The President of the Church holds the supreme authority. . . . He, it is, who holds the right of decision and the right of revelation for the Priesthood and for the Church" (*Church History and Modern Revelation,* 1:311–12).

If Frederick G. Williams Is Faithful in His Ministry, He Shall Have Eternal Life
DOCTRINE AND COVENANTS 81:3–7

81:3 *I acknowledge him and will bless him.* The Lord promised the Prophet Joseph Smith that he would inspire him "to move the cause of Zion in mighty power for good" (D&C 21:7).

81:6 *If thou art faithful.* No salvation is found in the holding of a particular office. All officers in the Church must work out their salvation
"with fear and trembling" according to the same terms and covenants as
all other members. In the Church and kingdom of God all are equal as to
their rights to draw upon the blessings and powers of heaven.

The story of Jesse Gause is instructive. This man, called to a position
of trust, simply did not answer the call. Invited to stand among the noble
and great ones, he simply refused. Today his name is remembered by none
but those who have a special love for the details of the history of the
Church. Jesse Gause is no different from countless others who have also
been called to write their names in the Lamb's book of life, thereby ensur-
ing themselves a place of honor among their posterity, but who also
refused the call.

Of Jesse Gause we know that he had been a member of the Shaker
communities in Hancock near Pittsfield, and possibly in North Union,
Ohio. No record of his baptism or ordination to the priesthood has survived. It was not until 8 March 1832, when he was called to be a counselor
to Joseph Smith, that his name even appeared in extant Church records.
The notation in the "Kirtland Revelation Book" reads: "March 8, 1832.
Chose this day and ordained brother Jesse Gause and Broth[er] Sidney to
be my councellors of the ministry of the presidency of the high
Priesthood."

The following week a revelation confirmed Gause's calling, giving fur-
ther direction to him. Two manuscript copies of this revelation exist: one
in the "Kirtland Revelation Book," located in the Church Historical
Department; the other in the library of the Reorganized Church of Jesus
Christ of Latter Day Saints. In both these revelations Jesse Gause's name
has been crossed out and Frederick G. Williams's name written above it.
Since that time, all published copies of this revelation list Frederick G.
Williams as the one to whom it was directed. Since this revelation contains
instructions, duties, and promised blessings to the one called as counselor
to the Prophet, the revelation rightly belonged to the one holding the
office.

"After Jesse Gause was ordained, he appeared in a leading role in the
Church for only a short time. In April 1832, he accompanied Joseph
Smith, Newel K. Whitney, and Peter Whitmer Jr. on a trip to Missouri.
They arrived 24 April and began holding conferences with the Saints in
Zion on the 26th. In the minutes of a meeting of the Literary Firm held
on Monday, 30 April, Jesse Gause was listed as a counselor to Joseph

Smith. Joseph left Independence that day to return again to Kirtland, and Jesse Gause remained behind to conduct further business. On his return trip home he stopped at North Union, Ohio, to retrieve his wife from the society of the Shakers there. An elder of this Shaker community, Matthew Houston, wrote a letter to his friend, Seth Y. Wells, who was a member of the Shaker bishopric at New Lebanon, about Jesse Gause's vain attempt to reunite with his wife. Part of his letter reads as follows:

"'And sure enough I presume you was acquainted with Jesse Gause from Hancock he was here a few days since after his wife Minerva—she utterly refused being his slave any longer—he had to go away without her. altho he tryed what the law could do for him he was very much inraged threatened to take away Minerva's child—she presented it to him but he went away without it and her—he is yet a Mormon—& and is second to the Prophet or Seer—Joseph Smith—this state of exaltation may tend to steady him or keep him away from us a little longer—for which I am heartily glad for he is certainly the meanest of men.—

"'But Minerva certainly conducts herself cleverly so far We find no fault with her—at any rate she cut off Old Jesse verry handsomely—& he felt it to his gizzard.'

"One important item in the letter is the reference to Jesse Gause's being 'second to the Prophet or Seer—Joseph Smith.'

"Upon his return to Kirtland, Jesse was called to serve a mission with Zebedee Coltrin. They began their journey on 1 August 1832, and traveled until the 19th, at which time Coltrin decided to return to Kirtland because of severe pains in his head. After praying with and for each other, they parted. Jesse Gause continued east and walked right out of the history of the Church, never again to return. There appears to be no other record of the man either in or out of the Church" (Woodford, "Notes and Comments," 363–64).

DOCTRINE AND COVENANTS 82

DATE: 26 APRIL 1832
PLACE: JACKSON COUNTY, MISSOURI

In obedience to the Lord's command to "sit in council with the saints which are in Zion" (D&C 78:9), the Prophet Joseph Smith, Sidney Rigdon, Newel K. Whitney, and Jesse Gause arrived in Jackson County, Missouri, 24 April 1832. The purpose of this visit was to establish a branch of the United Firm in Missouri according to the Lord's command (see commentary on D&C 78:3–4). At this time Joseph met with the brethren in a council of high priests. After the Prophet "Joseph Smith [was] acknowledged by the High Priests in the land of Zion to be President of the High Priesthood" (Cannon and Cook, *Far West Record*, 44), Sidney Rigdon read the commandment of God to organize the United Firm in both Ohio and Missouri. The Prophet recorded that "during the intermission, a difficulty or hardness which had existed between Bishop Partridge and Elder Rigdon, was amicably settled, and when we came together in the afternoon, all hearts seemed to rejoice and I received the following" (Smith, *History of the Church*, 1:267).

Where Much Is Given, Much Is Required
DOCTRINE AND COVENANTS 82:1–4

82:1 *Inasmuch as you have forgiven one another your trespasses.* The Lord taught, "Blessed are the merciful: for they shall obtain mercy" (Matthew 5:7). "For if ye forgive men their trespasses who trespass against you," the Savior taught further, "your heavenly Father will also forgive you; but if ye forgive not men their trespasses, neither will your heavenly Father forgive you your trespasses" (JST Matthew 6:16).

As mentioned in the introduction, prior to the reception of this revelation Sidney Rigdon and Bishop Partridge were reconciled after months of misunderstanding and hard feelings. The previous November, Brother Rigdon had written a letter to Saints in Missouri, charging Bishop Partridge with defrauding funds, insulting the Prophet, and assuming authority over him. Bishop Partridge confessed his faults in a special conference in Missouri, 10 March 1832. At his request, the council of high priests of the Church in Missouri wrote a letter to Brother Rigdon answering the charges and asking for forgiveness of those whom the bishop had offended, with assurance that he would confess his errors to Sidney when the occasion presented itself (Cannon and Cook, *Far West Record*, 40–42).

82:2 *Refrain from sin, lest sore judgments fall upon your heads.* The Spirit of the Lord cannot dwell in unclean tabernacles. "He that repents not," the Lord declared, "from him shall be taken even the light which he has received; for my Spirit shall not always strive with man" (D&C 1:33). Those that sin will always reap as they have sown. So it was that the Saints in Zion were warned that if they did not repent the Lord would visit them according to their works with "sore affliction, with pestilence, with plague, with sword, with vengeance, with devouring fire" (D&C 97:26).

A critical spirit that embraced evil speaking of the Lord's anointed became common, as evidenced by the following letter written by the Prophet to W. W. Phelps after his return to Ohio. "We received a letter from brother John Carl [Corrill] by the hand of Broth[er] [Sidney] Gilbert after we arrived home from Indiana who arrived here before us, but what did it contain . . . we learned by Broth[er] John's letter that the devil had set to work to reward us by stirring up your hearts (I mean those who were engaged in this wickedness) by raking every fault, which those eyes that are filled with beams could see in looking for motes in the eyes of those who are laboring with tender and prayerful hearts continually for their salvation" (Jessee, *Personal Writings of Joseph Smith*, 245; spelling standardized).

Such problems among the Saints eventually led to their expulsion from Jackson County, Missouri. Although the brethren in Zion appeared to have repented of their ill feelings against the Prophet Joseph Smith and the leaders in Ohio, they did not heed the Lord's warning in this revelation and allowed Satan to have influence over them. A later revelation warned "that they shall repent of their former evil works; for they are to be upbraided for their evil hearts of unbelief, and your brethren in Zion for their rebellion against you at the time I sent you" (D&C 84:76). Orson Hyde and Hyrum Smith identified the particulars of the problems in a letter they wrote to Church leaders in Missouri: "At the time Joseph, Sidney, and Newel left Zion, all matters of hardness and misunderstanding were

settled and buried (as they supposed), and you gave them the hand of fellowship; but, afterwards, you brought up all these things again, in a cen-
sorious spirit, accusing Brother Joseph in rather an indirect way of seeking
after monarchial power and authority. . . . We are sensible that this is not
the thing Brother Joseph is seeking after, but to magnify the high office
and calling whereunto he has been called and appointed by the command
of God, and the united voice of this Church" (in Smith, *History of the
Church*, 1:318–19). This spirit of faultfinding and ill feelings eventually
contributed to the expulsion of the Saints from Zion. Once the spirit of
evil entered the hearts of the Saints and prompted them to speak against
the Prophet, it also led the Missouri Saints to find fault with each other.
The Lord referred to these problems in a parable concerning a people who
failed to build a watch tower, explaining why the Saints suffered such
severe persecutions in Jackson County, which were "sore judgments"
indeed: "And while they were at variance one with another they became
very slothful, and they hearkened not unto the commandments of their
lord" (D&C 101:50). The judgments of God did fall upon the Missouri
Saints and gravely chastened them. The Lord's counsel in this verse serves
as a sober warning to all Saints of any day that the Lord is not pleased
with those who misjudge the motives of others and harbor bad feelings in
their hearts, preventing the Spirit of the Lord from abiding with them.

82:3–4 "Members of the Church are sometimes guilty of the same
sins that afflict fallen man generally," said Elder Bruce R. McConkie.
"When they are, their condemnation is greater than it otherwise would
be because of their greater light and knowledge. In addition, many acts
become sinful for the saints that would not be so considered had they not
taken upon themselves the obligations of the gospel" (*New Witness*, 225).
Concerning those who sin against greater light, the Book of Mormon
teaches, "Thus we can plainly discern, that after a people have been once
enlightened by the Spirit of God, and have had great knowledge of things
pertaining to righteousness, and then have fallen away into sin and transgression, they become more hardened, and thus their state becomes worse
than though they had never known these things" (Alma 24:30).

Darkness Reigns in the World
DOCTRINE AND COVENANTS 82:5–7

82:5 *The adversary spreadeth his dominions.* This is a day of great
iniquity as Satan seeks to extend his power throughout the world in

opposition to the kingdom of God. Speaking of the latter days, Nephi wrote: "At that day shall he rage in the hearts of the children of men, and stir them up to anger against that which is good. And others will he pacify, and lull them away into carnal security, that they will say: All is well in Zion; yea, Zion prospereth, all is well—and thus the devil cheateth their souls, and leadeth them away carefully down to hell" (2 Nephi 28:20–21).

82:7 *Unto that soul who sinneth shall the former sins return.* Elder Spencer W. Kimball explained: "To return to sin is most destructive to the morale of the individual and gives Satan another hand-hold on his victim. Those who feel that they can sin and be forgiven and then return to sin and be forgiven again and again must straighten out their thinking. Each previously forgiven sin is added to the new one and the whole gets to be a heavy load.

"Thus when a man has made up his mind to change his life, there must be no turning back. Any reversal, even in a small degree, is greatly to his detriment" (*Miracle of Forgiveness*, 170).

The Lord Is Bound When We Do What He Says
DOCTRINE AND COVENANTS 82:8–10

82:10 Both parties must meet the terms agreed upon for a covenant to be of efficacy and force. If one of the parties should break the covenant, the other party is under no obligation to honor the promises made. If the Saints are to receive the blessings of establishing Zion, they must be obedient to that law upon which those blessings are predicated.

Zion Must Increase in Beauty and Holiness
DOCTRINE AND COVENANTS 82:11–16

82:11 The next day the council of brethren to whom this revelation was given reconvened and determined that the names of the branches of the United Firm in Ohio and Missouri would be "Gilbert, Whitney & Company in Zion. And Newel K. Whitney & Company in Kirtland Geauga Co. Ohio" (Cannon and Cook, *Far West Record*, 45).

Beginning with the first printing of this revelation in 1835, the names of the individuals in this verse were not published. Their identities were veiled by the use of unusual names in place of their own. Elder Orson Pratt explained, "The names that were incorporated when it was printed, did not exist there when the manuscript revelations were given, for I saw them myself. Some of them I copied. And when the Lord was about to have the Book of Covenants given to the world, it was thought wisdom, in consequence of the persecutions of our enemies in Kirtland and some of the regions around, that some of the names should be changed" (*Journal of Discourses*, 16:156). Editions of the Doctrine and Covenants prior to 1981 gave the following names in place of those of the brethren: Alam (Edward Partridge); Ahashdah (Newel K. Whitney); Mahalaleel (Sidney Gilbert); Pelagoram (Sidney Rigdon); Gazelam (Joseph Smith); Horah (John Whitmer); Olihah (Oliver Cowdery); Shalemmanasseh (W. W. Phelps); Mahemson (Martin Harris).

Except judgment shall immediately follow. See commentary on Doctrine and Covenants 78:12.

82:13 *A stake to Zion.* This is the first designation of a stake to Zion in the Restoration. "In prophetic imagery," explained Elder McConkie, "Zion is pictured as a great tent upheld by cords fastened securely to stakes. Thus Isaiah, envisioning the latter-day glory of Israel, gathered to her restored Zion, proclaimed: 'Enlarge the place of thy tent, and let them stretch forth the curtains of thine habitations: spare not, lengthen thy cords, and strengthen thy stakes; For thou shalt break forth on the right hand and on the left. . . . For a small moment have I forsaken thee; but with great mercies will I gather thee.' (Isa. 54:2–7.) And of the millennial Zion, Isaiah exulted: 'Look upon Zion, the city of our solemnities: . . . a tabernacle that shall not be taken down; not one of the stakes thereof shall ever be removed, neither shall any of the cords thereof be broken.' (Isa. 33:20.)

"In keeping with this symbolism, the great areas of church population and strength, which sustain and uphold the restored Zion, are called stakes. They are the rallying points and the gathering centers for the remnants of scattered Israel" (*Mormon Doctrine*, 764). See commentary on Doctrine and Covenants 94:1, "The city of the stake of Zion."

82:14 Isaiah's words were "awake, awake; put on thy strength, O Zion; put on thy beautiful garments, O Jerusalem, the holy city" (Isaiah 52:1). In a later revelation the Lord explained that Isaiah "had reference to those whom God should call in the last days, who should hold the power of priesthood to bring again Zion, and the redemption of Israel; and to put on her strength is to put on the authority of the priesthood, which she, Zion, has a right to by lineage; also to return to that power which she had lost" (D&C 113:8). For the borders of Zion to be enlarged is to have the kingdom of God extend beyond its current boundaries. See commentary on Doctrine and Covenants 105:5.

Every Man Should Seek the Interest of His Neighbor
DOCTRINE AND COVENANTS 82:17–24

82:17–19 The redemption of Zion awaits a truly covenant people. To be such we must come to the understanding that we are not saved separately or singly. Salvation is a community affair. We must learn to bear one another's burdens, strengthen each other, and use the talents and means with which the Lord has blessed us to bless others. We must come to realize that we have no sins that affect only ourselves, for each of our shortcomings detracts from the strength of the whole. Only in unity can we create a Zion community.

82:20 *An everlasting order unto you, and unto your successors.* The principles upon which a Zion society rest are everlastingly the same. It matters not whether we live in the days of Enoch, Joseph Smith, or the future, the principles remain unchanged.

82:21 *According to the laws of my church.* "He that sinneth and repenteth not shall be cast out" of the Church (D&C 42:28).

Delivered over to the buffetings of Satan. See commentary on Doctrine and Covenants 78:12.

82:22 *Make unto yourselves friends with the mammon of unrighteousness.* In all of our interaction with those not of our faith we seek to make friends. Until he, whose right it is to reign, returns with equity and justice, laws and ordinances that affect the Church's ability to accomplish its mission will be administered by worldly people. We will be much more successful in the work of the Lord as friends to these people than as their enemies. Certainly, the Lord was not commanding us to partake of the wicked and dishonest practices of the world in this admonition. Rather, we are to freely associate with others in our business and social transactions, exhibiting the light of the gospel in all our dealings.

DOCTRINE AND COVENANTS 83

DATE: 30 APRIL 1832
PLACE: INDEPENDENCE, MISSOURI

"On the 27th, we transacted considerable business for the salvation of the Saints, who were settling among a ferocious set of mobbers, like lambs among wolves. It was my endeavor to so organize the Church, that the brethren might eventually be independent of every incumbrance beneath the celestial kingdom, by bonds and covenants of mutual friendship, and mutual love.

"On the 28th and 29th, I visited the brethren above Big Blue river, in Kaw township, a few miles west of Independence, and received a welcome only known by brethren and sisters united as one in the same faith, and by the same baptism, and supported by the same Lord. The Colesville branch, in particular, rejoiced as the ancient Saints did with Paul. It is good to rejoice with the people of God. On the 30th, I returned to Independence, and again sat in council with the brethren, and received the following" (Smith, *History of the Church*, 1:269).

Women and Children Have Claim upon Their Husbands and Fathers for Their Support
DOCTRINE AND COVENANTS 83:1–4

83:1 *In addition to the laws of the church.* See commentary on Doctrine and Covenants 42:30–39.

83:2–4 *Women have claim on their husbands . . . children have claim upon their parents for their maintenance.* The apostle Paul wrote: "If any provide not for his own, and specially for those of his own house, he hath denied the faith, and is worse than an infidel" (1 Timothy 5:8). "This is the divine right of a wife and mother," explained President Ezra Taft Benson. "While she cares for and nourishes her children at home, her husband earns the living for the family, which makes this nourishing possible.

"In a home where there is an able-bodied husband, he is expected to

583

be the breadwinner. Sometimes we hear of husbands who, because of economic conditions, have lost their jobs and expect the wives to go out of the home and work, even though the husband is still capable of providing for his family. In these cases, we urge the husband to do all in his power to allow his wife to remain in the home caring for the children while he continues to provide for his family the best he can, even though the job he is able to secure may not be ideal and family budgeting may have to be tighter" (Conference Report, October 1987, 60).

President Howard W. Hunter gave further counsel to the brethren of the Church: "You who hold the priesthood have the responsibility, unless disabled, to provide temporal support for your wife and children. No man can shift the burden of responsibility to another, not even to his wife. The Lord has commanded that women and children have claim on their husbands and fathers for their maintenance (D&C 83; 1 Timothy 5:8.) President Ezra Taft Benson has stated that when a husband encourages or insists that his wife work out of the home for their convenience, 'not only will the family suffer in such instances, . . . but (his) own spiritual growth and progression will be hampered.'

"We urge you to do all in your power to allow your wife to remain in the home, caring for the children while you provide for the family the best you can. We further emphasize that men who abandon their family and fail to meet their responsibility to care for those they have fathered may find their eligibility for a temple recommend and their standing in the Church in jeopardy. In cases of divorce or separation, men must demonstrate that they are meeting family support payments mandated by law and obligated by the principles of the Church in order to qualify for the blessings of the Lord" (Conference Report, October 1994, 69).

83:3 *They may remain upon their inheritances according to the laws of the land.* In the original manuscript copies of this revelation, transgressors were not allowed to retain property that was received as a stewardship from the Church. As done previously, instructions in this revelation were adapted to the laws of the land. See commentary on Doctrine and Covenants 51:5.

Widows and Orphans Have Claim upon the Church for Their Support
DOCTRINE AND COVENANTS 83:5–6

83:5 *They have claim upon the church.* These instructions have particular application within the laws of consecration as practiced at that time.

Children were expected to provide for their own temporal welfare when sufficiently mature to do so. If their parents had means to provide an inheritance for them, they were to receive property from them. Those that entered into adulthood without any means of providing for themselves had claim upon the properties of the Church to receive an inheritance within the law of consecration.

"When one comes to a bishop and asks for assistance because of his or her straitened circumstances," explained Joseph F. Smith, "the first thing the bishop should do is to inquire if he or she is a tithe-payer. He should know whether the name is on the book of the law of the Lord, and if not on the book, if he or she has been derelict and negligent in relation to this principle of tithing, he or she has no claim upon the bishop, neither have their children; and if, under those circumstances, the bishop assists him, it will simply be out of pure charity and not because such have any claim upon the Church. That is why the widow who receives assistance from the Church should pay her tithing, so that her name may be on the records of the Church. It is not a law that is applicable to one and not to another. If the rich may not receive blessings because their names are not on the record, then neither shall the poor receive blessings in the house of God, if their names are not recorded. So long as a poor person receives his or her support through the tithings of the people, they should be willing to observe the law themselves in order that they may be entitled to what they receive. They should show by their observance of the law that they are law-keepers and not law-breakers. Our children, as soon as they become old enough to earn means, should be taught to pay their tithing, that their names may be written in the book of the law of the Lord, so that if perchance their father die and they are left orphans, their names as well as the names of their parents, will be found upon the records and they will, as God lives, be entitled to their support and to their education. It is our duty to look after these children and see that they have an equal chance with those who are most favored with parents to look after them" (*Gospel Doctrine*, 231).

83:6 *Widows and orphans shall be provided for.* "Pure religion and undefiled before God and the Father is this," wrote James, "to visit the fatherless and widows in their affliction" (James 1:27). In ancient Israel the Lord commanded that special care be given to looking after the needs of widows. Those who provided for the widow were promised that they would be blessed in all of their affairs (Deuteronomy 14:29).

DOCTRINE AND COVENANTS 84

DATE: 22 AND 23 SEPTEMBER 1832
PLACE: KIRTLAND, OHIO

The Prophet Joseph Smith designated as a revelation on priesthood the revelation now recorded in Doctrine and Covenants 84. Any account of the restoration of the Melchizedek Priesthood, if the Prophet left one, is lost to us. We do not know what instruction, explanation, or direction Peter, James, and John gave Joseph Smith and Oliver Cowdery when this priesthood was conferred upon them. Thus, section 84 becomes the first great revelation on the nature and purpose of the Melchizedek Priesthood for our dispensation. In the first edition of the Doctrine and Covenants, section 20—which directs the organization of the Church and discusses the duties of elders, priests, teachers, and deacons—constituted section 1; the revelation we have now in section 84 came next, followed by what is known today as section 107, which also deals with matters pertaining to the priesthood. Clearly, this arrangement points to the importance of the organization of the Church and of the restoration of the authority upon which it is founded.

Section 84 gives us a meaningful understanding of what took place anciently regarding the priesthood and dramatizes that ours is truly a restored church, possessing the authority held by prophets of Old and New Testament times. This revelation centers on the restoration of the priesthood to Moses and his desire to give the fulness of its blessings to his people, who refused it and thus had it taken from them.

The Lord sent Moses down into Egypt not simply to liberate an enslaved people but to create a holy nation. Surely there was reason to wonder if leaving the fertile valley of the Nile for the furnace of Sinai was any kind of liberation. But it was at Sinai that the Lord announced his intention to make of them a kingdom of priests and a holy nation (Exodus 19:5–6). They, like their ancient fathers, were to be a covenant people. Abraham, Isaac, and Jacob had stood in God's divine presence and received the promise of a continuation of their seed throughout the

586

endless expanses of eternity. Likewise, the Lord manifested himself to their children and extended the same promise to them. Thus it was that Moses was to sanctify the children of Israel and prepare them to stand in the presence of the Lord.

Not willing to fully sanctify themselves, the children of Israel refused to come into the presence of God and thus lost the privilege of holding the priesthood given to prepare them for that purpose. The Lord, therefore, took the Melchizedek Priesthood from them and left them to be governed by the Aaronic or Levitical Order.

In our day the Melchizedek Priesthood has been restored for the same purpose. Under the direction of a modern Moses, Israel is once again to be gathered that she might be offered the blessings the Lord sought to give her fathers at Sinai. The place of the gathering is the New Jerusalem, where the mountain of the Lord's house is to be built. Here, the gathered hosts of Israel can sanctify themselves that they might stand where their forefathers would not: in the presence of their God.

The New Jerusalem and the Temple to Be Built in Missouri
DOCTRINE AND COVENANTS 84:1–5

84:2 Two reasons are given in this text for the organization of the Church: (1) for the gathering of Israel as promised by ancient prophets, and (2) for the gathering of the Saints to "stand upon Mount Zion," the New Jerusalem. That is, Israel must be gathered or returned to the covenants and promises made to her faithful fathers. According to prophecy, the Lord's people are to build temples in both the New Jerusalem and the Jerusalem of old. Then the prophecy of Isaiah will find fulfillment that "out of Zion shall go forth the law, and the word of the Lord from Jerusalem" (Isaiah 2:3; 2 Nephi 12:3). Revelation directs that they "who are among the Gentiles flee unto Zion. And let them who be of Judah flee unto Jerusalem, unto the mountains of the Lord's house" (D&C 133:12–13).

84:3 Orson Pratt explained: "God gave commandment to His people in the summer of 1831 that they should gather up from the Eastern lands, New York, the New England States, Pennsylvania and the Middle States, from Ohio and various parts of the United States, upon the western frontiers of Missouri; that is, that they should continue to gather, but not let their flight be in haste, and let all things be prepared before them. God led forth the Prophet that He had raised up to the western part of

Missouri, and pointed out, by His own finger, where the great city of Zion should stand in the latter days, the great city of the New Jerusalem that should be built up on the American continent. I say He pointed out these things and gave direction to His people to gather to that land, and commanded them to lay the corner stone of a great and magnificent temple that was to be built during the generation in which the people then lived. The corner stone was laid in the summer of 1831, in Jackson County, State of Missouri" (*Journal of Discourses*, 13:359–60).

84:4–5 It is through the faith of the Latter-day Saints that these words will yet find a literal fulfillment. "The Latter-day Saints have as firm faith and rely upon this promise," stated Orson Pratt, "as much as they rely upon the promise of forgiveness of sins when they comply with the first principles of the Gospel. We just as much expect that a city will be built, called Zion, in the place and on the land which has been appointed by the Lord our God, and that a temple will be reared on the spot that has been selected, and the corner-stone of which has been laid, in the generation when this revelation was given; we just as much expect this as we expect the sun to rise in the morning and set in the evening; or as much as we expect to see the fulfillment of any of the purposes of the Lord our God, pertaining to the works of his hands" (*Journal of Discourses*, 14:275).

Confusion, however, has centered on the meaning of the word *generation*, as used in these verses. Speaking to Joseph Smith, the Lord said, "This generation shall have my word through you" (D&C 5:10). In this instance, as in the present, the word *generation* is being used as a synonym for the word *dispensation*. Similarly, when the Lord said that it is "a wicked and adulterous generation" that seeks after signs (Matthew 16:4), he was not confining the principle to the period of time between parents' births and the birth of their children. In the case of the temple in Jackson County, *generation* means dispensation.

To explain why the Saints were unable to build the temple in Missouri during Joseph Smith's lifetime, the Lord said: "When I give a commandment to any of the sons of men to do a work unto my name, and those sons of men go with all their might and with all they have to perform that work, and cease not their diligence, and their enemies come upon them and hinder them from performing that work, behold, it behooveth me to require that work no more at the hands of those sons of men, but to accept of their offerings. And the iniquity and transgression of my holy laws and commandments I will visit upon the heads of those who hindered my work, unto the third and fourth generation, so long as they repent not, and hate me, saith the Lord God. Therefore, for this cause have I accepted the offerings of those whom I commanded to build up a city and a house unto my name, in Jackson county, Missouri, and were hindered by their enemies, saith the Lord your God. And I will answer judgment, wrath, and indignation, wailing, and anguish, and gnashing of teeth upon their heads, unto the third and fourth generation, so long as they repent not, and hate me, saith the Lord your God. And this I make an example unto you, for your consolation concerning all those who have been commanded to do a work and have been hindered by the hands of their enemies, and by oppression, saith the Lord your God" (D&C 124:49–53).

84:5 *A cloud shall rest upon it.* The cloud is a sign attesting to both the glory and the presence of the Lord. "And the Lord will create upon every dwelling place of mount Zion," prophesied Isaiah, "and upon her assemblies, a cloud and smoke by day, and the shining of a flaming fire by night: for upon all the glory shall be a defence" (Isaiah 4:5). Here Isaiah compares the homes of the Saints to the temple, thus emphasizing the sanctity of Zion and her people in this marvelous day (Parry, Parry, and Peterson, *Understanding Isaiah*, 49; Exodus 16:10; 24:15–16; 34:5; 2 Chronicles 5:13–14).

Priesthood of Moses Traced to Adam
DOCTRINE AND COVENANTS 84:6–17

84:6–17 Properly, all who profess to act in the name of God may be required to show proof of their having been so ordained. Thus, priesthood, which embraces the authority to speak in the name of Deity and to perform the ordinances of salvation, must, if legitimate, be traceable to God himself. In illustration, the priesthood of Moses is here traced through the generations back to father Adam, who received it from God himself even while in the Garden of Eden (Abraham 1:2–4; Facsimile 2, Explanation, Figure 3).

84:6 *Jethro.* When Moses fled from Egypt after killing Pharaoh's overseer, he lived with Jethro, a prince and priest of Midian. Moses married Jethro's daughter Zipporah and tended his sheep (Exodus 2:11–22; 3:1). Joseph Fielding Smith said: "Remember that the priesthood was not confined solely to the descendants of Jacob. Moses got his priesthood from Jethro who was not a descendant of Jacob, but was a descendant of

Abraham. The blessings of Abraham are to be given to the Gentiles who repent and receive the gospel, and by adoption they become of the seed of Abraham" (*Doctrines of Salvation*, 3:87).

84:12–13 *Esaias.* Following the pattern given in Doctrine and Covenants 107:40–53, Esaias received the holy priesthood from God (or one who had authority), then, at a subsequent time, received the fulness of the blessings of the priesthood under the hand of Abraham. This may suggest that when Melchizedek and his city were taken up (JST Genesis 14:33–34), Abraham succeeded him as the head of the dispensation.

84:14 It has frequently been taught that Melchizedek and Shem are one and the same. The argument traces back to Jewish traditions, more particularly to those who could not countenance the idea that Abraham, the father of the Semitic race, would bow down to or be subservient to someone not of that lineage. Melchizedek is an enigma to the scholars of the world who often think that he is a Canaanite priest. These verses lay that tradition to rest with the revelation that Melchizedek traced his priesthood through the "fathers even till Noah," the father of Shem. If it is reasoned that Melchizedek is the son of Noah, it would also follow, by such a reading of these verses, that Noah was the son of Enoch (v. 15). See commentary on Joseph Smith Translation Genesis 14:26–40, page 331.

84:16 *Abel.* Joseph Smith tells us that Abel held the keys of his dispensation (*Teachings of the Prophet Joseph Smith*, 169), while Adam held the keys over all dispensations. Thus, in killing Abel, Cain took the life of the Lord's anointed. In later generations it was held by certain apostates that "the blood of the righteous Abel was shed for sins" (JST Genesis 17:7).

Conspiracy of his brother. A conspiracy is a secret agreement for harmful purposes. Cain was not alone in the murder of his brother. In the book of Moses we learn that "Satan said unto Cain: Swear unto me by thy throat, and if thou tell it thou shalt die; and swear thy brethren by their heads, and by the living God, that they tell it not; for if they tell it, they shall surely die; and this that thy father may not know it; and this day I will deliver thy brother Abel into thine hands. And Satan sware unto Cain that he would do according to his commands. And all these things were done in secret" (Moses 5:29–30).

Adam, who was the first man. The revelations of the Restoration declare that Adam "was the son of God" (Moses 6:22), that he was the "firstborn" of all men (Abraham 1:3), and that he was in the "image of his

[God's] own body" (Moses 6:9). Lehi referred to Adam and Eve as "our first parents" and said that they brought forth "the family of all the earth" (2 Nephi 2:15, 20). The present text affirms that he "was the first man." Holy writ does not countenance the notion of pre-Adamites.

84:17 The church of God in all generations. Matthew 16:18 is the first reference to the word *church* in the Bible. It is commonly argued in the sectarian world that no church organization existed prior to the Savior's ministry. Here we are assured that not only was there a church in Old Testament times but also that the Church of God existed "in all generations," meaning dispensations (D&C 107:4).

The Greater Priesthood Administers the Gospel
DOCTRINE AND COVENANTS 84:18–25

84:19 This greater priesthood administereth the gospel. All that is done in the Church and kingdom of God is and must be done under the direction of the priesthood. The priesthood can exist without the Church, but the Church cannot exist without the priesthood. "It shall not be given to any one to go forth to preach my gospel, or to build up my church," the Lord declared, "except he be ordained by some one who has authority, and it is known to the church that he has authority and has been regularly ordained by the heads of the church" (D&C 42:11). A legal and binding baptism requires proper priesthood authority. Teaching the doctrine of baptism requires that same authority. Men have no more right to go forth preaching the gospel without having been properly commissioned than they have the right to represent the governments of men without such a commission.

The key of the mysteries of the kingdom. In the context of theology, "mysteries" are those singular truths that can be known only by revelation, or those doctrines revealed only to the initiated. They are, in a way, knowledge obtained through participation in sacred rites. Thus we are told that the priesthood holds the "key of the mysteries," meaning the authority to unlock to our understanding truths that cannot be known in any other way.

Even the key of the knowledge of God. It is the purpose of the high or holy priesthood to bring the children of God back into his presence both in this life and in the world to come. The ordinances (rites or rituals) of the priesthood are designed to prepare both men and women to stand in the presence of God.

84:20 *In the ordinances thereof.* In the broad and general sense, an ordinance is a law or statute of God. In a more particular and specific sense, an ordinance may be a ritual or rite, something designed to establish a union between heaven and earth.

84:21 When the authority of God is available to a people, they must comply with its laws and ordinances if they are going to be accounted worthy of either his power or his presence.

84:22 *Without this.* Reference is to the "power of godliness." As we read in the verses that follow, it was Moses' intent to bring the children of Israel into the divine presence. There is no thought here of excluding women or children; rather, it is the unsanctified who were to be excluded from God's presence.

The doctrine was well understood in Bible times that no unclean thing could enter into the presence of the Lord or his divinely sent messengers. Gideon, for instance, realizing he had seen an angel of the Lord, expected to die and found comfort only in the assurance from the Lord that he would not (Judges 6:22–23). Manoah, the father of Samson, was overwhelmed by the appearance of an angel to him and his wife and responded by saying, "We shall surely die, because we have seen God" (Judges 13:22). It was for this reason that Isaiah, when he discovered that he had been brought to stand in the heavenly council, said, "Woe is me! for I am undone [that is "I am lost" or "doomed"]; because I am a man of unclean lips, and I dwell in the midst of a people of unclean lips: for mine eyes have seen the King, the Lord of hosts" (Isaiah 6:5). A ritual of purification immediately followed, and Isaiah was told that his sins had been purged. Moses also had an experience in which the Lord told him: "Thou canst not see my face at this time, lest mine anger be kindled against thee also, and I destroy thee, and thy people; for there shall no man among them see me at this time, and live, for they are exceeding sinful. And no sinful man hath at any time, neither shall there be any sinful man at any time, that shall see my face and live" (JST Exodus 33:20).

So it was that after the children of Israel heard the Lord speak to Moses on Sinai and "saw the thunderings, and the lightnings, and the noise of the trumpet, and the mountain smoking" that they retreated some distance from the mountain and said to Moses, "Speak thou with us, and we will hear: but let not God speak with us, lest we die" (Exodus 20:18–19).

84:23 *To sanctify his people.* To sanctify a people is to set apart, ordain, or consecrate them for sacred purposes. The act of sanctification centers in a ritual purification and a covenant to remain free from sin. Whenever the Lord has had a people that he acknowledged as his own, he has demanded that they be a sanctified people, that is a holy people, or as was the case anciently, a holy nation. Thus, as the army of Israel would sanctify itself before going into battle in ancient times, so are Latter-day Saint missionaries sanctified before being sent forth to herald the news of the Restoration to the nations of the earth (Joshua 3:5; D&C 43:15; 95:8).

84:23–24 The Lord did not send Moses to Pharaoh simply to liberate the children of Israel from their Egyptian bondage. They were not to be taken to the beautiful beaches of the Mediterranean for a much-deserved rest; rather, Moses was directed to take them to the refining furnace of a desert. There it was that they were to meet their God and become a covenant and chosen people. Sinai, "the holy mountain," was the place where their nation was to be forged. Here it was that a covenant would be made that would distinguish them from all other nations and peoples. Here it was that the Lord said to them, "If ye will obey my voice indeed, and keep my covenant, then ye shall be a peculiar treasure unto me above all people: for all the earth is mine: And ye shall be unto me a kingdom of priests, and an holy nation." For this reason Moses was directed to sanctify his people that they might stand in the presence of their God (Exodus 19:5–6, 10–11).

Joseph Smith's situation constitutes a striking parallel to that of Moses. Moses liberated his people from their Egyptian bondage. Because of Joseph Smith and the restoration of the gospel, all who will listen are liberated from the bondage of ignorance and priestcraft. Moses took his people out of Egypt to a wilderness temple, where it was the purpose of God to make of them a "kingdom of priests, and an holy nation." Joseph Smith worked to gather liberated Israel to the wilderness of Jackson County, Missouri, where they were to build a temple to their God. The Lord invited ancient Israel to receive the fulness of the gospel and the blessings of the priesthood as known to Abraham, Isaac, and Jacob. Those same blessings and promises would be granted to those who gathered under the direction of Joseph Smith, the modern Moses (D&C 28:2; 103:15–18; 105:16, 27; 107:91–92).

Moses did not seek to establish an Aaronic order of things, for that order would not bring his people into the presence of God. The Aaronic order came only after the children of Israel had rejected the invitation to stand in God's presence. The "kingdom of priests," to which reference is made, is clearly a kingdom of high priests. What the Lord sought to institute through Moses was a nation of men who had been ordained both "priests and kings" (D&C 76:56).

As we are told in this revelation, the children of Israel hardened their hearts and refused the privileges that were offered to them. This, combined with their foolish rebellion when Moses ascended the holy mount, resulted in having these promised blessings taken from them. In the Joseph Smith Translation we read, "And the Lord said unto Moses, Hew thee two other tables of stone, like unto the first, and I will write upon them also, the words of the law, according as they were written at the first on the tables which thou brakest; but it shall not be according to the first, for I will take away the priesthood out of their midst; therefore my holy order, and the ordinances thereof, shall not go before them; for my presence shall not go up in their midst, lest I destroy them. But I will give unto them the law as at the first, but it shall be after the law of a carnal commandment; for I have sworn in my wrath, that they shall not enter into my presence, into my rest, in the days of their pilgrimage" (JST Exodus 34:1–2).

84:25 *He took Moses out of their midst.* From the book of Alma we learn that Moses was translated (Alma 45:19).

And the Holy Priesthood also. Although the higher or holy priesthood was taken from the children of Israel, Joseph Smith told us that "all the prophets had the Melchizedek Priesthood and were ordained by God himself" (*Teachings of the Prophet Joseph Smith*, 181).

The Lesser Priesthood Administers the Preparatory Gospel
DOCTRINE AND COVENANTS 84:26–32

84:26 *Key of the ministering of angels.* The Melchizedek Priesthood is empowered to bring us into the presence of God. The Aaronic Priesthood possesses the authority by which we may receive the ministering of angels. Thus, it is the right of those holding this priesthood to be instructed and blessed by angels. It is also their right to perform those ordinances that entitle those who do not hold the priesthood to also enjoy the ministering of angels.

Wilford Woodruff illustrates the principles here involved with the following experience: "I was once moved upon to go and warn old Father Hakeman, living on Petty-John Creek, Arkansas. He had been in Jackson County during the persecution period. His wife died there. His family consisted of five sons, all over six feet tall. Most of them had been whipped with hickory gads by mobs, and he went south into Arkansas, taking his sons with him. We went a good deal out of our way for the purpose of visiting Father Hakeman. I had a vision the night previous, in which was manifested to me the trouble that lay before us, but that the Lord would deliver us. We arrived at his house on Sunday morning. He was taking breakfast. We had had breakfast at the place where we stayed overnight. I saw a Book of Mormon on his shelf. He did not seem to pay any attention to us, or to take any interest in us. I took up the Book of Mormon, and said, 'You have a very good book here.'

"'Yes,' said he, 'but it is a book that came from the devil.'

"That opened my eyes. He had been an elder; he had been in Zion; had been persecuted there and driven out; but I found that he had apostatized, and he was our enemy. I saw he would do anything he could against us.

"We left him and went to Brother Hubbard's and stayed with him three weeks, during which we took our axes and cleared some land for him. I was strongly impressed three times to go up and warn Father Hakeman. At last I did so, according to the commandment of God to me. The third time I met with him, his house seemed to be full of evil spirits, and I was troubled in spirit at the manifestation. When I finished my warning, I left him. He followed me from his house with the intention of killing me. I have no doubt about his intention, for it was shown to me in vision. When he came to where I was, he fell dead at my feet, as if he had been struck with a thunderbolt from heaven. I was then a priest, but God defended me and preserved my life. I speak of this because it is a principle that has been manifest in the church of God in this generation as well as in others. I had the administration of angels while holding the office of a priest. I had visions and revelations" (*Discourses of Wilford Woodruff*, 297–98).

To this Wilford Woodruff added, "I went out as a priest, and my companion as an elder, and we traveled thousands of miles, and had many things manifested to us. I desire to impress upon you the fact that it does not make any difference whether a man is a priest or an apostle, if he magnifies his calling. A priest holds the key of the ministering of angels. Never in my life, as an apostle, as a seventy, or as an elder, have I ever had more of the protection of the Lord than while holding the office as a priest. The Lord revealed to me by visions, by revelations, and by the Holy Spirit, many things that lay before me" (*Discourses of Wilford Woodruff*, 300).

84:27 The "preparatory gospel" was had among the Jews from the time of Moses to the ministry of John the Baptist. Thus the promise of salvation could be extended to none save those who were obedient to its principles. There was nothing new in the ordinance of baptism when John came out of the wilderness and commenced preaching to them. Nor was there anything new in the doctrines of faith in Christ and the necessity of repentance. John, however, came to introduce a new dispensation, which of necessity required a new covenant and thus a new baptism.

John was the rightful heir to the office once held by Aaron and traced his authority to him (D&C 68:15–18; 107:16, 70, 76). Even while in his mother's womb, he enjoyed the companionship of the Holy Ghost (Luke 1:15).

84:28 *Baptized . . . in his childhood.* John was baptized "in his childhood," not in his infancy. He that "supposeth that little children need baptism is in the gall of bitterness and in the bonds of iniquity" (Moroni 8:14) and denies the atonement of Christ, according to Mormon (v. 20). In the days of Abraham, the Lord said, "Thou mayest know for ever that children are not accountable before me until they are eight years old" (JST Genesis 17:11).

It would be equally far from the mark to suppose that John had priesthood conferred upon him when he was eight days old. The text certainly does not say this. What Doctrine and Covenants 84:28 says is that he was "ordained . . . *unto this power,* to overthrow the kingdom of the Jews, and to make straight the way of the Lord before the face of his people, to prepare them for the coming of the Lord" (emphasis added). It would appear that the giving of such a blessing required the higher priesthood, which Zacharias did not hold. Having, as did his son, the companionship of the Holy Ghost, Zacharias could and did prophesy relative to his ministry (Luke 1:67–80), but he did not seek to bless him. If what was taking place was a matter of conferring the Aaronic Priesthood, Zacharias could have done that. Indeed, as the rightful heir of the office of Aaron, it would have been his right and responsibility to do so. Suffice it to say, angels simply don't come to do what the Lord has already commissioned someone else to do.

It should also be noted that the Aaronic Priesthood in that day was not conferred upon a man until he was thirty years of age (Numbers 4:1–3).

To overthrow the kingdom of the Jews. The kingdom of the Jews centered in the temple priesthood and the great Sanhedrin in Jerusalem.

When he came on the scene, John "was the only legal administrator in the affairs of the kingdom there was then on the earth" (*Teachings of the Prophet Joseph Smith*, 276). By rejecting him and his authority, the leaders of the Jews closed salvation's door to themselves. In their rejection of Christ, they sealed their own doom and that of their nation. "Because of priestcrafts and iniquities," Jacob said, "they at Jerusalem will stiffen their necks against him, that he be crucified. Wherefore, because of their iniquities, destructions, famines, pestilences, and bloodshed shall come upon them; and they who shall not be destroyed shall be scattered among all nations" (2 Nephi 10:5–6).

84:29 *The high priesthood.* The phrase "high priesthood" has been used to refer to the Melchizedek Priesthood and the office of a high priest in that priesthood. As used here, and in many of the early documents of the Restoration, it refers to the office of high priest rather than the Melchizedek Priesthood. Thus, in the present text, we are being told that the offices of "elder" and "bishop" are appendages to the office of high priest. It would be redundant to say that they were appendages to the Melchizedek Priesthood, as all priesthood offices are appendages to the priesthood. It naturally follows that no office or combination of offices in the priesthood could be greater than the priesthood itself.

In like manner, section 107 also uses the phrase "high priesthood" in reference to the office of high priest. There we read that "there must needs be presiding *elders* to preside over those who are of the office of an elder; and also priests to preside over those who are of the office of a priest; and also teachers to preside over those who are of the office of a teacher, in like manner, also the deacons—wherefore, from deacon to teacher, and from teacher to priest, and from priest to *elder*, severally as they are appointed, according to the covenants and commandments of the church. Then comes the *High Priesthood*, which is the greatest of all" (D&C 107:60–64; emphasis added). The text having listed the offices of deacon through elder says, "Then [after these offices] comes the High Priesthood, which is the greatest of all." Given that the purpose of the text is to place the offices of the priesthood in their respective order, not to distinguish the obvious fact that the Melchizedek Priesthood is greater than the Aaronic, we can only conclude that its purpose is to tell us that the office of a high priest "is the greatest of all," which would be in harmony with the previous direction that if high priests and elders are both present the high priests are to preside (D&C 107:10–11). See commentary on Doctrine and Covenants 20:67, "President of the high priesthood."

A review of the history of the office of high priest in our dispensation along with a review of how that office has functioned in past dispensations, brings meaning to the present text and to the office itself.

The first high priests were ordained at a conference convened at Kirtland, Ohio, on 3 June 1831. Describing this event in the *History of the Church*, Joseph Smith declared, "The Melchizedek Priesthood [meaning the fulness of that priesthood as found in its highest office] was manifested and conferred for the first time upon several of the Elders [those already holding the Melchizedek Priesthood]" (Smith, *History of the Church*, 1:176). The Prophet explained further: "The duty of a High Priest is to administer in spiritual and holy things, and to hold communion with God; but not to exercise monarchial government, or to appoint meetings for the Elders without their consent. And again, it is the High Priests' duty to be better qualified to teach principles and doctrines, than the Elders; for the office of Elder is an appendage to the High Priesthood and it concentrates and centers in one" (*History of the Church*, 1:338).

Church historian John Whitmer recorded these events thus: "June 3 1831, A general conference was called, and a blessing promised, if the elders were faithful, and humble before him [the Lord]. Therefore the elders assembled from the East and the West, from the North and the South. And also many members.

"Conference was opened by prayer and exhortation by Joseph Smith Jr. the Revelator. After the business of the church was attended to according to the covenants. The Lord made manifest to Joseph that it was necessary that such of the elders as were considered worthy, should be ordained to the high priesthood" ("Book of John Whitmer," 65–66).

William E. McLellin, a participant in these events, recorded that "a number of Elders were ordained to the High-Priesthood of the Holy order of God among whom though I felt unworthy I was ordained and took upon me the high responsibility of that office" (*Journals of William E. McLellin*, 45; spelling and syntax standardized).

Of this same event, Elder George A. Smith said: "Among the early baptisms in Northern Ohio, was a Methodist minister by the name of Ezra Booth. He was present when the Elders first received the ordination of the High Priesthood. They met together in June, 1831, in a log school house in Kirtland, a room about eighteen feet by twenty. While they were there, the manifestation of the power of God being on Joseph, he set apart some of the Elders to the High Priesthood" (*Journal of Discourses* 11:4).

Thereafter, at least to the time of President David O. McKay, the phrase "high priesthood" has often been used to describe the office of a high priest. Illustrations are as follows:

1. "Elias and Isaac Higbee, and Jesse Hitchcock, [all of whom were elders] were ordained to the High Priesthood" (Smith, *History of the Church*, 2:141).

2. "After one hour's adjournment of the Council, Elder Don Carlos Smith was nominated to be ordained to the High Priesthood, also to offi-ciate as President, to preside over that body in Kirtland" (Smith, *History of the Church*, 2:370).

3. "Another subject of vital importance to the Church, was the estab-lishing of the grades of the different quorums. It was ascertained that all but one or two of the presidents of the Seventies were High Priests, and when they had ordained and set apart any from the quorum of Elders, into the quorum of Seventies, they had conferred upon them the High Priesthood, also. This was declared to be wrong, and not according to the order of heaven. New presidents of the Seventies were accordingly ordained to fill the places of such of them as were High Priests, and the ex-officio presidents, and such of the Seventies as had been legally ordained to be High Priests, were directed to unite with the High Priests' quorum [6 April 1837]" (Smith, *History of the Church*, 2:476).

4. "A letter was read from presidents of the Seventies, wishing for an explanation of the steps, which the High Council had taken, in remov-ing Elder F. G. Bishop from the quorum of the Seventies to that of the High Priests, without any other ordination than he had when in the Seven-ties, and wished to know whether those ordained into the Seventies at the same time F. G. Bishop was, had a right to the High Priesthood, or not. After observations on the case by different individuals, the president gave a statement of the authority of the Seventies, and stated that they were Elders and not High Priests, and consequently Brother F. G. Bishop had no claim to that office. It was then unanimously resolved that Elder F. G. Bishop be placed back again into the quorum of the Seventies" (Smith, *History of the Church*, 4:105).

5. Of his own father, Joseph Smith Sr., the Prophet wrote, "He removed with his family to Kirtland in 1831; was ordained Patriarch and President of the High Priesthood . . . on the 18th of December, 1833" (*History of the Church*, 4:190).

6. "Thursday morning April 8th: at an early hour this morning the dif-ferent quorums, who had previously been organized, came to the ground

and took their seats as follows: the First Presidency, with the presidents of the quorums on the stand; the High Council, on the front of the stand; the High Priesthood on the front to the right of the stand; the Seventies immediately behind the high priesthood; the Elders in the front, to the left; the Lesser Priesthood on the extreme right" (*Times and Seasons*, 2:387).

7. "Br. Sidney Rigdon said it was the privilege of those Elders present to be ordained to the High Priesthood" (Cannon and Cook, *Far West Record*, 25).

8. Parley P. Pratt, in describing the business attended to at a conference of the Church in Manchester, England, held 6 July 1840, noted that three persons were "ordained to the high Priesthood" and that seven others were "ordained to the lesser Priesthood" (*Autobiography*, 269). Of the conference held on 6 April 1841 he said, "Eleven persons were chosen and ordained to the High Priesthood during this Conference, and twelve persons were ordained Elders" (Pratt, *Autobiography*, 275).

9. John Taylor observed, "There is a matter that has of late become a subject of a good deal of conversation, and it occurs to my mind to refer to it, namely that of the High Priesthood, or the place and calling of a High Priest" (*Journal of Discourses*, 19:242).

10. Again John Taylor said, "The high priesthood, as you are aware, differs from the priesthood of the seventies in this respect—the high priests are expected to preside. It is a part of their office and calling to do that (*Gospel Kingdom*, 183).

11. George Q. Cannon stated that "an Elder is not a High Priest until he is ordained to the 'High Priesthood,' that is, is made a High Priest" (*Gospel Truth*, 1:243).

12. Responding to questions about why members of the First Quorum of Seventy had been ordained high priests, President David O. McKay explained, "It should be sufficient for you who have the Spirit of the Lord to know that the work today is required of those members of the First Council of the Seventy which needs the High Priesthood. They do not join the high priests' quorum, but they are sent out by the Council of the Twelve Apostles to set in order the Church in the stakes and missions, and they should be given authority to set apart a president of a stake, a high councilman, a bishop of a ward, which requires the High Priesthood" (Conference Report, October 1961, 90).

A review of the revelations of the Restoration relative to the office of a high priest sustains its distinctive place among the offices of the priesthood. Chief among them would be Alma 13 and Abraham 1. In Alma we read of those who became "high priests forever, after the order of the Son, the Only Begotten of the Father." Concerning "the holy order, or this high priesthood," we are told that "there were many who were ordained and became high priests of God; and it was on account of their exceeding faith and repentance, and their righteousness before God" that they were "called after this holy order, and were sanctified, and their garments were washed white through the blood of the Lamb." We learn that in so doing, they became like Melchizedek (King of Righteousness), who had also taken upon him that "high priesthood forever," and like him became both priests and kings (Alma 13:9–11, 14).

Similarly, we read in the book of Abraham that Abraham also "sought for the blessings of the fathers and the right whereunto I should be ordained to administer the same," which we would understand to be the keys or right of presidency. He was already "a follower of righteousness" but desired "to be a greater follower of righteousness, and to possess a greater knowledge, and to be a father of many nations, a prince of peace, and . . . to receive instructions, and to keep the commandments of God." He tells us he "became a rightful heir, a High Priest, holding the right belonging to the fathers." This right, he said, came down from the fathers from the beginning of time and reached back even before the foundations of the earth. "I sought," he said, "for mine appointment unto the Priesthood according to the appointment of God unto the fathers concerning the seed" (Abraham 1:2, 4).

In his labor on the Joseph Smith Translation, the Prophet had already learned that Melchizedek "was a man of faith, who wrought righteousness" and "having been approved of God, he was ordained an high priest after the order of the covenant which God made with Enoch, it being after the order of the Son of God," which order "was delivered unto men by the calling of his own voice, according to his own will, unto as many as believed on his name" (JST Genesis 14:26–29).

We are told that Adam gathered those who were "high priests, with the residue of his posterity who were righteous, into the valley of Adam-ondi-Ahman" and there bestowed his last blessing upon them, after which the Lord appeared to them (D&C 107:53). The great revelation on the degrees of glory describe those who will receive the celestial kingdom, saying, "They are they who are priests [meaning high priests] and kings, who have received of his fulness, and of his glory; and are priests of the Most

High, after the order of Melchizedek, which was after the order of Enoch, which was after the order of the Only Begotten Son" (D&C 76:56–57).

In more recent years, the distinctiveness relative to the office of high priest has been replaced with an emphasis magnifying the particular office and calling that one has. We have often been told that it is not where we serve but how we serve that merits the pleasure of heaven. This principle is a true one. The elder who magnifies his priesthood works out his salvation as readily as does the apostle who in like manner magnifies his office. It is how one honors the office he holds that counts; it matters not what honor comes to man due to his office. To this is appended the scriptural assurance that every man who so honors the offices to which he is called will be privileged, like Melchizedek for whom the priesthood is named, to eventually become both priest and king.

A bishop, whose calling is an office in the Aaronic Priesthood, must also preside over his ward (which would have other Melchizedek Priesthood holders in it). To do so he must hold the office of a high priest and be set apart as the presiding high priest in the ward. He does not preside by virtue of the office of bishop or that of an elder, for these offices are appendages to the office of a high priest. The bishop presides because he holds the office of high priest and has been given the necessary keys to do so. These keys are not given to an elder nor are they given to a bishop who has not first been ordained a high priest.

84:30 The offices of teacher and deacon "are necessary appendages" to the Aaronic or lesser priesthood. This explanation is given because these offices were not a part of the Aaronic or Levitical Priesthood in Old Testament times. The equivalent duties of a teacher or deacon would have been filled by those known anciently as Levites.

84:31 Both the sons of Moses and of Aaron are to present an acceptable offering in the house of the Lord. As part of the restoration of all things, the sons of Aaron will bring the offering prophesied by Malachi and promised by John the Baptist when he restored the keys of the Aaronic Priesthood (Malachi 3:1–4; D&C 13), which could be nothing other than animal sacrifice. Explaining this promise, Joseph Smith said: "It is generally supposed that sacrifice was entirely done away when the Great Sacrifice [i.e.,] the sacrifice of the Lord Jesus was offered up, and that there will be no necessity for the ordinance of sacrifice in future; but those who assert this are certainly not acquainted with the duties, privileges and authority of the Priesthood, or with the Prophets.

"The offering of sacrifice has ever been connected and forms a part of the duties of the Priesthood. It began with the Priesthood, and will be continued until after the coming of Christ, from generation to generation. We frequently have mention made of the offering of sacrifice by the servants of the Most High in ancient days, prior to the law of Moses; which ordinances will be continued when the Priesthood is restored with all its authority, power and blessings . . .

"These sacrifices, as well as every ordinance belonging to the Priesthood, will, when the Temple of the Lord shall be built, and the sons of Levi be purified, be fully restored and attended to in all their powers, ramifications, and blessings. This ever did and ever will exist when the powers of the Melchizedek Priesthood are sufficiently manifest; else how can the restitution of all things spoken of by the Holy Prophets be brought to pass. It is not to be understood that the law of Moses will be established again with all its rites and variety of ceremonies; this has never been spoken of by the prophets; but those things which existed prior to Moses' day, namely, sacrifice, will be continued.

"It may be asked by some, what necessity for sacrifice, since the Great Sacrifice was offered? In answer to which, if repentance, baptism, and faith existed prior to the days of Christ, what necessity for them since that time? The Priesthood has descended in a regular line from father to son, through their succeeding generations" (*Teachings of the Prophet Joseph Smith*, 172–73).

Holders of the Aaronic Priesthood cannot participate in the sealing ordinances of the temple. Of necessity their offering will differ from that of those holding the Melchizedek Priesthood. The Prophet identifies the "acceptable offering" to be made by the sons of Moses—those holding the greater priesthood—as "a book containing the records of our dead" (D&C 128:24). That book will contain the list of those of our progenitors for whom we have stood as proxies in the performance of the ordinances of salvation. This is done that they might accept those labors performed in their behalf and obtain all the promises associated with them. See commentary on Doctrine and Covenants 128:24.

This generation, upon the consecrated spot. See commentary on verses 4–5.

84:32 *Mount Zion.* See commentary on Doctrine and Covenants 76:66.

To build up my church. The servants of the Lord are sent forth "to build up the kingdom of God, and to establish his righteousness" (JST Matthew

6:38). That is, they are sent forth to build, lift, encourage, teach, edify, but not to do otherwise.

This verse returns to the announcement in verse 2 that the Church has been restored in order that Israel might be returned to the covenants that God made with her fathers anciently. In the true and proper sense, the gathering of Israel is to those sacred covenants made in the house of the Lord.

The Oath and Covenant of the Priesthood
DOCTRINE AND COVENANTS 84:33–44

84:33–44 The Melchizedek Priesthood comes with an oath and covenant. The oath is on God's part, for he alone has the authority to swear oaths. The covenant is between God and the priesthood holder. Those receiving the priesthood covenant to magnify the office conferred upon them and to sustain those called to preside over them. They are to "live by every word that proceedeth forth from the mouth of God" (v. 44). God in turn covenants to accept the faithful priesthood holder as his heir and thus to make him equal in power, might, and dominion. This promise—that one can become as God—is so far beyond the imagination of man that God, to affirm the reality of it, seals it with an oath.

Joseph Fielding Smith explained: "To swear with an oath is the most solemn and binding form of speech known to the human tongue; and it was this type of language which the Father chose to have used in the great Messianic prophecy about Christ and the priesthood. Of him it says: 'The Lord hath sworn, and will not repent, Thou art a priest for ever after the order of Melchizedek.' (Ps. 110:4.)

"In explaining this Messianic prophecy, Paul says that Jesus had 'an unchangeable priesthood,' and that through it came 'the power of an end-less life.' (See Heb. 7:24, 16.) Joseph Smith said that 'all those who are ordained unto this priesthood are made like unto the Son of God, abid-ing a priest continually,' that is, if they are faithful and true" (Conference Report, October 1970, 92).

The doctrine of the priesthood centers in the understanding that God, contrary to all the creeds of men, is a personal being with body, parts, and passions. Indeed, he is an exalted, glorified man. He is literally the Father of our spirits and lives in the family unit. He possesses all attributes of godliness in their perfection.

Exaltation consists in our becoming like God. It is to become equal with him in power, might, and dominion. For this purpose, God endows his children with power from on high.

In the doctrine of the priesthood, we can enter an order of the priesthood named the new and everlasting covenant of marriage (D&C 131:2), named also the patriarchal order, because of which order we can create eternal family units of our own, patterned after the family of our Heavenly Father.

Thus, Elder Bruce R. McConkie explained, we obtain "power, by faith, to govern and control all things, both temporal and spiritual; to work miracles and perfect lives; to stand in the presence of God and be like him because we have gained his faith, his perfections, and his power, or in other words the fulness of his priesthood" (Conference Report, April 1982, 50).

84:33 *Magnifying their calling.* Nowhere in scripture are men charged to magnify the priesthood; rather, they are charged to magnify their particular office or calling in the priesthood. To be entrusted with priesthood is an honor beyond that which either men or nations can confer. Men can add neither authority nor power to God; they can, however, utilize the office that has been conferred upon them with dignity and honor. Thus the elder must do the work and labor of an elder, the high priest that of a high priest, the apostle the labor of an apostle, and so forth. Each must labor to magnify his own office and his own calling (D&C 84:109; 107:99–100).

To labor faithfully sanctifies the soul. It has both a purifying effect and the power to bring about a remission of sins (James 5:19–20; D&C 4:4; 62:3; 84:61; 108:1; 132:50). See commentary on Doctrine and Covenants 20:31.

84:34 In a figurative sense, those who magnify their callings in the Aaronic Priesthood become the sons of Aaron, while those who magnify their callings in the Melchizedek Priesthood become the sons of Moses; all such are the seed of Abraham and the "elect of God."

84:38 *All that my Father hath.* See commentary on Doctrine and Covenants 76:94–95.

84:42 *Wo unto all those who come not unto this priesthood.* To receive the promise of salvation, a man must hold the higher priesthood and receive the blessings associated with the house of the Lord. To refuse the priesthood is to refuse those promises and blessings.

With equal propriety it could also be said to every woman, "Wo unto all those who come not unto this priesthood," meaning "wo" to those who do not choose to receive all the blessings of salvation under the hands of the priesthood.

A man cannot enjoy the fulness of the blessings of the priesthood without a woman who has been sealed to him for time and eternity. As there is no salvation for a man independent of the blessings of the priesthood, so there is no salvation for a woman independent of those blessings. They must magnify the callings that come to them, sustain those called to preside over them, and hearken unto every word of the Lord.

The Spirit of Christ Enlightens Men and Leads Them to the Father

DOCTRINE AND COVENANTS 84:45–53

84:45–53 This text affirms that the path of salvation is the same for all. Those who love light and truth will be led to greater light and greater truth. All such will, in the course of time, be brought to the knowledge of the Fatherhood of God and the covenant of salvation. By contrast, those who refuse such a course place themselves in bondage to both sin and darkness. Teaching this principle, Alma said: "It is given unto many to know the mysteries of God; nevertheless they are laid under a strict command that they shall not impart only according to the portion of his word which he doth grant unto the children of men, according to the heed and diligence which they give unto him. And therefore, he that will harden his heart, the same receiveth the lesser portion of the word; and he that will not harden his heart, to him is given the greater portion of the word, until it is given unto him to know the mysteries of God until he know them in full. And they that will harden their hearts, to them is given the lesser portion of the word until they know nothing concerning his mysteries; and then they are taken captive by the devil, and led by his will down to destruction. Now this is what is meant by the chains of hell" (Alma 12:9–11).

84:45–46 We are taught that all men are born with the capacity to know and recognize the truths of salvation. Such truths are not incomprehensible mysteries! They are to be known, to be felt, and to be believed by all of God's children. Their understanding is within the grasp of every soul that desires to know them. No one is justified in rejecting the revelations of heaven. All revelations carry within them the evidence of their authenticity, and all children of God—be their station high or low, be they young or old—are divinely endowed with the capacity to see the light and feel its warmth.

The Saints Are to Testify of That Which They Have Received

DOCTRINE AND COVENANTS 84:54–62

84:54–62 The Saints were chastened for treating lightly that which they had received. Considering all that they had been given, it is not surprising that they—notwithstanding all the difficulties they had faced—were spoiled by God's goodness to them. Earth's history knows no time when so many of heavens' treasures have been dispensed to so few in such a short period. Consider the events that had taken place between May 1829 and this revelation, which was recorded in September 1832. John the Baptist had come to restore the Aaronic Priesthood; Peter, James, and John had come to restore the Melchizedek Priesthood; the Book of Mormon, containing more than five hundred pages of scripture, had been printed; the Church was organized; the Joseph Smith Translation had commenced; more than eighty revelations had been given to the Saints; and the place of the New Jerusalem had been identified. It would be difficult to argue that those of us living in this century have yet grown up into an understanding and an appreciation of the flood of light granted during these few short years.

84:57 *The new covenant, even the Book of Mormon.* We have come to think of the Bible as consisting of the Old and New Testaments. Elder Jeffery Holland explained the division of the ancient record: "The words *testament* and *covenant* are virtually synonymous in their theological usage, the Latin definition of *testamentum* being 'a covenant with God, holy scripture.' Thus, the Old and New Testaments, as we commonly refer to them, are written testimonies or witnesses (the Latin *testis* meaning 'witness') of the covenants between God and man in various dispensations. Furthermore, such covenants always deal with the central issue between perfect, immortal God and imperfect, mortal man—why they are separated and how they can again unite. The Latin root for *covenants* is *convenire*, 'to agree, unite, come together.' In short, all covenants, all testaments, all holy witnesses since the beginning have essentially been about one thing—the atonement of Jesus Christ, the *at-one-ment* provided every man, woman, and child if they will but receive the witness, the *testimony* of the prophets and apostles, and honor the terms of that coming together, that *convenire*, or covenant, whose central feature is always the atoning sacrifice of the Son of God himself" (*Christ and the New Covenant*, 7–8). So it is that in the Book of Mormon the Lord has given the world one last covenant or testament relative to the hope of salvation that is found in him. Thus, the Book of Mormon becomes God's "new covenant" with gathering Israel.

The former commandments which I have given them. Reference is to revelations given those in Zion (Missouri) through Joseph Smith. The counsel and instruction found therein was not being properly heeded. This caused the Spirit of the Lord to withdraw and opened the door to the spirit of contention, which quickly took its place. Some of their number had gone to Zion unprepared and without permission; others who had means to donate to the bishop in Missouri had refused to do so. See also Doctrine and Covenants 84:59 and 76.

84:58 *Otherwise there remaineth a scourge and judgment to be poured out upon the children of Zion.* This warning was to find both immediate and literal fulfillment the following year (1833) in the mob action against the Church in Independence.

84:60 *Hear my words, which are my voice.* See commentary on Doctrine and Covenants 18:36.

84:61 Here the Lord promises the Saints a remission of sins if they will be true to the message of the Restoration. If they will declare with boldness those singular truths that the Lord has revealed for the benefit of the children of men in this dispensation, they will find a purifying power therein. Their testimony would, of course, center in the Book of Mormon. See commentary on Doctrine and Covenants 31:4; 49:1–3; 75:4.

Signs Follow Them That Believe
DOCTRINE AND COVENANTS 84:63–76

84:63 *You are mine apostles.* The office of an apostle had not yet been restored. It would be another two and half years before this would take place (D&C 107). An apostle is a messenger or an emissary for someone else. In the context of the gospel, he is a special witness of the Lord and his gospel. Those to whom reference is made in this verse were high priests who had proven faithful in both delivering the message of the restored gospel and in testifying of its verity; thus, the Lord refers to them as both his friends and as apostles. See commentary on Doctrine and Covenants 35:8.

84:64–72 The promise that signs would follow them that believe was given by the Savior to the Twelve in both the Old World and the New (Mark 16:15–18; Mormon 9:23–25). Significantly, it is restored to our dispensation in a revelation on the priesthood, one which differs from the earlier texts by repeating the phrase "in my name" four times (D&C 84:66–69). This is the equivalent of saying, "By the authority of the priesthood" you will be able to do wonderful works, cast out devils, heal the sick, open the eyes of the blind and unstop the ears of the deaf, and so on. The present text also improves on its older counterparts by noting that the gift of the Holy Ghost follows baptism.

"When faith comes," Joseph Smith explained, "it brings its train of attendants with it—apostles, prophets, evangelists, pastors, teachers, gifts, wisdom, knowledge, miracles, healings, tongues, interpretation of tongues, etc. All these appear when faith appears on the earth, and disappear when it disappears from the earth; for these are the effects of faith, and always have attended, and always will, attend it. For where faith is, there will the knowledge of God be also, with all things which pertain thereto—revelations, visions, and dreams, as well as every necessary thing, in order that the possessors of faith may be perfected, and obtain salvation; for God must change, otherwise faith will prevail with him. And he who possesses it will, through it, obtain all necessary knowledge and wisdom, until he shall know God, and the Lord Jesus Christ, whom he has sent—whom to know is eternal life" (*Lectures on Faith*, 7:20). See commentary on Lectures on Faith, page 806.

84:73 A sense of sacredness attends the blessings of heaven and the manner in which the priesthood is used. In the days of Christ and his disciples, signs and wonders were given in a very public fashion to aid in the announcement that the gospel had been restored. Here we are commanded not to boast in the miracles we see or have performed for us. This is not to suggest that such miracles are to cease. Miracles are ever to be numbered among the fruits of the gospel. The public miracles that announce the Restoration to the world in our age are the revelations of the Restoration as found in the Book of Mormon and the Doctrine and Covenants. This revelation centers our attention on the importance of bearing testimony to that which was revealed through the Prophet Joseph Smith (vv. 54–61; D&C 24:13–14).

The Lord Will Care for the Needs of His Servants
DOCTRINE AND COVENANTS 84:77–91

84:76 Your brethren in Zion [*are to be upbraided*] for their rebellion against you. See commentary on Doctrine and Covenants 82:2, "Refrain from sin, lest sore judgments fall upon your heads."

84:77–91 Here the promise of divine protection is placed on those called to declare the message of the Restoration to the world. Fulfillment of this promise can be found in the experiences of virtually every missionary called to serve (Matthew 6:25–34; Luke 12:22–30).

84:78 *I suffered them not to have purse or scrip.* In the early part of his ministry, Jesus sent his disciples out without purse or scrip (Mark 6:8; Luke 10:4). Later he charged them to take both food and money with them (Luke 22:35–36). As conditions change, the instruction given for the protection and wellbeing of missionaries will also change. "All of which shows," said Elder Bruce R. McConkie, "the need of continuing revelation so the Lord's people will always know how to act in the circumstances confronting them at any given moment" (*Doctrinal New Testament Commentary*, 1:771; see also D&C 24:18).

84:79 *The laborer is worthy of his hire.* The servant of the Lord is a rightful heir to the blessings promised in these verses. Through faithful service he gains the promise of salvation (D&C 4:4).

Plagues and Cursings Await Those Who Reject the Gospel
DOCTRINE AND COVENANTS 84:92–97

84:92–97 There are no blessings to be had in rejecting the gospel or the servants of the Lord. To reject the opportunity to be baptized for the remission of sins is to drown in sin. To refuse the light of heaven is to remain in the dark. To give no heed to the warning voice is to reap the disaster against which it warned. There is no neutrality where the principles of heaven are concerned. Eventually, all must choose to stand with Christ or against him. They must choose to embrace his principles or stand in opposition to them. All such will be rewarded according to their works.

84:92 *Cleanse your feet.* See commentary on Doctrine and Covenants 24:15.

The New Song of the Redemption of Zion

DOCTRINE AND COVENANTS 84:98–102

84:98–102 This is a hymn of great rejoicing. For century after century the scattered remnants of Israel have wandered the earth longing for that promised day when they would be gathered home again. Addressing the resurrected Christ, the meridian Twelve asked, "Wilt thou at this time restore again the kingdom to Israel?" But theirs was not the promised day, and he responded, saying, "It is not for you to know the times or the seasons, which the Father hath put in his own power" (Acts 1:6–7). Indeed, we are told that they would come to look upon the long absence of their spirits from their bodies as a bondage before their posterity, and even those who were "afar off" both in time and place would come to realize the promised blessings (D&C 45:17; Acts 2:39).

In that great day, Satan will be bound, for righteousness and truth will have swept the earth as a flood to gather out the elect from its four quarters into the New Jerusalem. The city of Enoch will return. Its inhabitants will fall upon their necks in rejoicing, and they will kiss each other. "And there shall be mine abode," the Lord said, "and it shall be Zion" (Moses 7:64).

Isaiah foretold the time when the scattered remnants of Israel would awake once again to the things of the Spirit, shed the rags of filth in which she was clothed, and put on the "beautiful garments" to which she had right by birth (Isaiah 52:1). Commenting on the words of the ancient seer, Joseph Smith said, "He had reference to those whom God should call in the last days, who should hold the power of priesthood to bring again Zion, and the redemption of Israel; and to put on her strength is to put on the authority of the priesthood, which she, Zion, has a right to by lineage; also to return to that power which she had lost" (D&C 113:8).

84:100 *Satan is bound and time is no longer.* See commentary on Doctrine and Covenants 88:110.

Let Every Man Stand in His Own Office

DOCTRINE AND COVENANTS 84:103–10

84:104 *The bishop in Zion.* Reference is to Edward Partridge. See commentary on Doctrine and Covenants 72:5–6.

The bishop in Ohio. Reference is to Newel K. Whitney (D&C 72:8).

84:109–10 In harmony with the oath and covenant of the priesthood, it becomes the duty of the elder to do the work and labor of an elder, the high priest the labor of a high priest and so forth. All are to labor as they have been called, free from envy and free from the spirit of criticism. The great principle being, it is not where you serve but how you serve that brings forth the promises of heaven.

Proclaiming the Abomination of Desolation
DOCTRINE AND COVENANTS 84:111–20

84:114 Shortly after this revelation was received, the Prophet accompanied Bishop Whitney on a hurried journey to Albany, New York City, and Boston. While in New York City he wrote his beloved wife, Emma, describing his feelings.

"My Dear Wife

"This day I have been walking through the most splendid part of the City of New Y—the buildings are truly great and wonderful to the astonishing of every beholder and the language of my heart is like this can the great God of all the Earth maker of all things magnificent and splendid be displeased with man for all these great inventions sought out by them my answer is no it can not be seeing these works are calculated to make men comfortable wise and happy therefore not for the works can the Lord be displeased only against man is the anger of Lord Kindled because they Give him not the Glory therefore their iniquities shall be visited upon their heads and their works shall be burned up with unquenchable fire the inequity of the people is printed in every countenance and nothing but the dress of the people makes them look fair and beautiful all is deformity there is something in every countenance that is disagreeable with few exceptions Oh how long Oh Lord Shall this order of things exist and darkness cover the Earth and gross darkness cover the people after beholding all that I had any desire to behold I returned to my room to meditate and calm my mind and behold the thoughts of home of Emma and Julia [Murdock, the adopted baby] rushes upon my mind like a flood and I could wish for a moment to be with them my breast is filled with all the feelings and tenderness of a parent and a Husband and could I be with you I would tell you many things yet when I reflect upon this great city like Ninevah not discerning their right hand from their left yea more then two hundred thousand souls my bowels is filled with compassion towards them and I am determined to lift up my voice in this City and leave the Event with God who holdeth all things in his hands and will not suffer an hair of our heads unnoticed to fall to the ground there is but few Cases of the cholera in this City now and if you should see the people you would not know that they had ever heard of the cholera I hope you will excuse me for writing this letter so soon after writing for I feel as if I wanted to say something to you to comfort you in your peculiar trial and present affliction [Emma was expecting her fourth child] I hope God will give you strength that you may not faint I pray God to soften the hearts of those around you to be kind to you and take the burden off your shoulders as much as possible and not afflict you I feel for you for I know your state and that others do not but you must comfort yourself knowing that God is your friend in heaven and that you have one true and living friend on Earth your Husband, Joseph Smith Jr" (Jessee, *Personal Writings of Joseph Smith*, 252–53; spelling standardized; punctuation as in original).

New York . . . Albany . . . Boston. Wilford Woodruff prophesied that New York would be destroyed by an earthquake, that Boston would be swept into the sea, and Albany would be destroyed by fire (Cook, *Revelations,* 177)

84:117 *The desolation of abomination.* The term is the same as abomination of desolation (Matthew 24:15; Joseph Smith–Matthew 1:12, 32), and the "abomination that maketh desolate" (Daniel 12:11; 9:27). The conditions of desolation, born of abomination and wickedness, as spoken of by Daniel, are destined to occur twice. The first occurrence centered in the destruction of Jerusalem in 70 A.D.; the second occurrence will be when these events repeat themselves in the last days. Drawing upon this imagery, this text uses the phrase "desolation of abomination" to describe the latter-day terrors that will be poured out upon the wicked wherever they may be.

That the pure and honest in heart may escape these desolations, the Lord sends his missionaries to raise a warning voice (D&C 84:114, 117). To this end President Joseph Fielding Smith observed: "When we become ripe in iniquity, then the Lord will come. I get annoyed sometimes at some of our elders who when speaking say the Lord will come when we all become righteous enough to receive him. The Lord is not going to wait for us to get righteous. When he gets ready to come, he is going to come—when the cup of iniquity is full—and if we are not righteous then, it will be just too bad for us, for we will be classed among the ungodly, and we will be as stubble to be swept off the face of the earth, for the Lord says wickedness shall not stand.

"Do not think the Lord delays his coming, for he will come at the appointed time, not the time which I have heard some preach when the earth becomes righteous enough to receive him. . . . Christ will come in the day of wickedness, when the earth is ripe in iniquity and prepared for the cleansing, and as the cleanser and purifier he will come, and all the wicked will be as stubble and will be consumed" (*Doctrines of Salvation*, 3:3).

DOCTRINE AND COVENANTS 85

DATE: 27 NOVEMBER 1832

PLACE: KIRTLAND, OHIO

This section is an extract from a letter written by Joseph Smith in Kirtland, Ohio, to William W. Phelps, who was in Missouri. Elder Phelps was troubled about problems associated with the manner in which the law of consecration was being administered. The Prophet wrote, "I fancy to myself that you are saying or thinking something similar to these words:—'My God, great and mighty art Thou, therefore show unto Thy servant what shall become of those who are essaying to come up unto Zion, in order to keep the commandments of God, and yet receive not their inheritance by consecrations, by order of deed from the Bishop, the man that God has appointed in a legal way, agreeably to the law given to organize and regulate the Church, and all the affairs of the same.'

"Brother William," the Prophet continued, "in the love of God, having the most implicit confidence in you as a man of God, having obtained this confidence by a vision of heaven, therefore I will proceed to unfold to you some of the feelings of my heart, and to answer the question" (Smith, *History of the Church,* 1:298). What follows in this revelation is the Lord's answer to the questions troubling Elder Phelps.

Inheritances in Zion Are to Be Received through Consecration
DOCTRINE AND COVENANTS 85:1–5

85:1 *The Lord's clerk.* Reference is to John Whitmer, the Church historian. In addition to keeping the history of the Church, he was to keep a record of all that took place in Zion and a record of all persons who legally consecrated properties with the bishop of Zion, who was Edward Partridge (D&C 42:30–36).

85:2 It would be foolish on our part to suppose that all who embrace gospel covenants will keep them. There will always be those who fall short or quit before the journey is complete. We would suppose that every gospel dispensation has known its Judas. Special instructions were given concerning those who received property as a stewardship and then apostatized (D&C 51:4–6; 54:4–5).

85:3–5 The Lord directs that those who do not receive their inheritance by consecration, according to his law, are not to have their names enrolled with those who are to be known as his people. Neither they nor their fathers nor their children are to be acknowledged as having place among the children of the covenant. See commentary on verses 11–12.

85:3 *Tithe his people.* The law of tithing as understood in the Church today was not revealed until 8 July 1838. References to tithing prior to that time (D&C 64:23; 97:11–12) appear to be general in nature and simply refer to contributions or offerings. In this instance, those who have tithed are those who had consecrated their properties.

One Mighty and Strong Shall Give the Saints Their Inheritance in Zion
DOCTRINE AND COVENANTS 85:6–12

85:6 *Apostates who apostatize.* All revelations do not come with the same clarity or the same power. Writing to Timothy, Paul said, "Now the Spirit speaketh expressly" (1 Timothy 4:1), thus suggesting that in other instances that same Spirit speaks less expressly. In like manner, the Prophet, in this text, observes that "often times" the Spirit makes his "bones to quake," though this is not always the case.

The phrase "still small voice," which is used in only two other scriptural texts, refers to the Holy Ghost (1 Kings 19:12; 1 Nephi 17:45).

85:7–8 *One mighty and strong.* The leader of virtually every cult or apostate group that has broken with the Church has claimed to be the "one mighty and strong" spoken of by the Lord who is to set the Church in order. As early as 1905, President Joseph F. Smith and his counselors, John R. Winder and Anthon H. Lund, issued a statement on this text:

"It is to be observed first of all that the subject of this whole letter, as also the part of it subsequently accepted as a revelation, relates to the affairs of the Church in Missouri, the gathering of the Saints to that land and obtaining their inheritances under the law of consecration and stewardship; and the Prophet deals especially with the matter of what is to become of those who fail to receive their inheritances by order or deed from the bishop. . . .

"It was while these conditions of rebellion, jealousy, pride, unbelief and hardness of heart prevailed among the brethren in Zion—Jackson county, Missouri—in all of which Bishop Partridge participated, that the words of the revelation taken from the letter to William W. Phelps, of the 27th of November, 1832, were written. The 'man who was called and appointed of God' to 'divide unto the Saints their inheritance'—Edward Partridge—was at that time out of order, neglecting his own duty, and putting 'forth his hand to steady the ark'; hence, he was warned of the judgment of God impending, and the prediction was made that another, 'one mighty and strong,' would be sent of God to take his place, to have his bishopric—one having the spirit and power of that high office resting upon him, by which he would have power to 'set in order the house of God, and arrange by lot the inheritance of the Saints'; in other words, one who would do the work that Bishop Edward Partridge had been appointed to do, but had failed to accomplish. . . .

". . . The Lord said, some three years later, that he was well pleased with Edward Partridge. The word of the Lord came to the Prophet to this effect, on the 7th of November, 1835:

"'Behold, I am well pleased with my servant Isaac Morley, and my servant Edward Partridge, because of the integrity of their hearts in laboring in my vineyard, for the salvation of the souls of men. Verily I say unto you, their sins are forgiven them, therefore, say unto them in my name, that it is my will that they should tarry for a little season, (in Kirtland) and attend the school and also the solemn assembly, for a wise purpose in me. Even so. Amen. (*History of the Church*, [2:302–3]).' . . .

". . . Inasmuch as through his repentance and sacrifices and suffering, Bishop Edward Partridge undoubtedly obtained a mitigation of the threatened judgment against him of falling 'by the shaft of death, like as a tree that is smitten by the vivid shaft of lightning,' so the occasion for sending another to fill his station—'one mighty and strong to set in order the house of God, and to arrange by lot the inheritances of the Saints'—may also be considered as having passed away and the whole incident of the prophecy closed" (Clark, *Messages*, 4:112, 115–17).

85:8 *Steady the ark.* At the time of Eli, the ark of the covenant stood in the sanctuary at Shiloh (1 Samuel 3:3). Thereafter it fell into the hands of the Philistines (1 Samuel 4:10–11). Discovering that its possession only brought them misfortunes, they sent it back to Israel (1 Samuel 6). It was brought first to Beth Shemesh in the tribe of Judah, near the borders of the Philistines and soon after to Kiriath-jearim, about 7.5 miles northwest of Jerusalem. From there, David went with thirty thousand men to bring the ark to Jerusalem. As they were doing so the oxen stumbled, and Uzzah, who drove the cart on which the ark was being carried, put forth his hand to prevent the ark from falling. "And the anger of the Lord was kindled against Uzzah; and God smote him there for his error; and there he died by the ark of God" (2 Samuel 6:7). Levites had been forbidden by the Lord to touch the ark on pain of death (Numbers 4:15–20).

However well intended Uzzah's efforts were, the Lord made it plain that he needed neither the help of Uzzah nor any other man to sustain his affairs. Thus, the direction not to steady the ark constituted sober warning to Edward Partridge to follow the counsel of the Prophet rather than seek to counsel him.

85:11–12 "The children of the priests . . . sought their register among those that were reckoned by genealogy, but they were not found: therefore were they, as polluted, put from the priesthood" (Ezra 2:61–62).

The conclusion of the Prophet's letter to W. W. Phelps is counsel we should heed: "Now, Brother William, if what I have said is true, how careful men ought to be what they do in the last days, lest they are cut short of their expectations, and they that think they stand should fall, because they keep not the Lord's commandments; whilst you, who do the will of the Lord and keep His commandments, have need to rejoice with unspeakable joy, for such shall be exalted very high, and shall be lifted up in triumph above all the kingdoms of this world" (Smith, *History of the Church*, 1:299).

85:11 *High Priesthood.* See commentary on Doctrine and Covenants 84:29.

DOCTRINE AND COVENANTS 86

DATE: 6 DECEMBER 1832
PLACE: KIRTLAND, OHIO

Doctrine and Covenants 86 appeared as the fifth section in the first publication of the Doctrine and Covenants. It was labeled as a revelation on priesthood and immediately followed what are now known as sections 107 and 84, which are also revelations on the priesthood. Though it is not generally thought of as an important revelation on priesthood in our day, it was considered to be such in the lifetime of the Prophet Joseph Smith. It affirms that the Apostasy took place after the death of the meridian Twelve and that the restoration of the gospel centered in restoring the priesthood to the descendants of Abraham.

It is not clear whether this revelation preceded or followed inspired corrections made by the Prophet in the Bible parable of the wheat and tares. On a third editing of that manuscript, he appended a note to the parable that the wheat was to be gathered into the Lord's barn before the tares were to be bound and burned. That understanding probably came in the receipt of this revelation (Matthews, *Plainer Translation*, 82).

The Lord Interprets the Parable of the Wheat and the Tares
DOCTRINE AND COVENANTS 86:1–7

86:1 *Concerning the parable.* The use of parables in scripture always raises the question of whether their purpose is to reveal or to conceal. In the New Testament, for instance, Jesus did not begin to teach in parables until opposition to his teaching had developed and it became necessary for him to be very guarded about what he saying. To the Twelve he said, "Unto you it is given to know the mysteries of the kingdom of God," while he spoke "to others in parables; that seeing they might not see, and hearing they might not understand" (Luke 8:10; Matthew 13:10–17; Mark 4:11–12). So it is that the full meaning of the parable of the wheat and the tares can be had only by revelation. As Christ in his day explained the meaning of his parables privately, with those who had eyes to see and ears to hear—his chosen servants—so he does today. Thus the meaning of the parable is not given openly to all the world but privately to his servants—those who sustain the prophet he has called.

86:2 *The apostles.* Christ alone ("a man") appears to be the sower of the seed in the New Testament parable (Matthew 13:24–30). Here we learn that the apostles were "the sowers of the seed," meaning those whose testimony gave spiritual life to others.

The seed. In this parable "the seed" is not the word or the gospel as is the case in the parable of the sower (Matthew 13:3–8). Christ said, "The good seed are the children of the kingdom; but the tares are the children of the wicked one" (Matthew 13:38).

86:3 After the death of the apostles (those holding the keys of the priesthood), the enemy of Christ in the form of Babylon (sophistry and worldliness) sowed tares, meaning it mingled the philosophies of men with the truths of the gospel. These tares in turn choked the wheat (those things taught by Christ and the Twelve) and drove the Church into the wilderness (a state of apostasy).

The apostate, the whore. In a revelation recorded three weeks after this one (27 December 1832), the tares are identified as "that great church, the mother of abominations, that made all nations drink of the wine of the wrath of her fornication, that persecuteth the saints of God, that shed their blood—she who sitteth upon many waters, and upon the islands of the sea" (D&C 88:94).

86:4 *The Lord is beginning to bring forth the word.* This was a prophecy to the early Saints that there was yet much to be revealed.

The blade . . . is yet tender. The faithful member of the Church is likened to a tender blade that has just broken ground after a long, cold winter. Church members need protection and the light of heaven if they are to grow and bring forth good fruits.

86:5 *Angels are . . . ready . . . to reap down the fields.* President Wilford Woodruff said: "I want to ask this congregation a question: When I have the vision of the night opened continually before my eyes, and can see the mighty judgments that are about to be poured out upon this world, when I know these things are true, and are at the door of Jew and Gentile; while I know they are true and while I am holding this position before God and this world, can I withhold my voice from lifting up a warning to this people, and to the nations of the earth? I may never meet with this people again; I cannot tell how that may be. But while I live and see these things continually before my eyes I shall raise my warning voice. Now, the question I wanted to ask you is this: We have millions of people on this earth, and over them all there hangs a cloud of darkness almost entirely upon their shoulders. Can you tell me where the people are who will be shielded and protected from these great calamities and judgments which are even now at our doors? I'll tell you. The priesthood of God who honor their priesthood, and who are worthy of their blessings are the only ones who shall have this safety and protection. They are the only mortal beings. No other people have a right to be shielded from these judgments. They are at our very doors; not even this people will escape them entirely. They will come down like the judgments of Sodom and Gomorrah. And none but the priesthood will be safe from their fury. God has held the angels of destruction for many years, lest they should reap down the wheat with the tares. But I want to tell you now, that those angels have left the portals of heaven, and they stand over this people and this nation now, and are hovering over the earth waiting to pour out the judgments. And from this very day they shall be poured out. Calamities and troubles are increasing in the earth, and there is a meaning to these things. Remember this, and reflect upon these matters. If you do your duty, and I do my duty, we'll have protection, and shall pass through the afflictions in peace and in safety" (*Discourses of Wilford Woodruff*, 229–30). See commentary on Joseph Smith–History 1:37, page 23.

86:6–7 The single great sign of the times is the extent to which Israel has been gathered. Christ will not return until the scattered remnants of Israel have been brought forth from those of every nation, kindred, tongue and people (Joseph Smith–Matthew 1:31, 37). The promise given here is that Israel (the wheat) will be gathered into the barn (the kingdom of God on earth) before the tares are bound to be burned (JST Matthew 13:29). The gathering spoken of here will not preclude the greater gathering that will take place after the return of Christ and the introduction of the millennial era (3 Nephi 21–22).

86:7 *The wheat and the tares grow together until the harvest.* The "harvest," as identified in this text, represents the time of Christ's return. Until that day evil will hold its place in this fallen, or telestial, world. Righteousness and evil will be neighbors, and even among the Saints much will parade in the name of goodness and in the name of the Lord which is an abomination in his sight (D&C 50:4).

Promises to the Lawful Heirs of the Priesthood

DOCTRINE AND COVENANTS 86:8–11

86:8–10 In these verses a transition is made between the revealed explanation of the parable of the wheat and the tares and a revelation on the priesthood. The bridge between the two subjects is the word "therefore," with which verse eight begins. The word implies that because there was an apostasy and because the house of Israel has been scattered and lost for many centuries, those who have by birth the right to the priesthood and all of its blessings have not been able to claim them. Nevertheless they have not been lost to God. Indeed, they have been hidden by him to come forth at this time as "lawful heirs, according to the flesh"; as the literal descendants of Abraham they have claim on the promises given to their father. The Lord has looked after them even in their lost and fallen state. The promise to the priesthood has not been lost to Abraham's sons down through the generations. They are the seed of Abraham and the elect of God spoken of in Doctrine and Covenants 84:34. This has been known to all the holy prophets since the world began. All holy prophets have known that salvation is a family affair; it requires the blessings of the priesthood, which belong by birthright to the family of Abraham. Such was the promise that God made with our ancient father, adding a provision for the adoption of any who desired these blessings who were not naturally his seed (Abraham 2:9–11).

86:11 *A light unto the Gentiles, . . . a savior unto my people Israel.* This phrase combines the prophetic language of Isaiah and Obadiah (Isaiah 42:6; 49:6; 60:3; Obadiah 1:21). It identifies the destiny of Israel, meaning those who hold the priesthood restored to the Prophet Joseph Smith, which is to gather the scattered remnant of Abraham's seed and bring them to the covenant God made with their ancient father. It foreshadows the role that those gathering Israel will play in the house of the Lord as they perform ordinances for their kindred dead. It was not until Nauvoo, however—where the revelations were received relative to the sealing powers and the eternal nature of the family unit—that the Saints began to understand the implications of this revelation.

DOCTRINE AND COVENANTS 87

DATE: 25 DECEMBER 1832
PLACE: KIRTLAND, OHIO

This revelation, given through Joseph Smith on Christmas day in 1832, is generally remembered as the prophecy that foretold the Civil War. In fact, this revelation reaches far beyond that sorrowful conflict that pitted brother against brother and father against son to be as prophetic for those of our day as it was when first recorded. It identifies the beginning of the Civil War as the time when peace would be taken from the earth. From that time forth, we are told, war will be poured out upon all nations. To that bloodshed, the heavens will add the testimony of famine, plague, earthquake, thunder, and vivid lightning, all of which will testify against her wickedness. Also foreshadowed in this revelation is the evil and bitterness that will greet the gospel as it goes forth to the nations of the earth as the blood of the Saints will have cause to cry forth to the Lord of Sabaoth for vengeance. Only then will the consumption decreed make a full end of all nations and the millennial reign of Christ be ushered in. Until that day the Saints are warned to stand in holy places.

War between Northern and Southern States Foretold
DOCTRINE AND COVENANTS 87:1–4

87:1 On 2 April 1843 Joseph Smith said: "I prophesy, in the name of the Lord God, that the commencement of the difficulties which will cause much bloodshed previous to the coming of the Son of Man will be in South Carolina. It may probably arise through the slave question. This a voice declared to me, while I was praying earnestly on the subject, December 25th, 1832" (D&C 130:12–13).

Concerning the wars. This is not a prophecy of the Civil War alone but rather a warning that there will be "wars" and undoubtedly rumors of war in greater profusion than has ever been known in earth's history.

Terminate in the death and misery of many souls. Nothing in the history of our nation has matched the Civil War for "death and misery."

The aggregate of those killed in this war was 618,000 (360,000 from the North and 258,000 from the South). The next highest U.S. casualty figure is for World War II, when 318,000 were killed. The third highest figure is for World War I at 115,000. Other wars include the American Revolution: 4,044; the War of 1812: 2,200; the Mexican War: 13,270; the Korean War: 33,000; and Vietnam: 46,616 (Cannon, *Studies in Scripture*, 1:337).

87:2 *Beginning at this place.* The place is South Carolina, where, on 12 April 1861, the first shot of the war was fired by General Beauregard against Fort Sumter. On 1 November 1831 the Lord had said, "For I am no respecter of persons, and will that all men shall know that the day speedily cometh; the hour is not yet, but is nigh at hand, when peace shall be taken from the earth, and the devil shall have power over his own dominion" (D&C 1:35).

87:3 "In 1861 the South sent commissioners abroad to France, England, Belgium, and Holland in an endeavor to get these nations to recognize the Confederate States" (Sperry, *Doctrine and Covenants Compendium*, 419). The prophecy then says that, in turn, the nations called upon by the Southern States (France, England, Belgium, and so on) would call upon other nations to aid them. This prediction found literal fulfillment in World War II, when each of these nations sought help from other nations—chiefly the United States.

87:4 *Slaves shall rise up.* Though this happened, at least in some measure, during the Civil War, the statement as here given refers to events yet future. Presiding Bishop Joseph L. Wirthlin suggested in a 1958 general conference talk that this text could be making reference to peoples in countries where the citizens were both slaves to the government and without freedom of religion (see Conference Report, October 1958, 32). We anticipate that the day will yet come, as it has at least in some measure in Russia, that the peoples of all such nations will rise up and throw off the schackles of oppressive and corrupt governments, demanding the freedom that will allow the gospel to be taught to them.

Calamities to Come
DOCTRINE AND COVENANTS 87:5–8

87:5 *The remnants who are left.* This text is often thought to be tied to Micah's prophecy that in the last days "the remnant of Jacob shall be among the Gentiles in the midst of many people as a lion among the beasts of the forest, as a young lion among the flocks of sheep: who, if he go through, both treadeth down, and teareth in pieces, and none can deliver" (Micah 5:8). If the remnant here is one and the same with the remnant spoken of by Micah, then we can anticipate that this prophecy will find fulfillment through events involving all twelve tribes of Israel and encompassing the whole earth.

87:6 *A full end of all nations.* This phrase, "a full end of all nations," does not of necessity mean that all nations will be destroyed. During the Millennium all man-made governments will be dissolved to make place for the kingdom of God. Christ will rule as Lord of lords and King of kings.

87:7 *The blood of the saints.* In a prophecy that reaches to the ends of the earth in the promise of calamity among the wicked and divine warn-ings among those of every nation, kindred, tongue, and people, we can but suppose that his reference to the blood of the Saints bespeaks the sad reality that the gospel will not go forth unopposed and that there will yet be martyrs for the gospel cause among virtually all people (Revelation 16:6; 17:6; 18:24; 2 Nephi 28:10; Mormon 8:27, 41). This conclusion is sustained in Doctrine and Covenants 88:94, wherein we read that the "mother of abominations, that made all nations drink of the wine of the wrath of her fornication," is the same "that persecuteth the saints of God, that shed their blood—she who sitteth upon many waters, and upon the islands of the sea."

Lord of Sabaoth. Christ is the Lord of Sabaoth (Isaiah 1:9; Romans 9:29; James 5:4; D&C 88:2; 98:2). *Sabaoth* is a Hebrew word meaning hosts or armies; thus, Jehovah Sabaoth means the Lord of Hosts. Also, as revealed to the Prophet, "The Lord of Sabaoth . . . is by interpretation, the creator of the first day, the beginning and the end" (D&C 95:7).

87:8 *Stand ye in holy places.* See commentary on Doctrine and Covenants 45:32.

DOCTRINE AND COVENANTS 88

DATE: 27 AND 28 DECEMBER 1832 AND 3 JANUARY 1833
PLACE: KIRTLAND, OHIO

The revelation recorded in Doctrine and Covenants 88 was given through the Prophet Joseph Smith at Kirtland, Ohio, in the translating room of the Whitney store. Receipt of the revelation spanned three days, 27 through 28 December 1832, and 3 January 1833. Fredrick G. Williams, who recorded the revelation and kept the minutes of this conference, wrote as follows:

"A conference of High Priests assembled in the translating room in Kirtland Ohio on the 27th day of Dec. A.D. 1832 . . . Bro Joseph arose and said, to receive revelation and the blessing of Heaven it was necessary to have our minds on God and exercise faith and become of one heart and of one mind. Therefore he recommended all present to pray separately and vocally to the Lord for [Him] to reveal His will unto us concerning the upbuilding of Zion & for the benefit of the saints and for the duty and employment of the Elders. Accordingly we all bowed down before the Lord, after which each one arose and spoke in his turn his feelings and determination to keep the commandments of God. And then proceeded to receive a revelation [D&C 88] concerning the duty [not legible] above stated. [At] 9 o'clock P.M., the revelation not being finished, the conference adjourned and commenced by prayer [and] thus proceeded to receive the residue of the above revelation. And it being finished and there being no further business before [the council], the conference closed the meeting by prayer, in harmony with the brethren and gratitude to our Heavenly Father for the great manifestation of His Holy Spirit during the setting of the conference" (*Kirtland Council Minute Book*, 3–4; spelling standardized).

The revelation was designated by the Prophet as "the 'olive leaf' which we have plucked from the Tree of Paradise, the Lord's message of peace to us" (Smith, *History of the Church*, 1:316). Verses 127 through 141 were received 3 January 1833.

Faithful Saints to Receive Another Comforter
DOCTRINE AND COVENANTS 88:1–5

88:1 *You who have assembled.* Meeting with the Prophet on this occa-sion were Joseph Smith Sr., Sidney Rigdon, Orson Hyde, Hyrum Smith, Samuel H. Smith, Newel K. Whitney, Frederick G. Williams, Ezra Thayer, and John Murdock, all of whom were high priests (Cook, *Revelations*, 181).

88:2 *The alms of your prayers.* Alms, meaning works of righteousness, open the heavens and bring the ministering of angels, revelations, and all manner of spiritual blessings (Acts 10:4).

The Lord of Sabaoth. See commentary on Doctrine and Covenants 87:7.

The book of the names of the sanctified. The book of life, meaning the book in which the names of those who will inherit eternal life, is here called "the book of the names of the sanctified." The names of the faith-ful are recorded here even while they are in mortality (*Teachings of the Prophet Joseph Smith*, 9) and blotted out in the event of wickedness (Revelation 13:8; 17:8; 22:19). In the instance of this verse, it appears that their prayers are also recorded there. And if prayers are recorded there, then we might wonder if sermons would also be so recorded. And if sermons were recorded there, we would suppose that all their works of righteousness would be so recorded.

88:3 *Another Comforter, . . . the same that I promised unto my disciples, as is recorded in the testimony of John.* This and the following verse are con-fusing because in the "testimony of John" Christ promised his disciples two Comforters. The Comforter known to the generality of mankind as the first Comforter, or the Holy Ghost, was promised to them as "another Comforter" (John 14:16), because during their ministry he had been their Comforter. He then promised them a second Comforter, having reference to his personal appearance (John 14:18–23). In a subsequent revelation the Prophet stated, "John 14:23—The appearing of the Father and the Son, in that verse, is a personal appearance; and the idea that the Father and the Son dwell in a man's heart is an old sectarian notion, and is false" (D&C 130:3).

This verse draws upon the language of John 14:16, in which the phrase "another Comforter" has reference to the Holy Ghost. "The word *another* literally means 'another of the same kind,' that is, 'someone like Jesus Himself who will take His place and do His work.' The Greek word translated in the King James Version as Comforter is *paraclete*, 'one called to stand along side of.' Other meanings include 'a friend, especially a legal friend.' The word refers to 'a counselor who supports a defendant at a trial. The Spirit, then, will be the great defender of the disciples.' Other translations render the passage as 'another Helper' (New King James Version), 'another Counselor' (New International Version), and even 'another Advocate' (New Revised Standard Version; see also Revised English Bible). Although ultimately Christ is our Advocate with the Father (see D&C 45:3–5), the Savior has sent his Spirit to convict us of sin, convince us of the truth, and direct us toward righteousness (see John 16:8–11). The *paraclete* was 'any person who helped someone in trouble with the law. The Spirit will always stand by Christ's people.' The Holy Ghost, 'one called alongside to help,' would be that member of the Godhead who 'encourages and exhorts' the Saints" (Millet, "Ministry of the Holy Ghost," 180).

The Holy Spirit of promise. See commentary on Doctrine and Covenants 76:53.

88:5 *Church of the Firstborn.* See commentary on Doctrine and Covenants 76:54.

All Things Are Governed by the Light of Christ
DOCTRINE AND COVENANTS 88:6–13

88:6–13 Joseph Smith is the great revelator of Christ for our dispensation. We learn more about our eternal Father, his Only Begotten Son, and of the laws that govern the endless expanses of eternity from his lips than from any other man who ever lived. In this revelation that was plucked, as he said, from the Tree of Paradise, we read a breathtaking testimony of Christ and the light that emanates from him. Where else are we told that Christ is the light of the sun, the moon, and the stars? Where else do we read that there are no laws save he gave them? No power save it is his? No knowledge or intelligence save it comes from him! No power for good save it comes of him! How puny the views of men who would have us believe that he obtained his exalted status by mastery of laws when the testimony of holy writ is that he is source and author of them all. How lame the notion that he is endlessly learning when the words of revelation assure us that he is the source of all knowledge, all wisdom, all understanding, that he is above all, and in all, and through all! Indeed, all things testify of him—for without him they are not.

We do not even begin to comprehend the length or breadth, the majesty or greatness of his power. Nevertheless, this we do know:

His light fills the immensity of space—it is in greater or lesser measure everywhere present.

Light is the source of his power and the law by which all things are governed.

His light is the power that gives life to all things.

His light enlightens the mind and quickens the understanding of every person born into this world.

The light of Christ strives with men (the Holy Ghost testifies but does not strive) unless and until they rebel against light and truth, at which time it ceases to strive and withdraws from them.

Those who follow that light will receive more light and that light will grow brighter and brighter until the perfect day.

Resurrection Comes through the Redemption
DOCTRINE AND COVENANTS 88:14–16

88:14 *Redemption.* We are released from the bondage of death and sin through the obedience and sacrifice of Christ; hence, he alone is our Redeemer.

Resurrection. Resurrection is the inseparable union of body and spirit.

88:15 *Soul.* In most instances in scripture the word *soul* is used as a synonym for spirit. Our unembodied spirits in the premortal life are called souls (Abraham 3:23) as are our disembodied spirits awaiting the day of resurrection in paradise or hell (Alma 40:11–14). The mortal body is also called a soul (Abraham 5:7). This text gives yet another definition, defining a soul as a resurrected being.

The Law We Live Dictates the Glory We Receive
DOCTRINE AND COVENANTS 88:17–31

88:17 *The poor and the meek of the earth shall inherit it.* This promise given by the Savior in the Sermon on the Mount (Matthew 5:5) is also found in the writings of the psalmists (37:11, 29–30), who promised that the meek (meaning righteous) would obtain an everlasting inheritance on the earth. The idea that the meek inherit the earth would generally be thought of as a metaphorical expression. Latter-day Saints, however, knowing that the resurrection is corporeal and that the earth is destined to obtain celestial glory (vv. 18–20) understand this promise to be literal. See commentary on Doctrine and Covenants 38:18–20.

88:18 *Sanctified from all unrighteousness.* From the writings of Enoch we learn that he "looked upon the earth; and he heard a voice from the bowels thereof, saying: Wo, wo is me, the mother of men; I am pained, I am weary, because of the wickedness of my children. When shall I rest, and be cleansed from the filthiness which is gone forth out of me? When will my Creator sanctify me, that I may rest, and righteousness for a season abide upon my face?" (Moses 7:48). In the days of Noah the earth was cleansed with a baptism of water; and again in the last days—when it is consumed with wickedness—it will be cleansed by the baptism of fire (Malachi 4:1–6).

The cleansing of the earth will take place in two stages, both of which are described as a new heaven and new earth. First it will be returned to that state of sanctity and purity known to it before the Fall. The tenth Article of Faith promises that "the earth will be renewed and receive its paradisiacal glory." In this millennial state all that is of a telestial order will have been destroyed. "Every corruptible thing, both of man, or of the beasts of the field, or of the fowls of the heavens, or of the fish of the sea, that dwells upon all the face of the earth, shall be consumed; and also that of element shall melt with fervent heat; and all things shall become new, that my knowledge and glory may dwell upon all the earth" (D&C 101:24–25). Thereafter the earth will die, be resurrected, and obtain its celestial glory (D&C 88:26). All that is terrestrial will be removed. Only that which is of a celestial nature may remain. "When the thousand years are ended, and men again begin to deny their God, then will I spare the earth but for a little season; and the end shall come, and the heaven and the earth shall be consumed and pass away, and there shall be a new heaven and a new earth. For all old things shall pass away, and all things shall become new, even the heaven and the earth, and all the fulness thereof, both men and beasts, the fowls of the air, and the fishes of the sea" (D&C 29:22–24). See commentary on Doctrine and Covenants 77:12.

88:21–24 With the help of the Joseph Smith Translation we learn that this same principle was taught by the apostle Paul. The principle was so obvious to him that he felt it was foolish to ask what kind of a body a man would have in the resurrection. To make the point, he likened the resurrection to the day of harvest, noting that one harvested what they planted. He simply reasoned that if you wanted to harvest wheat then you planted wheat, if you wanted to harvest beans that you planted beans, and so forth. Likewise, the nature of your body in the resurrection will reflect the law you chose to live in mortality. Those living a telestial law, he held, would receive a telestial body, those living a terrestrial law would inherit a terrestrial body, and those complying with the celestial law would obtain a celestial body. In making the point, Paul also asked what the various members of the animal kingdom would be in the resurrection? Again the point being that in the resurrection a bear has no hope of becoming a bird or a bird a bear. Fish will be resurrected as fish and skunks as skunks. Everything coming forth according to its order, which is according to the law it chose to obey (JST 1 Corinthians 15:37, 46).

88:26 *It shall die, it shall be quickened again.* The revelations of the Restoration take us far beyond what is known to us by science relative to the creation of the earth. By revelation we know that the earth is a living thing. Further, we know that all living things were created first as spirits (Moses 3:5) and as such existed long before they obtained the physical tabernacles known to them in this mortal state. Because of the fall of Adam, the earth is subject to corruption and will yet die. In like manner, because of the atonement of Christ, the earth will be resurrected and obtain a celestial glory and become the abiding place of all things that lived upon it and also abided by that same order.

88:27 *Spiritual body.* Alma describes a resurrected body as immortal, one that can die no more, and in which body and spirit are united, never to be divided. "Thus," he said, the whole becomes "spiritual and immortal" and cannot "see corruption" (Alma 11:45). In like manner, Paul spoke of a natural body—a body subject to corruption—and a spiritual body—one not subject to corruption (1 Corinthians 15:44). In accord with this pattern, the present text also tells us that the union of the natural body with the spirit becomes "a spiritual body"—a body that is not subject to death or corruption. The bodies of Adam and Eve prior to the Fall are properly referred to as "spiritual" bodies and the creation as a physical-spiritual event.

88:28 *The same body which was a natural body.* The resurrected body will be the same body inherited in mortality. In the resurrection Christ took up the very body that died upon the cross and had been laid in the tomb. To emphasize this fact, when he appeared to his disciples after his resurrection he showed them the marks of the wounds in his hands, feet, and side (Luke 24:36–40; John 20:26–27). In the resurrection our bodies will come forth from the grave as they were laid down. President Joseph F.

Smith declared: "It was revealed from God, the fountain of truth, through Joseph Smith the prophet, in this dispensation, that in the resurrection of the dead the child that was buried in its infancy will come up in the form of the child that it was when it was laid down; then it will begin to develop. From the day of the resurrection, the body will develop until it reaches the full measure of the stature of its spirit, wheter it be male or female" (*Gospel Doctrine*, 24).

The body received in mortality is an eternal inheritance. Some question the literalness of resurrecting with the same body, or the same elements that made up the mortal body before the corruption of the flesh destroyed it in the grave. Apparently, a similar comment was included in a talk given by Orson Pratt during the Church's April 1843 general conference in Nauvoo. "To a remark of Elder Orson Pratt's, that a man's body changes every seven years, President Joseph Smith replied: There is no fundamental principle belonging to a human system that ever goes into another in this world or in the world to come; I care not what the theories of men are. We have the testimony that God will raise us up, and he has the power to do it. If any one supposes that any part of our bodies, that is, the fundamental parts thereof, ever goes into another body, he is mistaken" (Smith, *History of the Church*, 5:339). There are many elements of the earth that pass through our bodies as we gain and lose flesh; however, the fundamental parts of our bodies, referred to by the Prophet, will rise with us in the resurrection. Further, our resurrected bodies will be composed of the same particles that were incorporated in our system during mortality (Alma 11:43–44; 40:32).

88:28 *Your glory shall be that glory by which your bodies are quickened.* It is the spirit of an individual that will quicken the body in the resurrection. It follows that the light and glory received by the spirit determines the glory that quickens the body. Further, the law that the spirit has come to abide determines the glory it receives, whether that be celestial, terrestrial, or telestial. Those who abide celestial law receive a fulness of the glory of the Father, as did the Savior (D&C 93:3–7, 22).

88:28–31 To be "quickened by a portion of the celestial glory" appears to mean that if the major thrust of one's life has been in harmony with a celestial standard, that person will come forth in a celestial resurrection and thereafter be able to grow up into a fulness of that glory. The same principle would apply to those who come forth in the terrestrial and telestial resurrections.

Those Who Are Filthy Still
DOCTRINE AND COVENANTS 88:32–35

88:32 *They who remain shall also be quickened.* After all who are to inherit a degree of glory—be it celestial, terrestrial, or telestial—have come forth from the grave in an inseparable union of body and spirit, those unworthy of any glory—elsewhere referred to as sons of perdition—will also be resurrected.

88:35 *Filthy still.* These have committed the unpardonable sin and, though they are resurrected, they remain "filthy still" and thus are unable to inherit even the least of the degrees of glory.

All Kingdoms Are Governed by God's Law
DOCTRINE AND COVENANTS 88:36–41

88:36 *All kingdoms have a law given.* Well might the Lord ask of us, as he did of Job so many years ago, "Knowest thou the ordinances of heaven?" (Job 38:33). Do you know the laws that govern the planetary systems and all the endless expanses of the eternities? Can you account for the difference of their motions, and the influences by which they are retained and revolve in their orbits? Sir Isaac Newton, considered by many to be the greatest scientist of all time, identified the law of universal gravitation. Yet, in response to the question, From whence is gravity? he could neither explain nor comprehend. No man, unaided by the power of God, can comprehend "the ordinances of heaven." The God we worship is not a divine scientist. He did not discover law and then harness it for righteous purposes. He is the author and creator of all "the ordinances of heaven and earth" (Jeremiah 33:25; D&C 88:42).

88:37–38 There is no place in the eternities where God is without authority. There is no border that one can cross to escape his justice or hide from his wrath. He stands supreme. There is no space that is not governed by his law.

88:39 To be justified is to be judged to be in compliance with the law. Elder Bruce R. McConkie explained: "Once a law has been ordained, it thereafter operates automatically; that is, whenever there is compliance with its terms and conditions, the promised results accrue. The law of gravitation is an obvious example. Similarly, compliance with the law of faith always brings the gifts of the Spirit. By obedience to celestial law men automatically qualify for a celestial inheritance in eternity; by open rebellion against law, they automatically assure themselves of a place in a kingdom which is not a kingdom of glory" (*Mormon Doctrine*, 433). This would be according to and in compliance with the law of justification.

88:40 All things produce after their own kind. Love begets love, goodness results in goodness, and kindness is reciprocated with kindness. Conversely, hatred begets hatred, one evil incites another, and a mean act will be matched by another. Doves beget doves and snakes beget snakes. As people who seek light and truth are led to it, so will those who seek darkness and evil in like manner find that which they seek.

Judgment goeth before the face of him who sitteth upon the throne. God is not nonjudgmental. Without judgment—that is the approving of one thing and the disapproving of another—there could be no virtue, no goodness, no righteousness, and no kingdom of light and truth. All that is good stands opposed by that which is not good. All that is true stands opposed by that which is not true. To suppose that God does not discriminate between the two is to deny the very existence of God and all the attributes of godliness. Thus we are commanded to discern spirits by the Spirit and to make righteous judgments (JST Matthew 7:1–3).

88:41 *He comprehendeth all things.* The announcement here is not simply that God knows all things but that he constitutes the source of their existence. All things are an expression of the existence of God. Every truth, every law, every form of existence—all evidence the hand of God. He created them all; there is nothing relative to them that he does not know. Thus he is above all things, he is the source of life to all things, and governs all things. Again, to suppose that there is place or knowledge that is presently beyond God is to suppose that in some place or in some matter God is other than, indeed less than, God. God himself testifies that this is not the case.

God Both Knows and Governs All Things

DOCTRINE AND COVENANTS 88:42–45

88:42 *He hath given a law unto all things.* A common Latter-day Saint heresy is that we become as God is through education or the mastery of laws. The notion being that God became God by identifying the laws of nature and learning how to live in harmony with them and how to harness them for his purposes. Our present text (see also v. 36) refutes such a notion. God is the author of law, not the co-partner with it. We do not

worship law. Law, like the sectarian god, is without body, parts, and passions; it knows nothing of justice or mercy, or of good or evil. It has no
power to determine or change its own course.

But, says one, is it not by obedience to law that Christ became as his
Father and that we become as God is? To which the answer is, Yes, of
course, but Christ followed only laws that had been ordained by the
Father. His salvation rested in doing the will of the Father, not in discovering laws that govern in the universe and attempting to comply with
them. So it is with us. We seek salvation in the teachings of the prophets,
not that of scholars.

It is righteousness of which the scriptures speak, not scholarship.
Exaltation is obtained by faith in Christ, repentance from sin, compliance
with the ordinances of salvation, and enjoying the companionship of the
Holy Ghost, not by the mastery of math and science. By obedience to
gospel principles, Christ obtained the fulness of his Father. Having
obtained that fulness, he became the personification of the Father and
thus became a perfect expression of the mind and will of the Father. The
power and authority of the Father thus became his and so we say of him
(as we say of the Father) that he is in and through all things, that nothing
is greater than he is, for he and the Father are one. The idea that God
became such by the mastery of the laws of nature is a modern tower of
Babel built on a college campus. It gets men no closer to heaven than its
ancient counterpart. By contrast, revelation tells us, "The powers of
heaven cannot be controlled nor handled only upon the principles of righteousness" (D&C 121:36).

Man Will Yet Comprehend God
DOCTRINE AND COVENANTS 88:46–50

88:47 All created things bear witness of a Creator. As the existence
of a watch attests to the existence of the watchmaker, so must all life
forms trace to a source of life. A single cell, it has been learned, contains
more information than all the volumes of the *Encyclopedia Britannica* put
together. And with this knowledge comes the haunting suspicion that in
future years, when our ability to see and understand has been extended,
we may also find that the intelligence found within that cell has expanded
proportionately. Among the great discoveries of modern times is the
immense extension of the universe in space. In comparison to what we
see and know today, the Cosmos of the ancient world was but a jeweled

cup found floating on the ocean. As our ability to see increases, the immensity of space increases. In it all, from great to small, we see the majesty of God and find the constant assurance that all things testify of him.

88:48 *He who came unto his own was not comprehended.* Introducing his testament of Christ, John the Beloved wrote: "He was in the world, and the world was made by him, and the world knew him not. He came unto his own, and his own received him not. But as many as received him, to them gave he power to become the sons of God, even to them that believe on his name" (John 1:10–12).

88:49 *The day shall come when you shall comprehend even God.* The god of the philosophers transcends the ability of man to comprehend. He is unknown and unknowable, inexpressible, immovable, invisible, and unapproachable. Thus it is improper to ascribe to him form, movement, place, attributes, or names. Such is the god adopted in the creeds of historical Christianity. By contrast, Christ chided the woman of Samaria for not knowing the God she worshipped, saying to her, "Ye worship ye know not what: *we know what we worship.*" The time had come, he said, for those having the truth to "*worship* the Father in spirit and *in truth:* for the Father seeketh such to worship him" (John 4:22–23; emphasis added). As he offered the great intercessory pray to the Father, Christ said, "And this is life eternal, that they might know thee the only true God, and Jesus Christ, whom thou has sent" (John 17:3). In that same spirit Joseph Smith said, "It is the first principle of the Gospel to know for a certainty the Character of God, and to know that we may converse with him as one man converses with another" (*Teachings of the Prophet Joseph Smith*, 345). The promise given in this text is that in a future day, when the power of God has been placed upon us, we will be able to see, know, and understand the nature of God. See commentary on King Follett Discourse 4:4, page 1086.

The Parable of the Servants in the Field Being Visited
DOCTRINE AND COVENANTS 88:51–61

88:51–61 This parable, given in the context of a discussion about the endless expanses of eternity, is one of the plainest assertions in scripture that there are other inhabited worlds, each of which will be visited by Christ. In each instance the pattern is the same: Christ chooses his servant, appoints to him his labor, and gives the attendant promise that he will, at the appropriate time and season, visit him, which he does. The parable does not suggest that Christ made appearances to anyone other than his appointed servant in each of these worlds. That the resurrected Christ appeared to great multitudes on the various planets following the pattern of his appearance among the Nephites and among various groups of the lost tribes seems a reasonable assumption. It is not, however, the purpose of this parable to make that point. See commentary on Doctrine and Covenants 76:23–24.

The Faithful to See the Face of the Lord
DOCTRINE AND COVENANTS 88:62–76

88:62 *My friends.* Here Christ calls the ten men involved in the receipt of this revelation his friends. In principle the expression extends to all his faithful servants. Similarly, he referred to the meridian Twelve as "my brethren" (John 20:17).

88:63 *Draw near unto me and I will draw near unto you.* To his people in the days of Malachi, the Lord said, "Return unto me, and I will return unto you" (Malachi 3:7). Our relationship with the Lord is conditional.

88:64–65 No one enjoys being in a situation in which a friend asks something of him that is either improper or inappropriate. Such a request may strain or seriously impair their relationship. The same principles apply in our relationship with our divine Father. The invitation to ask of him has obvious bounds or limits. We ask only for that which is right, proper, expedient, necessary, that which edifies and for which the Spirit directs. To pray improperly is to take the Lord's name in vain, but to trifle with that which is sacred may well, as this text warns, bring "condemnation" (D&C 8:10; 18:18; 75:10; 3 Nephi 18:20; James 4:3).

88:66 *My voice is Spirit.* To hear the quiet whisperings of the Spirit is to hear the voice of the Lord. Reading the words of scripture in company with the Spirit is also to hear that voice (D&C 18:35; 84:60). It can also be our privilege to hear the audible voice of the Lord (D&C 130:14–15; Helaman 5:29–33; 3 Nephi 11:3–7).

88:67 The chain of thought here is simple and direct: "That which is of God is light; and he that receiveth light, and continueth in God, receiveth more light; and that light groweth brighter and brighter until the perfect day" (D&C 50:24). As the immediate text notes, to be filled with light is to comprehend all things. God is light, and to be filled with the Spirit of God is to possess the wisdom and knowledge of God. Such would be the case with messengers that come from his presence known to us as angels of light. Teaching this principle, Brigham Young observed, "God is the source, the fountain of all intelligence, no matter who possesses it, whether man upon the earth, the spirits in the spirit-world, the angels that dwell in the eternities of the Gods, or the most inferior intelligence among the devils in hell. All have derived what intelligence, light, power, and existence they have from God—from the same source from which we have received ours" (*Journal of Discourses*, 8:205).

88:68 *Sanctify yourselves.* See Doctrine and Covenants 88:74.

You shall see him. The promise here given was that Christ would manifest himself to these, the "first laborers," after they had sanctified themselves (for the fulfillment of this promise see commentary on verses 74–75).

88:69 *The great and last promise.* In the concluding chapter of his Gospel, Luke gives an account of the appearance of Christ to the Twelve in the upper room shortly before his ascension. Having instructed them, he said, "I send the promise of my Father upon you: but tarry ye in the city of Jerusalem, until ye be endued with power from on high" (Luke 24:49). Luke begins his next epistle, known to us as the book of Acts, at the same point. He reminds Theophilus, to whom he is writing, that Christ had appeared to the Twelve and commanded them not to depart Jerusalem until they had received "the promise of the Father. . . . Ye shall receive power, after that the Holy Ghost is come upon you: and ye shall be witnesses unto me both in Jerusalem, and in all Judaea, and in Samaria, and unto the uttermost part of the earth" (Acts 1:4, 8). During the infancy of the Church, while the Saints were still in New York, the Lord commanded them to go to Ohio, saying, "There I will give unto you my law; and there you shall be endowed with power from on high" (D&C 38:32). Returning to this instruction in another revelation, given three days later, the Lord said, "And inasmuch as my people shall assemble themselves at the Ohio, I have kept in store a blessing such as is not known among the children of men, and it shall be poured forth upon their heads. And from thence men shall go forth into all nations" (D&C 39:15). After their arrival in Ohio the Lord said: "Ye are to be taught from on high. Sanctify yourselves and ye shall be endowed with power, that ye may give even as I have spoken" (D&C 43:16). In a revelation that came after the present text, the Lord said, "I gave unto you a commandment that you should build a house [the Kirtland Temple], in the which house I design to endow those whom I have chosen with power from on high;

for this is the promise of the Father unto you; therefore I command you to tarry, even as mine apostles at Jerusalem" (D&C 95:8–9).

The promise given to the Twelve at the time of Christ centered in a ritual endowment of power that was to be theirs before they took the gospel of Christ to the nations of the earth. The gospel requires the same endowment of power in our day. The brethren assembled at the time this revelation was received were to be among the first to participate in that ordinance which would be restored and which is called "the great and last promise" (D&C 88:69, 74–75).

Cast away your idle thoughts. Of those called to labor in his behalf, the Lord requires the full measure of their heart, mind, might, and strength. Idleness has no place in the Lord's kingdom.

Your excess of laughter. The text directs the avoidance of "excess," not of laughter. Laughter is an essential ingredient of good health. In excess, any virtue or wholesome thing becomes a vice. No light-mindedness was to exist in the School of the Prophets (D&C 88:121).

88:70 *Call a solemn assembly.* Solemn assemblies are meetings of a particularly solemn or sacred nature. Their attendance is limited by both worthiness and invitation. They are not for the world. Generally they are of three kinds: a temple dedication, the sustaining of a new presidency of the Church, and special priesthood leadership meetings held in temples. In the context of this revelation, two special solemn assemblies were anticipated. First, the meetings at which the "first laborers" would be washed and anointed prior to the dedication of the Kirtland Temple; and second, the dedication of the temple itself.

Of the first of these solemn assemblies the Prophet explained, "We must have all things prepared, and call our solemn assembly as the Lord has commanded us, that we may be able to accomplish His great work, and it must be done in God's own way. The house of the Lord must be prepared, and the solemn assembly called and organized in it, according to the order of the house of God; and in it we must attend to the ordinance of washing of feet. It was never intended for any but official members. It is calculated to unite our hearts, that we may be one in feeling and sentiment, and that our faith may be strong, so that Satan cannot overthrow us, nor have any power over us here.

"The endowment you are so anxious about, you cannot comprehend now, nor could Gabriel explain it to the understanding of your dark minds; but strive to be prepared in your hearts, be faithful in all things, that when we meet in the solemn assembly, that is, when such as God shall name out of all the official members shall meet, we must be clean every whit. Let us be faithful and silent, brethren, and if God gives you a manifestation, keep it to yourselves; be watchful and prayerful, and you shall have a prelude of those joys that God will pour out on that day. Do not watch for iniquity in each other, if you do you will not get an endowment, for God will not bestow it on such. But if we are faithful, and live by every word that proceeds forth from the mouth of God, I will venture to prophesy that we shall get a blessing that will be worth remembering, if we should live as long as John the Revelator; our blessings will be such as we have not realized before, nor received in this generation. The order of the house of God has been, and ever will be, the same, even after Christ comes; and after the termination of the thousand years it will be the same; and we shall finally enter into the celestial kingdom of God, and enjoy it forever.

"You need an endowment, brethren, in order that you may be prepared and able to overcome all things; and those that reject your testimony will be damned. The sick will be healed, the lame made to walk, the deaf to hear, and the blind to see, through your instrumentality. But let me tell you, that you will not have power, after the endowment to heal those that have not faith, nor to benefit them, for you might as well expect to benefit a devil in hell as such as are possessed of his spirit, and are willing to keep it: for they are habitations for devils, and only fit for his society. But when you are endowed and prepared to preach the Gospel to all nations, kindreds, and tongues, in their own languages, you must faithfully warn all, and bind up the testimony, and seal up the law, and the destroying angel will follow close at your heels, and exercise his tremendous mission upon the children of disobedience; and destroy the workers of iniquity, while the Saints will be gathered out from among them, and stand in holy places ready to meet the Bridegroom when he comes" (*Teachings of the Prophet Joseph Smith*, 91–92).

88:74–75 In all dispensations and generations the faithful servants of the Lord have been endowed with power from on high and commissioned to raise the warning voice in order that they not be responsible for the sins of those they failed to teach (Jacob 1:19). In this process they sanctify themselves that they might receive the blessings of heaven.

"All who are prepared, and are sufficiently pure to abide the presence of the Savior, will see Him in the solemn assembly," said Joseph Smith (*Teachings of the Prophet Joseph Smith*, 92). The solemn assembly was held in the Kirtland Temple, 30 March 1836, three days after it had been dedicated. The *History of the Church* records the events of that day, according to Joseph Smith.

A Commandment to Teach Each Other the Doctrine of the Kingdom
DOCTRINE AND COVENANTS 88:77–80

88:77–80 Ignorance and the gospel are as antithetical as light and darkness. Schools and learning can no more be separated from the principles of salvation than faith and repentance. Here the command is given that we teach one another. True it is that in the pursuit of an education, many of our teachers will not be people of faith. We anxiously receive whatever light they have, but we do not look to them to set the perimeters of our faith or to determine our standards. The curriculum in which Latter-day Saints should be conversant, according to the Lord, includes things in the heavens, things on the earth and under the earth, things which have been and which are, things which must shortly come to pass, things at home, and things abroad. This, the Lord said, will prepare us "to magnify" our callings to take the message of salvation to all that will hear it.

It is important that Latter-day Saints not lose sight of the Lord's purpose for directing his Saints to be conversant in secular subjects. There is no implication in this revelation that we will find salvation in secular learning. Salvation comes only through the atonement of Christ and our obedience to the laws and ordinances he has instituted for that purpose. No amount of secular learning will ever substitute for that faith or those principles. For this reason, this revelation includes the direction to first teach doctrine, "the law of the gospel," that which is "expedient," that we might understand the order of things in the kingdom of God.

All Who Have Been Warned Are to Warn Their Neighbors
DOCTRINE AND COVENANTS 88:81–85

88:81 *It becometh every man who hath been warned to warn his neighbor.* All who have been warned of an impending danger have an obligation to warn others. This is true regardless of whether they choose to heed the warning or not. If I have been warned of the necessity of repentance and baptism and choose not to comply, I still have the obligation to warn family and friends that they must repent and be baptized.

88:84 *Go forth among the Gentiles for the last time.* Ours is the final gospel dispensation. According to prophecy, the gospel is to go first to the Gentiles and then to the Jews a "last time" before the day of calamity and judgment (1 Nephi 13:42; D&C 1:17–23).

As many as the mouth of the Lord shall name. The Good Shepherd "calleth his own sheep by name, and leadeth them." "My sheep hear my voice, and I know them, and they follow me: and I give unto them eternal life; and they shall never perish, neither shall any man pluck them out of my hand" (John 10:3, 27–28). See commentary on Doctrine and Covenants 50:41–42.

To bind up the law and seal up the testimony. The language is Isaiah's, coming from a description of those of both houses of Israel, who would reject Christ and his gospel. Isaiah charged servants of the Lord to "bind up the testimony, seal the law among my disciples" (Isaiah 8:16).

All disciples "go forth" with power given them "to seal both on earth and in heaven, the unbelieving and rebellious; Yea, verily, to seal them up unto the day when the wrath of God shall be poured out upon the wicked without measure" (D&C 1:8–9). Of these wicked and unbelieving ones, the revealed word says: "Behold, and lo, there are none to deliver you; for ye obeyed not my voice when I called to you out of the heavens; ye believed not my servants, and when they were sent unto you ye received them not. Wherefore, they sealed up the testimony and bound up the law, and ye were delivered over unto darkness. These shall go away into outer darkness, where there is weeping, and wailing, and gnashing of teeth" (D&C 133:71–73).

Elder Bruce R. McConkie explained: "The gospel brings blessings or curses. Both are administered to men by the Lord's agents. Those whom they bless are blessed, and those whom they curse are cursed (D&C 124:93). The Lord's servants go forth 'to bind up the law and seal up the testimony, and to prepare the saints for the hour of judgment which is to come' (D&C 88:84). The crowning blessing bestowed is: 'And of as many as the Father shall bear record, to you shall be given power to seal them up unto eternal life' (D&C 68:12)" (*Promised Messiah*, 174; see Doctrine and Covenants 109:46).

88:85 *The desolation of abomination which awaits the wicked.* See commentary on Joseph Smith–Matthew 1:32, page 349; Doctrine and Covenants 45:19, 47.

The first elders. The reference is to the presiding officers of the Church (D&C 20:1–2; 105:7).

Signs, Upheavals of the Elements, and Angels Prepare the Way for the Return of Christ
DOCTRINE AND COVENANTS 88:86–94

88:86 *Abide ye in the liberty wherewith ye are made free.* Servants of the Lord must be free from the bondage of sin, the slavery of addiction, the darkness of ignorance, the meanness of prejudice, the shallowness of idleness, the stench of uncleanness, and all things that would be offensive to the light of Christ and the companionship of the Holy Ghost. The servants of the Lord should not take as their companion any spirit unworthy of the message they bear.

88:87–94 This section of the revelation bears a striking similarity to chapters seven through twenty-two in the book of Revelation. The events spoken of by the Revelator are obviously being summarized here so that we might see and understand them in the light of the Restoration. The writings of the Revelator prophetically describe the destruction and calamity that is to precede the return of Christ. The wickedness and destruction described here are soul depressing; but standing behind them is the ultimate promise of the return of Christ. Righteousness will prevail, good will conquer evil, and the enemies of light and truth will be vanquished.

Gospel scholar Robert J. Matthews observed: "The Prophet had been involved for many months with making an initial draft of an inspired translation of the New Testament, concluding with the book of Revelation in March 1832. In the process of making the translation, many important things were revealed to him about the gospel and in this case about future events to take place on the earth (D&C 45:60–62). The history of the earth, the ministry of seven angels who play a prominent part in the final judgment scenes, and the opening of the seven seals are significant aspects of the Revelation of John. These were reiterated and partially explained in Doctrine and Covenants 77 as a consequence of the translation and were further enlarged upon in these verses from section 88. Thus we regard this part of section 88 as a further clarification and explanation of the Revelation of John. These are eschatological items—the winding-up events to take place on the earth before it is prepared for the celestial glory. All nations must hear the proclamation of the gospel and be informed of the means of redemption. The earth must die and wickedness be cleansed from off its face. There will be a resurrection of all mankind and a final judgment. Through faith in Jesus the Saint will have gained the victory over sin and death and will be crowned with eternal glory (vv. 106–7). The calamities and convulsive quaking of the earth, the wars and the pestilences spoken of in these verses are the 'details' involved in the larger concept of the earth being prepared for its eternal celestial destiny" ("Olive Leaf," 352).

88:92 *Angels shall fly through the midst of heaven.* Every priesthood, key, power, or authority known to the ancients has been restored by those who held them. It is for us to complete the labor that they commenced. "The Son of Man shall come," we have been promised, "and he shall send his angels before him with the great sound of a trumpet, and they shall gather together the remainder of his elect from the four winds, from one end of heaven to the other" (Joseph Smith–Matthew 1:37).

88:93 *A great sign in heaven.* Speaking of the signs of the times, Joseph Smith said: "There will be wars and rumors of wars, signs in the heavens above and on the earth beneath, the sun turned into darkness and the moon to blood, earthquakes in divers places, the seas heaving beyond their bounds; *then will appear one grand sign of the Son of Man in heaven.* But what will the world do? They will say it is a planet, a comet, etc. But the Son of [M]an will come as the sign of the coming of the Son of Man, which will be as the light of the morning cometh out of the east" (*Teachings of the Prophet Joseph Smith*, 286–87; emphasis added).

88:94 *That great church, the mother of abominations.* History has seen no shortages of false and even devilish churches. Indeed, there never has been a time—even from before the earth began—when false churches have not stood in opposition to the Church and kingdom of God. Elder Bruce R. McConkie wrote: "The church of the devil is the world; it is all the carnality and evil to which fallen man is heir; it is every unholy and wicked practice; it is every false religion, every supposed system of salvation which does not actually save and exalt man in the highest heaven of the celestial world. It is every church except the true church, whether parading under a Christian or a pagan banner. As Moroni will say in a later era of Nephite history, and as we shall ascertain in our evaluation of Rev. 18:1–24, it is 'secret combinations,' oath-bound societies, and the great world force of Godless communism (Ether 8:14–26)" (*Doctrinal New Testament Commentary*, 3:541).

Angelic Trumps Call Forth the Dead Each in Their Order
DOCTRINE AND COVENANTS 88:95–102

88:95–102 These verses set forth the order of the resurrection, affirming that it is universal—all will be resurrected—and that all will be called forth according to the obedience they rendered to the law of heaven. Thus, resurrection begins with the most righteous (Christ) and ends with those who were most wicked (those who are perdition). Those who are to inherit the celestial kingdom will be the first resurrected, then those obtaining terrestrial glory, telestial glory, and perdition, in that order.

88:95 *There shall be silence in heaven for the space of half an hour.* Elder Bruce R. McConkie wrote: "What is meant by the half hour of silence has not yet been revealed. If it is to be reckoned on the basis of 'the Lord's time' of 1000 years to a day, the duration would be some 21 of our years (Abraham 3:4; 2 Peter 3:8)" (*Doctrinal New Testament Commentary,* 3:498). The phrase comes from Revelation 8:1.

The face of the Lord shall be unveiled. Apparently, this is the time referred to by the Lord when he said, "All flesh shall see me together" (D&C 101:23; Revelation 1:7).

88:96 Here we are told that at Christ's return the Saints that are upon the earth "who are alive" will be caught up to meet him. This seems to imply that those who have died are also upon the earth. Joseph Smith said, "The spirits of the just . . . are not far from us, and know and understand our thoughts, feelings, and motions, and are often pained therewith" (*Teachings of the Prophet Joseph Smith,* 326). See verse 104.

88:97–98 Those who lived according to a celestial law will join Christ when he comes. Those Saints who are alive at the time of his coming, those awaiting the day of resurrection in the spirit world, and those who were resurrected with Christ will all join him at the time of his return. "The dead in Christ shall rise first," taught the apostle Paul. "Then we which are alive and remain shall be caught up together with them in the clouds, to meet the Lord in the air: and so shall we ever be with the Lord" (1 Thessalonians 4:16–17).

88:99 *The second trump.* Joseph Fielding Smith said: "After the Lord and the righteous who are caught up to meet him have descended upon the earth, there will come to pass another resurrection. This may be considered as a part of the first, although it comes later" (*Doctrines of Salvation,* 2:296–97). Those who rejected Christ while in the flesh but accepted him in the world of the spirits will come forth in this resurrection to inherit the terrestrial kingdom. See commentary on Doctrine and Covenants 76:73.

88:100 *The third trump.* At the sounding of the third trump, those who will inherit the telestial kingdom will be resurrected. This will take place at the end of the Millennium.

88:102 *The fourth trump.* After all who inherit a degree of glory have been resurrected, then those who receive no glory or remission of sins but remain "filthy still" will be resurrected. These are they who are perdition.

Angelic Trumps Proclaim the Restoration of the Gospel, the Fall of Babylon, and the Battle of the Great God
DOCTRINE AND COVENANTS 88:103–16

88:103 *The fifth angel.* This appears to be Moroni (Revelation 14:6–7).

88:104 When the fifth angel sounds his trump, all the inhabitants of heaven and earth will bow the knee and confess that the kingdom is Christ's and that judgment rests with him. See commentary on Doctrine and Covenants 133:36–45.

88:105 When the sixth angel sounds his trump, the judgment on the mother of abominations, the great apostate church, will be carried out. "Babylon is fallen! is fallen!" (Revelation 14:8). Nephi gave the following prophetic description of these events: "And the blood of that great and abominable church, which is the whore of all the earth, shall turn upon their own heads; for they shall war among themselves, and the sword of their own hands shall fall upon their own heads, and they shall be drunken with their own blood. And every nation which shall war against thee, O house of Israel, shall be turned one against another, and they shall fall into the pit which they digged to ensnare the people of the Lord. And all that fight against Zion shall be destroyed, and that great whore, who hath perverted the right ways of the Lord, yea, that great and abominable church, shall tumble to the dust and great shall be the fall of it. . . . For the time speedily shall come that all churches which are built up to get gain, and all those who are built up to get power over the flesh, and those who are built up to become popular in the eyes of the world, and those who seek the lusts of the flesh and the things of the world, and to do all manner of iniquity; yea, in fine, all those who belong to the kingdom of the devil are they who need fear, and tremble, and quake; they are those who must be brought low in the dust; they are those who must be consumed as stubble; and this is according to the words of the prophet" (1 Nephi 22:13–14, 23).

88:106–7 When the seventh angel, who is Michael (v. 112), sounds his trump, the triumphant cry will ascend to heaven and reverberate through the universe, "It is finished!" The plan of redemption as announced by the Father in the Grand Council of Heaven, including the appointment of the Firstborn to come as a ransom for us all, will now have been accomplished in every detail. Then shall the angels be crowned with glory, and the Saints receive their celestial inheritance "and be made equal" with the Almighty God "in power, and in might, and in dominion" (D&C 76:95).

88:107 *Be made equal with him.* See commentary on Doctrine and Covenants 76:94–95.

88:108–10 Again the seven angels will sound their trumps, each representing one of the seven seals as seen by the Revelator, each seal representing a thousand years of the temporal history of the earth (D&C 77:7, 12). From each seal the secret acts of men will be revealed and the mighty acts of God.

88:110 *There shall be time no longer.* The phrase "there should be time no longer" comes from Revelation 10:6. Both the Living New Testament translation and the Revised Standard translation render it, "There should be no more delay," and the Amplified translation records, "There should be no more waiting or delay" (*Layman's Parallel New Testament*, 908–9). The idea here is not that time will cease but rather that the righteous will have waited and implored the Lord long enough. Satan will be bound, and the time of persecution and evil will have ended.

Satan shall be bound. Bruce R. McConkie explained: "What does it mean to bind Satan? How is he bound? Our revelation says: 'And in that day Satan shall not have power to tempt any man' (D&C 101:28). Does this mean that power is withdrawn from Satan so that he can no longer entice men to do evil? Or does it mean that men no longer succumb to his enticements because their hearts are so set on righteousness that they refuse to forsake that which is good to follow him who is evil? Clearly it means the latter. Satan was not bound in heaven, in the very presence of God, in the sense that he was denied the right and power to preach false doctrine and to invite men to walk away from that God whose children they were; nay, in this sense, he could not have been bound in heaven, for even he must have his agency.

"How, then, will Satan be bound during the Millennium? It will be by the righteousness of the people. Thus Nephi says: 'The time cometh speedily that Satan shall have no more power over the hearts of the children of men; for the day soon cometh that all the proud and they who do wickedly shall be as stubble; and the day cometh that they must be burned.' The destruction of the wicked sets the stage for millennial righteousness. When the wicked are burned, those who are left will not be susceptible to the promptings from beneath. 'And the time cometh speedily that the righteous must be led up as calves of the stall, and the Holy One of Israel must reign in dominion, and might, and power, and great glory.' During the Millennium, when the Lord reigns, children will grow up in an environment of righteousness. No longer will the calves of Abraham's herds and the lambs of Jacob's flocks be lost in the deserts of sin; no longer will they forage for food by the wayside and drink water from stagnant pools; no longer will they be pulled down by the evils and designs of conspiring men. In the millennial day, in the household of faith, children will be brought up in the nurture and admonition of the Lord, as calves in the stall, as lambs in the sheepcote" (*Millennial Messiah*, 668–69).

88:111 *A little season.* "After the Millennium plus a little season—perhaps itself another thousand years—during which men turn again to wickedness, then cometh the end, not of the world, which occurred at the Second Coming, but the end of earth. Then the final battle against Gog and Magog, the battle of the Great God, will be fought. Michael will lead the armies of heaven and Lucifer the legions of hell" (McConkie, *Millennial Messiah*, 22).

88:112 *Michael . . . the archangel.* Michael is Adam, who holds the "keys of salvation" (D&C 78:16) or the "keys of the universe" (*Teachings of the Prophet Joseph Smith*, 157). From the time of Satan's rebellion in premortal councils through the final winding up scenes Michael will lead the armies of the Lord in their battles against Satan.

88:114 *The battle of the great God.* After the Millennium, Satan, who has been bound, will be loosed for a little season. He will gather his armies together as will Michael, the seventh angel, even the archangel. Then will come "the battle of the great God" in which the devil and his armies will "be cast away into their own place," no longer to have any power over the Saints of God. "This final great battle, in which evil spirits, mortal men, and resurrected personages all participate, will be the end of war as far as this earth is concerned. Then the earth shall be celestialized and become the abode of the righteous forever (D&C 88:16–31, 116)" (McConkie, *Mormon Doctrine*, 75).

Seek Learning, Build the Temple, Be Charitable

DOCTRINE AND COVENANTS 88:117–26

88:117 *Call your solemn assembly.* See commentary on verses 70, 74–75.

88:118 *As all have not faith.* The knowledge of God and those things associated with him must precede faith. We cannot exercise faith in that of which we have no knowledge. Therefore, the Saints are to teach one another that faith might increase among their number. It naturally follows that there is no place in a Church classroom for that which is not productive of faith.

Seek ye out of the best books. The Lord's people are to be a literate people. They should be constantly reading good books. As to "the best books," men and women of faith and goodness will always write them.

Seek learning, even by study and also by faith. Much learning would come to Latter-day Saints were they to couple their study with greater faith. For instance, the revelations of the Restoration—including the Book of Mormon, the Doctrine and Covenants, the Pearl of Great Price and the Joseph Smith Translation—can unlock an immeasurable amount of knowledge about the teachings of the Old and New Testaments if we have the faith to allow them to do so. Were we as a people less concerned with having everything that we are told by revelations conform to the findings of the science of our day, our understanding of the origin of man and life beyond the grave would be greatly enhanced. We too are entitled to that same Spirit and the same knowledge known to Joseph Smith and the great prophets of dispensations past in which they, clothed in the robes of righteousness, have had the mysteries of heaven unfolded to them.

88:119 *Establish a house.* It is the Kirtland Temple to which reference is made. At first it was referred to as a "house of God," or a "school." Extant evidence suggests that the Prophet initially conceived the primary function of this sacred edifice to be that of a schoolhouse for missionaries. It was to have two levels—the lower being for preaching and public meetings, the upper for classes and study. It was not until Nauvoo that the full endowment was revealed and a temple built primarily for the administering of sacred ordinances. See commentary on Doctrine and Covenants 95.

88:121 The spirit one feels in the temple or other sacred places is the spirit they take with them. No divine endowment will compensate for our failure to have prepared properly. Further, the presence of those who have not properly prepared will restrain that which others present might have enjoyed. See commentary on Doctrine and Covenants 59:15.

88:122 The direction here is that one be appointed as the teacher (for it was not expected that Joseph Smith do all the teaching) and that all be given the opportunity to be heard. There is nothing here that suggests everyone in the School of the Prophets was equal in understanding or that in a class the teacher was obligated to call on those who had not prepared themselves to contribute. This was the School of the Prophets, and all that were in attendance were expected to have the spirit of prophecy. See Doctrine and Covenants 88:134.

The Order of the School Set Forth and Ordinances Instituted
DOCTRINE AND COVENANTS 88:127–41

88:131 *The everlasting covenant.* The composite of all covenants essential for salvation constitutes the "everlasting covenant."

88:139 *The ordinance of the washing of feet.* Here the washing of feet as instituted by the Savior with the Twelve at the Last Supper is identified as an ordinance. For Jesus to kneel and wash his disciples' feet, as slaves did for their masters, was not simply a gesture of humility on his part. It was an ordinance of salvation that he performed; that is, it was a rite without which they could have no part in his Father's kingdom. Be it recalled that Peter, the first to have his feet washed, objected, saying to the Savior, "Thou shalt never wash my feet," to which Jesus responded, "If I wash thee not, thou hast no part with me" (John 13:8). That same ordinance was being restored anew to those invited to be a part of the School of the Prophets.

Orson Pratt gives this description of the ordinances performed in the Kirtland Temple: "When the temple was built, the Lord did not see proper to reveal all the ordinances of the Endowments, such as we now understand. He revealed little by little. . . . These administrations in the Kirtland Temple were revealed, little by little, corresponding with what I have already been saying, that the Lord does not give the fullness at once, but imparts to us according to his own will and pleasure" (*Journal of Discourses*, 19:16).

88:140 All ordinances must be done under the direction of those who have been given the keys or presidency over them.

DOCTRINE AND COVENANTS 89

DATE: 27 FEBRUARY 1833
PLACE: KIRTLAND, OHIO

Recalling the circumstances that precipitated this revelation, Brigham Young said: "I think I am as well acquainted with the circumstances which led to the giving of the Word of Wisdom as any man in the Church, although I was not present at the time to witness them. The first school of the prophets was held in a small room situated over the Prophet Joseph's kitchen, in a house which belonged to Bishop Whitney, and which was attached to his store, which store probably might be about fifteen feet square. In the rear of this building was a kitchen, probably ten by fourteen feet, containing rooms and pantries. Over this kitchen was situated the room in which the Prophet received revelations and in which he instructed his brethren. The brethren came to that place for hundreds of miles to attend school in a little room probably no larger than eleven by fourteen. When they assembled together in this room after breakfast, the first [thing] they did was to light their pipes, and, while smoking, talk about the great things of the kingdom, and spit all over the room, and as soon as the pipe was out of their mouths a large chew of tobacco would then be taken. Often when the Prophet entered the room to give the school instructions he would find himself in a cloud of tobacco smoke. This, and the complaints of his wife at having to clean so filthy a floor, made the Prophet think upon the matter, and he inquired of the Lord relating to the conduct of the Elders in using tobacco, and the revelation known as the Word of Wisdom was the result of his inquiry" (*Journal of Discourses*, 12:158).

A Word of Wisdom Given to the Saints
DOCTRINE AND COVENANTS 89:1–3

89:1–3 As the Prophet received it, the revelation began with the fourth verse as it is now rendered. The first three verses were simply an introduction that he gave to the revelation. The revelation was directed particularly to the brethren attending the School of the Prophets in Kirtland. The Saints in Missouri and in the Church generally were also invited to conform to the prohibitions of the revelation.

89:1 *Council of high priests.* The organizational structure of the Church unfolded gradually. It is evident from the beginning that the Church was to be governed by councils. Even before the first stake high council was formed or the Quorum of the Twelve was called, decisions were made in councils formed from among those holding the office of high priest. The reference in this revelation to the "council of high priests, assembled in Kirtland" is to those involved in the School of the Prophets, which met in the upper room of the Whitney store.

The saints in Zion. This refers to those members of the Church who had already gone to Missouri.

89:2 *Not by commandment or constraint.* As originally given, the Word of Wisdom was not binding on the Church as a commandment. The Lord, in his wisdom, was patient in allowing a time and season for his people to grow up into the commandment. President Joseph F. Smith offered this explanation, "The reason undoubtedly why the Word of Wisdom was given—as not by 'commandment or restraint' was that at that time, at least, if it had been given as a commandment it would have brought every man, addicted to the use of these noxious things, under condemnation; so the Lord was merciful and gave them a chance to overcome, before He brought them under the law" (Conference Report, October 1913, 14). Since the early 1930s, however, the prohibitions of the commandment— refraining from the use of alcohol, tea, coffee, and tobacco—have been viewed as binding on the faithful Saint. Adherence to the same is considered a prerequisite for baptism and for entrance into the temple.

The Church has often been criticized for such an unyielding standard. "It keeps thousands of good people out of the Church," one woman bitterly complained to the writer. Such a complaint rather misses the point. Were the Church to announce today that its members were no longer expected to abide by the standards of this revelation, all who ceased to do so would forfeit the blessings promised those who adhere to its standards. Nothing short of compliance to its standards will bring the promised blessings.

89:3 *A principle with promise.* The Word of Wisdom, like many other principles, has specific and particular blessings promised to those who live it. See verses 18–21.

Weakest of all saints. The thought being conveyed with this expression is that all who desire to live the commandment will be blessed with the ability to do so.

Use of Alcohol, Tobacco, Tea, and Coffee Prohibited
DOCTRINE AND COVENANTS 89:4–9

89:4 *Evils and designs . . . in the hearts of conspiring men.* In today's world evil abounds. Greedy and conspiring men seek wealth and power, marketing prostitution, pornography, weapons, drugs, vulgar music, and entertainment offensive to the light of Christ. A prime target for their avarice will always be our children. The tobacco industry markets an addictive and killing poison, knowing it to be such. Profit is their only concern. We have found it necessary to pass numerous laws that protect consumers in the supermarket, yet all manner of destructive influences are available on the streets, in our schools, and even in our homes through television and the Internet.

There is no form of wickedness that someone will not make available for a price. To give their evil designs some sense of respectability, they hide them behind weak phrases: "If it offends you, don't buy it." We in turn are expected to be so foolish as to suppose that if we don't buy that which is evil or offensive we will be spared its effects. The logic is threadbare. Our choice not to operate a smelter will not protect us against another man's choice to do so. We all breathe the same air; nonsmoking sections in a restaurant provide precious little protection to the nonsmoker. Again, one man's choice not to use alcohol will hardly protect him from drunk drivers.

Gratefully, the spirit and direction of the revelations of the Restoration are such that not only are we warned against the designs of evil men, but a path of safety is marked so that we can—to the extent possible—protect ourselves from their destructive influence in our society. See commentary on verses 18–21.

89:6 *Pure wine.* Convincing arguments can be presented to sustain the idea that the phrase "pure wine" refers simply to grape juice or to a wine with a low level of intoxicant in it. The language of this revelation leaves the impression that a wine with a low level of intoxicant is intended. See commentary on Doctrine and Covenants 27:2–3.

89:7 *Strong drinks are not for the belly.* "Strong drink" is a biblical phrase used to mean intoxicating drinks (Leviticus 10:9; Numbers 6:3; Deuteronomy 14:26; 29:6). It is not simply drunkenness that is prohibited here, but indulgence in any drink that has the capacity to intoxicate—regardless of how moderate that use may be—with the exception of the sacrament.

"The Lord has told us that 'Strong drinks are not good,' who is it that will say they are?" asked Hyrum Smith, "when the Lord says they are not. That man who says 'I can drink wine or strong drink, and it not hurt me,' is not wise. But some will say, 'I know that it did me good, for I was fatigued, and feeble, on a certain occasion, and it revived me, and I was invigorated thereby, and that is sufficient proof for me:' It may be for you, but it would not be for a wise man, for every spirit of this kind will only produce a greater langor when its effects cease to operate upon the human body. But you know that you are benefited, yes, so does the man who has mortgaged his property, know that he is relieved from his present embarrassments; but his temporary relief only binds the chords of bondage more severely around him" (*Times and Seasons*, 3:800).

Washing of your bodies. Alcohol is a very helpful agent for cleansing wounds and abrasions.

89:8 *Tobacco . . . is an herb for bruises and all sick cattle*. Applied with skill, a tobacco poultice can be useful in healing cuts and bruises on cattle.

89:9 *Hot drinks*. This language is contemporary to the days in which the revelation was given. Hyrum M. Smith and Janne M. Sjodahl observe in their commentary that "'Hot drinks' means tea and coffee, as those two beverages were the only ones in common use among the members of the Church, and drunk at a high temperature, at the time when the Revelation was given. The reason why those beverages were condemned was because they contained a habit-forming drug, rather than because of the temperature at which they were swallowed; although liquids taken into the stomach at too high a temperature, frequently and in large quantities, would be hurtful. But the chief objection to tea and coffee is the drug they contain. It follows logically that any other beverage which contains a hurtful drug or element, is open to the same objection, regardless of the temperature at which it is taken" (*Doctrine and Covenants Commentary*, 573).

Herbs, Fruits, Meat, and Grain Were Given by God for the Use of Men

DOCTRINE AND COVENANTS 89:10–17

89:11 *In the season thereof*. Illustrating the meaning of this phrase, Joseph Fielding Smith said: "Some have stumbled over the meaning of the expression . . . and have argued that grains and fruits should only be used in the season of their growth and when they have ripened. This is not the intent, but any grain or fruit is out of season no matter what part of the year it may be, if it is unfit for use. The apple under the tree bruised and decaying is out of season while the good fruit is waiting to be plucked from the tree" (*Church History and Modern Revelation*, 1:385).

89:11–13 *Flesh also of beasts and of the fowls of the air.* The eating of meat is not prohibited by this or any other revelation from God. This revelation does direct, however, that meat be used with "prudence," with "thanksgiving," "sparingly," and preferably "in times of winter, or of cold, or famine."

Previous revelations had already addressed issues relative to the use of meat by the Saints. The first announced that anyone who forbade the use of meat did so without the authority of God, for "the beasts of the field and the fowls of the air" had been "ordained" by God "for the use of man for food and for raiment" (D&C 49:19). In the second revelation on the matter, the Lord told the Saints that "the fulness of the earth is yours, the beasts of the field and the fowls of the air, and that which climbeth upon the trees and walketh upon the earth," all these were created for the "benefit and the use of man," as "food" to "strengthen the body and to enliven the soul." As with all things that the Lord has given us, these are to be used "with judgment, not to excess" (D&C 59:16, 18–20). "Wo be unto man that sheddeth blood or that wasteth flesh and hath no need," the Lord warned (D&C 49:21). In the Joseph Smith Translation of Genesis 9:8–11, we learn that after the Flood "God blessed Noah and his sons, and said unto them, Be fruitful and multiply, and replenish the earth. And the fear of you, and the dread of you shall be upon every beast of the earth, and upon every fowl of the air, upon all that moveth upon the earth, and upon all the fishes of the sea; into your hand are they delivered. Every moving thing that liveth shall be meat for you; even as the green herb have I given you all things. But, the blood of all flesh which I have given you for meat, shall be shed upon the ground, which taketh life thereof, and the blood ye shall not eat. And surely, blood shall not be shed, only for meat, to save your lives; and the blood of every beast will I require at your hands."

89:13 *They should not be used.* When this revelation was first printed in the Doctrine and Covenants (1835), there was no comma after this phrase. The addition of the comma clarifies the meaning of the text, thus dramatizing the importance of proper punctuation. The addition of the comma is in harmony with the context of the revelation, which is that meat should be used sparingly.

Blessings Promised to the Obedient
DOCTRINE AND COVENANTS 89:18-21

89:18 *All saints.* Saints who abide by the principles given in this revelation are rightful heirs to its promises. This assumes, as the verse states, that they are walking in obedience to all the commandments. The promise of blessings is not extended to those who keep the Word of Wisdom in isolation of that covenant obligation. Those other than the "saints" who abide the principles of health here espoused will be rewarded for doing so but have no claim to the blessings that are associated with living this principle in harmony with the fulness of the gospel law.

Health in their navel and marrow to their bones. Symbolically, the navel represents the original source of nourishment and strength to every soul born into this world. Marrow represents the source of strength to the bones. The metaphor is rooted in one of the Proverbs. It reads: "Be not wise in thine own eyes: fear the Lord, and depart from evil. It shall be health to thy navel, and marrow to thy bones" (Proverbs 3:7–8). In this expressive way, the ancient sage reminds us that obedience to the commands of God brings a healthy body. The chain of thought being that to trust God brings peace of mind, this in turn fosters good health, which in its turn brings a long and happy life.

89:19 *Wisdom . . . knowledge . . . hidden treasures.* It is spiritual wisdom and knowledge to which reference is being made in this text. The revelation does not concern itself with the wisdom and knowledge of the world. Moral cleanliness, purity of soul, and the recognition that the body is a divine temple and is not to be polluted with that which is unclean or subjected to addictions are not requisites to study in the great universities of men. They are, however, quite necessary for those who desire to obtain that knowledge that comes only by the spirit of revelation. It was the need for those brethren attending the School of the Prophets in Kirtland to measure up to the standard that called forth this revelation. In doing so they prepared their hearts and minds to receive truths and understanding that would have remained hidden to them otherwise.

We understand observance of the Word of Wisdom to be an essential key in obtaining a knowledge and understanding of spiritual truths. It is not simply a health law. There would be little purpose in extending someone's life if it were not replete with light and truth. To avoid cancer, for example, as marvelous as that may be, is not as important as being able to dream dreams, entertain angels, or get answers to your prayers.

89:20 *Run and not be weary . . . walk and not faint.* The promise given in this verse is couched in the language of Isaiah, who wrote as follows: "Hast thou not known? hast thou not heard, that the everlasting God, the Lord, the Creator of the ends of the earth, fainteth not, neither is weary? there is no searching of his understanding. He giveth power to the faint; and to them that have no might he increaseth strength. Even the youths shall faint and be weary, and the young men shall utterly fall: But they that wait upon the Lord . . . shall mount up with wings as eagles; they shall run, and not be weary; and they shall walk, and not faint" (Isaiah 40:28–31). Here Isaiah reminds us that God does not tire, nor does he sleep, and his knowledge is infinite. This is the God who gave us the breath of life and of whom we should seek the strength to sustain it. Isaiah reminds us that those who "wait upon the Lord," those found "walking in obedience to the commandments," will "renew their strength," they will run and not be weary and walk and not faint. With the aid of this revelation we can also say that there will be "no searching" their understanding, for theirs is the promise of "wisdom," of "knowledge," and of "hidden treasures"—all things reserved for the obedient.

89:21 *The destroying angel shall pass by them.* Is this reference to the destroying angel in this text to be understood figuratively or literally? The answer, it would appear, is both. Certainly there have been those whose lives were destroyed by their failure to comply with the principles given in the Word of Wisdom. There will yet be others who will lose their lives in like manner. Given also that this revelation cannot, in the proper sense, be lived in isolation of all the commandments of the Lord and thus all the promises of the Lord, we would also think that the time must surely come when the angels of heaven will take vengeance on the wicked as they did among the firstborn of the Egyptians (Exodus 12:23, 29).

DOCTRINE AND COVENANTS 90

DATE: 8 MARCH 1833
PLACE: KIRTLAND, OHIO

This revelation came in response to the prayers of the Prophet and his brethren and centers in the organization of the First Presidency, which would take place ten days later. On that occasion (18 March 1833) Sidney Rigdon and Frederick G. Williams were set apart by the Prophet as his counselors in the presidency of the high priesthood. On that occasion "many of the brethren saw a heavenly vision of the Savior, and concourses of angels" (Smith, *History of the Church*, 1:335).

Keys of the Kingdom Committed to Joseph Smith
DOCTRINE AND COVENANTS 90:1-5

90:2 *Keys of the kingdom.* See commentary on Doctrine and Covenants 81:2.

Which kingdom is coming forth for the last time. There have been many dispensations of the gospel, or, in other words, many instances in which the truths of salvation have been dispensed anew from the heavens. Ours, however, is the dispensation of the fulness of all past dispensations. It represents the last time the gospel will be restored before Christ comes in judgment upon the wicked and commences to rule and reign personally upon the earth (Daniel 2:35, 44; Jacob 5:62-64, 71, 75-76; D&C 24:19; 33:3; 39:17).

90:3 Earlier revelations had stated that only Joseph Smith could receive revelations for the whole Church. These revelations, however, contained the provision that this was to be the case unless the Lord placed another in his stead. Were that to happen, however, even the revelation identifying Joseph Smith's successor must come through him (D&C 28:7; 35:18; 43:3). The present text does not contain that provision; but rather, it promises that Joseph Smith will hold the keys of the kingdom both in life and in death. Thus it appears that the Prophet was on probation for a time and that having proven himself that season had now ended.

90:5 *Oracles of God*. An oracle is a brief utterance. An oracle of God is that which has been spoken by way of divine revelation. It is the right of the First Presidency "to receive the oracles [the word of God] for the whole church" (D&C 124:126). We occasionally refer to those through whom the word of God comes as oracles.

Sidney Rigdon and Frederick G. Williams Called to Serve in the First Presidency
DOCTRINE AND COVENANTS 90:6–7

90:6 *Accounted as equal . . . in holding the keys*. The principle here established is that counselors in a presidency can act in the stead of the president when they do so under his direction. It is not intended to suggest that counselors are equal in authority with the president; but rather that they are to be "accounted as equal" when they act by his authority. It is for this reason that they are set apart as counselors and not as presidents. "I laid my hands on Brothers Sidney and Frederick," recounted the Prophet, "and ordained them to take part with me in holding the keys of this last kingdom, and to assist in the Presidency of the High Priesthood, as my Counselors" (Smith, *History of the Church*, 1:334).

Be it remembered that it was Joseph Smith who was told that he would hold the keys of the kingdom in this world and in the world to come, not his counselors (v. 3). It will also be remembered that the release of a president brings with it the release of his counselors. The same principle is involved in the presidencies of the various auxiliaries to the priesthood. In each instance, the counselor is empowered to act for the president when doing so under the president's direction; and in each instance, the counselor is released with the release of the president.

90:7 *The school of the prophets*. See commentary on Doctrine and Covenants 88:119.

Gospel to Be Preached to the Nation of Israel and to Gentiles and Jews
DOCTRINE AND COVENANTS 90:8–11

90:8 *The nations of Israel*. The nations of Israel—that is, the twelve tribes of Israel—are at the present time scattered among all the nations of the earth. Missionaries, armed with the Book of Mormon, will yet go to those of every nation, kindred, tongue, and people to "show unto the remnant of the House of Israel what great things the Lord hath done for their fathers; and that they may know the covenants of the Lord, that they are not cast off forever." The message of the Restoration is also to go to both Jew and Gentile, that they too might know that Jesus is the Christ, the author and source of salvation (Preface to the Book of Mormon).

90:9 *Gentiles first, and then . . . the Jews.* Because the gospel went first to the Jews in the meridian dispensation and they rejected it, by the justice of the Lord, in this the dispensation of the fulness of times it is to go first to the Gentiles and only then to the Jews. Thus it is said that the first shall be last and the last shall be first. Nephi, speaking some six hundred years before Christ was to be born among the Jews, prophesied, saying, "And the time cometh that he shall manifest himself unto all nations, both unto the Jews and also unto the Gentiles; and after he has manifested himself unto the Jews and also unto the Gentiles, then he shall manifest himself unto the Gentiles and also unto the Jews, and the last shall be first, and the first shall be last" (1 Nephi 13:42; Luke 13:30).

90:10 *When the arm of the Lord shall be revealed in power.* See Doctrine and Covenants 43:25.

The heathen nations. Reference is to those nations unacquainted with the true God.

The house of Joseph. The house of Joseph consists of the tribes of Ephraim and Manasseh. Of Joseph's house Moses said, "His glory is like the firstling of his bullock [meaning the birthright is his], and his horns [a symbol for authority] are like the horns of unicorns: with them he shall push [gather] the people together to the ends of the earth: and they are the ten thousands of Ephraim, and they are the thousands of Manasseh" (Deuteronomy 33:17). See commentary on Doctrine and Covenants 133:26–32.

90:11 *In his own tongue.* Not only are we promised that the gospel will go to those of every nation, kindred, tongue, and people but that it will go to them in their "own tongue." Further, Alma tells us, "The Lord doth grant unto all nations, of their own nation and tongue, to each his word, yea, in wisdom, all that he seeth fit that they should have" (Alma 29:8). Nephi assured us that the great winding-up scene will not take place until there are congregations of the Saints "upon all the face of the earth" (1 Nephi 14:12), to which John the Revelator tells us that there will also be those who have been ordained "kings and priests" (Revelation 5:9–10) in the house of the Lord among all the nations of the earth.

The First Presidency to Set the Church in Order
DOCTRINE AND COVENANTS 90:12–18

90:13 *Translation of the prophets.* In the Hebrew canon, or Old Testament, the Major Prophets are followed by a collection of smaller prophetic oracles that are commonly designated as the Twelve Minor Prophets. It is to these books that reference is being made here. The Prophet had returned to labor on these books after completing his work on the New Testament on 2 February 1833 (Smith, *History of the Church,* 1:324). Section 91, which was received the next day, indicated that the Prophet had now come to that portion of the Old Testament known as the Apocrypha, which his copy of the Bible contained, hence his inquiry about whether it should be translated.

The school. The reference is to the School of the Prophets. See commentary on Doctrine and Covenants 88:119.

90:14 *From time to time.* No one lives in a constant deluge of revelation. The treasures of heaven are not dispersed cheaply.

Mysteries of the kingdom. See commentary on Doctrine and Covenants 76:7.

90:15 *Set in order the churches.* Reference is to the various congregations of the Church. At the time of this revelation the Church was less than three years of age, and such geographic divisions as wards, stakes, and missions did not exist.

Study and learn. It is expected that the Lord's people will be conversant with all good books and that they will be students of literature, art, history, languages, and music. Indeed, all that enlightens the mind has its proper place in the gospel of Jesus Christ. Nor is that the end of the matter, for it should be their lot also to write the best books, produce the finest art, compose the most edifying and inspiring music, and do well all else that lifts and ennobles humankind. See commentary on Doctrine and Covenants 88:77–80, 118.

90:16 *To preside in council.* The first presidency, to whom this revelation was given, would preside not only in council meetings as this revelation directs but in any Church meeting that they attended.

Diverse Instruction
DOCTRINE AND COVENANTS 90:19–37

90:24 *Search diligently, pray always, and be believing.* It is for us to search the word of the Lord that we might obtain a clear understanding of the principles of eternal life, for it is in harmony with those principles that all the blessings of heaven are obtained. Such a search cannot be conducted without prayer and the companionship of the Lord's Spirit. Those who search in faith are rewarded in kind; while the unbelieving, those who refuse to seek after the things of the Spirit, become more narrow and restricted in their thoughts and understanding, for they begin to lose even the light which they once had.

In similar language, Moroni counseled that we "ask the Father in the name of Jesus for what things soever ye shall stand in need. Doubt not, but be believing, and begin as in times of old, and come unto the Lord with all your heart, and work out your own salvation with fear and trembling before him" (Mormon 9:27).

Remember the covenant wherewith ye have covenanted one with another. We are not saved separately and singly. No one who understands the gospel of Jesus Christ would say, "I have been saved," suggesting that they, independent of their relationship with the community of Saints, have obtained salvation. A church organization is essential in the declaration of the gospel and the performances of the ordinances of salvation. We do not baptize ourselves; the most righteous of men cannot confer the priesthood upon himself, nor can either a man or a woman endow themselves. All gospel covenants are community covenants. In baptism, for instance, we covenant to mourn with those that mourn and to comfort those that stand in need of comfort (Mosiah 18:9). Moses took the children of Israel to Sinai that the Lord might make of them a covenant people, a kingdom of priests, and a holy nation, not a kingdom of individuals (Exodus 19:5–6). This has been the pattern for those seeking salvation in all gospel dispensations.

90:25–27 This instruction is directed to the heads of households. It has nothing to do with the number of children born to them. It is an expression of concern about the size of their extended family, which often included friends, who sought shelter and succor from them. For them to be overly generous would hinder their ability to accomplish those things the Lord had called upon them to do. Joseph Smith Sr., because of his kindly nature, was particularly cautioned.

This same principle has to guide us in the affairs of the Church. Though we always desire to help those in need, it would not be wisdom that all of the Church's means be given to the poor and thus deprive it of the ability to accomplish its greater mission of building temples and proclaiming the gospel throughout the nations of the earth.

90:28 *Vienna Jaques.* "Vienna Jaques, a woman who had been kind to the Prophet and had cared for his wants when in need and had helped the elders, was now by revelation to be helped with means so that she could gather with the Saints in Zion" (Smith, *Church History and Modern Revelation,* 1:391).

DOCTRINE AND COVENANTS 91

DATE: 9 MARCH 1833
PLACE: KIRTLAND, OHIO

Doctrine and Covenants 91 was revealed one day after section 90. The Prophet was at that time engaged in the revision of the Bible (D&C 90:13). The Bible from which he was making his corrections contained the Apocrypha. Thus he inquired of the Lord as to whether he should revise those books. This revelation indicated that it was not necessary for him to do so.

The Apocrypha Need Not Be Translated
DOCTRINE AND COVENANTS 91:1–3

91:1–3 "An apocryphal writing," explained Hugh Nibley, "is one that had been accepted as inspired scripture by any Christian or Jewish group at any time. When such texts are brought together and examined, they are found almost without exception to reveal all the characteristics of real scripture. The manuscripts that contain them are just as old as and sometimes older than many of those of the canonical books, i.e., the books of the Bible; they are found in the same places and conditions; they were anciently put to the same uses; they talk about the same things in the same terms and make the same claim to divine origin. It is clear, for example, that the Qumran community considered the Book of Jubilees, the Testament of the Twelve Patriarchs, the Apocalypse of Baruch, the Assumption of Moses, the Psalms of Solomon, and many other writings just as sacred as anything in the Bible. So closely in fact do these documents resemble the scriptures and each other that to this day there is no agreement among their pious readers or among the specialists who study them as to what is really 'apocryphal' in the Bible and what is really biblical in the Apocrypha" (*Approach to the Book of Mormon*, 194–95).

We would suppose that no age has been spared its spiritual charlatans and counterfeiters. Nephi told us that many plain and precious things were taken from the Bible (1 Nephi 13:26–29). This revelation affirms that the workers of such mischief also freely added to the sacred books.

91:1 *Apocrypha*. The word *apocrypha* has been used so differently that its proper meaning is often confused. This confusion arises partly from the ambiguity of the ancient usage of the word and partly from its modern application to a group of books associated with the inter-testament period. Etymologically the word means "secret or hidden." Some have suggested that the content of these books is of such a nature that they ought to be kept hidden because they contain mysteries or esoteric lore too profound or sacred to be trusted to the uninitiated (2 Esdras 14:45–46). Others have suggested that the term was used by those who held that such books should be kept hidden because of their spurious or heretical nature. Thus the term had both an honorable and a derogatory meaning appended to it.

According to general usage today, "the Apocrypha" is the designation given to a collection of fourteen or fifteen books written during the last two centuries before Christ and the first century of the Christian era (Bible Dictionary, 610–11). None of these books is included in the Hebrew canon. All of them, however, with the exception of 2 Esdras, are found in the Greek version of the Old Testament known as the Septuagint.

91:2 *Interpolations*. "The act of foisting [to pass off something worthless as genuine] a word or passage into a manuscript or book" (Webster, *Dictionary*, 1828).

Those Enlightened by the Spirit Can Benefit from Study of the Apocrypha
DOCTRINE AND COVENANTS 91:4–6

91:4–6 While it does warn against things that have been added to the Apocrypha by designing men, this revelation does not reject it as being untrue. It simply states that it must be discerned by the Spirit. This principle applies to the reading of scripture as well as all other books.

DOCTRINE AND COVENANTS 92

DATE: 15 MARCH 1833
PLACE: KIRTLAND, OHIO

Frederick G. Williams, who had been called to be a member of the first presidency (D&C 90:6), is here called to hold place in the United Firm, or united order, which in turn has responsibility to oversee the business dealings of the Church.

A Commandment Relative to Admission to the United Order

DOCTRINE AND COVENANTS 92:1–2

92:1 *The united order, organized agreeable to the commandment previously given.* See commentary on Doctrine and Covenants 78:3–4.

What I say unto one I say unto all. The Lord was speaking to all members of the United Firm in commanding them to receive Frederick G. Williams as a member of their cooperative business firm.

92:2 *You shall be a lively member in this order.* Brother Williams was not to hold back in contributing to the order because he was the newest member. Likewise, all new members of the Church are received into full fellowship and are expected to be "lively members" in serving in the kingdom.

DOCTRINE AND COVENANTS 93

DATE: 6 MAY 1833
PLACE: KIRTLAND, OHIO

Section 93 is one of the greatest doctrinal revelations given in this dispensation. The historical record gives no indication as to what precipitated it. The language in the early part of the revelation reflects John's Gospel, while the testimony of the Baptist relative to the baptism of Christ is also quoted. The heart of the revelation deals with an extract from a record, apparently written by John the Baptist, with the promise that it will yet be restored to the Saints. From that extract we are instructed on the matters of how we are to worship and what we are to worship.

All Who Are Faithful Shall See the Lord
DOCTRINE AND COVENANTS 93:1-5

93:1 *Shall see my face and know that I am.* With the restoration of the gospel comes an understanding of its purpose, which has long been lost to the sectarian world. Christ atoned for our sins so that we might be reconciled to God and receive of his fulness. When the principle of revelation and the authority of the Priesthood was restored, we learned that the privilege of communication with our divine Father is not limited to the world to come, nor is the privilege of standing in his presence, as attested by the experience of many prophets in ancient days.

93:2 "The Spirit of Christ is given to every man, that he may know good from evil" (Moroni 7:16). In this manner, the light of Christ illuminates the course of everyone born into this world. Thus all are accountable to accept and live gospel principles. All are born with the ability to discern right from wrong, light from darkness (D&C 84:46–54; 88:5–13).

93:3 *The Father and I are one.* To know Jesus Christ is to know the Father. The Father is manifested through the Son by means of his attributes and perfection. The Savior explained to his disciples: "If ye had known me, ye should have known my Father also. . . . he that hath seen me hath seen the Father. . . . the words that I speak unto you I speak not of myself: but the Father that dwelleth in me, he doeth the works" (John 14:7, 9–10). The words and works of the Son are the same words that the Father would utter and the same works that the Father would do in the same circumstances. They are one in that they have the same purpose in all things: to "bring to pass the immortality and eternal life of man" (Moses 1:39).

93:4 *The Father because he gave me of his fulness.* Jesus Christ is the Father because in all things he is one with the Father, because he enjoys the power and knowledge of the Father, because he is in the image and likeness of the Father, because he has received the fulness of the Father. This verse is a summary statement of Abinadi's teaching in Mosiah 15:1–7. See commentary on Lectures on Faith 5:2–3, page 842.

The Son because I . . . made flesh my tabernacle. Before the Savior was born into mortality, he was identified as "the Father *of* the heavens and of the earth, and all things that in them are" (Ether 4:7; emphasis added). Note that he was not spoken of as our Father *in* heaven, but, rather, the Father *of* heaven. He is spoken of as Father because of his role in the Creation. Hence, he was known as "Christ the Lord, who is the very Eternal Father" to Book of Mormon prophets (Mosiah 16:15). Yet, when he took upon him a mortal body, he was spoken of as "Jesus Christ, the Son of God, the Father of heaven and earth, the Creator of all things from the beginning" (Mosiah 3:8). He did not cease to be the Father, but because he came into mortality, he became the Only Begotten Son of God in the flesh. Christ was referred to as the Only Begotten before his mortal birth because of his foreordained mission as the Savior of the world (Moses 1:6, 5:7; Alma 5:48).

How the Son of God Obtained the Fulness of His Father
DOCTRINE AND COVENANTS 93:6–11

93:6 *John saw and bore record of the fulness of my glory.* In this revelation John the Baptist tells of a vision in which he was shown the power, acts, and glory of Christ in the premortal realms. Likewise, Abraham saw in vision the noble and great spirits whom God appointed to be his rulers "and there stood one among them that was like unto God" (Abraham 3:24). Christ was the most intelligent of all of the heavenly hosts of our Father's children. Indeed, he was like unto God the Father in intelligence and glory, knowing all truth. His knowledge extended to comprehending "things as they are, and as they were, and as they are to come" (v. 24).

The Prophet Joseph Smith taught: "The great Jehovah contemplated the whole of the events connected with the earth, pertaining to the plan of salvation, before it rolled into existence, or ever 'the morning stars sang together' for joy; the past, the present, and the future were and are, with Him, one eternal 'now;' He knew of the fall of Adam, the iniquities of the antediluvians, of the depth of iniquity that would be connected with the human family, their weakness and strength, their power and glory, apostasies, their crimes, their righteousness and iniquity; He comprehended the fall of man, and his redemption; He knew the plan of salvation and pointed it out; He was acquainted with the situation of all nations and with their destiny; He ordered all things according to the council of His own will; He knows the situation of both the living and the dead, and has made ample provision for their redemption, according to their several circumstances, and the laws of the kingdom of God, whether in this world, or in the world to come" (*Teachings of the Prophet Joseph Smith*, 220).

This same Christ, Creator and Redeemer of the earth, took upon him a tabernacle of flesh and became a citizen of a fallen world. Here he "descended below all things"; here he was "despised and rejected of men"; here he became "a man of sorrows, and acquainted with grief"; here "he was bruised for our iniquities"; and here he advanced, as each one of us must advance, from one grace to a greater grace until he obtained the resurrection and thus became an heir to the fulness of the glory of his Father (D&C 88:6; Isaiah 53:3, 5).

John's record. It appears that the record being spoken of was written by John the Baptist. Similarities between this revelation and the testimony of the Gospels, especially that of the apostle John, indicate that the Gospel writers may have included some of John the Baptist's record with their own (Matthew 3:13–17; Mark 1:4–11; Luke 3:1–22; John 1:1–14, 29–34).

Bruce R. McConkie noted: "From latter-day revelation we learn that the material in the forepart of the gospel of John (the Apostle, Revelator, and Beloved Disciple) was written originally by John the Baptist. By revelation the Lord restored to Joseph Smith part of what John the Baptist had written and promised to reveal the balance when men became sufficiently faithful to warrant receiving it (D&C 93: 6–18) . . .

"Even without revelation, however, it should be evident that John the Baptist had something to do with the recording of events in the forepart of John's gospel, for some of the occurrences include his conversations with the Jews and a record of what he saw when our Lord was baptized—all of which matters would have been unknown to John the Apostle whose ministry began somewhat later than that of the Baptist's. There is little doubt but that the Beloved Disciple had before him the Baptist's account when he wrote his gospel. The latter John either copied or paraphrased what the earlier prophet of the same name had written. The only other possibility is that the Lord revealed to the gospel author the words that had been recorded by the earlier messenger who prepared the way before him" (*Doctrinal New Testament Commentary*, 1:70–71).

Both John Taylor and Orson Pratt joined in the opinion that it is the record of the Baptist for which we look rather than another record written by John the Revelator as some have supposed (Taylor, *Mediation and Atonement*, 55; and *Journal of Discourses*, 16:58).

93:8 *He was the Word.* God the Father committed into Christ's hands the responsibility to bring to pass the plan of salvation. Jesus Christ is the God of our fathers. He revealed to them the means by which they could be saved and return to live in the presence of the Father. The message of salvation comes only through him and those servants that he appoints to declare his word. The meaning of his being "the Word" is illustrated by the Father's declaration: "*This is My Beloved Son. Hear Him*" (Joseph Smith–History 1:17; JST Matthew 3:46; Matthew 17:5; Mark 9:7; Luke 9:35; 3 Nephi 11:7). We could quite properly say that the gospel is *the word,* and because the gospel (or *the word*) comes to us through Christ, he becomes the personification of the gospel or the Word.

The messenger of salvation. This is an equivalent expression to that of Malachi, who stated: "The Lord, whom ye seek, shall suddenly come to his temple, even the *messenger of the covenant,* whom ye delight in" (Malachi 3:1; emphasis added). We properly say that salvation is in Christ, that it is in the covenant, or that it is in the word. In each instance we are essentially saying the same thing, which is that all things that pertain to our salvation center in Christ.

93:9 *The Spirit of truth.* Christ is here spoken of as "the Spirit of truth," a title given to him in the premortal life. Thus he is the revealer and dispenser of all the truths of salvation. "My voice," he said, "is Spirit; *my Spirit is truth;* truth abideth and hath no end; and if it be in you it shall abound" (D&C 88:66; emphasis added). The resurrected Christ declared, "The Spirit of truth is of God. I am the Spirit of truth, and John bore record of me saying: He received a fulness of truth, yea, even of all truth" (D&C 93:26).

It should be noted that holy writ also applies this name title to the Holy Ghost to identify his mission in guiding the truth seeker to the light of the gospel (Moroni 10:5). The Holy Ghost is the "Comforter . . . the Spirit of truth; whom the world cannot receive" (John 14:16–17), for he manifests himself only to those who keep the commandments. His mission is to testify of Christ (John 15:26).

"When he, the Spirit of truth, is come," our Lord said to the apostles of old, "he will guide you into all truth: for he shall not speak of himself; but whatsoever he shall hear, that shall he speak: and he will shew you things to come. He shall glorify me: for he shall receive of mine, and shall shew it unto you" (John 16:13–14; D&C 6:15).

93:10 *Men were made by him.* Regarding the creation of man, the Lord revealed: "And I, God, said unto mine Only Begotten, which was with me from the beginning: Let us make man in our image, after our likeness" (Moses 2:26). In all other works of creation the Savior acted with the noble and great spirits under the delegated authority of the Father (Abraham 3:22–24). However, in the act of creating the first man and woman there was no delegation to the Son and his fellow servants. Moses was taught, "And I, God, created man in mine own image, in the image of mine Only Begotten created I him; male and female created I them" (Moses 2:27). That is to say, "All human beings—male or female—are created in the image of God. Each is a beloved spirit son or daughter of heavenly parents, and, as such, each has a divine nature and destiny" ("Family: A Proclamation to the World"). Christ is not the father of our spirits or our earthly bodies, these were fathered by God. Thus, when our text says "men were made by him," having reference to Christ, we understand this to be an expression of the doctrine of divine investiture of authority by which Christ or those holding the holy priesthood are invited to stand in the place or stead of our eternal Father.

All things were made by him, and through him, and of him. Referring to his infinite creations, God revealed to Moses: "Worlds without number have I created . . . and by the Son I created them, which is mine Only Begotten" (Moses 1:33). The vision shown to Abraham tells us that others were involved in creating the world under the direction of the Savior. After being shown many of the great and noble spirits, Abraham saw that "there stood one among them that was like unto God, and he said unto those who were with him: We will go down, for there is space there, and we will take of these materials, and we will make an earth whereon these may dwell" (Abraham 3:24). Thus, Christ, acting under the direction of the Father, directed the council of the Gods in the creation of the heavens and the earth.

John Bore Record That the Son of God Went from Grace to Grace Until He Received a Fulness of the Glory
DOCTRINE AND COVENANTS 93:12–18

93:12 *He received not of the fulness at the first.* The apostle Paul wrote concerning the Lord's condescension to mortality: "Let this mind be in you, which was also in Christ Jesus: Who, being in the form of God, thought it not robbery to be equal with God: But made himself of no reputation" (Philippians 2:5–7). Here, the English translation of "He made himself of no reputation" is a derivative of the Greek word *kenosis,* which means "to make empty." Bible scholars render Paul's writings to literally say that Jesus "emptied himself" (Jerusalem Bible and Revised Standard Version), or "laid aside his mighty power and glory" (*Living New Testament*). When Jesus was born into mortality, "over His mind had fallen the veil of forgetfulness common to all who are born to earth," wrote Elder James E. Talmage, "by which the remembrance of primeval existence is shut off" (*Jesus the Christ,* 111). "When Jesus lay in the manger, a helpless infant" further attested President Lorenzo Snow, "He knew not that He was the Son of God, and that formerly He created the earth. When the edict of Herod was issued, He knew nothing of it; He had not power to save Himself; and His father and mother had to take Him and fly into Egypt to preserve Him from the effects of that edict. Well, He grew up to manhood, and during His progress it was revealed unto Him who He was, and for what purpose He was in the world. The glory and power He possessed before He came into the world was made known unto Him" (Conference Report, April 1901, 3).

Received grace for grace. The grace of which John the Baptist wrote is that which comes and grows in doing the work of God. The Savior bore witness to Nicodemus, "He that doeth truth cometh to the light, that his deeds may be made manifest, that they are wrought in God" (John 3:21). Grace is divine help, or in other words, enabling power and strength that comes from God. The Savior increased in grace as he lived the commandments of God and blessed the lives others. His growth was accelerated above that of his fellowmen because of the reciprocal nature of receiving strength of the Spirit when extending grace. That is, he called upon his Father for power and strength to bless others in their need. In answer to his prayers, he was empowered and grew beyond his previous abilities, thus, receiving grace *for* grace. Christ was foremost in reaching out in compassion to others. Therefore, he received greater grace from God in his efforts than any other person. He increased his capacity to give with each experience, continuing "from grace *to* grace" (D&C 93:13; emphasis added).

93:13 *Until he received a fulness.* The point of emphasis here is that Christ came into mortality as a helpless infant, knowing no more than any other child at birth. It was then for him to grow up into a perfect knowledge of the principles of salvation, doing so in such a manner as to mark the path that all others seeking the same end could follow.

93:15 "And Jesus when he was baptized, went up straightway out of the water; *and John saw,* and lo, the heavens were opened unto him, and he saw the Spirit of God descending like a dove and lighting upon *Jesus.* And lo, *he heard* a voice from heaven, saying, This is my beloved Son, in whom I am well pleased. *Hear ye him*" (JST Matthew 3:45–46; emphasis added).

The Holy Ghost descended upon him in the form of a dove. The Holy Ghost is a spirit son of God and as such "is a personage of Spirit" (D&C 130:22). Joseph Smith said: "The Holy Ghost is a personage, and is in the *form* of a personage. It [he] does not confine itself [himself] to the form of the dove, but in *sign* of the dove. The Holy Ghost cannot be transformed into a dove; but the sign of a dove was given to John to signify the truth of the deed, as the dove is an emblem or token of truth and innocence" (*Teachings of the Prophet Joseph Smith,* 276). John saw the Holy Ghost descend upon Christ in "a bodily shape like a dove" (Luke 3:22), that is, the personage of the Holy Ghost descended upon Christ with the grace of a dove, which imagery is chosen because the dove was present—it being the visible or outward sign of the presence of the Holy Ghost.

93:16 It was only in and through the resurrection that Christ was able to obtain the fulness of the Father. In the Sermon on the Mount, he gave the command, "Be ye therefore perfect, even as your Father which is in heaven is perfect" (Matthew 5:48). In the New World counterpart of this sermon, which followed his resurrection, he said, "I would that ye should be perfect even as I, or your Father who is in heaven is perfect" (3 Nephi 12:48).

93:18 Orson Pratt explained: "John the Baptist is said by the highest authority to be one of the greatest Prophets ever born of a woman; but we have very little written in the Jewish record concerning him. We have a revelation in the Doctrine and Covenants concerning the record of John, that great Prophet. And we are promised that if we are faithful as a people, the fullness of the record of John shall hereafter be revealed to us. When we get this, I think we shall have still more knowledge in regard to doctrine and principle, and things that are great and marvelous, of which we know very little, if anything about" (*Journal of Discourses,* 19:218). See commentary on Doctrine and Covenants 93:6.

Faithful Men, Going from Grace to Grace, Shall Also Receive the Fulness of the Father
DOCTRINE AND COVENANTS 93:19–20

93:19–20 The preceding verse contains a brief extract from a Gospel written by the Baptist. The thoughtful student must ask, Why did the Lord think it necessary for us to have this extract restored to us during the very infancy of the restored Church? The answer is found in verses 19 and 20. Here we are told that the foregoing was restored so that we might know "what" it is that we worship and "how" it is that we are to worship. From these verses it could be said that we worship the Father, who sent his Son to mark the path that we are to follow if we desire to obtain—as Christ did—the fulness of the Father. That path embraces the ordinances of baptism and the receipt of the Holy Ghost. It also includes our advancing from grace to grace as the Savior did. Thus, both the "what" and "how" of worship center in our being followers of Christ, in emulating his example, in learning to think as he thinks, believe as he believes, do as he would do, and thus experience what he would experience. As Latter-day Saints we are to understand that salvation is not to be found in the profession of Christ alone, nor is it to be found in compliance with certain sacraments or ordinances, but rather in our following the path marked by the Savior. We must advance from grace to grace, we must become as "a smooth and polished shaft in the quiver of the Almighty" through laboring for the gospel cause. Ours must be lives consecrated to the blessing of family and the building up of the kingdom of God (*Teachings of the Prophet Joseph Smith,* 304).

"Here, then, is eternal life—to know the only wise and true God," explained the Prophet Joseph Smith; "and you have got to learn how to be Gods yourselves, and to be kings and priests to God, the same as all

Gods have done before you, namely, by going from one small degree to another, and from a small capacity to a great one; from grace to grace, from exaltation to exaltation. . . . To inherit the same power, the same glory and the same exaltation, until you arrive at the station of a God, and ascend the throne of eternal power, the same as those who have gone before. What did Jesus do? Why; I do the things I saw my Father do when worlds came rolling into existence. My Father worked out his kingdom with fear and trembling, and I must do the same. . . .

"When you climb up a ladder, you must begin at the bottom, and ascend step by step, until you arrive at the top; and so it is with the principles of the Gospel—you must begin with the first, and go on until you learn all the principles of exaltation. But it will be a great while after you have passed through the veil before you will have learned them. It is not all to be comprehended in this world; it will be a great work to learn our salvation and exaltation even beyond the grave" (*Teachings of the Prophet Joseph Smith*, 346–48). See commentary on King Follett Discourse 6:2, page 1090.

Those Who Are Begotten through Christ Are the Church of the Firstborn
DOCTRINE AND COVENANTS 93:21–22

93:21 *In the beginning.* In scripture this phrase is consistently used to refer to our premortal estate.

The Firstborn. In 1909 the First Presidency stated: "Jesus . . . is the firstborn among all the sons of God—the first begotten in the spirit, and the only begotten in the flesh. He is our elder brother, and we, like Him are in the image of God" (Clark, *Messages*, 4:203).

93:22 *Church of the Firstborn.* See commentary on Doctrine and Covenants 77:11.

Christ Received a Fulness of All Truth, and Man by Obedience May Do Likewise
DOCTRINE AND COVENANTS 93:23–28

93:23 *Ye were also in the beginning with the Father.* The announcement here is that Jesus existed before this mortal life, and so did we—all the children of men lived first in a premortal estate. "I made the world, and men," the Lord declared, "before they were in the flesh" (Moses 6:51; v. 29).

93:24 Our word *true* is derived from the Old English *treowe*, which meant "faithful," "trustworthy," or "covenant" (Partridge, *Origins*, 740). To be true was to be "constant," "steadfast," and "faithful." The standard dictionary of Joseph Smith's day stated that "the primary sense of the root is to make close and fast, to set, or to stretch, strain, and thus make straight and close." (Webster, *Dictionary*, 1828). This understanding gives greater meaning to the testimony of Nephi, in which he speaks of the words of Christ as being "true and faithful" (2 Nephi 31:15), or to the testimony of the Lord himself in which he declares that the prophecies and promises in the Doctrine and Covenants "are true and faithful" (D&C 1:37). That is, they are trustworthy; and obedient acceptance of them constitutes a covenant with God that he cannot break (D&C 82:10).

In the Hellenistic or Greek tradition, *truth* comes from a root meaning "to be hidden" and came to signify the unveiling of reality. In Semitic tradition, however, it meant to be solid or stable; one who was truthful was one who could be trusted. For the Greek, the opposite of truth was error or deception. But for the household of faith, truth was light; and its opposite consisted of the breaking of covenants with God. Truth was something to be done rather than something to be learned. Thus, we find the Savior reasoning that he who does evil "hateth the light, neither cometh to the light," that his deeds might be hidden, while "he that *doeth* truth cometh to the light, that his deeds may be made manifest, that they are wrought in God" (John 3:20–21; emphasis added). Again, John writes: "God is light, and in him is no darkness at all. If we say that we have fellowship with him, and walk in darkness, we lie, and *do not* the truth" (1 John 1:5–6; emphasis added).

Of the Gospel writers, it is John who uses the word *truth* in its highest spiritual sense. John, for instance, preserves the Savior's self-characterization that he is "the way, the truth, and the life" and that no man can come unto the Father but through him (John 14:6). The testimony of John's Gospel is that Christ is light, that light is truth, that salvation is in truth, and that we obtain salvation by acquiring light and truth. Thus, salvation is the process of becoming Christlike; it is the process of learning to think as he thought, feel as he felt, and do as he did.

The scholar can define the gospel as "all truth," but the prophet cannot. Prophetic knowledge is not the result of abstract learning. It is not a mastery of theosophic principles or subtle theories. It is something found more naturally in service than in sequestered study. It is more the product of callused hands than of a furrowed brow. It is more the child of the simple heart than the sire of eloquence of speech. It is something that rests closer to the heart than to the intellect.

93:25 *Whatsoever is more or less than this is the spirit of that wicked one.* The idea here is that divine truth is neither to be embellished nor pruned. It is not in the province of man to add to or take from the gospel message. The revelation continues by stating that no man can receive the fulness of such truths without keeping the commandments. The person who keeps the commandments is promised that he receiveth "truth and light" until he is "glorified in truth and knoweth all things" (vv. 27–28). It is an experiential knowledge of which the revelation speaks. Just as we cannot describe colors to a man born blind, so we cannot convey the truths of heaven to those who have not been born of the Spirit.

If, by *truth*, we have in mind merely "accurate information," truth is as much the servant of sin as it is the friend of righteousness. As there are no wars in which brothers have not been called upon to fight each other, so the great conflict between the sons of darkness and the sons of light finds such *truth* (information) a weapon common to both armies. Soldiers in both camps quote scriptures, profess a love of God, and claim a heritage of dreams and revelations, of prophets and angels. Regarding angels, we know that the scriptures generally assume the responsibility to identify an angel's nature. This is particularly true of the Bible texts. The scriptural pattern is to say that "an angel of the Lord," "an angel of God," or "an angel of his presence" has appeared with a message. It is not enough that it be an angel; it must be an angel from the divine presence. So it is with truth. Truth alone has no salvation in it. Again, we note from the scriptural pattern that truth must have its proper companions. Common scriptural phrases include the following:

"goodness and truth"
"sincerity and truth"
"kindness and truth"
"mercy and truth"
"right and truth"
"peace and truth"
"light and truth"
"truth and meekness"
"truth and uprightness"
"faithfulness and truth"
"truth and righteousness"
"grace and truth"

"spirit and in truth"

"truth and soberness"

"truth in the law"

"truth and holiness"

"goodness, righteousness, and truth"

"grace, equity, and truth"

"wisdom, mercy, and truth"

Accurate information is one thing; the *truths* of salvation are entirely another. Those who interpret the marvelous statement "the glory of God is intelligence" to mean that salvation is found in living in harmony with correct principles have missed the point of the revelation. Let us read it again: "The glory of God is intelligence, *or, in other words, light and truth. Light and truth forsake that evil one*" (vv. 36–37; emphasis added). The *truths* of salvation do not stand alone. Paul said, "Neither is the man without the woman, neither the woman without the man, in the Lord" (1 Corinthians 11:11). It might also be said, "Neither is truth without light, nor light without truth, in the Lord." Joseph Smith taught that one cannot have faith without its "train of attendants"—meaning "apostles, prophets, evangelists, pastors, teachers, gifts, wisdom, knowledge, miracles, healings, tongues, interpretation of tongues, and so on. It may also be said that one cannot have truth without *its* train of attendants— meaning goodness, mercy, peace, uprightness, faithfulness, grace, holi- ness, light, and so on.

93:26 *He received a fulness of truth, yea, even of all truth.* Christ received the fulness of his Father, and so must we. Teaching this same principle, Paul said that Christ "gave some, apostles; and some, prophets; and some, evangelists; and some, pastors and teachers; for the perfecting of the saints, for the work of the ministry, for the edifying of the body of Christ: Till we all come in the unity of the faith, and of the knowledge of the Son of God, unto a perfect man, unto the measure of the stature of the fulness of Christ" (Ephesians 4:11–13). The salvation of which Paul here speaks to the Ephesian Saints is one in which they are to advance from grace to grace, obtaining a perfection in Christ or the "fulness of Christ" that they with him might enjoy the fulness of the Father as the present text suggests.

In John 3:36 we read, "He that believeth on the Son hath everlast- ing life: and he that believeth not the Son shall not see life; but the wrath of God abideth on him." The idea here being that salvation centers in our belief in Christ. We note an interesting amplification of the text in the

Joseph Smith Translation of this verse. There it reads: "And he who believeth on the Son hath everlasting life; *and shall receive of his fulness. But he who believeth not the Son, shall not receive of his fulness*; for the wrath of God is upon him" (emphasis added). This concept of salvation is expanded from that of belief to that of receiving or becoming as Christ and God are.

Man Was in the Beginning with God
DOCTRINE AND COVENANTS 93:29–32

93:29 *Man was also in the beginning with God.* Reference is to our first estate, or the premortal life, where we were schooled and trained for the experiences that would be ours in mortality.

Intelligence, or the light of truth, was not created or made. "Some of our writers have endeavored to explain what an intelligence is," observed Joseph Fielding Smith, "but to do so is futile, for we have never been given any insight into this matter beyond what the Lord has fragmentarily revealed. We know, however, that there is something called intelligence which always existed. It is the real eternal part of man, which was not created nor made. This intelligence combined with the spirit constitutes a spiritual identity or individual" (*Progress of Man,* 11).

The God of the Latter-day Saints, unlike the God of the sectarian world, cannot and did not create anything out of nothing. In the creative act he gave form and order to extant element (D&C 131:6–7; King Follett Discourse 10:3, page 1095).

93:30 *All truth is independent in that sphere in which God has placed it.* Once God has created a particular thing and placed it in its intended sphere of activity, it functions independently. It needs no supervision. We take as an illustration the law of gravity. Having been designed by God to function in a particular way on this earth, it does so in an absolutely consistent manner. It remains unchanged by the light of day or the dark of night. It functions with indifference to the season of the year or the attention or lack of attention given to it. Neither righteousness nor wickedness has any effect on it. Unlike the mechanical devices of men, it will not wear out nor do we need to concern ourselves with the possibility of it breaking down. All truths of salvation function with the same undeviating consistency. They are irrevocable; when we comply with them we have claim upon their blessings, which no power in heaven or on earth can deny to us. To violate them is to be left without such a promise (D&C 130:20–21; 82:10).

Otherwise there is no existence. The existence of all things requires opposites. Explaining this principle, Lehi said: "For it must needs be, that there is an opposition in all things. If not so . . . righteousness could not be brought to pass, neither wickedness, neither holiness nor misery, neither good nor bad. Wherefore, all things must needs be a compound in one; wherefore, if it should be one body it must needs remain as dead, having no life neither death, nor corruption nor incorruption, happiness nor misery, neither sense nor insensibility. Wherefore, it must needs have been created for a thing of naught; wherefore there would have been no purpose in the end of its creation. Wherefore, this thing must needs destroy the wisdom of God and his eternal purposes, and also the power, and the mercy, and the justice of God" (2 Nephi 2:11–12).

This verse appears to be a summary statement of the principles taught by Lehi in 2 Nephi 2:11–13.

93:31 *That which was from the beginning is plainly manifest unto them.* No one in this mortal sphere will ever be taught any principle of truth that was not first known to him or her in the premortal estate. Individuals are not converted, for example, in the sense that they surrender old views for new and better ones. What happens is that the missionaries declare the truths of salvation to people who innately respond by saying, "Yes, that is right! It is what I have always believed." They do so because its truths have been planted in their hearts and, upon hearing them again, it is like recognizing an old friend. The conversion process would be better described as "a coming home," "an awakening," or "a distant memory." The gospel brings with it a familiar spirit attended with warm feelings, which take us back to a time long before our births when we were first taught its principles and vowed to live by them.

93:32 *To reject the light is to be left with darkness.* To reject the truth is to be left with falsehood. To reject the blessings of heaven is to be left with condemnation.

The Elements Are Eternal, and Man May Receive a Fulness of Joy in the Resurrection
DOCTRINE AND COVENANTS 93:33–35

93:33 *For man is spirit.* The Gospel of John says, "God is a spirit" (John 4:24). A more accurate or literal translation would be "God is spirit," in the same sense "man is spirit," meaning that both are spirit beings. This does not preclude the fact that both have bodies of flesh and bones.

The elements are eternal. The Prophet Joseph Smith declared, "Anything created cannot be eternal; and earth, water, etc., had their existence in an elementary state, from eternity" (*History of the Church,* 3:387; D&C 93:29; 131:6–7).

Spirit and element, inseparably connected, receive a fulness of joy. Only in a resurrected state—that is, the inseparable union of body and spirit—can we become as God is, and only in the state of godhood can we experience the fulness of joy (D&C 138:50).

93:35 *The elements are the tabernacle of God.* This declaration refutes the sectarian heresy that God is without body or parts. All living things have body, parts, form, and substance.

Man is the tabernacle of God. Man is in the image and likeness of his creator. As God is a personage of tabernacle, so are we.

The Glory of God Is Intelligence
DOCTRINE AND COVENANTS 93:36–37

93:36 This text is often used out of context to sustain the idea that the glory of God is in obtaining an education or gaining knowledge. Intelligence as used here is a synonym for "light and truth." Thus, what the text is really telling us is that the glory of God is found in righteousness, purity, and goodness, which virtues stand independent of the learning of men. It is the light of the Spirit to which reference is made here, light that can be had only by obedience to the order of heaven.

93:37 It was Brigham Young who said that light and darkness will never meet, that Christ and Satan will never shake hands (*Journal of Discourses,* 1:364).

Children Are Innocent before God Because of the Redemption of Christ
DOCTRINE AND COVENANTS 93:38–40

93:38 All the spirit children of God were innocent at the time of their spirit birth and again at the time of their entry into mortal life. This means that they were free from guilt or sin. At the time of birth, be it as a spirit or into mortality, the infant child knows neither good nor evil. As the infant becomes a child and the child an adult, innocence is lost in the countless choices that must be made. Alma describes the premortal estate as one in which both good and evil existed and in which all were called upon to exercise faith (Alma 13:3–9). A great division came among the spirits when Lucifer rebelled against God and sought to depose him and destroy the plan of salvation. A third part of the hosts of heaven chose to follow him. These were cast out of heaven, losing the right to obtain a body or the blessings of salvation. Those that kept their first estate—that is, those who were true to God—were granted the privilege of mortality. All such were born into a state of innocence predicated on the atonement of Christ.

93:39 The two greatest enemies of light and truth are disobedience and false traditions. Disobedience causes the light to withdraw; and, thus, what truths are left become distorted by dark shadows. "He that repents not," the Lord said, "from him shall be taken even the light which he has received; for my Spirit shall not always strive with man, saith the Lord of Hosts" (D&C 1:33). False traditions are also antithetical to truth, providing a convenient place to hide from the responsibility to listen, see, and know, thus ostensibly freeing the spiritually lethargic from the responsibility that inevitably follows knowledge of the truth.

The Leading Brethren Are Commanded to Set Their Families in Order
DOCTRINE AND COVENANTS 93:41–53

93:41–50 There is no office or calling in the Church and kingdom of God that excuses either a father or mother from their responsibilities as a parent. "'No other success can compensate for failure in the home,'" said David O. McKay (quoted in Conference Report, April 1935, 116). Harold B. Lee said, "Remember always that the most important of the Lord's work you and I will ever do will be within the walls of our own homes" (*Stand Ye in Holy Places*, 255).

In this revelation all three members of the First Presidency are chastened for their failure to properly teach their own children. Paul admonished Timothy that a bishop must be "one that ruleth well his own house, having his children in subjection with all gravity; (for if a man know not how to rule his own house, how shall he take care of the church of God?)" (1 Timothy 3:4–5).

93:53 *Hasten to translate my scriptures*. At this time Joseph Smith was engaged in the inspired translation of the Old Testament. Earlier, he had interrupted that effort to complete the translation of the New Testament. On 2 February 1833 he began to translate the books between Proverbs and Malachi. At present we are unable to determine exactly where in the Old Testament the Prophet Joseph Smith was working when this revelation was received. That same day, the Lord instructed that a house be built "for the work of the printing of the translation of my scriptures" (D&C 94:10). Some two months later, 2 July 1833, the First Presidency wrote from Kirtland to the brethren in Zion: "We are exceedingly fatigued, owing to a great press of business. We this day finished the translating of the Scriptures, for which we returned gratitude to our Heavenly Father" (Smith, *History of the Church*, 1:368).

Obtain a knowledge of history, and of countries. See commentary on Doctrine and Covenants 88:77–80.

DOCTRINE AND COVENANTS 94

DATE: 6 MAY 1833
PLACE: KIRTLAND, OHIO

On 23 March 1833 a council was called to appoint a committee to purchase land in Kirtland to which the Saints could gather in a city-stake of Zion. The committee was appointed and some large farms purchased (Smith, *History of the Church*, 1:335–36). Once the land had been purchased, a city plat was surveyed, and the Saints began to gather to it. Two days before this revelation was given, Joseph Smith wrote: "A conference of High Priests assembled in Kirtland, to take into consideration the necessity of building a school house, for the accommodation of the Elders, who should come together to receive instruction preparatory for their missions, and ministry, according to a revelation on that subject, given March 8, 1833 [D&C 90], and by unanimous voice of the conference; Hyrum Smith, Jared Carter, and Reynolds Cahoon were appointed a committee to obtain subscriptions, for the purpose of erecting such a building. (*History of the Church*, 1:342–43).

The building designed to house the "school of the prophets" (D&C 90:7) or "the school of mine apostles," as the Lord called it, was the Kirtland Temple.

A Commandment Relative to the Erection of a House for the Work of the Presidency
DOCTRINE AND COVENANTS 94:1–9

94:1 *Stake of Zion.* See commentary on Doctrine and Covenants 82:13.

The city of the stake of Zion. Each city of the stake of Zion was to be built according to the pattern of the city of Zion in Jackson County, Missouri. Therefore, like the center place in Independence, a stake begins with Saints gathering together in strength, enabling them to build houses for the purpose of furthering the work of the Lord. The Prophet Joseph

Smith sent a plat of the city of the New Jerusalem to Independence, Missouri, which served as a model for the cities of the stakes of Zion. He explained that the city stake of the Saints would center on a fifteen-acre block containing "twenty-four buildings to supply them with houses for public worship and schools. These buildings will be temples," each of which was to be of identical dimensions and two stories high. Ten-acre blocks containing twenty equal lots for homes were to extend from the central block, filling the city until it equaled one mile square and providing for fifteen to twenty thousand people. "Lands on the north and south of the city will be laid off for barns and stables for the use of the city," wrote the Prophet, "so there will be no barns or stables in the city among the homes of the people." This allowed everyone, families of businessmen and farmers alike, to enjoy the benefits of public schools, social refinements, worship, and ease of access to commerce. "When this square is thus laid off and supplied, lay off another in the same way," wrote the Prophet to those to whom the city plat was sent, "and so fill up the world in these last days, and let every man live in the city, for this is the city of Zion" (Roberts, *Comprehensive History of the Church*, 1:311–12).

Beginning at my house. The city was to be laid out with the temple as the starting point, and the rest of the city being built in relation to it. This pattern was followed by Brigham Young in laying out Salt Lake City. He first identified the spot upon which the temple would be built and paralleled all the streets out from what is called Temple Square.

94:3 *A house for the presidency.* This building was intended to be the administrative headquarters of the Church. Here the First Presidency would have a place to conduct their business and to communicate with the Lord. Today, administrative buildings in Salt Lake City fill this function, while ward houses and stake centers provide offices for stake presidencies and bishoprics to accomplish similar purposes in the discharge of their duties.

94:4–5 These dimensions are the same as those of the Kirtland Temple (D&C 95:15–17).

94:6 *Dedicated unto the Lord from the foundation thereof.* To be dedicated to the Lord is to be consecrated or set apart for his purpose. Thus, the "temples"—those buildings to be used as schools or for other public purposes in a city of Zion—were to be dedicated "from the foundation" or from their very inception to the purposes of the Lord. Formal dedicatory services are held at the ground breaking and completion of such buildings. There is also a formal ceremony for the laying of the corner-stone at the dedication of temples.

According to the order of the priesthood. "If the strict order of the Priest-hood were carried out in the building of Temples," explained the Prophet Joseph Smith, "the first stone would be laid at the south-east cor-ner, by the First Presidency of the Church. The south-west corner should be laid next. The third, or north-west corner next; and the fourth, or north-east corner last. The first Presidency should lay the south-east cor-ner stone and dictate who are the proper persons to lay the other corner stones.

"If a Temple is built at a distance, and the First Presidency are not present, then the Quorum of the Twelve Apostles are the persons to dic-tate the order for that Temple; and in the absence of the Twelve Apostles, then the Presidency of the Stake will lay the south-east corner stone; the Melchisedec Priesthood laying the corner stones on the east side of the Temple, and the Lesser Priesthood those on the west side" (*History of the Church,* 4:331).

94:8 *Ye shall not suffer any unclean thing to come in unto it.* This is the first reference in the Restoration that entrance to sacred buildings is to be restricted to worthy individuals. The leaders of the Church have taken this responsibility seriously. One purpose of temple recommends is to meet the obligations the Lord has placed on the Saints to see that the unworthy do not inhibit the Spirit of God from being poured out on those in the Lord's house.

My presence. The Spirit of the Lord is referred to in this verse as his glory and presence. Anciently, the presence of the Lord was marked by the fire of the burning bush or a bright cloud that attended the appear-ance of the Lord and dwelt between the mercy seat of the ark of the covenant in the Holy of Holies (Exodus 3:1–6; 24:15–18; Leviticus 16:2).

A Printing House to Be Built

DOCTRINE AND COVENANTS 94:10–12

94:10–12 The printing office described was never built. The Lord commanded that before this or the office for the presidency be built, the Kirtland Temple be finished. Debts, apostasy, and persecution pre-vented any further building in Kirtland in fulfillment of this revelation. However, before the temple in Kirtland could be finished, it was decided in council "to erect a house for the printing office, which is to be thirty by thirty-eight on the ground; the first story to be occupied for the School of the Prophets this winter [1833], and the upper story for the printing press" (Smith, *History of the Church*, 1:418), located near the temple. The reason for this decision appears to be the destruction of the printing office and theft of the Church's press in Independence, Missouri (see commentary on D&C 98). Stewardship for the printing office was given to Oliver Cowdery and Frederick G. Williams (D&C 104:28–29).

"The second lot south of this building was to be dedicated for the building of another house where the printing for the Church could be done and the translation of the scriptures, on which the Prophet had been working off and on for many months, could be published. . . . This house also was to be dedicated to the service of the Lord, and set apart for the printing" (Smith, *Church History and Modern Revelation*, 1:404).

94:11–12 See commentary on verses 4 through 6 for similar instructions regarding the office of the presidency and the printing office.

Certain Inheritances Are Assigned
Doctrine and Covenants 94:13–17

94:15 *To be a committee to build mine houses.* Hyrum Smith, Reynolds Cahoon, and Jared Carter were appointed as a committee to oversee the completion of the "temples" or buildings spoken of in this revelation. To aid them in their assignment, the Lord gave them land adjacent to the temple lot.

Because the building of the Kirtland Temple exhausted the means of the Church in Kirtland, the office for the First Presidency and the building to print the Joseph Smith Translation were never built.

94:16 The temple in Kirtland was to be built before the house for the presidency or the printing office.

DOCTRINE AND COVENANTS 95

DATE: 1 JUNE 1833
PLACE: KIRTLAND, OHIO

On 1 June 1833 the Prophet Joseph Smith wrote that "great preparations were making to commence a house of the Lord; and notwithstanding the Church was poor, yet our unity, harmony and charity abounded to strengthen us to do the commandments of God. The building of the house of the Lord in Kirtland was a matter that continued to increase in its interest in the hearts of the brethren, and the building committee issued . . . [a] circular to the different branches of the Church" calling for contributions to build the temple in Kirtland (*History of the Church,* 1:349). That same day, by revelation, the Lord chastened the Saints for their neglect in building his house that he might fulfill the promise of the Father unto them.

The Saints Are Chastened for Their Failure to Build the House of the Lord
DOCTRINE AND COVENANTS 95:1–6

95:1 *Whom I love I also chasten.* To chasten in love is a divine characteristic born of genuine love and concern for others. It is required of all parents that they discipline their children. So it is that when we err, the Lord chastens us. The Lord stated in the preface to the Book of Commandments that his revelations were given in part to make known error, offer instruction, and chasten those that sin, that they might repent (D&C 1:25–27). We ought to take to heart the words of Eliphaz to Job: "Behold, happy is the man whom God correcteth: therefore despise not thou the chastening of the Almighty" (Job 5:17).

Teaching this principle, Spencer W. Kimball said, "We are concerned that too many times the interviewing leader in his personal sympathies for the transgressor, and in his love perhaps for the family of the transgressor, is inclined to waive the discipline which that transgressor demands.

"Too often a transgressor is forgiven and all penalties waived when that person should have been disfellowshipped or excommunicated. Too often a sinner is disfellowshipped when he or she should have been excommunicated. . . .

"Do you remember what was said by the prophet Alma? 'Now,' he said, 'repentance could not come unto men except there were a punishment.' (Alma 42:16.)

"Ponder on that for a moment. Have you realized that? There can be no forgiveness without real and total repentance, and there can be no repentance without punishment. This is as eternal as is the soul. . . .

"Please remember these things when somebody comes before you who has broken the laws of God.

"It is so easy to let our sympathies carry us out of proportion; and when a man has committed sin, he must suffer. It's an absolute requirement—not by the bishop—but it's a requirement by nature and by the very part of a man" (Conference Report, April 1975, 116).

Brigham Young said: "At times I may to many of the brethren appear to be severe. I sometimes chasten them; but it is because I wish them to so live that the power of God, like a flame of fire, will dwell within them and be round about them. These are my feelings and desires" (*Journal of Discourses*, 8:62).

With the chastisement I prepare a way for their deliverance. Leaun G. Otten and C. Max Caldwell explained: "We learn from this revelation that when the chastisement ceases, the chastiser is responsible to show the one who has erred how to proceed to correct his mistake. . . . It is one thing to tell a person that he is wrong. It is quite another to show him how to do things right.

"When the saints failed to begin to build the Kirtland temple, the Lord not only chastised them for their failure, but He also revealed to them how to proceed in the accomplishment of their assigned task (see D&C 95:13–17)" (*Sacred Truths*, 2:151).

95:4 *I design to prepare mine apostles.* "Apostles" as used in this text has reference to those who go forth at the direction of the Lord to testify of his restored gospel. It does not refer to the office of apostle, which had not yet been restored. It was in the Kirtland Temple that the elders were instructed in the principles of the gospel and endowed with the power of

God. Both experiences were fundamental to their preparation to represent the Lord.

Prune my vineyard for the last time. This phrase alludes to Zenos's allegory of the olive trees. The last pruning of the vineyard represented the final call to Israel to return to the true Messiah before the burning of the vineyard, or the burning of the wicked at the second coming of Christ (Jacob 5).

That I may bring to pass my strange act. The language is that of Isaiah (Isaiah 28:21–22). It was quoted by Moroni to Joseph Smith on their first meeting. The idea that it conveys is that the gospel will appear "strange," and the things the Lord does or has his people do will appear as a "strange act" to those so given up to the things of the world that they have lost all spiritual discernment or sensitivity.

That I may pour out my Spirit upon all flesh. The Spirit testifies of truth. Thus, the Lord pours out his Spirit when the gospel is taught. Given that the truth of the gospel must fill the earth, the Lord through his servant Joel said, "And it shall come to pass afterward, that I will pour out my spirit upon all flesh; and your sons and your daughters shall prophesy, your old men shall dream dreams, your young men shall see visions: And also upon the servants and upon the handmaids in those days will I pour out my spirit" (Joel 2:28–29).

95:5–6 *But few of them are chosen.* See commentary on Doctrine and Covenants 121:34.

95:6 *Walking in darkness at noon-day.* The rebuke here centers in the failure to complete the temple in Kirtland. Again, the temple was to perform two important functions for those called to the ministry: (1) they were to attend the School of the Prophets, where they could be more thoroughly instructed in the doctrines of the kingdom, and (2) they were to be endowed with power from on high. To proceed without such light would be to walk in "darkness at noon-day."

Christ Is the Lord of Sabaoth
DOCTRINE AND COVENANTS 95:7–10

95:7 *The Lord of Sabaoth.* The Hebrew meaning of Sabaoth is literally "hosts." Often the word is used in conjunction with hosts of soldiers organized for war. Bible scholars explain that "since the realms of earth and heaven were closely related in ancient thought, it was believed that the same kind of organized military array was found in the heavenly sphere" (*Interpreter's Dictionary of the Bible*, 2:655). This text expands our understanding of those who marched in the heavenly army. It describes the Lord of Sabaoth as the "creator of the first day, the beginning and the end." In earlier revelations Christ is referred to as "the Great I Am, Alpha and Omega, the beginning and the end, the same which looked upon the wide expanse of eternity, and all the seraphic hosts of heaven, before the world was made" (D&C 38:1). Again, we are told to give "ear to him who laid the foundation of the earth, who made the heavens and all the hosts thereof" (D&C 45:1). We would understand the heavenly host to be the righteous spirits who had marched in the army of the Lord against Lucifer and his legions (D&C 29:36).

95:8–9 *I command you to tarry, even as mine apostles at Jerusalem.* See commentary on Doctrine and Covenants 39:15, "And from thence men shall go forth into all nations."

95:10 *The school of the prophets.* This school was organized by command of the Lord on 23 January 1833 (D&C 88:127–41). The brethren involved met in a room above the Newel K. Whitney store in Kirtland, Ohio. It was here that the Lectures on Faith were given.

The House Is to Be Dedicated As a Place of Worship and for the School of the Apostles
DOCTRINE AND COVENANTS 95:11–17

95:11 *If you keep my commandments you shall have power to build it.* The building of temples is never without opposition. From the laying of the foundation of the Lord's house in Kirtland to the present day, this has always been the case. The announcement of the temple in Missouri had the anticipated effect: Satan unleashed his wrath against the Saints there. Mobs drove the Saints from their property in Missouri and effectively stopped any work on the temple. Those in Kirtland and the surrounding regions, including the Prophet Joseph Smith, were called upon to march to Zion, where they would reclaim the lands from which their fellow Saints had been driven. This delayed the building of the temple there. Upon the return of those that traveled to Zion, the Saints in Kirtland had to exert every effort to accomplish the task given to them by the Lord to build his house.

At this time the brethren were laboring night and day to build the house of the Lord. Heber C. Kimball recorded: "Our women were engaged in spinning and knitting in order to clothe those who were laboring at the building; and the Lord only knows the scenes of poverty, tribulation and distress which we passed through to accomplish it. My wife had toiled all summer in lending her aid towards its accomplishment. She took a hundred pounds of wool to spin on shares, which, with the assistance of a girl, she spun, in order to furnish clothing for those engaged in building the temple; and although she had the privilege of keeping half the quantity of wool for herself, as a recompense for her labor, she did not reserve even so much as would make a pair of stockings, but gave it for those who were laboring at the house of the Lord. She spun and wove, and got the cloth dressed and cut and made up into garments, and gave them to the laborers on the temple. Almost all the sisters in Kirtland labored in knitting, sewing, spinning, etc., for the same purpose; while we went up to Missouri to endeavor to reinstate our brethren on the lands from which they had been driven.

"Elder Rigdon, when addressing the brethren upon the importance of building this house, spake to this effect: That we should use every effort to accomplish this building by the time appointed; if we did the Lord would accept it at our hands; and on it depends the salvation of the Church, and also of the world. Looking at the sufferings and poverty of the Church, he frequently went upon the walls of the building, both by night and day, and wept, crying aloud to the Almighty to send means whereby we might accomplish the building.

"After we returned from our journey to the West, the whole Church united in this great undertaking, and every man lent a helping hand. Those who had not teams went to work in the stone quarry and prepared the stones for drawing to the house.

"The Prophet being our foreman, would put on his tow frock and tow pantaloons and go into the quarry. The Presidency, High Priests, and Elders all alike assisting. Those who had teams assisted in drawing the stone to the house. These all laboring one day in the week, brought as many stones to the house as supplied the masons through the whole week. We continued in this manner until the walls of the house were reared. The committee who were appointed by revelation to superintend the building were Hyrum Smith, Reynolds Cahoon, and Jared Carter. They used every exertion in their power to forward the work" (Whitney, *Life of Heber C. Kimball*, 67–69). The Lord was true to his promise, and the Saints were able to finish the temple in Kirtland before Satan again exerted his influence, and they were driven from Ohio.

95:12 The Savior told his disciples, "If ye love me, keep my commandments" (John 14:15). Their love for him would be measured by their obedience. In turn he said, "He that hath my commandments, and keepeth them, he it is that loveth me: and he that loveth me shall be loved of my Father, and I will love him, and will manifest myself to him" (John 14:21). "He that is righteous is favored of God," Nephi declared (1 Nephi 17:35).

95:14 *Built after the manner which I shall show unto three of you.* If the house is the Lord's, the design must be his also. Anciently, he commanded Moses regarding the holy tabernacle, saying: "Let them make me a sanctuary; that I may dwell among them. According to all that I shew thee, after the pattern of the tabernacle" (Exodus 25:8–9). In fulfillment of the Lord's promise, the First Presidency were shown in vision the temple they had been commanded to build. Concerning the construction, Truman O. Angell, an early convert to the Church, recorded in his journal: "About this time Frederick G. Williams, one of President Smith's counselors, came into the Temple when the following dialogue took place in my presence:

"Carpenter Rolph said, 'Doctor, what do you think of the House?' He answered, 'It looks to me like the pattern precisely.' He then related the following:

"'Joseph received the word of the Lord for him to take his two counselors, [Frederick G.] Williams and [Sidney] Rigdon, and come before the Lord and He would show them the plan or model of the House to be built. We went upon our knees, called on the Lord, and the Building [Kirtland Temple] appeared within viewing distance. I being the first to discover it. Then all of us viewed it together. After we had taken a good look at the exterior, the Building seemed to come right over us, and the Makeup of this Hall seemed to coincide with what I there saw to a minutia'" ("His Journal," [1967] 198).

The Prophet Joseph Smith's mother, Lucy Mack Smith, wrote regarding a council meeting held to discuss the building of the house of the Lord in Kirtland: "In this council Joseph requested each of the brethren to rise and give his views, and when they were through, he would give his opinion concerning the matter. They all spoke. Some thought that it would be better to build a frame house. Others said that a frame house was too costly, and the majority concluded upon putting up a log house and made their calculations about what they could do towards building it. Joseph rose and reminded them that they were not making a house for themselves or any other man, but a house for God. 'And shall we, brethren, build a house for our God of logs? No, I have a better plan than that. I have the plan of the house of the Lord, given by himself. You will see by this the difference between our calculations and his idea of things.'

"He then gave them the full plan of the house of the Lord at Kirtland" (*History of Joseph Smith*, 1996, 321–22).

95:15–17 The temple at Kirtland was mainly a house of worship. Ordinances such as endowments, sealings, baptisms, and other vicarious work for the dead were not revealed until the Saints were commanded to build a temple in Nauvoo, Illinois. In addition, the Kirtland Temple was built that the keys for performing these ordinances might be restored. The physical layout of the temple met the purpose for which it was built. The lower part of the Lord's house in Kirtland, or the main floor, was used for church services similar to the chapels in church buildings today. Congregations met to worship and partake of the sacrament. The congregational seating of the building followed the custom of the day, which included enclosed pews. The benches in the pews were movable, allowing the congregation to sit facing either direction. The distinction that separates this building apart from other church meetinghouses is the three tiers of pulpits at each end of the inner court, each row set a little higher than the previous one. In addition, the pulpits had three seats behind an enclosed breastwork, with a fourth row on ground level behind a hinged table that extended when lifted and upon which the emblems of the sacrament were placed. The west pulpits were designated for the presiding officers of the Higher, or Melchizedek, Priesthood. Those on the east were for the presidencies of the Lesser, or Aaronic, Priesthood. The breastwork of the pulpits at each end had lettering that designated the proper seating for the various offices.

The second floor had pulpits at each end similar to those on the main floor. This was a visible designation that the activities of the school held there were under the direction of the priesthood (D&C 90:7, 13–15). It was unusual for the times to have a school as part of a church building. This floor served a missionary training center at which secular as well as religious instruction was offered. The third floor was in the attic of the building. It was divided into five rooms, which were utilized as offices for the presiding quorums and officers. See commentary on Doctrine and Covenants 88:77–81.

95:16 *Dedicated unto me*. Elder Boyd K. Packer has written: "Consider the definition of the word *dedication* as it applies to temples. When a developer prepares a tract of land for the building of homes, he makes provision for streets. But the streets will not be the property of home-owners. These are deeded to the community. The process of deeding that property to the community is called dedication. A street that is 'dedicated' becomes the property of the community, which has some responsibility to maintain it and to set the conditions under which the public might use it. In simple terms, the developer gives his ownership of that property to the community.

"Something similar to that happens when we dedicate a temple. While members of the Church may have contributed the money to build the temple and may themselves have labored to construct it, it is not theirs once it is dedicated. The dedication of a temple, in a real way, gives the building and all of the landscaping and structures related to the temple site to the Lord. The temple itself becomes literally the house of the Lord. The word *temple* comes from the word *templum*, which is defined as the abode of Deity or simply the house of the Lord.

"Elder James E. Talmage defines the temple as 'a building constructed for and exclusively devoted to sacred rites and ceremonies' (Talmage, *The House of the Lord*, 1).

"After a temple is dedicated we do not feel we own it. It is the Lord's house. He directs the conditions under which it may be used. He has revealed the ordinances that should be performed therein and has estab-lished the standards and conditions under which we may participate in them" (*Holy Temple*, 34–35).

Orson Pratt explained: "By and by we will have Temples, with a great many things contained in them which we now have not; for with them, as with all other things, the Lord begins little by little; he does not reveal everything all at once. He gave the pattern of these things in Kirtland, Ohio, as the beginning; but there were not rooms for the wash-ings, no rooms such as we have now, and such as were prepared in the Nauvoo Temple; and in other respects, there was something added to the Nauvoo Temple. Why; Because we had greater experience, and were prepared for greater things. There was no font in the basement story of the Kirtland Temple, for baptismal purposes in behalf of the dead? Why not! Because that principle was not revealed. But in the Nauvoo Temple this font was prepared, which was something in advance of the Kirtland Temple. We have, of late, constructed a Temple at St. George. Blessings have been administered in that Temple, that were totally unknown in the two former Temples, namely, endowments for the dead. Again, by and by, we build a Temple in Jackson County, Missouri. Will it be built according to the pattern of our present Temples? No. There will be, according to the progress of this people, and the knowledge they receive, and the greatness of the work that is before them, many things, pertaining to the pattern, that will then be given, which will differ materially, or will be, at least, in addition to that which is in these Temples now built. I think if you will go and search in the Church Historian's office, you will find a plan of a Temple, that is to be built in Jackson County, which will be very different from the little Temples we now build" (*Journal of Discourses*, 19:19).

95:17 *Son Ahman*. See commentary on Doctrine and Covenants 78:20.

DOCTRINE AND COVENANTS 96

DATE: 4 JUNE 1833
PLACE: KIRTLAND, OHIO

As more and more Saints gathered to the Kirtland area, the need arose to purchase lands for their settlement. In April 1833 the Church purchased a 103-acre farm from Peter French. This farm extended south from the Kirtland flats, near the Newel K. Whitney home and store, and rose up the hill to the lot upon which the Kirtland Temple now stands. The Prophet Joseph Smith wrote: "A conference of High Priests convened in the translating room in Kirtland . . . and took into consideration how the French farm should be [distributed]. The conference could not agree who should take charge of it, but all agreed to inquire of the Lord; accordingly we received the following" (*History of the Church*, 1:352). The revelation deals with concerns that were specific to the historical context in which it was received.

The Kirtland Stake of Zion Is to Be Made Strong
DOCTRINE AND COVENANTS 96:1

96:1 *This stake that I have set for the strength of Zion.* In this scriptural imagery Zion is likened to a tent with stakes as its support. If the stakes are driven securely into the ground the stake will be secure. The expression comes from Isaiah, who wrote, "Look upon Zion, the city of our solemnities: thine eyes shall see Jerusalem a quiet habitation, a tabernacle that shall not be taken down; not one of the stakes thereof shall ever be removed, neither shall any of the cords thereof be broken" (Isaiah 33:20). And again the ancient prophet wrote, "Enlarge the place of thy tent, and let them stretch forth the curtains of thine habitations: spare not, lengthen thy cords, and strengthen thy stakes" (Isaiah 54:2).

Responding to the misuse of this imagery among the Saints, Joseph Fielding Smith reminded us: "Isaiah speaks of Zion as a tent, or tabernacle, having in mind the Tabernacle which was built and carried in the wilderness in the days of Moses, and the cords are the binding cables and extend from the tent, or tabernacle, to the stakes which are fastened in the ground. Now the Lord revealed that Zion was to be built and surrounding her would be the stakes helping to bind and keep her in place. This figure of speech has almost been lost through the intervening years, but it retains its significance, or beauty. To speak of Zion, the New Jerusalem, or even that section where the city will be built, as a stake of Zion, is a sad mistake. Zion is the tent, the stakes of Zion are the binding pegs that support her. Zion, therefore, cannot be a stake, it would be as improper to call a tent a stake as to apply this term to Zion" (*Church History and Modern Revelation*, 1:321–22). See commentary on Doctrine and Covenants 94:1.

The Bishop Is to Divide the Inheritances for the Saints
DOCTRINE AND COVENANTS 96:2–5

96:2 Newel K. Whitney was the bishop in Kirtland and as such would have responsibility there similar to that of Edward Partridge, who was the bishop of the Church in Independence, Missouri. They were the only two bishops in the Church at that time and functioned in their respective stakes much as the presiding bishop would today. See commentary on Doctrine and Covenants 58:17.

96:4 *Mine order, for the purpose of bringing forth my word.* The reference is to the Literary Firm, which was composed of Church leaders given stewardship over the revelations and their publication. The needs of those who labored for the Literary Firm were to be provided for so that their labors could continue expeditiously. See commentary on Doctrine and Covenants 70:3.

96:5 *My word should go forth unto the children of men.* The greatest of truths are of no value as long as they remain unknown. It is the primary responsibility of the Church and its members to do all within their power to share the truths of the restored gospel. This makes the publication of the revelations of the Restoration of paramount importance.

Preaching of the word of the Lord has a great "tendency to lead the people to do that which [is] just—yea, it [has] more powerful effect upon the minds of the people than the sword, or anything else" (Alma 31:5). Likewise, the Spirit of God attends the written word and is able to influence readers to do good.

John Johnson Is to Be a Member of the United Order
DOCTRINE AND COVENANTS 96:6–9

96:6 *My servant John Johnson.* Prior to this revelation, the Prophet Joseph Smith and his wife, Emma, had lived with John and his wife, Elsa, on their farm in Hiram, Ohio. It was on this farm that the leading elders of the Church met in conference and determined to publish a selection of the revelations which had been received, known as the Book of Commandments (D&C 67). It was there that Joseph Smith and Sidney Rigdon received the visions of the three degrees of glory while engaged in the translation of the Bible (D&C 76) and were later tarred and feathered. See commentary on Doctrine and Covenants 78:9.

96:7 *He is a descendant of Joseph.* Reference is to Joseph of Egypt, who received the promise that it would be his posterity that would assume the responsibility to gather Israel in the last days and who would lead them again to the temple of the Lord and the covenants that God had made with their fathers (Deuteronomy 33:13–17; JST Genesis 50:24–38; Isaiah 2:2–3; D&C 133:26–34).

96:8 *He should become a member of the order.* The order of which John Johnson was to become a member was composed of some of the leading elders of the Church and was referred to as the united order, or United Firm. Members of this order oversaw Church-owned properties. As members of the order, they covenanted to consecrate their surplus property and business profits for the poor and needy of the Church. See commentary on Doctrine and Covenants 78:3–4.

96:9 *He shall seek diligently to take away incumbrances.* At this time, as indicated in the introduction, the Church had negotiated the purchase of a farm from Peter French, which included a house or inn. The Lord commanded John Johnson to supply funds to help pay the debt the United Firm incurred in the purchase of the farm.

This simple passage in the Doctrine and Covenants had a profound influence in the life of John Johnson and the history of the Church. John gave liberally of his means for the building of the kingdom and eventually sold his home and farm in Hiram, Ohio, as part of honoring the covenant he had made as a member of the order. His offerings were combined with the money of the order and used to pay the mortgage on the Peter French farm. It was upon a portion of this land that the Kirtland Temple was built. This temple and the resulting blessings, namely the preparatory endowment ordinances (washings and anointings), many great spiritual manifestations, and the long awaited restoration of priesthood keys held by Moses, Elias, and Elijah were made possible due, in part, to this one man's offering.

The house named among you. Refers to the Peter French Inn, located on the Kirtland flats on the lot south of Newel K. Whitney's home.

Doctrine and Covenants 97

DATE: 2 AUGUST 1833
PLACE: KIRTLAND, OHIO

On 20 July 1833 an armed mob, approved by the state Lieutenant
Governor Lilburn W. Boggs, demanded that all Mormons remove from
Jackson County, Missouri. They ransacked the home of William W.
Phelps and destroyed the unbound sheets of the Book of Commandments
that were in the printing office above his home. The printing press was
destroyed, and Brother Phelps's personal belongings were plundered.
Bishop Edward Partridge and another member, Charles Allen, were taken
into the county courthouse square where they were stripped of their clothing, tarred, and feathered. Sidney Gilbert was forced to agree to close his
mercantile store. Three days later, leaders among the Saints signed a
treaty with the mob that they would leave the county.

During the summer of 1833 the Saints in Kirtland had devoted much
of their attention to building the temple, as commanded by the Lord. On
23 July, the very day that the treaty was signed in Missouri, "the corner
stones of the Lord's House were laid in Kirtland, after the order of the
Holy Priesthood" (Smith, *History of the Church*, 1:400). The Prophet, who
was in Kirtland, was without knowledge of what was happening in
Missouri. On 2 August he received the following revelation, which
warned the inhabitants of Zion to observe the commandments or be visited "with sore affliction, with pestilence, with plague, with sword, with
vengeance, with devouring fire" (D&C 97:26).

Many of the Saints in Zion (Jackson County, Missouri) Are Blessed for Their Faithfulness
DOCTRINE AND COVENANTS 97:1–9

97:3 *I, the Lord, am well pleased that there should be a school in Zion.*
Concerning his labors in the School of the Elders in Zion, Parley P. Pratt
wrote: "In the latter part of the summer and in the autumn [1833], I

devoted almost my entire time ministering among the churches; holding meetings; visiting the sick; comforting the afflicted, and giving counsel. A school of Elders was also organized, over which I was called to preside. This class, to the number of about sixty, met for instruction once a week. The place of meeting was in the open air, under some tall trees, in a retired place in the wilderness, where we prayed, preached and prophesied, and exercised ourselves in the gifts of the Holy Spirit. Here great blessings were poured out, and many great and marvelous things were manifested and taught. The Lord gave me great wisdom, and enabled me to teach and edify the Elders, and comfort and encourage them in their preparations for the work which lay before us. I was also much edified and strengthened. To attend this school I had to travel on foot, and sometimes with bare feet at that, about six miles. This I did once a week, besides visiting and preaching in five or six branches a week" (*Autobiography*, 75–76).

97:5 *I will bless him with a multiplicity of blessings, in expounding all scriptures and mysteries.* It is the privilege of those appointed to teach in the kingdom to receive inspiration from God and, if they are faithful in teaching the scriptures, to have the mysteries of godliness unfolded to them. The blessing extends to all who are called to teach, whether it be in Primary, Sunday School, Relief Society, the quorums of the priesthood, or the Church Educational System. The promise extends to tens, even hundreds of thousands who have been so called. According to the apostle Paul, these teachers rank second only to apostles and prophets in their importance in the Church. "And God hath set some in the church, first apostles, secondarily prophets, thirdly teachers" (1 Corinthians 12:28).

There is no thought here that the right to teach or to receive the appropriate revelation for the particular teaching assignment to which one has been called is limited to those holding high office or position. All who have been baptized and had the gift of the Holy Ghost conferred upon them have received not just the right but the responsibility to receive revelation. Joseph Smith said, "No man can receive the Holy Ghost without receiving revelations" (*Teachings of the Prophet Joseph Smith*, 328).

97:7 *The axe is laid at the root of the trees.* John the Baptist used this expression in his condemnation of the Pharisees and Sadducees, who viewed with scorn the doctrine he taught and the baptism he performed. To them he said, "Bring forth therefore fruits meet for repentance: and think not to say within yourselves, We have Abraham to our father: for I say unto you, that God is able of these stones to raise up children unto

Abraham. And now also the axe is laid unto the root of the trees: there-fore every tree which bringeth not forth good fruit is hewn down, and cast into the fire" (Matthew 3:8–10; Luke 3:8). That is, the axe is laid to the tree of formalism and Mosaic performances, to the tree of tortured inter-pretations of the scriptures, and self-serving religious observances, for all trees that bring not forth good fruit will be cut down and burned. So it was that John had been sent to overthrow the corrupt kingdom of the Jews (D&C 84:28).

Thus, those in the School of the Elders who, like their ancient counterparts in the nation of the Jews, had not brought forth good works, whose private lives did not match their public professions, stood in danger of being cut down and destroyed.

A House Is to Be Built in Zion in Which the Pure in Heart Shall See God
DOCTRINE AND COVENANTS 97:10–17

97:10 *A house should be built unto me in the land of Zion.* See com-mentary on Doctrine and Covenants 57:3.

Like unto the pattern which I have given you. The instructions sent to Zion indicate that the temple to be built at this time in Independence, Missouri, was identical in style to the temple in Kirtland, Ohio, except that the dimensions were larger (Roberts, *Comprehensive History*, 1:359). See commentary on Doctrine and Covenants 95:15–17.

97:11 *By the tithing of my people.* See commentary on Doctrine and Covenants 64:23.

97:12 *For the salvation of Zion.* Because the Saints in Zion had not lived worthily of the Lord's blessing, they were unable to build the temple in Jackson County as they had been commanded. Rather than redeem Zion according to the ancient promises, they were driven from it.

Bruce R. McConkie said: "Time and time again the early saints in this dispensation were offered the precious privilege of building up Zion, of estab-lishing the New Jerusalem, and of crowning that Holy City with the temple of temples. But always the promises were conditional. Always the divine pro-visos set forth the need for faith, obedience, righteousness, and complete conformity to the high, holy, and heavenly law. Sad to say, the Lord's people failed to gain the promised blessing. Obeying only in part, they received only a partial reward. Failing to live the fulness of the divine law, they were denied an inheritance in the Holy City in the days of their mortal probation.

"It was with the Latter-day Saints as it had been with their ancestors in the days of Moses. The Lord Jehovah offered ancient Israel the fulness of his eternal gospel; by the mouth of Moses and others of the prophets, he pled with his people to sanctify themselves and receive the fulness of his glory while in the wilderness and again after they entered their promised Canaan. A few in Israel gained wondrous gifts and powers, but the generality of the people, obeying only in part, rose no higher in spiritual stature than provided for in the lesser law. And yet in that law, always and everlastingly, there was a call to higher things. The very law itself was a schoolmaster to prepare the people for the fulness of the gospel.

"And so it has been among us. Though the newly called saints of the nineteenth century failed to build their promised Zion, yet they retained the glorious gospel, with all its hopes and promises. They were left in that state which now exists among us. What we now have is a schoolmaster to prepare us for that which is yet to be. We are now seeking to build Zion in our hearts by faith and personal righteousness as we prepare for the day when we will have power to build the city whence the law will go forth when He rules whose right it is" (*New Witness*, 610–11). See commentary on Doctrine and Covenants 103.

97:13–17 Instructions and promises regarding the house of the Lord in Kirtland were repeated for the Saints in Missouri (D&C 88:68, 77–78, 118–19; 94:15–17). Regarding the promises to those in Kirtland, the Prophet Joseph Smith wrote: "You will see that the Lord commanded us, in Kirtland, to build a house of God, and establish a school for the Prophets, this is the word of the Lord to us, and we must, yea, the Lord helping us, we will obey: as on conditions of our obedience He has promised us great things; yea, even a visit from the heavens to honor us with His own presence. We greatly fear before the Lord lest we should fail of this great honor, which our Master proposes to confer on us; we are seeking for humility and great faith lest we be ashamed in His presence" (*Teachings of the Prophet Joseph Smith*, 19).

97:13 *A place of instruction.* The temple in the New Jerusalem was, like the Kirtland Temple, to house the School of the Prophets, or the School of the Elders. It was in effect to perform the function now assumed in our Missionary Training Centers.

97:16 *All the pure in heart that shall come into it shall see God.* The psalmist asked, "Who shall ascend into the hill of the Lord? or who shall stand in his holy place?" (Psalm 24:3). His response: "He that hath clean hands, and a pure heart; who hath not lifted up his soul unto vanity, nor sworn deceitfully. He shall receive the blessing from the Lord, and righteousness from the God of his salvation. This is the generation of them that seek him, that seek thy face" (Psalm 24:4–6). After recounting the visions received by prophets of past ages, Joseph Smith taught, "And, fellow sojourners upon earth, it is your privilege to purify yourselves and come up to the same glory, and see for yourselves, and know for yourselves" (*Teachings of the Prophet Joseph Smith*, 13). The promise is given to the pure in heart that enter the house of the Lord that they shall see him. Those entering the temple with a pure heart have been baptized and have so lived as to receive a remission of sins. They have had hands laid upon their heads and been commanded to receive the Holy Ghost and have responded to that command. Thus they have been baptized by fire as the dross of sin has been purged from their souls. In the temple they have been washed and anointed and properly clothed so that they might stand in the presence of the Holy One, which becomes their privilege as they prepare themselves for it. See commentary on Doctrine and Covenants 88:68; 93:2.

Zion Is the Pure in Heart
DOCTRINE AND COVENANTS 97:18–21

97:18 *Very terrible.* "And it shall be said among the wicked: Let us not go up to battle against Zion, for the inhabitants of Zion are terrible; wherefore we cannot stand" (D&C 45:70).

97:21 *This is Zion—the pure in heart.* Zion is a state of being, a state of purity of heart that entitles one to be known as a member of the household of faith. President Brigham Young spoke of the Saints having Zion in their hearts: "Unless the people live before the Lord in the obedience of His commandments," he said, "they cannot have Zion within them." Further, "As to the spirit of Zion, it is in the hearts of the Saints, of those who love and serve the Lord with all their might, mind, and strength" (Young, *Journal of Discourses*, 2:253).

Zion Shall Escape the Lord's Scourge If She Is Faithful
DOCTRINE AND COVENANTS 97:22–28

97:25–28 A few months previous to receiving this revelation, the Prophet Joseph Smith had written to William W. Phelps concerning the Saints in Missouri: "The Lord will have a place whence His word will go forth, in these last days, in purity; for if Zion will not purify herself, so

as to be approved of in all things, in His sight, He will seek another people; for His work will go on until Israel is gathered, and they who will not
hear His voice, must expect to feel His wrath. Let me say unto you, seek
to purify yourselves, and also the inhabitants of Zion, lest the Lord's anger
be kindled to fierceness.

"Repent, repent, is the voice of God to Zion; and strange as it may
appear, yet it is true, mankind will persist in self-justification until all
their iniquity is exposed, and their character past being redeemed, and
that which is treasured up in their hearts be exposed to the gaze of
mankind. I say to you (and what I say to you I say to all), hear the warning voice of God, lest Zion fall, and the Lord swear in His wrath the
inhabitants of Zion shall not enter into His rest.

"The brethren in Kirtland pray for you unceasingly, for, knowing the
terrors of the Lord, they greatly fear for you. . . . Our hearts are greatly
grieved at the spirit which is breathed both in your letter and that of
Brother Gilbert's, the very spirit which is wasting the strength of Zion like
a pestilence; and if it is not detected and driven from you, it will ripen
Zion for the threatened judgments of God. Remember God sees the secret
springs of human action, and knows the hearts of all living" (*Teachings of
the Prophet Joseph Smith*, 18–19).

97:25 *Zion shall escape if.* God's designs always honor the agency of
his children. Although the Lord foreordained that Zion in all her beauty
should fill the earth, he has not predestined such to be the course for any
particular set of people. The early Saints were given a choice; they could
participate in the building up of Zion in her glory or suffer affliction,
pestilence, plague, and the sword. The determining factor was obedience
to all of God's commands, for the Lord "cannot look upon sin with the
least degree of allowance" (D&C 1:31). The inhabitants of geographical
Zion cannot be accepted simply because of the location of their earthly
dwelling place. They must live the laws of Zion. Satan had stirred up the
hearts of the citizens of Jackson County in anger against the Saints.
Apparently, there was a window of opportunity still available to the
Saints in which the Lord could turn away the wrath of their enemies. It
required immediate and complete obedience to the laws and covenants
the Lord had given them. We may never know before the Lord comes
and reveals all things what the history of Zion might have been had the
Saints hearkened to the Lord's Spirit and word at this time.

DOCTRINE AND COVENANTS 98

DATE: 6 AUGUST 1833
PLACE: KIRTLAND, OHIO

Seventeen days after the mobbing of the Saints in Missouri the Prophet received this revelation in which the Lord said that the prayers of the Saints were heard in heaven, and counsel was given them to be patient in their afflictions and not seek vengeance against their enemies. Although some news of the problems in Missouri had undoubtedly reached the Prophet in Kirtland (nine hundred miles away), he could have known the seriousness of the situation at this time only by the revelation. See introduction to Doctrine and Covenants 97.

Afflictions of the Saints Shall Be for Their Good
DOCTRINE AND COVENANTS 98:1–3

98:2 *Your prayers have entered into the ears of the Lord.* Given that we have repetitiously been commanded to pray to the Father in the name of the Son, this text raises the question as to why it would be said that our prayers were being heard by "the Lord" rather than his Father? Though our petitions in prayer are directed to the Father and answers come from him alone, this does not preclude Christ from having a perfect knowledge of all the desires of our hearts. As our advocate and intercessor with the Father, Christ must be fully aware of our petitions, desires, and needs.

Lord of Sabaoth. See commentary on Doctrine and Covenants 95:7.

98:3 *All things wherewith you have been afflicted shall work together for your good.* We came to the earth to be tested. This does not occur so that God will know how to judge us, for his knowledge of all things—past, present, and future—is perfect, but so that we can gain the strength and faith that comes from the test. Chief among those things that will rise with us in the resurrection will be the wisdom and strength gained in affliction. Well might it be said that affliction is a master teacher. It was Paul who said, "Tribulation worketh patience; and patience, experience;

and experience, hope" (Romans 5:3–4). See commentary on Doctrine and Covenants 122:7.

The Saints Are to Befriend the Constitutional Law of the Land
DOCTRINE AND COVENANTS 98:4–8

98:4–7 As Latter-day Saints, "We believe in being subject to kings, presidents, rulers, and magistrates, in obeying, honoring, and sustaining the law" (Article of Faith 12). The "law" to which reference is made in this verse is that law established by the Constitution of the United States. The question may well be asked, What is the duty of a Latter-day Saint when the law of the land is in conflict with the law of God? To which we would respond: To have saving power, the authority and doctrines of the Church must stand independent of the laws of men; until that millennial day when Christ himself will rule and reign, there must be a strict separation of church and state. We need no other reminder of the importance of this principle than the rebellion of Lucifer in the councils of heaven when he sought to control the hearts and minds of all of the hosts of heaven by using the authority of the priesthood to force compliance with his designs and desires. The moment compulsion begins, true religion ends.

Regarding the relationship of the Church and the state, none have stated the matter better than James E. Talmage, who wrote: "In the case of a conflict between the requirements made by the revealed word of God, and those imposed by the secular law, which of these authorities would the members of the Church be bound to obey? In answer, the words of Christ may be applied—it is the duty of the people to render unto Caesar the things that are Caesar's and unto God the things that are God's. At the present time the kingdom of heaven as an earthly power, with a reigning King exercising direct and personal authority in temporal matters, has not been established upon the earth. The branches of the Church as such, and the members composing the same, are subjects of the several governments within whose separate realms the Church organizations exist. In this day of comparative enlightenment and freedom there is small cause for expecting any direct interference with the rights of private worship and individual devotion; in all civilized nations the people are accorded the right to pray, and this right is assured by what may be properly called a common law of humankind. No earnest soul is cut off from communion with his God; and with such an open channel of communication, relief from burdensome laws and redress for grievances may be sought from the power that holds control of nations.

"Pending the overruling by Providence in favor of religious liberty, it is the duty of the saints to submit themselves to the laws of their country. Nevertheless, they should use every proper method, as citizens or subjects of their several governments, to secure for themselves and for all men the boon of freedom in religious service. It is not required of them to suffer without protest imposition by lawless persecutors, or through the operation of unjust laws; but their protests should be offered in legal and proper order. The saints have practically demonstrated their acceptance of the doctrine that it is better to suffer evil than to do wrong by purely human opposition to unjust authority. And if by thus submitting themselves to the laws of the land, in the event of such laws being unjust and subversive of human freedom, the people be prevented from doing the work appointed them of God, they are not to be held accountable for the failure to act under the higher law" (*Articles of Faith*, 422–23).

While imprisoned at Liberty Jail, the Prophet Joseph Smith wrote: "The Constitution of the United States is a glorious standard; it is founded in the wisdom of God. It is a heavenly banner; it is to all those who are privileged with the sweets of liberty, like the cooling shades and refreshing waters of a great rock in a thirsty and weary land. It is like a great tree under whose branches men from every clime can be shielded from the burning rays of the sun" (*Teachings of the Prophet Joseph Smith*, 147). See commentary on Doctrine and Covenants 58:21–23.

98:5 *Principle of freedom . . . belongs to all mankind.* "It is one of the first principles of my life," said Joseph Smith, "and one that I have cultivated from my childhood, having been taught it by my father, to allow every one that liberty of conscience. I am the greatest advocate of the Constitution of the United States there is on the earth. In my feelings I am always ready to die for the protection of the weak and oppressed in their just rights" (*Teachings of the Prophet Joseph Smith*, 326).

98:8 *I, the Lord God, make you free.* Without freedom there can be no salvation. To compel choice is to deny choice. Agency, which is the power to act on choices that have been freely made, was the gift of God to each of his spirit children at the time of their spirit birth (Moses 4:3) and is the God-given right of every soul born into this world (2 Nephi 2:26–27). It can be set down as an eternal principle that that which enhances the freedom of choice comes from God and that which enslaves and limits the power of action comes from the prince of darkness.

The law also maketh you free. Every law that has come from God and every wise and just law found in the governments of men has been established to preserve and protect the freedom of those for whom it was given.

Honest, Wise, and Good Men Should Be Supported for Secular Offices

DOCTRINE AND COVENANTS 98:9–10

98:9–10 As a book cannot exceed the wisdom and spirit of its writer, so will the system of government given a particular people never rise above the character of those chosen to lead. This principal was emphasized by King Mosiah when he related that monarchy is a good form of government if the king is righteous: "Therefore, if it were possible that you could have just men to be your kings, who would establish the laws of God, and judge this people according to his commandments, yea, if ye could have men for your kings who would do even as my father Benjamin did for this people—I say unto you, if this could always be the case then it would be expedient that ye should always have kings to rule over you" (Mosiah 29:13). On the other hand, he also emphasized the power of a wicked king: "He enacteth laws, and sendeth them forth among his people, yea, laws after the manner of his own wickedness; and whosoever doth not obey his laws he causeth to be destroyed; and whosoever doth rebel against him he will send his armies against them to war, and if he can he will destroy them; and thus an unrighteous king doth pervert the ways of all righteousness" (Mosiah 29:23).

In an official statement of the First Presidency, issued January 1928, President Heber J. Grant and his counselors proclaimed: "Laws which are enacted for the protection of society have no value except when they are administered in righteousness and justice, and they cannot be so administrated if dishonest men occupy administrative offices.

"The Lord says: 'When the wicked rule, the people mourn.' Wise men, good men, patriotic men are to be found in all communities, in all political parties, among all creeds. None but such men should be chosen.

"Without beneficent laws, righteously administered, the foundations of civilization crumble, anarchy reigns, decay and dissolution follow.

"We call upon all members of The Church of Jesus Christ of Latter-day Saints throughout the world to honor the laws of God, and obey and uphold the law of the land; and we appeal to good men and women every-where, regardless of creed, party affiliation, race or condition, to join with us in an effort to put into operation the words of Lincoln, the great eman-cipator, that our country may continue to be a light to the world, a loyal, law-abiding, God-fearing Nation" (Clark, *Messages*, 5:258).

Those Who Lay Down Their Lives in the Lord's Cause Shall Have Eternal Life
DOCTRINE AND COVENANTS 98:11–15

98:11 *Forsake all evil*. The command is to forsake "all evil," for, regardless of how small or innocuous it may appear, evil is a disease that both grows and fosters other evils.

Live by every word. See commentary on Doctrine and Covenants 84:45–46.

98:12 All must grow up into the principles of the gospel. The house of our understanding must be built one brick at a time. The process proves a trial for many. In teaching this principle, Mormon tells the reader of the Book of Mormon that he wrote only the "lesser part of the things" which Christ taught the nation of the Nephites. This, he said, was "expedient that they should have first, *to try their faith*, and if it shall so be that they shall believe these things then shall the greater things be made manifest unto them. And if it so be that they will not believe these things, then shall the greater things be withheld from them, unto their condemnation. Behold, I was about to write them, all which were engraven upon the plates of Nephi, but the Lord forbade it, saying: *I will try the faith of my people*" (3 Nephi 26:8–11; emphasis added).

98:13 *Whoso layeth down his life in my cause . . . shall find . . . life eternal*. The promise of eternal life is given to those who become martyrs for the faith. It does not apply to the likes of Joseph and Hyrum Smith alone—who sealed their testimonies with their blood in the Carthage Jail—but also to the faithful pioneers who lost their lives crossing the plains or those who lost or endangered their lives to rescue them. Brigham Young teaches this principle in the following: "Contrary to the anticipa-tion of these poorly clad people, the fall and early winter of 1856 were unusually stormy and merciless. A winter blizzard broke upon Willie's Company at the Sweetwater, and it struck Martin's group that was strug-gling across the alkaline waste lands above the last crossing of the Platte.

"The frigid, two-day storm, covering the country with more than a foot of snow, smashed tents and wagon covers. Ten, twelve, and some-times as many as fifteen deaths came in a day. Shallow graves were scraped out. At night packs of marauding wolves howled or fought at the burial places. From all appearances these two companies were doomed to perish on the eastern slopes of the Rockies, three hundred miles from Zion.

"When the storm subsided, the companies made a fresh start but moved only a few miles a day. It was under these trying conditions that two horsemen, riding ahead of the rescue parties from Salt Lake City, met Willie's Company October 28, 1856 on the Sweetwater River.

"John Chislett, a member of Willie's Company, expressing his over-whelming joy, exclaimed:

"'More welcome messengers never came from the courts of glory than these two young men were to us. They lost no time, after encouraging us all they could to press forward, but sped further to convey their glad news to Edward Martin, the fifth handcart company, who had left Florence about two weeks after us, and who it was feared were even worse off than we were. As they went from our view, many a hearty "God bless you," fol-lowed them.'

"Dan W. Jones, one of the rescuing party, gives a distressing picture of Martin's company: 'The train was strung out for three or four miles. There were old men pulling and tugging at their carts, and children, six and eight years of age, struggling through the snow and mud. As night came on the mud and snow froze to their clothing.'

"After Martin's Company had lost almost one fourth of its number in 'Martin's Ravine,' it moved forward to the Sweetwater River—a hun-dred feet wide, waist deep, and filled with floating ice. At the sight of this barrier, many Saints sank by their carts. In this helpless condition they were found by three sturdy young men who had pushed ahead of the sup-ply wagons. These brawny rescuers heroically waded the river and began carrying the sick and feeble across. This human fording continued back and forth, trip after trip through those chilling waters until every person and his cart had been safely landed upon the opposite shore.

"President Young, upon learning of this valorous service, wept freely. And while reporting it to the Saints in General Conference, pre-dicted: 'That act alone will insure David P. Kimball, George W. Grant, and C. Allen Huntington an everlasting salvation in the Celestial Kingdom of God, worlds without end.'

"With the coming of 104 relief outfits from Salt Lake City, the emi-grants abandoned their carts. Those who were unable to walk were loaded into the wagons. Death from freezing and exposure, nevertheless, continued daily. Before the last survivors arrived in Salt Lake City, Sunday, November 30, 222 of these valiant pioneers had found graves by the roadside" (Bennion, Conference Report, April 1954, 99–100).

In like manner Joseph Smith is recorded as having given the promise of salvation to the many martyrs who lost their lives that we might have the privilege of owning and reading the Bible. Edward Stevenson records the Prophet as saying "I have, by the aid of the Urim and Thummin, seen those martyrs, and they were honest, devoted followers of Christ, according to the light they possessed, and they will be saved" (Stevenson, *Reminiscences of Joseph, the Prophet*, 6).

98:14 *I will prove you in all things.* Dallin H. Oaks said: "Satan uses every possible device to degrade and enslave every soul. He attempts to distort and corrupt everything created for the good of man, sometimes by diluting that which is good, sometimes by camouflaging that which is evil. We generally think of Satan attacking us at our weakest spot. Elder Spencer W. Kimball of the Quorum of the Twelve described this technique when he said: 'Lucifer and his followers know the habits, weaknesses, and vulnerable spots of everyone and take advantage of them to lead us to spiritual destruction' . . .

"But weakness is not our only vulnerability. Satan can also attack us where we think we are strong—in the very areas where we are proud of our strengths. He will approach us through the greatest talents and spiritual gifts we possess. If we are not wary, Satan can cause our spiritual downfall by corrupting us through our strengths as well as by exploiting our weaknesses" ("Our Strengths," 12).

Renounce War and Proclaim Peace
DOCTRINE AND COVENANTS 98:16–18

98:16 *Turn the hearts of the children to their fathers.* The Latter-day Saint of our generation associates this language with the sealing ordinances of the temple. This, however, is not the way the text is being used in this instance. In 1833 when this revelation was received, the Lord had not yet revealed anything to them on that subject. The thought here is one of establishing a spirit of harmony and peace among all peoples and in all families that they might see in the actions of the Saints a fulfillment of the promises and prophecies made by the ancient fathers (patriarchs) and prophets.

Gabriel appropriated the same kind of language ("the hearts of the fathers to the children") to describe the ministry of John the Baptist in preparing the way for Christ. John's mission was to point the attention of the "disobedient" children of the prophets to the wisdom of their "just" fathers, who had prophesied the ministry of Christ (Luke 1:17). Elder Bruce R. McConkie wrote: "The hearts of the fathers—the prophets and patriarchs of former ages—had been centered on their children when these great Messianic prophecies were recorded. Such of the children of the prophets as believed the witness of John and the utterances of their inspired ancestors would attain unity of heart with their forebears. The hearts of all men, of whatever age, who believe and obey the same everlasting gospel truths are always united perfectly in one, whether those men are on earth, in the paradise of God, or in the kingdoms of glory" (*Doctrinal New Testament Commentary*, 1:80).

98:17 As with the preceding verse, the language is that of Malachi. The command is for the Jews to turn their hearts to the promises made to their fathers. They were to return to the land of their ancient inheritance where the temple of the Lord was once again to be built and the ordinances of salvation performed therein lest the "whole earth be cursed." See commentary on Joseph Smith–History 1:38–39, page 24; Doctrine and Covenants 133:7–16.

The Saints in Kirtland Are Reproved and Commanded to Repent
DOCTRINE AND COVENANTS 98:19–22

98:19–22 Here the Lord assures the Saints in Missouri that he is no respecter of persons and that their counterparts in Ohio are accountable to the same standard that they are. If the Ohio Saints do not repent they will reap the same devastation that the Missouri Saints are experiencing.

98:20 *The pride of their hearts, and their covetousness.* See commentary on Doctrine and Covenants 104:4, "Broken the covenant through covetousness."

The Lord Reveals His Laws Governing the Persecutions and Afflictions Imposed on His People
DOCTRINE AND COVENANTS 98:23–32

98:23 *Bear it patiently and revile not against them.* At least some of the Saints in Missouri were willing to endure their afflictions not only "patiently" but also courageously. One such was Edward Partridge, who recalled, "I was taken from my house by the mob, George Simpson being their leader, who escorted me about half a mile, to the court house, on the public square in Independence; and then and there, a few rods from said court house, surrounded by hundreds of the mob, I was stripped of my hat, coat and vest and daubed with tar from head to foot, and then had a quantity of feathers put upon me; and all this because I would not agree to leave the county, and my home where I had lived two years.

"Before tarring and feathering me I was permitted to speak. I told them that the Saints had suffered persecution in all ages of the world; that I had done nothing which ought to offend anyone; that if they abused me, they would abuse an innocent person; that I was willing to suffer for the sake of Christ; but, to leave the country, I was not then willing to consent to it. By this time the multitude made so much noise that I could not be heard: some were cursing and swearing, saying, 'call upon your Jesus,' etc.; others were equally noisy in trying to still the rest, that they might be enabled to hear what I was saying.

"Until after I had spoken, I knew not what they intended to do with me, whether to kill me, to whip me, or what else I knew not. I bore my abuse with so much resignation and meekness, that it appeared to astound the multitude, who permitted me to retire in silence, many looking very solemn, their sympathies having been touched as I thought; and as to myself, I was so filled with the Spirit and love of God, that I had no hatred towards my persecutors or anyone else" (*History of the Church*, 1:390–91).

Three years later, after the Saints had resettled in Clay County, Missouri, new troubles arose with the inhabitants of that county. The Prophet Joseph Smith and other leaders of the Church wrote in counsel: "We are sorry that this disturbance has broken out, but we do not consider it our fault. You are better acquainted with circumstances than we are, and, of course, have been directed by wisdom in your moves relative to leaving the county. . . . We advise that you be not the first aggressors. Give no occasion, and if the people will let you, dispose of your property, settle your affairs, and go in peace. . . . You know our feelings relative to not giving the first offense, and also of protecting your wives and little ones in case a mob should seek their lives. . . . Be wise; let prudence dictate all your counsels; preserve peace with all men, if possible; stand by the Constitution of your country; observe its principles; and above all, show yourselves men of God, worthy citizens, and we doubt not, the community, ere long, will

do you justice, and rise in indignation against those who are the instiga-
tors of your sufferings and afflictions" (*History of the Church*, 2:455–56).
See commentary on Doctrine and Covenants 19:30.

98:25–32 Those standing for the truth will always be countered by
those who oppose it. In every age and dispensation the Saints have been
called on to suffer for their faith (D&C 138:12–13). This revelation
restores to us the revealed principles by which they were to govern their
response to the actions of their enemies. Of the Nephites Mormon
recorded: "Nevertheless, the Nephites were inspired by a better cause, for
they were not fighting for monarchy nor power. . . . And they were doing
that which they felt was the duty which they owed to their God; for the
Lord had said unto them, and also unto their fathers, that: Inasmuch as
ye are not guilty of the first offense, neither the second, ye shall not suffer
yourselves to be slain by the hands of your enemies. . . . Ye shall defend
your families even unto bloodshed. Therefore for this cause were the
Nephites contending with the Lamanites, to defend themselves, and their
families, and their lands, their country, and their rights, and their religion"
(Alma 43:46–47).

It was not intended that the Saints in Missouri allow their enemies
to destroy them. They were to defend their lives against mob-armies that
came against them. Like the Nephites, they were "to defend themselves
against their enemies, even to the shedding of blood if it were necessary;
yea, and they were also taught never to give an offense, yea, and never to
raise the sword except it were against an enemy, except it were to preserve
their lives" (Alma 48:14).

War Is Justified Only When the Lord Commands It
DOCTRINE AND COVENANTS 98:33–38

98:33–38 The covenant people of the Old Testament are often
viewed as "cruel and vengeful, but the Lord says they went out to battle
when they were guided by prophets and the spirit of revelation when the
Lord commanded them. If any nation, tongue or people, came against
them they first lifted up a standard of peace, and if this standard was not
accepted the first, second or third time, these testimonies stood against
their enemies. The fourth time the Lord justified his people in going to
battle. This law is given 'as an ensample' unto us" (Smith, *Church History*

and Modern Revelation, 1:435). In the meager record we have of the Lord's words to ancient Israel, he declared: "When thou comest nigh unto a city to fight against it, then proclaim peace unto it. And it shall be, if it make thee answer of peace, and open unto thee, then it shall be, that all the people that is found therein shall be tributaries unto thee, and they shall serve thee. And if it will make no peace with thee, but will make war against thee, then thou shalt besiege it" (Deuteronomy 20:10–12).

During World War II, President David O. McKay reminded the Saints that they were to renounce war and proclaim peace.

"There are, however, two conditions which may justify a truly Christian man to enter—mind you, I say enter, not begin—a war: (1) An attempt to dominate and to deprive another of his free agency, and, (2) Loyalty to his country. Possibly there is a third, viz., Defense of a weak nation that is being unjustly crushed by a strong, ruthless one.

"Paramount among these reasons, of course, is the defense of man's freedom. An attempt to rob man of his free agency caused dissension even in heaven. Scriptures tell us: 'Michael and his angels fought against the dragon; and the dragon fought and his angels, And prevailed not; neither was their place found any more in heaven. And the great dragon was cast out, that old serpent, called the Devil, and Satan, which deceiveth the whole world: he was cast out into the earth, and his angels were cast out with him . . .'

"So fundamental in man's eternal progress is his inherent right to choose, that the Lord would defend it even at the price of war. Without freedom of thought, freedom of choice, freedom of action within lawful bounds, man cannot progress. . . .

"As a Church: 'We believe that all men are justified in defending themselves, their friends, and property, and the government from the unlawful assaults and encroachments of all persons in times of exigency, where immediate appeal cannot be made to laws, and relief afforded' (D&C 134:11).

"Even though we sense the hellish origin of war, even though we feel confident that war will never end war, yet under existing conditions we find ourselves as a body committed to combat this evil thing. With other loyal citizens we serve our country as bearers of arms, rather than to stand aloof to enjoy a freedom for which others have fought and died" (Conference Report, April 1942, 72–73).

The Saints Are to Forgive Their Enemies, Who, If They Repent, Shall Also Escape the Lord's Vengeance

DOCTRINE AND COVENANTS 98:39–48

98:39–42 See commentary on Doctrine and Covenants 64:8–9.

98:44 *They shall not be blotted out until he repent and reward thee four-fold.* True repentance requires restitution for the wrongs committed. Both the victim of the offense and the perpetrator need to do all within their power to mend the wrongs that have occurred between them. The victim should not refuse just offers for recompense made by the offender. The erring party must show contrition and desire to repair all wrongs and injuries. An example of such restitution is illustrated in the Lord's command to ancient Israel: "If a man shall steal an ox, or a sheep, and kill it, or sell it; he shall restore five oxen for an ox, and four sheep for a sheep" (Exodus 22:1). In following this law, the repentant Zacchaeus, chief publican in Jericho, said unto the Lord, "Behold, Lord, the half of my goods I give to the poor; and if I have taken any thing from any man by false accusation, I restore him fourfold" (Luke 19:8).

98:46–47 Children are responsible for their own transgressions and not the sins of their fathers. However, wounds from wrongs of previous generations may be passed from one generation to another. To heal these wounds, it is often necessary that the children acknowledge and make reparation for the wrongs of their parents. This principle is illustrated in the course followed by the Lamanites converted by the sons of Mosiah. Their king declared the necessity of reconciliation between his people and the Nephites after generations of hatred and wars. "We will go down unto our brethren," he said, "and we will be their slaves until we repair unto them the many murders and sins which we have committed against them" (Alma 27:8).

DOCTRINE AND COVENANTS 99

DATE: 29 AUGUST 1832
PLACE: HIRAM, OHIO

This revelation called John Murdock to serve as a missionary in the eastern states. He had joined the Church in 1830, having been baptized by Parley P. Pratt. He would yet be a part of Zion's Camp and serve on the high council in both Far West, Missouri, and in the Salt Lake Valley. He was ordained a bishop in Nauvoo in 1842. He opened the mission in Australia and served as a patriarch.

This section is out of chronological order in the Doctrine and Covenants due to an error in the 1876 edition in which the date was listed as August 1833. If it were in its proper place it would have been placed between sections 83 and 84.

John Murdock Is Called to Proclaim the Gospel, and Those Who Receive Him Receive the Lord and Shall Obtain Mercy
DOCTRINE AND COVENANTS 99:1–8

99:1 *The eastern countries.* Reference is to the eastern states.

99:2 *Who receiveth you receiveth me.* See commentary on Doctrine and Covenants 39:5.

You shall have power . . . in the demonstration of my Holy Spirit. The gospel is a living thing, not simply a list of precepts. Although we speak of the Bible and the Book of Mormon as containing the fulness of the gospel, in the true and proper sense the gospel can be found only in the lives of those who live it. We would not attempt to argue that a particular society had laws simply because they had a book on law. In like manner, we would not say that by giving a man who was incarcerated a copy of the Constitution we had given him freedom. The laws of which we speak exist only if they are lived, music exists only if it is heard, freedom exists only to those who enjoy the same. So it is with the gospel. It is a living thing. Thus we find the apostle Paul writing to the Thessalonian Saints, saying, "For our gospel came not unto you in word only, but also in power, and in the Holy Ghost, and in much assurance; as ye know what manner of men we were among you for your sake" (1 Thessalonians 1:5). That is, we have taken the gospel to a people only when they have a faith and power that lives. We cannot take the gospel to a people without taking the power to communicate with the heavens and receive revelation, entertain angels, heal the sick, administer the ordinances of salvation, work miracles, and raise the dead. All such activities are inseparably associated with the companionship of the Holy Ghost.

99:4 *Cleanse your feet in the secret places by the way for a testimony against them.* See commentary on Doctrine and Covenants 1:8; 24:15.

99:5 *As it is written of me in the volume of the book.* This appears to be a reference to the Bible, wherein are written the judgments that are to come upon the wicked.

99:6 *Sent up kindly.* The word *kindly* at the time of Joseph Smith meant more than just to perform an act with kindness. It meant "in the way suitable or appropriate . . . ; properly, fittingly." It also meant to do something "with natural affection" or "in a way that is pleasant or agreeable to the recipient or object" (*Oxford English Dictionary*, s. v. "kindly").

John Murdock, at the time of this missionary call, was a widower left to bring up five children at the death of his wife, Julia, who had died in giving birth to twins. About this same time, Emma Smith had also given birth to twins, both of whom died within hours. John, having no relatives who had accepted the fulness of the restored gospel and to whom he could entrust the babies, took his motherless twins to Emma for her to nurse and rear as her own. The twins, a baby boy and a baby girl, were named Joseph and Julia. By the time this revelation was received in August 1832, the baby Joseph had become the first martyr for the gospel (see commentary on D&C 78:9). John Murdock was on a mission at the time. When he returned, he recorded in his journal: "[I] arrived in Ohio, in the Church in the month of June, about 12 months after leaving my children. . . . arrived there about the 1st of June, found my little son Joseph had died. I had left my eldest son Orrice with Benjamin Bragg and John with Philo Judd and Phebe with Syrenus Burnet. I had to pay them all full price for keeping my children during my absence. But my daughter was still doing well with Bro. [Brother] Joseph, the Prophet."

At this time, Orrice was seven years; John, six years; and Phebe four years old. These then were the children whom, in obeying the instructions contained in the revelation, John Murdock was to send to Zion to stay with the family of Bishop Edward Partridge. Again, referring to John's journal: "I then continued with the church preaching to them and strengthening them and regaining my health till the month of Aug. when I received the Revelation recorded in the Book of Covenants [Doctrine and Covenants], page 206, at which time I immediately commenced to arrange my business and provide for my children and send them up to the Bishop in Zion."

John Murdock was commanded to leave his three young motherless children in the care of Bishop Partridge. The children also sacrificed that their father might faithfully fulfill his mission. They were among those driven out of Jackson County by the Missouri mobs. When the Lord called for an army to march to Missouri to aid the Saints who had been driven from their homes and property (D&C 103:22, 29–30), John Murdock quickly volunteered, hoping to reunite with his children, whom he had not seen in more than a year. When those enlisted in Zion's Camp were discharged, John wrote the following: "On the 30th [of June, 1834] word came to me that my daughter Phebe was sick nigh unto Death, of Cholera, and Bro. [Brother] A. [Algernon] S. [Sidney] Gilbert with whom she lived was dead. I immediately went and took care of her till July 6th when the Spirit left the body just at the break of day, being 6 years 3 months 27 days old" (Murdock, "Journal," 25). She is worthy of the Lord's promise: "Whoso layeth down his life in my cause, for my name's sake, shall find it again, even life eternal" (D&C 98:13). The two older boys lived to adulthood and served faithfully in the Church. His youngest, John Jr., served as a stake president in Beaver, Utah. He was the last surviving member of the Church to have actually lived in Jackson County during the initial settlement of Zion.

DOCTRINE AND COVENANTS 100

DATE: 12 OCTOBER 1833
PLACE: PERRYSBURG, NEW YORK

One week previous to receiving this revelation, at a time when the enemies of the Church in Missouri were preparing for an assault on the Church there, the Lord inspired Joseph Smith to leave Kirtland, Ohio, to do missionary work in the eastern states and in Canada. The Prophet recorded that Sidney Rigdon and Freeman Nickerson, who hailed from Perrysburg, New York, were his companions. The day previous, Joseph had recorded in his journal: "I feel very well in my mind. The Lord is with us, but have much anxiety about my family" (Smith, *History of the Church*, 1:419 n). In this revelation the Lord responded to the Prophet and Sidney's concern for their families and gave them additional instructions.

Joseph and Sidney to Preach the Gospel
for the Salvation of Souls
DOCTRINE AND COVENANTS 100:1–4

100:3–4 The Lord knows the hearts of all people. As difficult as it may have been for the Prophet Joseph Smith to leave his family at this time, it was necessary that he and Sidney proclaim the gospel and open the doors for missionaries in this area of New York and in Canada. Milton Backman recounted that "on Sunday, October 13, Joseph and Sidney preached to a 'large congregation' in western New York. The next day they continued their journey, arriving three days later at Mount Pleasant, upper Canada, at the home of Eleazer Nickerson, the second son of Freeman Nickerson. During the remainder of the week, with the land covered with a fresh mantle of snow, the two missionaries sought to spread the warmth of the gospel, teaching and preaching in Mount Pleasant, Brantford, Colburn, and Weathersford.

"One of the highlights of this missionary experience occurred on Sunday, October 27, after Joseph and Sidney had preached to a group gathered in the Nickerson home. Twelve converts were baptized, including Freeman Nickerson's two adult sons, Moses and Eleazer, and Lydia Bailey, who later married Newel Knight in Kirtland. That evening, the Prophet conducted a confirmation meeting. After partaking of the sacrament, the missionaries laid their hands on the heads of the converts and bestowed the gift of the Holy Ghost. The success of the missionaries' labors continued the following day when they baptized two additional converts and confirmed them near the water's edge. That night they held their last meeting in the area, during which they ordained Eleazer Nickerson an elder and witnessed one of the sisters speaking in tongues. . . .

"Missionary work in upper Canada continued after Joseph Smith and Sidney Rigdon left that region. Writing to Sidney Rigdon on December 20, 1833, Moses Nickerson observed: 'Your labors while in Canada have been the beginning of a good work: there are 34 members attached to the Church at Mt. Pleasant, all of whom appear to live up to their profession, five of whom have spoken in tongues and three sing in tongues: and we live at the top of the mountain. For my part, I feel that I cannot be thankful enough for that which I have received: the scriptures have been opened to my view beyond account.'

"Moses Nickerson requested that other missionaries be sent to that area, and John P. Greene was called to serve there. Writing to the editor of the *Messenger and Advocate,* he reported that he had been received by the Saints with expressions of joy, and many were desirous to be instructed more perfectly in the word of the Lord. 'I labored in this region about two months with a good degree of satisfaction,' he stated, 'and preached the gospel to many hundreds of souls'" (*Heavens Resound,* 117–18).

This missionary experience left Joseph Smith with a special love for the Saints in Mount Pleasant, Canada: "I remember Brother Freeman and wife, Ransom also, and Sister Lydia, and little Charles, with all the brethren and sisters. I entreat for an interest in all your prayers before the throne of mercy, in the name of Jesus. I hope the Lord will grant that I may see you all again, and above all that we may overcome, and sit down together in the kingdom of our Father" (*Teachings of the Prophet Joseph Smith,* 29–30).

It Shall Be Given Them in the Very Hour
What They Shall Say
DOCTRINE AND COVENANTS 100:5–8

100:5 *Speak the thoughts that I shall put into your hearts.* The admonition given here to Joseph Smith and Sidney Rigdon applies alike to all who have been called to labor in the Lord's name. It is a perfect expression of how the spirit of revelation operates. In Doctrine and Covenants 8 the spirit of revelation was defined as that which the Lord tells us in our minds and in our hearts (vv. 2–3). Precious few of the revelations given in the history of humankind have involved the audible voice of the Lord or personal instruction from angels. For the most part, the Lord places thoughts and feelings in our hearts, leaving the manner in which they are clothed in words to our discretion. Many of these revelations, like the scriptures we have already been given, go unheeded because we lack the courage to trust the Spirit and respond to its prompting. The more closely we learn to listen the more frequently the Spirit will take the occasion to speak.

100:6 "Neither take ye thought beforehand what ye shall say; but treasure up in your minds continually the words of life, and it shall be given you in the very hour that portion that shall be meted unto every man" (D&C 84:85).

100:7 *In the spirit of meekness.* See commentary on Doctrine and Covenants 52:15–21.

100:8 When we speak those truths the Lord has given us to declare to all the nations of the earth and when we speak those things the Lord places in our hearts to say, then we have the assurance that the Holy Ghost will carry our words to the hearts of those to whom we speak. They in turn will know of the truthfulness of that which we have spoken. Indeed, it is not an uncommon thing for those who give a listening ear to the words of the servants of the Lord to hear more than was said and to hear it more eloquently than it was spoken.

Sidney Is to Be a Spokesman and Joseph Is to Be a
Revelator and Mighty in Testimony
DOCTRINE AND COVENANTS 100:9–12

100:9 *Sidney, should be a spokesman.* With time and experience Joseph Smith became a powerful orator, though he was not always such. In a revelation given the day the Church was organized, the Lord called Oliver Cowdery "the first preacher of this church unto the church, and before the world, yea, before the Gentiles" (D&C 21:12). Thus, he, and not Joseph Smith, preached the first gospel discourse of this dispensation. The Prophet relied heavily upon him particularly in the early months after the Church's organization. When Sidney Rigdon joined the Church, he was a powerful and articulate speaker. The Lord felt to take full advantage of his experience and ability. In these early years of the Church's history, both Oliver Cowdery and Sidney Rigdon were better public speakers than the Prophet.

The calling of Sidney Rigdon to be the spokesman for the Prophet is often associated with a prophecy relative to a spokesman made by Joseph of Egypt and quoted by Lehi in the Book of Mormon (2 Nephi 3:18–19). A closer reading of the text suggests that Joseph Smith is the spokesman to whom reference is being made, not Sidney Rigdon.

The prophecy in question speaks of one who is to assume a special role in writing the word of the Lord and another who is to play a special role in proclaiming that which has been written. To Joseph of old, the Lord said, "I will raise up unto the fruit of thy loins; and I will make for him a spokesman" (2 Nephi 3:18). Just as Moses wrote and Aaron proclaimed the law given in the Old World, so too was someone in the New World—someone of the seed of Joseph—to write the Lord's law, and another, "a spokesman," was to declare it. Bruce R. McConkie explained: "In this case the writer and the spokesman are not identified by name; rather, we are left, based on our knowledge of what has transpired in this and previous dispensations, to identify those whose missions were of such import as to have them revealed thousands of years before the events transpired. Mormon wrote the Book of Mormon, quoting, condensing, and summarizing from many ancient records as the Spirit directed. And Joseph Smith translated the ancient word by the gift and power of God and proclaimed it to all men, and to the seed of Joseph in particular, as the mind and will and voice of Him by whom salvation comes.

"With this in mind, note these words of the Lord: 'And I, behold, I will give unto him [Mormon] that he shall write the writing of the fruit of thy loins [the Nephites], unto the fruit of thy loins [the Lamanites]; and the spokesman of thy loins [Joseph Smith] shall declare it.' That is, Mormon wrote the Book of Mormon, but what he wrote was taken from the writings of the Nephite prophets; and these writings, compiled into one book, were translated by Joseph Smith and sent forth by him unto the Lamanites unto whom, as the title page of the Book of Mormon attests, they were originally written. And further, they are sent forth to all the seed of Joseph, whether in the Lamanite branch of Israel or not.

"'And the words which he [Mormon] shall write shall be the words which are expedient in my wisdom should go forth unto the fruit of thy loins.' They were selected by inspiration, and they contain that portion of the word that is designed to bring fallen Israel again into the true sheepfold, where they will be taught the deeper doctrines, including the mysteries of the kingdom. 'And it shall be as if the fruit of thy loins [the Nephites] had cried unto them [their Lamanite brethren, in particular] from the dust; for I know their faith.' Many were the ancient Book of Mormon prophets who pled with the Lord that the gospel might go in due course and in his providences to the remnant of Lehi's seed.

"'And they [the Nephites] shall cry from the dust [for as a nation they have been destroyed and have no living voice with which to speak]; yea, even repentance unto their brethren, even after many generations have gone by them. And it shall come to pass that their cry [in the Book of Mormon] shall go, even according to the simpleness of their words. Because of their faith their words [in the Book of Mormon] shall proceed forth out of my mouth'—the Book of Mormon is the word of the Lord; it is as though the words fell from his own lips—'unto their brethren [the Lamanites] who are the fruit of thy [Joseph's] loins; and the weakness of their words will I make strong in their faith, unto the remembering of my covenant which I made unto thy fathers.' (2 Nephi 3:4–21.) With Joseph's fathers—Abraham, Isaac, and Jacob—the Lord covenanted that in them and in their seed all generations shall be blessed. These blessings are now available to the seed of Joseph because of the coming forth of the Book of Mormon and the restoration of the gospel" (*New Witness*, 425–27).

100:10–11 Sidney was to be blessed with the gift to testify of the truths of the Restoration with great power. Joseph, in turn, who as the prophet, seer, and revelator stood at the head of the Church and kingdom of God, was the one through whom those truths were to be revealed.

The Lord Will Raise Up a Pure People, and the Obedient Shall Be Saved
DOCTRINE AND COVENANTS 100:13–17

100:13 *Zion shall be redeemed.* The gospel could not be restored without asking those who gathered to its standard to redeem Zion and to build the long promised New Jerusalem and the great temple that is to crown the Holy City. All promises to this effect are of course conditional. Only a worthy and obedient people can accomplish such a work. The city of God cannot be built upon any principles other than those that come from God. These early attempts to build Zion fell short, for far too many Saints had their hearts set too much upon the things of the world. These were eventually betrayed by their avarice and pettiness of soul. Obeying only in part, they received only in part. The fulness of God's blessings can be given only to those who live the fulness of his law.

It was with modern Israel as it had been with their ancient counterparts in the days of Moses. The God of heaven offered ancient Israel the fulness of his gospel by the mouth of a great prophet who had stood in his presence. This prophet pleaded with his people to sanctify themselves and receive the fulness of God's glory while in the wilderness and again after they entered their promised Canaan. A few obeyed, but most declared such blessings to be too much for them and opted for a lesser law in their stead, a lesser law whose purpose was to prepare them for something greater. As it was then, so it has been in our day.

Though the early Saints of our day failed to redeem Zion, they yet retained the gospel with all its hopes and promises. Although we have grown in understanding and stability over the ensuing years, we still fall short of the faith and devotion necessary to lay claim to those promises. Thus we remain, as did ancient Israel, under a schoolmaster. We labor to find the faith to redeem families and wards. The day may come when we can redeem stakes and regions and thus gain rightful claim to the inheritance promised our great-grandfathers.

"Thus, on February 24, 1834, after the Saints had been scattered and driven from their lands in Jackson County, the Lord gave these words of comfort and counsel to his people: 'I will give unto you a revelation and commandment . . . concerning the salvation and redemption of your brethren, who have been scattered on the land of Zion; being driven and smitten by the hands of mine enemies, on whom I will pour out my wrath without measure in mine own time.' Those who persecute the Saints and oppose the cause in which they are engaged are the enemies of God. Whether their opposition is directed against the Lord or against his servants, it is the same. And when the great and dreadful day arrives and the Lord returns to take vengeance upon the ungodly, then his wrath will be poured out upon them without measure" (McConkie, *New Witness*, 610–12).

"I cannot learn from any communication by the Spirit to me," Joseph
Smith said, "that Zion has forfeited her claim to a celestial crown,
notwithstanding the Lord has caused her to be thus afflicted, except it
may be some individuals, who have walked in disobedience, and forsaken
the new covenant; all such will be made manifest by their works in due
time. I have always expected that Zion would suffer some affliction, from
what I could learn from the commandments which have been given. But
I would remind you of a certain clause in one which says, that after much
tribulation cometh the blessing. By this, and also others, and also one
received of late, I know that Zion, in the due time of the Lord, will be
redeemed; but how many will be the days of her purification, tribulation,
and affliction, the Lord has kept hid from my eyes; and when I inquire
concerning this subject, the voice of the Lord is: Be still, and know that I
am God; all those who suffer for my name shall reign with me, and he that
layeth down his life for my sake shall find it again" (*Teachings of the
Prophet Joseph Smith*, 34).

    100:14 Soon after Oliver Cowdery arrived from Missouri in late
August or early September with news of mob action in Independence,
"arrangements were made to dispatch Elders Orson Hyde and John Gould
to Jackson county, Missouri, with advice to the Saints in their unfortu-
nate situation, through the late outrage of the mob" (Smith, *History of the
Church*, 1:407). After arriving, "Elders W. W. Phelps and Orson Hyde
were dispatched to the Governor of Missouri, residing at Jefferson City,
the capital of the state," with a petition for aid from Governor Daniel
Dunklin (Smith, *History of the Church*, 1:410).

DOCTRINE AND COVENANTS 101

DATE: 16 DECEMBER 1833
PLACE: KIRTLAND, OHIO

Following the mob violence of July 1833 (see introduction to D&C 97), the Saints petitioned the governor of Missouri for aid in protecting their lives and property in Jackson County, Missouri. They complied with his instructions to obtain legal counsel to aid them in their quest for justice. Upon learning that the Saints intended to appeal to law, their enemies responded with further illegal outrage, which resulted in further loss of life and property.

The *History of the Church* records: "Thursday, November 7th, the shores of the Missouri river began to be lined on both sides of the ferry, with men, women and children; goods, wagons, boxes, chests, and provisions; while the ferrymen were busily employed in crossing them over. When night again closed upon the Saints, the wilderness had much the appearance of a camp meeting. Hundreds of people were seen in every direction; some in tents, and some in the open air, around their fires, while the rain descended in torrents. Husbands were inquiring for their wives, and women for their husbands; parents for children, and children for parents. Some had the good fortune to escape with their families, household goods, and some provisions; while others knew not the fate of their friends, and had lost all their effects. The scene was indescribable, and would have melted the hearts of any people upon earth, except the blind oppressor, and the prejudiced and ignorant bigot. Next day the company increased, and they were chiefly engaged in felling small cottonwood trees, and erecting them into temporary cabins, so that when night came on, they had the appearance of a village of wigwams, and the night being clear, the occupants began to enjoy some degree of comfort" (Smith, *History of the Church*, 1:437).

The Prophet Joseph Smith learned of the Saints' grave situation from Elders Orson Hyde and John Gould when they returned to Kirtland from Missouri and from letters by Church leaders in Missouri. Joseph repeatedly petitioned the Lord for answers concerning the reasons for the

Saints' sufferings. Earlier he wrote: "Now, there are two things of which I
am ignorant; and the Lord will not show them unto me, perhaps for a wise
purpose in Himself—I mean in some respects—and they are these: Why
God has suffered so great a calamity to come upon Zion, and what the
great moving cause of this great affliction is; and again, by what means He
will return her back to her inheritance, with songs of everlasting joy upon
her head" (*Teachings of the Prophet Joseph Smith*, 34). Finally, on 16
December 1833 he wrote, "I received the following . . ." (Smith, *History of
the Church*, 1:458).

The Saints Are Chastened and Afflicted
Because of Their Transgressions
DOCTRINE AND COVENANTS 101:1–8

101:2 *They have been afflicted, in consequence of their transgressions.*
Had the Lord not chastened the Saints for their transgressions, he would
have denied justice. Earlier, he had warned: "Zion shall escape if
she observe to do all things whatsoever I have commanded her. But if she
observe not to do whatsoever I have commanded her, I will visit her
according to all her works, with sore affliction, with pestilence, with
plague, with sword, with vengeance, with devouring fire" (D&C
97:25–26). The Saints were responsible for their behavior. Parents contribute to the delinquency of their children when they warn them but
then fail to follow through on their warning after their children's disobedience. The Lord is a caring parent. He did not condone the actions of
the Missouri mobs, but neither did he excuse the transgressions of those
who were called by his name. The strivings of the Spirit had not penetrated the hearts of the transgressors to turn them to the Lord. Like the
children of Israel in Moses' day, they required chastening to teach them
that only a pure people can build Zion.

101:3 *In that day when I shall come to make up my jewels.* This phrase
comes from Malachi 3:17. It means that the Lord, in the day of his return,
will set apart the faithful among his people as special treasures. To the wicked
he will come as a judge; to the righteous he will come as a loving father.

101:4 *Chastened.* To make pure by correction.

Tried, even as Abraham. If we are to receive the blessings of Abraham,
we must first have the faith of Abraham. Bible history accords no more
soul-wrenching test than that given our ancient father when God commanded him to offer his son, Isaac, in place of a ram as a sacrifice. Surely

every feeling of Abraham's heart must have cried out in protest and anguish. This cannot be so! This is not right! This violates every principle of heaven! And yet Abraham schooled his feelings and offered to the Lord not just his son but his own heart and soul. He held nothing back. All his hopes and dreams lay with Isaac upon an altar built to his God. In the providence of heaven, Abraham's hand was withheld. His son and his hopes were returned to him, and he received an inheritance that reaches to the endless bounds of eternity.

Why was such a test necessary? Was it to amuse God or to bless Abraham? Of this there can be no question. To Abraham was given the promise of eternal life and an endless seed. To him was given the promise that his posterity would find in its numbers all who would follow him as faithful witnesses of the God of heaven and all who would hold the priesthood and be called upon to declare the gospel of salvation to the nations of the earth. Abraham's faith was to become their faith, and his promises were to become their promises. See commentary on Doctrine and Covenants 110:12.

101:6 "Those who cannot endure persecution," stated the Prophet Joseph Smith, "and stand in the day of affliction, cannot stand in the day when the Son of God shall burst the veil, and appear in all the glory of His Father, with all the holy angels" (*Teachings of the Prophet Joseph Smith*, 42).

101:7 The Saints in Missouri reaped as they had sown. They ignored the Lord's warnings and now he would ignore their petitions. Abinadi taught this principle to King Noah's people, saying, "Except this people repent and turn unto the Lord their God, they shall be brought into bondage; and none shall deliver them, except it be the Lord the Almighty God. Yea, and it shall come to pass that when they shall cry unto me I will be slow to hear their cries; yea, and I will suffer them that they be smitten by their enemies. And except they repent in sackcloth and ashes, and cry mightily to the Lord their God, I will not hear their prayers, neither will I deliver them out of their afflictions; and thus saith the Lord" (Mosiah 11:23–25).

The Lord's People Will Be Gathered and Comforted
DOCTRINE AND COVENANTS 101:9–15

101:9–11 The Lord looked compassionately upon his children in their suffering. He had cleansed the inner vessel first, even though the outer vessel was more filthy by comparison. The Saints were first chastened for their transgressions, even though mob members in Jackson County were more filthy than the Saints. The day of judgment was not far distant for the Saints' enemies, as the Civil War would witness.

101:9 *I will not utterly cast them off.* The covenant people had not been cast off by the Lord; rather, they were cast out of Zion by the mobs, who represented the chastening hand of the Lord. The Lord had dealt similarly with ancient Israel. Through the prophet Isaiah he declared, "O Assyrian, the rod of mine anger, and the staff in their hand is mine indignation. I will send him against an hypocritical nation" (Isaiah 10:5–6). The ten tribes of Israel were taken from the land of their inheritance by the Assyrians and scattered among all the nations of the earth. Yet the Lord covenanted that they would be gathered in the latter days, when they would again return to him. Like their ancestors of old, the Saints will suffer the rod of the Lord's chastening hand until they learn obedience by the things they suffer (Hebrews 5:8). Only then can they obtain their inheritance in Zion.

101:10 *The decree hath gone forth by a former commandment.* See Doctrine and Covenants 1:13.

101:12 This text considers all the covenant people to be watchmen upon the tower; all have a responsibility to their neighbor. "It becometh every man who hath been warned to warn his neighbor" (D&C 88:81).

Zion and Her Stakes Will Be Established
DOCTRINE AND COVENANTS 101:16–21

101:17 *Zion shall not be moved out of her place.* The place of Zion remains the same, and in some future day the Saints of the Almighty will possess it.

101:18 *They that remain, and are pure in heart, shall return.* Lands of inheritance are an everlasting possession and as such will be the rightful possession of the "pure in heart" in the eternal world. See commentary on Doctrine and Covenants 88:17.

101:20 *There is none other place appointed.* See commentary on Doctrine and Covenants 57:1–3.

101:21 *They shall be called stakes.* The kingdom of God has continued to grow and be organized throughout the earth. Wherever sufficient numbers of Saints have gathered together, geographical areas have been appointed as stakes of Zion, and presiding officers have been designated and set apart. See commentary on Doctrine and Covenants 82:13; 101:63–67.

The Nature of Life during the Millennium Is Set Forth
DOCTRINE AND COVENANTS 101:22–31

101:22 *Worship me according to mine everlasting gospel.* It is not for men to ordain the system of worship or to determine the conditions of salvation. It is the Lord's church, and he runs it. The terms of salvation are not negotiable. We are neither to add to, nor take from, the word of the Lord.

Gather together, and stand in holy places. The holy places are the stakes of Zion to which the pure in heart have gathered. See commentary on Doctrine and Covenants 45:32.

101:23 *The veil of the covering of my temple.* Anciently, a veil hung between the two holy chambers of the tabernacle (Exodus 26:31–33). Its presence in Herod's temple is supported by the statement in each of the synoptic gospels that at the time of Christ's death the veil of the temple was rent from top to bottom (Matthew 27:51; Mark 15:38; Luke 23:45). Christ, by his sacrificial death, opened a way for the faithful to enter the holiest place, meaning the celestial kingdom, "through the veil, that is to say, his flesh" (Hebrews 10:20). The present text, drawing on this imagery, suggests that the veil separating us from the presence of the Lord will be rent, and all will be able to see what otherwise would remain hidden to them.

101:24–25 When the Lord comes again, "the earth will be renewed and receive its paradisiacal glory" (Article of Faith 10). Isaiah prophesied of "a new earth" during the Millennium (Isaiah 65:17). All that is corruptible—everything of a telestial order—will be destroyed, for a terrestrial or Edenic law will rule during the Millennium. This text affirms that when Adam fell, the whole earth fell—including everything in the plant and animal kingdoms. Prior to the fall of Adam there was neither death nor corruption of any sort in these kingdoms or in any other place in the world that Adam inhabited. With the return of Christ, all things will return to a state like that known in Eden.

101:26 Men will learn peace, and all men and animals will live together in harmony. Further, "there will be no wild animals," explained Bruce R. McConkie. "The coyote will not stalk the deer, and the wolf will not kill the sheep, and all forms of life will be the friends and servants of men.

"Isaiah gives us these poetically phrased particulars about animal life during the Millennium. 'The wolf and the lamb shall feed together,' he says, 'and the lion shall eat straw like the bullock.' Implicit in this pronouncement is the fact that man and all forms of life will be vegetarians in the coming day; the eating of meat will cease, because, for one thing, death as we know it ceases. There will be no shedding of blood, because man and beast are changed (quickened) and blood no longer flows in their veins. 'And dust shall be the serpent's meat,' meaning, as we suppose, that they shall no longer eat mice and vermin and animal life. 'They shall not hurt nor destroy in all my holy mountain, saith the Lord' (Isaiah 65:25). And further: 'The wolf also shall dwell with the lamb, and the leopard shall lie down with the kid; and the calf and the young lion and the fatling together; and a little child shall lead them. And the cow and the bear shall feed; their young ones shall lie down together: and the lion shall eat straw like the ox. And the suckling child shall play on the hole of the asp, and the weaned child shall put his hand on the cockatrice' [adders'] den. They shall not hurt nor destroy in all my holy mountain' (Isaiah 11:6–9)" (*Millennial Messiah*, 658).

101:27 "And it shall come to pass, that before they call, I will answer; and while they are yet speaking, I will hear" (Isaiah 65:24).

101:28 *Satan shall not have power to tempt any man.* A change will come upon the inhabitants of the earth similar to that experienced by the three Nephite disciples who were translated. By revelation Mormon learned that "there was a change wrought upon them, insomuch that Satan could . . . not tempt them; and they were sanctified in the flesh, that they were holy" (3 Nephi 28:39). See commentary on Doctrine and Covenants 43:17.

101:29 *There is no death.* Those on the earth during the Millennium will be like the Three Nephites, for "there must needs be a change wrought upon their bodies, or else it needs be that they must taste of death; Therefore, that they might not taste of death there [will be] a change wrought upon their bodies, that they might not suffer pain nor sorrow" (3 Nephi 28:37–38). Those living during the Millennium will live in a state akin to translation: their bodies will be changed so that they are not subject to disease or death as we know it.

101:30 *The age of a tree.* Isaiah identified this as one hundred years (Isaiah 65:20).

101:31 *Changed in the twinkling of an eye.* No graves will be dug during the Millennium. Death and suffering as we now know them will not exist. The body and the spirit will no longer separate for a long period of time. For now the body returns to the dust while the spirit awaits in a world of spirits for the day of its reunion with a perfected body, but in that day the body will not see corruption, and the spirit will not go to a spirit world. The separation of body and spirit will be virtually instantaneous and their reunion inseparable. "Children shall grow up until they become old; old men shall die; but they shall not sleep in the dust, but they shall be changed in the twinkling of an eye" (D&C 63:51). The Lord told the Three Nephites: "Ye shall never endure the pains of death; but when I shall come in my glory ye shall be changed in the twinkling of an eye from mortality to immortality; and then shall ye be blessed in the kingdom of my Father" (3 Nephi 28:8).

Shall be caught up. Those changed "in the twinkling of an eye" will not remain on the earth. The Prophet Joseph Smith recorded: "Christ and the resurrected Saints will reign over the earth during the thousand years. They will not probably dwell upon the earth, but will visit it when they please, or when it is necessary to govern it" (*Teachings of the Prophet Joseph Smith,* 268). Some people will not be caught up after their death. Joseph taught, "There will be wicked men on the earth during the thousand years. The heathen nations who will not come up to worship will be visited with the judgments of God, and must eventually be destroyed from the earth" (*Teachings of the Prophet Joseph Smith,* 268–69). The wicked will not be caught up to a glorious rest. Isaiah prophesied that during the Millennium "there shall be no more thence an infant of days, nor an old man that hath not filled his days: for the child shall die an hundred years old; but the sinner being an hundred years old shall be accursed" (Isaiah 65:20).

Elder Bruce R. McConkie explained: "Isaiah's description of life and death during the Millennium seems to preserve the concept that even then—even in that blessed day when Satan is bound and righteousness overflows—even then men are free to come out in open rebellion and, as sinners, suffer the fate reserved for the sons of perdition. Manifestly, they, being accursed, would die the death with which we are familiar, for their resurrection is destined to be in that final day when those shall come forth 'who shall remain filthy still' (D&C 88:102)" (*Millennial Messiah,* 646).

The Saints Shall Be Blessed and
Rewarded in the Millennium
DOCTRINE AND COVENANTS 101:32–42

101:32–34 During the Millennium the mysteries of creation will be revealed. It is apparent from these verses that men will not know the answers to questions concerning creation before that time. In large measure such questions will answer themselves. When we live in a terrestrial or paradisiacal world—a world in which there is no death, aging, decay, or disease—we will, by mere observation, be able to deduce much relative to the true nature of creation. This will be a world much like that known to Adam and Eve before the Fall. Whereas our earth now abides a telestial law, millennial earth will abide a much higher order. It is possible that many scientific conclusions based on our telestial order will have no meaning or relevance there.

Until the day comes when "the earth shall be full of the knowledge of the Lord, as the waters cover the sea" (Isaiah 11:9), it would be wise for us to hearken to the counsel of Elder Harold B. Lee: "I appeal to you again as teachers, let's use those three precious words that ought to be used more often by teachers of religion, 'I don't know.' And we don't know very much because the Lord has not told us. We have these speculations, these theories that if you want to have them in your mind as something to ponder, and something that you never can find a full answer to, go ahead and think about them, but label them for what they are, and do not teach them as facts until the Lord tells us about the details, which presently must be considered in the realm of theory" (*Teachings of Harold B. Lee*, 456).

101:38 *Seek the face of the Lord always.* See commentary on Doctrine and Covenants 93:1.

101:39–40 Salt that has lost its savor, we are told, is good for nothing but to be cast out and trodden under foot. Salt does not dissipate with age; it carries no expiration date. Savor is lost through mixture and contamination—only diluting salt with impure substances can cause it to lose its capacity to season food.

In ancient times salt was acquired in its natural state. It had to be washed before it could be used for seasoning food or for other purposes. After it had been cleansed, the residue or tailings were tossed upon walkways to be trodden down by the feet of men. How powerful the imagery! Once we have been gathered, we are washed and cleansed and our impurities are discarded. As Saints, we have a duty to serve as a savor, to bring out the best, to elicit all that is good. This is a power lost to us only if we choose to contaminate ourselves with things of the world.

101:41 *But not all.* Regarding the faithful among the suffering Saints in Missouri, the Prophet wrote: "When I contemplate upon all things that have been manifested, I am aware that I ought not to murmur, and do not murmur, only in this, that those who are innocent are compelled to suffer for the iniquities of the guilty; and I cannot account for this, only on this wise, that the saying of the Savior has not been strictly observed: 'If thy right eye offend thee, pluck it out, and cast it from thee; or if thy right arm offend thee, cut it off, and cast it from thee.' Now the fact is, if any of the members of our body is disordered, the rest of our body will be affected with it, and then all are brought into bondage together; and yet, notwithstanding all this, it is with difficulty that I can restrain my feelings when I know that you, my brethren, with whom I have had so many happy hours—sitting, as it were, in heavenly places in Christ Jesus; and also, having the witness which I feel, and ever have felt, of the purity of your motives—are cast out, and are as strangers and pilgrims on the earth, exposed to hunger, cold, nakedness, peril, sword—I say when I contemplate this, it is with difficulty I can keep from complaining and murmuring against this dispensation; but I am sensible that this is not right, and may God grant that notwithstanding your great afflictions, and sufferings, there may not anything separate us from the love of Christ" (*Teachings of the Prophet Joseph Smith*, 34–35).

Parable of the Nobleman and the Olive Trees, Signifying the Troubles and Eventual Redemption of Zion
DOCTRINE AND COVENANTS 101:43–62

101:43–62 In this parable the Lord is the nobleman and his vineyard is Zion, or Jackson County, Missouri. The servants are the Saints who have settled in Zion, and their settlements are the olive trees. Had they built the tower—or temple—as directed, it would have been a spiritual watchtower. From it Church leaders could have seen by revelation the movements of the enemy from afar and gained foreknowledge that would have saved Zion when the enemy attacked. But because the Saints had a spirit of discord, they were unable to build either the temple or Zion.

While the Saints in Missouri procrastinated, the enemy came and drove them from the land of their inheritance. The Lord rebuked the

Saints but commanded one of his servants, Joseph Smith (v. 55; D&C 103:21), to gather the "strength of mine house" and rescue the lands and possessions of those driven from Jackson.

Two months later the Lord revealed further instruction concerning these verses. "Let my servant Joseph Smith, Jun., say unto the strength of my house, my young men and the middle aged—Gather yourselves together unto the land of Zion, upon the land which I have bought with money that has been consecrated unto me" (D&C 103:22). An assembly of brethren known as Zion's Camp was instructed to try to obtain land in Missouri without using force. Zion's Camp, if necessary, was to be the power of the priesthood.

The parable states that all things will be fulfilled "after many days" (v. 62), indicating that a long period of time will pass before the redemption of Zion. Though Zion was not redeemed at the time of Zion's Camp, we may look for its redemption in the due time of the Lord (D&C 136:18).

101:56–58 See commentary on Doctrine and Covenants 105:23–30.

The Saints Are Commanded to Continue Gathering Together
DOCTRINE AND COVENANTS 101:63–75

101:63–67 The gathering to the holy places, or stakes of Zion, is likened to wheat that is gathered in bundles. After the wheat has ripened, it is gathered together and bound. Likewise, as the kingdom gains sufficient strength throughout the world, stakes are organized. This is done in preparation for the redemption of Zion in Independence, Missouri, and for the burning of the earth at the Second Coming. The gathering embraces participation in the ordinances of salvation. As the work of the Lord spreads throughout the world, many stakes will yet be organized and many temples will be built wherein the faithful will be "secured in the garners to possess eternal life" (v. 65).

101:68 *Let not your gathering be in haste.* See commentary on Doctrine and Covenants 63:24.

101:70–71 See commentary on Doctrine and Covenants 57:4.

101:72–74 During the few years immediately following this revelation, failure to abide the Lord's counsel in these verses led to many Saints gathering far too quickly in Kirtland, Ohio. The large numbers gathering to Kirtland led to rising real estate prices as the demand for property increased. The possibility of becoming rich tempted the Saints with speculative land ventures. Covetousness entered the Church and infected members of even the presiding quorums with its debilitating spirit. A similar scenario occurred in northern Missouri, resulting in the Saints' being sorely tried by opportunities to seek riches in real estate. John Whitmer and W. W. Phelps, members of the presidency of the Church at Far West, embezzled Church funds to purchase lands, hoping to make a profit selling the land to the gathering Saints. Their covetous desires took them out of the Church; both were excommunicated.

The Lord Established the Constitution of the United States
DOCTRINE AND COVENANTS 101:76–80

101:77–80 Without freedom of religion, there is no salvation. The war in heaven raged over the principle of free choice (Moses 4:1–3). Governments that restrict their citizens' freedom of choice do so under satanic influence. The Lord foreordained the establishment of a nation that granted freedom of religion in the latter days. He fired the heart of Columbus to set out to sea in a quest that brought knowledge of the ancient promised land to Europeans. He inspired men and women to seek religious liberty and planted in their breasts the desire to seek that freedom in the Americas. He sent to mortality choice spirits who craved freedom of conscience for all mankind so they could exert their influence in establishing laws guaranteeing freedom to all citizens. President Ezra Taft Benson explained: "Before the gospel could again shine forth its resplendent light, religious and political freedom first had to be restored. This land had been preserved as a continent apart from the religious oppression, tyranny, and intolerance of Europe. In time, emigrants came to the new land and established colonies. By and large, they were a God-fearing people. A war was fought for their independence, and by God's intervention, victory was achieved. (See 1 Nephi 13:16–19.) By that same omnipotent power the Constitution was born (see D&C 101:80), which guaranteed religious and political liberty (see D&C 98:5–8). Only then was the time propitious for the kingdom of God—that 'stone cut out without hands' to be restored (see Daniel 2:34)" (*Teachings of Ezra Taft Benson*, 109). See commentary on Doctrine and Covenants 98:4–8.

101:78 *Moral agency.* A moral agent is someone who is obligated to act morally. To act morally is more than being moral. All infants are moral beings; they simply cannot knowingly do things that are wrong. They are not, however, moral agents because they do not have power to act or to change their behavior based on an understanding of right and wrong. The more mature children are, the greater their agency. They grow into the ability to act for themselves and to make their own choices.

Similarly, as we grow in intelligence (light and knowledge), obedience, and faith, our agency grows proportionately. To increase in faith and knowledge of spiritual things is to increase in agency. God is the perfect example of a moral agent. No one has greater power to act in a responsible and moral manner than he.

Salvation can only be granted to moral agents. Only moral agents have the ability to distinguish between right and wrong, and they alone have the capacity to be righteous.

101:79 Agency, which is the power to act for ourselves, is, next to life itself, the greatest gift of God. Only with unfettered freedom of choice can we become as God is. Slavery in any form, be it physical, mental, or spiritual, is antithetical to salvation in the kingdom of God. See commentary on Doctrine and Covenants 134:12.

101:80 *I established the Constitution of this land.* "In recognizing God as the source of their rights," taught President Ezra Taft Benson, "the Founding Fathers declared Him to be the ultimate authority for their basis of law. This led them to the conviction that people do not make law but merely acknowledge preexisting law, giving it specific application. The Constitution was conceived to be such an expression of higher law. And when their work was done, James Madison wrote: 'It is impossible for the man of pious reflection not to perceive in it a finger of that Almighty hand which has been so frequently and signally extended to our relief in the critical stage of the revolution' (The Federalist, no. 37)" (*Constitution: A Heavenly Banner*, 23).

Wise men whom I raised up unto this very purpose. Brigham Young declared: "We consider that the men in the Revolution were inspired, by the Almighty, to throw off the shackles of the mother government, with her established religion. For this cause were Adams, Jefferson, Franklin, Washington, and a host of others inspired to deeds of resistance to the acts of the King of Great Britain, who might also have been led to those aggressive acts, for aught we know, to bring to pass the purposes of God, in thus establishing a new government upon a principle of greater freedom, a basis of self-government allowing the free exercise of religious worship.

"It was the voice of the Lord inspiring all those worthy men who bore influence in those trying times, not only to go forth in battle, but to exercise wisdom in council, fortitude, courage, and endurance in the tented field, as well as subsequently to form and adopt those wise and efficient measures which secured to themselves and succeeding generations, the blessing of a free and independent government" (*Journal of Discourses*, 2:170).

The Saints Are to Importune for the Redress of Grievances
DOCTRINE AND COVENANTS 101:81–101

101:86–89 "We believe that men should appeal to the civil law for redress of all wrongs and grievances, where personal abuse is inflicted or the right of property or character infringed, where such laws exist as will protect the same; but we believe that all men are justified in defending themselves, their friends, and property, and the government, from the unlawful assaults and encroachments of all persons in times of exigency, where immediate appeal cannot be made to the laws, and relief afforded" (D&C 134:11).

101:89 *Vex the nation.* The cold disregard of human rights among government officials who rejected the Latter-day Saint appeal for redress in Missouri did much to bring about the Civil War.

101:95 See commentary on Doctrine and Covenants 95:4, "That I may bring to pass my strange act."

101:99 The Prophet Joseph Smith wrote to the Saints in Missouri: "It is better in the eyes of God that you should die, than that you should give up the land of Zion, the inheritances which you have purchased with your moneys; for every man that giveth not up his inheritance, though he should die, yet, when the Lord shall come, he shall stand upon it, and with Job, in his flesh he shall see God. Therefore, this is my counsel, that ye retain your lands, even unto the uttermost, and employ every lawful means to seek redress of your enemies; and pray to God, day and night, to return you in peace and in safety to the lands of your inheritance: and when the judge fail you, appeal unto the executive; and when the executive fail you, appeal unto the president; and when the president fail you, and all laws fail you, and the humanity of the people fail you, and all things else fail you but God alone, and you continue to weary Him with your importunings, as the poor woman did the unjust judge, He will not fail to execute judgment upon your enemies, and to avenge His own elect that cry unto Him day and night" (*Teachings of the Prophet Joseph Smith*, 35–36).

101:101 Of the millennial day Isaiah wrote: "And they shall build houses, and inhabit them; and they shall plant vineyards, and eat the fruit of them. They shall not build, and another inhabit; they shall not plant, and another eat: for as the days of a tree are the days of my people, and mine elect shall long enjoy the work of their hands. They shall not labour in vain, nor bring forth for trouble; for they are the seed of the blessed of the Lord, and their offspring with them" (Isaiah 65:21–23).

And again, "Upon the land of my people shall come up thorns and briers; yea, upon all the houses of joy in the joyous city: Because the palaces shall be forsaken; the multitude of the city shall be left; the forts and towers shall be for dens for ever, a joy of wild asses, a pasture of flocks; Until the spirit be poured upon us from on high, and the wilderness be a fruitful field, and the fruitful field be counted for a forest. Then judgment shall dwell in the wilderness, and righteousness remain in the fruitful field. And the work of righteousness shall be peace; and the effect of righteousness quietness and assurance for ever. And my people shall dwell in a peaceable habitation, and in sure dwellings, and in quiet resting places" (Isaiah 32:13–18).

DOCTRINE AND COVENANTS 102

DATE: 17 FEBRUARY 1834
PLACE: KIRTLAND, OHIO

Doctrine and Covenants 102 consists of the minutes of the meeting at which the first stake high council was organized. It is not a revelation, though the principles out of which it grows were revealed to the Prophet.

In ancient times the Church, or earthly kingdom of God, was governed by councils. This system of government was patterned after the order of heaven. It was essential in the restoration of all things that this divinely ordained system be restored in this dispensation. As the Church grew in numbers, the necessity of a system of governing the Saints grew with it. As early as 1832, the Lord had directed that a stake be organized in Kirtland, Ohio (D&C 82:13). With the organization of this first stake, the idea was formalized for a council of high priests assembled to settle difficult matters. A council of twelve high priests had assembled for this purpose previously, though it had served only on an *ad hoc* basis (*Journal of Discourses*, 11:7).

On 17 February 1834 approximately sixty members of the Church gathered at the home of Joseph Smith in a special meeting to call twelve high priests to serve as members of the high council in what was the first stake organized in this dispensation.

The minutes of the meeting include the following: "Bro Joseph then said he would show the order of councils in ancient days as shown to him by vision. The law by which to govern the Council in the Church of Christ. Jerusalem was the seat of the Church Council in ancient days. The apostle Peter was the president of the Council and held the keys of the Kingdom of God on the earth. [He] was appointed to this office by the voice of the Savior and acknowledged in it by the voice of the Church. . . . It was not the order of heaven in ancient councils to plead for and against the guilty as in our judicial courts (so called) but that every councilor when he arose to speak, should speak precisely according to evidence and according to the teaching of the Sprit of the Lord, that no councilor

743

should attempt to screen the guilty when his guilt was manifest. That the person accused before the High Council had a right to one half the members of the council to plead his cause, in order that his case might be fairly presented before the president that a decision might be rendered according to truth and righteousness. . . . Bro Joseph said that this organization was an ensample to the high priests in their councils abroad. . . . It was then voted by all present that they desired to come under the present order of things which they all considered to be the will of God" (*Kirtland Council Minute Book*, 24–25; spelling and punctuation as in original).

In a meeting held five days earlier the Prophet had observed: "In ancient days councils were conducted with such strict propriety, that no one was allowed to whisper, be weary, leave the room, or get uneasy in the least, until the voice of the Lord, by revelation, or the voice of the council by the Spirit, was obtained, which has not been observed in this Church to the present time. It was understood in ancient days, that if one man could stay in council, another could; and if the president could spend his time, the members could also; but in our councils, generally, one will be uneasy, another asleep; one praying, another not; one's mind on the business of the council, and another thinking on something else.

"Our acts are recorded, and at a future day they will be laid before us, and if we should fail to judge right and injure our fellow-beings, they may there, perhaps, condemn us; there they are of great consequence, and to me the consequence appears to be of force, beyond anything which I am able to express. Ask yourselves, brethren, how much you have exercised yourselves in prayer since you heard of this council; and if you are now prepared to sit in council upon the soul of your brother" (Smith, *History of the Church*, 2:25–26).

The High Council Is to Settle Important Difficulties that Arise in the Church
DOCTRINE AND COVENANTS 102:1–8

102:3 *Joseph Smith, Jun., Sidney Rigdon and Frederick G. Williams were acknowledged presidents by the voice of the council.* "The Kirtland high council was a unique body in the history of the Church, not only because it was the first—and for a while the only—high council, but also because the First Presidency served as the stake presidency of this 'standing' high council. Later the Quorum of the Twelve Apostles was formed as a 'traveling' high council, and on July 7, 1834, the Prophet organized a second high council in Clay County, Missouri, with David Whitmer as president and William W. Phelps and John Whitmer as counselors. These first two high councils were constituted before there were wards and before stake presidents presided over bishops and quorums of high priests" (Backman, *Heavens Resound*, 245).

A standing council. A "standing council" is a council that has authority in a specified area, in this instance the Kirtland Stake. A "traveling council" is not confined by such boundaries. Today we refer to those whose authority is not limited to a specific area as "general authorities" or general officers of the Church.

102:5 These forty-three people, chosen from the sixty who attended the meeting held at the home of the Prophet on 17 February, in turn nominated the twelve men who were called to serve as the first high council in the Church.

102:6 The high council has no authority to act unless seven of the twelve members are present.

102:7 As an illustration of the procedure being announced here, if some members of a stake high council could not attend a church disciplinary council, other worthy high priests could be invited to substitute for them.

Procedures for Hearing Cases
DOCTRINE AND COVENANTS 102:9–18

102:9 *The president of the church, who is also the president of the council.* Today all high councils are presided over by the president of their respective stakes.

102:11 Counselors to a president may preside in the absence of the president if they have been directed to do so by the president. Counselors have no authority independent of the president. When the president is released they are also released.

102:12–17 In a Church disciplinary council, the members of the high council draw lots. Those drawing even numbers (2, 4, 6, 8, 10, and 12) assume the obligation to look after the interests of the one for whom the council is being held. Those drawing odd numbers (1, 3, 5, 7, 9, and 11) assume the obligation to look after the interests of the Church. This, however, does not suggest that an adversarial relation exists. We misunderstand the spirit of the council if we suppose that half its members act as prosecutors while the other half act as defenders. Rather, all twelve men, in concert with the presiding three members of the presidency, unite as one to determine truth and establish right or justice.

102:18 In 1840 the Prophet gave this counsel relative to the holding of church disciplinary councils: "That the Council should try no case without both parties being present, or having had an opportunity to be present; neither should they hear one person's complaint before his case is brought up for trial; neither should they suffer the character of any one to be exposed before the High Council without the person being present and ready to defend him or herself; that the minds of the councilors be not prejudiced for or against any one whose case they may possibly have to act upon" (Smith, *History of the Church*, 4:154).

The President of the Council Renders the Decision and Appellate Procedure Set Forth
DOCTRINE AND COVENANTS 102:19–34

102:19–23 The principles here stated, if followed, will assure that what is right and proper and in the best interest of both the accused and the Church will be made manifest. Church disciplinary councils do not center on an effort to define points of law but rather in a quest for the direction of the Spirit to assure the preservation of justice and truth.

102:23 *Obtain the mind of the Lord.* The decision of every disciplinary council should be sustained by the Spirit of revelation. It is customary in such councils for the presiding officers of the council to retire for prayer, in which they seek the confirmation of heaven on their decision.

102:24–26 Where stakes of Zion have been established throughout the world, this instruction would be obsolete.

102:27 Those against whom judgment is rendered in a Church disciplinary council are always accorded the right of appeal to the First Presidency of the Church.

102:30–32 The Prophet added these verses to this section in the 1835 edition of the Doctrine and Covenants. Their purpose is to place the newly formed Quorum of the Twelve above the stake high council in authority. The Twelve have the right to review and overturn, if necessary, decisions of a stake high council.

DOCTRINE AND COVENANTS 103

DATE: 24 FEBRUARY 1834
PLACE: KIRTLAND, OHIO

During the first week of November 1833 the Saints were driven across the Missouri River from Jackson County to Clay County, where they were received with some degree of kindness. Parley P. Pratt recalled: "After making our escape into the county of Clay—being reduced to the lowest poverty—I made a living by day labor, jobbing, building, or wood cutting, till some time in the winter of 1834, when a general Conference was held at my house, in which it was decided that two of the Elders should be sent to Ohio, in order to counsel with President Smith and the Church at Kirtland, and take some measures for the relief or restoration of the people thus plundered and driven from their homes. The question was put to the Conference: 'Who would volunteer to perform so great a journey?'

"The poverty of all, and the inclement season of the year made all hesitate. At length Lyman Wight and myself offered our services, which were readily accepted. I was at this time entirely destitute of proper clothing for the journey; and I had neither horse, saddle, bridle, money nor provisions to take with me; or to leave with my wife, who lay sick and helpless most of the time" (*Autobiography*, 87).

Elder Wight, responding to Bishop Partridge's inquiry about his situation, said "his wife lay by the side of a log in the woods with a child three days old, and he had three days' provisions on hand; so he thought he could go very well" (*Millennial Star*, 27:455).

Continuing his account of these events, Elder Pratt said, "Nearly all had been robbed and plundered, and all were poor. As we had to start without delay, I almost trembled at the undertaking; it seemed to be all but an impossibility; but 'to him that believeth all things are possible.' I started out of my house to do something towards making preparation; I hardly knew which way to go, but I found myself in the house of brother John Lowry, and was intending to ask him for money; but as I entered his miserable cottage in the swamp, amid the low, timbered bottoms of the

747

Missouri river, I found him sick in bed with a heavy fever, and two or three others of his family down with the same complaint, on different beds in the same room. He was vomiting severely, and was hardly sensible of my presence. I thought to myself, 'well, this is a poor place to come for money, and yet I must have it; I know of no one else that has got it; what shall I do?' I sat a little while confounded and amazed. At length another Elder happened in; at that instant faith sprung up in my heart; the Spirit whispered to me, 'is there anything too hard for the Lord?' I said to the Elder that came in: 'Brother, I am glad you have come; these people must he healed, for I want some money of them, and must have it.'

"We laid hands on them and rebuked the disease; brother Lowry rose up well; I did my errand, and readily obtained all I asked. This provided in part for my family's sustenance while I should leave them. I went a little further into the woods of the Missouri bottoms, and came to a camp of some brethren, by the name of Higbee, who owned some horses; they saw me coming, and, moved by the Spirit, one of them said to the other, 'there comes brother Parley; he's in want of a horse for his journey—I must let him have old Dick;' this being the name of the best horse he had. 'Yes,' said I, 'brother, you have guessed right; but what will I do for a saddle?' 'Well,' says the other, 'I believe I'll have to let you have mine.' I blessed them and went on my way rejoicing.

"I next called on Sidney A. Gilbert, a merchant, then sojourning in the village of Liberty—his store in Jackson County having been broken up, and his goods plundered and destroyed by the mob. 'Well,' says he, 'brother Parley, you certainly look too shabby to start a journey; you must have a new suit; I have got some remnants left that will make you a coat,' etc. A neighboring tailoress and two or three other sisters happened to be present on a visit, and hearing the conversation, exclaimed, 'Yes, brother Gilbert, you find the stuff and we'll make it up for him.' This arranged, I now lacked only a cloak; this was also furnished by brother Gilbert.

"Brother Wight was also prospered in a similar manner in his preparations. Thus faith and the blessings of God had cleared up our way to accomplish what seemed impossible. We were soon ready, and on the first of February we mounted our horses, and started in good cheer to ride one thousand or fifteen hundred miles through a wilderness country. We had not one cent of money in our pockets on starting.

"We travelled every day, whether through storm or sunshine, mud, rain or snow; except when our public duties called us to tarry. We arrived in Kirtland early in the spring, all safe and sound; we had lacked for nothing on the road, and now had plenty of funds in hand. President Joseph Smith and the Church in Kirtland received us with a hospitality and joy unknown except among the Saints; and much interest was felt there, as well as elsewhere, on the subject of our persecution" (*Autobiography*, 87–89).

Elders Wight and Pratt left Clay County on 12 January and arrived in Kirtland on 22 February 1834. After receiving their report of the conditions and sufferings of the Saints in Missouri, the Prophet received this section, which, alluding to the parable in section 101, directed him to organize a body of men to journey to Missouri to redeem the land. Eight men, mentioned in verses 37–40, were to enlist volunteers to make the trip to Missouri.

Heber C. Kimball described the situation thus: "Brother Joseph received a revelation concerning the redemption of Zion, part of which remains yet to be fulfilled. He sent Messengers to the East and to the West and to the North and to the South, to gather up the Elders, and He gathered together as many of the brethren as he conveniently could, with what means they could spare to go up to Zion, to render all the assistance that we could to our afflicted brethren. We gathered clothing and other necessaries to carry up to our brethren and sisters who had been plundered; and putting our horses to the wagons and taking our firelocks and ammunition, we started on our journey; leaving only Oliver Cowdery, Sidney Rigdon and a few aged workmen who were engaged at the Temple; so that there were very few men left in Kirtland" (cited in Cook, *Revelations*, 209).

Why the Lord Permitted the Saints in Jackson County to Be Persecuted
Doctrine and Covenants 103:1–4

103:3 *That they might fill up the measure of their iniquities.* We learn by revelation that the Lord allows atrocities on the part of wicked people that they might merit the judgment he has in store for them. When the wicked inhabitants of Ammonihah destroyed faithful women and children by fire, Amulek asked Alma whether they should exercise power to save them. "The Spirit constraineth me that I must not stretch forth mine hand;" answered Alma, "for behold the Lord receiveth them up unto himself, in glory; and he doth suffer that they may do this thing, or that the people may do this thing unto them, according to the hardness of their hearts, that the judgments which he shall exercise upon them in his wrath may be just; and the blood of the innocent shall stand as a witness against them, yea, and cry mightily against them at the last day" (Alma 14:11).

The wicked determine the severity of their own suffering. The Lord has declared that "the things which they are willing to bring upon others, and love to have others suffer" will come upon them "to the very uttermost" (D&C 121:13).

103:4 *Chastened for a little season.* See commentary on Doctrine and Covenants 101:2.

The Saints Will Prevail If They Keep the Commandments
DOCTRINE AND COVENANTS 103:5–10

103:5–10 Here the Saints are promised that if they will heed the counsel of the Lord they will prevail over all the kingdoms of the world, even to subduing them under their feet until the earth becomes their rightful inheritance. Refusal to heed the Lord's counsel, however, reverses the promise, and it will be their lot, like salt that has lost its savor, to be trodden under the foot of those they sought to emulate. The principle is eternal: To follow the counsel of the Lord is to enjoy the protection of the Lord; to refuse his counsel is to become the heir of all the sorrows and difficulties from which the Lord seeks to protect them.

The Redemption of Zion Will Come by Power, and the Lord Will Go before His People
DOCTRINE AND COVENANTS 103:11–20

103:11–20 Elder Joseph Fielding Smith wrote: "In this instruction the Lord gave them [the Saints driven out of Jackson County] the opportunity to obtain the redemption of Zion and for the exiles to be reinstated in their possessions. Had they remained faithful he would have fulfilled his promise to them. They understood the warnings and that through their continued unfaithfulness the redemption would have to be postponed and they themselves would be thrown down. There have been some who have criticized this, and other revelations, claiming that the word of the Lord failed, for he promised them that if they would gather their forces and go to Zion, he would fight their battles and they would be reinstated and the redemption would immediately come. This promise is not found in any of these revelations. To the contrary, the promise is made that they would have to be obedient in all things and keep inviolate their covenants, or these blessings would be indefinitely postponed. The fact that the Lord declared here once again that the redemption was not to come until after much tribulation indicates that he was fully aware that the time for Zion's redemption had not come, although it could have come if the commandments were fulfilled" (*Church History and Modern Revelation*, 1:483).

The redemption of Zion will come only when the Saints are worthy of the Lord's divine power. On 21 January 1836, after attending to the ordinance of anointing in the upper west school room of the Kirtland Temple, the Prophet Joseph Smith recorded that he "beheld the redemption of Zion. . . . My scribe also received his anointing with us, and saw, in a vision, the armies of heaven protecting the Saints in their return to Zion, and many things which I saw" (Smith, *History of the Church*, 2:381). It is also important to note that throughout all of the revelations concerning inheritances in Zion the Lord indicated that the Saints were to obtain them by purchase (D&C 42:35; 45:65–66; 48:4–5; 57:4–6; 58:49–52; 63:27–30; 101:70–71; 103:23; 105:28–30).

103:12 *After much tribulation . . . cometh the blessing.* See commentary on Doctrine and Covenants 58:3–5.

103:16 *Like as Moses.* The Lord revealed that "the President of the office of the High Priesthood is [called] to preside over the whole church, and to be like unto Moses" (D&C 107:91). When the day comes that the Saints are permitted to redeem their inheritances in Zion, it will be under the direction of the president of the Church.

103:18 *As your fathers were led . . . even so shall the redemption of Zion be.* The initial thought upon reading such a prophesy is that a modern Moses will lead the army of Israel back to their promised inheritance, with the powers of heaven attending as they did Moses at the parting of the Red Sea, bringing water from a rock, and feeding the people with manna from heaven. Such thinking, however, misses the point of this and the attendant revelations that deal with the eventual redemption of Zion. Moses took his people to Sinai and there sought to sanctify them that they might stand in the presence of their God. His people, however, proved themselves emotionally, mentally, and spiritually unready for such an experience and refused it. The Lord in response took from them the Melchizedek, or higher, Priesthood with its attendant ordinances and blessings. They were then consigned to wander in the wilderness for forty years before a new generation could arise with sufficient faith to follow their leaders into the promised land. In likening the events of our day to those of Moses' day, we as a people still appear unwilling and unready to redeem Zion. We have not yet sanctified ourselves that we might stand in the presence of God, and we have not obtained the discipline and faith necessary to live the law of consecration. When a sanctified generation comes, the Lord will call a modern Moses who will lead the armies of Israel with the same power in his priesthood as that known to his ancient counterpart from whom we received the keys of the gathering of Israel.

103:20 *In time ye shall possess the goodly land.* "It appears from this declaration that the redemption of Zion was not to come immediately," explained Joseph Fielding Smith, "but was to be postponed to some future day. Moreover, that day would not come until the members of the Church were willing to keep their covenants and walk unitedly, for until the members of the Church learn to walk in full accord and in obedience with all of the commandments, this day cannot come. It may be necessary in order to bring this to pass for the Lord to use drastic measures and cleanse the Church from everything that offends. This he has promised to do when he is ready to redeem Zion" (*Church History and Modern Revelation*, 1:484).

The Saints Are to Gather to Zion, and Those Who Lay Down Their Lives Will Find Them Again
DOCTRINE AND COVENANTS 103:21–28

103:21–28 These verses call to arms the young and middle-aged men of the Church, directing them to gather upon the land of Zion and "avenge" the Lord of his "enemies" (v. 25). See Doctrine and Covenants 101:55.

103:24 *Ye shall curse them.* See commentary on Doctrine and Covenants 24:15.

103:24–26 While the members of Zion's Camp marched nearer to Jackson County, Missouri, the mob element there met to propose means of stopping them from entering the district. The Prophet Joseph Smith recorded several instances in which the power of the Lord was manifest. "The Jackson mob to the number of about fifteen, with Samuel C. Owens and James Campbell at their head, started for Independence, Jackson county, to raise an army sufficient to meet me, before I could get into Clay county. Campbell swore, as he adjusted his pistols in his holsters, 'The eagles and turkey buzzards shall eat my flesh if I do not fix Joe Smith and his army so that their skins will not hold shucks, before two days are passed.' They went to the ferry and undertook to cross the Missouri river after dusk, and the angel of God saw fit to sink the boat about the middle of the river, and seven out of twelve that attempted to cross, were drowned. Thus, suddenly and justly, went they to their own place. Campbell was among the missing. He floated down the river some four or five miles, and lodged upon a pile of drift wood, where the eagles, buzzards, ravens, crows, and wild animals ate his flesh from his bones, to fulfill his own words, and left him a horrible example of God's vengeance. He was discovered about three weeks after by one Mr. Purtle. Owens saved his life only, after floating four miles down the stream, where he lodged upon an island, 'swam off naked about day light, borrowed a mantle to hide his shame, and slipped home rather shy of the vengeance of God'" (Smith, *History of the Church*, 2:99–100).

Two days after the recording of the previous incident, the Prophet wrote further: "During this day, the Jackson county mob, to the number of about two hundred, made arrangements to cross the Missouri river, above the mouth of Fishing river, at Williams' ferry, into Clay county, and be ready to meet the Richmond mob near Fishing river ford, for our utter destruction; but after the first scow load of about forty had been set over the river, the scow in returning was met by a squall, and had great difficulty in reaching the Jackson side by dark.

"When these five men were in our camp, swearing vengeance, the wind, thunder, and rising cloud indicated an approaching storm, and in a short time after they left the rain and hail began to fall. The storm was tremendous; wind and rain, hail and thunder met them in great wrath, and soon softened their direful courage, and frustrated all their designs to 'kill Joe Smith and his army.' Instead of continuing a cannonading which they commenced when the sun was about one hour high, they crawled under wagons, into hollow trees, and filled one old shanty, till the storm was over, when their ammunition was soaked, and the forty in Clay county were extremely anxious in the morning to return to Jackson, having experienced the pitiless pelting of the storm all night; and as soon as arrangements could be made, this 'forlorn hope' took the 'back track' for Independence, to join the main body of the mob, fully satisfied, as were those survivors of the company who were drowned, that when Jehovah fights they would rather be absent. The gratification is too terrible.

"Very little hail fell in our camp, but from half a mile to a mile around, the stones or lumps of ice cut down the crops of corn and vegetation generally, even cutting limbs from trees, while the trees, themselves were twisted into withes by the wind. The lightning flashed incessantly, which caused it to be so light in our camp through the night, that we could discern the most minute objects; and the roaring of the thunder was tremendous. The earth trembled and quaked, the rain fell in torrents, and, united, it seemed as if the mandate of vengeance had gone forth from the God of battles, to protect His servants from the destruction of their enemies, for the hail fell on them and not on us, and we suffered no harm, except the blowing down of some of our tents, and getting wet; while our enemies had holes made in their hats, and otherwise received damage, even the breaking of their rifle stocks, and the fleeing of their horses through fear and pain.

"Many of my little band sheltered in an old meetinghouse through this night, and in the morning the water in Big Fishing river was about forty feet deep, where, the previous evening, it was no more than to our ankles, and our enemies swore that the water rose thirty feet in thirty minutes in the Little Fishing river. They reported that one of their men was killed by lightning, and that another had his hand torn off by his horse drawing his hand between the logs of a corn crib while he was holding him on the inside. They declared that if that was the way God fought for the Mormons, they might as well go about their business" (Smith, *History of the Church*, 2:103–5).

103:27–28 The Savior declared, "Greater love hath no man than this, that a man lay down his life for his friends" (John 15:13). Those who volunteered to march to Missouri placed their lives on the line to help the Saints in Zion. See commentary on Doctrine and Covenants 98:11–14; 105:19.

Various Brethren Are Called to Organize Zion's Camp
DOCTRINE AND COVENANTS 103:29–40

103:29–40 "Parley P. Pratt and Lyman Wight, the messengers from the land of Zion, were commanded not to return until they had obtained companies to go up unto the land of their brethren. The companies were to be by tens, or by twenties, or by fifties, or by hundreds, until they had obtained the number of five hundred men. If they could not obtain five hundred, they were to seek diligently to get three hundred, and if they could not obtain three hundred, then they were to obtain one hundred. They were not, however, to go up to the land of Zion until they had obtained at least one hundred. The Prophet Joseph was to go up with them and preside in their midst, for, 'all victory and glory is brought to pass unto you through your diligence, faithfulness and prayer of faith.' Parley P. Pratt was to go with Joseph Smith the Prophet; Lyman Wight with Sidney Rigdon; Hyrum Smith with Frederick G. Williams; Orson Hyde with Orson Pratt, on this mission to raise funds and volunteers to undertake this journey to assist their exiled brethren in the land of Zion" (Smith, *Church History and Modern Revelation*, 1:485). This assembled army is known today as Zion's Camp.

The assigned brethren traveled throughout the branches of the Church and raised a sizeable army to redeem Zion. The Prophet Joseph Smith led a group to Missouri and eventually presided over the united army. By the time all the companies met together, Zion's Camp consisted of "207 men, 11 women, 11 children, and 25 baggage wagons" (*Church History in the Fulness of Times*, 143). After the small army reached Fishing River, the Lord revealed to Joseph Smith that the Saints were not yet prepared spiritually to redeem Zion (D&C 105:1–10), and the camp was disbanded.

103:35 *Establish the children of Zion upon the laws and commandments.* See commentary on Doctrine and Covenants 103:20.

DOCTRINE AND COVENANTS 104

DATE: 23 APRIL 1834
PLACE: KIRTLAND, OHIO

Destruction of the Saints' property in Jackson County, Missouri, by lawless mobs contributed to a financial crisis for the Church. Earlier the Lord had given responsibility for the Church's properties to leaders within an organization known as the United Firm. Members of the United Firm were called by revelation and included prominent Saints in both Ohio and Missouri. See commentary on Doctrine and Covenants 78:3–4.

At a meeting of the United Firm on 30 April 1832 in Independence, Missouri, it was "resolved that the firm [secure a] loan [of] fifteen thousand dollars for five years or longer at six per cent annually or semi-annually . . . , and that N. K. Whitney & Co. be appointed to negotiate the same" (Cannon and Cook, *Far West Record*, 48). In late October 1832 the Prophet Joseph Smith and Newel K. Whitney traveled together to New York City. Brother Whitney purchased goods on credit for the mercantile businesses of the United Firm. These goods were used to stock the Newel K. Whitney store in Kirtland, Ohio, and, most probably, the A. Sidney Gilbert store in Independence, Missouri (D&C 57:8; 63:42–43; 64:26). In addition, the United Firm incurred debt for the purchase of the Peter French farm in Kirtland, Ohio (D&C 96), and possibly for land in Jackson County, Missouri. Profits from Church-owned businesses and consecrated funds from the Saints were to pay off these debts. This plan met with difficulties in the fall of 1833 when the Saints in Missouri, specifically members of the United Firm, were unable to contribute financially to the Church because mobs had driven them from their farms and businesses in Jackson County. See introduction to commentary on Doctrine and Covenants 97 and 101.

In addition, in Kirtland, Ohio, an apostate named Philastus Hurlburt brought a lawsuit against Hyrum Smith to obtain property owned by the United Firm. As a result, funds of the United Firm were further drained to pay court costs and lawyer fees, as well as travel expenses. The Prophet Joseph Smith felt that he could not journey to Missouri at the head of Zion's

Camp until the problems concerning the United Firm's debts were resolved. But he realized that "if I do not go [to Missouri], it will be impossible to get my brethren in Kirtland, any of them, to go" (Smith, *History of the Church*, 2:48). Thus, the success of Zion's Camp in restoring the Saints' property in Jackson County, Missouri, was connected to the needs of the United Firm.

Donations were sought from members of the Church, but it soon became evident that sufficient funds would not be raised to pay the notes that were due. Members of the Firm in Kirtland had been meeting for months, counseling with one another and petitioning the Lord to show the way whereby they might free themselves from debt. On 7 April the Prophet wrote, "Bishop Whitney, Elder Frederick G. Williams, Oliver Cowdery, Heber C. Kimball, and myself, met in the council room, and bowed down before the Lord, and prayed that He would furnish the means to deliver the Firm from debt, that they might be set at liberty; also, that I might prevail against that wicked man, Hurlburt, and that he might be put to shame" (Smith, *History of the Church*, 2:47–48). Three days later the Prophet recorded that "it was agreed that the Order should be dissolved, and each one have his stewardship set off to him" (Smith, *History of the Church*, 2:49). By such a plan the property of the Church managed by the United Firm could be protected. The creditors would have claim on property held by the United Firm, not on property owned by individuals. This move was not made to escape responsibility for paying debts but rather to give the Church more time to gather needed funds and to allow the Prophet to travel with Zion's Camp to Missouri.

The actual division of the property was postponed for two weeks in the hope that such a course might not be necessary. When the council met again on 23 April, the Lord confirmed by revelation that he approved their decision to assign properties to individuals, but rather than allow the council to dissolve the United Firm, the Lord commanded that they reorganize into two separate orders in Ohio and Missouri. He also gave instructions regarding the Church's assets and the obligation of members of the United Firm to pay their debts.

Saints Who Transgress against the United Order Shall Be Cursed

DOCTRINE AND COVENANTS 104:1–10

104:1 *The order which I commanded to be organized and established.* This reference is to the literary and mercantile establishments organized under the titles of Literary Firm and United Firm. See commentary on Doctrine and Covenants 70:3; 78:3–4.

104:4 *Inasmuch as some of my servants have not kept the commandment.* Apparently the commandment referred to here is recorded in section 98, which reads: "Behold, I, the Lord, am not well pleased with many who are in the church at Kirtland; For they do not forsake their sins, and their wicked ways, the pride of their hearts, and their covetousness, and all their detestable things, and observe the words of wisdom and eternal life which I have given unto them. Verily I say unto you, that I, the Lord, will chasten them and will do whatsoever I list, if they do not repent and observe all things whatsoever I have said unto them. And again I say unto you, if ye observe to do whatsoever I command you, I, the Lord, will turn away all wrath and indignation from you, and the gates of hell shall not prevail against you" (D&C 98:19–22).

Broken the covenant through covetousness. The kingdom of God can only be built on the principles of selflessness and sacrifice. "Covetousness" and "detestable things" can have no place in such a kingdom. Those entering into a covenant community such as those established by the Saints in Ohio and Missouri were required to do so with all their heart and soul. Such people must "seek first the kingdom of God and its righteousness" with the confidence that in pursuing such a course their own needs would be met. Those entering a united order for personal gain inevitably found reason to be disgruntled and unhappy. The spirit of such people is not difficult to identify, as illustrated by the following recollection of Brigham Young.

"In the fall of 1833, many of the brethren had gathered to Kirtland, and not finding suitable employment, and having some difficulty in getting their pay after they had labored, several went off to Willoughby, Painesville, and Cleveland. I told them I had gathered to Kirtland because I was so directed by the Prophet of God, and I was not going away to Willoughby, Painesville, Cleveland, nor any where else to build up the Gentiles, but I was going to stay here and seek the things that pertained to the kingdom of God by listening to the teachings of his servants, and I should work for my brethren and trust in God and them that I would be paid" (Watson, *Manuscript History of Brigham Young*, 7).

The Saints in Missouri brought upon themselves the tribulations suffered at the hands of mobs in Jackson County because of their "covetous desires" (D&C 101:6). Nephi, speaking to those of our day, taught that "the laborer in Zion shall labor for Zion; for if they labor for money they shall perish" (2 Nephi 26:31).

A. Sidney Gilbert, manager of the mercantile branch of the United Firm in Independence, Missouri, was specifically warned of the punishments that would befall him if he did not repent of his covetousness. On 14 January 1833, Orson Hyde and Hyrum Smith wrote in behalf of a conference of twelve high priests in Kirtland to Bishop Partridge and the Saints in Zion: "There is manifestly an uneasiness in Brother Gilbert, and a fearfulness that God will not provide for His Saints in these last days, and these fears lead him on to covetousness. This ought not so to be; but let him do just as the Lord has commanded him, and then the Lord will open his coffers, and his wants will be liberally supplied. But if this uneasy, covetous disposition be cherished by him, the Lord will bring him to poverty, shame, and disgrace" (Smith, *History of the Church*, 1:319).

Feigned words. Words spoken falsely for personal gain.

I have cursed them with a very sore and grievous curse. God's law dictates prosperity for those who keep the commandments; for those who disobey, he warned, "Instead of blessings, ye, by your own works, bring cursings, wrath, indignation, and judgments upon your own heads, by your follies, and by all your abominations, which you practise before me, saith the Lord" (D&C 124:48).

104:5 *He shall be cursed in his life.* As the keeping of covenants brings the blessings of heaven, so the breaking of covenants brings sorrows of all kinds. And as affirmed by a host of scriptures, the curses that flow from disobedience are both temporal and spiritual. They include famine, sickness, pestilence, slavery, poverty, war, and death. Those who disobey God hardly need wait for the world to come to reap as they have sown.

104:6–10 Here the Lord reaffirms and amplifies the warning given when the United Firm was first organized. See commentary on Doctrine and Covenants 78:12.

The Lord Provides for His Saints in His Own Way
DOCTRINE AND COVENANTS 104:11–16

104:11 *Appoint every man his stewardship.* This command indicated that the United Firm was to be reorganized with individuals receiving stewardships over specific Church-owned property. In so doing the Lord approved of the decisions made by members of the Firm in earlier council meetings (see introduction to this section). Each person was accountable to make his stewardship profitable. The income from Church-owned property was used for printing scriptures and purchasing lands of inheritance for the Saints. In addition, with this command the Lord reemphasized that he was the master of the earth and the Saints were his stewards.

104:14 *Stretched out the heavens.* This phrase, which comes from Isaiah, conveys the idea that the Lord took of extant materials and created the sun, the moons, and the stars, and placed them in their courses in the heavens (Isaiah 42:5; 45:12).

Built the earth. The notion common to the theology of the historical Christian world is that the universe was brought into being out of nothing by the free act of God. Here the Lord testifies that he "built the earth," that is, it was organized of "chaotic matter," or element that is eternal (*Teachings of the Prophet Joseph Smith*, 351; Abraham 3:24).

All things therein are mine. "The earth is the Lord's, and the fulness thereof; the world, and they that dwell therein" (Psalm 24:1). All accountable souls are stewards of what the Lord chooses to give them during their mortal sojourn. Each of us will be called upon to give an accounting of what we did with the talents, abilities, opportunities, and earthly wealth given to us to bless others.

104:16 The Lord's means of providing for his Saints was revealed to the Prophet Joseph Smith when he arrived in Kirtland, Ohio, in February 1831 and constitutes the "law of the Church" (*History of the Church*, 1:148). The Saints were commanded to consecrate all their property to the Lord and to receive stewardships from the bishop of the Church. The portion of the Lord's law governing earthly property is known as the law of consecration and stewardship. See commentary on Doctrine and Covenants 42:30–39.

The poor shall be exalted, in that the rich are made low. Explaining this phrase, Elder Harold B. Lee observed that to be exalted, the poor have to be "stimulated to success and pride, and uplifted because the rich have been made low, or in other words, because the rich have been made humble and willing to give of their substance, their time, and their talent, and their wisdom, and their example that the poor might be thus guided and directed" (Conference Report, October 1941, 113).

Gospel Law Governs Care of the Poor
DOCTRINE AND COVENANTS 104:17–18

104:17–18 The earth was created by an all-knowing God who assures us that this world is rich enough to feed, clothe, and house all his children. Standing opposite this declaration are such notions as social Darwinism (survival of the fittest) and the prophets of doom who preach against our having more than one or two children. The testimony of heaven is that the earth is capable of providing the necessities of life for all its inhabitants.

God holds his children responsible for their management and distribution of the earth's riches. Were this done according to gospel principles, there would be no poor or needy, except by choice, among all the nations of the earth.

Having created the earth and placed Adam and Eve on it, the Lord blessed them and said, "Be fruitful, and multiply, and replenish the earth, and subdue it: and have dominion over the fish of the sea, and over the fowl of the air, and over every living thing that moveth upon the earth" (Genesis 1:28).

To those of our dispensation the Lord said, "For, behold, the beasts of the field and the fowls of the air, and that which cometh of the earth, is ordained for the use of man for food and for raiment, and that he might have in abundance. But it is not given that one man should possess that which is above another, wherefore the world lieth in sin" (D&C 49:19–20).

"The precepts of men would have you believe that by limiting the population of the world, we can have peace and plenty," Ezra Taft Benson observed. "That is the doctrine of the devil. Small numbers do not insure peace; only righteousness does. After all, there were only a handful of men on the earth when Cain interrupted the peace of Adam's household by slaying Abel. On the other hand, the whole city of Enoch was peaceful; and it was taken into heaven because it was made up of righteous people. . . .

"A major reason why there is famine in some parts of the world is because evil men have used the vehicle of government to abridge the freedom that men need to produce abundantly.

"True to form, many of the people who desire to frustrate God's purposes of giving mortal tabernacles to his spirit children through worldwide birth control are the very same people who support the kinds of government that perpetuate famine. They advocate an evil to cure the results of the wickedness they support" (Conference Report, April 1969, 12).

104:18 *Impart not his portion, according to the law of my gospel.* Having admonished the Saints of his day to be generous with all who were in need, King Benjamin then cautioned that they do so "in wisdom and order" (Mosiah 4:27). The gospel plan requires all to labor according to their ability. Honest toil and labor are as much a part of the gospel as faith and repentance. Any system of giving to those who claim need that reinforces indolence or idleness stands contrary to the gospel plan and will result in evil. Part of the preparation given the Savior for his ministry was to learn a trade at the hand of his earthly father, Joseph. All men, in like manner, should learn to provide for their own, for many of life's greatest lessons will be learned in this process.

He shall, with the wicked, lift up his eyes in hell. The rich who covet their property and keep it from those in need are in danger of damnation. They misuse the trust God placed in them by granting them the riches of the earth.

The language of this verse comes from the Savior's parable of Lazarus and the rich man. After his death, angels carried Lazarus to the bosom of Abraham. "The rich man also died, and was buried; And in hell he lift up his eyes, being in torments" (Luke 16:22–23). For the rich, a great test of character is their willingness to give of their abundance to those in need. See commentary on Doctrine and Covenants 56:16, "Your riches will canker your souls."

Stewardships and Blessings of Various Brethren Are Designated
DOCTRINE AND COVENANTS 104:19–46

104:19–46 The instructions found in these verses replaced previous direction concerning assignments of property to the Church building committee in section 94. By assigning the responsibility to manage Church-owned properties, the Lord emphasized what he had previously taught: those who manage property are his stewards. All individuals who received stewardships over property were members of the United Firm. For years the names of those receiving stewardships and the property that they received were published with substitute names and descriptions. This protected the property from being taken from members of the United Firm before they could obtain means to pay their debts. The original manuscripts of the revelation contained the names and properties as they have been published since the 1981 edition of the Doctrine and Covenants. From 1876 to 1981 the correct names followed the substitute names in parentheses.

104:20 Prior to joining the Church, Sidney Rigdon made his living as a tanner and Protestant preacher. The Lord utilized Sidney's talents to bless the Church.

104:26 Martin Harris, as a member of the Literary Firm, was responsible, with other Firm members, for printing the scriptures and other Church publications (D&C 70:1–4). Martin was commanded to use his wealth to see that the revelations were printed, as he had earlier done in the publishing of the Book of Mormon (D&C 19:26).

104:28–29 Following the mob violence in Jackson County, Missouri, W. W. Phelps no longer had a printing press to publish the *Book of Commandments* or the Church newspaper, *The Evening and the Morning Star*. The Church purchased a second printing press for use in the printing office in Kirtland, Ohio. Along with Oliver Cowdery, Frederick G. Williams received stewardship over the printing office and became the editor of another Church newspaper, the *Star*, which succeeded the newspaper in Independence, Missouri.

104:34–35 John Johnson received most of the property purchased from Peter French. See introduction to Doctrine and Covenants 96.

104:39–40 Bishop Newel K. Whitney received as a stewardship the properties he had originally consecrated to the Church. These included his home, store, and an ashery, where soap was made.

104:43 The Prophet Joseph Smith held title to the lot upon which the Kirtland Temple was built. He received a home, located near the temple lot, in which he had been living. Later, the title of the Kirtland Temple, following its completion, was put in his name.

The United Order in Kirtland and the Order in Zion Are to Operate Separately
DOCTRINE AND COVENANTS 104:47–53

104:47–53 "The Lord . . . commanded that there should be a separation of the United Order in Zion from the Order in Kirtland," explained Joseph Fielding Smith. "Each was to act henceforth independently of the other. Distance was too great between these places for unity of purpose in all things. Each order was to be organized in the names of the brethren residing in each place, and to do business in their own names. This separation and dissolving of the former order came about also because of transgression and covetousness on the part of some" (*Church History and Modern Revelation*, 1:489).

The Sacred Treasury of the Lord Is Set Up
for the Printing of the Scriptures
DOCTRINE AND COVENANTS 104:54–66

104:58 *Even to print my words, the fulness of my scriptures.* The Lord's mention of "the fulness of my scriptures" refers to the Prophet Joseph Smith's inspired translation of the Bible. At the time the Prophet received this revelation, the work of translation was already completed. On 2 July 1833 the First Presidency wrote from Kirtland to the brethren in Zion: "We are exceedingly fatigued, owing to a great press of business. We this day finished the translating of the Scriptures, for which we returned gratitude to our Heavenly Father" (Smith, *History of the Church*, 1:368). In June 1835 the Prophet Joseph Smith wrote to the Saints: "We are now commencing to prepare and print the New Translation, together with all the revelations which God has been pleased to give us in these last days, and we are in want of funds to go on with so great and glorious a work, brethren, [we] want you [to] donate and loan us all the means or money you can that we may be enable[d] to accomplish the work as a great means towards the salvation of men" (Jessee, *Personal Writings of Joseph Smith*, 343–44). The new translation was to be published as a single volume. The Prophet Joseph Smith wrote to W. W. Phelps, editor of *The Evening and the Morning Star*: "It is not the will of the Lord to print any of the New Translation in the *Star*; but when it is published, it will all go to the world together, in a volume by itself; and the New Testament and the Book of Mormon will be printed together" (*History of the Church*, 1:341). Lack of financial support from the Saints, persecution, and pressing temporal concerns prevented the new translation of the Bible from being printed during the Prophet's lifetime.

The revelations which I have given unto you. This refers to the revelations given through the Prophet Joseph Smith up to this time, many of which are printed in the Doctrine and Covenants.

The revelations . . . which I shall, hereafter, from time to time give unto you. Latter-day Saints do not believe in a closed canon. "We believe all that God has revealed, all that He does now reveal, and we believe that He will yet reveal many great and important things pertaining to the Kingdom of God" (Article of Faith 9). Seeing our day, Nephi addressed those who seek to close the heavens to revelation and silence God, saying: "Wo be unto him that shall say: We have received the word of God, and we need no more of the word of God, for we have enough! For behold, thus saith the Lord God: I will give unto the children of men line upon line, precept upon precept, here a little and there a little; and blessed are those who hearken unto my precepts, and lend an ear unto my counsel, for they shall learn wisdom; for unto him that receiveth I will give more; and from them that shall say, We have enough, from them shall be taken away even that which they have" (2 Nephi 28:29–30).

104:60–66 The Lord commanded that profits generated from the sale of the scriptures be placed into a special treasury, named by him "the sacred treasury of the Lord" (v. 66). The funds in this treasury were to remain separate from other contributions for the building up of the kingdom of God. This command preserves the sacred purpose of publishing books of scripture. No individual or people are to profit from publishing the word of God.

104:63 Funds to print the scriptures were to be generated by individual stewardships, which this revelation assigned to members of the United Firm. Earlier, funds were to be generated by the combined efforts of the United Firm. On 25 June 1833 the Prophet Joseph Smith wrote to the Saints in Missouri, "The order of the Literary Firm is a matter of stewardship, which is of the greatest importance; and the mercantile establishment God commanded to be devoted to the support thereof" (*History of the Church*, 1:365–66). Although stewardships for Church properties were given into the hands of individuals at this time, the responsibility of the members of the United Firm remained the same: they were to generate profits that could be used to publish the word of the Lord.

The General Treasury of the United Order Is to Operate on the Basis of Common Consent
DOCTRINE AND COVENANTS 104:67–77

104:67–76 Members of the United Firm placed profits they earned from managing Church-owned properties into the second treasury mentioned in these verses. No individual had any claim to the profits generated from these stewardships. Members of the United Firm determined, as a council, the use of treasury funds. The funds were used to improve the Church's properties or for further purchases made in behalf of the Church.

Those in the United Order Are to Pay All Their Debts
DOCTRINE AND COVENANTS 104:78–86

104:78–81 See the introduction to this section concerning loans secured from creditors in New York City.

104:78 *You shall pay all your debts.* Latter-day Saints are to be honest in all their dealings. Those who contract financial obligations should make every effort to meet their obligations. The debts specifically referred to in this revelation were incurred by loans secured in behalf of the Church. The name of the Church must not be held in disrepute because those stewards responsible for Church finances secure loans that go unpaid. Regardless of who contracted debt as an agent of the Lord, all his agents are responsible to pay the debt incurred.

Those who were later called to positions of trust similar to that of members of the United Firm assumed the debts and obligations entered into by their predecessors. Brigham Young accepted responsibility for the Prophet Joseph Smith's debts. "Joseph was doing business in Kirtland," Brigham explained, "and it seemed as though all creation was upon him, to hamper him in every way, and they drove him from his business, and it left him so that some of his debts had to be settled afterwards; and I am thankful to say that they were settled up; still further, we have sent East to New York, to Ohio, and to every place where I had any idea that Joseph had ever done business, and inquired if there was a man left to whom Joseph Smith, Jun., the Prophet, owed a dollar, or a sixpence. If there was we would pay it. But I have not been able to find one. I have advertised this through every neighborhood and place where he formerly lived, consequently I have a right to conclude that all his debts were settled" (*Journal of Discourses*, 18:242).

104:83 *Your bondage.* Debt places an individual in bondage to the creditor every bit as much as the children of Israel were in bondage to Pharaoh in Egypt.

104:84 *A chance to loan money.* This phrase refers to securing a loan, not to loaning money to someone else. The United Firm was without money to loan. Here the Lord gave the United Firm permission to use Church-owned properties as collateral for needed funds.

DOCTRINE AND COVENANTS 105

DATE: 22 JUNE 1834
PLACE: FISHING RIVER, MISSOURI

During the spring of 1834 Joseph Smith led an army of more than two hundred of his brethren, known as Zion's Camp, from Kirtland, Ohio, to Clay County, Missouri—a distance of one thousand miles. Their objective was to help the Missouri Saints reclaim their homes and property in Jackson County, from which they had been driven by mobs (D&C 103). While the Prophet's party was encamped on Fishing River, he received this revelation.

Zion's Camp left Kirtland on 5 May 1834 with a pledge from Governor Dunklin of Missouri that the state would give those who had been driven from their homes and lands a military escort back to reclaim that which was rightfully theirs. The plan was published and sent to the eastern branches of the Church.

Zion's Camp crossed the Mississippi River in early June, arriving at the Salt River Branch of the Church in Monroe County, Missouri, on 7 June 1834. After a short rest there the camp resumed its march on 12 June. Three days later Orson Hyde and Parley P. Pratt brought the message to the camp that Governor Dunklin was refusing to fulfill his promise to help the Saints reclaim their homes, which he did to avert action he believed would escalate into civil war.

Because Zion's Camp was intended only to work in concert with the authority of the state, the governor's refusal frustrated the camp's designs. As a result, the camp moved to Clay County, where the refugees from Jackson County had gathered to consider what to do. The Prophet received this revelation after their arrival in that county.

Zion Shall Be Built Up by Conformity to Celestial Law
DOCTRINE AND COVENANTS 105:1–5

105:3 *Do not impart of their substance, as becometh saints.* One of the most fundamental of all virtues is to care for the needy. When asked by the people how they could "bring forth . . . fruits worthy of repentance," John the Baptist answered, "He that hath two coats, let him impart to him that hath none; and he that hath meat, let him do likewise" (Luke 3:8, 11). King Benjamin taught his people that to retain a remission of sins "ye yourselves will succor those that stand in need of your succor; ye will administer of your substance unto him that standeth in need; and ye will not suffer that the beggar putteth up his petition to you in vain, and turn him out to perish" (Mosiah 4:16).

In contrast to these teachings, some of the Saints in Missouri would not even care for the sick of Zion's Camp. An example of this disobedience occurred shortly before the camp disbanded. At the end of their thousand-mile journey, the men of Zion's Camp stayed temporarily on the land of a Brother Burgett. Heber C. Kimball said: "While we were here, the brethren being in want of some refreshment, Brother Luke Johnson went to Brother Burgett to get a fowl, asking him for one to make a broth for Elder Wilcox and others [who were stricken with cholera]; but Brother Burgett denied him it, saying, 'In a few days we expect to return back into Jackson County, and I shall want them when I get there.' When Brother Johnson returned he was so angry at Burgett for refusing him, he said, 'I have a great mind to take my rifle and go back and shoot his horse.' I told Luke to never mind; that such actions never fail to bring their reward.

"Judge how we felt, after having left the society of our beloved families, taking our lives in our hands and traveling about one thousand miles through scenes of suffering and sorrow, for the benefit of our brethren, and after all to be denied of a small fowl to make a little soup for brethren in the agonies of death. Such things never fail to bring their reward, and it would do well for the Saints never to turn away a brother who is penniless and in want, or a stranger, lest they may one day or other want a friend themselves" (Whitney, *Life of Heber C. Kimball*, 62).

105:4 Zion cannot be redeemed save it be by a "Zion" people. When Enoch took his city into heaven, he took a people worthy of a heavenly home. Avarice, greed, selfishness, and meanness of spirit in any of its forms can have no place among such a people. A perfect love, manifesting itself in concern for others, must prevail. The spirit and nature of such a community must be one and the same with what we would expect to find in celestial realms. Of such a spirit, Alma taught those gathered at the waters of Mormon "that there should be no contention one with another, but that they should look forward with one eye, having one faith and one baptism, having their hearts knit together in unity and in love one towards another" (Mosiah 18:21). To those of our day the Lord said, "Be one; and if ye are not one ye are not mine" (D&C 38:27). Of those of Enoch's city the Lord said, "They were of one heart and one mind" (Moses 7:18).

Brigham Young explained: "The Savior sought continually to impress upon the minds of his disciples that a perfect oneness reigned among all celestial beings—that the Father and the Son and their minister, the Holy Ghost, were one in their administration in heaven and among the people pertaining to this earth. Between them and all the heavenly hosts there can be no disunion, no discord, no wavering on a suggestion, on a thought or reflection, on a feeling or manifestation; for such a principle would differ widely from the character of Him who dictates them, who makes his throne the habitation of justice, mercy, equity, and truth. If the heavenly hosts were not one, they would be entirely unfit to dwell in the eternal burnings with the Father and Ruler of the universe" (*Journal of Discourses*, 7:276).

105:5 Zion is a celestial city; it is the earthly abode of the Lord. Zion can be built upon only one standard: those that inhabit her must be worthy to behold the face of the Lord. Before this earth can be "crowned with glory, even with the presence of God the Father" (D&C 88:19), cities of Zion must fill the breadth and width of her lands. Each time a stake of Zion was organized under the direction of Joseph Smith, a city of Zion was prepared to which the Saints were to gather. The next phase of establishing Zion is that of perfecting the Saints who live within the geographical boundaries of a stake. The earth cannot roll back into the presence of God until we have learned to build a celestial kingdom founded on the laws given by the Lord to sanctify and purify us. The labor is spiritual in nature and made possible through the atoning blood of Jesus Christ. Each individual citizen of Zion must be washed clean and be able to abide the law of a celestial kingdom (D&C 88:22).

Redemption of Zion Deferred for a Little Season
DOCTRINE AND COVENANTS 105:6–13

105:6–10 After citing these verses, President Lorenzo Snow said: "Hence we learn that the Saints in Jackson County and other localities, refused to comply with the order of consecration, consequently they were allowed to be driven from their inheritances; and should not return until they were better prepared to keep the law of God, by being more perfectly taught in reference to their duties, and learn through experience the necessity of obedience. And I think we are not justified in anticipating the privilege of returning to build up the center stake of Zion, until we shall have shown obedience to the law of consecration. One thing, however, is certain, we shall not be permitted to enter the land from whence we were expelled, till our hearts are prepared to honor this law, and we become sanctified through the practice of the truth.

"The Lord required that those lands in Missouri should be obtained, not by force, but by purchase, through the consecrations of the properties of the Saints; and the manner was pointed out how these consecrations should be made, but it was disregarded" (*Journal of Discourses*, 16:276).

105:7 *First elders.* See commentary on Doctrine and Covenants 20:2.

105:8 The phrase "churches abroad" refers to the various branches of the restored Church of Jesus Christ outside of Kirtland, Ohio. The Prophet Joseph Smith sent word to these branches that money was needed to help the afflicted Saints in Missouri. The Saints donated little in response to his plea. He wrote concerning the Saints' refusal to help pay the debts of the United Firm (see introduction to commentary on D&C 104) and aid those driven from their homes in Missouri:

"If this Church, which is essaying to be the Church of Christ will not help us, when they can do it without sacrifice, with those blessings which God has bestowed upon them, I prophesy—I speak the truth, I lie not—God shall take away their talent, and give it to those who have no talent, and shall prevent them from ever obtaining a place of refuge, or an inheritance upon the land of Zion; therefore they may tarry, for they might as well be overtaken where they are, as to incur the displeasure of God, and fall under His wrath by the way side, as to fall into the hands of a merciless mob, where there is no God to deliver, as salt that has lost its savor, and is thenceforth good for nothing, but to be trodden under foot of men" (Smith, *History of the Church*, 2:48).

105:9 *Wait for a little season for the redemption of Zion.* When this revelation was given, the "little season" was to end 11 September 1836 (see commentary on Doctrine and Covenants 105:23–26). Because the Saints did not obey the Lord's counsel by imparting to those in need, the little season has lengthened to however much time passes before the Saints learn to live according to the principles of the celestial kingdom.

105:11 *Until mine elders are endowed with power from on high.* The endowment referred to is administered in temples. The ordinances associated with the endowment were received in this dispensation in the Kirtland Temple. These included washings and anointings, as well as a pouring out of the Lord's Spirit as on the day of Pentecost in Acts 2. The fulness of the endowment as administered in temples today was not available until the Nauvoo Temple was built.

The Lord Will Fight the Battles of Zion
DOCTRINE AND COVENANTS 105:14-19

105:14 *I will fight your battles.* The Saints were not required and will not be required to cleanse the area of Independence, Missouri, of wickedness. The Lord will secure the lands for the building of the temple and the inheritances of the righteous in his own way. To this end he instructed the Saints to purchase the lands of their inheritance (vv. 28–30). The Prophet clarified that the Lord never did intend that the Saints in Zion's Camp would battle the Missourians. See commentary on Doctrine and Covenants 105:19.

105:15 In the *Comprehensive History of the Church*, Elder B. H. Roberts documents the destruction that took place in Missouri during the Civil War. Many of the citizens of Jackson County and the surrounding regions were expelled from their homes as opposing Union and Confederate militias raided their lands. Citing a work by the Reverend W. M. Leftwich in *Martyrdom in Missouri*, Brother Roberts wrote, "The warfare at home [Missouri] presented scenes of outrage and horror unsurpassed by anything in the annals of civilized warfare, if, indeed, there can be such a thing as civilized warfare, for everything about it is intensely savage.

"Between the 'jayhawkers' of Kansas and the 'bushwackers' of Missouri some whole counties were plundered, some were desolated by fire and sword, and some were almost depopulated" (*Comprehensive History of the Church*, 1:547).

"Most Missourians were Southern in origin and culture," observed Albert Castel in his work on William Quantrill, one of the bloodiest of the Missouri bushwackers. "Although relatively few of them owned slaves, and most of these few did not own many, like the vast majority of Southerners they regarded the antislavery crusade in the North as a monstrous threat to their whole way of life. Negro slavery was to them much more than a mere economic matter. It was above all a system of race control and social order, the very basis of White Supremacy and of Southern Civilization. Consequently 'abolitionism' was a dread specter which aroused the deepest emotions of fear and wrath in their breasts. . . .

"Missourians joined the dark passions of the South to the rough turbulence of the West. Violent feelings, violent words, and violent deeds came naturally to them" (Castel, *William Clark Quantrill*, 2–3). He held this to be especially true of those counties that had so violently driven the Saints from their borders a few years earlier.

So it was that these western counties became a "seething hell" that produced the bloodiest men in our nation's history. Brawls, brutal whippings, shootings, and lynchings became daily occurrences. These men drove from the borders of their state those opposed to slavery, only to find the favor returned as they too were eventually driven from their homelands. "The outbreak of civil war in Missouri gave the Kansas jayhawkers the chance of their lifetime. Not only would the divided and strife-torn Missourians be unable to offer them any effective resistance, but they would now be able to steal horses, plunder farms, and liberate slaves in the name of the Union and under the guise of suppressing rebellion" (Castel, *William Clarke Quantrill*, 52).

This provided the Missourians with a greater reason to hate, to remember the wrongs committed against them, and to seek revenge. Their answer to their neighbors' depredations came in the form of bushwackers who more than returned the favor. Thus the state of Missouri became the devil's host as the bitter hostility between unionists and secessionists was overshadowed by guerilla warfare fought on the principle that one must kill or be killed. So dark did the scene become that "by the end of the war there was to be far more killing of Missourians by Missourians than by Kansans" (Castel, *William Clarke Quantrill*, 61–62).

On 21 August 1863 William Quantrill led his Missouri bushwackers on the "single most atrocious event of the entire Civil War." In an attack on Lawrence, Kansas, he left two hundred bodies littered in yards, doorways, and sidewalks and a hundred homes in flames. In response, Brigadier General Thomas Ewing Jr. of the Union Army issued his famous General Order No. 11, announcing that everyone living in Jackson, Cass, and Bates Counties was to leave their homes by 9 September. If they established their loyalty with the commanding officer nearest their residence, they would be permitted to remove to any military station in the district, or to any part of Kansas other than the eastern border counties. All others were to remove themselves from the areas involved. The order was enforced by military action (Castel, *William Clarke Quantrill*, 145).

The next two weeks witnessed a mass exodus from the border counties. Only a few families were permitted to stay. Thousands loaded their household goods onto wagons, gathered what stock they could take with them, and either crossed into northern Missouri or began trekking southward. A unionist living near Kansas City recorded that "poor people, widows and children, who, with little bundles of clothing, are crossing the river to be subsisted by the charities of the people amongst whom they might find shelter." Another reported that "women, barefooted and shivering in the cold, were driving oxen and riding upon miserable broken-down horses without saddles." And still another recorded, "A desolated country and men & women and children, some of them all most naked. Some on foot and some in old wagons. Oh God" (as quoted in Castel, *William Clarke Quantrill*, 145–46).

"Most of the soldiers enforcing the order were vengeance-minded Kansans who welcomed such a splendid opportunity to punish the Missourians. In addition, gangs of Red Legs swarmed into the depopulated area, looting, burning, and murdering indiscriminately" (Castel, *William Clarke Quantrill*, 146).

"If Missouri in the preceding generation had sown to the wind, when the Latter-day Saints were the victims of their cruel lawlessness, Missouri in the Civil War period reaped the whirlwind," noted B. H. Roberts. "The measure they had meted out to the saints was surely meted out to them again, pressed down and running over more than a hundred fold was the measure increased unto her. . . .

"The Missourians lived to see the outbreak of a 'civil war' in their state that was one of the most appalling men ever witnessed; and Missouri, when all things are considered, and especially western Missouri, suffered more than any other state of the Union. In other states the war lasted at most but four years; but counting her western border warfare in the struggle for Kansas, the war was waged in western Missouri from 1855 to 1865, ten years; and for many years after the close of the Civil War, a guerrilla warfare was intermittently carried on by bands of outlaws harbored in western Missouri—especially in Jackson, Ray, Caldwell and Clay counties—that terrorized the community and shocked the world by the daring and atrocity of their crimes—including bank robberies in open day, express train wrecking and robberies, and murders. . . .

"But what immeasurably added to her suffering, and especially to the suffering of western Missouri, was the spirit of lawlessness, rapine, murder and mobocracy engendered in the minds of the inhabitants of that section of the state, by their treatment of the Latter-day Saints, and the course the state pursued with reference to them.

"It is in no spirit of gloating exultation that the foregoing facts in Missouri's history are referred to here. It gives no gratification to the writer to recount the woes of Missouri, and his hope is that it will give none to the reader. These facts of history are set down only because they are valuable for the lesson they teach. It may be that visible retribution does not always follow in the wake of state or national wrong-doing; but it is well that it should sometimes do so, lest men should come to think that Eternal Justice sleeps, or that she may be thwarted, or, what would be worst of all, that she does not exist. I say it is well, therefore, that sometimes visible retribution should follow state and national as well as individual transgressions, that the truth of the great principle that 'as men sow, so shall they reap,' may be vindicated. Missouri in her treatment of the Latter-day Saints during the years 1833–9, sowed the wind; in the disastrous events which overtook her during the years 1855–1880, she reaped the whirlwind. Let us hope that in those events Justice was fully vindicated so far as the state of Missouri is concerned; and that the lessons of her sad experience may not be lost to the world" (*Comprehensive History of the Church*, 1:551–59).

105:17 The Lord called for five hundred brethren to march with Zion's Camp (D&C 103:30). Only 205 responded.

105:18 *I have prepared a blessing and an endowment for them.* Members of Zion's Camp were the first to receive the preparatory ordinances of the temple endowment in Kirtland, Ohio. See commentary on verses 33–36.

105:19 *For a trial of their faith.* The Lord knew before he called upon the Saints to raise an army of men to redeem Zion that they were not yet ready to live the laws necessary for her redemption. Yet the Lord had purpose in his command that they travel to Missouri as an army of Saints. Only 205 brethren volunteered to journey with Zion's Camp. Before leaving their homes in the eastern states, many feared that they might lose their lives in battle against the Missouri mobs. The journey to Missouri itself was a trial of faith that tested their mettle. Following the disbanding of Zion's Camp, a few of its numbers became critical of Joseph Smith and left the faith. The rest appear to have found great spiritual strength in the experience.

On 14 February 1835 the Prophet Joseph Smith called a meeting "of those who journeyed last season to Zion for the purpose of laying the foundation of its redemption, together with as many other of the brethren and sisters as were disposed to attend.

"President Joseph Smith, Jun., presiding, read the 15th chapter of John, and said: Let us endeavor to solemnize our minds that we may receive a blessing, by calling on the Lord. After an appropriate and affecting prayer, the brethren who went to Zion [in Zion's camp] were requested to take their seats together in a part of the house by themselves.

"President Smith then stated that the meeting had been called, because God had commanded it; and it was made known to him by vision and by the Holy Spirit. He then gave a relation of some of the circumstances attending us while journeying to Zion—our trials, sufferings: and said God had not designed all this for nothing, but He had it in remembrance yet; and it was the will of God that those who went to Zion, with a determination to lay down their lives, if necessary, should be ordained to the ministry, and go forth to prune the vineyard for the last time" (*History of the Church*, 2:181–82).

On that day the Quorum of the Twelve Apostles was organized with nine of its members coming from those who marched with Zion's Camp. Two weeks later the First Quorum of Seventy was organized. All seven presidents of the First Council of Seventy and sixty-three of the seventy members of the quorum were chosen from among those who had journeyed with Zion's Camp.

"Elder Joseph Young in his 'History of the Organization of the Seventies,' (page 14) says that the following sentiment was delivered by the Prophet Joseph Smith in an address to the Elders assembled in Kirtland soon after the Seventies were organized: 'Brethren, some of you are angry with me, because you did not fight in Missouri; but let me tell you, God did not want you to fight. He could not organize His kingdom with twelve men to open the Gospel door to the nations of the earth, and with seventy men under their direction to follow in their tracks, unless He took them from a body of men who had offered their lives, and who had made as great a sacrifice as did Abraham. Now the Lord has got His Twelve and His Seventy, and there will be other quorums of Seventies called, who will make the sacrifice, and those who have not made their sacrifices and their offerings now, will make them hereafter'" (Smith, *History of the Church*, 2:182).

Other Saints were similarly valiant. After cholera broke out among

Zion's Camp, fourteen Saints died. They too passed the trial of their faith. On 8 February 1835 "the Prophet Joseph Smith called Elders Brigham and Joseph Young to the chamber of his residence, in Kirtland, Ohio, it being on the Sabbath day. After they were seated and he had made some preliminaries, he proceeded to relate a vision to these brethren, of the state and condition of those men who died in Zion's Camp, in Missouri. He said, 'Brethren, I have seen those men who died of the cholera in our camp; and the Lord knows, if I get a mansion as bright as theirs, I ask no more.' At this relation he wept, and for some time could not speak" (Smith, *History of the Church*, 2:181). Earlier, the Lord revealed, "I will try you and prove you herewith. And whoso layeth down his life in my cause, for my name's sake, shall find it again, even life eternal. Therefore, be not afraid of your enemies, for I have decreed in my heart, saith the Lord, that I will prove you in all things, whether you will abide in my covenant, even unto death, that you may be found worthy" (D&C 98:12–14).

The Saints Are to Be Wise and Not Boast of Mighty Works As They Gather
DOCTRINE AND COVENANTS 105:20–26

105:23–26 These instructions offered the Saints another opportunity to regain their lands in Zion after a little season. In addition to the personal purification required of the Saints, they were to make friends of the nonmembers in Clay County and surrounding regions. If they did so, the Lord promised them success in being reinstated to their inheritances in Zion. The endowment of power required before the Saints would be fully prepared to redeem Zion was administered in the Kirtland Temple in early 1836. The Prophet wrote to the Church leaders in Missouri that they should be ready to move into Jackson County on 11 September 1836, "which is the appointed time for the redemption of Zion. If—verily I say unto you—if the Church with one united effort perform their duties; if they do this, the work shall be complete—if they do not this in all humility, making preparation from this time forth, like Joseph in Egypt, laying up store against the time of famine, every man having his tent, his horses, his chariots, his armory, his cattle, his family, and his whole substance in readiness against the time when it shall be said: To your tents, O Israel! Let not this be noised abroad; let every heart beat in silence, and every mouth be shut.

"Now, my beloved brethren, you will learn by this we have a great work to do, and but little time to do it in; and if we do not exert ourselves to the utmost in gathering up the strength of the Lord's house that this thing may be accomplished, behold there remaineth a scourge for the Church, even that they shall be driven from city to city, and but few shall remain to receive an inheritance; if those things are not kept, there remaineth a scourge also; therefore, be wise this once, O ye children of Zion! and give heed to my counsel, saith the Lord" (Smith, *History of the Church*, 2:145–46).

The Prophet Joseph Smith, writing from Kirtland, Ohio, continued to send instructions and counsel to the Saints in Missouri. Referring to these verses, he and other presiding high priests of the Church wrote to Hezekiah Peck: "It is wisdom that the church should make but little or no stir in that region, and cause as little excitement as possible and endure their afflictions patiently until the time appointed—and the Governor of Mo. fulfills his promise in settling the church over upon their own lands. . . .

"Let them remember the commandment which says, 'talk not of Judgment,' we are commanded not to give the children's bread unto the dogs; neither cast our pearls before swine, least they trample them under their feet, and turn again and rend you. Therefore let us be wise in all things, and keep all the commandments of God, that our salvation may be sure; having our armour ready and prepared against the time appointed, and having on the whole armor of righteousness, we may be able to stand in that trying day. We say also that if there are any doors open for the Elders to preach the first principles of the gospel, let them not keep silence; rail not against the sects, neither talk against their tenets. But preach Christ and him crucified, love to God and love to man, observing always to make mention of our republican principles, thereby if possible, we may allay the prejudice of the people, be meek and lowly of heart, and the Lord God of our fathers shall be with you for evermore Amen" (Jessee, *Personal Writings of Joseph Smith*, 347–48).

When the appointed time arrived, the Saints in Clay County, Missouri, had not heeded the commands of God. Without regard to the feelings of their neighbors, the Saints had gathered in great numbers to Clay County. "As the gathering heightened," explained Max Parkin, "some Saints did not follow counsel and were viewed as speaking with inordinate zeal for their home in exile. Friendly Joseph Thorpe lamented over what he saw as boasts of some of the Saints. '[The Latter-day Saints] with all their experience in Jackson, began to tell the citizens of Clay the same old tale; that this country was theirs by gift of the Lord, and it was folly for them to improve their lands, they would not enjoy the fruits of their labor; that it would finally fall into the hands of the saints.' After reviewing a conversation with a zealous Latter-day Saint, Thorpe unsympathetically reflected: 'This kind of talk, with their insolence and impudent behavior, so enraged the citizens that they began to consult about the best course to take to rid themselves of a set of religious fanatics.' Thus, lingering dissatisfaction by some old settlers of Clay County erupted into animosity against the Latter-day Saints.

"Adverse sentiment heightened by late spring 1836. On 29 June, friendly leading citizens at Liberty held a public meeting to help prevent violence by issuing suggestions and where they felt needful to file complaints against the Latter-day Saints. 'Their rapid emigration,' the committee report said of the Saints, 'their large land purchases,' and their claims that Clay County was 'destined by heaven to be theirs' were some of the objections they noted" ("Latter-day Saint Conflict," 254–55). The citizens of Clay County requested that the Saints move from the region and settle in Wisconsin. Instead, the Saints moved to relatively uninhabited lands north of Ray County, Missouri, at the advice of the Prophet Joseph Smith, who counseled them that "if [they] could stop short [of Wisconsin], in peace, [they] had better do so" (*History of the Church*, 2:455). The land they settled was later incorporated into Caldwell County, Missouri.

Lands in Jackson County and Adjoining Counties Should Be Purchased
DOCTRINE AND COVENANTS 105:27–30

105:28 *Purchasing of all the lands in Jackson county that can be purchased.* See commentary on Doctrine and Covenants 57:4, "The land should be purchased by the saints."

105:29 *My saints should possess them according to the laws of consecration.* To consecrate something is to dedicate it for sacred purposes. Lands that have been consecrated are lands dedicated to the Lord for building up his kingdom on earth. Those who possess such lands must in like manner be consecrated to the Lord if they are to bring forth the lands' riches.

105:30 This verse mentions things that were part of the provisional promise given to those who had been driven out of Jackson County. The

Saints lost the opportunity to lay claim to their property because of their failure to live according to the standard required of a Zion people.

The Elders Are to Receive an Endowment in the House of the Lord in Kirtland and to Be Sanctified
DOCTRINE AND COVENANTS 105:31–37

105:31 *Fair as the sun, and clear as the moon.* See commentary on Doctrine and Covenants 5:14, "Clear as the moon, and fair as the sun, and terrible as an army with banners."

105:32 At a future day—most probably the Millennium—the kingdoms of this world will come to acknowledge the greatness of Zion, its people, and her laws and will seek to unite with the Saints of God. "The worthiness of the Lord's people, their sanctified state, their purity and uprightness before him—these are the things that will enable them to build the New Jerusalem, for Zion is the City of Holiness," said Elder Bruce R. McConkie. "When it is built, as it was in Enoch's day, its grandeur and glory and power must be such that those in all nations, from one end of the earth to the other, standing in awe, will feel inclined to be subject to such a mighty city, whence comes such a perfect law" (*New Witness*, 618–19). At that time Isaiah's words will find yet another fulfillment, for "many people shall go and say, Come ye, and let us go up to the mountain of the Lord, to the house of the God of Jacob; and he will teach us of his ways, and we will walk in his paths" (Isaiah 2:3).

105:33–36 The day after he received this revelation, the Prophet Joseph Smith recorded: "A council of High Priests assembled in fulfillment of the revelation given the day previous, and the following individuals were called and chosen, as they were made manifest unto me by the voice of the Spirit and revelation, to receive their endowments" (*History of the Church*, 2:112). He then recorded that the following brethren "were called and chosen, to go to Kirtland and receive their endowment with power from on high" (Smith, *History of the Church*, 2:113): Edward Partridge, William W. Phelps, Isaac Morley, John Corrill, John Whitmer, David Whitmer, Algernon Sidney Gilbert, Peter Whitmer Jr., Simeon Carter, Newel Knight, Parley P. Pratt, Christian Whitmer, Solomon Hancock, Thomas B. Marsh, and Lyman Wight.

105:36 *They shall be sanctified.* See commentary on Doctrine and Covenants 84:23.

105:37 Originally, the Saints were promised that they could reenter

Jackson County 11 September 1836 (see commentary on D&C 57:4; 105:23–26). Failure to prepare themselves for this blessing resulted in its being taken from them.

Today the Saints await the Lord's instructions concerning the redemption of the City of Zion. Until that time, our responsibility is to establish and build up stakes of Zion among every nation, kindred, tongue, and people so that the whole earth can receive the blessings of the Holy City.

Saints Are to Lift an Ensign of Peace to the World
DOCTRINE AND COVENANTS 105:38–41

105:38–39 The mission of the Church is to teach the inhabitants of the earth how to live in peace and harmony. The ensign that is held up for the world to see is the fulness of the gospel of Christ. It teaches that every man is to esteem his brother as himself (D&C 38:24–25).

DOCTRINE AND COVENANTS 106

DATE: 25 NOVEMBER 1834
PLACE: KIRTLAND, OHIO

Following the disbanding of Zion's Camp at Fishing River, Missouri (D&C 105), the Prophet Joseph Smith and many of those who had marched with him returned to Ohio. The Saints then renewed their labors in building the temple in Kirtland. As membership in the Church grew, the Prophet gave attention to branches outside the Kirtland area. On 16 November 1834, he and several others left Kirtland to visit the Saints in Michigan. He recorded: "After preaching, and teaching the Saints in Michigan as long as our time would allow, we returned to Kirtland, greatly refreshed from our journey, and much pleased with our friends in that section of the Lord's vineyard.

"It now being the last of the month, and the Elders beginning to come in, it was necessary to make preparations for the school for the Elders, wherein they might be more perfectly instructed in the great things of God, during the coming winter. A building for a printing office was nearly finished, and the lower story of this building was set apart for that purpose, (the school) when it was completed. So the Lord opened the way according to our faith and works, and blessed be His name.

"No month ever found me more busily engaged than November; but as my life consisted of activity and unyielding exertions, I made this my rule: *When the Lord commands, do it.* . . . I continued my labors daily, preparing for the school, and received the following" (Smith, *History of the Church*, 2:169–70).

Warren A. Cowdery Is Called As a Local Presiding Officer
DOCTRINE AND COVENANTS 106:1–3

106:1 *Warren A. Cowdery.* Warren Cowdery was an older brother to Oliver. He learned of the Book of Mormon and the Restoration from his younger brother and had been baptized in 1831.

A presiding high priest. This designation referred to an appointment to direct the labors of the Church within a particular geographical area. Today, bishops are set apart as the presiding high priests in their respective wards. Similarly, a stake president is set apart as the "presiding high priest" in his stake.

The land of Freedom. Warren Cowdery was called to preside over the Saints in branches of the Church in the area of Freedom, Cattaraugus County, New York. In early March 1834, about eight months before receiving this revelation, the Prophet Joseph Smith served a mission that took him to this area of New York, where he established the Freedom branch. The Prophet recorded that on "Sunday, March 9.—We preached in a school house, and had great attention. We found a few disciples who were firm in the faith; and, after meeting found many believing and could hardly get away from them, and appointed a meeting in Freedom for Monday the 10th, and stayed at Mr. Warren A. Cowdery's, where we were blessed with a full enjoyment of temporal and spiritual blessings, even all we needed, or were worthy to receive" (Smith, *History of the Church,* 2:42).

The Prophet's companion on this journey was Parley P. Pratt, who described this experience: "President Joseph Smith and myself journeyed together. We had a pleasant and prosperous mission among the churches, and some very interesting times in preaching to the public. We visited Freedom, Catteraugus County, N.Y.; tarried over Sunday, and preached several discourses, to which the people listened with great interest; we were kindly and hospitably entertained among them. We baptized a young man named Heman Hyde; his parents were Presbyterians, and his mother, on account of the strength of her traditions, thought that we were wrong, and told me afterwards that she would much rather have followed him to an earthly grave than to have seen him baptized.

"Soon afterwards, however, herself, her husband, and the rest of the family, with some thirty or forty others, were all baptized and organized into a branch of the Church—called the Freedom branch—from which nucleus the light spread and souls were gathered into the fold in all the regions round. Thus mightily grew the word of God, or the seed sown by that extraordinary personage, the Prophet and Seer of the nineteenth century" (*Autobiography,* 89).

106:2–3 Warren A. Cowdery's calling was to preside over the branch in Freedom and to declare the gospel full time there and in the adjoining counties. His calling was similar to that of a mission president today.

Having no time to provide for his family, he was directed by the Lord to receive his support from the Church.

The Second Coming Shall Not Overtake the Children of Light As a Thief
DOCTRINE AND COVENANTS 106:4–5

106:4 Those who are of the world will no more know when Christ is to return than they know when the thief will strike. Spiritually, they have retired to their beds for the "slumber of death" (Jacob 3:11). It is as though they are asleep and unaware of the events taking place around them. While their sleeping eyes are closed to the signs of the times, they dream of iniquity, unaware of their danger. By contrast, the Lord told the "children of light" (v. 5) that they will "know the signs of the times, and the signs of the coming of the Son of Man" (D&C 68:11).

106:5 *The children of light.* To accept the gospel and live by its standard is to come out of darkness into the light (1 Peter 2:9), thus becoming children of light (John 12:36; Colossians 1:12) and followers of light and truth. The commandment given to the Saints of all ages is to "walk as children of light" (Ephesians 5:8).

That day shall not overtake you as a thief. Paul warned the Thessalonian Saints, "For yourselves know perfectly that the day of the Lord so cometh as a thief in the night. For when they shall say, Peace and safety; then sudden destruction cometh upon them, as travail upon a woman with child; and they shall not escape. But ye, brethren, are not in darkness, that that day should overtake you as a thief" (1 Thessalonians 5:2–4). Those who have treasured up the Lord's word shall not be deceived (Joseph Smith–Matthew 1:37) but will know of the nearness of the Lord's coming. The prophesied signs will indicate the generation in which the Son of Man will appear in glory.

The Saints ought to look forward to the Savior's return and be anxiously engaged in preparing the world for that great event. If the Saints will prepare for the Lord's return, sleep will flee from their eyes as they wait in eager anticipation for the coming of the Bridegroom. While the wicked slumber, the children of light will be alert and aware that with each passing year the time of the Lord's promised return draws closer.

Commenting on Paul's warning to the Thessalonians, the Prophet Joseph Smith explained: "It is not the design of the Almighty to come upon the earth and crush it and grind it to powder, but he will reveal it to His servants the prophets. Judah must return, Jerusalem must be rebuilt, and the temple, and water come out from under the temple, and the waters of the Dead Sea be healed. It will take some time to rebuild the walls of the city and the temple, &c.; and all this must be done before the Son of Man will make His appearance. There will be wars and rumors of wars, signs in the heavens above and on the earth beneath, the sun turned into darkness and the moon to blood, earthquakes in divers places, the seas heaving beyond their bounds; then will appear one grand sign of the Son of Man in heaven. But what will the world do? They will say it is a planet, a comet, &c. But the Son of Man will come as the sign of the coming of the Son of Man, which will be as the light of the morning cometh out of the east" (*Teachings of the Prophet Joseph Smith*, 286–87).

Great Blessings Follow Faithful Service in the Church
DOCTRINE AND COVENANTS 106:6–8

106:6 *There was joy in heaven.* As the heavens wept when Satan and his legions were lost, so they rejoice when children of our Eternal Father choose the course that will enable them to return to his presence. The text suggests that angels are aware of what their earthly counterparts are doing (D&C 62:3).

106:8 *If he continue to be a faithful witness.* Warren A. Cowdery moved his family to Kirtland in February 1836. There he was active in Church affairs until he became disaffected with the leadership of the Church in 1838. This same year his brother Oliver was excommunicated. When the Lord commanded the Saints to move to Far West, Missouri, Warren remained behind (D&C 115:17). He died in Kirtland on 23 February 1851 while still disaffected (Cook, *Revelations*, 215).

DOCTRINE AND COVENANTS 107

DATES: 28 MARCH 1835, NOVEMBER 1831, 18 DECEMBER 1833
PLACE: KIRTLAND, OHIO

Doctrine and Covenants 107 weaves together revelations received at different times. The primary date is 28 March 1835, when the first fifty-two verses and verses 56–58 were given in response to the request of the newly ordained apostles for instruction relative to their office and calling. Verses 53–55 were extracted from the blessing given to Joseph Smith Sr. when he was ordained Church patriarch by the Prophet on 18 December 1833 (*Teachings of the Prophet Joseph Smith*, 38–40). Verses 59 to 100 (with the exception of verses 61, 70, 73, 76–77, 88, 90, 93–98) were given in November 1831 (*Kirtland Record Book*). The verses in the latter part of the revelation not received in 1831 were added by the Prophet when he prepared this section for inclusion in the 1835 edition of the Doctrine and Covenants.

On 14 February 1835 the Quorum of the Twelve Apostles was organized for the first time in this dispensation. The Twelve were chosen, according to revelation, by the Three Witnesses of the Book of Mormon (D&C 18). The Prophet met periodically with the Twelve after their organization to instruct them. On 12 March 1835 the Prophet called the Twelve on their first mission to the eastern states and the Atlantic Coast, instructing them to hold meetings with various branches of the Church along the way. In preparation for their departure, the Twelve met again on the afternoon of 28 March. Orson Hyde and William E. McLellin, who recorded the minutes of that meeting, observed that "on reviewing our past course we are satisfied, and feel to confess also, that we have not realized the importance of our calling to that degree that we ought; we have been light-minded and vain, and in many things have done wrong. For all these things we have asked the forgiveness of our heavenly Father; and wherein we have grieved or wounded the feelings of the Presidency, we ask their forgiveness. The time when we are about to separate is near; and when we shall meet again, God only knows; we therefore feel to ask of him whom we have acknowledged to be our Prophet and Seer, that he inquire of God for us, and obtain a revelation, (if consistent) that we may look upon it when we are separated, that our hearts may be comforted. Our worthiness has not inspired us to make this request, but our unworthiness. We have unitedly asked God our heavenly Father to grant unto us through His Seer, a revelation of His mind and will concerning our duty the coming season, even a great revelation, that will enlarge our hearts, comfort us in adversity, and brighten our hopes amidst the powers of darkness" (Smith, *History of the Church*, 2:209). In response to that request, Joseph Smith inquired of the Lord and received the first fifty-eight verses, excluding verses 53–55.

There Are Two Priesthoods: Melchizedek and Aaronic
DOCTRINE AND COVENANTS 107:1–6

107:1 *Two priesthoods.* Joseph Smith stated, "There are two Priesthoods spoken of in the Scriptures, viz., the Melchizedek and the Aaronic or Levitical. Although there are two Priesthoods, yet the Melchizedek Priesthood comprehends the Aaronic or Levitical Priesthood, and is the grand head, and holds the highest authority which pertains to the priesthood, and the keys of the Kingdom of God in all ages of the world" (*Teachings of the Prophet Joseph Smith*, 166). On another occasion the Prophet said, "All Priesthood is Melchizedek" (*Teachings of the Prophet Joseph Smith*, 180), meaning that the Melchizedek Priesthood embraces the Aaronic or lesser priesthood and that those who hold it can function in all the offices and duties of the Aaronic Priesthood (vv. 5, 14).

107:2 *Melchizedek.* See commentary on Joseph Smith Translation Genesis 14:26–40, page 331.

107:4 *The church, in ancient days.* This phrase affirms that a church organization existed in Old Testament times. See commentary on Doctrine and Covenants 84:17.

107:5 *Appendages to this priesthood.* "The priesthood is greater than any of its offices. No office adds any power, dignity, or authority to the priesthood. All offices derive their rights, prerogatives, graces, and powers from the priesthood. This principle may be diagramed by dividing a circle into segments. The priesthood is the circle; the segments of the circle are the callings or offices in the priesthood. Anyone who serves in a segment of the circle must possess the power of the whole circle. No one can hold an office in the priesthood without first holding the priesthood" (McConkie, *Mormon Doctrine*, 595–96).

107:6 *Aaronic or Levitical Priesthood.* As the higher priesthood was named after Melchizedek, so the lesser priesthood was named after Aaron, the brother Moses. Aaron was the high priest, meaning presiding priest, over the Aaronic order, in which capacity he served for nearly forty years. This priesthood is also called the Levitical Priesthood because Aaron was a descendant of Levi, the third son of Jacob and Leah, whose descendants were given the birthright to this priesthood. They properly performed its functions from the time of Moses and Aaron to the coming of Christ.

Some argue that the Aaronic and Levitical Priesthoods are different priesthoods. This revelation, however, does not support such a distinction.

Those Holding the Melchizedek Priesthood Have Power to Officiate in all the Offices of the Church

Doctrine and Covenants 107:7–12

107:8 *The right of presidency.* The right of presidency—commonly referred to as holding keys—is the right to preside, direct, or govern. When someone becomes a member of the Quorum of the Twelve, for instance, all the keys of the kingdom are conferred upon him. Wherever he goes in the Church, a member of the Twelve is the presiding officer, unless a more senior member of the Twelve is also present. In a sense, the Twelve hold every office in the Church, for they preside over all offices and auxiliaries. They do not preside because they hold priesthood but because they have been given the keys or "right of presidency."

107:9 *Presidency of the High Priesthood.* The "Presidency of the High Priesthood," meaning the First Presidency of the Church, presides over all other offices and officers in the Church. Joseph Smith taught that "revelations of the mind and will of God to the Church, are to come through the Presidency" (*History of the Church*, 2:477). Of necessity the First Presidency holds all the keys of the kingdom (D&C 90:2). Keys are the "right of presidency," and priesthood is used properly only when it is used under the direction of those who hold its keys. For instance, holders of the Melchizedek Priesthood can confer that priesthood upon others. They can do so, however, only under the direction of those holding the keys of the priesthood. To act independent of the direction of those holding the keys is to lose the priesthood. An ordinance not performed under their direction counts for nothing in the Church and kingdom of God.

107:10 Under the direction of the First Presidency high priests can be called to positions of presidency and to administer spiritual things. This revelation notes that their office encompasses that of an elder in the Melchizedek Priesthood and the offices of priest, teacher, and deacon in the Aaronic Priesthood. It does not include the office of seventy, which belongs to the Melchizedek Priesthood, or the office of bishop, which belongs to the Aaronic Priesthood. The suggestion here is that seventies were to hold general authority status rather than be a part of the local organization. It was not necessary to include the office of bishop in this verse because a bishop, which is an office in the Aaronic Priesthood, must also be a high priest (D&C 68:19).

107:11 In the absence of those called to preside, high priests can act in their stead. In the absence of high priests, the responsibility falls to the elders.

A Bishopric Is to Preside over the Aaronic Priesthood
DOCTRINE AND COVENANTS 107:13–17

107:13 *The Priesthood of Aaron.* From the days of Aaron to the time of Christ, the only priesthood known generally among the house of Israel in the Old World was the Aaronic, or Levitical, Priesthood. The right to hold this priesthood was limited to those who were of the tribe of Levi. With the coming of the gospel in the meridian day came the restoration of the Melchizedek Priesthood. The Aaronic Priesthood was retained, with the right to hold it again extended to all the tribes of Israel. Following the same pattern, both priesthoods have been restored in our day. Notwithstanding the fact that both priesthoods can be held by all worthy males, regardless of the tribe of Israel from which they descend, the promises given to those of the tribe of Levi "throughout all their generations" are still remembered and will be honored as a part of the restoration of all things. See Doctrine and Covenants 68:13–21; 84:31; 107:69–71.

107:14 *An appendage to the greater.* In all things the Aaronic Priesthood acts under the direction of the Melchizedek Priesthood. Those holding the higher priesthood can function in all the offices and capacities of the lesser priesthood; it is unnecessary to have received the Aaronic Priesthood before receiving the higher priesthood.

Outward ordinances. See Doctrine and Covenants 107:20.

107:15 *The bishopric is the presidency of this priesthood.* This refers to the presiding bishop of the Church and his counselors. Ward bishoprics did not function as we now know them until after the Saints had moved west. This is a specialized usage of the word *bishopric* peculiar to Latter-day Saints. More generally the word simply refers to an office or calling (see Acts 1:20; D&C 114:2). According to this revelation, the presiding bishop and his counselors hold the keys restored by John the Baptist to Joseph Smith and Oliver Cowdery and thus give direction and leadership to all who hold the Aaronic Priesthood.

107:16–17 See commentary on Doctrine and Covenants 68:15–18.

The Keys of All Spiritual Blessings
DOCTRINE AND COVENANTS 107:18–20

107:18 *The keys of all the spiritual blessings.* Earlier in this section (vv. 8–10; 15), "keys" are equated with the "right of presidency," meaning the authority to preside. In the present text the emphasis shifts to unlocking things that would otherwise remain hidden. As used here "keys" become an individual possession by which sacred truths are revealed and divine promises obtained. "Without this priesthood power, men are lost," President Spencer W. Kimball explained. "Only through this power does man 'hold the keys of all the spiritual blessings of the church,' enabling him to receive 'the mysteries of the kingdom of heaven, to have the heavens opened' unto him (see D&C 107:18–19), enabling him to enter the new and everlasting covenant of marriage and to have his wife and children bound to him in an everlasting tie, enabling him to become a patriarch to his posterity forever, and enabling him to receive a fullness of the blessings of the Lord" (*Teachings of Spencer W. Kimball*, 494).

107:19 The promises enumerated in this verse are not the exclusive providence of prophets but are intended for all faithful Saints. All are to obtain the key of understanding. To receive it, men must first receive the higher priesthood, and both men and women must embrace the fulness of the new and everlasting covenant. See Doctrine and Covenants 132:19–24.

To enjoy the . . . presence of God the Father, and Jesus. The Melchizedek Priesthood was restored in order that the children of God might once again be brought into his presence. It is not future worlds to which this promise is directed but to the mortal and corruptible state in which we now reside. See commentary on Doctrine and Covenants 84:19–25.

107:20 *Keys of the ministering of angels.* See commentary on Joseph Smith–History 1:69, page 118.

To administer in outward ordinances. Baptism of water is described here as an "outward ordinance," or "the letter of the gospel." By contrast, the baptism of fire, meaning the Spirit or Holy Ghost, could be referred to as an "inward" or spiritual ordinance. The first can be performed by those holding the Aaronic Priesthood, the second only by those holding the higher or Melchizedek Priesthood. A primary charge given to the Aaronic Priesthood is to tend to temporal things, while the primary charge given the higher priesthood is to tend to spiritual things.

Agreeable to the covenants and commandments. The articles and covenants of the Church are set forth in Doctrine and Covenants 20 and 22.

The Presiding Quorums of the Church
DOCTRINE AND COVENANTS 107:21–38

107:21 *Presiding officers.* Where there is priesthood there of necessity must be discipline and order. Indeed, such is implicit in the very name of the priesthood as restored to us in this revelation: *"the Holy Priesthood, after the Order of the Son of God"* (v. 3). It is not the divine plan that every man walk in his own way after the image of a god of his own making (see D&C 1:16). To reach its destination, every ship requires both a captain and crew that know their duty and stand in the office to which they have been appointed. Of necessity there must be presiding officers, and over these officers is one greater to whom they too must report.

107:22 *Three Presiding High priests.* This refers to the members of the First Presidency of the Church, who constitute its leading quorum.

Chosen by the body. Though somewhat ambiguous as used in this verse, "the body" is the newly formed Quorum of the Twelve to which this revelation was given. Precedence accords that at the death of the president of the Church, his counselors are released and the quorum of the First Presidency is dissolved. "The body" responsible to form the new presidency of the Church is the Quorum of the Twelve.

When the First Presidency is dissolved by the death of its president, the Quorum of the Twelve then becomes the leading quorum in the Church. Its president, the senior apostle of God on earth, presides over the Church by virtue of the fact that he presides over its leading quorum.

No other man on earth has the right to lead. Indeed, the Quorum of the Twelve cannot even meet unless the senior apostle calls a meeting. When such a meeting is called, he presides over it. If revelation is to come, it must, according to the order of the Church, come through him. At the death of the President of the Church, the president of the Quorum of the Twelve automatically succeeds him. He is the mouthpiece of the Lord to the Church; no one else has a rightful claim to that privilege. From Brigham Young to the present day, this has always been the case.

Can the Lord change that order if he wants to? Of course; it's his Church and he runs it. But should he choose to change the order he has established, he must, according to his word, do it through the channels he has ordained. The only man on earth who can receive a revelation that the president of the quorum of the Twelve should not lead the Church is the president of that quorum. No other individual or quorum can receive that revelation until it has come through the channel the Lord has ordained. If a man is worthy and capable of presiding over the Quorum of the Twelve, he is certainly worthy and capable of presiding over the Church. What if the senior apostle is serving as a counselor in the First Presidency at the death of the president of the Church rather than as president of the Quorum of the Twelve? A senior apostle serving in the First Presidency is sustained as a member of the First Presidency *and* as president of the Quorum of the Twelve. The next senior apostle is sustained as "acting president" over that quorum. When the First Presidency is dissolved by the death of its president, the counselor who is the senior apostle assumes his rightful position as the president of the Twelve.

The system of succession in the presidency of the Church is but one of many illustrations of the Lord's genius. No room exits for contention, aspirations of the unworthy, or uncertainty. Nor is the Church left without inspired leadership for so much as a moment, for with his last breath one prophet bequeaths the office to another according to a system instituted by the God of heaven himself.

Upheld by the confidence, faith, and prayer of the church. No man can preside in the Church without the sustaining faith and goodwill of those over whom he presides. As the membership of the Church is edified and blessed by those who have been called as its leaders, so those in positions of leadership are edified and blessed by those who serve under their direction. As the husband is a strength to the wife and the wife to the husband, so both leader and follower strengthen each other through prayer and faithful service.

107:23 *Witnesses of the name of Christ in all the world.* While many have gone forth to testify of Christ, the charge given to the apostles is to testify of "the name of Christ." What, then, is the meaning of such a phrase and how does testifying of "the name of Christ" differ from the testimony of Christ? Much is embraced in the idea of the "name" of Christ. For instance, the Lord told Abraham, "I will lead thee by my hand, and I will take thee, to put upon thee my name, even the Priesthood of thy father, and my power shall be over thee" (Abraham 1:18). To testify of the name of Christ is to testify of his priesthood, his power, his holy order, and the system of government and laws and ordinances he has instituted. Little by way of obligation and commitment is associated with professing to believe in Christ and to testify that salvation is found in him. Testifying of his name embraces discipline, order, and the sacrifice of all things. The difference between the two testimonies is the difference between a pebble and a mountain. One suggests salvation on an individual basis, the other that salvation grows out of faithful participation in the covenant community. One represents a restoration of the principles and faith known to the Saints of ages past, the other a religion in which man dictates the terms of salvation. One calls upon us to consecrate all we have to the service of God, the other views such works as a denial of God's grace.

It becomes the role of the Twelve to travel throughout the world, placing in order the various branches of the Church, giving direction to the priesthood, teaching the principles of salvation, and showing how all that is associated with the same combines to testify of Christ (see verses 33, 35).

107:24 Elder Hyrum M. Smith and Janne M. Sjodahl explained that "there can never be two or three quorums of equal authority at the same time; therefore in the revelation where it reads that the Twelve Apostles form a quorum equal in authority with the First Presidency, and that the Seventies form a quorum equal in authority with the Twelve, it should be understood that this condition of equality could prevail only when the ranking quorum is no longer in existence, through death or otherwise. When the First Presidency becomes disorganized on the death of the President, then the Apostles become the presiding quorum, or council, of the Church with all the power to organize again the First Presidency, when they fall back again as the second ranking quorum of the Church.

So with the Seventies, they would become equal only on the condition that the first two quorums ceased to exist. In regard to the Seventies, this provision, of course, concerns the first quorum of the Seventies" (*Doctrine and Covenants Commentary*, 700). If through some catastrophe the two leading quorums of the Church were dissolved, the First Quorum of the Seventy would become the leading quorum in the Church. It would be that quorum's responsibility to reorganize the Quorum of the Twelve, which in turn would reorganize the First Presidency.

107:25 The office of a seventy is to teach the gospel in all the world. The Seventy are of necessity general officers of the Church. Though it took some time for the Church to grow up into the provisions of this revelation, it now follows this pattern.

On this matter John Taylor received a significant revelation while he presided over the Church. On Saturday, 14 April 1883, in answer to the question: *"Show unto us Thy will, O Lord, concerning the organization of the Seventies,"* he received the following: "Thus saith the Lord unto the First Presidency, unto the Twelve, unto the Seventies and unto all my holy Priesthood, let not your hearts be troubled, neither be ye concerned about the management and organization of my Church and Priesthood and the accomplishment of my work. Fear me and observe my laws and I will reveal unto you, from time to time, through the channels that I have appointed, everything that shall be necessary for the future development and perfection of my Church, for the adjustment and rolling forth of my kingdom, and for the building up and the establishment of my Zion. For ye are my Priesthood and I am your God. Even so Amen" (Clark, *Messages*, 2:354).

107:26 *Equal in authority.* See commentary on verse 24.

107:27 *The unanimous voice.* The Church is not a democracy, nor is there any notion that the majority rules. Where scripture declares that there is but one God, the design is not to teach a mathematical principle but rather to emphasize the necessity of unity in the plan of salvation. We are saved to the extent that we have learned to think as God thinks, feel as he feels, and act as he would act. It is expected that this principle will find expression in the decisions of church councils. There is a spirit, power, and strength in unity that cannot otherwise be enjoyed. There is no place for politics where the souls of men and principles of salvation are concerned. Vigorous discussion will have its place in the councils of the Church, but contention and quarreling will not. A unity of purpose should bring with it decisions that are unanimous.

107:29 *Three presidents . . . anciently.* An identifying characteristic of the true Church is that no officer or leader presides alone. Such has been the order from ancient times. The concept of a presidency of three not only complies with the law of witnesses but also constitutes an earthly type and shadow of the heavenly presidency, which consists of the Father, the Son, and the Holy Ghost.

107:30–31 See commentary on Doctrine and Covenants 4:6.

107:32 A decision by any of the three leading quorums of the Church made in unrighteousness may be reviewed before a general assembly of the several quorums, which constitute the spiritual authorities of the Church. Explaining such an action, President Joseph F. Smith said, "There can be no appeal from the decision of the First Presidency of the Church, except their decision be rendered in unrighteousness, and without love, and charity, etc., and in that case the appeal would have to be taken to the assembled bodies of the Priesthood. It means that when the Twelve Apostles are acting as Presidents of the Church, and they render a decision affecting the welfare of the Church, or on doctrine, there is absolutely no appeal from their decision, excepting it is rendered in unrighteousness. And the same would apply, of necessity, to a decision rendered by the Seventy in the absence of the First Presidency and Twelve—if such a thing could be thought of at all" (*Collected Discourses,* 5:287).

107:33–35 Though the Twelve are commissioned to travel throughout the world to build up the Church and regulate its affairs, they do so only under the direction of the First Presidency. The Seventy, in like manner, act under the direction of the Twelve. In declaring the gospel to the world, the charge given to those of both quorums is that they go first to the Gentiles and then to the Jews. This is a reversal of the charge given by Christ to the Twelve and Seventy in the meridian of time. In that day the gospel was taken first to the Jews and then to the Gentiles (see Acts 13:46–48; Romans 11:7–26).

107:36 The instruction in this verse can only be understood in the context in which it was given. At that time only two high councils existed in the Church, one which had been organized in Kirtland, Ohio, on 17 February 1834, and the other in Missouri on 3 July of the same year. With the exception of a few scattered branches, these two stakes covered and governed the whole Church. The First Presidency of the Church also served as the presidency of the stake in Kirtland. If both councils came to the same determination on a matter, that decision would for all practical purposes govern the Church. This circumstance was, of course, temporary and could not be expected to apply in a Church destined to include thousands upon thousands of stakes. Describing this situation, John Taylor observed:

"In Kirtland, Ohio, a great many things were revealed through the Prophet. There was then a First Presidency that presided over the High Council, in Kirtland; and that High Council and another which was in Missouri, were the only High Councils in existence. As I have said, the High Council in Kirtland was presided over by Joseph Smith and his Counselors; and hence there were some things associated with this that were quite peculiar in themselves. It is stated that when they were at a loss to find out anything pertaining to any principles that might come before them in their councils, that the presidency were to inquire of the Lord and get revelation on those subjects that were difficult for them to comprehend. And I would make a remark here in relation to these things, that all High Councils, and all Presidents of Stakes and Bishops, and in fact all men holding the Priesthood, who are humble and faithful and diligent and honest and true to the principles of our religion, if they seek unto God with that faith that he requires of us, he will give them wisdom under all circumstances and on all occasions, and the Holy Spirit will never fail to indicate the path they should pursue" (*Journal of Discourses*, 19:241).

107:37 Today the same pattern of organization is used in every stake in the Church. The authority of one high council is equal to that of all other high councils. That authority enables each high council to make decisions suited to its differing circumstances.

107:38 *The traveling high council.* This passage refers to the Quorum of the Twelve, which is to call upon the Seventy to aid them as circumstances warrant (see v. 34).

Patriarchal Order Traced from Adam to Noah

DOCTRINE AND COVENANTS 107:39-52

107:39 *All large branches of the church.* The Church today uses many terms with a precision of meaning unknown in its early history. This is particularly true of terms used to describe the division of the Saints into various congregations or ecclesiastical units: *wards, stakes, branches,* and *districts*. As used at the time of this revelation the term *branches* would best equate with that of *stakes* today.

Evangelical ministers. "An Evangelist is a Patriarch," stated the Prophet, "even the oldest man of the blood of Joseph or of the seed of Abraham. Wherever the Church of Christ is established in the earth, there should be a Patriarch for the benefit of the posterity of the Saints, as it was with Jacob in giving his patriarchal blessing unto his sons, etc. (June 27, 1839)" (*Teachings of the Prophet Joseph Smith*, 151).

107:40 *The order of this priesthood.* This verse refers to the patriarchal order of the priesthood (*Teachings of the Prophet Joseph Smith*, 322–23). The authority of the patriarchal order is found within the Melchizedek Priesthood. Were this not the case, the Twelve who have not received any priesthood but the Melchizedek Priesthood could not confer the office of patriarch upon others as they were directed to do in the previous verse. Because of the expanded duties of the Twelve in our day, the authority to ordain patriarchs has been given to stake presidents. The matter of approving or choosing patriarchs, however, remains with the Twelve.

Defining the nature of the office of patriarch, John Taylor asked, "Does not the patriarch stand in the same relationship to the church as Adam did to his family, and as Abraham and Jacob did to theirs?" His response was an emphatic No! "Adam," he explained, "was the *natural* father of his posterity, who were his family and over whom he presided as patriarch, prophet, priest, and king. Both Abraham and Jacob stood in the same relationship to their families." This, of course, was not the case with Joseph Smith Sr., the first church patriarch in this dispensation or any of his successors in that office. "They were not the natural fathers of the church, and could not stand in the same capacity as Adam, Abraham, or Jacob; but inasmuch as there had been none to bless for generations past, according to the ancient order, they were ordained and set apart for the purpose of conferring patriarchal blessings, to hold the keys of this priesthood, and unlock the door, that had long been closed upon the human family: that blessings might again be conferred according to the ancient order, and those who were orphans, or had no father to bless them, might receive it through a patriarch who should act as proxy for their father, and that fathers might again be enabled to act as patriarchs to their families, and bless their children. For like all other ordinances in the church, this had been neglected and must needs be restored" (Taylor, *Gospel Kingdom*, 148).

A year after this revelation was received, the keys held by Abraham and Elijah were restored (see commentary on D&C 110:12–16). With them came the right to perform eternal marriages and bind families together throughout the eternities. Thus the most important part of the patriarchal order, meaning the new and everlasting covenant of marriage, was restored (see commentary on D&C 131:1–4). In and through this order, a man becomes a natural patriarch to his own family, thus imitating the ancient order of things. President John Taylor taught: "Every father, after he has received his patriarchal blessing, is a patriarch to his own family, and has the right to confer patriarchal blessings upon his family; which blessings will be just as legal as those conferred by any patriarch of the church: in fact it is his right; and a patriarch in blessing his children, can only bless as his mouthpiece" (*Gospel Kingdom*, 146). Elder Bruce R. McConkie added this insight: "He means every father who is married in the celestial order and has thereby received the blessings of Abraham so as to be a natural patriarch" ("Eternal Family Concept," 89).

Confirmed to be handed down from father to son. "From Adam to Noah the presiding representative of the Lord on earth held the joint office of patriarch and high priest—a calling conferred successively from father to son. Abraham, Isaac, Jacob, and other patriarchs held similar rights in their respective days. Abraham was promised that from his day on all who received the gospel would be accounted his seed and that his descendants after him would have right, by lineage, to the same priesthood he had gained (Abraham 2:6–11). Certain righteous persons were thus destined to receive the priesthood because they were 'lawful heirs according to the flesh' (D&C 86:8–10). It was their birthright.

"Special birthright blessings and priesthood pre-eminence have remained in the lineage of Jacob. Reuben, his firstborn, lost the birthright because of iniquity, and it passed to Joseph (1 Chron. 5:1–2) and through him to Ephraim. 'I am a father to Israel,' the Lord said, 'and Ephraim is my firstborn' (Jer. 31:9). This preferential status enjoyed by Ephraim among his fellow tribes in Israel has continued to our day. Predominantly Ephraim, among all the tribes of Israel, has so far been gathered into the fold of the true Shepherd. When the lost tribes return, they shall come to the children of Ephraim to receive their crowns of glory (D&C 133:26–34).

"From Aaron to the coming of John the Baptist, the high priests in Israel served in their presiding offices (of the Aaronic order) because they were descendants of Aaron. The office of Presiding Bishop in the Church today is of comparable hereditary nature, although the Lord has not so far designated the lineage in which the right to such office rests (D&C 68:14–24). The right to hold the Levitical Priesthood anciently was limited to the sons of Levi, who thus gained their priesthood prerogatives by birth. In the meridian of time our Lord altered this system and spread this Aaronic order of authority among worthy male members of the Church generally (1 Tim. 3:1–13)" (McConkie, *Mormon Doctrine*, 87–88).

Rightly. The right referred to here is obtained by birth. It belongs to all who are born under the covenant.

Literal descendants of the chosen seed. See Abraham 2:9–11 and commentary on Doctrine and Covenants 110:12–16.

The promises were made. The promise is that of the continuation of the family unit throughout time and eternity. In all gospel dispensations this promise stands at the heart of the plan of salvation.

The Ancient Saints Assembled at Adam-ondi-Ahman, Where the Lord Appeared to Them

DOCTRINE AND COVENANTS 107:53–57

107:53–55 These verses were taken from the blessing given by Joseph Smith to his father, Joseph Smith Sr., when he was ordained the first patriarch in this dispensation on 18 December 1833. The blessing is as follows: "Blessed of the Lord is my father, for he shall stand in the midst of his posterity and shall be comforted by their blessings when he is old and bowed down with years, and shall be called a prince over them, and shall be numbered among those who hold the right of Patriarchal Priesthood, even the keys of that ministry: for he shall assemble together his posterity like unto Adam; and the assembly which he called shall be an example for my father, for thus it is written of him: Three years previous to the death of Adam, he called Seth, Enos, Cainan, Mahalaleel, Jared, Enoch and Methuselah, who were High Priests, with the residue of his posterity, who were righteous, into the valley of Adam-ondi-Ahman, and there bestowed upon them his last blessing. And the Lord appeared unto them, and they rose up and blessed Adam, and called him Michael, the Prince, the Archangel. And the Lord administered comfort unto Adam, and said unto him, I have set thee to be at the head: a multitude of nations shall come of thee, and thou art a Prince over them forever.

"So shall it be with my father: he shall be called a prince over his posterity, holding the keys of the patriarchal Priesthood over the kingdom of God on earth, even the Church of the Latter-day Saints, and he shall sit in the general assembly of Patriarchs, even in council with the Ancient of Days when he shall sit and all the Patriarchs with him and shall enjoy his right and authority under the direction of the Ancient of Days. . . .

"And again, blessed is my father, for the hand of the Lord shall be over him, and he shall be full of the Holy Ghost; for he shall predict whatsoever shall befall his posterity unto the latest generation, and shall see the affliction of his children pass away, and their enemies under their feet: and when his head is fully ripe he shall behold himself as an olive tree whose branches are bowed down with much fruit. Behold, the blessings of Joseph by the hand of his progenitor, shall come upon the head of my father and his seed after him, to the uttermost, even he shall be a fruitful bough; he shall be as a fruitful bough, even a fruitful bough by a well whose branches run over the wall, and his seed shall abide in strength, and the arms of their hands shall be made strong by the hands of the mighty God of Jacob, and the God of his fathers: even the God of Abraham, Isaac and Jacob, shall help him and his seed after him: even the Almighty shall bless him with blessings of heaven above and his seed after him, and the blessings of the deep that lieth under: and his seed shall rise up and call him blessed. He shall be as the vine of the choice grape when her clusters are fully ripe: and he shall also possess a mansion on high, even in the Celestial Kingdom. His counsel shall be sought for by thousands, and he shall have place in the house of the Lord; for he shall be mighty in the council of the elders, and his days shall yet be lengthened out: and when he shall go hence he shall go in peace, and his rest shall be glorious; and his name shall be had in remembrance to the end. Amen" (*Teachings of the Prophet Joseph Smith*, 38–40).

107:53 Each of the seven patriarchs named in this verse received the priesthood at the hands of Adam. Of Mahalaleel, Jared, and Enoch we are told that Adam at a subsequent time also blessed them. Thereafter, we are told that Enoch "saw the Lord." In this verse we learn that they were all high priests. Joseph Smith told us that Adam blessed his posterity because "he wanted to bring them into the presence of God" (*Teachings of the Prophet Joseph Smith*, 159). Here we are told that Adam gave them and "the residue of his posterity who were righteous" his "last blessing." After he did so the Lord appeared to them (D&C 107:54). All that we are told here conforms to the pattern given earlier in this revelation (vv. 18–19) and in Doctrine and Covenants 84:19. Perhaps Adam-ondi-Ahman, like a general conference of the Church, consisted of different meetings; everyone may not have participated in all of them. See commentary on Doctrine and Covenants 27:5–14.

Adam-ondi-Ahman. See commentary on Doctrine and Covenants 116.

107:54 *Michael, the prince, the archangel.* The great patriarch Adam was known to us in our premortal estate as Michael, who led the armies of the Lord against Lucifer when he and a third of the host of heaven rebelled against the Father and the Son. See commentary on Doctrine and Covenants 78:16.

107:57 *The book of Enoch.* We understand this text to be a promise that in a future day we will receive scriptural records written by Enoch. A number of ancient manuscripts attributed to Enoch are extant today. These manuscripts are generally classified as pseudepigraphic (meaning falsely named) at least in part because the scholarly world does not believe that a written language existed at the time of Enoch. Nonetheless, the Book of Moses assures us that Adam and his children had a "language that was pure and undefiled" and that this same language was known to Enoch (Moses 6:6, 46–47). Commenting on the extant Enoch manuscripts, Elder Bruce R. McConkie observed: "In the pseudepigraphic writings of Enoch we find visions, prophecies, exhortations, and doctrinal expositions relative to the Second Coming and the Millennium; the names and functions of the seven angels (including Raphael, Michael, and Gabriel); the separation of the spirits of righteous and wicked men as they await the day of judgment; the coming judgment of the wicked; the attainment of salvation by the righteous and elect; the bringing of the Son of Man before 'the head of days' (meaning, obviously, the Ancient of Days); the resurrection of the dead and the separation by the Judge of the righteous and the wicked; the translation of Enoch; preexistence and the creation of the souls of all men before the foundation of the world; the war in heaven and the casting out of Satan; the dividing of the eight-thousand-year history of the earth into the first six thousand years, to be followed by one thousand years of rest, after which would come another one thousand years, and then the end; a list of beatitudes, not far removed in wisdom from those of Jesus himself; personal responsibility for sin; the salvation of animals; the state of eternal life for those who keep the commandments; and much, much more.

"It will be observed that the matters here recited, though taught in part and by inference in the canonical scriptures of that and our day, are in fact known only in plainness and purity by latter-day revelation. It is far more than coincidence that doctrines attributed to Enoch in the pseudepigraphic writings are the very ones the Lord saw fit to restore in plainness in our dispensation. Unfortunately, the whole of these ancient writings cannot be accepted as the mind and will and voice of Him from whom revelation comes. As with the study of the apocryphal books, so it is with the study of the pseudepigraphic writings: the seeker after revealed wisdom must be guided by the power of the Holy Spirit" (*Mortal Messiah*, 1:274–75).

We fully expect all of Enoch's writings to be restored to us in the purity in which he originally recorded them.

The Twelve Are to Set the Officers of the Church in Order
DOCTRINE AND COVENANTS 107:58–67

107:58 At this point in this section a revelation given in November 1831 in Cuyahoga County, Ohio, on priesthood is added to that which had been received on 28 March 1835. Some additions to this revelation were made before it appeared in the 1835 edition of the Doctrine and Covenants. (Verses 61, 70, 73, 76–77, 88, 90, 93, 98 were added to the original revelation.)

107:61 *Priests to preside over . . . priests.* This verse was added to the 1831 revelation by the Prophet in 1835. As the Church is organized today, priests are presided over by their bishop, who holds the presidency of the Aaronic Priesthood in the ward. When these verses were recorded, wards did not yet exist and priests were men of full maturity.

107:63 *According to the covenants and commandments of the church.* In the 1831 revelation this read, "According to the Church Articles and Covenants," which referred to what is known today as Doctrine and Covenants 20.

107:64 *Then comes the High Priesthood.* The phrase "High Priesthood" as used here refers to the office of high priest. The previous verse speaks of an elder (an office in the higher priesthood); this verse follows, noting that after the elder comes "the High Priesthood." See commentary on Doctrine and Covenants 84:29.

107:65–66 The president of the Church is the presiding high priest in the Church. He holds all the keys of the kingdom, and all priesthood quorums function under his direction.

The Office of Bishop Defined
DOCTRINE AND COVENANTS 107:68–76

107:68–76 From the time of Aaron to John the Baptist, the high priest in Israel (according to the Aaronic order) presided over the priesthood and the temple. It is not surprising, therefore, that with the restoration of that office in this dispensation there would be some confusion as to just what authority was appended to this position. We are told that this office—known to us today as the presiding bishop—is not equal to that of the president of the high priesthood but rather is to preside over temporal things. To hold the keys of this office one must be either a high priest or a literal descendant of Aaron. This office of bishop also carries with it the responsibility to be a judge in Israel. "Other bishops" are also spoken of who are to function in their designated area of authority after the pattern of the presiding bishop. Following the pattern announced in this revelation, a ward bishop functions as the president of the Aaronic Priesthood, as the presiding high priest in his ward, as a judge in Israel, and as having charge over temporal affairs. Further, we are told that the bishop is to be guided in his duties "by the Spirit of truth" (v. 71). See commentary on Doctrine and Covenants 68:15–16.

107:70 *Literal descendant of Aaron.* See commentary on Doctrine and Covenants 68:15–16.

The First Presidency Constitute the Highest Court in the Church
DOCTRINE AND COVENANTS 107:77–84

107:77–84 As long as there is such a thing as right and wrong, as long as God continues to be a God of laws, and as long as the membership of the Church embraces mortal beings, there will be a necessity for church disciplinary councils. As every member of the Church is to work out his or her salvation with fear and trembling (Philippians 2:12), so all are subject to the order and discipline of the Church. No one is above the law. It is not to historical Christianity that one turns to find such principles, for historical Christianity is seriously marred by supposed spiritual leaders who held themselves above the law—be it man's or God's laws—and whose actions have been in many cases "enough to make hell itself shudder, and to stand aghast and pale, and the hands of the very devil to tremble and palsy" (D&C 123:10). It is but another evidence of the purity of purpose of the Prophet Joseph Smith that in establishing a system of government for the church of which he was the presiding officer that he would make himself subject to every law and ordinance of the gospel by which others were also to abide.

The supreme tribunal in the Church is here denominated as the

Common Council of the Church. It consists of the First Presidency and twelve high priests chosen by them to assist as counselors. This council has the final word on all matters of controversy that involve the Church or a member's standing in it. As noted, no one stands above this council. Should the president of the Church transgress, his actions are to be judged by this body. This revelation specifies that in such an instance the council would be presided over by the presiding bishop and, we can only suppose, the Quorum of the Twelve. Their decision is the end of the controversy concerning him.

We note in passing that charges were preferred against Joseph Smith by Sylvester Smith, a member of the first high council in Kirtland. George A. Smith gave this recollection of what happened: "I remember well in Zion's Camp, Levi W. Hancock made a fife, from a joint of sweet elder, Sylvester Smith marched his company to the music of that fife. That fife may be considered almost the introduction of martial music among the 'Mormons.' A dog came out and barked, when Sylvester Smith was going to kill the dog. Joseph said he was a good watch dog, Sylvester became wrathy and threatened; finally Joseph reproved him sharply, showing him that such a spirit would not conquer or control the human family, that he must get rid of it, and predicted that if he did not get rid of it, the day would come when a dog would gnaw his flesh, and he not have the power to resist it. Some months after the return to Kirtland, Sylvester Smith preferred a charge against Joseph the Prophet, for having prophesied lies in the name of the Lord, and undertook to substantiate that charge on the ground that the Prophet had said a dog should bite him, if he did not get rid of that spirit, when he had not power to resist. They were three days and parts of nights, with the High Council in Kirtland, in investigating this charge; one person spoke three hours in behalf of the Prophet. Sylvester published a confession which can be seen in the Church History, acknowledging his fault" (*Journal of Discourses*, 11:7).

Presidents Govern Their Quorums
DOCTRINE AND COVENANTS 107:85–100

107:85–88 The four offices in the Aaronic Priesthood, as that priesthood is to function in this dispensation, are here specified as deacon, teacher, priest, and bishop. The number of priesthood holders in each quorum is also given: twelve deacons to a quorum; twenty-four teachers; and forty-eight priests, all of whom labor under the presidency of the bishopric with the bishop also presiding as the president of the priests quorum. Each quorum president is responsible for teaching quorum members their respective duties as "given according to the covenants," meaning Doctrine and Covenants 20. The only officers on the ward level who hold keys are the deacons quorum president, the teachers quorum president, the bishop and the elders quorum president.

107:91 *Like unto Moses.* Moses, who is a classic type for Christ, is here held up as the pattern to be followed by the man who stands at the head of the Church.

107:92 *Having all the gifts.* See commentary on Doctrine and Covenants 46:29.

107:93 *According to the vision showing the order of the Seventy.* "Now, if he [Joseph Smith] saw the Seventies in vision," reasoned Orson F. Whitney, "why not the Apostles? Why not the First Presidency? Why not the stakes and wards, with their presiding officers, and even the auxiliary organizations? Who can say that he did not see them? Who can say that these quorums of the Priesthood, these auxiliary societies and associations, the Church of God in its entirety as it exists upon the earth, is not a reflex of the Church of God in heaven, so far as it is adapted to our present conditions, so far as it has been found necessary to organize it here; the eventual outcome to be a perfect Church, corresponding in every particular to the Church of the First Born; and this that the will of God may be done upon earth even as it is done in heaven?" (Conference Report, April 1912, 51).

107:93–98 Some time and effort were necessary to allow the Church to grow up into the revelation as it describes the duties of a seventy. In accord with the direction of scripture, those who serve as seventies today are General Authorities who labor under the direction of the Twelve throughout the world (v. 38).

107:99–100 This great revelation on the priesthood concludes with a charge given to every priesthood holder to learn his duty and act with diligence in the office to which he has been called. The call is to magnify offices, not priesthood (Romans 11:13; Jacob 1:19, 2:2; D&C 24:3, 9; 66:11; 88:80). "We speak loosely of magnifying our priesthood," observed Joseph Fielding Smith, "but what the revelations speak of is magnifying our callings in the priesthood, as elders, seventies, high priests, patriarchs, and apostles" (Conference Report, October 1970, 91).

Every man must work out his salvation in the office to which he has been called. Elders must do the work of elders and high priests the work of high priests if they seek to be saved. To envy the office of another while neglecting the one to which we have been called is to sow the seeds of sorrow. John Taylor said it was a simple thing to respond to the question, "Who was the greater, the seventy or the high priest? It is the man who magnifies his office" (*Gospel Kingdom*, 152). As to the responsibility in the office and calling that is ours, President Joseph Fielding Smith gave this reminder: "The Council of the Twelve did not place them upon you; the Presidency of the Church did not place them upon you—it is true that they, or their representatives, called you and ordained you to this ministry—but the responsibility to perform this labor came to you from the Son of God! You are his servants. You will be held accountable to him for your stewardship, and unless you magnify your callings and prove your-selves worthy and faithful in all things, you will not stand blameless before him at the last day" (*Doctrines of Salvation*, 3:118).

LECTURES ON FAITH

PLACE: KIRTLAND, OHIO
DATE PUBLISHED: 17 AUGUST 1835

The preface to the first edition of the Doctrine and Covenants (1835) begins with this explanation: "The first part of the book will be found to contain a series of Lectures as delivered before a Theological class in this place [Kirtland, Ohio], and in consequence of their embracing the important doctrine of salvation, we have arranged them into the following work.

"The second part contains items or principles for the regulation of the church, as taken from the revelations which have been given since its organization, as well as from former ones" (iii).

The book entitled Doctrine and Covenants then consisted of two parts: the first dealing with its doctrines, which are set forth in a series of seven lectures known to us today as the Lectures on Faith; and second, the covenants, which are represented by a selection of revelations given to the Prophet Joseph Smith. The name came from the idea that the doctrines of the Church were found in the Lectures on Faith and the covenants in the revelations given to the Prophet.

The preface to the book concluded by stating: "We do not present this little volume with any other expectation than that we are to be called to answer to every principle advanced, in that day when the secrets of all hearts will be revealed, and the reward of every man's labor be given him" (iv). It then bore the names of the First Presidency: Joseph Smith Jr., Oliver Cowdery, Sidney Rigdon, and F. G. Williams.

By revelation the Lord directed that a "School of the Prophets" be established to prepare the elders of Israel to more fully magnify their callings in declaring the message of salvation among all the peoples of the earth (D&C 88:74–80, 127; 90:7). This school was organized in Kirtland, Ohio, in February 1833 and continued until April of that year. Of this period the Prophet said, "Great joy and satisfaction continually beamed in the countenances of the School of the Prophets, and the Saints, on account of the things revealed, and our progress in the knowledge of God" (*History of the Church*, 1:334).

The expulsion of the Saints from Jackson County, Missouri, in the fall of 1833 appeared to prevent the continuation of the school in Kirtland during the winter of 1833 and 1834. In November 1834, however, preparations were made for the reopening of the school. The Prophet wrote: "It now being the last of the month, and the Elders beginning to come in, it was necessary to make preparations for the school for the Elders, wherein they might be more perfectly instructed in the great things of God, during the coming winter" (Smith, *History of the Church*, 2:169).

On 1 December 1834, the Prophet further said: "Our school for the Elders was now well attended, and with the lectures on theology, which were regularly delivered, absorbed for the time being everything else of a temporal nature. The classes, being mostly Elders gave the most studious attention to the all-important object of qualifying themselves as messengers of Jesus Christ, to be ready to do His will in carrying glad tidings to all that would open their eyes, ears and hearts" (Smith, *History of the Church*, 2:175–76).

It was during the winter of 1834 to 1835 that the Lectures on Faith were delivered. "During the month of January," the Prophet recorded, "I was engaged in the school of the Elders, and in preparing the lectures on theology for publication in the book of Doctrine and Covenants, which the committee appointed last September were now compiling" (Smith, *History of the Church*, 2:180).

The breadth of these lectures is as follows: lecture one explains what faith is; lecture two describes how mankind comes to know about God; lectures three and four identify the attributes of Deity and affirm that they are unchanging; lecture five deals with the nature of God the Father, his Son Jesus Christ, and the Holy Ghost; lecture six proclaims that the willingness to sacrifice all things is necessary to gaining faith unto salvation; and lecture seven identifies both the fruits of faith that must always be present among the Lord's people and the path by which they obtain the fulness of the Father.

Various editions of the Doctrine and Covenants have appeared through the years with appropriate additions and deletions being made. For instance, in the 1876 edition twenty-six sections were added and Oliver Cowdery's article on marriage was dropped. The Lectures on Faith were not included in the 1921 edition and have not been included in the Doctrine and Covenants since that time. By way of explanation it was noted that the lectures, while profitable for doctrine, are not scripture. The introduction to that edition reads thus: "Certain lessons, entitled 'Lectures on Faith,' which were bound in with the *Doctrine and Covenants* in some of its former issues [all of them], are not included in this edition. Those lessons were prepared for use in the School of the Elders, conducted in Kirtland, Ohio, during the winter of 1834–1835; but they were never presented to nor accepted by the Church as being otherwise than theological lectures or lessons" (1921 edition, v).

Doctrinal works, like doctrinal teachers, never enjoy a shortage of critics. Certainly this has been the case with the Lectures on Faith over the years. Perhaps because the lectures did not enjoy the immunity accorded to scripture—much of which is more difficult to understand or defend than anything in these seven lectures—it was felt best to drop them from inclusion in a book accepted as canon. Given, however, that the purpose of this work is to acquaint the reader with the natural development of Latter-day Saint theology, it would be a serious oversight not to include the lectures here. Indeed, they are a most instructive document, and, in the judgment of the writers, those few matters viewed by some as stumbling stones become, when polished by a thoughtful second or third look, rather bright and precious gems of truth.

A matter of some moment among particular critics of the lectures is that of authorship. Critics seem to feel that a word, a phrase, a thought, an idea that did not fall directly from the pen or lips of the Prophet cannot be approved by him, nor is it to be trusted by us. This idea is a little strained. It is similar to arguing that only the prophet should address the Saints at conference. From the beginning of the Restoration, Joseph Smith was quick to establish the idea that neither man nor woman was to serve without counselors and that the order of heaven was that the Church be governed by councils. That Joseph Smith was not the sole author of the Lectures on Faith but that they were written by a committee over which he presided seems quite compatible with that order. Let it suffice to say that the doctrinal ideas found in the lectures trace back to Joseph Smith; others helped in their expression; the final approval of all that was written rested with him.

It has also been argued that the ideas in these lectures are Protestant in tone and that, at least in some instances, they represent a concept of God which Joseph Smith would in the coming years throw off. In fact, each of the lectures centers on one or more basic ideas that are directly offensive to traditional or historical Christian theology. And one of the important roles played by the lectures in the early years of the Church's history was to distance Latter-day Saint theology from doctrines rooted in either Protestantism or Catholicism.

The first lecture concerns the nature of faith and the assurance we have of the reliability of what the Prophet called the "science of theology." The essence of the principle here involved is that faith and works are inseparably connected and that when we receive any blessing from heaven it is obtained by obedience to the law upon which it is predicated. Salvation cannot be obtained by grace alone any more that it can be obtained by compliance to any other gospel principle alone. No principle standing alone has any saving power in it.

The second lecture centers on the reality of a corporeal being who walked and talked with Adam and Eve in Eden and of whom they testified to their children and their children's children down through the generations. This is not the incorporeal essence of sectarian creeds. This lecture also taught that Adam had the gospel of Jesus Christ, which he received at the hands of angels, by revelation, and by the voice of the Father. Again, such doctrine hardly accords to traditional Christian beliefs.

The third lecture deals with the character of Deity. In sharp contrast with the idea espoused by historical Christianity that God is an incomprehensible mystery, this lecture declares that our faith in God cannot exceed our knowledge of him. To exercise faith in God we must first have "a *correct* idea of his character, perfections, and attributes," the Prophet declared (Lecture 3:4). First, it is stated that man must know that God was God before the world was created and that he is the same God now. Second, it must be understood that he is merciful and gracious and that he has been from everlasting and will be to everlasting. Third, it must be understood that he does not change. All attributes and characteristics of God are absolute and eternal. Fourth, it must be known that he is a God of truth, that he cannot lie. Fifth, God is no respecter of persons, meaning that all his children in all ages will be taught the same gospel and granted the same privilege to enjoy its blessings. And sixth, God is love.

Similarly, the fourth lecture centers on the attributes of Deity, stating that without a knowledge of God's attributes we cannot exercise faith in him. Attributes to consider are his perfect knowledge of all things, his power, justice, judgment, mercy, and truth. The lecture again rejects the notion of God as an incomprehensible or transcendental being.

The fifth lecture centers faith in a Godhead consisting of three separate beings and the idea that we advance from grace to grace to become "heirs of the heavenly kingdom, and joint heirs with Jesus Christ" (Lecture 5:2). Thus as the Son partakes of the fulness of the Father, so may we become partakers—through righteousness—of that same fulness. As stated in a revelation that had already been given to the Prophet, the doctrine of heirship embraced the idea that we could become equal with God in power, in might, and in dominion, an idea far beyond the reach of sectarian theology (D&C 76:95).

The sixth lecture centers on the idea that an actual or personal knowledge that the course we are pursuing is approved of by God is necessary to exercise sufficient faith unto salvation. In so doing, this lecture rejects the sectarian notion that the heavens are sealed to immediate and personal revelation. This lecture also declares that as a covenant people we must posses a willingness to sacrifice all for the gospel cause. There is no cheap grace here; we must be willing to lay all that we have upon the altar.

The seventh lecture defines salvation as our being as Christ is. Further, it declares Christ to have been like his Father in all things. Thus salvation is defined as being assimilated into the likeness of God. This returns us to the central thought of the fifth lecture, that those of the house of faith are to be heirs of God, joint heirs with Christ (Romans 8:15–17). Though this doctrine did not find its full expression until the King Follett Discourse, it is certainly foundational for the understanding that we can become as God is, an idea most offensive to sectarian theology.

Following is presented the complete text of the Lectures on Faith, with each lecture followed by commentary.

Lecture One

1. Faith being the first principle in revealed religion, and the foundation of all righteousness, necessarily claims the first place in a course of lectures which are designed to unfold to the understanding the doctrine of Jesus Christ.

2. In presenting the subject of faith, we shall observe the following order—

3 First, faith itself—what it is.

4. Secondly, the object on which it rests. And,

5. Thirdly, the effects which flow from it.

6. Agreeable to this order we have first to show what faith is.

7. The author of the epistle to the Hebrews, in the eleventh chapter of that epistle and first verse, gives the following definition of the word faith:

8. Now faith is the substance (assurance) of things hoped for, the evidence of things not seen."

9. From this we learn that faith is the assurance which men have of the existence of things which they have not seen, and the principle of action in all intelligent beings.

10. If men were duly to consider themselves, and turn their thoughts and reflections to the operations of their own minds, they would readily discover that it is faith, and faith only, which is the moving cause of all action in them; that without it both mind and body would be in a state of inactivity, and all their exertions would cease, both physical and mental.

11. Were this class to go back and reflect upon the history of their lives, from the period of their first recollection, and ask themselves what principle excited them to action, or what gave them energy and activity in all their lawful avocations, callings, and pursuits, what would be the answer? Would it not be that it was the assurance which they had of the existence of things which they had not seen as yet? Was it not the hope which you had, in consequence of your belief in the existence of unseen things, which stimulated you to action and exertion in order to obtain them? Are you not dependent on your faith, or belief, for the acquisition of all knowledge, wisdom, and intelligence? Would you exert yourselves to obtain wisdom and intelligence, unless you did believe that you could obtain them? Would you have ever sown, if you had not believed that you would reap? Would you have ever planted, if you had not believed that you would gather? Would you have ever asked, unless you had believed that you would receive? Would you have ever sought, unless you had believed that you would have found? Or, would you have ever knocked, unless you had believed that it would have been opened unto you? In a word, is there anything that you would have done, either physical or mental, if you had not previously believed? Are not all your exertions of every kind, dependent on your faith? Or, may we not ask, what have you, or what do you possess, which you have not obtained by reason of your faith? Your food, your raiment, your lodgings, are they not all by reason of your faith? Reflect, and ask

yourselves if these things are not so. Turn your thoughts on your own minds, and see if faith is not the moving cause of all action in yourselves; and, if the moving cause in you, is it not in all other intelligent beings?

12. And as faith is the moving cause of all action in temporal concerns, so it is in spiritual; for the Saviour has said, and that truly, that "He that believeth and is baptized, shall be saved." Mark 16:16.

13. As we receive by faith all temporal blessings that we do receive, so we in like manner receive by faith all spiritual blessings that we do receive. But faith is not only the principle of action, but of power also, in all intelligent beings, whether in heaven or on earth. Thus says the author of the epistle to the Hebrews 11:3—

14. Through faith we understand that the worlds were framed by the word of God; so that things which are seen were not made of things which do appear."

15. By this we understand that the principle of power which existed in the bosom of God, by which the worlds were framed, was faith; and that it is by reason of this principle of power existing in the Deity, that all created things exist; so that all things in heaven, on earth, or under the earth exist by reason of faith as it existed in Him.

16. Had it not been for the principle of faith the worlds would never have been framed neither would man have been formed of the dust. It is the principle by which Jehovah works, and through which he exercises power over all temporal as well as eternal things. Take this principle or attribute—for it is an attribute—from the Deity, and he would cease to exist.

17. Who cannot see, that if God framed the worlds by faith, that it is by faith that he exercises power over them, and that faith is the principle of power? And if the principle of power, it must be so in man as well as in the Deity? This is the testimony of all the sacred writers, and the lesson which they have been endeavouring to teach to man.

18. The Saviour says (Matthew 17:19, 20), in explaining the reason why the disciples could not cast out the devil, that it was because of their unbelief—"For verily I say unto you" (said he), "if ye have faith as a grain of mustard seed, ye shall say unto this mountain, 'Remove hence to yonder place,' and it shall remove; and nothing shall be impossible unto you."

19. Moroni, while abridging and compiling the record of his fathers,

has given us the following account of faith as the principle of power. He says, page 597, that it was the faith of Alma and Amulek which caused the walls of the prison to be rent, as recorded on the 278th page; it was the faith of Nephi and Lehi which caused a change to be wrought upon the hearts of the Lamanites, when they were immersed with the Holy Spirit and with fire, as seen on the 443rd page; and that it was by faith the mountain Zerin was removed when the brother of Jared spake in the name of the Lord. See also 599th page.

20. In addition to this we are told in Hebrews 11:32, 33, 34, 35, that Gideon, Barak, Samson, Jephthah, David, Samuel, and the prophets, through faith subdued Kingdoms, wrought righteousness, obtained promises, stopped the mouths of lions, quenched the violence of fire, escaped the edge of the sword; out of weakness were made strong, waxed valiant in fight, turned to flight the armies of the aliens, and that women received their dead raised to life again, &c., &c.

21. Also Joshua, in the sight of all Israel, bade the sun and moon to stand still, and it was done. Joshua 10:12.

22. We here understand, that the sacred writers say that all these things were done by faith. It was by faith that the worlds were framed. God spake, chaos heard, and worlds came into order by reason of the faith there was in Him. So with man also; he spake by faith in the name of God, and the sun stood still, the moon obeyed, mountains removed, prisons fell, lions' mouths were closed, the human heart lost its enmity, fire its violence, armies their power, the sword its terror, and death its dominion; and all this by reason of the faith which was in him.

23. Had it not been for the faith which was in men, they might have spoken to the sun, the moon, the mountains, prisons, the human heart, fire, armies, the sword, or to death in vain!

24. "Faith, then, is the first great governing principle which has power, dominion, and authority over all things; by it they exist, by it they are upheld, by it they are changed, or by it they remain, agreeable to the will of God. Without it there is no power, and without power there could be no creation nor existence!

Commentary

LF 1:1–24 The definition of faith given in this lecture—which is the power of action by which God does all things—appears to conflict with

that of Alma wherein he suggests that when we exercise faith in a particular thing and thereby obtain the assurance that it is so, the knowledge
that we have obtained supplants the faith with which we began and thus
our faith is dormant on that matter. Alma's idea is that if we had a perfect knowledge of all things we would have no need for faith (Alma
32:33–34). Because it was through Joseph Smith that we obtained the
writings of Alma, we can be quite confident that he was familiar with
what Alma had said. The apparent difference between the two men centers in the spiritual maturity of those to whom they speak. Alma is
instructing those of little understanding, Joseph Smith, on the other
hand, is addressing the School of the Prophets. One defines from the perspective of the immediate moment, the other from that of the eternities.
Both men define faith according to the level of understanding of those to
whom they speak. To those who have relatively little experience in spiritual things, Alma says to exercise faith and you will obtain knowledge.
(Such knowledge, however, cannot stand independent of the faith by
which it was obtained, for if that faith is lost, the knowledge obtained by
it will be lost also.) To those who are more mature and experienced, we
say that it is the perfection of God's faith that enables him to do all that
he does, and when we obtain the same faith we in like manner will be
able to do all things.

In the questions and answers that followed this lecture, the Prophet
defined theology as "revealed science." In the lecture it is reasoned that
just as faith is the moving cause in all that we do in the temporal world, so
is it the moving cause in the spiritual world also (vv. 11–12). In a future
day, this principle would find expression in this language, "There is a law,
irrevocably decreed in heaven before the foundations of this world, upon
which all blessings are predicated—And when we obtain any blessing
from God, it is by obedience to that law upon which it is predicated"
(D&C 130:20–21). It is this concept of the inseparable relationship
between faith and works—that is, the need for us to be obedient to the
laws of heaven in order to obtain the blessings of heaven—that separates
us from the Protestant concept of salvation by grace alone. Mormonism
holds that grace cannot stand alone. No gospel principle stands alone!
Just as the Lord declared that man was not to be without woman, so did
he declare that faith was not to be without works, that baptism was not
to be without repentance, that the Fall was not to be without the
Atonement, that mercy was not to be without justice, that agency was
not to be without accountability, and so on. Each principle of the gospel

is an inseparable part of the whole, with none in and of itself constituting the gospel or the way to salvation.

Lecture Two

1. Having shown in our previous lecture "faith itself—what it is," we shall proceed to show, secondly, the object on which it rests.

2. We here observe that God is the only supreme governor and independent being in whom all fullness and perfection dwell; who is omnipotent, omnipresent and omniscient; without beginning of days or end of life; and that in him every good gift and every good principle dwell; and that he is the Father of lights; in him the principle of faith dwells independently, and he is the object in whom the faith of all other rational and accountable beings center for life and salvation.

3. In order to present this part of the subject in a clear and conspicuous point of light, it is necessary to go back and show the evidences which mankind have had, and the foundation on which these evidences are, or were, based since the creation, to believe in the existence of a God.

4. We do not mean those evidences which are manifested by the works of creation which we daily behold with our natural eyes. We are sensible that, after a revelation of Jesus Christ, the works of creation, throughout their vast forms and varieties, clearly exhibit his eternal power and Godhead. Romans 1:20: "For the invisible things of him from the creation of the world are clearly seen, being understood by the things that are made, even his eternal power and Godhead;" but we mean those evidences by which the first thoughts were suggested to the minds of men that there was a God who created all things.

5 We shall now proceed to examine the situation of man at his first creation. Moses, the historian, has given us the following account of him in the first chapter of the book of Genesis, beginning with the 20th verse, and closing with the 30th. We copy from the new translation:

6. "And I, God, said unto mine Only Begotten, which was with me from the beginning, 'Let us make man in our image, after our likeness;' and it was so.

7. "And I, God, said, 'Let them have dominion over the fishes of the

sea, and over the fowl of the air, and over the cattle, and over all the earth, and over every creeping thing that creepeth upon the earth.'

8. "And I, God, created man in mine own image, in the image of mine Only Begotten created I him; male and female created I them. And I, God, blessed them, and said unto them, 'Be fruitful, and multiply, and replenish the earth, and subdue it; and have dominion over the fish of the sea, and over the fowl of the air, and over every living thing that moveth upon the earth.'

9. "And I, God, said unto man, 'Behold, I have given you every herb bearing seed, which is upon the face of all the earth, and every tree in the which shall be the fruit of a tree yielding seed; to you it shall be for meat.'"

10. Again, Genesis 2:15, 16, 17, 19, 20: "And I, the Lord God, took the man, and put him into the garden of Eden, to dress it and to keep it. And I, the Lord God, commanded the man saying, 'Of every tree of the garden thou mayest freely eat; but of the tree of knowledge of good and evil thou shalt not eat of it; nevertheless thou mayest choose for thyself, for it is given unto thee; but remember that I forbid it, for in the day thou eatest thereof thou shalt surely die.'

11. "And out of the ground I, the Lord God, formed every beast of the field, and every fowl of the air, and commanded that they should come unto Adam, to see what he would call them. And whatsoever Adam called every living creature, that should be the name thereof. And Adam gave names to all cattle, and to the fowl of the air, and to every beast of the field."

12. "From the foregoing we learn man's situation at his first creation, the knowledge with which he was endowed, and the high and exalted station in which he was placed—lord or governor of all things on earth, and at the same time enjoying communion and intercourse with his Maker, without a vail to separate between. We shall next proceed to examine the account given of his fall, and of his being driven out of the garden of Eden, and from the presence of the Lord.

13. Moses proceeds—"And they" (Adam and Eve) "heard the voice of the Lord God, as they were walking in the garden, in the cool of the day; and Adam and his wife went to hide themselves from the presence of the Lord God amongst the trees of the garden. And I, the Lord God, called unto Adam, and said unto him, 'Where goest thou?'

And he said, 'I heard thy voice in the garden, and I was afraid, because I beheld that I was naked, and I hid myself.'

14. "And I, the Lord God, said unto Adam, 'Who told thee thou wast naked? Hast thou eaten of the tree whereof I commanded thee that thou shouldst not eat? If so, thou shouldst surely die.' And the man said, 'The woman whom thou gavest me, and commandedst that she should remain with me, gave me of the fruit of the tree, and I did eat.'

15. "And I, the Lord God, said unto the woman, 'What is this thing which thou hast done?' And the woman said, 'The serpent beguiled me, and I did eat.'

16. "And again, the Lord said unto the woman, 'I will greatly multiply thy sorrow, and thy conception. In sorrow thou shalt bring forth children; and thy desire shall be to thy husband, and he shall rule over thee.'

17. "And unto Adam, I, the Lord God, said, 'Because thou hast hearkened unto the voice of thy wife, and hast eaten of the fruit of the tree of which I commanded thee, saying, Thou shalt not eat of it! cursed shall be the ground for thy sake; in sorrow thou shalt eat of it all the days of thy life. Thorns also, and thistles shall it bring forth to thee, and thou shalt eat the herb of the field. By the sweat of thy face shalt thou eat bread, until thou shalt return unto the ground—for thou shalt surely die—for out of it wast thou taken: for dust thou wast, and unto dust shalt thou return.'" This was immediately followed by the fulfillment of what we previously said—Man was driven or sent out of Eden.

18. Two important items are shown from the former quotations. First, after man was created, he was not left without intelligence or understanding, to wander in darkness and spend an existence in ignorance and doubt (on the great and important point which effected his happiness) as to the real fact by whom he was created, or unto whom he was amenable for his conduct. God conversed with him face to face. In his presence he was permitted to stand, and from his own mouth he was permitted to receive instruction. He heard his voice, walked before him and gazed upon his glory, while intelligence burst upon his understanding, and enabled him to give names to the vast assemblage of his Maker's works.

19. Secondly, we have seen, that though man did transgress, his transgression did not deprive him of the previous knowledge with

which he was endowed relative to the existence and glory of his Creator; for no sooner did he hear his voice than he sought to hide himself from his presence.

20. Having shown, then, in the first instance, that God began to converse with man immediately after he "breathed into his nostrils the breath of life," and that he did not cease to manifest himself to him, even after his fall, we shall next proceed to show, that though he was cast out from the garden of Eden, his knowledge of the existence of God was not lost, neither did God cease to manifest his will unto him.

21. We next proceed to present the account of the direct revelation which man received after he was cast out of Eden, and further copy from the new translation—

22. After Adam had been driven out of the garden, he "began to till the earth, and to have dominion over all the beasts of the field, and to eat his bread by the sweat of his brow, as I the Lord had commanded him." And he called upon the name of the Lord, and so did Eve, his wife, also. "And they heard the voice of the Lord, from the way toward the garden of Eden, speaking unto them, and they saw him not, for they were shut out from his presence; and he gave unto them commandments that they should worship the Lord their God, and should offer the firstlings of their flocks for an offering unto the Lord. And Adam was obedient unto the commandments of the Lord.

23. "And after many days an angel of the Lord appeared unto Adam, saying, 'Why dost thou offer sacrifices unto the Lord?' And Adam said unto him, 'I know not; save the Lord commanded me.'

24. "And then the angel spake, saying 'This thing is a similitude of the sacrifice of the Only Begotten of the Father, who is full of grace and truth. And thou shalt do all that thou doest in the name of the Son, and thou shalt repent and call upon God in the name of the Son for evermore.' And in that day the Holy Ghost fell upon Adam, which beareth record of the Father and the Son."

25. This last quotation, or summary, shows this important fact, that though our first parents were driven out of the garden of Eden, and were even separated from the presence of God by a vail, they still retained a knowledge of his existence, and that sufficiently to move them to call upon him. And further, that no sooner was the plan of redemption revealed to man, and he began to call upon God, than the Holy Spirit was given, bearing record of the Father and Son.

26. Moses also gives us an account, in the fourth of Genesis, of the transgression of Cain, and the righteousness of Abel, and of the revelations of God to them. He says, "In process of time, Cain brought of the fruit of the ground an offering unto the Lord. And Abel also brought of the firstlings of his flock, and of the fat thereof. And the Lord had respect unto Abel, and to his offering; but unto Cain and to his offering he had not respect. Now Satan knew this, and it pleased him. And Cain was very wroth, and his countenance fell. And the Lord said unto Cain, 'Why art thou wroth? Why is thy countenance fallen? If thou doest well, thou shalt be accepted. And if thou doest not well, sin lieth at the door, and Satan desireth to have thee; and except thou shalt hearken unto my commandments, I will deliver thee up, and it shall be unto thee according to his desire.'

27. "And Cain went into the field, and Cain talked with Abel, his brother. And it came to pass that while they were in the field, Cain rose up against Abel, his brother, and slew him. And Cain gloried in that, which he had done, saying, 'I am free; surely the flocks of my brother falleth unto my hands.'

28. "But the Lord said unto Cain, 'Where is Abel, thy brother?' And he said, 'I know not. Am I my brother's keeper?' And the Lord said, 'What hast thou done? the voice of thy brother's blood cries unto me from the ground. And now, thou shalt be cursed from the earth which hath opened her mouth to receive thy brother's blood from thy hand. When thou tillest the ground, it shall not henceforth yield unto thee her strength. A fugitive and a vagabond shalt thou be in the earth.'

29. "And Cain said unto the Lord, 'Satan tempted me because of my brother's flocks. And I was wroth also; for his offering thou didst accept and not mine; my punishment is greater than I can bear. Behold thou hast driven me out this day from the face of the Lord, and from thy face shall I be hid; and I shall be a fugitive and a vagabond in the earth; and it shall come to pass that he that findeth me will slay me because of mine iniquities, for these things are not hid from the Lord.' And the Lord said unto him, 'Whosoever slayeth thee, vengeance shall be taken on him sevenfold.' And I the Lord set a mark upon Cain, lest any finding him should kill him."

30. The object of the foregoing quotations is to show to this class the way by which mankind were first made acquainted with the existence of a God; that it was by a manifestation of God to man, and that God continued, after man's transgression, to manifest himself to him and

to his posterity; and, notwithstanding they were separated from his immediate presence that they could not see his face, they continued to hear his voice.

31. Adam, thus being made acquainted with God, communicated the knowledge which he had unto his posterity; and it was through this means that the thought was first suggested to their minds that there was a God, which laid the foundation for the exercise of their faith, through which they could obtain a knowledge of his character and also of his glory.

32. Not only was there a manifestation made unto Adam of the existence of a God; but Moses informs us, as before quoted, that God condescended to talk with Cain after his great transgression in slaying his brother, and that Cain knew that it was the Lord that was talking with him, so that when he was driven out from the presence of his brethren, he carried with him the knowledge of the existence of a God; and, through this means, doubtless, his posterity became acquainted with the fact that such a Being existed.

33. From this we can see that the whole human family in the early age of their existence, in all their different branches, had this knowledge disseminated among them; so that the existence of God became an object of faith in the early age of the world. And the evidences which these men had of the existence of a God, was the testimony of their fathers in the first instance.

34. The reason why we have been thus particular on this part of our subject, is that this class may see by what means it was that God became an object of faith among men after the fall; and what it was that stirred up the faith of multitudes to feel after him—to search after a knowledge of his character, perfections and attributes, until they became extensively acquainted with him, and not only commune with him and behold his glory, but be partakers of his power and stand in his presence.

35. Let this class mark particularly, that the testimony which these men had of the existence of a God, was the testimony of man; for previous to the time that any of Adam's posterity had obtained a manifestation of God to themselves, Adam, their common father, had testified unto them of the existence of God, and of his eternal power and Godhead.

36. For instance, Abel, before he received the assurance from heaven that his offerings were acceptable unto God, had received the

important information of his father that such a Being did exist, who had created and who did uphold all things. Neither can there be a doubt existing on the mind of any person, that Adam was the first who did communicate the knowledge of the existence of a God to his posterity; and that the whole faith of the world, from that time down to the present, is in a certain degree dependent on the knowledge first communicated to them by their common progenitor; and it has been handed down to the day and generation in which we live, as we shall show from the face of the sacred records.

37. First, Adam was 130 years old when Seth was born. Genesis 5:3. And the days of Adam, after he had begotten Seth, were 800 years, making him 930 years old when he died. Genesis 5:4, 5. Seth was 105 when Enos was born (v. 6); Enos was 90 when Cainan was born (v. 9); Cainan was 70 when Mahalaleel was born (v. 12); Mahalaleel was 65 when Jared was born (v. 15); Jared was 162 when Enoch was born (v. 18); Enoch was 65 when Methuselah was born (v. 21); Methuselah was 187 when Lamech was born (v. 25); Lamech was 182 when Noah was born (v. 28).

38. From this account it appears that Lamech, the 9th from Adam, and the father of Noah, was 56 years old when Adam died; Methuselah, 243; Enoch, 308; Jared, 470; Mahalaleel, 535; Cainan, 605; Enos, 695; and Seth, 800.

39. So that Lamech the father of Noah, Methuselah, Enoch, Jared, Mahalaleel, Cainan, Enos, Seth, and Adam, were all living at the same time, and beyond all controversy, were all preachers of righteousness.

40. Moses further informs us that Seth lived after he begat Enos, 807 years, making him 912 years old at his death. Genesis 5:7, 8. And Enos lived after he begat Cainan, 815 years, making him 905 years old when he died (vv. 10–11). And Cainan lived after he begat Mahalaleel, 840 years, making him 910 years old at his death (vv. 13–14). And Mahalaleel lived after he begat Jared, 830 years, making 895 years old when he died (vv. 16–17). And Jared lived after he begat Enoch, 800 years, making him 962 years old at his death (vv. 19–20). And Enoch walked with God after he begat Methuselah 300 years, making him 365 years old when he was translated (vv. 22–23). And Methuselah lived after he begat Lamech, 782 years, making him 969 years old when he died (vv. 26–27). Lamech lived after he begat Noah, 595 years, making him 777 years old when he died (vv. 30–31).

41. Agreeable to this account, Adam died in the 930th year of the world; Enoch was translated in the 987th, Seth died in the 1042nd; Enos in the 1140th; Cainan in the 1235th; Mahalaleel in the 1290th; Jared in the 1422nd; Lamech in the 1651st; and Methuselah in the 1656th, it being the same year in which the flood came.

42. So that Noah was 84 years old when Enos died, 176 when Cainan died, 234 when Mahalaleel died, 366 when Jared died, 595 when Lamech died, and 600 when Methuselah died.

43. We can see from this that Enos, Cainan, Mahalaleel, Jared, Methuselah, Lamech, and Noah, all lived on the earth at the same time; and that Enos, Cainan, Mahalaleel, Jared, Methuselah, and Lamech, were all acquainted with both Adam and Noah.

44. From the foregoing it is easily to be seen, not only how the knowledge of God came into the world, but upon what principle it was preserved; that from the time it was first communicated, it was retained in the minds of righteous men, who taught not only their own posterity but the world; so that there was no need of a new revelation to man, after Adam's creation to Noah, to give them the first idea or notion of the existence of a God; and not only of a God, but the true and living God.

45. Having traced the chronology of the world from Adam to Noah, we will now trace it from Noah to Abraham. Noah was 502 years old when Shem was born; 98 years afterwards the flood came, being the 600th year of Noah's age. And Moses informs us that Noah lived after the flood 350 years, making him 950 years old when he died. Genesis 9:28, 29.

46. Shem was 100 years old when Arphaxad was born. Genesis 11:10. Arphaxad was 35 when Salah was born (11:12); Salah was 30 when Eber was born (11:14); Eber was 34 when Peleg was born, in whose days the earth was divided (11:16); Peleg was 30 when Reu was born (11:18); Reu was 32 when Serug was born (11:20); Serug was 30 when Nahor was born (11:22); Nahor was 29 when Terah was born (11:24); Terah was 70 when Haran and Abraham were born (11:26).

47. There is some difficulty in the account given by Moses of Abraham's birth. Some have supposed that Abraham was not born until Terah was 130 years old. This conclusion is drawn from a variety of scriptures, which are not to our purpose at present to quote. Neither is it a matter of any consequence to us whether Abraham

was born when Terah was 70 years old, or 130. But in order that there may no doubt exist upon any mind in relation to the object lying immediately before us, in presenting the present chronology we will date the birth of Abraham at the latest period, that is, when Terah was 130 years old. It appears from this account that from the flood to the birth of Abraham, was 352 years.

48. Moses informs us that Shem lived after he begat Arphaxad, 500 years (11:11); this added to 100 years, which was his age when Arphaxad was born, makes him 600 years old when he died. Arphaxad lived, after he begat Salah, 403 years (11:13); this added to 35 years, which was his age when Salah was born, makes him 438 years old when he died. Salah lived after he begat Eber, 403 years (11:15); this added to 30 years, which was his age when Eber was born, makes him 433 years old when he died. Eber lived after he begat Peleg, 430 years (11:17); this added to 34 years, which was his age when Peleg was born, makes him 464 years old. Peleg lived after he begat Reu, 209 years (11:19); this added to 30 years, which was his age when Reu was born makes him 239 years old when he died. Reu lived after he begat Serug 207 years (11:21); this added to 32 years, which was his age when Serug was born, makes him 239 years old when he died. Serug lived after he begat Nahor, 200 years (11:23); this added to 30 years, which was his age when Nahor was born, makes him 230 years old when he died. Nahor lived after he begat Terah, 119 years (11:25); this added to 29 years, which was his age when Terah was born, makes him 148 years when he died. Terah was 130 years old when Abraham was born, and is supposed to have lived 75 years after his birth, making him 205 years old when he died.

49. Agreeable to this last account. Peleg died in the 1996th year of the world, Nahor in the 1997th, and Noah in the 2006th. So that Peleg, in whose days the earth was divided, and Nahor, the grand-father of Abraham, both died before Noah—the former being 239 years old, and the latter 148; and who cannot but see that they must have had a long and intimate acquaintance with Noah?

50. Reu died in the 2026th year of the world, Serug in the 2049th, Terah in the 2083rd, Arphaxad in the 2096th, Salah in the 2126th, Shem in the 2158th, Abraham in the 2183rd, and Eber in the 2187th, which was four years after Abraham's death. And Eber was the fourth from Noah.

51. Nahor, Abraham's brother, was 58 years old when Noah died,

Terah 128, Serug 187, Reu 219, Eber 283, Salah 313, Arphaxad 344, and Shem 448.

52. It appears from this account, that Nahor, brother of Abraham, Terah, Nahor, Serug, Reu, Peleg, Eber, Salah, Arphaxad, Shem, and Noah, all lived on the earth at the same time; and that Abraham was 18 years old when Reu died, 41 when Serug and his brother Nahor died, 75 when Terah died, 88 when Arphaxad died, 118 when Salah died, 150 when Shem died, and that Eber lived four years after Abraham's death. And that Shem, Arphaxad, Salah, Eber, Reu, Serug, Terah, and Nahor, the brother of Abraham, and Abraham, lived at the same time. And that Nahor, brother of Abraham, Terah, Serug, Reu, Eber, Salah, Arphaxad, and Shem, were all acquainted with both Noah and Abraham.

53. We have now traced the chronology of the world agreeable to the account given in our present Bible, from Adam to Abraham, and have clearly determined, beyond the power of controversy, that there was no difficulty in preserving the knowledge of God in the world from the creation of Adam, and the manifestation made to his immediate descendants, as set forth in the former part of this lecture; so that the students in this class need not have any doubt resting on their minds on this subject, for they can easily see that it is impossible for it to be otherwise, but that the knowledge of the existence of a God must have continued from father to son, as a matter of tradition at least; for we cannot suppose that a knowledge of this important fact could have existed in the mind of any of the before-mentioned individuals, without their having made it known to their posterity.

54. We have now shown how it was that the first thought ever existed in the mind of any individual that there was such a Being as a God, who had created and did uphold all things: that it was by reason of the manifestation which he first made to our father Adam, when he stood in his presence, and conversed with him face to face, at the time of his creation.

55. Let us here observe, that after any portion of the human family are made acquainted with the important fact that there is a God, who has created and does uphold all things, the extent of their knowledge respecting his character and glory will depend upon their diligence and faithfulness in seeking after him, until, like Enoch, the brother of Jared, and Moses, they shall obtain faith in God, and power with him to behold him face to face.

56. We have now clearly set forth how it is, and how it was, that God became an object of faith for rational beings; and also, upon what foundation the testimony was based which excited the inquiry and diligent search of the ancient saints to seek after and obtain a knowledge of the glory of God; and we have seen that it was human testimony, and human testimony only, that excited this inquiry, in the first instance, in their minds. It was the credence they gave to the testimony of their fathers, this testimony having aroused their minds to inquire after the knowledge of God; the inquiry frequently terminated, indeed always terminated when rightly pursued, in the most glorious discoveries and eternal certainty.

Commentary

LF 2:2 *God is the only supreme governor and independent being in whom all fullness and perfection dwell.* How, it is asked, can we say that "God is the only *supreme governor* . . . in whom all fullness and perfection dwell," on the one hand and claim that we can become as God is on the other? The answer rests in the patriarchal chain so essential to salvation. In yet another world it might be an individual's privilege to obtain all knowledge and all power, yet neither that knowledge nor that power will ever change the simple truth that his father is still his father and will "govern" his family as such. Throughout the endless eternities the members of that family will always love, honor, and respect him as such. Indeed, they would have no claim upon a place in the patriarchal chain were their feelings other than they are. If there are weak links in that family chain as it reaches back to Father Adam, they will be dropped and the joining links bound together. So it is that each of us as heirs of God and joint heirs with Christ will endlessly honor our Eternal Father, which we do by becoming equal with him in power, might, and dominion.

LF 2:5 *At his first creation.* Reference is to the first man created, Father Adam.

We copy from the new translation. Reference is to the Joseph Smith Translation. See Moses 2:26–29.

LF 2:12 *Without a vail to separate between.* The veil of separation between our Maker and us did not exist in Eden prior to the fall. There Adam and Eve freely walked and talked with their heavenly parents.

LF 2:15–18 In these verses we have as perfect an expression of the nature of Adam and his relationship with the Father as known to the pen of man. Of a certainty he is not the end product of evolution, nor is his father a spirit essence that fills the immensity of space. He is a son who walked and talked with his father even as we walked and talked with our own parents and as our children do with us.

LF 2:19–22 No prophet has ever walked the earth who knew God more perfectly than did Father Adam or enjoyed a more intimate association with him. That knowledge was not lost to him in the Fall nor did that association cease with the Fall.

It was not intended that man dwell in darkness. Long before the first of our race was placed upon the earth the Lord had given the command: "Let there be light" (Genesis 1:3). Nor was it intended that Adam wander in doubt or uncertainty relative to the nature and purpose of his creation or the being to whom he was answerable for his conduct. "God conversed with him face to face. In his presence he was permitted to stand, and from his own mouth he was permitted to receive instruction. He heard his voice, walked before him and gazed upon his glory, while intelligence burst upon his understanding, and enabled him to give names to the vast assemblage of his Maker's works" (Lecture 2:18).

Obviously Adam's transgression did not deprive him of the knowledge with which he had previously been endowed (Lecture 2:19). Upon hearing God's voice, Adam, knowing his shame, sought to hide himself. The expulsion of Adam and Eve from the Garden of the Divine Presence did not bring an end to communion with their Father (Lecture 2:20). Their circumstance in the lone and dreary world immediately evoked the desire for divine assistance. Their prayers did not go unheeded, for we read, "And they heard the voice of the Lord from the way toward the Garden of Eden, speaking unto them, and they saw him not; for they were shut out from his presence. And he gave unto them commandments, that they should worship the Lord their God, and should offer the firstlings of their flocks, for an offering unto the Lord. And Adam was obedient unto the commandments of the Lord. And after many days an angel of the Lord appeared unto Adam, saying: Why dost thou offer sacrifices unto the Lord? And Adam said unto him: I know not, save the Lord commanded me. And then the angel spake, saying: This thing is a similitude of the sacrifice of the Only Begotten of the Father, which is full of grace and truth. Wherefore, thou shalt do all that thou doest in the name of the Son, and thou shalt repent and call upon God in the name of the Son forevermore. And in that day the Holy Ghost fell upon Adam, which beareth record of the Father and the Son" (Moses 5:4–9).

The quotation clearly establishes two points: first, the Fall did not cause Adam and Eve to lose their knowledge of God; and second, "no sooner was the plan of redemption revealed to man, and he began to call upon God, than the Holy Spirit was given, bearing record of the Father and Son" (Lecture 2:25). How then did the family of Adam obtain a knowledge of God? Adam and Eve communicated that knowledge to them (Lecture 2:31). How did Adam and Eve obtain that knowledge? God manifested himself to them in the Garden and he continued to speak to them after their transgression and expulsion from Eden (Lecture 2:30). Thus it was for Adam and Eve, as special witnesses, to plant the first seeds of testimony in the hearts of their children and their children's children for many generations. Thus man learned to have faith in God after the Fall.

Adam and Eve established the pattern to be followed in all subsequent dispensations and in all generations. This pattern is that the posterity of Adam in all ages first learns of God or has the seeds of faith planted in their hearts by special witnesses chosen of God for that purpose. It is for one man to plant the seed in the heart of another. Most properly, it is for parents to plant the seed in the hearts of their children, for previous to the time that any of "Adam's posterity had obtained a manifestation of God to themselves, Adam, their common father, had testified unto them of the existence of God, and of his eternal power and Godhead" (Lecture 2:35).

Thus the whole human family partakes of the fruit of the tree of faith because Father Adam planted the tree. Each dispensation in its turn has had its special witness or witnesses—its "Adams"—but in all cases it has been "human testimony, and human testimony only" that motivated man's initial investigation concerning God. It has been the belief exercised in "the testimony of their fathers" that has aroused their minds to "inquire after the knowledge of God; the inquiry frequently terminated, indeed always terminated when rightly pursued, in the most glorious discoveries and eternal certainty" (Lecture 2:56).

Though one may plant the seed in the heart of another, each must nourish the seed for himself. The Prophet said that after any members of the human family "are made acquainted with the important fact that there is a God, who has created and does uphold all things, the extent of their knowledge respecting his character and glory will depend upon their diligence and faithfulness in seeking after him, until, like Enoch, the brother of Jared, and Moses, they shall obtain faith in God, and power with him to behold him face to face" (Lecture 2:55).

Lecture Three

1. In the second lecture it was shewn how it was that the knowledge of the existence of God came into the world, and by what means the first thoughts were suggested to the minds of men that such a Being did actually exist; and that it was by reason of the knowledge of his existence that there was a foundation laid for the exercise of faith in him, as the only Being in whom faith could center for life and salvation; for faith could not center in a Being of whose existence we have no idea, because the idea of his existence in the first instance is essential to the exercise of faith in him. Romans 10:14: "How then shall they call on him in whom they have not believed? and how shall they believe in him of whom they have not heard? and how shall they hear without a preacher (or one sent to tell them)? So, then, faith comes by hearing the word of God." (New Translation).

2. Let us here observe, that three things are necessary in order that any rational and intelligent being may exercise faith in God unto life and salvation.

3. First, the idea that he actually exists.

4. Secondly, a *correct* idea of his character, perfections, and attributes.

5. Thirdly, an actual knowledge that the course of life which he is pursuing is according to his will. For without an acquaintance with these three important facts, the faith of every rational being must be imperfect and unproductive; but with this understanding it can become perfect and fruitful, abounding in righteousness, unto the praise and glory of God the Father, and the Lord Jesus Christ.

6. Having previously been made acquainted with the way the idea of his existence came into the world, as well as the fact of his existence, we shall proceed to examine his character, perfections, and attributes, in order that this class may see, not only the just grounds which they have for the exercise of faith in him for life and salvation, but the reasons that all the world, also, as far as the idea of his existence extends, may have to exercise faith in him, the Father of all living.

7. As we have been indebted to a revelation which God made of himself to his creatures, in the first instance, for the idea of his existence, so in like manner we are indebted to the revelations which he has given to us for a correct understanding of his character, perfections, and attributes; because without the revelations which he has

given to us, no man by searching could find out God. Job. 11:7, 8, 9. 1 Corinthians 2:9, 10, 11. "But as it is written, eye hath not seen, nor ear heard, neither have entered into the heart of man, the things which God hath prepared for them that love him; but God hath revealed them unto us by his Spirit, for the Spirit searcheth all things, yea, the deep things of God. For what man knoweth the things of a man, save the spirit of man which is in him? Even so, the things of God knoweth no man but the Spirit of God."

8. Having said so much we proceed to examine the character which the revelations have given of God.

9. Moses gives us the following account in Exodus 34:6: "And the Lord passed by before him, and proclaimed, 'The Lord God, the Lord God, merciful and gracious, long-suffering and abundant in goodness and truth.'" Psalms 103:6, 7, 8: "The Lord executeth righteousness and judgment for all that are oppressed. He made known his ways unto Moses, his acts unto the children of Israel. The Lord is merciful and gracious, slow to anger and plenteous in mercy." Psalms 103:17, 18: "But the mercy of the Lord is from everlasting to everlasting upon them that fear him, and his righteousness unto children's children, to such as keep his covenant, and to those that remember his commandments to do them." Psalms 90:2: "Before the mountains were brought forth, or ever thou hadst formed the earth and the world, even from everlasting to everlasting thou art God." Hebrews 1:10, 11, 12: And thou, Lord, in the beginning, hast laid the foundation of the earth; and the heavens are the works of thine hands; they shall perish, but thou remainest; and they all shall wax old as doth a garment; and as a vesture shalt thou fold them up, and they shall be changed; but thou art the same and thy years shall not fail." James 1:17: "Every good gift and every perfect gift is from above, and cometh down from the Father of lights, with whom is no variableness, neither shadow of turning." Malachi 3:6: "For I am the Lord, I change not; therefore ye sons of Jacob are not consumed."

10. Book of Commandments 3:2: "For God does not walk in crooked paths, neither does he turn to the right hand or the left, or vary from that which he has said, therefore his paths are straight, and his course is one eternal round." Book of Commandments 35:1: "Listen to the voice of the Lord your God, even Alpha and Omega, the beginning and the end, whose course is one eternal round, the same yesterday, to-day, and forever."

11. Numbers 23:19: "God is not a man that he should lie, neither the

son of man that he should repent." 1 John 4:8: "He that loveth not, knoweth not God, for God is love." Acts 10:34, 35: "Then Peter opened his mouth and said, 'Of a truth I perceive that God is no respecter of persons, but in every nation he that feareth God and worketh righteousness is accepted with him.'"

12. From the foregoing testimonies we learn the following things respecting the character of God:

13. First, that he was God before the world was created, and the same God that he was after it was created.

14. Secondly, that he is merciful and gracious, slow to anger, abundant in goodness, and that he was so from everlasting, and will be to everlasting.

15. Thirdly, that he changes not, neither is there variableness with him; but that he is the same from everlasting to everlasting, being the same yesterday, to-day, and for ever; and that His course is one eternal round, without variation.

16. Fourthly, that he is a God of truth and cannot lie.

17. Fifthly, that he is no respecter of persons: but in every nation he that fears God and works righteousness is accepted of him.

18. Sixthly, that he is love.

19. An acquaintance with these attributes in the divine character, is essentially necessary, in order that the faith of any rational being can center in him for life and salvation. For if he did not, in the first instance, believe him to be God, that is, the Creator and upholder of all things, he could not *center* his faith in him for life and salvation, for fear there should be greater than he who would thwart all his plans, and he like the gods of the heathen, would be unable to fulfill his promises; but seeing he is God over all, from everlasting to everlasting, the Creator and upholder of all things, no such fear can exist in the minds of those who put their trust in him, so that in this respect their faith can be without wavering.

20. But secondly; unless he was merciful and gracious, slow to anger, long-suffering and full of goodness, such is the weakness of human nature, and so great the frailties and imperfections of men, that unless they believed that these excellencies existed in the divine character, the faith necessary to salvation could not exist; for doubt would take the place of faith, and those who know their weakness

and liability to sin would be in constant doubt of salvation if it were not for the idea which they have of the excellency of the character of God, that he is slow to anger and long-suffering, and of a forgiving disposition, and does forgive iniquity, transgression, and sin. An idea of these facts does away doubt, and makes faith exceedingly strong.

21. But it is equally as necessary that men should have the idea that he is a God who changes not, in order to have faith in him, as it is to have the idea that he is gracious and long-suffering; for without the idea of unchangeableness in the character of the Deity, doubt would take the place of faith. But with the idea that he changes not, faith lays hold upon the excellencies in his character with unshaken confidence, believing he is the same yesterday, to-day, and forever, and that his course is one eternal round.

22. And again, the idea that he is a God of truth and cannot lie, is equally as necessary to the exercise of faith in him as the idea of his unchangeableness. For without the idea that he was a God of truth and could not lie, the confidence necessary to be placed in his word in order to the exercise of faith in him could not exist. But having the idea that he is not man, that he cannot lie, it gives power to the minds of men to exercise faith in him.

23. But it is also necessary that men should have an idea that he is no respecter of persons, for with the idea of all the other excellencies in his character, and this one wanting, men could not exercise faith in him; because if he were a respecter of persons, they could not tell what their privileges were, nor how far they were authorized to exercise faith in him, or whether they were authorized to do it at all, but all must be confusion; but no sooner are the minds of men made acquainted with the truth on this point, that he is no respecter of persons, than they see that they have authority by faith to lay hold on eternal life, the richest boon of heaven, because God is no respecter of persons, and that every man in every nation has an equal privilege.

24. And lastly, but not less important to the exercise of faith in God, is the idea that he is love; for with all the other excellencies in his character, without this one to influence them, they could not have such powerful dominion over the minds of men; but when the idea is planted in the mind that he is love, who cannot see the just ground that men of every nation, kindred, and tongue, have to exercise faith in God so as to obtain eternal life?

25. From the above description of the character of the Deity, which is given him in the revelations to men, there is a sure foundation for the exercise of faith in him among every people, nation, and kindred, from age to age, and from generation to generation.

26. Let us here observe that the foregoing is the character which is given of God in his revelations to the Former-day Saints, and it is also the character which is given of him in his revelations to the Latter-day Saints, so that the saints of former days and those of latter days are both alike in this respect; the Latter-day Saints having as good grounds to exercise faith in God as the Former-day Saints had, because the same character is given of him to both.

Commentary

LF 3:4 A correct *idea of his character, perfections, and attributes.* The basic premise of this lecture is that we can exercise faith in God only to the extent that we know him. It stands in sharp contrast to the dogma of traditional Christianity that God is an incomprehensible mystery. To such, Joseph Smith would respond that to say that God is incomprehensible is at the same time to say that we cannot exercise faith in him.

LF 3:7 *Without the revelations . . . no man by searching could find out God.* God stands revealed or remains forever unknown. All the philosophical speculation in the world relative to the nature of God does not have the value of a feather carried away by the wind. Man himself is a marvelous revelation as to the nature of his Creator, but even this, the most obvious of truths, can be known only by revelation.

LF 3:13 *He was God before the world was created, and the same God . . . after.* The crowning revelation of the ministry of Christ is the fatherhood of God. Coupled with the understanding that he was the same God before the creation of the world as he was after, we can but conclude that he was our God and our Father in that first estate. Surely that is what he professes himself to be to men and women on the earth.

LF 3:14 *He is merciful and gracious.* Much has been said by those who do not have a proper understanding of the restored gospel about the angry and vengeful God of the Old Testament as contrasted with the God of love revealed to us in the New Testament. It is as if the ill-tempered old Man had retired, leaving the shop to his more mild-mannered and loving Son. The notion is ridiculous. By definition God must have all godly characteristics and attributes in their perfection, and his mercy and graciousness must be enjoyed in equal measure by the children of men irrespective of when they lived.

LF 3:15 *He changes not.* The testimony of the Book of Mormon prophets was that "God is the same yesterday, today, and forever, and in him there is no variableness neither shadow of changing." For if he were to do so "he would cease to be God" (Mormon 9:9, 19).

LF 3:16 *He is a God of truth.* "The Spirit of truth is of God. I am the Spirit of truth, and John bore record of me, saying: He received a fulness of truth, yea, even of all truth; And no man receiveth a fulness unless he keepeth his commandments. He that keepeth his commandments receiveth truth and light, until he is glorified in truth and knoweth all things" (D&C 93:26–28).

LF 3:17 *He is no respecter of persons.* God does not discriminate according to gender, age, nationality, or social standing; rather, he grants the blessings to all, on condition of their willingness to serve him (Lecture 7:17).

LF 3:18 *He is love.* Russell M. Nelson observed, "If I were to ask which characteristic of his life [Christ's] you would identify first, I think you might name his attribute of love. That would include his compassion, kindness, charity, devotion, forgiveness, mercy, justice, and more. Jesus loved his Father and loved his mother. He loved his family and the Saints. He loved the sinner, without excusing the sin. And he taught us how we can show our love for him. He said, 'If you love me, keep my commandments.' Then to underscore that his love was not *unconditional,* he added: 'If ye keep my commandments, ye shall abide in my love; even as I have kept my Father's commandments, and abide in his love' [John 15:10]" ("Gratitude," 4; emphasis in original).

LF 3:26 The Saints of all ages have known the same God, shared the same truths, participated in the same ordinances, withstood the same temptations, suffered the same rejection of the world, and obtained the promise of the same rewards.

Lecture Four

1. Having shown, in the third lecture, that correct ideas of the character of God are necessary in order to the exercise of faith in him unto life and salvation; and that without correct ideas of his character the minds of men could not have sufficient power with God to the exercise of faith necessary to the enjoyment of eternal life; and

that correct ideas of his character lay a foundation, as far as his character is concerned, for the exercise of faith, so as to enjoy the fullness of the blessing of the gospel of Jesus Christ even that of eternal glory; we shall now proceed to show the connection there is between correct ideas of the attributes of God, and the exercise of faith in him unto eternal life.

2. Let us here observe, that the real design which the God of heaven had in view in making the human family acquainted with his attributes, was, that they, through the ideas of the existence of his attributes, might be enabled to exercise faith in him, and through the exercise of faith in him, might obtain eternal life; for without the idea of the existence of the attributes which belong to God, the minds of men could not have power to exercise faith in him so as to lay hold upon eternal life. The God of heaven, understanding most perfectly the constitution of human nature, and the weakness of men, knew what was necessary to be revealed, and what ideas must be planted in their minds in order that they might be enabled to exercise faith in him unto eternal life.

3. Having said so much, we shall proceed to examine the attributes of God, as set forth in his revelations to the human family, and to show how necessary correct ideas of his attributes are to enable men to exercise faith in him; for without these ideas being planted in the minds of men it would be out of the power of any person or persons to exercise faith in God so as to obtain eternal life. So that the divine communications made to men in the first instance were designed to establish in their minds the ideas necessary to enable them to exercise faith in God, and through this means to be partakers of his glory.

4. We have, in the revelations which he has given to the human family, the following account of his attributes:

5. First—Knowledge. Acts 15:18: "Known unto God are all his works from the beginning of the world." Isaiah 46:9, 10: "Remember the former things of old: for I am God, and there is none else; I am God, and there is none like me, *declaring the end from the beginning,* and from ancient time the things that are not yet done, saying 'My counsel shall stand, and I will do all my pleasure.'"

6. Secondly—Faith or power. Hebrews 11:3: "Through faith we understand that the worlds were framed by the word of God." Genesis 1:1: "In the beginning God created the heaven and the earth." Isaiah 14:24, 27: "The Lord of hosts hath sworn, saying,

'Surely as I have thought, so shall it come to pass: and as I have purposed so shall it stand. For the Lord of Hosts hath purposed, and who shall disannul it? and his hand is stretched out, and who shall turn it back?'"

7. Thirdly—Justice. Psalm 89:14: "Justice and judgment are the habitation of thy throne." Isaiah 45:21: "Tell ye, and bring them near; yea, let them take counsel together: who hath declared this from the ancient time? have not I the Lord? and there is no God else beside me; a just God and a Saviour." Zephaniah 3:5: "The just Lord is in the midst thereof." Zechariah 9:9: "Rejoice greatly, O daughter of Zion; shout, O daughter of Jerusalem; behold thy King cometh unto thee: he is just and having salvation."

8. Fourthly—Judgment. Psalm 89:14: "Justice and judgment are the habitation of thy throne." Deuteronomy 32:4: "He is the Rock, his work is perfect; for all his ways are judgment: a God of truth and without iniquity, just and right is he." Psalm 9:7: "But the Lord shall endure for ever. He hath prepared his throne for judgment." Psalm 9:16: "The Lord is known by the judgment which he executeth."

9. Fifthly—Mercy. Psalm 89:14: "Mercy and truth shall go before his face." Exodus 34:6: "And the Lord passed by before him, and proclaimed, 'The Lord, the Lord God, merciful and gracious.'" Nehemiah 9:17: "But thou art a God ready to pardon, gracious and merciful."

10. And sixthly—Truth. Psalm 89:14: "Mercy and truth shall go before thy face." Exodus 34:6: "Long-suffering and abundant in goodness and truth." Deuteronomy 32:4: "He is the Rock, his work is perfect; for all his ways are judgment: a God of truth and without iniquity, just and right is he." Psalm 31:5: "Into Thine hand I commit my spirit: thou hast redeemed me, O Lord God of Truth."

11. By a little reflection it will be seen that the idea of the existence of these attributes in the Deity is necessary to enable any rational being to exercise faith in him; for without the idea of the existence of these attributes in the Deity men could not exercise faith in him for life and salvation; seeing that without the knowledge of all things, God would not be able to save any portion of his creatures; for it is by reason of the knowledge which he has of all things, from the beginning to the end, that enables him to give that understanding to his creatures by which they are made partakers of eternal life; and if it

were not for the idea existing in the minds of men that God had all knowledge it would be impossible for them to exercise faith in him.

12. And it is not less necessary that men should have the idea of the existence of the attribute power in the Deity; for unless God had power over all things, and was able by his power to control all things, and thereby deliver his creatures who put their trust in him from the power of all beings that might seek their destruction, whether in heaven, on earth, or in hell, men could not be saved. But with the idea of the existence of this attribute planted in the mind, men feel as though they had nothing to fear who put their trust in God, believing that he has power to save all who come to him to the very uttermost.

13. It is also necessary, in order to the exercise of faith in God unto life and salvation, that men should have the idea of the existence of the attribute justice in him; for without the idea of the existence of the attribute justice in the Deity, men could not have confidence sufficient to place themselves under his guidance and direction; for they would be filled with fear and doubt lest the judge of all the earth would not do right, and thus fear or doubt, existing in the mind, would preclude the possibility of the exercise of faith in him for life and salvation. But when the idea of the existence of the attribute justice in the Deity is fairly planted in the mind, it leaves no room for doubt to get into the heart, and the mind is enabled to cast itself upon the Almighty without fear and without doubt, and with the most unshaken confidence, believing that the Judge of all the earth will do right.

14. It is also of equal importance that men should have the idea of the existence of the attribute judgment in God, in order that they may exercise faith in him for life and salvation; for without the idea of the existence of this attribute in the Deity, it would be impossible for men to exercise faith in him for life and salvation, seeing that it is through the exercise of this attribute that the faithful in Christ Jesus are delivered out of the hands of those who seek their destruction; for if God were not to come out in swift judgment against the workers of iniquity and the powers of darkness, his saints could not be saved; for it is by judgment that the Lord delivers his saints out of the hands of all their enemies, and those who reject the gospel of our Lord Jesus Christ. But no sooner is the idea of the existence of this attribute planted in the minds of men, than it gives power to the mind for the exercise of faith and confidence in God, and they are

enabled by faith to lay hold on the promises which are set before them, and wade through all the tribulations and afflictions to which they are subjected by reason of the persecution from those who know not God, and obey not the gospel of our Lord Jesus Christ, believing that in due time the Lord will come out in swift judgment against their enemies, and they shall be cut off from before him, and that in his own due time he will bear them off conquerors, and more than conquerors, in all things.

15. And again, it is equally important that men should have the idea of the existence of the attribute mercy in the Deity, in order to exercise faith in him for life and salvation; for without the idea of the existence of this attribute in the Deity, the spirits of the saints would faint in the midst of the tribulations, afflictions, and persecutions which they have to endure for righteousness' sake. But when the idea of the existence of this attribute is once established in the mind it gives life and energy to the spirits of the saints, believing that the mercy of God will be poured out upon them in the midst of their afflictions, and that he will compassionate them in their sufferings, and that the mercy of God will lay hold of them and secure them in the arms of his love, so that they will receive a full reward for all their sufferings.

16. And lastly, but not less important to the exercise of faith in God, is the idea of the existence of the attribute truth in him; for without the idea of the existence of this attribute the mind of man could have nothing upon which it could rest with certainty—all would be confusion and doubt. But with the idea of the existence of this attribute in the Deity in the mind, all the teachings, instructions, promises, and blessings, become realities, and the mind is enabled to lay hold of them with certainty and confidence, believing that these things, and all that the Lord has said, shall be fulfilled in their time; and that all the cursings, denunciations, and judgments, pronounced upon the heads of the unrighteous, will also be executed in the due time of the Lord: and, by reason of the truth and veracity of him, the mind beholds its deliverance and salvation as being certain.

17. Let the mind once reflect sincerely and candidly upon the ideas of the existence of the before-mentioned attributes in the Deity, and it will be seen that, as far as His attributes are concerned, there is a sure foundation laid for the exercise of faith in him for life and salvation. For inasmuch as God possesses the attribute knowledge, he can make all things known to his saints necessary for their salvation,

and as he possesses the attribute power, he is able thereby to deliver them from the power of all enemies; and seeing, also, that justice is an attribute of the Deity, he will deal with them upon the principles of righteousness and equity, and a just reward will be granted unto them for all their afflictions and sufferings for the truth's sake. And as judgment is an attribute of the Deity also, His saints can have the most unshaken confidence that they will, in due time, obtain a perfect deliverance out of the hands of their enemies, and a complete victory over all those who have sought their hurt and destruction. And as mercy is also an attribute of the Deity, his saints can have confidence that it will be exercised towards them, and through the exercise of that attribute towards them comfort and consolation will be administered unto them abundantly, amid all their afflictions and tribulations. And, lastly, realizing that truth is an attribute of the Deity, the mind is led to rejoice amid all its trials and temptations, in hope of that glory which is to be brought at the revelation of Jesus Christ, and in view of that crown which is to be placed upon the heads of the saints in the day when the Lord shall distribute rewards unto them, and in prospect of that eternal weight of glory which the Lord has promised to bestow upon them, when he shall bring them in the midst of his throne to dwell in his presence eternally.

18. In view, then, of the existence of these attributes, the faith of the saints can become exceedingly strong, abounding in righteousness unto the praise and glory of God, and can exert its mighty influence in searching after wisdom and understanding, until it has obtained a knowledge of all things that pertain to life and salvation.

19. Such, then, is the foundation which is laid, through the revelation of the attributes of God, for the exercise of faith in him for life and salvation; and seeing that these are attributes of the Deity, they are unchangeable—being the same yesterday, to-day, and for ever—which gives to the minds of the Latter-day Saints the same power and authority to exercise faith in God which the Former-day Saints had; so that all the saints, in this respect, have been, are, and will be, alike until the end of time; for God never changes, therefore his attributes and character remain forever the same. And as it is through the revelation of these that a foundation is laid for the exercise of faith in God unto life and salvation, the foundation, therefore, for the exercise of faith was, is, and ever will be, the same; so that all men have had, and will have, an equal privilege.

Commentary

LF 4:1 *Correct ideas of the character of God are necessary in order to the exercise of faith in Him.* True faith cannot be exercised in principles that are false. If we plant wheat, we harvest wheat. If we plant corn, we harvest corn. But we cannot plant wheat and expect to harvest corn. If we could change the law of the harvest through the exercise of faith—that is, if we could call forth corn by the power of faith when we had planted wheat—we would rob the world of order. No longer could the divine law be trusted that all things were to bring forth after their own kind. If things no longer brought forth after their own kind we could not trust that righteousness would bring forth the blessings of heaven or that wickedness would close the window of blessings to us. Faith exists because truth exists, and where there is no truth there can be no faith. One could worship as God a stone, a tree, or the clouds of heaven, expending all the energy of their souls in so doing, yet such efforts will call forth only those blessings that stones, trees, or clouds are capable of dispensing. It cannot be argued that God will reward the sincerity of our prayers, for then the sincere prayer that the planting of wheat might yield a harvest of corn must also be honored. And by so doing, God would, as we have seen, suspend the necessity of truth which in turn would destroy all possibility of exercising faith.

How then, the question is asked, does the God of heaven turn water to wine? Does that not alter a law of nature that is of his own making? We answer: all laws are ordained of him and function according to his command for his purpose. Can such laws be altered or suspended by a greater law? Certainly. Were this not the case, God would be the servant of law rather than its author. Thus all laws bear witness of him—the law of nature in its place and the greater law that suspends nature in its place. Both the greater and the lesser law must testify of the same God. Both must respond to his command and both must respect the order of the kingdom of which they are a part. Both must be appended to truth, for the point cannot be surrendered that God is a God of truth. No prayer can be answered independent of truth, and no blessing can be granted that is in disharmony with the order of heaven. All miracles involve the suspension of certain laws and all miracles are in harmony with the greater purpose or law of heaven, none contradict truth and none sustain error or mistruth.

LF 4:2 Faith is born of righteousness and truth and cannot be exercised in a God who is not a god of righteousness and truth. Thus the exercise of faith requires the assurance that the focus of our worship is a Being possessed of all the attributes of godliness in their perfection. How could one be expected to exercise faith in a god who lacked virtue, was dishonest, or unjust, or who lacked wisdom? No honorable person would worship such a being, nor could they be expected to exercise faith in him (Lecture 4:11).

LF 4:11 Countless scriptural texts attest to the fact that the Father, Son, and Holy Ghost know all things both in heaven and on earth. The plainness of these lectures, particularly in verses 11 and 17 of this lecture and again in verse 9 of the seventh lecture, is much easier to ignore than to uproot.

The whole system and plan of salvation as represented in these lectures appears to be an extension of the principles announced in Doctrine and Covenants 93, which assure that salvation consists in our receiving a "fulness of truth," which is one and the same with the "fulness of the Father" (D&C 93:19, 26–28).

LF 4:19 *God never changes.* If we begin with the idea that God by definition possess all the attributes of godliness in their perfection and that if he did not he could not be God, then to suggest that he is to change is to suggest that he will cease to be God. If God did lack knowledge, power, justice, judgment, mercy, or truth, to that same extent he would fall short of being God and thus of being worthy of our worship.

Lecture Five

1. In our former lectures we treated of the being, character, perfections, and attributes, of God. What we mean by perfections is, the perfections which belong to all the attributes of his nature. We shall, in this lecture, speak of the Godhead—we mean the Father, Son, and Holy Spirit.

2. There are two personages who constitute the great, matchless, governing, and supreme power over all things, by whom all things were created and made, that are created and made, whether visible or invisible, whether in heaven, on earth, or in the earth, under the earth, or throughout the immensity of space. They are the Father and the Son—the Father being a personage of spirit, glory, and power, possessing all perfection and fulness, the Son, who was in the bosom of the Father, a personage of tabernacle, made or fashioned like unto man, being in the form and likeness of man, or rather man was

formed after his likeness and in his image; he is also the express image and likeness of the personage of the Father, possessing all the fulness of the Father, or the same fulness with the Father; being begotten of him, and ordained from before the foundation of the world to be a propitiation for the sins of all those who should believe on his name, and is called the Son because of the flesh, and descended in suffering below that which man can suffer; or, in other words, suffered greater sufferings, and was exposed to more powerful contradictions than any man can be. But, notwithstanding all this, he kept the law of God, and remained without sin, showing thereby that it is in the power of man to keep the law and remain also without sin; and also, that by him a righteous judgment might come upon all flesh, and that all who walk not in the law of God may justly be condemned by the law, and have no excuse for their sins. And he being the Only Begotten of the Father, full of grace and truth, and having overcome, received a fulness of the glory of the Father, possessing the same mind with the Father, which mind is the Holy Spirit, that bears record of the Father and the Son, and these three are one; or, in other words, these three constitute the great, matchless, governing and supreme power over all things; by whom all things were created and made that were created and made, and these three constitute the Godhead, and are one; The Father and the Son possessing the same mind, the same wisdom, glory, power, and fulness—filling all in all; the Son being filled with the fulness of the mind, glory, and power; or, in other words, the spirit, glory, and power, of the Father, possessing all knowledge and glory, and the same kingdom, sitting at the right hand of power, in the express image and likeness of the Father, mediator for man, being filled with the fulness of the mind of the Father; or, in other words, the Spirit of the Father, which Spirit is shed forth upon all who believe on his name and keep his commandments; and all those who keep his commandments shall grow up from grace to grace, and become heirs of the heavenly kingdom, and joint heirs with Jesus Christ; possessing the same mind, being transformed into the same image or likeness, even the express image of him who fills all in all; being filled with the fulness of his glory, and become one in him, even as the Father, Son and Holy Spirit are one.

3. From the foregoing account of the Godhead, which is given in his revelations, the saints have a sure foundation laid for the exercise of faith unto life and salvation, through the atonement and mediation of Jesus Christ; by whose blood they have a forgiveness of sins, and

also a sure reward laid up for them in heaven, even that of partaking of the fullness of the Father and the Son through the Spirit. As the Son partakes of the fullness of the Father through the Spirit, so the saints are, by the same Spirit, to be partakers of the same fullness, to enjoy the same glory; for as the Father and the Son are one, so, in like manner, the saints are to be one in them. Through the love of the Father, the mediation of Jesus Christ, and the gift of the Holy Spirit, they are to be heirs of God, and joint heirs with Jesus Christ.

Commentary

LF 5:2–3 *The Father being a personage of spirit . . . the Son . . . a personage of tabernacle.* Much of the criticism directed at the Lectures on Faith is pointed at this description of the Father as "a personage of spirit." The principle stated here is simply a restatement of the teachings of Abinadi as found in Mosiah 15:1–7. That text reads as follows:

"And now Abinadi said unto them: I would that ye should understand that God himself shall come down among the children of men, and shall redeem his people.

"And because he dwelleth in flesh he shall be called the Son of God, and having subjected the flesh to the will of the Father, being the Father and the Son—

"The Father, because he was conceived by the power of God; and the Son, because of the flesh; thus becoming the Father and Son—

"And they are one God, yea, the very Eternal Father of heaven and of earth.

"And thus the flesh becoming subject to the Spirit, or the Son to the Father, being one God, suffereth temptation, and yieldeth not to the temptation, but suffereth himself to be mocked, and scourged, and cast out, and disowned by his people.

"And after all this, after working many mighty miracles among the children of men, he shall be led, yea, even as Isaiah said, as a sheep before the shearer is dumb, so he opened not his mouth.

"Yea, even so he shall be led, crucified, and slain, the flesh becoming subject even unto death, the will of the Son being swallowed up in the will of the Father."

If we carefully follow Abinadi's teachings, the meaning of the Prophet's words in lecture five becomes clear. "God himself shall come down among the children of men, and shall redeem his people," Abinadi declares. It is Christ of whom Abinadi is speaking. Thus we know that

Abinadi understood Christ to be his God or, as we might say today, the God of the Old Testament. Abinadi explains that because Christ would dwell in the flesh, he would be called the Son of God. This, of course, is literally so; he is, indeed, the Son of the Eternal Father. Abinadi adds that the Son would subject "the flesh to the will of the Father." He would conquer the appetites of the flesh and do the will of the Father in all things. Thus, Abinadi says, Christ will be the Father *and* the Son.

Though Christ is the Son, he fully represents the Father by doing what the Father would do in all cases. There is nothing particularly confusing in saying that someone is both father and son; for all fathers are also sons, and most sons will someday become fathers. In this instance, however, Abinadi explains his meaning. He says Christ will be the Father "because he was conceived by the power of God." Because God is literally his father, Christ will inherit his nature and likeness. This is as it was with Adam and Seth: "He (Seth) was a perfect man, and his likeness was the express likeness of his father, insomuch that he seemed to be like unto his father in all things" (D&C 107:43).

Abinadi says that Christ will be the Son "because of the flesh," returning to the fact that he previously had not possessed a physical body, which is obviously one of the reasons he came to the earth. Thus, Abinadi explains, Christ is both Father and Son. "And they [Christ and the Father] are one God [they are perfectly united in all things], yea, the very Eternal Father of heaven and of earth" (Mosiah 15:4).

To assure that he has been understood, Abinadi then says, "Thus the flesh becoming subject to the Spirit, or [and now the explanation so you cannot miss his meaning] the Son [the flesh] to the Father [the Spirit]" (Mosiah 15:5). A description of Christ's mortal ministry follows, and Abinadi concludes by returning to the major theme of development, that being "the will of the Son being swallowed up in the will of the Father."

Abinadi makes two major points here: (1) the crowning revelation of the Father is spirit and (2) the crowning revelation of the Son is flesh. The great principle to be learned about the Father is that his power and influence, like the light and law that come from him, emanate everywhere. The great principle to be learned about the Son is that he became flesh—he received a body so that he could work out his own salvation and so that he could offer his life as an atoning sacrifice for us all.

Abinadi's teachings echo those in Doctrine and Covenants 93:3–4, where Christ says he and the Father are one: "The Father [Christ is the Father here] because he [Christ's Father] gave me of his fulness, and the

Son because I was in the world and made flesh my tabernacle [I came and clothed my spirit with a physical body], and dwelt among the sons of men."

At the conclusion of verse 3 in this fifth lecture, we are told that "the Son partakes of the fullness of the Father through the Spirit." This is the key to all that both Abinadi and the Prophet Joseph were teaching. The whole system and plan of salvation centers in this principle. Christ can be as his Father is through the light of the Spirit. Advancing far beyond the thinking of the historical Christian world, the Prophet Joseph Smith, in this lecture, said, "The saints are, by the same Spirit, to be partakers of the same fullness" and thus to enjoy "the same glory; for as the Father and the Son are one, so, in like manner, the saints are to be one in them."

Again, this follows the doctrine found in Doctrine and Covenants 93, where we are told that Christ did not receive the fulness of his Father's glory at first but that he advanced from one grace to a greater grace until he received "a fulness of the glory of the Father; and he received all power, both in heaven and on earth, and the glory of the Father was with him, for he dwelt in him" (vv. 16–17). The same doctrine is then extended to all who follow Christ in receiving grace for grace, for they have the promise that in due time they will also receive of his fulness. "The Spirit of truth is of God [it comes originally from the Father]. I [Christ is now speaking] am the Spirit of truth, and John bore record of me, saying: He received a fulness of truth, yea, even of all truth; and no man receiveth a fulness unless he keepeth his commandments. He that keepeth his commandments receiveth truth and light, until he is glorified in truth and knoweth all things" (D&C 93:16–17, 19, 26–28).

Both Doctrine and Covenants 93 and the fifth Lecture on Faith are clear to us; as members of the Church we read them through the lens Joseph Smith crafted for us in his King Follett Discourse in April 1844, when he told us that God was an exalted, glorified man. Without the aid of the King Follett Discourse, few would see the length and breadth of what is written in this lecture and in Doctrine and Covenants 93. All who were a part of the household of faith at the time this lecture was given would be challenged to grow up into the full implications of this doctrine. The extent of their understanding at the time this lecture was delivered may not be clear to us but it rather misses the point to confuse the God described here as a "personage of spirit" with the god of the creeds of Christendom.

Reference to the Father as spirit and the Son as flesh is simply an expansion of what had already been taught by Abinadi in Mosiah 15 and by the Lord in Doctrine and Covenants 93. If the latter two scriptural expressions constitute good doctrine, then the restatement of them in this lecture is also good doctrine.

Being begotten of him. Christ was the biological Son of God the Father. When this simple but sublime truth is lost, all other principles in the plan of salvation are lost with it.

He kept the law of God . . . showing thereby that it is in the power of man to keep the law and remain also without sin. In his birth into mortality, Christ, like all men, was subject to the carnal nature of the flesh. He too needed sleep and food, he too tired at the end of a long day, and he too knew the feel of aching muscles. Sickness and pain were not unknown to him, sorrow and heartache were his common lot (Isaiah 53:3–4). In a prophetic description of the Savior's ministry, Alma said, "He shall go forth, suffering pains and afflictions and temptations of every kind; and this that the word might be fulfilled which saith he will take upon him the pains and the sicknesses of his people. And he will take upon him death, that he may loose the bands of death which bind his people; and he will take upon him their infirmities, that his bowels may be filled with mercy, according to the flesh, that he may know according to the flesh how to succor his people according to their infirmities" (Alma 7:11–12). Thus it was that Christ was spared no temptation and rightfully showed all men that they too could live beyond sin and rise above the fallen world into which they were born.

Which mind is the Holy Spirit. A better statement could have been made relative to the nature of the Holy Ghost, though this statement is certainly the equal of anything in the Bible on the nature of the third member of the Godhead. Eleven days before his death, the Prophet in a public discourse said, "I have always [taught] in all congregations when I have preached, it has been the plurality of Gods. It has been preached fifteen years. I have always declared God to be a distinct personage, Jesus Christ a separate and distinct personage from God the Father. The Holy Ghost was a distinct personage and or spirit, and these three constitute three distinct personages, and three Gods" (Ehat and Cook, *Words of Joseph Smith*, 378; syntax standardized). Verse two does identify the Holy Ghost as a member of the eternal presidency, stating that "these three constitute the great, matchless, governing and supreme, power over all things; by whom all things were created and made that were created and made, and these three constitute the Godhead." In January 1843, the

Prophet said: "The Holy Ghost is a personage, and is in the form of a personage. It [He] does not confine itself to the *form* of the dove, but in *sign* of the dove. The Holy Ghost cannot be transformed into a dove; but the sign of a dove was given to John to signify the truth of the deed, as the dove is an emblem or token of truth and innocence" (*Teachings of the Prophet Joseph Smith*, 276). Again in April of the same year, he said, "The Holy Ghost has not a body of flesh and bones, but is a personage of Spirit" (D&C 130:22).

In the summary or review of the lecture, the question is asked, "How many personages are there in the Godhead?" To which the answer is, "Two: the Father and the Son." By this we would understand the text to be saying two tangible or corporeal personages, because the question is also asked, "Do the Father, Son, and Holy Spirit constitute the Godhead?" To which the answer is, "They do."

Lecture Six

1. Having treated in the preceding lecture of the ideas, of the character, perfections, and attributes of God, we next proceed to treat of the knowledge which persons must have, that the course of life which they pursue is according to the will of God, in order that they may be enabled to exercise faith in him unto life and salvation.

2. This knowledge supplies an important place in revealed religion; for it was by reason of it that the ancients were enabled to endure as seeing him who is invisible. An actual knowledge to any person, that the course of life which he pursues is according to the will of God, is essentially necessary to enable him to have that confidence in God without which no person can obtain eternal life. It was this that enabled the ancient saints to endure all their afflictions and persecutions, and to take joyfully the spoiling of their goods, knowing (not believing merely) that they had a more enduring substance. Hebrews 10:34.

3. Having the assurance that they were pursuing a course which was agreeable to the will of God, they were enabled to take, not only the spoiling of their goods, and the wasting of their substance, joyfully, but also to suffer death in its most horrid forms; knowing (not merely believing) that when this earthly house of their tabernacle was dissolved, they had a building of God, a house not made with hands, eternal in the heavens. 2 Corinthians 5:1.

4. Such was, and always will be, the situation of the saints of God, that unless they have an actual knowledge that the course they are pursuing is according to the will of God they will grow weary in their minds, and faint; for such has been, and always will be, the opposition in the hearts of unbelievers and those that know not God against the pure and unadulterated religion of heaven (the only thing which insures eternal life), that they will persecute to the uttermost all that worship God according to his revelations, receive the truth in the love of it, and submit themselves to be guided and directed by his will; and drive them to such extremities that nothing short of an actual knowledge of their being the favorites of heaven, and of their having embraced the order of things which God has established for the redemption of man, will enable them to exercise that confidence in him, necessary for them to overcome the world, and obtain that crown of glory which is laid up for them that fear God.

5. For a man to lay down his all, his character and reputation, his honor, and applause, his good name among men, his houses, his lands, his brothers and sisters, his wife and children, and even his own life also—counting all things but filth and dross for the excellency of the knowledge of Jesus Christ—requires more than mere belief or supposition that he is doing the will of God; but actual knowledge, realizing that, when these sufferings are ended, he will enter into eternal rest, and be a partaker of the glory of God.

6. For unless a person does know that he is walking according to the will of God, it would be offering an insult to the dignity of the Creator were he to say that he would be a partaker of his glory when he should be done with the things of this life. But when he has this knowledge, and most assuredly knows that he is doing the will of God, his confidence can be equally strong that he will be a partaker of the glory of God.

7. Let us here observe, that a religion that does not require the sacrifice of all things never has power sufficient to produce the faith necessary unto life and salvation; for, from the first existence of man, the faith necessary unto the enjoyment of life and salvation never could be obtained without the sacrifice of all earthly things. It was through this sacrifice, and this only, that God has ordained that men should enjoy eternal life; and it is through the medium of the sacrifice of all earthly things that men do actually know that they are doing the things that are well pleasing in the sight of God. When a man has offered in sacrifice all that he has for the truth's sake, not even

withholding his life, and believing before God that he has been called to make this sacrifice because he seeks to do his will, he does know, most assuredly, that God does and will accept his sacrifice and offering, and that he has not, nor will not seek his face in vain. Under these circumstances, then, he can obtain the faith necessary for him to lay hold on eternal life.

8. It is in vain for persons to fancy to themselves that they are heirs with those, or can be heirs with them, who have offered their all in sacrifice, and by this means obtain faith in God and favor with him so as to obtain eternal life, unless they, in like manner, offer unto him the same sacrifice, and through that offering obtain the knowledge that they are accepted of him.

9. It was in offering sacrifices that Abel, the first martyr, obtained knowledge that he was accepted of God. And from the days of righteous Abel to the present time, the knowledge that men have that they are accepted in the sight of God is obtained by offering sacrifice. And in the last days, before the Lord comes, he is to gather together his saints who have made a covenant with him by sacrifice. Psalm 1:3, 4, 5: "Our God shall come, and shall not keep silence: a fire shall devour before him, and it shall be very tempestuous round about him. He shall call to the heavens from above, and to the earth, that he may judge his people. Gather my saints together unto me; those that have made a covenant with me by sacrifice."

10. Those, then, who make the sacrifice, will have the testimony that their course is pleasing in the sight of God; and those who have this testimony will have faith to lay hold on eternal life, and will be enabled, through faith, to endure unto the end, and receive the crown that is laid up for them that love the appearing of our Lord Jesus Christ. But those who do not make the sacrifice cannot enjoy this faith, because men are dependent upon this sacrifice in order to obtain this faith: therefore, they cannot lay hold upon eternal life, because the revelations of God do not guarantee unto them the authority so to do, and without this guarantee faith could not exist.

11. All the saints of whom we have account, in all the revelations of God which are extant, obtained the knowledge which they had of their acceptance in his sight through the sacrifice which they offered unto him; and through the knowledge thus obtained their faith became sufficiently strong to lay hold upon the promise of eternal life, and to endure as seeing him who is invisible; and were enabled, through faith, to combat the powers of darkness, contend against the

wiles of the adversary, overcome the world, and obtain the end of their faith, even the salvation of their souls.

12. But those who have not made this sacrifice to God do not know that the course which they pursue is well pleasing in his sight; for whatever may be their belief or their opinion, it is a matter of doubt and uncertainty in their mind; and where doubt and uncertainty are there faith is not, nor can it be. For doubt and faith do not exist in the same person at the same time; so that persons whose minds are under doubts and fears cannot have unshaken confidence; and where unshaken confidence is not there faith is weak; and where faith is weak the persons will not be able to contend against all the opposition, tribulations, and afflictions which they will have to encounter in order to be heirs of God, and joint heirs with Christ Jesus; and they will grow weary in their minds, and the adversary will have power over them and destroy them.

Commentary

LF 6:1–3 To explain the doctrine of faith, the author of the epistle to the Hebrews wrote about those ancient prophets who had an actual knowledge that the course they were pursuing was according to the will of God. "By faith Abel offered unto God a more excellent sacrifice than Cain, *by which he obtained witness that the was righteous*" (Hebrews 11:4; emphasis added). And further: "by faith Enoch was translated that he should not see death; and was not found, because God translated him: for *before his translation he had this testimony, that he pleased God*" (Hebrews 11:5; emphasis added). These and others from Adam down to the Saints living on the earth today go forth in faith, or in the assurance that they are on the Lord's errand and are doing his will. Most importantly, the Savior Jesus Christ exercised such great faith because he knew that the words he spoke, the acts he performed, and the atoning sacrifice he suffered were all according to the will of God. He too received the witness: "This is my beloved Son, *in whom I am well pleased*" (Matthew 3:17, emphasis added; 17:5; also 3 Nephi 11:7; Joseph Smith–History 1:17).

LF 6:4 *The favorites of heaven*. This lecture argues that an actual knowledge that the course one is pursuing is according to the will of God is necessary to endure faithfully to the end. Those who have obtained that knowledge are referred to here as "the favorites of heaven," which phrase is not suggesting that God is a respecter of persons—for heaven's favor is accessible to all on the same terms—but rather that "he that is righteous is favored of God" (1 Nephi 17:35).

LF 6:7 *A religion that does not require the sacrifice of all things never has power sufficient to produce the faith necessary.* Significantly, none have had greater faith than Abraham, of whom the greatest of sacrifices was asked. Faith is the fruit of sacrifice and cannot be born of easy labors nor found on the path not fraught with difficulties and seemingly insurmountable obstacles.

Seek his face. The idea of seeking the face of God or standing in his presence is quite literal. This idea had been repetitiously developed in the revelations of the Restoration. "Verily, thus saith the Lord: It shall come to pass that every soul who forsaketh his sins and cometh unto me, and calleth on my name, and obeyeth my voice, and keepeth my commandments, shall see my face and know that I am" (D&C 93:1; D&C 76:116–19; 84:19–24; 88:68; 107:18–19; 130:3; 132:19, 26).

Lecture Seven

1. In preceding lessons we treated of what faith was, and of the object on which it rested. Agreeable to our plan, we now proceed to speak of its effects.

2. As we have seen in our former lectures that faith was the principle of action and of power in all intelligent beings, both in heaven and on earth, it will not be expected that we shall, in a lectures of this description, attempt to unfold all its effects; Neither is it necessary to our purpose so to do, for it would embrace all things in heaven and on earth, and encompass all the creations of God, with all their endless varieties; for no world has yet been framed that was not framed by faith, neither has there been an intelligent being on any of God's creations who did not get there by reason of faith as it existed in himself or in some other being; nor has there been a change or a revolution in any of the creations of God, but it has been effected by faith; neither will there be a change or a revolution, unless it is effected in the same way, in any of the vast creations of the Almighty, for it is by faith that the Deity works.

3. Let us here offer some explanation in relation to faith, that our meaning may be clearly comprehended. We ask, then, what are we to understand by a man's working by faith? We answer—we understand that when a man works by faith he works by mental exertion instead of physical force. It is by words, instead of exerting his

physical powers, with which every being works when he works by faith. God said, "Let there be light, and there was light." Joshua spake, and the great lights which God had created stood still. Elijah commanded, and the heavens were stayed for the space of three years and six months, so that it did not rain: he again commanded and the heavens gave forth rain. All this was done by faith. And the Savior says: "If you have faith as a grain of mustard seed, say to this mountain, 'Remove,' and it will remove; or say to that sycamine tree, 'Be ye plucked up, and planted in the midst of the sea;' and it shall obey you." Faith, then, works by words; and with these its mightiest works have been, and will be, performed.

4. It surely will not be required of us to prove that this is the principle upon which all eternity has acted and will act, for every reflecting mind must know that it is by reason of this power that all the hosts of heaven perform their works of wonder, majesty, and glory. Angels move from place to place by virtue of this power; it is by reason of it that they are enabled to descend from heaven to earth; And were it not for the power of faith they never could be ministering spirits to them who should be heirs of salvation, neither could they act as heavenly messengers, for they would be destitute of the power necessary to enable them to do the will of God.

5. It is only necessary for us to say that the whole visible creation, as it now exists, is the effect of faith. It was faith by which it was framed, and it is by the power of faith that it continues in its organized form, and by which the planets move round their orbits and sparkle forth their glory. So, then, faith is truly the first principle in the science of THEOLOGY, and, when understood, leads the mind back to the beginning, and carries it forward to the end; or, in other words, from eternity to eternity.

6. As faith, then, is the principle by which the heavenly hosts perform their works, and by which they enjoy all their felicity, we might expect to find it set forth in a revelation from God as the principle upon which his creatures here below must act in order to obtain the felicities enjoyed by the saints in the eternal world; and that, when God would undertake to raise up men for the enjoyment of himself, he would teach them the necessity of living by faith, and the impossibility there was of their enjoying the blessedness of eternity without it, seeing that all the blessings of eternity are the effects of faith.

7. Therefore it is said, and appropriately too, that "Without faith it is impossible to please God." If it should be asked—Why is it

impossible to please God without faith? the answer would be—because without faith it is impossible for men to be saved; and as God desires the salvation of men, he must, of course, desire that they should have faith; and he could not be pleased unless they had, or else he could be pleased with their destruction.

8. From this we learn that the many exhortations which have been given by inspired men, to those who had received the word of the Lord to have faith in him, were not mere common-place matters, but were for the best of all reasons, and that was—because without it there was no salvation, neither in this world nor in that which is to come. When men begin to live by faith they begin to draw near to God; and when faith is perfected they are like him; and because he is saved they are saved also; for they will be in the same situation he is in, because they have come to him; And when he appears they shall be like him, for they will see him as he is.

9. As all the visible creation is an effect of faith, so is salvation also—we mean salvation in its most extensive latitude of interpretation, whether it is temporal or spiritual. In order to have this subject clearly set before the mind, let us ask what situation must a person be in in order to be saved? or what is the difference between a saved man and one who is not saved? We answer, from what we have before seen of the heavenly worlds, they must be persons who can work by faith and who are able, by faith, to be ministering spirits to them who shall be heirs of salvation; and they must have faith to enable them to act in the presence of the Lord, otherwise they cannot be saved. And what constitutes the real difference between a saved person and one not saved is—the difference in the degree of their faith—one's faith has become perfect enough to lay hold upon eternal life, and the other's has not. But to be a little more particular, let us ask—Where shall we find a prototype into whose likeness we may be assimilated, in order that we may be made partakers of life and salvation? or, in other words, where shall we find a saved being? for if we can find a saved being, we may ascertain without much difficulty what all others must be in order to be saved. We think that it will not be a matter of dispute, that two beings who are unlike each other cannot both be saved; for whatever constitutes the salvation of one will constitute the salvation of every creature which will be saved; and if we find one saved being in all existence, we may see what all others must be, or else not be saved. We ask, then, where is the prototype? or where is the saved being? We conclude, as to the answer of this question, there will be no dispute among those who

believe the Bible, that it is Christ: all will agree in this, that he is the prototype or standard of salvation; or, in other words, that he is a saved being. And if we should continue our interrogation, and ask how it is that he is saved? the answer would be—because he is a just and holy being; and if he were anything different from what he is, he would not be saved; for his salvation depends on his being precisely what he is and nothing else; for if it were possible for him to change, in the least degree, so sure he would fail of salvation and lose all his dominion, power, authority and glory, which constitute salvation; for salvation consists in the glory, authority, majesty, power and dominion which Jehovah possesses and in nothing else; and no being can possess it but himself or one like him. Thus says John in his first epistle, third chapter, second and third verses: "Beloved, now are we the sons of God, and it doth not yet appear what we shall be; but we know that, when he shall appear, we shall be like him, for we shall see him as he is. And every man that hath this hope in him, purifieth himself, even as he is pure." Why purify themselves as he is pure? Because if they do not, they cannot be like him.

10. The Lord said unto Moses, "Speak unto all the congregation of the children of Israel, and say unto them, 'Ye shall be holy: for I the Lord your God am holy.'" And Peter says, first epistle, 1:15, 16: "But as he which hath called you is holy, so be ye holy in all manner of conversation; because it is written, 'Be ye holy; for I am holy.'" And the Savior says, Matthew 5:48: "'Be ye therefore perfect, even as your Father which is in heaven is perfect.'" If any should ask, why all these sayings? the answer is to be found from what is before quoted from John's epistle, that when he (the Lord) shall appear, the saints will be like him; and if they are not holy, as he is holy, and perfect, as he is perfect, they cannot be like him; for no being can enjoy his glory without possessing his perfections and holiness, no more than they could reign in his kingdom without his power.

11. This clearly sets forth the propriety of the Savior's saying, recorded in John's testimony, 14:12: "Verily, verily, I say unto you, he that believeth on me, the works that I do shall he do also; and greater works than these shall he do, because I go unto my Father." This taken in connection with some of the sayings in the Savior's prayer, recorded in the seventeenth chapter, gives great clearness to his expressions. He says in the 20, 21, 22, 23, and 24th verses: "Neither pray I for these alone, but for them also who shall believe on me through their words; that they all may be one; as thou, Father, art in me, and I in thee, that they also may be one in us; that the world may

believe that thou hast sent me. And the glory which thou gavest me I have given them; that they may be one, even as we are one: I in them, and thou in me, that they may be made perfect in one; and that the world may know that thou hast sent me, and hast loved them, as thou hast loved me. Father, I will that they also, whom thou hast given me, be with me where I am; that they may behold my glory, which thou hast given me: for thou lovedst me before the foundation of the world."

12. All these sayings put together give as clear an account of the state of the glorified saints as language could give—the works that Jesus had done they were to do, and greater works than those which he had done among them should they do, and that because he went to the Father. He does not say that they should do these works in time; but they should do greater works, because he went to the Father. He says in the 24th verse: "Father, I will that they also, whom thou hast given me, be with me where I am; that they may behold my glory." These sayings, taken in connection, make it very plain that the greater works which those that believed on his name were to do were to be done in eternity, where he was going and where they should behold his glory. He had said, in another part of his prayer, that he desired of his Father that those who believed on him should be one in him, as he and the Father were one in each other. "Neither pray I for these [the apostles] alone, but for them also who shall believe on me through their words, that they all may be one"; that is, they who believe on him through the apostles' words, as well as the apostles themselves, "that they all may be one, as thou, Father, are in me and I in thee; that they also may be one in us."

13. What language can be plainer than this? The Savior surely intended to be understood by his disciples, and he so spake that they might understand him; for he declares to his Father, in language, not to be easily mistaken, that he wanted his disciples, even all of them, to be as himself and the Father, for as he and the Father were one so they might be one with them. And what is said in the 22nd verse is calculated to more firmly establish this belief; if it needs anything to establish it. He says: "And the glory which thou gavest me I have given them, that they may be one, even as we are one." As much as to say that unless they have the glory which the Father had given him they could not be one with them; for he says he had given them the glory that the Father had given him that they might be one; or, in other words, to make them one.

14. This fills up the measure of information on this subject, and shows most clearly that the Savior wished his disciples to understand that they were to be partakers with him in all things, not even his glory excepted.

15. It is scarcely necessary here to observe what we have previously noticed, that the glory which the Father and the Son have is because they are just and holy beings; and that if they were lacking in one attribute or perfection which they have, the glory which they have never could be enjoyed by them, for it requires them to be precisely what they are in order to enjoy it; and if the Savior gives this glory to any others, he must do it in the very way set forth in his prayer to his Father—by making them one with him as he and the Father are one. In so doing he would give them the glory which the Father has given him; and when his disciples are made one with the Father and Son, as the Father and Son are one, who cannot see the propriety of the Savior's saying—"The works which I do, shall they do; and greater works than these shall they do, because I go to my Father."

16. These teachings of the Savior most clearly show unto us the nature of salvation, and what he proposed unto the human family when he proposed to save them—that he proposed to make them like unto himself, and he was like the Father, the great prototype of all saved beings; and for any portion of the human family to be assimilated into their likeness is to be saved; and to be unlike them is to be destroyed; and on this hinge turns the door of salvation.

17. Who cannot see, then, that salvation is the effect of faith? for, as we have previously observed, all the heavenly beings work by this principle; and it is because they are able so to do that they are saved, for nothing but this could save them. And this is the lesson which the God of heaven, by the mouth of his holy prophets, has been endeavoring to teach to the world. Hence we are told, that "Without faith it is impossible to please him God"; and that salvation is of faith, that it might be by grace, to the end the promise might be sure to all the seed. Romans 4:16. And that Israel, who followed after the law of righteousness, has not attained to the law of righteousness. Wherefore? Because they sought it not by faith, but as it were by the works of the law; for they stumbled at that stumbling stone. And Jesus said unto the man who brought his son to him, to get the devil who tormented him cast out: "If thou canst believe, all things are possible to him that believeth." Mark 9:23. These with a multitude of other scriptures which might be quoted plainly set forth the light

in which the Savior, as well as the Former-day Saints, viewed the
plan of salvation. That it was a system of faith—it begins with faith,
and continues by faith; and every blessing which is obtained in relation to it is the effect of faith, whether it pertains to this life or that
which is to come. To this all the revelations of God bear witness. If
there were children of promise, they were the effects of faith, not
even the Savior of the world excepted. "Blessed is she that believed,"
said Elizabeth to Mary, when she went to visit her, "for there shall be
a performance of those things which were told her from the Lord."
Luke 1:45. Nor was the birth of John the Baptist the less a matter of
faith; for in order that his father Zacharias might believe he was
struck dumb. And through the whole history of the scheme of life
and salvation, it is a matter of faith: every man received according to
his faith—according as his faith was, so were his blessings and privileges; and nothing was withheld from him when his faith was sufficient to receive it. He could stop the mouths of lions, quench the
violence of fire, escape the edge of the sword, wax valiant in fight,
and put to flight the armies of the aliens; women could, by their faith,
receive their dead children to life again; in a word, there was nothing
impossible with them who had faith. All things were in subjection to
the Former-day Saints, according as their faith was. By their faith
they could obtain heavenly visions, the ministering of angels, have
knowledge of the spirits of just men made perfect, of the general
assembly and church of the first born, whose names are written in
heaven, of God the judge of all, of Jesus the Mediator of the new
covenant, and become familiar with the third heavens, see and hear
things which were not only unutterable, but were unlawful to utter.
Peter, in view of the power of faith, second epistle, first chapter, second and third verses, says to the Former-day Saints: "Grace and peace
be multiplied unto you, through the knowledge of God, and of Jesus
our Lord, according as his divine power hath given unto us all things
that pertain unto life and godliness, through the knowledge of him
that hath called us to glory and virtue." In the first epistle, first chapter, third, fourth, and fifth verses he says: "Blessed be the God and
Father of our Lord Jesus Christ, which, according to his abundant
mercy, hath begotten us again unto a lively hope by the resurrection
of Jesus Christ from the dead, to an inheritance incorruptible and
undefiled, and that fadeth not away, reserved in heaven for you, who
are kept by the power of God through faith unto salvation, ready to
be revealed in the last time."

18. These sayings put together show the apostle's views most clearly,

so as to admit of no mistake on the mind of any individual. He says that all things that pertain to life and godliness were given unto them through the knowledge of God and our Savior Jesus Christ. And if the question is asked, how were they to obtain the knowledge of God? (for there is a great difference between believing in God and knowing him—knowledge implies more than faith. And notice, that all things that pertain to life and godliness were given through the knowledge of God) the answer is given—through faith they were to obtain this knowledge; and, having power by faith to obtain the knowledge of God, they could with it obtain all other things which pertain to life and godliness.

19. By these sayings of the apostle, we learn that it was by obtaining a knowledge of God that men got the knowledge of all things which pertain to life and godliness, and this knowledge was the effect of faith; so that all things which pertain to life and godliness are the effects of faith.

20. From this we may extend as far as any circumstances may require, whether on earth or in heaven, and we will find it the testimony of all inspired men, or heavenly messengers, that all things that pertain to life and godliness are the effects of faith and nothing else; all learn-ing, wisdom and prudence fail, and every thing else as a means of sal-vation but faith. This is the reason that the fishermen of Galilee could teach the world—because they sought by faith, and by faith obtained. And this is the reason that Paul counted all things but filth and dross—what he formerly called his gain he called his loss; yea, and he counted all things but loss for the excellency of the knowl-edge of Christ Jesus the Lord. Philippians 3:7, 8, 9, and 10. Because to obtain the faith by which he could enjoy the knowledge of Christ Jesus the Lord, he had to suffer the loss of all things. This is the rea-son that the Former-day Saints knew more, and understood more, of heaven and of heavenly things than all others beside, because this information is the effect of faith—to be obtained by no other means. And this is the reason that men, as soon as they lose their faith, run into strifes, contentions, darkness, and difficulties; for the knowledge which tends to life disappears with faith, but returns when faith returns; for when faith comes it brings its train of attendants with it—apostles, prophets, evangelists, pastors, teachers, gifts, wisdom, knowledge, miracles, healings, tongues, interpretation of tongues, etc. All these appear when faith appears on the earth, and disappear when it disappears from the earth; for these are the effects of faith, and always have attended, and always will, attend it. For where faith

is, there will the knowledge of God be also, with all things which
pertain thereto—revelations, visions, and dreams, as well as every
necessary thing, in order that the possessors of faith may be perfected,
and obtain salvation; for God must change, otherwise faith will prevail with him. And he who possesses it will, through it, obtain all
necessary knowledge and wisdom, until he shall know God, and the
Lord Jesus Christ, whom he has sent—whom to know is eternal life.
Amen.

Commentary

LF 7:2 *Faith was the principle of action and of power in all intelligent
beings, both in heaven and on earth.* Faith is as essential to the gods as it is to
mortals. It is, as here stated, the principle of action and power in all intelligent beings. As "no world has yet been framed that was not framed by
faith," so no man has been resurrected save it were by faith, and no deed
of God ever performed independent of this principle. Indeed, "all the
blessings of eternity are the effects of faith" (Lectures 7:6).

LF 7:8 Salvation consists in our becoming like God. Thus we are
saved to the extent that we are like him.

LF 7:9 The reasoning used in this verse is an important extension of
the announcement in Lecture 4:11, which declares that God has all
knowledge. Those arguing that God is eternally progressing in knowledge
and understanding are not only arguing that he is infinitely ignorant but
also that he is forever changing, which would, if it were possible, mean
that the requirements of salvation would be in eternal flux, for salvation
consists in becoming like him. One man would become as God is by complying with one set of principles; while another would be assimilated into
his likeness by complying with still other principles, thus the order of
heaven would change with the seasons.

Here the Prophet explains that were it possible for God to change
even in the "least degree, so sure he would fail of salvation and lose all his
dominion, power, authority and glory, which constitute salvation; for salvation consists in the glory, authority, majesty, power and dominion
which Jehovah possesses and in nothing else; and no being can possess it
but himself or one like him."

LF 7:16 *On this hinge turns the door of salvation.* Salvation is not as
the world supposes—they will not find themselves in a state of rapture in
which they stand forever gazing in awe and wonderment on the grandeur,
glory, and greatness of God. Such a notion leaves us to suppose that God

finds pleasure in being worshiped by beings inferior to himself, beings that he created for that very purpose. Would it not do greater honor to God to suppose that he could not and would not create that which was less than godly? The work and glory of God is "to bring to pass the immortality and eternal life of man" (Moses 1:39), to exalt his family that they too might share in the glory, power, and dominion that is his.

LF 7:18 *There is a great difference between believing in God and knowing him.* The great thrust of thought in this lecture is that God can only be known to the extent that we are like him. To the extent that we are holy, we understand his holiness. To the extent that we are just or merciful, we understand his justice and mercy. To the extent that our natures are contrary to his, we are blind to his nature and his purposes.

LF 7:20 *Train of attendants.* If we plant the same seeds as did the ancients, we will harvest the same fruits. Thus the Lord says to those of all dispensations, "These signs follow them that believe," for the signs are everlastingly the same. That faith that opened the heavens to the ancients will open the heaven to those of our day and will bring the same dreams, the same visions, the same understanding, the same faith, and the same exaltation.

DOCTRINE AND COVENANTS 108

DATE: 26 DECEMBER 1835
PLACE: KIRTLAND, OHIO

Doctrine and Covenants 108 records a personal revelation given to Lyman Royal Sherman, confidant and friend of the Prophet Joseph Smith. He, his wife, Delcena Johnson, and others of her family joined the Church in January 1832 in Vermont. Lyman and Delcena moved to Kirtland, Ohio, in 1833.

In 1834 Lyman Sherman marched with Zion's Camp and upon his return from Missouri was ordained one of the seven presidents of the original Quorum of Seventy, 28 February 1835. He was released from this position in April 1837 because he had previously been ordained a high priest.

The day after Christmas in 1835, while in conversation with the Prophet, Lyman said, "I have been wrought upon to make known to you my feelings and desires, and was promised that I should have a revelation which should make known my duty" (Smith, *History of the Church*, 2:345). The revelation recorded in section 108 was given in response to that request.

Shortly after receiving this revelation, Sherman participated with those of his quorum in several meetings in the Kirtland Temple in early 1836 wherein anointings and blessings were given.

After Joseph Smith's flight to Missouri in early 1838, dissenters in Kirtland sought to use the printing office and materials to foster opposition to the Prophet. To thwart their designs, Lyman secretly burned the press. He moved to Missouri sometime prior to October 1838 and was made a temporary member of the high council in Far West on 13 December 1838.

In a revelation given to Joseph Smith while the Prophet was incarcerated in the Liberty Jail, Lyman Sherman was called to fill a vacancy in the Quorum of the Twelve. Unfortunately he died of illness at the age of thirty-five without learning that this sacred trust had been accorded him (Cook, "Lyman Sherman," 123–24).

Lyman Sherman Forgiven of His Sins

DOCTRINE AND COVENANTS 108:1–3

108:1 Lyman Sherman, a man of great spiritual integrity, was responding to the direction the Lord had given to him in coming to seek counsel from the Prophet (D&C 122:2). The Prophet knew nothing of the direction the Lord had given Lyman to seek counsel at his hand. It is a significant lesson for all that he received a remission of sins not in this instance for attending required meetings, but rather for being responsive to the personal directions of the Lord to him.

108:2 *Let your soul be at rest concerning your spiritual standing.* Forgiveness of sins brings "peace of conscience" (Mosiah 4:3), in which guilt is swept away (Enos 1:6). The soul is cleansed from the effects of wickedness and finds rest in the Lord without anguish for wrongs committed. Alma explained to his son Helaman that when forgiven, "I was harrowed up by the memory of my sins no more" (Alma 36:19).

Resist no more my voice. The voice of the Lord is heard in promptings of the Spirit. These proddings must be heeded if we are to receive the blessings the Lord has in store for us. Regarding such promptings, Amulek testified to the people of Ammonihah: "I did harden my heart, for I was called many times and I would not hear" (Alma 10:6). How long Lyman Sherman had been receiving promptings from the Lord to visit with the Prophet is not known. It is evident, however, that his anxiety over his spiritual standing could have been of a shorter length if he had not earlier resisted the Lord's voice to go to the Prophet. In like manner there are members today who resist visiting with their priesthood leaders concerning their spiritual standing, even though the Lord has prompted them to do so many times. How sweet is the comforting solace that comes from meeting with one's bishop and receiving the assurance that one can be at peace concerning his or her spiritual standing before the Lord.

He Is to Be Numbered with the Leading Elders of the Church

DOCTRINE AND COVENANTS 108:4–5

108:4 *The solemn assembly.* The purpose of a solemn assembly of the Saints is for worship. Joel spoke of the nature of these assemblies:

"Sanctify ye a fast, call a solemn assembly, gather the elders and all the inhabitants of the land into the house of the Lord your God, and cry unto the Lord" (Joel 1:14).

This revelation informed Lyman Sherman that he was to be numbered among the first to receive the endowment. These were those who had proven themselves worthy of such an honor in Zion's Camp. Preparation for the endowment occupied much of the Church leaders' time during the early months of 1836. Those selected to participate in this sacred ritual met regularly in the Kirtland Temple during January and February of 1836.

Of these preparations Joseph Smith said: "We must have all things prepared, and call our solemn assembly as the Lord has commanded us, that we may be able to accomplish His great work, and it must be done in God's own way. The house of the Lord must be prepared, and the solemn assembly called and organized in it, according to the order of the house of God; and in it we must attend to the ordinance of washing of feet. It was never intended for any but official members. It is calculated to unite our hearts, that we may be one in feeling and sentiment, and that our faith may be strong, so that Satan cannot overthrow us, nor have any power over us here" (*Teachings of the Prophet Joseph Smith*, 91).

On Monday, 5 October 1835, the Prophet recorded, "I returned home, being much fatigued from riding in the rain. Spent the remainder of the day in reading and meditation, and in the evening attended a Council of the Twelve Apostles; had a glorious time, and gave them much instruction concerning their duties for time to come; told them that it was the will of God they should take their families to Missouri next season; also this fall to attend the solemn assembly of the first Elders, for the organization of the School of the Prophets; and attend to the ordinance of the washing of feet; and to prepare their hearts in all humility for an endowment with power from on high; to which they all agreed with one accord, and seemed to be greatly rejoiced. May God spare the lives of the Twelve to a good old age, for Christ the Redeemer's sake. Amen" (Smith, *History of the Church*, 2:287; see also 308, 345).

You shall be remembered with the first of mine elders. At this time, Elder Sherman was one of the seven presidents of the Seventy. The reference to "the first of mine elders" does not refer to the office of an elder in the Melchizedek Priesthood but rather to the presiding quorums of the Church. The blessing promised to them was that they would be the first elders in this dispensation to be endowed with power in the Kirtland Temple (D&C 105:7, 33).

108:5 *The Promise of the Father.* See commentary on verse 6.

He Is Called to Preach the Gospel and Strengthen His Brethren
DOCTRINE AND COVENANTS 108:6–8

108:6 *Right to preach my gospel wheresoever I shall send you.* It was not until after the elders of the Church were endowed with power from on high that they were to go forth to preach the gospel to the nations of the world. The same was true of the Savior's disciples in Palestine. The risen Lord instructed them, "But tarry ye in the city of Jerusalem, until ye be endued with power from on high" (Luke 24:49). The Prophet Joseph Smith explained, "The endowment was to prepare the disciples for their missions unto the world" (*Teachings of the Prophet Joseph Smith,* 274). In like manner the Savior commanded the Saints to "build a house, in the which house I design to endow those whom I have chosen with power from on high; For this is the promise of the Father unto you; therefore I command you to tarry, even as mine apostles at Jerusalem" (D&C 95:8–9). "And from thence," the Lord instructed, "whosoever I will shall go forth among all nations" (D&C 38:33). Following the endowment of power, Lyman Sherman, as well as other endowed brethren, had the right to take the gospel to the entire world. See commentary on Doctrine and Covenants 39:15, "And from thence men shall go forth into all nations."

108:7 *Strengthen your brethren in all your conversation.* Following the entry "conversation" in the dictionary of Joseph Smith's day we read: "General course of manners; behavior; deportment; especially as it respects morals" (Webster, *Dictionary,* 1828). This usage accords with that of the King James Translation of the New Testament. For instance, Paul says, "For ye have heard of my conversation in time past in the Jews' religion, how that beyond measure I persecuted the church of God, and wasted it" (Galatians 1:13). As noted in the footnote in the LDS edition of the Bible, Paul's reference is not to his speech but rather to his "conduct" (Ephesians 2:3; 1 Timothy 4:12; 1 Peter 1:15–16).

DOCTRINE AND COVENANTS 109

DATE: 27 MARCH 1836
PLACE: KIRTLAND, OHIO

In preparation for the dedication of the Kirtland Temple, the Prophet Joseph Smith, Sidney Rigdon, and Oliver Cowdery, as well as Warren A. Cowdery and Warren Parrish, who acted as scribes for the Prophet, met the day previous to the dedication "to make arrangements for the solemn assembly; this business occupied the remainder of the day" (Smith, *History of the Church*, 2:409). During this meeting the dedicatory prayer for the temple was written down. It is likely that Warren A. Cowdery and Warren Parris recorded the prayer because they served the Prophet as his scribes and personal secretaries. Oliver Cowdery recorded in his journal: "This day our school did not keep, We prepared for the dedication of the Lord's house. I met in the presidents room pres. J. Smith, jr. S Rigdon, my brother W. A. Cowdery & Elder W. Parrish, and assisted in writing a prayer for the dedication of the house" (cited in Cook, *Revelations*, 218; spelling and punctuation as in original).

On the day of the dedication, the Prophet Joseph Smith recorded: "The congregation began to assemble at the Temple, at about seven o'clock, an hour earlier than the doors were to be opened. Many brethren had come in from the regions round about, to witness the dedication of the Lord's House and share in His blessings; and such was the anxiety on this occasion that some hundreds (probably five or six) assembled before the doors were opened. The presidents entered with the doorkeepers, and stationed the latter at the inner and outer doors; also placed our stewards to receive donations from those who should feel disposed to contribute something to defray the expense of building the House of the Lord. We also dedicated the pulpits, and consecrated them to the Lord.

"The doors were then opened. Presidents Rigdon, Cowdery and myself seated the congregation as they came in, and, according to the best calculation we could make, we received between nine and ten hundred, which were as many as could be comfortably seated. We then informed the doorkeepers that we could receive no more, and a multitude were deprived of the benefits of the meeting on account of the house not being sufficiently capacious to receive them; and I felt to regret that any of my brethren and sisters should be deprived of the meeting, and I recommended them to repair to the schoolhouse and hold a meeting, which they did, and filled that house also, and yet many were left out. . . .

"At nine o'clock A.M. President Sidney Rigdon commenced the services of the day by reading the 96th and 24th Psalms" (*History of the Church*, 2:410–11). This was followed by hymns, an opening prayer, sermons, and sustaining of Church officers. In the afternoon the Prophet Joseph Smith read the dedicatory prayer given by revelation.

The Thursday after the dedication of the temple, the dedicatory services were repeated "for the benefit of those who could not get into the house on the preceding Sabbath. . . . The services of the day were commenced, prosecuted and terminated in the same manner as at the former dedication, and the Spirit of God rested upon the congregation, and great solemnity prevailed" (Smith, *History of the Church*, 2:433).

Kirtland Temple Built As a Place for the Son of Man to Visit
DOCTRINE AND COVENANTS 109:1–5

109:1 The only other dedicatory prayer for a temple found in holy writ is the one offered by Solomon at the dedication of his temple (1 Kings 8:23–61). The language of this verse comes from the first verse of that prayer. It reads, "Lord God of Israel, there is no God like thee, in heaven above, or on earth beneath, who keepest covenant and mercy with thy servants that walk before thee with all their heart."

The language used in this prayer may cause concern as to who the Prophet Joseph Smith was addressing, God, the Father, or his Son, Jesus Christ (vv. 1, 4, 31, 34, 68, and 77). The Savior taught, "Ye must always pray unto the Father in my name" (3 Nephi 18:19). With regard to those verses that call upon Jehovah, it is part of the divine program to use the form and language of prayer in crying Hallelujah, which means praise Jehovah, or praise the Lord, or praise Christ who is Jehovah. These expressions of joy are uttered in the spirit of prayer and of thanksgiving. They arise from every believing heart because of all that Christ the Lord has done in bringing to pass the immortality and eternal life of man. Such cries or shouts or expressions of praise to Jehovah, and also a formal prayer to the Father, given in the true and proper sense of the word, are perfectly linked together in the revealed dedicatory prayer of the Kirtland Temple. With joy and in the spirit of exultation, the revelation begins: "Thanks be to thy name, O Lord God of Israel, who keepest covenant and showest mercy unto thy servants who walk uprightly before thee, with all their hearts [that is, thanks be to Christ whose arm of mercy is over his saints]— 'Thou who hast commanded thy servants to build a house to thy name in this place [Kirtland]. And now thou beholdest, O Lord, that thy servants have done according to thy commandment" (vv. 1–3). The command to build the house came from the Lord Jesus. He conveyed the Father's will and gave the direction. It was his voice that spoke to Joseph Smith.

"The dedicatory prayer is addressed to the Father, as all prayers should be; it is addressed to the One whose original command it was that the house be built, which direction had been revealed to the builders by the Son through whom all revelation comes" (McConkie, *Promised Messiah*, 561–62).

Who keepest covenant. The Lord's people have always been a covenant people. Thus it naturally follows that they are temple building people because the temple is the place of the covenant. To have claim upon his blessings, they must abide with exactness the covenants they have made with him. Thus it is properly said that the God of Israel "keepest covenant" with those who "walk uprightly" before him.

Showest mercy unto thy servants who walk uprightly. Only those who choose to "walk uprightly" have rightful claim upon the mercies of heaven. It is an irrevocable principle that all the blessings of heaven are predicated on obedience and the keeping of covenants (D&C 130:20).

109:2 The commandment to build the temple in Kirtland, Ohio, was first given in Doctrine and Covenants 88:119.

109:4 *In whose name alone salvation can be administered to the children of men.* There are no alternative plans outside the gospel of Jesus Christ to enable us to enter into the presence of God. Jesus Christ is the Way, the Truth, and the Life: no man comes unto the Father, but by him (John 14:6). No amount of misplaced faith in false religions can save a soul. Teachings which proclaim that prayers are to be offered to or through so-called saints of days' past are the doctrines of men but not the doctrines of heaven (D&C 46:7). An angel of God declared to King Benjamin, "There shall be no other name given nor any other way nor means whereby salvation can come unto the children of men, only in and through the name of Christ, the Lord Omnipotent" (Mosiah 3:17).

Accept of this house. One week later, Sunday, 3 April 1836, the Savior appeared in the Kirtland Temple, declaring, "Let the hearts of all my people rejoice, who have, with their might, built this house to my name. For behold, I have accepted this house, and my name shall be here; and I will manifest myself to my people in mercy in this house" (D&C 110:6–7). See commentary on Doctrine and Covenants 109:26.

The workmanship of the hands of us. The Kirtland Temple was a unique building constructed according to the Lord's instructions. See commentary on Doctrine and Covenants 95:15–17.

109:4–5 Many of the Saints that gathered to Kirtland sacrificed their means to build the temple even before they paused to build homes for themselves. They sought to build a place worthy of the presence of God and angels. For three years the Saints sacrificed to build the temple in Kirtland, Ohio. Sister Eliza R. Snow, who was living in Kirtland at the time the temple was built, wrote: "At that time the Saints were few in number, and most of them very poor; and had it not been for the assurance that God had spoken, and had commanded that a house should be built to His name, of which He not only revealed the form, but also designated the dimensions, an attempt towards building that Temple, under the then existing circumstances, would have been, by all concerned, pronounced preposterous . . .

"From the day the ground was broken for laying the foundation of the Temple, until its dedication on the 27th of March, 1836, the work was vigorously prosecuted.

"With very little capital except brain, bone, and sinew, combined with unwavering trust in God, men, women, and even children worked with their might. While the brethren labored in their departments, the sisters were actively engaged in boarding and clothing workmen not otherwise provided for—all living as abstemiously as possible, so that every cent might be appropriated to the grand object, while their energies were stimulated by the prospect of participating in the blessing of a house built by the direction of the Most High, and accepted by Him" (as cited in Talmage, *House of the Lord*, 96–97). See commentary on Doctrine and Covenants 97:16.

It Is to Be a House of Prayer, Fasting, Faith, Learning, Glory, and Order, and a House of God
DOCTRINE AND COVENANTS 109:6–21

109:6 *Call your solemn assembly, as I have commanded you.* The commandment referred to in this text was given to those the Lord called the "first laborers," or his "friends," whom he directed to hold a "solemn assembly" (D&C 88: 70, 117; 108:4). The solemn assembly to whom this reference was made was the School of the Prophets, where the elders would be instructed and endowed with power from on high. The dedication of a temple is also a solemn assembly as noted in Doctrine and Covenants 109:10.

The pattern of such assemblies would follow that of the Lord's people in ancient times. Solemn assemblies included the gathering of his servants in a state of ritual purity for sacred purposes and holy convocations such as the Festival of Unleavened Bread (Deuteronomy 16:8, 16) or the eighth day of the Festival of Booths (Leviticus 23:36; Numbers 29:35; 2 Chronicles 7:9; Nehemiah 8:18).

109:7–9 See commentary on Doctrine and Covenants 88:118–20.

109:11 *To secure a fulfillment of the promises.* With the command to move to Ohio, the Lord promised his Saints, "There you shall be endowed with power from on high" (D&C 38:32). The Savior revealed that this endowment of power was "the promise of the Father unto you [the Saints]" (D&C 95:9). It was with that hopeful expectation that the Saints had gathered to dedicate this temple.

109:12 *That thy glory may rest down upon thy people.* See commentary on verses 35–37.

That thy holy presence may be continually in this house. If no unclean thing defiles the temple, it will have the right to the constant presence of God or the Spirit of God within its walls.

109:13 Everything that the Lord does bears witnesses of him. No one who is susceptible to the Spirit of the Lord can go to the house of the Lord and not sense and know that his Spirit resides there.

109:14 The Kirtland Temple, unlike the temples we attend today, was also intended to serve as the meeting place for the School of the Prophets. Here the elders of Israel were to be instructed in virtually any subject that enhanced their ability to present the gospel message (D&C 88:78–80).

109:15 *Receive a fulness of the Holy Ghost.* As we grow up into an understanding of the scriptures and the gospel, so we grow up into an understanding of the spirit of revelation and of the companionship of the Holy Ghost. Spencer W. Kimball explained: "The Holy Ghost comes to you as you grow and learn and make yourselves worthy. It comes a little at a time as you merit it. And as your life is in harmony, you gradually receive the Holy Ghost in a great measure" (*Teachings of Spencer W. Kimball*, 114).

109:19 *With holy hands, uplifted to the Most High.* See Doctrine and Covenants 88:120.

109:20 Those who participated in the ordinances performed in the temple in Kirtland did so by invitation. These rites were performed on the third floor of the temple. It was not this area that was polluted by apostates who sought to depose the Prophet. Their activities took place in the assembly room on the main floor which was open to the public (D&C 95:16–17). Notwithstanding, their actions were sufficient to offend the Spirit of the Lord and pollute his house.

Similarly, the Nauvoo Temple was built with the idea that the lower floors of the temple would be available for public meetings and activities. Ordinances were performed in the upper rooms or attic where those who desired to participate in the temple ritual were required to first pass through an "examination area," or room, of which there were two presumably: one for men and the other for women (Brown, "Sacred Departments," 3:369). It was only after temples were built in the territory of Utah that recommends signed by priesthood leaders were required of those desiring to enter the temple.

May the Unrepentant Who Oppose the Lord's People Be Confounded
DOCTRINE AND COVENANTS 109:22–33

109:22–33 18 These verses are descriptive, in part, of the blessings that attend the endowment.

109:22 *Armed with thy power.* The missionary experiences of David Patten, one of the first apostles of this dispensation, are an illustration of the principle of being armed with the Spirit. Wilford Woodruff records the following experience had by Elder Patten when arrested for teaching the gospel in Tennessee in 1835.

"June 19th. About forty men armed with deadly weapons, led by Sheriff Robert C. Petty, and a Colonel and Major, with some other officers, and a Methodist priest with a gun on his shoulder; the Sheriff informed the brethren that he had a States' warrant for D. [David] W. [Warren] Patten, W. Parrish and W. Woodruff, issued on complaint of Mathew Williams the Methodist priest, who swore that those brethren had put forth the following false and pretended prophecy: 'That Christ

REVELATIONS OF THE RESTORATION

would come the second time before this generation passed away,' and 'That four individuals should receive the Holy Ghost within twenty-four hours.' After examination brothers Patten and Parrish were bound over to appear on June 22nd under $2000 bonds.

"Early on the 22nd Elders [David] Patten and [Warren] Parrish had their trial. The mob gathered to the number of 100 all fully armed, they took from brother Patten his walking stick and a penknife; they went through with a mock trial, but would not let the defendants produce any witnesses, and without suffering them to say a word in defence, the Judge pronounced them guilty of the charges preferred.

"Brother [David] Patten being filled with the Holy Ghost rose to his feet and by the power of God bound them fast to their seats until he addressed them. He rebuked them sharply for their wicked and unjust proceedings. Brother Parrish afterwards said, 'my hair stood up strait on my head for I expected to be killed.' When Patten closed, the judge addressed him saying, 'you must be armed with concealed weapons, or you would not treat an armed court as you have this.' Patten replied, 'I am armed with weapons you know not of, and my weapons are the Holy Priesthood and the power of God. God is my friend, and he permits you to exercise all the power you have, and he bestows on me all the power I have.' The Court finally concluded to let the brethren go if they would pay the cost of court, and leave the country in ten days" (*Millennial Star*, 26:439).

That thy name may be upon them. In the waters of baptism we covenant to take upon ourselves the name of Christ (D&C 18:21–22). We renew that covenant when we partake of the sacrament (D&C 20:77). We take that name upon us in the anointing associated with the temple endowment. The Greek form of the word *anointed* is *Christos* (Christ). See commentary on Doctrine and Covenants 20:77.

For Christ to place his name upon someone is for him to identify them as his. Thus those bearing his name are rightfully endowed with his power and authority. "Their arm," the Lord said, "shall be my arm, and I will be their shield and their buckler; and I will gird up their loins, and they shall fight manfully for me; and their enemies shall be under their feet; and I will let fall the sword in their behalf, and by the fire of mine indignation will I preserve them" (D&C 35:14; see also v. 26).

Thine angels have charge over them. To those who have received the Melchizedek Priesthood, the Lord said, "I have given the heavenly hosts and mine angels charge concerning you" (D&C 84:42). And again he said, "And whoso receiveth you, there I will be also, for I will go before your face. I will be on your right hand and on your left, and my Spirit shall be in your hearts, and mine angels round about you, to bear you up" (D&C 84:88). "Angels are our associates," explained Heber C. Kimball, "they are with us and round about us, and watch over us, and take care of us, and lead us, and guide us, and administer to our wants in their ministry and in their holy calling unto which they are appointed" (*Journal of Discourses*, 2:222).

However, none of this should be construed to mean that individuals are assigned guardian angels with the sole responsibility of following us around "silent notes taking;" which is not good doctrine (*Hymns*, no. 237). Such a thought is demeaning to both the living and the dead. It demeans the living in the assumption that they need constant watching, a divine baby-sitter, as it were. It demeans the dead in the assumption that they have no greater work or labor to do. That simply is not the case. Were it so, we would be left to wonder why we had been given the companionship of the Holy Ghost and a blessing of protection as part of the endowment.

109:24 Those who are worthy to enter the temple of the Lord and participate in its sacred rituals will be blessed in and through their families throughout endless generations.

109:25 *No weapon formed against them shall prosper.* See commentary on Doctrine and Covenants 71:9.

He who diggeth a pit for them shall fall into the same himself. Nephi prophesied: "Every nation which shall war against thee, O house of Israel, shall be turned one against another, and they shall fall into the pit which they digged to ensnare the people of the Lord. And all that fight against Zion shall be destroyed, and that great whore, who hath perverted the right ways of the Lord, yea, that great and abominable church, shall tumble to the dust and great shall be the fall of it" (1 Nephi 22:14).

109:26 *Upon whom thy name shall be put in this house.* Similarly, King Solomon pled to the Lord in the dedicatory prayer of the temple at Jerusalem "that thine eyes may be open toward this house night and day, even toward the place of which thou has said, My name shall be there" (1 Kings 8:29). Dallin H. Oaks explained: "All of these references to ancient and modern temples as houses for 'the name' of the Lord obviously involve something far more significant than a mere inscription of his sacred name on the structure. The scriptures speak of the Lord's putting his name in a temple because he gives authority for his name to be used in the sacred ordinances of that house. That is the meaning of the

Prophet's reference to the Lord's putting his name upon his people in that holy house" (Conference Report, April 1985, 103).

Endowed servants of the Lord enjoy a special blessing of protection. Of their enemies the Lord has said, "Their bounds are set, they cannot pass" (D&C 122:9). The experience of tens of thousands of missionaries attests to the reality of this promise.

109:28 *Thou wilt fight for thy people as thou didst in the day of battle.* The world of the Old Testament was one of warfare. Much of the history recorded therein finds the Lord's people either locked in battle or preparing to go to battle. For the children of Israel, war was a sacred event. Nowhere is this more evident than in the holy war by which she obtained possession of her land of promise. This was warfare undertaken at God's command and in his presence. Going to battle was approached much like worship in the sanctuary. Sacrifices were made to God (1 Samuel 13), soldiers consecrated themselves to him (Joshua 3:5), while the war camp was maintained in a state of ritual purity (Deuteronomy 23:9–14).

The leader of the army of Israel, often the Lord's prophet, was expected to be instructed by God as to how to conduct the impending battle (Judges 20:28). When Israel marched against Jericho, a procession of priests and the ark of the covenant, symbolizing the presence of God, marched at the head of Israel's army (Joshua 6:4). "Fear not" was the watchword of the Lord's army, for they knew in whose name they marched and the source of the strength that was theirs (Exodus 14:13–14).

109:30–33 To have evil spoken of is the heritage of the Saints of God in all ages. Such will not end until that great day in which Satan is bound and his tongue silenced. Nevertheless, we have the assurance that truth will prevail and the promise of Moroni that the Church will increase the more it is opposed (*Messenger and Advocate*, 2:199).

109:30 *Swept away by the hail.* The hail appears to refer to the great hailstorm that the Lord revealed would destroy the crops of the earth. See commentary on Doctrine and Covenants 29:16.

May the Saints Go Forth in Power to Gather the Righteous to Zion

DOCTRINE AND COVENANTS 109:34–42

109:34 "All have sinned, and come short of the glory of God" (Romans 3:23).

109:35 *Let the anointing of thy ministers be sealed upon them.* Preparatory to the anticipated outpouring of the Spirit at the dedication of the temple, the Prophet and the "first elders" were washed and anointed. Joseph Smith records as follows, on 21 January 1836: "About three o'clock, P.M., I dismissed the school, and the Presidency retired to the attic story of the printing office, where we attended the ordinance of washing our bodies in pure water. We also perfumed our bodies and our heads, in the name of the Lord.

"At early candle-light I met with the Presidency at the west school room, in the Temple, to attend to the ordinance of anointing our heads with holy oil; also the Councils of Kirtland and Zion met in the two adjoining rooms, and waited in prayer while we attended to the ordinance. I took the oil in my left hand, Father Smith being seated before me, and the remainder of the Presidency encircled him round about. We then stretched our right hands towards heaven, and blessed the oil, and consecrated it in the name of Jesus Christ.

"We then laid our hands upon our aged Father Smith, and invoked the blessings of heaven. I then anointed his head with the consecrated oil, and sealed many blessings upon him. The Presidency then in turn laid their hands upon his head, beginning at the oldest, until they had all laid their hands upon him, and pronounced such blessings upon his head, as the Lord put into their hearts, all blessing him to be our Patriarch, to anoint our heads, and attend to all duties that pertain to that office. The Presidency then took the seat in their turn, according to their age, beginning at the oldest, and received their anointing and blessing under the hands of Father Smith. And in my turn, my father anointed my head" (*History of the Church,* 2:379–80). During the weeks that preceded the dedication of the temple, others of the brethren participated in the biblical ritual of washing and anointing.

109:36–37 The day of Pentecost took place fifty days after Passover as mandated by the law of Moses (Exodus 23:15–16; 34:22; Leviticus 23:16). The first day of Pentecost following the resurrection of Christ was of particular importance. The Lord directed his disciples to "tarry . . . in the city of Jerusalem, until ye be endued with power from on high" (Luke 24:49). "And when the day of Pentecost was fully come, they were all with one accord in one place. And suddenly there came a sound from heaven as of a rushing mighty wind, and it filled all the house where they were sitting. And there appeared unto them cloven tongues like as of fire, and it sat upon each of them. And they were all filled with the Holy

Ghost, and began to speak with other tongues, as the Spirit gave them utterance" (Acts 2:1–4).

Writing of that occasion, President Joseph F. Smith and his counselors in the First Presidency stated: "We read that Jesus, after His resurrection, breathed upon His disciples and said, 'Receive ye the Holy Ghost.' But we also read that He said, 'Behold, I send the promise of my father upon you: but tarry ye in the city of Jerusalem, until ye be endued with power from on high.' (John 20:22; Luke 24:49.) We read further, 'For the Holy Ghost was not yet given: because that Jesus was not yet glorified.' (John 7:39.) Thus the promise was made, but the fulfilment came after, so that the Holy Ghost sent by Jesus from the Father did not come in person until the day of Pentecost, and the cloven tongues of fire were the sign of His coming. This manifestation was repeated in this dispensation at the endowment in the Kirtland Temple, in the month of January, 1836" (Clark, *Messages*, 5:4).

The Prophet recorded that following the closing hymn and benediction at the dedicatory service: "President Brigham Young gave a short address in tongues, and David W. Patten interpreted, and gave a short exhortation in tongues himself, after which I blessed the congregation in the name of the Lord, and the assembly dispersed a little past four o'clock, having manifested the most quiet demeanor during the whole exercise.

"I met the quorums in the evening and instructed them respecting the ordinance of washing of feet, which they were to attend to on Wednesday following; and gave them instructions in relation to the spirit of prophecy, and called upon the congregation to speak, and not to fear to prophesy good concerning the Saints, for if you prophesy the falling of these hills and the rising of the valleys, the downfall of the enemies of Zion and the rising of the kingdom of God, it shall come to pass. Do not quench the Spirit, for the first one that opens his mouth shall receive the Spirit of prophecy.

"Brother George A. Smith arose and began to prophesy, when a noise was heard like the sound of a rushing mighty wind, which filled the Temple, and all the congregation simultaneously arose, being moved upon by an invisible power; many began to speak in tongues and prophesy; others saw glorious visions; and I beheld the Temple was filled with angels, which fact I declared to the congregation. The people of the neighborhood came running together (hearing an unusual sound within, and seeing a bright light like a pillar of fire resting upon the Temple), and were astonished at what was taking place. This continued until the meeting closed at eleven p. m." (Smith, *History of the Church*, 2:428).

The Pentecostal season continued for weeks after the dedication of the temple. The Prophet Joseph Smith recorded a week later: "I left the meeting in the charge of the Twelve, and retired about nine o'clock in the evening. The brethren continued exhorting, prophesying, and speaking in tongues until five o'clock in the morning. The Savior made His appearance to some, while angels ministered to others, and it was Pentecost and an endowment indeed, long to be remembered, for the sound shall go forth from this place into all the world, and the occurrences of this day shall be handed down upon the pages of sacred history, to all generations: as the day of Pentecost, so shall this day be numbered and celebrated as a year of jubilee, and time of rejoicing to the Saints of the Most High God" (*History of the Church*, 2:432–33).

109:38 *Put upon thy servants the testimony of the covenant.* Those upon whom a true testimony of the covenant rests will always be numbered among those who are faithful and valiant. Addressing this issue in general conference, Elder M. Russell Ballard said: "Somehow we need to instill in our hearts the powerful testimony of the gospel of Jesus Christ like unto that of our pioneer forefathers. Remember when Nauvoo fell in September of 1846 and the unbearable conditions of the Saints in the poor camps. When word reached Winter Quarters, Brigham Young immediately called the brethren together. After explaining the situation and reminding them of the covenant made in the Nauvoo Temple that no one who wanted to come, no matter how poor, would be left behind, he gave them this remarkable challenge:

"'Now is the time for labor,' he said. '*Let the fire of the covenant* which you made in the House of the Lord, *burn in your hearts, like flame unquenchable.*' . . . Within a few days, in spite of near-destitute conditions at Winter Quarters, many wagons were rolling eastward to rescue the Saints in the poor camps along the Mississippi River" (Conference Report, April 1999, 112–13; emphasis added).

Seal up the law. See commentary on verse 46.

109:39 *Come forth to Zion, or to her stakes.* Elder Bruce R. McConkie explained: "The law of gathering as given to us has varied to meet the needs of an ever-growing Church that one day will have dominion over all the earth. In 1830 the saints were commanded to assemble in 'one place.' (D&C 29:8). How could it have been otherwise? They were told to 'assemble together at the Ohio' (D&C 37:3) and to go forth to Zion in 'the western countries' (D&C 45:64). In 1833 they were told to gather in the Zion of Missouri, 'Until the day cometh when there is found no more room for them; and then I have other places which I will appoint unto them,' saith the Lord, 'and they shall be called stakes, for the curtains or the strength of Zion.' They were to worship the Lord 'in holy places.' (D&C 101:21–22.) In the revealed prayer dedicating the Kirtland Temple (1836), the Prophet importuned for the righteous, 'that they may come forth to Zion, or to her stakes, the places of thine appointment, with songs of everlasting joy.' (D&C 109:39.) In 1838 the Lord spoke of 'the gathering together upon the land of Zion, and upon her stakes.' (D&C 115:6.) In 1844 the prophetic word acclaimed: 'The whole of America is Zion itself from north to south, and is described by the Prophets, who declare that it is the Zion where the mountain of the Lord should be, and that it should be in the center of the land.' (*Teachings of the Prophet Joseph Smith*, 362.)

"We now have stakes of Zion in many nations, in Europe and Asia and South America and upon the islands of the sea. Before the Lord comes, there will be stakes in all lands and among all peoples. Any portion of the surface of the earth that is organized into a stake of Zion—a City of Holiness, as it were—becomes a part of Zion. A stake of Zion is a part of Zion—it is just that simple. And every stake becomes the place of gathering for the saints who live in the area involved" (*Millennial Messiah*, 294–95).

109:42 *Cleanse them from their blood.* When servants of the Lord are commissioned to declare the message of salvation to a particular people, they cannot be held guiltless when they, through their own negligence, fail to do so. Only in raising the warning voice can they cleanse themselves from the blood and sins of those whom they have been given the responsibility to teach.

Teaching this principle, Jacob, brother of Nephi said, "We did magnify our office unto the Lord, taking upon us the responsibility, answering the sins of the people upon our own heads if we did not teach them the word of God with all diligence; wherefore, by laboring with our might their blood might not come upon our garments; otherwise their blood would come upon our garments, and we would not be found spotless at the last day" (Jacob 1:19).

May the Saints Be Delivered from the Terrible Things to Be Poured Out upon the Wicked in the Last Days

DOCTRINE AND COVENANTS 109:43–53

109:46 *Seal up the law, and bind up the testimony.* Isaiah 8:16 reads, "Bind up the testimony, seal the law among my disciples." The imagery is idiomatic to the ancient day. After a parchment or papyrus scroll had been used, it was tied with a cord and sealed to preserve it until future use. Thus the thought expressed in this verse is "tie up the evidence," or "seal the admonition," it will be brought forth again in the day of judgment. In the context of this revelation, the servants of the Lord are to be endowed with power and sent to the nations of the earth, there they are to raise the warning voice, bind or seal up their testimonies, which will stand as evidence against those whom they have taught come the day of judgment (*Interpreter's Bible*, 12:227). See commentary on Doctrine and Covenants 88:84, "To bind up the law and seal up the testimony."

109:49 *A display of thy testimony.* In early records this is written as "a display of thy power" (Woodford, *Historical Development*, 1451).

109:50–53 *Have mercy, O Lord, upon the wicked mob.* The revealed utterance of the Holy Ghost in this prayer is in harmony with the Savior's instructions: "Love your enemies, bless them that curse you, do good to them that hate you, and pray for them which despitefully use you, and persecute you; That ye may be the children of your Father which is in heaven" (Matthew 5:44–45). This righteous prayer also voiced the truth that mercy is available only upon conditions of repentance (v. 1). Divine justice cannot be denied for the wicked that drove the Saints from their homes in Jackson County, Missouri.

109:52 *Wasted away, both root and branch.* The words are similar to those revealed to Malachi concerning the destruction of the wicked at the Second Coming: "For, behold, the day cometh, that shall burn as an oven; and all the proud, yea, and all that do wickedly, shall be stubble: and the day that cometh shall burn them up, saith the Lord of hosts, that it shall leave them neither root nor branch" (Malachi 4:1). The root and branch refer to the familial associations of grandparents, parents, brothers, sisters, and children. The Saints prayed that the wicked mobs who had driven them from Zion might have the day of judgment moved forward, if they would not repent. In this way the redemption of Zion would not need to wait for the burning of the wicked; the wicked would waste away, without family, parents, or children to carry out their evil designs against the Saints. In the eternal sense, the wicked will be left without familial association in eternity. For more on the destruction in Missouri, see commentary on Doctrine and Covenants 105:15.

May Nations and Peoples and Churches Be Prepared for the Gospel

DOCTRINE AND COVENANTS 109:54–58

109:54–58 Knowing that the adversary would seek to prevent the ambassadors of the Lord from entry into the various communities, cities, states, and nations to which the gospel must go, this inspired prayer called upon the Lord to open the way for the restored gospel to be taught to all peoples. The prayer recognizes that the leaders of nations are the gates through which missionaries must pass to enter their countries. The Prophet Joseph Smith pled with the Lord to soften their hearts so that the message might be taught.

109:56 *That their prejudices may give way before the truth.* Prejudice is a preconceived judgment that closes the hearts and minds of people to light and truth. Self-inflicted bondage robs hosts of people of associations and knowledge that would greatly edify and bless them. It finds perfect expression in those who reject the Book of Mormon without reading it, the story of the First Vision without praying about it, and the message of the Restoration out of fear of change or being thought different. It is a tool of the devil and is always associated with apostasy and spiritual darkness.

109:57 The test of true discipleship is found in the ability to accept and follow the living oracles of the Lord. The religious world has always been full of people who reject the living prophets in the name of loyalty to the prophets of earlier dispensations. Describing the same in his poem *A Vision*, the Prophet wrote:

> These are they that came out for Apollos and Paul;
> For Cephas and Jesus, in all kinds of hope;
> For Enoch and Moses, and Peter and John;
> For Luther and Calvin, and even the Pope.
> For they never received the gospel of Christ,
> Nor the prophetic spirit that came from the Lord;
> Nor the covenant neither, which Jacob once had;
> They went their own way, and they have their reward.
> (*Times and Seasons*, 4:85)

Compare Doctrine and Covenants 109:70–71. See commentary on Doctrine and Covenants 76:70–71.

109:58 *The sons of Jacob.* Refers to literal descendants of Jacob, whom the Lord named Israel.

May the Jews, the Lamanites, and All Israel Be Redeemed
DOCTRINE AND COVENANTS 109:59–67

109:59 *Appoint unto Zion other stakes besides this one.* The Lord appoints by revelation through the Quorum of the Twelve Apostles, under the direction of the First Presidency, the "building up [of] the church" (D&C 107:33), including the formation of stakes throughout the world. Today the Lord has appointed stakes unto Zion numbering in the thousands.

Thy work may be cut short in righteousness. The Saints of latter days are commanded to preach repentance to the world and to invite them to come unto Christ. Those who hearken to the message of the Restoration are commanded to gather to the stakes of Zion before the wicked are destroyed. "For I, the Almighty, have laid my hands upon the nations, to scourge them for their wickedness. And plagues shall go forth, and they shall not be taken from the earth until I have completed my work, which shall be cut short in righteousness—Until all shall know me, who remain" (D&C 84:96–98). As the prophesied destruction of the last days gets closer, the Lord will prosper the preaching of the gospel to all nations. Doors now locked to our missionaries will be opened. The Lord's work will be hastened by the blessings that he bestows upon the earth that all might know the truth. The Lord's work being cut short in righteousness will happen according to a divinely predetermined timetable.

109:60 *Identified with the Gentiles.* As used in the Bible, the word *Gentile* means nation—a collective body. It is used in the same manner in the Book of Mormon. As a Jew is a Jewish national, so is a Gentile a citizen of a gentile nation. Thus, Joseph Smith, a pure-blooded Israelite, is referred to as a Gentile; and the gospel, it is prophesied, will be restored in a gentile nation. By this definition Latter-day Saints are Israelites by descent but Gentile by culture. Any nation that does not have prophets at its head, revelation as its constitution, and the Messiah as its king is a gentile nation.

109:61–64 As part of the promises of the Lord to be fulfilled before the coming of the Son of Man, the Prophet Joseph Smith taught that "the tribe of Judah will return to old Jerusalem" (*Teachings of the Prophet Joseph Smith*, 17). In this inspired prayer dedicating the Kirtland Temple, the

Prophet was moved upon by the Holy Ghost to ask that the long-awaited day of Judah's return to Jerusalem be hastened. Jerusalem had not been under Jewish control since the Roman destruction of the holy city in 70 AD. The Lord covenanted with Abraham that the land of Palestine was to be given to him and his seed after him forever (Genesis 13:14–15). Preparations for that promise to be fulfilled were enacted with the gathering of the Jewish remnant to Palestine and the establishment of the nation of Israel following World War II.

The keys for gathering Judah to Jerusalem were restored by Moses to the Prophet Joseph Smith and Oliver Cowdery as part of the keys of the gathering of Israel (D&C 110:11). In 1841, under the direction of the Prophet Joseph Smith, Elder Orson Hyde traveled to Palestine and dedicated the land of Israel for the gathering of the Jews. He knelt on the Mount of Olives to the east of the city and dedicated the land for that purpose. Concerning the return of the Jews to their ancient homeland, he prayed: "Let the large ships of the nations bring them from the distant isles; and let kings become their nursing fathers, and queens with motherly fondness wipe the tear of sorrow from their eye.

"Thou, O Lord, did once move upon the heart of Cyrus to show favor unto Jerusalem and her children. Do Thou now also be pleased to inspire the hearts of kings and the powers of the earth to look with a friendly eye towards this place, and with a desire to see Thy righteous purposes executed in relation thereto. Let them know that it is Thy good pleasure to restore the kingdom unto Israel—raise up Jerusalem as its capital, and constitute her people a distinct nation and government, with David Thy servant, even a descendant from the loins of ancient David to be their king" (Smith, *History of the Church*, 4:457). Christ, when he returns in glory as the promised David of the millennial kingdom, will claim his right to reign over the house of Israel, including Judah (D&C 45:43–53).

109:65 *The remnants of Jacob, who have been cursed and smitten.* This verse refers to the descendants of Lehi identified with the Indian nations of North America. They bore the curse of their ancestors who rejected the fulness of the gospel and had been smitten by the Gentiles that came to the Americas from across the Atlantic Ocean. Because of apostasy, they had no knowledge of the Holy One of Israel, even though they are descendants of the house of Israel. They have been promised that in the last days they will be restored to a knowledge of the true Messiah, believe in his gospel, and blossom as a rose (D&C 3:16–19; 49:24).

109:67 The Book of Mormon emphatically and repetitiously teaches that the gathering must in all instances be first to Christ and then, and only then, to lands of inheritance. No true prophecy is filled by someone claiming possession of a particular land with the idea in mind that salvation is a matter of homesteading the right piece of property. It is the truths of salvation, as noted in this text, to which the lost and fallen remnant of Israel must first return.

May the Saints Be Crowned with Glory and Honor and Gain Eternal Salvation
DOCTRINE AND COVENANTS 109:68–80

109:71 *Remember . . . all the presidents of thy church.* This reference is not to those who have succeeded Joseph Smith in the office of president of the Church but rather to those who stood with him in the presidency of the Church at that time and those who presided in the presidency of the two stakes of Zion that had been organized by that point in time.

109:72 *The kingdom, which thou hast set up without hands.* See commentary on Doctrine and Covenants 65.

109:73 *Fair as the moon, clear as the sun, and terrible as an army with banners.* See commentary on Doctrine and Covenants 5:14, "Clear as the moon, and fair as the sun, and terrible as an army with banners."

109:74 *Mountains to flow down at thy presence.* See commentary on Doctrine and Covenants 133:22–24.

109:75 *Shall be caught up.* See commentary on Doctrine and Covenants 88:96; 101:31, "Shall be caught up."

109:76 This language in which clothing is used to represent the righteousness of the Saints is taken from Isaiah. "I will greatly rejoice in the Lord," he declared, "my soul shall be joyful in my God; for he hath clothed me with the garments of salvation, he hath covered me with the robe of righteousness" (Isaiah 61:10). Similarly, John the Revelator described those who would be exalted as "a great multitude, which no man could number, . . . clothed with white robes, and palms in their hands" (Revelation 7:9).

Garments may be pure. Symbolically, as the garment is clean, so is the soul. Alma taught, "There can no man be saved except his garments are washed white; yea, his garments must be purified until they are cleansed from all stain, through the blood of him of whom it has been spoken by our fathers, who should come to redeem his people from their sins" (Alma

5:21). Speaking of high priests, Alma taught: "Therefore they were called after this holy order, and were sanctified, and their garments were washed white through the blood of the Lamb. Now they, after being sanctified by the Holy Ghost, having their garments made white, being pure and spotless before God, could not look upon sin save it were with abhorrence; and there were many, exceedingly great many, who were made pure and entered into the rest of the Lord their God" (Alma 13:11–12).

With palms in our hands. The palm leaf is a symbol of victory and peace (John 12:13; Revelation 7:9).

Crowns of glory upon our heads. The crowns represent those that reign as kings and queens over their posterity in eternity. They have been married in "the new and everlasting covenant, and it is sealed unto them by the Holy Spirit of promise. . . . [They] shall inherit thrones, kingdoms, principalities, and powers" (D&C 132:19).

109:79 *That we may mingle our voices with those bright, shining seraphs . . . singing.* "The veil is very thin in the temples," explained Dallin H. Oaks, "especially when we join in worshiping through music. At temple dedications I have seen more tears of joy elicited by music than by the spoken word. I have read accounts of angelic choirs joining in these hymns of praise, and I think I have experienced this on several occasions. In dedicatory sessions featuring beautiful and well-trained choirs of about thirty voices, there are times when I have heard what seemed to be ten times thirty voices praising God with a quality and intensity of feeling that can be experienced but not explained. Some who are listening today will know what I mean" (Conference Report, October 1994, 11).

Shining seraphs. See commentary on Doctrine and Covenants 38:1.

With acclamations of praise, singing Hosanna to God and the Lamb! William W. Phelps wrote a dedicatory hymn for this occasion, "The Spirit of God Like a Fire Is Burning," which has been sung at all latter-day temple dedications. The words of the first verse and chorus express the sentiments of the dedicatory prayer and are familiar to Latter-day Saints. The fifth verse, which is particularly fitting for a temple dedication, is no longer sung.

We'll wash and be washed, and with oil be anointed,
Withal not omitting the washing of feet;
For he that receiveth his penny appointed
Must surely be clean at the harvest of wheat.
(Smith, *History of the Church*, 2:426)

Hosanna. The word *Hosanna* is "of Hebrew origin, meaning literally, save now, or save we pray, or save we beseech thee—[and] is both a chant of praise and glory to God and an entreaty for his blessings" (McConkie, *Mormon Doctrine*, 368). At the dedication of the Kirtland Temple, a pattern for all subsequent temple dedications, the proceedings of the day were sealed "by shouting hosanna, hosanna, hosanna to God and the Lamb, three times, sealing it each time with amen, amen, and amen" (Smith, *History of the Church*, 2:427–28).

DOCTRINE AND COVENANTS 110

DATE: 3 APRIL 1836
PLACE: KIRTLAND, OHIO

This revelation, which records some of the most significant events of this dispensation, indeed, of the history of the earth, took place in the Kirtland Temple one week after its dedication. These events set the Kirtland Temple apart in the story of the Restoration and in the annals of temple building. Its purpose was not like that of other temples. It was built primarily as a place for prophets of past dispensations to restore the keys, powers, and authorities distinctive to their dispensations and ministries. The restoration of these keys brought about a "fulness of gospel ordinances" (Smith, *Doctrines of Salvation*, 2:242).

Were it not for the authority restored in the Kirtland Temple, the entire purpose for which the earth was created would have come to naught (Malachi 4:5–6; D&C 2). Here the authority to gather Israel from her long dispersion and to lead "the ten tribes from the land of the north" was restored by Moses; here the authority to perform eternal marriages and bind families together for eternity was given anew by the Elias from Abraham's dispensation (see commentary on D&C 110:12); and the sealing power, by which all gospel ordinances are sealed for both the living and the dead, was restored by Elijah.

Introducing this revelation, Joseph Smith recorded the following:

"Sunday, 3.—attended meeting in the Lord's House, and assisted the other Presidents of the Church [members of the first presidency] in seating the congregation, and then became an attentive listener to the preaching from the stand. Thomas B. Marsh and David W. Patten spoke in the forenoon to an attentive audience of about one thousand persons. In the afternoon, I assisted the other Presidents in distributing the Lord's Supper to the Church, receiving it from the Twelve, whose privilege it was to officiate at the sacred desk this day. After having performed this service to my brethren, I retired to the pulpit, the veils being dropped, and bowed myself, with Oliver Cowdery, in solemn and silent prayer. After rising from prayer, the following vision was opened to both of us—" (*History of the Church*, 2:434–35).

The Lord Appears to Accept the
Kirtland Temple As His House
DOCTRINE AND COVENANTS 110:1–10

110:1 *The veil was taken from our minds.* When the spirit children of God leave the realms of heaven and come to the earth to obtain a body, a veil is drawn across their minds, taking from them both the memory of their divine origin and the ability to see and comprehend the things of heaven. Elder James E. Talmage explained that "though the veil of mortality, with all its thick obscurity, may shut the light of the divine presence from the sinful heart, that separating curtain may be drawn aside and the heavenly light may shine into the righteous soul. By the listening ear, attuned to the celestial music, the voice of God has been heard declaring His personality and will; to the eye that is freed from the motes and beams of sin, single in its search after truth, the hand of God has been made visible; within the soul properly purified by devotion and humility the mind of God has been revealed" (*Articles of Faith*, 298). Such was the experience of Joseph Smith and Oliver Cowdery on this occasion as the veil was lifted, allowing them to stand in the presence of the God of Israel and receive his instruction (Alma 19:6).

110:2 *We saw the Lord.* Like Joseph and Oliver, John Murdock also saw the Lord. He recorded: "The visions of my mind were opened, and the eyes of my understanding were enlightened, and I saw the form of a man, most lovely! The visage of his face was sound and fair as the sun. His hair, a bright silver gray, curled in most majestic form, His eyes, a keen penetrating blue, and the skin of his neck a most beautiful white, and He was covered from the neck to the feet with a loose garment, pure white, whiter than any garment I have ever before seen. His countenance was most penetrating, and yet most lovely! And while I was endeavoring to comprehend the whole personage, from head to feet, it slipped from me, and the Vision was closed up. But it left on my mind the impression of love, for months, that I never before felt, to that degree" (quoted in Anderson, *Joseph Smith's Kirtland*, 109–10).

110:3 *The voice of Jehovah.* Jesus of Nazareth identifies himself here as the great Jehovah of the Old Testament and as our advocate with the Father (v. 4).

110:5 *Your sins are forgiven you.* Had Joseph and Oliver not been clean and pure they could not have taken part in these visionary experiences.

You are clean before me. Anciently it was understood that one must be sanctified to stand in the presence of the Lord or perform any sacred function. Accordingly, Joseph Smith and Oliver Cowdery had prepared themselves for such an experience through the ordinances of washing and anointing in the Kirtland Temple (D&C 84:23; 88:37–41; 109:34–35). See commentary on Doctrine and Covenants 137.

110:7 *My name shall be here.* The "name" of the Lord signifies his priesthood and power (Abraham 1:18). To say that his name will be found in the temple is to say that his Spirit and power will manifest itself there.

I will manifest myself to my people in mercy in this house. This promise is twofold: to manifest himself is to reveal his mind and will to his people; it is also to reveal himself physically just as he is here doing with Joseph Smith and Oliver Cowdery (D&C 110:8).

In the dedicatory prayer for the Kirtland Temple, an appeal was made for three particular blessings—namely, that the Lord would accept the Temple as his house; that his name would be there; and that he would manifest himself to his people in that place (D&C 109:4–5). In this verse the Lord affirms his willingness to do all three.

110:8 *Do not pollute this holy house.* "Like the Temple of Solomon and those which succeeded that grand structure in Jerusalem, the Kirtland temple was polluted and ceased to be a sanctuary to the name of the Lord. Even today, if it had remained undefiled it could hardly be used for the performance of the essential ordinances which are received in temples, for it was not built for them. . . .

"It is not a sacred temple today—not by any means. It is no more a temple than an adobe building, and is not recognized by the Lord any more. It filled the measure of its creation, then fell into the hands of wicked men, and the Lord ceased to consider that building as a house built unto his name, and in the 124th section of the Doctrine and Covenants [v. 28] he says so" (Smith, *Doctrines of Salvation*, 2:242–43).

Eliza R. Snow later described in part how the Kirtland Temple became polluted: "During the time my brother [Lorenzo Snow] was on this, his first mission, a great change had been going on in Kirtland, in the midst of the Saints. A spirit of speculation had crept into the hearts of some of the Twelve, and nearly, if not every quorum was more or less infected. Most of the Saints were poor, and now prosperity was dawning upon them—the Temple was completed, and in it they had been recipients of marvelous blessings, and many who had been humble and faithful to the performance of every duty—ready to go and come at every call of the Priesthood, were getting haughty in their spirits, and lifted up in the pride of their hearts. As the Saints drank in the love and spirit of the world, the Spirit of the Lord withdrew from their hearts, and they were filled with pride and hatred toward those who maintained their integrity. They linked themselves together in an opposing party—pretended that they constituted the Church, and claimed that the Temple belonged to them, and even attempted to hold it.

"Warren Parrish, who had been a humble, successful preacher of the Gospel, was the ringleader of this apostate party. One Sabbath morning, he, with several of his party, came into the Temple armed with pistols and bowie-knives, and seated themselves together in the Aaronic pulpits, on the east end of the Temple, while Father Smith and others, as usual, occupied those of the Melchisedec Priesthood on the west. Soon after the usual opening services, one of the brethren on the west stand arose, and just after he commenced to speak, one on the east interrupted him. Father Smith, presiding, called to order—he told the apostate brother that he should have all the time he wanted, but he must wait his turn—as the brother on the west took the floor and commenced first to speak, he must not be interrupted. A fearful scene ensued—the apostate speaker becoming so clamorous, that Father Smith called for the police to take that man out of the house, when Parrish, John Boynton . . . saying he would blow out the brains of the first man who dared to lay hands on him. Many in the congregation, especially women and children, were terribly frightened—some tried to escape from the confusion by jumping out of the windows. Amid screams and shrieks, the policemen, in ejecting the belligerents, knocked down a stovepipe, which fell helter-skelter among the people; but, although bowie-knives and pistols were wrestled from their owners, and thrown hither and thither to prevent disastrous results, no one was hurt, and after a short, but terrible scene to be enacted in a Temple of God, order was restored, and the services of the day proceeded as usual" (cited in Smith, *Biography and Family Record of Lorenzo Snow*, 20–21).

110:9 *The endowment.* The Lord directed his Saints to gather in the Ohio Valley to receive the endowment (D&C 38:15). "In January, 1836, over two months before the dedication, the first ceremonies of endowment were given in the temple," explained Joseph Fielding Smith. "They were not as complete as are the ceremonies today, but nevertheless, it was the beginning of the revealing and bestowing of the heavenly blessings in this dispensation. Washings and anointings were given, and the Prophet saw wonderful visions of the celestial kingdom. . . .

"The greater manifestations and endowment came, however, after the dedication of the temple. At that time all the elders who were out preaching the gospel were ordered to come to Kirtland to receive their endowment. The Lord said in June, 1834: 'Verily I say unto you, it is expedient in me that the first elders of my church should receive their endowment from on high in my house, which I have commanded to be built unto my name in the land of Kirtland' (see D&C 105:33). For this reason they were assembled at Kirtland at the dedication.

"This prophetic utterance about the elders obtaining an endowment in the temple at Kirtland is of double meaning. First, there were to come from on high essential blessings for the saints, which up to that time had not been revealed. Second, the elders were to receive greater powers that they might be better qualified to teach. It was made known by many manifestations of divine power at the dedication that the temple had been accepted as the house of the Lord" (*Doctrines of Salvation*, 2:241–42).

In an address given at the laying of the cornerstone of the Salt Lake Temple, Brigham Young explained that Joseph Smith was given a commandment to build a temple in Kirtland, Ohio: "Joseph not only received revelation and commandment to build a temple, but he received a pattern also, as did Moses for the tabernacle, and Solomon for his temple; for without a pattern, he could not know what was wanted, having never seen one, and not having experienced its use.

"Without revelation, Joseph could not know what was wanted, any more than any other man, and, without commandment, the Church were too few in number, too weak in faith, and too poor in purse, to attempt such a mighty enterprise. But by means of all these stimulants, a mere handful of men, living on air, and a little hominy and milk, and often salt or no salt, when milk could not be had; the great Prophet Joseph, in the stone quarry, quarrying rock with his own hands; and the few then in the Church, following his example of obedience and diligence wherever most needed; with laborers on the walls, holding the sword in one hand to protect themselves from the mob, while they placed the stone and moved the trowel with the other, the Kirtland temple—the second house of the Lord, that we have any published record of on the earth, was so far completed as to be dedicated. And those first Elders who helped to build it, received a portion of their first endowments, or we might say more clearly, some of the first, or introductory, or initiatory ordinances, preparatory to an endowment.

"The preparatory ordinances there administered, though accompanied by the ministrations of angels, and the presence of the Lord Jesus, were but a faint similitude of the ordinances of the house of the Lord in their fulness; yet many, through the instigation of the Devil, thought they had received all, and knew as much as God; they have apostatized, and gone to hell. But be assured, brethren, there are but few, very few of the Elders of Israel, now on earth, who know the meaning of the word endowment. To know, they must experience; and to experience, a temple must be built.

"Let me give you a definition in brief. Your endowment is, to receive all those ordinances in the house of the Lord, which are necessary for you, after you have departed this life, to enable you to walk back to the presence of the Father, passing the angels who stand as sentinels, being enabled to give them the key words, the signs and tokens, pertaining to the holy Priesthood, and gain your eternal exaltation in spite of earth and hell" (*Discourses of Brigham Young*, 415–16).

Moses and Elias Appear and Commit
Their Keys and Dispensations
DOCTRINE AND COVENANTS 110:11–12

110:11 *Keys of the gathering of Israel from the four parts of the earth.* Keys are the "right of presidency" (D&C 107:8), meaning the right to preside. When Moses gave the keys of the gathering of Israel to Joseph Smith and Oliver Cowdery, it meant that they alone held the presidency over this event. Thus everything that happens relative to the gathering of Israel that constitutes the fulfillment of prophecy must take place under their direction, or under that of their legal and lawful successors as possessors of those keys, or that presidency.

Their authority embraces the whole earth and is to be used to gather the twelve tribes of Israel, which have been scattered to the four winds, or the "four parts of the earth" (2 Nephi 10:8). They are gathered by missionaries sent forth for that purpose. To be gathered is to be baptized for the remission of sins (D&C 137:6; 3 Nephi 21:6). It is to embrace the testimony that Joseph Smith is a prophet, that the Father and the Son appeared to him in the Sacred Grove, and that the fulness of truth and

eternal salvation are found only in The Church of Jesus Christ of Latter-
day Saints. Mormon prophesies of this gathering: "I am Mormon, and a
pure descendant of Lehi. I have reason to bless my God and my Savior
Jesus Christ, that he brought our fathers out of the land of Jerusalem, (and
no one knew it save it were himself and those whom he brought out of
that land) and that he hath given me and my people so much knowledge
unto the salvation of our souls. Surely he hath blessed the house of Jacob,
and hath been merciful unto the seed of Joseph. And insomuch as the
children of Lehi have kept his commandments he hath blessed them and
prospered them according to his word. Yea, and surely shall he again bring
a remnant of the seed of Joseph to the knowledge of the Lord their God.
And as surely as the Lord liveth, will he gather in from the four quarters of
the earth all the remnant of the seed of Jacob, who are scattered abroad
upon all the face of the earth. And as he hath covenanted with all the
house of Jacob, even so shall the covenant wherewith he hath covenanted
with the house of Jacob be fulfilled in his own due time, unto the restoring
all the house of Jacob unto the knowledge of the covenant that he hath
covenanted with them. And then shall they know their Redeemer, who is
Jesus Christ, the Son of God; and then shall they be gathered in from the
four quarters of the earth unto their own lands, from whence they have
been dispersed; yea, as the Lord liveth so shall it be. Amen" (3 Nephi
5:20–26).

   Leading of the ten tribes from the land of the north. Elder Bruce R.
McConkie explained: "'We believe in the literal gathering of Israel and
in the restoration of the Ten Tribes' (A of F 10). This inspired language
leaves the clear impression that the gathering of Israel is one thing and
the restoration of the Ten Tribes is another. Why this distinction? Are not
the Ten Tribes a part of Israel? And if Israel is to be gathered, surely in the
very nature of things this would include the gathering of the major portion of that ancient and favored people.

   "An immortal Moses, appearing in resurrected glory on the 3rd day
of April, 183[6], in the Kirtland Temple, committed unto his mortal
fellowservants, Joseph Smith and Oliver Cowdery, 'the keys of the gathering of Israel from the four parts of the earth, and the leading of the ten
tribes from the land of the north' (D&C 110:11). Again there is a distinction between Israel as a whole and the Ten Tribes who are the dominant portion of Jacob's seed. All scripture comes by the power of the Holy
Ghost and is verily true. When special and unusual language is used, there
is a reason. Holy writ is not idle chatter; it is the mind and will of the

Lord; it says what he wants said. And so it now behooves us to learn why it is one thing to gather Israel from the four parts of the earth and yet another to lead the Ten Tribes from the land of the north.

"We have already seen that all Israel, including specifically and pointedly the Ten Tribes, is scattered in all the nations of the earth, upon all the islands of the sea, and among every people who dwell on this planet. . . .

"We are also aware that the Ten Tribes were first taken as a body into Assyria; that they went out from Assyria, northward, in a body, under prophetic guidance; and that they were then splintered and driven and scattered into all places and among all peoples. These Ten Tribes, no matter where they are located, are in nations and places known in the days of Isaiah and Jeremiah and the ancient prophets as the north countries. Hence, their return to Palestine at least will be from the land of the north.

"The tribe of Ephraim is one of the Ten Tribes; and her people became wanderers in the nations, where they now reside and where they are now being found and gathered, one of a city and two of a family, into the stakes of Zion in those nations. This gathering of Israel is not to an American Zion; it is not to Palestine and the ancient holy land; it is not to any central place or location. Rather, it is to the holy places of safety that are now being set up in all nations as rapidly as our strength and means permit. As we have seen, this gathering of Ephraim falls in the category of the gathering of Israel and not of the leading of the Ten Tribes from the land of the north. This gathering of Ephraim is into the stakes of Zion in all the nations of the earth. There are, of course, isolated and unusual instances of people from the other lost tribes gathering with Ephraim, but these are few and far between. The gathering of these other tribes is not yet, but by and by. . . .

" . . . But with the Ten Tribes, in part at least, it will be another thing. They are destined to return (at least in large and representative numbers) to the same soil where the feet of their forebears walked during the days of their mortal pilgrimage. They are to return to Palestine. At least a constituent assembly will congregate there in the very land given of God to Abraham their father. Others will, of course, be in America and in all lands, but the formal return, the return from the north countries, will be to the land of their ancient inheritance" (*Millennial Messiah*, 319–21).

110:12 *Elias*. Discussions about the identity and mission of Elias demand attention and a careful reading of the texts involved. Two doctrines and a number of prophets are involved. First, Elias is a title properly given to a prophet whose office or calling is that of a forerunner, that is, one who prepares the way for something greater. The Aaronic Priesthood, for instance, could be called the Priesthood of Elias because it is a preparatory priesthood. It prepares the way for that which is greater (JST Matthew 17:11, 13). Second, there is a doctrine of Elias that pertains to restoration rather than preparation (JST Matthew 17:9–10). Scripture speaks of John the Baptist as an Elias of preparation (Luke 1:16–17; JST John 1:21–22) and Christ as an Elias of restoration (JST John 1:26–28). The name Elias can also be a title for those prophets who play a part in the restoration of all things. For instance, John the Revelator is referred to as Elias in section 77 (vv. 9 and 14); in the present text another prophet is identified as an Elias restoring keys from the dispensation of Abraham. In section 27 we are told that Gabriel (whom the Prophet Joseph Smith identified as Noah) holds the keys of the restoration of all things (*Teachings of the Prophet Joseph Smith,* 157; D&C 27:5–6).

The identity of the Elias in the present text is not entirely certain. It could have been Abraham himself or Melchizedek, either of whom could have restored keys from that dispensation. It is frequently said that it was Noah, because he is identified as an Elias in Doctrine and Covenants 27:5–6. This, however, seems unlikely, as Noah's life did not overlap that of Abraham (Bible Dictionary, 636). It is something of a strain on the order of heaven to suppose that Noah would restore the keys of a dispensation in which he did not live. Further, the text from which this conclusion is made identifies Noah as holding the keys of the restoration of all things. This seems to mean that all the Eliases who came to restore keys in this dispensation (or in the meridian of time) did so under Noah's direction, not that he restored all the keys (McConkie, *Millennial Messiah,* 103–4, 115–21; McConkie, *Mormon Doctrine,* 219–22).

The dispensation of the gospel of Abraham. The gospel of Abraham is that power and authority distinctive to Abraham and the covenant that God made with him. A "dispensation" of that gospel is the giving of it anew, or its restoration to those willing to enter into a like covenant. Thus all promises made to Abraham relative to his seed—the endless continuation of his family and his eternal relationship with his wife Sarah— are granted to all who receive that same gospel. The keys to perform the ordinances were restored by the Elias spoken of in this verse; the keys to seal this and all gospel ordinances were restored by Elijah.

In us and our seed all generations after us should be blessed. The promises given to Abraham, Isaac, and Jacob are here given to Joseph Smith and Oliver Cowdery. Through these keys the priesthood can be extended to any who are married by this authority in the house of the Lord. Among the blessings of temple marriage are the promise of eternal increase and the promise that the seed of those so married will have right to the priesthood and will be called upon to take the blessings of salvation and eternal life to all nations (Abraham 2:9, 11).

Elijah Returns and Confers the Keys of His Dispensation
DOCTRINE AND COVENANTS 110:13–16

110:13–14 *Elijah the prophet . . . before the great and dreadful day.* The Old Testament ends with the promise that Elijah the prophet would visit the earth prior to "the great and dreadful day" of the Lord's return (Malachi 4:5). Though there may be no plainer prophecy in all of holy writ, its meaning has been entirely lost to most Christians, who assume that this prophecy was fulfilled with Elijah's appearance on the Mount of Transfiguration (Matthew 17:1–13). This event, in which Peter, James, and John, who were with Christ on the Mount, were charged to keep secret (Matthew 17:9), hardly fits the description of a "great and dreadful day." Not even the faithful members of the Church in that day knew of it, nor would it generally be known for generations to come. Further, the context in which the prophecy is given is the destruction of the wicked by fire while the righteous inherit the millennial earth, which assuredly did not take place at that time (Malachi 4:1–3). See commentary on Joseph Smith–History 1:37, page 23.

110:15 *Hearts of the fathers.* That separation known to us as death brings with it a heightened concern for our children and our children's children throughout their generations. Those in the spirit world have a great interest in and concern for their progeny yet in the flesh.

Children to the fathers. As the hearts of the fathers turn to their children, so will the hearts of the children turn to their fathers. This is evidenced by members of the Church going to the house of the Lord to perform vicarious ordinances in behalf of their kindred dead. As the dead accept those ordinances, they assure themselves of a place in an eternal family.

Smitten with a curse. Moroni rendered this "utterly wasted" when he appeared to Joseph in September 1823 (D&C 2:3). The world will be saved in family units. Since salvation centers in the Abrahamic covenant, to fail to enter into that covenant through marriage and the eternal sealing of family units is to squander the purpose of mortality. The earth was created to facilitate the natural and proper love between a man and a woman. In marriage they are to become "one flesh," the Lord said, "and all this that the earth might answer the end of its creation; And that it might be filled with the measure of man, according to his creation before the world was made" (D&C 49:16–17). Simply stated, salvation is a family affair. In subsequent years Joseph Smith learned how this authority restored by Elijah applied as well to our kindred dead. Moreover he learned that they—after the gospel was preached to them in the world of spirits—could by proxy have all the ordinances of salvation performed for them in the house of the Lord. See commentary on Doctrine and Covenants 127, 128, and 138.

110:16 *The keys of this dispensation are committed into your hands.* These are the keys of the sealing power by which gospel ordinances for both the living and the dead are sealed. This explains Moroni's statement that God would reveal the priesthood, meaning the purpose and function of the priesthood (see D&C 2:1), through Elijah. The authority restored by Elijah binds or seals every ordinance so that it is of "efficacy, virtue, or force in and after the resurrection from the dead" (D&C 132:7). Further, because of that authority restored by Elijah, ordinances can be performed for our kindred dead whereby the same blessings and promises can extend to those who died without the opportunity to receive them while in the flesh.

DOCTRINE AND COVENANTS 111

DATE: 6 AUGUST 1836
PLACE: SALEM, MASSACHUSETTS

Following the pentecostal season associated with the dedication of the Kirtland Temple, it was necessary that the Saints attend to the temporal needs of the Church. Heavy debt hung over the Church because of loans secured to procure land (see commentary on D&C 104) and to build the temple.

Ebenezer Robinson, an early member of the Church who served for a time as the Prophet's scribe, reported on a possible solution that had presented itself. "There came to Kirtland a brother by the name of Burgess who stated that he had knowledge of a large amount of money secreted in the cellar of a certain house in Salem, Massachusetts, which had belonged to a widow (then deceased), and thought he was the only person who had knowledge of it, or of the location of the house" (Roberts, *Comprehensive History*, 1:411).

The Prophet Joseph Smith wrote: "On . . . July 25th, in company with Sidney Rigdon, Brother Hyrum Smith, and Oliver Cowdery, I left Kirtland" to travel to New York City. These brethren met with creditors in New York for four days. "From New York we continued our journey to Providence, on board a steamer," the Prophet further wrote, "from thence to Boston, by steam cars, and arrived in Salem, Massachusetts, early in August, where we hired a house, and occupied the same during the month, teaching the people from house to house, and preaching publicly, as opportunity presented; visiting occasionally, sections of the surrounding country, which are rich in the history of the Pilgrim Fathers of New England, in Indian warfare, religious superstition, bigotry, persecution, and learned ignorance" (*History of the Church*, 2:463–64). The day after arriving in Salem the Prophet received the revelation recorded as section 111.

The outcome of the journey is recorded in B. H. Roberts's *Comprehensive History*: "Burgess, according to [Ebenezer] Robinson, met the brethren in Salem, but claimed that time had wrought such changes in the town that he could not for a certainty point out the house 'and soon left'" (*Comprehensive History*, 1:411).

The Lord Had Treasure in Salem
DOCTRINE AND COVENANTS 111:1–11

111:1 *Not displeased with your coming this journey.* Lest discouragement overtake these brethren after the disappointing news that Brother Burgess could not tell them the location of the treasure, the Lord revealed that he was not angry with their efforts in seeking solutions to their debts.

Notwithstanding your follies. The Prophet's folly lay less in the fanciful hope of finding a treasure than it did in his failure to counsel with the Lord. A little over two years earlier he had received direction from the Lord about the Church's indebtedness. At that time the Saints were told that if they would humble themselves and be prayerful and diligent that he would send means for their deliverance (D&C 104:78–80). The trip to Salem was a venture of their own design, not one of divine direction.

111:2 *I have much treasure in this city.* The hidden treasure in Salem, that which is of greatest worth to God, was his children (v. 10). In the Old Testament the house of Israel was referred to as the Lord's "peculiar treasure" (Exodus 19:5; Psalm 135:4). The references here to his gathering them out for "the benefit of Zion" suggest that the city was rich in the blood of Israel.

Through your instrumentality. The Prophet Joseph Smith and his companions did not have success in preaching the gospel in Salem. However, five years later to the day, Elder Erastus Snow began his missionary labors there. The result of his efforts included the organization of a branch numbering about a hundred members, many of whom later joined the Saints in Nauvoo, Illinois.

111:4 *I will give this city into your hands.* In some future day, perhaps in the Millennium, the city of Salem (meaning the city of Peace) will be governed by righteous men holding the priesthood of God. These will have the necessary power and authority to draw upon its wealth to the blessing of all of its inhabitants.

They shall not discover your secret parts. This is a Hebrew idiom meaning embarrassment or shame (Isaiah 3:17). Their embarrassment centered in the financial plight that brought them to Salem in search of treasures.

111:5 *Your debts.* This refers to the debt incurred by the Prophet Joseph Smith and other Church leaders as agents for the Church in buying land, building the Kirtland Temple, and stocking Church-owned mercantile establishments. Most of the debt was in the form of contracts, which had been entered into for the purpose of purchasing property and goods received on credit from merchants. It is difficult from extant records to determine the exact amount of accumulative debt contracted at this time.

111:9 *This place you may obtain by hire.* The brethren rented a house in Salem for a month (Smith, *History of the Church,* 2:464).

Inquire diligently concerning the more ancient inhabitants and founders of this city. This revelation, which directs an interest in their kindred dead, comes some years before the principles associated with temple work had been revealed. It was given in Salem, the county seat of Essex County, Massachusetts. Robert Smith, the first of the Prophet Joseph Smith's family in America, had settled here. Similarly, record of many of the progenitors of the early families in the Church would later be found here.

DOCTRINE AND COVENANTS 112

DATE: 23 JULY 1837
PLACE: KIRTLAND, OHIO

This revelation was given during some of the darkest days in the history of the Church. As night follows the day, so the light and glory that surrounded the dedication of the Kirtland Temple was supplanted by darkness and evil. In the summer of 1837, members of the Quorum of the Twelve, witnesses to the Book of Mormon, and other key priesthood leaders met in the upper room of the temple to dispose of Joseph Smith as the prophet of the Lord. Their plan was to organize a new Church, with David Whitmer at its head. They had determined to reject the Prophet, the Book of Mormon, and the priesthood, while seeking to unite the Christian world around repentance, baptism, and the Bible (George A. Smith, *Journal of Discourses*, 11:11).

In the midst of this darkness, Joseph Smith said, "God revealed to me that something new must be done for the salvation of His Church" (*History of the Church*, 2:489). Heber C. Kimball reported that the Prophet Joseph Smith came to him while he was in the Kirtland Temple and said, "Brother Heber, the Spirit of the Lord has whispered to me: 'Let my servant Heber go to England and proclaim my Gospel, and open the door of salvation to that nation'" (Whitney, *Life of Heber C. Kimball*, 104).

Section 112 was given on the day the gospel was first preached in England. It was directed to Thomas B. Marsh, then the president of the Quorum of the Twelve and the man thus entitled to a revelation on the duties of that quorum. This revelation is of singular importance in identifying the rights and authority of the Twelve in declaring the gospel to the nations of the earth and in specifying their relationship to the First Presidency.

The Twelve Are to Take the Gospel to All Nations and People

DOCTRINE AND COVENANTS 112:1–10

112:1 *Thine alms have come up as a memorial before me.* These same words were spoken by the angel of the Lord who appeared to Cornelius, a

898

Gentile, directing him to send for Peter, from whom he and his family received the gospel (Acts 10:1–4). It was, the angel said, Cornelius's alms, meaning good works, that opened the heavens and its blessings to him. In like manner the Lord spoke to Lehi in a dream, saying, "Blessed art thou Lehi, because of the things which thou hast done; and because thou hast been faithful and declared unto this people the things which I commanded thee" (1 Nephi 2:1). This principle, often repeated in scripture, is that the heavens are opened to those whose works are works of righteousness.

Were chosen to bear testimony of my name. In the revelation given to the Twelve at the time they were called, the Lord said, "The twelve traveling councilors are called to be the Twelve Apostles, or special witnesses of the name of Christ in all the world—thus differing from other officers in the church in the duties of their calling" (D&C 107:23).

112:4 *Thou shalt bear record of my name.* It is the office and calling of an apostle to testify of Christ and of all that properly bears his name, that is, all that is done under the direction of the priesthood. It is the duty of the Twelve to both teach the gospel among the nations of the earth and to see that the affairs of the Church are properly regulated wherever it had been organized.

112:5 *Contend thou.* In the early nineteenth century, this phrase meant to "use earnest efforts to obtain, or to defend and preserve" (Webster, *Dictionary*, 1828, s.v. "contend").

112:6 *Publishing my name.* The Twelve are to make the gospel known among all men.

112:7 *Let thy feet be shod.* To have one's feet shod meant to have one's shoes on and to be ready to travel. To show that they were ready for their journey, the Israelites were commanded to eat the Passover with their shoes on (Exodus 12:11). Similarly, Christ commanded his disciples to be "shod with sandals" (Mark 6:9) that they might be ready to go and publish the gospel. The Lord here directs Thomas B. Marsh to stand ready to travel in the duty of his office.

Thy path lieth among the mountains. Isaiah wrote, "How beautiful upon the mountains are the feet of him that bringeth good tidings, that publisheth peace; that bringeth good tidings of good, that publisheth salvation; that saith unto Zion, Thy God reigneth!" (Isaiah 52:7). The revelations of the Restoration use the same imagery to announce glad tidings, particularly of the going forth of the Book of Mormon (D&C 128:19).

112:8 See Luke 1:52.

112:10 Thomas B. Marsh's failure to heed the counsel given him in this verse caused the Spirit of the Lord eventually to withdraw from him. George A. Smith, Heber C. Kimball, and Orson Hyde all relate interesting experiences regarding Elder Marsh's rejection of the Lord's admonitions and his apostasy from the Church. George A. Smith tells the story: "The wife of Thomas B. Marsh, who was then President of the Twelve Apostles, and sister Harris concluded they would exchange milk, in order to make a little larger cheese than they otherwise could. To be sure to have justice done, it was agreed that they should not save the strippings, but that the milk and strippings should all go together. Small matters to talk about here, to be sure, two women's exchanging milk to make cheese.

"Mrs. Harris, it appeared, was faithful to the agreement and carried to Mrs. Marsh the milk and strippings, but Mrs. Marsh, wishing to make some extra good cheese, saved a pint of strippings from each cow and sent Mrs. Harris the milk without the strippings.

"Finally it leaked out that Mrs. Marsh had saved strippings, and it became a matter to be settled by the Teachers. They began to examine the matter, and it was proved that Mrs. Marsh had saved the strippings, and consequently had wronged Mrs. Harris out of that amount. An appeal was taken from the Teacher to the Bishop, and a regular Church trial was had. President Marsh did not consider that the Bishop had done him and his lady justice, for they decided that the strippings were wrongfully saved, and that the woman had violated her covenant.

"Marsh immediately took an appeal to the High Council, who investigated the question with much patience, and I assure you they were a grave body. Marsh being extremely anxious to maintain the character of his wife, as he was the President of the Twelve Apostles, and a great man in Israel, made a desperate defence, but the High Council finally confirmed the Bishop's decision.

"Marsh, not being satisfied, took an appeal to the First Presidency of the Church, and Joseph and his Counsellors had to sit upon the case, and they approved the decision of the High Council.

"This little affair, you will observe, kicked up a considerable breeze, and Thomas B. Marsh then declared that he would sustain the character of his wife, even if he had to go to hell for it.

"The then President of the Twelve Apostles, the man who should have been the first to do justice and cause reparation to be made for wrong, committed by any member of his family, took that position, and what next? He went before a magistrate and swore that the 'Mormons' were hostile towards the State of Missouri.

"That affidavit brought from the government of Missouri an exterminating order, which drove some 15,000 Saints from their homes and habitations" (*Journal of Discourses*, 3:283–84).

Heber C. Kimball reported that "about the time he [Thomas B. Marsh] was preparing to leave this Church, he received a revelation in the Printing Office. He retired to himself, and prayed, and was humble, and God gave him a revelation, and he wrote it. There were from three to five pages of it; and when he came out, he read it to brother Brigham [Young] and me. In it God told him what to do, and that was to sustain brother Joseph and to believe that what brother Joseph had said was true. But no; he took a course to sustain his wife and oppose the Prophet of God, and she led him away" (*Journal of Discourses*, 5:28).

Last, we learn from Orson Hyde, who partook of the spirit of apostasy with Thomas B. Marsh, "During our temptation, David W. Patten was shot by the enemy, and several days afterward while Thos. B. and myself were sitting in a log cabin together in silent meditation, some being smote him on the shoulder, and said, with a countenance full of deepest anxiety and solicitude, 'Thomas! Thomas! why have you so soon forgotten?' Thomas told me it was David W. Patten, with whom, he not long before, had made a covenant to remain true and faithful until the end" (cited in Anderson, "Being Valiant," 42).

Revelation Given to Thomas B. Marsh
on the Duties of the Twelve
DOCTRINE AND COVENANTS 112:11–15

112:12 *Let them be admonished for all their sins.* No good man has ever escaped the attention of the adversary. Satan, who confronted the Savior face to face, can be expected to show like attention to all who have been called to bear witness of his name. To the Nephite Twelve the Savior said, "Verily, verily, I say unto you, ye must watch and pray always, lest ye be tempted by the devil, and ye be led away captive by him" (3 Nephi 18:15). Apostles labor with the same temptations and frailties as do all other men.

112:13 *After their temptations, and much tribulation.* Of these difficult times in Kirtland, John Taylor wrote, "There was a very bitter feeling gotten up by a number of men who had apostatized. Parley P. Pratt was one who was affected. He, however, did not go to the length that some did; and Orson Pratt had partaken more or less of that spirit" (*Gospel Kingdom*, 189). As a measure of his integrity, Elder Pratt recounted this experience in his autobiography, saying, "About this time, after I had returned from Canada, there were jarrings and discords in the Church at Kirtland, and many fell away and became enemies and apostates. There were also envy-ings, lyings, strifes, and divisions, which caused much trouble and sorrow. By such spirits I was also accused, misrepresented, and abused. And at one time, I also was overcome by the same spirit in a great measure, and it seemed as if the very powers of darkness which war against the Saints were let loose upon me. But the Lord knew my faith, my zeal, my integrity of purpose, and he gave me the victory.

"I went to Brother Joseph Smith in tears, and, with a broken heart and contrite spirit, confessed wherein I had erred in spirit, murmured, or done or said amiss. He frankly forgave me, prayed for me, and blessed me. Thus, by experience I learned more fully to discern and to contrast the two spirits, and to resist the one and cleave to the other. And, being tempted in all points, even as others, I learned how to bear with, and excuse, and succor those who are tempted" (Pratt, *Autobiography*, 144).

We are told that Orson Hyde had come close to defecting but per-chance walked in on the meeting in which Heber C. Kimball was being set apart for his mission to England. Humbled by the spirit that he felt, he acknowledged his faults to the Prophet, sought forgiveness, and asked to accompany Elder Kimball on his mission. The Prophet set him apart to that calling, and he later played a significant role in that mission that proved to be the salvation of the Church (Talbot, *Acts of the Modern Apostles*, 37).

Many others did not repent. Luke S. Johnson, Lyman E. Johnson, and John F. Boynton were dropped from the Quorum of the Twelve in the conference held on 3 September 1837, less than a month and a half after this revelation was given. See commentary on verse 15, "Rebel not against my servant Joseph."

They shall be converted. As this refers to the Quorum of the Twelve Apostles, it thus raises the question: How could men be called to the apostleship and at the same time not be converted? First, it should be noted that having a testimony and being converted are not necessarily the same thing. A testimony comes by the witness of the Spirit and leaves one with the knowledge that something is true. Conversion, on the other hand, is the fruit, or reward, of acting on the witness of the Spirit.

Conversion comes only in discipleship, in living the gospel. To be converted is to be born again, to put off the world and walk with the Saints. It comes by putting off the natural man and putting on Christ. Thus true conversion is a process and comes only in the course of time.

The apostle Peter is the classical illustration of a convert. After he accepted Jesus as the Messiah, after he was baptized, after he spent three full years in almost constant companionship with the Son of God, after he was ordained an elder and an apostle, after he went forth on a mission healing the sick and performing other miracles, after he walked on the water amid the tempestuous waves of the Galilean sea, after he bore a fervent witness of the Savior's divinity, after all this and more, Jesus said to him: "When thou art converted, strengthen thy brethren" (Luke 22:32). It was only then that Peter was reconciled to God and became a new creature by the power of the Holy Ghost. Peter's conversion was manifest in his valiant actions from the time of the first Pentecost after the death of Christ until he, too, died upon a Roman cross (John 21:18).

112:14 *Take up your cross.* See commentary on Doctrine and Covenants 23:7.

Follow me. This divine injunction, repeatedly given to the Twelve in the meridian of time, marks the true path of salvation. Salvation is not merely found in professing Christ but rather in following, or emulating, him (v. 26).

112:15 *Exalt not yourselves.* The primary charge of apostleship is to teach the gospel of Jesus Christ. All their time, talents, and interests are to be centered in that ministry. All else is secondary. They are personal ambassadors of Christ. Thus it is not their purpose to promote themselves nor a personal point of view. The apostles are to know the gospel of him for whom they have been called to speak. To go beyond that gospel is a usurpation of stewardship.

Rebel not against my servant Joseph. The spirit of darkness in Kirtland in 1837 was so pervasive that no quorum of the priesthood could escape it. Nor was this mist of darkness quick to lift. "At the quarterly conference assembled at Far West, April 7, 1838, David W. Patten declared that, as a member of the Quorum of the Twelve, he could confidently recommend Thomas B. Marsh, Brigham Young, Heber C. Kimball, Orson Hyde, Parley P. Pratt, and Orson Pratt as being men of God. However, in a spirit of discernment rather than of disparagement, he stated that he somewhat doubted William Smith, and that he could not recommend William E. McLellin, Luke S. Johnson, Lyman E. Johnson, or John F.

Boynton. As time was to prove, Elder Patten's discernments were valid" (Talbot, *Acts of the Modern Apostles*, 40).

John Taylor, who would be called to fill the place of one of the fallen apostles in December the following year, had occasion to counsel Parley P. Pratt, also an apostle and the missionary who had converted him (see commentary on v. 13, "After their temptations, and much tribulation"). Elder Taylor recounted part of that dialogue thus: "I am surprised to hear you speak so, Brother Parley. Before you left Canada you bore a strong testimony to Joseph Smith being a Prophet of God, and to the truth of the work he has inaugurated; and you said you knew these things by revelation, and the gift of the Holy Ghost. You gave me a strict charge to the effect that though you or an angel from heaven was to declare anything else I was not to believe it. Now Brother Parley, it is not man that I am following but the Lord. The principles you taught me led me to Him, and I now have the same testimony that you then rejoiced in. If the work was true six months ago, it is true today: if Joseph was then a prophet, he is now a prophet" (Roberts, *Life of John Taylor*, 40).

The keys . . . shall not be taken from him. See commentary on Doctrine and Covenants 90:3.

Those Who Receive the First Presidency Receive the Lord
DOCTRINE AND COVENANTS 112:16–20

112:16–18 Each member of the Quorum of the Twelve holds all the keys of the kingdom, which they receive at the time of their ordination to that quorum. Nevertheless, they use those keys—which constitute the right of presidency—only under the direction of the First Presidency and their own quorum president. Such discipline is essential if the Lord's house is to remain a house of order.

112:17 In this verse the First Presidency is announced as consisting of Joseph Smith, Sidney Rigdon, and Hyrum Smith. Perhaps the earliest manuscript of this revelation was recorded by Fredrick G. Williams (Woodford, *Historical Development*, 1479). What makes this of special interest is that Elder Williams was the second counselor in the presidency at the time. Various sources help us understand the context of the receiving of this revelation:

1. From the *Kirtland Council Minute Book* we learn that on 29 May (about two months before this revelation was received) complaints had been brought before the Kirtland High Council against Fredrick G.

Williams, David Whitmer, Parley P. Pratt, Lyman Johnson, and Warren Parrish. Elder Williams disputed the council's authority according to "the Book of Covenants" to try him because as a member of the First Presidency he was to be tried by a "Bishop's Court," meaning a court presided over by the presiding bishop as specified in the revelation on priesthood given 28 March 1835 (D&C 107:82). It was rightly agreed that the council did not have the authority to try him and charges against him were dismissed (*Kirtland Council Minute Book*, 181–84).

2. It was apparently in July that Joseph Smith learned that money was missing from the Kirtland Safety Society. He went immediately to Fredrick G. Williams, the appointed magistrate, to obtain a search warrant. In her history the Prophet's mother, Lucy Mack Smith, says this was "flatly refused" and then records the following dialogue between the Prophet and his counselor: "'If you will give me a warrant, I can get the money, but if you do not, I will break you of your office.'

"'Well, break it is then,' said Williams, 'and we will strike hands upon it.'

"'Very well,' said Joseph, 'from henceforth I drop you from my quorum, in the name of the Lord,' and Williams in wrath replied, 'Amen.'

"Joseph entered a complaint against him, for neglect of duty as an officer of justice, on which account his ministry was taken from him, and given to Oliver Cowdery" (Smith, *History of Joseph Smith*, 335–36).

3. Ezra Granger Williams, son of Fredrick G. Williams, claims to have been present on the occasion when his father and Joseph Smith verbally crossed swords and Joseph dropped him as a counselor. As he tells the story, Joseph wanted to borrow money and his father would not authorize it. Shortly thereafter he said the Prophet returned and "on bended knees, crying like a child, humbly asked my father's forgiveness, admitting that he was wrong and that my father was right. He pleaded with him to still be friends and to continue by his side as usual. My father gladly forgave him, but answered, 'No, as the people would never have the confidence in him again that they had had before'" (Williams, "Frederick Granger Williams," 256).

4. Though the Prophet's contrition in the above account seems exaggerated, it certainly was in character for him to freely acknowledge errors if he felt that he had made them. Assuming this to be the case in this instance, it would not have been unusual for Fredrick G. Williams to return to his aid in recording this revelation and at the same time not to

be offended or surprised when Hyrum Smith was named as a counselor in the presidency in his stead.

5. At a conference held 3 September 1837, "President Smith . . . presented Sidney Rigdon and Frederick G. Williams as his counselors, and to constitute with himself the three first Presidents of the Church. Voted unanimously in the affirmative, except for Frederick G. Williams, which was not carried unanimously.

"President Smith then introduced Oliver Cowdery, Joseph Smith, Sen., Hyrum Smith, and John Smith for assistant counselors. These last four, together with the first three, are to be considered the heads of the Church. Carried unanimously" (Smith, *History of the Church*, 2:509).

6. "At a conference of the Church held 7 November 1837, at Far West, the proposal to sustain President Williams in the presidency again met with opposition, and, after a lengthy debate, Hyrum Smith was nominated to take his place" (Williams, "Frederick Granger Williams," 256–57).

7. President Joseph Fielding Smith notes that on 8 July 1838 the Prophet received a revelation for the benefit of Frederick G. Williams and William W. Phelps. Of Elder Williams, President Joseph Fielding Smith observed, "The Prophet loved him dearly and wrote in his record: 'Brother Frederick G. Williams is one of those men in whom I place the greatest confidence and trust, for I have found him ever full of love and brotherly kindness. He is not a man of many words, but is ever winning, because of his constant mind.' (*D.H.C.* 1:444.) He partook of the rebellious spirit in Kirtland and had to be released from his high calling and lost his standing in the Church. He was baptized again, however, August 5, 1838, upon a show of repentance" (*Church History and Modern Revelation*, 2:99).

The revelation the Prophet received for the benefit of Frederick G. Willilams and Willliam W. Phelps reads as follows:

"Verily, thus saith the Lord, in consequence of their transgressions their former standing has been taken away from them, and now, if they will be saved, let them be ordained as Elders in my Church to preach my Gospel and travel abroad from land to land and from place to place, to gather mine elect unto me, saith the Lord, and let this be their labors from henceforth. Amen" (Smith, *History of the Church*, 3:46n).

112:20 To accept the Lord is to accept his word, it is to find his will and do it. Conversely, to reject his word—the revelations he gives through his anointed servants—is to reject him. Just as we cannot with consistency say we love the Father while rejecting the Son, neither can we profess to love the Son while rejecting those whom he has sent in his name to do his bidding. To accept his servants is to accept him, to reject them is to reject him.

Trials in Kirtland Separated the Wicked from the Righteous
DOCTRINE AND COVENANTS 112:21–29

112:21 *Send them.* See Doctrine and Covenants 84:107–8; 107:33–34.

112:23–26. In the imagery of a New Testament parable, the gospel net had been cast out and all kinds of fish had been gathered in (Matthew 13:47–50). The failure of the Kirtland Anti-Banking Society would result in a sorting of the good fish from the bad, as it were. This separation did much to cleanse the Church of those who would not have the faith to accept that which would be revealed in Nauvoo and to make the journey West. These verses also apply to a future day when the true Saints will be separated from those who only profess to be Saints.

112:23 A world blinded by sin is not able to see the light of the gospel. In the "Preface" to the Doctrine and Covenants (section 1), the Lord declared, "He that repents not, from him shall be taken even the light which he has received; for my Spirit shall not always strive with man" (v. 33). Later, he said, "That wicked one cometh and taketh away light and truth, through disobedience, from the children of men (D&C 93:39).

112:26 *Blasphemed agains me in the midst of my house.* See commentary on Doctrine and Covenants 110:8. "Do not pollute this holy house."

The Keys of the Kingdom are Held by the First Presidency and the Twelve
DOCTRINE AND COVENANTS 112:30–34

112:30–32 These verses teach that each member of the Quorum of the Twelve Apostles and the First Presidency holds all the keys of the kingdom. That is, each member of these two quorums would hold all the keys of the kingdom. For this reason we now sustain the members of these two quorums as prophets, seers, and revelators. This, however, was not the case when this revelation was given. It was not until the end of Joseph Smith's ministry in Nauvoo that all the keys had been restored in fulness to the Twelve.

Wilford Woodruff described the time bestowal of these keys: "In the winter of 1843–4, Joseph Smith, the Prophet of God, called the Twelve Apostles together in the City of Nauvoo, and spent many days with us in giving us our endowments, and teaching us those glorious principles which God had revealed to him. And upon one occasion he stood upon his feet in our midst for nearly three hours declaring unto us the great and last dispensation which God had set His hand to perform upon the earth in these last days. The room was filled as if with consuming fire; the Prophet was clothed upon with much of the power of God, and his face shone and was transparently clear, and he closed that speech, never-to-be-forgotten in time or in eternity, with the following language:

"'Brethren, I have had great sorrow of heart for fear that I might be taken from the earth with the keys of the Kingdom of God upon me, without sealing them upon the heads of other men. God has sealed upon my head all the keys of the Kingdom of God necessary for organizing and building up of the Church, Zion, and Kingdom of God upon the earth, and to prepare the Saints for the coming of the Son of Man. Now, brethren, I thank God I have lived to see the day that I have been enabled to give you your endowments, and I have now sealed upon your heads all the powers of the Aaronic and Melchizedek Priesthoods and Apostleship, with all the keys and powers thereof, which God has sealed upon me; and I now roll off all the labor, burden and care of this Church and Kingdom of God upon your shoulders, and I now command you in the name of the Lord Jesus Christ to round up your shoulders, and bear off this Church and Kingdom of God before heaven and earth, and before God, angels and men; and if you don't do it you will be damned'" (Clark, *Messages*, 3:134).

112:30 *Priesthood given, for . . . the last time.* Various dispensations have required a restoration of the priesthood with all its keys, powers, and authority. Ours is the last such dispensation. As foreseen by the prophet Daniel, the restored gospel and the reestablished Church would never again be lost or left to "other people" (Daniel 2:44). These verses assured the Saints that those who sought to overthrow the Church in Kirtland would not be successful.

112:31 See commentary on Doctrine and Covenants 128:15, 18.

112:34 *I come quickly.* This description of the Lord's return tells how the Lord will come rather then when. Although no man knows the day or hour of his coming, this phrase teaches that when he appears it will be suddenly, catching the wicked unawares.

DOCTRINE AND COVENANTS 113

DATE: MARCH 1838 (AFTER 14 MARCH)
PLACE: FAR WEST, MISSOURI

In the story of the Restoration, the most trying of circumstances consistently brought forth the richest treasures of heaven. As the spirit of apostasy continued to grow in Kirtland, it became necessary for the Prophet to flee for his own safety. Of January 1838 Joseph Smith recorded, "A new year dawned upon the Church in Kirtland in all the bitterness of the spirit of apostate mobocracy; which continued to rage and grow hotter and hotter, until Elder Rigdon and myself were obliged to flee from its deadly influence, as did the Apostles and Prophets of old, and as Jesus said, 'when they persecute you in one city, flee to another.' On the evening of the 12th of January, about ten o'clock, we left Kirtland, on horseback, to escape mob violence, which was about to burst upon us under the color of legal process to cover the hellish designs of our enemies, and to save themselves from the just judgment of the law. . . .

"The weather was extremely cold, we were obliged to secrete ourselves in our wagons, sometimes, to elude the grasp of our pursuers, who continued their pursuit of us more than two hundred miles from Kirtland, armed with pistols and guns, seeking our lives. They frequently crossed our track, twice they were in the houses where we stopped, once we tarried all night in the same house with them, with only a partition between us and them; and heard their oaths and imprecations, and threats concerning us, if they could catch us; and late in the evening they came in to our room and examined us, but decided we were not the men. At other times we passed them in the streets, and gazed upon them, and they on us, but they knew us not. One Lyons was one of our pursuers" (*History of the Church*, 3:1–3).

On 14 March the Prophet arrived at Far West, Missouri, where he was welcomed by the Saints. On that day or shortly thereafter, he received the following revelation. The particular circumstances that called it forth are not known. We do know, however, that Isaiah 11 was of particular interest to Joseph Smith because it was one of the chief passages quoted to him by Moroni when Moroni initially came to instruct him (Joseph Smith–History 1:40).

The Stem, Rod, and Root of Jesse Are Identified
DOCTRINE AND COVENANTS 113:1–6

113:1–4 The text referred to in Isaiah reads: "And there shall come forth a rod out of the stem of Jesse, and a Branch shall grow out of his roots: And the spirit of the Lord shall rest upon him, the spirit of wisdom and understanding, the spirit of counsel and might, the spirit of knowledge and of the fear of the Lord; and shall make him of quick understanding in the fear of the Lord: and he shall not judge after the sight of his eyes, neither reprove after the hearing of his ears: but with righteousness shall he judge the poor, and reprove with equity for the meek of the earth: and he shall smite the earth with the rod of his mouth, and with the breath of his lips shall he slay the wicked. And righteousness shall be the girdle of his loins, and faithfulness the girdle of his reins" (Isaiah 11:1–5). The Prophet Joseph Smith indicated that on the night of 21 September 1823 Moroni "quoted the eleventh chapter of Isaiah, saying that it was about to be fulfilled" (Joseph Smith–History 1:40).

113:1 The last two verses of Isaiah 10 speak of the Lord, or the forester, trimming and thinning the trees in the forest. These trees represent the power and glory of foreign rulers and, of course, their nations. Thus the dead wood and overgrowth is removed to prepare the way for a new shoot or "stem" to grow out of the stump of Jesse. Through this imagery we are invited to look at the stump of a once great tree to see a new branch spring forth. In other words, after the great dynasty or tree of David is cut down a new branch of the royal family will spring forth. The intent of this imagery is, in a veiled way, to say that Christ will be a descendant of Jesse, the father of David, and that from that "stem" will come a "rod" who will be the great prophet of the Restoration.

113:3 *The rod . . . that should come of the Stem of Jesse.* As indicated in the following verse, the rod represents a servant of Christ. The rod (Hebrew, *choter*) grows as an offshoot from the stem or trunk of the tree. It is allowed to grow into a sturdy branch that, when cut from the tree, is used as a shepherd's staff. The point of attachment to the tree is taken with the branch and worked into a thick knot on the head of the staff, which the shepherd uses both as a weapon against predators and to direct his flock. Isaiah's imagery is a perfect description of a rod that "is a servant in the hands of Christ" (v. 4), the Good Shepherd.

113:3–6 This revelation must have been a source of great consolation to Joseph Smith particularly in the time and circumstances that called it forth. Both the "rod" and the "root" in the Isaiah prophecy refer to the Prophet. We would assume both innate modesty and the sacred implications of this prophecy precluded any more direct expression from Joseph than that which the revelation contains.

By revelation the Saints had already been told that Joseph Smith had claim to the priesthood through the lineage of his fathers (D&C 86:8–10). That he held the keys of the kingdom was also known to them (D&C 27:13; 35:17–18; 65:2; 81:2; 90:3; 112:32). That he held these keys by right, meaning birthright, was affirmed in the patriarchal blessing given him by his father. That blessing reads as follows:

"'A marvelous work and a wonder' has the Lord wrought by thy hand, even that which shall prepare the way for the remnants of his people to come in among the Gentiles, with their fulness, as the tribes of Israel are restored. I bless thee with the blessings of thy fathers Abraham, Isaac and Jacob; and even the blessings of thy father Joseph, the son of Jacob. Behold, he looked after his posterity in the last days, when they should be scattered and driven by the Gentiles, and wept before the Lord; he sought diligently to know from whence the Son should come who should bring forth the word of the Lord, by which they might be enlightened, and brought back to the true fold, and his eyes beheld thee, my son; his heart rejoiced and his soul was satisfied and he said, As my blessings are to extend to the utmost bounds of the everlasting hills; as my father's blessing prevailed, over the blessings of his progenitors, and as my branches are to run over the wall, and my seed are to inherit the choice land whereon the Zion of God shall stand in the last days, from among my seed, scattered with the Gentiles, shall a choice Seer arise, whose bowels shall be a fountain of truth, whose loins shall be girded with the girdle of righteousness, whose hands shall be lifted with acceptance before the God of Jacob to turn away his anger from his anointed, whose heart shall mediate great wisdom, whose intelligence shall circumscribe and comprehend the deep things of God, and whose mouth shall utter the law of the just . . . and he shall feed upon the heritage of Jacob his father: Thou (Joseph Smith, Jr.) shall hold the keys of this ministry, even the presidency of this Church, both in time and in eternity, and thou shalt stand on Mount Zion when the tribes of Jacob come shouting from the north, and with thy brethren, the Sons of Ephraim, crown them in the name of Jesus Christ" ("Seed of Joseph," 23:175).

That the labors of Joseph Smith stand as an "ensign" to which the nations of the earth gather is also a matter of scriptural promise known to the Saints. "Zion shall flourish, and the glory of the Lord shall be upon her; And she shall be an ensign unto the people, and there shall come unto her out of every nation under heaven. And the day shall come when the nations of the earth shall tremble because of her, and shall fear because of her terrible ones" (D&C 64:41–43).

The Scattered Remnants of Zion Have a Right to the Priesthood and Are Called to Return to the Lord
DOCTRINE AND COVENANTS 113:7–10

113:7–10 This revealed commentary on Isaiah's prophecy about the redemption of Israel in the last days restores to the ancient text the understanding and perspective that is always lost in times of apostasy. First, we note that it is for God to call those who will labor in his behalf. There is no suspicion here that it is the prerogative of the worker to hire himself or herself. Second, we note the importance of priesthood in the whole story of the gathering. Israel is to be gathered under the direction of and by the power and authority of the priesthood. Without priesthood there can be no gathering. Third, we note that the gathering of Israel is always first a return to faith in Christ. There can be no true redemption of Israel without the true Redeemer. And finally, we are reminded of the importance of revelation. There never has been a people that the Lord acknowledged as his own to whom he would not speak. Revelation that is immediate and personal is always a part of true religion.

113:9 Isaiah's words were: "Shake thyself from the dust; arise, and sit down, O Jerusalem: loose thyself from the bands of thy neck, O captive daughter of Zion" (Isaiah 52:2).

113:10 *Return to the Lord.* The scattering of ancient Israel was spiritual as well as temporal. Assyria was allowed to take Israel into captivity because they had forsaken the Lord, their God. As a result, over the centuries the children of Israel were literally "scattered upon all the face of the earth, and also among all nations" (1 Nephi 22:3). Because of wickedness and apostasy, they were as branches broken off from the trunk of an olive tree. They were driven out of the land of their inheritance in

Palestine. In latter days Israel must first return to the Lord spiritually before they will be restored to the lands of their inheritance.

The bands of her neck are the curses of God upon her. When the inhabitants of Israel were taken captive and led away into other lands, bands of enslavement were placed upon them. In addition to binding them physically, these bands also symbolized the spiritual bondage and captivity that lay ahead of them. The spiritual decline that began in Palestine with forsaking the Lord in worship of false gods continued to accelerate as the children of Israel lived among the Gentiles. There were no prophets among them to receive the word of the Lord. They lost their identity and royal heritage as the covenant people and became slaves to the false beliefs and precepts of men.

Nephi recorded that he was shown in vision "the nations and kingdoms of the Gentiles. And it came to pass that I saw among the nations of the Gentiles the formation of a great church. And the angel said unto me: Behold the formation of a church which is most abominable above all other churches, which slayeth the saints of God, yea, and tortureth them and bindeth them down, and yoketh them with a yoke of iron, and bringeth them down into captivity. And it came to pass that I beheld this great and abominable church; and I saw the devil that he was the founder of it" (1 Nephi 13:3–6). The doctrines of devils and men became the creeds of Israel. The chains of hell held them captive from knowledge of the true Messiah and the covenants that God made with their fathers.

Isaiah promised that the bands upon the neck of Zion would be loosed, or the curses of God removed, when the Lord spoke again from the heavens to descendants of ancient Israel in the last days. The restoration of the gospel through the Prophet Joseph Smith fulfills this promise. The word of the Lord through Isaiah, as referred to in this verse, was that when such took place: "My people shall know my name: therefore they shall know in that day that I am he that doth speak: behold, it is I. How beautiful upon the mountains are the feet of him that bringeth good tidings, that publisheth peace; that bringeth good tidings of good, that publisheth salvation; that saith unto Zion, Thy God reigneth! Thy watchmen shall lift up the voice; with the voice together shall they sing: for they shall see eye to eye, when the Lord shall bring again Zion" (Isaiah 52:6–8).

DOCTRINE AND COVENANTS 114

DATE: 17 APRIL 1838
PLACE: FAR WEST, MISSOURI

This revelation was given to David W. Patten, one of the original members of the Quorum of the Twelve. For some time prior to this he and Thomas B. Marsh were the steadying influence of the Church in Missouri, where the three men who had been called to preside there—David Whitmer, William W. Phelps, and John Whitmer—had become disaffected with the Church.

To these problems was added the persecution of the Saints by mobs. In October of 1838, a mob of some forty men took three of the brethren prisoner, threatening that they would kill them and return the next morning to burn the rest of the Saints out. Joseph Smith appointed David Patten to lead a group of volunteers against this mob, hoping to rout them without bloodshed and free the prisoners. The prisoners were freed but not without bloodshed. Among others, Elder Patten was shot in the stomach and died that night.

Of this fearless servant of the Lord, Joseph Smith said, "Brother David Patten was a very worthy man, beloved by all good men who knew him. He was one of the Twelve Apostles, and died as he had lived, a man of God, and strong in the faith of a glorious resurrection, in a world where mobs will have no power or place. One of his last expressions to his wife was—'Whatever you do else, O! do not deny the faith'" (*History of the Church*, 3:171).

Church Positions Held by Those Who Are Not Faithful Shall Be Given to Others

DOCTRINE AND COVENANTS 114:1–2

114:1 *Perform a mission unto me next spring, in company with others, even twelve.* The Quorum of the Twelve were to take a mission to Great Britain in the spring of 1839. By that time David Patten had been killed and Thomas B. Marsh, William E. McLellin, Luke S. Johnson, John F. Boynton and Lyman E. Johnson had all apostatized and lost their membership in the Quorum and in the Church. The newly called members of the Twelve were John Taylor, John E. Page, Wilford Woodruff, and Willard Richards (D&C 118:6). Orson Hyde was dropped from the Quorum in May of 1839 and restored June 27 of the same year. He and John E. Page were redirected to Jerusalem to dedicate the land of Palestine for the return of the Jews. William Smith, one of the original members of the Quorum of the Twelve, failed to keep his calling, leaving Brigham Young, Heber C. Kimball, Parley P. Pratt, Orson Pratt, John Taylor, Wilford Woodruff, and Willard Richards (who already was in England) to fill this commandment.

114:2 *There are those among you who deny my name.* To partake of the spirit of apostasy is to deny the name of Christ. Specific reference is made in this instance to those men who lost the spirit of their calling and thus their place as "Apostles, or special witnesses of the name of Christ" (D&C 107:23).

Receive their bishopric. The Greek word for bishopric is *episkope*, meaning "overseership," or "office." It was not originally used in reference to religious callings and can properly be used to describe any of a variety of duties. Peter referred to the place of Judas among the Twelve Apostles as a "bishoprick" (Acts 1:20). Here it is used in reference to the office of an apostle.

DOCTRINE AND COVENANTS 115

DATE: 26 APRIL 1838
PLACE: FAR WEST, MISSOURI

The Prophet identified this as a "Revelation given at Far West making known the will of God concerning the building up of that place, and of the Lord's House" (Smith, *History of the Church*, 3:23). Far West, Missouri, had become the focal point of gathering in Missouri after the Saints were petitioned to depart from Clay County, which had served as a temporary refuge following mob action that had driven them from Jackson County.

This section is best known as the revelation that gives the official name of the Church: The Church of Jesus Christ of Latter-day Saints. In the early years of its existence the Church was called "The Church of Christ," "The Church of Jesus Christ," and "The Church of God." This caused some problems for missionaries because many congregations used these names. To distinguish themselves, members began to refer to the Church as "The Church of Latter-day Saints."

This section was first published in the *Elders' Journal* in August of 1838. It was included in the 1876 edition of the Doctrine and Covenants.

The Lord Names His Church The Church of Jesus Christ of Latter-day Saints
DOCTRINE AND COVENANTS 115:1–4

115:1 At this time Sidney Rigdon and Hyrum Smith were first and second counselors, respectively, to the Prophet Joseph Smith in the First Presidency of the Church. Hyrum was set apart as second counselor in the place of Frederick G. Williams, 7 November 1837. See commentary on Doctrine and Covenants 112:17.

And your counselors who are and shall be appointed hereafter. In addition to the three members of the First Presidency mentioned in this revelation, assistant counselors had previously been called in a conference in

Kirtland, Ohio, on 3 September 1837. The minutes of that meeting read: "President Smith then introduced Oliver Cowdery, Joseph Smith, Sen., Hyrum Smith, and John Smith for assistant counselors. These last four, together with the first three, are to be considered the heads of the Church. Carried unanimously" (Smith, *History of the Church*, 2:509). By the time this revelation was received, neither Hyrum Smith nor Oliver Cowdery was still serving as assistant counselor in the First Presidency. Hyrum, as this revelation notes, was serving as second counselor in the First Presidency. Oliver Cowdery had lost his membership in the Church.

Doctrine and Covenants 107:22 established that the First Presidency was to consist of a quorum of three. Additional counselors became counselors *to* that quorum, not counselors *in* that quorum. Those who have served as counselors to that quorum include the following: John C. Bennett (1841–42), Amasa M. Lyman (1843–44), Joseph F. Smith (1866–77), Lorenzo Snow (1873–77), Brigham Young Jr. (1873–77), Albert Carrington (1873–77), John W. Young (1873–77), George Q. Cannon (1873–77), Hugh B. Brown (1961), Joseph Fielding Smith (1965–70), H. Thorpe B. Isaacson (1965–70), Alvin R. Dyer (1968–70), and Gordon B. Hinckley (1981–82) (*1999–2000 Church Almanac*, 16, 47–55).

115:2 *Edward Partridge, and his counselors.* Edward Partridge was the bishop in Zion; his counselors were Isaac Morley and Titus Billings. John Corrill, who had been his second counselor, was released the previous August to serve as a Church historian.

115:4 Elder B. H. Roberts explained the significance of the Lord naming his Church in this revelation: "Previous to this the Church had been called 'The Church of Christ,' 'The Church of Jesus Christ,' 'The Church of God,' and by a conference of Elders held at Kirtland in May, 1834 (see [Smith, *History of the Church*, 2:62–63]), it was given the name 'The Church of the Latter-day Saints.' All these names, however, were by this revelation brushed aside, and since then the official name given in this revelation has been recognized as the true title of the Church, though often spoken of as 'The Mormon Church,' the 'Church of Christ,' etc. The appropriateness of this title is self evident, and in it there is a beautiful recognition of the relationship both of the Lord Jesus Christ and of the Saints to the organization" (Smith, *History of the Church*, 3:23–24n). See commentary on Doctrine and Covenants 20:1, "The Church of Christ."

Zion and Her Stakes Are Places of Refuge for the Saints
DOCTRINE AND COVENANTS 115:5–6

115:5 *That thy light may be a standard for the nations.* See commentary on Doctrine and Covenants 105:32.

115:6 This text affirms that in the last days the whole earth is to feel the chastening hand of the Almighty. When that day comes, two places of safety for the faithful Saints are identified: first, the "land of Zion," meaning Jackson County, Missouri; and second, the stakes of Zion, which will be scattered throughout the earth. Much must yet transpire before Zion is redeemed and becomes the administrative headquarters of the Church. In the meantime the safety known to the general body of the Church will center in its stakes. That these stakes will dot the whole earth suggests that the safety of the Saints will center not in a particular location but rather through the garment of protection that rests upon them in and through keeping their covenants with exactness and honor. The safety of the Saints will revolve around unity, love, concern, and support given to one another and upon their right to draw on the powers of heaven to protect their interests.

As the stakes of Zion spread across the face of the earth, we expect temples to follow. The hope is that in some not too far distant day every faithful Latter-day Saint will find themselves within some reasonable proximity of a temple. "Let us . . . recite the crowning reason for gathering to Zion or to her stakes," taught Elder Bruce R. McConkie. "It is to receive the blessings found in the temples of the Lord. There and there only are the saints endowed with power from on high after the ancient pattern. There and there only can they enter into the same eternal covenants that Jehovah made with Abraham, Isaac, and Jacob, that through celestial marriage they might have a continuation of the seeds forever and ever. There and there only can they perform the ordinances of salvation and exaltation for their ancestors who died without a knowledge of the gospel, but who would have received it with all their hearts had it come to them in their day . . .

"Indeed, all of the places appointed for the gathering of the saints are holy places, and the center and crown of each place is that sacred sanctuary, that holy temple, wherein the fulness of the blessings of heaven may be received" (*New Witness*, 574–75).

Wrath when it shall be poured out without mixture. The imagery of plagues being poured out upon the earth, like liquid from vials, comes from the book of Revelation (Revelation 16:1–21). To describe the wrath of God as liquid being "without mixture" is to say that the plagues will not be diluted or watered down. That is, the fulness of the wrath of God will be poured out upon the wicked of the earth.

The Saints Are Commanded to Build a House
of the Lord in Far West

DOCTRINE AND COVENANTS 115:7–16

115:7 *For the ground upon which thou standest is holy.* It will be recalled that when Moses approached the burning bush on the side of Mount Sinai, he was commanded to take off his shoes for, he was told, "the place whereon thou standest is holy ground" (Exodus 3:5). In like manner, Jerusalem is referred to in holy writ as the "holy city" unto which in a future day the uncircumcised and the unclean will not come (Isaiah 52:1). Indeed, all places appointed for the gathering of the Saints are holy, "and the center and crown of each place is that sacred sanctuary, that holy temple, wherein the fulness of the blessings of heaven may be received" (McConkie, *New Witness*, 575).

That the spirit of revelation can flow with greater freedom in some places than others is evident from the Lord's instruction to Enoch, who, when he stood upon "the place Mahujah, and cried unto the Lord," heard "a voice out of heaven, saying Turn ye, and get ye upon the mount Simeon. And it came to pass that I turned and went up on the mount; and as I stood upon the mount, I beheld the heavens open, and I was clothed upon with glory; and I saw the Lord; and he stood before my face, and he talked with me, even as a man talketh one with another, face to face" (Moses 7:2–4). Why the Lord would appear to Enoch on Mount Simeon but not in the place Mahujah we are not told. It appears, however, that one place was holy, whereas the other was not.

All that was associated with the place known to us as Far West, Missouri, in ancient times is not known to us. It seems evident, however, that this was a place made holy by events that have transpired there.

Recounting one of the unusual and sacred experiences that Joseph Smith had at Far West, Joseph Fielding Smith recalled, "The Prophet Joseph Smith contended with the devil face to face for some time, upon the occasion of the power of evil menacing one of his children in the

Prophet's home just west of the temple site. Lucifer declared that Joseph had no right to be there, that this was his place. Whereupon the Prophet rebuked Satan in the name of the Lord, and he departed and did not touch the child again" (Smith and Stewart, *Life of Joseph Fielding Smith*, 340).

115:10 *Let the beginning be made on the fourth day of July next.* Concerning the events of that day, the Prophet Joseph Smith wrote: "The day was spent in celebrating the Declaration of Independence of the United States of America, and also by the Saints making a 'Declaration of Independence' from all mobs and persecutions which have been inflicted upon them, time after time, until they could bear it no longer; having been driven by ruthless mobs and enemies of truth from their homes, and having had their property confiscated, their lives exposed, and their all jeopardized by such barbarous conduct. The corner stones of the Houses of the Lord, agreeable to the commandments of the Lord unto us, given April 26, 1838, were laid.

"Joseph Smith, Jun., was president of the day; Hyrum Smith, vice-president; Sidney Rigdon, orator; Reynolds Cahoon, chief marshal; George M. Hinkle and J. Hunt, assistant marshals; and George W. Robinson, clerk.

"The order of the day was splendid. The procession commenced forming at 10 o'clock A.M., in the following order: First, the infantry (militia); second, the Patriarchs of the Church; the president, vice-president, and orator; the Twelve Apostles, presidents of the stakes, and High Council; Bishop and counselors; architects, ladies and gentlemen. The cavalry brought up the rear of the large procession, which marched to music, and formed a circle, with the ladies in front, round the excavation. The southeast corner stone of the Lord's House in Far West, Missouri, was then laid by the presidents of the stake, assisted by twelve men. The southwest corner, by the presidents of the Elders, assisted by twelve men. The northwest corner by the Bishop, assisted by twelve men. The northeast corner by the president of the Teachers, assisted by twelve men. This house is to be one hundred and ten feet long, and eighty feet broad" (*History of the Church*, 3:41–42).

115:11 See commentary on Doctrine and Covenants 118:4–5.

115:13 This command came on the heels of debt shackling the Church incurred from building the Kirtland Temple. Elder Heber C. Kimball explained, "This building [Kirtland Temple] the Saints commenced in 1833, in poverty, and without means to do it. In 1834 they completed the walls, and in 1835–6 they nearly finished it. The cost was between sixty and seventy thousand dollars. A committee was appointed to gather donations; they traveled among the churches and collected a considerable amount, but not sufficient, so that in the end they found themselves between thirteen and fourteen thousand dollars in debt" (Whitney, *Life of Heber C. Kimball*, 88). It has been the policy of the Church for many years that no church building is dedicated until it is paid for in full.

115:14–16 The plan or pattern for the temple in Far West, Missouri, was to be given by revelation. Elder Joseph Fielding Smith wrote: "We have good reason to believe that his plan contemplated many changes not found in the house in Kirtland. The keys for the sealing of both the living and the dead had been revealed since the Kirtland Temple was built. The doctrine of salvation for the dead had been hinted at, but not yet clearly revealed. The Lord certainly intended to place in this new temple if it should be built according to his plan, the provisions which were found in the Nauvoo Temple and all the other temples erected since that day so that the ordinance of baptism for the dead, and all the ordinances of the gospel could be given to both the living and the dead, as outlined by the Lord to the Prophet, January 19, 1841" (*Church History and Modern Revelation*, 2:87).

Joseph Smith Holds the Keys of the Kingdom of God on Earth
DOCTRINE AND COVENANTS 115:17–19

115:18–19 Stakes may be designated and established only under the direction of the President of the Church, he holding the keys of the kingdom. The Prophet Joseph Smith received revelation explaining the proper order for organizing a stake of Zion: "Revelation Given . . . January 12th 1838, upon an inquiry being made of the Lord, whether any branch of the Church of Christ of Latter Day Saints can be concidered a Stake of Zion, until they have acknowledged the authority of the first Presidency by a vote of Such Church

"Thus Saith the Lord, Verily I Say unto you Nay.

"No Stake Shall be appointed, Except by the first Presidency, and this Presidency be acknowledged, by the voice of the Same, otherwise it Shall not be Counted as a Stake of Zion and again except it be dedicated by this presidency it cannot be acknowledged as a Stake of Zion. For unto this End have I appointed them in Laying the foundation of and Establishing my Kingdom Even So Amen" ("Scriptory Book of Joseph Smith," 52–53, cited in Cook, *Revelations*, 333).

DOCTRINE AND COVENANTS 116

DATE: UNCERTAIN, EITHER 19 MAY OR 11 JUNE 1838

PLACE: SPRING HILL, MISSOURI

Doctrine and Covenants 116 is an extract from the journal of the Prophet Joseph Smith. It was first included in the 1876 edition of the Doctrine and Covenants. The Prophet, in company with Sidney Rigdon, Thomas B. Marsh, David W. Patten, Bishop Partridge, Elias Higbee, and a good number of others had left Far West and headed north in search of a place where they could lay out the beginnings of a city-stake of Zion similar to that at Far West (D&C 115). According to the divine pattern, at the center of a city-stake was to be a temple. The site where the Saints intended to build the temple at Adam-ondi-Ahman is not known.

Earlier, a few Saints had settled in Daviess County in 1837, and by 28 June 1838 a stake was organized, frequently referred to as the Diahman stake. John Smith was called as president, with Reynolds Cahoon and Lyman Wight as counselors. Vinson Knight was appointed as bishop, and in a subsequent revelation Newel K. Whitney was called to move from Kirtland, Ohio, to "come up to the land of Adam-ondi-Ahman, and be a bishop unto my people" (D&C 117:11). After the Saints were driven from the state of Missouri in early 1839, the area became known as Cravensville, named for John Cravens. The community ceased to exist by the early 1870s after most of the inhabitants had moved away.

During the second day that the Prophet Joseph Smith and his companions explored this area he noted the following: "Saturday, 19.—This morning we struck our tents and formed a line of march, crossing Grand River at the mouth of Honey Creek and Nelson's Ferry. Grand River is a large, beautiful, deep and rapid stream, during the high waters of Spring, and will undoubtedly admit of navigation by steamboat and other water craft. At the mouth of Honey Creek is a good landing. We pursued our course up the river, mostly through timber, for about eighteen miles, when we arrived at Colonel Lyman Wight's home. He lives at the foot of Tower Hill (a name I gave the place in consequence of the remains of an old

Nephite altar or tower that stood there), where we camped for the Sabbath.

"In the afternoon I went up the river about half a mile to Wight's Ferry, accompanied by President Rigdon, and my clerk, George W. Robinson, for the purpose of selecting and laying claim to a city plat near said ferry in Daviess County, township 60, ranges 27 and 28, and sections 25, 36, 31, and 30, which the brethren called 'Spring Hill,' but by the mouth of the Lord it was named Adam-ondi-Ahman, because, said He, it is the place where Adam shall come to visit his people, or the Ancient of Days shall sit, as spoken of by Daniel the Prophet" (*History of the Church*, 3:34–35).

Adam-ondi-Ahman and the Ancient of Days
DOCTRINE AND COVENANTS 116:1

116:1 *Adam-ondi-Ahman.* Elder Orson Pratt explained the meaning of this name: "We have then an understanding that [Adam-ondi-Ahman] was the place where Adam dwelt. Perhaps you may be anxious to know what 'Ondi-Ahman' means. It means the place where Adam dwelt. 'Ahman' signifies God. The whole term means Valley of God, where Adam dwelt. It is in the original language spoken by Adam, as revealed to the Prophet Joseph" (*Journal of Discourses*, 18:342–43). At the end of his life, Adam called all of his righteous posterity to gather to "the valley of Adam-ondi-Ahman and there bestowed upon them his last blessing" (D&C 107:53). See commentary on Doctrine and Covenants 107:53–55.

The Lord revealed to the Prophet Joseph Smith, as indicated in Doctrine and Covenants 116, that the clearer meaning of *Adam-ondi-Ahman* as applied to the area known in the 1830s as Spring Hill, Missouri, refers not to a place that Adam dwelt in past ages but to the area of a future visit that Adam will make to this region.

It is the place where Adam shall come to visit his people. Before Christ's appearance in glory to the world, Adam—the mighty Prince, the Archangel—will hold a great conference at Adam-ondi-Ahman. Joseph Smith said that Adam "will call his children together and hold a council with them to prepare them for the coming of the Son of Man. He (Adam) is the father of the human family, and presides over the spirits of all men, and all that have had the keys must stand before him in this grand council. This may take place before some of us leave this stage of action. The Son of Man stands before him, and there is given him glory and dominion. Adam delivers up his stewardship to Christ, that which was delivered to him as holding the keys of the universe, but retains his standing as head of the human family" (*Teachings of the Prophet Joseph Smith*, 157).

The phrase "the Ancient of Days" in the sectarian world is thought to be Christ. This revelation makes it clear that Daniel used this term in reference to Adam. The Prophet Joseph Smith explained that Daniel was referring to Father Adam as the oldest or the first man (*Teachings of the Prophet Joseph Smith*, 157).

As spoken of by Daniel the Prophet. Daniel recorded a vision wherein the degenerate kingdoms of the earth were represented by four beasts. Each had their season of dominion, which was taken away by the succeeding kingdom until the Lord God set up a kingdom never to be destroyed. Describing his vision of these events, Daniel said, "I beheld till the thrones were cast down, and the Ancient of days [Adam] did sit, whose garment was white as snow, and the hair of his head like the pure wool: his throne was like the fiery flame, and his wheels as burning fire" (Daniel 7:9–10). This description of Adam is similar to that given of the Savior during his appearance to Joseph Smith and Oliver Cowdery in the Kirtland Temple (see D&C 110:1). It seems that Daniel saw Father Adam as a glorified resurrected being.

Daniel continued: "A fiery stream issued and came forth from before him: thousand thousands ministered unto him, and ten thousand times ten thousand stood before him [Adam]: the judgment was set, and the books were opened" (Daniel 7:10). By revelation we have been told that Adam holds "the keys of salvation under the direction of the Holy One" (D&C 78:16) and presides under Christ in directing the work of the priesthood of God, including judgment.

Daniel further wrote: "I saw in the night visions, and, behold, one like the Son of man came with the clouds of heaven, and came to the Ancient of days, and they brought him [Adam] near before him [Christ]. And there was given him [Christ] dominion, and glory, and a kingdom, that all people, nations, and languages, should serve him: his dominion is an everlasting dominion, which shall not pass away, and his kingdom that which shall not be destroyed" (Daniel 7:13–14).

Daniel further wrote: "I beheld, and the same horn [the last kingdom to have dominion] made war with the saints, and prevailed against them; until the Ancient of days came, and judgment was given to the saints of the most High; and the time came that the saints possessed the kingdom"

(Daniel 7:21–22). It appears that the assembly to be held at Adam-ondi-Ahman may include several meetings or sessions and convene at various times. It may well include the promised sacrament meeting spoken of by the Savior to his disciples at the Last Supper: "And he took the cup, and gave thanks, and gave it to them, saying, Drink ye all of it. For this is in remembrance of my blood of the new testament, which is shed for as many as believe on my name, for the remission of their sins. . . . But I say unto you, I will not drink henceforth of this fruit of the vine, until that day when I shall come and drink it new with you in my Father's kingdom" (JST Matthew 26:23–26). The Lord revealed to the Prophet Joseph Smith that during this sacrament meeting he would partake with Joseph and with Moroni, Elias, John the Baptist, Elijah, Joseph, Jacob, Isaac, Abraham, Adam, Peter, James, John, "and also with all those whom my Father hath given me out of the world" (D&C 27:5–14).

It is likely that the gatherings will be held during the great tribulations that will precede the Savior's appearance to the Jewish remnant on the Mount of Olives (see commentary on D&C 45:43–52) and his appearance in glory to the world. Daniel places the return of Adam before the desolation of abomination that will take place at Jerusalem (see Joseph Smith–Matthew 1:32). "And at that time shall Michael stand up," an angel revealed to Daniel, "the great prince which standeth for the children of thy people: and there shall be a time of trouble, such as never was since there was a nation even to that same time: and at that time thy people shall be delivered, every one that shall be found written in the book" (Daniel 12:1).

DOCTRINE AND COVENANTS 117

DATE: 8 JULY 1838
PLACE: FAR WEST, MISSOURI

When the Lord commanded that "the city of Far West should be built up speedily by the gathering of my saints" (D&C 115:17), the five years of retaining "a stronghold in the land of Kirtland" (D&C 64:21) came to an end. The Prophet Joseph Smith and others had fled Kirtland earlier in the year. On 6 July 1838, a group of 529 Saints, known as the Kirtland Camp, made their exodus from Kirtland, Ohio, to travel to Missouri. It appears that only 260 completed that journey, the others having been scattered 'to the four winds.' Conspicuously missing from this camp were Bishop Newel K. Whitney and William Marks. Both of these brethren chose to remain behind in Kirtland because they were concerned about securing their properties before leaving. President Joseph Fielding Smith said, "It is quite evident that these two brethren had fallen under the spell of speculation and temptation so rife in Kirtland in 1837, and which was the downfall of so many of the leading brethren of the Church" (*Church History and Modern Revelation*, 2:96).

Although the decision of these two leaders to remain in Kirtland would have been unknown to the Prophet Joseph Smith, who was a thousand miles away, yet the Lord was aware of their actions. Two days after the exodus of the Kirtland Camp, the Lord expressed his displeasure with these two men in this revelation and appointed Oliver Granger as an agent to transact business of Church-owned properties.

This revelation was one of four published in the Doctrine and Covenants that were received on the same day (D&C 118, 119, 120).

The Lord's Servants Should Not Covet Temporal Things, for "What Is Property unto the Lord?"

DOCTRINE AND COVENANTS 117:1–9

117:1–9 To the disciples of his day the Savior said, "Seek not the things of this world but seek ye first to build up the kingdom of God, and

927

to establish his righteousness, and all these things shall be added unto you" (JST Matthew 6:38). A great deal of toil and energy were given to build up the stake in Kirtland. Now, however, it was time to let go of the property attained there and to build up the kingdom of God in Far West, Missouri. It must be remembered that the Church is not made of land and buildings. These are but means to meet the temporal needs of its members. Of the many buildings erected in dispensations past, not one has remained for use by the Saints of our day. Principles are eternal, not the wealth of men.

The command to abandon Kirtland was but one occasion on which our faithful forefathers were required to leave home and lands behind to follow their faith. As early as January 1831, the Lord had commanded the New York Saints to gather to Ohio (D&C 38:37). Now in moving to Far West the Kirtland Saints would be joining their Missouri counterparts who had been driven from Jackson County to Clay County and from Clay County to Caldwell County. Together these Saints would yet be driven from the state of Missouri to take up their abode in Illinois, where they would build Nauvoo, the "city beautiful," from whence they would be driven outside the boundaries of the United States to the Great Basin.

Surely the Lord was sifting his people that he might build his kingdom with the strongest of stock. Many of their number would yet be able to say, as did Brigham Young and Heber C. Kimball, that they had seen their houses burned to the ground five times and it was nothing to them as compared to the truths they obtained in Mormonism (Brigham Young, *Journal of Discourses*, 10:316).

117:7 In each instance the Lord caused the unwanted, solitary places that were inhabited by the Saints, ranging from swamps to deserts, "to bud and . . . to bring forth in abundance."

117:8 *The plains of Olaha Shinehah.* Joseph Fielding Smith said, "The plains of Olaha Shinehah, or the place where Adam dwelt, must be a part of, or in the vicinity of Adam-ondi-Ahman. This name Olaha Shinehah, may be, and in all probability is, from the language of Adam. We may without great controversy believe that this is the name which Adam gave to this place, at least we may venture this as a probable guess. Shinehah, according to the Book of Abraham, is the name given to the sun. (Abraham 3:13.) . . . Elder Janne M. Sjodahl commenting on the name, Olaha Shinehah, has said: 'Shinehah means sun, and Olaha is possibly a variant of the word Olea, which is "the moon." (Abraham 3:13.) If so the plains of Olaha Shinehah would be the Plains of the Moon and the Sun, so called, perhaps because of astronomical observations there made.' We learn from the writings of Moses that the Lord revealed to the ancients great knowledge concerning the stars, and Abraham by revelations and through the Urim and Thummim received wonderful information concerning the heavens and the governing planets, or stars. It was also revealed by the Prophet Joseph Smith that Methuselah was acquainted with the stars as were others of the antediluvian prophets including Adam. So it may be reasonable that here in this valley important information was made known anciently in relation to the stars of our universe" (*Church History and Modern Revelation*, 2:97–98).

They Are to Forsake Littleness of Soul, and Their Sacrifices Shall Be Sacred unto the Lord
DOCTRINE AND COVENANTS 117:10–16

117:10 William Marks was called to serve as president of the Far West Missouri Stake. However, before he arrived in Missouri the Saints were being driven out by the state militia under Governor Lilburn W. Boggs's extermination order. Elder Marks was later called to serve as president of the stake in Nauvoo. Unfortunately, he allied himself with Sidney Rigdon in his false claims to guardianship of the Church after the martyrdom of the Prophet and his brother, Hyrum. In his apostasy Elder Marks wandered among various groups that had broken away from the Church and was still outside the kingdom at the time of his death in 1872.

117:11 *Littleness of soul.* This expression was directed to the lack of faith and spiritual strength on the part of Bishop Whitney in remaining behind in Kirtland, Ohio, to regulate his business instead of heeding the Lord's call to come to Missouri. Joseph Smith wrote the following in his journal regarding Bishop Newel K. Whitney, giving insight into Brother Whitney's weaknesses and strengths: "Blessed of the Lord is Brother Whitney, even the Bishop of the Church of Latter-day Saints, for the Bishopric shall never be taken away from him while he liveth. And the time cometh that he shall overcome all the narrow-mindedness of his heart, and all his covetous desires that so easily beset him; and he shall deal with a liberal hand to the poor and the needy, the sick and afflicted, the widow and the fatherless. And marvelously and miraculously shall the Lord his God provide for him, even that he shall be blessed with a fullness of the good things of this earth, and his seed after him from generation to generation. And it shall come to pass, that according to the measure that he meteth out with a liberal hand to the poor, so shall it be measured to him again by the hand of his God, even an hundred fold" (*History of the Church*, 2:288).

Nicolaitane band. In the revelation of the apostle John, the Nicolaitans are identified as those that "cast a stumblingblock before the children of Israel, to eat things sacrificed unto idols, and to commit fornication" (Revelation 2:14). These abominations were in direct contradiction to the counsel issued to the new gentile converts by Peter and the apostles at the conference at Antioch (Acts 15:22–29). As stated earlier, the Saints in Kirtland had been counseled to remove to Missouri; Bishop Whitney remained behind to secure his property. Thus, he put his desires to retain his property above the Lord's command to gather speedily to Far West, Missouri (D&C 115:17). In so doing he took the same course of opposing the counsel of the presiding authority of the Church that the Nicolaitans had pursued in the first century after Christ.

Because of his tardiness in arriving in Missouri his calling as bishop at Adam-ondi-Ahman was never fulfilled. As with his equally tardy companion, William Marks, Brother Whitney arrived in Missouri only to find the Saints being driven from the state.

117:12–15 The Prophet Joseph Smith fled from Kirtland, Ohio, without being able to settle the debts he had incurred there. He wrote: "As I was driven away from Kirtland without the privilege of settling my business, I had, previous to this, employed Colonel Oliver Granger as my agent, to close all my affairs in the east; and as I have been accused of 'running away, cheating my creditors,' etc., I will insert one of the many cards and letters I have received from gentlemen who have had the best opportunity of knowing my business transactions, and whose testimony comes unsolicited: A Card.

"PAINSVILLE, October 19, 1838.

"We, the undersigned, being personal acquaintances of Oliver Granger, firmly believe that the course which he has pursued in settling the claims, accounts, etc., against the former citizens of Kirtland township, has done much credit to himself, and all others that committed to him the care of adjusting their business with this community, which also furnishes evidence that there was no intention on their part of defrauding their creditors. [Signed] THOMAS GRIFFITH, JOHN S. SEYMOUR" (Smith, *History of the Church*, 3:164–65).

The service that Oliver Granger rendered to put his business talents to work on behalf of the First Presidency later led to another blessing. At a conference held at Quincy, Illinois, 4–6 May 1839, he was "appointed to go to Kirtland and take the charge and oversight of the House of the Lord, and preside over the general affairs of the Church in that place" (Smith, *History of the Church*, 3:345).

In an expression of gratitude, the First Presidency wrote a letter of recommendation for Brother Granger: "We have always found President Oliver Granger to be a man of the most strict integrity and moral virtue; and in fine, to be a man of God.

"We have had long experience and acquaintance with Brother Granger. We have entrusted vast business concerns to him, which have been managed skilfully to the support of our characters and interest as well as that of the Church; and he is now authorized by a general conference to go forth and engage in vast and important concerns as an agent for the Church, that he may fill a station of usefulness in obedience to the commandment of God, which was given unto him July 8, 1838, which says, 'Let him (meaning Brother Granger) contend earnestly for the redemption of the First Presidency of my Church, saith the Lord'" (Smith, *History of the Church*, 3:350).

117:13 *Let him contend earnestly for the redemption of the First Presidency.* Oliver Granger performed a great service in settling the financial affairs of the First Presidency and thus restoring their good name.

His sacrifice shall be more sacred unto me than his increase. Being a man of sound business sense and reputation, Oliver Granger might have become a very wealthy man. The sacrifice of opportunity for wealth made by his servants is known to the Lord. As the Lord assured Oliver Granger, "his sacrifice shall be more sacred unto me than his increase," so is it true in the lives of countless others in the Church today. Their worth to the Lord is in that which they have given up, not that which they have accumulated.

117:16 *Overthrow the moneychangers.* Even before the Prophet Joseph Smith fled from Kirtland, apostates asserted that they should have control of the temple. The Lord likened them to the moneychangers that polluted the temple in Jerusalem. He declared at that time: "It is written, My house shall be called the house of prayer; but ye have made it a den of thieves" (Matthew 21:13).

DOCTRINE AND COVENANTS 118

DATE: 8 JULY 1838

PLACE: FAR WEST, MISSOURI

The revelation recorded in Doctrine and Covenants 118 was received the same day as sections 117, 119, and 120. The Prophet Joseph Smith recorded that it was received "in answer to the question, Show us thy will O Lord concerning the Twelve" (*History of the Church*, 3:46).

The Lord Will Provide for the Families of the Twelve
DOCTRINE AND COVENANTS 118:1–3

118:1 *Let a conference be held immediately.* In obedience to this command, a conference was held the very next day. The following minutes of the conference pertain to business transacted according to the word of the Lord in this revelation: "July 9, 1838, a conference of the Twelve Apostles assembled at Far West, agreeable to the revelation, given July 8, 1838. Present, Thomas B. Marsh, David W. Patten, Brigham Young, Parley P. Pratt and William Smith: T. B. Marsh, presiding.

"Resolved 1st. That the persons who are to fill the places of those who are fallen, be immediately notified to come to Far West; as also, those of the Twelve who are not present.

"Resolved 2nd. That Thomas B. Marsh notify Wilford Woodruff, that Parley P. Pratt notify Orson Pratt, and that President Rigdon notify Willard Richards, who is now in England.

"Voted that President Marsh publish the same in next number of *The Elders' Journal*.

"President Rigdon gave some counsel concerning the provisions necessary to be made for the families of the Twelve, while laboring in the cause of their Redeemer, advising them to instruct their converts to move without delay to the places of gathering, and there to strictly attend to the law of God" (Smith, *History of the Church*, 3:47).

118:2 *To publish my word.* President Marsh was appointed printer and publisher of the *Elders' Journal* in Zion, or Missouri. This was a continuation of the same responsibilities that he had in Kirtland, Ohio. The Prophet Joseph Smith was the editor of the journal, which served as the official voice of the Church.

The Apostles Depart on Their Mission
DOCTRINE AND COVENANTS 118:4–6

118:4–5 President Wilford Woodruff explained the conditions that prevailed at the time the Twelve were to leave Far West, Missouri, in accordance with this revelation: "The mission then mentioned was one of much interest to the Twelve, if not to the Church. The whole of that mission to England, from the beginning to the end, placed the apostles in such a position that they had to walk by faith from first to last. The Lord gave a revelation, with date, day, month and year, when they were to go up to lay the corner-stone in Caldwell county, Far West, Missouri. When that revelation was given all was peace and quietude, comparatively, in that land. But when the time came for the Twelve Apostles to fulfill that revelation, the Saints had all been driven out by the exterminating order of Governor Boggs, and it was as much as a man's life was worth, especially one of the Twelve, to be found in that State; and when the day came on which we were commanded by the Lord in that revelation to go up and lay the corner-stone of that Temple, and there take the parting hand with the Saints, to cross the waters to preach the gospel in England, the inhabitants of Missouri had sworn that if all the revelations of 'old Joe Smith' were fulfilled, that should not be, because it had a day and date to it.

"President Young asked the Twelve who were with him—'What shall we do with regard to the fulfillment of this revelation?' He wanted to know their feelings. Father Smith, the Patriarch, said the Lord would take the will for the deed; others said the Lord could not expect the Twelve Apostles to go up and sacrifice their lives to fulfill that revelation; but the Spirit of the Lord rested upon the twelve, and they said—'The Lord God has spoken, and we will fulfill that revelation and commandment;' and that was the feeling of President Young and of those who were with him. We went through that State, and we laid that cornerstone. George A. Smith and myself were ordained to the Apostleship on that corner-stone upon that day. We returned in safety, and not a dog to move his tongue, and no man shed our blood" (*Journal of Discourses*, 18:123).

On another occasion President Woodruff related events that

transpired following the Twelve's departure from Far West: "The devil, however, tried to kill us, for before we started for England everyone of the Twelve was taken sick, and it was about as much as we could do to move or stir. I had travelled in Tennessee, Mississippi, Kentucky and Arkansas for two or three years, and that, too, during the sickly season, where they were not well enough to take care of the sick, and I had never had the ague. But upon this occasion I was taken with the ague, the first time in my life. All the Twelve had something the matter with them. But we had to travel sick; we had to travel by faith in order to fulfil the mission to which we had been called by revelation. But the Lord sustained us; He did not forsake us" (*Journal of Discourses*, 13:159–60).

118:5 *On the building-spot of my house.* In other words, from the lot dedicated for the building of the temple in Far West, Missouri.

118:6 *To fill the places of those who have fallen.* See commentary on Doctrine and Covenants 114:2, "There are those among you who deny my name."

DOCTRINE AND COVENANTS 119

DATE: 8 JULY 1838
PLACE: FAR WEST, MISSOURI

Attempts by the Saints to live the law of consecration had not provided for the expenses of building up the kingdom of God. The Lord forbade the First Presidency from building the temple in Far West with materials received on credit as had been done with the temple in Kirtland, Ohio (D&C 115:13). Thus, the Prophet Joseph Smith "inquired of the Lord, 'O Lord! Show unto thy servant how much thou requirest of the properties of thy people for a tithing,' and received the following answer, which was also read in public" (*History of the Church*, 3:44). This revelation was received the same day as sections 117, 118, and 120.

The Saints Are to Pay Their Surplus Property and Then Give, as Tithing, One-Tenth of Their Interest Annually
DOCTRINE AND COVENANTS 119:1–5

119:1–5 This revelation restored the ancient law of tithing to our dispensation as part of the restoration of all things. We know that this law was practiced during the dispensations of Abraham and Moses. We suppose, further, that it was revealed to Adam and was known and obeyed by those that lived during the dispensations of Enoch and Noah. The earliest mention of tithing in the Old Testament is the account of Abraham paying tithes to Melchizedek (Genesis 14:20). Later, Jacob renewed the covenant of tithing with the Lord at Beth-el (Genesis 28:20–22). The children of Israel were commanded that all of the tithes of the fruits of the land and of their flocks were the Lord's (Leviticus 27:30–34; Malachi 3:8–10).

Though it is little known, the command that the Saints pay one-tenth of their increase annually required a greater sacrifice of property than that required by the law of consecration and stewardship, as practiced in the early days of this dispensation. In the law of consecration, after the Saints put their substance and properties before the bishop, they received a stewardship to provide for their needs. Later, if from their stewardship they had more than was necessary for their support (D&C 42:33), or in other words, a residue or a surplus, then they would contribute surplus to the Church. The great difference in the law of tithing is that it requires the Saints to pay a tenth of their income before any expenses are met, not from their surplus after their needs have been satisfied.

Because the law of tithing requires an act of faith *before* the day of harvest, it provides a greater promise of blessing than that found in the law of consecration as it was applied to temporal stewardships in the early 1830s. President Joseph F. Smith taught: "The Bishop should encourage every man, woman and child, who earns and receives in return for labor, to honor the Lord and to prove obedient to the law of God by giving the one-tenth of that which he or she receives, as the Lord requires, so that they may have their names enrolled on the book of the law of the Lord, that their genealogies may be had in the archives of the Church, and that they may be entitled to the privileges and blessings of the house of God.

"I recollect most vividly a circumstance that occurred in the days of my childhood. My mother was a widow, with a large family to provide for. One spring when we opened our potato pits, she had her boys get a load of the best potatoes and she took them to the tithing office; potatoes were scarce that season. I was a little boy at the time, and drove the team. When we drove up to the steps of the tithing office, ready to unload the potatoes, one of the clerks came out and said to my mother, 'Widow Smith, it's a shame that you should have to pay tithing,' . . . and he chided my mother for paying her tithing, called her anything but wise or prudent; and said there were others who were strong and able to work that were supported from the tithing office. My mother turned upon him and said: 'William, you ought to be ashamed of yourself. Would you deny me a blessing? If I did not pay my tithing, I should expect the Lord to withhold his blessings from me. I pay my tithing, not only because it is a law of God, but because I expect a blessing by doing it. By keeping this and other laws, I expect to prosper and to be able to provide for my family.' Though she was a widow, you may turn to the records of the Church from the beginning unto the day of her death, and you will find that she never received a farthing from the Church to help her support herself and her family; but she paid in thousands of dollars in wheat, potatoes, corn, vegetables, meat, etc. The tithes of her sheep and cattle, the tenth pound of her butter, her tenth chicken, the tenth of her eggs, the tenth pig, the tenth calf, the tenth colt—a tenth of everything she raised was paid. Here sits my brother who can bear testimony to the truth of what I say, as can others who knew her. She prospered because she obeyed the laws of God. She had abundance to sustain her family" (*Gospel Doctrine*, 228–29).

Thus, the kingdom of God is built up by the faithful tithes and offerings of the poor, as well as by those who have been blessed beyond their needs with a surplus. The millions of poor in the Church who give their tithes to the Lord follow the path taken by the widow in Christ's day who gave two mites in her poverty, not out of her abundance but out of her faith (Mark 12:41–44).

Consecration is a higher law only when it extends beyond that which is temporal and involves dedicating all of one's time, talent, and energies that may be needed to building up the Lord's kingdom (D&C 105:3–5). The consecration of property was the Lord's means to teach the Saints that all things are his. In reality very little revenue was generated from the surplus that could be used for the building up of the kingdom of God.

The Lord's wisdom in giving the law of tithing at this time is evidenced by history. Very few of the Saints at the time of this revelation had much, if any, surplus goods, and of those that did, very few considered their property to be surplus. President Brigham Young described the response of the Saints to this revelation as follows: "The brethren wished me to go among the Churches, and find out what surplus property the people had, with which to forward the building of the Temple we were commencing at Far West. I accordingly went from place to place through the country. Before I started, I asked brother Joseph, 'Who shall be the judge of what is surplus property?' Said he, 'Let them be the judges themselves, for I care not if they do not give a single dime. So far as I am concerned, I do not want anything they have.'

"Then I replied, 'I will go and ask them for their surplus property;' and I did so; I found the people said they were willing to do about as they were counselled, but, upon asking them about their surplus property, most of the men who owned land and cattle would say, 'I have got so many hundred acres of land, and I have got so many boys, and I want each one of them to have eighty acres, therefore this is not surplus property.' Again, 'I have got so many girls, and I do not believe I shall be able to give them more than forty acres each.' 'Well, you have got two or three hundred acres left.' 'Yes, but I have a brother-in-law coming on, and he will depend on me for a living; my wife's nephew is also coming on, he is poor, and I shall have to furnish him a farm after he arrives here.' I would go on to the next one, and he would have more land and cattle than he could make use of to advantage. It is a laughable idea but is nevertheless true, men would tell me they were young and beginning the world, and would say, 'We have no children, but our prospects are good, and we think we shall have a family of children, and if we do, we want to give them eighty acres of land each; we have no surplus property.' 'How many cattle have you?' 'So many.' 'How many horses, &c?' 'So many, but I have made provisions for all these, and I have use for every thing I have got.'

"Some were disposed to do right with their surplus property, and once in a while you would find a man who had a cow which he considered surplus, but generally she was of the class that would kick a person's hat off, or eyes out, or the wolves had eaten off her teats. You would once in a while find a man who had a horse that he considered surplus, but at the same time he had the ringbone, was broken-winded, spavined in both legs, had the pole evil at one end of the neck and a fistula at the other, and both knees sprung" (Journal of Discourses, 2:306–7).

119:2 *Debts of the Presidency of my Church.* This has no reference to personal indebtedness, but, rather, those debts incurred for purchasing and managing Church-owned property. See introduction to Doctrine and Covenants 104.

119:4 *Those who have thus been tithed.* Reference to tithing as used in this revelation included all offerings given to the Church.

One-tenth of all their interest annually. The definition of the Hebrew word for *tithe* is "one-tenth." Some discussion is had among the Saints as to the use and meaning of the word *interest* in this revelation. Interest means income—the profit that is gained on any investment of time or money. The term *tithing* did not carry the official definition of being one-tenth of an individual's increase until this revelation was received. In December 1837, at Far West, Missouri, Bishop Partridge met with John Corrill and Isaac Morley as a committee to determine how the expenses of the kingdom could be sustained. They proposed "a plan whereby the church of Latter Day Saints may voluntarily raise means by tithing themselves to be a fund ready at all times to assist the poor" and appointed that a tithe of "five mills could be raised upon the dollar which every man is worth" (Cannon and Cook, *Far West Record*, 129–30). This plan consisted of the Saints estimating their total assets in property and goods and paying two cents on the dollar. A further proposition was that widows and those "families not worth over seventy-five dollars, each should not be required to tithe themselves and yet retain an honorable standing in the church" (Cannon and Cook, *Far West Record*, 129).

The idea of a tithing consisting of ten percent of an individual's income was not an entirely new concept to the Saints in 1838. The Prophet recorded that "on the evening of the 29th of November [1834]; . . . after commencing and rejoicing before the Lord on this occasion, we agreed to enter into the following covenant with the Lord, viz.:

"That if the Lord will prosper us in our business and open the way before us that we may obtain means to pay our debts; that we be not troubled nor brought into disrepute before the world, nor His people; after that, of all that He shall give unto us, we will give a tenth to be bestowed upon the poor in His Church, or as He shall command; and that we will be faithful over that which he has entrusted to our care, that we may obtain much; and that our children after us shall remember to observe this sacred and holy covenant; and that our children, and our children's children, may know of the same, we have subscribed our names with our own hands (Signed) Joseph Smith, Jun. Oliver Cowdery" (*History of the Church*, 2:174–75).

119:4–5 The law of tithing separates those Saints who are committed to the kingdom of God and those who are not. Today it serves as one of the determining factors of worthiness to enter the temples of God and receive the holy ordinances administered therein. President Joseph F. Smith taught, "By this principle the loyalty of the people of this Church shall be put to the test. By this principle it shall be known who is for the kingdom of God and who is against it. By this principle it shall be seen whose hearts are set on doing the will of God and keeping His commandments, thereby sanctifying the land of Zion unto God, and who are opposed to this principle and have cut themselves off from the blessings of Zion. There is a great deal of importance connected with this principle, for by it it shall be known whether we are faithful or unfaithful. In this respect it is as essential as faith in God, as repentance of sin, as baptism for the remission of sin, or as the laying on of hands for the gift of the Holy Ghost" (Conference Report, April 1900, 47).

Such a Course Will Sanctify the Land of Zion
DOCTRINE AND COVENANTS 119:6–7

119:6 *By this law sanctify the land of Zion.* President Joseph F. Smith explained to those of latter-day Israel: "If you will sanctify the land of Zion unto the Lord through the observance of this law, it shall be a land of Zion unto you. The Lord will bless the land and make it fruitful unto you, as He did the land of the children of Israel. In ancient times the Lord blessed the earth for those who observed the law of tithing (2 Chronicles 31:5). This law was given to the children of Israel, and when they obeyed it they were prospered and had abundance; when they disobeyed it, they were afflicted with drought, with mildew, with rust, with the devouring insect, and they were impoverished and destroyed because they did not observe the law" (Conference Report, April 1900, 49).

Through the prophet Malachi, the Lord commanded ancient Israel: "Bring ye all the tithes into the storehouse, that there may be meat in mine house, and prove me now herewith, saith the Lord of hosts, if I will not open you the windows of heaven, and pour you out a blessing, that there shall not be room enough to receive it. And I will rebuke the devourer for your sakes, and he shall not destroy the fruits of your ground; neither shall your vine cast her fruit before the time in the field, saith the Lord of hosts. And all nations shall call you blessed: for ye shall be a delightsome land, saith the Lord of hosts" (Malachi 3:10–12). The renewing and sanctifying of the land is symbolic of the spiritual renewal of the Lord's people.

DOCTRINE AND COVENANTS 120

DATE: 8 JULY 1838
PLACE: FAR WEST, MISSOURI

In connection with receiving the revelation on tithing recorded in Doctrine and Covenants 119, the Prophet Joseph Smith wrote: "Revelation . . . making known the disposition of the properties tithed as named in the preceding revelation" (*History of the Church*, 3:44).

DOCTRINE AND COVENANTS 120:1

120:1 *Disposed of by a council.* In accordance with the Lord's instructions in this revelation, all "expenditures of Church funds . . . [are] authorized by the Council on the Disposition of the Tithes according to written policies. The Council is composed of the First Presidency, the Quorum of the Twelve Apostles, and the Presiding Bishopric" (Conference Report, April 1999, 26).

By mine own voice unto them. The expenditure of tithes is a sacred trust. The monies contributed come from both the poor and the wealthy. The Lord indicated that through revelation to members of the Council on the Disposition of Tithes he determines the use of these sacred funds.

DOCTRINE AND COVENANTS 121

DATE: 20 MARCH 1839
PLACE: JAIL AT LIBERTY, MISSOURI

On 27 October 1838, Governor Lilburn W. Boggs issued his infamous extermination order. Writing to General John B. Clark, commander of the state militia, he said, "The Mormons must be treated as enemies and must be exterminated or driven from the state, if necessary for the public good. Their outrages are beyond all description" (Smith, *History of the Church*, 3:175). Three days later a mob under the leadership of Colonel William O. Jennings, who had not yet received the governor's order, attacked a little settlement of Saints at Haun's Mill, killing seventeen and severely wounding others. At the same time, the mob-militia, about two thousand strong, under the command of Samuel D. Lucas, arrived near Far West as its citizens made preparations for its defense.

On Wednesday, 31 October, the Prophet was informed by Colonel Hinkle, a fellow Saint, that the officers of the militia wished to have a conference with him and several of the leaders of the Church. "I immediately complied with the request," wrote the Prophet, "and in company with Elders Sidney Rigdon and Parley P. Pratt, Colonel Wight and George W. Robinson, went into the camp of the militia. But judge of my surprise, when, instead of being treated with that respect which is due from one citizen to another, we were taken as prisoners of war, and treated with the utmost contempt. The officers would not converse with us, and the soldiers, almost to a man, insulted us as much as they felt disposed, breathing out threats against me and my companions. I cannot begin to tell the scene which I there witnessed. The loud cries and yells of more than one thousand voices, which rent the air and could be heard for miles, and the horrid and blasphemous threats and curses which were poured upon us in torrents, were enough to appall the stoutest heart. In the evening we had to lie down on the cold ground, surrounded by a strong guard, who were only kept back by the power of God from depriving us of life. We petitioned the officers to know why we were thus treated, but they utterly refused to give us any answer, or to converse with us. . . .

"[The next day] Brothers Hyrum Smith and Amasa Lyman were brought prisoners into camp. The officers of the militia held a court martial, and sentenced us to be shot, on Friday morning, on the public square of Far West as a warning to the 'Mormons'" (Smith, *History of the Church*, 3:188–90).

The lives of the Prophet and his companions were spared when General Alexander Doniphan courageously refused to carry out the illegal and immoral order. The prisoners were taken to Independence and then to Richmond, Missouri, for trial. The judge ordered that they be bound over for further trial and placed in the jail at Liberty, Missouri. Here it was that they were incarcerated in the dungeon on the bottom floor in miserable circumstances for the next four months. During this time word reached the prisoners of the atrocities committed against the Saints in Far West and other places.

During this period the Prophet communicated with the Saints by letter. Excerpts from one of those letters, dated 25 March 1839, constitute what we know today as sections 121, 122, and 123, and were first included in the Doctrine and Covenants in the 1876 edition.

"To the Church of Latter-day Saints at Quincy, Illinois, and Scattered Abroad, and to Bishop Partridge in Particular.

"Your humble servant, Joseph Smith, Jun., prisoner for the Lord Jesus Christ's sake, and for the Saints, taken and held by the power of mobocracy, under the exterminating reign of his excellency, the governor, Lilburn W. Boggs, in company with his fellow prisoners and beloved brethren, Caleb Baldwin, Lyman Wight, Hyrum Smith, and Alexander McRae, send unto you all greeting. . . .

" . . . Inasmuch as we know that the most of you are well acquainted with the wrongs and the high-handed injustice and cruelty that are practiced upon us; whereas we have been taken prisoners charged falsely with every kind of evil, and . . . a strong guard, who continually watch day and night as indefatigable as the devil does in tempting and laying snares for the people of God.

"Therefore, dearly beloved brethren, we are the more ready and willing to lay claim to your fellowship and love. For our circumstances are calculated to awaken our spirits to a sacred remembrance of everything, and we think that yours are also, and that nothing therefore can separate us from the love of God and fellowship one with another; and that every species of wickedness and cruelty practiced upon us will only tend to bind our hearts together and seal them together in love. We have no need to say to you that we are held in bonds without cause, neither is it needful that you say unto us, We are driven from our homes and smitten without cause. We mutually understand that if the inhabitants of the state of Missouri had let the Saints alone, and had been as desirable of peace as they were, there would have been nothing but peace and quietude in the state unto this day; we should not have been in this hell, surrounded with demons (if not those who are damned, they are those who shall be damned) and where we are compelled to hear nothing but blasphemous oaths, and witness a scene of blasphemy, and drunkenness and hypocrisy, and debaucheries of every description.

"And again the cries of orphans and widows would not have ascended up to God against them. Nor would innocent blood have stained the soil of Missouri. But oh! the unrelenting hand! The inhumanity and murderous disposition of this people! It shocks all nature; it beggars and defies all description; it is a tale of woe; a lamentable tale; yea a sorrowful tale; too much to tell; too much for contemplation; too much for human beings; it cannot be found among the heathens; it cannot be found among the nations where kings and tyrants are enthroned; it cannot be found among the savages of the wilderness; yea, and I think it cannot be found among the wild and ferocious beasts of the forest—that a man should be mangled for sport! women be robbed of all that they have—their last morsel for subsistence, and then be violated to gratify the hellish desires of the mob, and finally left to perish with their helpless offspring clinging around their necks. . . .

"They practice these things upon the Saints, who have done them no wrong, who are innocent and virtuous; who loved the Lord their God, and were willing to forsake all things for Christ's sake. These things are awful to relate, but they are verily true. It must needs be that offenses come, but woe unto them by whom they come" (Smith, *History of the Church*, 3:289–91).

The Prophet Pleads with the Lord for the Suffering Saints
DOCTRINE AND COVENANTS 121:1–6

121:1–6 These verses, which constitute a prayer, do not reflect a faith that is wavering, but rather a soul wearied with concern for the suffering of the innocent. The Prophet wrote with a heart sickened "with grief, because of the sufferings of the poor and much injured Saints. And we need not say to you that the floodgates of our hearts were lifted and our eyes were a fountain of tears" (Smith, *History of the Church*, 3:293).

121:1 *The pavilion that covereth thy hiding place.* A pavilion symbolizes the heavenly tabernacle or temple where the Most High dwells. The "thick clouds" which surround this holy residence signify the glory of God. God's pavilion is hidden from the eyes of mortal man (Psalm 18:11; 27:5; D&C 121:1, 4). Reference to the Lord's "hiding place" is not intended to suggest that God is an absentee landlord but rather that his presence is hidden from the wicked (D&C 101:89).

121:4 *The dark and benighted dominion of Sheol.* Sheol is a Hebrew rendering of the English word *hell*. It represents the kingdom of the devil and those who follow him.

The Lord Speaks Peace to Joseph Smith
DOCTRINE AND COVENANTS 121:7–10

121:7–10 At a particularly dreary time, letters from Emma and others at home encouraged the Prophet and prompted these verses. The Prophet Joseph Smith wrote that one token of friendship can work so that "all enmity, malice, and hatred, and past differences, misunderstandings and mismanagements are slain victorious at the feet of hope; and when the heart is sufficiently contrite, then the voice of inspiration steals along and whispers, My son, peace be to thy soul; thine adversity and thine afflictions shall be but a small moment . . . " (*History of the Church*, 3:293).

121:8 *If thou endure it well, God shall exalt thee on high.* To the Saints of his day, Peter said, "Beloved, think it not strange concerning the fiery trial which is to try you, as though some strange thing happened unto you; But rejoice, inasmuch as ye are partakers of Christ's sufferings; that, when his glory shall be revealed, ye may be glad also with exceeding joy" (1 Peter 4:12–13).

This period of confinement for the Prophet proved to be a school in which his soul was sanctified. Mercy and compassion, which often are best learned by personal suffering, are characteristics that all exalted beings must possess. Three months after recording these words, the Prophet wrote: "After a person has faith in Christ, repents of his sins, and is baptized for the remission of his sins and receives the Holy Ghost, (by the laying on of hands), which is the first Comforter, then let him continue to humble himself before God, hungering and thirsting after righteousness, and living by every word of God, and the Lord will soon say unto him, Son, thou shalt be exalted. When the Lord has thoroughly proved him, and finds that the man is determined to serve Him at all hazards, then the man will find his calling and his election made sure" (*Teachings of the Prophet Joseph Smith*, 150; D&C 132:49). See commentary on Doctrine and Covenants 131:5, "More sure word of prophecy."

121:9 *Thy friends do stand by thee.* Those that were incarcerated in Liberty Jail received with the utmost appreciation the words of friends in letters. Joseph and his companions wrote, "Those who have not been enclosed in the walls of prison without cause or provocation, can have little idea how sweet the voice of a friend is; one token of friendship from any source whatever awakens and calls into action every sympathetic feeling" (Smith, *History of the Church*, 3:293).

121:10 *Thou art not yet as Job.* Among other things, this text affirms that the scriptural story of Job is not fictional, as many have supposed. He was not a mythical character but rather a real man of exemplary faith. Unlike Job, whose wife and friends became his accusers, the Prophet Joseph Smith was loved and supported by his wife, family, and friends.

Cursed Are All Those Who Raise False Cries of Transgression against the Lord's Anointed
DOCTRINE AND COVENANTS 121:11–17

121:11–12 "From apostates the faithful have received the severest persecutions," declared the Prophet Joseph Smith. "Judas was rebuked and immediately betrayed his Lord into the hands of his enemies because Satan entered into him. There is a superior intelligence bestowed upon such as obey the Gospel with full purpose of heart, which, if sinned against, the apostate is left naked and destitute of the Spirit of God, and he is, in truth, nigh unto cursing, and his end is to be burned. When once that light which was in them is taken from them, they become as much darkened as they were previously enlightened, and then, no marvel, if all their powers should be enlisted against the truth and they, Judas like, seek the destruction of those who were their greatest benefactors" (*Teachings of the Prophet Joseph Smith*, 67).

Like Cain, the wicked are deceived into believing that they are so intelligent and crafty that they can hide their abominations and outwit the laws of justice (Moses 5:31–33). Secret combinations of wickedness breed pride and cause the wicked to become blind to threats of their own destruction. The proud and the wicked will be cut down like mighty trees of a forest that boast of themselves before the small, seemingly powerless axe in the hands of the Lord's servants.

121:11 *As the hoar frost.* The moisture that gathers on the ground during the cool of the evening to form a thin white covering is referred to as hoar frost, due to its white color.

121:15 *Their posterity shall be swept from under heaven.* See commentary on Doctrine and Covenants 105:15.

Not one of them is left to stand by the wall. This is a modern rendition of an idiom from Old Testament times that refers to the destruction of the entire male population among a family or people (1 Kings 16:11).

121:16 *Those that shall lift up the heel against mine anointed.* This phrase refers to those that fight against Jesus Christ, the Anointed One. The psalmist foretold the treachery of Judas, "Yea, mine own familiar friend, in whom I trusted, which did eat of my bread, hath lifted up his heel against me" (Psalm 41:9). To fight against those who come in the name of the Lord is to fight against the Lord's anointed. Traitors from among the Saints had betrayed those held captive in Liberty Jail and had given testimony against them, as they had spoken similar words against the Church.

121:16–17 Those who speak out against leaders of the Church do so in an attempt to hide their own sins. They become like their father Lucifer, who was and is "the accuser of our brethren" (Revelation 12:10). They project their own desires into the actions of others and show the darkness of their souls in the manner in which they speak evil against the Lord's anointed. Harold B. Lee observed: "There are some who look upon the leaders of this Church and God's anointed as men who are possessed of selfish motives. By them the words of our leaders are always twisted to try to bring a snare to the work of the Lord. Mark well those who speak evil of the Lord's anointed for they speak from impure hearts. . . .

" . . . I want to bear you my testimony that the experience I have had has taught me that those who criticize the leaders of this Church are showing signs of a spiritual sickness which, unless curbed, will bring about eventually spiritual death. I want to bear my testimony as well that those who in public seek by their criticism, to belittle our leaders or bring them into disrepute, will bring upon themselves more hurt than upon those whom they seek thus to malign. I have watched over the years, and I have read of the history of many of those who fell away from this Church, and I want to bear testimony that no apostate who ever left this Church ever prospered as an influence in his community thereafter" (Conference Report, October 1947, 67).

They Shall Not Have Right to the Priesthood
and Shall Be Damned
DOCTRINE AND COVENANTS 121:18–25

121:18 *Those who swear falsely against my servants.* Though the principle here stated is an eternal one, it had a very specific application at the time of this writing (see commentary on v. 22). "While all of these troubles with mobs were going on," commented President Joseph Fielding Smith, "and the members of the Church living in DeWitt and other settlements were being robbed and driven from their homes, other evils developed that tried the Prophet's soul. Thomas B. Marsh, who had been honored by being called to the apostleship and as the oldest member in that council was chosen as the president of the twelve, suddenly left Far West and went to Richmond in a fit of anger in October 1838. It was only a trivial matter that had caused him to be offended but he permitted it to interfere with his faith and standing in the Church. Arriving in Richmond he went before Henry Jacobs, justice of the peace, and made an affidavit consisting of the vilest slanders against the Prophet and the Church. A few days earlier, Orson Hyde had also gone to Richmond, leaving a letter with one of the brethren stating that it would reveal the secret of his leaving" (*Church History and Modern Revelation*, 2:120–21). Commenting on Thomas B. Marsh, the Prophet Joseph Smith wrote: "He had been lifted up in pride by his exaltation to office and the revelations of heaven concerning him, until he was ready to be overthrown by the first adverse wind that should cross his track, and now he has fallen, lied and sworn falsely, and is ready to take the lives of his best friends. Let all men take warning by him, and learn that he who exalteth himself, God will abase. Orson Hyde was also at Richmond and testified to most of Marsh's statements" (*History of the Church*, 3:167).

121:20 *They themselves shall be despised by those that flatter them.* In a previous letter written from Liberty Jail, the Prophet Joseph Smith had written concerning those who bore false testimony against the Saints: "Renegade 'Mormon' dissenters are running through the world and spreading various foul and libelous reports against us, thinking thereby to gain the friendship of the world, because they know that we are not of the world, and that the world hates us; therefore they [the world] make a tool of these fellows [the dissenters]; and by them try to do all the injury they can, and after that they hate them worse than they do us, because they find them to be base traitors and sycophants" (*History of the Church,* 3:230).

121:21 Righteous male descendants of Abraham have a right by birth to hold the priesthood (Abraham 2:11; D&C 132:30–31; see commentary on D&C 86:8–11). This right passes naturally to their male descendants from generation to generation. This promise, which is fundamental to the Abrahamic covenant, is renewed with every couple that enters into the new and everlasting order of marriage. When someone so blessed pursues a course to dishonor the priesthood—for instance, those priesthood holders who lift up the heel against the Lord's anointed—he will have that priesthood taken from him and will forfeit in the process his place in the family of Abraham or the family of the faithful. No longer a part of that family, he cannot bequeath to his posterity the promises reserved for the seed of Abraham, including the right to the priesthood or any of its blessings.

121:22 From the Liberty Jail, the Prophet Joseph Smith wrote concerning those that apostatized from the Church and bore false witness against the Saints: "We have waded through an ocean of tribulation and mean abuse, practiced upon us by the ill bred and the ignorant, such as Hinkle, Corrill, Phelps, Avard, Reed Peck, Cleminson, and various others, who are so very ignorant that they cannot appear respectable in any decent and civilized society, and whose eyes are full of adultery, and cannot cease from sin. Such characters as McLellin, John Whitmer, David Whitmer, Oliver Cowdery, and Martin Harris, are too mean to mention; and we had liked to have forgotten them. Marsh and 'another,' whose hearts are full of corruption, whose cloak of hypocrisy was not sufficient to shield them or to hold them up in the hour of trouble, who after having escaped the pollutions of the world through the knowledge of their Lord and Savior Jesus Christ, became again entangled and overcome—their latter end is worse than the first. But it has happened unto them according to the word of the Scripture: 'The dog has returned to his vomit, and the sow that was washed to her wallowing in the mire.'

"Again, if men sin wilfully after they have received the knowledge of the truth, there remaineth no more sacrifice for sin, but a certain fearful looking for of judgment and fiery indignation to come, which shall devour these adversaries. For he who despised Moses' law died without mercy under two or three witnesses. Of how much more severe punishment suppose ye, shall he be thought worthy, who hath sold his brother, and denied the new and everlasting covenant by which he was sanctified, calling it an unholy thing, and doing despite to the Spirit of grace.

"And again we say unto you, that inasmuch as there is virtue in us, and the Holy Priesthood has been conferred upon us—and the keys of the kingdom have not been taken from us, for verily thus saith the Lord, 'Be of good cheer, for the keys that I gave unto you are yet with you'—therefore we say unto you, dear brethren, in the name of the Lord Jesus Christ, we deliver these characters unto the buffetings of Satan until the day of redemption, that they may be dealt with according to their works; and from henceforth their works shall be made manifest" (*History of the Church*, 3:232).

After being released from Liberty Jail and again enjoying the company of his family and the Saints, the Prophet Joseph Smith further instructed: "O ye Twelve! and all Saints! profit by this important Key— that in all your trials, troubles, temptations, afflictions, bonds, imprisonments and death, see to it, that you do not betray heaven; that you do not betray Jesus Christ; that you do not betray the brethren; that you do not betray the revelations of God, whether in Bible, Book of Mormon, or Doctrine and Covenants, or any other that ever was or ever will be given and revealed unto man in this world or that which is to come. Yea, in all your kicking and flounderings, see to it that you do not this thing, lest innocent blood be found upon your skirts, and you go down to hell. All other sins are not to be compared to sinning against the Holy Ghost, and proving a traitor to the brethren" (*Teachings of the Prophet Joseph Smith*, 156).

121:24–25 Additional information is given here concerning the appointed time for death. In the wisdom of God, an individual's life may be lengthened because of righteousness (2 Kings 20:1–11) or cut short because of wickedness (Jacob 7:1–20). See commentary on Doctrine and Covenants 122:9, "Thy days are known, and thy years shall not be numbered less."

Glorious Revelations Promised Those Who Endure Valiantly
DOCTRINE AND COVENANTS 121:26–32

121:26–32 These verses and those that follow are excerpted from the letter containing this section of the Doctrine and Covenants and follow the preceding verses by several paragraphs. They are written as inspired instruction and counsel. The Prophet Joseph Smith promised to instruct the Saints regarding "whether there be one God or many gods" (v. 28); the laws and times of the sun, moon, and stars; and "the Council of the Eternal God of all other gods" (v. 32). The Prophet Joseph Smith wrote from Liberty Jail: "It has been the plan of the devil to hamper me and distress me from the beginning, to keep me from explaining myself to them [the Saints]; and I never have had opportunity to give them the plan that God has revealed to me" (*History of the Church*, 3:286). These doctrines were clarified for the Saints in some degree through the translation of the book of Abraham. Although the Saints had purchased the papyri containing writings of Abraham in 1835, it was not until 1842 that the Prophet's translation was published in the *Times and Seasons*. It was not until the latter months of his life that the Prophet Joseph Smith revealed the endowment administered in holy temples and unfolded the doctrine of the plurality of gods by preaching in plainness to the Saints in Nauvoo. See commentary on the King Follett Discourse, page 1078.

121:26 *God shall give unto you knowledge by his Holy Spirit.* "No man can receive the holy ghost without receiving revelations. The Holy Ghost is a revelator," the Prophet said (*Teachings of the Prophet Joseph Smith*, 328).

121:28 *Whether there be one God or many gods.* The crowning truths of the Restoration are those truths that deal with the nature of God. From the First Vision in the spring of 1820 to his last public discourse on 18 June 1844, Joseph Smith enhanced the Saints understanding of the God of heaven. That there are more Gods than one we learned in the First Vision, where the Father and the Son stood separate and distinct as exalted men. That we can become as God was affirmed in Joseph's final public remarks as he challenged the Saints to "hold out to the end, and we shall be resurrected and become like Gods, and reign in celestial kingdoms, principalities, and eternal dominions" (Smith, *History of the Church*, 6:500).

"I will preach on the plurality of Gods," he said on 16 June 1844. "I have selected this text for that express purpose. I wish to declare I have always and in all congregations when I have preached on the subject of the Deity, it has been the plurality of Gods. It has been preached by the Elders for fifteen years.

"I have always declared God to be a distinct personage, Jesus Christ a separate and distinct personage from God the Father, and the Holy Ghost was a distinct personage and a Spirit: and these three constitute three distinct personages and three Gods. If this is in accordance with the New Testament, lo and behold! we have three Gods anyhow, and they are plural; and who can contradict it?

"Our text says, 'And hath made us kings and priests unto God and His Father.' The Apostles have discovered that there were Gods above, for Paul says God was the Father of our Lord Jesus Christ. My object was to preach the scriptures, and preach the doctrine they contain, there being a God above, the Father of our Lord Jesus Christ. I am bold to declare I have taught all the strong doctrines publicly, and always teach stronger doctrines in public than in private.

"John was one of the men, and apostles declare they were made kings and priests unto God, the Father of our Lord Jesus Christ. It reads just so in the Revelation. Hence, the doctrine of a plurality of Gods is as prominent in the Bible as any other doctrine. It is all over the face of the Bible. It stands beyond the power of controversy. A wayfaring man, though a fool, need not err therein.

"Paul says there are Gods many and Lords many. I want to set it forth in a plain and simple manner; but to us there is but one God—that is pertaining to us; and he is in all and through all. But if Joseph Smith says there are Gods many and Lords many, they cry, 'Away with him! Crucify him! crucify him!'

"Mankind verily say that the scriptures are with them. Search the scriptures, for they testify of things that these apostates would gravely pronounce blasphemy. Paul, if Joseph Smith is a blasphemer, you are. I say there are Gods many and Lords many, but to us only one, and we are to be in subjection to that one, and no man can limit the bounds or the eternal existence of eternal time. Hath he beheld the eternal world, and is he authorized to say that there is only one God? He makes himself a fool if he thinks or says so, and there is an end of his career or progress in knowledge. He cannot obtain all knowledge, for he has sealed up the gate to it" (Smith, *History of the Church*, 6:474–75).

121:29 Those that will receive thrones and principalities have entered into the new and everlasting covenant of marriage and it has been sealed unto them by the Holy Spirit of promise. See Doctrine and Covenants 132:19.

121:30–31 By means of the Urim and Thummim, Abraham was shown the manner of the creation, times, revolutions, and reckoning of the sun, moon, and stars (Abraham 3:1–13).

121:32 *The Council of the Eternal God of all other gods.* "The Eternal

God of all other gods" is our Eternal Father, meaning the father of our spirits. The psalmist declared, "Ye are gods; and all of you are children of the most High" (Psalm 82:6). When we assembled in council with our Eternal Father, we sat in the council of the Gods; all who assembled there were of the family of the gods. The Prophet Joseph Smith explained, "In the beginning the head of the Gods called a council of the Gods; and they came together and concocted a plan to create the world and people it" (*Teachings of the Prophet Joseph Smith*, 349).

Why Many Are Called and Few Are Chosen
DOCTRINE AND COVENANTS 121:33–40

121:34 *Many called, but few are chosen.* If we live beneath our privileges, blessings go unclaimed, calls go unmagnified, and opportunities are lost. To be chosen is to have chosen to honor every opportunity to serve the Lord and to stand in defense of the gospel cause.

121:34–40 The Prophet Joseph Smith drew upon the experiences of the previous months to pen these inspired words. These thoughts reflect the sorrow of seeing friends become traitors and then war against the Saints. They were given by way of explanation as to how those who had been sustained as presiding authorities of the Church could apostatize and become enemies of the kingdom of God. It was a difficult lesson for the Saints to endure—that wickedness may be found even among those of high and holy station. The Three Witnesses to the Book of Mormon, the presidency of the Church in Missouri, and six members of the Quorum of the Twelve Apostles had lost their rights to and the authority of the priesthood. Foremost among those who betrayed the Saints was Thomas B. Marsh, former president of the Quorum of the Twelve Apostles. After the Saints had been driven from Nauvoo, Illinois, and settled in the Rocky Mountains, he went to Salt Lake City, where he confessed to the wrongs he had committed and pleaded for forgiveness. He was called on to speak to the Saints at the Tabernacle. Marsh stated: "Many have said to me, 'How is it that a man like you, who understood so much of the revelations of God as recorded in the Book of Doctrine and Covenants, should fall away?' . . .

"I have sought diligently to know the Spirit of Christ since I turned my face Zionward, and I believe I have obtained it. I have frequently wanted to know how my apostasy began, and I have come to the conclusion that I must have lost the Spirit of the Lord out of my heart.

"The next question is, 'How and when did you lose the Spirit?' I became jealous of the Prophet, and then I saw double, and overlooked everything that was right, and spent all my time in looking for the evil; and then, when the Devil began to lead me, it was easy for the carnal mind to rise up, which is anger, jealousy, and wrath. I could feel it within me; I felt angry and wrathful; and the Spirit of the Lord being gone, as the Scriptures say, I was blinded, and I thought I saw a beam in brother Joseph's eye, but it was nothing but a mote, and my own eye was filled with the beam; but I thought I saw a beam in his, and I wanted to get it out; and, as brother Heber says, I got mad, and I wanted everybody else to be mad. I talked with Brother Brigham and Brother Heber, and I wanted them to be mad like myself; and I saw they were not mad, and I got madder still because they were not. Brother Brigham, with a cautious look, said, 'Are you the leader of the Church, brother Thomas?' I answered, 'No.' 'Well then,' said he, 'Why do you not let that alone?'

"Well, this is about the amount of my hypocrisy—I meddled with that which was not my business" (*Journal of Discourses*, 5:206–7).

For details concerning the events that led to the apostasy of Thomas B. Marsh, see commentary on Doctrine and Covenants 112:10.

121:36 *The rights of the priesthood are inseparably connected with the powers of heaven.* Authority in the priesthood is obtained by the laying on of hands and must always be traceable to one who had it and was properly authorized to confer it upon the one laying claim to it. Authority functions in such a manner that every priest in the Church has the same authority as every other priest in the Church. One priest cannot perform a baptism that has greater effect than any other priest, nor can anyone holding any other priesthood office perform a baptism that is more efficacious or binding than a baptism performed by a priest. In like manner every elder in the Church has the same authority as every other elder in the Church. Thus there would be no difference found in any ordinances performed that required the office of an elder or one holding any office in the Melchizedek Priesthood.

Power in the priesthood differs from authority in the priesthood in that it does not come by the laying on of hands but rather through righteousness, faith, and knowledge. Thus, no two priesthood holders have the same power in their priesthood. To give, for instance, a patriarchal blessing, one must both hold the office of a patriarch and be so living as to enjoy a rich outpouring of the spirit of revelation. The office comes by ordination; the inspiration or ability to receive revelation comes through the companionship of the Holy Ghost, having a clear understanding of the principles of the gospel, and experience in responding to the direction of the Spirit.

121:38 *Kick against the pricks.* This imagery comes from the direction of the Lord to Saul on the road to Damascus (Acts 9:1–5). The image elicited is of an ox resisting its owner's sharp goading stick by kicking back against it, only to drive the sharp point into its hoof. The message is that those who fight against the Lord or his people destroy themselves with self-inflicted wounds.

121:39 The priesthood bears the name *Melchizedek,* which means "king of righteousness." The priesthood holder is expected to be a king, one who rules and reigns in righteousness. Anything that is unrighteous stands outside the bounds, or dominion, of his kingdom.

The Priesthood Should Be Used Only in Righteousness
DOCTRINE AND COVENANTS 121:41–46

121:41–46 These verses are the foundation of power to preside in the priesthood in time and in eternity, and reveal how God the Father exercises power and authority. Each of the approaches and characteristics mentioned reveal his nature. The doctrine of the priesthood contained herein includes truths by which we may become like him. He is a "Man of Holiness" (Moses 6:57). Through the spirit of truth, he invites his children to do good without force or compulsion (Moroni 7:16). He is long-suffering as he waits for them to discover and learn the exactness and veracity of his doctrines. He is gentle and meek in teaching them truth and allowing them to make it part of their lives. He does not seek his own good but does all things out of pure love for his children. He does not feign love as a disguise for manipulating and controlling them. Even in his chastisement, his motive is pure love (D&C 95:1). He does not seek to dominate by virtue of his fatherhood. In the words of Alma, he asks his children to "give place" in their hearts for the truths he teaches them (Alma 32:27). He is virtuous in thought and deed, possessing perfect purity. We know that we may put our everlasting trust and faith in him. All who give him dominion over them do so with the utmost confidence in his sincere and fatherly intent to bring to pass their immortality and eternal life. The grand secret of presiding in the priesthood is that there is power in righteousness. Virtuous beings will freely give honor and glory to their Father, who is in every respect a "Man of Holiness."

The guidelines in these verses are given as truths that cannot be trampled upon. Each priesthood bearer must learn them and make them part of his character if he is to ever preside over a family in righteousness. Likewise, those who are called to presiding offices in the Church should govern upon these principles of righteousness. By doing so they will also receive power in the priesthood within their sphere of teaching and presiding over the Saints.

121:43 Those who cherish truth know that chastening may be a manifestation of love (D&C 95:1). "A frank and open rebuke provoketh a good man to emulation," the Prophet Joseph Smith wrote from Liberty Jail; "and in the hour of trouble he will be your best friend" (*History of the Church*, 3:295). "If you are ever called upon to chasten a person," President Brigham Young counseled, "never chasten beyond the balm you have within you to bind up" (*Journal of Discourses*, 9:124–25).

121:45 *The doctrine of the priesthood.* "What then is the doctrine of the priesthood? And how shall we live as the servants of the Lord?" asked Elder Bruce R. McConkie. "This doctrine is that God our Father is a glorified, a perfected, and an exalted being who has all might, all power, and all dominion, who knows all things and is infinite in all his attributes, and who lives in the family unit.

"It is that our Eternal Father enjoys this high status of glory and perfection and power because his faith is perfect and his priesthood is unlimited.

"It is that priesthood is the very name of the power of God, and that if we are to become like him, we must receive and exercise his priesthood or power as he exercises it.

"It is that he has given us an endowment of heavenly power here on earth, which is after the order of his Son and which, because it is the power of God, is of necessity without beginning of days or end of years.

"It is that we can enter an order of the priesthood named the new and everlasting covenant of marriage (see D&C 131:2), named also the patriarchal order, because of which order we can create for ourselves eternal family units of our own, patterned after the family of God our Heavenly Father.

"It is that we have power, by faith, to govern and control all things, both temporally and spiritual; to work miracles and perfect lives; to stand in the presence of God and be like him because we have gained his faith, his perfections and his power, or in other words the fulness of his priesthood.

"This, then, is the doctrine of the priesthood, than which there neither is nor can be anything greater. This is the power we can gain through
faith and righteousness.

"Truly, there is power in the priesthood—power to do all things!

"If the world itself was created by the power of the priesthood, surely
that same power can move mountains and control the elements.

"If one-third of the hosts of heaven were cast down to earth by the
power of the priesthood, surely that same power can put at defiance the
armies of nations or stay the fall of atomic bombs.

"If all men shall be raised from mortality to immortality by the power
of the priesthood, surely that same power can cure the diseased and the
dying and raise the dead.

"Truly there is power in the priesthood—a power which we seek to
acquire to us, a power which we devoutly pray may rest upon us and upon
our posterity forever" (Conference Report, April 1982, 50).

121:46 All eternal relationships are based on free choice. Our Father
in Heaven will not force any of his sons or daughters to embrace any
covenant or any truth contrary to their will. God derives his power from
the allegiance given him because his children love and honor him. His
unfailing love and unselfish efforts to bless his children are his only means
of drawing them to him. There is no compulsion in the kingdom of
heaven.

Thy scepter an unchanging scepter of righteousness and truth. A scepter
is a staff or rod, which, like a throne or a crown, is a symbol of kingship
and its accompanying authority and power. In this text we are told that
the authority and power of the Melchizedek Priesthood centers in the
principles of "righteousness and truth." The word *righteousness* literally
means "to move in a straight line," it is to be "up right," and "virtuous."
Truth, as used here, carries the idea of conformity to correct principles or
doctrines. Thus, the authority and power of the priesthood centers in the
"up right" or "virtuous" application of eternal principles or the light of
heaven. This meaning is captured in the name *Melchizedek,* by which the
priesthood is known. It naturally follows that the priesthood of God will
never be found conscribing agency. All that is done in the Church and
kingdom of God must represent free will and be accomplished by "persuasion, by long-suffering, by gentleness and meekness, and by love
unfeigned" (v. 41).

DOCTRINE AND COVENANTS 122

DATE: BETWEEN 20 AND 25 MARCH 1839
PLACE: JAIL AT LIBERTY, MISSOURI

This revelation contains the word of the Lord to Joseph Smith the Prophet while he, his brother Hyrum, Sidney Rigdon, Lyman Wight, Caleb Baldwin, and Alexander McRae were held prisoners in the jail at Liberty, Missouri. See introduction to commentary on Doctrine and Covenants 121.

The Ends of the Earth Shall Inquire after the Name of Joseph Smith

DOCTRINE AND COVENANTS 122:1–4

122:1–2 As Latter-day Saints, our commission is to bear witness of the restored gospel to all the peoples of the earth. Central to that testimony is the announcement that Joseph Smith was the man chosen by God to stand at the head of this dispensation. We cannot be true to that commission independent of the testimony that Joseph Smith is the great prophet of the Restoration. If the adversary can get us to substitute something for that message, the victory is his. It is not our purpose to convert people to programs, to activities, or to a Latter-day Saint culture. Nor can we modify the message the Lord gave us in an attempt to be more acceptable. To make such things the focus of our efforts is to lose sight of our destiny and purpose and will eventually cause us to lose our own way. There is power in such a testimony, and every effort is made by the adversary to keep us from bearing it. Perhaps his most effective ploy is the notion that we should not testify about Joseph Smith for fear that people will think we worship him instead of Christ. The hope here is to gain respectability in the eyes of professing Christians by emphasizing our faith in Christ while avoiding reference to Joseph Smith. We cannot follow such a course without offending the Spirit. Joseph Smith is the great revelator of Christ for this dispensation. It is through him—that is, the revelations given him—that we have learned every truth about Christ we have been commissioned to teach the nations of the earth.

We can no more disassociate our message from Joseph Smith than we can disassociate Moses from the law that bears his name, John from the baptism he performed, or the Revelator from the book he wrote. We cannot accept Christ without accepting those he has sent in his name. We cannot declare the message of the Restoration without telling the story of the First Vision. If God did not speak to Joseph Smith and if he did not send the ancient prophets to him to give him the keys, powers, and authorities that were theirs, we have no message to bear. Our testimony is like that of Brigham Young, who said, "There is not a man or woman that loves the truth, who has heard the report of the Book of Mormon, but the Spirit of the Almighty has testified to him, or her of its truth; neither has any man heard the name of Joseph Smith, but the Spirit has whispered to him—'He is a true Prophet'" (*Journal of Discourses*, 1:93).

122:1 *Thy name.* See commentary on Joseph Smith–History 1:33, page 19.

Hell shall rage against thee. Every truth of salvation is attested to by two witnesses: (1) the sweet, quiet whisperings of the Spirit and (2) the loud, ugly, and rancorous hollering of the adversary. If the prince of darkness and his legions do not oppose a doctrine, fighting and warring against it, we can have every assurance it is not a principle of salvation. The importance of a doctrine can always be measured in Satan's opposition to it. Standing opposite the greatest doctrines may always be found the greatest heresies. Further, it is the practice among people of evil disposition that when they cannot refute a person's doctrine they attack their character.

Had Satan chosen to leave Joseph Smith and the Latter-day Saint people alone, we would have every reason to hold them suspect as far as their claim to possessing the truths of salvation is concerned. Such was never their lot, for as the Prophet observed, "As for the perils which I am called to pass through, they seem but a small thing to me, as the envy and wrath of man have been my common lot all the days of my life; and for what cause it seems mysterious, unless I was ordained from before the foundation of the world for some good end, or bad, as you may choose to call it" (D&C 127:2).

122:4 Though the influence of traitors caused Joseph Smith much difficulty and resulted in considerable suffering, their names today are virtually unknown—and then only for their pitiful wickedness. But the name Joseph Smith is had in great honor by millions upon millions of faithful Latter-day Saints. To him was given the promise that his voice would be more terrible in the midst of his enemies than the fierce lion. The expression is reminiscent of the prophesy of Micah, which was quoted three times by the Savior to the nation of the Nephites as he described the events of the last days. "And the remnant of Jacob shall be among the Gentiles in the midst of many people as a lion among the beasts of the forest, as a young lion among the flocks of sheep: who, if he go through, both treadeth down, and teareth in pieces, and none can deliver" (Micah 5:8; 3 Nephi 16:15; 20:16; 21:12). With graphic imagery, the text assures that truth will prevail and that the gospel restored by Joseph Smith and carried with power by missionaries who testify that he was a prophet will lay waste to all that opposes it. All who opposed the Prophet will be confounded, and victory will be the Lord's.

All His Perils and Travails Shall Give Joseph Smith Experience and Be for His Good
DOCTRINE AND COVENANTS 122:5–9

122:7 *All these things shall give thee experience, and shall be for thy good.* Difficulty faced well rewards its subjects with greater strength. Greatness of character can come only from the rigors of experience in which it is forged. There is a purifying and sanctifying power that grows out of suffering that cannot, perhaps, be gained in any other way.

122:9 *Their bounds are set, they cannot pass.* The reference is to those who held Joseph Smith and his companions captive in the dungeon of Liberty Jail. Angels stood as companions to their captive brethren. They would assure that the bounds the Lord had set for the fiends that held his servants captive would not be traduced.

Thy days are known, and thy years shall not be numbered less. "For there is a time appointed for every man, according as his works shall be" (D&C 121:25). As to those of the Saints who suffer with sickness or affliction, the Lord said, "It shall come to pass that he that hath faith in me to be healed, and is not appointed unto death, shall be healed" (D&C 42:48). At the funeral of Richard L. Evans, a member of the Quorum of the Twelve, Joseph Fielding Smith, then president of the Church, said, "No righteous man is taken before his time" (unpublished funeral address, text in possession of authors). Joseph Smith had the sure promise that he would not be taken until his work had been completed.

DOCTRINE AND COVENANTS 123

DATE: MARCH 1839
PLACE: JAIL AT LIBERTY, MISSOURI

This section is an excerpt of the same letter from which the previous two sections of the Doctrine and Covenants were selected. The letter was written by the Prophet Joseph Smith while he was illegally incarcerated in Liberty, Missouri. See introduction to Doctrine and Covenants 121.

The Saints Should Collect and Publish an Account of Their Sufferings and Persecutions
DOCTRINE AND COVENANTS 123:1–6

123:1–6 Dr. Clark V. Johnson, professor of Church history and doctrine at Brigham Young University, compiled and published over 700 redress petitions of the Saints regarding the conflicts in Missouri. He has written: "As an outgrowth of the Mormon War, Joseph Smith spent the winter of 1838–39 confined to jail in Liberty, Missouri. While imprisoned, he instructed the Saints to assemble all their grievances against Missouri, to organize a committee, and to present the information to the U.S. government (D&C 123:1–6). Joseph sent word to the Saints to prepare affidavits of their recent experiences with the design of securing redress from the federal government for the losses they had suffered in Missouri at the hands of mobocrats. In 1839 Church members commenced writing affidavits of their Missouri experiences and swearing to their authenticity before civil authorities, including justices of the peace, clerks of the court, clerks of the circuit court, clerks of county commissioner's courts, and notary publics in two counties in Iowa and ten counties in Illinois. Thus the Saints took every precaution to send sworn, legal documents authenticated by the seals of local government officials. They even sent documents authenticating the officials themselves. During the ensuing years the Mormons presented these documents to the federal government in an effort to obtain reparation for their sufferings in Missouri.

"The petitions indicate that the Nauvoo Saints made at least three and probably four separate attempts to obtain redress from Congress. . . . Church leaders made the first appeal beginning late in 1839. . . . Joseph Smith led the Mormon delegation, which originally consisted of Elias Higbee, Sidney Rigdon, and Orrin Porter Rockwell; Robert Foster later joined the group as a physician to Sidney Rigdon. The Prophet and Higbee were the first members of the delegation to reach Washington, D.C., arriving 28 November 1839. On the following day they met with President Martin Van Buren, who showed some sympathy but offered no assistance. By 23 December 1839, Rigdon, Foster, and Rockwell had arrived in Washington, D.C. Together the five members of this delegation made every effort to place the Mormon cause before the U.S. Congress. Besides the introductory memorial signed by Joseph Smith, Sidney Rigdon, and Elias Smith, they presented 491 individual claims to Congress (Smith, *History of the Church*, 4:74). Nothing came from these attempts. Frustrated by their lack of success, Joseph, Porter Rockwell, and Dr. Foster left Washington late in February 1840 (Smith, *History of the Church*, 4:81). Rigdon and Higbee remained in Washington a few weeks more continuing the effort. However, nothing came of this final attempt, and Higbee returned to Nauvoo, followed shortly by Rigdon" (Clark, *Mormon Redress Petitions*, xix-xxi).

123:2 The petitions for redress ranged from terse to tedious. Stephen Blackman, for example, was very concise in his written statement: "State of Missouri Dr [due] to Stephen Blackman For damage and loss of property by burning and being driven from the State $150 For damage by loss of Son there is no earthly consideration can compensate" (Clark, *Mormon Redress Petitions*, 143).

123:6 *Claim that promise which shall call him forth from his hiding place.* After the Saints were driven from Jackson County, Missouri, the Lord gave them instructions to importune at the feet of the judge, the governor, and the president for redress (D&C 101:86–89). It was only after the Saints had done their part to follow the procedures of justice delineated in the Constitution of the United States and were not upheld in their rights that the Lord would "arise and come forth out of his hiding place, and in his fury vex the nation" (D&C 101:89). In order for the Saints to have claim on the Lord's promise they needed to obey his commands concerning the presentation of affidavits to the government leaders (D&C 82:10). That the Lord did come out in his fury against the nation is evidenced by the Civil War. See commentary on Doctrine and Covenants 105:15; 121:1.

The Same Spirit That Established False Creeds Also Leads to Persecution of the Saints
DOCTRINE AND COVENANTS 123:7–10

123:7–10 The Prophet Joseph Smith attributes the persecutions of the Saints to the religious bigotry of the Missourians. Regardless of historical commentary attributing the conflict between the Saints and the old settlers to cultural differences, political power, or economic advantage, the main complaint that the Missourians had against the Saints was their religion. For example, Captain Samuel Bogart, who led a company of Caldwell County Militia against the Saints, was a Methodist minister. He and two other ministers, Neil Gilliam and Sashel Woods, led much of the opposition to the Saints. The theme of religious persecution is borne out even more plainly by the fact that many Saints were given the opportunity to remain in Missouri if "they would deny their faith or their religion" (Clark, *Mormon Redress Petitions*, 158).

123:7 *The most damning hand of murder.* The Savior referred to those of his day that sought to kill him as having the devil for their father (John 8:44). Murderers will be "thrust down to hell . . . [and] shall not be redeemed from the devil until the last resurrection" (D&C 76:84–85). The Prophet Joseph Smith taught the Saints, "your friends who have been murdered for the truth's sake in the persecutions shall triumph gloriously in the celestial world, while their murderers shall welter for ages in torment, even until they shall have paid the uttermost farthing" (*Teachings of the Prophet Joseph Smith*, 359).

The fathers, who have inherited lies. Jeremiah prophetically described the day of Restoration saying, "O Lord, my strength, and my fortress, and my refuge in the day of affliction, the Gentiles shall come unto thee from the ends of the earth, and shall say, Surely our fathers have inherited lies, vanity, and things wherein there is no profit. Shall a man make gods unto himself, and they are no gods? Therefore, behold, I will this once cause them to know, I will cause them to know mine hand and my might; and they shall know that my name is the Lord" (Jeremiah 16:19–21).

123:7–8 It would be hard to overstate the wickedness or the darkness that has been spawned by the creeds of historical Christianity. By their very nature they deny the principle of revelation, enshrining in its stead the philosophical vagaries of men. They are the banners of tyrants and the colors under which the enemies of agency, and freedom of religion have marched. They have been the source of license by which the Saints of God have been hounded, pillaged, tortured, and slain in one generation after another. They are the children of priestcraft born to mystify the simple truths of heaven in such a manner as to convince the honest truth seeker that only those who have been baptized in the sophistry of men can understand them. Thus by blocking the light of heaven they cause a spiritual eclipse and establish themselves as the way the truth and the light. Wherever creeds are found one can also expect to find a paid clergy, the simple truths of the gospel cloaked in the dark robes of mystery, religious intolerance, and a history of bloodshed.

Many among All Sects Will Yet Receive the Truth
DOCTRINE AND COVENANTS 123:11–17

123:11–17. The need has never been greater for publishing the truth to all of the world. Satan has set up a kingdom whose doctrines include all manner of lies concerning the Lord's people and his church. Many people among the religions of the world know instinctively that the creeds of their faith are incorrect. They know by the Spirit of God that they are his children and that they were created in his image. The apostasy left the world barren of the fruits of truth. The Restoration of the fulness of the gospel provided the truths that the honest in heart seek. Yet they are left to wander the earth seeking the word of the Lord (Amos 8:11–12). We are stewards of the Restoration and must do all within our power to publish the glad tidings of truth. Thus, the answer to attacks against the truthfulness of the Book of Mormon is to flood the earth with copies of that volume, allowing all people to judge for themselves as they read and pray concerning its testimony of Jesus Christ. Likewise, the answer to every attack against the kingdom of God is to publish the truth as far and wide as our means will permit through members, full-time missionaries, books, newspapers, magazines, the Internet, videos, television and radio interviews, and any other means at our disposal through which the Spirit of God might witness to the heart of those who are seeking the truth. See commentary on Doctrine and Covenants 71:1–4.

DOCTRINE AND COVENANTS 124

DATE: 19 JANUARY 1841
PLACE: NAUVOO, ILLINOIS

This revelation was given during a brief period of respite that followed the expulsion of the Saints from Missouri and included the escape of the Prophet and his companions from their imprisonment in the Liberty Jail. It preceded the expulsion of the Saints from the state of Illinois and their great westward movement. Along with matters that dealt with the building of the city of Nauvoo, this revelation directed the Saints once again to build a temple to their God. This was done at the cost of all the energy, strength, faith, and means available to them. For which in turn they were granted the crowning revelations of the Restoration. It is in this revelation that the doctrine of baptism for the dead is first announced. This was followed almost immediately by the revelation of the fulness of the ordinances of the temple. Surely it can be said that the revelations received during this period constitute the strength, power, glory, and genius of Mormonism. Truly the spirit of Mormonism is the spirit of Nauvoo.

Joseph Smith Is Commanded to Make a Solemn Proclamation of the Gospel to the President of the United States, the Governors, and the Rulers of All Nations
DOCTRINE AND COVENANTS 124:1–14

124:1 *That I might show forth my wisdom through the weak things of the earth.* See commentary on Doctrine and Covenants 1:19.

124:2 *This stake which I have planted to be a cornerstone of Zion.* It is the city of Nauvoo to which reference is made here. Today a new stake is organized when there are sufficient people in a given geographic area to provide leadership and to sustain the various priesthood and auxiliary programs of the Church. In the early history of the Church a city-stake, Kirtland for instance, was laid out first and then the people came to live in it. Nauvoo was such a city-stake. A plan for the city was created and then people purchased lots and commenced to build up Zion, or the city. Thus, to say that Nauvoo is or was "a cornerstone of Zion" is to say that the city was built according to the master plan by which all city-stakes were to be built.

The "corner-stone" of the temple, an important civic edifice, has provided rich scriptural imagery. It is used in at least three different ways: first, it is that upon which the rest of that which is built is to rest (Job 38:6); second, it ties two walls together, thus keeping them straight and true, or just and right (Isaiah 28:16); and third, it describes the function performed by a keystone, or capstone, which holds the other stones in the building in place (Psalm 118:22). In each instance the imagery fits the city-stake of Nauvoo. The city represented the capstone of the ministry of the Prophet Joseph Smith. The revelations received here hold everything in place that was restored or revealed to him. The power with which the Saints were endowed in its temple enabled them to go west in the faith that they could do the impossible, which they did. Thereafter the doctrines of Nauvoo become the theological foundation upon which all subsequent generations have built.

Shall be polished with the refinement which is after the similitude of a palace. The Saints were to build up cities that, as stakes of Zion, reflected the glory of God. The spirit of this counsel is found in the instruction given by Brigham Young to the Saints as they colonized the West. He charged them saying, "Let the people build good houses, plant good vineyards and orchards, make good roads, build beautiful cities in which may be found magnificent edifices for the convenience of the public, handsome streets skirted with shade trees, fountains of water, crystal streams, and every tree, shrub and flower that will flourish in this climate, to make our mountain home a paradise and our hearts wells of gratitude to the God of Joseph, enjoying it all with thankful hearts, saying constantly, 'not mine but thy will be done, O Father'" (Young, *Journal of Discourses*, 10:3–4).

124:2–14 *Make a solemn proclamation of my gospel.* The Prophet Joseph Smith was killed before he could write this proclamation. Initially, his efforts were hindered by the death of his assistant, Robert B. Thompson, who died 27 August 1841. Later efforts were hampered by the apostasies of John C. Bennett and William Law, both of whom were called to assist the Prophet in issuing the proclamation (vv. 16–107). Following the death of brother Thompson, further efforts were made to write the proclamation 22 December 1841. The Prophet Joseph Smith recorded: "This evening I commenced giving instructions to the scribe [Willard

Richards] concerning writing the proclamation to the kings of the earth, mentioned in the revelation given January 19, 1841" (*History of the Church*, 4:483–84). Other concerns intervened with these efforts until finally in November 1843 the Prophet Joseph Smith "instructed Elders Richards, Hyde, Taylor, and Phelps to write a 'Proclamation to the Kings of the Earth'" (*History of the Church*, 6:80). But again other concerns took the Prophet's immediate attention, particularly the building of the Nauvoo Temple. The need to fulfill this responsibility was still upon his mind, however (Smith, *History of the Church*, 6:176–77). William W. Phelps reported that he did write a twenty-two-page manuscript under the direction of the Prophet Joseph Smith in the spring of 1844, but that he stopped after the martyrdom. A 16-page pamphlet was written in behalf of the Twelve Apostles by Parley P. Pratt and published in 1845 by Wilford Woodruff in Liverpool, England, entitled "Proclamation of the Twelve to the Kings of the World," which ultimately fulfilled the Lord's command in this revelation (Smith, *History of the Church*, 7:558).

Hyrum Smith, David W. Patten, Joseph Smith Sen., and Others Are Blessed for Their Integrity and Virtues

DOCTRINE AND COVENANTS 124:15–21

124:15 *Hyrum Smith.* Hyrum Smith was described by his Prophet brother as having "the mildness of a lamb, and the integrity of a Job, and in short, the meekness and humility of Christ" (Smith, *History of the Church*, 2:338). When John Taylor looked upon Hyrum's slain body, he reflected, "He was a great and good man, and my soul was cemented to his. If ever there was an exemplary, honest, and virtuous man, an embodiment of all that is noble in the human form, Hyrum Smith was its representative" (Smith, *History of the Church*, 7:107).

124:16 *John C. Bennett.* In 1840 Bennett arrived in Nauvoo offering to help the Saints obtain a city charter and joined the Church shortly thereafter. A man of some ability he was called to serve as an assistant to the Prophet while Sidney Rigdon struggled with bad health and was also elected the first mayor of Nauvoo in 1841. In May of 1842 he apparently intended to do harm to the Prophet during a sham battle conducted by the Nauvoo Legion. After "the gentle breathings of [the] Spirit [whispered to the Prophet Joseph Smith] that there was mischief concealed in that sham battle," Bennett's conduct was investigated (Smith, *History of the*

Church, 5:4). The inquiry found him guilty of adultery and of teaching that his illicit sexual behavior was condoned by Church leaders.

His behavior having been exposed, he sought to even the score and in 1842 published *The History of the Saints; or, An Exposé of Joe Smith and Mormonism* in which he charged Joseph Smith with being "one of the grossest and most infamous impostors that ever appeared upon the face of the earth" (Bennett, *History of the Saints*, 3).

124:18 *Lyman Wight.* A companion of the Prophet Joseph Smith in Liberty Jail, Lyman Wight was chosen to fill the vacancy in the Quorum of the Twelve created by the death of David W. Patten. After the Prophet's death he refused to acknowledge the right of Brigham Young or the Quorum of the Twelve to preside over him. Contrary to their direction he led a group of Saints from Wisconsin to settle in Texas. He was excommunicated 3 December 1848.

Bear him up as on eagle's wings. Speaking of those who "wait upon the Lord," Isaiah said, they "shall renew their strength; they shall mount up with wings as eagles; they shall run, and not be weary; and they shall walk, and not faint" (Isaiah 40:31). The same promise is given those who keep the Word of Wisdom (D&C 89:19–20).

124:19 The three men named in this verse—David W. Patten (thirty-eight), of the Quorum of the Twelve; Edward Partridge (forty-six), first bishop of the Church; and Joseph Smith Sr. (sixty-nine), first patriarch to the Church—all died as a result of the Missouri persecutions.

John Taylor commented: "There is something said concerning Joseph Smith, Sen., the father of the Prophet Joseph Smith, of whom it is said that he sitteth with Abraham, at his right hand. (See D & C 124:19.) Who was Abraham? A patriarch. Who was Father Joseph Smith? A patriarch. It is quite fitting, therefore, that he should associate with Abraham, who was and is also a patriarch" (*Gospel Kingdom*, 184).

124:20–21 George Miller was the first man in the history of the Church to serve as a bishop over a ward. Earlier Edward Partridge and Newel K. Whitney served as regional or traveling bishops (D&C 20:66). Bishop Partridge served the Saints in Missouri and the surrounding areas; Bishop Whitney received responsibility for Ohio and the eastern states.

At the suggestion of the Prophet Joseph Smith, the City council divided Nauvoo into four political divisions called wards on 1 March 1841 (Smith, *History of the Church*, 4:305–6). Consequently, four bishops, Newel K. Whitney, George Miller, Isaac Higbee, and Vinson Knight (D&C 124:141), were assigned to preside over these areas. As part of their stewardship they were responsible to receive the consecrations, or tithes and offerings, of the Saints living within those ward boundaries. Their responsibilities dealt primarily with temporal concerns, whereas spiritual matters were administered through the Melchizedek Priesthood. On 20 August 1842 the Nauvoo Stake High Council determined, "that the city of Nauvoo be divided into ten [ecclesiastical] wards, according to the division made by the temple committee; and that there be a bishop appointed over each ward; and also that other bishops be appointed over such districts immediately out of the city and adjoining thereto as shall be considered necessary" (Smith, *History of the Church*, 5:119).

This pattern of geographical areas being assigned bishops to preside over the temporal needs of the members continued as the Saints moved to Winter Quarters during the exodus from Nauvoo and as they settled the Great Basin. On 6 April 1847, Newel K. Whitney was sustained as the presiding bishop of the Church. Others were called as bishops within stakes of Zion, which practice has continued to the present day.

The Saints Are Commanded to Build Both a House for the Entertainment of Strangers and a Temple in Nauvoo
DOCTRINE AND COVENANTS 124:22–28

124:23 *A house that strangers may come from afar to lodge therein.* It was not intended that the Latter-day Saints isolate themselves from the world. This revelation called for the building of what is called the Nauvoo House to provide comfortable lodgings for visitors to their city. Joseph Smith explained, "It is important that the Nauvoo House should be finished, that we may have a suitable place wherein to entertain the great ones of the earth, and teach them the truth" (*History of the Church*, 5:137).

The Prophet Joseph Smith emphasized the significance of the Nauvoo House in bringing the Church out of obscurity in the April 1843 general conference. He stated: "It is necessary that this conference give importance to the Nauvoo House. A prejudice exists against building it, in favor of the Temple; and the conference is required to give stress to the building of the Nauvoo House. This is the most important matter for the time being; for there is no place in this city where men of wealth, character and influence from abroad can go to repose themselves, and it is necessary we should have such a place. The Church must build it or abide the result of not fulfilling the commandment" (Smith, *History of the Church*, 5:328).

The Nauvoo House was never completed as originally designed. After the martyrdom of the Prophet, his wife, Emma, inherited the unfinished building (v. 56). She later married Lewis C. Bidamon, who tore down one wing of the Nauvoo House to complete a smaller two-story house on the southwest corner of the original building.

124:26–27 These verses, which refer to the building of a temple in Nauvoo, extend the invitation to scattered Israel to return as their fathers did anciently, bringing with them their rich treasures that they might aid in the building of the house of the Lord. John Snyder (v. 22) was appointed to receive funds and materials for the building of the temple. The *History of the Church* under 22 December 1841 reads, "The word of the Lord came unto Joseph the Seer, verily thus saith the Lord, let my servant John Snyder take a mission to the eastern continent, unto all the conferences now sitting in that region; and let him carry a package of epistles, that shall be written by my servants the Twelve making known unto them their duties concerning the building of my houses which I have appointed unto you, saith the Lord, that they may bring their gold and their silver, and their precious stones, and the box-tree, and the fir-tree, and all fine wood to beautify the place of my sanctuary, saith the Lord; and let him return speedily with all means which shall be put into his hands, even so. Amen" (Smith, *History of the Church*, 4:483).

124:27 *Build a house to my name.* In the general conference October, 1840 the Saints appointed a committee to build the House of the Lord (Smith, *History of the Church*, 4:186, 205).

124:28 *Restore again that which was lost.* Latter-day Saints could hardly claim to be in possession of the faith of ancient Israel and not at the same time claim to have received as a part of that restoration the concept of temple worship. Whenever the Lord has had a people that he acknowledged as his own, they have been a temple-building people. Thus from the days of Adam to the time of Christ temples existed in which sacred ceremonies and ordinances were performed, revelations were given, and the Lord manifested himself to the faithful. That the blessings of the holy temple were available to the former-day Saints is made clear in the Prophet's translation of the Egyptian papyri. We are told that one particular figure represents "God, sitting upon his throne, clothed with power and authority; with a crown of eternal light upon his head; representing also the grand Key-words of the Holy Priesthood, as revealed to Adam in the Garden of Eden, as also to Seth, Noah, Melchizedek, Abraham, and all to whom the Priesthood was revealed" (Facsimile 2, Explanation, Figure 3; see also D&C 124:38–39).

The fulness of the priesthood. In a broad sense the fulness of the priesthood includes the authority to administer the ordinances of the house of the Lord for both the living and the dead. The keys of the fulness of the priesthood were conferred upon the Prophet Joseph Smith and Oliver Cowdery in the Kirtland Temple by Moses, Elias, and Elijah (D&C 110:11–16). More specifically, to receive the fulness of the priesthood is to receive the highest ordinances of the temple. The Prophet Joseph Smith taught, "Those holding the fulness of the Melchizedek Priesthood are kings and priests of the Most High God, holding the keys of power and blessings" (*Teachings of the Prophet Joseph Smith,* 322). A man can receive the fulness of the priesthood only after he has entered into the new and everlasting covenant of marriage. That marriage covenant must be sealed "by the Holy Spirit of promise, by him who is anointed" (D&C 132:19). To this the Prophet Joseph Smith added, "If a man gets a fullness of the priesthood of God he has to get it in the same way that Jesus Christ obtained it, and that was by keeping all the commandments and obeying all the ordinances of the house of the Lord" (*Teachings of the Prophet Joseph Smith,* 308).

William Clayton recorded these additional instructions from Brigham Young, while the Twelve were preparing the temple and the ordinances to be administered therein: "We have been ordained to the Melchisedeck (sic) Priesthood, which is the highest order of Priesthood, and it has many branches or offices. And those who have come in here and have received their washing and anointing will be ordained Kings and Priests, and will then have received the fullness of the Priesthood, all that can be given on earth, for Brother Joseph said he had given us all that could be given to man on earth" (Smith, *Intimate Chronicle,* 234).

"In setting forth as much as can, with propriety, be spoken outside of the temple," explained Elder Bruce R. McConkie, "the Lord says that 'the fulness of the priesthood' is received only in the temple itself. This fulness is received through washings, anointings, solemn assemblies, oracles in holy places, conversations, ordinances, endowments, and sealings. (D&C 124:40.) It is in the temple that we enter into the patriarchal order, the order of priesthood that bears the name 'the new and everlasting covenant of marriage'" (*New Witness,* 315).

Baptisms for the Dead Are to Be Performed in Temples
DOCTRINE AND COVENANTS 124:29–36

124:29 *My saints, may be baptized for those who are dead.* The revelation on baptism for the dead came while the Twelve were laboring in the British Isles. Joseph Smith wrote to them saying: "I presume the doctrine of 'baptism for the dead' has ere this reached your ears, and may have raised some inquiries in your minds respecting the same. I cannot in this letter give you all the information you may desire on the subject; but aside from knowledge independent of the Bible, I would say that it was certainly practiced by the ancient churches; and St. Paul endeavors to prove the doctrine of the resurrection from the same, and says, 'Else what shall they do which are baptized for the dead, if the dead rise not at all? Why are they then baptized for the dead?'

"I first mentioned the doctrine in public when preaching the funeral sermon of Brother Seymour Brunson: and have since then given general instructions in the Church on the subject. The Saints have the privilege of being baptized for those of their relatives who are dead, whom they believe would have embraced the Gospel, if they had been privileged with hearing it, and who have received the Gospel in the spirit, through the instrumentality of those who have been commissioned to preach to them while in prison" (*Teachings of the Prophet Joseph Smith*, 179). See commentary on Doctrine and Covenants 127; 128.

With the announcement of the doctrine of baptism for the dead it became apparent for the first time in this dispensation that the priesthood can be used to perform the ordinances of salvation for those who passed from this life without the opportunity to receive them. In so doing priesthood bearers act upon the same principle as that governing the atonement of Christ. In his atoning sacrifice Christ did for us that which we could not do for ourselves. So it is that in the performance of vicarious ordinances we do for others that which they were unable to do for themselves. Thus we can stand in the stead of those who died without the opportunity to be baptized in the performance of that sacred ordinance and make that covenant in their behalf. It then becomes their right to accept or reject that which was done in their behalf.

124:30 *This ordinance belongeth to my house.* "It was the design of the councils of heaven before the world was, that the principles and laws of the priesthood should be predicated upon the gathering of the people in every age of the world. Jesus did everything to gather the people, and they would not be gathered, and He therefore poured out curses upon them. Ordinances instituted in the heavens before the foundation of the world, in the priesthood, for the salvation of men, are not to be altered or changed. All must be saved on the same principles.

"It is for the same purpose that God gathers together His people in the last days, to build unto the Lord a house to prepare them for the ordinances and endowments, washings and anointings, etc. One of the ordinances of the house of the Lord is baptism for the dead. God decreed before the foundation of the world that that ordinance should be administered in a font prepared for that purpose in the house of the Lord" (*Teachings of the Prophet Joseph Smith*, 308).

Thus only in their poverty when they are unable to do otherwise does the Lord permit his people to perform this sacred ordinance some place other than a temple. Even then, the ordinances performed outside the temple, are generally redone after a temple becomes available.

124:31–35 Before the Nauvoo temple was completed, the baptismal font for the dead was dedicated by the Prophet Joseph Smith. Concerning these verses Elder Joseph Fielding Smith wrote: "In the months when the saints were without a Temple the Lord granted them the privilege of baptizing for their dead in the Mississippi River, but with the understanding that this was a special privilege which would end when they had been given sufficient time to prepare a place in the Temple where this ordinance could be performed. For baptism for the dead, as well as other ordinances for the dead, are to be performed in a house built to the name of the Lord and for that holy purpose. Therefore we find the members of the Church engaging in baptisms for the dead in the river from the time the privilege was granted until the time arrived when the font in the house of the Lord was prepared for that ordinance, and when that time arrived all baptisms for the dead in the river ceased by divine command. The Lord said: [D&C 124:32–33].

"And if ye do not these things at the end of the appointment [v. 32], obviously does not mean 'if ye do not build a temple at the end of the appointment,' as our critics infer it does, but it refers to the ordinances that were to be performed in the Temple, and the failure on the part of the Saints to perform these ordinances for their dead was the thing that would cause their rejection with their dead, and not the failure to build the Temple, which was merely the edifice in which the saving principles were to be performed. This is in harmony with the teachings of the Prophet Joseph Smith, who said that if we neglect the salvation of our dead, we do it at the peril of our own salvation! Why? Because we without them cannot be made perfect [D&C 128:15]" (quoted in Doxey, *Latter-day Prophets*, 4:265–66).

124:36 This is a marvelously prophetic verse. Not only does it fore-shadow a day when temples will be common to the stakes of Zion, as we now see happening with the building of smaller temples, but it also fore-sees the building of a temple in which baptisms for the dead will be per-formed in Jerusalem. Some have supposed that the temple prophesied to be built in Jerusalem in the last days can be built by a people other than the Latter-day Saints. This could hardly be the case if it is to be built to accommodate the performance of baptisms for the dead and by implica-tion other vicarious ordinances.

The Lord's People Always Build Temples for the Performance of Holy Ordinances
DOCTRINE AND COVENANTS 124:37–44

124:37–38 Such ordinances as baptisms for the dead (vv. 32–33) are to be performed in a temple but may be performed elsewhere for a given time and season when the Lord's people are unable to build a temple. Such circumstances, however, are expected to be only temporary. Thus the Lord commanded the children of Israel to build a tabernacle or portable temple that they could carry with them in the wilderness. When they obtained their promised land, however, it was understood that the tabernacle would be replaced with a temple.

The ordinances performed in the holy edifice of the Lord, be it a tabernacle or the temple, were first taught to us in the councils of heaven. They are as eternal as the covenants and promises associated with them.

124:39 Ordinances had been administered and solemn assemblies held in the Kirtland Temple. They were placed in their proper order as part of the endowment in Nauvoo. See commentary on Doctrine and Covenants 109:6, 35.

Memorials for your sacrifices by the sons of Levi. According to the prom-ise of Malachi and in conjunction with the authority restored to Joseph Smith and Oliver Cowdery by John the Baptist, the sons of Levi, as a part of the restoration of all things, are to offer again the same offering that they offered anciently (*Teachings of the Prophet Joseph Smith*, 172–73). See commentary on Joseph Smith–History 1:68–75, page 117.

Oracles in your most holy places. Revelations or prophecy.

You receive conversations. The 1828 Webster's Dictionary defines *conversation* as a "familiar discourse" or as "unrestrained talk."

Your statutes and judgments. Statutes are laws, and the covenants made in the temple include promises to keep the laws of God. Elder James E. Talmage explained: "The ordinances of the endowment embody certain obligations on the part of the individual, such as covenant and promise to observe the law of strict virtue and chastity, to be charitable, benevolent, tolerant and pure; to devote both talent and material means to the spread of truth and the uplifting of the race; to maintain devotion to the cause of truth; and to seek in every way to contribute to the great preparation that the earth may be made ready to receive her King—the Lord Jesus Christ. With the taking of each covenant and the assuming of each obligation a promised blessing is pronounced, contingent upon the faithful observance of the conditions" (*House of the Lord,* 84).

Those who receive the endowment understand to a greater degree the justice and judgments of God according to the faithfulness given to his commandments. The judgment sought being that one is worthy and acceptable before the Lord to enter into his rest or into his presence (D&C 84:19–24).

Elder James E. Talmage further commented: "The Temple Endowment, as administered in modern temples, comprises instruction relating to the significance and sequence of past dispensations, and the importance of the present as the greatest and grandest era in human history. This course of instruction includes a recital of the most prominent events of the creative period, the condition of our first parents in the Garden of Eden, their disobedience and consequent expulsion from that blissful abode, their condition in the lone and dreary world when doomed to live by labor and sweat, the plan of redemption by which the great transgression may be atoned, the period of the great apostasy, the restoration of the Gospel with all its ancient powers and privileges, the absolute and indispensable condition of personal purity and devotion to the right in present life, and a strict compliance with Gospel requirements" (*House of the Lord,* 83–84).

My holy house, which my people are always commanded to build unto my holy name. See commentary on Doctrine and Covenants 124:28, "Restore again that which was lost."

In the fear that he might be killed before the Nauvoo Temple was completed, the Prophet was prompted to administer the ordinances of the temple to the Quorum of the Twelve and a few other trusted Saints before construction of the temple was completed. These ordinances were first administered in the upper room of the Red Brick Store in Nauvoo. For instance, we read the following entry in Joseph's journal for the 4th of May in 1842. "I spent the day in the upper part of the store, that is in my private office (so called because in that room I keep my sacred writings, translate ancient records, and receive revelations) and in my general business office, or lodge room (that is where the Masonic fraternity meet occasionally, for want of a better place) in council with General James Adams, of Springfield, Patriarch Hyrum Smith, Bishops Newel K. Whitney and George Miller, and President Brigham Young and Elders Heber C. Kimball and Willard Richards, instructing them in the principles and order of the Priesthood, attending to washings, anointings, endowments and the communication of keys pertaining to the Aaronic Priesthood, and so on to the highest order of the Melchisedek Priesthood, setting forth the order pertaining to the Ancient of Days, and all those plans and principles by which any one is enabled to secure the fullness of those blessings which have been prepared for the Church of the First Born, and come up and abide in the presence of the Eloheim in the eternal worlds. In this council was instituted the ancient order of things for the first time in these last days. And the communications I made to this council were of things spiritual, and to be received only by the spiritual minded: and there was nothing made known to these men but what will be made known to all the Saints of the last days, so soon as they are prepared to receive, and a proper place is prepared to communicate them, even to the weakest of the Saints; therefore let the Saints be diligent in building the Temple, and all houses which they have been, or shall hereafter be, commanded of God to build; and wait their time with patience in all meekness, faith, perseverance unto the end, knowing assuredly that all these things referred to in this council are always governed by the principle of revelation" (*History of the Church*, 5:1–2).

124:41 The Prophet Joseph Smith taught: "The dispensation of the fullness of times will bring to light the things that have been revealed in all former dispensations; also other things that have not been before revealed" (*Teachings of the Prophet Joseph Smith*, 193; see also D&C 128:18).

124:41–42 During the April 1844 conference of the Church the Prophet said, "The declaration this morning is, that as soon as the Temple and baptismal font are prepared, we calculate to give the Elders of Israel their washings and anointings, and attend to those last and more impressive ordinances, without which we cannot obtain celestial thrones.

But there must be a holy place prepared for that purpose. There was a proclamation made during the time that the foundation of the Temple was laid to that effect, and there are provisions made until the work is completed, so that men may receive their endowments and be made kings and priests unto the Most High God, having nothing to do with temporal things, but their whole time will be taken up with things pertaining to the house of God. There must, however, be a place built expressly for that purpose, and for men to be baptized for their dead. It must be built in this central place; for every man who wishes to save his father, mother, brothers, sisters and friends, must go through all the ordinances for each one of them separately, the same as for himself, from baptism to ordination, washing and anointings, and receive all the keys and powers of the Priesthood, the same as for himself" (*Teachings of the Prophet Joseph Smith*, 362–63).

124:43 *Ye shall build it on the place where you have contemplated building it.* A site had already been chosen for the temple on the crest of the hill rising to the east above the flats of Nauvoo.

The Saints Are Excused from Building the Temple in Jackson County Because of Oppression by Their Enemies
DOCTRINE AND COVENANTS 124:45–55

124:45–48 These verses return us to the fact that the Lord requires that we become a covenant people or a covenant community; we are not simply a community of covenant individuals. We do not work out our salvation separately and singly but rather together. If one man chooses to pollute the water it is not he alone who suffers. All who drink it, regardless of how innocent they may be, will be poisoned. While if another man choose to raise the blinds so that the light of heaven might enter the otherwise darkened room, all within the room are thereby enabled to see. All of us have been both blessed and cursed by that which others have done. These verses return us to both the promises and warnings of Jackson County and Kirtland, Ohio (D&C 101:1–8; 112:24–26). Nauvoo is to be to them a place of refuge and safety if the Saints abide in the counsels of the Lord, but if some of their number choose to pursue another course, all will suffer, and again as history attests such was the case.

124:49–55 Though Zion and its temple were not built within the appointed generation, and though the early Saints were excused from this labor, these things will yet come to fruition. On 8 March 1833, the Lord promised: "I, the Lord, will contend with Zion, and plead with her strong ones, and chasten her until she overcomes and is clean before me. For she shall not be removed out of her place" (D&C 90:36–37). All that has been prophesied must yet be fulfilled and every labor assigned the Saints of this dispensation must be accomplished.

124:52 See commentary on Doctrine and Covenants 105:15.

Directions Are Given for the Building of the Nauvoo House
DOCTRINE AND COVENANTS 124:56–83

124:56–60 See commentary on Doctrine and Covenants 124:23.

124:58 *Joseph: In thee and in thy seed shall the kindred of the earth be blessed.* See commentary on Doctrine and Covenants 110:12.

124:61 *Plants of renown, and as watchmen upon her walls.* Those the Lord has chosen to lead his people are here referred to in the imagery of the Bible as "plant[s] of renown" (Ezekiel 34:29), and as "watchmen upon [her] walls" (Isaiah 62:6).

124:62–83 George Miller, Lyman Wight, John Smith, and Peter Haws were appointed as "the quorum of the Nauvoo House" (D&C 124:119). As such they were given the responsibility to oversee the building of the boarding house for strangers that the Lord commanded to be built in Nauvoo (v. 23). Although it was to be a boarding house for strangers, the Lord revealed that the Nauvoo House was to "be built unto my name" (v. 24). It was to be a place where the weary traveler could "contemplate the word of the Lord . . . [and] the glory of Zion" (vv. 23, 60). Due to the sacred nature of the building, the Lord commanded that each individual who held stock in the Nauvoo House must be "a believer in the Book of Mormon" and the revelations given to Joseph Smith (v. 119). Those mentioned as worthy to hold stock in this sacred enterprise were Joseph Smith, Vinson Knight, Hyrum Smith, Isaac Galland, William Marks, Henry Sherwood, and William Law (vv. 56, 74, 77–78, 80–82).

124:83 *I, the Lord, will build up Kirtland, but . . . have a scourge prepared for the inhabitants thereof.* See Doctrine and Covenants 112:23–26.

Hyrum Smith Is Called to Be a Patriarch and to Receive Keys and Stand in the Place of Oliver Cowdery
DOCTRINE AND COVENANTS 124:84–96

124:84 Almon Babbitt, a very capable man, was caught up in his own importance and thought he ought be the one who stood at the head of the Church. Writing to Oliver Granger about Almon Babbitt, Joseph Smith said, "It is in consequence of aspiring men that Kirtland has been forsaken. How frequently has your humble servant been envied in his office by such characters, who endeavored to raise themselves to power at his expense, and seeing it impossible to do so, resorted to foul slander and abuse, and other means to effect his overthrow. Such characters have ever been the first to cry out against the Presidency, and publish their faults and foibles to the four winds of heaven. . . .

"When I think that others who have lately come into the Church should be led to Kirtland instead of to this place, by Elder Babbitt; and having their confidence in the authorities lessened by such observations as he (Elder Babbitt) has thought proper to make, as well as hearing all the false reports and exaggerated accounts of our enemies—I must say that I feel grieved in spirit, and cannot tolerate such proceedings—neither will I; but will endeavor to disabuse the minds of the Saints, and break down all such unhallowed proceedings.

"It was something new to me when I heard there had been secret meetings held in the Lord's House, and that some of my friends—faithful brethren—men enjoying the confidence of the Church, should be locked out. Such proceedings are not calculated to promote union, or peace, but to engender strife; and will be a curse instead of a blessing. To those who are young in the work, I know they are calculated to be, and must be, injurious. Those who have had experience, and who should know better than to reflect on their brethren—there is no excuse for them.

"If Brother Babbitt and the other brethren wish to reform the Church, and come out and make a stand against sin and speculation, &c., they must use other weapons than lies, or their object can never be effected; and their labors will be given to the house of the stranger, rather than to the House of the Lord.

"Proceedings of Brother Babbitt were taken into consideration at a meeting of the Church at this place, when it was unanimously resolved, that fellowship should be withdrawn from him until he make satisfaction for the course he has pursued: of which circumstance I wish you to apprise him without delay, and demand his license" (*History of the Church*, 4:166–67).

After regaining his membership in the Church, Almon Babbitt moved to Ramus, Illinois, and presided over a branch of the Church there. He crossed the plains to Salt Lake City and was elected as a delegate to Congress in Washington, D.C., to request statehood for the territory of Deseret. On his return trip, he refused to heed the counsel to travel with a large group across the plains and was killed by Indians.

124:86 Those faithful Saints who die "are received into a state of happiness, which is called paradise, a state of rest, a state of peace, where they shall rest from all their troubles and from all care, and sorrow" (Alma 40:12). This does not mean, however, that they cease to labor in the kingdom of God. Rather, "faithful elders of this dispensation, when they depart from mortal life, continue their labors in the preaching of the gospel . . . in the great world of the spirits of the dead" (D&C 138:57).

124:87 *Cease to fear . . . because of the sickness of the land.* When the Saints first settled the city of Commerce, Illinois, later renamed Nauvoo, it was a place of sickness. During the first two years many of the Saints died due to the ague, or malaria, especially those who were weakened from their cruel expulsion from Missouri.

124:91–97 These verses have been the source of much discussion, and like those verses describing the legal right of a descendant of Aaron to claim the office of presiding bishop, they have been, and undoubtedly yet will be, used to sustain spurious claims to the office of Church patriarch. Thus it may not be inappropriate to remind the reader that The Church of Jesus Christ of Latter-day Saints is governed by the Spirit of revelation as it rests on its living oracle rather than the revelations given one of his predecessors. It would be our understanding that the promises here given to Hyrum Smith belong to him alone.

124:91 *Let my servant William be appointed, ordained, and anointed.* The reference in this text is to William Law who is being called to take the place of Hyrum Smith as the second counselor in the First Presidency of the Church. Having been "appointed" by revelation he was then "ordained" or as we use terms today "set apart" to his office. He was "anointed," or endowed on 4 May 1842, in the Red Brick Store.

Rejecting the principles revealed in Doctrine and Covenants 132, William Law became an avowed enemy of Joseph Smith. After his excommunication in April of 1844, Law fought openly against the Prophet, seeking even the destruction of Nauvoo. In league with his brother Wilson and other apostates, he organized a short-lived church with himself as its president. These same men published a slanderous newspaper called the *Nauvoo Expositor.* It was the decision of the Nauvoo city council to destroy this paper that precipitated the arrest and murder of Joseph and Hyrum Smith in Carthage. Willard Richards, who was with the Prophet at the time of his death, identified Wilson Law as part of the Carthage mob.

Hyrum may take the office of Priesthood. Hyrum Smith, in turn, is called to "take the office of Priesthood," which had previously been held by Oliver Cowdery. Oliver had been excommunicated from the Church at Far West in 1838. This office was peculiar to Joseph and Oliver, and centers in the fact that these two men were present whenever keys or authority were restored. That two men should always be present on such occasions was necessitated by the law of witnesses. By virtue of this office, Oliver functioned as an Assistant or Associate President of the Church and as such stood above the counselors in the First Presidency and the members of the Quorum of the Twelve. Had Joseph Smith died while Oliver Cowdery was still in good standing, it would have been Oliver's right and responsibility to assume the leadership of the Church (D&C 124:94–95).

And Patriarch, which was appointed unto him by his father, by blessing and also by right. In addition to "the office of Priesthood," meaning his position as associate president of the Church, Hyrum was to hold the office of Church Patriarch. He had a double claim upon this office, it being his by blessing and by birthright. As one of his last mortal acts, Hyrum's father, Joseph Smith Sr., laid his hands upon his head and said, "My son, Hyrum, I seal upon your head your patriarchal blessing which I placed on your head before, for that shall be verified. In addition, I now give you my dying blessing. You shall have a season of peace, so that you shall have a sufficient rest to accomplish the work which God has given you to do. You shall be as firm as the pillars of heaven unto the end of your days. I seal upon your head the patriarchal power, and you shall bless the people. This is my dying blessing upon your head in the name of Jesus. Amen" (Smith, *History of Joseph Smith,* 433–34).

In a blessing previously given to his brother Hyrum, the Prophet had said, "He shall stand in the tracks of his father and be numbered among those who hold the right of Patriarchal Priesthood, even the Evangelical Priesthood and power shall be upon him" (*Teachings of the Prophet Joseph Smith,* 40). This is the same office and priesthood held by the ancient patriarchs of which our revelation states, "order of this priesthood was confirmed to be handed down from father to son, and rightly belongs to the literal descendants of the chosen seed, to whom the promises were made" (D&C 107:40).

In addition to this blessing by his father, Hyrum had a right by birth to the office of patriarch as his oldest surviving son. Joseph Smith Sr. laid claim to the patriarchal office as the oldest lineal descendant of Joseph of Egypt (D&C 107:40; Smith, *History of the Church*, 3:381). The only other lineal office in the Church is that of presiding bishop when that office is held by a direct lineal descendant of Aaron (D&C 68:16–21).

124:92 *He shall hold the keys of the patriarchal blessings.* "Two different usages of the term *keys* are found in the revelations. One has reference to the directive powers whereby the Church or kingdom and all its organizations are governed, the *keys of the kingdom* being the powers of presidency. The other usage refers to the means provided whereby something is revealed, discovered, or made manifest" (McConkie, *Mormon Doctrine*, 409–10). As used in this text the term *keys* is not intended to refer to the right to govern or direct. The Church patriarch does not preside over a quorum of patriarchs nor is it his right to give direction or instruction to them save he does so under the direction of the First Presidency or the Twelve. The patriarch holds keys in the sense that he can unlock the mysteries of heaven by way of the Spirit of revelation and in the instance of Hyrum Smith in the sense that he is here promised the authority by which the fulness of temple blessings are conferred (v. 124). Joseph Smith explained that, "Those holding the fulness of the Melchizedek Priesthood are kings and priests of the Most High God, holding the keys of power and blessings" (*Teachings of the Prophet Joseph Smith*, 322).

124:95 *That he might act in concert with my servant Joseph.* In assuming the office held by Oliver Cowdery it was necessary for Hyrum Smith to both receive the keys which he held and to share the testimony that Oliver Cowdery had of those events. "Thus, according to promise, the Lord opened to the vision of Hyrum Smith and showed to him those things which were necessary to qualify him for this exalted position, and upon him were conferred by Joseph Smith all the keys and authorities by which he, Hyrum Smith, was able to act in concert with his younger brother as a prophet, seer and revelator, and president of the Church, 'as well as my servant Joseph'" (Smith, "Patr. Hyrum G. Smith," 23:51–52).

Elder Joseph Fielding Smith explained: "The Lord conferred upon Hyrum Smith, however, another important and special honor, in making him as well as Joseph Smith a holder of the keys of authority in this dispensation of the fulness of times. These are the words of that appointment: 'And from this time forth I appoint unto him that he may be a prophet, and a seer, and a revelator unto my church, as well as my servant Joseph.'

"This was a special blessing given to Hyrum Smith, and in accepting it he took the place of Oliver Cowdery, upon whom these keys had previously been bestowed. It should be remembered that whenever the Lord revealed priesthood and the keys of priesthood from the heavens, Oliver Cowdery stood with Joseph Smith in the presence of the heavenly messengers, and was a recipient, as well as Joseph Smith, of all this authority. They held it conjointly, Joseph Smith as the first and Oliver Cowdery as the second elder of the Church.

"Thus the law pertaining to witnesses was fully established, for there were two witnesses standing with authority, keys, and presidency, at the head of this the greatest of all dispensations. When through transgression Oliver Cowdery lost this wonderful and exalted blessing, Hyrum Smith was chosen by revelation of the Lord to take his place" (*Doctrines of Salvation*, 3:165–66).

The keys whereby he may ask and receive. This promise, also given to William Law (D&C 124:97), is directed to the system of importuning the heavens, which we now associate with temple worship.

William Law and Others Are Counseled in Their Labors
DOCTRINE AND COVENANTS 124:97–122

124:102 William Law and Hyrum Smith were appointed to travel to the eastern states. They left Nauvoo, 4 September 1842, to counter false statements of John C. Bennett and to attend a conference of the Church in Philadelphia (Smith, *History of the Church*, 5:146). They returned on 4 November (Smith, *History of the Church*, 5:183).

124:103–4 Like many of the Saints, Sidney Rigdon was very concerned about the poor health conditions along the Mississippi River. Despite this he remained in Nauvoo for a time in accordance with the Lord's counsel in this revelation. At a conference held 20 August 1842, he testified that God had miraculously raised his daughter, Eliza, from the dead. Hyrum Smith, who spoke after him, "cited Elder Rigdon's mind back to the revelation concerning him, that if he would move into the midst of the city and defend the truth, he should be healed, &c.; and showed that what Elder Rigdon felt in regard to the improvement in his health was a fulfillment of the revelation" (Smith, *History of the Church*, 5:123).

124:119 The principle that all those who contributed to the building of the Nauvoo House be founded upon a testimony of the Book of

Mormon found a rather literal expression in the building itself. Ebenezer Robinson, one-time editor of the *Times and Seasons*, recalled: "After the brethren had assembled at the southeast corner of the foundation, where the cornerstone was to be laid, President Joseph Smith said: 'Wait, brethren, I have a document I wish to put in that stone,' and started for his house, which was only a few rods away, across Main Street. I went with him to the house, and also one or two other brethren. He got a manuscript copy of the Book of Mormon, and brought it into the room where we were standing, and said: 'I will examine to see if it is all here.' and as he did so I stood near him, at his left side, and saw distinctly the writing, as he turned up the pages until he hastily went through the book and satisfied himself that it was all there . . . It was written on foolscap paper, and formed a package, as the sheets lay flat, of about two or two and a half inches thick, I should judge. It was written mostly in Oliver Cowdery's handwriting, with which I was intimately acquainted, having set many pages of type from his handwriting, in the church printing office at Kirtland, Ohio. Some parts of it were written in other handwriting. He took the manuscript and deposited it in the cornerstone of the Nauvoo House, together with other papers and things, including different pieces of United States coin" (Roberts, *Comprehensive History of the Church*, 1:159–60n).

Years after the Saints made their exodus from Nauvoo to the Rocky Mountains, they acquired much of the original manuscript of the Book of Mormon from Lewis Bidamon, Emma's second husband. He came across the cornerstone box while tearing down the walls of the eastern wing of the Nauvoo House. He graciously imparted pages of the manuscript to interested parties over a number of years. The pages were forwarded to Salt Lake City, where they are now preserved in the Church historians office (Jessee, "Original Book of Mormon Manuscript," 264–72).

General and Local Officers Are Named, Along with Their Duties and Quorum Affiliations
DOCTRINE AND COVENANTS 124:123–45

124:124 A patriarch has sealing power only so far as can be pronounced in patriarchal blessings. He does not have authority as a patriarch to administer ordinances of salvation and exaltation. He is under the direction of those who preside over him. In the case of the patriarch to the Church, the First Presidency and the Quorum of the Twelve preside over him. In the case of a patriarch in a stake of Zion, the stake president presides over him as the president of the high priests quorum. Hyrum Smith was unique among those who have been ordained patriarchs because he was also set apart as the Assistant President of the Church and had been given keys to preside over the entire Church under the direction of the Prophet Joseph Smith. See commentary on verses 91–97.

124:125 *A translator, a revelator, a seer, and a prophet.* See commentary on Doctrine and Covenants 21:1, "Seer" and "A prophet."

124:127 Because of the apostasy and excommunication of Thomas B. Marsh, who had been the president of the Quorum of the Twelve Apostles, and the death of Elder David W. Patten, who was second in seniority in that quorum, Brigham Young became its president. The keys he held as president of the Quorum of the Twelve made him the presiding officer in the Church at the deaths of Joseph Smith and his brother Hyrum. Thus the responsibility falls to the president of the Quorum of the Twelve to preside over the Church at the death of the prophet.

124:130 *David Patten I have taken unto myself.* See commentary on Doctrine and Covenants 114; 124:19.

Another may be appointed. According to the Lord's instructions in conference 8 April 1841, "President Smith observed that it was necessary that someone should be appointed to fill the Quorum of the Twelve Apostles, in the room of the late Elder David W. Patten; whereupon President Rigdon nominated Elder Lyman Wight to that office; and he was unanimously accepted. Elder Wight stated that it was an office of great honor and responsibility, and he felt inadequate to the task; but, inasmuch as it was the wish of the authorities of the Church that he should take that office, he would endeavor to magnify it" (Smith, *History of the Church,* 4:341). See commentary on verse 18.

124:131–32 See introduction to commentary on Doctrine and Covenants 102.

124:133–36 Today the stake president presides over the high priest quorum in his stake. Thus he is a "standing officer," meaning that he has no authority outside the boundaries of his stake (vv. 133–34). Explaining the responsibilities of high priests, John Taylor said: "It is the duty of High Priests to preside; the principle of Presidency is connected with them . . . What is the duty of that quorum? To meet together to instruct one another in regard to the principles of the government of the church and

kingdom of God; that its members may understand the various organizations of the Church, the laws, and the principles of government thereof,
and the various duties they may be called upon to fill; it may be to occupy
the position of a President of a Stake; it may be a Counselor to the
President; it may be a High Counselor; it may be a Bishop or his
Counselor. There are divers positions that High Priests are called to
occupy, as deaths and other changes often transpire, and new Stakes and
Wards are being organized" (*Journal of Discourses*, 24:33–34).

124:137 Elders quorums are organized within wards and stakes of
Zion. The presidency of the quorum direct and train the elders over
whom they preside. The elders themselves may travel to preach the gospel
abroad as missionaries to the world. However, they remain members of
the elders quorum from which they left for their missions.

124:138–40 The Seventies' quorum is a presiding quorum. Today
members of the First and Second Quorum of the Seventy are considered
General Authorities in that wherever they travel throughout the earth,
they preside over the local officers of the Church.

124:144 *Approve of those names which I have mentioned, or else disap-*
prove of them. The Church and kingdom of God is governed by the law of
common consent. Even the prophet himself cannot preside without first
having received the sustaining vote of the Church. Accordingly, Church
officers are selected by the Spirit of revelation as it rest upon those
appointed to choose them, but before any officers may serve in the offices
to which they have been called they must receive a formal sustaining vote
of the people over whom they are to preside. See commentary on
Doctrine and Covenants 26:2.

124:145 The upper floor or attic of the Nauvoo Temple contained
12 rooms for offices, as the Lord directed in this revelation. They were
located on each side of the inner court, consisting of the examination,
waiting, creation, garden, telestial, terrestrial, and celestial rooms, which
were set aside for administering the endowment (Brown, "Sacred
Departments," 368–69). President Brigham Young recorded: "The main
room of the attic story is eighty-eight feet two inches long and twenty-
eight feet eight inches wide. It is arched over, and the arch is divided into
six spaces by cross beams to support the roof. There are six small rooms
on each side about fourteen feet square. The last one on the east end on
each side is a little smaller.

"The first room on the south side beginning on the east is occupied
by myself, the second by Elder Kimball, the third by Elders Orson Hyde,

Parley P. Pratt and Orson Pratt; the fourth by John Taylor, George A. Smith, Amasa Lyman and John E. Page; the fifth by Joseph Young and Presidents of Seventies: the sixth, a preparation room.

"On the north side, the first east room is for Bishop Whitney and the lesser priesthood, the second is for the high council, the third and fourth for President George Miller and the high priests' quorum, the fifth the elders' room, and the sixth the female preparation room" (Smith, *History of the Church*, 7:542).

DOCTRINE AND COVENANTS 125

DATE: MARCH 1841
PLACE: NAUVOO, ILLINOIS

In June 1839, shortly after land was purchased for the settlement of the Saints in Illinois, the Prophet Joseph Smith negotiated the purchase of land across the Mississippi River in Iowa Territory (Smith, *History of the Church*, 3:378). At the October 1839 general conference of the Church, a stake was appointed for the gathering of the Saints at Commerce (Nauvoo), Illinois. At that same time a stake was appointed on the "west side of the river, in Iowa Territory; over which Elder John Smith was appointed President" (Smith, *History of the Church*, 4:12). However, after the announcement that a temple was to be built in Nauvoo the question was raised about the propriety of those living in Iowa leaving their settlements there to gather to Nauvoo. "About this time I received a revelation," recorded the Prophet Joseph Smith, "given in the City of Nauvoo, in answer to the following interrogatory—'What is the will of the Lord, concerning the Saints in the Territory of Iowa?'" (*History of the Church*, 4:311).

The Saints Are to Build Cities and to Gather to the Stakes of Zion
DOCTRINE AND COVENANTS 125:1–4

125:2 *Let them gather themselves together unto the places which I shall appoint unto them by my servant Joseph.* See commentary on Doctrine and Covenants 115:18–19; 124:2.

125:3 *Zarahemla.* The name *Zarahemla* is taken from the Book of Mormon. Zarahemla was the name of the leader of a people that "came out from Jerusalem at the time that Zedekiah, king of Judah, was carried away captive into Babylon" (Omni 1:15). The place in America where they settled was called the land of Zarahemla.

125:4 *Nashville.* "A little town, pleasantly situated on the Mississippi

River, at the head of Des Moines Rapids, in Lee County, Iowa, three miles by rail southeast of Montrose and eight miles north of Keokuk, [which] was purchased by the Church, together with 20,000 acres of land adjoining it, June 24th 1839, . . . It continued to exist as a 'Mormon' town until the general exodus in 1846" (quoted in Brewster, *Doctrine and Covenants Encyclopedia*, 375).

DOCTRINE AND COVENANTS 126

DATE: 9 JULY 1841
PLACE: NAUVOO, ILLINOIS

Brigham Young was born to teach the gospel. His missionary zeal and love of truth knew no bounds. Almost immediately after his baptism, he went on a mission to Canada, in company with his brother, Joseph, to declare the restored gospel. Shortly after his return he joined Zion's Camp in their march from Kirtland, Ohio to the Fishing River in Missouri. He and his brother were known as the "sweet singers" of the Camp, always cheerful and true. In February of 1835 he was named one of the first Apostles of this dispensation. Early in May of that year he commenced his first apostolic mission in the Eastern States. In 1836, after having attended the solemn assembly at Kirtland and receiving the promised endowment, he went on another mission to the Eastern States, traveling through New York, Vermont, Massachusetts, and Rhode Island, returning to Kirtland in the fall of the year. In 1840, Brigham Young, accompanied by Heber C. Kimball, Parley P. Pratt, Orson Pratt, George A. Smith, and Reuben Hedlock, left New York for a mission to Great Britain, where he labored with great success. On 20 April, 1841, he set sail for New York on his return journey. While in the British mission field, he had been instrumental in performing a great work. Of that missionary experience he said, "Through the mercy of God we have gained many friends, established churches in almost every noted town and city in the Kingdom of Great Britain, baptized between seven and eight thousand souls, printed 5000 Books of Mormon, 3000 Hymn Books, 2500 volumes of the Millennial Star, and 50,000 tracts" (Young, "History," 1). It was shortly after his return to Nauvoo that Joseph Smith visited Brigham's humble log cabin where his family were in near destitute conditions to give Brigham Young the revelation recorded here.

At a conference held at Nauvoo 16 August 1841, the Prophet Joseph, with this revelation in mind, said that "the time had come when the Twelve should be called upon to stand in their place next to the First

Presidency, and attend to the settling of emigrants and the business of the Church at the stakes, and assist to bear off the kingdom victoriously to the nations" (Smith, *History of the Church*, 4:403). The time had come for Brigham Young to stand more watchfully in the shadow of Joseph Smith that he might be fully prepared when the time came for him to bear the Prophet's mantle.

Brigham Young Is Commended for His Labors and Is Relieved of Future Travel Abroad
DOCTRINE AND COVENANTS 126:1–3

126:1–3 Recounting his experience in those early days Brigham Young said: "I came into this Church in the spring of 1832. Previous to my being baptized, I took a mission to Canada at my own expense; and from the time that I was baptized until the day of our sorrow and afflic- tion, at the martyrdom of Joseph and Hyrum, no summer passed over my head but what I was traveling and preaching, and the only thing I ever received from the Church, during over twelve years, and the only means that were ever given me by the Prophet, that I now recollect, was in 1842, when brother Joseph sent me the half of a small pig that the brethren had brought to him, I did not ask him for it; it weighed 93 pounds. And that fall, previous to my receiving that half of a pig, brother H. C. Kimball and myself were engaged all the time in pricing property that came in on tithing, and we were also engaged in gathering tithing, and I had an old saddle valued at two dollars presented to me, and brother Heber was cred- ited two dollars in the Church books for one day's services, by brother Willard Richards who was then keeping those books. Brother Heber said, 'Blot that out, for I don't want it.' I think it was crossed out, and so was the saddle, for I did not want it, even had it been given to me. These were the only articles I ever received in the days of Joseph, so far as I recollect.

"I have traveled and preached, and at the same time sustained my family by my labor and economy. If I borrowed one hundred dollars, or fifty, or if I had five dollars, it almost universally went into the hands of brother Joseph, to pay lawyers' fees and to liberate him from the power of his enemies, so far as it would go. Hundreds and hundreds of dollars that I have managed to get, to borrow and trade for, I have handed over to Joseph when I came home. That is the way I got help, and it was good for me; it learned me a great deal, though I had learned, before I heard of 'Mormonism,' to take care of number one.

"For me to travel and preach without purse or scrip, was never hard; I never saw the day, I never was in the place, nor went into a house, when I was alone, or when I would take the lead and do the talking, but what I could get all I wanted. Though I have been with those who would take the lead and be mouth, and been turned out of doors a great many times, and could not get a night's lodging. But when I was mouth I never was turned out of doors; I could make the acquaintance of the family, and sit and sing to them and chat with them, and they would feel friendly towards me; and when they learned that I was a 'Mormon' Elder, it was after I had gained their good feelings.

"When the brethren were talking about starting a press in New York, and how it has been upheld, I did wish to relate an incident in my experience. In company with several of the Twelve I was sent to England in 1839. We started from home without purse or scrip, and most of the Twelve were sick; and those who were not sick when they started were sick on the way to Ohio; brother Taylor was left to die by the road-side, by old father Coltrin, though he did not die. I was not able to walk to the river, not so far as across this block, no, not more than half as far; I had to be helped to the river, in order to get into a boat to cross it. This was about our situation. I had not even an overcoat; I took a small quilt from the trundle bed, and that served for my overcoat, while I was traveling to the State of New York, when I had a coarse sattinet overcoat given to me. Thus we went to England, to a strange land to sojourn among strangers.

"When we reached England we designed to start a paper, but we had not the first penny to do it with. I had enough to buy a hat and pay my passage to Preston, for from the time I left home, I had worn an old cap which my wife made out of a pair of old pantaloons; but the most of us were entirely destitute of means to buy even any necessary article.

"We went to Preston and held our Conference, and decided that we would publish a paper; brother Parley P. Pratt craved the privilege of editing it, and we granted him the privilege. We also decided to print three thousand hymn books, though we had not the first cent to begin with, and were strangers in a strange land. We appointed brother Woodruff to Herefordshire, and I accompanied him on his journey to that place. I wrote to brother Pratt for information about his plans, and he sent me his prospectus, which stated that when he had a sufficient number of subscribers and money enough in hand to justify his publishing the paper, he would proceed with it. How long we might have waited for that I know not, but I wrote to him to publish two thousand papers, and I would foot the bill. I borrowed two hundred and fifty pounds of sister Jane Benbow, one hundred of Brother Thomas Kington, and returned to Manchester, where we printed three thousand Hymn Books, and five thousand Books of Mormon, and issued two thousand *Millennial Stars* monthly, and in the course of the summer printed and gave away rising of sixty thousand tracts. I also paid from five to ten dollars per week for my board, and hired a house for brother Willard Richards and his wife who came to Manchester, and sustained them; and gave sixty pounds to brother P. P. Pratt to bring his wife from New York. I also commenced the emigration in that year.

"I was there one year and sixteen days, with my brethren the Twelve and during that time I bought all my clothing, except one pair of pantaloons, which the sisters gave me in Liverpool soon after I arrived there, and which I really needed. I told the brethren, in one of my discourses, that there was no need of their begging, for if they needed anything the sisters could understand that. The sisters took the hint, and the pantaloons were forthcoming.

"I paid three hundred and eighty dollars to get the work started in London, and when I arrived home, in Nauvoo, I owed no person one farthing" (*Journal of Discourses*, 4:34–35).

THE BOOK OF ABRAHAM

DATE: MARCH AND APRIL 1842

PLACE: NAUVOO, ILLINOIS

The book of Abraham is a translation of ancient records purchased by the Church in Kirtland, Ohio, in 1835. It was first published in Nauvoo, Illinois, in the *Times and Seasons* in the spring of 1842.

This work was translated by the Prophet Joseph Smith from a papyrus record taken from the catacombs of Egypt. Abraham was the original author of that portion of the papyrus that is known to us by his name. The papyrus was purchased in behalf of the Church from Michael H. Chandler, a traveling entrepreneur from Pennsylvania. It had been exhumed on the west bank of the Nile River opposite the ancient city of Thebes (Luxor), sometime between 1817 and 1821.

Joseph Smith began translation soon after the purchase of the manuscript in 1835. As a prophet and seer he did not use conventional methods of translation, but, as with the Book of Mormon, he accomplished the labor of translation by the "gift and power of God." The book of Abraham was first printed in three issues of the *Times and Seasons* in the spring of 1842. Harassment by his enemies prevented the Prophet from publishing more of the record. It was formally canonized as part of the Pearl of Great Price in a general conference of the Church in October 1980.

It would be hard to overstate the doctrinal significance of the Book of Abraham. It is falsely supposed by many that what Joseph Smith restored was a New Testament Church. The idea of returning to New Testament Christianity was more than common on the American frontier. It was from such movements that many of the early converts to the Church came. The gospel restored by Joseph Smith was clearly rooted in the Old Testament as a review of the keys that were restored to him illustrates. He received the Aaronic Priesthood from John the Baptist who was the last of the Old Testament prophets and who traced his authority to Aaron (D&C 84:27). He received the higher priesthood from Peter, James, and John, but that which they brought him was the priesthood and authority known to and held by Melchizedek. Every other angelic ministrant who came to him to restore keys and authority came from that period known to us as the Old Testament.

What Joseph Smith restored, and this is in perfect accord with the purpose and message of the Book of Mormon, was the Abrahamic covenant. It rather misses the point to suppose that the purpose of the Restoration was to reestablish the organization of the New Testament church. Salvation is not found in the organizational structure of a church. We should not argue that we are the only true and living church on the face of the earth because we claim the same offices that existed in the primitive Church. This would be to argue against the salvation of those who lived in Old Testament times. Salvation is found in covenants, not offices or organizational structure. Indeed, salvation is a family affair that centers in the Abrahamic covenant. The genius of the Restoration is the restoration of that principle. It centers in restoring a knowledge of that covenant and the authority by which one receives it. Our schoolmaster in these principles is the Book of Abraham; from it we learn how father Abraham sought after and received the fulness of these blessings. In short, it gives us our most perfect rendering of the Abrahamic covenant. These principles, first restored to the Prophet in Kirtland, Ohio, become the foundation for all that would follow when the Saints turn to Nauvoo in search of the same promises and blessings sought and received by Abraham.

Abraham Seeks the Blessings of the Patriarchal Order
ABRAHAM 1:1–5

Abraham 1:1–5 In these verses we read that Abraham sought for "the blessings of the fathers" to which he was a rightful heir notwithstanding the apostate condition of his own immediate "fathers."

He identifies himself in these verses as "a follower of righteousness," who desired to possess greater knowledge and to be "a greater follower of righteousness," which he identifies as one who is "a father of many nations," and a "prince of peace." Thus he said he became a "High Priest, holding the right belonging to the fathers." All of which is to say that Abraham sought after and received "the patriarchal order," including what we would know as the "fulness of the priesthood" or the fulness of temple blessings.

Tracing these blessings back to Abraham's righteous fathers takes us all the way back to father Adam. Adam and Eve knew of the fulness of the gospel and taught it to their children. Because our first parents were faithful in all things, the Lord said to them, "Thou art after the order of him who was without beginning of days or end of years, from all eternity to all eternity" (Moses 6:67). Of the events that followed, President Ezra Taft Benson said, "Three years before Adam's death, a great event occurred. He took his son Seth, his grandson Enos, and other high priests who were his direct-line descendants, with others of his righteous posterity, into a valley called Adam-ondi-Ahman. There Adam gave to these righteous descendants his last blessing.

"The Lord then appeared to them.

"The vast congregation rose up and blessed Adam and called him Michael, the prince and archangel. The Lord himself declared Adam to be a prince forever over his own posterity.

"Then Adam in his aged condition rose up and, being filled with the spirit of prophecy, predicted 'whatsoever should befall his posterity unto the latest generation.' [See D&C 107:53–56.]

"The Prophet Joseph Smith said that Adam blessed his posterity because 'he wanted to bring them into the presence of God' [Smith, *Teachings of the Prophet Joseph Smith*, 159]" ("What I Hope," 8–9). President Benson then quoted from Section 107 as follows: "The order of this priesthood was confirmed to be handed down from father to son, and rightly belongs to the literal descendants of the chosen seed, to whom the promises were made. This order was instituted in the days of Adam, and came down by lineage in [order] . . . that his posterity should be the chosen of the Lord, and that they should be preserved unto the end of the earth" (vv. 40–42).

President Benson then asked, "How did Adam bring his descendants into the presence of the Lord?" to which he responded, "The answer: Adam and his descendants entered into the priesthood order of God. Today we would say they went to the House of the Lord and received their blessings . . .

"But this order is otherwise described in modern revelation as an order of family government where a man and woman enter into a covenant with God—just as did Adam and Eve—to be sealed for eternity, to have posterity, and to do the will and work of God throughout their mortality" ("What I Hope," 9).

Abraham 1:3 *The firstborn, or the first man, who is Adam.* The text affirms that Adam was "born," not simply created. See Moses 6:22.

Or first father. In earlier editions of the Pearl of Great Price this text read "our" first father rather than "or" father. The correction, which comes from a more careful reading of original handwritten documents, affirms that the name *Adam* means "first father." Brigham Young taught, "In the first place the name of the man is given, a new name, Adam, signifying the first man, or Eve, the first Woman. Adam's name was more ancient than he was. It was the name of a man long before him, who enjoyed the Priesthood" (Smith, *Intimate Chronicle*, 238). Thus, the name Adam represents the first man or the first father of all.

False Priests Attempt to Kill Abraham, He Is Saved by Jehovah
ABRAHAM 1:6–17

Abraham 1:6–17 The idolaters of Abraham's day embraced the practice of offering up their own children to the supposed pleasure of dumb idols. Abraham himself was so offered. "The priests laid violence upon me, that they might slay me also," he attests. He further testified that it was only by the hand of Jehovah that he was spared such a fate. Surely such an experience must have made the great Abrahamic test wherein he was commanded to offer his son, Isaac, as a sacrifice all the more difficult. The knowledge that he had been delivered once, however, would surely increase his trust in the Lord's purposes and that all would be right.

Origins and Government of Egypt
ABRAHAM 1:18–31

Abraham 1:25–27 When Abraham writes saying that Pharaoh, a righteous man, sought "to imitate that order established by the fathers in the first generations," even that order established in the days of Adam, he had reference to the very order by which he sought and obtained the promise that he could become the "father of many nations," and "a prince of peace," which right he could obtain only as "a High Priest." Pharaoh had been blessed by Noah with "the blessings of the earth and with the blessings of wisdom," but he had been "cursed" as "pertaining to the Priesthood." Where we are told that Abraham had "right" to the Priesthood, we are now told that Pharaoh was of that lineage by which he had no "right of Priesthood." The seeming injustice of this caused Abraham's father, Terah, to reject God in preference to idolatry.

Abraham 1:31 *The records of the fathers . . . concerning the right of*

Priesthood. "We talk frequently about the fact that the Melchizedek Priesthood is not reserved for a particular lineage, which is true in the sense in which we quote the revelations and use them," observed Elder Bruce R. McConkie, "but there is another sense in which the Melchizedek Priesthood *is* reserved for a particular lineage." The revelation in which Joseph Smith and the early brethren of this dispensation were told that they were "lawful heirs, according to the flesh" was cited by Elder McConkie.

"We talk about Aaronic Priesthood. Aaronic Priesthood anciently came by lineage. That is the perfect system of Aaronic Priesthood. The expression that the ancients would have used was that the Aaronic Priesthood came to one because of father and because of mother—in other words through birth. You got it automatically if you were a Levite 30 years of age. To contrast the Melchizedek Priesthood with that order of priesthood which came to people because they were Levites, Paul said the Melchizedek priesthood was 'without father, without mother, without descent, having neither beginning of days, nor end of life.' (Hebrews 7:3.) This is the contrast between the Aaronic and the Melchizedek Priesthoods. The Melchizedek Priesthood comes because of faithfulness and righteousness and not because you are born into the tribe of Levi, as was the case anciently with the Aaronic Priesthood. We tend to emphasize that the Melchizedek Priesthood comes by righteousness, and sometimes we overlook the fact that there is a chosen and select and foreordained lineage who are entitled as of right to the Melchizedek Priesthood. That lineage is Abraham and his descendants. The Lord says to Abraham, 'Your descendants have a right to the priesthood.' Then the Lord says to Joseph Smith, 'You are a descendant of Abraham, and you are a lawful heir according to the flesh of the priesthood that I promised Abraham, your father, you would inherit'" ("Eternal Family," 4–5).

I shall endeavor to write . . . for the benefit of my posterity. This record was not written as a missionary tract to all the world nor do we use it as such. It was written by Abraham for the benefit of his posterity, that is, it was written for those with believing blood. Bruce R. McConkie explains, "The concept of a chosen and favored people, a concept scarcely known in the world and but little understood even by the saints of God, is one of the most marvelous systems ever devised for administering salvation to all men in all nations in all ages. Israel, the Lord's chosen people, were a congregation set apart in the preexistence. In large measure, the spirit children of the Father who acquired a talent for spirituality, who chose to heed the divine word then given, and who sought, above their fellows, to do good and work righteousness—all these were foreordained to be born in the house of Israel. They were chosen before they were born. This is the doctrine of election. They were true and faithful in the premortal life, and they earned the right to be born as the Lord's people and to have the privilege, on a preferential basis, of believing and obeying the word of truth. Believing blood, the blood of Abraham, flows in their veins. They are the ones of whom Jesus said: 'My sheep hear my voice, and I know them, and they follow me: And I give unto them eternal life; and they shall never perish, neither shall any man pluck them out of my hand' (John 10:27–28)" (*Millennial Messiah*, 182–83).

Appropriately, Joseph Smith, to whom this record rather miraculously found its way, for the purpose of translation had already been told by revelation that he was a literal descendant of Abraham (D&C 132:30).

The Lord Covenants with Abraham
ABRAHAM 2:1–11

Abraham 2:6 *An everlasting possession*. The promise of an "everlasting possession" is quite literal, given that in a future day this earth is destined to become a celestial planet and that those inheriting that glory will live on it and will enjoy their inheritance everlastingly. See commentary on Doctrine and Covenants 88:17.

When they hearken to my voice. The Lord promised the land from the river of Egypt to the Euphrates to Abraham and his seed as an everlasting possession (Genesis 15:18). Jew and Arab have fought over this land for thousands of years, forgetting that it was promised only to those who hearken to the voice of Jehovah, the God of Abraham. Only those who embrace the same God, the same faith, and the same covenants as did Abraham can lay claim to the same land and to the same promises.

Abraham 2:9–11 These verses represent the most perfect expression of the Abrahamic covenant extant in holy writ, placing it in the context of priesthood and the gospel. That gospel, these verses declare, is to be taken to all the families of the earth by the literal seed of Abraham who alone have right to the priesthood. Those not of the seed of Abraham who embrace the gospel are through that process adopted into it. Thus salvation becomes a family affair, with Abraham marking the true path to Christ and salvation.

Abraham 2:9 *They shall bear this ministry and Priesthood unto all* *nations.* The right to the priesthood belongs exclusively to the posterity of Abraham. With that right goes the responsibility to take the authority of that priesthood to all nations. See commentary on Abraham 1:1–5, page 995.

Abraham 2:10 The principle being announced here is the doctrine of adoption. Joseph Smith said that when a Gentile (meaning someone who was not a literal descendant of Abraham) received the Holy Ghost that an "actual" change would take place in their blood that they might be numbered among the seed of Abraham (*Teachings of the Prophet Joseph Smith*, 149–50).

Abraham 2:11 The Church and kingdom of God requires legal administrators. Here we are told once again that all such must be the literal seed of Abraham. No one else has the authority to declare the doctrines of salvation or perform the ordinances through which we are granted the promise of eternal life.

Kolob and Christ
ABRAHAM 3:1–17

Abraham 3:1–17 Through the use of the Urim and Thummim, Abraham learned about the sun, moon, and stars, their rotations, order, and relationship to each other. The order that exists among these heavenly bodies constitutes a remarkable allegory for the order of heaven. Comparing the characteristics of Kolob with spiritual descriptions of Christ and the characteristics of stars with those of spirits shows that Kolob is a type for Christ and the stars of the heavens are types for spirits.

Stars and Spirits
ABRAHAM 3:18–28

The stars or planets in Abraham 3, with their various rotations, provide a natural parallel with the "noble and great ones" described in the latter part of the chapter. We can summarize this likeness as follows concerning the nature and order of the planets:

1. "The stars . . . were very great" (v. 2). There were "many great ones . . . near unto" Kolob (Christ) (v. 2).

2. These stars were the "governing ones" (v. 3).

3. All stars are to sustain or be governed by "the great one" (v. 3). Each ruling star has a "set time" for its revolutions.

KOLOB	JESUS CHRIST
"The name of the great one is Kolob, because it is near unto [God]" (v. 3).	Is "the Great I Am" (D&C 29:1).
Is "after the manner" or in the likeness of the Lord (v. 4).	Is in the "brightness" of God's "glory, and the express image of his person" (Hebrews 1:3).
Is the "first creation" (v. 2; Facsimile 2, Figure 1).	Said, "I was in the beginning with the Father, and am the Firstborn" (D&C 93:21).
Is the "nearest unto the throne of God" (v. 2; Fac. 2:1).	Is described as being "in the bosom of the Father" (D&C 76:25).
Is "first in government" (Facsimile 2, Figure 1) and is "to govern all those which belong to the same order" (v. 3).	Has promised, "I will be your ruler when I come" (D&C 41:4); prophesying of the Lord's coming, Isaiah said, "The government shall be upon his shoulder" (Isaiah 9:6). He is "Lord of lords, and King of kings" (Revelation 17:14).
Holds "the key of power" (Facsimile 2, Figure 2).	Holds the keys of all power. All who hold keys in the kingdom of God here on earth received them under his direction (D&C 132:45), and an accounting of how all keys and authority have been used will yet be made to him (Daniel 7:9–14).
There are "many great ones" near Kolob; these are the governing ones (vv. 2–3).	Joseph and Hyrum Smith, along with Brigham Young, John Taylor, and Wilford Woodruff, are specifically mentioned as being "among the noble and great ones who were chosen in the beginning to be rulers in the Church of God" (D&C 138:55).
Is the source of light for others (Facsimile 2, Figure 5).	Is the source of "light which is in all things, which giveth life to all things, which is the law by which all things are governed" (D&C 88:13).
"Is the greatest of all the Kokaubeam [stars] . . . because it is nearest unto [God]" (v. 16).	Was the greatest of all the premortal spirits. He is described as being "like unto God" (Abraham 3:24).

4. The star with the longer "set time" rules above the star with the lesser "set time" (vv. 4–7).

5. Anytime there is a star with a set time that has another star above it, then there will be another "planet whose reckoning of time shall be longer still" (v. 8). That is, for every star there is a greater star until we come to Kolob (Christ), for Kolob (Christ) "is set nigh unto the throne of God, to govern all those planets which belong to the same order" (v. 9).

6. To Abraham the Lord said: "It is given unto thee to know the set time of all the stars that are set to give light, until thou come near unto the throne of God" (v. 10).

Now note what Abraham is taught concerning the premortal spirits:

1. Abraham was shown that among the great hosts of premortal spirits many had—through "exceeding faith and good works" (Alma 13:3)—merited the designation "noble and great" (v. 22).

2. Of these "noble and great" spirits the Lord said, "These I will make my rulers" (v. 23).

3. Those spirits who rebelled at the choice of Christ as their Redeemer were cast out (vv. 27–28).

4. Abraham was also told that whenever there were two spirits, one more intelligent than the other, then "there shall be another more intelligent than they" (v. 19).

5. Though it is not recorded for us, Abraham undoubtedly had revealed to him some knowledge of the destiny and mission of his fellow prophets. Such experiences were common to the ancient seers.

The Creation
ABRAHAM 4 AND 5

Abraham 4 and 5 detail the story of the creation of the earth. They differ from the account in Genesis (or its Joseph Smith Translation equivalent as found in Moses 2 and 3) in that they are an account of the council of the Gods at which the plan for the creation of the earth was made. Commonly referred to as the blueprint of creation, these accounts make constant reference to the "Gods" who sat in council together and who would do the labor of creation. These references to the "Gods" traces back to the noble and great ones referred to in Abraham 3:22–23, thus suggesting that at least the valiant among the premortal host were involved in the work of creation.

WENTWORTH LETTER

DATE: 1 MARCH 1842
PLACE: NAUVOO, ILLINOIS

What has become known as the Wentworth Letter was written by the Prophet Joseph Smith to a Mr. John Wentworth, editor of the *Chicago Democrat*, one of the state's leading newspapers. Mr. Wentworth indicated that his request had come in turn from a Mr. George Bastow, a friend who was writing a history of New Hampshire. What was desired was a brief history of the Church and a statement of its doctrines. At the conclusion of his letter the Prophet penned thirteen statements of belief, known today as the Articles of Faith.

No evidence exists that this history or the Articles of Faith were ever published by Mr. Wentworth in his newspaper, though a number of issues from that period were destroyed by the great fire of 1871. Mr. Bastow made no reference to Joseph Smith or the Mormons in his *History of New Hampshire*. The letter was published, however, in the *Times and Seasons* (1 March 1842), and in 1844 by I. Daniel Rupp in his work *An Original History of the Religious Denominations At Present Existing in the United States*. We have taken the liberty to divide this letter into sections and verses.

Section One

1. I have written the following sketch of the rise, progress, persecution, and faith of the Latter-day Saints, of which I have the honor, under God, of being the founder.

2. I was born in the town of Sharon Windsor co., Vermont, on the 23rd of December, A.D. 1805.

3. When ten years old my parents removed to Palmyra New York, where we resided about four years, and from thence we removed to the town of Manchester.

4. My father was a farmer and taught me the art of husbandry.

5. When about fourteen years of age I began to reflect upon the importance of being prepared for a future state, and upon enquiring [about] the plan of salvation I found that there was a great clash in religious sentiment;

6. if I went to one society they referred me to one plan, and another to another; each one pointing to his own particular creed as the summum bonum of perfection:

7. considering that all could not be right, and that God could not be the author of so much confusion I determined to investigate the subject more fully,

8. believing that if God had a church it would not be split up into factions, and that if he taught one society to worship one way, and administer in one set of ordinances, he would not teach another principles which were diametrically opposed.

9. Believing the word of God I had confidence in the declaration of James; "If any man lack wisdom let him ask of God who giveth to all men liberally and upbraideth not and it shall be given him,"

10. I retired to a secret place in a grove and began to call upon the Lord.

11. While fervently engaged in supplication my mind was taken away from the objects with which I was surrounded, and I was enwrapped in a heavenly vision and saw two glorious personages who exactly resembled each other in features, and likeness, surrounded with a brilliant light which eclipsed the sun at noon-day.

12. They told me that all religious denominations were believing in incorrect doctrines, and that none of them was acknowledged of God as his church and kingdom.

13. And I was expressly commanded "to go not after them,"

14. at the same time receiving a promise that the fulness of the gospel should at some future time be made known unto me.

Family History and the First Vision
WENTWORTH LETTER 1

It is a significant guide to those involved in missionary work that the Prophet in telling the story and teaching the doctrines of the Restoration chooses to begin with what we have come to call the First Vision.

Evidence suggests that this was his pattern. At present we have nine contemporary reports of his doing so. As the circumstances in which the story was told were different, so his telling of the story differs in length and detail. As would be expected, the richest view of what he experienced is obtained by a careful reading of each of these accounts. In order they are (1) An account apparently in the handwriting of John Whitmer, then the Church historian. This 1832 account indicates that the search that led Joseph Smith to the Sacred Grove was three or four years in length. (2) A Church secretary's account of a conversation the Prophet had with a visitor in Kirtland calling himself Joshua and claiming to be a Jewish minister. In this account the Prophet tells us that he saw many angels in the vision. (3) The formal account now found in the Pearl of Great Price and in common use in missionary pamphlets. (4) Orson Pratt's publication of the vision in Edinburgh, Scotland, in 1842. (5) Orson Hyde's revision of Elder Pratt's pamphlet published in 1842 in Frankfurt, Germany. (6) The Wentworth Letter here being considered. (7) A terse diary entry by Levi Richards written in Nauvoo. (8) A newspaper interview published in the fall of 1843. (9) A very rough but moving account written in the diary of Alexander Neibaur, a German convert in Nauvoo. (For a consideration of these accounts see Anderson, "Joseph Smith's Testimony," 10–21). See commentary on Joseph Smith–History 1:1–26, page 3.

WL 1:7–8 *Considering that all could not be right.* See commentary on Joseph Smith–History 1:6, "A scene of great confusion," page 6.

Section Two

1. On the evening of the 21st of September, A.D. 1823, while I was praying unto God, and endeavoring to exercise faith in the precious promises of scripture on a sudden a light like that of day, only of a far purer and more glorious appearance, and brightness burst into the room,

2. indeed the first sight was as though the house was filled with consuming fire; the appearance produced a shock that affected the whole body;

3. in a moment a personage stood before me surrounded with a glory yet greater than that with which I was already surrounded.

4. This messenger proclaimed himself to be an angel of God sent to bring the joyful tidings, that the covenant which God made with

ancient Israel was at hand to be fulfilled, that the preparatory work for the second coming of the Messiah was speedily to commence;

6. that the time was at hand for the gospel, in all its fulness to be preached in power, unto all nations that a people might be prepared for the millennial reign.

7. I was informed that I was chosen to be an instrument in the hands of God to bring about some of his purposes in this glorious dispensation.

8. I was also informed concerning the aboriginal inhabitants of this country, and shown who they were, and from whence they came;

9. A brief sketch of their origin, progress, civilization, laws, governments, of their righteousness and iniquity, and the blessings of God being finally withdrawn from them as a people was made known unto me:

10. I was also told where there was deposited some plates on which were engraven an abridgment of the records of the ancient prophets that had existed on this continent.

11. The angel appeared to me three times the same night and unfolded the same things.

12. After having received many visits from the angels of God unfolding the majesty, and glory of the events that should transpire in the last days, on the morning of the 22d of September A.D. 1827, the angel of the Lord delivered the records into my hands.

13. These records were engraven on plates which had the appearance of gold, each plate was six inches wide and eight inches long and not quite so thick as common tin.

14. They were filled with engravings, in Egyptian characters and bound together in a volume, as the leaves of a book with three rings running through the whole.

15. The volume was something near six inches in thickness, a part of which was sealed.

16. The characters on the unsealed part were small, and beautifully engraved. The whole book exhibited many marks of antiquity in its construction and much skill in the art of engraving.

17. With the records was found a curious instrument which the

ancients called "Urim and Thummim," which consisted of two transparent stones set in the rim of a bow fastened to a breastplate.

18. Through the medium of the Urim and Thummim I translated the record by the gift, and power of God.

19. In this important and interesting book the history of ancient America is unfolded, from its first settlement by a colony that came from the tower of Babel, at the confusion of languages to the beginning of the fifth century of the Christian era.

20. We are informed by these records that America in ancient times has been inhabited by two distinct races of people. The first were called Jaredites and came directly from the tower of Babel. The second race came directly from the city of Jerusalem, about six hundred years before Christ. They were principally Israelites, of the descendants of Joseph.

21. The Jaredites were destroyed about the time that the Israelites came from Jerusalem, who succeeded them in the inheritance of the country. The principal nation of the second race fell in battle towards the close of the fourth century. The remnant are the Indians that now inhabit this country.

22. This book also tells us that our Saviour made his appearance upon this continent after his resurrection,

23. that he planted the gospel here in all its fulness, and richness, and power, and blessing;

24. that they had apostles, prophets, pastors, teachers and evangelists; the same order, the same priesthood, the same ordinances, gifts, powers, and blessing, as was enjoyed on the eastern continent,

25. that the people were cut off in consequence of their transgressions,

26. that the last of their prophets who existed among them was commanded to write an abridgment of their prophecies, history &c., and to hide it up in the earth, and that it should come forth and be united with the bible for the accomplishment of the purposes of God in the last days. . . .

27. As soon as the news of this discovery was made known, false reports, misrepresentation and slander flew as on the wings of the wind in every direction,

28. the house was frequently beset by mobs, and evil designing

persons, several times I was shot at, and very narrowly escaped, and every device was made use of to get the plates away from me,

29. but the power and blessing of God attended me, and several began to believe my testimony.

The Coming Forth of the Book of Mormon
WENTWORTH LETTER 2

WL 2:4 *The covenant which God made with ancient Israel was at hand to be fulfilled.* This statement is of considerable importance in understanding the message of the Restoration. Joseph Smith was not restoring a New Testament Church nor is the necessity to do so the message of the Book of Mormon. Rather, Joseph Smith was the instrument in the hands of the Lord by which the "promises made to the fathers," will find fulfillment. The great promise of the Book of Mormon is that Israel will return to Christ, to his Church, and to the covenants of salvation that she might once again have rightful claim upon her ancient lands of promise.

WL 2:12 *Having received many visits from the angels of God.* In addition to Moroni, Joseph Smith's tutors included ancient prophets and apostles of both hemispheres. Among those who instructed him who had known Christ during their earthly ministries were Adam (*Journal of Discourses*, 18:336; 9:41; Smith, *History of the Church*, 2:247); John the Baptist (D&C 13; Joseph Smith–History 1:68–72); Peter, James, and John (D&C 27:12; *Journal of Discourses*, 18:326); and the Three Nephites (Andrus, *Joseph Smith*, 95). Other ancient prophets to whom Christ had manifested himself during their mortal ministries and who in turn tutored Joseph Smith were: Seth (Smith, *History of the Church*, 5:24; 6:30); Enoch (*Journal of Discourses*, 21:94; Moses 7:4); Noah (*History of the Church*, 3:386; Moses 8:27); Abraham (*Journal of Discourses*, 21:94; Abraham 3:11); Jacob (*Journal of Discourses*, 21:94; Genesis 32:30); Moses (D&C 110:11; Moses 1:1–11); Nephi (*Journal of Discourses*, 21:161; 2 Nephi 11:2–3); Paul (*Teachings of the Prophet Joseph Smith*, 180; 2 Corinthians 12:1–4); and Mormon (*Journal of Discourses*, 17:374; Mormon 1:15).

WL 2:18 *Through the medium of the Urim and Thummim.* This may have been Joseph Smith's last written expression about how the Book of Mormon was translated. Contrary to the argument of some of our modern historians that he translated by the use of a seer stone, the Prophet consistently maintained that he did the labor of translation by use of the Urim and Thummim. See commentary on Doctrine and Covenants 6–9.

WL 2:20 *The descendants of Joseph.* Indeed the Book of Mormon is the stick of Joseph.

WL 2:24 *They had Apostles.* Here the Prophet tells us that the Twelve chosen by Christ in the New World were "apostles" in every sense of the word, not simply "disciples." In the text of the Book or Mormon, Moroni refers to "miracles wrought by the hands of the apostles." We would think that in doing so he had reference to the apostles who labored among this people in the New World, for no record of the labors of the apostles in the Old World would have been available to him (Mormon 9:18). Again, he encouraged his readers to "seek this Jesus of whom the prophets and apostles have written" (Ether 12:41), leaving us to suppose that he was referring to those known in the account he was writing. Still again, he speaks of Christ giving the Nephite apostles the authority to confer the gift of the Holy Ghost (Moroni 2:2).

Nephi explained that the Old World Twelve would judge the twelve tribes of Israel, including the Nephite Twelve (1 Nephi 12:8–9). Mormon added the understanding that the New World Twelve would be responsible, under the Old World Twelve, to judge their own people (Mormon 3:18–19).

Section Three

1. On the 6th of April, 1830, the "Church of Jesus Christ of Latter-day Saints," was first organized in the town of Manchester, Ontario co., state of New York.

2. Some few were called and ordained by the spirit of revelation, and prophecy, and began to preach as the spirit gave them utterance, and though weak, yet were they strengthened by the power of God,

3. and many were brought to repentance, were immersed in the water, and were filled with the Holy Ghost by the laying on of hands.

4. They saw visions and prophesied, devils were cast out and the sick healed by the laying on of hands.

5. From that time the work rolled forth with astonishing rapidity, and churches were formed in the states of New York, Pennsylvania, Ohio, Indiana, Illinois and Missouri;

6. in the last named state a considerable settlement was formed in Jackson co.; numbers joined the church and we were increasing rapidly; we made large purchases of land, our farms teemed with plenty,

and peace and happiness was enjoyed in our domestic circle and throughout our neighborhood;

7. but as we could not associate with our neighbors who were many of them of the basest of men and had fled from the face of civilized society, to the frontier country to escape the hand of justice, in their midnight revels, their sabbath breaking, horseracing, and gambling,

8. they commenced at first to ridicule, then to persecute, and finally an organized mob assembled and burned our houses, tarred, and feathered, and whipped many of our brethren

9. and finally drove them from their habitations; who houseless, and homeless, contrary to law, justice and humanity, had to wander on the bleak prairies

10. till the children left the tracks of their blood on the prairie, this took place in the month of November, and they had no other covering but the canopy of heaven, in this inclement season of the year;

11. this proceeding was winked at by the government and although we had warrantee deeds for our land, and had violated no law we could obtain no redress.

12. There were many sick, who were thus inhumanly driven from their houses, and had to endure all this abuse and to seek homes where they could be found.

13. The result was, that a great many of them being deprived of the comforts of life, and the necessary attendances, died; many children were left orphans; wives, widows; and husbands widowers.

14. Our farms were taken possession of by the mob, many thousands of cattle, sheep, horses, and hogs, were taken and our household goods, store goods, and printing press, and type were broken, taken, or otherwise destroyed.

15. Many of our brethren removed to Clay where they continued until 1836, three years; there was no violence offered but there were threatenings of violence.

16. But in the summer of 1836, these threatenings began to assume a more serious form, from threats, public meetings were called, resolutions were passed, vengeance and destruction were threatened, and affairs again assumed a fearful attitude,

17. Jackson county was a sufficient precedent, and as the authorities

in that county did not interfere, they boasted that they would not in this; which on application to the authorities we found to be too true,

18. and after much violence, privation and loss of property we were again driven from our homes.

19. We next settled in Caldwell, and Daviess counties, where we made large and extensive settlements, thinking to free ourselves from the power of oppression, by settling in new counties, with very few inhabitants in them;

20. but here we were not allowed to live in peace, but in 1838 we were again attacked by mobs an exterminating order was issued by Gov. Boggs, and under the sanction of law an organized banditti ranged through the country, robbed us of our cattle, sheep, horses, hogs &c.,

21. many of our people were murdered in cold blood, the chastity of our women was violated, and we were forced to sign away our property at the point of the sword,

22. and after enduring every indignity that could be heaped upon us by an inhuman, ungodly band of marauders, from twelve to fifteen thousand souls men, women, and children were driven from their own fire sides,

23. and from lands that they had warrantee deeds of, houseless, friendless, and homeless (in the depth of winter,) to wander as exiles on the earth or to seek an asylum in a more genial clime, and among a less barbarous people.

24. Many sickened and died, in consequence of the cold, and hardships they had to endure; many wives were left widows, and children orphans, and destitute.

25. It would take more time than is allotted me here to describe the injustice, the wrongs, the murders, the bloodshed, the theft, misery and woe that has been caused by the barbarous, inhuman, and lawless, proceedings of the state of Missouri.

26. In the situation before alluded to we arrived in the state of Illinois in 1839, where we found a hospitable people and a friendly home; a people who were willing to be governed by the principles of law and humanity.

27. We have commenced to build a city called "Nauvoo" in Hancock co., we number from six to eight thousand here besides vast numbers in the county around and in almost every county of the state.

28. We have a city charter granted us and a charter for a legion the troops of which now number 1,500.

29. We have also a charter for a university, for an agricultural and manufacturing society, have our own laws and administrators, and possess all the privileges that other free and enlightened citizens enjoy.

30. Persecution has not stopped the progress of truth, but has only added fuel to the flame, it has spread with increasing rapidity,

31. proud of the cause which they have espoused and conscious of their innocence and of the truth of their system amidst calumny and reproach have the elders of this church gone forth, and planted the gospel in almost every state in the Union;

32. it has penetrated our cities, it has spread over our villages, and has caused thousands of our intelligent, noble, and patriotic citizens to obey its divine mandates, and be governed by its sacred truths.

33. It has also spread into England, Ireland, Scotland and Wales: in the year 1839 where a few of our missionaries were sent over five thousand joined the standard of truth,

34. there are numbers now joining in every land. Our missionaries are going forth to different nations, and in Germany, Palestine, New Holland, the East Indies, and other places, the standard of truth has been erected:

35. no unhallowed hand can stop the work from progressing,

36. persecutions may rage, mobs may combine, armies may assemble, calumny may defame, but the truth of God will go forth boldly, nobly, and independent

37. till it has penetrated every continent, visited every clime, swept every country, and sounded in every ear,

38. till the purposes of God shall be accomplished and the great Jehovah shall say the work is done (*Times and Seasons*, 3:706–9).

The Church Is Organized and Converts Made
WENTWORTH LETTER 3

WL 3:1 *6th of April.* See commentary on Doctrine and Covenants 20:1–2.

WL 3:4 *They saw visions . . . devils were cast out.* Joseph Smith records that after the Church was organized, he "went on a visit to the residence of Mr. Joseph Knight, of Colesville, Broome county, New York. . . . Mr. Knight and his family were Universalists, but were willing to reason with me upon my religious views, and were, as usual, friendly and hospitable. We held several meetings in the neighborhood; we had many friends, and some enemies. Our meetings were well attended, and many began to pray fervently to Almighty God, that He would give them wisdom to understand the truth.

"Amongst those who attended our meetings regularly, was Newel Knight, son of Joseph Knight. He and I had many serious conversations on the important subject of man's eternal salvation. We had got into the habit of praying much at our meetings, and Newel had said that he would try and take up his cross, and pray vocally during the meeting; but when we again met together, he rather excused himself. I tried to prevail upon him, making use of the figure, supposing that he should get into a mud-hole, would he not try to help himself out? And I further said that we were willing now to help him out of the mud-hole. He replied, that provided he had got into a mud-hole through carelessness, he would rather wait and get out himself, than to have others help him; and so he would wait until he could get into the woods by himself, and there he would pray. Accordingly, he deferred praying until next morning, when he retired into the woods; where, according to his own account afterwards, he made several attempts to pray, but could scarcely do so, feeling that he had not done his duty, in refusing to pray in the presence of others. He began to feel uneasy, and continued to feel worse both in mind and body, until, upon reaching his own house, his appearance was such as to alarm his wife very much. He requested her to go and bring me to him. I went and found him suffering very much in his mind, and his body acted upon in a very strange manner; his visage and limbs distorted and twisted in every shape and appearance possible to imagine; and finally he was caught up off the floor of the apartment, and tossed about most fearfully.

"His situation was soon made known to his neighbors and relatives, and in a short time as many as eight or nine grown persons had got together to witness the scene. After he had thus suffered for a time, I succeeded in getting hold of him by the hand, when almost immediately he spoke to me, and with great earnestness requested me to cast the devil out of him, saying that he knew he was in him, and that he also knew that I could cast him out.

"I replied, 'If you know that I can, it shall be done;' and then almost unconsciously I rebuked the devil, and commanded him in the name of Jesus Christ to depart from him; when immediately Newel spoke out and said that he saw the devil leave him and vanish from his sight. This was the first miracle which was done in the Church, or by any member of it; and it was done, not by man, nor by the power of man, but it was done by God, and by the power of godliness; therefore, let the honor and the praise, the dominion and the glory, be ascribed to the Father, Son, and Holy Spirit, for ever and ever. Amen.

"This scene was now entirely changed, for as soon as the devil had departed from our friend, his countenance became natural, his distortions of body ceased, and almost immediately the Spirit of the Lord descended upon him, and the visions of eternity were opened to his view. So soon as consciousness returned, his bodily weakness was such that we were obliged to lay him upon his bed, and wait upon him for some time. He afterwards related his experience as follows:

"I now began to feel a most pleasing sensation resting on me, and immediately the visions of heaven were opened to my view. I felt myself attracted upward, and remained for some time enwrapt in contemplation, insomuch that I knew not what was going on in the room. By and by, I felt some weight pressing upon my shoulder and the side of my head, which served to recall me to a sense of my situation, and I found that the Spirit of the Lord had actually caught me up off the floor, and that my shoulder and head were pressing against the beams.

"All this was witnessed by many, to their great astonishment and satisfaction, when they saw the devil thus cast out, and the power of God, and His Holy Spirit thus made manifest. As may be expected, such a scene as this contributed much to make believers of those who witnessed it, and finally the greater part of them became members of the Church. . . .

"On the ninth day of June, 1830, we held our first conference as an organized Church. Our numbers were about thirty, besides whom many assembled with us, who were either believers or anxious to learn. Having opened by singing and prayer, we partook together of the emblems of the body and blood of our Lord Jesus Christ. We then proceeded to confirm several who had lately been baptized, after which we called out and ordained several to the various offices of the Priesthood. Much exhortation and instruction was given, and the Holy Ghost was poured out upon us in a miraculous manner—many of our number prophesied, whilst others had the heavens opened to their view, and were so overcome that we had to lay them on beds or other convenient places; among the rest was Brother Newel Knight, who had to be placed on a bed, being unable to help himself. By his own account of the transaction, he could not understand why we should lay him on the bed, as he felt no sense of weakness. He felt his heart filled with love, with glory, and pleasure unspeakable, and could discern all that was going on in the room; when all of a sudden a vision of the future burst upon him. He saw there represented the great work which through my instrumentality was yet to be accomplished. He saw heaven opened, and beheld the Lord Jesus Christ, seated at the right hand of the majesty on high, and had it made plain to his understanding that the time would come when he would be admitted into His presence to enjoy His society for ever and ever. When their bodily strength was restored to these brethren, they shouted hosannas to God and the Lamb, and rehearsed the glorious things which they had seen and felt, whilst they were yet in the spirit" (*History of the Church*, 1:81–85).

WL 3:11 *We could obtain no redress.* Be it remembered that these events took place in the 1830s and that it was not until after the Civil War and the passage of the 14th Amendment that states were forbidden to deny their citizens the protections guaranteed them in the Bill of Rights. Section 1 of this amendment defined citizenship and provided that "No State shall make or enforce any law which shall abridge the privileges or immunities of citizens of the United States; nor shall any State deprive any person of life, liberty, or property, without due process of law; nor deny to any person within its jurisdiction the equal protection of the laws" (as quoted in Melville, "Joseph Smith," 73). The 14th Amendment extended for the first time the protection of the federal government around the rights of life, liberty, and property which the states of Missouri had ignored in allowing the Latter-day Saints to be pillaged and driven from her borders.

The 14th Amendment was passed at the cost of the Civil War. Intended to protect the rights of Black-Americans against unfavorable legislation by the states, it assures that the federal government can never again sit by as an accessory to their crimes of proclaiming as did Martin Van Buren when Joseph Smith presented the case of the Saints to him, "Your cause is just, but I can do nothing for you" (Smith, *History of the Church*, 4:80).

WL 3:34–38 *The Standard of Truth has been erected.* This powerful expression, known to us today as "The Standard of Truth," is quite appropriately often memorized and quoted by missionaries. It centers in the sure promise of the Lord that the gospel will yet go to all who are willing to hear it. Prophecy is of two kinds: conditional and unconditional. Most prophecies have conditions attached, their fulfillment is predicated upon the righteousness of those to whom they are given or their wickedness as the case may be. Virtually all the promises given in patriarchal blessings are conditioned on the worthiness of those to whom they are given. In like manner the calamities prophesied to come upon the nations of the earth prior to the return of Christ assume that they will reject those he has sent in his name. These dire events could all be averted if people choose, accept, and live according to his gospel. By contrast unconditional prophecies such as the return of Christ, the resurrection, and the judgment are all certain. Nothing can or will change them. Chief among the unconditional prophecies is the promise that the restored gospel will go to those of every nation, kindred, tongue, and people. Daniel assured us that the kingdom of God, when restored in the last days, "shall never be destroyed," and that it "shall not be left to other people," that is, no other dispensation of the gospel will be necessary and no other people will have to be raised up to take the place of those to whom it would be given. In likening the restored gospel to a stone, he said it would roll forth to fill the whole earth. His prophecy, he said, "is certain, and the interpretation thereof sure" (Daniel 2:45). See commentary on Doctrine and Covenants 65.

The stone spoken of by Daniel, we are told, was "cut out of the mountain without hands," meaning that it is not the work of men but that of God, and that as it goes forth it will do so by his power and the authority of his priesthood, not by the authority of men or nations (Daniel 2:45). The gospel, this proclamation declares, will go forth "boldly and independent." That is, it will go forth without making any earthly alliances as did historical Christianity when she joined hands with Constantine and Rome and brought upon humankind a thousand years of darkness, as opposed to the thousand years of light and glory promised as a part of Christ's millennial reign.

The Articles of Faith

DATE: 1 MARCH 1842
PLACE: NAUVOO, ILLINOIS

As a conclusion to his brief history of the rise of the Church addressed to Mr. Wentworth, Joseph Smith wrote thirteen single-sentence statements of doctrinal beliefs held by the Latter-day Saints. They subsequently appeared in various forms and on occasion had other expressions of beliefs added to them to respond to other questions of the day. Publishing them in a missionary tract, Orson Pratt added an article to testify of the literal nature of the resurrection. Orson Hyde, in a publication directed to the Saints, added an expression about avoiding idleness. After the Saints had established themselves in the Salt Lake Valley, George A. Smith published them with an additional statement pertaining to patriarchal or plural marriage. In 1851, when Franklin D. Richards published them in his mission publication (a paperback book he titled *A Pearl of Great Price*), he had them printed as they appeared in the original *Times and Seasons* article. Thirty years later, in October 1880, this publication was accepted as one of the standard works of the Church. Thus these thirteen statements by the Prophet Joseph Smith, first called the Articles of Faith in the 1888 publication of the Pearl of Great Price, have become a part of the standard works of the Church.

Before the Wentworth Letter, other accounts of the coming forth of the Church had been prepared and published. They too contained brief statements of our beliefs. For example, in the October 1834 *Latter-day Saints' Messenger and Advocate*, Oliver Cowdery penned a brief letter wherein he stated eight items of our belief, centered around the doctrines restored by the Prophet Joseph Smith. Elder Orson Pratt published a tract in 1842 in Scotland, entitled *An Interesting Account of Several Remarkable Visions and of the Late Discovery of Ancient American Records*. It contained an account of the First Vision and the coming forth of the Book of Mormon. At the conclusion of the pamphlet he also presented a number of articles or statements of belief designed to demonstrate the distinctiveness of Latter-day Saint beliefs. The writings of both Elder Cowdery and Elder Pratt are similar to the Articles of Faith later written by Joseph Smith.

Drawing on these earlier references as evidence, some authors have mistakenly attempted to show that Joseph Smith was not the author of the Articles of Faith. It need only be remembered that both Oliver Cowdery and Orson Pratt were writing for the purpose of testifying that Joseph Smith had restored the doctrines about which they wrote. Similarly, some scholars have argued that Christ was not the author of the gospel of Jesus Christ because they have found similar ideas, teachings, proverbs, prayers, beatitudes, blessings, and expressions in earlier sources. What they have overlooked is that it was Jesus Christ who gave these very truths to the prophets and righteous men in those earlier dispensations. So it was with Oliver and Orson. They wrote of that which they had been taught by the Prophet Joseph Smith.

Articles of Faith
1–13

The Articles of Faith were written by Joseph Smith in response to often-asked questions about the faith of the Mormon people. His purpose in writing them was to clearly silhouette the doctrines of the Restoration against the confusion and darkness common to historical Christianity. There was no thought in their writing that they constituted either a statement of creed or that they represented a comprehensive summary of Latter-day Saint beliefs. For instance, they say nothing about resurrection, judgment, or eternal rewards. They make no mention of temples or the ordinances performed in them. Doctrines distinctive to Mormonism— such as a universal apostasy, premortal life, the teaching of the gospel to those who have died, and the various degrees of glory after the resurrection—go unmentioned. Similarly, such teachings as the Word of Wisdom, temple marriage, a lay priesthood, and full-time missionary service are also not included. This is not a matter of oversight nor does it suggest that the doctrines and practices that are not mentioned are of less importance than those that were. The Prophet simply addressed those things he thought to be of greatest interest to those to whom he was writing.

The principles outlined by the Prophet are quite adequate to give the inquirer after truth a concise and meaningful understanding of the distinctiveness of the restored gospel. They established our reverence for the faith of those spoken of in the Bible while freeing us from the heresies that typified the Apostasy. In Article of Faith 1 the Prophet separates the Latter-day Saints from Trinitarians and the idea of a God who is without body, parts, and passions. In Article of Faith 2 he refutes the idea of original sin; in Article of Faith 3 he rejects Calvinism and the idea of salvation by grace without obedience to the laws of the gospel; in Articles of Faith 4 though 10 the Prophet emphasizes the restoration of the faith known to the ancients; and Articles of Faith 11 through 13 respond to the charges commonly levied by enemies of The Church that the Latter-day Saints are neither law abiding or honorable.

DOCTRINE AND COVENANTS 127

DATE: 1 SEPTEMBER 1842
PLACE: NAUVOO, ILLINOIS

No more perfect illustration that historical Christianity is without the authority to speak for God could be given than the inability to adequately answer the question about what becomes of those who died without having heard of Christ and his gospel. It is only in the doctrine of baptism for the dead that we find a soul-satisfying answer to this dilemma. This revelation contains instruction on how baptisms for the dead are to be performed.

In May 1838 the Prophet responded to a series of questions about Mormonism. One of the questions was, "If the Mormon doctrine is true, what has become of all those who died since the days of the Apostles?" Joseph Smith replied: "All those who have not had an opportunity of hearing the Gospel, and being administered unto by an inspired man in the flesh, must have it hereafter, before they can be finally judged" (*Teachings of the Prophet Joseph Smith,* 121).

The first public discourse on the subject of baptism for the dead had been given on 15 August 1840 at the funeral of Seymour Brunson, who had been a member of the high council in Nauvoo. Simon Baker made an account of what Joseph Smith had said on that occasion. "He [the Prophet] read the greater part of the 15th chapter of Corinthians and remarked that the Gospel of Jesus Christ brought glad tidings of great joy, and then remarked that he saw a widow in that congregation that had a son who died without being baptized, and this widow in reading the sayings of Jesus 'except a man be born of water and of the spirit he cannot enter the kingdom of heaven,' and that not one jot nor tittle of the Savior's words should pass away, but all should be fulfilled. He then said that this widow should have glad tidings in that thing. He also said the apostle [Paul] was talking to a people who understood baptism for the dead, for it was practiced among them. He went on to say that people could now act for their friends who had departed this life, and that the plan of salvation was calculated to save all who were willing to obey the requirements of the law of God" (Ehat and Cook, *Words of Joseph Smith*, 49).

Persecution and Tribulation
DOCTRINE AND COVENANTS 127:1–4

127:1 By the summer of 1842, the enemies of the Prophet were hounding him to the point that he was forced into hiding for the preservation of his life. This revelation was recorded in an epistle written by the Prophet in the home of John Taylor's father, a resident of Nauvoo, where the Prophet was hiding at the time. Before this revelation was communicated to the Saints, an attempt had been made on the life of Lilburn Boggs, former governor of Missouri. With no evidence other than their own bitterness, enemies of the Prophet in Missouri accused Orrin Porter Rockwell, bodyguard and faithful friend of the Prophet's, as being the hapless would-be assassin, with Joseph Smith as his accessory. They hoped to extradite Joseph to Missouri to answer the charge so that they could get him back into the hands of the Missouri mobbers. Rockwell's response to the charge was that if he had taken aim at the former governor, he would not have missed.

Responding to the question as to why the Prophet was constantly subjected to such harassment, Brigham Young said, "Why was he hunted from neighborhood to neighborhood, from city to city, from State to State, and at last suffered death? Because he received revelations from the Father, from the Son, and was ministered to by holy angels, and published to the world the direct will of the Lord concerning his children on the earth. Again, why was he persecuted? Because he revealed to all mankind a religion so plain and so easily understood, consistent with the Bible, and so true. It is now as it was in the days of the Savior; let people believe and practise these simple, Godlike truths and it will be as it was in the old world, they will say, if this man be let alone he will come and take away our peace and nation" (*Journal of Discourses*, 18:231).

Falsehood of the blackest dye. Brigham Young observed that "Joseph, our Prophet, was hunted and driven, arrested and persecuted, and although no law was ever made in these United States that would bear against him, for he never broke a law, yet to my certain knowledge he was defendant in forty-six lawsuits, and every time Mr. Priest was at the head of and led the band or mob who hunted and persecuted him. And when

Joseph and Hyrum were slain in Carthage jail, the mob, painted like Indians, was led by a preacher" (*Journal of Discourses*, 14:199).

127:2 *I was ordained from before the foundation of the world.* "Every man who has a calling to minister to the inhabitants of the world was ordained to that very purpose in the Grand Council of heaven before this world was," declared the Prophet Joseph Smith, "I suppose I was ordained to this very office in that Grand Council" (*Teachings of the Prophet Joseph Smith*, 365).

I shall triumph over all my enemies. On another occasion the Prophet said, "I shall triumph over my enemies: I have begun to triumph over them at home, and I shall do it abroad. All those that rise up against me will surely feel the weight of their iniquity upon their own heads. Those that speak evil of me and the Saints are ignorant or abominable characters, and full of iniquity. All the fuss, and all the stir, and all the charges got up against me are like the jack-a-lantern, which cannot be found" (*Teachings of the Prophet Joseph Smith*, 258).

127:3 *A just recompense.* Jedediah M. Grant explained, "It is good that all men in the different dispensations of the Almighty, each in his situation, calling, capacity, and sphere of action, are to be, and of right should be, rewarded according to his works. We do not wish to reverse this law in relation to our enemies, we only wish them to be rewarded according to their works; we do not desire to warp the law in the least.

"I am aware that many suppose that we entertain some unchristian feelings to those out of the Church, but this is a mistake; we only wish that persons who have shed the blood of our Apostles may be rewarded just according to their works. And we expect that, sooner or later, they will have meted out to them that reward which the Almighty actually knows that they deserve. When speaking of governors, rulers, kings, emperors, judges, and officers of nations and states, would we wish to reverse the general law that every person shall be rewarded according to their works? No. It would not do to have some men die as soon as many might desire, for they would not meet their proportionate reward on the earth" (*Journal of Discourses*, 3:126).

127:4 It can justly be said that the revelations received in Nauvoo and the ordinances performed in its temple rank among the most important events in earth's history. Events of such spiritual grandeur require a matching expression of faith. The building and completion of the Nauvoo Temple constituted evidence sufficient for all the hosts of heaven to know that the Lord had indeed raised up a people worthy of the endowment of power that he deigned to put upon them. In the labor of building that temple, the nation of Israel was born anew and the announcement made to all the world that the stone seen by Daniel had commenced to roll forth and that there was no power in heaven or on earth that could stop it.

Records of Baptisms for the Dead Must Be Kept
DOCTRINE AND COVENANTS 127:5–12

127:6 Baptism is an ordinance of salvation by which men obtain entrance into the kingdom of heaven. Of necessity it must be performed by one having authority—one properly commissioned to act—and of equal necessity others sharing that same authority must act as witnesses of the event. They are also to see that proper records are kept. Such is the order of heaven.

127:8 It was in Nauvoo that the fulness of the priesthood was restored. Here the keys of the kingdom were given to those who would succeed Joseph Smith in this great latter-day work. Here the Twelve received the rights of the priesthood and all the powers and blessing of the temple. Here thousands of Latter-day Saints were clothed in the blessings of the priesthood and endowed with power from on high. Those sensitive to the things of the Spirit cannot walk the streets where old Nauvoo stood without the sense that they walk on sacred ground, the staging place for great events of our dispensation.

127:11 *The prince of this world cometh, but he hath nothing in me.* These words come from John 14:30 and were spoken by the Savior to the disciples at the Last Supper. In the Joseph Smith Translation this passage reads, "For the prince of darkness, who is of this world, cometh, but hath no power over me, but he hath power over you [meaning the Twelve]."

DOCTRINE AND COVENANTS 128

DATE: 6 SEPTEMBER 1842
PLACE: NAUVOO, ILLINOIS

The circumstances under which Doctrine and Covenants 128 was written were the same as those noted for section 127. "Brother Joseph was hid up in my house from his enemies from Missouri," wrote Edward Hunter. "During that time, Joseph revealed the last part of the baptism for our dead. I was present with William Clayton" (Carter, *Our Pioneer Heritage* 6:323).

Recorders Must Certify Facts for Baptisms for the Dead
DOCTRINE AND COVENANTS 128:1–5

128:2–4 Rudger Clawson explained that "in the early days of the Church, some baptisms for the dead that were not properly witnessed and recorded, were rejected of the Lord, and the work had to be done over again. We know that great care and attention is given to this matter today in our Temples and that efficient help must be secured to do this. . . . Truly it is a great and marvelous work, and not the least important thing about it is that these ordinances are all carefully recorded in the books and are filed away in the archives of the Temple, to be brought forth in due time. From these records the people who have gone to that house will be judged. Nothing that is done in that Temple will be accepted of the Lord, except it is properly witnessed and recorded" (Conference Report, April 1900, 43–44).

128:2 Reference is to Doctrine and Covenants 127.

128:5 *By conforming to the ordinance and preparation that the Lord ordained and prepared before the foundation of the world.* The Prophet Joseph Smith declared that the Lord contemplated all things regarding the plan of salvation before the earth was ever created. "He knows the situation of both the living and the dead," he taught further, "and has made ample provision for their redemption, according to their several circumstances, and the laws of the kingdom of God, whether in this world, or in the world to come" (*Teachings of the Prophet Joseph Smith,* 220). Wilford Woodruff recorded the following from a talk given by Joseph Smith on 11 June 1843: "A large assembly of Saints met at the Temple & were addressed by President Joseph Smith[.] He took for the foundation of his discourse the words of Jesus to the Jews how oft would I have gatherd you togetherd as a hen gathereth her chickens under wings But ye would not &c. He then asked what was the object of Gathering the Jews together or the people of God in any age of the world, the main object was to build unto the Lord an house whereby he could reveal unto his people the ordinances of his house and glories of his kingdom & teach the peopl the ways of salvation for their are certain ordinances & principles that when they are taught and practized, must be done in a place or house built for that purpose this was purposed in the mind of God before the world was & it was for this purpose that God designed to gather together the Jews oft but they would not it is for the same purpose that God gathers togethe the people in the last days to build unto the Lord an house to prepare them for the ordinances & endowment washings & anointing &c. one of the ordinances of the house of the Lord is Baptism for the dead, God decreed before the foundation of the world that that ordinance should be administered in a house prepared for that purpose. If a man gets the fulness of God he has to get [it] in the same way that Jesus Christ obtain it & that was by keeping all the ordinances of the house of the Lord" (Ehat and Cook, *Words of Joseph Smith,* 212–13).

The dead who should die without a knowledge of the gospel. "In the same world there are also the spirits of Catholics and Protestants of every sect who all have need to be taught and to come to the knowledge of the true, unchangeable gospel, in its fulness and simplicity, that they may be judged the same as if they had been privileged with the same in the flesh. There is also the Jew, the [Muslim], the infidel who did not believe in Christ while in the flesh. All these must taught, must come to the knowledge of the crucified and risen Redeemer, and must hear the glad tiding of the gospel.

"There are also all the varieties of the heathen spirits: the noble and refined philosopher, poet, patriot, or statesmen of Rome or Greece; the enlightened Socrates, Plato, and their like; together with every grade of spirits down to the most uncultivated of the savage world. All these must be taught, enlightened, and bow the knee to the eternal King, for the decree hath gone forth that unto him every knee shall bow and every tongue confess.

"O what a field of labor, of benevolence, of missionary enterprise now opens to the apostles and elders of the Church of the Saints! As this field opens they will begin to realize more fully the extent of their divine mission, and the meaning of the great command to *'preach the gospel to every creature.'* (D&C 68:8.)

"In this vast field of labor, holders of the priesthood are, in a great measure, occupied during their sojourn in the world of spirits while awaiting the resurrection of the body; and at the same time they themselves are edified, improved, and greatly advanced and matured in the science of divine theology" (Pratt, *Key*, 81–82; emphasis added).

Records Binding on Earth and in Heaven
DOCTRINE AND COVENANTS 128:6–9

128:6 *The books were opened.* "What books? The Standard Works of the Church, the holy scriptures wherein the law of the Lord is recorded and the instruction given as to how men should walk in this mortal probation; also, the records of the Church wherein are recorded the faith and good works of the saints—the records of their baptism, celestial marriage, tithe paying, missionary service, and their acts of devotion and worship" (McConkie, *Doctrinal New Testament Commentary*, 3:578).

The book of life. "What is it? Figuratively, it is our own life, and being, the record of our acts transcribed in our souls, an account of our obedience or disobedience written in our bodies. Literally, it is the record kept in heaven of the names and righteous deeds of the faithful" (McConkie, *Doctrinal New Testament Commentary*, 3:578).

128:7 *The dead were judged out of those things which were written in the books.* The dead are judged by the law of the gospel as found in the scripture known to them and out of the records attesting to the nature of their works.

The book of life is the record which is kept in heaven. Heaven too keeps its record of all that we do. This record will stand as a second witness with the record kept on earth in the determination of our standing before God.

128:8 *The nature of this ordinance consists in the power of the priesthood.* A knowledge of the priesthood is essential to understanding the true meaning of Old and New Testament prophecy. In this text the Prophet ties the prophecy of the Revelator about our being judged by our works to the power of the priesthood to bind on earth and bind in heaven or to loose on earth and loose in heaven. See Revelation 20:12.

128:9 *Those men did in authority.* Never in earth's history has the gospel been taught or its saving ordinances practiced save these things were done under the direction of the priesthood (D&C 84:19). As gospel principles are everlastingly the same, so is the priesthood. Thus we read this prophecy restored to the book of Genesis in the Joseph Smith Translation, "Now this same Priesthood, which was in the beginning, shall be in the end of the world also" (Moses 6:7; JST Genesis 6:7). For that to be the case, a restoration of priesthood and keys had to take place, for both had been lost to the world.

It is not without significance that the purpose and place of priesthood ranks chief among the plain and precious things taken from the Old Testament by evil and designing men. Independent of a knowledge of the priesthood, the biblical texts lose much of their meaning while for the same reason the Bible-believing world wanders in confusion.

The revelations of the Restoration are consistent in restoring to us an understanding of priesthood. From the Joseph Smith Translation of Genesis 14, we learn much about how the priesthood was used "in the beginning" or in the early years of earth's history. Similarly, the first two chapters of the book of Abraham restore much to our understanding of the workings of the priesthood in that ancient day. Moroni placed the prophecy relative to the return of Elijah in the context of revealing to us an understanding of the purposes of the priesthood (D&C 2). By revelation the Prophet placed the events associated with the gathering of Israel and the redemption of Zion as prophesied by Isaiah in the context of priesthood direction (D&C 113), while in this epistle the Prophet assures us that Malachi had his eye on the restoration of the priesthood (D&C 128:17).

A Baptismal Font in Similitude of the Grave
DOCTRINE AND COVENANTS 128:10–14

128:10 *Thou art Peter.* The name *Peter* (*petros*) means "small rock"; Christ is using a subtle word play here. When he says "upon this rock" (*petra*), meaning bedrock, "I will build my church," he is telling Peter that he will be a revelator and that the Church will be founded upon the principle of revelation. At the time of their first meeting, Christ told Peter that he would be called "Cephas," which is by interpretation a "seer," or a "stone" (JST John 1:42).

Upon this rock. Here the Prophet quotes the classic New Testament text dealing with the doctrine of the keys of the kingdom. The text itself is one over which there has been much argument and debate among the various sects of Christendom. One of the traditional arguments holds that Christ was telling Peter that he was the rock upon which the Church was to be built, with the bishops of Rome as his successors in that authority. Three observations ought be made in response to this supposition. First, the argument itself did not appear before the 5th century and grows out of the struggle to determine whether the highest bishop of the church would be the bishop of Rome or the bishop of Constantinople. Today the argument is retained by Roman Catholics and rejected by the Eastern Orthodox churches. Second, the issue can be settled by simply noting to whom Christ gave the keys of the kingdom. It was not to Peter alone that the keys were given but to all of the Twelve (Matthew 18:18–20). Third, the Church was not and cannot be founded on a man. "If it be called in the name of a man then it [the Church] be the church of a man; but if it be called in my name then it is my church, if it so be that they are built upon my gospel" (3 Nephi 27:8).

The rock to which reference is made is of course the rock of revelation, more especially and particularly the revelation that Jesus is the Christ. All who legitimately profess Christ must know him to be such by the spirit of revelation, and "if it be some other way it is not of God" (D&C 50:20). It is of particular importance that as members of The Church of Jesus Christ of Latter-day Saints we embrace no doctrine that has not come to us by direct revelation. It is our testimony to all the world that to deny revelation, meaning revelation that is immediate to our day, is to deny the very foundation upon which all true Christianity must rest. Further, we testify that to reject the living voice of God as given to those of our day in the name of loyalty to such revelations as given to those of ages past is to represent the spirit of apostasy as it has fought against the truth in ages past. Significantly, every argument against Joseph Smith and the message of the Restoration is borne of that dark spirit.

"What then is the principle upon which the Lord has built up his Church and established his kingdom in all ages?" asked Bruce R. McConkie. "Always, invariably, eternally, exclusively, Deity has and does operate upon the principle of revelation. By revelation his mind and will is made known and his kingdom established; without it he becomes an unknown God, an immaterial nothing; without it men substitute their own creeds and theories for his plans and purposes. Adam, Enoch, Noah, Abraham, Moses, the Brother of Jared, Nephi, Joseph Smith, and every prophet through whom the God of heaven set up his earthly kingdom, received their commission and direction by revelation. Where there is revelation, there is the kingdom of God on earth; where there is no revelation, there the kingdom of God is not" (*Doctrinal New Testament Commentary*, 1:386). See commentary on Doctrine and Covenants 18:4, "My gospel, and my rock."

My Church. "There is and can be only one true Church, even as there is only one true science of mathematics or chemistry. Two different churches, teaching conflicting doctrines, cannot both be true. If one group of religionists affirms that God is a personal being in whose image man is created, and that he has a body of flesh and bones which is as tangible as man's; and if another assembly of so-called believers professes to think that Deity is a spirit essence which fills the immensity of space, an immaterial nothingness that is everywhere and nowhere in particular present, a spirit that is incorporeal, uncreated, immaterial and unknowable (all of which is found in the false creeds of Christendom)—then both of these concepts cannot be true. Two and two cannot be four and also be three" (McConkie, *Doctrinal New Testament Commentary*, 1:388).

The gates of hell shall not prevail. As used in scripture, hell has reference to the place of departed spirits (Bible Dictionary, 699). In some passages, though certainly not all, it refers to the place of torment or the abiding place of wicked spirits. The point of this passage of scripture is that the keys being promised to Peter will have power to open such gates. A gate prevails when it keeps something in or out of a particular place. For keys to prevail is for them to either lock or unlock such a gate so that people can enter or leave the gated area.

Those who obey the laws and ordinances of the gospel have the promise that the gates of hell shall not prevail against them (D&C 10:69; 17:8; 21:4–6; 98:22). This is generally thought to mean that they are safe from the threat of ending up in the place of torment when they die. It is also generally supposed that in the context of the present text it is saying that hell or the devil will not prevail against Peter. In fact, what is being said is that Peter will have power to direct the ministering of the gospel in the world of the spirits and that he, and for that matter all faithful Saints acting under his direction, will have the power to move freely from one part of the spirit world to another.

The keys of the kingdom of heaven. "Keys are the right of presidency, the directing, controlling, governing power. The *keys of the kingdom* are the power, right, and authority to preside over the kingdom of God on earth (which is the Church) and to direct all of its affairs" (McConkie, *Mormon Doctrine*, 411; emphasis in original). "These keys include the sealing power, that is, the power to bind and seal on earth, in the Lord's name and by his authorization, and to have the act ratified in heaven. Thus if Peter performed a baptism by the authority of the sealing power here promised him, that ordinance would be of full force and validity when the person for whom it was performed went into the eternal worlds, and it would then admit him to the celestial heaven. Again, if Peter used these sealing keys to perform a marriage, then those so united in eternal marriage would continue as husband and wife forever. When they attained their future heaven, they would find themselves bound together in the family unit the same as they were on earth" (McConkie, *Doctrinal New Testament Commentary*, 1:389–90).

128:11 The man standing at the head of the Church and Kingdom of God, the prophet, seer, and revelator, to whom the keys of the kingdom have been given, has the right to unlock the heavens and obtain whatever intelligence is necessary to direct the sealing work in our temples or to direct the teaching of the gospel and the performance of gospel ordinances among any who dwell upon the earth. Of the Prophet Joseph Smith the Lord said, "I have given unto him the keys of the mystery of those things which have been sealed, even things which were from the foundation of the world, and the things which shall come from this time until the time of my coming" (D&C 35:18). See commentary on Doctrine and Covenants 84:19, "Even the key of the knowledge of God."

128:12–13 According to the plan of heaven—even before the creation of the earth—all gospel ordinances were instituted as types to testify of Christ and the principles of his gospel. Relative to baptism, Paul testified to the Saints in Rome, saying, "Know ye not, that so many of us as were baptized into Jesus Christ were baptized into his death? Therefore we are buried with him by baptism into death: that like as Christ was raised up from the dead by the glory of the Father, even so we also should walk in newness of life. For if we have been planted together in the likeness of his death, we shall be also in the likeness of his resurrection. Knowing this, that our old man is crucified with him, that the body of sin might be destroyed, that henceforth we should not serve sin" (Romans 6:3–6).

In harmony with this symbolism, the baptismal font in which baptisms are performed for the dead in our temples is always to be placed below the surface of the earth. Thus, those for whom we are baptized are symbolically invited to come forth from their grave into the kingdom of God.

128:14 As noted in the previous verse, the Prophet here quotes 1 Corinthians 15:46–48. Verse 46 reads more clearly in the Joseph Smith Translation: "Howbeit, that which is natural first, and not that which is spiritual; but afterwards, that which is spiritual." The thrust here is simply to say that that which is natural will become spiritual, meaning immortal. See Moses 3:5, 7.

The keys of the kingdom, which consist in the key of knowledge. See Doctrine and Covenants 128:11.

Elijah Restored Power Relative to Baptism for the Dead
DOCTRINE AND COVENANTS 128:15–17

128:15 No one is saved separately and singly. Salvation is a community affair, and the covenant of salvation is made with the community of Saints rather than with people individually. The Lord had Moses lead the children of Israel to Sinai that he might make of them a holy nation. To Moses he said, "If ye will obey my voice indeed, and keep my covenant, then ye shall be a peculiar treasure unto me above all people: for all the earth is mine: and ye shall be unto me a kingdom of priests, and an holy nation. These are the words which thou shalt speak unto the children of Israel" (Exodus 19:5–6).

So it was that covenants were made between the generations long before we were born to do a work and labor for each other. Elder John A. Widtsoe explained: "In our preexistent state . . . we made a certain agreement with the Almighty. The Lord proposed a plan. . . . We accepted it. Since the plan is intended for all men, we became parties to the salvation of every person under that plan. We agreed, right then and there, to be not only saviors for ourselves but . . . saviors for the whole human family. We went into a partnership with the Lord. The working out of the plan became then not merely the Father's work, and the Savior's work, but also our work. The least of us, the humblest, is in partnership with the Almighty in achieving the purpose of the eternal plan of salvation.

"That places us in a very responsible attitude towards the human race. By that doctrine, with the Lord at the head, we become saviors on Mount Zion, all committed to the great plan of offering salvation to the untold numbers of spirits. To do this is the Lord's self-imposed duty, this great labor his highest glory. Likewise, it is man's duty, self-imposed, his pleasure and joy, his labor, and ultimately his glory" ("Worth of Souls," 25:189).

Illustrating the covenants made before we were born that exist between the generations, Wilford Woodruff bore the following testimony, "I am going to bear my testimony to this assembly, if I never do it again in my life, that those men who laid the foundation of this American Government and signed the Declaration of Independence were the best spirits the God of Heaven could find on the face of the earth. They were choice spirits, not wicked men. George Washington and all the men that labored for the purpose were inspired of the Lord. Another thing I am going to say here, because I have a right to say it. Every one of those men that signed the Declaration of Independence with General Washington called upon me, as an Apostle of the Lord Jesus Christ, in the Temple at St. George two consecutive nights, and demanded at my hands that I should go forth and attend to the ordinances of the house of God for them. Men are here, I believe, that know of this—Brothers J. D. T. McAllister, David H. Cannon and James C. Bleak. Brother McAllister baptized me for all these men, and I then told these brethren that it was their duty to go into the Temple and labor until they got endowments for all of them. They did it. Would those spirits have called upon me, as an Elder in Israel, to perform that work if they had not been noble spirits before God? They would not. I bear this testimony because it is true. The spirit of God bore record to myself and the brethren while we were laboring in that way" (cited in Lundwall, *Temples of the Most High*, 82). To President Woodruff they said, "You have had the use of the Endowment House for a number of years and yet nothing has ever been done for us. We laid the foundation of the government you now enjoy, and we never apostatized from it, but we remained true to it and were faithful to God" (*Journal of Discourses*, 19:229). See commentary on verse 18.

128:17 *This most glorious of all subjects.* The specific reference is to the ordinance of baptism for the dead. In the broad and general sense, reference would be to all the ordinances of the house of the Lord as they are made available to both the living and the dead. It is evident that more will have the opportunity to be baptized and receive these ordinances vicariously than will ever be given the opportunity to receive baptism for themselves while in mortality. The salvation of God's children is predicated upon the ordinances performed for them by others in their behalf.

He shall turn the heart of the fathers. On a subsequent occasion, the Prophet told us that the word "turn" in this text could have been translated as "bind," or "seal" (*Teachings of the Prophet Joseph Smith*, 330). See commentary on Doctrine and Covenants 2; Joseph Smith–History 1:37–39, page 23.

Keys, Powers, and Authorities of Past Dispensations Have Been Restored

DOCTRINE AND COVENANTS 128:18–21

128:18 A . . . *welding together of dispensations.* Having quoted this text, Elder Orson F. Whitney observed that "Paul the apostle also referred to this great and final period as one in which God would gather together all things in Christ, both in heaven and upon earth.

"Involved in this mighty scheme of bringing together all things that are Christ's, is the gathering of the scattered house of Israel, the children of Abraham, Isaac and Jacob, the chosen people, through whom God has worked from the beginning for the salvation and betterment of mankind; and Joseph Smith, a descendant of that Joseph who was sold into Egypt, was the divinely appointed instrument for lifting up the ensign for the gathering of Israel in the last days.

"And what is the object in view? Why all this stupendous labor and sacrifice? Why must the house of Israel be assembled? Why must the gospel dispensations—links of a mighty chain extending from the creation down to the end of time—be bound together in one? It is because God is coming down upon the earth, and the way must be prepared before him. Jesus Christ is coming to reign as King of kings, to inaugurate the millennial era of universal freedom, righteousness and peace; and in order that his coming, which is designed as a blessing, may not prove a curse, a calamity, through the unpreparedness of his people and the world at large, he has set his hand in these days to perform the marvelous work and wonder that the Prophet Isaiah foretold. Israel must be gathered because this God who is coming is the God of Israel, and no other people have the right to receive him. He will come to his own as he came anciently, but his own will not reject him as they did before. Neither will he come again as a lamb led to the slaughter; he will come as the Lion of the tribe of Judah, to sit upon the throne of David and reign for a thousand years, sanctifying the earth and preparing it for future glory, when it will become a heaven, a celestial abode for the righteous. God raised up Joseph Smith and revealed to him anew the everlasting gospel, and conferred upon him the powers of the eternal Priesthood, that he might lift up the ensign as a rallying center for the tribes of Israel, that a people might be ready to receive the Lord when he comes" (Conference Report, April 1918, 74–75).

128:19 *Truth out of the earth.* "Truth" is the name by which the Nephite record known to us as the Book of Mormon was spoken of in prophecy. For instance, Enoch speaking for the Lord prophetically described the final gospel dispensation, saying, "And righteousness will I send down out of heaven; and *truth will I send forth out of the earth,* to bear testimony of mine Only Begotten; his resurrection from the dead; yea, and also the resurrection of all men; and righteousness and truth will I cause to sweep the earth as with a flood, to gather out mine elect from the four quarters of the earth, unto a place which I shall prepare, an Holy City" (Moses 7:62; emphasis added). Drawing on this text, the psalmist wrote, "Truth shall spring out of the earth; and righteousness shall look down from heaven" (Psalm 85:11).

Glad tidings for the dead; a voice of gladness for the living and the dead. Though the coming forth of the Book of Mormon would certainly be a cause for rejoicing among those who faithfully compiled this record that it might in some future day come into the hands of their descendants (D&C 10:46–48), we would understand this text to mean that as the Book of Mormon is destined to gather Israel among the living so it is destined to be used in like manner among the dead. If they are to be judged according to men in the flesh (1 Peter 4:6; D&C 138:10), they too must be called upon to accept or reject the testimony of scripture.

How beautiful upon the mountains are the feet of those that bring glad tidings. This phrase comes from an Isaiah prophesy about the latter-day redemption of Zion (Isaiah 52:7). It is an expression of the love that those who are brought into the faith have for the missionaries who found them and taught the gospel to them.

128:20 *The fulfilment of the prophets.* No subject was of greater interest to Israel's prophets than the latter-day gathering and redemption of Israel. This was a dominant theme with both the prophets of the Old Testament and the prophets of the Book of Mormon. The coming forth of the Book of Mormon signaled the beginning of these long-looked-for events.

A voice of the Lord in the wilderness of Fayette, Seneca county. It was not far from the log home of Peter Whitmer Sr. that Moroni appeared to the Three Witnesses of the Book of Mormon. In addition to that shown them by Moroni, they heard the audible voice of the Lord attesting to the truth of the book (Testimony of Three Witnesses, in the introductory pages of the Book of Mormon). See commentary on Doctrine and Covenants 17.

Michael . . . detecting the devil when he appeared as an angel of light. No account has been preserved of the occasion when Michael, or Adam, appeared to aid the Prophet in detecting the devil when he appeared as an angel of light. Lehi, in his great discourse on the Atonement, refers to the fact that the devil attempted to deceive Adam and Eve in the same manner (2 Nephi 9:9). This may suggest that Adam by virtue of his own experience in such things came to aid the Prophet as a mentor on this occasion. See introduction to commentary on Doctrine and Covenants 129.

The voice of Peter, James, and John. Reference is to the occasion on which Peter, James, and John restored the Melchizedek Priesthood. See commentary on Doctrine and Covenants 27:12.

In the wilderness between Harmony, Susquehanna county, and Colesville, Broome county. Though no formal account exists of the restoration of the Melchizedek Priesthood, we have two reminiscences that bear examination. Addison Everett in a letter to Oliver B. Huntington written in 1881 states as follows: "I heard the following conversation between Joseph & Hyrum a few days before they were martyred. . . .

" . . . Oliver Cowdery was spoken of and Joseph went on to state that 'at Coalville [Colesville] he & Oliver were under arrest on charge of Deceiving the people & in court he stated that the first miracle done was to create this earth.' About that time his attorney told the court that he wanted to see Mr. Smith alone a few moments. When alone Mr. Reid said that there was a mob in front of the house & hosting [hoisting] the window, Joseph & Oliver went to the woods in a few rods, it being night, and they traveled until Oliver was exhausted & Joseph almost carried him through mud and water. They traveled all night and just at the break of day Olive[r] gave out entirely and exclaimed 'O! Lord! How long Brother Joseph have we got to endure this thing,'

"Brother Joseph said that at that very time Peter, James & John came to them and Ordained them to the Apostleship.

"They had 16 or 17 miles to travel to get back to Mr. Hales his father in law and Oliver did not complain anymore of fatigue" (Porter, "Priesthood Restored," 403).

Elements of this account can be accepted but only with some reservation. John Reid was involved in Joseph Smith's June-July 1830 trial, which took place a year later than Brother Everett is remembering it. In relation to the fleeing from enemies, however, Erastus Snow gave a similar account in an address given at a conference held in Logan, Utah, in 1882:

"In due course of time, as we read in the history which he [Joseph] has left, Peter, James and John appeared to him—it was at a period when they were being pursued by their enemies and they had to travel all night, and in the dawn of the coming day when they were weary and worn, who should appear to them but Peter, James and John, for the purpose of conferring upon them the Apostleship, the keys of which they themselves had held while upon the earth, which had been bestowed upon them by the Savior. This Priesthood conferred upon them by those three messengers embraces within it all offices of the Priesthood from the highest to the lowest" (*Journal of Discourses*, 23:183).

128:21 *The voice of God in the chamber of old Father Whitmer.* It was in the chamber or upper room of the Whitmer home that Joseph and Oliver labored on much of the translation of the Book of Mormon. It was here too that the revelation was given directing that they proceed with the organization of the Church.

Gabriel, and of Raphael. The Prophet learned by revelation that Gabriel was Noah (*Teachings of the Prophet Joseph Smith*,157). Raphael may have been Enoch. This conclusion is deduced by listing the six major gospel dispensations prior to our own—Adam's, Enoch's, Noah's, Abraham's, Moses', and the meridian of time, and then noting that we can identify someone coming to restore keys from each of them except Enoch's. Since we have both a name and a dispensation unaccounted for, the answer may be found in putting the two together.

All declaring their dispensation. The genius of the Lord is evident in the return of all of these ancient prophets to restore the keys and authority that were peculiar to their dispensation. In this process all are united in the same great redemptive work. Their having come creates a link and a tie between the faithful of their day and the faithful of our day. No gospel dispensation can stand independent of the others, and we cannot be saved separately and singly. From the first man to the last, all must be saved by the very same truths and the very same powers.

In an earlier revelation, the Lord had said that the powers of the priesthood were being given "for the last days and for the last time, in the which is the dispensation of the fulness of times. Which power you hold," he told Joseph Smith and his counselors in the first presidency, "with all those who have received a dispensation at any time from the beginning of the creation; for verily I say unto you, the keys of the dispensation, which ye have received, have come down from the fathers, and last of all, being sent down from heaven unto you" (D&C 112:30–32).

Glad Tidings Acclaimed for the Living and the Dead
DOCTRINE AND COVENANTS 128:22–25

128:22 *For the prisoners shall go free.* In a marvelous Messianic prophecy, Isaiah spoke in behalf of the promised Messiah, saying, "The Spirit of the Lord God is upon me; because the Lord hath anointed me to preach good tidings unto the meek; he hath sent me to bind up the broken hearted, to proclaim liberty to the captives, *and the opening of the prison to them that are bound;* to proclaim the acceptable year of the Lord, and the day of vengeance of our God; to comfort all that mourn" (Isaiah 61:1–2; emphasis added). Some 750 years later, Jesus would quote these same words in the synagogue at Nazareth to identify himself as the promised Messiah and formally begin his ministry among men (Luke 4:16–21). Following his crucifixion, and while his body lay in the borrowed tomb of Joseph of Arimathea, Christ visited the spirits in prison to announce that through his resurrection all might eventually be freed from that prison. There he commissioned missionaries to teach the gospel to those bound by sin and ignorance that they too might be free to stand in the light of the gospel. Only with the restoration of the gospel is the true meaning of such text made known to us. See commentary on Doctrine and Covenants 138.

128:24 This verse is often misused and misunderstood. In its first sentence, it simply draws upon the language of Malachi relative to the role to be played by the literal sons of Levi in the last days. Joseph Smith identified this as animal sacrifice (*Teachings of the Prophet Joseph Smith,* 172–73). In the second sentence, the Prophet says that since the sons of Levi are going to make their offering, let us also make our offering. Our sacrifice is to center in the labor we do in behalf of our kindred dead in the house of the Lord. That is, if the sons of Levi are going to be true to their office and calling, let us in like manner be true to ours. See commentary on Doctrine and Covenants 84:31.

DOCTRINE AND COVENANTS 129

DATE: 9 FEBRUARY 1843
PLACE: NAUVOO, ILLINOIS

True religion, according to the Prophet Joseph Smith, is one of individual participation. If one man can dream dreams, see visions, entertain angels, or stand in the presence of God, so can all others by complying with the same principles. Thus, it was necessary to educate the Saints that they not be deceived by counterfeit revelations or by the devil appearing as an angel of light. As previous revelations had been given to teach the Saints how to distinguish a true revelation from a false one, this revelation announced principles or keys by which the devil or one of his own could be discerned when posing as a messenger from God.

When the Prophet first learned these principles is not known. We can be confident, however, that it was some time before this section was recorded. Given that all priesthood and keys restored in this dispensation were conferred upon the Prophet by angelic ministrants, and given Satan's insatiable desire to deceive, the keys of discernment must have been given to Joseph Smith quite early. As it is presently found in the Doctrine and Covenants, this section comes from the journal of William Clayton. He recorded it as the Prophet gave it in conversation with Parley P. Pratt, who had just returned from a mission in England. It was first included in the 1876 edition of the Doctrine and Covenants (Cook, *Revelations*, 286).

Wilford Woodruff had recorded the following in his journal on 27 June 1839 as part of the instruction given to the Twelve by the Prophet prior to their departure for a mission to England:

"In order to detect the devel when he transforms himself nigh unto an angel of light. When an angel of God appears unto man face to face in personage & reaches out his hand unto the man & he takes hold of the angels hand & feels a substance the Same as one man would in shaking hands with another he may then know that it is an angel of God, & he should place all Confidence in him Such personages or angels are Saints with there resurrected Bodies, but if a personage appears unto man &

offers him his hand & the man takes hold of it & he feels nothing or does not sens[e] any substance he may know it is the devel, for when a Saint whose body is not resurrected appears unto man in the flesh he will not offer him his hand for this is against the law given him" (Ehat and Cook, *Words of Joseph Smith*, 6).

On 2 July of the same year, the Prophet taught that "an angel of God never has wings. Some will say that they have seen a spirit; that he offered them his hand, but they did not touch it. This is a lie. First, it is contrary to the plan of God; a spirit cannot come but in glory; an angel has flesh and bones; we see not their glory. The devil may appear as an angel of light. Ask God to reveal it; if it be of the devil, he will flee from you; if of God, He will manifest Himself, or make it manifest" (*Teachings of the Prophet Joseph Smith*, 162).

The version of the Prophet Joseph Smith's instructions contained in this section was given for the benefit of Elder Parley P. Pratt. The Prophet's earlier instructions to the Twelve in late June and early July 1839 concerning the keys to discern angels of God and angels of the devil had been given after Joseph and his fellow prisoners were set free from Liberty Jail but while Elder Pratt was still in the jail at Richmond, Missouri, so he missed this instruction. Following his return from England, where he had remained a year and a half longer than the other apostles, presiding over the Saints there and serving as editor of the Church publication, the *Millennial Star*, Elder Pratt and the Prophet Joseph visited for the better part of the afternoon. The following day, when these instructions were given, the Prophet Joseph Smith recorded in his journal: "Spent most of the day in conversation with Parley P. Pratt and others" (*History of the Church*, 5:267). As part of these instructions, the Prophet told of a man who came to him "in Kirtland," saying he had seen an angel and described his dress. "I told him," the Prophet said, "he had seen no angel, and that there was no such dress in heaven. He grew mad, and went into the street and commanded fire to come down out of heaven to consume me. I laughed at him, and said, You are one of Baal's prophets; your God does not hear you; jump up and cut yourself: and he commanded fire from heaven to consume my house" (Smith, *History of the Church*, 5:267–68).

Even earlier than this the Prophet acknowledged, "There have also been ministering angels in the Church which were of Satan appearing as an angel of light. A sister in the state of New York had a vision, who said it was told her that if she would go to a certain place in the woods, an angel would appear to her. She went at the appointed time, and saw a glorious personage descending, arrayed in white, with sandy colored hair; he commenced and told her to fear God, and said that her husband was called to do great things, but that he must not go more than one hundred miles from home, or he would not return; whereas God had called him to go to the ends of the earth, and he has since been more than one thousand miles from home, and is yet alive. Many true things were spoken by this personage, and many things that were false. How, it may be asked, was this known to be a bad angel? By the color of his hair; that is one of the signs that he can be known by, and by his contradicting a former revelation" (*Teachings of the Prophet Joseph Smith*, 214–15).

The Prophet recorded that Michael (Adam) appeared to him "on the banks of the Susquehanna, detecting the devil when he appeared as an angel of light!" (D&C 128:20). It would appear that this experience took place while Joseph was translating the Book of Mormon in Harmony, Pennsylvania. It was here that John the Baptist restored to the Prophet and Oliver Cowdery the "keys of the ministering of angels" (Joseph Smith–History 1:69; D&C 13:1). Thus, the right to receive the ministration of angels and the ability to discern true messengers of God from counterfeits came before the Church was organized.

Perhaps it is of more than passing interest that we have ancient stories that have been preserved for us in what is known as the Book of Adam and Eve, or The Conflict of Adam and Eve with Satan, in which Satan constantly tries to deceive our first parents in order to obtain the garments they had received from the Lord in Eden. In one of those episodes, Satan "took the form of an angel, and with him two others" in order to imitate a threesome who had come to them from the presence of the Lord. In this story Adam and Eve were initially deceived by them "because, when they came to Adam the first time, there came upon him from them, peace and joy, through their bringing him good tokens; so Adam thought that they were come a second time to give him other tokens for him to rejoice withal. For he did not know it was Satan; therefore did he receive them with joy and companied with them" (*Lost Books of the Bible*, 49).

It appears that the recording of the three revelations in our current edition of the Doctrine and Covenants (sections 128, 129, 132), along with the translation of the Book of Abraham, all took place in the Prophet's office on the upper floor of the Red Brick Store in Nauvoo. It was there that the ordinances of the temple were restored and first practiced in this dispensation (Launius and McKiernan, *Joseph Smith, Jr.'s Red Brick Store*, 26–29). These events appear to tie closely with the recording of this revelation. Speaking to the newly formed Relief Society on 28 April 1842, the Prophet said that the Church would not be fully organized until the temple was complete. He further spoke of the sisters receiving the "keys," or knowledge through the priesthood, by which they could "detect everything false" if they would sustain their husbands and those the Lord had called to lead his Church. The Prophet further promised the sisters that in the temple they would learn how to ask of God and how to receive answers. "If you live up to your privileges," the Prophet promised them, "the angels cannot be restrained from being your associates." Women, he added, "if they are pure and innocent, can come in the presence of God" (Smith, *History of the Church*, 4:603–7).

Speaking to the Saints in the grove on Sunday, 1 May 1842, the Prophet said, "The keys are certain signs and words by which false spirits and personages may be detected from true, which cannot be revealed to the Elders till the Temple is completed. . . . There are signs in heaven, earth and hell; the Elders must know them all, to be endowed with power, to finish their work and prevent imposition" (Smith, *History of the Church*, 4:608).

This revelation was added to the Doctrine and Covenants along with twenty-five other sections in 1876.

Messengers from God May Be Either Resurrected Beings or Unembodied Spirits
DOCTRINE AND COVENANTS 129:1–3

129:1–3 In a subsequent revelation, we learn that "there are no angels who minister to this earth but those who do belong or have belonged to it" (D&C 130:5). The angels who ministered to father Adam and those of his dispensation of necessity would have been unembodied spirits, that is, righteous men yet to be born on this earth. In Old Testament times there would have been no angels who were resurrected beings. During that period it appears that translated beings played a larger role as divine messengers than they do in our dispensation. In stating that there are "two kinds of beings in heaven," which it names as resurrected beings and just men made perfect, this revelation seems to be suggesting that unembodied or premortal spirits are not sent to those of our dispensation. Translated beings who have remained upon the earth (and thus are not "in heaven") also continue to minister to us and can be discerned by the same keys as resurrected beings or just men made perfect.

129:1 *In heaven*. As used in this revelation, the phrase "heaven" has reference to the abiding places of the righteous dead, be it a degree of glory or paradise.

129:3 *Just men made perfect*. The righteous dead in paradise who in the resurrection will inherit the fulness of the Father are referred to as "just men made perfect." David Patten, one of the Twelve, had been killed in the Battle of Crooked River in Missouri in 1838. He is used here as an illustration of a "Just man made perfect." It had been stated at the funeral of Seymour Brunson in August of 1840 that Elder Patten was the spirit who came to escort him to his rightful place in the spirit world (Cook, *Revelations*, 345). See commentary on Doctrine and Covenants 76:69.

Keys by Which True Messengers Can Be Known
DOCTRINE AND COVENANTS 129:4–9

129:4–9 Why would Satan or one of his angels extend his hand knowing that so doing would unveil his true identity? The answer is found in understanding the authority of God in establishing laws by which all things, including the devil and his angels, are governed (D&C 88:36–38, 42). As mortals we are bound by the law of gravity and find physical objects a hindrance. Angels know no such limitations, and yet they are not free to converse with mortals, save it be according to the order of heaven. Similarly, evil spirits have bounds beyond which they cannot pass (D&C 122:9). The laws given to the prince of darkness and his legions include the sign of the dove, which the Prophet tells us was "instituted before the creation of the world, a witness for the Holy Ghost, and the devil cannot come in the sign of a dove" (*Teachings of the Prophet Joseph Smith*, 276). We know that it "is not given unto Satan to tempt little children, until they begin to become accountable" before the Lord (D&C 29:47). In like manner Nephi tells us that Satan cannot tempt translated beings and that he has no power over them (3 Nephi 28:39). Thus, God, who governs all things, has placed limits and bounds on the adversary as to what he can and cannot do. In the instance here cited, Satan, or those acting in his name, must either extend his hand or withdraw, and in either case he will be detected. William Clayton recorded the Prophet as saying in 1840 that "if an angel or spirit appears, offer him your hand; if he is a spirit from God, he will stand still and not offer you his hand. If from the Devil, he will either shrink back from you or offer his hand, which if he does you will feel nothing, but be deceived.

"A good Spirit will not deceive.

"Angels are beings who have bodies and appear to men in the form of man" (Ehat and Cook, *Words of Joseph Smith*, 44; syntax and spelling standardized).

129:9 *Three grand keys.* As used in this context, "keys" consist of the knowledge necessary to discern the true messenger of God from angels of the devil when they appear as angels of light in an attempt to deceive.

129:1–9 *You may know whether any administration is from God.* As found in Joseph Smith's diary, this revelation reads thus: "There are 3 administrater[s]: Angels, Spirits, [and] Devils. One [manner of] dress in heaven. Angels [are] the spirits of Just men made perfect. Innumerable co[mpany] of angels and spirits of Just men made perfect. [If] an Angel appears to you how will you prove him? Ask him to shake hands. If he has flesh and bones he is an angel. 'Spirit hath not flesh and bones.' Spirit of a Just man made perfect. Person[age] in its tabernacle could [not] hide its glory. If David Patten or the Devil come how would you determine? Should you take hold of his hand you would not feel it. If it were a false administrater he would not do it. True spirit will not give his hand. The Devil will. 3 keys" (Faulring, *American Prophet's Record*, 300).

Doctrine and Covenants 130

Date: 2 April 1843
Place: Ramus, Illinois

On 1 April 1843 Joseph Smith, Orson Hyde, and William Clayton traveled from Nauvoo to Ramus, twenty miles to the east, where they spent the evening with Benjamin F. Johnson. Of the events of the next day, Joseph Smith recorded the following: "Sunday, 2.—Wind N. E. Snow fell several inches, but melted more or less.

"At ten a. m. went to meeting. Heard Elder Orson Hyde preach, comparing the sectarian preachers to crows living on carrion, as they were more fond of lies about the Saints than the truth. Alluding to the coming of the Savior, he said, 'When He shall appear, we shall be like Him, &c. He will appear on a white horse as a warrior, and maybe we shall have some of the same spirit. Our God is a warrior (John 14:23). It is our privilege to have the Father and Son dwelling in our hearts, &c.'

"We dined with my sister Sophronia McCleary, when I told Elder Hyde that I was going to offer some corrections to his sermon this morning. He replied, 'They shall be thankfully received'" (*History of the Church*, 5:323).

The following were among items of instruction given by the Prophet that day.

The Father and the Son May Appear Personally to Men
Doctrine and Covenants 130:1–3

130:1 *When the Savior shall appear we shall see him as he is.* When the resurrected Christ ascended into heaven, two angels stood by testifying to the Twelve who were with him, "Ye men of Galilee, why stand ye gazing up into heaven? This same Jesus, which is taken up from you into heaven, shall so come in like manner as ye have seen him go into heaven" (Acts 1:11). It was a man with "flesh and bones" who ascended from their sight that day, one whom they had embraced and felt the warmth of his body, one with whom they had taken meat, walked, talked, and shared the sociality known to them before his death upon the cross. "That which is without body, parts and passions is nothing," the Prophet declared. "There is no other God in heaven but that God who has flesh and bones" (*Teachings of the Prophet Joseph Smith,* 181).

130:2 *That same sociality which exists among us here will exist among us there.* The whole system and plan of salvation centers in the idea that we are the children of a loving father and mother from whom we have been temporarily separated and to whose society we seek to return. It embraces the idea that our family relationships here in mortality are intended to be eternal, that the love a mother feels for her children is as endless as God himself, and that the love of a man and woman is as timeless as eternity. All other descriptions of heaven leave the soul as empty as a life without love and as cold as the grave.

130:3 *John 14:23.* This verse (John 14:23) is part of the discourse about two comforters that the Savior gave to the meridian Twelve. "Now what is this other Comforter?" asked the Prophet Joseph Smith. "It is no more nor less than the Lord Jesus Christ Himself; and this is the sum and substance of the whole matter; that when any man obtains this last Comforter, he will have the personage of Jesus Christ to attend him, or appear unto him from time to time, and even He will manifest the Father unto him, and they will take up their abode with him, and the visions of the heavens will be opened unto him, and the Lord will teach him face to face, and he may have a perfect knowledge of the mysteries of the Kingdom of God; and this is the state and place the ancient Saints arrived at when they had such glorious visions—Isaiah, Ezekiel, John upon the Isle of Patmos, St. Paul in the three heavens, and all the Saints who held communion with the general assembly and Church of the Firstborn" (*Teachings of the Prophet Joseph Smith,* 150–51).

Angels Reside in a Celestial Sphere
DOCTRINE AND COVENANTS 130:4–7

130:4 *The reckoning of . . . time.* Time is a relative measurement of duration that enables us to think and speak in terms of past, present, and future. Its meaning is subject to constant change. The period of time we measure as a year passes relatively slowly for children and quickly for adults. The same unit of time passes slowly when we are waiting, particularly when associated with anxiety, and quickly when we are busy or having an enjoyable experience. The measurement of time as known to us in our premortal estate was very different than known to us in this mortal world. Eons, as we measure time, were involved in our preparation prior to coming to this earth. Abraham told us that "Kolob [the planet nearest to that upon which God resides] was after the manner of the Lord, according to its times and seasons in the revolutions thereof; that one revolution was a day unto the Lord, after his manner of reckoning, it being one thousand years according to the time appointed unto that whereon thou standest. This is the reckoning of the Lord's time, according to the reckoning of Kolob" (Abraham 3:4).

The present text suggests a difference in the spectrum of time between prophets and men. This would have to have reference to the measurement of time as seen by a prophet when giving prophetic descriptions of future events. For instance, Joseph Smith said, "Now it is called today until the coming of the Son of Man" (D&C 64:23) and in 1836 he said, "The great and dreadful day of the Lord is near, even at the doors" (D&C 110:16).

130:5 *Angels who administer to this earth . . . belong to it.* It is interesting that, while only those who have lived or will live upon this earth can be ministering spirits to it, some from this earth will be permitted to minister to those on other planets. The Prophet said, "Many have supposed that the doctrine of translation was a doctrine whereby men were taken immediately into the presence of God, and into an eternal fullness, but this is a mistaken idea. Their place of habitation is that of the terrestrial order, and a place prepared for such characters He held in reserve to be ministering angels unto many planets, and who as yet have not entered into so great a fullness as those who are resurrected from the dead" (*Teachings of the Prophet Joseph Smith,* 170).

President Joseph F. Smith taught: "We are told by the Prophet Joseph Smith, that 'there are no angels who minister to this earth but those who do belong or have belonged to it.' Hence, when messengers are sent to minister to the inhabitants of this earth, they are not strangers, but from the ranks of our kindred, friends, and fellow-beings and fellow-servants. The ancient prophets who died were those who came to visit their fellow creatures upon the earth. . . . In like manner our fathers and mothers, brothers, sisters, and friends who have passed away from this earth, having been faithful, and worthy to enjoy these rights and privileges, may have a mission given them to visit their relatives and friends upon the earth again, bringing from the divine Presence messages of love, of warning, or reproof and instruction, to those whom they had learned to love in the flesh" (Smith, *Gospel Doctrine*, 435–36).

The Celestial Earth Will Be a Great Urim and Thummim
DOCTRINE AND COVENANTS 130:8–9

130:9 *This earth in its sanctified and immortal state.* Brigham Young said, "This earth, when it becomes purified and sanctified, or celestialized, will become like a sea of glass; and a person, by looking into it, can know things past, present, and to come; though none but celestialized beings can enjoy this privilege. They will look into the earth, and the things they desire to know will be exhibited to them, the same as the face is seen by looking into a mirror" (*Journal of Discourses*, 9:87).

"If the people could fully understand this matter," Brigham Young said, "they would perceive that it is perfectly reasonable and has been the law to all worlds. And this world, so benighted at present, and so lightly esteemed by infidels, as observed by Brother Clements, when it becomes celestialized, it will be like the sun, and be prepared for the habitation of the Saints, and be brought back into the presence of the Father and the Son. It will not then be an opaque body as it now is, but it will be like the stars of the firmament, full of light and glory; it will be a body of light. John compared it, in its celestialized state, to a sea of glass" (*Journal of Discourses*, 7:163).

Will be made like unto crystal. See commentary on Doctrine and Covenants 77:1.

A White Stone Is Given to All Who Enter the Celestial World
DOCTRINE AND COVENANTS 130:10–11

130:10–11 Revelation 2:17 states: "He that hath an ear, let him hear what the Spirit saith unto the churches; To him that overcometh will I give to eat of the hidden manna, and will give him a white stone, and in the stone a new name written, which no man knoweth saving he that receiveth it." Those "who overcome by faith" (D&C 76:53) inherit the celestial kingdom. Such have received the "hidden manna" or the revealed knowledge of Christ and his gospel. To them will be given a white stone symbolizing their innocence and purity before God. On the white stone will be written "a new name," which symbolically suggests that they are ready to enter into a new life on a higher stage of existence.

130:10 *The white stone.* The custom observed by judges in ancient times in announcing their decision as to guilt or innocence was to give the accused either a white or black stone. The white stone meant they had been pardoned or found innocent. The black stone meant guilt and condemnation. (Clarke, *Clarke's Commentary*, 3:979). One commentator described the white stone as "the imperishable token of acquittal, like . . . the pebble used in contemporary courts of justice in rendering a favorable verdict" (Alleman, *New Testament Commentary*, 687).

130:11 *The new name is the key word.* A new name implies entrance into a new life—the one receiving it is to enter into a higher stage of existence (Dummelow, *Commentary on the Bible*, 1075). Ancient tradition holds that possession of the "white stone" (viewed as an amulet having magical powers) could, by use of the name written on it, "secure entrance into heaven." One commentator notes that "the power of a secret name to open closed portals and to give the user supernatural powers was widespread" (Eiselen, et al., *Abingdon Bible Commentary*, 1374).

The Time of the Second Coming Is Withheld from the Prophet
DOCTRINE AND COVENANTS 130:12–17

130:12–13 See introduction to commentary on Doctrine and Covenants 87.

130:14–17 In Matthew 24:36, the Savior is recorded as saying of the time of his own return, "But of that day and hour knoweth no man, no, not the angels of heaven, but my Father only." Recording the same expression, Mark states that neither man or angels would know, not even "the Son," but only the Father (Mark 13:32). The Joseph Smith Translation rendering of this text deletes the words "neither the Son," suggesting that Christ and the Father know the time of his return. That no man was to know the time of his return was affirmed for the Prophet in a revelation given him in March of 1831. Thus, it appears that the Prophet was knowingly asking for something for which he should not have asked. It also appears that the Lord was deliberately giving a response that the Prophet could not interpret.

Intelligence Gained in This Life Rises with Us in the Resurrection

DOCTRINE AND COVENANTS 130:18–19

130:19 *Knowledge and intelligence . . . through . . . diligence and obedience.* It is not the knowledge obtained from textbooks that rises with us in the resurrection. The learned professor will have no advantage over the unschooled Saint through his mastery of human knowledge. The intelligence that rises with us in the resurrection is equated in scripture with "light and truth" (D&C 93:36). Such knowledge is obtained only by obedience, and remains forever unknown to those who are impure (2 Timothy 3:7). Those who worship at the shrine of their own intellect have chosen a rather foolish god, one who has no authority to bestow blessings in the world to come. None have articulated the principles here involved better than Jacob who said, "O that cunning plan of the evil one! O the vainness, and the frailties, and the foolishness of men! When they are learned they think they are wise, and they hearken not unto the counsel of God, for they set it aside, supposing they know of themselves, wherefore, their wisdom is foolishness and it profiteth them not. And they shall perish. But to be learned is good if they hearken unto the counsels of God" (2 Nephi 9:28–29). To which Nephi added, "Cursed is he that putteth his trust in man, or maketh flesh his arm, or shall hearken unto the precepts of men, save their precepts shall be given by the power of the Holy Ghost" (2 Nephi 28:31). That intelligence that rises with us in the resurrection comes only when we forsake evil, come to the Lord, call on his name, obey his voice, and keep his commandments (D&C 93:1–2, 28, 37). This same intelligence is lost through disobedience and loyalty to false traditions (D&C 93:39).

All Blessings Come by Obedience to Law

DOCTRINE AND COVENANTS 130:20–21

130:20–21 The question is asked, What effect did our premortal life have on our position and condition in this life? To which the answer is, The same effect that what we do in this life will have on who and what we are in the world to come. If there is a God in heaven, it can be no other way. We begin each day where we left off the previous day. The principle is immutable. We cannot begin a journey from where we are not or from where we wish were. All journeys must begin from where we are;

all that we learn is based upon what we already know; all that we can do will be the result of what we have previously done. So it was in our pre-mortal life, so it is here, and so it will be in the worlds to come.

The Father and the Son Have Bodies of Flesh and Bones
DOCTRINE AND COVENANTS 130:22–23

130:22 *The Father has a body of flesh and bones as tangible as man's; the Son also.* The crowning revelation of the New Testament is the Fatherhood of God. In every recorded instance in which Christ addressed the God of heaven, he called him "Father." He used such expressions as "my Father," "our Father," and "the Father," but it was always the "Father" that he addressed. With the restoration of the gospel through the Prophet Joseph Smith comes the knowledge that in so doing Christ was not simply using a pleasant metaphor as believed in historical Christianity but rather had in mind the plain and simple meaning of the word. Our testimony to all the world is that "Jesus Christ is the Son of God in the most literal sense," said President Ezra Taft Benson. "The body in which He per-formed His mission in the flesh was sired by that same Holy Being we wor-ship as God, our Eternal Father. Jesus was not the son of Joseph, nor was He begotten by the Holy Ghost. He is the Son of the Eternal Father!" (*Come unto Christ*, 4). So it was that in every recorded instance in which the Father addressed the Savior in scripture, it was as "Son." Again, through the restoration of the gospel, we have come to know that what was intended in his so doing is found in the plain and simple meaning of the word. Christ is the Son of God in the same sense that we are the sons of our fathers. As we obtained tangible bodies through the process of mor-tal birth, so did he; and as he suffered death through the separation of the body and the spirit, so will we; and as his body and spirit were inseparably united in the Resurrection, so it will be with us. Joseph Smith testified that "God himself was once as we are now, and is an exalted man, and sits enthroned in yonder heavens! That is the great secret. If the veil were rent today, and the great God who holds this world in its orbit, and who upholds all worlds and all things by his power, was to make himself visible,—I say, if you were to see him today, you would see him like a man in form—like yourselves in all the person, image, and very form as a man; for Adam was created in the very fashion, image and likeness of God, and received instruction from, and walked, talked and conversed with him, as one man talks and communes with another" (*Teachings of the Prophet*

Joseph Smith, 345). See commentary on King Follett Discourse 4:2, "God
. . . is an exalted Man," page 1085.

The Holy Ghost . . . is a personage of Spirit. The Holy Ghost is a spirit
man, a spirit son of God the Father. Joseph Smith taught that an "everlasting covenant was made between three personages before the organization of this earth, and relates to their dispensation of things to men on
the earth; these personages . . . are called God the first, the Creator; God
the second, the Redeemer, and God the third, the witness or Testator"
(*Teachings of the Prophet Joseph Smith*, 190). "The Holy Ghost as a personage does not inhabit the bodies of mortal men, but that member of the
Godhead dwells in a man in the sense that his promptings, the whisperings of the Spirit, find lodgment in the human soul. When the Holy Spirit
speaks to the spirit in man, the Holy Ghost is thereby dwelling in man,
for the truths that man then gives forth are those which have come from
the Holy Ghost" (McConkie, *Doctrinal New Testament Commentary*,
1:738).

Those present when the prophet made this statement affirmed that
he taught that the Holy Ghost, as a personage, cannot enter into a man's
heart (Ehat and Cook, *Words of Joseph Smith*, 170).

130:23 *It may descend upon him and not tarry with him.* Man can neither predict nor program the Spirit of the Lord. To suggest that a sequence
of deeds or performances will always result in an unusual outpouring of
the Spirit, or to teach that spiritual gifts may be had through following a
carefully constructed list of steps, may be misleading. The Lord knows best
our spiritual capacity and is thus able to decide perfectly what measure of
spiritual experience we should receive. Although he grants to the children of men according to their desires and their works, he does so "in his
own time, and in his own way, and according to his own will" (D&C
88:68). We simply cannot force spiritual things. Further, we cannot
restrain the Spirit from determining the times of his comings and goings.
"The presentation or 'gift' of the Holy Ghost," President Joseph F. Smith
explained, "simply confers upon a man the right to receive at any time,
when he is worthy of it and desires it, the power and light of truth of the
Holy Ghost, although he may often be left to his own spirit and judgment" (*Gospel Doctrine*, 60–61). That is to say, the Holy Ghost "may be
conferred upon men, and he may dwell with them for a while, or he may
continue to dwell with them in accordance with their worthiness, and he
may depart from them at his will" (Smith, *Gospel Doctrine*, 466).

Doctrine and Covenants 131

Date: 16 and 17 May 1843
Place: Ramus, Illinois

Doctrine and Covenants 131 consists of three different doctrinal statements made by the Prophet Joseph Smith while visiting members of the Church in Ramus, Illinois. They were recorded by his personal scribe, William Clayton, who was among those who accompanied him. The *History of the Church* reads as follows:

"Tuesday, 16.—At eleven o'clock, with George Miller, William Clayton, Eliza and Lydia Partridge and J. M. Smith, I started for Carthage where we tarried about half-an-hour conversing with different individuals, when we started for Ramus; arrived about half-past three, p. m., and stayed at William G. Perkins for the evening; then went to Benjamin F. Johnson's with William Clayton to sleep. Before retiring, I gave Brother and Sister Johnson some instructions on the priesthood; and putting my hand on the knee of William Clayton, I said: Your life is hid with Christ in God, and so are many others. Nothing but the unpardonable sin can prevent you from inheriting eternal life for you are sealed up by the power of the Priesthood unto eternal life, having taken the step necessary for that purpose.

"Except a man and his wife enter into an everlasting covenant and be married for eternity, while in this probation, by the power and authority of the Holy Priesthood, they will cease to increase when they die; that is, they will not have any children after the resurrection. But those who are married by the power and authority of the priesthood in this life, and continue without committing the sin against the Holy Ghost, will continue to increase and have children in the celestial glory. The unpardonable sin is to shed innocent blood, or be accessory thereto. All other sins will be visited with judgment in the flesh, and the spirit being delivered to the buffetings of Satan until the day of the Lord Jesus.

"The way I know in whom to confide—God tells me in whom I may place confidence" (Smith, *History of the Church*, 5:391–92). Then followed verses 1 through 4 as found in Doctrine and Covenants 131.

Celestial Marriage Is Essential to Exaltation
DOCTRINE AND COVENANTS 131:1–4

131:1–3 In this revelation we learn that in the celestial kingdom there are three degrees of glory and that eternal marriage is required to enter into the highest of those degrees.

131:2 *This order of the priesthood.* Joseph Smith explained that there are "three grand orders of priesthood" (not three priesthoods—but three orders of the priesthood); they are the Levitical order, the Melchizedek order, and the patriarchal order as spoken of in this verse (*Teachings of the Prophet Joseph Smith*, 322). "All priesthood," he said, "is Melchizedek" (*Teachings of the Prophet Joseph Smith*, 180).

"What was the power of Melchizedek?" the Prophet inquired, "'Twas not the Priesthood of Aaron which administers in outward ordinances, and the offering of sacrifices. Those holding the fulness of the Melchizedek Priesthood are kings and priests of the Most High God, holding the keys of power and blessings. In fact, that Priesthood is a perfect law of theocracy, and stands as God to give laws to the people, administering endless lives to the sons and daughters of Adam.

"Abraham says to Melchizedek, I believe all that thou hast taught me concerning the priesthood and the coming of the Son of Man; so Melchizedek ordained Abraham and sent him away. Abraham rejoiced, saying, Now I have a priesthood" (*Teachings of the Prophet Joseph Smith*, 322–23).

As to what is involved in the patriarchal order of the priesthood, Elder Bruce R. McConkie observed, "Joseph Smith says that in the temple of God there is an order of priesthood that is patriarchal. 'Go to the temple,' he says, 'and find out about this order.' So I went to the temple, and I took my wife with me, and we kneeled at the altar. There on that occasion we entered, the two of us, into an 'order of the priesthood,' When we did it, we had sealed upon us, on a conditional basis, every blessing that God promised Father Abraham—the blessings of exaltation and eternal increase. The name of that order of priesthood, which is patriarchal in nature, because Abraham was a natural patriarch to his posterity, is the New and Everlasting Covenant of Marriage" ("Eternal Family," 7).

Meaning the new and everlasting covenant of marriage. Responding to

the question, "What is the new and everlasting covenant?" President
Joseph Fielding Smith said, "I regret to say that there are some members of
the Church who are misled and misinformed in regard to what the new
and everlasting covenant really is. The new and everlasting covenant is
the sum total of all gospel covenants and obligations, and I want to prove
it. In the 66th section of the Doctrine and Covenants, verse 2, I read:
'Verily I say unto you, blessed are you for receiving mine everlasting
covenant, even the fulness of my gospel, sent forth unto the children of
men, that they might have life and be made partakers of the glories which
are to be revealed in the last days, as it was written by the prophets and
apostles in days of old.'

"More definitely stated is the definition of the new and everlasting
covenant given to us in section 132 of the Doctrine and Covenants. Now
I am going to say before I read this that marriage is not the new and everlasting covenant. If there are any here that have that idea I want to say
that right to them. Baptism is not the new and everlasting covenant.
Ordination to the priesthood is not the new and everlasting covenant. In
section 22 of the Doctrine and Covenants the Lord says that baptism is
'a new and an everlasting covenant, even that which was from the beginning.' Marriage in the temple of the Lord for time and for eternity is 'a'
new and everlasting covenant" (*Doctrines of Salvation*, 1:156).

131:4 *He cannot have an increase.* "Except a man and his wife enter
into an everlasting covenant and be married for eternity, while in this
probation, by the power and authority of the Holy Priesthood, they will
cease to increase when they die; that is, they will not have any children
after the resurrection" (*Teachings of the Prophet Joseph Smith*, 300–301).

Being Sealed unto Eternal Life
DOCTRINE AND COVENANTS 131:5–6

131:5 *More sure word of prophecy.* Joseph Smith taught: "After a person has faith in Christ, repents of his sins, and is baptized for the remission of his sins and receives the Holy Ghost (by the laying on of hands),
which is the first Comforter, then let him continue to humble himself
before God, hungering and thirsting after righteousness, and living by
every word of God, and the Lord will soon say unto him, Son, thou shalt
be exalted. When the Lord has thoroughly proved him, and finds that the
man is determined to serve Him at all hazards, then the man will find his
calling and election made sure, then it will be his privilege to receive the

other Comforter" (*Teachings of the Prophet Joseph Smith*, 151). For a man to receive the other Comforter is to have Christ appear to him and to see the visions of eternity.

131:6 *It is impossible for a man to be saved in ignorance.* Though it is certainly true that there is no salvation in ignorance, meaning ignorance of the saving truths of the gospel of Jesus Christ, contextually this statement is an extension of the previous verse and as such means that there is no salvation independent of participation in the necessary ordinances of salvation.

All Spirit Is Matter
DOCTRINE AND COVENANTS 131:7–8

131:7–8 "The laws of *truth* are omnipotent and unalterable—no power in heaven or on earth can break them in the least degree. Among these laws we find that two and two make just four—that five from eight leave three, and that nothing added to nothing is nothing still. And ten thousand nothings multiplied together cannot increase the amount.

"If it still be argued that something can be made from nothing, we would inquire how many solid feet of nonentity it would require to make one solid foot of material substance? The very idea is the climax of absurdity.

"Therefore we argue that it is a self-evident fact, clearly manifested to every reflecting mind, that the elements of matter are eternal. That the earth was formed out of the eternal elements, and man's body out of the earth. These facts are not only proven from scripture, reason and philosophy, but are also demonstrated or confirmed by daily experience. The work of creation has been proceeding in every age up to the present time upon the same unchangeable principles. That is, all material organization in our world is produced from the earth, or from its own elements, as we daily witness while there is not a single instance of a thing, or being, produced from nothing, so far as has come within the sphere of man's observation. . . .

"But to return to the main thread of our subject, viz: the impossibility of the annihilation of matter, we would inquire in the first place what the scriptures reveal on the subject.

"The Psalmist declares that the heavens and the earth shall be folded as a vesture and that they shall be changed.

"Isaiah and other prophets testify that they will be burned; and pass away and there will be a new heavens and a new earth.

"The Apostles adopt the same language on this subject with this addition that the *'elements shall melt with fervent heat.'* And finally the Lord declares by the mouth of John saying: 'Behold, I make *all things new.'* Now every one the least acquainted with terms, must know that none of these expressions convey the least idea of annihilation; but on the contrary they clearly reveal the destiny of the material world, viz: that the elements are to be melted, changed, purified, and renewed; even ALL THINGS. And it is further said, the new heaven and the new earth shall endure forever.

"Therefore the scriptures decide in the most definite terms that nothing will be annihilated; but that *all things* will be made new.

"The science of chemistry serves to illustrate the subject in the most clear and lucid manner. For instance, by burning or melting any substance, not one particle is annihilated, they are only separated, decomposed, analyzed and changed, and could the whole operation be reversed they would be restored to their former state without the loss of a single particle.

"If then, we find ourselves composed of, and associated with material substance, which is eternal in its elementary principles, and inseparably connected with all organized existence in all worlds, past, present, and to come, we must feel the same interest in, and the same solicitation for the salvation, exaltation, and perfection of our bodies that we do for our souls, or spirits" (Pratt, *Writings*, 29–33; emphasis in original).

DOCTRINE AND COVENANTS 132

DATE: 12 JULY 1843
PLACE: NAUVOO, ILLINOIS

The principles here recorded, though not committed to writing until 12 July 1843, were revealed to Joseph Smith in 1831 while he was working on his inspired translation of the Bible. The question as to how the Old Testament patriarchs were justified in having many wives would naturally arise during that labor, and it would be natural that Joseph Smith would inquire about it at that time.

It will be profitable for the student of this revelation to give careful consideration to the way the Lord answered the Prophet when he asked this question. The Lord first establishes himself as a God of law and order who deals with men by way of covenant. Thus his people have always been a covenant people. All such covenants, we are told, were decreed before the world was and are neither to be added to or taken from in this mortal sphere. Further, all such covenants must be performed by the authority of the priesthood, by someone holding the appropriate keys or presidency, and must be sealed by the Holy Spirit of Promise to be of efficacy, virtue, or force after men are dead. The composite of all the covenants of salvation is identified as the "new and everlasting covenant."

The Lord then takes the principle of marriage to illustrate what he is teaching. Marriage was ordained in the councils of heaven to be eternal but will be such only if it complies with the order there established. Again, it must be performed by the authority of the priesthood, it must be done by someone holding the proper keys, and it must be ratified or sealed by the Holy Spirit of promise, which is to say that the Holy Ghost must affirm that both the man and the woman have abided by the terms of their covenant. To ensure that this is understood, the Lord uses three case studies: first, a marriage which was not intended to be binding in the world to come (vv. 15–17); second, a marriage in which the hope of an eternal union was expressed though the marriage was performed without the authority of the priesthood, or having been performed by the priesthood was not ratified by the Holy Ghost (v. 18); and third, a marriage that complies with the order established in this revelation with a description of the blessings that will attend it (v. 19). A brief discussion of exaltation and the doctrine of eternal lives (meaning the endless continuation of seed) follows (vv. 20–25). Then comes a warning of the depths of suffering that will come to those who have received such sacred covenants and promises and then turned against them (vv. 25–27).

Having taught the principles here announced, the Lord tells Joseph Smith that he is going to give him "the law of my Holy Priesthood" (v. 28), which law is the promise of exaltation and eternal increase. In teaching this law, the Lord takes Abraham as his illustration. The revelation then identifies Joseph Smith as a descendant of Abraham and thus an heir of the promises made to Abraham relative to his posterity (vv. 30–31). If, however, he is to receive these promises, he must do the "works of Abraham" (v. 32), that is, he must comply with the same law given to our ancient father (v. 33).

After these principles have been established, the Lord begins, in verse 34, to answer the question with which the revelation began: Why did some of the faithful in ages past have plural wives? The temple of our understanding has now been "fitly framed" by an understanding of the law of the Holy Priesthood. We now see that the plurality of wives—as with all the principles that come from the throne of heaven—is governed by law, and is acceptable to God only according to that law and those covenants agreed upon before the foundations of the earth. The plurality of wives, which practice was discontinued by Wilford Woodruff in 1890, is an appendage to the greater principle of eternal marriage. The principle of eternal marriage, being a law of heaven, is inseparably associated with the holy priesthood—thus, where there is no holiness, the other principles will not be found either. The exaltation of the man and the woman consists in the eternal preservation of the roles unique to their gender. It is in fatherhood and motherhood that the glories of eternity are found. Only in the sacred institution of marriage can we find exaltation.

Exaltation Is Gained through the New and Everlasting Covenant
DOCTRINE AND COVENANTS 132:1–6

132:1 *Solomon.* See commentary on verse 38.

Concubines. As relates to the ancient patriarchs, a concubine was a legal and lawful plural wife of a lower social order than the primary wives.

132:3 *All those who have this law revealed unto them must obey the same.* No law of God can be ignored with impunity. When any truth from heaven is revealed, we are obligated to accept and live it. There is no salvation to be found in picking and choosing among the commandments of God or the truths of salvation, supposing that we can live some and ignore others. We cannot, for instance, profess to accept the Bible while rejecting the Book of Mormon, or accept the Book of Mormon while rejecting the direction of our living prophets. Thus, those to whom the law of the priesthood, or eternal marriage, has been revealed are obligated to live the same. It would be equally improper to assume offices to which we had not been called or to claim privileges to which we have not been ordained. Some have attempted to find justification for the practice of polygamy in this verse. It simply is not there. The law to which reference is made is that of eternal marriage, not the plurality of wives. There is but one man on earth at a time who can authorize the performance of such marriages: the president of The Church of Jesus Christ of Latter-day Saints (v. 7).

132:4–6 Marriage, when performed by the authority of God, is here announced to be "a" new and "an" everlasting covenant. In like manner, baptism is "a" new and "an" everlasting covenant (D&C 22:1) as are all other "covenants, contracts, bonds, obligations, oaths, vows, performances, connections, associations, or expectations" intended to be of "efficacy, virtue, or force in and after the resurrection" (v. 7). The composite or sum of these individual covenants is "the" new and everlasting covenant. See commentary on Doctrine and Covenants 22:1.

132:5 *The law which was appointed for that blessing.* "There is a law, irrevocably decreed in heaven before the foundations of this world, upon which all blessings are predicated—And when we obtain any blessing from God, it is by obedience to that law upon which it is predicated" (D&C 130:20–21). "The law" to which reference is made in this revelation is the law of the holy priesthood (v. 38), or eternal marriage.

The conditions thereof, as were instituted from before the foundation of the world. Referring to our premortal life, President Spencer W. Kimball said, "We committed ourselves to our Heavenly Father, that if He would send us to the earth and give us bodies and give to us the priceless opportunities that earth life afforded, we would keep our lives clean and would marry in the holy temple and would rear a family and teach them righteousness. This was a solemn oath, a solemn promise" ("Be Ye Therefore Perfect," 2).

132:6 *It was instituted for the fulness of my glory.* It is in and through the new and everlasting covenant that we obtain the fulness of God's glory. There is no salvation independent of such a covenant (v. 31).

The Terms and Conditions of the New and Everlasting Covenant
DOCTRINE AND COVENANTS 132:7–14

132:7 *Sealed by the Holy Spirit of promise.* See commentary on Doctrine and Covenants 76:53.

Of him who is anointed. This refers to Joseph Smith and, by implication, his rightful successors in the office of president of the high priesthood, or president of the Church. Though the First Presidency and the Quorum of the Twelve all hold the keys of the kingdom, they can exercise those keys only under the direction of their president, who is referred to repeatedly in this revelation as "him who is anointed."

Keys of this priesthood. Applying the principle here stated to plural marriage, Joseph Smith observed: "In the afternoon, rode . . . to show some of the brethren some land. Evening, at home, and walked up and down the streets with my scribe. Gave instructions to try those persons who were preaching, teaching, or practicing the doctrine of plurality of wives; for, according to the law, I hold the keys of this power in the last days; for there is never but one on earth at a time on whom the power and its keys are conferred; *and I have constantly said no man shall have but one wife at a time, unless the Lord directs otherwise* [5 October 1843]" (*History of the Church,* 6:46; see D&C 132:45–47).

In the worlds to come, only those ordinances which were ordained of God, performed by his priesthood, sealed by him who is anointed, and ratified by the Holy Ghost will be of "efficacy, virtue, or force."

132:8–11 Having announced that his house is one of order, the Lord here asks three questions to illustrate the point. "Will I," he asks, "accept of an offering that is not made in my name?" Were he to do so, he would negate the purpose of priesthood authority. Priesthood authority is either necessary or it is not, we cannot have it both ways. If everyone had the right to act in the name of the Lord, then salvation would simply be an individual matter. There could be no collective salvation, or kingdom of God, in the worlds to come, for there would be no universal standard as to who could be admitted and who must be excluded. There could be neither good nor evil, right nor wrong. The idea denies the very existence of

God for, as Lehi explained, "If ye shall say there is no law, ye shall also say there is no sin. If ye shall say there is no sin, ye shall also say there is no righteousness. And if there be no righteousness there be no happiness. And if there be no righteousness nor happiness there be no punishment nor misery. And if these things are not there is no God. And if there is no God we are not, neither the earth; for there could have been no creation of things, neither to act nor to be acted upon; wherefore, all things must have vanished away" (2 Nephi 2:13).

In the second of his three questions, the Lord asks, "Will I receive that . . . which I have not appointed?" To respond in the affirmative would be to liken the system of salvation to a flea market where we barter and trade for the blessings of salvation. The price of such blessings would be subject to inflation or deflation; one man could pay for them with his life, while another might obtain them for simply saying, "Praise the Lord, I believe."

The third question emphasizes the eternal nature of the gospel. The Lord asks, "Will I appoint unto you anything that did not accord with the laws and ordinances of the gospel as they have existed since before the world was created?" If God were at liberty to change the terms that constitute the covenant of salvation as he may choose, we would be without any sure knowledge that the course we were following was approved by him. The example of one man would be of no value to another in such a circumstance, nor would there be any particular value in scripture, for the word of the Lord may prove to be of no more worth than that of a scheming scoundrel.

Only the knowledge that God is constant, that he changes not, that all principles that flow from him are everlastingly the same, enables us to exercise faith in him. If God is not a God of order, he is no God at all.

Celestial Marriage and the Continuation of the Family Unit Enables Us to Obtain Exaltation
DOCTRINE AND COVENANTS 132:15–20

132:15–20 Marriage was ordained of God, and it is expected that where possible, at the appropriate age, members of the Church seek the opportunity to find a worthy and suitable spouse. Further, it is expected that all such marriages be entered into in accordance with the laws of the land. Such temporal unions, however, are dissolved at death because the authority to marry for eternity belongs exclusively to the priesthood.

Agreements—be they private or public—to extend a marriage beyond death are without authority. As far as the eternities are concerned, all marriages performed by the authority of men have at the same time a built-in divorce clause, often expressed with the phrase, "Till death do ye part." Only those marriages performed by priesthood authority in the manner prescribed in this revelation will be binding in the world to come.

Those who accept the gospel of Jesus Christ—in this life or the next—will be given the opportunity to go to the house of the Lord with the companion of their choice and be married for time and eternity. Those who reject that opportunity are destined to "remain separately and singly" throughout the endless eternities. These, we are told, will be "ministering servants" to those who have been married for time and eternity.

132:17 *They cannot be enlarged.* These will not be exalted; they "cannot have an increase" (D&C 131:4); they will not enjoy the "continuation of the lives" (v. 22), that is they will not enjoy the privileges of the family unit nor will they be able to have posterity. As Malachi said, they will be left with neither "root nor branch" (Malachi 4:1).

In their saved condition. As generally used in the scriptures, the terms "saved" or obtain "salvation" are synonymous with exaltation or eternal life (McConkie, *Mormon Doctrine,* 670). This is not the case in the present text, where the term carries much the same meaning as immortal life in some condition less than exaltation.

132:19 *And it shall be sealed unto them.* Elder Bruce R. McConkie referred to verses 19 and 26 as the "most difficult and least understood" verses among all the revelations of the Restoration. These verses speak simultaneously of eternal marriage and having one's calling and election made sure. The promised blessings require both. The chain of thought is as follows: a man and woman must be married according to the law of the Lord, meaning they must enter into the eternal covenant of marriage. They must then go forth and so live that they can receive the promise through the Lord's anointed that they will come forth in the first resurrection to inherit thrones and kingdoms. Having received that promise, which is certainly not given to them at the time of their marriage, their salvation is sure, unless they so transgress that they become perdition (v. 26). With that promise, they have received all that is necessary to their exaltation as long as they do not commit the unpardonable sin (v. 26).

And it shall be said . . . next resurrection. The order of resurrection is from most righteous to most wicked. Those who are celestial will come forth before those who are terrestrial, and so forth. Thus, all who are celestial will come forth in a "first resurrection." It was a first resurrection that brought forth the righteous dead from Adam to Christ (Mosiah 15:21; Alma 40:16). The righteous dead from our dispensation will also come forth in a first resurrection (D&C 88:98). Those who live on into the millennium or the "next resurrection," as referred to in this verse, will also be part of a first resurrection.

Lamb's Book of Life. "The book of life, or Lamb's book of Life, is the record kept in heaven which contains the names of the faithful and an account of their righteous covenants and deeds (D. & C. 128:6–7; Ps. 69:28; Rev. 3:5; 21:27). The book of life is the book containing the names of those who shall inherit eternal life; it is the book of eternal life (Dan. 12:1–4; Heb. 12:23; D. & C. 76:68; 132:19). It is "the book of the names of the sanctified, even them of the celestial world" (D. & C. 88:2). Names of faithful saints are recorded in the book of life while they are yet in mortality (Luke 10:20; Philip. 4:3; *Teachings of the Prophet Joseph Smith*, 9). But those names are blotted out in the event of wickedness (Rev. 13:8; 17:8; 22:19)" (McConkie, *Mormon Doctrine*, 97).

Commit no murder whereby to shed innocent blood. See commentary on verse 27.

They shall pass by the angels, and the gods, which are set there, to their exaltation. "Your endowment," explained Brigham Young, "is to receive all those ordinances in the House of the Lord, which are necessary for you, after you have departed this life, to enable you to walk back to the presence of the Father, passing the angels who stand as sentinels, being enabled to give them the key words, the signs and tokens, pertaining to the Holy Priesthood, and gain your eternal exaltation in spite of earth and hell" (*Journal of Discourses*, 2:31).

Which glory shall be a fulness and a continuation of the seeds forever and ever. The explanation of this text as it applies to faithful women was given by President Joseph F. Smith: "Some of you will understand when I tell you that some of these good women who have passed beyond have actually been anointed queens and priestesses unto God and unto their husbands, to continue their work and to be the mothers of spirits in the world to come. The world does not understand this—they cannot receive it— they do not know what it means, and it is sometimes hard for those who ought to be thoroughly imbued with the spirit of the gospel—even for some of us, to comprehend, but it is true" (*Gospel Doctrine*, 461).

132:20 *Therefore shall they be from everlasting to everlasting, because they continue.* Everlasting to everlasting means from eternity past to eternity future. It is from the premortal life through the temporal (mortal) life to the eternity following the resurrection (Smith, *Answers*, 2:127). It can properly be said of those obtaining exaltation that they are from eternity to eternity or from everlasting to everlasting.

The Strait and Narrow Way That Leads to Eternal Lives
DOCTRINE AND COVENANTS 132:21–25

132:22 *Continuation of the lives.* To obtain eternal life is also to obtain eternal "*lives*," that is, the continuation of seed throughout eternity. Similar terms are "increase" (D&C 131:4), "enlarged" (v. 17), and "a continuation of the seeds" (v. 19).

132:25 *The deaths.* "If a man is deprived of the 'continuation of the lives' for ever—and not to have these blessings is referred to as leading to the deaths, or the lack of the continuation of the lives, or increase—then he cannot 'worlds without end' reach the celestial glory; for the celestial glory is the continuation of the lives or increase eternally; it is to be gods, even the sons of God" (Smith, *Doctrines of Salvation*, 2:33).

The Law Relative to Blasphemy against the Holy Ghost
DOCTRINE AND COVENANTS 132:26–27

132:26 *He or she shall commit any sin or transgression of the new and everlasting covenant.* This verse is a brief restatement of what was said in verse 19. A superficial reading of the verse has led some to suppose that it is saying that those who have entered into the eternal covenant of marriage are assured salvation as long as they do not commit murder wherein they shed innocent blood. This simply is not the case. The promises here given apply exclusively to those who, having been married for time and eternity, advance to that station wherein they have had their calling and election made sure. On this matter, President Joseph Fielding Smith observed, "Verse 26, in section 132, is the most abused passage in any scripture. The Lord has never promised any soul that he may be taken into exaltation without the spirit of repentance. While repentance is not stated in this passage, yet it is, and must be, implied. It is strange to me that everyone knows about verse 26, but it seems that they have never read or heard of Matthew 12:31–32, where the Lord tells us the same thing in substance as we find in verse 26, section 132" (*Doctrines of Salvation*, 2:95).

"The Lord said by his own mouth: And he that endureth not unto the end, the same is he that is also hewn down and cast into the fire, from whence they can no more return, because of the justice of the Father. And this is the word which he hath given unto the children of men. And for this cause he fulfilleth the words which he hath given, and he lieth not, but fulfilleth all his words. And no unclean thing can enter into his kingdom; therefore nothing entereth into his rest save it be those who have washed their garments in my blood, because of their faith, and the repentance of all their sins, and their faithfulness unto the end.

"So we must conclude that those spoken of in verse 26 are those who, having sinned, have fully repented and are willing to pay the price of their sinning, else the blessings of exaltation will not follow. Repentance is absolutely necessary for the forgiveness, and the person having sinned must be cleansed" (Smith, *Doctrines of Salvation*, 2:95–96).

Shed innocent blood. See commentary on verse 27.

Destroyed in the flesh. "To be 'destroyed in the flesh' means exactly that. We cannot destroy men in the flesh, because we do not control the lives of men and do not have power to pass sentences upon them which involve capital punishment. In the days when there was a theocracy on the earth, then this decree was enforced. What the Lord will do in lieu of this, because we cannot destroy in the flesh, I am unable to say, but it will have to be made up in some other way" (Smith, *Doctrines of Salvation*, 2:96–97).

Delivered unto the buffetings of Satan unto the day of redemption. "To be turned over to the buffetings of Satan is to be given into his hands; it is to be turned over to him with all the protective power of the priesthood, of righteousness, and of godliness removed, so that Lucifer is free to torment, persecute, and afflict such a person without let or hindrance. When the bars are down, the cuffs and curses of Satan, both in this world and in the world to come, bring indescribable anguish typified by burning fire and brimstone. The damned in hell so suffer" (McConkie, *Mormon Doctrine*, 108).

Commenting on this verse, Joseph Fielding Smith said, "Here is something which those who contend that the Lord has granted immunity from their sins to some [the claim is made by some who have been married in the temple], if they have received certain sealings by the Holy Spirit of promise, have overlooked in this passage. I call attention to these two things. If covenants are broken and enormous sins are committed, but not unto death, there are certain punishments to be inflicted. The mere confession is not enough; the sinners are: 1—to 'be destroyed in the flesh'; and 2—to 'be delivered unto the buffetings of Satan unto the day of redemption.'

"Who in the world is so foolish as to wish to sin with the hope of forgiveness, if such a penalty is to be inflicted? No one but a fool! . . .

"Who wishes to endure such torment? No one but a fool! I have seen their anguish. I have heard their pleadings for relief and their pitiful cries that they cannot endure the torment. This was in *this* life. Add to that, the torment in the spirit world before the redemption comes—all of this, mark you, coming *after severe and humble repentance!*" (*Doctrines of Salvation*, 2:96–97).

132:27 *Blasphemy against the Holy Ghost.* What is "blasphemy against the Holy Ghost"? Having quoted this verse, Elder Bruce R. McConkie said: "The unpardonable sin consists in denying Christ, in fighting the truth, in joining hands with those who crucified him, knowing full well, and with a perfect knowledge, that he is the Son of God; it means pursuing this course after gaining a perfect knowledge, given of the Holy Ghost, that he is Lord of all. The innocent blood thus shed is his blood; those who so sin become murderers by assenting unto his death, an assent that is given with a full and perfect knowledge of his divinity.

"Paul tells us that these rebellious ones who choose to become sons of perdition (or angels of the devil) cannot repent. 'It is impossible for those who were once enlightened,' he says, 'and [who] have tasted of the heavenly gift, and were made partakers of the Holy Ghost, and have tasted the good word of God, and the powers of the world to come, if they shall fall away, to renew them again unto repentance; seeing they crucify to themselves the Son of God afresh, and put him to an open shame' (Hebrews 6:4–6). And also: 'If we sin willfully after that we have received the knowledge of the truth there remaineth no more sacrifice for sins, but a certain fearful looking for of judgment and fiery indignation, which shall devour the adversaries. He that despised Moses' law died without mercy under two or three witnesses: of how much sorer punishment, suppose ye, shall he be thought worthy, who hath trodden under foot the Son of God, and hath counted the blood of the covenant, wherewith he was sanctified an unholy thing, and hath done despite unto the Spirit of grace?' (Hebrews 10:26–29)" (*New Witness*, 232–33).

Shed innocent blood, and assent unto my death. "The innocent blood is that of Christ; and those who commit blasphemy against the Holy Ghost, which is the unpardonable sin (Matt. 12:31–32), thereby 'crucify to themselves the Son of God afresh, and put him to an open shame' (Heb. 6:6). They are, in other words, people who would have crucified Christ, having the while a perfect knowledge that he was the Son of God" (McConkie, *Doctrinal New Testament Commentary*, 3:345). Not being in a position to crucify Christ, those of this spirit seek the blood of those upon whom he has placed his name, that is, his anointed servants.

The Promise of Eternal Increase and Exaltation Had by the Saints of All Ages
DOCTRINE AND COVENANTS 132:28–39

132:28 *The law of my Holy Priesthood.* The law of the priesthood centers in the promise that a man and his wife are to be sealed together for time and eternity and that they have claim upon the promise of eternal increase. From the days of Adam, this has been the order of things among all who possessed the holy priesthood. The question is often asked, Did the prophets and Saints in the Book of Mormon have eternal marriage? To suppose that they had the holy priesthood without eternal marriage would be akin to supposing that someone could have the gospel without faith, repentance, and baptism, or without the knowledge and testimony of Christ. Affirming this conclusion, the heading given to these verses in the chapter summary at the beginning of the revelation reads, *"Promises of eternal increase and exaltation made to prophets and saints in all ages."* No other explanation can be given to explain the concern of the Book of Mormon prophets for their posterity, generations unborn to whom they wrote and with whom they had undoubtedly made covenants in the premortal councils. So it was that Samuel prophesied that unless the Nephites repented, their descendants some four hundred years later would be smitten with "the sword and with famine and with pestilence" (Helaman 13:9). Unless there was some understanding of the importance of the family unit, it would sound strange to be warned by a prophet that unless they repented their children's children, some four hundred years removed, would be destroyed.

Consider Mormon's lament as he views his people slain by the swords of the Lamanites:

"O ye fair ones, how could ye have departed from the ways of the Lord! O ye fair ones, how could ye have rejected that Jesus, who stood with open arms to receive you!

"Behold, if ye had not done this, ye would not have fallen. But behold, ye are fallen, and I mourn your loss.

"O ye fair sons and daughters, ye fathers and mothers, ye husbands and wives, ye fair ones, how is it that ye could have fallen!

"But behold, ye are gone, and my sorrows cannot bring your return.

"And the day soon cometh that your mortal must put on immortality, and these bodies which are now moldering in corruption must soon become incorruptible bodies; and then ye must stand before the judgment-seat of Christ, to be judged according to your works; and if it so be that ye are righteous, then are ye blessed with your fathers who have gone before you" (Mormon 6:17–21).

Mormon also observed that his people "were married, and given in marriage, and were blessed according to the multitude of the promises which the Lord had made unto them" (4 Nephi 1:11).

Ordained . . . before the world was. All gospel ordinances were ordained in the councils of heaven (v. 11), thus marriage and the family were ordained as central to the plan of salvation. This leads to the thought that families were organized and covenants and promises were made among the faithful in the premortal councils.

132:29 *Abraham received all things . . . by revelation.* One of the evidences that Abraham was indeed a prophet of the Lord is the frequency with which his actions have been criticized by both Bible students and Bible scholars. Here we are told that he has entered into his exaltation and sits upon his throne. Thus, it is his right to rule and reign as a king and a priest (Revelation 5:10) as he lays claim to all the promises spoken of in Doctrine and Covenants 132:19 and 20.

132:30–31 At this point in the revelation, the Lord turns Joseph Smith's attention to the covenant or promises that He made anciently with Abraham. Given that all "covenants, contracts, bonds, obligations, oaths, vows," are part of the new and everlasting covenant, it naturally follows that the new and everlasting covenant embraces the covenant made with Abraham. The Abrahamic covenant, or "dispensation of the gospel of Abraham" as it was described when it was restored to the Prophet (D&C 110:12), centers in the principle of eternal marriage and the endless continuation of the family unit. The Lord, in effect, says to Joseph Smith, I appeared to you because you are a descendant of Abraham and as such are a rightful heir of the priesthood and promises given to that ancient patriarch.

The two great witnesses of Christ for this dispensation are Joseph

Smith and the Book of Mormon. Christ appeared to Joseph Smith, and he appeared to the peoples in the Book of Mormon. Joseph Smith is the source through which the purity of the gospel of Christ has been restored to us, and so is the Book of Mormon. Joseph Smith received these privileges because he was a descendant of Abraham, and those privileges were accorded the peoples of the Book of Mormon because they were Abraham's seed. When Christ appeared among the Nephites, he said, "Ye are the children of the prophets; and ye are of the house of Israel; and ye are of the covenant which the Father made with your fathers, saying unto Abraham: And in thy seed shall all the kindreds of the earth be blessed. The Father having raised me up unto you first, and sent me to bless you in turning away every one of you from his iniquities; and this because ye are the children of the covenant" (3 Nephi 20:25–26). Earlier he had explained that they were those of whom he said, "Other sheep I have, which are not of this fold: them also I must bring, and they shall hear my voice" (John 10:16). In the Old World, he said, they had supposed that he was making reference to the Gentiles, but "The Gentiles," he explained, "should not at any time hear my voice—that I should not manifest myself unto them save it were by the Holy Ghost. But behold, ye have both heard my voice, and seen me; and ye are my sheep, and ye are numbered among those whom the Father hath given me" (3 Nephi 15:23–24).

As the seed of Abraham, Joseph Smith was a rightful heir to the blessings of the priesthood and the manifestations of heaven. This heirship, is eternal, meaning that it cannot be dissolved by death. Those unable to lay claim to its blessings in this life will have the opportunity to do so in the world to come, for, as the revelation states, these promises continue "both in the world and out of the world."

132:31 *By this law is the continuation of the works of my Father, wherein he glorifieth himself.* It is the work and labor of God to exalt his children (Moses 1:39). This can only be done in the family unit. Thus, the law of eternal marriage, as given to Abraham, becomes the law by which God glorifies both his children and himself.

132:32–33 The law referred to was referred to earlier as "the law of my Holy Priesthood" (v. 28). It is the new and everlasting covenant of marriage. No reference has been made to this point in the revelation to the plurality of wives. It would be to seriously misunderstand all that has been said in the first thirty-three verses of this revelation to impose on them something they have not said. The purpose of the revelation to this point is to declare as plainly and as emphatically as it possibly can be done that a man and his wife can only receive the promise of eternal life in and through the ordinance of marriage. The cultist idea that such a promise can only be obtained in plural marriage finds no justification in the text.

132:34 *Because this was the law.* The patriarchal practice of having more than one wife was in keeping with customs that were widespread in Abraham's day. A variety of ancient texts indicate that it was an accepted practice for a man to have a second wife if his first wife could not give him children. Thus, the command of the Lord to Abraham and Sarah was in accordance with the custom or law of the day. For instance, in the *Laws of Hammurabi* (1792 to 1750 B.C.), king of Old Babylon, we read, "If a man marries a *nadītu*, and she does not provide him with children, and that man then decides to marry a *šugītu*, that man may marry the *šugītu* and bring her to his house: that *šugītu* should not aspire to equal status with the *nadītu*" (Roth, *Law Collections*, 109).

Contrary to the impression given in Genesis 16:2–3 that Sarah instructed her husband of her own accord, the Lord commanded Abraham to take Hagar to wife after instructing Sarah. She consented out of reverence for the law of the Lord and loyalty and obedience to God and his priesthood representative.

132:37 *Concubines.* See commentary on verse 1.

As Isaac also. The Old Testament, as we presently have it, makes no reference to Isaac having taken any wives but Rebekah (Genesis 25:20). This text seems to suggest that he, like his father Abraham and his son Jacob, also took plural wives.

They have entered into their exaltation, according to the promises. Reference is to the promises accorded to Abraham in the Abrahamic covenant (Abraham 2:9–11) and in Doctrine and Covenants 132:19.

132:38 *In nothing did they sin save in those things which they received not of me.* There can be no sin in doing that which God has commanded. Thus, David and Solomon committed no sin in taking to themselves those wives the Lord had given them. To do other than that would clearly be sin, which is what both of the men here involved committed. In the book of Kings we read the following:

"But king Solomon loved many strange women, together with the daughter of Pharaoh, women of the Moabites, Ammonites, Edomites, Zidonians, and Hittites;

"Of the nations concerning which the Lord said unto the children of

Israel, Ye shall not go in to them, neither shall they come in unto you: for surely they will turn away your heart after their gods: Solomon clave unto these in love.

"And he had seven hundred wives, princesses, and three hundred concubines: and his wives turned away his heart.

"For it came to pass, when Solomon was old, that his wives turned away his heart after other gods: and his heart was not perfect with the Lord his God, as was the heart of David his father.

"For Solomon went after Ashtoreth the goddess of the Zidonians, and after Milcom the abomination of the Ammonites.

"And Solomon did evil in the sight of the Lord, and went not fully after the Lord, as did David his father" (1 Kings 11:1–6).

Our text tells us that Solomon had a thousand wives and that the Lord was offended with what he had done. In Deuteronomy we read:

"When thou art come unto the land which the Lord thy God giveth thee, and shalt possess it, and shalt dwell therein, and shalt say, I will set a king over me, like as all the nations that are about me;

"Thou shalt in any wise set him king over thee, whom the Lord thy God shall choose: one from among thy brethren shalt thou set king over thee: thou mayest not set a stranger over thee, which is not thy brother.

"But he shall not multiply horses to himself, nor cause the people to return to Egypt, to the end that he should multiply horses: forasmuch as the Lord hath said unto you, Ye shall henceforth return no more that way.

"Neither shall he multiply wives to himself, that his heart turn not away: neither shall he greatly multiply to himself silver and gold" (Deuteronomy 17:14–17).

What Solomon had done was clearly wrong. He had married outside the covenant, or the Church, and he had taken a great host of wives that he should not have taken. What he had done was simply absurd and represented gross apostasy. The book of Jacob describes what David and Solomon had done as "abominable" in the sight of the Lord (Jacob 2:23–24). This, however, has nothing to do with the law of plural marriage as revealed to these men by the Lord.

132:39 *Nathan . . . and others of the prophets who had the keys of this power.* Here we are told that Nathan and other prophets of the day had the same authority to perform eternal marriages as known to the Church today. This is a marvelous addition to our understanding of the gospel as known to the Saints of the Old Testament. In addition to this, we learn that David's sin centered not in the plurality of wives but in committing adultery and then in allowing Uriah to be killed so that David could take Bathsheba to himself.

He hath fallen from his exaltation. David is perhaps the most loved of all the men in the Old Testament. Nevertheless, the laws of God are as applicable to him as they are to any other man.

"As to the fact that the sealing power cannot seal a man up unto eternal life if he thereafter commits murder and thereby sheds innocent blood (not in this case the blood of Christ, but the blood of any person slain unlawfully and with malice) the Prophet says: 'A murderer, for instance, one that sheds innocent blood, cannot have forgiveness. David sought repentance at the hand of God carefully with tears, for the murder of Uriah; but he could only get it through hell; he got a promise that his soul should not be left in hell.

"'Although David was a king, he never did obtain the spirit and power of Elijah and the fullness of the priesthood; and the priesthood that he received, and the throne and kingdom of David is to be taken from him and given to another by the name of David in the last days, raised up out of his lineage' (*Teachings of the Prophet Joseph Smith*, 339). Thus, even though a man's calling and election has been made sure, if he then commits murder, all of the promises are of no effect, and he goes to a telestial kingdom (Revelation 21:8; D&C 76:103), because when he was sealed up unto eternal life, it was with a reservation. The sealing was not to apply in the case of murder" (McConkie, *New Testament Commentary*, 3:347).

Joseph Smith Is Given the Power to Bind and Seal on Earth and in Heaven
DOCTRINE AND COVENANTS 132:40–47

132:40 *I gave unto thee, my servant Joseph, an appointment.* It is with this language that the Lord charges the Prophet Joseph Smith to use the priesthood and keys that he has been given to authorize and perform plural marriages.

And restore all things. The restoration of all things must of necessity include the new and everlasting covenant of marriage as known to all gospel dispensations and the plurality of wives as practiced when the Saints were so directed by the Lord.

It shall be given unto you according to my word. Such was the trust that Christ had in the Twelve in his day, that he promised them that

"Whatsoever ye shall ask in my name, that will I do, that the Father may be glorified in the Son. If ye shall ask any thing in my name, I will do it" (John 14:13–14). Similarly, we read that the Lord told Nephi, son of Helaman, that because of his "unwearyingness" in his service he would make him "mighty in word and in deed, in faith and in works; yea, even that all things shall be done unto thee according to thy word, for thou shalt not ask that which is contrary to my will. Behold, thou art Nephi, and I am God. Behold, I declare it unto thee in the presence of mine angels, that ye shall have power over this people, and shall smite the earth with famine, and with pestilence, and destruction, according to the wickedness of this people. Behold, I give unto you power, that whatsoever ye shall seal on earth shall be sealed in heaven; and whatsoever ye shall loose on earth shall be loosed in heaven; and thus shall ye have power among this people" (Helaman 10:5–7). The same promise is given here to the Prophet Joseph Smith, in whom the Lord had the same trust that he had in the noble and great ones of past dispensations. See Doctrine and Covenants 132:59.

132:41–44 In these verses the Lord returns to the question with which the revelation began: the question as to the justification of the early patriarchs in having a plurality of wives. Plural marriage performed by or under the direction of the man standing at the head of the Church of Jesus Christ of Latter-day Saints—which authority was rescinded through President Wilford Woodruff in 1890—was not adultery. To violate the marriage covenant is to commit that sin, the penalty being destruction (vv. 41, 52), but it is for God himself to execute that judgment (v. 54).

132:45 *I have conferred upon you the keys and power of the priesthood.* In September 1830 Joseph Smith was told that he held "the keys of the mysteries, and the revelations which are sealed," with the obvious idea that through him and his office they would be revealed (D&C 28:7). In December of that year, the Lord said, "I have sent forth the fulness of my gospel by the hand of my servant Joseph; and in weakness have I blessed him; and I have given unto him the keys of the mystery of those things which have been sealed, even things which were from the foundation of the world, and the things which shall come from this time until the time of my coming" (D&C 35:17–18). We are also told that "for him to whom these keys are given there is no difficulty in obtaining a knowledge of facts in relation to the salvation of the children of men, both as well for the dead as for the living" (D&C 128:11). Thus, by revelation the "keys of the kingdom" are also designated as the "key of knowledge" (D&C 128:14) or the "keys of access to God" (Ehat and Cook, *Words of Joseph Smith*, 54).

In Nauvoo, when Joseph Smith received revelation and direction relative to the ordinances of the temple, he began to refer to the keys of the kingdom in still a third sense. In a talk to the Relief Society given 28 April 1842, he spoke of their receiving "the keys of the Priesthood" or the "keys of the kingdom" with their husbands and of their learning how to ask the Lord questions and receive answers. The following Sunday, 1 May 1842, speaking to the assembled Saints in the grove, the Prophet referred to the keys of the kingdom as "certain signs and words by which false spirits and personages may be detected." These keys, he said, could not be revealed to the elders until the temple was completed and they had been endowed (Ehat and Cook, *Words of Joseph Smith*, 119). Perhaps his crowning discourse on this subject was given on 10 March 1844, when he referred to the "power of Elijah and the keys of the kingdom of Jehovah" (*Teachings of the Prophet Joseph Smith*, 338).

The symbolism associated with the keys of the kingdom is threefold. As it pertains to the government of the Church, the priesthood embraces the power and authority to lock or unlock, to open or close, to bind or loose—that is, to grant promises and blessings or to preclude the same. It is the authority that disciplines and marshals the priesthood. As to doctrinal matters, the keys of the mysteries of the kingdom constitute the authority by which the heavens are opened and the channel through which God's revelations flow. Finally, in a combination of the two previous definitions, the keys embrace that authority restored by the prophet Elijah whereby men and women are sealed up to eternal life and receive the fulness of the priesthood.

132:46 *Whatsoever you seal on earth shall be sealed in heaven.* See commentary on Doctrine and Covenants 128:10.

132:47 *Whomsoever you curse I will curse.* See Doctrine and Covenants 1:9; 24:15; 60:15; 75:20; 84:92–94; 133:71–73.

The Lord Seals upon Joseph His Exaltation
DOCTRINE AND COVENANTS 132:48–50

132:48 *Shall be visited with blessings not cursings.* The sealing power used by the Prophet Joseph Smith would prove a marvelous blessing to those sealed, but it has also been a blessing of immeasurable worth to the

Church, as the descendants of these marriages have stood in the forefront of the leadership of the Church and have been numbered among those of valor in the defense of the faith.

132:49 *I seal upon you your exaltation.* See commentary on Doctrine and Covenants 131:5.

With Abraham your father. We do not speak metaphorically when we say that Abraham is the father of the faithful. The great majority of people who are baptized into the Church are direct descendents of Abraham, as affirmed by their patriarchal blessings. Those not naturally of the blood of the ancient patriarch are adopted into his family, in which process, the Prophet told us, there was an "actual" change in their blood so that they too become his "actual" or "literal" seed (*Teachings of the Prophet Joseph Smith*, 149–50; Abraham 2:9–11). We speak advisedly, knowing that such a statement finds no support in the world of science, but neither does the idea that a drop of consecrated oil on the head of the sick has a healing effect or that looking upon a snake raised on a brazen pole could heal.

132:50 *I make a way for your escape.* An example of one such escape is here recorded. "Early in the spring of 1844, the Prophet was apprised by two young men, Denison L. Harris and Robert Scott, the latter living in the family of William Law, of a secret movement then on foot to take his life, and the lives of several other leading men of the church; among them the Prophet's brother, Hyrum. These young men were invited to the secret meetings by the conspirators, but before going conferred with the Prophet, who told them to go, but to take no part in the proceedings of these wicked men against himself. They carried out his instructions, and at the risk of their lives attended the secret meetings three times, and brought to President Smith a report of what they had witnessed—the hatching of plots to take the life of the Prophet and his brother Hyrum" (Roberts, *Comprehensive History of the Church*, 2:223–24).

Emma Smith Is Counseled to Be Faithful and True
DOCTRINE AND COVENANTS 132:51–57

132:54 *She shall be destroyed.* There is no threat here of physical harm. The intent of the word "destroyed" is the same as that found in the prophecy of Moses relative to those who would reject Christ. "A prophet shall the Lord your God raise up unto you of your brethren, like unto me; him shall ye hear in all things whatsoever he shall say unto you. And it shall come to pass, that every soul, which will not hear that prophet, shall be *destroyed* from among the people" (Acts 3:22–23; emphasis added). This same prophecy as translated in the Book of Mormon was rendered "cut off from among the people" (1 Nephi 22:20), or perhaps most correctly, "cut off from among my people who are of the covenant" (3 Nephi 21:11; see also Alma 30:46).

Laws Governing Marriage Are Set Forth
DOCTRINE AND COVENANTS 132:58–66

132:58 *The law of the priesthood.* This phrase is used to refer to the Lord's law of marriage. As a man cannot be exalted without priesthood, so he cannot be exalted without his spouse. Thus, in the context of this revelation, "the law of the priesthood" and the "law of marriage" are one and the same.

132:59 *The keys of the power of this priesthood.* If a man has been called of God and by the voice of his Son and he has been endowed with the powers of heaven—"the keys of the power of this priesthood"—that which he does in the name of the Lord with the authority so given him will be honored by the Lord.

132:61 *The law of the priesthood.* For a man to take a second wife—doing so under the direction of the keys of the priesthood—is legal and lawful according to the government of heaven. For him to do so without the sanction of those keys or that authority is quite another matter.

132:63 *For herein is the work of the Father continued.* This verse affirms that marriage as an eternal part of the gospel plan was decreed before the foundations of the earth were laid. It also affirms that the glory of God is extended through his righteous posterity and that it was for this purpose that this earth was created.

132:64 *If any man have a wife, who holds the keys of this power.* The reference is to Joseph Smith, who held the keys referred to here (vv. 7, 45–47). If a man holding the keys of this power teaches these principles to his wife and she chooses to oppose him, she will lose the Spirit of the Lord. If she remains unrepentant, she will eventually destroy her own soul and lose her own salvation.

132:65 *He is exempt from the law of Sarah.* In the context of the principles announced in the previous verses, it is lawful, if a wife does not receive this law, for her husband to receive all things that God chooses to give him. In that case his wife would be the transgressor, and thus her husband is exempt from the law of Sarah who gave heed to Abraham when the Lord commanded him to take Hagar to wife. The principle is certain: Those who follow the commandments of the Lord and keep their covenants will be blessed; those who refuse to do so will not share those blessings. A woman can still lay claim to the blessings of the sealing power given to her in the temple even if her husband chooses to pursue a path that leaves him unworthy of them. Similarly, if a man or woman dies without having had the opportunity to enter into a particular covenant in this life but was worthy to do so, that privilege and blessing will be granted to that person in the world to come (*Teachings of Lorenzo Snow*, 138).

132:66 *Let this suffice for the present.* This revelation ends with the promise that more instruction will be given on this matter.

THE KING FOLLETT DISCOURSE

DATE: 7 APRIL 1844
PLACE: NAUVOO, ILLINOIS

The greatest discourse ever delivered by the Prophet Joseph Smith is known to us as the King Follett Discourse. It was a commemorative oration for Brother King Follett, a faithful elder in Nauvoo, who had been crushed to death when a bucket of rocks fell on him while he was walling up a well. The address was given on Sunday, 7 April 1844, at a general conference of the Church held in a grove near the temple. The congregation was said to have numbered twenty thousand, and the effort expended to be heard by so large a group was so taxing that the Prophet was unable to do more than speak for a few moments the following day, his lungs still being exhausted.

Amasa Potter, who was present when this discourse was delivered, recalled the circumstances thus:

"The subject of baptism for the dead was dwelt upon, and when he had spoken about thirty minutes there came up a heavy wind and storm. The dust was so dense that we could not see each other at any distance, and some of the people were leaving when Joseph called out to them to stop and let their prayers ascend to Almighty God that the winds may cease blowing and the rain stop falling, and it should be so. In a very few minutes the winds and rains ceased and the elements became calm as a summer's morning. The storm divided and went on the north and south of the city, and we could see in the distance the trees and shrubs waving in the wind, while where we were it was quiet for one hour, and during that time one of the greatest sermons that ever fell from the Prophet's lips was preached on the great subject of the dead" (*Juvenile Instructor*, 29:132).

Our account of the sermon comes from notes written by Willard Richards, Wilford Woodruff, William Clayton and Thomas Bullock at the time the sermon was given. In 1855, Jonathan Grimshaw, a clerk in the Church historian's office, amalgamated their notes, thus providing us with a more complete and detailed account of the Prophet's discourse.

The greatness of the discourse lies in the spirit and power of the doctrines taught. In it the Prophet declares the character and nature of God and of man, his offspring. We have taken the liberty of dividing into sections and paragraphs the text of the King Follett Discourse, which follows.

Section One

1. Beloved Saints, I will call the attention of this congregation while I address you on the subject of the dead. The decease of our beloved brother, Elder King Follett, who was crushed in a well by the falling of a tub of rock, has more immediately led me to that subject. I have been requested to speak by his friends and relatives, but inasmuch as there are a great many in this congregation who live in this city as well as elsewhere, who have lost friends, I feel disposed to speak on the subject in general, and offer you my ideas, so far as I have ability, and so far as I shall be inspired by the Holy Spirit to dwell on this subject.

2. I want your prayers and faith that I may have the instruction of Almighty God and the gift of the Holy Ghost, so that I may set forth things that are true and which can be easily comprehended by you, and that the testimony may carry conviction to your hearts and minds of the truth of what I shall say. Pray that the Lord may strengthen my lungs, stay the winds, and let the prayers of the Saints to heaven appear, that they may enter into the ears of the Lord of Sabaoth, for the effectual prayers of the righteous avail much. There is strength here, and I verily believe that your prayers will be heard.

3. Before I enter fully into the investigation of the subject which is lying before me, I wish to pave the way and bring up the subject from the beginning, that you may understand it. I will make a few preliminaries, in order that you may understand the subject when I come to it. I do not intend to please your ears with superfluity of words or oratory, or with much learning; but I intend to edify you with the simple truths from heaven.

4. In the first place, I wish to go back to the beginning—to the morn of creation. There is the starting point for us to look to, in order to understand and be fully acquainted with the mind, purposes and decrees of the Great Elohim, who sits in yonder heavens as he did at the creation of this world. It is necessary for us to have an understanding of God himself in the beginning. If we start right, it is easy to go right all the time; but if we start wrong, we may go wrong, and it be a hard matter to get right.

5. There are but a very few beings in the world who understand rightly the character of God. The great majority of mankind do not comprehend anything, either that which is past, or that which is to come, as it respects their relationship to God. They do not know, neither do they understand the nature of that relationship; and consequently they know but little above the brute beast, or more than to eat, drink and sleep. This is all man knows about God or his existence, unless it is given by the inspiration of the Almighty.

6. If a man learns nothing more than to eat, drink and sleep, and does not comprehend any of the designs of God, the beast comprehends the same things. It eats, drinks, sleeps, and knows nothing more about God; yet it knows as much as we, unless we are able to comprehend by the inspiration of Almighty God. If men do not comprehend the character of God, they do not comprehend themselves. I want to go back to the beginning, and so lift your minds into a more lofty sphere and a more exalted understanding than what the human mind generally aspires to.

The Character of God
THE KING FOLLETT DISCOURSE 1

KFD 1:1 *Elder King Follett.* King Follett, for whom this commemorative discourse was given, was born July 24, 1877 in Vermont. As a youth he moved to Cuyahoga County, Ohio. It was there that, in the spring of 1831, he met the Mormon missionaries and was baptized. He moved with the Saints from Ohio to Missouri. He was among those imprisoned in Richmond, Missouri, in April of 1839 on a charge of robbery. As Parley P. Pratt, also arrested at that time, explained, they had taken a keg of powder from a gang of ruffians who planned to use it against the Saints (*Autobiography*, 193). King Follett was acquitted and released six months later. With his wife and family he became one of the early settlers in Nauvoo.

KFD 1:2 *Stay the winds.* See the quotation from Amasa Potter in the introduction to this discourse, page 1078.

KFD 1:3 *I intend to edify you with the simple truths from heaven.* How singular it is that the God of Joseph Smith could be understood by a child while the God of historical Christianity is incomprehensible to even the greatest of scholars. The 1844 edition of *Buck's Theological Dictionary*, a book known to Joseph Smith, under the heading "God" it states: "As the

Divine Being possess[es] a nature far beyond the comprehension of any of his creatures, of course that nature is inexplicable." Then by way of clarification and emphasis it adds, "All our knowledge of invisible objects is obtained by analogy; that is, by the resemblance which they bear to visible objects; but as there is in nature no exact resemblance of the nature of God, an attempt to explain the divine nature is absurd and impracticable. All similitudes, therefore, which are used in attempting to explain it must be rejected."

Thomas Aquinas had declared many years before, "We cannot know what God is." By way of explanation, he said, "One reaches the highest point of one's knowledge about God when one knows that one does not know him" (Davies, *Thoughts of Thomas Aquinas*, 54). Augustine put it thus, "If you can understand it, it's not God" (McGrath, *Understanding the Trinity*, 111).

KFD 1:4 *The Great Elohim*. Elohim is a Hebrew word meaning "gods." It is commonly used by the Saints as a title for God the Father.

KFD 1:5 All knowledge of God and the principles of salvation must have revelation as their source. Historical Christianity, having sealed the heavens and thus denied God the right to communicate with his children, bases its theology on philosophical speculations (McConkie, *Sons and Daughters of God*, 84–118). Joseph Smith had no source for his understanding save it be the revelations of heaven. What he knew of God, he learned from God. This made Joseph Smith the most authoritative and competent witness and teacher about Christ on the face of the earth.

KFD 1:6 *If men do not comprehend the character of God, they do not comprehend themselves.* The God of the sectarian world is described as "a force or power behind the universe" or as "a dynamic, pulsating activity" (McGrath, *Understanding the Trinity*, 111). "'The true God,'" they tell us, "'has neither sex, age, nor definite corporeal members'" (Scaevola, as quoted in Augustine, *City of God*, 203). He is a silent mystery, "beyond all inference and imagination," and "is quite indecipherable, incomprehensible, unknow[able]" (Lash, *Believing Three Ways in One God*, 93). We are left to ask how one is expected to emulate such a God? What inspiration is to be found in the realization that no meaningful description or understanding can be had about him?

Section Two

1. I want to ask this congregation, every man, woman and child, to answer the question in their own heart, what kind of a being God is? Ask yourselves; turn your thoughts into your hearts, and say if any of you have seen, heard, or communed with him. This is a question that may occupy your attention for a long time. I again repeat the question—What kind of a being is God? Does any man or woman know? Have any of you seen him, heard him, or communed with him? Here is the question that will, peradventure, from this time henceforth occupy your attention. The Scriptures inform us that "This is life eternal that they might know thee, the only true God, and Jesus Christ whom thou hast sent."

2. If any man does not know God, and inquires what kind of a being he is—if he will search diligently his own heart—if the declaration of Jesus and the apostles be true, he will realize that he has not eternal life; for there can be eternal life on no other principle.

3. My first object is to find out the character of the only wise and true God, and what kind of a being he is; and if I am so fortunate as to be the man to comprehend God, and explain or convey the principles to your hearts, so that the Spirit seals them upon you, then let every man and woman henceforth sit in silence, put their hands on their mouths, and never lift their hands or voices, or say anything against the man of God or the servants of God again. But if I fail to do it, it becomes my duty to renounce all further pretensions to revelations and inspirations, or to be a prophet; and I should be like the rest of the world—a false teacher, be hailed as a friend, and no man would seek my life. But if all religious teachers were honest enough to renounce their pretensions to godliness when their ignorance of the knowledge of God is made manifest, they will all be as badly off as I am, at any rate; and you might as well take the lives of other false teachers as that of mine, if I am false. If any man is authorized to take away my life because he thinks and says I am a false teacher, then, upon the same principle, we should be justified in taking away the life of every false teacher, and where would be the end of blood? And who would not be the sufferer?

What Kind of Being Is God?

THE KING FOLLETT DISCOURSE 2

KFD 2:1–2 How do we worship a God who is incomprehensible and unknowable? What honor can God bestow upon those who worship him in ignorance or untruth? Can we expect salvation to be found in error and falsehood? Surely there can be salvation in no principles other than truth and righteousness.

KFD 2:3 *Should [I] be like the rest of the world—a false teacher, [I would] be hailed as a friend.* The world loves its own. Those who seek the truths of God but know not where to find them need only follow the spirit of bitterness and persecution, for that spirit will always be found opposing the truths of heaven. The greater the truth, the greater the opposition to it. No principle in the so-called Christian world has been more darkened by the philosophies of men than those truths dealing with the nature and character of God. The creeds of Christendom have robbed God of his gender, of his fatherhood, of his body, of his speech, and of his passion, or love, for his children. In his stead they have given us an incomprehensible mystery to which they have given the title God.

Section Three

1. But meddle not with any man for his religion: and all governments ought to permit every man to enjoy his religion unmolested. No man is authorized to take away life in consequence of difference of religion, which all laws and governments ought to tolerate and protect, right or wrong. Every man has a natural, and, in our country, a constitutional right to be a false prophet, as well as a true prophet. If I show, verily, that I have the truth of God, and show that ninety-nine out of every hundred professing religious ministers are false teachers, having no authority, while they pretend to hold the keys of God's kingdom on earth, and was to kill them because they are false teachers, it would deluge the whole world with blood.

2. I will prove that the world is wrong, by showing what God is. I am going to enquire after God; for I want you all to know him, and to be familiar with him; and if I am bringing you to a knowledge of him, all persecutions against me ought to cease. You will then know that I am his servant; for I speak as one having authority.

The Privilege of Religious Freedom
THE KING FOLLETT DISCOURSE 3

KFD 3:2 *I speak as one having authority.* It was Joseph Smith's right to speak as one having authority. Let us take the Bible as an illustration. Save Jesus only, no man ever walked the face of the earth that had greater knowledge of the Bible than Joseph Smith had. A library containing every whit the world knows about the book would not rival his understanding. It is one thing to read a book and quite another to be instructed by its authors. Who among the world's theologians and scholars can boast of having stood face to face with Adam, Enoch, Noah, Abraham, Moses, John the Baptist, Peter, James, and John? While the religious leaders of the day testified that the heavens were sealed, Joseph Smith was personally tutored by ancient prophets who laid their hands upon his head and conferred upon him the power, keys, and authority they held.

Joseph Smith knew the God of whom he spoke. As with the ancients, he had stood with him face to face and been instructed by him. Joseph did not testify of that which he had learned in books, but of that which he had learned directly. His testimony was not of hearsay but of that which he had seen and that which had been revealed to him. He never suggested that our understanding should be limited to that which we learned from him. He saw himself as a guide. That which he had seen, all were entitled to see. He would point the way (D&C 84:19–24; 88:68; 93:1).

Section Four

> 1. I will go back to the beginning before the world was, to show what kind of being God is. What sort of a being was God in the beginning? Open your ears and hear, all ye ends of the earth, for I am going to prove it to you by the Bible, and to tell you the designs of God in relation to the human race, and why He interferes with the affairs of man.

> 2. God himself was once as we are now, and is an exalted man, and sits enthroned in yonder heavens! That is the great secret. If the veil were rent today, and the great God who holds this world in its orbit, and who upholds all worlds and all things by his power, was to make himself visible,—I say, if you were to see him today, you would see him like a man in form—like yourselves in all the person, image, and very form as a man; for Adam was created in the very fashion, image

and likeness of God, and received instruction from, and walked, talked and conversed with him, as one man talks and communes with another.

3. In order to understand the subject of the dead, for consolation of those who mourn for the loss of their friends, it is necessary we should understand the character and being of God and how he came to be so; for I am going to tell you how God came to be God. We have imagined and supposed that God was God from all eternity. I will refute that idea, and take away the veil, so that you may see.

4. These are incomprehensible ideas to some, but they are simple. It is the first principle of the Gospel to know for a certainty the Character of God, and to know that we may converse with him as one man converses with another, and that he was once a man like us; yea, that God himself, the Father of us all, dwelt on an earth, the same as Jesus Christ himself did; and I will show it from the Bible.

God Is an Exalted Man
THE KING FOLLETT DISCOURSE 4

KFD 4:1 *I am going to prove it to you by the Bible.* The crowning revelation of the New Testament, that is the principle most distinctive and unique to the ministry of Christ, is the fatherhood of God. All of the nearly 240 references in which Christ addresses the God of heaven use the title "Father," while each instance in which the God of heaven addressed himself to Jesus of Nazareth, he calls him "Son."

KFD 4:2 *God . . . is an exalted man.* Latter-day Saints are the only people in the Bible-believing world who truly understand why the New Testament refers to God as our "Father in Heaven." Outside of Mormonism this nomenclature is universally held to be nothing more than a metaphor, while for the Latter-day Saint its literalness becomes the very foundation of our faith. For us the announcement that Adam and Eve were created in the image and likeness of God is understood to be literally so. By contrast, *Buck's Theological Dictionary* defines "Anthropomorphites" as "A sect of ancient heretics, who, taking everything spoken of God in the scripture in a literal sense, particularly that passage of Genesis in which it is said, 'God made man after his own image,' maintained that God had a human shape." To sectarian Christianity the idea that we are the literal offspring of Deity—even if only as spirits—is blasphemy. To the Latter-day Saint, the idea could hardly be otherwise. Could a God do anything unworthy of his own nature, we would ask? Could his children—those of his own family—be made of lesser stuff than he? Thus we might ask if true blasphemy would not be the failure to recognize so simple a truth?

God himself was once as we are now, and is an exalted man. On 5 January 1841 the Prophet said, "That which is without body, parts and passions is nothing. There is no other God in heaven but that God who has flesh and bones. John 5:26: 'As the Father hath life in himself; even so hath he given to the Son to have life in himself.' God the Father took life unto himself precisely as Jesus did" (*Teachings of the Prophet Joseph Smith,* 181). To say that God of necessity must have a body of "flesh and bones," and that he "took life . . . precisely as Jesus did" is in effect to say that he was once a man as we are and continues to be a personage of flesh and bones in his exalted state. That which appears obvious to us, however, was not obvious to those of Joseph Smith's day. The implication of such a statement simply had not dawned on them. The experience of Lorenzo Snow illustrates the point. Four years earlier, while en route to his assigned mission in England, this principle was revealed to him. He captured what he had learned in the now-often-quoted couplet, "As man now is, our God once was; / As now God is, so man may be" (Snow, "Devotion to a Divine Inspiration," 22:660). At that time he shared his experience with only two people, his sister, Eliza R. Snow, and Brigham Young, who was his mission president. President Young advised him to keep the matter to himself until he had heard it taught by the Prophet (Jenson, *LDS Biographical Encyclopedia,* 1:27–28).

KFD 4:4 *It is the first principle of the Gospel to know for a certainty the Character of God.* There is no gospel truth that is not rooted in the doctrine of the fatherhood of God or that can be properly understood without an understanding of his nature. We cite but one illustration: the sonship of Christ. Surely it cannot be the same thing to say that Christ is the son of a spirit essence that fills the immensity of space, being at the same time everywhere and nowhere present, and saying that he is the literal son of a divine father and a mortal woman whose name was Mary. In the first instance, his resurrection simply means that he, like water poured into the ocean, becomes of the same essence with that ever existent body. In the second instance, he continues his existence as a man living in a material but exalted state. In that glorified state he, like his father, could, with a spouse at his side, continue in an eternal family relationship, and his children could become like him, just as he had become as his father was.

We may converse with him as one man converses with another. How simple the truth. God is our father, and thus we can converse with him as a son or daughter converses with a father. By contrast Origen, who did much to design the theology of historical Christianity, observed that having no body, God could have no speech. Since speech is defined as vibrated air or a percussion of air cause by the voice box of one person, which in turn acts upon the eardrum of another, God having neither voice box or eardrum would neither speak nor hear in ways known to man.

Section Five

1. I wish I was in a suitable place to tell it, and that I had the trump of an archangel, so that I could tell the story in such a manner that persecution would cease for ever. What did Jesus say? (Mark it, Elder Rigdon!) The Scriptures inform us that Jesus said, As the Father hath power in Himself, even so hath the Son power—to do what? Why, what the Father did. The answer is obvious—in a manner to lay down His body and take it up again. Jesus, what are you going to do? To lay down my life as my Father did, and take it up again. Do we believe it? If you do not believe it, you do not believe the Bible. The Scriptures say it, and I defy all the learning and wisdom and all the combined powers of earth and hell together to refute it.

2. Here, then, is eternal life—to know the only wise and true God; and you have got to learn how to be Gods yourselves, and to be kings and priests to God, the same as all Gods have done before you, namely, by going from one small degree to another, and from a small capacity to a great one; from grace to grace, from exaltation to exaltation, until you attain to the resurrection of the dead, and are able to dwell in everlasting burnings, and to sit in glory, as do those who sit enthroned in everlasting power. And I want you to know that God, in the last days, while certain individuals are proclaiming his name, is not trifling with you or me.

Power of the Father and the Son
THE KING FOLLETT DISCOURSE 5

KFD 5:1 *Jesus, what are you going to do? To lay down my life as my Father did.* Joseph Smith's purpose is to show that the Bible teaches that our Father in Heaven was once mortal, as we are. To do so he takes John 5:19 as a text. Here the Savior said, "The Son can do nothing of himself, but what he seeth the Father do: for what things soever he doeth, these also doeth the Son likewise." The Prophet then reasons that it is Christ's purpose to lay down his life and take it up again. Thus, if Christ can do only that which his father did, his father must also have been subject to death, he must have died and then taken up his life again as a resurrected being. From this statement of the Prophet, many have attempted to reason that he was saying that his father was also a savior for those of another world and thus that all worlds require their own saviors. The Prophet never taught such a thing and was not alluding to it here. His remarks centered on the doctrine of resurrection, not the salvation of God's endless creations. The Prophet had already clearly taught that the atonement of Christ—which was infinite—embraced all that he had created under the direction of the Father (see commentary on D&C 76:23–24). Responding to those who wanted to argue that there is a special strain of savior gods, Elder Bruce R. McConkie often asked, "What earthly good could possibly come from teaching such a thing?"

KFD 5:2 *You have got to learn how to be Gods yourselves.* At this point in this discourse, the Prophet introduces the doctrine of plurality of Gods. The fact that we worship but one God does not negate the verity that there are in reality many Gods. The Godhead consists of three separate Gods, the Father, the Son, and the Holy Ghost, which in itself affirms the idea of a plurality of Gods. It also leaves us to ask, If two of God's sons can obtain the station of a God, why in justice is that privilege not accorded to all of his children? The answer found in the plan of salvation is that this is the very purpose for which we were created. Now, if there have been worlds without number, there must from among their populations be Gods without number also (Deuteronomy 10:17; Joshua 22:22; Psalm 82:1; Acts 17:24–29; 1 Corinthians 8:5; D&C 121:28).

The whole purpose of the plan of salvation is to make us equal with God in power, might, and dominion (D&C 76:95). Thus, when John says that it is life eternal to know God (John 17:3), we understand him to be saying that we know God to the extent that we are like him or are one with him.

To be kings and priests to God. See commentary on Doctrine and Covenants 76:56.

From exaltation to exaltation. From the book of Moses we learn that it is the work and glory of God to save his children (Moses 1:39). God advances from one exaltation (or glory) to another through the exaltation of his posterity (D&C 132:63).

Dwell in everlasting burnings. See King Follett Discourse, 20:1, page 1104.

Section Six

1. These are the first principles of consolation. How consoling to the mourners when they are called to part with a husband, wife, father, mother, child, or dear relative, to know that, although the earthly tabernacle is laid down and dissolved, they shall rise again to dwell in everlasting burnings in immortal glory, not to sorrow, suffer, or die any more; but they shall be heirs of God and joint heirs with Jesus Christ. What is it? To inherit the same power, the same glory and the same exaltation, until you arrive at the station of a God, and ascend the throne of eternal power, the same as those who have gone before. What did Jesus do? Why; I do the things I saw my Father do when worlds came rolling into existence. My Father worked out his kingdom with fear and trembling, and I must do the same; and when I get my kingdom, I shall present it to my Father, so that he may obtain kingdom upon kingdom, and it will exalt him in glory. He will then take a higher exaltation, and I will take his place, and thereby become exalted myself. So that Jesus treads in the tracks of his Father, and inherits what God did before; and God is thus glorified and exalted in the salvation and exaltation of all his children. It is plain beyond disputation, and you thus learn some of the first principles of the Gospel, about which so much hath been said.

2. When you climb up a ladder, you must begin at the bottom, and ascend step by step, until you arrive at the top; and so it is with the principles of the Gospel—you must begin with the first, and go on until you learn all the principles of exaltation. But it will be a great while after you have passed through the veil before you will have learned them. It is not all to be comprehended in this world; it will be a great work to learn our salvation and exaltation even beyond the grave. I suppose I am not allowed to go into an investigation of anything that is not contained in the Bible. If I do, I think there are so many over-wise men here, that they would cry "treason" and put me to death. So I will go to the old Bible and turn commentator today.

The Righteous to Dwell in Immortal Glory
THE KING FOLLETT DISCOURSE 6

KFD 6:1 *He may obtain kingdom upon kingdom, and it will exalt him.* Latter-day Saints use the phrase "eternal progression." If by that we mean that Gods are everlastingly ignorant and thus of necessity everlastingly learning, we are at odds with both reason and scripture. If, however, we have in mind that the work and glory of God are in the exaltation of his children and theirs, in turn, in the exaltation of their children in a never-ending cycle, we are in accord with the doctrine being taught here by the Prophet (Moses 1:39).

KDF 6:2 *It will be a great while after you have passed through the veil before you will have learned them.* It would be foolish to suppose that we can learn all that is necessary to stand equal with God in our short sojourn in mortality. An earlier revelation states that "in due time" we will receive the fulness of the Father (D&C 93:19). Here the Prophet tells us that it will be a long time—as men measure it—after we leave this life until we will obtain our exaltation.

Section Seven

1. I shall comment on the very first Hebrew word in the Bible; I will make a comment on the very first sentence of the history of creation in the Bible—*Berosheit.* I want to analyze the word. *Baith*—in, by, through, and everything else. *Rosh*—the head. *Sheit*—grammatical termination. When the inspired man wrote it, he did not put the *baith* there. An old Jew without any authority added the word; he thought it too bad to begin to talk about the head! It read first, "The head one of the Gods brought forth the Gods." That is the true meaning of the words. *Baurau* signifies to bring forth. If you do not believe it, you do not believe the learned man of God. Learned men can teach you no more than what I have told you. Thus the head God brought forth the Gods in the grand council.

2. I will transpose and simplify it in the English language. Oh, ye lawyers, ye doctors, and ye priests, who have persecuted me, I want to let you know that the Holy Ghost knows something as well as you do. The head God called together the Gods and sat in grand council to bring forth the world. The grand councilors sat at the head in yonder heavens and contemplated the creation of the worlds which were created at the time. When I say doctors and lawyers, I mean the doctors and lawyers of the Scriptures. I have done so hitherto without explanation, to let the lawyers flutter and everybody laugh at them. Some learned doctors might take a notion to say the Scriptures say thus and so; and we might believe the Scriptures; they are not to be altered. But I am going to show you an error in them.

3. I have an old edition of the New Testament in the Latin, Hebrew,

German and Greek languages. I have been reading the German, and find it to be the most [nearly] correct translation, and to correspond nearest to the revelations which God has given to me for the last fourteen years. It tells about Jacobus, the son of Zebedee. It means Jacob. In the English New Testament it is translated James. Now, if Jacob had the keys, you might talk about James through all eternity and never get the keys. In the 21st of the fourth chapter of Matthew, my old German edition gives the word Jacob instead of James.

4. The doctors (I mean doctors of law, not physic) say, "If you preach anything not according to the Bible, we will cry treason." How can we escape the damnation of hell, except God be with us and reveal to us? Men bind us with chains. The Latin says Jacobus, which means Jacob; the Hebrew says Jacob, the Greek says Jacob and the German says Jacob; here we have the testimony of four against one. I thank God that I have got this old book; but I thank him more for the gift of the Holy Ghost. I have got the oldest book in the world; but I [also] have the oldest book in my heart, even the gift of the Holy Ghost. I have all the four Testaments. Come here, ye learned men, and read, if you can. I should not have introduced this testimony, were it not to back up the word *rosh*—the head, the Father of the Gods. I should not have brought it up, only to show that I am right.

Meaning of the Hebrew Scriptures
THE KING FOLLETT DISCOURSE 7

KFD 7:1 *If you do not believe it.* As the faith of those in the days of Christ limited what he was able to give them, so the faith of the Saints in Nauvoo—many of whom were still bound to one degree or another by the traditions of their fathers—prevented them from accepting pure revelation if it reached beyond the Bible. What, we are left to wonder, would the Prophet have been able to teach if the faith of those there assembled had not been limited by such an artificial boundary?

KFD 7:2 *Oh, ye lawyers, ye doctors, and ye priests . . . the Holy Ghost knows something as well as you.* With tongue in cheek, it could be observed that Latter-day Saints have no serious difficulties with the way the Bible has been translated before the first verse of Genesis. Joseph Smith's translation in this instance is arguably correct, though it goes beyond traditional usage and is more a product of revelation than linguistics. It accords perfectly with what he learned from the translation of the Abraham manuscript (Abraham 4–5).

KFD 7:3 *The most nearly correct translation.* No book in earth's history has been subject to as much tampering and mischief as has the Bible. Further, in no age has it been free from the blatant reworking of its text. "The English Bible in America" during the nineteenth century "was never a simple, uniform entity. When scholars have noted the presence of the Bible in American culture, they have treated it as a volume containing a kind of mythic core text, entirely overlooking the reality that the different English translations, commentaries, illustrations, and bindings significantly complicate any understanding of the Bible's influence in American society. Once it began to be printed in the United States, it soon underwent a great many textual revisions and changes in format, as different editors and publishers appropriated it to meet a wide range of changing ideologic and economic demands. By 1880, nearly two thousand different editions of the Bible were available to Americans" (Gutjahr, *American Bible*, 3).

Jacob . . . is translated James. James is an English form of the Hebrew name Jacob. The name James was preferred to that of Jacob because the translators courted the favor of King James to obtain the necessary support to see their labors printed.

KFD 7:4 *I also have the oldest book in my heart, even the gift of the Holy Ghost.* For those who enjoy the spirit of revelation, having their understanding of the things of God confined to what can be found in the Bible would be the same as being bound in chains. "The best way to obtain truth and wisdom," the Prophet said, "is not to ask it from books, but to go to God in prayer, and obtain divine teaching" (*Teachings of the Prophet Joseph Smith*, 191). Of his youthful experience in search of truth he said, "The teachers of religion of the different sects understood the same passages of scripture so differently as to destroy all confidence in settling the question by an appeal to the Bible" (Joseph Smith–History 1:12).

Section Eight

1. In the beginning, the head of the Gods called a council of the Gods; and they came together and concocted a plan to create the world and people it. When we begin to learn this way, we begin to learn the only true God, and what kind of a being we have got to worship. Having a knowledge of God, we begin to know how to approach him, and how to ask so as to receive an answer. When we understand the character of God, and how to come to him, he begins to unfold

the heavens to us, and to tell us all about it. When we are ready to come to him, he is ready to come to us.

2. Now, I ask all who hear me, why the learned men who are preaching salvation, say that God created the heavens and the earth out of nothing? The reason is, that they are unlearned in the things of God, and have not the gift of the Holy Ghost; they account it blasphemy in any one to contradict their idea. If you tell them that God made the world out of something, they will call you a fool. But I am learned, and know more than all the world put together. The Holy Ghost does, anyhow, and He is within me, and comprehends more than all the world: and I will associate myself with Him.

A Council of the Gods
THE KING FOLLETT DISCOURSE 8

KFD 8:1 *When we are ready to come to him, he is ready to come to us.* See Doctrine and Covenants 88:63.

KFD 8:2 *Why learned men . . . say God created the heaven and the earth out of nothing.* Scholars of the history of Christian doctrine tell us that the idea of creation *ex nihilo* is a product of the hellenistic Christian era. Gerhard May in his work *Creatio ex Nihilo: The Doctrine of 'Creation out of Nothing' in Early Christian Thought* concludes that "in the second half of the second century the theological development begins which leads directly to the formulation of the church doctrine of *creatio ex nihilo*"; by "the beginning of the third century [it was] regarded as a fundamental tenet of Christian theology" (*Creatio ex Nihilo*, 148, 179). Of necessity the doctrine traces itself to Greek philosophy, having originated after traditional Christianity claims revelation to have ceased.

Section Nine

1. You ask the learned doctors why they say the world was made out of nothing; and they will answer, "Doesn't the Bible say He *created* the world?" And they infer, from the word create, that it must have been made out of nothing. Now, the word create came from the word *baurau* which does not mean to create out of nothing; it means to organize; the same as a man would organize materials and build a ship. Hence, we infer that God had materials to organize the world out of chaos—chaotic matter, which is element, and in which dwells all the glory. Element had an existence from the time he had. The

pure principles of element are principles which can never be destroyed; they may be organized and re-organized, but not destroyed. They had no beginning, and can have no end.

Meaning of the Word *Create*
THE KING FOLLETT DISCOURSE 9

KFD 9:1 *Baurau*. The Hebrew word *baurau* rendered "created" in the Genesis account of the story of creation means "to form or to fashion." There is no thought in the word of the creation of something from nothing.

The principles of element are principles which can never be destroyed. By revelation the Prophet stated: "There is no such thing as immaterial matter. All spirit is matter, but it is more fine or pure, and can only be discerned by purer eyes; We cannot see it; but when our bodies are purified we shall see that it is all matter" (D&C 131:7–8).

Section Ten

1. I have another subject to dwell upon, which is calculated to exalt man; but it is impossible for me to say much on this subject. I shall therefore just touch upon it, for time will not permit me to say all. It is associated with the subject of the resurrection of the dead— namely, the soul—the mind of man—the immortal spirit. Where did it come from? All learned men and doctors of divinity say that God created it in the beginning; but it is not so: the very idea lessens man in my estimation. I do not believe the doctrine; I know better. Hear it, all ye ends of the world; for God has told me so; and if you don't believe me, it will not make the truth without effect. I will make a man appear a fool before I get through; if he does not believe it. I am going to tell of things more noble.

2. We say that God himself is a self-existent being. Who told you so? It is correct enough; but how did it get into your heads? Who told you that man did not exist in like manner upon the same principles? Man does exist upon the same principles. God made a tabernacle and put a spirit into it, and it became a living soul (Refers to the old Bible). How does it read in the Hebrew? It does not say in the Hebrew that God created the spirit of man. It says "God made man out of the earth and put into him Adam's spirit, and so became a living body."

3. The mind or the intelligence which man possesses is co-equal with God himself. I know that my testimony is true; hence, when I talk to these mourners, what have they lost? Their relatives and friends are only separated from their bodies for a short season: their spirits which existed with God have left the tabernacle of clay only for a little moment, as it were; and they now exist in a place where they converse together the same as we do on the earth.

4. I am dwelling on the immortality of the spirit of man. Is it logical to say that the intelligence of spirits is immortal, and yet that it had a beginning? The intelligence of spirits had no beginning, neither will it have an end. That is good logic. That which has a beginning may have an end. There never was a time when there were not spirits; for they are co-equal [co-eternal] with our Father in heaven.

5. I want to reason more on the spirit of man; for I am dwelling on the body and spirit of man—on the subject of the dead. I take my ring from my finger and liken it unto the mind of man—the immortal part, because it has no beginning. Suppose you cut it in two; then it has a beginning and an end; but join it again, and it continues one eternal round. So with the spirit of man. As the Lord liveth, if it had a beginning, it will have an end. All the fools and learned and wise men from the beginning of creation, who say that the spirit of man had a beginning, prove that it must have an end; and if that doctrine is true, then the doctrine of annihilation would be true. But if I am right, I might with boldness proclaim from the house-tops that God never had the power to create the spirit of man at all. God himself could not create himself.

6. Intelligence is eternal and exists upon a self-existent principle. It is a spirit from age to age, and there is no creation about it. All the minds and spirits that God ever sent into the world are susceptible of enlargement.

The Immortal Spirit
THE KING FOLLETT DISCOURSE 10

KFD 10:1–6 Again, by revelation the Prophet stated that "intelligence, or the light of truth, was not created or made, neither indeed can be" (D&C 93:29); he also taught that "the elements are eternal, and spirit and element, inseparably connected, receive a fulness of joy" (D&C 93:33).

Section Eleven

1. The first principles of man are self-existent with God. God himself, finding he was in the midst of spirits and glory, because he was more intelligent, saw proper to institute laws whereby the rest could have a privilege to advance like himself. The relationship we have with God places us in a situation to advance in knowledge. He has power to institute laws to instruct the weaker intelligences, that they may be exalted with himself, so that they might have one glory upon another, and all that knowledge, power, glory, and intelligence, which is requisite in order to save them in the world of spirits.

2. This is good doctrine. It tastes good. I can taste the principles of eternal life, and so can you. They are given to me by the revelations of Jesus Christ; and I know that when I tell you these words of eternal life as they are given to me, you taste them, and I know that you believe them. You say honey is sweet, and so do I. I can also taste the spirit of eternal life. I know it is good; and when I tell you of these things which were given me by inspiration of the Holy Spirit, you are bound to receive them as sweet, and rejoice more and more.

The Power to Advance in Knowledge
THE KING FOLLETT DISCOURSE 11

KFD 11:1 *Institute laws whereby the rest could have a privilege to advance like himself.* God is omnipotent. He is not the servant of law nor does he maintain his place in the heavens because of his ability to live in harmony with laws that are independent of him. He is the creator of all law. He is "above all things, and in all things, and is through all things, and is round about all things; and all things are by him, and of him, even God, forever and ever" (D&C 88:41). See commentary on Doctrine and Covenants 88:36.

KFD 11:2 *I can taste the principles of eternal life.* Similarly, the psalmist wrote, "The law of the Lord is perfect, converting the soul: the testimony of the Lord is sure, making wise the simple. The statutes of the Lord are right, rejoicing the heart: the commandment of the Lord is pure, enlightening the eyes. The fear of the Lord is clean, enduring for ever: the judgments of the Lord are true and righteous altogether. More to be desired are they than gold, yea, than much fine gold: sweeter also than honey and the honeycomb" (Psalm 19:7–10).

Section Twelve

1. I want to talk more of the relation of man to God. I will open your eyes in relation to your dead. All things whatsoever God in his infinite wisdom has seen fit and proper to reveal to us, while we are dwelling in mortality, in regard to our mortal bodies, are revealed to us in the abstract, and independent of affinity of this mortal tabernacle, but are revealed to our spirits precisely as though we had no bodies at all; and those revelations which will save our spirits will save our bodies. God reveals them to us in view of no eternal dissolution of the body, or tabernacle. Hence the responsibility, the awful responsibility, that rests upon us in relation to our dead; for all the spirits who have not obeyed the Gospel in the flesh must either obey it in the spirit or be damned. Solemn thought!—dreadful thought! Is there nothing to be done?—no preparation—no salvation for our fathers and friends who have died without having had the opportunity to obey the decrees of the Son of Man? Would to God that I had forty days and nights in which to tell you all! I would let you know that I am not a "fallen prophet."

The Relation of Man to God
THE KING FOLLETT DISCOURSE 12

KFD 12:1 *Awful responsibility, that rests upon us in relation to our dead.* See commentary on Doctrine and Covenants 137:7–9.

Section Thirteen

1. What promises are made in relation to the subject of the salvation of the dead? and what kind of characters are those who can be saved, although their bodies are mouldering and decaying in the grave? When his commandments teach us, it is in view of eternity; for we are looked upon by God as though we were in eternity. God dwells in eternity, and does not view things as we do.

2. The greatest responsibility in this world that God has laid upon us is to seek after our dead. The Apostle says, "They without us cannot be made perfect;" (Hebrews 11:40) for it is necessary that the sealing power should be in our hands to seal our children and our dead for the fulness of the dispensation of times—a dispensation to meet the promises made by Jesus Christ before the foundation of the world for the salvation of man.

3. Now, I will speak of them. I will meet Paul half way. I say to you, Paul, you cannot be perfect without us. It is necessary that those who

are going before and those who come after us should have salvation in common with us; and thus hath God made it obligatory upon man. Hence, God said, "I will send you Elijah the prophet before the coming of the great and dreadful day of the Lord: and he shall turn the heart of the fathers to the children, and the heart of the children to their fathers, lest I come and smite the earth with a curse" (Malachi 4:5).

Our Greatest Responsibility
THE KING FOLLETT DISCOURSE 13

KFD 13:1–3 The Prophet teaches the Saints about the redemption of the dead.

Section Fourteen

1. I have a declaration to make as to the provisions which God hath made to suit the conditions of man—made from before the foundation of the world. What has Jesus said? All sin, and all blasphemies, and every transgression, except one, that man can be guilty of, may be forgiven; and there is a salvation for all men, either in this world or the world to come, who have not committed the unpardonable sin, there being a provision either in this world or the world of spirits. Hence God hath made a provision that every spirit in the eternal world can be ferreted out and saved unless he has committed that unpardonable sin which cannot be remitted to him either in this world or the world of spirits. God has wrought out a salvation for all men, unless they have committed a certain sin; and every man who has a friend in the eternal world can save him, unless he has committed the unpardonable sin. And so you can see how far you can be a savior.

A Salvation for Men
THE KING FOLLETT DISCOURSE 14

KFD 14:1 *There is a salvation for all men . . . who have not committed the unpardonable sin.* In scripture "salvation" is generally a synonym for exaltation. In a few instances, however, it simply means that someone has been redeemed from death and hell and has inherited a degree of glory. The Prophet uses the term in that manner in this text.

The unpardonable sin. The unpardonable sin, which the Prophet discusses in that which immediately follows, is that sin which is so grievous that there is no forgiveness for it in this world or in the world to come. It falls outside the veil of Christ's mercy and his atonement. Those who have committed this sin will be perdition, which means hopelessly or irredeemably lost.

Section Fifteen

1. A man cannot commit the unpardonable sin after the dissolution of the body, and there is a way possible for escape. Knowledge saves a man; and in the world of spirits no man can be exalted but by knowledge. So long as a man will not give heed to the commandments, he must abide without salvation. If a man has knowledge, he can be saved; although, if he has been guilty of great sins, he will be punished for them. But when he consents to obey the Gospel, whether here or in the world of spirits, he is saved.

2. A man is his own tormenter and his own condemner. Hence the saying, They shall go into the lake that burns with fire and brimstone. The torment of disappointment in the mind of man is as exquisite as a lake burning with fire and brimstone. I say, so is the torment of man.

3. I know the Scriptures and understand them. I said, no man can commit the unpardonable sin after the dissolution of the body, nor in this life, until he receives the Holy Ghost; but they must do it in this world. Hence the salvation of Jesus Christ was wrought out for all men, in order to triumph over the devil; for if it did not catch him in one place, it would in another; for he stood up as a Savior. All will suffer until they obey Christ himself.

4. The contention in heaven was—Jesus said there would be certain souls that would not be saved; and the devil said he could save them all, and laid his plans before the grand council, who gave their vote in favor of Jesus Christ. So the devil rose up in rebellion against God, and was cast down, with all who put up their heads for him (Moses 4:1–4; Abraham 3:23–28).

The Unpardonable Sin
THE KING FOLLETT DISCOURSE 15

KFD 15:1 *A man cannot commit the unpardonable sin after the dissolution of the body.* Why, it is asked, if one could become perdition as a spirit in the premortal life, could one not also become perdition in the spirit world after death? The answer rests in the fact that before someone could become perdition in this life, he or she must have received the fulness of all temple blessings (D&C 132:19–28). All who have arrived at that station would in death find themselves in paradise, and no one can apostatize from paradise. Satan has no power in paradise; all who are there have kept their second estate and have obtained the promise that they will have glory added upon them forever and ever (Abraham 3:26).

KFD 15:3 *All will suffer until they obey Christ himself.* In the vision on the degrees of glory, the Prophet learned that even the inhabitants of the telestial kingdom must bow the knee and confess Christ. See Doctrine and Covenants 76:109–10.

Section Sixteen

1. All sins shall be forgiven, except the sin against the Holy Ghost; for Jesus will save all except the sons of perdition. What must a man do to commit the unpardonable sin? He must receive the Holy Ghost, have the heavens opened unto him, and know God, and then sin against Him. After a man has sinned against the Holy Ghost, there is no repentance for him. He has got to say that the sun does not shine while he sees it; he has got to deny Jesus Christ when the heavens have been opened unto him, and to deny the plan of salvation with his eyes open to the truth of it; and from that time he begins to be an enemy. This is the case with many apostates of the Church of Jesus Christ of Latter-day Saints.

2. When a man begins to be an enemy to this work, he hunts me, he seeks to kill me, and never ceases to thirst for my blood. He gets the spirit of the devil—the same spirit that they had who crucified the Lord of Life—the same spirit that sins against the Holy Ghost. You cannot save such persons; you cannot bring them to repentance; they make open war, like the devil, and awful is the consequence.

3. I advise all of you to be careful what you do, or you may by-and-by find out that you have been deceived. Stay yourselves; do not give way; don't make any hasty moves, you may be saved. If a spirit of bitterness is in you, don't be in haste. You may say, that man is a sinner. Well, if he repents, he shall be forgiven. Be cautious: await. When you find a spirit that wants bloodshed—murder, the same is not of God, but is of the devil. Out of the abundance of the heart of man the mouth speaketh.

The Forgiveness of Sins
THE KING FOLLETT DISCOURSE 16

KFD 16:1–2 Here we are told that one cannot become perdition unless he or she has received the Holy Ghost (which comes only after baptism), has received revelations, and more particularly has experienced the manifestation of God, meaning, we learn from Doctrine and Covenants 76:43 and 130:3, both the Father and the Son. Then with full knowledge and full accountability for what they are doing, such persons deny what they have seen and heard and come out in open rebellion against God, thirsting after the blood of his anointed.

KFD 16:1 *This is the case with many apostates of the Church.* It has been said that those who will become sons of perdition can be numbered on the fingers on your hand. This could hardly be the case if Joseph Smith could say at that time that there were "many" who would become such.

Section Seventeen

1. The best men bring forth the best works. The man who tells you words of life is the man who can save you. I warn you against all evil characters who sin against the Holy Ghost; for there is no redemption for them in this world nor in the world to come.

2. I could go back and trace every subject of interest concerning the relationship of man to God, if I had time. I can enter into the mysteries; I can enter largely into the eternal worlds; for Jesus said, "In my Father's house are many mansions; if it were not so, I would have told you. I go to prepare a place for you" (John 14:2). Paul says, "There is one glory of the sun, and another glory of the moon, and another glory of the stars; for one star differeth from another star in glory. So also is the resurrection of the dead" (1 Cor. 15:41). What have we to console us in relation to the dead? We have reason to have the greatest hope and consolations for our dead of any people on the earth; for we have seen them walk worthily in our midst, and seen them sink asleep in the arms of Jesus; and those who have died in the faith are now in the celestial kingdom of God. And hence is the glory of the sun.

"In My Father's House"
THE KING FOLLETT DISCOURSE 17

KFD 17:2 *Those who have died in the faith are now in the celestial kingdom.* The glory promised the faithful being assured, the Prophet speaks of it as if they had already obtained it. He then notes that they will have to "await until the resurrection of the dead," which we know will not take place until Christ returns. See commentary on Doctrine and Covenants 88:97–98.

Section Eighteen

1. You mourners have occasion to rejoice, speaking of the death of Elder King Follett; for your husband and father is gone to wait until the resurrection of the dead—until the perfection of the remainder; for at the resurrection your friend will rise in perfect felicity and go to celestial glory, while many must wait myriads of years before they can receive the like blessings; and your expectations and hopes are far above what man can conceive; for why has God revealed it to us?

2. I am authorized to say, by the authority of the Holy Ghost, that you have no occasion to fear; for he is gone to the home of the just. Don't mourn, don't weep. I know it by the testimony of the Holy Ghost that is within me; and you may wait for your friends to come forth to meet you in the morn of the celestial world.

3. Rejoice, O Israel! Your friends who have been murdered for the truth's sake in the persecutions shall triumph gloriously in the celestial world, while their murderers shall welter for ages in torment, even until they shall have paid the uttermost farthing. I say this for the benefit of strangers.

4. I have a father, brothers, children, and friends who have gone to a world of spirits. They are only absent for a moment. They are in the spirit, and we shall soon meet again. The time will soon arrive when the trumpet shall sound. When we depart, we shall hail our mothers, fathers, friends, and all whom we love, who have fallen asleep in Jesus. There will be no fear of mobs, persecutions, or malicious lawsuits and arrests; but it will be an eternity of felicity.

Righteous Mourners Rejoice
THE KING FOLLETT DISCOURSE 18

KFD 18:1–4 The Prophet teaches that we will come forth in the resurrection as men and women, husband and wife, father and mother, son or daughter, with all the proper and wholesome feelings innate to us here.

Following the example of *Teachings of the Prophet Joseph Smith,* we have omitted the paragraph dealing with the resurrection of little children. It is evident that this part of the Prophet's discourse was not recorded properly. See *History of the Church,* 4:556–57 and notes.

Section Nineteen

1. I will leave this subject here, and make a few remarks on the subject of baptism. The baptism of water, without the baptism of fire and the Holy Ghost attending it, is of no use; they are necessarily and inseparably connected. An individual must be born of water and the Spirit in order to get into the kingdom of God. In the German, the text bears me out the same as the revelations which I have given and taught for the last fourteen years on that subject. I have the testimony to put in their teeth. My testimony has been true all the time. You will find it in the declaration of John the Baptist. (Reads from the German.) John says, "I baptize you with water, but when Jesus comes, who has the power (or keys), he shall administer the baptism of fire and the Holy Ghost." Where is now all the sectarian world? And if this testimony is true, they are all damned as clearly as anathema can do it. I know the text is true. I call upon all you Germans who know that it is true to say, Aye. (Loud shouts of "Aye.")

2. Alexander Campbell, how are you going to save people with water alone? For John said his baptism was good for nothing without the baptism of Jesus Christ. "Therefore, not leaving the principles of the doctrine of Christ, let us go on unto perfection; not laying again the foundation of repentance from dead works, and of faith toward God, of the doctrine of baptisms, and of laying on of hands, and of resurrection of the dead, and of eternal judgment. And this will we do, if God permit" (Heb. 6:1–3).

3. There is one God, one Father, one Jesus, one hope of our calling, one baptism. * * * Many talk of baptism not being essential to salvation; but this kind of teaching would lay the foundation of their damnation. I have the truth, and am at the defiance of the world to contradict me, if they can.

4. I have now preached a little Latin, a little Hebrew, Greek, and German; and I have fulfilled all. I am not so big a fool as many have taken me to be. The Germans know that I read the German correctly.

Baptism

THE KING FOLLETT DISCOURSE 19

KFD 19:2 *Alexander Campbell.* Mr. Campbell was a leader in the Disciples of Christ movement, which started in the late 1820s. He held that the "Kingdom of God" was not set up on the earth until the day of

Pentecost. Thus, he argued that the Book of Mormon and the Book of Moses could not be true because of their reference to the ordinance of baptism before that time. He denounced Joseph Smith as an impostor. Some of the converts from Campbell's movement found it difficult to surrender such views.

Section Twenty

1. Hear it, all ye ends of the earth—all ye priests, all ye sinners, and all men. Repent! repent! Obey the Gospel. Turn to God; for your religion won't save you, and you will be damned. I do not say how long. There have been remarks made concerning all men being redeemed from hell; but I say that those who sin against the Holy Ghost cannot be forgiven in this world or in the world to come; they shall die the second death. Those who commit the unpardonable sin are doomed to *Gnolom*—to dwell in hell, worlds without end. As they concoct scenes of bloodshed in this world, so they shall rise to that resurrection which is as the lake of fire and brimstone. Some shall rise to the everlasting burnings of God; for God dwells in everlasting burnings, and some shall rise to the damnation of their own filthiness, which is as exquisite a torment as the lake of fire and brimstone.

2. I have intended my remarks for all, both rich and poor, bond and free, great and small. I have no enmity against any man. I love you all; but I hate some of your deeds. I am your best friend, and if persons miss their mark it is their own fault. If I reprove a man, and he hates me, he is a fool; for I love all men, especially these my brethren and sisters.

3. I rejoice in hearing the testimony of my aged friends. You don't know me; you never knew my heart. No man knows my history. I cannot tell it: I shall never undertake it. I don't blame any one for not believing my history. If I had not experienced what I have, I could not have believed it myself. I never did harm any man since I was born in the world. My voice is always for peace.

4. I cannot lie down until all my work is finished. I never think any evil, nor do anything to the harm of my fellow-man. When I am called by the trump of the archangel and weighed in the balance, you will all know me then. I add no more. God bless you all. Amen. (April 6, 1844).

A Call to Repentance
THE KING FOLLETT DISCOURSE 20

KFD 20:1 *Gnolom.* In his translation of the book of Abraham the Prophet added the word *gnolaum* (Abraham 3:18), which means "eternal," to the vocabulary of the Latter-day Saints. Here he adds the word "gnolom," which appears to come from the same root and to mean essentially the same thing.

KFD 20:3 *No man knows my history.* Heber C. Kimball reports that Joseph Smith said, "Would to God, brethren, I could tell you who I am! Would to God I could tell you what I know! But you would call it blasphemy, and there are men upon this stand who would want to take my life" (Whitney, *Life of Heber C. Kimball,* 322). We assume this to be an allusion to the same principle revealed in Doctrine and Covenants 113. See commentary on Doctrine and Covenants 113:3–6.

DOCTRINE AND COVENANTS 133

DATE: 3 NOVEMBER 1831
PLACE: HIRAM, OHIO

Doctrine and Covenants 133 is the companion revelation to section 1, the preface to the compilation of revelations that were to be published in the Book of Commandments, and it was given at the same conference. Though the press for the Book of Commandments was destroyed before Doctrine and Covenants 133 was printed, it was included in the 1835 edition of the Doctrine and Covenants as the Appendix.

This revelation deals with the return of Christ and those events that will precede that great and glorious day. It weaves together scores of Bible prophecies, either announcing their fulfillment or shining greater light on them. It was given, Joseph Smith said, because the Elders "desired to know relative to preaching the Gospel to the inhabitants of the earth, and concerning the gathering; and in order to walk by the true light, and be instructed from on high" (*History of the Church,* 1:229).

This revelation was published for the first time in the *The Evening and Morning Star,* introduced as follows: "It affords us joy to lay before the saints, an article fraught with so much heavenly intelligence. . . .

"We hope that while they read it, they will remember, that it is a voice from him who spake as never man spake. We hope that while they are blessed with revelation upon revelation, with commandment upon commandment, and with precept upon precept, they will remember to do them. We hope that while they are thus blessed with the precious word of their Lord from heaven, in these last days, to fulfill that which was spoken in days of old, they will hearken to his counsels and lend an ear to all his precepts.

"Indeed it is a source of joy to us, to know, that all the prophecies and promises which are contained in them, which have not been fulfilled, will come to pass. The saints may lift up their heads and rejoice, for their redemption will soon be perfected. Soon the curtain of heaven will be

1106

unfolded, as a scroll is unfolded after it is rolled up, and they will see their Lord face to face. In view of these coming scenes, they may lift up their heads and rejoice, and praise his holy name, that they are permitted to live in the days when he returns to his people his everlasting covenant, to prepare them for his presence" (*The Evening and Morning Star*, 1:89).

The Saints Are Commanded to Prepare for the Second Coming
DOCTRINE AND COVENANTS 133:1–6

133:1 *The word of the Lord concerning you.* The glory of Mormonism is that we have a God who speaks! Surely the events that will attend his second coming are of greater concern to us than they were to the ancient Saints. Yet, the historical Christian world is dependent upon the record of revelations—to the extent that accounts of them have been preserved—that were spoken to people thousands of years ago and were suited to their circumstances. To be entirely reliant upon these revelations, as marvelous as they are, could be likened to taking as one's guide for life a patriarchal blessing given to one's ancient progenitors. Certainly it would contain inspired counsel, yet it is not ours and will not contain direction that will be specific to us. Such is the instruction and blessing that we receive in the verses that follow.

133:2 *The Lord who shall suddenly come to his temple.* This language, which comes from the prophecy of Malachi (3:1–3), affirms that in the last days the temple will still be the focal point of worship among the Lord's people. This prophecy seems to embrace the idea that the Savior will make appearances in many of his temples before the great and dreadful day comes.

133:3 *He shall make bare his holy arm in the eyes of all the nations.* Explaining this prophecy, which comes from the writings of Isaiah (Isaiah 52:10), Nephi said, "All the kindreds of the earth cannot be blessed unless he shall make bare his arm in the eyes of the nations. Wherefore, the Lord God will proceed to make bare his arm in the eyes of all the nations, in bringing about his covenants and his gospel unto those who are of the house of Israel. Wherefore, he will bring them again out of captivity, and they shall be gathered together to the lands of their inheritance; and they shall be brought out of obscurity and out of darkness; and they shall know that the Lord is their Savior and their Redeemer, the Mighty One of Israel" (1 Nephi 22:10–12).

And all the ends of the earth shall see the salvation of their God. Again the words are those of Isaiah (52:10). The word *salvation* is used to render the Hebrew *yshuw'ah*, which means deliverance or victory. Thus, the point of the text is that in the teaching of the gospel to the nations of the earth and in the gathering and redemption of Israel, the victory will rest with the Lord. Despite all darkness and evil in the world, his purposes will be accomplished and his promises fulfilled.

133:4 *Sanctify yourselves; gather ye together.* Reference is to the endowment that is received in the house of the Lord. The endowment is a ritual cleansing and is requisite to being sanctified. It is for this purpose that the Saints had at that time been commanded to gather in Kirtland, Ohio, where they would build the first temple in this dispensation. "And that ye might escape the power of the enemy, and be gathered unto me a righteous people, without spot and blameless—Wherefore, for this cause I gave unto you the commandment that ye should go to the Ohio; and there I will give unto you my law; and there you shall be endowed with power from on high; And from thence, whosoever I will shall go forth among all nations, and it shall be told them what they shall do; for I have a great work laid up in store, for Israel shall be saved, and I will lead them whithersoever I will, and no power shall stay my hand" (D&C 38:31–33).

The land of Zion. The immediate reference is to Missouri, where the Saints were then preparing to go. Later, the Prophet defined Zion as all of north and south America (*Teachings of the Prophet Joseph Smith*, 362).

Commanded to tarry. See commentary on Doctrine and Covenants 101:21; 105:23–26.

Be ye clean that bear the vessels of the Lord. See commentary on Doctrine and Covenants 38:42.

133:6 *Call your solemn assemblies.* See commentary on Doctrine and Covenants 88:70.

Let every man call upon the name of the Lord. See commentary on Doctrine and Covenants 1:20.

All Men Are Commanded to Flee Babylon and Come to Zion

DOCTRINE AND COVENANTS 133:7–16

133:7–16 The second coming of Christ will not take place until the message of the Restoration has been declared to all the nations of the earth. The best measure of how close we are to the day of the Savior's return is the extent to which the gospel has been declared among the nations of the earth. When this revelation was given, the direction of the Lord was that people leave Babylon (the world) and flee to the place of Zion in Jackson County, Missouri. Initially it was necessary for those of faith—regardless of the sacrifice required—to leave their homelands and immigrate to Zion where they could join with those of like faith.

As they gathered together, the Saints could build the temples where the keys and power of the priesthood could be restored. First came the Kirtland Temple, where Moses, an Elias from Abraham's day, and Elijah each restored keys and left blessings upon the Lord's people. Here the Saints were washed and anointed preparatory to receiving the full endowment in Nauvoo. In the Nauvoo Temple, the full endowment was administered for the first time, and couples were sealed together for time and eternity.

All of this was accomplished despite the greatest of opposition. It was well known to Satan and his legions that once temples had been built and the Saints endowed with power from on high, the work of the Lord could not be rooted up but would go forth to fill the whole earth as the waters do the sea. So it was that the nations of the earth made their offerings to the Lord, sending the best of their faith—men and women of courage—to aid in laying the foundations of Zion. Many hands were needed for this work: hands that were strong and callused, hands of skilled artisans, and hands into which the revelations of the Restoration could be placed to carry them to wherever the honest in heart might be found. From these early members would come, in future generations, a great army of missionaries in whom the spirit of their forebears would brood. These missionaries, following the trails blazed by their progenitors, would take the gospel to the scattered remnants of Israel that they might be returned to the covenants God had made with their fathers.

133:13 *Mountains of the Lord's house.* Mountains are nature's temples. They served so frequently as the meeting place between God and man that in ancient times they were thought of as temples. Here two temples are spoken of, both in a prophetic sense: the temple yet to be built in the Jerusalem of old and the temple to be built in the New Jerusalem.

In our day the call is no longer to flee Babylon for Zion but rather to establish Zion among all the nations of the earth. Ours is a day in which those of the house of faith are charged to enlarge the tent of Israel and stretch the curtains of the Lord's habitations (meaning the number of his temples) among all peoples so that they too can gather to the covenant and receive in full measure the blessings of salvation.

Christ Shall Stand on Mount Zion, the Continents Shall Become One Land, and the Lost Tribes Shall Return

DOCTRINE AND COVENANTS 133:17–35

133:17 *Prepare ye the way of the Lord.* See commentary on Doctrine and Covenants 65:1, 3.

133:18 *Having his Father's name written on their foreheads.* The text quotes Revelation 14:1. The Mount Zion to which reference is made is the New Jerusalem (D&C 84:2). The one hundred and forty-four thousand who have their father's name written on their foreheads are high priests who through the holy anointing have received the promise that they will become as God is. See commentary on Doctrine and Covenants 77:11.

133:19 *The coming of the Bridegroom.* Again the text draws upon New Testament imagery. The wedding customs of Jesus' day called for the bridegroom and his friends, in processional array, to call for the bride and to take her to the home of the bridegroom where the wedding feast was to be held. As the procession returned to the home of the groom, friends of the bride, in groups, joined the party to go to the wedding feast. As weddings were celebrated at night, those awaiting the bridegroom and his festal party needed to carry lamps.

In the parable of the ten virgins, Jesus is the bridegroom. The marriage feast is to be celebrated when he returns to take the Church as his bride (Revelation 21:2; 21:9; 22:17). The ten virgins represent those Church members who are looking for the bridegroom to come, and the oil-filled lamps are symbolic of the Holy Spirit which lights the way before the Saints.

133:20 *For behold, he shall stand.* The second coming of Christ to the world will be preceded by a host of other comings. These preparatory comings will be to his servants charged to make his paths straight; these will be those worthy to stand in his presence and bear his name. The number of these comings and the places where he will appear suggest the numerical strength the Church will enjoy in that day. This text lists the Mount of Olives, the mighty ocean, the islands of the sea, and the land of Zion. To these we can add visits to his temples which will dot the earth and the great meeting yet to be held in Adam-ondi-Ahman. See commentary on Doctrine and Covenants 27:5–14.

133:21 *He shall utter his voice out of Zion, and he shall speak from Jerusalem.* This verse is rooted in the words of Isaiah, "And it shall come to pass in the last days, that the mountain of the Lord's house shall be established in the top of the mountains, and shall be exalted above the hills; and all nations shall flow unto it. And many people shall go and say, Come ye, and let us go up to the mountain of the Lord, to the house of the God of Jacob; and he will teach us of his ways, and we will walk in his paths: for out of Zion shall go forth the law, and the word of the Lord from Jerusalem" (Isaiah 2:2–3). Bible commentators assume that the Zion spoken of here is one and the same with the Jerusalem of old. From the context of the Restoration, it is clear that Isaiah saw two great capitals—the Old and New Jerusalems—administering the affairs of the Lord. The events here described are millennial, for only then will Christ rule and give direction to the whole earth. At that time church and state will be one, nevertheless laws, order, and government will be necessary; the Lord will establish both a political and an ecclesiastical kingdom. "But even then, as we suppose, administrative affairs will be departmentalized, for the law will go forth from Zion (in Jackson County), and the word of the Lord from Jerusalem (in Palestine). But, nonetheless, once again the government of the earth will be theocratic. God will govern. This time he will do it personally as he reigns over all the earth. And all of this presupposes the fall of Babylon, and the death of false religions, and the fall of all earthly governments and nations. And these things, as we are aware, shall surely come to pass" (McConkie, *Millennial Messiah,* 596).

133:22–24 Commenting on these verses, Elder Bruce R. McConkie said: "Knowing as we do from latter-day revelation that the islands and continents were once joined in one landmass and will yet again be joined, we find new meaning in allusions and comments found in the ancient scriptures. As part of a description of the Second Coming, John tells us: 'And the heaven departed as a scroll when it is rolled together; and every

mountain and island were moved out of their places.' (Rev. 6:14). In connection with the greatest earthquake of the ages, John says: 'And every
island fled away, and the mountains were not found.' (Rev. 16:20). Also in
a Second Coming setting John speaks of the voice of the Lord 'as the
voice of many waters, and as the voice of a great thunder.' (Rev. 14:2).
This is the identical language used by the Lord in telling Joseph Smith
that the mountains and valleys shall not be found, that the great deep
(apparently the Atlantic Ocean) will be driven back into the north countries, 'and the islands shall become one land.' (D&C 133:22–23). The
voice of many waters and of a great thunder could well be the thunder-
ous surging of a whole ocean moving half an earth's distance from where
it now is. And all of this gives deep meaning to John's account, which
says: 'And I saw a new heaven and a new earth: for the first heaven and
the first earth were passed away; and there was no more sea.' (Rev. 21:1).
The apparent meaning of this is that the sea, or ocean, that separates the
continents will cease to be, for their great landmasses will be joined
together again" (*Millennial Messiah*, 623–24).

133:26 *Their prophets shall hear his voice.* The Lord's people always
have been and always will be led by prophets. Confusion has been associated with this passage because of the idea that somehow the lost tribes
are together as a group with their prophets at their head waiting for the
call to return. This notion is fraught with serious difficulties, including
the following:

First, a host of scriptural passages attest that the tribes of Israel have
been scattered among all the nations of the earth. We cite but one classic
illustration from 3 Nephi:

"As surely as the Lord liveth, will he gather in from the four quarters
of the earth all the remnant of the seed of Jacob, who are scattered abroad
upon all the face of the earth. And as he hath covenanted with all the
house of Jacob, even so shall the covenant wherewith he hath covenanted
with the house of Jacob be fulfilled in his own due time, unto the restoring
all the house of Jacob unto the knowledge of the covenant that he hath
covenanted with them. And then shall they know their Redeemer, who is
Jesus Christ, the Son of God; and then shall they be gathered in from the
four quarters of the earth unto their own lands, from whence they have
been dispersed; yea, as the Lord liveth so shall it be. Amen" (5:24–26).

No other statement in all of holy writ begins and ends with the
announcement that if what is being written is not so, then God no longer
lives! More emphatic language is simply not possible. The text then

assures us that the tribes of Israel have been scattered to the four quarters of the earth and that they will remain in their scattered condition until they come to the knowledge of the covenant that God made with their fathers and the knowledge that Jesus is the Christ and the Son of God. Now, we would ask, How is it possible for a people to have prophets at their head and yet not have heard of the covenant of salvation or that Jesus is the Christ and the Son of God?

Second, Why would God send Moses to Joseph Smith to give him the keys by which Israel was to be gathered if some other prophets had already accomplished the task?

Third, Why would John the Baptist, and then Peter, James and John restore priesthood to Joseph Smith and Oliver Cowdery if that priesthood and its keys were already on the earth?

Fourth, What of the statements the Lord made to Joseph Smith stating that he stood at the head of "the only true and living church upon the face of the whole earth" (D&C 1:30). If priesthood, prophets, and covenants were already to be found upon the earth what truth can be found in such a statement?

Fifth, If we are to accept the standard established in the revelations of the Restoration, we must maintain that none have the right to act in the name of the Lord (and surely that would include leading the tribes of Israel) save they have been "ordained by some one who has authority, and it is known to the church that he has authority and has been regularly ordained by the heads of the church" (D&C 42:11). The Doctrine and Covenants accepts none as prophets save those who have been called, ordained, and received the sustaining vote of the Church. The Lord's house is and always has been a house of order.

Is it not wholly harmonious with the revelations and all we know about the Lord's system of governing his people to suppose that the prophets called to lead the tribes of Israel back to the lands of their inheritance will be elders of Israel who trace their priesthood to Joseph Smith and Oliver Cowdery and through them to Peter, James, and John?

133:27 *An highway shall be cast up in the midst of the great deep.* In his prophetic description of the return of Israel in the last days, Isaiah said, "An highway shall be there, and a way, and it shall be called The way of holiness; the unclean shall not pass over it; but it shall be for those: the wayfaring men, though fools, shall not err therein. No lion shall be there, nor any ravenous beast shall go up thereon, it shall not be found there; but the redeemed shall walk there: and the ransomed of the Lord shall return, and come to Zion with songs and everlasting joy upon their heads: they shall obtain joy and gladness, and sorrow and sighing shall flee away" (Isaiah 35:8–10).

133:30 *Rich treasures.* When Abraham and Sarah returned after their trial in Egypt to that sacred land promised them, they were "rich in cattle, in silver, and in gold." They went first to Beth-el—"the house of God" (Genesis 28:19a)—and its altar that they might call upon the name of the Lord (Genesis 13:2–4). Similarly, before the children of Israel left Egypt to return to the promised land to rebuild their temple and call upon God, they were directed to "borrow" (meaning ask) from the Egyptians their "jewels of silver, and jewels of gold" (Exodus 11:2; 2a). When the Jews were freed from their captivity in Babylon to return to Palestine to rebuild the Holy City and its temple, the treasure houses of that great nation were opened to them and they returned laden with silver and gold (Ezra 7:15–21). Thus, when Israel returns in the last days to claim the blessings of the temple, we look to them to follow the pattern of their progenitors and bring with them their rich treasures. We would suppose that such treasures would be used in the building of temples and the spreading of the gospel to all the nations of the earth.

We have frequently heard it said that the rich treasures spoken of in this verse were scriptural records. There are a number of serious difficulties associated with such an interpretation. The priesthood is the ordained channel through which the revelations of heaven are to come. The very reason the scattered remnants of Israel are being gathered is to return them to the priesthood and its blessings. We do not expect to receive our scripture or revelations from those who have been lost and have not known where the truths of salvation are to be found. The time will come when we will have scriptural records from the various tribes of Israel, but they must come to us through the channels the Lord has ordained. The Lamanites did not bring the Book of Mormon with them, rather, we took it to them. Indeed, the Book of Mormon was ordained in the councils of heaven for the very purpose of gathering the lost tribes of Israel. If the prophecies are to be fulfilled, the stick of Judah and the stick of Joseph will be the books that actuate the gathering (Ezekiel 37:15–21). Then, at the appropriate time, other scripture will be given to those of the house of faith. Such scripture will come to us from he whom we sustain as prophet, seer, and revelator.

Parley P. Pratt provides a wonderful commentary on the reference to "rich treasures" as used in this text in his hymn "An Angel from on High."

> Lo, Israel filled with joy
> Shall now be gathered home,
> Their wealth and means employ
> To build Jerusalem,
> While Zion shall arise and shine
> And fill the earth with truth divine,
> While Zion shall arise and shine
> And fill the earth with truth divine.
> (*Hymns,* no. 328)

133:31 *Boundaries of the everlasting hills.* This refers to the Rocky Mountain range. When Jacob blessed his son Joseph, he said, "The blessings of thy father have prevailed above the blessings of my progenitors unto the utmost bound of the everlasting hills: they shall be on the head of Joseph, and on the crown of the head of him that was separate from his brethren" (Genesis 49:26). Moses, in like manner, placed a blessing upon the tribe of Joseph, saying: "And for the chief things of the ancient mountains, and for the precious things of the lasting hills . . . let the blessing come upon the head of Joseph and upon the top of the head of him that was separated from his brethren" (Deuteronomy 33:15–16). Again, Jacob referred to Joseph as "a fruitful bough, . . . by a well, whose branches run over the wall" (Genesis 49:22). It was affirmed to Joseph Smith in his own patriarchal blessing that these references were directed to the Americas. As Joseph of old was separated from his brethren by their choice, so by the will of the Lord he received a greater blessing and, besides his inheritance in Palestine, he also received as an inheritance the land of Zion—America—separated from the inheritance of the other tribes. His blessing which his father gave him "prevailed above the blessings of his [Jacob's] progenitors" in that the Lord gave to him the choicest of all lands to possess with his seed forever.

133:32 *Crowned with glory . . . by the hands of . . . the children of Ephraim.* It is for the blessings of the temple that the tribes of Israel return to Zion. It is there that they will be crowned with glory by the children of Ephraim.

The Gospel Restored through Joseph Smith
Is to Be Preached in All the World
DOCTRINE AND COVENANTS 133:36–39

133:36–39 These verses pick up the language of Revelation 14:6–7 relative to the angel that John promised would return to the earth in the last days to restore the everlasting gospel. They announce that the Revelator's prophecy has been fulfilled. Thus, these verses confirm that it was Moroni and the Book of Mormon of which John wrote. Having done so, they then affirm that it is the very gospel restored by Moroni in the Book of Mormon that must go to those of every nation, kindred, tongue, and people. Sending the Bible to the nations of the earth will not do, nor will sending the testimony of Christ as it comes from that record. As marvelous as the New Testament Gospels are, many people have professed to accept the Gospels' testimony of Christ while rejecting baptism, the need for revelation, the place of living prophets, the need for priesthood authority, the ordinances of the house of the Lord, and the fulfillment of the Revelator's promise. The simple truth is that without such principles there is no salvation.

The Lord Will Come in Vengeance upon the Wicked
DOCTRINE AND COVENANTS 133:40–51

133:40–45 These verses are rooted in Isaiah 64:1–5, which constitute the prayer of Israel for the Second Coming and the salvation that will be enjoyed by the faithful at that time. The oft-asked question is, Would one, knowing the calamities that are to befall the world at the time of Christ's return long to be a part of such events or should one pray to be spared such an experience? The answer to such a question is entirely dependant upon who asks it. The universal plea of the righteous is, "Thy kingdom come. Thy will be done in earth, as it is in heaven" (Matthew 6:10). While among the wicked the promise is, "Woe unto you that desire the day of the Lord! to what end is it for you? The day of the Lord is darkness, and not light. As if a man did flee from a lion, and a bear met him; or went into the house, and leaned his hand on the wall, and a serpent bit him. Shall not the day of the Lord be darkness, and not light? even very dark, and no brightness in it?" (Amos 5:18–20).

In these verses the voice of Isaiah and Joseph Smith become one in painting a dramatic word picture of the vengeance and the love that the

Lord will manifest at the time of his return. Both must stand together, for he cannot save the righteous without damning the wicked; he cannot reward the obedient without condemning the rebellious; he cannot be a God of mercy save he is also a God of justice. So it is that we find in the revelations of the Restoration a second witness of all that the Lord said to the ancient prophets about the day of his wrath. These revelations speak of "the day when the wrath of God shall be poured out upon the wicked without measure" (D&C 1:9). In them he says: "Hear the word of him whose anger is kindled against the wicked and rebellious. . . . Let the wicked take heed, and let the rebellious fear and tremble; and let the unbelieving hold their lips, for the day of wrath shall come upon them as a whirlwind, and all flesh shall know that I am God" (D&C 63:2, 6). "Behold, the day has come, when the cup of the wrath of mine indignation is full," saith the Lord (D&C 43:26). "For behold, mine anger is kindled against the rebellious, and they shall know mine arm and mine indignation, in the day of visitation and of wrath upon the nations" (D&C 56:1).

For those who have walked in carnal paths, it will be a most dreadful day. "The time is soon at hand that I shall come in a cloud with power and great glory," saith the Lord. "And it shall be a great day at the time of my coming, for all nations shall tremble" (D&C 34:7–8). "For when the Lord shall appear he shall be terrible unto them, that fear may seize upon them, and they shall stand afar off and tremble. And all nations shall be afraid because of the terror of the Lord, and the power of his might" (D&C 45:74–75).

And so we ask, Will there be no hope for those called upon to abide that day? Our answer, There is for those who are true and faithful. As Elder Bruce R. McConkie stated, "For them, whether in life or in death, it will be a time of glory and renown. Will they escape the outpouring of divine wrath and avoid the vengeance with which the wicked will be smitten? They will. They are the true Israel who yearn for the restoration to them of the ancient kingdom. They are the ones who shall abide the day and who shall live and reign on earth with their Lord for the space of a thousand years. And blessed are they, for they shall inherit the earth" (*Millennial Messiah*, 505).

133:40 *Rend the heavens.* To "rend the heavens" is to tear the veil so that God can be seen.

Mountains might flow down. At the return of Christ, "Every valley shall be exalted, and every mountain and hill shall be made low: and the crooked shall be made straight, and the rough places plain" (Isaiah 40:4).

133:41 *Melting fire.* This is a fire of such heat that it melts the very elements of the earth. All that is telestial on this earth at the time of Christ's return must be destroyed. "Every corruptible thing, . . . that dwells upon all the face of the earth, shall be consumed; and also that of element shall melt with fervent heat" (D&C 101:24–25).

133:43 *Terrible things.* The power of God will be so manifest that it will show itself to be greater than that of either man or nature.

133:46–48 These verses parallel Isaiah 63:1–2, which read as follows: "Who is this that cometh from Edom, with dyed garments from Bozrah? this that is glorious in his apparel, travelling in the greatness of his strength? I that speak in righteousness, mighty to save. Wherefore art thou red in thine apparel, and thy garments like him that treadeth in the winefat?" Edom was a land in the ancient Near East; Bozrah was its capital. It was also referred to as Idumea, which, like Babylon or Egypt, is a scriptural symbol for that which is unclean, or the world (D&C 1:36).

"This picture is a familiar one in Israel. The wine is trampled from the grapes in great vats, staining the garments of the laborers as though with blood. But in this case the second coming of Christ is involved, the one harvesting the crop is the Lord himself, and the winepress is full of the wrath of God. Thus John heard a command given to one of the angels of God in heaven. It was: 'Thrust in thy sharp sickle, and gather the clusters of the vine of the earth; for her grapes are fully ripe.' It is the day of harvest. 'And the angel thrust in his sickle into the earth, and gathered the vine of the of the earth, and cast it into the great winepress of the wrath of God. And the winepress was trodden without the city, and blood came out of the winepress' (Rev. 14:18–20)" (McConkie, *Millennial Messiah*, 503).

133:49 *So great shall be the glory of his presence.* This text comes from Isaiah 13:10. See commentary on Doctrine and Covenants 45:42.

It Shall Be the Year of His Redeemed
DOCTRINE AND COVENANTS 133:52–56

133:52 *The year of my redeemed.* The phrase "year of my redeemed" is used to describe the time of Christ's return and the ushering in of his millennial kingdom.

133:53 *The angel of his presence saved them.* This verse is rooted in

Isaiah 63:9. Israel has but one Savior and that is the Lord himself (Deuteronomy 4:35), he is "the angel of his presence" (Abraham 1:15–16). Moses proclaimed the same blessing in Exodus 33:12–17.

133:54–55 This text affirms that Enoch (and those of his city), Moses, and Elijah, all of whom as translated beings were taken into heaven without tasting death, nonetheless died that they might be resurrected with Christ. Their death and resurrection must have been a change that occurred in the twinkling of an eye (D&C 63:51).

133:56 *The graves of the saints shall be opened.* As all who were in the graves who were worthy of a celestial resurrection were called forth to meet Christ following his resurrection, so once again at the time of his return those worthy of a celestial resurrection will be called forth to join him (D&C 88:97–98). It appears from this text that those in Mount Zion, or the Jerusalem of old, will be called forth first and then those in the New Jerusalem, each when he makes his appearance to them (verses 20–21).

They shall sing the song of the Lamb. In honor of the Lamb, a great choir of 100,000,000 voices of the redeemed shall sing this new song (Revelation 5:9–13; D&C 84:99–102):

> Thou wast slain,
> And hast redeemed us to God by
> thy blood
> Out of every kindred, and tongue,
> and people, and nation;
> And hast made us unto our God
> kings and priests:
> And we shall reign on the earth. . . .
> Worthy is the Lamb that was slain
> To receive power, and riches, and
> wisdom,
> And strength, and honour, and
> glory, and blessing. . . .
> Blessing, and honour, and glory,
> and power,
> Be unto him that sitteth upon the
> throne,
> And unto the Lamb for ever and
> ever.

The Gospel Is to Be Sent Forth to Save the Saints and to Condemn the Wicked

DOCTRINE AND COVENANTS 133:57–74

133:57 *The fulness of the gospel, his everlasting covenant.* The fulness of the gospel and the everlasting covenant are one and the same (D&C 45:9). There is no gospel without covenants and there are no covenants (with the Lord) without the gospel. Thus, in the proper sense of the word, a covenant people are and must always be a people who have and live the gospel of Jesus Christ.

133:58 *The little one become a strong nation.* The "little one" is the Church. Early in the Kirtland period of Church history, Wilford Woodruff attended a meeting in a log cabin above the Morley farm. Of that occasion he recalled the following: "On Sunday night the Prophet called on all who held the Priesthood to gather into the little log school house they had there. It was a small house, perhaps 14 feet square. But it held the whole of the Priesthood of the Church of Jesus Christ of Latter-day Saints who were then in the town of Kirtland. . . . When we got together . . . the Prophet said, 'Brethren I have been very much edified and instructed in your testimonies here tonight. But I want to say to you before the Lord, that you know no more concerning the destines of this Church and kingdom than a babe upon its mother's lap. You don't comprehend it.' I was rather surprised. He said, 'It is only a little handfull of Priesthood you see here tonight, but this Church will fill North and South America—it will fill the world'" (Conference Report, April 1898, 57).

Two shall put their tens of thousands to flight. "Out of Armageddon will come great blessings, in the eternal sense, to those Jews and others who abide the day. 'In that day'—when all nations are gathered together against Jerusalem and she has become a cup of trembling unto all the people—'shall the Lord defend the inhabitants of Jerusalem; and he that is feeble among them at that day shall be as David; and the house of David shall be as God, as the angel of the Lord before them.' This is the day when two shall put their tens of thousands to flight, when divine intervention will scatter the hosts of the wicked, when in weakness and by faith the Lord's people will wax valiant and put to flight the armies of the aliens" (McConkie, *Millennial Messiah*, 467).

133:59 *The weak things of the earth shall thrash the nations.* See commentary on Doctrine and Covenants 35:13–14; see also Doctrine and Covenants 1:19; 124:1.

133:60 *Now are to go forth unto all flesh.* Reference is to the Book of Commandments. It was determined to publish this book of revelations at the conference where this revelation was received.

Should any question exist in the mind of anyone relative to the place the revelations in the Doctrine and Covenants (the successor to the Book of Commandments) are to play in our declaring the message of the Restoration to the world it is answered here—they are to "go forth unto all flesh." See Doctrine and Covenants 1 and 67.

133:63 *Cut off from among the people.* This statement traces to an often repeated Messianic prophecy first given to Moses (Deuteronomy 18:15–18). It was quoted by Peter as he spoke of the day of restoration (Acts 3:22–23), by Nephi in his interpretation of Isaiah 48 and 49 (1 Nephi 22:21), and by Moroni to Joseph Smith (Joseph Smith—History 1:40). Christ also quoted it to the Nephites, telling them that in the last days those who would not accept his words as they would be found in the Book of Mormon would "be cut off from among my people who are of the covenant" (3 Nephi 21:11).

133:64 *It shall leave them neither root nor branch.* Those who are cut off from the people of the covenant as spoken of in the preceding verse will be left with neither "root nor branch" according to the words of Malachi, meaning they will have no family ties in the world to come (Malachi 4:1–6).

133:73 *Outer darkness.* "So complete is the darkness prevailing in the minds of these spirits [those rejecting the gospel message], so wholly has gospel light been shut out of their consciences, that they know little or nothing of the plan of salvation, and have little hope within themselves of advancement and progression through the saving grace of Christ. Hell is literally a place of outer darkness, darkness that hates light, buries truth, and revels in iniquity" (McConkie, *Mormon Doctrine*, 551–52).

DOCTRINE AND COVENANTS 134

DATE: 17 AUGUST 1835
PLACE: KIRTLAND, OHIO

On 17 August 1835, a conference of the Church was held in Kirtland, Ohio, to examine and approve the compilation of revelations that had been prepared for publication in the Doctrine and Covenants of the Church.

After the priesthood quorums and the congregation had voted unanimously to accept these revelations for publication, W. W. Phelps arose and read an article on marriage. This was voted on and ordered to be published with the revelations. Then Oliver Cowdery arose and read the article on laws and governments that constitutes this section. It too was accepted for publication in the Doctrine and Covenants. Neither article was accepted as a revelation or thought to be other than a general expression of belief. Oliver Cowdery was the author of both articles.

Joseph Smith was not present at this conference. He and Frederick G. Williams were on a short mission to Michigan. He did not learn about the inclusion of these two articles until his return. He did not approve of either action but chose to respect the vote of the conference (Smith, *Doctrines of Salvation*, 3:195). The article "Marriage," which was written before the revelation known to us as Doctrine and Covenants 132 was committed to writing, was dropped from the Doctrine and Covenants in the 1876 edition. Section 132, which contains the Lord's law of eternal marriage, was added at that time.

Governments Should Preserve Freedom of Conscience and Worship
DOCTRINE AND COVENANTS 134:1–4

134:1 *We believe that governments were instituted of God for the benefit of man.* The supposition that all governments—as this statement implies—"were instituted of God for the benefit of man" is simply not defensible. Certainly we believe that the government known to Adam was given of God, as was that given on Sinai to Moses. We believe that the Founding Fathers of the government of the United States of America were inspired in what they did, but in the context of world history, such governments constitute precious few among countless governments formed by uninspired and conspiring men. Although the principles of righteous government were instituted of God, those principles are not often found in the many forms of government instituted by mankind.

134:4 *We believe that religion is instituted of God.* If this statement is taken at face value there would have been no need for Joseph Smith and the Restoration. We could simply join the great chorus of voices that tell us that as all roads in the ancient world led to Rome, so all faiths are capable of leading us to salvation. Again, true religion and true worship were instituted by God in the beginning, while man-made philosophies masquerading as religion are not the work of God.

All Men Owe Respect and Deference to Law
DOCTRINE AND COVENANTS 134:5–8

134:5–8 As Latter-day Saints, we believe ourselves to be accountable to God in all our actions. We also believe ourselves to be accountable to our fellow men insomuch that we honor and obey the laws of the society of which we are a part, nor is it our thought that we will isolate ourselves from society. Our role is to be a light to all, that we might take the message of the gospel to them.

The Saints Did Not Believe It Prudent to Meddle with Slaves
DOCTRINE AND COVENANTS 134:9–12

134:12 *We do not believe it right to interfere with bond servants.* This verse was intended to appease slaveholders and avoid placing the Saints in the crossfire between the Southern and Northern states over the issue of slavery, though there was very little sympathy in the Church for the same. The Church had enjoyed some missionary success in the Southern states, particularly, Virginia, Tennessee, and Kentucky, and it was feared that if they came out against slavery it would invoke persecution similar to that which they had experienced in Jackson County. "For you will see," wrote one Mormon, "that if madam rumor, with her thousand poisoned tongues, was once to set afloat the story that this society had come out in favor of the doctrines of Abolitionism, there would be no safety for one of us in the South" (*Messenger and Advocate*, 2:313). The Prophet Joseph Smith sensed the precariousness of the situation and took measures to avoid trouble; he and other Church leaders during the spring of 1836 used the *Messenger and Advocate* to voice disapproval of the abolition movement. "I do not believe that the people of the North have any more right to say that the South *shall* not hold slaves, than the South have to say the North *shall*," he wrote (*Messenger and Advocate*, 2:289), though he taught that the slave master must treat his slaves "with kindness before God."

In the spring of 1844, in order to give the Saints a candidate for whom they could vote in good conscience, the Prophet announced his candidacy for the presidency of the United States. In so doing he also announced a most enlightened platform with included a provision for Congress to pay slaveholders a reasonable price for their slaves with money obtained from the sale of public lands, and from deduction of pay from the members of Congress. The idea, which was ignored, received wide public acclaim eleven years later when it was proposed by Ralph Waldo Emerson. The Prophet continued, "The southern people are hospitable and noble. They will help to rid so free a country of every vestige of slavery whenever they are assured of an equivalent for their property" (Smith, *History of the Church*, 6:207).

DOCTRINE AND COVENANTS 135

DATE OF MARTYRDOM: 27 JUNE 1844
PLACE OF MARTYRDOM: CARTHAGE, ILLINOIS

This is a historical account of the martyrdom of the Prophet Joseph Smith and his brother Hyrum. It was penned by John Taylor who, with Willard Richards, survived that event. Joseph Smith, who stood at the head of the Church and kingdom of God, and his brother Hyrum, who held the office of assistant or associate president of the Church, both holding all the keys of the kingdom, sealed their testimonies with their blood. Two men sealed their testimonies with their lives, and two men— all ordained apostles of the Lord—survived to tell the story. In the providence of the Lord, the ancient law of witnesses had been complied with perfectly.

The martyrdom took place in the jail at Carthage, Illinois, on 27 June 1844. This document is a testimony of the Prophet and his brother and a brief commentary on the greatness of their lives. Written by the spirit of revelation, it will ever stir the souls of all who are of the household of faith.

Briefly, the events leading to the martyrdom were as follows:

Monday, 24 June 1844: "Joseph and Hyrum Smith, accompanied by seventeen friends, started for Carthage, to submit to another trial, under pledge of protection from Gov. Thos. Ford. On the way they received a demand from the governor to surrender the State arms in possession of the Nauvoo Legion; Joseph returned and complied with the request, and then proceeded to Carthage."

Tuesday, 25 June: "Joseph Smith and his brethren surrendered themselves to a constable at Carthage and submitted to a trial, after which they were, contrary to law, remanded to prison."

Wednesday, 26 June: "Gov. Thos. Ford had a long interview with the prisoners in Carthage jail. He renewed his promises of protection and said, if he went to Nauvoo, he would take them with him."

Thursday, 27 June: "Gov. Thos. Ford went to Nauvoo, leaving the prisoners in jail to be guarded by their most bitter enemies, the 'Carthage Greys.' About 5:20 p. m. an armed mob with blackened faces surrounded and entered the jail, and murdered Joseph and Hyrum Smith in cold blood; Apostle John Taylor was severely wounded, while Apostle Willard Richards only received a slight wound on his ear" (Jenson, *Church Chronology*, 25–26).

Joseph and Hyrum Martyred in Carthage Jail
DOCTRINE AND COVENANTS 135:1–2

135:1 *To seal the testimony of this book and the Book of Mormon.* It is our intent to go among those of every nation, kindred, tongue, and people to testify that Joseph Smith was and is the great prophet of the Restoration. We accept it as a principle binding upon all who would bear such a testimony that he who asserts must prove. That is, the burden of evidence rests with the one making the assertion. It is for us to prove our testimony. The proof we bring is both tangible and spiritual. We bring it in the form of two volumes of scripture, one ancient, the other modern, one named the Book of Mormon and the other titled the Doctrine and Covenants. Each contains countless truths that could not have been known to Joseph Smith except by the spirit of revelation. Each in its own way attests perfectly that Joseph Smith was indeed the prophet of the Lord, the man chosen to stand at the head of this the last great dispensation of the gospel to men before the return of him whose gospel it is.

These two books go hand in hand, for each testifies of the truthfulness of the other. It was not intended that they stand alone any more than it was intended that Adam be without Eve, that there be a fall without a redemption, or that the Bible stand independent of the Book of Mormon. It was ordained in the councils of heaven that the Book of Mormon be the book that would gather scattered Israel in the last days. In like manner it was also ordained in those same councils that the Doctrine and Covenants contain the announcement of the restoration of the priesthood and the organization of the Church and kingdom of God once again upon the earth. It is from this book that men learn that the authority to baptize and perform all the ordinances of salvation have been restored. It is from this book that men are to learn of the order of the priesthood and of the manner in which the earthly kingdom of the Lord is to be governed. Neither message is to stand independent of the other. They, with the record of the Jews, were intended to be one in the hand of the messenger of truth, as testimony that the Father, Son, and Holy Ghost are one.

Among the irrevocable decrees of heaven are those laws that guard every man's right to receive the message of salvation through channels ordained by God himself and to have that message attested to by two or more witnesses. Even the testimony of the Son of God himself could not stand alone. This law was well known to the ancients, and it was for this reason that the Pharisees challenged Christ, saying, "Thou bearest record of thyself; thy record is not true." Jesus, John tells us, answered, saying, "Though I bear record of myself, yet my record is true . . . for I am not alone. . . . It is written in your law, that the testimony of two men is true. I am one that bear witness of myself, and the Father that sent me beareth witness of me" (John 8:13–18).

This principle assures us that the heavenly presidency or godhead must consist of three separate persons, two to testify of the third. Teaching this principle to the Nephites, Christ said, "I bear record of the Father, and the Father beareth record of me, and the Holy Ghost beareth record of the Father and me" (3 Nephi 11:32). True it is that all will not be privileged to hear the audible voice of the Father bear witness of the Son, though certainly some have; yet, as Christ explained, his was the doctrine of the Father of which he bore record, "And whoso believeth in me believeth in the Father also; and unto him will the Father bear record of me, for he will visit him with fire and with the Holy Ghost. And thus will the Father bear record of me, and the Holy Ghost will bear record unto him of the Father and me; for the Father, and I, and the Holy Ghost are one [meaning all testify as one]" (3 Nephi 11:35–36).

No man complied more perfectly with the law of witnesses than did the Prophet Joseph Smith. He gave us the Book of Mormon to stand as a second witness of the Bible. He gave us a modern volume of scripture to stand as a second witness of the truths taught by ancient prophets. As they entertained angels, he entertained angels. As they performed miracles, he performed miracles. As they saw visions and penned revelations, he saw visions and penned revelations. As they spoke in the name of the Lord and performed the ordinances of salvation, so he spoke in the name of the Lord and performed the ordinances of salvation. As they sealed their testimonies with their blood, so he sealed his testimony with his blood (v. 6). See commentary on Doctrine and Covenants 6:28; 17).

Martyrdom. The word *martyr* comes from a Greek word meaning "to bear witness," "to be a witness," or "to testify." In a theological sense, it is generally held to mean one who voluntarily submits to death for the Christian faith, but in a broader sense it is used to describe one who has experienced great suffering or death on account of loyalty to the gospel. Critics of the Church like to argue that Joseph Smith was not a martyr because he made an effort to defend himself when he was killed. The purpose of the argument is to avoid giving credence, honor, or respect to the Prophet, who willingly submitted himself to arrest on false charges and went to Carthage knowing he would die there (v. 4). The idea that a true martyr cannot resist an attempt to take his or her life grows out of the false zeal associated with the early Christian era. Many of the so-called martyrs of that day sought death. Their efforts grew out of the apostate notion that the body was to be eschewed, that it was a prison in which the spirit had been confined by the fall of Adam, and that to rid themselves of it was a matchless good. Latter-day Saints reject such theological travesty while granting the title of martyr to those who have experienced great suffering and dangers associated with being true to the faith and who have eventually lost their lives in that cause. See commentary on Doctrine and Covenants 136:39.

The martyrdom of Joseph Smith the Prophet, and Hyrum Smith the Patriarch. In compliance with the divine law of witnesses, it was necessary for the two men who jointly held all of the keys of the kingdom and who stood at the head of the Church to seal their testimonies with their blood. Joseph was the prophet, seer, and revelator and stood at the head. Hyrum stood next to him as the assistant or associate president of the Church. Had the wisdom of God called for Hyrum to survive Carthage, the presidency of the Church would have rested with him. Explaining these principles, President Joseph Fielding Smith taught: "The Prophet Joseph Smith conferred upon Hyrum Smith all the keys, authority and gifts of the priesthood which he, the Prophet, held, and which were formerly held by Oliver Cowdery. The Lord also revealed to Hyrum Smith all that was necessary to make him completely and to the full degree, a witness with his brother Joseph, as a prophet, seer, revelator and president of the Church, and to stand through all time and all eternity at the head of this dispensation with his brother Joseph, a witness for Jesus Christ.

"Thus, we see, Hyrum Smith became a president of the Church with Joseph Smith, which place Oliver Cowdery might have held had he not wavered and fallen from his exalted station. I am firmly of the opinion that had Oliver Cowdery remained true to his covenants and obligations as a witness with Joseph Smith, and retained his authority and place, he, and not Hyrum Smith, would have gone with Joseph Smith as a prisoner and to martyrdom at Carthage.

"The sealing of the testimony through the shedding of blood would not have been complete in the death of the Prophet Joseph Smith alone; it required the death of Hyrum Smith who jointly held the keys of this dispensation. It was needful that these martyrs seal their testimony with their blood, that they 'might be honored and the wicked might be condemned'" (*Doctrines of Salvation*, 1:218–19).

135:2 *John Taylor and Willard Richards, two of the Twelve . . . escaped.* In the providence of the Lord, as it was necessary for two men to seal their testimonies with their blood at Carthage, so it was necessary for two men to escape. Had Joseph and Hyrum been alone then, the only accounts that we would have of the events of that day would have been those written by men with the blood of the Lord's anointed on their hands. Had but one man survived, his testimony would have been refuted. So it was, in the wisdom of him who foreknows all things, that two men, whose reputation for truth was such that it could not be refuted, survived to tell the story. "Dr. Richards' escape was miraculous; he being a very large man, and in the midst of a shower of balls, yet he stood unscathed, with the exception of a ball which grazed the tip end of the lower part of his left ear. His escape fulfilled literally a prophecy which Joseph made over a year previously, that the time would come that the balls would fly around him like hail, and he should see his friends fall on the right and on the left, but that there should not be a hole in his garment" (Smith, *History of the Church*, 6:619).

Preeminent Position of the Prophet Acclaimed
DOCTRINE AND COVENANTS 135:3

135:3 *Joseph Smith . . . has done more, save Jesus only, for the salvation of men . . . than any other man that ever lived.* How Joseph Smith ranks among the prophets, both past and future, we know not, nor do we think there is any particular merit in weighing the faithful labors of one servant of the Lord against those of another. However, we know that among all those chosen of God to labor in his name, none have been privileged to do a labor that would have a greater effect on more of our Father's children than that of the prophet Joseph Smith. Illustrating this point, President Wilford Woodruff commented, "Why, did he [the Lord] call him

[Joseph Smith] into the spirit world? Because he held the keys of this dispensation, not only before he came to this world and while he was in the flesh, but he would hold them throughout the endless ages of eternity (D&C 90:3). He held the keys of past generations—of the millions of people who dwelt on the earth in the fifty generations that had passed and gone who had not the law of the gospel, who never saw a prophet, never saw an Apostle, never heard the voice of any man who was inspired of God and had power to teach them the gospel of Christ, and to organize the church of Christ on earth. He went to unlock the prison doors to these people, as far as they would receive his testimony, and the Saints of God who dwell in the flesh will build temples unto the name of the Lord, and enter these temples and perform certain ordinances for the redemption of the dead. This was the work of Joseph the prophet in the spirit world" (Conference Report, April 1880, 8–9).

Joseph Smith stands at the head of the gospel dispensation that may include the majority of the premortal host. More people will learn of Christ and his gospel by missionaries who trace both their commission to teach and their understanding of Christ through the Prophet Joseph Smith than will be the case in any other dispensation or with any other prophet who ever lived.

The Innocent Blood of Joseph and Hyrum Testifies of the Divinity of the Restored Gospel
DOCTRINE AND COVENANTS 135:4–7

135:7 *The innocent blood of all the martyrs under the altar that John saw.* Reference is to the vision seen by John the Revelator in the book of Revelation. He saw under the altar of the temple "the souls of them that were slain for the word of God, and for the testimony which they held: and they cried with a loud voice, saying, How long, O Lord, holy and true, dost thou not judge and avenge our blood on them that dwell on the earth? And white robes were given unto every one of them; and it was said unto them, that they should rest yet for a little season, until their fellowservants also and their brethren, that should be killed as they were, should be fulfilled" (Revelation 6:9–11).

John sees the blood of those who died for Christ as being—like the blood of the sacrificial lambs—Christ's blood, for these were his servants and acted in his name. As he was to be honored with crowns of glory, so will they be honored.

DOCTRINE AND COVENANTS 136

DATE: 14 JANUARY 1847
PLACE: OMAHA NATION, WEST BANK OF THE MISSOURI RIVER,
NEAR COUNCIL BLUFFS, IOWA

The autumn of 1846 found fifteen thousand exiled Latter-day Saints making temporary homes at what was known as Winter Quarters of the Camp of Israel, on the banks of the Missouri River in the Omaha Nation, near where the cities of Omaha and Council Bluffs now stand. They had been driven from Nauvoo, the city they had built, their Prophet and his beloved brother Hyrum had been killed by a mob while held captive in Carthage Jail, and their temple had been burned. They sought a place of peace and refuge. Before his death, Joseph Smith had told them that they would only find peace in the Rocky Mountains, where they were destined to become a mighty people.

This revelation was given to Brigham Young who, as the president of the Quorum of the Twelve at the death of the Prophet and his brother Hyrum, was the man responsible to lead the Lord's people. The revelation was received at a meeting held at Heber C. Kimball's home. At this meeting the manner of the westward migration was considered, and President Young received this revelation, known as the "Word and Will of God concerning the Camp of Israel."

How the Camp of Israel Was to Be Organized for Its Westward Journey
DOCTRINE AND COVENANTS 136:1–16

136:1–11 Salvation is a covenant affair. We can no more be saved alone than the Saints could have journeyed west and conquered the wilderness acting singly. Their strength came in a unity of faith and purpose, their covenant was not only with their God but also with each other. Such has ever been the system of salvation among the Lord's people. Thus, the spirit of the instruction given here contains the reminder of the importance of caring for "the widows, the fatherless, and the families of those who have gone into the army," that none will have cause to feel neglected or forgotten by their God. That concern for each other brought with it a strength and spiritual power unknown to other companies and groups that went west.

136:1 *The Camp of Israel.* With little more to clothe themselves in than the faith known to their ancient father Abraham, his children assembled from the nations of the earth and readied themselves for their march into the wilderness. They sought a modern Sinai, the mountain of the Lord's house, where they too could hear the voice of the God of Israel and be endowed with power. As the body of Joseph, son of Jacob, was carried before their ancient counterparts as they left Egypt, so they were lead by the spirit of the man to whom Moses had committed the keys of the gathering of Israel and the leading of the ten tribes from the lands of the north. To him the Lord had said, "I will raise up unto my people a man, who shall lead them like as Moses led the children of Israel. For ye are the children of Israel, and of the seed of Abraham, and ye must needs be led out of bondage by power, and with a stretched-out arm." So it was that Brigham would become their leader, the modern Moses, and to those who followed him the Lord said, "And as your fathers were led at the first, even so shall the redemption of Zion be. Therefore, let not your hearts faint, for I say not unto you as I said unto your fathers: Mine angel shall go up before you, but not my presence. But I say unto you: Mine angels shall go up before you, and also my presence, and in time ye shall possess the goodly land" (D&C 103:16–20).

All that here took place had been known to the ancient counterparts of modern Israel who gave prophetic description of it. We cite the words of Jeremiah:

"For there shall be a day, that the watchmen upon the mount Ephraim shall cry, Arise ye, and let us go up to Zion unto the Lord our God.

"For thus saith the Lord; Sing with gladness for Jacob, and shout among the chief of the nations: publish ye, praise ye, and say, O Lord, save thy people, the remnant of Israel.

"Behold, I will bring them from the north country, and gather them from the coasts of the earth, and with them the blind and the lame, the woman with child and her that travaileth with child together: a great company shall return thither.

"They shall come with weeping, and with supplications, will I lead them: I will cause them to walk by the rivers of waters in a straight way, wherein they shall not stumble: for I am a father to Israel, and Ephraim is my firstborn.

"Hear the word of the Lord, O ye nations, and declare it in the isles afar off, and say, He that scattered Israel will gather him, and keep him, as a shepherd doth his flock.

"For the Lord hath redeemed Jacob, and ransomed him from the hand of him that was stronger than he.

"Therefore they shall come and sing in the height of Zion, and shall flow together to the goodness of the Lord, for wheat, and for wine, and for oil, and for the young of the flock and of the herd: and their soul shall be as a watered garden; and they shall not sorrow any more at all.

"Then shall the virgin rejoice in the dance, both young men and old together: for I will turn their mourning into joy, and will comfort them, and make them rejoice from their sorrow.

"And I will satiate the soul of the priests with fatness, and my people shall be satisfied with my goodness, saith the Lord (Jeremiah 31:6–14).

136:2 *With a covenant and promise.* Of the Lord's promise that latter-day Israel would "walk by the rivers of waters in a straight way," Elder LeGrand Richards said, "In their trek from Nauvoo across the great American desert to the Great Salt Lake Valley, the Saints traveled about six hundred miles (1,000 kilometers) along the North Platte River, as Jeremiah had seen" (*Marvelous Work and a Wonder*, 225–26). To this Bruce R. McConkie added a spiritual interpretation, saying, "The way is straight and the course is narrow, but the Lord shall be a father to all who heed the call of Ephraim and walk therein" (*Millennial Messiah*, 195). It was not a series of emigrant wagon trains going west to find and cultivate new lands of which Jeremiah spoke. Rather it was the gathering remnant of Israel coming together from the various nations of the earth in fulfillment of the promises made to their ancient fathers. It was a people seeking a place of refuge where they could build a temple to their God.

136:3 *Let the companies be organized.* To Moses the Lord had said, "Thou shalt provide out of all the people able men, such as fear God, men of truth, hating covetousness; and place such over them, to be rulers of thousands, and rulers of hundreds, rulers of fifties, and rulers of tens" (Exodus 18:21; see also D&C 136:12–14).

136:4 *The ordinances of the Lord.* Reference is not only to rites but rather to all the commandments and revelations the Lord has given.

136:8 *The poor, the widows, the fatherless.* These have the same claim on the blessings of heaven as the physically strong and financially able. The strength of each company was to be found in its concern for those less able. They would go together or they would not go.

Into the army. Twelve days after the arrival of President Brigham Young on the banks of the Missouri River, Captain James Allen of the United States Army arrived at Mount Pisgah with a call from the government for four or five companies of volunteers to serve in the Mexican War. He was advised to go to Council Bluffs to see President Young, with whom he met on 30 June 1846.

President Young assured him that the volunteers would be furnished. A battalion of five hundred men was raised. Though not called upon to fight, the Mormon Battalion acquitted themselves honorably, and the pay for their service, which went to their families going west was as manna from heaven.

136:10 *Every man use all his influence.* This was the true principle of consecration. All "influence," that is all property, all talents, all strength, all that a soul had were to be enlisted in the cause of Zion.

136:12 *Ezra T. Benson and Erastus Snow.* Six months before this revelation was received, Ezra T. Benson had been called by Brigham Young to fill a vacancy in the Quorum of the Twelve. Thirty-six years of age at this time, he was a Massachusetts native who had followed impressions to move west. He and his wife learned of the Church while in Quincy, Illinois, and were baptized in 1840. Six months later he was called to serve in the presidency of the Quincy Stake.

Erastus Snow, then twenty-eight years of age, would, with Orson Pratt, who had baptized him at the age of fourteen, become the first of the vanguard company of pioneers to enter the Great Salt Lake Valley. He was called to the Quorum of the Twelve a month after this revelation was received.

136:13 *Orson Pratt and Wilford Woodruff.* Orson Pratt, thirty-five years of age, had been ordained to the Quorum of the Twelve at the age of twenty-three. He is revered as one of the great intellects of the Church and as one of its greatest missionaries.

Wilford Woodruff, destined to become the fourth president of the Church, was ordained an apostle in April 1839. He stands uncontested as the greatest missionary of our dispensation.

136:14 *Amasa Lyman and George A. Smith.* Amasa Lyman, baptized at nineteen years of age, traveled seven hundred miles to meet the

Prophet Joseph Smith. He was called as an apostle in August 1842 and served as a counselor to the Prophet the year prior to Joseph's death. He was thirty-four years of age at this time.

Called as an apostle at the age of twenty-two, George A. Smith was a first cousin of the Prophet's. He would later serve as a counselor to Brigham Young. He was thirty years of age when this revelation was given.

The Saints Are Commanded to Live Gospel Standards
DOCTRINE AND COVENANTS 136:17–27

136:18 *Zion shall be redeemed in my own due time.* Reference is to the New Jerusalem and the temple to be built there. As certainly as we have now gone back to Nauvoo to rebuild our temple there, so the Saints will return to Jackson County, Missouri, to build a temple to their God and to fulfill all the associated promises. As Joseph Fielding Smith said, "When the Lord gets ready for it to be accomplished, he will command his people, and the work will be done" (*Doctrines of Salvation*, 3:79).

136:24 *Cease drunkenness.* Though the Word of Wisdom was given in February of 1833, it was given as wise counsel and not as a commandment. It was only after the Saints had come west that it was accepted as a commandment binding upon them.

The Saints Are to Sing, Dance, Pray, and Learn Wisdom
DOCTRINE AND COVENANTS 136:28–33

136:30 *Fear not thine enemies for they are in mine hands.* Counseling the Saints in their grief at the death of their beloved Prophet, Brigham Young said on behalf of the Twelve, "We are sensible that the account of the death of the Prophet and Patriarch of the church will be painful to your hearts: it is to ours. We feel and mourn their loss, but they have sealed their testimony with their blood; they have not counted their lives as dear unto themselves as the lives of the church; they have died in the Lord and their works will follow them.

"The eyes of the Lord are upon those who have shed the blood of the Lord's anointed, and he will judge them with a righteous judgment" (Smith, *History of the Church*, 7:199).

Prophets Are Slain That They Might Be Honored and the Wicked Condemned
DOCTRINE AND COVENANTS 136:34–42

136:34 *Thy brethren have rejected you . . . even the nation that has driven you out.* As Christ was rejected by his own, so Joseph Smith and the Latter-day Saint people were rejected by those who should have been their brothers in Christ. They would now be forced outside the territory of the United States in the hopes that they would perish in a desert wasteland.

136:35 *Now cometh the day of their calamity.* This prophecy finds at least partial fulfillment in the Civil War, which began fifteen years later.

136:39 *It was needful that he should seal his testimony with his blood.* The chorus of the hymn "Praise to the Man," written by William W. Phelps, responds in part to the question as to why it was necessary for the Prophet to die:

> Hail to the Prophet, ascended to heaven!
> Traitors and tyrants now fight him in vain.
> Mingling with Gods, he can plan for his brethren;
> Death cannot conquer the hero again.
> (*Hymns*, no. 27)

Having established a dispensation of the gospel here and having conferred all of the keys, powers, and authorities that he held upon the Twelve, the Prophet in his death then took those same powers with him into the world of the spirits where he commenced a dispensation of the gospel there (D&C 90:2–3). Teaching this principle, Charles W. Penrose said, "When the Prophet Joseph and his brother Hyrum were slain for the testimony of Jesus it was in the providence of God; it was with His permission. They went to open the door of the kingdom in the spirit world, and thus a marvelous work and a wonder has begun there also. When we get there we will find out the magnitude of it; for we will see that the Elders of Zion who have tabernacled in the flesh are laboring there, under the direction of him who holds the keys of the last dispensation, and the Gospel is being preached to millions upon millions of spirits, and a far greater work is to be accomplished there than among men in the flesh" (Conference Report, April 1902, 52–53).

DOCTRINE AND COVENANTS 137

DATE: 21 JANUARY 1836
PLACE: KIRTLAND TEMPLE, KIRTLAND, OHIO

This revelation was received in the west school room on the third floor of the Kirtland Temple. Church leaders from Kirtland and Missouri had assembled to be anointed as part of the endowment of power to be bestowed upon the "first elders" in connection with the dedication of the temple. Two separate meetings were held the evening of 21 January, the latter continuing into the morning hours. During the first meeting, Joseph Smith, his father, and his brother Hyrum, along with members of the First Presidency (Sidney Rigdon and Frederick G. Williams and Oliver Cowdery, associate president of the Church), the presidency of the Church in Missouri (David Whitmer, William W. Phelps, and John Whitmer), the bishoprics in Kirtland and Missouri, and the Prophet's scribe (Warren Parrish), anointed each other with "holy oil" and offered prayers that the anointing blessings would be accepted. "The second meeting was not unlike the first, except that those being anointed were members of the Church high councils in Kirtland and Missouri. Although visions and spiritual manifestations were witnessed during both cere-monies, section 137 was received during the first anointing session" (Cook, *Revelations*, 303).

Oliver Cowdery made the following entry in his diary for the day: "Thursday, the 21st, this morning, at 15 minutes past nine, my little daughter is 5 months old. O Lord, I thank thee that thou hast thus been merciful and spared my only child. At about three o'clock P.M. I assembled in our office garret, having all things prepared for the occasion, with presi-dents Joseph Smith, jr. F. G. Williams, Sidney Rigdon Hyrum Smith, David Whitmer, John Whitmer and elder John Corrill, and washed our bodies with pure water before the Lord, preparatory to the annointing with the holy oil. After we were washed, our bodies were perfumed with a sweet smelling oderous wash. At evening the presidents of the Church, with the two bishops and their counsellors, and elder Warren Parrish, met in the presidents' room, the high cou[n]cils of Kirtland and Zion in their rooms. Those named in the first room were annointed with the same kind of oil and in the man[ner] that were Moses and Aaron, and those who stood before the Lord in ancient days, and those in the other rooms with annointing oil prepared for them. The glorious scene is too great to be described in this book, therefore, I only say, that the heavens were opened to many, and great and marvelous things were shown" (Arrington, "Oliver Cowdery's Kirtland," 418–19).

Though consisting of but ten verses this is one of the most significant revelations in the Doctrine and Covenants. It lays the doctrinal foundation upon which rests the whole concept of our labors in behalf of our kindred dead. It clearly separates this doctrine from any notion that the living can neglect their responsibilities in this life, believing that they can attend to them or have someone else attend to them when they have died.

The Prophet Sees His Brother Alvin in the Celestial Kingdom

DOCTRINE AND COVENANTS 137:1–6

137:1 *The heavens were opened upon us.* Virtually every revelation received by Joseph Smith and recorded in the Doctrine and Covenants was received in the presence of others. In this instance those present included the Prophet's father, Joseph Smith Sr., who was the Church patriarch; the counselors in the First Presidency; the presidency of the stake in Missouri; the bishoprics from Kirtland and Missouri; and Warren Parrish, the Prophet's scribe.

Whether in the body or out I cannot tell. This was the language used by the apostle Paul to describe a vision in which he also was permitted to see the celestial kingdom (2 Corinthians 12:2–3). For Joseph Smith it was not an out of body experience and we would suppose it was not for Paul either. Apparently what is being described transcends normal mortal experience. For instance, Moses described his experience on the high mountain, saying, "Now mine own eyes have beheld God; but not my natural, but my spiritual eyes, for my natural eyes could not have beheld; for I should have withered and died in his presence; but his glory was upon me; and I beheld his face, for I was transfigured before him" (Moses 1:11).

137:5 *I saw . . . my Father and my mother: my brother Alvin.* In this most remarkable vision, the Prophet was not shown things as they were in the celestial kingdom but rather as they yet would be. This would have been immediately evident to him as he saw in that vision his own father and mother. As already noted, his father was present in the room with him when the vision was received, and his father and mother lived for some years after this event. Each of the persons shown in the vision appears to have been deliberately chosen to emphasize that salvation is a family affair and that it centers in the promises made to our ancient fathers. In addition to seeing the Father and the Son, the Prophet saw Adam, the father of all humankind; Father Abraham, the father of the faithful; and his own father and mother reunited with his brother Alvin, who had died twelve years earlier at age twenty-five.

137:6 *And marveled how it was that he had obtained an inheritance in that kingdom.* To this point, 21 January 1836, so far as we have record, Joseph Smith had been taught nothing about the doctrine of salvation for the dead. The thought that his brother Alvin, who died without baptism, could be in the celestial kingdom caused him to "marvel."

A proper understanding of gospel principles requires that they be learned in their proper order. It is for the living to save themselves before they attempt to save the dead. The idea that the living can somehow defer obedience to the laws and ordinances of the gospel to some future world has no place in the gospel of Jesus Christ.

So that no such notion could be a part of his thinking, Joseph Smith was carefully taught while translating the Book of Mormon that mortality is the time appointed by God for people to accept the gospel. Only those who do not have the opportunity to receive its fullness will be granted that opportunity in the world of spirits.

Joseph Smith had been carefully tutored by the prophets of the Book of Mormon. He understood that "this life is the time for men to prepare to meet God," the time for them "to perform their labors," and that we can "not procrastinate the day" of our repentance until death, "for after this day of life, which is given us to prepare for eternity, behold, if we do not improve our time while in this life, then cometh the night of darkness wherein there can be no labor performed" (Alma 34:32–33).

In the book of Helaman, we learn that Samuel the Lamanite testified against the Nephites, saying, "But behold, your days of probation are past; ye have procrastinated the day of your salvation until it is everlastingly too late, and your destruction is made sure; yea, for ye have sought all the days of your lives for that which ye could not obtain; and ye have sought for happiness in doing iniquity, which thing is contrary to the nature of that righteousness which is in our great and Eternal Head" (Helaman 13:38). The Savior is recorded as saying, "Come unto me and be ye saved; for verily I say unto you, that except ye shall keep my commandments, which I have commanded you *at this time*, ye shall in no case enter into the kingdom of heaven" (3 Nephi 12:20; emphasis added).

To gather Israel the second time. This text teaches that to be "gathered" is to be baptized, or to become a member of the restored Church. By quoting his father, Nephi taught the same principle: "After the house of Israel should be scattered they should be gathered together again; or, in fine, after the Gentiles had received the fulness of the Gospel, the natural branches of the olive-tree, or the remnants of the house of Israel, should be grafted in, or come to the knowledge of the true Messiah, their Lord and their Redeemer"(1 Nephi 10:14). "They shall be restored to the true church and fold of God" (2 Nephi 9:2).

The Doctrine of Salvation for the Dead Revealed
DOCTRINE AND COVENANTS 137:7–9

137:7–9 In these verses the principles upon which the doctrine of salvation for the dead rests are announced for the first time in this dispensation. They are: first, that the doctrine applies only to those who "died without a knowledge" of the gospel; second, that God must read the hearts of those concerned and affirm that had the gospel come to them in mortality they would have accepted it; and third, that God must judge that not only would they have accepted the gospel but that they would have done so "with all their hearts," meaning that they would have endured valiantly and faithfully to the end. These principles accord perfectly with the promise of Peter that those who receive the gospel in the spirit world must do so in such a manner that they "might be judged according to men in the flesh" (1 Peter 4:6), which is to say that the price in faith and works to receive the gospel in the spirit world is the same as the price appended to receiving it in mortality.

The question could well be asked as to why it was that Alvin would be chosen to represent these truths? The answer is that he is the perfect example of the kind of person to whom these principles apply. Alvin died in November of 1823. His passing had been a matter of considerable sorrow to the Smith family and to the young woman to whom he was engaged. Their wounded souls had been cut to the core at his funeral by the unfeeling remarks of the Presbyterian minister who had consigned

Alvin to hell because he had not been baptized or involved in that church.

Despite his relative youth, Alvin was a man of unusual spiritual propensity. Before his death, he called each of his brothers and sisters in turn to his bedside and gave them a parting admonition. To his eighteen-year-old brother, Joseph, he said: "Be a good boy, and do everything that lies in your power to obtain the record [the Book of Mormon]. Be faithful in receiving instruction and in keeping every commandment that is given you" (Smith, *History of Joseph Smith*, 1996, 116). Mother Smith stated that "Alvin had ever manifested a greater zeal and anxiety, if it were possible, than any of the rest with regard to the record which had been shown to Joseph, and he always showed the most intense interest concerning the matter. With this before our minds, we could not endure to hear or say one word upon that subject, for the moment that Joseph spoke of the record it would immediately bring Alvin to our minds with all his kindness, his affection, his zeal, and piety. And when we looked to his place and realized that he was gone from it, to return no more in this life, we all wept with one accord over our irretrievable loss, and we could 'not be comforted, because he was not'" (Smith, *History of Joseph Smith*, 1996, 119).

Nearly twenty years later, Joseph Smith recounted his feelings at the time of Alvin's death, saying: "I remember well the pangs of sorrow that swelled my youthful bosom and almost burst my tender heart when he died. He was the oldest and noblest of my father's family. . . . He lived without spot from the time he was a child. . . . He was one of the soberest of men, and when he died the angel of the Lord visited him in his last moments" (*History of the Church*, 5:126–27). See commentary on Doctrine and Covenants 10:67; 18:4.

137:9 *I, the Lord, will judge all men according to their works, according to the desires of their hearts.* The scales of justice used in the realms of heaven can be depended upon to render that perfect equity and judgment known only to an all-wise God. Our works will be placed in one of the pans of balance and the desires of our heart in the other. Where our works are lacking because of circumstances beyond our control, the desires of our hearts can compensate. For instance, if someone did not marry in the temple because the opportunity to do so was not afforded but in the judgment of God that person would have taken that opportunity with all his or her heart, then the scales are balanced. That individual is rewarded as if he or she had complied with the commandment. On the other hand, impressive works may hide evil desires left unfulfilled only because the opportunity to act on them did not come. Again, the reward will accord with the desires of the heart. Though men may deceive each other, none will deceive God. Nor will there be so much as a single soul from one end of eternity to the other who will be denied the blessings of heaven because of circumstances beyond his or her control.

Little Children Who Die Before the Years of Accountability Are Saved in the Kingdom of Heaven
DOCTRINE AND COVENANTS 137:10

137:10 *All children who die . . . are saved in the celestial kingdom.* Little children shall live! What more perfect evidence of an omniscient and loving God than the doctrine which proclaims that little children who die are heirs of celestial glory! From these no blessing shall be withheld and to such no opportunities will be denied. The testimony of the Book of Mormon and the latter-day oracles is certain and clear: children who die before the age of accountability shall come forth in the resurrection of the just and go on to enjoy all of the privileges associated with eternal life and the family unit.

As a result of his vision of the celestial kingdom, the Prophet Joseph Smith recorded, "I also beheld that all children who die before they arrive at the years of accountability are saved in the celestial kingdom of heaven" (D&C 137:10). This idea was not entirely new to the Prophet, for he had learned from the Book of Mormon and previous revelations of the Lord's disposition in regard to the status of children. An angel explained to King Benjamin that "the infant perisheth not that dieth in his infancy" (Mosiah 3:18). After having described the nature of those who come forth in the first resurrection, Abinadi said simply, "And little children also have eternal life" (Mosiah 15:25). A revelation given in September of 1830 specified that "little children are redeemed from the foundation of the world through mine Only Begotten" (D&C 29:46).

DOCTRINE AND COVENANTS 138

DATE: 3 OCTOBER 1918
PLACE: SALT LAKE CITY, UTAH

This revelation, generally known as the vision of the redemption of the dead, was given to Joseph F. Smith, sixth president of the Church, the day before the October conference of 1918. It was received in the Beehive House, where the president of the Church and his family lived. After the conference he dictated it to his son and namesake, Joseph Fielding Smith Jr., then a member of the Quorum of the Twelve, who in turn became the tenth president of the Church. On 31 October it was submitted to President Smith's counselors, the Quorum of the Twelve, and the patriarch, and was unanimously accepted by them. It was not, however, added to the canon of scripture until 1978. Before that time it had been available to the Saints for many years in the book *Gospel Doctrine*, a compilation taken from President Smith's sermons.

President Smith had been ill for the five months before the October 1918 general conference and undoubtedly had pondered his own passing (which took place the following month) and wondered about the nature of the ministry that would be his in the spirit world. In January of that year he had witnessed what seemed the untimely death of his son Hyrum Mack Smith, then only forty-five years of age and also a member of the Quorum of the Twelve. This was a source of grief to President Smith, who also sought understanding about why Hyrum had been taken and the nature of his labors in the world of spirits.

In the opening session of that conference, President Joseph F. Smith said, "I will not, I dare not, attempt to enter upon many things that are resting upon my mind this morning, and I shall postpone until some future time, the Lord being willing, my attempt to tell you some of the things that are in my mind, and that dwell in my heart. I have not lived alone these five months. I have dwelt in the spirit of prayer, of supplication, of faith and of determination; and I have had my communication with the Spirit of the Lord continuously" (Conference Report, October 1918, 2).

Peter's References to Christ's Visit to the Spirits in Prison
DOCTRINE AND COVENANTS 138:1–10

138:3 *Love made manifest by the Father and the Son.* In all things the restored gospel outreaches the gospel known to historical Christianity. Where they speak of being saved by the grace of Christ, a more perfect understanding embraces the knowledge that we are saved by the grace of both the Father and Son. By the grace of the Father we were born as his spirit offspring, given the gift of agency, and provided with a plan whereby we might obtain the fulness of all that he has. By the grace of Christ, we can obtain a remission of sins, be resurrected, and return to the presence of our Father.

138:5 *The writings of Peter.* One of the most difficult theological questions facing the historical Christian world is what becomes of those who died without the opportunity to accept Christ while they lived. What has to be of particular interest to Latter-day Saints is the historical Christians' near universal refusal to give credence to the references made by Peter to the visit of Christ to the world of the spirits and his statement that those in the spirit world are to be judged according to men in the flesh. They also refuse a place in their thought to the many historical references to the faith of the meridian Saints that the faithful in this life would be involved in teaching the gospel to those who died without hearing it.

Early commentary on the statement in Hebrews that "they without us should not be made perfect" (Hebrews 11:40) holds that the passage referred to the Old Testament Saints who were trapped in Hades awaiting the help of their New Testament counterparts and that Christ held the keys that would "open the doors of the Underworld to the faithful souls there" (MacCulloch, *Harrowing of Hell*, 48–49). Significantly, Justin Martyr in his work *Dialogue with Trypho* cites an apocryphon which he claims was deleted from Jeremiah but is still found in some synagogue copies. It read: "The Lord God remembered His dead people of Israel who lay in the graves; and He descended to preach to them His own salvation" (MacCulloch, *Harrowing of Hell*, 84–85.) Irenaeus is also recorded as saying, "The Lord descended to the parts under the earth, announcing to them also the good news of his coming, there being remission of sins for such as believe on him" (Irenaeus, *Against Heresies*, 499).

Another of the early Christian documents that linked the writings of Peter on the teaching of the gospel in the spirit world with those of Paul on baptism for the dead (1 Corinthians 15:29) is the "Shepherd of Hermas" which states that "these, the apostles and the teachers who preached the name of the Son of God, after they had fallen asleep in the power and faith of the Son of God, preached also to them that had fallen asleep before them, and themselves gave unto them the seal of the preaching. Therefore they went down with them into the water, and came up again. But these went down alive [and again came up alive]; whereas the others that had fallen asleep before them, went down dead and came up alive. So by their means they were quickened into life, and came to the full knowledge of the name of the Son of God" (Lightfoot, *Apostolic Fathers*, 232).

Christ's Ministry among the Spirits in Paradise
DOCTRINE AND COVENANTS 138:12–24

138:12–14 These three verses, which constitute two sentences, provide greater understanding of the faith of those who lived before the coming of Christ than can be found in the voluminous writings of the world's best Old Testament scholars. By revelation we learn that, when gathered together, the faithful Saints in Old Testament times constituted an "innumerable company," which in turn suggests that the message of salvation was much more extensively known among the nations of the earth than has been thought. We also have it affirmed for us that they knew of Christ and were faithful to their testimony of him, for which testimony they suffered tribulation. Further, we are told that they knew Christ to be "the Son of God" and the source of their redemption from the effects of Adam's fall. We learn that they fully understood the symbolism and purpose of the law of sacrifice. Further still, we learn that they understood that salvation came to them through the grace of God, whom they knew to be their Father and through the grace of his Son, Jesus Christ, who was the Only Begotten of the Father in the flesh. None of these truths can be understood from the Old Testament as it has come to us, none of them are a part of the understanding of the scholarly world, yet all of them are fundamental to an understanding of the fulness of the gospel that we as Latter-day Saints know these ancient Saints to have had.

138:12 *Gathered together in one place.* The place referred to is paradise. The meeting could be likened to a general conference of the Church, one to which only those who died in the faith are admitted.

An innumerable company. All faithful and righteous souls who had lived from the days of Adam to the time of Christ's death were assembled. Speaking more than a hundred years earlier, Alma said, "There were many, exceedingly great many, who were made pure and entered into the rest of the Lord their God" (Alma 13:12). They are spoken of in verse 18 as a "vast multitude."

138:15 *Joy and gladness . . . rejoicing.* The message of salvation, or gospel of Jesus Christ, often referred to as "glad tidings," has ever been attended by a spirit of joy and gladness. It was greeted by us and our kindred spirits in the councils of heaven with songs of praise and shouts of joy (Job 38:7). Jacob, as spokesman for all who have carefully pondered the goodness of the gospel, expressed such praise as, "O the wisdom of God, his mercy and grace!" "O how great the goodness of our God," and "O how great the plan of our God!" (2 Nephi 9:8, 10, 13).

138:16 *Awaiting the advent of the Son of God . . . to declare their redemption.* Redemption from the bands of death. See Doctrine and Covenants 138:18.

138:17 *Its perfect frame.* Only Alma 11:45 can rival this text as a definition of resurrection. Alma explains, "Now, behold, I have spoken unto you concerning the death of the mortal body, And also concerning the resurrection of the mortal body. I say unto you that this mortal body is raised to an immortal body, that is from death, even from the first death unto life, that they can die no more; their spirits uniting with their bodies, never to be divided; thus the whole becoming spiritual and immortal, that they can no more see corruption."

138:18 *The chains of death.* All who descend from Adam, no matter how many generations removed, must die. All are subject to the effects of his fall, and in death the righteous as well as the wicked are said to go to "spirit prison" because they are yet to be redeemed from their fallen state. Thus, scripture refers to the righteous dead as being subject to the "bands of death" (v. 16) or "the chains of death," and as being "captives" waiting the day of their "liberty."

Declaring liberty to the captives. As Jesus began his mortal ministry, he quoted the great prophet Isaiah who states that Christ would "bind up the brokenhearted," "proclaim liberty to the captives," and open "the prison to them that are bound" (Isaiah 61:1). It is significant that Jesus proclaimed his mission as one that extended beyond death. He was called not only to heal and comfort the living but "to comfort all that mourn" (Isaiah 61:2), including the captives of the spirit world.

138:19 *He preached unto them the everlasting gospel.* Having just completed a week of unmatched drama with which he could have held his listeners spellbound, Christ chose simply to teach the "everlasting gospel." To the likes of Adam, Enoch, Isaiah, Jeremiah, Nephi, Jacob, and Alma, he taught the doctrine of "resurrection and the redemption of mankind from the fall."

138:20–21 Among the disembodied spirits, only those who had proven themselves true and faithful, only those who had complied with the laws and ordinances of the gospel while in the flesh, were among those assembled to greet Christ and to be taught by him. Such is the pattern. The resurrected Christ did not appear to Caiaphas and the Sanhedrin or to the Jews who jeered and rejected him or to the soldiers who mocked and ridiculed him. Rather, he appeared to his humble followers in the upper room and later, Paul tells us, to above 500 of the faithful in Galilee (1 Corinthians 15:6). His appearance to those in the New World was only to the faithful, for the wicked were destroyed before his visitations there. Such we understand will be the case until that great and dreadful day when, clothed in red, he comes to take vengeance upon the wicked (D&C 133:48; 138:37).

138:24 *Sang praises unto his holy name.* From premortal councils to the splendor of the eternal worlds, the song of the righteous will be one of praise for their God.

The Beginning of Missionary Work in the Spirit World
DOCTRINE AND COVENANTS 138:25–37

138:27 *The brief time intervening between the crucifixion and his resurrection.* From the time Christ "gave up the ghost" on Friday afternoon (Mark 15:37) to the time of his resurrection on Sunday morning—three days as the Jews measure time—would have spanned thirty-eight to forty hours.

138:30 *He organized his forces and appointed messengers.* It is a sacred privilege to teach the gospel. It is a right that one does not arrogate to oneself. To those of our dispensation, the Lord said, "Again I say unto you, that it shall not be given to any one to go forth to preach my gospel, or to build up my church, except he be ordained by some one who has authority" (D&C 42:11). This principle is as eternal as the gospel itself.

Similarly, none could lay claim to the gospel without a legal administrator. This too is as eternal as the gospel. Thus, though there was a great host, including prophets and righteous men in the world of spirits, men who had preached the gospel while in the flesh with great power and force, before the arrival of the Savior none had been commissioned to take the gospel to those who did not have it.

138:31 *To declare the acceptable day of the Lord.* This is a phrase from Isaiah (Isaiah 61:2), which could be rendered "the time of the Lord's favor," which we would understand to mean the day in which his promise is to be fulfilled.

Unto all who would repent of their sins. Repentance is as much a part of the gospel in the spirit world as it is in mortality.

138:32 *Thus the gospel was preached to those who had died.* Both those who died without hearing the gospel in mortality and those who rejected the words of the prophets while in the flesh are to hear the gospel in the spirit world. That is to say the gospel will be taught to all who will listen. Those who had the opportunity to receive the gospel in this life (God being their judge) and who rejected it, may accept it in the spirit world to their blessing but not to their exaltation (see commentary on D&C 76:73–74; 137:7–9). This is not to suggest that there is no repentance in the spirit world. This revelation states that "the dead who repent will be redeemed, through obedience to the ordinances of the house of God. And after they have paid the penalty of their transgressions, and are washed clean, shall receive a reward according to their works, for they are heirs of salvation" (D&C 138:58–59).

138:33–34 Death makes no change in gospel principles. The plan of salvation is the same for the living as it is for the dead. To know the gospel in our second estate is to know the gospel in the spirit world and in the resurrection. Our revelations promise that "whatever principle of intelligence we attain unto in this life, it will rise with us in the resurrection" (D&C 130:18).

The question is often asked as to whether it is harder or easier to accept the gospel in the spirit world. If those in that sphere are to be "judged according to men in the flesh," it must of necessity require the same degree of faith and courage to accept and live the gospel there as here. For those who have accorded their lives with gospel principles, accepting the gospel will be a natural step in their progression. Those whose lives were devoted to debauchery, wickedness, and warring against light and truth will have the greatest of difficulty in changing their course.

138:37 *That they might carry the message of redemption unto all the dead.* Relative to the manner in which the gospel will be taught in the spirit world, President Joseph F. Smith explained, "Now, among all these millions of spirits that have lived on the earth and have passed away, from generation to generation, since the beginning of the world, without the knowledge of the gospel—among them you may count that at least one-half are women. Who is going to preach the gospel to the women? Who is going to carry the testimony of Jesus Christ to the hearts of the women who have passed away without a knowledge of the gospel? Well, to my mind, it is a simple thing. These good sisters who have been set apart, ordained to the work, called to it, authorized by the authority of the Holy Priesthood to minister for their sex, in the House of God for the living and for the dead, will be fully authorized and empowered to preach the gospel and minister to the women while the elders and prophets are preaching it to the men. The things we experience here are typical of the things of God and the life beyond us. There is a great similarity between God's purposes as manifested here and his purposes as carried out in his presence and kingdom. Those who are authorized to preach the gospel here and are appointed here to do that work will not be idle after they have passed away, but will continue to exercise the rights that they obtained here under the Priesthood of the Son of God to minister for the salvation of those who have died without a knowledge of the truth" (*Gospel Doctrine*, 461).

Even Paradise Is a Bondage to the Righteous Dead
DOCTRINE AND COVENANTS 138:38–52

138:50 *A bondage.* "The elements are eternal, and spirit and element, inseparably connected, receive a fulness of joy; and when separated, man cannot receive a fulness of joy" (D&C 93:33–34).

A Second Vision of the Spirit World, Including Great Leaders from Our Dispensation
DOCTRINE AND COVENANTS 138:53–60

138:53–60 Having witnessed the visit of the Savior to the world of spirits while his body lay in the borrowed tomb of Joseph of Arimathaea, the scene now changes so that President Joseph F. Smith is invited to view things in the spirit world as they were at the time he received this vision in October of 1918. There is no justification in the supposition that premortal spirits (Joseph Smith, Hyrum Smith, Brigham Young, John Taylor, and Wilford Woodruff) mingled with the disembodied spirits during the visit of Christ to them in the meridian of time. Those described as being present included the faithful from Adam to Malachi (vv. 38–46) and the Book of Mormon prophets (v. 49), all of whom had complied with the law of sacrifice as practiced in the Old Testament (vv. 12–14) and had received the power of resurrection (v. 51).

It is common for a vision of this sort to change scenes, including time and place. The vision of John the Revelator in the book of Revelation, that of Nephi in 1 Nephi 11–14, and that of the Prophet Joseph Smith in Doctrine and Covenants 76 are classic examples. What President Smith now sees is a vision of those who had been "reserved to come forth in the fulness of times" to lay the foundation of the "great latter-day work." Having completed their labors in the flesh, they now continued them in the spirit world. Verses 55 and 56 may well be a flashback to our first estate.

138:57 *I beheld that the faithful elders of this dispensation.* President Wilford Woodruff explained that in the spirit world "every Apostle, every Seventy, every Elder, etc., who has died in the faith as soon as he passes to the other side of the vail, enters into the work of the ministry, and there is a thousand times more to preach [to] there than there is here" (*Journal of Discourses*, 22:334).

138:59 *After they have paid the penalty of their transgressions.* In the previous verse we are assured that the dead can repent. We know that there is no true repentance without suffering (Alma 42:16–18). It naturally follows that those in the spirit world who repent will be involved in the same process that they would have been involved in had they lived to do their repenting in this life. If they are to be judged according to men in the flesh, they too must pay "the penalty of their transgressions." One illustration of this principle could include those who, in a state of despondency, commit suicide. While not negating the seriousness of this transgression, it would be our hope that there will be those who, in the course of time, having "paid the penalty" will be able to right their lives (Ballard, *Suicide*, 52–54).

OFFICIAL DECLARATIONS

Through the years the First Presidency and Quorum of the Twelve have issued official documents for governing the Church or making announcements to the world. Generally, documents issued for governing the Church are called official declarations, whereas documents directed to the world are called proclamations. Two official declarations are included in the canonized scriptures of the Church. These declarations bear directly on key doctrines of the kingdom. A historical introduction explaining the circumstances that precipitated each document has been provided.

OFFICIAL DECLARATION 1

DATE: 24 SEPTEMBER 1889
PLACE: SALT LAKE CITY, UTAH

On 16 May 1843, in Ramus, Illinois, the Prophet Joseph Smith, said: "Except a man and his wife enter into an everlasting covenant and be married for eternity, while in this probation, by the power and authority of the Holy Priesthood, they will cease to increase when they die; that is, they will not have any children after the resurrection. But those who are married by the power and authority of the priesthood in this life, and continue without committing the sin against the Holy Ghost, will continue to increase and have children in the celestial glory. . . . In the celestial glory there are three heavens or degrees; and in order to obtain the highest, a man must enter into this order of the priesthood [meaning the new and everlasting covenant of marriage]; and if he does not, he cannot obtain it. He may enter into the other, but that is the end of his kingdom; he cannot have an increase" (*Teachings of the Prophet Joseph Smith,* 300–301; D&C 131:1–4).

On 12 July 1843, the Prophet dictated the revelation on the eternity of the marriage covenant, including plurality of wives, to his scribe William Clayton in Nauvoo. In addition to teaching the necessity of marriage for time and eternity as performed by the proper priesthood authority, this revelation announced the conditions under which the Lord permitted his servants to take plural wives.

The keys to perform both eternal marriages and to authorize a plurality of wives had been given to Joseph Smith: "I have appointed unto my servant Joseph to hold this power in the last days, and there is never but one on the earth at a time on whom this power and the keys of this priesthood are conferred" (D&C 132:7). Any ceremony to bind man and woman together beyond the period of mortal life or to give the right to take plural wives which is not done under the direction of this authority will be of no efficacy or force when people are out of the world.

"There is but one person on the earth at a time upon whom the keys of this sealing ordinance are conferred. That man is the Presiding High Priest, the President of the Church. He is the bearer of this authority, which he may exercise personally or he may commission others to exercise it under his jurisdiction, for such time, long or short, up to the end of his life, as he may desire.

"It was after the revelation of July, 1843, which provided that under certain conditions, which are clearly defined, a man may receive more than one woman to be his wife, that plural marriage became a recognized doctrine of the Church. Under this system family ties were established and relationships entered into which were held sacred and binding, not alone by those who accepted and entered into the order of plural marriage, but by all who had become members of the Church" (Clark, *Messages*, 5:319).

The years that followed witnessed ceaseless criticism of the Church and relentless persecution of those who had entered into the relationship of plural marriage. Legislation regarding plural marriage was enacted by the Congress of the United States during the years 1862 to 1887 in three successive acts known as the Morrill Act, the Edmunds Act, and the Edmunds-Tucker Act.

"Under the provisions of the Edmunds-Tucker law the Church of Jesus Christ of Latter-day Saints was disincorporated, the Perpetual Emigration Fund Company was dissolved, and all property belonging to the Church, with the exception of buildings used exclusively for religious worship, was escheated to the government.

"Hundreds of men who had contracted plural marriages were heavily fined, and imprisoned. All persons who could not subscribe to a test oath which was provided especially for those who practiced or believed in the practice of plural marriage, were disfranchised.

"It became obvious that no human power could prevent the disintegration of the Church, except upon a pledge by its members to obey the laws which had been enacted prohibiting the practice of polygamy" (Clark, *Messages*, 5:320).

It was under these circumstances that Wilford Woodruff, then the president of the Church, announced the Official Declaration to the Church and to the People of the United States, commonly referred to as the Manifesto. President Woodruff wrote in his journal: "I have arrived at a point in the history of my life as the President of the Church of Jesus Christ of Latter-day Saints where I am under the necessity of acting for the temporal salvation of the Church. . . . and after praying to the Lord and feeling inspired, I have issued the following proclamation which is sustained by my counselors and the Twelve Apostles" (Clark, *Messages*, 3:192).

After reviewing the enactment of the law prohibiting the practice of plural marriage and the effects of its enforcement, President Woodruff, in this declaration, said: "Inasmuch as laws have been enacted by Congress forbidding plural marriages, which laws have been pronounced constitutional by the Court of last resort, I do hereby declare my intention to submit to those laws, and to use all my influence with the members of the church over which I preside to have them do likewise. . . . And I now publicly declare that my advice to the Latter-day Saints is to refrain from contracting any marriage forbidden by the laws of the land" (Clark, *Messages*, 3:193).

The Manifesto was signed by President Woodruff as president of the Church. A motion in the October conference of that year called for the members of the Church to sustain what President Woodruff had done:

"I move that, recognizing Wilford Woodruff as the President of the Church of Jesus Christ of Latter-day Saints, and the only man on the earth at the present time who holds the keys of the sealing ordinances, we consider him fully authorized by virtue of his position to issue the manifesto which has been read in our hearing, and which is dated September 24th, 1890, and that as a Church in General Conference assembled, we accept his declaration concerning plural marriages as authoritative and binding" (Clark, *Messages*, 3:195).

The vote to sustain the motion was unanimous.

Soon afterward, on 1 November 1891, President Woodruff provided additional understanding relative to the Manifesto:

"I saw exactly what would come to pass if there was not something done. I have had this spirit upon me for a long time. But I want to say this: I should have let all the temples go out of our hands; I should have gone to prison myself, and let every other man go there, had not the God of heaven commanded me to do what I did do; and when the hour came that I was commanded to do that, it was all clear to me. I went before the Lord, and I wrote what the Lord told me to write. I laid it before my brethren—such strong men as Brother George Q. Cannon, Brother Joseph F. Smith, and the Twelve Apostles. I might as well undertake to turn an army with banners out of its course as to turn them out of a course that they considered to be right. These men agreed with me, and ten thousand Latter-day Saints also agreed with me. Why? Because they were moved upon by the Spirit of God and by the revelations of Jesus Christ to do it" (*Discourses of Wilford Woodruff*, 217).

OFFICIAL DECLARATION 2

DATE: 1 JUNE 1978
PLACE: SALT LAKE TEMPLE

On Thursday, 1 June 1978, President Spencer W. Kimball, while meeting with his counselors in the First Presidency and the Twelve in the Salt Lake Temple, indicated that for months he had been giving prayerful consideration to the matter of conferring the priesthood upon those of all races and that he felt the need for divine guidance. He explained that he had spent many hours in the upper room in the temple pleading with the Lord for counsel and direction. He indicated his hope that the Lord would give a revelation and resolve the matter. He further stated that if it was the mind and will of the Lord that the Church continue in the present course, he was willing to sustain and support that decision and defend it to the death. He said he hoped for a clear affirmation so there would be no question in anyone's mind.

All present were invited to express their views on the matter, which they did. A strong spirit of unity existed. At the conclusion of this discussion, President Kimball asked his counselors in the presidency and the Quorum of the Twelve to join with him in prayer. President Kimball then importuned the Lord with great fervor and faith. The prayer offered by President Kimball was dictated by the Holy Ghost.

"On this occasion," recalled one of those who was present, "because of the importuning and the faith, and because the hour and the time had arrived the Lord in his providences poured out the Holy Ghost upon the First Presidency and the Twelve in a miraculous and marvelous manner, beyond anything that any then present had ever experienced. The revelation came to the President of the Church; it also came to each individual present. There were ten members of the Council of the Twelve and three of the First Presidency there assembled. The result was that President Kimball knew, and each one of us knew, independent of any other person, by direct and personal revelation to us, that the time had now come to extend the gospel and all its blessings and all its obligations, including the priesthood and the blessings of the house of the Lord, to those of every nation, culture, and race, including the black race. There was no question whatsoever as to what happened or as to the word and message that came" (McConkie, *Sermons and Writings*, 166–67).

In what is perhaps the most perfect illustration of the law of witnesses in this dispensation, the marvelous outpouring of the Holy Ghost—described by some present as "cloven tongues of fire"—fell upon the prophet who stood at the head of the Church and twelve other prophets, seers, and revelators. When he ceased to pray, there was a great Pentecostal outpouring of the Spirit such as none of those present had ever before experienced. The experience cannot be confined to words. It was something that could only be felt in the hearts of the recipients and which can only be understood by the power of the Spirit. The announcement was carried in the *Deseret News* of Friday, 9 June 1978, without editorial comment.

Following is the letter that appeared over the signature of the First Presidency:

"June 8, 1978

"To all general and local priesthood officers of The Church of Jesus Christ of Latter-day Saints throughout the world:

"Dear Brethren:

"As we have witnessed the expansion of the work of the Lord over the earth, we have been grateful that people of many nations have responded to the message of the restored gospel, and have joined the

Church in ever-increasing numbers. This, in turn, has inspired us with a desire to extend to every worthy member of the Church all of the privileges and blessings which the gospel affords.

"Aware of the promises made by the prophets and presidents of the Church who have preceded us that at some time, in God's eternal plan, all of our brethren who are worthy may receive the priesthood, and witnessing the faithfulness of those from whom the priesthood has been withheld, we have pleaded long and earnestly in behalf of these, our faithful brethren, spending many hours in the Upper Room of the Temple supplicating the Lord for divine guidance.

"He has heard our prayers, and by revelation has confirmed that the long-promised day has come when every faithful, worthy man in the Church may receive the holy priesthood, with power to exercise its divine authority, and enjoy with his loved ones every blessing that flows there from, including the blessings of the temple. Accordingly, all worthy male members of the Church may be ordained to the priesthood without regard for race or color. Priesthood leaders are instructed to follow the policy of carefully interviewing all candidates for ordination to either the Aaronic or the Melchizedek Priesthood to insure that they meet the established standards for worthiness.

"We declare with soberness that the Lord has now made known his will for the blessing of all his children throughout the earth who will hearken to the voice of his authorized servants, and prepare themselves to receive every blessing of the gospel.

"Sincerely Yours,

"Spencer W. Kimball

"N. Eldon Tanner

"Marion G. Romney

"The First Presidency"

("LDS Church Extends Priesthood to All Worthy Members," 1A; Tanner, "Revelation on the Priesthood," 16).

This letter was read in the October general conference of that year, and the vote to "accept this revelation as the word and will of the Lord" was unanimous in the affirmative.

In Conclusion

The Lord has never had a people he acknowledged as his own to whom he would not speak. Revelation is the sure sign of the true Church; it is the foundation upon which the kingdom of God must rest. God stands revealed, or he remains forever unknown. "The testimony of Jesus is the spirit of prophecy" (Revelation 19:10). Revelation must be the root of every principle of salvation. Jesus of Nazareth stated the principle thus: "Every plant, which my heavenly Father hath not planted, shall be rooted up" (Matthew 15:13).

The revelation of which we speak must be our own. Our hope of salvation cannot rest on the divine promises given to another people in ages long past. As their baptism will not remit our sins, so their sins will not bar us from a place in the kingdom of God. We stand independent. If it was required of them to know of Christ by the spirit of revelation, then it must be required of us to know of him in like manner.

The revelation of which we speak must be both institutional and personal. Universal truths, those principles that apply alike to all of God's children, must be revealed through him whom the Lord has chosen to be his covenant spokesman. It then becomes the burden of the children of the covenant to herald those truths to the ends of the earth. And, as the Church that houses those truths must be directed by the spirit of revelation, so must the individual homes of each of its members. As baptism is the covenant of membership, so the receipt of the Holy Ghost is the seal placed upon each member. No one, Joseph Smith explained, can receive the Holy Ghost without receiving revelations (*Teachings of the Prophet Joseph Smith*, 328). Thus, as the body of the Church is to be directed by the spirit of revelation, so must the lives of each of its members be directed. "What power shall stay the heavens? As well might man stretch forth his puny arm to stop the Missouri river in its decreed course, or to turn it up stream, as to hinder the Almighty from pouring down knowledge from heaven upon the heads of the Latter-day Saints" (D&C 121:33).

This volume constitutes a brief commentary on revelations received by Joseph Smith and some of his successors in the presidency of The Church of Jesus Christ of Latter-day Saints. Within each revelation is found the evidence of its authenticity, and all honest truth seekers may be endowed with a sufficient portion of the Spirit of the Lord to find it. Thus, within the Doctrine and Covenants is to be found a veritable avalanche of evidence that Joseph Smith is the great prophet of the Restoration and that in and through him the Church and kingdom of God have again been established upon the earth.

The revelations contained herein span the length and breadth of the eternities. They embrace the great and the small, the timely and the timeless; they open the heavens to things both past, present, and future. They speak of worlds without number that have been blessed with the saving principles of the gospel; they speak of our premortal existence, of the world of departed spirits, and of the various glories that await us in the worlds to come. They also record counsel and direction as it was given to people who would be long forgotten were it not for the devotion and faith of those who preserved these records for us. It is then for us in that same spirit of faith and devotion to come to know and understand the voice of the Lord as he has spoken to those of our day. In so doing we prepare ourselves to hear that same voice as it speaks to us.

We conclude this volume with the testimony that ours is not a mute God. His voice is quite audible to all who will listen. He has spoken, he does speak, and "he will yet reveal many great and important thing pertaining to the Kingdom of God" (Article of Faith 9). We further attest that he will yet reveal many great and important things to each father, mother, son, and daughter of the household of faith as they seek to obtain his word and live by it.

SOURCES

Alleman, Herbert C., ed. *New Testament Commentary*. Philadelphia, Pa.: Board of Publication of the United Lutheran Church in America, 1944.

Anderson, A. Gary. "Being Valiant by Following the Lord's Anointed." In *The Heavens Are Open: 1992 Sperry Symposium on the Doctrine and Covenants and Church History*. Salt Lake City: Deseret Book, 1993.

Anderson, Karl R. *Joseph Smith's Kirtland: Eyewitness Accounts*. Salt Lake City, Utah: Deseret Book, 1996.

Anderson, Richard L. "'By the Gift and Power of God.'" *Ensign*, September 1977, 79–85.

———. "The Impact of the First Preaching in Ohio." *Brigham Young University Studies* 11, no. 4 (1971): 474–96.

———. *Investigating the Book of Mormon Witnesses*. Salt Lake City: Deseret Book, 1981.

———. "Joseph Smith's Testimony of the First Vision." *Ensign*, April 1996, 10–21.

Andrus, Hyrum L. *Joseph Smith: The Man and the Seer*. Salt Lake City: Deseret Book, 1960.

Angell, Truman O. "His Journal." In *Our Pioneer Heritage*. Compiled by Kate B. Carter. 20 vols. Salt Lake City, Utah: Daughters of the Utah Pioneers, 1958–77.

Arrington, Leonard J., Feramorz Y. Fox, and Dean L. May. *Building the City of God: Community and Cooperation among the Mormons*. Urbana and Chicago: University of Illinois Press, 1992.

Arrington, Leonard J. "Oliver Cowdery's Kirtland, Ohio, 'Sketch Book.'" *Brigham Young University Studies* 12, no. 4 (1972): 410–26.

Augustine. *The City of God*. Vol. 18 of *Great Books of the Western World*. Edited by Robert Maynard Hutchings. Chicago: William Benton, 1952.

Backman, Milton V., Jr. *The First Vision*. Salt Lake City: Bookcraft, 1980.

———. *The Heavens Resound: A History of the Latter-day Saints in Ohio, 1830–1838*. Salt Lake City: Deseret Book, 1983.

———. "A Non-Mormon View of the Birth of Mormonism in Ohio." In James B. Allen, ed., "The Historian's Corner," *Brigham Young University Studies* 12, no. 3 (1972): 306–11.

Backman, Milton V., Jr., and Richard O. Cowan. *Joseph Smith and the Doctrine and Covenants*. Salt Lake City: Deseret Book, 1992.

Ballard, M. Russell. Conference Report, April 1999.

———. *Suicide: Some Things We Know, Some Things We Do Not*. Salt Lake City: Deseret Book, 1993.

Bavinck, Herman. *The Doctrine of God*. Translated by William Hendriksen. Edinburgh: The Banner of Truth Trust, 1977.

Bellville, Peter K. "A Year without a Summer." *Ensign*, January 1983, 65.

Bennett, John C. *History of the Saints; or, an Expose of Joe Smith and Mormonism*. Boston: Leland & Whiting, 1842.

Bennion, Adam S. Conference Report, April 1954.

Benson, Ezra Taft. *Come unto Christ*. Salt Lake City: Deseret Book, 1983.

———. Conference Report, April 1969, October 1987.

———. *The Constitution: A Heavenly Banner*. Salt Lake City: Deseret Book, 1986.

———. *The Teachings of Ezra Taft Benson*. Salt Lake City: Bookcraft, 1988.

———. *This Nation Shall Endure*. Salt Lake City: Deseret Book, 1977.

———. "What I Hope You Will Teach Your Children about the Temple." *Ensign*, August 1985, 6–10.

Brewster, Hoyt W., Jr. *Doctrine and Covenants Encyclopedia*. Salt Lake City: Bookcraft, 1988.

Brown, Lisle G. "The Sacred Departments for Temple Work in Nauvoo: The Assembly Room and the Council Chamber." *Brigham Young University Studies* 19, no. 3 (1979): 361–74.

Buck, Charles. *Buck's Theological Dictionary*. Philadelphia: JJ Woodward, 1844.

Bushman, Richard L. *Joseph Smith and the Beginnings of Mormonism*. Urbana and Chicago: University of Illinois Press, 1984.

Cannon, Donald Q., and Lyndon W. Cook, eds. *The Far West Record*. Salt Lake City: Deseret Book, 1983.

Cannon, Donald W. "A Prophecy of War (D&C 87)." In *The Doctrine and Covenants*. Edited by Robert L. Millet and Kent P. Jackson. Vol. 1 of *Studies in Scripture* series. Salt Lake City: Deseret Book, 1989.

Cannon, George Q. *Gospel Truth*. Compiled by Jerreld L. Newquist. 2 vols. Salt Lake City: Deseret Book, 1974.

Carter, Jared. "Journal." Typescript. Special Collections. Harold B. Lee Library, Brigham Young University. Provo, Utah.

Carter, Kate B. *Our Pioneer Heritage*. 20 vols. Salt Lake City: Daughters of the Utah Pioneers, 1958–77.

Castel, Albert. *William Clark Quantrill*. Norman, Okla.: University of Oklahoma Press, 1999.

Church History in the Fulness of Times. Salt Lake City: The Church of Jesus Christ of Latter-day Saints, 1989.

Clark, J. Reuben, Jr. Conference Report, October 1936.

Clark, James R., ed. *Messages of the First Presidency of The Church of Jesus Christ of Latter-day Saints*. 6 vols. Salt Lake City: Bookcraft, 1965–75.

Clarke, Adam. *Clarke's Commentary on the Bible*. 3 vols. Nashville: Abingdon, n.d.

Clawson, Rudger. Conference Report, April 1900.

Collected Discourses. Edited by Brian H. Stuy. 5 vols. Burbank, California, and Woodland Hills, Utah: B. H. S. Publishing, 1987–92.

The Compact Oxford English Dictionary. 2d ed. Oxford: Clarendon Press, 1989.

Conference Reports. Salt Lake City: The Church of Jesus Christ of Latter-day Saints. 1880–1999.

Cook, Lyndon W. *Joseph Smith and the Law of Consecration*. Provo: Grandin Book, 1985.

———. "Lyman Sherman—Man of God, Would-Be Apostle." *Brigham Young University Studies* 19, no. 1 (1979): 121–24.

———. *Revelations of the Prophet Joseph Smith*. Salt Lake City: Deseret Book, 1985.

———, ed. *David Whitmer Interviews: A Restoration Witness*. Orem, Utah: Grandin Book, 1991.

Davies, Brian. *The Thoughts of Thomas Aquinas*. Oxford: Clarendon Press, 1993.

Davis, Ted E. Church Audit Committee Report. Conference Report, April 1999.

Deseret Semi-Weekly News, 23 January 1894.

Dibble, Philo. "Philo Dibble's Narrative." In *Early Scenes in Church History: Eighth Book in the Faith-Promoting Series*. Salt Lake City: Juvenile Instructor Office, 1882.

———. "Recollections of the Prophet Joseph Smith." *Juvenile Instructor* 27, no. 10 (15 May 1892): 303–4.

Doxey, Roy W. *The Latter-day Prophets and the Doctrine and Covenants*. 4 vols. Salt Lake City: Deseret Book, 1963–65.

Dummelow, J. R., ed. *A Commentary on the Bible*. New York: Macmillan, 1908.

Ehat, Andrew F., and Lyndon W. Cook, eds. *The Words of Joseph Smith*. Provo, Utah: Religious Studies Center, Brigham Young University, 1980.

Ehrman, Bart D. *The New Testament and Other Early Christian Writings: A Reader*. New York: Oxford University Press, 1998.

Eiselen, Fredrick Carl, Edwin Lewis, and David George Downey, eds. *Abingdon Bible Commentary*. New York: Abingdon Press, 1929.

Evans, Beatrice C., and Janath R. Cannon, eds. *Cannon Family Historical Treasury*. Salt Lake City: George Cannon Family Association, 1967.

Evening and Morning Star (Independence, Missouri, and Kirtland, Ohio), 1832–1833, 1834–1836.

"The Family: A Proclamation to the World." *Ensign*, November 1985, 102.

Faulring, Scott H., comp. and ed. *An American Prophet's Record: The Diaries and Journals of Joseph Smith*. 2d ed. Salt Lake City: Signature Books, 1987.

Faust, James E. "Keeping Covenants and Honoring the Priesthood." *Ensign*, November 1993, 36–39.

Foster, Lawrence. "Lee, Ann." In *Encyclopedia of Religion*. Edited by Mircea Eliade. 16 vols. New York: Macmillan, 1987.

Garrett, H. Dean. "The Coming Forth of the Doctrine and Covenants." In *Ohio*. Edited by Milton V. Backman Jr. Regional Studies in Latter-day Saint Church History series. Provo, Utah: Department of Church History and Doctrine, Brigham Young University, 1990.

———. "Ziba Peterson: From Missionary to Hanging Sheriff." In *Nauvoo Journal* 9, no. 1 (Spring 1997): 28–42.

Gibbon, Edward. *The Decline and Fall of the Roman Empire*. Edited by Dero A. Saunders. New York: Penguin Books, 1985.

"Golden Bible," *Painesville Telegraph*, 22 September 1829.

Grant, Heber J. Conference Report, October 1936, 1940.

Gutjahr, Paul C. *An American Bible: A History of the Good Book in the United States, 1777–1880*. Stanford, Calif.: Stanford University Press, 1999.

Hancock, Levi. "Autobiography of Levi Ward Hancock." Typescript. Special Collections. Harold B. Lee Library, Brigham Young University, Provo, Utah.

Hatch, Edwin. *Influence of Greek Ideas on Christianity*. 1890. Reprint, Gloucester, Mass.: Peter Smith, 1970.

Holland, Jeffrey R. *Christ and the New Covenant*. Salt Lake City: Deseret Book, 1997.

Homer, William Harrison. "The Passing of Martin Harris." *Improvement Era* 29 (March 1926): 468–72.

Hunter, Howard W. Conference Report, October 1994.

Hymns of The Church of Jesus Christ of Latter-day Saints. Salt Lake City: The Church of Jesus Christ of Latter-day Saints, 1985.

The International Standard Bible Encyclopedia. Edited by James Orr. 5 vols. Grand Rapids, Mich.: William B. Eerdmans, 1939.

The Interpreter's Dictionary of the Bible. Edited by George A. Buttrick. 4 vols. New York: Abingdon Press, 1962.

Irenaeus. *Against Heresies.* In *The Ante-Nicene Fathers.* Edited by Rev. Alexander Roberts and James Donaldson. Grand Rapids, Mich.: William B. Eerdmans, 1985.

Ivins, Anthony W. Conference Report, October 1925.

Jenson, Andrew. *Church Chronology.* Salt Lake City: Deseret News, 1914.

———. *Latter-day Saint Biographical Encyclopedia: A Compilation of Biographical Sketches of Prominent Men and Women in the Church of Jesus Christ of Latter-day Saints.* 4 vols. Salt Lake City: A. Jenson History Company and Deseret News, 1901–36.

Jerusalem Bible. Garden City, N.Y.: Doubleday and Company, 1968.

Jessee, Dean C. "Joseph Knight's Recollection of Early Mormon History." *Brigham Young University Studies* 17, no. 1 (1976): 30–39.

———. "The Original Book of Mormon Manuscript." *Brigham Young University Studies* 10, no. 3 (1970): 259–78.

———. *Personal Writings of Joseph Smith.* Salt Lake City: Deseret Book, 1984.

———, ed. *The Papers of Joseph Smith.* 2 vols. Salt Lake City: Deseret Book, 1989, 1992.

Johnson, Clark V., ed. *Mormon Redress Petitions: Documents of the 1833–1838 Missouri Conflict.* Vol. 16 of Religious Studies Center Monograph series. Provo, Utah: Religious Studies Center, Brigham Young University, 1992.

"Joseph Smith, the Prophet." *Young Woman's Journal* 17, no. 12 (December 1906): 537–48.

Journal of Discourses. 26 vols. Liverpool: Latter-day Saints' Book Depot, 1854–86.

Journals of William E. McLellin, 1831–1836. Edited by Jan Shipps and John W. Welch. Provo, Utah: Brigham Young University Studies, Brigham Young University; Urbana and Chicago: University of Illinois Press, 1994.

Juvenile Instructor. Vol. 29. Salt Lake City: George Q. Cannon & Sons, 1894.

Kimball, Spencer W. "Be Ye Therefore Perfect." Address to Salt Lake City Institute of Religion, University of Utah, 10 January 1975.

———. "The Blessings and Responsibilities of Womanhood." *Ensign,* March 1976, 70–73.

———. Conference Report, April 1974, 1975.

———. *Love Versus Lust.* Brigham Young University Speeches of the Year. Provo, 5 January 1965.

———. *Miracle of Forgiveness.* Salt Lake City: Bookcraft, 1969.

———. "Planning for a Full and Abundant Life." *Ensign,* May 1974, 86–89.

———. *The Teachings of Spencer W. Kimball.* Edited by Edward L. Kimball. Salt Lake City: Bookcraft, 1982.

"Kirtland Council Minute Book." Typescript. Special Collections, Harold B. Lee Library, Brigham Young University, Provo, Utah.

"Kirtland Revelation Book." Typescript. Special Collections, Harold B. Lee Library, Brigham Young University, Provo, Utah.

Lash, Nicholas. *Believing Three Ways in One God*. Notre Dame, Ind.: University of Notre Dame Press, 1992.

Launius, Roger D., and F. Mark McKiernan. *Joseph Smith, Jr.'s Red Brick Store*. Macomb: Western Illinois University, 1985.

Layman's Parallel New Testament. Grand Rapids, Mich.: Zondervan Bible Publishers, 1970.

"LDS Church Extends Priesthood to All Worthy Members." *Deseret News*, 9 June 1978.

Lee, Harold B. Conference Report, April 1973, October 1941, 1947, 1970, 1972.

———. *Stand Ye in Holy Places: Selected Sermons and Writings of President Harold B. Lee*. Salt Lake City: Deseret Book, 1976.

———. *The Teachings of Harold B. Lee*. Edited by Clyde J. Williams. Salt Lake City: Bookcraft, 1996.

Lightfoot, Joseph B. *The Apostolic Fathers*. Edited and compiled by J. R. Harmer. Originally published as *The Apostolic Fathers*. London: Macmillan, 1891. Reprint, Grand Rapids, Mich.: Baker Book House, 1987.

Lindsey, Robert. *A Gathering of Saints*. New York: Simon and Schuster, 1988.

The Living New Testament. Wheaton, Ill.: Tyndale House Foundation, 1967.

Lost Books of the Bible and The Forgotten Books of Eden. Cleveland: World Publishing, 1927.

Lundwall, N. B. *Temples of the Most High*. Salt Lake City: Bookcraft, 1993.

MacCulloch, J. A. *The Harrowing of Hell*. Edinburgh: T. & T. Clark, 1930.

Matthews, Robert J. *A Bible! A Bible!* Salt Lake City: Bookcraft, 1990.

———. *A Burning Light: the Life and Ministry of John the Baptist*. Provo, Utah: Brigham Young University Press, 1972.

———. "The Olive Leaf." In *The Doctrine and Covenants*. Edited by Robert L. Millet and Kent P. Jackson. Vol. 1 of *Studies in Scripture* series. Salt Lake City: Deseret Book, 1989.

———. "*A Plainer Translation:*" Joseph Smith's Translation of the Bible, a History and Commentary. Provo, Utah: Brigham Young University Press, 1975.

Maxwell, Neal A. Conference Report, October 1984, 1985, 1988.

———. *That My Family Should Partake*. Salt Lake City: Deseret Book, 1974.

May, Gerhard. *Creatio ex Nihilo*. Translated by A. S. Worrall. Edinburgh: T. & T. Clark, 1994.

McConkie, Bruce R. Conference Report, April 1971, 1978, 1982, 1985.

———. *Doctrinal New Testament Commentary*. 3 vols. Salt Lake City: Bookcraft, 1965, 1970, 1973.

———. "The Doctrinal Restoration." In *The Joseph Smith Translation: The Restoration of Plain and Precious Things*. Edited by Monte S. Nyman and Robert L. Millet. Provo, Utah: Religious Studies Center, Brigham Young University, 1985.

———. "Eternal Family Concept." Address given at Priesthood Genealogical Research Seminar. Brigham Young University, Provo, Utah, 23 June 1967.

———. Letter to Mr. Thomas B. McAffee. 18 October 1978.

———. *The Millennial Messiah*. Salt Lake City: Deseret Book, 1982.

———. *Mormon Doctrine*. 2d ed. Salt Lake City: Bookcraft, 1966.

———. *The Mortal Messiah*. 4 vols. Salt Lake City: Deseret Book, 1978–81.

———. *New Witness for the Articles of Faith*. Salt Lake City: Deseret Book, 1985.

———. *The Promised Messiah*. Salt Lake City: Deseret Book, 1978.

———. *Sermons and Writings of Bruce R. McConkie*. Edited by Mark L. McConkie. Salt Lake City: Bookcraft, 1998.

————. "This Generation Shall Have My Word through You." *Ensign*, June 1980, 54–59.

McConkie, Joseph Fielding. *Sons and Daughters of God*. Salt Lake City: Bookcraft, 1994.

McConkie, Joseph Fielding, and Robert L. Millet. *Joseph Smith, the Choice Seer*. Salt Lake City: Bookcraft, 1996.

McConkie, Mark L. *The Father of the Prophet*. Salt Lake City: Bookcraft, 1993.

McGrath, Alister. *Understanding the Trinity*. Eastbourne, Great Britain: Kingsway Publications, 1987.

McKay, David O. Conference Report, April 1935, 1942, October 1961.

Melville, J. Keith. "Joseph Smith, the Constitution, and Individual Liberties." In *Speeches of the Year, 1987*. Provo: Brigham Young University Press, 1988.

Messenger and Advocate, Latter Day Saints' (Kirtland, Ohio). 1834–37.

Millennial Star (Liverpool, England). 1840–present.

Millet, Robert L. "The Ministry of the Holy Ghost." In *The Testimony of John the Beloved*. Edited by Daniel K Judd, Craig J. Ostler, and Richard D. Draper. Salt Lake City: Deseret Book, 1998.

Murdock, John. "Journal." Typescript. Special Collections. Harold B. Lee Library, Brigham Young University. Provo, Utah.

Nelson, Russell M. "Gratitude for the Mission and Ministry of Jesus Christ." Address given at Brigham Young University Education Week, Provo, Utah, 18 August 1998.

Nibley, Hugh W. *An Approach to the Book of Mormon*. 3d ed. Vol. 6 of The Collected Works of Hugh Nibley. Salt Lake City: F.A.R.M.S. and Deseret Book, 1988.

1999–2000 Church Almanac. Salt Lake City, Utah: Deseret News, 1998.

Oaks, Dallin H. Conference Report, April 1985, October 1994, 1998.

————. "Our Strengths Can Become Our Downfall." *Ensign*, October 1994, 11–19.

————. "Revelation." *New Era*, September 1982, 38–46.

————. "Sin and Suffering." *Ensign*, July 1992, 70–74.

————. "Sins, Crimes, and Atonement." Address to employees of the Church Educational System, Salt Lake City, 7 February 1992.

Olson, Earl E. "The Chronology of the Ohio Revelations." *Brigham Young University Studies* 11, no. 3 (1971): 329–49.

Otten, L. G., and C. Max Caldwell. *Sacred Truths of the Doctrine and Covenants*. 2 vols. Springville, Utah: LEMB, 1982–83.

Oxford Dictionary of the Christian Church. Edited by F. L. Cross. Oxford: Oxford University Press, 1990.

Packer, Boyd K. "Balm of Gilead." *Ensign*, November 1987, 16–18.

————. *The Holy Temple*. Salt Lake City: Bookcraft, 1980.

Palmyra New York Courier. 31 May 1872.

Parkin, Max. "Latter-day Saint Conflict in Clay County." In *Missouri*. Edited by Arnold K. Garr and Clark V. Johnson. Regional Studies in Latter-day Saint Church History series. Provo, Utah: Department of Church History and Doctrine, Brigham Young University, 1994.

Parry, Donald W., Jay A. Parry, and Tina M. Peterson. *Understanding Isaiah*. Salt Lake City: Deseret Book, 1998.

Partridge, Eric. *Origins: A Short Etymological Dictionary of Modern English*. New York: Greenwich House, 1983.

Penrose, Charles W. Conference Report, April 1902.

Porter, Larry C. "The Colesville Branch and the Coming Forth of the Book of Mormon." *Brigham Young University Studies* 10, no. 3 (1970): 365–86.

———. "The Priesthood Restored." In *The Pearl of Great Price*. Edited by Robert L. Millet and Kent P. Jackson. Vol. 2 of *Studies in Scripture* series. Salt Lake City: Randall Book, 1985.

———. "A Study of the Origins of The Church of Jesus Christ of Latter-day Saints in the States of New York and Pennsylvania, 1816–1831." Ph.D. diss., Brigham Young University, 1971.

Pratt, Parley P. *Autobiography of Parley P. Pratt*. Salt Lake City: Deseret Book, 1985.

———. *Key to the Science of Theology*. Classics in Mormon Literature series. Salt Lake City: Deseret Book, 1978.

———. *Writings of Parley Parker Pratt*. Edited by Parker P. Robison. Salt Lake City: Deseret News Press, 1952.

Revised Standard Version of the Holy Bible.

Reynolds, George, and Janne M. Sjodahl. *Commentary on the Pearl of Great Price*. Salt Lake City: Deseret Book, 1965.

Richards, LeGrand. Conference Report, April 1941.

———. *A Marvelous Work and a Wonder*. Salt Lake City: Deseret Book, 1976.

Roberts, B. H. *A Comprehensive History of The Church of Jesus Christ of Latter-day Saints*. 6 vols. Salt Lake City: The Church of Jesus Christ of Latter-day Saints, 1930. Reprint. Provo, Utah: Brigham Young University Press, 1976–77.

———. Conference Report, October 1926.

———. *The Life of John Taylor*. Salt Lake City: Bookcraft, 1963.

———. *New Witnesses for God*. 3 vols. Salt Lake City: Deseret News, 1911, 1950, 1951.

Robinson, Stephen E. "Eternities That Come and Go." *Religious Studies Center Newsletter* 8, no. 3 (May 1994): 1–4.

Romney, Marion G. Conference Report, October 1945.

Roth, Martha T. *Law Collections from Mesopotamia and Asia Minor*. 2d ed. Vol. 6 of *Writings of the Ancient World*. Atlanta, Ga.: Scholars Press, 1997.

The Saints Herald (Independence, Missouri), 1860–.

"The Seed of Joseph." *Utah Genealogical and Historical Magazine* 23 (October 1932): 173–76.

Shakespeare, William. *Henry VIII*.

Shelley, Bruce L. *Church History in Plain Language*. 2d ed. Dallas: Word Books, 1996.

Smith, Eliza R. Snow. *Biography and Family Record of Lorenzo Snow*. Salt Lake City: Deseret News, 1884.

Smith, George D., ed. *An Intimate Chronicle: The Journals of William Clayton*. Salt Lake City: Signature Books, 1995.

Smith, Hyrum M., and Janne M. Sjodahl. *Doctrine and Covenants Commentary*. Salt Lake City: Deseret Book, 1951.

Smith, Joseph. *History of The Church of Jesus Christ of Latter-day Saints*. Edited by B. H. Roberts. 2d ed. rev. 7 vols. Salt Lake City: The Church of Jesus Christ of Latter-day Saints, 1932–51.

———. *Lectures on Faith*. Salt Lake City: Deseret Book, 1985.

———. *Teachings of the Prophet Joseph Smith*. Selected by Joseph Fielding Smith. Salt Lake City: Deseret Book, 1976.

Smith, Joseph F. Conference Report, April 1900, 1909, October 1913, 1918.

————. *Gospel Doctrine*. Salt Lake City: Deseret Book, 1986.

Smith, Joseph Fielding. *Answers to Gospel Questions*. 5 vols. Salt Lake City: Deseret Book, 1957, 1958, 1960, 1963, 1972.

————. *Church History and Modern Revelation*. Salt Lake City: The Council of The Twelve Apostles of The Church of Jesus Christ of Latter-day Saints, 1953.

————. Conference Report, April 1967, October 1918, 1970.

————. *Doctrines of Salvation*. Edited by Bruce R. McConkie. 3 vols. Salt Lake City: Bookcraft, 1954–56.

————. *Essentials in Church History*. Salt Lake City: Deseret Book, 1950.

————. "Patr. Hyrum G. Smith." *Utah Genealogical and Historical Magazine* 23 (April 1932): 49–53.

————. *The Progress of Man*. Salt Lake City: Deseret News Press, 1936.

————. *The Restoration of All Things*. Salt Lake City: Deseret Book, 1973.

————. Unpublished funeral address, 1 November 1971.

————. *The Way to Perfection*. Salt Lake City: Deseret Book, 1975.

Smith, Joseph Fielding, Jr., and John J. Stewart. *The Life of Joseph Fielding Smith*. Salt Lake City: Deseret Book, 1972.

Smith, Lucy Mack. *History of Joseph Smith*. Edited by Preston Nibley. Salt Lake City: Bookcraft, 1979.

————. *History of Joseph Smith*. Edited by Preston Nibley. Revised edition edited by Scot Facer Proctor and Maurine Jensen Proctor. Salt Lake City: Bookcraft, 1996.

Smith, William. *Dictionary of the Bible*. Revised and edited by H. B. Hackett. 4 vols. New York: Hurd and Houghton, 1868–70.

Smith, William P. Interview by J. W. Peterson and W. S. Pender. *The Rod of Iron* 1, no. 3 (February 1924): 7.

Snow, Lorenzo. Conference Report, April 1901.

————. "Devotion to a Divine Inspiration." *Improvement Era* 22 (June 1919): 653–62.

————. *Teachings of Lorenzo Snow*. Edited by Clyde J. Williams. Salt Lake City: Bookcraft, 1984.

Sperry, Sidney B. *Doctrine and Covenants Compendium*. Salt Lake City: Bookcraft, 1960.

Stevenson, Edward. *Reminiscences of Joseph, the Prophet and the Coming Forth of the Book of Mormon*. Salt Lake City: Edward Stevenson, 1893.

Talbot, Wilburn D. *The Acts of the Modern Apostles*. Salt Lake City: Randall Book, 1985.

Talmage, James E. *The Articles of Faith*. 12th ed., rev. Salt Lake City: The Church of Jesus Christ of Latter-day Saints, 1978.

————. Conference Report, April 1916, 1930.

————. *The House of the Lord*. Salt Lake City: Deseret Book, 1976.

————. *Jesus the Christ*. 3d ed. Salt Lake City: Deseret Book, 1976.

Tanner, N. Eldon. "Revelation on Priesthood Accepted, Church Officers Sustained." *Ensign*, November 1978, 16–17.

Taylor, John. Conference Report, April 1880.

————. *The Gospel Kingdom*. Edited by G. Homer Durham. Salt Lake City: Bookcraft, 1987.

————. *The Government of God*. Liverpool: S. W. Richards, 1852.

————. *Mediation and Atonement*. Salt Lake City: Deseret News, 1882.

Times and Seasons (Nauvoo, Illinois). 1839–46.

Tucker, Pomeroy. *Origin, Rise and Progress of Mormonism*. New York: D. Appleton and Company, 1867.

Tuckett, Madge H., and Belle H. Wilson. *The Martin Harris Story*. Provo, Utah: Vintage Books, 1983.

Tuttle, Theodore. Conference Report, October 1974.

Van Orden, Bruce. "'By That Book I Learned the Right Way to God': The Conversion of William W. Phelps." In *New York*. Edited by Larry C. Porter, Milton V. Backman Jr., and Susan Easton Black. Regional Studies in Latter-day Saint Church History series. Provo, Utah: Department of Church History and Doctrine, Brigham Young University, 1992.

Watson, Elden J., ed. *Manuscript History of Brigham Young, 1801–1844*. Salt Lake City: Smith Secretarial Service, 1968.

———, ed. *The Orson Pratt Journals*. Salt Lake City: E. J. Watson, 1975.

Webster, Noah. *Dictionary of the English Language*. 1828. Reprint, San Francisco: Foundation for American Christian Education, 1980.

Whitmer, John. "Book of John Whitmer." Typescript. Brigham Young University Archives and Manuscripts. Provo, Utah.

Whitney, Orson F. Conference Report, April 1912, 1917, 1918, 1927.

———. *Life of Heber C. Kimball: An Apostle—The Father and Founder of the British Mission*. 2d ed. Revised by Spencer W. Kimball. Salt Lake City: Bookcraft, 1945.

Widtsoe, John A. *Joseph Smith: Seeker After Truth, Prophet of God*. Salt Lake City: Deseret News Press, 1951.

———. "The Worth of Souls." *Utah Genealogical and Historical Magazine* 25 (October 1934): 189–92.

Williams, Frederick G. "Frederick Granger Williams of the First Presidency of the Church." *Brigham Young University Studies* 12, no. 3 (1972): 243–60.

Wirthlin, Joseph L. Conference Report, October 1958.

Woodford, Robert J. "The Articles and Covenants of the Church of Christ and the Book of Mormon." In *Doctrines for Exaltation: 1989 Sidney B. Sperry Symposium on the Doctrine and Covenants*. Edited by H. Dean Garrett and Rex C. Reeve Jr. Salt Lake City: Deseret Book, 1989.

———. "The Historical Development of the Doctrine and Covenants." Ph.D. diss., Brigham Young University, 1974.

———. "Notes and Comments." *Brigham Young University Studies* 15, no. 3 (1975): 362–64.

Woodruff, Wilford. Conference Report, April 1880, 1898.

———. *The Discourses of Wilford Woodruff*. Edited by G. Homer Durham. Salt Lake City: Bookcraft, 1946.

Wright, Dennis A. "The Hiram Page Stone: A Lesson in Church Government." In *The Doctrine and Covenants: A Book of Answers*. Edited by Leon R. Hartshorn, Craig J. Ostler, and Dennis A. Wright. Salt Lake City: Deseret Book, 1996.

Young, Brigham. *Discourses of Brigham Young*. Compiled by John A. Widtsoe. Salt Lake City: Bookcraft, 1978.

———. "History." *Deseret News*. 10 March 1858.

Young, Emily. "Reminiscences of Emily Dow Young Partridge." Typescript. Special Collections. Harold B. Lee Library, Brigham Young University. Provo, Utah.

INDEX

Aaron (brother of Moses), 86–88, 130, 208, 356, 406, 490, 602, 605, 725, 797, 802, 980

Aaronic Priesthood: restoration of, 84, 112, 117–21, 166–67; keys of, 118, 491; during time of Moses, 593–94; administers preparatory gospel, 594–604; is part of Melchizedek Priesthood, 786, 788; bishops preside over, 788–89; presided over temple anciently, 801–2; as priesthood of Elias, 892; anciently, came by lineage, 998

Abel: offers sacrifice, 227; obtains witness, 228; and priesthood, 230, 590; is murdered, 230, 453

Abinadi, 532, 842–45

Abolitionism, 772

Abomination of desolation, 612–14, 642

Abraham: promises made to, 24, 25, 58, 85, 203, 283, 395, 892–93; rightful heirs of, 47; knew plan of salvation, 161; and Melchizedek, 331, 334; covenant of, 421, 880, 999–1000; blessings of, 590, 730–31; on high priests, 601; descendants of, 622; saw noble and great spirits, 668; gospel of, 892; knew astronomy, 929; seed of, 949; seeks blessings of patriarchal order, 995–97; false priests attempt to kill, 997; on Kolob, 1046; has plural wives, 1058; receives all things, 1068

Accountability, 242, 463, 493, 1142

Adam: fall of, 11, 23, 108, 164, 213, 215, 216, 219, 220, 221–22, 226, 507, 733; and sacrifice, 119; knew plan of salvation, 160–61; knew mode of baptism, 172; as Michael, 203, 237–38, 648; as first flesh, 215, 590–91; offers sacrifice and serves God, 224–27; is

taught to pray, 225; blessed of God, 226; transgression of, 226, 826; as Ancient of Days, 235, 567; land cursed for, 441; serves under Jesus Christ, 566–68; as Son Ahman, 568–69; priesthood lineage of, 589–91; gathers high priests, 601; and meeting of patriarchs, 798–99; as great patriarch, 800; and keys to resurrection, 926; appears to Joseph Smith, 1040; angels minister to, 1041. See also Michael

Adam and Eve: transgression of, 150; temptation of, 212; became natural, 214; were married, 217; are sent from Garden, 222–23; bring forth children, 224; bodies of, 226; agency of, 423–24; in Garden of Eden, 431; as first parents, 591; freely associate with heavenly parents, 825–26; Satan attempts to deceive, 1035

Adams, James, 976

Addictions, 643

Adultery, 305–6, 320–21, 347, 448, 450–51, 461, 479, 1072

Adversary. See Satan

Agency, 198–99, 218–19, 240, 241, 272, 355, 422–24, 476, 739–40, 964

Alcoholic beverages, 200–1, 652–54, 1135

Allen, Charles, 701

Allen, James, 1134

Allen, Lucy Diantha Morley, 298

Alma: on small and simple things, 128; on worth of souls, 138; on endless torment, 145; on spiritual preparation, 152; on Adam's fall, 223; on mortal probation, 242, 465; on thoughts, 256; on being born again, 260; on consecration, 307; on death, 313–14; on soberness, 330; on prayer, 361–62; on mysteries of God, 452, 606; on

judgment of wicked, 234–35; on Ancient of Days (Adam), 238, 924, 925; prophecy of, 472–76; on salvation, 533; saw beasts, 553; vision of, 1016

Dartmouth Medical College, 5

Darwinism, 761

David, 618, 1072

Davidson, James, 187

Deacon, 602

Dead Sea, 784

Death: physical, 216, 223, 242; spiritual, 223, 242; of the faithful, 312–14; and faith, 367; is temporary separation, 417; second, 524–25; stops during Millennium, 734–35; chains of, 1146

Debts, 467, 766

Dedications, 685–86, 694–95, 864–83

Degrees of glory, 459, 539–40

Delaware Indians, 210

Deseret News, 402

Devil. *See* Satan

Dibble, Philo, 513

Didache, The, 384

Discernment, 255–56, 264, 367–68, 368, 379–80, 1038–43

Discipleship, 178, 325

Disciples of Christ. *See* Campbellites

Disciplinary councils, 322–23, 688–89, 745–46

Disfellowshipment, 689

Dispensations, 159, 201, 203, 273, 555, 588, 976, 1033–37

Divine dictation, 85

Divine investiture of authority, 226

Divining rods, 86

Divorce, 506

Docetists, 13

Doniphan, Alexander, 943

Dotrephes, 12

Dreams, 473

Drugs, 653

Dunklin, Daniel, 728, 767

Dusting of feet, 191–92

Dyer, Alvin R., 917

Earth: celestialization of, 237; curse upon, 284; during Millennium, 451; sanctification of, 551, 630; creator of, 760; will be great Urim and Thummim, 1047

Edification, 383–84

Edinburgh, Scotland, 1005

Edmunds-Tucker Act, 1152

Education, 404, 641

Egypt, 380, 441, 589, 593, 994, 997, 999, 1114

Eight Witnesses, 72, 114

Elders: office of, 154, 156, 197, 245; duties of, 166; are authorized to build up Church abroad, 301–2; are to bless the sick, 311–12, 367; are to warn and prepare men, 329; are assigned to travel together, 396; teaching of, 396; are to preach gospel, 436–37; are to preach and baptize all the world, 490; are to sit in judgment, 510–12; twenty-four, 554; presiding, 597; are endowed with power from on high, 770–71; are to receive endowment, 779–80; quorums of, 986

Elders' Journal, The, 932

Elect, 234, 344, 351–52

Eleventh hour, 256

Elias: has mission to gather tribes, 83; keys of, 202; appears in Kirtland Temple, 271, 889–93; will restore all things, 555–56

Elijah: Malachi's prophecy of, 23–24, 58; sealing power of, 23–24; appears in Kirtland Temple, 271; is given food, 327–28; on Mount of Transfiguration, 452; confers keys of his dispensation, 893–94; restores authority to baptize for the dead, 1031–33

Eliphaz, 688

Endless torment, 145

Endurance, 950–53

England, 898, 902, 914, 933, 934, 992, 1038

Enoch: power of, 83; prayed, 225; city of, 273–75, 278–79, 338–41, 357, 411, 611, 768; and Melchizedek, 332; society of, 377, 392; power of, 442; church of, 533–34; order of, 561; writings of, 630; book of, 800; and Raphael, 1036

Enos, 996

Ensign of peace, 780

suffering, 149–50; on test of discipleship, 178; on paradisiacal immortality, 221; on sacrifice of Christ, 224–25; on Cain, 229; on judgment of wicked, 234–35; on earth's curse, 284; on standing in holy place, 343–44; on signs, 350; on translation, 376; on Zion, 412, 779; on God the Father, 430; on testimony, 446; on wrath of God, 447; on sins, 451, 579; on preaching by Holy Ghost, 487; on receiving revelation, 517–18; on buffetings of Satan, 564–65; on stakes of Zion, 581, 918; on priesthood, 605; on continuing revelations, 610; on law of God, 633–34; on sealing up testimony, 642; on church of devil, 644; on half hour of silence, 645; on binding of Satan, 647–48; on John the Baptist's writings, 669–70; on building up of Zion, 703–4; on unity of heart, 714; on writers of revelation, 725–26; on Millennium, 733–34, 735; on writings of Enoch, 800–801; on law of gathering, 875–76; on ten tribes, 890–91; on priesthood, 956–57, 971, 998; on chosen and favored people, 998–99; on revelation, 1028–29; on patriarchal order, 1053; on eternal marriage, 1062; on Holy Ghost, 1066; on savior gods, 1088; on Second Coming, 1111–12; on wrath of God, 1117; on call of Ephraim, 1133

McIlwaine's Bend, 439

McIntyre, Dr., 33, 34

McKay, David O., 600, 682, 717

McLellin, Cinthia, 479

McLellin, William E., 142, 189–90, 477–80, 481, 482, 486, 509–10, 598, 785, 903, 915

McRae, Alexander, 943

Meat, eating of, 377, 654–56

Medicines, 310–11

Meekness, 266, 724

Meetings, 360–61, 432

Meibaur, Alexander, 10

Melchizedek (High Priest), 331–33, 333–34, 590

Melchizedek Priesthood: keys of, 84, 118; restoration of, 135, 156, 166–67, 203;

presidency in, 168; requires missionary service, 269–70; is divine channel, 331; exaltation through, 530; administers gospel, 591–94; encompasses Aaronic, 786, 788; officiates in all offices of Church, 787–88; angels have charge over holders of, 870–71; holders of, to be kings, 955; is not reserved for particular lineage, 998

Members, church: duties of, 169; role of, 176–77; to teach one another, 286; edify each other, 327; financial assistance from, 327–28; to provide for themselves, 397

Mental disabilities, 243

Mercy, 160, 518, 832, 866, 877, 886, 945

Messenger and Advocate, 26, 93, 723, 1124

Methodists, 5–6, 8, 206, 266, 598, 869, 963

Methuselah, 929

Mexican War, 624, 1134

Micah, 624–25, 960

Michael, 202, 203, 237, 385, 566–68, 646, 648, 800, 1035, 1040. *See also* Adam

Michigan, 781, 1122

Millennial Star, 261, 993, 1039

Millennium: sealed plates to come forth in, 38, 317–18; is near, 73; judgment follows, 144, 237, 558; destruction of wicked will precede, 234–36; will last a thousand years, 284–85; conditions of, 329–30; Enoch's city will return in, 338–41; Second Coming to usher in, 349, 455; Christ to reign during, 354–56; as Sabbath of earth, 434; earthly changes during, 451; all man-made governments will be dissolved in, 625; nature of life during, 733–35, 736–37

Miller, George, 968, 976, 978, 987, 1152

Miracles, 191, 264–65, 368, 385, 609

Miriam, 208

Missionaries: instructions for, 254; as weak things of world, 265; courage and faith of, 266; setting apart, 300; to go in companionships, 301; are to teach and warn, 328–29; will comb earth, 352; to Shakers, 374; invite all to attend marriage, 476; are to declare